Management and Organizational Behavior

Second Edition

Curtis W. Cook
San Jose State University

Phillip L. Hunsaker
University of San Diego

Robert E. Coffey
University of Southern California

IRWIN

Chicago • Bogotá • Boston • Buenos Aires • Caracas
London • Madrid • Mexico City • Sydney • Toronto

Irwin Book Team

Publisher: *Rob Zwettler*
Sponsoring editor: *Karen Mellon*
Editorial coordinator: *Christine Scheid*
Marketing manager: *Michael Campbell*
Project supervisor: *Karen J. Nelson*
Production supervisor: *Dina L. Genovese*
Designer: *Larry J. Cole*
Cover designer: Ellen Pettengell/Ellen Pettengell Design
Cover Art: Vasily Kandinsky, "Black Lines", December 1913.
        Solomon R. Guggenheim Museum, New York
Director, Prepress Purchasing: *Kimberly Meriwether David*
Compositor: *Times Mirror Higher Education Group, Inc., Imaging Group*
Typeface: *10/12 Baskerville*
Printer: *Von Hoffmann Press, Inc.*

Library of Congress Cataloging-in-Publication Data

Cook, Curtis W.
    Management and organizational behavior/Curtis W. Cook, Phillip L. Hunsaker,
        Robert E. Coffey.
        p.   cm.
    ISBN   0-256-20807-7
    Coffey's name appears first on the earlier edition.
    Includes bibliographical references and index.
    1. Management. 2. Organizational behavior. I. Title. II. Hunsaker, Phillip
L. III. Coffey, Robert E.
    HD31 .C583   1997
    658–dc21   96-44030

Printed in the United States of America
1 2 3 4 5 6 7 8 9 0 VH 3 2 1 0 9 8 7 6

The popular success of the first edition of *Management and Organizational Behavior* was a great stimulus as we reformulated the second edition. Our original goal was to pioneer a blended text between what historically has been taught as two separate fields—management plus organizational behavior (OB). We assumed two external forces would drive convergence of the fields: [1] curriculum reform encouraged by the American Assembly of Collegiate Schools of Business (AACSB), combined with [2] business expectations that students graduate with applied behavioral skills and a grounded understanding of how organizations function.

WHY INTEGRATE MANAGEMENT AND ORGANIZATIONAL BEHAVIOR?

Based on feedback from both professors and students who have used the text, we now know that our original assumptions were correct. Students readily learn applied skills and perspectives of OB when concepts and techniques are integrated into a management context; and conversely, essential management subjects come alive when infused with lessons and techniques from the behavioral sciences.

This second edition provides even more integration of the two fields starting with substantial rearrangement of content based on comments from many users. Edition two of the text deepens our commitment of responsiveness to two changing educational forces:

Student Needs. Our vision is that most students who use this text will be organizational contributors, not managers within, say, the next five years. Therefore they need to know how to be effective performers both individually and on teams within organizations. They also need to know how to work with managers and to begin preparing for the time when they are likely to assume managerial responsibilities. Nevertheless, part of their success requirements will be to understand the macro aspects of organizational behavior, which of necessity involves managerial skills and ways of thinking.

Curriculum Reform. By the mid-1990s, the AACSB had moved toward new institutionally-focused accreditation standards that abandoned 30 years of expecting business schools to look more alike than different. The new standards encourage faculties to critically review and redesign curricula by focusing on each school's unique mission. As a derivative of its mission statement, a school or college is expected to develop processes for curriculum review/reform and instructional enhancement that assure continuous improvement. In effect, accreditation now encourages curriculum innovation and integration. Faculties in progressive business schools have already completed or are engaged in the task of reconceptualizing curricula, which leads to a breaking away from strict discipline-based courses.

Given these forces, the merger of OB and management topics seems a natural one. Because OB will be students' dominant need, about two-thirds of the book's content is anchored in traditional and emergent OB subjects. About one-third focuses on issues and practices that every manager needs to know, although not necessarily presented from the traditional principles of management paradigm.

A Note to "Management" Faculty. While this book may have more the look and feel of an organizational behavior text, it clearly provides coverage of topics expected by management faculty. For those who prefer a management perspective, every business student should know practical skills associated with managerial success—say, how to engage in group-based planning, rather than just know managers are supposed to plan. In addition to management applications through skill-building lessons, examples, cases, and exercises, the text emphasizes managing through chapters that focus on:

- Strategy and behavioral approaches to planning and control (Chapter 2)
- Structure, as the organized community in which people work (Chapter 3)
- Job design, as part of applied motivation practices (Chapter 7)
- Teams, as a way to get work done using group techniques (Chapter 10)
- Conflict management, which overcomes the illusion of rationality (Chapter 11)
- Problem solving and decisions with an ethical perspective (Chapter 12)
- How leaders and managers differ, and what they do (Chapter 14)
- How managers promote change and organizational learning (Chapter 16)

A Note to "Organizational Behavior" Faculty. *Management and Organizational Behavior* provides a comfortable and contemporary feel for those who teach from an OB perspective. Of particular note are the behavioral exercises (two at the end of each chapter) and other pedagogy elements, such as the *Your Turn* instrument or personal evaluation found within every chapter. From the behavioral perspective, the text includes chapters on skill-building topics such as:

- Organizational culture, with a heavy infusion of values and expectations (Chapter 4)
- Personality and perception from a learning perspective (Chapter 5)
- Motivation fundamentals, which also build on a learning paradigm (Chapter 6)
- A practice-based survey of motivational applications (Chapter 7)
- Communication from the perspective of sharing and influencing (Chapter 8)
- Interpersonal relationships, which promote experiential explorations of OB (Chapter 9)
- How groups and teams function, and how to influence them (Chapter 10)
- The reality that power and organizational politics are critical to success (Chapter 13)
- An examination of the elements of stress and strategies for coping (Chapter 15)
- A venture into organizational change and learning (Chapter 16).

WHAT DO REVIEWERS SAY? (AN OVERVIEW OF THE TEXT)

To give you a brief overview of the text, we let the independent judgments of reviewers speak to select qualities of each chapter. Here is a quick review of the text through their collective thoughts.

Management and Organizational Behavior 2/e is divided into five parts. We begin with an overview of why management is necessary and how some of the big picture (macro) elements affect individual and collective behavior. The explanation then progresses through four stages of managing processes: managing people, managing relationships, managing the organization, and managing change.

Part I: What Managers and Organizations Do.

Chapter 1 Managers and Organizations. Arch Darrow of Bowling Green University sees the power in a first chapter that adds educational value beyond just setting the stage: "This is one of the few introductory chapters that I have ever read that actually has some substance. This chapter introduces a very good approach to studying organizations (systems), sets the tone for the rest of the book with the four themes (change, diversity, ethics, and international), and defines the initial and basic set of variables.

Chapter 2 Strategic Thinking, Planning and Control. Keirsten Moore recognizes the value of including these managerial concepts not normally included in OB texts: "This chapter addresses a more macro-oriented, strategic approach to OB and HRM which is often lacking in intro texts."

Chapter 3 Organizing Work Teams and Structures. Reviewers see strengths in "the details on the advantages and disadvantages of various designs" and "good use of practical examples to support concepts." "The section on multinational corporations and global structures gives students an understanding of the complexities of 'going international.' Finally, the tie-in of quality and flexible structures is an important one for students in today's work place to understand."

Chapter 4 Organizational Culture. Royce Abrahamson of Southwest Texas State University reports, "One of the best chapters I have read on the topic. (The) content and organization are excellent, refreshing, and complete." Arch Darrow sees the value of placing organizational culture up front: "I really like such an in-depth discussion of culture, especially at the beginning of the text. It serves to set the tone and direction for the rest of the book."

Part II: Managing People

Chapter 5 Perception, Learning, and Personality. Brian Niehoff of Kansas State University remarks, "I like the topics combined because they fit together well. . . . The coverage of Myers-Briggs and Kolb adds an educational focus to the chapter, which is relevant to learning. . . . I also like the integration of diversity management with the perceptual process—it's a good fit."

Chapter 6 Motivation, and Organizational Learning.
Mary Zalesny of Kent State University points out superior treatment of familiar topics combined with opportunities for application: "The section on expectancy is really good! The LRS exercise is a good opportunity for students to apply motivation theories."

Chapter 7 Motivational Methods and Applications. Steven Grover sees value in the dual treatment of motivation fundamentals and practices. He writes, "I like the way the authors have split topics between Chapters 6 and 7. The coverage of the applied motivation issues is engaging and succinct and flows well from topic to topic. . . . I am very happy with the balance of theory vs. empiricism. The authors have done a good job of separating the two and explaining that theories offer explanations but are not always true themselves."

Part III Managing Relationships

Chapter 8 Communications.　One reviewer writes, "The strength of pedagogical devices and the Your Turn exercise make the chapter a cut above other texts."

Chapter 9 Interpersonal Relations.　Keirsten Moore of Ohio State University also sees Chapter 9 as covering needed material lacking in most texts: "This chapter addresses a critical, practical need; interpersonal skills are critical to success in business, and training in this area is sorely lacking in business education."

Chapter 10 Building Groups and Teams.　Several reviewers see value in the integration of topics, especially the "integration of leadership, communication, and decision making." A reviewer from Kansas State University appreciates the way the chapter ties concepts together: "The inclusion of traditional literature (e.g., group development process, sources and consequences of cohesiveness, roles) is done very clearly and uses real-life examples to bring some of the concepts to life."

Chapter 11 Conflict Management and Intergroup Behavior.　"The opening section on types of intergroup relations is a powerful feature not found in most texts," writes Brian Niehoff. "The authors have taken a macro perspective of conflict and placed it into a micro text. By viewing conflict as conflict among groups, they take advantage of more extensive literature on the topic."

Part IV: Leading and Managing Practices (Managing the Organization)

Chapter 12 Problem Solving.　Mary Zalesny writes, "This is a well-balanced and well-written chapter. . . . Moreover, it incorporates many decision-making innovations—such as fishbone chart, group decision support systems—that I have not seen included in other comparable OB texts. I especially like that the focus is on problem solving and the role of decision making in organizations, rather than on decision making alone."

Chapter 13 Power and Organizational Politics.　Compared with coverage in other OB/management texts, Brian Niehoff acknowledges the balance of the familiar and the new: "The chapter mixes many traditional ideas about power and politics with some new and innovative taxonomies of politics. The moral/immoral/amoral management section is interesting, and the situational factors that alter power relationships is a new way to present this material."

Chapter 14 Leaders and Managers.　Royce Abrahamson enjoys the leadership chapter's clarifying appeal: "A major strength of this chapter is the section that helps the reader distinguish between leaders and managers." Writes Brian Niehoff, "This is a very well-written, inclusive chapter on leadership. The variety of theories and models are presented in a clear and interesting fashion."

Part V: Managing Change

Chapter 15 Stress at Work.　"Well written, more dynamic and interesting than (other texts)" is the conclusion of three reviewers. Keirsten Moore observes that it includes a "good section on personal coping strategies. The section on organizational coping strategies is more applied than in other texts."

Chapter 16 Change and Organizational Development. A reviewer states: "A delightful perspective on the challenges and methods of managing change."

Appendixes

Appendix A Origins and Methods of Management and OB Theories. Many professors, especially in the management field, like students to know about the history of management and organization theory, and about research methods. These two topics are covered in considerable detail in a compressed but very readable appendix.

Appendix B Managing Your Career. Because career realities of today's generation are going to be quite different from those of the past, Appendix B introduces students to many of the issues they need to consider if they are going to have some degree of personal control over what they do in the world of work.

WHAT MAKES THE TEXT A MULTIDIMENSIONAL LEARNING RESOURCE?

Thanks to the constructive feedback of more than 50 professors in North America at different stages of this project, *Management and Organizational Behavior* is a text designed to achieve several goals. The text and ancillaries are a learning package with a balance of concepts, examples, and practical applications. Included are pedagogy alternatives that help students develop personal skills and organizational insights. It also promotes an understanding of how organizations function and why they do the things they do within applied contexts that are highly visual and interesting to read.

Each chapter incorporates a repertoire of features and pedagogical aids aimed at holding reader interest and encouraging the student to bridge an understanding of concepts and theories with skill-building capabilities and applications. This multidimensional resource approach provides the professor with several options to use text features most compatible with his or her personal approach to stimulating learning. Chapters include the following features:

Learning Objectives

As an introductory overview, learning objectives help students quickly grasp the essentials they are expected to learn from each chapter. Objectives are reinforced by directly linking them to the study and discussion questions at the end of the chapter.

Opening Vignettes

To provoke preliminary thought about the practical lessons of the chapter, an opening real-world scenario or issue introduces students to the value of learning chapter material. For example, *Chapter 13 opens with an historic overview of the power struggles for control of the chief executive's position at Apple Computer.*

"Your Turn"

Students encounter self-reflective exercises designed to apply lessons of the chapter to themselves. The objective is to encourage the student to reflect upon personal preferences, behaviors, or other factors that reveal something about how he or she functions on one or more dimensions explained in the chapter. *In Chapter 10, students are asked to take a quick quiz to determine how well a team they are part of is working (page 347).*

Boxed Features

To enable students to grapple with real-world key issues facing managers and organizations, five types of boxes appear throughout the text. Four kinds of boxed material links the chapter content to the four emphasized themes: *diversity, ethics, change, and global perspectives.* Students are also given an opportunity to evaluate their own thoughts and ideas through *Your Turn* exercises within each chapter. Here's an up-close review of each type:

Dynamics of Diversity.   Details a situation in which factors of gender, race, ethnicity, or disability calls for managerial sensitivity and/or change. *The Diversity box in Chapter 11 discusses conflict resolution skills managers utilize to diffuse potentially litigious situations (page 375).*

Eye on Ethics.   Spotlights the ethical dilemmas or action situations facing managers who confront the ideological issues involved in choosing between right and wrong. *An Ethics box in Chapter 4 presents Hewlett-Packard's company-forming "HP Way" that puts forth ethical and behavioral principles (page 130).*

Challenge of Change.   Provides insights into how managers have approached the all pervasive task of managing change. *In Chapter 13, the Change box profiles challenges faced by Kid Rhino's director of marketing in creating a childrens' music market (page 443).*

World Watch.   Brings world events, people, and organizations into focus for the purpose of learning about life in other cultures, and to reduce the tendency to judge others through the filters of one's own culture. *The box in Chapter 7 discusses sweat shop practices in Latin American apparel factories (page 233).*

"A Second Look"

Because the chapter opener confronts readers with an example or situation before they have learned chapter concepts and techniques, at the end of each chapter we revisit the lead-off situation for a "second look." This closure typically extends the company experience to more complex levels and applies some of the tools of analysis to increase learning from the example.

Photo Essays and Content-Focused Captions

Today's students certainly learn from visual images. Each chapter contains several "photo essays," full-color pictures about people and organizations complete with captions that tie-in the photos with the topics discussed in the chapter.

The Use of Color

Learning by reading is no longer constrained by a black and white world. The artists and editors who have crafted the features of this text provide an engaging use of colors across the full spectrum of the rainbow. Color is a stimulus to learning throughout the book.

Exhibits

Tables, charts, and diagrams remain time-tested ways of summarizing comparative data, the relationships among variables, or the actions that lead to a desired outcome. Typically each chapter includes a half-dozen or so color-enhanced exhibits to provide the visual learner with a break from text reading and an easy summary of ideas conveyed in a graphical form.

Margin Definitions

The technical language of management and OB is summarized in key terms. These appear with definitions in the page margins beside the point in the text where they are introduced and discussed.

Summary

Some students find it helpful to turn from the chapter objectives immediately to review the summary. They then begin reading the text and features. Those who do will find that the summaries provide highlights that relate back to chapter objectives and key topics.

List of Key Concepts

At the end of each chapter is a list of key terms and the page on which each is introduced and defined.

Questions for Study and Discussion

Whenever appropriate, main headings within the chapters are presented as questions to be answered by reading the text, exhibits, boxes, and photo essays. End-of-chapter questions provide ways to help students ensure that chapter objectives are learned.

Experiential Exercises

Many OB faculty like to use selected in-class exercises as a way of encouraging students to learn from direct experiences. Two exercises at the end of each chapter provide considerable variety in terms of the unit of analysis (individuals, dyads, groups, the total class) and the type of activity used to stimulate experiential learning behaviors. *Chapter 9's exercise involves a team discussion of varying interpersonal needs, as assessed by an exercise earlier in the chapter (page 311).*

Cases

Business education has a long history of engaging students in discussions of cases as a way of learning from experience. End-of-chapter cases provide vivid descriptions of an organization's experience, followed by a few questions to encourage students to think critically about the case situation in relation to concepts explained in the text. *The case in Chapter 11 examines Kimberly Toy Company's goal to increase profits by 20 percent in one year.*

Reference Notes

For the research minded, chapter notes are collected at the end of the text, arranged by chapter.

SUPPLEMENTS FOR INSTRUCTORS

Video Series

Seeing is believing. Selective use of videos can be a powerful way to supplement lecture-discussion-exercise forms of in-class learning. We realize that most instructors view class time as a scarce resource; therefore, Irwin provides a carefully tailored series of six 10- to 12-minute videos to accompany this text. The video series on Marshall Industries is specifically designed to complement lessons in the text. By focusing on a single firm, students are able to analyze and synthesize how a variety of managerial and OB issues apply to a single organization. Each video was produced with a limited set of learning objectives in mind, which shaped the "script" and eventual action filming. A brief *Instructor's Video Manual* accompanies the series. The themes of the six segments are:

- Managing for quality performance
- Motivation and learning
- Leadership
- Effective groups
- Planning and controlling
- Managing change

Test Bank and Computerized Test Bank

The print and computerized testing support materials were designed to develop a variety of testing formats that get at learning beyond the simple concept recognition stage. Each chapter has 100 questions plus a 10-question quiz. Formats include:

- 60 multiple choice (including mini cases)
- 10 true-false
- 20 fill-in the blank
- 10 short essay

Not only is the answer included for each question with text page reference, but a rationale is provided for each. Questions are also identified by level of difficulty and linked back to the appropriate learning objective. The *Test Bank* has a preface on how to use it and a section on how to construct and add test questions.

The *Test Bank* is also available in a computerized version. Professors can quickly tailor their own quizzes and exams by using either the MS-DOS, Mac or Windows formatted computer disks.

Teletest

If using the keyboard to select questions and develop your own testing protocols is not for you, make use of Irwin's free customized exam preparation service. Select your desired questions form the *Test Bank,* then phone Irwin's Educational Software Services (ESS) at 1–800–331–5094. ESS will send you a master test with answer key within 24 hours of receiving your order.

Instructor's Manual

No *Instructor's Manual (IM)* is intended to supplant the creativity and perspectives on learning each professor brings to his or her class. However, instructors often find the *IM* a helpful guide in planning class sessions. Even in preparing the course syllabus, the *Instructor's Manual* provides alternative suggestions for management and/or OB focused courses. The *IM* also suggests short cuts in making decisions, for example, about which cases or exercises to assign, and how to sequence chapter assignments. To offer teaching suggestions, the *IM* provides the following elements for each chapter:

- Chapter overview
- Key terms from the text with definitions
- Learning objectives
- Answers to study and discussion questions
- Synopsis of the experiential exercise and debriefing questions/answers
- Synopsis of the case and answers to questions
- A summary of each boxed item
- A teaching note for each exhibit
- Supplemental handouts—an exercise, case, or self-assessment instrument
- Selected transparency masters from the text's exhibits

Transparency Acetates

Ten to 12 supplemental transparencies per chapter are included as color acetates. Some review each chapter's key points. Some include a self-quiz or a chapter quiz to use as a review. Some summarize key points likely to be taught as a mini lecture. Overall, the combination gives instructors considerable choice in drawing upon resources beyond those they have personally created for the classroom.

ACKNOWLEDGMENTS

We are indebted to all the reviewers and participants who helped define the domain, processes, and pedagogies we cover in bridging the fields conveyed in *Management and Organizational Behavior*.

Joel Baum, *New York University*
Scott Elston, *University of Iowa*
Joseph Foerst, *Georgia State University*
Brian Ganmore, *University of Texas, Austin*
Denny Gioia, *Pennsylvania State University*
Sonia Goltz, *University of Notre Dame*
Jean Gruby, *University of Wisconsin, Madison*
Don Hellriegel, *Texas A&M University*
John Lea, *Arizona State University*
Bonnie Lindemun, *University of Iowa*
James McElroy, *Iowa State University*
Marsha Miceli, *Ohio State University*
Charles Rudy Milton, *University of South Carolina*
Robert Quinn, *University of Michigan*
Ben Rosen, *University of North Carolina*
Richard Sevedra, *University of Minnesota*
William Snavely, *Miami University*
Barry Staw, *University of California, Berkeley*

John Wagner, *Michigan State University*
Ross Weber, *University of Pennsylvania*
Ellen Whitner, *University of Virginia*
Larry Williams, *Purdue University*
Jerry Young, *University of Florida*
Mary Zalesny, *Kent State University*

Focus Group Participants

Royce Abrahamson, *Southwest Texas State University*
J. Lynn Johnson, *University of North Texas*
Delany Kirk, *Drake University*
Raymond Read, *Baylor University*

Reviewers

Royce Abrahamson, *Southwest Texas State University*
Rudy Butler, *Trenton State College*
Arthur Darrow, *Bowling Green State University*
Joseph Foerst, *Georgia State University*
Steven Grover, *Indiana University*
Steve Iman, *California State Polytechnic University, Pomona*
Delaney Kirk, *Drake University*
Tony Martinez, *University of San Francisco*
Charles Rudy Milton, *University of South Carolina*
Keirsten Moore, *Ohio State University*
Barbara Neil, *NAIT, Edmonton, Canada*
Brian Niehoff, *Kansas State University*
Mike Stevens, *University of Texas, El Paso*
Linda Trevino, *Pennsylvania State University*

On the home front we are thankful for the tolerance of our wives, Ruth, Jo, and Helen, each an educator who at least cognitively understood our tenacity to dedicate long hours to this project over the past few years.

Management and Organizational Behavior and its ancillaries are intended to be a living compendium of learning materials. Just as the practice of managing organizational behavior is an on-going process, so is the refinement of the text in a continuous stage of quality improvement. As we prepare for the next edition, we invite your comments and feedback, whether professor or student. Only by listening and responding to our customers can we modify the text package so that it meets the unfolding needs of those who learn and practice its lessons.

Curtis W. Cook
San Jose
Phillip L. Hunsaker
San Diego
Robert E. Coffey
Los Angeles

Contents in Brief

Part I   **WHAT MANAGERS AND ORGANIZATIONS DO**   **1**

Chapter 1   Managers and Organizations   2

Chapter 2   Strategic Thinking, Planning, and Control   38

Chapter 3   Organizing Work Teams and Structures   74

Chapter 4   Organizational Culture   110

Part II   **MANAGING PEOPLE**   **145**

Chapter 5   Perception, Learning, and Personality   146

Chapter 6   Motivation and Organizational Learning   182

Chapter 7   Motivational Methods and Applications   216

Part III   **MANAGING RELATIONSHIPS**   **253**

Chapter 8   Communications   254

Chapter 9   Interpersonal Relations   286

Chapter 10   Building Groups into Teams   314

Chapter 11   Conflict Management and Intergroup Behavior   350

Part IV   **LEADING AND MANAGING PRACTICES**   **385**

Chapter 12   Problem Solving   386

Chapter 13   Power and Organizational Politics   424

Chapter 14   Leaders and Managers   460

Part V   **MANAGING CHANGE**   **495**

Chapter 15   Stress at Work   496

Chapter 16   Change and Organizational Development   528

Appendix A   Origins and Methods of Management and OB Theories   567

Appendix B   Managing Your Career   576

Contents

Part I

WHAT MANAGERS AND ORGANIZATIONS DO   1

Chapter 1

Managers and Organizations   2

Dan Logan, Code Trinity: The Spy Who Broke Away 3

What Purpose Do Organizations Serve? 5

    Business Firms Serve Themselves by Serving Customers 5

    Purpose Is Focused by Mission and Goals 7

    Organizations Work to Benefit Multiple Stakeholders 8

Why Study Management and Organizational Behavior? 9

    Organizational Behavior (OB) Provides a Road Map 9

    Management Provides Direction and Organization 10

    Knowledge Promotes Socially Responsible Behavior 11

    Beware the Law of Effect 12

How Do Organizations Behave as Systems? 12

    Systems Depend on Input-Transformation-Output Processes 12

    Organization Systems Are Open and Dynamic 15

    Systems Interact with Environmental Forces 15

What Do Successful Managers Do? 16

    The Rational View: Managers Plan, Organize, Direct, and Control 16

Your Turn: Do You Have the Right Stuff to Be a Manager? 17

    The Chaotic View: Managerial Life Is Intense, Fragmented, and Complex 18

    Managers Work in Multiple Roles 18

How Do Managers Influence Organization Systems? 21

    Select Options for Changing an Organization 21

    Anticipate Mutual Dependency among System Elements 23

    Achieve Balance among Essential Output Goals 23

What Is the Context for Managers and Organizations? 27

    Challenge of Change 27

    Globalization of Business 28

    Managing Diversity 29

    Promoting Ethical Behavior 29

Overview of the Book 30

Dan Logan, Code Trinity—A Second Look 31

Summary 32

    Questions for Study and Discussion 33

Experiential Exercise: Visioning McDonald's from Burgers to System 33

Experiential Exercise: Analyzing Joyce Johnson's System 34

Case: Who's in Charge of Purchasing at Reymont? 35

    Challenge of Change: The Battle Between Gates's Microsoft and Grove's Intel 6

    Eye on Ethics: Mark Whitacre—Competitors over Customers at Archer Daniels Midland? 13

    World Watch: Japanese Business Reinvented with Bullet-Train Thinking 24

    Dynamics of Diversity: Opportunity Is a Two-Way Street 28

Chapter 2

Strategic Thinking, Planning, and Control   38

Philip Morris: Addicted to Nicotine Sales? 39

How Does a Manager Begin to Think Strategically? 40

    Focus on Adding Value to Customers 40

    Craft a Mission to Define Common Purpose 42

Use a Vision to Set Direction for a Desired Future 43

Create Structures and Systems to Support Strategy 44

What Strategic Questions Should Every Manager Explore? 45

1. What Business Are We In? 45

2. What Are Our Internal Strengths and Weaknesses? 46

3. What External Opportunities and Threats Do We Face? 46

4. What Business Should We Be In? 47

5. How Do We Get There? 48

6. How Do We Know We're Still on the Right Course? 48

Results Are the Payoff 48

Your Turn: Strategically Planning Your Career 49

How Do Organizations Develop Competitive Advantage? 49

Assets and Skills Build Organizational Capabilities 50

Craft Strategic Actions to Win Competitive Advantage 50

Thinking Strategy before Action 53

Why Is Planning More about Learning Than Programming? 53

Planning Helps Reorient Vision and Direction 54

The Paradox of Managing by Ideology in the Information Age 56

Ideology Guides Environmental Scanning 57

How Can Group Processes Create a Shared Vision? 57

Organizing for Relational Planning 58

Guidelines for a Four-Step Group Process 59

Map Alternative Paths to Bridge the Future 62

Vision Planning Works Best under Fast-Changing Conditions 62

Why Should Managers Be Concerned about Control Systems? 63

Control Systems Help Close the Gap 63

Behaviors and Outcomes Are Measured and Evaluated 64

Use Social Expectations to Control Behavior 65

Managerial Values Influence Patterns of Control Systems 66

Philip Morris: Addicted to Nicotine Sales?— A Second Look 67

Summary 68

Questions for Study and Discussion 69

Experiential Exercise: Group Techniques for Vision Planning 70

Experiential Exercise: What's Your SWOT Analysis? 71

Case: Product Development at Oakmark Computer 72

World Watch: Asea Brown Boveri Reinvents Its Global Business Strategy 52

Eye on Ethics: Is GE's Simple Formula for Global Competitiveness Out of Control? 55

Challenge of Change: Norm Brodsky's Four Steps for Success in Business Start-Up Planning 58

Dynamics of Diversity: Japan's TDK Introduces Social Controls to Cope with Aging 65

Chapter 3

Organizing Work Teams and Structures   74

Ford Motor Co. Reorganizes Its Finance Function 75

Why Must the Design of Work and Organizational Structures Change Over Time? 76

Technology Is a Driver of Organization Change 77

Technology Creates Global Competition for Jobs and Skills 80

Why Design Work Around Self-Managing Teams? 80

Your Turn: What Type of Organization Do You Prefer? 81

Involvement and Innovation 82

Options for Participative Team Management 82

What Are the Basic Organizational Design Structures? 85

Purposes Served by Organizational Structure 85

Organizational Design by Function 86

Organizational Design by Geography 88

Organizational Design by Product Line 89

Organizational Design by Customer/Market Channel 90

Combining Designs over the Organizational Structure Life Cycle 91

What Are the Trade-Offs for Balancing Organizational Design? 92

Balancing Centralization and Decentralization 92

Balancing Autonomy, Control, and Coordination 93

Bureaucracy versus Organic Organizations 95

How Do Organizations Achieve Leaner, Flatter Structures? 98

Widen the Span of Control 99

Shift Control from Staff to Line 100

Cut Levels of Management 100

Reengineer from Vertical Flows to Horizontal Work Processes 101

Ford Motor Co. Reorganizes Its Finance Function—A Second Look 104

Summary 105

Questions for Study and Discussion 106

Experiential Exercise: Visualizing the Ideal Workweek 106

Experiential Exercise: Nominal Group Technique (NGT) Focuses Person–Organization Fit 107

Case: Metric Technology's Latin American Division 108

Eye on Ethics: Balancing Flexibility, Structure, and Responsibility at Johnson & Johnson (J&J) 86

Dynamics of Diversity: Entrepreneur Andrea Cunningham Moves from Control to Autonomy to Teams 95

Challenge of Change: Ships on a Stormy Sea: The Coming Death of Bureaucracy 98

Chapter 4

Organizational Culture 110

Wal-Mart's Culture Inspires Remarkable Growth 111

How Do Assumptions Give Meaning to Organizational Culture? 112

Organizational Assumptions Guide Behavior 112

Assumptions Define Relationships to the Environment 113

Assumptions Promote Learning and Communicating 114

Assumptions Tell about People and Relationships 115

Why Do Organizational Value Systems Differ? 115

Two Key Factors Define Organizational Value Systems 116

Your Turn: What Do You Value in Organizational Culture? 117

Four Alternative Value Systems Define Organizational Cultures 118

What Functions Does Organizational Culture Serve? 120

Culture Complements Rational Managerial Tools 120

Culture Supports (or Resists) Strategic Changes 121

Culture Helps Socialize New Members 122

Culture Promotes Expected Behaviors 123

Subcultures Allow Organizational Diversity 124

How Do Members Read Their Organization's Culture? 125

Observe Physical Settings and Artifacts 125

Find Meaning in Organizational Rites 126

Ask Questions and Observe Responses 127

How Do Leaders Build Flexible, Responsive Cultures? 128

First Generation Managers Develop a Culture 128

The Second Generation Adapts a Culture 129

Growth Promotes Revolutionary Shifts in Culture 130

Ethnic Diversity Sensitizes Organizational Cultures 131

How Do National Cultures Impact Global Business? 133

Culture Has International and Ethnic Implications 134

National Cultures Program Collective Learning 134

National Cultures Have Four Dimensions 135

National Cultures Adapt to Promote Business Activity 138

Wal-Mart's Culture Inspires Remarkable Growth—A Second Look 139

Summary 140

Questions for Study and Discussion 141

Experiential Exercise: Draw a Culture 142

Experiential Exercise: Oh Say Can You See an Organizational Culture? 142

Case: AT&T + NCR = Negative Synergy 143

Challenge of Change: Allied Signal CEO Refocuses Values to Emphasize Quality 119

World Watch: Rites of Passage in a Japanese Bank 123

Eye on Ethics: The Hewlett-Packard (H-P) Way 130

Challenge of Change: Childress Buick/Kia Shifts Its Culture to Keep People Informed 132

Dynamics of Diversity: Women, too, Manage Firefighting 137

Part II

MANAGING PEOPLE 145

Chapter 5

Perception, Learning, and Personality 146

Managing in Turbulent Times 147

What Are Person–Job Fit and the Psychological Contract? 148

Ability versus Aptitude 149

What Are Perceptions and Attributions? 150

Attention and Selection 151

Organization 152

Interpretation 155

Perceptual Distortions 155

Attribution 156

How Do People Learn? 158
  Behavioral Conditioning 160
  Social Learning Theory 161
  The Cognitive View: New Patterns of Thought 162
  Experiential Learning Styles 164
  The Need to Combine Skills and Styles 165
  Two Hemispheres of Learning 165
  Lifelong Learning 166
What Are Personal Values? 167
  Types of Values 167
Your Turn: Your Values 169
  Changes in Values 169
What Are Attitudes? 170
  Attitudes Drive Productivity 171
How Do Personalities Differ? 171
  Heredity and Learning Determine Personality 171
  The "Big Five" Personality Factors 172
  Different Psychological Types and Cognitive Styles 173
  Personality Traits 176
Managing in Turbulent Times—A Second Look 177
Summary 177
  Questions for Study and Discussion 179
Experiential Exercise: Exploring Stereotypes 180
Experiential Exercise: Diversity Dilemma : A Role Play 180
Case: The Crowder Company 181
▬ *Eye on Ethics:* Do Subliminal Messages Mess with the Mind? 154
▬ *Challenge of Change:* At H-P, Learning Moves Outside Existing Structures 159
▬ *Dynamics of Diversity:* A Woman's Role—Cultural Context Shapes Beliefs 168

Chapter 6

Motivation and Organizational Learning   182

Chuck Mitchell Opens Dispirited Hearts at GTO 183
How Do Needs Affect Approach–Avoidance Behaviors? 185
  Needs Trigger Approach–Avoidance Behaviors 185
Your Turn: Motivational Forces That Affect You 186
  Maslow's Hierarchy of Needs 187
  Existence, Relatedness, and Growth Needs 188

How Do Needs Affect Work-Related Motivation? 190
  Herzberg's Dual-Factor Theory 190
  McGregor's Theory X and Theory Y 192
  Limitations of Classic Need Theories 193
How Do Learned Motives Influence Work Behavior? 194
  Motives Are Learned from Experience 194
  Attributions and Learning Affect Motive Development 196
  Motives Help Predict Behavior 197
  Personal Ideology Promotes Motivational Consistency 198
How Do Expectations Affect Work Motivation? 199
  Expectancy Theory Raises Three Questions 199
  Motivational Implications of Intrinsic and Extrinsic Rewards 201
  Managing Motivational Expectancies 202
How Do Perceptions of Equity Affect Motivation? 204
  Perceptions of Equity Moderate Motivation 204
  Adjusting for Equity Gaps 204
  Fairness Involves Distributive and Procedural Justice 205
Should Motivation Focus on Individuals or Groups? 206
  Globally, Many Cultures Disregard Individual Motivation 206
  Innovation Goals Shift Motivation toward Teams 207
What Is the Interaction between Learning and Motivation? 207
  Learning Is Often at a Superficial Level 208
  Shifting Learning to Double-Loop Systems Questioning 209
  Organizations Become Learning Systems 209
Chuck Mitchell at GTO—A Second Look 210
Summary 211
  Questions for Study and Discussion 212
Experiential Exercise: What's Your Motive? 213
Experiential Exercise: Team Problem Solving: Lightning Rod Motivation 213
Case: Ralph Henry's Motivational Crisis 215
▬ *World Watch:* A Case of Misdirected Motivation in Mexico? 189
▬ *Challenge of Change:* Entrepreneurs: Finding Motivation the Second Time Around 198
▬ *Eye on Ethics:* Can Koreans Learn to Do Business without Bribes? 203
▬ *Dynamics of Diversity:* Mojo of the Oilers: An Uncomplicated Life Wins the Hearts of the Team 208

Chapter 7

Motivational Methods and Applications 216

The IPO 217

Why Do Goals Enhance Motivation? 219

Difficult Goals Stimulate Effort and Commitment 219

Intentions Combine Goals and Action Plans 220

Management by Objectives (MBO) Sets Priorities 221

Goals Should Be Clear, Specific, Challenging 224

How Does Reinforcement Modify Behavior? 225

Behavior Modification Follows an ABC Sequence 225

Managing Environments with Organizational Behavior Modification (OB Mod) 226

Beware the Folly of Rewarding *A* While Hoping for *B* 229

What Is the Link between Rewards and Behavior? 229

Performance Means Behavior Has Been Evaluated 230

The Concept of Pay-for-Performance Rewards 231

Merit Pay Ties Performance to Add-on Rewards 232

Your Turn: What Do You Want from Your Job? 235

Rewards As a Cafeteria of Benefits 235

Controversial Consequences of Incentives and Rewards 236

What Are the Key Factors in Job Design? 237

Task Scope and Task Depth 238

Combining Scope and Depth into Four Job Profiles 238

Changing Task Scope and Depth 239

How Does Job Design Affect Work Outcomes? 240

An Integrating Motivational Theory of Job Design 240

Interdisciplinary Approaches to Job Design 241

Strategies to Enhance Jobs through Redesign 243

How Are People Motivated by Empowerment? 244

Empowerment Enhances Self-Perceptions and Behavior 244

Empowerment Results in Personal Changes 246

Empowerment Alters Expectations 246

The IPO: A Motivational Tool for Innovation, from Samuel Adams to Netscape—A Second Look 247

Summary 248

Questions for Study and Discussion 249

Experiential Exercise: Team Feedback and Goal Setting 250

Experiential Exercise: How Does the Design of Jobs Affect People? 250

Case: Motivation at New United Motor Manufacturing, Inc. (NUMMI) 251

▬ *Eye on Ethics:* Saving Lives: Breed Automotive Bags the Big Three 222

▬ *Challenge of Change:* The Early Birds Get the Goods 229

▬ *World Watch:* Sweatshop Practices in Latin American Apparel Factories 233

Part III

MANAGING RELATIONSHIPS 253

Chapter 8

Communications 254

Coffee-Klatching with the CEO 255

What Is Communication? 256

The Importance of Communication to Organizational Effectiveness 256

The Communication Process 257

How Are Communication Channels Used in Organizations? 261

Formal Communication Channels 262

Informal Communication Channels 263

What Barriers to Communication Exist? 265

Frames of Reference 266

Semantics 267

Value Judgments 268

Selective Listening 268

Filtering 268

Distrust 269

How Can Messages Be Sent More Effectively? 269

Increase the Clarity of Messages 269

Develop Credibility 271

Obtain Feedback 271

How Can Messages Be More Accurately Received? 273

Ask Questions 273

Listen 274

Your Turn: Listening Inventory 275

Read Nonverbal Communication Cues 276

Improve Cross-Cultural Communication 277

Coffee-Klatching with the CEO—A Second Look 283

Summary 283

    Questions for Study and Discussion 284

Experiential Exercise: Listening to Understand Problems 284

Experiential Exercise: Attending to Help Listen 285

Case: The Team-Spirit Tailspin 285

- *Challenge of Change:* New Electronic Communication Increases Efficiency at Benetton 260

- *Eye on Ethics:* Electronic Spying on Employees: Performance Booster or Invasion of Privacy? 261

- *World Watch:* Meet Me at the Club: Horizontal Communication at Mitsubishi 263

- *Dynamics of Diversity:* Culture Clash at School and Work 266

- *Challenge of Change:* Changing Feedback to Improve Quality at Boeing 272

Chapter 9

Interpersonal Relations   **286**

Charm School for Managers: Improving Interpersonal Skills 287

What Influences Interpersonal Relations? 288

    The A-B Model 289

    Personality Factors 291

Your Turn: What Are Your Relationship Needs? 295

    Interaction Setting 296

Why Do People Have Different Styles of Relating? 299

    Differences in Self Presentation 300

    Different Behavioral Styles 302

    Male/Female Differences 305

    Different Communication Ethics 308

Charm School for Managers—A Second Look 308

Summary 309

    Questions for Study and Discussion 310

Experiential Exercise: Comparing Interpersonal Needs 311

Experiential Exercise: Getting to Know You: Connecting by Rubber Bands 311

Case: The Bill and Mary Show: Bendix to Morrison Knudsen 312

- *World Watch:* Rule Number 1: Don't Diss the Locals 289

- *Dynamics of Diversity:* Caution! Cultural Blinders at Work 292

- *Challenge of Change:* Battling Executives Seek Out Therapists 297

- *World Watch:* The Trusting Japanese 299

- *Eye on Ethics:* Obtaining and Using Interpersonal Information without Permission 309

Chapter 10

Building Groups into Teams   **314**

New Teams Enhance Quality at Chrysler 315

What Are Groups and What Functions Do They Perform? 316

    Formal Groups 317

    Informal Groups 319

How Do Groups Develop? 319

    The Five-Stage Model of Group Development 320

    Moderators to the Five-Stage Sequence of Group Development 322

How Are Groups Structured? 322

    Functional Group Roles 323

    Norms 323

    Status within Groups 325

    Cohesiveness 325

    Group versus Individual Problem Solving 328

What Are the Threats to Group Effectiveness? 328

    Inappropriate Conformity 328

    The Groupthink Phenomenon 329

    Social Loafing 330

    Group Composition 330

How Can Groups Become More Effective? 331

    Leadership Facilitation 331

    Meeting Guidelines 333

    Team Building 334

How Do Teams Differ from Groups? 335

    Types of Teams: Sports Analogies 335

    Types of Teams: Actions Taken 336

How Do Groups Develop into Teams? 337

    Team Values 338

    Organizational Conditions 338

    Member Skills 339

    Matching Team Roles and Preferences 340

    Team Work Roles 340

    Work Preferences 341

How Do Teams Maintain and Improve Their
Effectiveness? 342

    Maintaining Balanced Roles and Preferences 342

    Maintaining Trust and Openness 343

New Teams Enhance Quality at Chrysler—A Second Look 343

Summary 344

    Questions for Study and Discussion 345

Experiential Exercise: Analyzing Work Group Structure 346

Experiential Exercise: Working Together As a Problem-
Solving Team 346

Your Turn: How Well Do We Work Together As a
Team? 347

Case: Self-Directed Work Teams at the San Diego Zoo 348

■ *World Watch:* Japanese Quality Circles 318

■ *Dynamics of Diversity:* Support Groups for Homosexual
Employees 320

■ *Eye on Ethics:* Lunada Bay Pirates Guard Their Surf
Turf 327

■ *Challenge of Change:* Cross-Functional Advice Teams at
McCormick 338

Summary 378

    Questions for Study and Discussion 379

Experiential Exercise: Win As Much As You Can 380

Experiential Exercise: Used Car Negotiation 382

Case: Goal Setting at the Kimberly Toy Company 383

■ *Eye on Ethics:* General Dynamics Gives Execs Big-
Bucks Bonuses but Workers Get Pink Slips 356

■ *World Watch:* Task Forces Let Labor into the
Boardroom 371

■ *Challenge of Change:* Tracking Product Teams at
Hewlett-Packard 372

■ *Dynamics of Diversity:* Diversity Can Help Solve Cross-
Cultural Problems 375

Part IV

LEADING AND MANAGING PRACTICES 385

Chapter 11

Conflict Management and Intergroup
Behavior   350

Restructuring Promotes Quality at GM's Saturn Plant 351

What Is Conflict? 352

    The Conflict Process 352

    Functional versus Dysfunctional Conflict 353

Why Does Conflict Occur? 354

    Goal Incompatibility 354

    Structural Design 355

    Different Role Expectations 358

    Degenerative Climate 360

    Personal Differences 361

What Are the Consequences of Conflict? 362

    Functional Conflict 362

    Dysfunctional Conflict 364

How Can Conflict Be Managed? 365

    Interpersonal Conflict-Management Styles 365

    Approaches to Managing Intergroup Conflict 367

Your Turn: What is Your Conflict Management Style? 368

    Strategies for Preventing and Reducing Dysfunctional
    Intergroup Conflict 373

*Restructuring Promotes Quality at GM's Saturn Plant—
A Second Look 378*

Chapter 12

Problem Solving   386

Putting Porsche in the Pink. Banzai! 387

What Are the Steps for Rational Problem Solving? 388

    Problem Awareness 388

    Problem Definition 392

    Decision Making 395

    Action Plan Implementation 398

    Follow-Through 400

What Is Ethical Decision Making? 402

    Morality 405

    Moral Principles 405

What Are Individual Differences in Decision Styles? 408

    Amount and Focus of Information Processing 409

    The Five Dominant Decision Styles 410

    Backup Styles 411

When Is Participation Important for Decision Making? 411

    Degrees of Decision Participation 411

    Criteria for Participation 412

How Can Problems Be Solved More Effectively? 412

Encouraging Creativity 412

Your Turn: How Creative Are You? 414

    Brainstorming 415

    Nominal Group Technique 416

Delphi Technique 417

Group Decision Support Systems 417

Putting Porsche in the Pink—A Second Look 417

Summary 418

Questions for Study and Discussion 419

Experiential Exercise: Ethical Decision Making 420

Experiential Exercise: None of Us Is As Smart As All
of Us 422

Case: Dealing with Academic Dishonesty 423

▬ *Dynamics of Diversity:* Culture Clash in the L.A. Fire
Department 390

▬ *World Watch:* The Cuban Missile Crisis Revisited 399

▬ *Eye on Ethics:* Ethical Decision Making in
International Environments 403

▬ *Challenge of Change:* Electronic Brainstorming 416

Chapter 13

Power and Organizational Politics   424

Power Plays Take a Bite out of Apple Computer Inc. 425

What Is Power and How Do We Gain It? 427

Power Goes Beyond Influence 427

Power Often Comes with Organizational Position 428

Power Can Originate from Personal Behavior 430

Power Can Originate from Situational Forces 432

Power Can Be Enhanced by Empowerment 433

How Do Social Networks Affect a Manager's Power? 434

People Expect Social Control 434

Central Positions Enhance Power 435

Diversity Is Threatened by Power Relationships 436

Sexism Sustains Power Imbalances/Inequities 437

Biased Negotiations Limit Power Effectiveness 439

How Do Situational and Personal Factors Affect
Power? 439

Situational Factors Determine Power
Relationships 439

People Have Different Power Needs 442

Dual Face of the Power Motive 442

How Do People Engage in Organizational Politics? 444

Organizational Uncertainty Increases Conflict and
Politics 445

Important, Decentralized Decisions Invite Politics 445

Alternative Forms of Political Behavior 445

Political Tactics Are Learned Skills 447

Your Turn: A Checklist of Political Tactics 448

How Can Power and Politics Be Moral? 450

Morality and Power Are Not Mutually Exclusive 450

Pluralistic Positive Politics 452

*Power Plays Take a Bite out of Apple Computer Inc.—
A Second Look 452*

Summary 454

Questions for Study and Discussion 455

Experiential Exercise: Power Plays within Universal Care,
Inc.: A Role Play 456

Experiential Exercise: Triads Learn from Personal Power
Situations 457

Case: Power Tactics at Old Line Bank and Trust 458

▬ *Eye on Ethics:* Disney—World of Multimedia
Power? 431

▬ *Dynamics of Diversity:* Chinese Women Face Tough
Obstacles in Business 438

▬ *Challenge of Change:* Mary Mueller Builds Power from
Networking 443

▬ *World Watch:* Managing in Russia—Uneasy Transition
from Bear to Bull 453

Chapter 14

Leaders and Managers   460

Larry Bossidy: Growth Separates Winners from Losers 461

What Distinguishes Managers from Leaders? 462

Managers Have Authority to Be in Charge 463

Leaders Influence Others to Follow 463

Managers Do Things Right, Leaders Do the Right
Things 464

Your Turn: Are You Ready for Leadership? 465

Qualities That Distinguish Leaders from
Followers 466

Leaders May Be Perceived As Having Distinguishing
Personalities 466

Behavior As a Characteristic of Leadership 467

Leadership Style As a State of Mind 470

How Do Leaders and Managers Adjust to Situational
Contingencies? 471

Contingency Theory Variables 472

A Leader's Motives Predict Style and Effectiveness 474

A Leader's Behavior Should Be Matched to
Followers' Needs 475

Leaders Clarify the Path to a Goal 477

Decision Style Influences Group Behavior 480

How Do Leaders Transform Organizations? 481

Pathfinding Precedes Problem Solving and Implementing 482

Behavioral Strategies for Transformational Leaders 484

Transformation through Dedication and Continuous Improvement 485

Is Leadership Always Necessary? 487

Playing Favorites: Leader–Member Exchange Theory 487

There Are Substitutes for Leadership 488

The Dilemma of Women and Minorities in Leadership 488

Larry Bossidy's Growth Separates Winners from Losers— A Second Look 489

Summary 490

Questions for Study and Discussion 491

Experiential Exercise: What Does the Leader Do Now? (A Role-Play) 492

Experiential Exercise: Dividing Up Leadership (A Role-Play) 492

Case: Troubling Leadership Issues in the Panamanian Agency 494

▬ *World Watch:* Brazilian Firm "Hunts the Woolly Mammoth" 467

▬ *Eye on Ethics:* Steve Wozniak: Inventor, Educator, Humanitarian 469

▬ *Dynamics of Diversity:* One Woman Executive Shows Others the Paths to the Top 479

▬ *Challenge of Change:* GE's Jack Welch: The Pathfinder Personified 484

▬ *Challenge of Change:* Silicon Graphics Thrives on Fantasy and Chaos 486

Part V

MANAGING CHANGE   **495**

Chapter 15

Stress at Work   **496**

The Stress of Success 497

What Is Stress? 498

The General Adaptation Syndrome 498

Constructive versus Destructive Stress 500

Episodic versus Chronic Stress 500

What Causes Stress? 501

Personal Factors 501

Your Turn: Are You a Type A Personality? 503

Organizational Factors 505

Environmental Factors 509

Individual Stress Moderators 510

What Are the Consequences of Stress? 513

Physiological Consequences 513

Psychological Consequences 513

Behavioral Consequences 514

Organizational Costs 515

How Can Stress Be Managed Productively? 516

Individual Coping Strategies 516

Organizational Coping Strategies 519

The Stress of Success—A Second Look 522

Summary 523

Questions for Study and Discussion 524

Experiential Exercise: Diagnosing Stress and Its Causes 524

Experiential Exercise: Tensing Muscles Relaxation Technique 525

Case: A Hectic Day at Alcala Savings and Loan Association 526

▬ *World Watch:* Stressed to Death in Japan 505

▬ *Eye on Ethics:* Facing the Legalities of Job Stress 510

▬ *Challenge of Change:* The People Costs of a Balanced Budget 511

▬ *Eye on Ethics:* Stress on Wall Street 516

▬ *Challenge of Change:* Employees See Plays, Eat Brownies to Relieve Stress 523

Chapter 16

Change and Organizational Development   **528**

Ford Prospers by Embracing Change 529

What Factors Cause Change? 531

Why Is Change Often Resisted? 532

Why Individuals Resist Change 533

Your Turn: Are You Ready for Change? 534

Why Organizations Resist Change 536

Overcoming Resistance to Change 537

How Do Managers Prepare for Planned Change? 539

Goals of Planned Change 539

Performance Gaps between Present and Desired Future 540

Change Agents 540

Targets and Process of Change 540

Anticipating Organizational Consequences: The Systems Approach 541

What Are the Phases of Planned Change? 542

How Is the Planned Change Process Managed? 543

Recognizing the Need for Change 543

Diagnosing and Planning Change 544

Managing the Transition 546

Measuring Results and Maintaining Change 546

What Is Organizational Development (OD)? 546

The Nature of Organizational Development 547

OD Values 548

OD Practitioners 548

OD Processes 549

Example of OD in Action 550

OD Interventions 554

Ethical Concerns in Organizational Development 559

What Are Learning Organizations? 559

The Characteristics of Learning Organizations 560

Types of Organizational Learning 561

Creating Learning Organizations 561

*Auto Makers Prosper by Embracing Change—
A Second Look 562*

Summary 562

Questions for Study and Discussion 563

Experiential Exercise: Changing the Grading System 564

Experiential Exercise: Personal Force-Field Analysis 565

Case: Rebuilding Metro East's Department of Housing and Urban Development 566

World Watch: Motorola Participates in China's Changing Economy 532

Eye on Ethics: Inequality Lingers for Women at Work 533

Challenge of Change: OD Practices Revive Ailing Xerox 549

Appendix A: Origins and Methods of Management and OB Theories   567

Appendix B: Managing Your Career   576

Notes   590

Glossary   00

Name and Company Index   00

Subject Index   00

Part I

What Managers and Organizations Do

1   Managers and Organizations

2   Strategic Thinking, Planning, and Control

3   Organizing Work Teams and Structures

4   Organizational Culture

Chapter 1

Managers and Organizations

LEARNING OBJECTIVES

After studying this chapter, you should be able to:

- Explain how business firms attempt to balance the profit motive with serving customer needs.
- Understand how an organization's mission and superordinate goals guide employee behavior toward desired quality outcomes.
- Identify the key elements and relationships that characterize organizations as dynamic open systems.
- Explain a manager's interpersonal, informational, and decisional roles.
- Explain how managers can influence the five basic resources to transform their organizations.
- Defend the premise that international competition, quality, diversity, and ethical behavior are the major management issues of the 1990s.

DAN LOGAN, CODE TRINITY: THE SPY WHO BROKE AWAY

Dan Logan began professional life as a spy. Trained in military intelligence, Logan was expert in three ways of getting information: "elicitation (getting information out of people without them knowing you're trying to get it), observation, and penetration." Twenty years after leaving the spy business, Logan, as vice president of communications for The New England (TNE) insurance company, employed his intelligence gathering skills in a covert action within TNE. His personal mission: to break away his communications department from the conservative organizational culture of its parent, the oldest chartered mutual life insurance company in the United States.

Eight years earlier, F. Daniel Logan, Jr., had been recruited from a New York City advertising agency to start an internal communications department within TNE to handle its advertising, annual report presentation, training videos, and direct mail campaigns. His department had grown from 7 to 90 employees when in July 1992 he and all department heads were directed by senior management to find ways to cut costs. Given this opportunity, Logan conceived of a strategy that was more unconventional than the company had intended: Why not become an entrepreneur and spin off his department as an independent, employee-owned firm? For his strategy to work, Logan had to achieve two objectives: (1) demonstrate to TNE management that a breakaway start-up would be economically viable, and (2) show considerable cost savings with no loss of quality.

Before revealing his plan, Logan talked with his internal customers to gather information and to subtly plant the idea of "outsourcing" most communications jobs to an outside supplier rather than doing everything inside. He knew he would need partners, and he found three senior-level TNE employees intrigued by his idea. The four met secretly evenings and weekends over the next two months to detail their plan. To make it work, they would need to bring with them about 20 TNE employees. Nancy Michalowski, one of the partners, described the profile they wanted: "We were looking for people who were entrepreneurial by nature—who didn't need a lot of supervision or support staff, who were flexible, willing to learn and try new things, and chip in to get the job done."

The team of four shared a common vision. Jim Kerley, one of the partners, explained: "We wanted to take the things that worked well at TNE and improve or discard the ones that didn't." In the first category, they included putting an emphasis on training and technology, community involvement, and building in quality measures such as surveys of customer satisfaction and tracking the effects of each project on sales and profits. The new business would offer to TNE and other clients services that focused on creative communications functions; it would leave behind administrative jobs such as preparing the annual report. They agreed to have a flat organization, with no position titles for anyone, including the partners. Everyone would be subject to peer review evaluations, financial records would be open to all, and all employees would participate in stock ownership and bonuses.

TNE management accepted the proposal in September, and on January 1, 1993, the new business, Trinity Communications, opened its doors as a separate corporation. Trinity began with several advantages uncommon to most start-ups: a team of 21 proven performers from TNE, $100,000 worth of donated computers and office furniture, free access to TNE's lawyers and professional staff, and a $500,000 advance on a $2.2 million client contract for the first year. Within three months it had a second client, and it ended the first year with $3.5 million in revenues with pretax profits of $700,000. Trinity's performance history to date has been exceptional, with pretax profit margins of 20 percent to 25 percent (whereas the advertising industry overall averages 10 percent to 12 percent). It has yet to lose a customer, and it is projecting revenues of $7 million for 1997 with profits of $1.5 million. Dan Logan reflects on the healthy consequences of this breakaway that created a new organization: "I wake up in the morning and I look forward to going to work. At times in a [big] corporation, you don't feel that lightness. With Trinity, it's more of an intellectual challenge than a depressing burden. It's invigorating."

Source: Alessandra Bianchi, "Breaking Away," *Inc.* (November 1995), pp. 36–41.

Managers work to influence people and to develop organizational systems. Dan Logan was clearly able to influence people within The New England (TNE) insurance company.[1] First, he enticed 20 productive employees to join him in the vision of starting a new advertising business enterprise, a risky venture compared to the security of a 165-year-old insurance company. Second, he convinced senior managers and the major users of communication services within TNE that everyone would benefit if the internal communications department were to be disbanded and key communications services purchased from outside vendors—including Trinity Communications.

Beyond influencing people, as a manager Dan Logan also developed and changed organizational systems. First, he created systems and processes for the internal communications department he founded within TNE. Then he transformed the entire function of corporate communications by creating a totally new and different organization. In doing so, Logan and his three partners planned to create an enterprise that encouraged creativity and individual initiative to enable the new advertising agency to be competitive in recruiting and pleasing clients.

Logan and his three managerial partners designed an organization structure that was flat, without anyone holding titles, for titles always convey a pecking order of authority within a hierarchy. At the same time they created an organizational culture of informality that promoted risk taking with fast response and attentiveness to clients. Trinity's culture was a constellation of values and assumptions about doing business that differed substantially from the conservative, formal corporate mentality of TNE.

Trinity Communications, like other firms, depends on managers to develop organizational systems and practices that bring out the best in people and to apply human talents and the firm's other resources toward sustaining a competitive advantage over time. *Management and Organizational Behavior* provides examples, theories, insights, and practices that will help you achieve a productive and satisfying life within organizations, whether or not you aspire to be a manager. The emphasis is on helping you first to understand the range of human behavior and managerial practices in a variety of organizational contexts and second to develop the judgment and skills you need to succeed as an organizational performer both in managing your own behavior and at times managing to guide the behavior of others.

WHAT PURPOSE DO ORGANIZATIONS SERVE?

organization
A group of people working toward a common objective.

Organizations are the product of human ingenuity, created to serve one or more specific needs of a community, be it a neighborhood, a state, or multiple nations. An **organization** is a group of people working toward a common objective of providing value to the people served. Business organizations of even modest size create systems to use financial and technical resources to provide products, services, and/or experiences valued by one or more segment of society, including customers, owners, and employees.

So defined, the local McDonald's restaurant is an organization created to provide fast access to prepared food of consistent quality, at reasonable prices, in a clean and cheerful eating environment. McDonald's also provides employment for hundreds of thousands of people and rewards for its franchise owners and corporate investors. Although serving different purposes, the public school is an organization, as is the community bank, hospital, professional baseball team, and fire department. Churches, the Rotary, the NAACP, and fraternal service clubs are organizations that serve the spiritual or social needs of members and in the process often provide public services that create benefits for nonmembers.

Business Firms Serve Themselves by Serving Customers

Throughout this book, we will focus on organizations that are goal striving and that hire employees to serve the needs of customers or clients. By focusing on serving customers, organizations indirectly help society when they accomplish the purpose for which they were created. Management philosopher Peter Drucker identifies in simple terms the common purpose of private enterprise:

> *To know what a business is we have to start with its purpose. Its purpose must lie outside itself. In fact, it must lie in society since business enterprise is an organ of society. There is only one valid definition of business purpose: to create a customer.*[2]

When an organization is in its start-up phase, the founder or founders are usually fixated on one narrowly defined customer-focused goal. For Netscape, the goal is to become the browser of choice for navigating the Internet. For Dell, it is to be the premier maker of computers custom-outfitted to customer specifications through mail order. Nevertheless, simplistic goals and strategies—those that overemphasize the things that made a firm successful in its early history—are positively related with performance during the early stages of an organization's development, but detrimental as the firm grows. What happens is that the organization becomes preoccupied with a single goal and factor, such as marketing, to the neglect of other factors, such as R&D and manufacturing.[3]

During every organization's early years, energies and resources are focused on making viable the concept around which the organization was created. In the case of business firms, this means designing the technology or processes that create products and services of value to customers, finding financing, and working to secure a position in the market against competitors. Profits are the reward

Challenge of Change

The Battle Between Gates's Microsoft and Grove's Intel

Serendipity at times plays a role in organizational success. The successes of Microsoft and Intel were boosted by a decision IBM made in 1981. Rather than develop its own technology in personal computers, IBM made a deal to purchase the MS-DOS operating system from fledgling Microsoft and the microprocessor chip from Intel. IBM's contracts did not prevent either Microsoft or Intel from selling their products to other customers. Thus, hundreds of firms produced PC clones. Today Microsoft (in software) and Intel (in hardware) lead the pack in personal computing. IBM is a distant also ran with no competitive advantage (*Fortune* ranked IBM 997 of its largest 1000 companies in market value added— minus $8.9 billion from 1985–1995).

Gates was still twentysomething when he cofounded the Microsoft organization. Says Gates, "I think the success of Microsoft has come from knowing [that technology and business] have a relationship with each other. The two sides drive each other. I think business is very simple. Profit. Loss. Take the sales, subtract the costs, you get this big positive number. The math is quite straightforward." This simple approach to math has enabled thousands of Microsoft employees to become millionaires.

Although "soft" Bill Gates may be the richest person in America, "hard" Intel dominates the field of microprocessors and may displace the apparent supremacy of Microsoft. Through innovation Intel has grown into the biggest and richest chip maker in the world, a firm that sells two "Intel Inside" computers every

second. The Intel strategy is twofold: Create new demand for PCs, and preserve high profit margins by speeding up the shift from one generation of microprocessor to the next, making it difficult for competition to catch up. To improve margins and revenue, CEO Andy Grove moved Intel from simply making microprocessors (the chip that provides computing power) to providing the entire computer for computer marketers such as IBM, Compaq, and Dell to place inside their branded boxes.

By providing all the circuitry short of the software operating system, Intel has become arguably the most powerful force in the PC industry. Says the chairman of a big computer maker: "Everybody has been hassling Gates about Microsoft's monopoly [of software]. Microsoft doesn't have half the leverage that Intel has today." Grouses another PC executive: "If you want a system [that's state-of-the-art], you have one choice. You buy the Intel box because they're doing the chip, the board, the mechanicals, everything."

Software. Hardware. Who really dominates the PC industry? The name on the outside of the box seems to make little difference in this battle for what's inside and what the inside will do.

Sources: Robert D. Hof, "Intel Unbound," *Business Week* (October 9, 1995), pp. 148–154; William J. Cook with David Bowermaster, "The New Rockefeller," *U.S. News & World Report* (February 15, 1993), pp. 64–69; and "Microsoft May Lose Grip on Windows," *New York Times* (February 25, 1993).

and reinforcement for taking the risk in which enterprise managers bet they will be able to better serve customers than can competitors. If a firm is to create wealth for its investors, its profits must be greater than its cost of capital, otherwise the business destroys resources.[4] During the period from 1985 to 1995, Coca-Cola was the number one wealth generator, and General Motors was the biggest destroyer of wealth of the *Fortune 1000* companies.[5]

Bill Gates of Microsoft did a great job originally of commercializing MS-DOS and developing applications software to run on the DOS operating system platform and then later upgrading customers to advanced systems such as Windows 95.[6] But chip maker Intel seems to be gaining the upper hand in the competitive battle to dominate personal computing (see the Challenge of Change box). As to

Fortune's 1995 wealth-generation scorecard, Microsoft was number 5 (which made Gates the richest person in America) and Intel was number 18, fantastic rankings for relatively young organizations.

Once success for the emerging firm takes hold and growth takes off, managers often branch out to offer products or services beyond those that established the original business. The firm then runs the risk of becoming unfocused, of trying to be too many things to too many people. To survive the complexity brought on by growth, the firm's managers turn to focusing more on strategies for positioning products within the competitive marketplace. They design a rational organization structure, establish policies and procedures for consistent handling of recurrent events, and give attention to nurturing an organizational culture that embodies the beliefs and values on which they plan to build success. "In the past, organizations have been structured around largely autonomous, self-contained, traditional functions such as accounting, finance, human resources, law, marketing, strategic planning, and so on. While important, they are no longer the building blocks of today's organizations."[7] Such forces require that every organization periodically refocus its mission and goals.

Purpose Is Focused by Mission and Goals

mission
An organization's fundamental purpose, articulated to define the nature of the business and unify human and other resources.

An organization's **mission** articulates its fundamental purpose in such a way that it both defines the business of the enterprise and unifies the use of human, technical, and financial resources. A well-framed mission provides a sense of purpose and establishes parameters that focus effort and resources. For example, pharmaceutical giant Merck states its mission in life-enhancing terms: "We are in the business of preserving and improving human life. All of our actions must be measured by our success in achieving this." In the early days of Apple Computer, cofounder Steve Jobs articulated for the organization a lofty mission: "To make a contribution to the world by making tools for the mind that advance humankind." Clearly these missions focus on serving specific needs of society.[8]

Choosing a mission is not a one-time decision. Any organization's mission statement is open to change as needs shift and new technologies displace old products and services. Hewlett-Packard began business in a garage in 1938 with a focus on making more accurate measuring instruments; today its primary emphasis is on computing and imaging, and H-P is the world leader in computer printers. For many firms whose success in the 1980s was dependent on Department of Defense contracts, the quick thaw of the Cold War in the early 1990s caused them to search for ways of transferring their technological capabilities to civilian applications.

superordinate goals
The highest goals of an organization, fundamental desired outcomes that enable managers to assess performance relative to its mission.

Beyond defining its mission, founders and top managers are responsible for articulating the organization's fundamental values, goals, and guiding concepts. Such statements provide a sense of direction, conveying how the game of business is to be played by organization members. **Superordinate goals** are the highest goals of the organization—its fundamental desired outcomes stated in ways that enable managers to measure and assess specific performance targets relative to overall mission aspirations.

Favoring simplicity over complexity, General Electric Chief Executive John "Jack" Welch developed two key superordinate goals to help focus what had become an unwieldy diversified business. His goals: to achieve number one or two global market share in each of its lines of business and to be the low cost producer in each.[9] Welch lamented, "I saw businesses that were No. 5 in the marketplace, not even No. 3, that we were holding on to as a shrine to our past."[10] Welch's goals enabled GE to weed

■■■■■■ **EXHIBIT 1–1**

*Important Stakeholder
Groups*

All organizations interact
with various stakeholder
groups. Some of these
stakeholders or constituency
groups, such as employees
and managers, function as
insiders. Others are clearly
external and seek to
constrain the organizations's
behaviors, as do watchdog
advocacy groups and certain
government regulatory
agencies. Still others are both
internal and external, such
as alliances and joint
ventures with other firms
that may serve as suppliers or
customers or true partners in
producing a joint product.

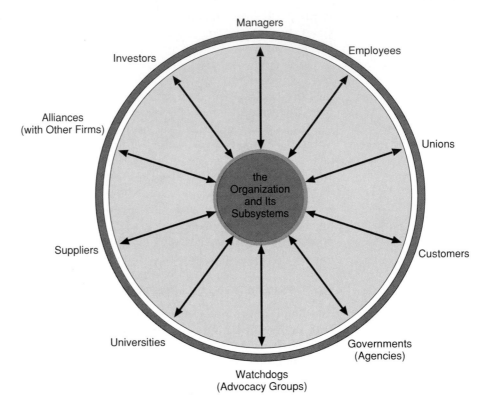

out weak, underperforming product lines to focus each product division as if it were
a small company. Welch wrote in one annual report, "What we are trying relentlessly
to do is get that small-company soul—and small-company speed—inside our big-
company body." So far under Welch's decade and a half of leadership, GE has
slashed employment by 100,000 and increased revenue and profits about fourfold
(and was *Fortune's* number two wealth generator in the 10 years up to 1995). GE
demonstrates that a clearly articulated superordinate goal simplifies understanding
of the organization's purpose and focuses employee behavior.

Organizations Work to Benefit Multiple Stakeholders

stakeholders
Members of identifiable
clusters of people who have
economic and/or social
interests in the behaviors
and performance of a
specific organization.

Formulating goals in organizations is complicated by the need to balance the interests of various groups who have a stake in its actions and outcomes. **Stakeholders** are definable clusters of people who have an economic and/or social interest
in the behavior and outcomes of the organization. Exhibit 1–1 identifies 10 stakeholder constituencies common to business firms. Stakeholders can be either
external or internal. External stakeholders include suppliers, customers, competitors, regulators, special-interest groups, government, and society. Managers and
employees are internal stakeholders. Investors in common stock might be either,
depending on their degree of influence over organizational actions and their investment goals.[11] Shareholders in large firms are usually outside investors.
Smaller firms tend to have more inside investors, so that owner and manager
goals coincide.

An important challenge for managers is to identify the relevant stakeholders and to operate the business in ways that optimize the returns to each group. Such decisions are often made in the context of considerable pressure and conflict created by each stakeholder group pursuing its own interests.[12] Owners/investors want to maximize wealth generation (nominally profits) and minimize costs, but employees want to maximize personal income and security, which is a cost paid as salaries, wages, bonuses, and fringe benefits. Sometimes the interests of these stakeholders are in conflict—external investors are concerned about financial performance, while managers may be more interested in surviving in a high-status, highly paid position. One way to balance these apparent conflicts is to work aggressively for continuous improvement, being ever mindful of adding value to customers.

WHY STUDY MANAGEMENT AND ORGANIZATIONAL BEHAVIOR?

As a person who has chosen to read this book, the chances are better than nine to one that over the next 30 to 40 years you will spend half your daylight hours (or evenings if you prefer) working for organizations. Whether or not you look forward to that prospect, the reality is that organizations of people working collectively for a common purpose long ago displaced individual toilers as the providers of goods and services. Organizations are the dominant generators of employment and economic wealth (in the case of business firms) or the re-allocators of income and wealth (in the case of governments).

The magnitude to which organizations have become center stage to the lives of people is a phenomenon of the past century or so, especially for women who for the most part were neither counted as part of the work force nor career-oriented until recently. Before and during the 1800s, people generally worked at agricultural tasks or were individual artisans and shopkeepers. While about half the world's population still live in villages largely unaffected by organizational life, as an educated adult the quality of your life will be dependent on the quality of organizations with whom you regularly interact.

Organizational Behavior (OB) Provides a Road Map

organizational behavior
OB for short, refers to the behaviors of individuals and groups within an organization, and the interactions between the organization and environmental forces.

Because organizations dominate society, you increase your odds of being meaningfully involved with organizations if you formally study how they function. In effect, the study of organizational behavior provides a road map to the many twists, turns, and detours that make life in organizations both complex and exciting. **Organizational behavior** (often referred to as **OB**) refers to the behavior of individuals and groups within organizations and the interaction between organizations and their external environments. Organizational behavior constitutes a behavioral science field of study that borrows its core concepts from disciplines such as psychology, sociology, social psychology, and anthropology. These behavioral science disciplines have extensive research foundations that explain human behavior using the scientific method as an investigative tool (see Appendix A at the end of the book).

People bring to their work in organizations their hopes and dreams as well as their fears and frustrations. Much of the time people around you may appear to be acting quite rationally, doing their fair share of work, and going about their tasks in a civil manner. But often, without warning, one or more of your colleagues may appear distracted, their work slips, and they become snappy or unpleasant. Worse,

Dilbert □ Scott Adams

Source: Reprinted with special permission of United Features Syndicate, Inc.

you may find that someone has taken advantage of you to further his own personal aims. Or your manager may not seem to be treating everyone fairly, and obviously singles out some for favored treatment. Occasionally you are likely to get caught up in organizational changes that may involve reassignments or even layoffs. Such a range of human behaviors makes life in organizations perplexing. But those who know what to look for and have some advance ideas about how to cope with the pressures caused by others are more likely to respond in ways that are functional, less stressful, and perhaps even career advancing.

Students of organizational behavior seek to improve the effectiveness of organizations through the application of behavioral science concepts and research. The assumption that organizational behavior can be improved by study and analysis is based on the premise that behavior is not completely random. Rather, it represents mutual dependencies or cause-and-effect links that can be anticipated, sometimes predicted, and often influenced within limits. A comprehensive knowledge of organizational behavior helps prepare managers or aspiring managers for the tasks of influencing and transforming organizational systems.

Management Provides Direction and Organization

management
The practice of organizing, directing, and developing people, technology, and financial resources to provide products and services through organizational systems.

The practice of management is thousands of years old. But the formal study of management and organizational behavior is a product of the twentieth century (see Appendix A). **Management** is the practice of directing, organizing, and developing people, technology, and financial resources in task-oriented systems that provide services and products to others. Managers are the ones who practice management. For the foreseeable future, two forces of change complicate the actions managers choose in their efforts to guide their organizations and keep them viable. First, the speed of change on practically all fronts is accelerating, from technological developments to competitive strategies. Second, the forces that affect organizational performance, such as governmental actions and the expectations and behavior of employees, are becoming more complex and thus less controllable.

The speed and complexity of change are what make life in organizations challenging and uncertain. However, as a partial offset to these forces of change, our knowledge of behavior in organizations has increased exponentially in the last half of the twentieth century. Knowledge of organizational behavior and management techniques enables managers and nonmanagerial professionals alike to be better informed and more prepared to cope with the challenges they encounter. Research provides clues as to why people behave as they do in organizational settings and creates a more systematic understanding of the factors that affect performance. Practical applications of behavioral research help managers improve the probability that their influence will be effective.

Knowledge Promotes Socially Responsible Behavior

Because organizations are a collection of human decisions and behaviors, none is perfect and 100 percent predictable. Unlike a finely tuned machine, the inputs to performance as well as performance itself vary over time. One source of variation that frustrates some is the clash between personal values (integrity) and the things that people are pressured to do on behalf of the organization. Employees may be more motivated to work diligently for organizations that fulfill socially desirable purposes than for firms whose managers define their principal objective as profit taking or engaging in practices that question ethical norms. Two contrasting examples underscore managerial values and the benefits of being socially responsible.

On the positive side, Solectron Corp., a contract manufacturer of high-tech components, is dedicated to serving its customers with fast, flexible, reliable products manufactured to their specifications. As explained by founding CEO Winston Chen, "Manufacturing is our number one priority. We learn the best skills, the best techniques in the whole world, from American companies, from Japanese companies. And we help our customers by letting them focus on what they do best [which is usually the design and marketing of products]."[13] This focused purpose and these guiding values enabled this Silicon Valley firm to be an early winner of the prestigious Malcolm Baldrige National Quality Award—the first California business to win this coveted prize. The Baldrige award, created by the Malcolm Baldrige National Quality Improvement Act of 1987, has been called "the most important catalyst for transforming American business" by encouraging process documentation and evaluation and continuously improving contributors to quality.[14]

In contrast, Sears, Roebuck and Co.—once the world's largest retailer in the era before Wal-Mart—sometimes compromises its responsibility to consumers. As growth slowed and Sears reported a net loss of $4 billion early in the 1990s, managers struggled to find ways to reposition the firm against competitors.[15] In its overemphasis on increasing revenue and profits, Sears was charged by the California attorney general for routinely performing unnecessary repairs on customers' autos. Sears agreed to an $8 million out-of-court settlement. The alleged practice of selling unnecessary repairs was apparently driven by a quota system—a sales maximization goal—imposed on its 72 auto repair centers in California.[16]

Ryder provides L'eggs Products with comprehensive transportation and distribution systems to efficiently and effectively deliver the hosiery manufacturer's products to clients. This supplier/customer relationship makes Ryder an external stakeholder in L'eggs and Sara Lee Corporation, L'egg's corporate parent. (Photo: Ryder Dedicated Logistics; and operating unit of Ryder Systems, Inc.)

Beware the Law of Effect

law of effect
People tend to behave in ways that enable them to attain the goals for which they are rewarded.

The **law of effect** is the behavioral tendency for people to persistently work to attain the goals for which they are rewarded.[17] But not all managerially imposed goals and rewards promote socially responsible behaviors. For Solectron, the goal of customer service and continuous improvement enhanced the total business system and increased value to all stakeholders. The Sears goal of meeting sales quotas diminished organizational performance and left numerous automotive repair customers worse off.

Moral judgments and ethical behavior occur within a complex, often politicized and pressure-driven organizational environment (see the Eye on Ethics box for Mark Whitacre's disturbing experience at Archer Daniels Midland). Employees who resist expediency pressures and continuously behave in socially responsible ways frame their ethical judgments on an awareness of how organizations function as dynamic open systems.

HOW DO ORGANIZATIONS BEHAVE AS SYSTEMS?

system
An integrated whole formed by a set of interrelated elements and interacting subsystems.

The basic model we use to help you understand how organizations behave is that of an integrated system. A **system** is a set of interrelated and interacting elements and subsystems that form an integrated whole. Consider a simple mechanical system. An automobile can be conceptualized as an integrated system providing personal transportation made up of elements such as metal and glass and various combustion, exhaust, and electrical subsystems. Each element or subsystem contributes to the whole; without each functioning effectively, the whole system will not work properly.

Systems Depend on Input-Transformation-Output Processes

organizations
Complex forms of social systems comprised of people, other resources and subsystems integrated for the purpose of transforming inputs into mission-relevant outputs.

Organizations are a form of *social system* made up of people and a variety of resources and subsystems integrated for the purpose of transforming inputs into mission satisfying outputs. For example, employee selection, training, evaluation, and

Eye on
Ethics

*Mark Whitacre—Competitors over Customers
at Archer Daniels Midland?*

Marc Whitacre was recruited from a chemical company to manage a new biochemical products division at Archer Daniels Midland Co. (ADM). With his Ph.D. degree in biochemistry and two degrees in animal science, Whitacre was a natural fit at ADM, a converter of farm products. Whitacre's goal was to manage ADM's entry into the business of making lysine and to become the world market leader in an industry dominated by two Japanese firms and with no U.S. producers. (Lysine is an amino acid derived from corn and used to promote lean muscle growth in livestock.)

Whitacre was attracted to ADM because of its lack of bureaucracy and reputation for speed in making decisions. With an investment of over $150 million, Whitacre and his team were able to design, engineer, and build a manufacturing facility near Decatur, Illinois, and get into production in less than a year and a half. To gain market share, Whitacre set up a worldwide sales and distribution system—then cut prices to win big orders. A price war broke out, with prices falling from $1.30 a pound to 60 cents a pound, causing ADM to lose several million dollars a month in its lysine business.

About a year after the business was into production, Mark Whitacre was approached by Mick Andreas (ADM's vice chairman) and Jim Randall (ADM's president) and told to take lessons from Terry Wilson. They said, "I should look to Terry as a mentor, someone to teach me some things about how ADM does business. It was phrased just that way: How ADM does business." On their first meeting, Wilson asked Whitacre to set up meetings with the two largest competitors. The first meetings were in Japan, then Hawaii, then Mexico City. By Mexico City, managers from the two Japanese firms had warmed up to their relationship with Wilson and Whitacre. After sharing data about production capacity, market size, pricing, and margins, Wilson concluded the three were losing $200 million because of the price cutting. Whitacre said Wilson then proposed:

"Well, gentlemen, there's $200 million that we're giving to our customers. In other words, the customer is benefiting, not the people who spent hundreds of millions of dollars building these plants."

Then he said something that was a common phrase around ADM, a phrase that turns up lots of times on the tapes [explained below]. It was our philosophy. And this was it: *"The competitor is our friend, and the customer is our enemy."* There are tapes of Mick Andreas quoting his father [ADM's chairman] as always saying this.

Back in Decatur, several people from Terry Wilson's division came up to Whitacre and said, half-jokingly, "Oh, you and Terry have been at one of your price-fixing meetings." Bothered by the apparent price-fixing implications of how ADM conducted business, Mark Whitacre became a mole for the FBI, later blowing the whistle on ADM. Embittered by the experience, he told *Fortune:*

For 2 1/2 years I worked undercover as an informer for the FBI. In numerous sessions, at which my bosses, colleagues, and competitors were present, I recorded conversations about fixing prices and about stealing technology from other companies. It's all there, all on the tapes. And it's already caused me more stress and grief than anything I ever could have imagined. I've been fired from my job and accused of stealing millions. My family has been threatened; we've been forced to move. My phones are probably tapped, and I have been hounded by the press.

Ethical dilemmas are seldom neat and tidy. Whose or what ethics do you question at ADM?

Source: Mark Whitacre as told to Ronald Henkoff, "My Life as a Corporate Mole for the FBI," *Fortune* (September 4, 1994), pp. 52–62.

EXHIBIT 1–2   *Model of an Open Systems Organization*

Assume the organization consists of the subsystems within the shaded box. Various inputs are imported from the environment, which are then transformed by the firm's subsystems into products and services. These are subsequently exported to different sectors of the environment in the form of outputs.

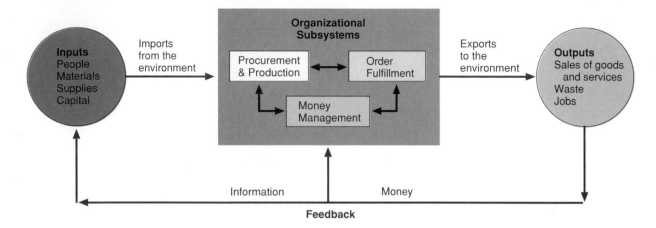

A furnace operator at U.S. Steel prepares slabs for rolling. As an open system, U.S. Steel faced enormous pressure from low-priced foreign competitors in the 1980s. As a dynamic system, it was able to change to meet the competition by investing in modern equipment and technology, improving quality, participating in joint ventures, closing unprofitable facilities, and trimming its work force. (Photo: Courtesy USX Corporation.)

rewards make up the processes performed by the human resource subsystem. The human resource subsystem in turn interacts with the product development, production, marketing, finance, and accounting subsystems.

Any business organization is an *input-transformation-output system* that takes in resources, converts them into goods and services, and passes along these outputs to customers and others. In the simplified model of Exhibit 1–2, each of the three functional subsystems in the shaded box represents several departments or work units that contribute to the transformation or conversion process. Inputs include resources such as people, capital, land, buildings, equipment, services, materials, and technology. Transformation involves the work of the firm's people and subsystems to produce or convert inputs into value-added outputs of products and services. Some of these outputs are sold to customers, and some must be disposed of as waste by-products.

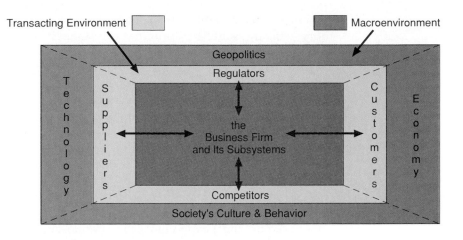

Key Environmental Forces That Affect Businesses

Business firms conduct exchanges directly with persons and entities in their immediate transacting environment. In the more distant macroenvironment are forces that indirectly influence the behavior of the firm by altering behavior of the transacting forces.

Organization Systems Are Open and Dynamic

closed systems
Systems that operate without environmental or outside disturbances.

open systems
Systems influenced by external pressures and inputs, making them more complex and difficult to control than closed systems.

dynamic system
Any system that changes over time as structures and functions adapt to external disturbances and conditions.

Systems can be either closed or open. **Closed systems** operate without interference from outside their boundaries. For example, within a building, we know that each time we flip a specific switch, the light on that circuit will turn on unless the bulb is burned out. **Open systems** are subject to pressures and inputs from outside their boundaries and thus are more complex and more difficult to control than closed systems.[18] A **dynamic system** changes over time—its essential elements, functions, and structures shift and adapt to external disturbances and conditions. All business organizations are thus open dynamic systems. As an open system, firms are subjected to outside forces by competitors, customers, suppliers, and regulators. As a dynamic system, a business can change its product mix, enter new markets, restructure its sources of financing, hire new managers, or redesign its compensation policy in anticipation of or response to outside forces.

Microsoft can be thought of as an open dynamic system continuously working to improve its line of software and computing services in an effort to stay ahead of competitors. Yet each Microsoft manager defines his or her own subsystem differently by selecting a boundary that makes sense in terms of his or her desired sphere of influence. A purchasing manager attends to a different set of external constituents than does a sales manager or engineer.

Systems Interact with Environmental Forces

Organizations are linked with environmental forces through exchanges or transactions. Exhibit 1–3 identifies the key environmental forces that impact any business system—suppliers, regulators, competitors, and customers. The exhibit also identifies the more distant macroenvironmental forces—those that indirectly influence behavior in any one organization, such as technology, the economy, geopolitical behavior, and social behavior.

boundary-spanning transactions
Those actions that link an organization to specific external sectors, exchanges that make the system dynamic and open.

Most links to the transacting forces occur through specialized subsystems and the people who hold those jobs. Purchasing agents transact with suppliers; salespeople with customers; corporate lawyers with regulators, customers, and vendors; and financial officers with bankers and investors. The management of open dynamic systems requires careful attention to these important **boundary-spanning transactions** that link the organization to specific external sectors. As circumstances change, the relative importance of boundary-spanning links will shift. In period 1 the critical need might be to maintain the supply of a critical component from vendors. With the shifting of priorities over time, in period 2 obtaining additional financing might be most critical.

An organizational system is interdependent with environmental forces because both are influenced by each other. To illustrate, imagine that BioInstruments, a manufacturer of medical diagnostic instruments, depends on a select few suppliers for the parts and components that go into its final assembled instruments. If even one supplier who is the sole source of a component interrupts the supply flow, then BioInstruments' production schedules are thrown off. Shipments of products ordered by hospitals and clinics will be delayed, which may lead to canceled orders or even layoffs if the delay stretches too long. In one study of customer transactions with supplier organizations, researchers found an interesting result: Customers who are more involved with their suppliers were more dissatisfied if the product performance did not meet expectations than were peripherally involved customers.[19]

In a different scenario, a competitor begins to market an improved model of a diagnostic tool at a lower price. Sales of the BioInstruments model drop precipitously, and unsold inventories begin to stockpile. This ties up working capital, adding to costs. Unless sales of alternative products take up the slack, the firm will begin to lay off employees to bring costs into line with reduced revenues. Morale will likely decline, and employee stress over future uncertainty will increase.

This latter scenario is common in plants designed to produce only one product, such as one automobile model. Such pressures make the manager's job challenging, forcing him or her to change roles throughout the day. Let's examine what managers do to carry out their task of analyzing and influencing the system.

WHAT DO SUCCESSFUL MANAGERS DO?

manager
A systems diagnoser and influencer who works with people and other resources to perform tasks that achieve goals.

A **manager** can be thought of as a systems diagnoser and influencer who works with people and other resources to carry out tasks and achieve goals. This implies that the manager must understand the totality of his or her organization and then influence system components such as tasks, technology, structure, and people to achieve desired outputs. Additionally, managers must be aware of the environments in which their systems operate and how external forces alter internal elements and processes. Managers engage in a dynamic search to align the organization with its changing environment and to arrange internal resources to fit that alignment.[20]

By describing managers as system influencers, we recognize that managers do not have total control over that part of the organization for which they are responsible. Many factors other than a manager's actions (often attempts to influence others) determine why organizational outcomes unfold as they do. No manager can absolutely predict and control environmental forces, and even internal forces that involve human behavior are often unpredictable and thwart attempts at influence by managers. Now to help you ponder some personal managerial issues, spend a couple of minutes completing the Your Turn exercise.

The Rational View: Managers Plan, Organize, Direct, and Control

"If you ask a manager what he does, he will most likely tell you that he plans, organizes, coordinates, and controls. Then watch what he does. Don't be surprised if you can't relate what you see to these four words."[21] This contradiction, observed by Henry Mintzberg, suggests two contrasting views of managers: the rational heroic view and the chaotic view.

YOUR TURN

Do You Have the Right Stuff to Be a Manager?

Envision yourself in a professional work environment. Which of the following would you like to experience at work? Check yes or no for each statement.

	Yes	No
1. To perform a great quantity of work at a hectic pace, driven to keep on top of changing demands.	☐	☐
2. A workday with a great variety of unrelated tasks, fragmented into brief encounters with a number of people.	☐	☐
3. To react to issues and problems that are largely unplanned and initiated by others.	☐	☐
4. To receive more information than you generate, and to spend as much time with people in other departments as you do with people in your department.	☐	☐
5. Verbal communication (whether face to face, in meetings, or on the phone) more than written reports, mail, and correspondence.	☐	☐
6. To feel that you are a puppet with others pulling on the strings, yet somehow you still manage to move in the direction you want to go.	☐	☐

Scoring: These six statements describe how typical managers actually work. If you checked yes 5 or 6 times, you have the personal characteristics that will enable you to feel comfortable with a manager's responsibilities. If you checked no 5 or 6 times, you are likely to feel uncomfortable with the demands of being a manager. With 3 or 4 yes answers, it's a mixed call. As you read the forthcoming section on the chaotic view of management, you'll discover why a manager is more likely to answer yes to all of the above.

Since the early writings of Henri Fayol, researchers have presented a picture of the manager as one who engages in reflective planning, takes time to carefully organize structures and systems, directs and coordinates an orchestrated flow of activities, and exercises timely control to keep critical elements in harmony.[22] (See Appendix A at the end of the book for historic perspectives on management.) According to this rational heroic view, the manager is expected to have an overall feel for where the unit is going, know what is going on, and accept responsibility for problem solving and the department's success or failure.

Such a rational heroic view of management may have been valid in slower and simpler times, but today's organizations are subjected to fast rates of change and increasing complexity. For example, managers in fast-changing, high-technology environments have learned to focus on concept development of new products and keep specifications as flexible as possible until late in a project so as to maintain flexibility and responsiveness.[23]

All forces considered, the rational heroic model places too much emphasis and responsibility on the manager and not enough on teams and nonmanagers within the organization. When managers act as if they should be the only ones "in control," they deprive subordinates of job challenges and create delays in decisions. Heroism sets up a self-defeating cycle: The more the manager commands responsibility for departmental success, the more likely subordinates will be to yield it. This leaves the manager with more to do, with fewer creative and problem-solving inputs from those who carry out the work.[24]

The Chaotic View: Managerial Life Is Intense, Fragmented, and Complex

Chaos well describes the circumstances under which today's managers flourish. Tom Peters devoted an entire book to the premise that managers and organizations "thrive on chaos."[25] *Fortune* magazine recently splashed across its cover the headline "Managing amid chaos: The corporate world seems to be going crazy, as companies cut costs but demand more."[26] Amid this environment of chaos, Henry Mintzberg found that instead of being the reflective and systematic planners described in traditional books on management, most managers are actually caught up in various intense, brief, disconnected activities. Few managers work for very long without interruption—by phone calls, people dropping by their office, impromptu meetings, and other fragmented events. In observations of chief executives, half of their activities lasted less than nine minutes. Over 90 percent of their verbal contacts were ad hoc—short, unplanned episodes that shifted quickly from one topic to another.

Managers prefer action to reflection, according to both Mintzberg and Kotter.[27] The "plans" of managers often exist largely in their heads. Managers have several informational media at their disposal (documents, telephone calls, scheduled meetings, unscheduled meetings, and observational tours). Of these options, they prefer oral mediums over written information. Mail and reports are usually dispensed with by a quick scan. Verbal contacts with others are the manager's principal source of information—gossip, ideas, opinions, and facts. From such contacts emerge a sense of direction and, ultimately, actions.

Managers Work in Multiple Roles

Whether CEO, vice president, supervisor, coach, bishop, dean, superintendent, or crew chief, all managers share common work characteristics. Writes Mintzberg, "All these managers are vested with formal authority over an organizational unit. From formal authority comes status, which leads to various interpersonal relations, and from these comes access to information. Information, in turn, enables the manager to make decisions and strategies for his unit."[28]

Having formal authority and status simply sets the stage for managerial activity, which is classified into 10 unique roles. Managerial roles are those distinct patterns of behavior that managers engage in while working at different tasks. As events and needs shift throughout the manager's working day, the roles keep changing as well. Exhibit 1–4 identifies Mintzberg's 10 specific managerial roles, classifying them as three primary dimensions: interpersonal, informational, and decisional.

The Interpersonal Roles.   Managers interact in different ways with people. Interpersonal roles involve three key functions served by managers when representing the organization and communicating with people: figurehead, leader, and liaison.

Figurehead.   All managers at times play a figurehead role by participating in ceremonial duties. Some of these duties are routine and have little if any apparent impact on work-unit performance, such as when the business school dean puts in an appearance at a university party honoring the retirement of the dean of science. But when the sales vice president has lunch with a sales manager and key customer, the figurehead role is important to goal achievement and work-unit performance.

First-level managers often assist workers with technical expertise. Here a Japanese technical advisor examines raw tire material with a technician at Bridgestone's La Vergne, Tennessee, works. (Photo: Milt and Joan Mann/Cammeramann International, Ltd.)

■■■■ **EXHIBIT 1–4**

Mintzberg's Ten Managerial Roles

The manager's job is far from routine. Mintzberg suggests that the job of manager can be broken into ten identifiable roles, each within one of three clusters. As the manager goes about performing his or her job, there is a general flow from interacting with people to handling information to making decisions.

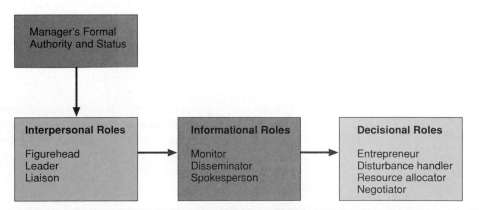

Source: Reprinted by permission of *Harvard Business Review*. An exhibit from "The Manager's Job: Folklore and Fact," by Henry Mintzberg (March–April 1990). Copyright © 1990 by the President and Fellows of Harvard College, all rights reserved.

Leader.   When acting as a leader, the manager focuses on exerting influence over people. As leaders, managers strive to motivate and encourage team members to follow their agenda and to develop their people. Often leader effort overlaps the activities of other roles. (Chapter 14 provides a thorough discussion of leadership.)

Liaison.   The liaison role encompasses the manager's interactions with others outside his or her vertical chain of reporting relationships. Liaison activities typically involve lateral contacts, or attempts to influence peers in other parts of the organization. Observational studies typically find about half a manager's time is filled by discussions with peers in other parts of the organization.

The Informational Roles.   All organizations depend on information as the basis for making decisions and taking action. In fact, information may well be the most critical resource in *post-industrial societies* like our own.[29] The informational roles of a manager involve obtaining or exchanging relevant information as monitor, disseminator, or spokesperson.

Monitor.   The monitor role means scanning the environment, asking questions, maintaining a network of contacts, and in general finding out what is going on. It places the manager in the role of information collector and assimilator.

Disseminator.   When managers share information with unit members—especially proprietary or goal directing information—they are fulfilling the disseminator role. Selective dissemination also helps the manager build a power base, which can be good or bad depending on how that influence is exercised. (Power is the subject of Chapter 13.)

Spokesperson.   Managers are at work in the spokesperson role when they share information with influential people outside the unit. Being a spokesperson ranges from the chief financial officer making a speech before a group of visiting security analysts to the director of computer systems keeping the divisional manager informed of progress on a system changeover.

The Decisional Roles.   Making decisions is the natural consequence of working with the output of informational roles. Decisional roles are exercised when the manager acts on information to commit the organization to new courses of action, whether as entrepreneur, disturbance handler, resource allocator, or negotiator. (Chapter 12 examines ethical decision-making and problem-solving techniques.)

Entrepreneur.   The entrepreneurial role involves attempting to adjust the organization to its environment. Entrepreneurial behavior includes modifying the product line or repositioning products for a new customer segment, converting operations to a new technology, or altering the compensation scheme for salaried professionals. Entrepreneurial behavior exists at all levels and in all functions, in the public as well as the private sector.

Disturbance Handler.   While the entrepreneurial role causes managers to act as agents of change, the disturbance handler role typically draws them in involuntarily. A major breakdown in a critical machine, a union work stoppage, the bankruptcy of a key vendor may all be relatively unanticipated events that call on the manager to restore functionality and performance.

Resource Allocator. Whether initiated through entrepreneurial foresight or the compelling need to handle a threatening disturbance, the resource allocator role is one all managers perform. Resource allocations can be as far reaching as restructuring the organization or authorizing a capital expenditure for a new plant, or as mundane (yet politically charged) as assigning one member of the work unit to a vacant office with a window.

Negotiator. None of the other roles by itself prevents conflict. Thus, the manager inevitably shifts into the negotiator role when bargaining with a union steward over an employee grievance or working out a solution to a new product design dispute between engineering and manufacturing. Negotiations and the management of conflict are a way of life for managers. (Chapter 9 discusses conflict in interpersonal relationships.)

The 10 roles we've just discussed span the work activities of the manager. They provide clues to the abilities managerial aspirants must learn if they are to succeed. Yet there is a danger in decomposing the manager's job into a series of discrete roles. Real managerial success comes from integrating the roles so that behavior flows naturally across roles. In practice, the relative emphasis given to different roles depends on where the manager is within the organizational hierarchy and the pressures felt at any point in time.[30] A first-line supervisor is dependent primarily on liaison, monitor, disturbance handler, and negotiator roles. At the top of the organization, a manager is consumed more by the figurehead, leader, spokesperson, and entrepreneur roles.

HOW DO MANAGERS INFLUENCE ORGANIZATION SYSTEMS?

A key function of managing is to adapt or transform system elements in pursuit of adding value within a dynamic environment. In dynamic open systems—especially those feeling the effects of weak performance—system variables become misaligned with environmental forces and need to be realigned or changed.[31] Managers need to understand and diagnose their systems and then influence select variables to transform system capabilities.

Select Options for Changing an Organization

The key resource variables or capabilities that managers seek to influence and transform include tasks, technology, organization, people, and organizational culture. Exhibit 1–5 shows a model of these change options within a general systems framework. The model is intended to simplify the complexity of a real organization and serves as a conceptual framework to help decide where and how to make changes. Managers evaluate these key internal system elements in planning how they will bring about organizational innovation and improvement.

Tasks. Tasks are the jobs or work people do in pursuit of enterprise purpose. Tasks begin with goals and can be designed to be simple or complex, easy or difficult, physical or mental, and so on. The job of carpenters who specialize in cutting and nailing drywall to studs is simpler and less mentally challenging than the jobs of carpenters responsible for framing, roofing, and installing exterior siding. How managers design tasks is crucial to motivating and helping people achieve desired outputs.

━━━━━ **EXHIBIT 1–5**   *Resource Elements for Transforming Organizational Systems*

Every organization uses a few basic internal resources to convert and transform external inputs into value-added outputs. The five resource elements (people, tasks, technology, organization, and culture) are dynamically interactive—a change in one potentially affects the others. Managers not only work to keep these resource elements in balance, but they also use them to trigger changes that transform the entire system. The leaders in many firms are now trying to bring about a transformation to total quality, using these resource elements as their instruments of change.

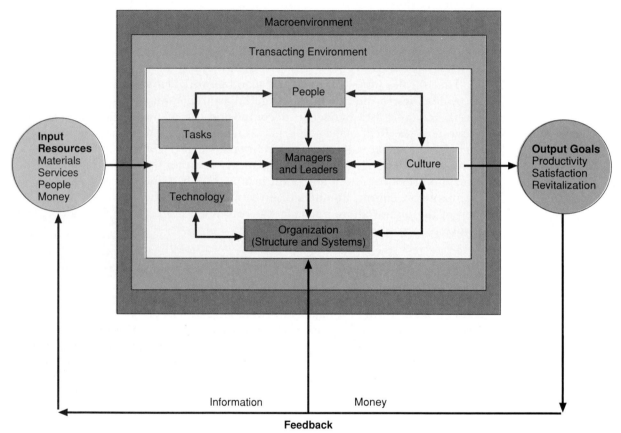

Technology.   Technology includes the knowledge, equipment, subsystems, and methods for accomplishing work tasks. In manufacturing, technology choices are matched to the expected quantity of outputs and methods for producing products, ranging from custom made to batch produced to systems for mass or continuous production. While computers, robots, and lasers are obvious examples, we also include the knowledge needed to use that hardware and software in our definition of *technology.*

People.   People energize and give life to systems. People make the fundamental decisions that influence system outputs. To begin with, managers have to decide how many people to employ in a certain task and what knowledge and skills they require. Managers are then responsible for selecting and training people who have or can develop the skills needed to achieve the organization's goals.

Organization. *Organization* as used here refers to a structural network and the processes that define and link key subsystems. It encompasses the communication and decision-making network among work units that guides and limits people's behavior within an organization's structure. An organization's structure is simplistically symbolized by a chart that depicts the authority and status relationships among people. Managers view structure in a broader way to include all those elements that help govern people's behavior at work. These include goals, plans, policies, and rules, as well as the authority network.

Organizational Culture. All of the foregoing elements combine to form a network of social systems, and from these evolve an organizational culture. By culture we mean the beliefs, values, and assumptions people have about their particular organization and the expected behavior within it. Culture includes the norms that influence the members' behavior and how they present themselves to the outside world.

Management—The Integrating Responsibility. In the center of this transformation network, we show *managers* and *leaders*. Traditionally, they are the ones responsible for planning, coordinating, organizing, controlling, and directing the other elements. They are responsible for ensuring that appropriate inputs are received and processed through the transformation system in timely ways. Managers are assessed in part on the extent to which their part of the system (typically a subsystem such as manufacturing or accounting) produces appropriate outputs that satisfy customers or users. At times, managers make significant breakthroughs in the way they go about analyzing systems and making change, as emphasized in the World Watch box on Japan's new bullet-train approach to product design.

Anticipate Mutual Dependency among System Elements

The planned changes managers make in a system to achieve intended results commonly lead to unintended second-order consequences. As part of its corporate restructuring in the early 1990s, General Motors executives decided to terminate the jobs of 240 machinists at its Lordstown, Ohio, parts plant and subcontract machining work to other firms. To send GM a message that management couldn't shift the cost of restructuring onto employees, the United Auto Workers union shut down the Lordstown plant with a 10-day strike. This caused nine auto assembly plants (including the only one making the popular Saturn) to close because of lack of parts, idling more than 43,000 workers.[32]

In the GM example, a planned change in one variable—organization—caused subsequent changes in tasks and technology. Because of its negative impact on people, machinists expanded the chain reaction, closing down the Lordstown plant and, through second-order consequences, nine other plants dependent on Lordstown for parts. When one system variable is changed, it is likely that some or all of the mutually dependent variables will also change.

Achieve Balance among Essential Output Goals

In diagnosing how and where to influence an organizational system, managers typically start with outputs because they are important to all organizations. For a business, outputs are goods and services that provide value to customers. All organizations try to produce outputs that meet the quality, quantity, and price expectations of customers. To do so, they need to set specific goals that address three output criteria: productivity, satisfaction, and revitalization.

**World
Watch**   *Japanese Business Reinvented with Bullet-Train Thinking*

In the 1980s, managers worldwide flocked to Japan's businesses to study techniques for bringing about continuous improvement leading to total quality management (TQM). But when Japan's economic bubble burst in 1991, and revenue growth stopped, managers scrambled to make radical cuts in costs. One firm made a major breakthrough that started a trend—bullet-train thinking.

Rather than provide ever more complex product features, the movement in Japan is now toward simplicity. Eiji Mikawa, president of Yokogawa Electric, a $1.7 billion revenue producer of industrial equipment, turned to the methods used to design and build *Shinkansen,* the bullet train of Japanese National Railways. *shinkansen* doubled speed by building a straight, wide, 311-mile track between Tokyo and Osaka and designing each car to be self-propelled. By designing train and track as a total system, travel time between Japan's largest cities was cut from six and one-half hours to three hours ten minutes.

By borrowing the concept of total redesign (rather than incremental improvement), Yokogawa discovered that how a product is designed can account for 80 percent of production costs. For its basic industrial recorder that oil refineries or paper mills use to measure temperature, flow rates, and pressure, a 22-member design team cut overall production costs 45 percent by simplifying features. A new die-casting method makes the hard plastic cover in just one piece—before it required 31 separate components. Redesigning the recorder's knobs eliminated 90 percent of the materials and 96 percent of the assembly-time requirements for these components. Reflects president Mikawa, "Like many Japanese companies, we had a tendency to make things too complicated. We were selling systems with features and accessories that our customers never used."

And who is now emulating Yokogawa's bullet-train design team concept? None other than General Electric, championed by GE's Chief Executive Jack Welch. At GE's jet engine division near Cincinnati, a total product redesign team produced efficiencies not possible by reengineering how engines were made. Because engineers were only looking at how engines were built, not designed, William Vareschi, vice president of finance, admitted: "We never, shamefully, even discussed that. We thought manufacturing productivity was just a manufacturing problem." Now teams are working to simplify everything about a product—that's the bullet-train approach.

Source: Ronald Henkoff, "New Management Secrets from Japan—Really," *Fortune* (November 27, 1995), pp. 135–146.

Productivity.   To put the concept of productivity into a managerial perspective, think of the output (product or service) that is the purpose for being in business. The output of IBM is principally computers, software, and computer-related services. For Citibank, output refers to the services of protecting deposits, providing loans and charge card accounts, and administering trusts. For Sears Roebuck, output is merchandising and selling apparel and household goods and services. As a starting point, productivity compares the level of output from one reporting period to another. For manufacturing, it is the number of units produced; for accounting, the information collected, organized, and disseminated; for research and development, the number of innovations patented and commercialized.

But in producing outputs, costs are incurred as inputs are consumed. Costs include both capital investments (in physical facilities) and operational expenses (which includes payroll and supplies or services consumed). Thus, a more mean-

Total quality management is not just for industry giants. Donald and Suzanne Sykes, co-founders of Marpac Industries, Inc. in Waldwick, New Jersey, instituted TQM in their small company, which manufactures plastic containers and dispensers. They stress to their 70-person staff that everything they make must be the best. They believe TQM has contributed significantly to the firm's ability to increase its customer base and sales despite the recession of the early 1990s. (Photo: © Alan Dorrow.)

productivity
Ratio of acceptable quality outputs to inputs consumed, a measure of how well the organization achieves its goals.

efficiency
Doing something right or getting the most output for the least input.

effectiveness
Producing the right output or doing things right to create value for stakeholders.

ingful concept of productivity refers to how outputs are achieved. **Productivity** is the ratio of outputs of acceptable quality to inputs consumed and is a measure of how well an organization attains its goals. Productivity depends on both efficiency and effectiveness.

Efficiency means doing things right, or getting the most output for the least input. Typical measures of efficiency are sales per employee, inventory turns per year, student-faculty ratios, and number of acceptable units produced per person-hour or per shift.

Effectiveness means producing the right outputs—those that are sufficiently valued by stakeholders to sustain the organization. For machine-tool company Cincinnati Milacron, producing robots proved not to be effective when its largest customer, General Motors, decided to make its own robots. For GM, producing the Saturn automobile has been effective for it pleases customers.

It is possible to have efficiency without effectiveness and vice versa. An accounting department might collect certain data very efficiently (at low cost), but it might not provide the data needed for managerial decision making. The ideal is to achieve a balance of effectiveness and efficiency, although effectiveness is usually more critical. Baldwin Locomotive was efficient at producing high-quality steam locomotives, but the firm stopped being effective (and went out of business) when it failed to shift to diesel technology. Compaq Computer had for years been losing sales to lower-cost rivals, when in 1992 it became committed to improving productivity by overhauling manufacturing methods, installing new information systems, and penetrating overseas sales markets. Within two years Compaq had leapt back to number one worldwide market share in personal computers.[33]

Satisfaction.   Another key goal of organizations is to keep stakeholders satisfied. **Satisfaction** refers to the overall positive feelings people have about an organization, whether as an employee, customer, supplier, or regulator.

Satisfaction can be measured informally by listening to people talk or by asking them how they feel about the organization. Satisfaction can also be measured by administering attitude surveys to employees, customers, and/or vendors. Or it can be inferred by studying employee data such as absenteeism, turnover, and number of grievances. Firms also measure customer satisfaction by examining trends in sales volume, number of product returns/complaints, or number of repeat purchases per customer.

One of the pervasive problems facing managers is to manage the relationship between productivity and satisfaction. Managers commonly think that happy people are productive people. However, research suggests otherwise, for the causality between satisfaction and productivity is low.[34] Instead, high productivity more often leads to satisfaction.[35] Here is clearly a case in which research overturns conventional beliefs.

Workers who are dissatisfied with their work and maybe even negative toward their employer can still be very productive. Assembly-line workers often typify this positive–negative combination. On the other hand, sometimes satisfied workers are not productive. You may know some tenured professors in this category! As you will study later on, research about empowerment and self-governing teams suggests that productivity and satisfaction often improve when management lightens up—less management can produce more results.[36]

Revitalization and Organizational Renewal.   A third major output criterion is the capacity of the organization to develop and renew itself. **Revitalization** refers to the ability to take care of tomorrow's problems as well as today's by renewing the strategies, resources, technology, and skills required for future success. Rather than deplete the resource base to get immediate results, companies must periodically or continually reinvest, renew, and reinvent.

Revitalization naturally occurs when a firm replaces worn-out or technically obsolete equipment. Revitalization also involves people, for without training and professional development of human resources, an organization slips in its capacity to compete. Reinvention occurs when firms invest in the research and development of new products and the improvement of internal processes (such as streamlining the number of steps required to pay accounts receivable).

Each of these output criteria—productivity, satisfaction, and revitalization—can be applied to individuals, groups, organizations, and even societies. The overall job of any manager is to identify clearly the output requirements of his or her system, to devise measures of efficiency and effectiveness, to develop core skills and capabilities within the organization to do the job well, to promote improvement and innovation, and to make changes when results fail to measure up.[37]

Both researchers and managers realize that the critical issues that affect organizational practices change with time. As issues emerge in the search for ways to improve organizational performance, some become the constant subject of discussions, conferences, workshops, and research agendas, and are eventually put into practice. Four such central themes concern managers who look beyond the 1990s to the twenty-first century.

WHAT IS THE CONTEXT FOR MANAGERS AND ORGANIZATIONS?

Every generation of managers faces a set of forces and issues that seems to dominate the context if not the content of many decisions. Most informed managers are aware that their organizations have to contend with external forces such as:

- The acceleration of technology that affects work processes as well as the development and positioning of products in the marketplace.
- The tenacity of competing interests, not just as rivals jockey to gain customers, but as constituent interest groups vie for resources or elevate conflict to dramatize their views.
- The swings in social behaviors that usually begin externally with shifts in expectations and values by one or more segments of society, whose members then affect organizations as employees, customers, suppliers, and regulators.
- The uncertainties of geopolitical and economic forces that in some situations flare up into aggressive hostilities and in others pull nations together in treaties and business relationships.

These broad forces of change take on greater specificity as they are perceived by managers to present immediate threats or opportunities to their organizations. As socio-techno-economic changes take on greater specificity, four thematic issues affect most managerial practices regardless of industry. The challenge of *managing change* has become a driving force affecting practically all organizational processes as pressures to change come from both external and internal sources. One force of change is *global business,* where organizations are caught up in global competition for customers and suppliers as the scope of business shifts to a worldwide stage. With the increased flow of people across national borders and pressures to safeguard the civil rights of all people, managers are expected to promote *human diversity* and equity. Finally, in spite of the complex pressures facing people in today's organizations, the expectation of *ethical behavior* is stronger today than in previous generations.

These four themes are woven throughout the fabric of this book. Detailed examples are provided in boxes under the headings of Challenge of Change, World Watch, Eye on Ethics and Dynamics of Diversity. You have already encountered examples of the first three. Now it's time for Dynamics of Diversity (see box). While each theme is a valid issue in its own right, there are threads of interdependency among them. Let's examine some of the forces within each.

Challenge of Change

For decades, Western firms have been driven by the belief that low cost was the route to increased market share, and that market share growth would transform economies of scale into higher profits. And yet the irony is that, on average, North American firms are more top heavy with layers of managers than, say, Asian firms. Thus, American costs are higher. Firms in the United States entered the 1990s with 1 manager per 8 workers, whereas in Japan the ratio was 1 in 27.[38] It is little wonder that so many U.S. organizations reacted to the high-cost lack of global competitiveness by laying off people earlier in this decade—a change reaction called *downsizing.*

By managing change through a combination of cutting costs and redesigning systems and products, North American firms have either regained lost markets (such as semiconductors, steel) or strengthened their worldwide market leadership

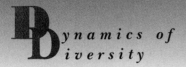

ynamics of iversity

Opportunity Is a Two-Way Street

Reginald D. Dickson is chief executive officer of Inroads Inc., a St. Louis–based organization that trains and develops minority professionals in business. What is it like to be a minority in corporate America? Dickson has a lot to say on the subject:

I love the capitalist system. Part of the reason is simply that I'm a businessperson at heart. My instincts are business instincts. But another part of the reason is that I was born black, poor, and illegitimate in the rural South and have a strong social commitment to minorities—especially disadvantaged minorities. In capitalism's focus on profit and competition, I have found and expanded a professional foothold for people of color.

Quite simply, business needs the best and the brightest, regardless of race and ethnic background, and to meet that need, corporate America is willing to make a place for diversity beyond anything we've ever seen before. There are great problems to overcome, of course, including a lot of lingering prejudice. There is also a condition—namely, that minority members must be able to give business what it needs, both in skills and in behavior. But the fact remains that U.S. corporate leaders want to recruit young people of color and want them to shatter the glass ceilings and rise to their levels of greatest competence . . .

If minorities like me want into the American mainstream, we have to stop being victims and adapt our talents to business needs and business norms . . . The fact is that minorities always have to adapt to the majority culture. And adapting to American corporate culture is easy compared with what most blacks have had to adapt to in the past.

Source: Reginald D. Dickson, "The Business of Equal Opportunity," *Harvard Business Review* 70 (January–February 1992), pp. 46–53.

(in software, aircraft, and entertainment). Pressures for continuous change are ever present, forcing companies to benchmark with firms known for best practices. Regardless of an organization's country of origin, organizations known for their best practices emphasize the management of relationships as instrumental to success.[39]

Globalization of Business

For most of the twentieth century, the United States was the dominant economic power in the world. In 1967, French historian Servan-Schreiber's best-selling book *The American Challenge* told Europeans to be aware that the United States would dominate the world economy in a short time because of its management expertise.[40] But the forces of change were at work as Servan-Schreiber was writing, and one soon negated his prediction—the rebirth of the Japanese economy.

Japan started anew in the second half of the twentieth century to develop the capital, technology, human resources, and management practices needed to become a dominant economic power. The 1950s, 1960s, and early 1970s were a time of mass markets in which customers were satisfied with highly standardized products that changed slowly. Japanese firms supplied mass quantities of items at low prices—products that were originally ridiculed as cheap imitations. But during the late 1970s and 1980s, ridicule turned to admiration and even envy. Through the process of continuous quality improvement, Japanese products in many industries became the world-class standards of quality and innovation. Then in the 1990s,

Japan's economy went into a tailspin. Banks were confronted with the reality that many of their loans, especially for real estate, were nonperforming. Japanese firms, from automobiles to consumer electronics, for the first time in decades experienced strong foreign competition that reduced their global market share. Japan's short-term history of wild swings from growth to stagnation is but one example of the instability of global competition.

Managing Diversity

People tend to feel more comfortable with people they see as similar. But people are different, and differences are at the root of diversity. Differences in gender, race, language, size, physical impairments, and age are clearly visible. Less visible are differences in education, religion, nationality, economic status, sexual orientation, learning disabilities, and domestic partner status.

The United States has long been recognized as a melting pot for its ability to assimilate people from other cultures into its own culture. Today the melting pot has melted—the United States has become multicultural. New immigrants are the fastest-growing segment of the population. During the 1960s, immigrants made up 11 percent of total population growth; during the 1970s, they accounted for 33 percent; and during the 1980s, 39 percent.[41] The verdict is still out on the 1990s, but increasingly companies located on the coasts and in Illinois find their employees were born in countries other than the one in which they are employed.[42]

Given accelerating diversity within the work force, it is unlikely that the nonwhite, nonanglo part of the population will be assimilated as fully into the dominant culture as in the past. Arthur Schlesinger's view is that the United States is unique in its ability to assimilate diverse peoples through their willingness to subsume their language and culture and accept the language and values common to all Americans. He forecasts that a movement away from the melting pot toward separateness and multiculturalism will lead to the disuniting and weakening of American society.[43] But at the organizational level, managers are learning to build on the strengths of differences among employees and customers.

Affirmative action and managing diversity are not the same. The goal of affirmative action is to ensure that people of both genders and all races, nationalities, religions, and ages are given a fair opportunity to be hired or admitted to organizations. Progress has been made in minority entry into organizations. Roosevelt Thomas, Jr., believes that affirmative action will "die a natural death" because "women and minorities no longer need a boarding pass, they need an upgrade."[44] The challenge today is less one of guaranteeing entry than of granting people of all kinds equal opportunities to reach their potential in all functions and at all levels of management and leadership. This means reducing barriers to equal opportunity and introducing progressive practices for taking advantage of diversity as a stimulus to innovation and market segment understanding.

Promoting Ethical Behavior

The fourth management theme is that of striving to inculcate norms of ethical behavior as a healthy and profitable way of conducting business. Pressures arising from international competition and accelerating diversity increase the complexities of organizational behavior. Too many self-centered people are not prepared to cope in ways that ensure fair and moral treatment of others. Many fail to anticipate how often people are injured by one person's or one firm's decisions.

The examples of probable wrongdoing are legion: Recall the Eye on Ethics box on Archer Daniels Midland, and in the recent past, the savings and loan debacle, the fraudulent practices in selling junk bonds, the mislabeling of products, the cover-up of tobacco's addictive power, Dow's breast implant, or the wrongful discharge of an employee. Unethical and even illegal actions can occur at all levels in organizations. In subsequent chapters we introduce ways of thinking systematically about making moral decisions and behaving with ethical integrity. Acting ethically promotes long-term benefits. Bowing to immediate pressures by dropping the ethical filter may seemingly solve one problem, but inevitably one bad decision creates many more serious ones. Being ethical is synonymous with practicing effective organizational behavior.

OVERVIEW OF THE BOOK

There are no easy answers to effectively managing organizational behavior. Nevertheless, this text exposes you to numerous issues, situations, research conclusions, and techniques that—if learned well—improve your chances of being an effective organizational performer. Your behavior should also be more efficient because you will have less need to learn by trial and error, having gained insights from your study of management and organizational behavior.

Exhibit 1–6 shows how the pieces of this book fit together, from Part I that sets the stage with a macro perspective of organizations, to the final linking together of managing stress and change strategies in Part V. The next chapter continues our broad overview of managing organizational behavior in Part I by focusing on one of the key elements to competitive positioning, that of crafting a mission and strategies and putting in motion comprehensive planning and control systems. With strategies in place, managers turn to designing work units and structures, and work indirectly to shape the organization's culture—its assumptions, values, and beliefs.

The focus shifts in Part II to the smallest unit of analysis—the individual and the tasks involved in managing people. Since people are the reason why life in organizations is interesting and challenging, you will study such fundamentals of individual behavior as personality and perception and learning and motivation and will learn how to engage motivational practices through empowering people, setting goals and objectives, designing jobs, and administering rewards.

In Part III you will learn about critical behaviors in managing relationships with others. Here you will begin to see how and why managers go about the process of influencing the thoughts and actions of others through communications, interpersonal relationships, and functioning in groups and teams. Because not everyone agrees with where the work unit should be headed or how it should function, managing conflict becomes critical to managerial success.

Part IV focuses squarely on the manager's exertion of influence and leadership. You will learn about problem solving and decision making within an ethical context. You will also get the opportunity to push back the veil of power and politics, a natural part of every organization. This part concludes with a review of what leaders do and the ways in which leadership helps groups achieve their performance expectations and transform entire organizations.

Finally, in Part V you will learn how managers manage change. Part of change management is to understand personal or individual stressors and how to cope with stress. At a higher level of organizational performance, managers lead the

━━━━━ **EXHIBIT 1.6**   *How the Parts of this Book Fit Together*

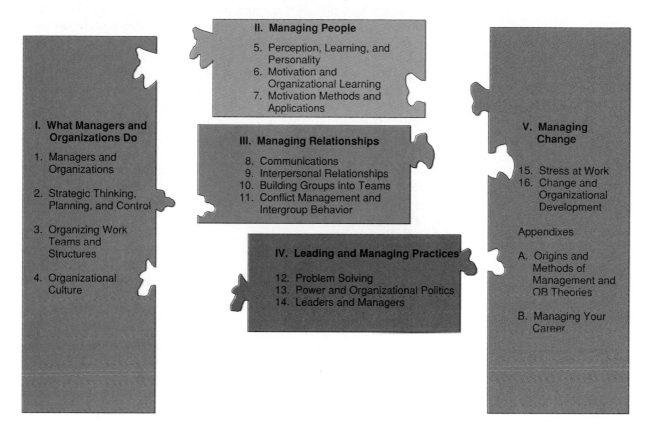

process of change and organizational learning. This ranges from modest changes in a work unit's internal processes to transforming large parts of an organization through substantial organizational development efforts.

Regardless of your intended career path, this book can help make your life in organizations more knowledgeable, controllable, meaningful, and satisfying. Appendix A brings you up to date on the history of management theory, and Appendix B leads you down the path of exploring career strategies. Enjoy the journey.

DAN LOGAN, CODE TRINITY—A SECOND LOOK

You may have thought initially that Dan Logan's covert operation within The New England (TNE) insurance firm was unethical. Why should any manager be secretive about gathering information and planning to break away his business unit. But two years before the cost cutting mandate led Logan to conceive of spinning off the communications business, TNE management gave him the added responsibility of heading up a program of continuous quality improvement within the firm. They sent him around the country to study the best practices of world-class "benchmark" firms such as Corning Glass and Federal Express. What he learned from this process was that it was tough to introduce radical ideas within a very tradition-bound firm. Senior management wanted to become modern, but they also wanted to keep operations consistent with their experience.

That is why the continuous improvement practice of outsourcing made perfect sense to Logan, his 20 colleagues in the new venture, and eventually to senior management. *Outsourcing* is the increasingly common practice of closing down nonessential internal operations unrelated to the core business and contracting with outside vendors to provide specialized services. Corporate communications was not core to the business of packaging and selling insurance. In fact, Logan had been recruited to TNE only eight years before to start an internal communications department—157 years after the business was founded. As an employee-owned private business, Trinity Communications was free to experiment in creative ways of becoming more efficient and effective than if kept as a service department within a conservative insurance company. The new employees got to run their own business, and TNE had more flexibility in obtaining lower cost, quality services. Everyone won.

Dan Logan, now entrepreneur as well as manager, notes that this freedom to operate as an independent organization is both a source of freedom and pressure: "You can move faster because there's no resistance to overcome. . . . [But] It's weird to start your year off knowing that you have more committed expenses than certain revenues. It's either get new business or go out of business—which adds a certain urgency and intensity to the importance of achieving our goals."[45]

SUMMARY

Organizations are open dynamic systems for transforming resource inputs into salable outputs (goods and services). They are created to provide useful products and services that satisfy the needs of customers and provide value to stakeholders. But the interests of various stakeholders (whether employees, customers, suppliers, or shareholders) are not always aligned. This places conflicting pressures and demands on managers.

At the highest organizational level, managers seek to navigate competitive environmental forces by developing a mission to define the firm's unique business purpose and crafting superordinate goals to challenge and guide employees. At all levels, managers function as systems diagnosers and influencers, seeking to align components of the organization's internal system, tempered by sensitivity to external forces of change. In performing their jobs, managers behave in different roles, frequently shifting emphasis among interpersonal, information, and decision-making roles.

To maintain organizational viability, managers work to achieve goals in the areas of productivity, satisfaction, and revitalization. One of the realities of life in organizations is that today's effective practices are not likely to suffice tomorrow. Whether pulled by the success of growth or jolted by crisis and downturn, managers must periodically transform the system to adapt to environmental realities. In the process of transformation, managers can target changes in the key internal resources such as tasks, technology, organization, people, and culture. Maintaining a dynamic balance among these resources is what organizational behavior (OB) is all about.

The study of organizational behavior is important because of the growing complexity and turbulence of the business environment and the related growth in research knowledge about behavior within organizations. For students who will be managers in the twenty-first century, four themes are paramount: the necessity of managing the challenges of change, functioning within a global environment, being sensitive to the diversity among people, and behaving with ethical integrity.

Key Concepts

organization, *p. 5*

mission, *p. 7*

superordinate goals, *p. 7*

stakeholders, *p. 8*

organizational behavior, *p. 9*

management, *p. 10*

law of effect, *p. 12*

system, *p. 12*

organizations, *p. 12*

closed systems, *p. 15*

open systems, *p. 15*

dynamic system, *p. 15*

boundary-spanning transactions, *p. 15*

manager, *p. 16*

productivity, *p. 25*

efficiency, *p. 25*

effectiveness, *p. 25*

satisfaction, *p. 26*

revitalization, *p. 26*

Questions for Study and Discussion

1. Critically challenge or defend the statement, "The mission of a business firm is to produce profits."

2. Identify the three primary clusters of managerial roles, and for each give examples of at least two specific roles within each cluster.

3. What key elements and relationships define a business as a dynamic open system? Provide an example of why a systems understanding of organizations and their environments is useful to managers.

4. What are the fundamental internal system elements managers commonly target in their change or transformation of organizations? Describe an example that demonstrates the potential interdependency among at least three change variables.

5. Think about the themes we characterize as the challenge of change, world watch, dynamics of diversity, and eye on ethics. Provide at least one reason why each is an important managerial issue for the 1990s.

EXPERIENTIAL EXERCISE

Visioning McDonald's from Burgers to System

Purpose. Everyone knows McDonald's, the hamburger chain that spans the globe. This in-class exercise gives students, working in groups, the opportunity to analyze a familiar business from a systems perspective. (Time required: about 25 minutes total.)

Materials. Newsprint pad and colored markers preferred.

Procedures. Organize the class into teams, each with four to six members.

1. Each team meets to share reflections about what members know about McDonald's. Express these observations and conjectures in *one or more diagrams that represent the system elements and interdependencies*

within a McDonald's restaurant (about 15 minutes). Use the various system diagrams within this chapter as clues for how you might go about presenting your analysis. But be specific to McDonald's. The following questions suggest elements you may want to include, but you are not bound to these—be creative:

- What are the major output goals? How might McDonald's evaluate performance?

- Who are the customers? How might customers be segmented into distinct product markets (on the basis of demographics)? What adds value to the customers' needs?

- What are the major resource inputs? What types of vendors might McDonald's need?

- Who are the stakeholders, and what do they want from their relationship with McDonald's?

- What are the principal work subsystems within the restaurant? How are the inputs transformed into salable outputs?

- How do the internal resource elements (tasks, technology, organization, people, culture, and managers) come together in an alignment that aids in accomplishing the mission?

- What changes or adjustments in the system would have to be made to accommodate a new cooked menu item?

2. Each group displays its systems design(s) or drawing(s) and discusses why it chose both the features and the mode of representation in its drawing(s).

3. Discuss and debrief by calling attention to similar and different elements across groups. Discuss the group process:

- What helped and what hindered the process of performing this task?

- How did you handle disagreements among members about how to format your presentation and what to include?

- In what ways did your group function as a mission-guided system? Or, did it dissolve into a variety of disconnected opinions?

EXPERIENTIAL EXERCISE

Analyzing Joyce Johnson's System

This is a team-based exercise that involves sequential analysis, prediction, and planning. Your task is to help Joyce Johnson, president of Johnson Controls Company, and to experience working as an impromptu team. (Time required: about 20 to 30 minutes.)

Procedure.   Form teams of three to five members each. Then, as a team, perform sequentially the tasks called for in each part of the exercise.

Part 1.   Joyce Johnson is president and general manager of a small aerospace parts manufacturing company that has been operating for nine years. Johnson Controls Company was profitable its second year, and in each of the succeeding five years sales and profits increased moderately. Two years ago, sales and profits peaked, but they have since been declining. During the decline, customers have complained that deliveries of Johnson parts are often delayed and the parts are sometimes of unacceptable quality and are no longer price competitive with two other competitors.

Johnson knows that two-thirds of her sales are to three key customers who value product quality, timely delivery, and price, in that order. Johnson also is aware that morale and commitment among her 125 employees are not strong and seem to be slipping with declining sales. Turnover of employees has risen from 2 percent to 15 percent over the past two years. Her key managers have been driving people to get more work out, but with little progress.

Joyce Johnson's goals have been to try to differentiate Johnson Controls Company from its competitors. The company has done this by identifying what the customer wants and then quickly agreeing to supply the desired parts at specified quality levels, by a specific delivery date, at a quoted price. Being relatively small, Johnson Controls historically has been able to respond to customer needs. Johnson thinks her strategy is appropriate but knows something has to change since competitiveness has slipped.

Before you go on to part 2, decide as a group on answers to the following three questions, and agree on a rationale for each answer:

1. Johnson needs more quality-control inspectors:
   ( ) Agree   ( ) Disagree
   Why? _____

2. Johnson needs to immediately get employee attention by doing something dramatic like promising bonuses for sales and profits improvements:
   ( ) Agree   ( ) Disagree
   Why? _____

3. Johnson should concentrate on reducing the production cycle time in order to make on-time deliveries:
   ( ) Agree   ( ) Disagree
   Why? _____

Part 2.   Before doing anything, Johnson thought she ought to diagnose her situation using a systems model framework. She began to list a series of questions to help guide her analysis. Johnson started with: Do we have the right kinds of resources? As a group, write out at least five other questions that would be most helpful to Johnson in analyzing her business system:

1. _____
2. _____
3. _____
4. _____
5. _____

As you reflect on your questions, does it appear that:

1. Most of Johnson's problems are people problems?

    ( ) Agree   ( ) Disagree

    Why? _____

2. Most likely Johnson has a number of interdependent systems problems that require transformation or change?

    ( ) Agree   ( ) Disagree

    Why? _____

Part 3.   Once Johnson has her list of system-guiding questions and begins seeking information to answer them, she discovers several areas that could be improved. In trying to understand why morale and commitment are declining, she finds many of the workers feel they benefit little from increasing output performance. Their pay stays the same, their opportunities for advancement in the small company are slight, and they expect continuing pressure to produce more regardless of the level of their output. Some find their jobs boring, and most think supervisors spend more time pressuring employees to produce more than showing appreciation for what has been produced.

Johnson also discovers that three key machines are old and frequently require repair. Machine operators feel frustrated using them, and production is held up when the machines are down for repairs. Also, Johnson finds that friction between production and quality-control people results in considerable loss of time and energy and causes considerable rework. Finally, it appears that the layout of the manufacturing process is not as efficient as employees believe it could be.

Although you do not have enough information to solve all of Johnson's problems, conclude this exercise by helping Johnson provide a big picture sense of direction to employees within the firm.

1. Write a one-sentence mission statement to appropriately guide Johnson Controls in its future behavior.

    _____

    _____

2. Write two or three superordinate goals that help employees focus on and support this mission.

    a. _____

    b. _____

    c. _____

Part 4.   As a total class, teams should share their output to each of the three parts to the exercise and discuss their similarities and differences. How well did your team work? Did you use disagreements and conflict to push for deeper insight into understanding the situation at Johnson Controls? Or, did your group agree to the first idea anyone expressed? How can a group benefit from having disagreements and differences of opinion among members?

CASE

Who's in Charge of Purchasing at Reymont?[46]

Clayton Erik, the Reymont Company's CEO, decided to move toward centralizing support functions and began with purchasing. He took this action to cut inventory management costs and out of fear that the economy was entering a phase of possible shortages and higher prices in some key supply sectors. Reymont had a tradition of promoting local autonomy among its divisions (they now number 14 in the Americas, 2 in Europe, and 4 in Asia). With its decentralization emphasis, purchasing practices had never been coordinated. Each plant (division) was left to procure whatever it needed from any source of supply. Each division provided monthly consolidated reports to the home office.

As part of his move toward centralization, Erik decided to create a new position, vice president of purchasing. Michelle Dupré had been a divisional purchasing manager before becoming a strategic planner for the chief financial officer. Well known throughout the company, she made known her aspirations for the position. Dupré was disappointed when she read a companywide e-mail that, with approval by the board of directors, Erik was appointing Seymour Rhodes into the newly created position. Rhodes had worked for 18 years with other firms, and to help his transition into Reymont, Erik appointed Dupré to be his assistant.

Although Reymont was diversified into several lines of business, most of the purchasing managers were entering their busiest season of the year, which would peak in about a month. The new vice president was aware of this and thought he would initiate his new appointment by announcing a policy calling for home office review of pending purchasing contracts. After some contemplation, Rhodes thought he would ask divisional purchasing managers to transmit to him copies of all pending contracts over $20,000. He planned to e-mail each of the 20 purchasing managers a copy of his new policy directive (which had been approved by Erik) but thought he would first test the communiqué on Dupré. Rhodes called Dupré into his office, handed her the draft, and asked, "What do you think of this as a way of getting started?" The message read:

MEMO TO: *Divisional Purchasing Managers*
FROM: *Seymour Rhodes, Vice President, Purchasing*
SUBJECT: *Implementation of a Review Policy on Pending*
                 Contracts

I'm sure you are all concerned about maintaining a steady flow of quality supplies and components at the best possible prices. As you know from the recent announcement, Mr. Erik has appointed me to coordinate purchasing among our 20 divisions. Therefore, to get started at this task I am initiating a change in policy with the approval of Mr. Erik and the board. As you negotiate contracts with values of $20,000 or more, please FAX or e-mail to the home office for my review a copy of each pending contract before it is signed.

With the forecast turmoil in supplier markets, I know you will appreciate the value of what we in the home office can do to assure the best prices and delivery terms. Realizing this is a busy time, I assure you that we will give a prompt response on all contracts. As we move into a new era of vendor relations, I count on your continued professionalism to help us get the most from our relations with suppliers.

Dupré read through the memo twice, then told Rhodes, "The policy change seems appropriate enough, but I'm not sure about sending an e-mail memo as the method of implementing it. Wouldn't you rather personally inform the purchasing managers of the necessity for this policy?"

Rhodes abruptly responded, "Haven't got time. There's too much to do in networking our key suppliers. If any questions arise, why don't you act as the point person and convince the purchasing managers this is in their best interest?"

Dupré decided to let it pass. Rhodes released the memo and had it transmitted immediately to the 20 plants. Within the next week he received several replies from the purchasing managers. Each said, in so many words, "I understand your policy and you can count on our cooperation."

Four weeks later, Rhodes had yet to receive a pending contract. During executive meetings in the home office, the other vice presidents reported that, during their visits to the plants, they found business to be booming and plants were producing at near-capacity levels.

Questions for Managerial Action

1. What concepts of management and organizational behavior do you see in this situation or infer from the case?

2. What thoughts could have possibly gone through Rhodes's mind as he contemplated sending out his new policy on contract reviews? Were there any system factors he should have analyzed but, based on his actions, probably did not?

3. What would you do if you were in Dupré's position once Rhodes sent his memo? What are the motivational implications of this situation for Dupré?

4. What would you do if you were one of the 20 divisional purchasing managers? In what ways might they have some leverage or power over Rhodes? What system forces impact on them as they consider what to do about the new policy?

5. What is your evaluation of Rhodes as a manager? As a leader? Why do you believe he took the action he did? What should he do at this point?

Chapter 2

Strategic Thinking, Planning, and Control

LEARNING OBJECTIVES

After studying this chapter, you should be able to:

- Describe the essential elements that help a manager to begin thinking strategically, including a vision and a mission with a focus on adding value to customers.

- Ask six questions that help you think strategically about planning actions, whether for an entire business or an organizational subunit.

- Conduct a SWOT analysis to better understand an organization's limitations and potential when you read a complex case or feature story.

- Explain how organizational capabilities translate into competitive advantage when linked to strategies for where and how to compete.

- Discuss why planning is more about organizational learning than about programming actions, and why a manager's ideology may be more useful than managing by information.

- Describe how group processes can create a shared vision through the use of planning tools such as an affinity map, a cause → effect diagram, and a radar chart.

- Differentiate among three managerial control orientations and explain whether control is influenced more through social expectations or output measurements.

PHILIP MORRIS: ADDICTED TO NICOTINE SALES?

Philip Morris, Inc. (PM), is a firm historically dedicated to making and selling cigarettes. Its Marlboro brand, introduced in 1924, is the world market leader and perhaps PM's greatest asset. Yet smokers in the United States are finding it increasingly difficult to light up. Health consciousness and strong regulatory restrictions have significantly reduced the domestic market for cigarettes.

Philip Morris's top managers remain staunch defenders of their right to sell cigarettes. But as strategic-minded planners, they have slowly repositioned the firm over the past three decades. As threats to the tobacco market have intensified, they have pursued opportunities in the larger food and beverage industry and in global markets. Strategically, PM has diversified by venturing into other lines of business and increasing its production and sales of cigarettes in international markets, where consumers have fewer health concerns about smoking. PM has acquired such firms as Miller Brewing, Kraft, General Foods, Oscar Mayer, and Louis Rich. In some years during the early 1990s, it acquired more than 20 firms annually. By making so many food-related acquisitions, Philip Morris is acting on a plan to shift its vision. In the words of its former CEO, Philip Morris aims to be "the largest consumer packaged goods company in the world."

Although cigarettes are still a mainstay of PM's profitability, management has restructured its systems and strategies in planning for better ways to add value to its customers and shareholders. In March 1991, Michael A. Miles, a nonsmoker and "nontobacco person," was appointed chairman and chief executive. Today Philip Morris is the leading innovator of new food products sold through supermarkets. The food business is organized into two major groups: North American Food and International Food. When Miles became CEO, he launched a consolidation process to reduce redundancies among the approximately 200 domestic food production plants and 70 distribution centers. Consolidation, which means eliminating duplicate operations, is a typical strategy for paring costs and streamlining efficiency following periods of rapid growth by acquisition. Although thousands of people were laid off, Miles explained his intended relationship between people and strategy: "The first of our strategies is to maintain the highest quality of people. We are, and will remain, dedicated to helping all our employees achieve their full career potential within Philip Morris Companies." By simplifying organization structures and using technology as productive tools, fewer people are needed to meet output requirements.

Sources: Tracy Robertson Kramer and Arthur A. Thompson, Jr., "Philip Morris Companies, Inc.," in A. A. Thompson, Jr., and A. J. Strickland III, *Strategic Management: Concepts and Cases* (Burr Ridge, IL: Irwin, 1995), pp. 703–751; Philip Morris, Inc., *Annual Report* (1989); and Bruce Horovitz, "Hot New Products Line Grocery Shelves," *USA Today* (February 16, 1995), p. 1B.

Strategic thinking, planning, and control are fundamental to every enterprise, even those that are not branching into diverse lines of business as Philip Morris has been doing. Whether pulling people together to publish a newspaper, film a movie, fight a war, or manufacture light bulbs, crafting strategies and planning are a part of all organized human activity. Having a vision and a mission and bringing people together to plan the actions necessary to carry out strategies are essential to achieving goals and bolstering organizational success.

However, not only the tangible "plans" are important. Also important is the process by which plans are developed, for increasingly managers are drawing in people at lower levels in the organization to participate in the planning process.[1] Everyone expects senior managers to be strategic thinkers. But if lower-level managers and technically experienced professionals will be engaged in business planning, they too need to develop the ability to think strategically.

HOW DOES A MANAGER BEGIN TO THINK STRATEGICALLY?

strategic thinking

A process of envisioning and planning to create a workable fit between organizational competencies (and limitations) and external opportunities (and threats) with the goal of better serving customers.

All organizational professionals improve their managerial skills by learning to think strategically. **Strategic thinking** involves envisioning and planning a workable fit between organizational competencies and limitations on the one hand and opportunities and threats on the other, with the aim of better serving customers. Thinking strategically means anticipating what actions are most likely to help the organization prosper in a changing environment. The strategic side of management is the craft of balancing stability and consistency over time with change when needed.[2] Much of the time, strategic decisions involve refining a basic way of doing business rather than abruptly charting a new course.[3]

Exhibit 2–1 shows how strategic elements fit within the typical functions of management. It suggests a flow of decisions throughout the organization. Senior managers make strategic decisions that seek to balance environmental forces with organizational capabilities. Strategies take shape through decisions within and across units throughout the organization. Typical of the classic functions of management, this flow of decisions involves a cycle of planning, organizing, activating, and controlling behaviors.

For Philip Morris, planning at the corporate level might involve evaluation of new businesses to acquire, whereas managers within a unit might plan to promote a product via a one-month television campaign. Integrating two newly acquired businesses may involve rearranging the structure of reporting relationships, whereas the promotional campaign requires assigning responsibilities to the appropriate people. Activating any plan means allocating resources, initiating operational decisions and actions, and keeping the organization on track toward its goals. Control systems then allow managers to monitor how well management's plans are succeeding and organizational goals are being met. All of these tasks draw on the manager's perception, learning, and problem-solving skills.

Focus on Adding Value to Customers

Business firms have a fundamental singlemindedness of purpose that distinguishes them from other types of organizations. If you took a microeconomics or finance course, you might have been taught that the unique purpose of business firms is to create profits, or to maximize shareholder wealth. True, the owners and managers of businesses expect that if they are successful, they will be profitable. Profits

▬▬▬ EXHIBIT 2–1

The Playing Field of Strategic Management

Managing strategically involves striking a balance among environmental forces and the available human, technical, and financial resources. Management at any organizational level is a process of working ideas and actions through a planning, organizing, activating, and controlling cycle while ensuring that unit performance supports the strategic vision of the enterprise.

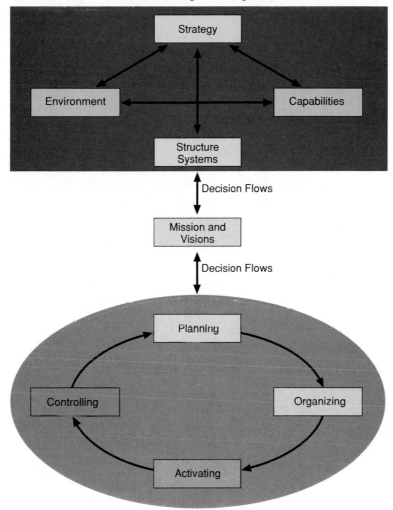

The Balancing of Strategic Fit

The Behavioral Management Process

become the ultimate goal called "the bottom line." But profits are the *result,* the outcome of doing things well. Profits are not to be confused with *purpose,* which focuses on serving customers well. To appreciate the fundamental purpose of a business firm, consider this classic definition by Peter Drucker:

> *To know what a business is we have to start with its purpose. Its purpose must lie outside itself. In fact, it must lie in society since business enterprise is an organ of society. There is only one valid definition of business purpose: to create a customer.[4]*

For manufacturing firms, the concept of creating a customer means bringing to market products that attract customers because they satisfy current or latent needs. A manufacturer of tennis rackets aims to create certain performance and design characteristics that appeal to a particular segment of tennis players. A software firm attempts to get ahead of the competition by introducing an application package that will enable potential users to do certain things more easily, quickly,

━━━━━ **EXHIBIT 2–2**

*Purposes Served by a Well-
Articulated Mission*

To be useful, a statement of mission should:

1. Articulate the vision that defines the business, what it is, what it is not, and what it should be in the future.
2. Communicate to internal members and external constituencies a clear sense of meaning and direction that is motivating and energizing.
3. Convey which customer wants or needs it will seek to satisfy, and the target markets it will serve.
4. Identify the value-adding functions it will perform, realizing its specific enabling actions will change over time while the purpose endures.
5. Be of bumper-sticker length—brief enough to be incorporated into corporate communications and easily remembered.

or accurately than they ever imagined. For the tennis player, the newly designed product may have satisfied a current need. The new software may have brought a latent need to the surface by suggesting that a product that will take the drudgery out of performing certain tasks is finally available.

A customer who believes Wal-Mart offers greater value than Sears will do more shopping at Wal-Mart. Similarly, one customer may see greater sport utility value in a Jeep Grand Cherokee than in a Ford Explorer. The value-added objective sometimes influences "customer" choices indirectly. For example, a family decides, despite considerable cost of time and money, to move from community A to community B because of better schools and public services, less crime, and other quality-of-life considerations. Whether an organization is designed for profit or for public service, aiming to satisfy customers is consistent with long-term quality goals. This emphasis on continuous improvement as the route to quality is woven throughout the text.

Craft a Mission to Define a Common Purpose

Whether a business firm, a not-for-profit organization, or a government agency, every organization has a mission, or cause, intended to unite and provide direction to its members. Some organizations are created out of community need. A police department is created to protect people within the community from careless or criminal acts. A hospital cares for the health needs of the community, from health maintenance to active treatment.

mission
The fundamental purpose of an enterprise that defines the nature of its business and provides strategic direction to unify the use of human and other resources.

The **mission** of an enterprise is its fundamental purpose, articulated to define the nature of its business and provide a unifying sense of strategic direction. A well-conceived mission answers the questions: Why do we exist and what do we do? Who are we and where are we headed? A mission should serve as a rallying cry to induce organizational members to take up its cause. This is epitomized by the Peace Corps' mission to attract idealistic young people wanting to help humanity or by Silicon Graphics' mission to bring three-dimensional image manipulation and simulation to the world of computing.

Exhibit 2–2 lists five essential functions of a well-framed mission statement. Once the mission statement is cast, it is expected to provide guidance for specific goals and strategies for years to come. But with the passage of time, mission statements may have to be reassessed and even reformulated. Managers of the three National Research Laboratories (Lawrence Livermore, Sandia, and Los Alamos) realize that the environmental conditions that had created the labs—the nuclear threat associated with the cold war between the United States and the former communist nations—no longer existed after the breakup of the Soviet Union in 1989. The United States no longer needed to build up its nuclear arsenal; thus, the mission that led to creation of the labs was no longer viable. The new mission is apparently to boost American industry and create jobs by conducting, at government expense, research and development for firms such as AT&T, Amoco, DuPont, General Motors, IBM, and others. Between 1990 and 1994, the National Labs subsidized $293 million in technical research for eight large corporations, but these same firms cut their U.S. work force by 329,000 people.[5] Is the new mission really working?

Buried in the graveyard of dead corporations are numerous firms that clung to what they knew best long after the need had vanished or after customers had switched to companies offering products that made life easier, more attractive, or less costly. Missions become complicated when a firm branches beyond its original line of business, as Philip Morris has done. The abundance of conglomerates—firms that sell unrelated products and services to a variety of markets—suggests that framing a meaningful, customer-focused mission is difficult in the absence of unifying themes. Originally a cigarette maker and marketer, Philip Morris maneuvered through several unsuccessful acquisitions before slowly beginning to focus on acquiring food companies. Although PM's cigarette business continues to create large profits, remaining in that business raises serious questions about the true value PM really adds to customers—and to society.

Use a Vision to Set Direction for a Desired Future

The concepts of mission and vision are often used interchangeably. While a mission statement should flow out of a vision, the mission is normally expected to provide direction that stretches beyond the foreseeable future. Visions occur more often, change more frequently, and can be specific to a product, program, or project. A **vision** incorporates current realities and expected future conditions to create a desired organizational image within a relevant time frame. "A vision belongs to what we may term a process of direction setting. Direction setting connotes the identification of something in the future (a vision), often the distant future, and a strategy for getting there."[6] Three elements are fundamental to a comprehensive, meaningful vision: a purpose, a goal, and an image of results.[7]

vision
A desired future image of the organization and its processes and products that integrates current realities and expected future conditions within a specific time frame.

A Statement of Purpose. First, ideology and core values are combined in an explicit *statement of purpose*. The purpose need not be meaningful to outsiders but should inspire and motivate insiders. The executives of Compression Labs, Inc., are able to appeal to both insiders and outsiders in their statement of purpose: "As the pioneer of compressed digital video technology, the Company makes and markets a variety of video communications products that allow people at different locations to see and interact with one another in a natural, intuitive manner."[8]

A Tangible Goal. The second element of a vision, *creation of a tangible goal*, begins with a vision statement that frames a clear, specific, and compelling goal that focuses people's efforts. A well-framed goal has a target and a time frame for its attainment. To achieve one of Wal-Mart's visions of maintaining consistent growth, founder Sam Walton gave employees their goal for the 1990s at the 1990 annual shareholders' meeting. The target was to double the number of stores and increase dollar volume per square foot 60 percent, and the time frame was to accomplish this by the year 2000. This is a very tangible and meaningful goal. Five years later, at the midpoint for realizing the goal, Wal-Mart was two-thirds of the way toward doubling the number of stores, and it had increased dollar volume per square foot by 45 percent (three-quarters of the way toward the goal).[9] At this rate, it will achieve the goal two to three years earlier than projected.

An Image of Results.   The final element is creating a *vivid image of the results*. The image should paint a compelling picture using crisp language, much as Henry Ford projected in his original vision for Ford: "I will build a motor car for the great multitude . . . It will be so low in price that no man making a good salary will be unable to own one . . . When I'm through everybody will be able to afford one, and everyone will have one. The horse will have disappeared from our highways, the automobile will be taken for granted." Ford's vision conveyed a clear picture of the future, and it was realized within two generations.

Although ideally a vision should contain these three elements, they are not necessarily found in most visions. To researchers, vision remains a "hypothetical construct" in the sense that a vision is not directly observable and may mean different things to different people.[10] To more fully understand the meaning of vision, researchers have investigated at least five alternative approaches: assessing (1) the content of what a vision says, (2) the process by which it is formulated and communicated, (3) its impact in providing strategic direction, (4) its meaning as a pattern of values embedded in organizational culture, and (5) the qualities of leaders who are considered visionary.[11] Despite these differences in meaning, one finding can be generalized: The faster an industry changes, the more the articulation of a vision needs to be communicated to insiders (the people who design, build, sell, and service products) to provide a sense of purpose and meaning in the projects and activities they undertake.[12]

Create Structures and Systems to Support Strategy

strategy
The planned fit between an organization's capabilities and its evolving environment, crafted to achieve a favorable position within the competitive marketplace.

Every organizational mission and the visions that emerge in pursuit of the mission call forth multiple strategies. **Strategy** is the process of planning a fit between an organization's capabilities and its evolving environment to achieve a favorable position within the competitive marketplace. Strategies pertain to those destiny-shaping decisions concerning the choice of technologies on which products are based; the development and release of new products; the processes for producing products and services; the way they are marketed, distributed, and priced; and the ways the firm responds to rivals. Even nonbusiness entities depend on strategies to help employees or members plan new programs or revitalize services so that constituencies are better served.

Federal Express was created by Richard Smith on the premise that organizations would pay for guaranteed next-day delivery of parcels, something that the U.S. Postal Service could not deliver at the time. Fundamental to this vision was the strategy of routing all aircraft through a single airport hub in Memphis. It meant that a package shipped from Minneapolis to Orlando on Tuesday afternoon would be sorted at Memphis during the night and then shipped aboard another plane to Orlando for delivery by Wednesday morning. To make the hub-and-spoke concept work in shipping packages, FedEx had to create a national network of airports, airplanes, trucks, and computers. FedEx also had to organize people into a structure and create systems to provide consistency.

structure
Organizational groupings of people and tasks into departments providing for coordination among workflows and decision authority.

Structure provides a way of grouping people and tasks into departments, then defines the linkages among departments so that work flows and decision authority are coordinated and communicated. At FedEx, a geographical structure had to be organized to connect managers and operations at terminals in each major airport city and to grant terminal managers the authority to organize employees into work groups to perform tasks in each location. Structures also had to be created for managing the logistics of scheduling aircraft and pilots, and for purchasing airplanes and trucks.

systems
Guidelines or structured processes for handling recurring transactions and events in a standardized or consistent way.

Systems provide guidelines or processes for handling recurring transactions and events in a standardized or consistent way. FedEx systems had to be developed and maintained, beginning with the computers and information system for routing and tracking parcels, accounts receivable, aircraft, and delivery vans and extending from accounting for employee time to purchasing bar code labels and billing corporate accounts.

What does all of this mean for the management of organizational behavior? An organization's mission provides constituencies (primarily employees, but also customers and vendors) with a sense of identity, values, and meaning about the organization. Visions, which change as new programs or projects emerge, provide people with a sense of purpose, a goal, and a direction. Most new visions require strategies, which allocate people and resources to make it happen. Structure and systems support strategy, and people's work lives are either limited or broadened by their position within the organization structure (and the managers with whom they work) and by the scope and number of systems and procedures intended to guide their everyday behavior. The interplay among visions, strategies, structures, and systems inevitably requires change, and much of the manager's job is to work with people to bring about needed change or to prevent unwanted change. During the 1990s, many organizations have attempted to evaluate and redesign how they are organized and how they function. Processes of corporate redesign require organizational learning and investing in new skills and knowledge bases, which often lead to cutbacks in staffing and a downsizing of the organization as the bureaucracy is scaled back.[13] Changes in people's work lives means that people on the firing line as well as those who are managers need to periodically ponder a series of strategic questions.

WHAT STRATEGIC QUESTIONS SHOULD EVERY MANAGER EXPLORE?

There are no hard-and-fast rules for thinking and managing strategically. Rather, the process is a way of analyzing, planning, and thinking that evaluates and anticipates the relationship between the organization and its environment. Leaders who effectively guide strategy formulation and implementation draw in others. Collectively they explore alternative responses to questions such as the six that follow.[14] These are the types of questions that a manager ponders while commuting or discusses with colleagues in the hallway, over lunch, or in conference rooms. Often the answers emerge over time as ideas and actions take shape. These six questions provide a basic framework for thinking strategically and for planning within an organizational network. When seriously explored, they promote organizational learning.[15]

1. What Business Are We In?

The most basic question any business must answer is, What product or service should we market? A related question is, Who is our customer, and how can we provide value to that customer? Some businesses have only one or a few customers, such as the Illinois coal-mining company that sinks its shafts adjacent to a coal-fired electrical utility. Others, such as Boeing, sell their aircraft to a hundred or so customers throughout the world. Still others, such as Procter & Gamble, sell thousands of consumer products to tens of thousands of retailers, which in turn sell them to millions of individual consumers.

This "What business are we in?" question should be asked by every manager. *Every unit must serve a customer,* regardless of the unit's level, function, or size. For most units, the customer is one or more other units within the organization that receives its output. Even then, however, the same dedication to increasing value for the customer should apply. For example, an MIS manager should work with other departments to find solutions to their information-processing needs. In effect, all managers of work units should think of themselves as entrepreneurs serving internal markets—and if they don't serve them well, other units are free to buy where they find the best deal. When Alcoa, the aluminum company, declared that all line and staff units were free to conduct business with outside companies, productivity and sales among line units doubled.[16]

2. What Are Our Internal Strengths and Weaknesses?

core capabilities
The critical skills and processes that an organization executes so well in carrying out its intended strategy that its reputation builds around them.

A firm (or a subunit within it) should be aware of its core capabilities and sources of competitive advantage.[17] A sustainable competitive advantage is created if a firm's core capabilities cannot be readily copied by competitors.[18] **Core capabilities** are the critical skills and processes that an organization executes so well that its reputation builds around them. Core capabilities develop if people consistently carry out the actions necessary to achieve the intended strategy.[19]

For example, there is nothing unique about the strategy of Marriott Corporation: simply attract travelers and diners by providing them with consistently excellent service. Marriott realizes it must ignite within each employee a deep commitment to outstanding customer service.[20] Employees are empowered to use their initiative in meeting customers' needs, backed by training and guidelines to make sure details are not overlooked. The housekeeping staff, for example, follows a 66-point guide in making up rooms; nothing is left to chance.

In addition to knowing its strengths, an organization must recognize its limitations. Whether limited by a poorly equipped production facility or a sales force that merely quotes prices and delivery dates, a business that acknowledges its weaknesses forces disciplined planning across business processes and levels of management. In some regions, Sears' automotive departments were recommending unnecessary repairs, driven by management goals to boost sales and margins. When confronted by state investigators, Sears at first denied the allegations, but eventually acknowledged that some departments were overzealous in meeting their goals and indifferent to customers. Some internal elements, such as a strong organizational culture or structure, act more as constraints rather than weaknesses. General Motors' strong hierarchy makes it difficult for managers and work teams to make fast decisions in response to competitors' actions. This contributed to GM's loss of more than $20 billion one year as it entered the 1990s, giving GM the infamous record of having the most unprofitable year of any corporation, surpassing IBM's previous record loss.[21]

3. What External Opportunities and Threats Do We Face?

External and internal environments present both driving and restraining forces. Opportunities may occur suddenly: A key supplier agrees to form a joint venture, a regulation is relaxed, or a competitor encounters a major problem (such as a

Agway is a farm supply cooperative in the Northeast serving farmers through direct deliveries and merchandise within its 600 stores. When the company began to lose money, senior management started to explore the basic planning questions. Initially, when asked what Agway should become, the top executives said different things. After reviewing its strategy the company decided to split up its retailing and commercial farm businesses. The result: Better service to farmers and the elimination of an entire layer of costs. (Photo: © Michael Greenlar.)

product recall). Conversely, managers need to be aware of looming threats and plan for them. Lawsuits, competitor product breakthroughs, and even industry-wide price cuts (common in the airline industry) all threaten a firm's current strategies. In unstable or hostile environments, managers need to plan for contingencies, adopting a "what will we do if" preparedness to respond to likely threats.

The combination of questions that assess internal *strengths* and *weaknesses* and external *opportunities* and *threats* are the keys to a process called the *situational audit,* or SWOT analysis. Managers perform a **SWOT analysis** whenever they assess conditions in their relevant environment in relation to internal resources and competence; that is, when they assess the relationships among strengths, weaknesses, opportunities, and threats.[22] Few experienced managers would think of planning strategies without making SWOT analysis part of the process.

SWOT analysis

An assessment of internal resources and competence (**S**trengths and **W**eaknesses) in relation to conditions in an organization's external environment (**O**pportunities and **T**hreats).

4. What Business Should We Be In?

With this question, managers seek to control their firm's destiny. This critical question encourages managers to infuse their own values, ideology, creativity, and desires into strategic planning, creating a vision of what the organization is capable of becoming. Even managers of functional departments (such as marketing or design engineering) are capable of drastically altering the types of services they provide.

In some firms, the vision of the future organizational unit may be simply one of continuous expansion of output with incremental improvements. In other organizations, the vision is one of branching out, of becoming more diversified by moving beyond current product lines into a broader offering of related products or services. Philip Morris took the diversification route when management realized that the market for cigarette sales in North America was declining. Over time PM has become a more diversified consumer products company by acquiring large food-related firms. In rare cases, a firm may abandon its original business and redirect its resources elsewhere. International Harvester did this when it discontinued its well-known line of tractors and agricultural machinery to compete only in the truck market under the new name Navistar.

5. How Do We Get There?

Responses to the preceding questions are transformed into the plans and actions managers generally think of as the strategies for achieving the firm's goals. Plans set the direction for obtaining and allocating resources, establishing systems and policies, and, when necessary, restructuring the organization. Often the key is to recognize emerging possibilities and help them take shape. Mintzberg claims, "The job of the manager is not just to preconceive specific strategies but also to recognize their emergence elsewhere in the organization and intervene when appropriate."[23]

For example, managers might extend a particular product line, drive down costs by simplifying product design (to reduce labor costs), streamline production, strengthen customer service, develop new channels of distribution, restructure the pricing policy, and perhaps simplify the organization. Strategies can also be changed to phase out products that no longer contribute to the core business, one of several changes BankAmerica made when it faced a crisis in the late 1980s.[24] To successfully carry out these operational strategies, the firm needs a planning process that identifies critical resources, events, and timetables for converting intentions into actions.

6. How Do We Know We're Still on the Right Course?

milestones
Future dates by which certain events are planned to occur.

Plans need to have milestones and controls to ensure that actions correspond to plans, or to evaluate whether intended actions and goals are still feasible. **Milestones** are future dates by which certain events are to occur. Milestones are useful when a plan has several distinct components, each of which must be completed at a specified time for the entire event to occur. Managers also use controls to evaluate efficiency by comparing actual with planned performance. Actual costs can be compared with budgeted costs, or the number of service calls handled within a targeted response time can be compared with set standards or to historical results.

A control system works if it prevents deviations from a well-conceived plan. If a deviation does occur, the control process should trigger actions to bring out-of-control elements back in line with the plan's goals and milestones. For example, if Great Plains Software of Fargo, North Dakota, does not return a customer's phone call within three hours, it gives the customer a price break on future orders.[25] Management monitors deviations from this callback policy and encourages employees to see how many thousands of calls they can return before the company misses the target.

Results Are the Payoff

results
An external acceptance or rejection of what an organization does—satisfied customers are the hallmark of positive results.

All of the plans, actions, milestones, goals, and controls managers use to shape business strategy culminate in performance results. Drucker emphasizes that **results** are an external acceptance or rejection of what the enterprise does:

> *The single most important thing to remember about any enterprise is that results exist only on the outside. The result of a business is a satisfied customer. The result of a hospital is a healed patient. The result of a school is a student who has learned something and puts it to work ten years later. Inside an enterprise, there are only costs.*[26]

The previous six questions, or variations of them, should not be asked only when a firm or an organizational unit is in trouble. Rather, they should be asked periodically to help managers look ahead to opportunities as well as threats. Such

To give you insights into strategically focusing your career, write answers to the following questions. Periodically thinking through such questions can keep your career from drifting.

1. What business are you in? What is your product (the service or value you create for others)? Who is your market (what type of employer or client is willing to buy your service)?

2. What are your strengths and weaknesses as an employee or self-employed provider of services? What are your core skills and competencies?

3. What external opportunities and threats do you anticipate? Where could you best use your competencies following graduation? What can go wrong in controling your career?

4. What business should you be in? Where would you like your career to be, say, 5 or 10 years from now? What vision do you value?

5. How do you get there? What actions do you need to undertake now to reach your career vision?
   a. What added education/training do you need?
   b. What organizational experiences do you need?
   c. What people are critical to your progress?

6. How do you know you are still on the right course? What milestones do you have for periodically checking up on your career progress?

Note: For additional help in planning your career, see Appendix B at the end of the book.

questions serve as the focus for management retreats, meetings, and conversations with peers. Together, they create an integrated way of thinking and acting strategically within an organization. You too can begin to think strategically by asking yourself similar questions. Take a couple of minutes now to complete the Your Turn exercise.

HOW DO ORGANIZATIONS DEVELOP COMPETITIVE ADVANTAGE?

In a practical sense, strategy is about making decisions about which markets to compete in and what products and services to provide so that customers' needs are met and their expectations are exceeded. Strategy also includes decisions about how much of the product the firm should make and how much it should buy from other firms.[27] Furthermore, strategy deals with the issues of whether to be technology or labor intensive, whether to distribute through independent dealers or a business-owned dealer network, whether to aim for high-volume economies of scale or achieve flexibility with short product life cycles and greater customized production, and whether to price to gain market share or to improve gross margins.[28] Exhibit 2–3 summarizes the key concepts that come into play when an enterprise seeks to sustain a competitive advantage.

■■■■■■ **EXHIBIT 2–3**

Key Concepts That Shape Competitive Advantage

Competitive advantage occurs whenever an organization is able to sustain an edge over its rivals in attracting customers and defending itself against competitive forces. Behind every organization that enjoys a superior competitive advantage are a unique set of core capabilities that develop with experience and focused use of resources. For diversified firms, these capabilities should limit the lines of business that make up the portfolio of corporate strategy. Within each business unit, managers craft competitive strategies that affect actions involving technology, production, product development, marketing, pricing, and other means of building a favorable position within the marketplace.

Corporate Strategy
Choice of lines of business

Core Capabilities
Unique human skills, technologies, and processes

Competitive Strategies
Business level actions for product-market position

Competitive Advantage

Results

Competitive Forces

Assets and Skills Build Organizational Capabilities

To achieve a strategic competitive advantage, all enterprises build their strategies around a core of physical assets and the skills and talents of its people. The critical question is how well assets and skills combine to endow the organization with unique capabilities. Remember that core capabilities provide the keys to long-term success by enabling the firm to combine assets and skills to do certain things better than competitors can.[29] Firms need to be cautious, however, that extreme success in combining technology with other capabilities may be viewed as restraint of trade—an issue that has confronted Microsoft.[30]

Some researchers conclude that the key to competitive success within manufacturing organizations is not in having the resources to access a certain technology or equipment but in "the ability to produce it [a product] efficiently, sell it efficiently, or advance it over time . . . Such superior organizational capabilities provide a competitive advantage that is much more sustainable than one based on something you can build or buy."[31] Skills and knowledge are also critical: "A company's capabilities are more than its physical assets. In fact, they are largely embodied in the collective skills and knowledge of its people and the organizational procedures that shape the way employees interact."[32] For Sun Microsystems, skill-based capabilities include rapid high-technology product development and rollout, and production flexibility. Tandy/Radio Shack has the capability to quickly and consistently spot market trends and shift products and production.[33]

Craft Strategic Actions to Win Competitive Advantage

competitive advantage
Occurs whenever a business is able to sustain an edge over its rivals by attracting customers and defending itself against competitive forces.

A business enjoys a **competitive advantage** whenever it is able to sustain an edge over its rivals by attracting customers and defending itself against competitive forces.[34] For decades Eastman Kodak Company was the undisputed market leader in chemical-based photography film. But externally, the combination of world competition in film (especially by Fuji) and the emergence of digital imaging stalled Kodak's growth and profitability. Internally, Kodak was hamstrung by a dysfunctional organizational culture and a dispirited work force.

In late 1993, George Fisher gave up his post as CEO of Motorola, Inc., to take the helm of Kodak. He reorganized and changed strategy to reposition the rapidly fading Kodak. Fisher sold off its unrelated Sterling Drug division so that management could refocus on imaging. He also slashed debt by $6 billion to save on interest costs, reignited photography growth in global markets (especially Asia), invested heavily in digital technology, and began shaking up the sluggish management system by stressing accountability, quality, and cycle time.[35] In short, he worked to restore and sustain Kodak's competitive advantage.

Corporate Strategy for Managing a Diversified Enterprise. For the firm as a whole, **corporate strategy** involves senior executive decisions about what lines of business to be in and how to manage them. The enterprise George Fisher took over at Kodak had been diversified into several business lines, from film, photographic paper, and chemicals to cameras, digital imaging, and pharmaceuticals. Diversified enterprises often branch beyond the core capabilities that define the product technologies and markets of the core businesses. But Porter's research on diversified firms found that competition occurs only at the business-unit level.[36] Consistent with this finding, one of Fisher's early corporate strategies was to refocus on photography and imaging, and to get out of the pharmaceuticals business where Kodak had no distinctive capabilities and thus no strong basis for competitive advantage.

> **corporate strategy**
> For multibusiness firms, the highest-level decisions and actions about what lines of business to be in and how to manage them.

Today many diversified (multibusiness) firms are using a couple of basic strategies to plan robust futures. One is to narrow their focus by downsizing and exercising control over fewer industries, but ones they know well—their core businesses.[37] Firms are unloading support services and activities that are not critical to core businesses; they are even outsourcing information technologies.[38] **Outsourcing** is the strategy of purchasing services or components from suppliers to prevent overextending the firm beyond its core capabilities. Managers are realizing that they must not lose strength in their core businesses; otherwise, their relative quality will be degraded. **Relative quality degradation** occurs when an enterprise's rate of improvement falls behind that of competitors. Even if product quality improves in an absolute sense, the rate of improvement relative to competitors determines growth or decline. It is better for an enterprise to be a world-class competitor in a few select lines of business than a second-class one in many.

> **outsourcing**
> The strategy of purchasing services or components from suppliers to prevent overextending the firm beyond its core capabilities.

> **relative quality degradation**
> Occurs when an enterprise's rate of improvement falls behind that of competitors, which relegates it to second-class performance.

A second basic strategy is to transform a hierarchical, bureaucratic organization into a series of internal enterprise units. The objective is to create internal markets among relatively small, semiautonomous enterprise units. Hewlett-Packard is an example of how internal enterprise units balance freedom with control:

> *Units are converted into enterprises by accepting controls on performance in return for freedom of operations. Hewlett-Packard (H-P) is famous for its entrepreneurial system that holds units accountable for results but gives them wide operating latitude. As one H-P executive described it, "The financial controls are very tight, what is loose is how [people] meet those goals."[39]*

The Swedish-Swiss firm ABB has excelled at stimulating innovation by granting local autonomy among its 4,500 semiautonomous profit centers, each a separate legal entity with its own financial statements (see the World Watch box). Especially for global enterprises like ABB, competitive advantage is created more by setting up businesses in locations that offer unique capabilities than by shifting production facilities in pursuit of low-cost labor.[40]

*World
Watch*

Asea Brown Boveri Reinvents Its Global Business Strategy

Asea Brown Boveri (ABB) is the result of a 1987 merger of two century-old firms, one Swedish, one Swiss. In the years since then, a wrenching process of consolidating and rationalizing (the European term for consolidation) has resulted in plant closings, layoffs, and product exchanges between countries. The evolving organizational network is truly transnational.

First the numbers: ABB generates more than $30 billion in annual revenues through the efforts of a quarter million employees. Operations are divided into approximately 1,200 companies, with an average of 200 people in each. These companies in turn are divided into over 4,500 semiautonomous profit centers, each averaging about 50 people. But the headquarters staff in Zurich numbers only 100—miniscule compared to most firms this size. They keep informed of results in profit centers through ABACUS (Asea Brown Boveri Accounting and Communication Systems) to ensure that every manager in the network takes advantage of the wealth of knowledge and trends accumulated within the system.

For ABB, plans for a global business rest on a series of three internal contradictions. Says CEO Percy Barnevik: "We want to be global and local, big and small, decentralized with centralized reporting." Within this fluid network, the 1,200 companies are clustered into 50 or so business areas (BAs), each responsible for optimizing a line of business on a global basis. The BA leader develops a global strategy, sets standards and monitors

costs and quality, allocates export markets to each company, and periodically rotates personnel to create cross-nationality teams. Parallel to the BA product structure is a country structure made up of national enterprises, each with its own president and financial statements. The job of the national enterprise president is to organize country efforts in ways that best serve and penetrate domestic markets. Separate sales companies may be created within a country to focus ABB's presence in a particular product line, regardless of where the product is manufactured.

In effect, ABB creates a strategic matrix of businesses and countries that creates dual reporting relationships, all woven into a loosely structured global network. ABB has thousands of internal enterprises, concurrently selling to other divisions and competing against them for the same customers. CEO Barnevik says, "The matrix is the framework through which we organize our activities. It allows us to optimize our businesses globally and maximize performance in every country in which we operate . . . As we learn to master the matrix, we get a truly multidomestic organization."

Sources: William Taylor, "The Logic of Global Business: An Interview with ABB's Percy Barnevik," *Harvard Business Review* 69 (March–April 1991), pp. 91–105; William E. Halal, "From Hierarchy to Enterprise: Internal Markets Are the New Foundation of Management," *Academy of Management Executive* 8 (November 1994), pp. 69–83; and Andrew C. Boynton, "Achieving Dynamic Stability through Information Technology," *California Management Review* 35 (Winter 1993), pp. 58–77.

competitive strategy
Actions at the level of a specific line of business intended to create a competitive advantage by planned actions about where to compete and how to compete.

Competitive Strategies at the Business-Unit Level.   Many firms compete across multiple lines of business. **Competitive strategy** is possible only within specific lines of business, where competitive advantage can be created through making choices about *where to compete* (the markets and segments, the type of rivals one goes up against) and *how to compete* (on the basis of product features, manufacturing, pricing, distribution, and so on).[41] Designing an integrated set of competitive strategies requires creativity and innovation in one or more spheres of business activity. In researching how companies succeed in international markets, Porter writes:

> *Companies achieve competitive advantage through acts of innovation. They approach innovation in its broadest sense, including both new technologies and new ways of doing things. They perceive a new basis for competing or find better means for competing in old ways.*[42]

National Competitiveness through Innovation.   On a global level, if one nation's firms in a once-dominant industry begin to lag behind competitors in another region of the world, that nation loses global market share. Once the decline begins, it often accelerates, as has occurred in North American markets for TVs, CDs, VCRs, and stereos. In contrast, when the U.S. semiconductor industry slipped to second place in global market share in the 1980s, firms such as Intel, AMD, and National Semiconductor invested heavily in innovation to regain their competitiveness. In the 1990s, the U.S. semiconductor industry overtook the Japanese industry to regain world market share leadership. One factor that helped U.S. firms regain the lead in semiconductors and microprocessors is access to a strong base of domestic semiconductor equipment manufacturers, such as Applied Materials, the world leader in its field.

After completing a four-year study in 10 countries, Porter concluded that "a nation's competitiveness depends on the capacity of its industry to innovate and upgrade." Furthermore, "Once a country achieves competitive advantage through an innovation, it can sustain it only through relentless improvement."[43] Such improvements come about by managers who are capable of strategic thinking and work through planning processes that help reinvent the organization. The objective is to create new lines of products and new markets, as well as to prevent relative quality degradation.

Think Strategy before Action

Strategy is the glue that holds the organization together by unifying plans throughout. Competitive strategy is the pattern of actions that focus an organization's resources and core competencies on achieving a sustained competitive advantage in its chosen environment. Managing strategically is a process of "making choices that best align the organization with environmental demands."[44] Every manager, regardless of position within the organization, needs to think strategically before initiating major strategy actions, for every organizational unit is responsible for strategy.

WHY IS PLANNING MORE ABOUT LEARNING THAN PROGRAMMING?

The preceding discussion suggests that planning should be a rational, analytical process based on "facts." In reality, planning is more about organizational learning than about programming a series of activities to attain an objective.[45] As the former head of planning at Royal Dutch/Shell noted, "The real purpose of effective planning is not to make plans but to change the . . . mental models that . . . decision makers carry in their heads." During the 1970s, senior executives got caught up in strategic planning as "the thing to do." But in this earlier approach to planning, planning was divorced from doing; it was something to assign to staff analysts. Thus, strategic planning became detailed analyses to support strategies managers had already envisioned.

Today planning is the responsibility of managers, and it involves participation, empowerment, and commitment more than it does making calculations. When managers plan, the emphasis is on strategic thinking, not on strategic planning. As Mintzberg emphasized:

> Strategic planning is not strategic thinking. *Indeed, strategic planning often spoils strategic thinking, causing managers to confuse real vision with the manipulation of numbers . . . Strategic thinking . . . is about* synthesis. *It involves intuition and creativity. The outcome of strategic thinking is an integrated perspective of the enterprise, a not-too-precisely articulated vision of direction.*[46]

In the mid-1980s Wabash National began producing truck trailers. Founder Donald J. Erlich's strategy has been to rely on a flexible work force and flexible manufacturing tools and techniques to allow limited production runs for customers with specialized needs. Another part of the strategy is to constantly root out inefficiencies to lower costs. A third is to raise profitability by linking the creation of specialized products to long-term joint ventures with customers. Erlich was named *Inc.* magazine's 1992 Entrepreneur of the Year. (Photo: © Bruce Zake. All rights reserved.)

Mintzberg's words are not an indictment of planning, but an encouragement not to treat it as a mechanistic, highly analytical, and formalized process to be delegated to staff. Organizations do need to plan, but planning begins when managers lead, rather than delegate, the process.

Planning Helps Reorient Vision and Direction

All firms that expect to grow or reposition themselves need to plan their strategic moves. After a few years of successful growth, most leaders latch onto a formula that seems to work; they develop core capabilities and learn how to be competitive. But most organizations encounter periods of crisis in which the winning formula that created success under one set of conditions no longer propels growth. Drucker refers to this as the need to "slough off yesterday" and reposition for the future.[47]

In part because of their size and past success, industry giants encounter difficulty when yesterday's collective decisions no longer fit new realities. Tom Peters declares bluntly, "Success breeds failure. The challenge of reinvention is absolutely required."[48] But the need to reinvent the future and slough off yesterday applies even to the smallest organizational unit. Any department or subunit needs to plan how it will continually revitalize its contribution. Otherwise, it may be absorbed into another unit or axed altogether.

American Airlines, BankAmerica, Caterpillar, General Motors, IBM, and Kodak have struggled in recent years to reorient their organizations to a future that differs from that of an earlier era. In some firms, management beliefs are too anchored to the past. In others, management is blind to internal weaknesses (such as too many layers of managers) or key environmental changes (such as shifting customer demands). In still others, plans are poorly conceived and executed, whether they focus on product development, acquisition, or defenses against antitrust litigation. Competent managers typically think of planning and implementation as a process, a responsive flow of values, information, goals, decisions, and resources

Is GE's Simple Formula for Global Competitiveness Out of Control?

To reduce the bureaucratic hierarchy and speed up the flow of strategic decisions at General Electric, the top 100 or so managers meet together as the corporate executive council (CEC) for two days every quarter. CEO Jack Welch at times asks leaders of GE's business units to reduce their analyses to one-page answers to each of five questions:

- What are your global market dynamics today; where are they going over the next few years?
- What actions have competitors taken in the last three years to upset those global dynamics?
- What have you done in the last three years to upset those global dynamics?
- What are the most dangerous things your competitor could do in the next three years to upset those dynamics?
- What are the most effective things you could do to bring your desired impact on those global dynamics?

Good questions. And the sharing allows everyone to know the basic game plan and plays across the 14 or so major lines of business. However, the push for profits ($4 billion annually) encourages managers to sometimes disregard normal operating procedures and to undertake risky transactions that could be unethical—or even illegal.

In 1994 GE was embarrassed with the scandal of reporting about $350 million in phony profits in its investment banking business, Kidder Peabody, a division headed by an executive not licensed by the Securities and Exchange Commission as required. A series of fiascoes in the early 1990s confirmed GE's need for stronger ethics: In 1993 GE's NBC News unit apologized on the air to General Motors (and paid GM $1 million for legal expenses) for staging a misleading simulated pick-up crash. In 1992 GE pled guilty to defrauding the Pentagon of more than $30 million in the bribed sale of jet engines to Israel (GE paid fines of $69 million). In 1990 GE paid $30 million in penalties for overcharging the Defense Department for a battlefield computer system.

These and other embarrassments raise the question, at what point does integrity take a holiday in the name of profits? Perhaps the emphasis ought to balance planning with control?

Sources: Noel Tichy and Ram Charan, "Speed, Simplicity, Self-Confidence: An Interview with Jack Welch," *Harvard Business Review* 67 (September–October 1989), p. 115; and Terence P. Paré, "Jack Welch's Nightmare on Wall Street," *Fortune* 130 (September 5, 1994), pp. 40–48.

throughout the organization. Although they periodically make major mistakes, the managers of General Electric have made significant progress in repositioning GE's many businesses through such processes (see the Eye on Ethics box).

Planning and controlling events, behaviors, and resources are critical parts of every manager's job. **Planning** is the process of establishing objectives and specifying how they are to be accomplished in an uncertain future. When it works well, planning helps individuals and groups visualize desired outcomes and anticipate the behaviors necessary to make them a reality. **Controlling** is the process of evaluating whether outcomes match objectives and, if not, analyzing why and taking corrective action. Control involves measuring and assessing performance to increase the probability that behaviors and resources support plans or that plans are reevaluated as circumstances change.

The dynamics of planning and managing strategically cannot be distilled into a predetermined set of steps. Nevertheless, managers draw on common elements to give direction and meaning to their plans. Effective managers combine ideology

planning
The process of establishing objectives and specifying how they are to be accomplished in a future that is uncertain.

controlling
The process of evaluating the degree to which outcomes match objectives; and when they do not, analyzing why and taking corrective action.

—————— **EXHIBIT 2–4**   *Elements Involved in Crafting a Firm's Plans*

Plans really take shape in the boxes under "levels of planning." Corporate strategy typically begins by top management defining the lines of business in which the enterprise will compete and the basis for being competitive. For each line of business, more refined strategies and plans shape how the product or service is to be produced, financed, and marketed. Finally, each individual department plans operational tactics to support business and/or corporate strategies and contribute to the mission and goals.

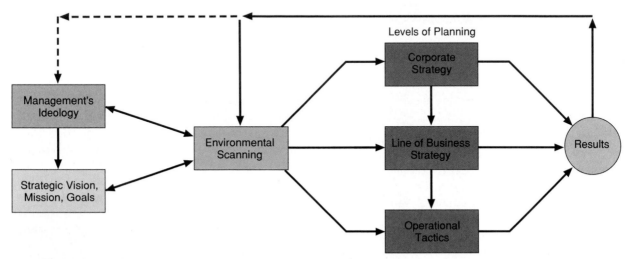

Source: Douglas C. Basil and Curtis W. Cook, *The Management of Change* (London: McGraw-Hill, 1974), pp. 135–140; and Henry Mintzberg, "Crafting Strategy," *Harvard Business Review* 65 (July–August 1987), pp. 66–75.

(their business beliefs and values) with environmental scanning perceptions (inferences about external conditions) to articulate a strategic vision. Although these factors vary among firms and managers, as shown in Exhibit 2–4, all managers rely on their ideology to interpret data and perceptions. A manager's **ideology** is his or her values and beliefs about how to succeed in business, which runs the gamut from economic assumptions to ethical ideals. A manager's ideology weaves its way into his or her approach toward planning as well as the outcomes of planning.

ideology
Beliefs and values held by a manager about how to succeed in business, encompasses economic assumptions and ethical ideals.

The Paradox of Managing by Ideology in the Information Age

Two systems of management have been identified by Larry Cummings, one based on information and the other on ideology.[49] Organizations that encourage *management by information* believe in developing clear, specific goals and plans. Managers analyze problems by studying cause-effect relationships. Thought processes are expected to be logical and directed toward well-defined systems and structures. Upper managers manipulate the symbols of success: promotions and bonuses, larger offices on higher floors, prestigious job titles, and so on. Lower managers are rewarded for passing relevant information upward and carrying out operational plans that emanate from higher up. Information is believed to be truth.

Does this sound like your ideal approach to management? If so, take comfort in the fact that for generations it was *the* way to get things done in organizations. But its emphasis on predictability makes information-driven planning limited. It is most applicable when environmental conditions are reasonably stable, which is increasingly atypical.

An alternative approach encourages self-expression and individuality among managers and professionals. *Management by ideology* means being sensitive to the attitudes and perceptions of participants. Managers are expected to "do what is right" in a situation rather than base decisions on information that may be inadequate, distorted, or outdated. Cummings sees value in basing plans on ideology: "Trust and credibility begin to center more on ideology, values, and basic beliefs, as opposed to . . . the accuracy and completeness of information. If one cannot trust others' information because of environmental change and turbulence, then one must trust others' values."[50]

Ideology Guides Environmental Scanning

Today's widespread use of sophisticated information systems might suggest that management by information is the way to go. Yet this is not necessarily so, even in information-rich organizations such as Intel, Wal-Mart, and General Electric. The combination of increased environmental turbulence and better-educated managers has made management by ideology more common. If ideology is the driver, information can be used creatively to reinvent the future. In part, this shift has occurred to help organizations respond to faster, more complex external changes:

> *In management by ideology, innovation is sought and positions are advocated that, in fact, reward innovative policies and structures. Contrary to the usual assumption, on the other hand, in management by information real innovation is to be avoided . . . Technological and information systems are designed to ensure the status quo or, at most, the gradual and incremental modification of organizational policies and designs."[51]*

By now it should be clear that management by ideology is a critical factor in planning and crafting strategies. Organizations led by people with a coherent ideology are able to use what they have learned in the past to make sense of all the conflicting information that surrounds them. Ideology filters the manager's environmental scanning perceptions of everything from external forces to internal dynamics. Managers who engage in **environmental scanning** monitor current events in the business environment and forecast future trends to combine quantitative data with qualitative perceptions.[52]

If a manager uses only ideology as a filter, data generated by scanning may not fit the manager's beliefs, and may be discounted as an aberration or ignored altogether. Active environmental scanning opens managers to a broader array of possibilities, especially if they evaluate data guided by ideology. Research found that hospital administrators who paid attention to environmental cues (signals) had a more reliable frame of reference to make decisions.[53] Therefore, they initiated more product and service improvements and performed better than those who paid less attention to their environments.

Another way to envision possible relationships with environmental forces is to engage others in group processes that lead first to shared visions and then to plans.

HOW CAN GROUP PROCESSES CREATE A SHARED VISION?

Regardless of whether an enterprise is a huge, diversified conglomerate (such as GE) or a start-up business, managers have to plan actions that promote the organization's prosperity. Such actions require periodically reinventing the organization to help it to better adapt to turbulent environments. To do so, managers are turning

environmental scanning
The monitoring of current and anticipated trends and events in the external environment through quantitative data and qualitative perceptions.

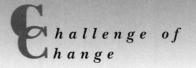

Challenge of Change

Norm Brodsky's Four Steps for Success in Business Start-Up Planning

Norm Brodsky has started six new businesses, three of which made the stats of the *Inc. 500,* with another on the threshold. After observing the business of budding entrepreneurs and checking out their performance numbers, he typically offers this advice for reorienting strategic thinking:

1. "Get a grip on your emotions and decide on your goals." He emphasizes goals that center on preserving capital and maintaining gross profit margins in early years.

2. "Make sure you understand what cash flow is and where it's going to come from." The centerpiece of a business plan is cash flow, and cash flow is about making the right kind of sales. Realize that capital is limited and make sure it lasts long enough to make the business viable (to where the business is generating the cash needed to cover expenses).

3. "Recognize the sales mentality before it's too late." Successful entrepreneurs fixate on making sales go up every day, week, month. Sales, rather than earnings, should be the early goal. But so as not to be foolish, entrepreneurs should also protect their capital, and go after the highest gross margin the business can sustain while keeping sales increasing.

4. "Learn to anticipate and recognize the changes in your business." The biggest change occurs once critical mass is attained. Critical mass is a threshold necessary for the business to take off, such as the size of the customer base. Critical mass is the point at which internally generated cash flow allows the business to grow without needing outside investment.

Even though your text focuses on understanding and influencing human behavior, in business, numbers remain important and cannot be ignored. For entrepreneur Brodsky, the numbers are fundamental to disciplining the mind of the manager. He advises would-be entrepreneurs:

> Sooner or later . . . you're going to wind up in trouble unless you stick to the rules [above] and stay on top of the numbers. Because the numbers help you balance your emotions, they keep success from going to your head. They remind you that, while your cash may be self-generated, it is not unlimited, and it can still run out.

Source: Bo Burlingham, "How to Succeed in Business in 4 Easy Steps," *Inc.* 17 (July 1995), pp. 30–42.

to planning as a group process—of building shared perceptions and organizational learning—not as a mechanical exercise of cranking out "what if" numbers. Let's walk through the details of a series of group planning processes for reinventing the organization.

Organizing for Relational Planning

Since planning usually links organizational activities to outside stakeholders, representative stakeholders are included in the process. For small start-ups, the collaborative planning may be as simple as the owner conferring with an experienced outsider, as suggested in the Challenge of Change box. In medium-sized to large organizations, the following series of techniques offer a "how to" process for planning a shared vision. They can be used with groups of 8 to 12 participants representing different stakeholders. Businesses commonly include vendors and customers as well as managers from several functional fields within the organization.

The processes described can be completed within a full day or in two half-day sessions, usually presented at an "off-site retreat" away from the office. It helps if the facilitator is an outsider—someone not ultimately responsible for carrying out the plan. Such participative techniques make visible key relationships for program planning, whether the organization is a corporation, a university, or a hospital.

Guidelines for a Four-Step Group Process

The following four-step group process is a favorite of Michael Cowley, former general manager of the Optoelectronics Division at Hewlett-Packard (H-P), who later administered H-P's worldwide quality review process.[54] To get started, a large conference room with ample wall space and plenty of floor space for walking around the table and chairs is needed. A flip chart on an easel and colored felt-tip markers are a must. Each participant will need part of a pad of 3 × 5-inch Post-it™ notes, a bold felt-tip pen such as a Sharpie®, and a dozen or more half-inch-diameter adhesive dots. Add refreshments and the participants are ready to plan.

1. Identify Stakeholder Needs and Requirements.   During the welcome, the lead manager informs participants about the general purpose of the planning meeting, usually to create innovative visions for strengthening a program or developing a new product and/or market. For small organizations, the purpose might be to reinvent the entire enterprise if its future appears threatened, off course, or on the threshold of a new opportunity.

As a warm-up activity, the group brainstorms a list of possible stakeholders affected by the project, with responses recorded on a flip chart. Next, participants brainstorm lists of the specific needs or requirements of any stakeholders with whom they have experience. From these overall impressions, participants are collectively asked to categorize (a) the strength of these needs and (b) the degree to which they are satisfied by the organization's current actions. Two columns (representing a and b) are marked off on the flip chart. Each stakeholder's needs are evaluated using the two criteria, with the group's consensus represented by symbols such as □ (strong), △ (medium), and ○ (weak). A comparison of needs and their fulfillment by the organization usually reveals unfilled needs. (See photo A in the six-picture photo essay.) Strong needs that are weakly satisfied at present are candidates for visioning new or corrective actions.

2. Initiate Visioning through an Affinity Map.   As defined earlier, a vision is a statement of elements that captures what planners want a business or program to look like in the future. The first step in crafting a vision via the group process is to identify the elements essential to make it happen. The second step is to define what the group wants the business to look like at some time in the future, say, three years. In effect, a plan becomes a bridge between the present state and the desired future state. Planners then proceed by (1) viewing the stakeholder analysis as a picture of the present state, (2) creating a vision of the future, and (3) working out details of the plan as the bridge between the present and future.

Participants are asked to write a series of statements, one item per Post-it, in response to the second item, creating a vision. For example, participants planning a business school program in technology management might be guided by the question "What will be the characteristics of a successful business school program in technology management three years from today?" As a prompt, the facilitator suggests that participants think about internal capabilities, customer needs, competition, the economic environment, obstacles to overcome, and opportunities to exploit.

Participants then post their statements randomly on a wall until everyone has exhausted his or her possibilities. Next comes the creative part. The group is asked to silently create "affinity maps" by individually and collectively arranging groupings in which individual statements appear to have a relationship to each other. They do this by moving all statements around on the wall to create thematic clusters. (See photo B.)

The affinity positioning often results in 8 to 12 clusters for most visioning tasks. The group then decides on a thematic heading for each affinity set, which is written on a Post-it with a border drawn around it to distinguish integrating themes from individual items.

3. Convert Cause → Effect Diagram to a Vision Statement.   A duplicate set of thematic labels is written and posted in a circle on a flip-chart sheet. The next group task is to evaluate the relationships (if any) between items in the circle. Connecting arrows are drawn to show cause → effect relationships. The group discusses each possible pairing: some relationships are easy to agree on; others generate controversy and a deeper probing of the interplay between forces. (See photo C.)

Once the network of cause → effect arrows has been completed, the group counts the number of incoming and outgoing arrows for each theme and tabulates scores beside the label (using $C = x$, where x is the number of causal elements; and $E = y$, where y is the number of effects). The group then labels the two or three thematic elements that have the largest number of outgoing arrows as *PC* for *primary cause.* The same is done for the *PE,* or *primary effect,* themes. (See photo D.)

For planning purposes, the primary cause (PC) elements are the ones that focus attention. If primary cause elements are acted on and strengthened, the primary effects will likely occur. From this cause → effect diagram, the group then collectively articulates a written *vision statement* of what the future should look like. Each stakeholder should be able to see its role in this vision. (See photo E.)

4. Use a Radar Chart to Show Vision-Reality Gaps.   One further refinement allows individual participants to evaluate each thematic element in a creative, graphic way. The facilitator draws a large circle on a blank flip-chart page, then places a "hub" dot in the center. Thematic labels are then placed around the outer circumference of the circle and a series of "spokes" are drawn, one for each theme.

Participants are told to let the hub represent a score of zero (0) on a theme—the complete absence of performance or lack of any value added. The point at which the spoke connects the outer circumference of the wheel represents a perfect score of ten (10)—the future state desired three years from now (or whatever the time horizon is). Each person then pastes an adhesive-backed dot on each spoke at the point where he or she judges the organization to be currently performing on that thematic element. Participants may differ in their evaluations; thus, a spoke may have dots pasted at several points along it, although typically a few spokes will have a tight clustering.

To tie results together, the facilitator asks the group to visually estimate the central tendency of dots on each thematic spoke. A hash mark is drawn to represent the estimated midpoint, or average score, and a number approximating its value (ranging from 0 to 10) is written beside the mark. Once midpoints are determined, connecting lines are drawn between midpoints of pairs of spokes. The results look like a web or radar display within the circle. The facilitator then shades in the inner portion of the web to represent distance already traveled in crossing the bridge to the future. This completes the "radar chart" (see photo F). The

Photo Essay of Group Planning Process

A. Brainstorming a list of stakeholders and evaluating how well their needs and requirements are being met.

B. Creating an affinity map to cluster planning elements into key affinity themes.

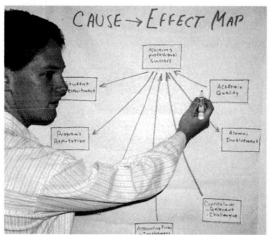

C. Starting to identify cause → effect relationships among key planning themes.

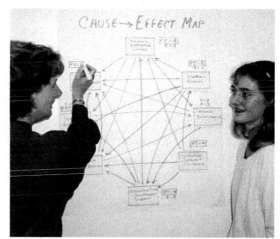

D. One group's completed cause → effect diagram shows a network of arrows used to identify primary causes and effects.

E. Results of the previous planning output is articulated into a comprehensive written vision statement.

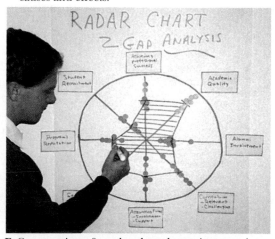

F. Construction of a radar chart dramatizes gaps in planning elements between the present and desired future.

unshaded area represents the *gap,* where future progress must be accomplished. Radar charts can also be constructed for principal competitors as a way to compare performance.

Map Alternative Paths to Bridge the Future

With this visual, graphic, intuitive-analytic work accomplished, participants have a shared sense of where they must concentrate planning efforts. They can now use their collective creativity to map out alternative routes for crossing the bridge between present and future.

One group of executives developed a matrix that listed for each element the number of "causes" (outward arrows) and the radar gap score (the difference between the current performance score and 10). They then multiplied the two scores for each element to come up with a weighted gap index. This process highlights the causal elements that most need to be improved, for those with both high causal impact and high gaps between present and desired future states are most critical to overall performance.

With causal-gap analysis completed, the group can determine where to concentrate its planning and action-taking energies. Since few organizations can be all things to all people, some elements with an overall low impact are usually discarded as not providing enough benefits for the resources expended. Subgroups can be formed to use the original affinity statements and other visualization outputs as a way to consider planning options. Most important, this interactive process usually energizes participants and gives them a broader shared vision of the project, which is difficult to accomplish when just one or two people sit down to plan. Such a group approach to planning emphasizes four *Ps: participation* of people in a series of *processes* that collectively produce a variety of visualization *products* that guide action taking to achieve *performance* results.

Vision Planning Works Best under Fast-Changing Conditions

Visual planning approaches (rather than the more traditional linear and quantitative forecasting methods of planning) are preferred by managers whose industries require fast, imaginative outlooks and decisions. Recent statistical interpretations (using factor analysis) of a survey of top executives confirms that the rate of industry change affects corporate visioning.[55] Twenty-two executives in one cluster who saw their industries as being slow to change also saw their visions as involving far-reaching but conservative strategic planning. These executives expressed little need for acceptance of their vision by others. In contrast, 97 executives in a second cluster characterized their firms as involved in rapid change. These executives embraced the belief that visions, in addition to providing strategic direction, should empower others and be widely accepted throughout the organization.

An executive who believes in vision planning is Ed McCracken, CEO of Silicon Graphics, the computer company that set the world benchmark in three-dimensional visual computing and simulation. McCracken anticipates a thousandfold improvement in computing within the next ten years. By comparison, the 1970s produced a tenfold increase, a combination of increased capacity, speed, and lower price. At a thousandfold rate of change, the industry will be thrown into chaos, with revolutionary leaps in technology. If this occurs, computing will probably transform those industries that enable people to learn, be entertained, and communicate.

Exerting control and being in control are not necessarily the same.

Calvin and Hobbes

According to McCracken, firms participating in the transformation of technology require long-term visioning but cannot tolerate long-range planning. He says, "If a product takes one year to design, the operational planning can be for no more than one year out." To sustain its technology leadership, Silicon Graphics relies more on "dynamic step-wise planning in which we do it [plan] at the last minute." With self-imposed limits placed on planning, Ed McCracken has no illusion about being in control of 6,000 talented employees. He prefers to "trust intuitive wisdom" in people throughout the organization. When technology changes so rapidly, people have "to make decisions quick, at the right level, and without concern over making mistakes."[56] In making such statements, McCracken personifies the competitive team orientation to systems control, the concept that concludes this chapter.

WHY SHOULD MANAGERS BE CONCERNED ABOUT CONTROL SYSTEMS?

Control is widely misunderstood by people in organizations because they think of it in narrow terms, as management through coercion and punishment. Even H. Ross Perot claimed, "People cannot be managed. Inventories can be managed, but people must be led."[57] This view implies that control should focus more on the activities or outcomes people produce than on people as individuals.

Control Systems Help Close the Gap

control

Any process to help align actions of people and systems with the goals and interests of the organization.

Although negative connotations persist, control systems are a must in organizations. A **control** is "any process that helps align the actions of individuals with the interests of their employing firm."[58] As dynamic, open social systems, organizations are efficient and effective when control systems are in place and working.[59] Unlike the thermostat control in a closed system that turns the furnace on and off within narrow temperature fluctuations, organizational control systems need not be mechanistic. And unless a work team is using statistical process controls (SPC) to monitor quality, controls are seldom initiated automatically in response to variance from standards.

Ann Blakeley is president of Earth Resources Corp., an environmental consulting and contracting firm in Ocosee, Florida. She uses weekly planning sessions with representatives of each department as a control system. In the sessions every contract, lead, and proposal that exceeds a certain probability is ranked in a forecasting log and updated against the previous week's model. This control system allows Blakeley and her managers to spot and correct potential problems. (Photo: © Bob Daemmrich.)

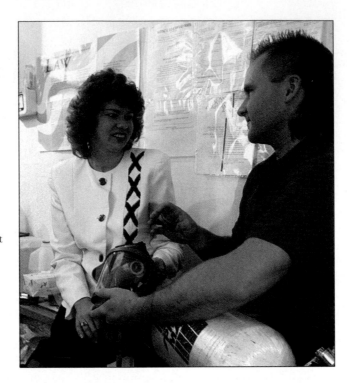

control system
Evaluative and feedback processes to let people know their managers are paying attention to what they do and can tell when undesired deviations occur.

A **control system** is "the knowledge that someone who knows and cares is paying close attention to what we do and can tell us when deviations are occurring."[60] Such a generalized definition does encompass formal control systems, such as those based on assembly-line fault tolerances, comparisons of expenses with budgets, or performance appraisals. However, it also includes behavioral sources of control, such as organizational culture and leadership.

For social system controls to work, people need to know that someone in authority knows what they are doing and is willing to call attention to gaps between performance and objectives. When Jan Carlzon took over as CEO of SAS Airline, one of his main concerns was the decline in on-time departures. To give ground and flight crews the message that on-time departures were important and had to increase, Carlzon made it known that he was personally monitoring the departure times of all flights. Within two years, the record had improved from 83 to 97 percent on-time departures.[61] Crews knew that Carlzon knew which flights were late, and they didn't want to be on his list. Less conventional social controls sometimes challenge historical practices, even in tradition-bound Japan (see the Dynamics of Diversity box).

Behaviors and Outcomes Are Measured and Evaluated

Control systems evaluate and, wherever possible, measure outcomes and/or behaviors. Measurement is preferred when outcomes can be quantified, which is the purpose of formalized control systems such as accounting. In sales, for example, outcomes are compared with each person's quota or target and to productivity measures such as sales per week, sales per customer, or orders per 10 calls. In manufacturing, controls may measure defects per million, output per shift, or on-time shipments.

**ynamics of
iversity**

Japan's TDK Introduces Social Controls to Cope with Aging

Traditions within Japan appear to be under attack. Even the presumed right to lifetime employment is no longer sacred. Japanese firms promote managers based on seniority, not performance or qualifications. As a result, managers have diminished incentive to continue being productive and innovative as they age, and there are no controls to prevent this decline. The economic downturn in the global electronics industry in the early 1990s provided TDK Corp. (the world's largest producer of magnetic tapes) a reason to lay off about 50 of its 250 middle managers over age 50.

Although TDK is regarded as a well-managed company, President Hiroshi Sato said some managers over age 50 are so steeped in the old ways that they

squash innovative ideas originating with younger managers. TDK risked having younger managers see older ones get paid to do nothing productive, which would inculcate the same slacking-off behaviors in another generation of managers. Instead, TDK took what is regarded as the most extreme action yet by a big company in Japan. To cope with the economic downturn and lack of motivation, it broke the cycle of traditional expectations that managers were not accountable for productivity. TDK took control of its work force and gave a clear performance message. The layoff shook up the complacent.

Source: "Japanese Execs Uneasy as TDK Discloses Layoff," *Washington Post* (September 13, 1992).

But for some activities, behaviors are more reliable assessments than output measures. Charles O'Reilly observes that it makes little sense to evaluate a nursing staff, based on, for example, whether patients get well, which is really a physician responsibility.[62] Assessments of behaviors make more sense—determining whether medical procedures are followed and whether medications are given or patient monitorings are made at appropriate times. In other environments, evaluation focuses on both behaviors and outcomes. In retail establishments, behaviors such as treatment of customers and promptness of processing orders are as important as sales volume per employee or gross margins.

Use Social Expectations to Control Behavior

One paradox of management is that social expectations conveyed within an organization's culture provide better controls over people than do formal measurement systems. O'Reilly states, "With formal systems, people often have a sense of external constraint which is binding and unsatisfying. With social controls, we often feel as though we have great autonomy, even though paradoxically we are conforming much more."[63]

The purpose of social controls is to get people to commit themselves to the organization. Commitments require actions, not just attitudes, even though the more a person likes a job, the more willing he or she is to stay with the organization. Maguire and Ouchi found that supervisors who focus on output increase employee satisfaction, but those who focus on close behavior monitoring do not.[64]

A summary of the effects of supervisory controls on employee commitment is captured in the statement, "We would expect that high output monitoring coupled with low behavioral control would lead to the greatest felt responsibility on the part of the worker."[65] Whether this condition leads to greater satisfaction depends on the extent to which the employee can handle the task. Overall, an important positive contribution of controls is that at least people know what is expected of them. If no one is willing to tell an employee what is expected, that employee is likely to receive little or no performance feedback and will not be particularly attentive to performance.

Managerial Values Influence Patterns of Control Systems

Control systems differ across organizations, and the patterns of variation can be traced to differences in managerial values. Let's examine the different approaches to control among financial executives. These managers are responsible for the accounting systems and resource policies that determine which units get what financial resources and what kinds of performances those resources will buy. The following control distinctions are based on observations of 805 executives.[66]

Three Control Orientations.   Managers differ in their philosophies of control. Keating and Jablonsky fit control styles into one of three "pure" orientations: competitive team, command and control, and conformance.[67] A **competitive team orientation** focuses on adding value to the market, with controls used to enhance the organization's core competence and strategic competitiveness. Information flows laterally and informally throughout the organization to help people make timely decisions.

The classic **command and control orientation** is used most often in firms that rely on a chain-of-command structure to emphasize operating efficiency and conservation of corporate resources. Controls focus on internal events, with vertical flows of information up the hierarchy for top management review and oversight.

Finally, the **conformance orientation** of control is found most often in organizations doing business with the government. Work is organized around a bureaucracy, with fixed control routines for processing information and externally reporting it in compliance with government regulations. The Internal Revenue Service (IRS) is the archetype of an organization focused on conformance control.

Two Managerial Control Profiles.   Because the traditional orientation is command and control, each of the other two can be thought of as alternatives. The competitive team and conformance orientations have nothing in common; each is either a variant or a rejection of command and control (see Exhibit 2–5). Notice that each leg in the exhibit contains a managerial control profile—behavior built on contrasting core values, either business advocate or corporate policeman.[68]

The **business advocate** approach to control builds on the core values of service and involvement, knowledge of the business, and internal customer service. Business advocates consider external competition to be the greatest threat to business success. The business advocate who emphasizes strategy most likely builds on a command and control orientation and is concerned with resource allocation and use. In contrast, those who identify more with supporting business activities in smaller business units exhibit more of a competitive team orientation. Their objective is to help increase market share. Business advocates with a competitive team orientation fit naturally into the emerging high-tech, spontaneous systems such as the World Wide Web (or Internet) or the telecommunications networks.[69]

In contrast, the more stereotypical view of control is seen in the core values of the **corporate policeman,** who emphasizes oversight and surveillance and administration of rules and procedures. Not surprisingly, corporate policemen at the corporate staff level consider internal line managers to be the greatest threat to

competitive team orientation
A manager's approach to control focused on adding value to the market by enhancing core competencies and strategic competitiveness.

command and control orientation
A manager's approach to control that emphasizes chain-of-command structures for operating efficiencies and conservation of resources.

conformance orientation
A manager's approach to control found in organizations doing business with governments where the emphasis is on compliance to rules and procedures.

business advocate
A control profile focused on competitiveness built upon core values of service and involvement.

corporate policeman
A control profile focused on budgets that emphasizes administering and checking up on rules and procedures.

Corporate Control Orientations and Profiles

Three control orientations prevail among managers. Between these extreme orientations are two possible managerial profiles (business advocate or corporate policeman) that embody the core values influencing the manager's control outlook.

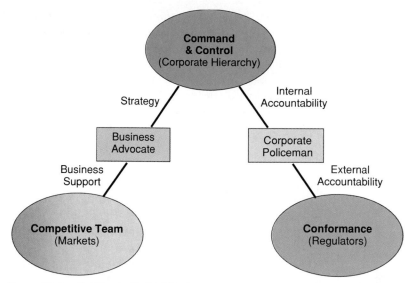

Source: Stephen F. Jablonsky, Patrick J. Keating, and James B. Heian, *Business Advocate or Corporate Policeman? Assessing Your Role as a Financial Executive* (Morristown, NJ: Financial Executives Research Foundation, 1993).

corporate performance. They stress calling attention to variances from budgets and apply rules and regulations as impersonal procedures.

While managers voice an intent to shift toward the business advocate profile and competitive team orientation, most have not made the transition.[70] Clearly, the focus of the business advocate is more consistent with the goals of quality management and continuous improvement. This control emphasis zeros in on customer satisfaction, which encourages risk taking and innovation. But whatever a manager's control orientation and profile, keep in mind how that set of beliefs is likely to translate into behaviors with co-workers. While organizational circumstances differ, the team-centered business advocate is more likely to use social expectations to foster commitment and self-accepted responsibility than the corporate policeman.

PHILIP MORRIS: ADDICTED TO NICOTINE SALES?—A SECOND LOOK

Although the official word from Philip Morris (PM) management continues to be that the nicotine in cigarettes is nonaddictive and not kept intentionally high, a few insiders have blown the whistle to the contrary. Two former scientists and a production manager presented evidence in affidavits to the Food and Drug Administration (FDA) that the strategy of Philip Morris USA has been to control nicotine levels to keep smokers hooked on cigarettes.[71] Said William A. Farone, former director of applied research at PM, "It is well recognized within the cigarette industry that there is one principal reason why people smoke—to experience the effects of nicotine." Added Ian L. Uydess, former PM research scientist, "Nicotine levels were routinely targeted and adjusted by Philip Morris."

At issue in the controversy is whether cigarettes sold in the United States will become regulated by the FDA. Philip Morris, as is true of most companies, aggressively fights regulation. The FDA claims that cigarettes are a drug-delivery device, sold for their drug effects, and thus should be regulated. If regulated, controls will be slapped on Philip Morris and other cigarette manufacturers to restrict their ability to sell, especially to minors. Any regulation that limits the sale of tobacco to young people and/or a cigarette's nicotine content will directly curb PM's ability to attract a steady stream of new, lifetime customers.

Could Philip Morris enjoy life without lighting up? Is their food and beverage business sound enough to sustain growth in sales and profits? In short, would PM be better off strategically and financially to give up on pushing cigarettes in North America and instead to sell tobacco products in countries unconcerned about health effects and focus on selling food products in North America? Organizational tradition, like an addictive habit, is tough to kick.

SUMMARY

You don't have to be an executive to benefit from learning to think like a strategist. Strategic thinking involves having a vision of a desired future that leads to a workable fit between the organization and its environment. Visions are crafted into an articulated mission, a statement of fundamental purpose that focuses on adding value to customers.

No matter what your position in the organization, you can use six all-encompassing questions to investigate, evaluate, and plan strategic actions. Two of these questions in combination enable managers to develop a SWOT analysis of internal strengths and weaknesses and external opportunities and threats. Because every work unit can be thought of as a business that creates value for others, thinking strategically through these questions can help any performance-minded person think and plan more effectively.

Managerial visions and organizational missions lead to strategies for choosing products and services that will give the firm a competitive advantage. Strategies build on organizational capabilities, the combination of assets and skills that enable one firm to do certain things better than competitors, usually by combining unique technology and employee talents into programs and services rivals cannot duplicate. Competitive strategies are possible only within lines of business where specific products jockey for position within a competitive market. For diversified businesses, corporate strategies are the choices senior executives make about what businesses to be in and how to compete.

Planning is not a mechanistic exercise of programming actions to attain objectives; rather it is a process for organizational learning. Managers draw on several elements to shape their plans. One is the manager's ideology, which shapes his or her environmental scanning perceptions as well as mission and goals.

Planning is often approached as a group exercise using a number of techniques to move from defining a vision to detailing specific actions. Affinity diagrams help pull ideas into clusters of related elements that frame a desired future state. These key themes can then be evaluated using a cause → effect diagram and a radar chart to identify gaps between current performance and future expectations.

Control systems help close the gap between performance and goals. Managers differ in their control orientation, most typically by identifying more closely with either command and control, competitive team, or conformance ideals. In between these approaches are two control profiles, business advocate and corporate policeman. Finally, managers are beginning to realize that social expectations actually provide better controls over people than do measurement systems.

Key Concepts

strategic thinking, *p. 40*

mission, *p. 42*

vision, *p. 43*

strategy, *p. 44*

structure, *p. 44*

systems, *p. 45*

core capabilities, *p. 46*

SWOT analysis, *p. 47*

milestones, *p. 48*

results, *p. 48*

competitive advantage, *p. 50*

corporate strategy, *p. 51*

outsourcing, *p. 51*

relative quality degradation, *p. 51*

competitive strategy, *p. 52*

planning, *p. 55*

controlling, *p. 55*

ideology, *p. 56*

environmental scanning, *p. 57*

control, *p. 62*

control system, *p. 63*

competitive team orientation, *p. 66*

command and control orientation, *p. 66*

conformance orientation, *p. 66*

business advocate, *p. 66*

corporate policeman, *p. 66*

Questions for Study and Discussion

1. Apply the six questions that form a basis for strategic thinking to the organization with which you are most experienced. What new insights into the organization do you gain by this process?

2. What is a SWOT analysis? How can a SWOT analysis be used to plan within a department of a larger organization? Give an example.

3. In what ways does management ideology influence the planning process? Why is managing by ideology more useful than managing by information within many organizations?

4. Describe what a group of managers would do to create an affinity map, a cause → effect diagram, and a radar chart. Explain how each device contributes to planning.

5. How do managers' command and control, conformance, and competitive team control orientations differ? Under which control orientation do you function most effectively? Why?

6. Why might an organization want its managers to appraise the behaviors of individual employees rather than rely only on absolute measures of performance?

≡ **EXPERIENTIAL EXERCISE**

≡ *Group Techniques for Vision Planning*

Purpose. This exercise enables in-class teams to develop skills for group-based vision planning by focusing on an organization that everyone knows. Specifically, the team task is to plan actions that would strengthen the academic program in which you are enrolled. The process engages teams in the hands-on experience of creating affinity maps, cause → effect diagrams, and radar charts. (Time required: about 75 minutes if students have read the chapter section on group processes for visioning.)

Materials Needed.
- One or two pads of Post-its™ per team (minimum size 3˝ × 3˝, preferably larger).
- Two or three sheets of blank newsprint per team.
- A roll of masking tape (for taping newsprint to wall).
- A felt-tip pen (such as a Sharpie®) for each person.
- About a dozen adhesive-backed dots for each person.

Procedures. Form teams of 7 to 10 persons each and hand out materials. Then work through tasks 1 to 4.

Task 1: Individual Visioning. Once teams have been assembled, each person should write brief responses to the question below. Write each response on a single Post-it, boldly enough to be read from a distance of six to eight feet. Write as many statements as you believe are relevant, but use only one theme or idea per Post-it. For planning purposes, focus on a time horizon of three years in the future. The following question is suggested as a way of focusing on a tangible task, although your instructor may present a different question:

As a student, you are concerned about the quality of the academic program in which you are enrolled. What practices or qualities should be part of this educational program three years from now to help students receive the greatest benefit from the experience? In effect, what features would enable this program to be truly excellent?

Task 2: Creation of a Team Affinity Map.

a. After three or four minutes of writing, members randomly post their responses on a wall, with each team's responses in one area.

b. Members arrange responses into clusters. This is a silent activity, with everyone working individually. Simply link themes based on any kind of affinity relationship that comes to mind. Feel free to break up groupings others have made.

c. As a group, decide on a brief title for each affinity cluster. Then write that title on a separate Post-it, draw a border or box around it, and post it at the top of the cluster.

Task 3: Creation of a Cause → Effect Diagram. Tape a sheet of newsprint to the wall near your affinity map (one for each team). Make a duplicate set of title labels and stick them to the newsprint in a large circle (similar to an analog clock face). Now draw arrows to show cause → effect relationships between each pair of themes where your group believes one has an impact on the other. Refer back to the photo essay and text for guidance if needed. (Your instructor will provide detailed instructions for tasks 3 and 4.)

Task 4: Creation of a Radar Chart for Gap Analysis. On another flip-chart sheet, draw a large circle and post another set of labels around the outer circumference. Place a hub and spokes using the text and photo essay as guides. With the circumference representing an ideal score of 10 and the hub 0, each person places an adhesive-backed dot on each spoke to spatially represent your institution's current performance. When completed, collectively determine the midpoint for each line of dots, draw a connecting line between the midpoints of each adjacent pair of spokes, and shade in the inner area. The white space represents the gap between performance now and the ideal future for the themes.

Debriefing. Reflect on the process and learning implications of this exercise by discussing questions such as:

a. What obstacles did you encounter, if any? What behaviors or processes seemed to help get the task done?

b. In what ways are your affinity maps, cause → effect diagrams, and radar charts more complex because they were developed by a group rather than by you alone? Do they more accurately represent reality? What do your answers say about whether planning should be done by individuals or teams?

c. If your school were to use this process for actual program planning, what other stakeholders or constituents would you want to include?

d. Now that you have identified cause → effect relationships and performed a gap analysis, what specific actions would you plan to bring about the vision created by your group?

▤ EXPERIENTIAL EXERCISE

▤ *What's Your SWOT Analysis?*

Purpose. This is a quickly administered small group exercise that gives students an in-class opportunity to apply the essentials of SWOT analysis. It provides a lively, practical application of one of the most widely used tools for strategic thinking. (Time required: 15 to 20 minutes.)

Materials: It makes total class sharing more dramatic if each group is provided a blank flip-chart sheet (or transparency) and a marker. Also needed is masking tape (or an overhead projector).

Procedure. Group into teams of 4 to 7 participants. With the guidance of your instructor, select an organization with which team members are familiar. We suggest that all teams focus on *your school* (or college or university); although if students are familiar with another organization (such as McDonald's, General Motors), then another organization can be chosen with instructor approval.

Step 1—Group Work. Now, as a group, invest about 10 minutes in developing a SWOT analysis of the organization your group has chosen (or been assigned). Recall from strategic questions 2 and 3 that a SWOT analysis involves: (a) an analysis of the organization's *strengths* and *weaknesses,* and (b) an assessment of the environmental *opportunities* and *threats* that the organization faces. Summarize the components of your analysis on the flip chart or transparency sheet by dividing it into four quadrants. See Exhibit 2–6 for an example of the beginnings of SWOT analysis applied to Philip Morris, the company featured in the opening vignette.

Step 2—Class Sharing. Each group shares its results with the class. If every team has focused on the same organization and summarized their results on a flip-chart page, simply tape these to the front of the room. If groups have chosen different organizations, then results can be shared sequentially with one member briefly summarizing team conclusions.

Step 3—Debriefing. Discuss issues such as:

1. In what ways did the four-factor analysis cause you to see critical elements about the organization that you probably would have overlooked if you were not using a structured framework?

2. To what extent does the profile of elements suggest any strategies that ought to be changed or initiated? To what extent does it reinforce the efficacy of current strategies?

3. What did you observe about the group process that made this a productive (or unproductive) exercise?

▤ EXHIBIT 2–6

Example of SWOT Analysis Applied to Philip Morris Companies

SWOT analysis provides a structured framework for assessing relevant internal and external factors affecting an organization's strategies. This PM example is highly abbreviated—your group may want to provide greater detail for each key element.

Strengths	Weaknesses
• High profits from tobacco • World's largest advertiser • Operational efficiencies • Etc....	• Dependence on tobacco • Some acquisition mismatch • Management blunders • Etc....
Opportunities	**Threats**
• Global tobacco markets • Many food companies for sale • Price power over ad media • Etc....	• Tobacco regulation as a drug • Customer product boycotts • Competitor retaliation • Etc....

CASE

Product Development at Oakmark Computer

Oakmark Computer produces and sells personal computers, software, and peripherals such as printers through a network of independent dealers. Oakmark is a major competitor but has recently experienced a decline in its North American market share from a high of 19 percent three years ago. George Clinton, president of one of the firm's four divisions, has concerns about several performance indicators and thinks the decline in competitiveness may be caused in part by what he believes to be an overly informal rather than planned approach to new-product development.

Clinton called in Dan Dole, a manager familiar with transforming concepts into products. He said, "Dan, I'm feeling increasingly uneasy about the way Oakmark brings new products to market. You know the ropes we go through to transform an idea into sales of new hardware and software. Write me a brief description of the activities we do, something I can use for examining and maybe changing the way we plan for product development."

The next day, Dole passed the following report to Clinton:

Report on Product Development at Oakmark
Recent products have been late to market, inadequately tested, and lacking in customer after-sale service and technical support. Engineers and computer programmers believe that doing research and development is their source of personal rewards, a way of thinking reinforced by the organization's values and practices that is becoming dated. Furthermore, we have yet to clarify the distinction between research and product development, which causes the commercialization of ideas to be engineering driven, undisciplined, and developed with little sensitivity to customer needs.

In an industry where the transformation of a product possibility into actual revenue is measured in months, we often take years to reach the market. At times products are created as a result of the personal needs and interests of the developer; in some cases, they are a reaction to something introduced by the competition that threatens to make an Oakmark product obsolete faster. All this occurs in an industry where being first to market with a new product goes hand in hand with market share.

To get a product to market in this firm an idea needs the support of a management champion. This champion must lobby people in various parts of the company that have the resources necessary to create the product. If some preliminary interest is shown, a "proof of concept" paper is written and circulated more broadly, until there is a critical mass of support voiced for the product possibility. Once political support is obtained, a formal product proposal is developed to identify the essential technical requirements and to propose a preliminary design.

If the formal proposal wins enough approvals, an engineering team is pulled together to develop a prototype. The working prototype then enables the concept to be evaluated in terms of its practicality, manufacturability, customer acceptance, price and function relative to our other products, investment payoff, legal implications, and other considerations. A product that passes this stage is then transferred to production engineering. At this stage, further changes may be made to accommodate manufacturing capability, placement in a suitable division within the firm, and feedback from customers who "beta test" the product. (A beta test allows a sample of customers to use the product under actual conditions and provide feedback about its performance prior to release of the product to the public.) If it still looks feasible, someone will give the go-ahead (it could be the CEO, the COO, a division president, or a divisional manager), and the project moves into production and distribution.

Once someone gets a vision of a product possibility that interests a potential champion, the process becomes one of working one's personal network—posturing, pleading, and confronting opposing and supporting views. At times similar work may be under way in other parts of the organization, but there is no systematic way of knowing. As a project advances, it is handed off from player to player or team to team until, if it survives, it finally appears on the sales force product and price sheets with a request for advertising and promotion.

Once a project has been handed off to production, teams involved at earlier stages of engineering development are disbanded and reassigned to other projects. If problems or questions arise from the product's use, a customer support group may have to reinvent solutions if the documentation and design specifications handed off after product development were incomplete. As the number of "proof of concept" papers and product proposals increases, people at all levels are beginning to wonder if the product development process needs to become more focused. Do we need to plan a better process?

Questions for Managerial Action
1. Draw a diagram of Oakmark's product development process. What are the strengths and weaknesses of Oakmark's current approach to product development?

2. Try to envision what might be going on in the competitive marketplace and how customers or users are likely to respond when Oakmark gets into channels of distribution with a new product offering. What external opportunities and threats is Oakmark likely to face in the marketplace?

3. From your SWOT analysis (responses to questions 1 and 2), what elements of product planning would you recommend that Oakmark keep? Which should it eliminate?

4. Evaluate Oakmark from the perspectives of planning and control systems. How does the filter-up approach fit into the concept of managing by strategic vision?

5. How would you improve Oakmark's product development? What would be your plan to speed up time to market and improve follow-through to customer service? To what degree should individual or team accountability become formalized? What kinds of controls might be reasonable for this high-tech firm?

Chapter 3

Organizing Work Teams and Structures

LEARNING OBJECTIVES

After studying this chapter, you should be able to:

- Explain why significant changes in the nature of jobs are occurring as a result of new technology.
- Compare the similarities and contrast the differences among quality circles, self-managed teams, and cross-functional teams.
- Sketch an organization chart of the four common structures and cite two advantages and disadvantages of each.
- Explain how the issues of autonomy, control, and coordination affect decisions about centralized versus decentralized authority.
- Contrast the characteristics, strengths, and weaknesses of bureaucracy with those of organic organizations.
- State how differences in span of control, hierarchical levels, and size yield flatter organizations.

FORD MOTOR CO. REORGANIZES ITS FINANCE FUNCTION

The power of Ford's central finance group has been legendary since the 1950s. Designed by Henry Ford II's whiz kids Robert McNamara (Secretary of Defense under Presidents Kennedy and Johnson) and J. Edward Lundy (CFO from 1962 through 1979), finance has been the venerable gatekeeper of profits at Ford, deciding which projects to fund and which to terminate. Such a structure made it difficult for operating people—those who design, build, and market cars—to trust the Dearborn, Michigan, headquarters staff. It led to a lot of second-guessing.

Ford self-promotes on an image of innovation with its "Ford has a better idea" campaign. In truth, smaller Chrysler has been the automotive innovation leader within North America, and by far the world-class leader in efficiency. In benchmarking profits per vehicle, in 1993 Chrysler earned $828 per vehicle to Ford's $323 (GM lost $189)—statistics that galled Ford executives as Ford spends $200 less in labor costs per vehicle. For over a decade Chrysler has been designing cars by starting with a target sticker price and giving rigorous attention to costs beginning with the early stages of design. Ford's finance didn't run the numbers until new designs were well along, almost too late to be really helpful.

Under the roadmap plan Ford 2000, all of its historic highly centralized structure was turned upside down. Ford had accounted for profits three ways, beginning with geography, then corporate function, followed by product line. With reorganization, product line became the first priority and geography dropped to third. Ford plans to become an integrated global auto maker during the last half of the 1990s by eliminating what has been four autonomous geographic divisions: North America, Europe, Asia, and Latin America. Says Murray Reichenstein, controller for worldwide automotive operations, "We're going to run our business the way the market looks at it. I promise you we'll be faster and more responsive." By the time 1999 models hit the showrooms, all regional boundaries will have disappeared along with several levels of the corporate hierarchy and $2 billion to $3 billion of related overhead costs.

The reorganization means the jobs of finance managers have to be redesigned and relearned. Most finance people will become members of operating teams, working alongside the rank-and-file in design, engineering, manufacturing, and marketing. By placing finance managers on product development teams, Ford aims to gain early advantage from up-front financial analysis, which should mean greater profits. Reichenstein sees the value in this control shift from corporate policeman to competitive team: "You have all ranges of choice in the beginning [of vehicle development]." A year or two later design and engineering decisions have been made that are difficult to overturn with delayed financial analysis. The change will also affect new college hires, says Reichenstein: "You want to put pressure on them so they get a lot of experience when they're very young. You want to move them across all kinds of functions—sales, treasury, central staff, and so on—so that they're not just manufacturing finance people, or just product development finance people."

Sources: S. L. Mintz, "Redesigning Finance at Ford," *CFO Magazine* (March 1995), pp. 26–34; and Robert L. Simpson and Neal Templin, "Ford Motor Co. Shakes Up Staff of Finance Unit," *The Wall Street Journal* (June 1, 1995), pp. A3, A6.

Organization is the architecture on which enterprises are built. As in any architectural design, there are trade-offs and compromises. But unlike the design of a vehicle or building, organization structures are expected to change substantially and fairly frequently to accommodate growth and keep the organization viable. Ford Motor Co. in the early 1990s began to realize that the structure built more than 30 years ago had become dysfunctional. It was acting more as a brake on technological innovation than as an accelerator. No longer was the automotive industry separated by oceans and continental land masses. It had become integrated into a global market with firms domiciled in any one country willing to battle for market share in any other country where people bought cars and trucks.

To respond to this changing world order, Ford took the bold step of reconfiguring both its organizational structure and the design of jobs for people throughout finance and other functions. The goal of Ford's reorganization was to speed up decision making, improve the efficiency of designing and building vehicles, cut administrative costs by eliminating management layers, shift the focus from regions to product lines, and literally break down the walls that separated people on the basis of the functional task they performed. In effect, Ford was redesigning the vehicle in which its people work, to give it more speed and responsiveness.

The focus of this chapter is on the interplay between technology, job tasks (or roles), and organizational structures as they impact people. Structures and jobs are intended to support and help people carry out the strategies of an enterprise. But structure can no longer be thought of as the static, mechanical arrangement of boxes and lines of reporting relationships that generations of employees have known as the "organization chart." Organization also involves the systems and processes managers put in place to guide behavior. Systems can be tightly structured to promote order, or they can be loosely structured to promote risk taking and creativity.

WHY MUST THE DESIGN OF WORK AND ORGANIZATIONAL STRUCTURES CHANGE OVER TIME?

Strategies require the orchestrated capabilities of people, resources, and systems to make them work in ways that produce a competitive advantage. For this to happen, managers engage and draw on the five principal options that typically are the *targets for internal change* within organizations: people, tasks, technology, structure, and culture. The arrows in Exhibit 3–1 show that potentially there can be complete interactions among these five variables that we call the "organization star." A change in one might affect one or more other variables.

Even though the primary focus of this book is on the people variable, a person's behaviors at work are not entirely based on free will. Surrounding situational factors present changing stimuli that either constrain or liberate what a person does

■■■■ EXHIBIT 3–1   *The Organizational Star Offers Organizational Targets for Change*

When managers seek to improve or change the internal behaviors of an organization, their decisions and actions focus on one or more of five options. The variables they can attempt to influence are tasks (including strategies, goals, and jobs), technology (as it affects the development of products and processes for getting work done), structure and internal systems, organizational culture (values and beliefs), and people (their numbers, attitudes, capabilities, and behaviors). Surrounding the organization (within the dashed border) are four forces comprising the transacting environment of the enterprise: vendors, customers, regulators, and competitors.

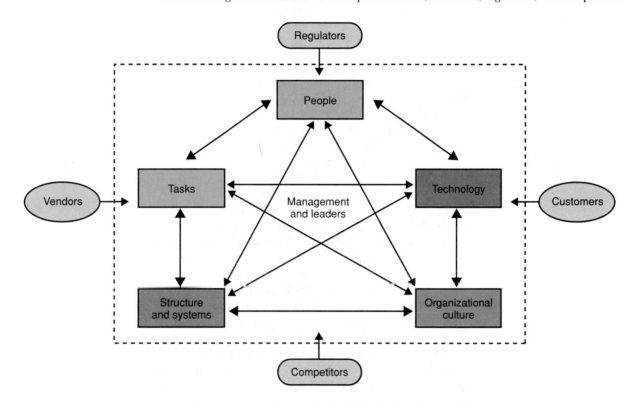

in carrying out a job. The designs of organization structures and teams are two of those situational factors we examine in this chapter, along with the contributing role of technology. (Organizational culture is explained in the next chapter and the design of individual jobs in Chapter 7).

Technology Is a Driver of Organization Change

A digital revolution, manifest by the combination of computer networking and telecommunications, is transforming work and organizations. People are united independently of time and distance through tools such as distributed databases, teleconferencing, e-mail, the Internet, and groupware. Corporate boundaries become transparent when vendors and customers are connected through a network of paperless transactions that puts everyone on the same screen instantaneously.

In a study of more than 75 networked companies, the researcher concluded: "Where work is carried out through networks, an organization's structure changes whether you want it to or not. I can't find a single case where it doesn't happen."[1] What happens is data now connect people to people directly, without the need of managers in a hierarchy to filter and pass along information and

▬▬▬ EXHIBIT 3–2

*Job Enhancement
Determines a Country's
Growth*

An expanded standard of
living allows increased
investments to be made in
education and training, but
only if educational
opportunity for all is valued.
Education and training drive
technology, and improved
application of technology
makes productivity increases
possible. Productivity gains
fuel improvements in the
country's living standards.
The bottom line: Jobs must
be enhanced by education,
training, and technology.

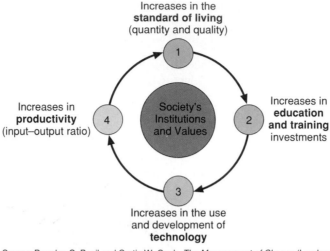

Source: Douglas C. Basil and Curtis W. Cook, *The Management of Change* (London: McGraw-Hill, Inc., 1974), pp. 35–37.
Reprinted with permission of McGraw-Hill, Inc.

technology
The scientific knowledge,
processes, systems and
equipment used to create
products and services and
to help people carry out their
tasks.

hand down decisions. Not only does information technology pressure an organization to flatten its hierarchy, it also pressures changes in jobs—including management. The traditional concept of the boss who knows more than his subordinates quickly fades when talented people have access to information—and through information, access to customers and vendors.

Technology encompasses the scientific knowledge, processes, systems, and equipment used to create products and services and to help people carry out their tasks. Technology is typically the motivating force behind improvements in what an organization produces and the means by which human productivity is increased. Some examples of technological processes that are transforming work methods include statistical process control (SPC), manufacturing resource planning (MRP II), just-in-time (JIT) inventory, management information systems (MIS), and computer-integrated manufacturing (CIM). For the individual worker, an upgrade in technology might be as basic as replacing a stand-alone computer with networked computing or a hand tool with an electrically powered one.

The Historic Impact of Technology on Transforming Work.   Our focus on technology largely examines how process improvements and new types of tools and systems alter the nature and organization of human work. But technology is also the engine that drives much of a firm's or industry's competitive and productivity gains, which collectively improve the standard of living for society. Future technology gains are possible, however, only by improving the quality of education and training of the work force, as symbolized in Exhibit 3–2.

When technology expands productivity over time, the nature of jobs changes dramatically. Before the American Civil War, about 90 percent of the population was engaged in agriculture. But with technology applied to the mechanization of farming and the development of land grant colleges (to conduct agricultural research and train farmers) in the late 1800s and early 1900s, farm productivity increased dramatically. Today the United States requires less than 3 percent of its working population to produce an abundant agricultural harvest—the most productive use of agricultural resources of any nation.

■■■■ **EXHIBIT 3–3**

Drucker Defines Five Skills for Improving the Person–Job Match

To improve the productivity of knowledge and service employees, Peter Drucker advises managers to develop *five types of skills:*

- First, ask, "What is the task? What are we trying to accomplish? Why do it at all?" In manufacturing and transportation jobs, the task is more observable; in knowledge and service jobs, tasks need to be evaluated frequently and changed. In any industry, the most profound route for improving performance and the person–job match is often to eliminate tasks altogether—to stop doing that which really does not need to be done.
- Second, take a hard look at the ways in which jobs add value. Where does real value occur? Many activities only add costs rather than value. Cost generators such as unnecessary meetings or reports written to impress higher managers should be candidates for elimination.
- Third, define performance in terms of what works. Quality only comes by analyzing the steps in the process that produce value-added performance. Managers then need to wipe out unnecessary steps and build in those that are necessary but lacking.
- Fourth, managers need to develop a partnership with people who hold potentially productive jobs and get them to improve the process. This means relying on jobholders to identify obstacles to improved performance and to build in corrective action. Drucker says quite simply, "To find out how to improve productivity, quality, and performance, ask the people who do the work."
- Finally, to sustain continuous learning, people at all levels need to teach. Drucker says, "The greatest benefit of training comes not from learning something new but from doing better what we already do well. Equally important . . . knowledge workers and service workers learn most when they teach."

Source: Peter F. Drucker, "The New Productivity Challenge," *Harvard Business Review* 69 (November–December 1991), pp. 69–79.

Similarly, the percentage of people required to manufacture the nation's industrial and consumer goods peaked in the 1950s (at almost 27 percent); today, manufacturing employs only about one-seventh of the work force.[2] In the short run, transformation of technology creates structural unemployment. In the long run, it frees up human resources to be shifted into more productive types of work—if education and training provide advanced skills.

Employment Shifts to New Technologies. In a perceptive view of our past and future, Alvin Toffler uses the metaphor of colliding waves to visualize three distinct, work-related changes transforming civilization. The waves shift from agriculture to industrial manufacturing to the current information and knowledge-based third wave, a new way of organizational life based on new technologies and new work patterns.[3] Electronics alone now employs considerably more people in the United States than steel, autos, and aerospace combined.[4] We all know that the technological push toward electronic miniaturization and doing more with less has enabled more power and speed to be packed into smaller microprocessor packages that control such products as computers, auto climate systems, watches, and video cameras. Even something as basic as long-distance telephone service requires fewer resources and yields an improved quality of service because of a shift in transmission from copper wires to hair-thin fiber-optic cable. It took one ton of coal to produce 90 miles of copper phone wire. The same ton of coal produces 80,000 miles of fiber-optic cable—today's standard for long-distance voice and data transmission.

The contemporary challenge is to increase productivity in the sectors employing most of the population, the knowledge and service sectors. In the knowledge sector, career opportunities are increasingly limited to people with advanced education. And yet those qualified to perform these knowledge-based jobs are outnumbered by people who lack the qualifications for anything but low-skilled service jobs.[5] With technology tools, managers must also learn skills that enable them to improve productivity among knowledge and service workers. Exhibit 3–3 offers several skill-building ideas from Peter Drucker.

To dramatize the impact of technology on changing the nature of clerical jobs and even organization structures, consider the improvements in productivity realized by changing the way customers' orders are processed at the checkout counter of retail stores. Within your lifetime retail clerks have shifted from keying in the dollar amount of each item in your purchase to essentially keeping their hands off the cash register keyboard and letting technology enter the data. Three technologies have been combined—optical scanning, bar codes, and databases—to simplify the job of the clerk and provide the customer with a faster, more accurate transaction. Most important, information technology "allows near instantaneous electronic transmission of sales and inventory information, enabling even the largest retailers to keep abreast of what customers want without communicating with them personally."[6] The retail chain has an electronic record of each item sold for use in inventory control, merchandising, analyzing profit contributions of each product, and comparing performance among stores. Because clerks represent the largest occupational group in developed nations, such applications of technology are having major impacts on transforming jobs and organizational designs.

Technology Creates Global Competition for Jobs and Skills

National boundaries still exist for political and ethnic reasons, but economically, the factory worker or clerk in Des Moines is competing as much with employees in Frankfurt, Seoul, or Tokyo as with workers in Atlanta or Ontario. Increasingly, products and services blend together, and often it is the service component that affords competitive advantage because it is not easily replicated. The objective is to create products that are specialized due to their high service component—service provided by what Labor Secretary Robert Reich calls "knowledge workers." Three *universal work skills* drive successful firms because each skill provides high value to the customer.

- Problem-solving skills, or the ability to put things together in unique ways, be they movie scripts, software, or semiconductor chips.
- The skills to help customers understand their needs and how those needs can best be met by taking advantage of the customized product offered.
- The skills to link problem solvers with problem identifiers, or the management and brokerage of ideas.[7]

Such skills reflect the changing organizational requirements that people must meet to be effective in a global labor market. They also apply directly to the increasing use of teams as the basic work unit, which slowly displace the emphasis of designing jobs around individual tasks (individual job design is explored in Chapter 7 on applied motivation). Before reading on, however, take a couple of minutes to reflect on the conditions you hope to find in your employing organization by answering the questions in the Your Turn exercise.

WHY DESIGN WORK AROUND SELF-MANAGING TEAMS?

To bring about continuous improvement and innovation, routine tasks of production and in-person service jobs are increasingly bundled into teams to work in harmony with technology. Firms are moving to abandon what have been narrowly defined job classifications. For example, "craft" boundaries in union shops historically have prevented a firm's carpenters from moving an electrical outlet or pipe when relocating a wall in a production facility. Such skill rigidities are dysfunctional to employees and to the enterprise.

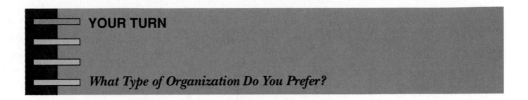

YOUR TURN

What Type of Organization Do You Prefer?

Describe the characteristics you prefer to experience in an organization. Use your personal beliefs and values as a guide to score each of the 12 characteristics on a 5-point scale, where 5 means "strongly agree" with the statement and 1 means "strongly disagree." Circle your preference.

	Agree			Disagree	
1. People should know where they fit in a well-defined hierarchy of explicit authority–status relationships.	5	4	3	2	1
2. Supervision, decisions, and controls should be exercised through a chain of command with clearly understood roles.	5	4	3	2	1
3. Codified systems of formal rules, policies, and procedures should simplify the handling of routine activities.	5	4	3	2	1
4. Division of labor should be refined through job specialization.	5	4	3	2	1
5. Technical competence and seniority should be the basis for job staffing.	5	4	3	2	1
6. Promotions and pay should be based on individual performance merit.	5	4	3	2	1
7. Roles should be fluid, changing with new goals and needs.	5	4	3	2	1
8. Planning should take place throughout the organization; plans should not simply be handed down from the top.	5	4	3	2	1
9. Personal involvement in challenging, complex tasks should be a greater source of motivation than management style or formal rewards.	5	4	3	2	1
10. Teams rather than individuals should be the primary source of output.	5	4	3	2	1
11. Primary work tasks should occur more in a horizontal work flow than within specialized functional departments with vertical responsibilities.	5	4	3	2	1
12. Performance should be measured more by external results (customer satisfaction) than by internal statistics (costs per hour).	5	4	3	2	1

Scoring and Interpretation:

Enter the sum of your scores to questions 1 through 6 here: _____ M
Enter the sum of your scores to questions 7 through 12 here: _____ O
Subtract the smaller score from the larger. If M is larger, on balance you prefer more mechanistic or bureaucratic organizations. If O is larger, your preference is for organic or flexible organizations. If the difference between your M and O score is 17 or greater, your preference is quite strong. If the difference between scores is 9 to 16, a moderate preference is indicated; if 1 to 8, your preference is slight. Obviously, a zero is neutral. As you read on in the chapter, you will understand the differences between these two organizational prototypes.

Involvement and Innovation

As an alternative, many organizations allow team members to be given greater discretion to define their jobs so they can respond to whatever challenge the group encounters. Teams now carry out many of the planning and problem-solving functions previously reserved for managers. Ford Motor Co. can produce as many autos today as it did in the late 1970s with half as many employees. The most important factor in this improvement is increased cooperation of the work force to help find ways to reduce costs.[8] Ford worked with union participation to eliminate work rules with narrow job classifications in the company's formerly least productive stamping plant, a change that saved $15 million per year.

The movement to give the work group or team more responsibility for performing tasks in the workplace is gaining momentum. Ed Lawler writes: "Despite the fact that individual enrichment has important advantages and should be used in certain situations . . . the preferred work design for most high-involvement situations is the team approach."[9] Propelling this trend is the growth of quality management and continuous improvement practices. Traditional organizational practices place responsibility for improvement on the manager. There is evidence, however, that managers often make erroneous assumptions about what is wrong, for example, with manufacturing quality.[10] Although managers may assume that quality problems stem from a poor work force, poor workmanship, and poor maintenance of production facilities and equipment, in reality the problems may be due to poor quality of incoming parts or poor design—factors that people doing the work contend with every day. Mitroff notes that "You can't get quality through blame or through fixing the wrong part of the whole system."[11] Participative teams are often more resourceful in bringing about continuous quality improvement.

Options for Participative Team Management

Although managerial authority still prevails in most organizations, the shift toward participation in decisions by nonmanagers is increasing. Managers are learning that to be competitive, they "should count on the ideas and judgment of production workers, as well as their physical effort."[12] American managers have been slower than their Japanese and Swedish counterparts to accept and learn from work teams. They fear potential power loss and often fail to perceive the value of potential improvements that are easily seen by those working in nonmanagerial jobs.[13]

Managers who wish to begin to allow nonmanagers to participate in making decisions face two questions: In what types of decisions should employees participate? How much latitude should they be granted to implement their recommendations? Exhibit 3–4 uses these two issues to identify a matrix of different participation possibilities. The three team-based participation models through which performers can influence work practices and policies are quality circles, self-managed work teams, and cross-functional teams.[14] Self-managed teams and cross-functional teams enjoy greater authority to act on their own recommendations than do quality circles. Quality circles essentially provide an analysis and advisory function. But since the move toward participation typically begins as a way of breaking away from traditional manager-focused practices, quality circles are often a starting point.

Quality Circles.   A movement to capture the creative power of workers using quality circles began in Japan in the 1960s.[15] Although the concept originated in the United States, in was not practiced here until introduced by Lockheed in 1974. A

▬▬▬ **EXHIBIT 3–4**

Participation in Decision Making

Not all decisions are equally participative. Once management moves beyond traditional management practices, in which decisions reside with managers, the intermediate step is usually joint decisions, where performers can make recommendations (as usually practiced by quality circles, consultative participation, and task forces). Only when decisions are completely delegated to the performers (as with self-managed teams and cross-functional teams) is participation at its highest level.

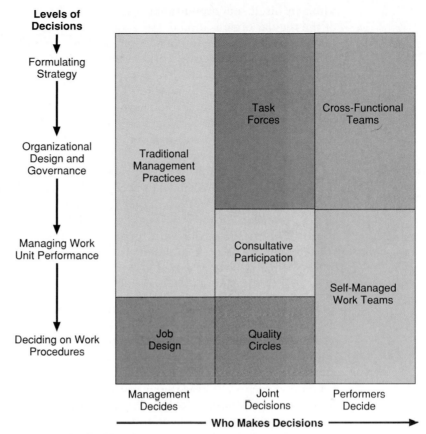

Levels of Decisions

↓

Formulating Strategy

↓

Organizational Design and Governance

↓

Managing Work Unit Performance

↓

Deciding on Work Procedures

	Task Forces	Cross-Functional Teams
Traditional Management Practices		
	Consultative Participation	
		Self-Managed Work Teams
Job Design	Quality Circles	

Management Decides — Joint Decisions — Performers Decide

Who Makes Decisions →

Source: Adapted from Edward E. Lawler III and Susan A. Mohrman, "Quality Circles: After the Honeymoon," *Organizational Dynamics* (Spring 1987).

quality circle (QC)
A group process that operates apart from but parallel to the traditional managerial structure by involving volunteers in analyzing problems and recommending solutions.

quality circle (QC) is a group process that operates parallel to the traditional managerial structure by involving volunteers in problem-solving recommendations. Quality circle members study ways to improve quality, although normally they do not have authority to implement changes. Instead, they sell the merits of group analysis and recommendations to management, in what is at best a form of joint decision making.

Quality circles provide a means for people in technical or operational capacities to become responsible for solving problems and improving practices. They learn that their ideas do make a difference, as did a nine-person team of physicians, technicians, and managers at Norfolk General Hospital when they eliminated 14 steps to cut X-ray processing time from an average 72.5 hours to 13.8 hours.[16] Because it trains participants and managers alike to share responsibility, the QC experience provides a positive skill-building prelude to true self-managed work teams.

self-managed team
A work unit whose members are granted responsibility and authority to take the decisions and actions necessary to produce a product or service.

Self-Managed Teams. Although work teams have existed for centuries, only recently have self-managed teams become a key approach to organizing work within large organizations. A **self-managed team** is a work unit whose members are granted responsibility and authority to make the decisions necessary to produce a product or service. Teams are given the right to be largely self-governing, to make decisions about scheduling and assigning tasks, to decide on work methods and who gets hired, and even in some cases to adjust rates of pay. Because they are part of the regular organizational system rather than a group that operates parallel to it (as QCs do), teams are intended to create high rates of member involvement.

Much of the pioneering work on teams originated from the Tavistock Institute in Great Britain. Tavistock conducted early experiments with work teams under the label of "sociotechnical systems design."[17] Ironically, what the Tavistock researchers observed in their pioneering study was how technology and work reorganization broke up naturally functioning self-managing teams of coal miners. These researchers reasoned that work organization needed to consider both the technical requirements (for equipment, tools, and work processes) and the social-system aspects of work if teams are to be motivated. The goal of **sociotechnical systems design** is to achieve a balanced fit between the technical system and the human system as a group. Whereas job design focuses on ways of achieving greater motivation and satisfaction for individual employees, sociotechnical systems design seeks these benefits for entire work groups. During a recent decade, researchers reported on over 130 examples of change toward sociotechnical systems design involving organizations as varied as a railway maintenance depot, auto manufacturing, textile mills, and pet food production.[18]

sociotechnical systems design
A systems approach to enhance motivation and productivity by structuring work groups to achieve a balance between technical and human subsystems.

Cross-Functional Teams.   Bringing new or improved products to market traditionally is organized as a series of sequential processes to transform ideas into products. Four or five separate functional groups are typically involved, each doing their own work and then handing it off to the next downstream group. To attack the cost of product introduction delays, some firms have moved to cross-functional teams.[19] **Cross-functional teams** pull together people from different functions or disciplines to coordinate separate but interrelated tasks that affect overall product or service quality. They often take the form of development teams who band together only long enough to complete a particular project and then disband.

cross-functional teams
A way of organizing that pulls people together from several different functions or disciplines to emphasize coordination of separate but interrelated tasks in achieving product and service quality.

Ford Motor Co. created the original Team Taurus when management decided to design and build the Taurus and Sable automobiles in the 1980s. The cross-functional team assembled designers, production specialists, engineers, customers, accountants, and others to generate a simultaneous flow of ideas about designs, cost estimates, organizational processes, and other aspects to speed development and production of the vehicles. "Before the first clay model was built, they knew how the car would be assembled. Under the previous system, manufacturing managers didn't see the cars they were going to build until eight or nine months before production started."[20] Taurus became the best-selling car in America by the early 1990s, but to make it attractive to younger buyers, a second Team Taurus assembled in the basement of Ford's Design Center, nicknamed "The Dungeon." Starting with 150 members in 1991, the team expanded to 700 before the new, redesigned 1996 model was introduced. *Business Week* writes:

> *Team Taurus (II) is Ford's biggest experiment with the team method Trotman (Ford Chairman) plans to make the cornerstone of Ford's global product-development process. Engineers handling chassis, engine, and manufacturing chores work alongside designers, marketers, bean counters, suppliers, and factory-floor workers to design and test the vehicle together. Says (team leader) Landgraff: "How we managed this program is as important to Ford as the vehicle we engineered."[21]*

WHAT ARE THE BASIC ORGANIZATIONAL DESIGN STRUCTURES?

Designing jobs and structuring teams are fundamental to organizing work. To pull jobs and teams together, all enterprises need a structure and governance process that divide up tasks and yet promote work toward a common cause. For start-up businesses and small enterprises, decisions about organization design are simple and easy to implement. Organizations of up to a hundred or so people typically have few basic departments structured around functions performed. Each has a supervisor or manager who is responsible directly to the chief executive. The owner or executive personally acts as leader, decision maker, and controller over the single line of business. But as a firm grows to employ tens of thousands, organization designs become complex, almost mazelike, changing periodically to accommodate growth or realignment needs.

Purposes Served by Organizational Structure

organizational structure
The networked arrangement of positions and departments through which the essential tasks of an enterprise are subdivided and grouped to create the systems, decision centers, and behavioral linkages that carry out business strategies.

organization chart
The symbolic structure of boxed titles and lines that represent positions and reporting of relationships.

organizational design
The process managers go through to create meaningful structures, decision and information networks, and governance systems.

An **organizational structure** is the hierarchical arrangement through which the essential tasks of an enterprise are subdivided and grouped to create the systems, decision centers, and behavioral network that carries out enterprise strategies. Organizational structures have been in use for over two thousand years as a means of getting large numbers of people to work toward a common goal, be it building a pyramid or fighting a war. An organization structure is more than the boxes and lines on an **organization chart**—the tangible symbols of the positions and reporting relationships throughout an enterprise. Organization affects human behavior because structure can make it easy or difficult for people in separate work units to talk and work with one another. Structure affects the way people size up situations, the way they interact with others, what they value and believe to be important, time horizons, and even management styles.[22]

The Eye on Ethics box describes how Johnson & Johnson, the pharmaceutical company, uses organizational design to balance creative, entrepreneurial needs of autonomous lines of business with ease of customer interaction with a unified organization. **Organizational design** is the process managers go through to create meaningful structures, decision and information networks, and governance systems. Organizational design provides for (1) the dividing and grouping of tasks; (2) networks to convey information; (3) a structure for locating decision centers, or authority; (4) processes for coordination, control, and conflict resolution; and (5) the means to link key work units with appropriate external stakeholders such as customers and suppliers.[23] Designing an organization involves deciding how the enterprise should be managed as much as it does creating structures to subdivide and allocate tasks.

Four basic structures have served as common approaches for grouping people and subunits within social systems, whether they be business firms, police departments, or the postal service. These four basic designs are by function, geography, product, and customer. Traditionally, the chosen structural arrangement is summarized as an organization chart, a symbolic picture of an organization that uses boxes to represent positions arranged by hierarchical level and connecting lines to indicate reporting relationships. Typically, enterprises are built around a dominant structural form, and then other forms are blended in for special purposes. This hybrid approach is logical because each basic structure has weaknesses as well

Eye on Ethics

Balancing Flexibility, Structure, and Responsibility at Johnson & Johnson (J&J)

How does a diversified pharmaceutical firm structure hundreds of product lines into an organization that maintains efficiency and also promotes ethical, entrepreneurial behavior? At Johnson & Johnson, the key is decentralization. Presidents of the 160 or so J&J business units are given reasonable autonomy to run their own businesses consistent with a code of ethics. The objective of these small, self-governing units is to make each manageable and ethically responsive to market forces.

Marvin Woodall, president of the 130-person J&J Interventional Systems unit, is typical of the independent thinkers at J&J: "I don't ask permission. I'm almost never distracted by J&J management." Distracted is an interesting word choice, for in many large firms senior management creates a lot of distractions for line managers. But at J&J, each independent business unit (with its unique product line and market) prepares its own budgets and marketing plans and often manages its own research and development.

Says CEO Ralph Larsen, the J&J way "provides a sense of ownership and responsibility for a business that you simply cannot get any other way." But no organization of this magnitude is static. Larsen is now working to fine-tune the balance of entrepreneurial spirit and organization structure. His goal is to cut out redundancies, share more services among units, and make it easier for J&J's largest customers to interact with a more unified organization rather than dozens of independent entities.

Larsen realizes the impact of organization design on ethical behavior: "Perhaps, in the past, decentralization went a bit too far. We're bringing it back. We will never give up the principle of decentralization, which is to give our operating executives ownership of a business. They are ultimately responsible." That ownership has created for J&J the reputation of being one of America's most aggressive marketers.

Source: Joseph Weber, "A Big Company That Works," *Business Week* (May 4, 1992), pp. 124–132.

as strengths. Edward Lawler emphasizes this contingency aspect of organizing in his remark: "Depending upon the choices about strategy that organizations make, different organizational designs and structures are appropriate, for one simple reason: different designs produce different behaviors and different outcomes."[24]

To illustrate the rationale and pros and cons for these four structures, we describe the organizational designs of Office Systems Design, Inc. (OSD), as it grows in complexity over time.[25] OSD was founded in St. Louis, Missouri, by Charles Simpson for the purpose of producing and selling customized office furniture. The business started small, with just a few craftsmen and Simpson handling the basic business functions, from selling to accounting. Its quality and promptness in delivering furniture exceeded customer expectations, so OSD became more specialized to accommodate growth and increased task complexity. The next few pages of text and organization charts describe how this firm used each of the four basic structures to cope with different strategies and task-grouping needs over time.

Organizational Design by Function

By the time Office Systems Design, Inc., reached $3 million in revenues, Charles Simpson had grouped essential activities into three key functional areas. A functional organizational design groups people into departments or subunits based on

━━━ **EXHIBIT 3–5**

Organizational Design by Function at OSD

Functional design structures the organization on the basis of the key functions (tasks or activities) to be performed. Each major group or subunit is responsible for performing a particular type of activity, such as production, sales, or the office administrative functions. The major functional managers in the OSD organization chart are also responsible for supervising the subfunctions reporting to them.

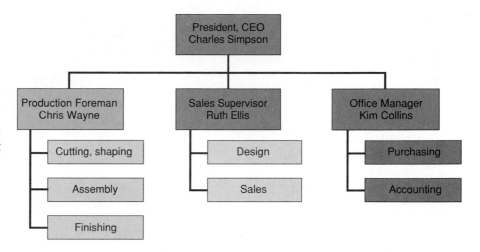

similar skills, expertise, and resource use. As a still small firm, OSD's key functions included production, sales, and office management. Exhibit 3–5 shows this simple structure, consisting of three supervisors, each responsible to the president for specialized activities common to the function under which they are grouped.

You might argue that the "design" specialty identified in the organization chart could logically fit under the production foreman because production must interpret the designer's drawings and specifications and make the product. But Simpson reasoned that it is the salesperson who comes directly into contact with the customer. To transfer a customer's vision of a customized desk or credenza into a deliverable product requires close coordination between the salesperson and the designer. Therefore, Simpson opted to link design more directly with sales than with production subfunctions such as cutting, assembly, or finishing.

Advantages and Disadvantages of Design by Function.[26] Organizations dominated by a functional architecture work best when a company has a single line of business and/or is relatively small. A functional structure is ideally suited to encourage specialization and prompt people to keep up with the latest technical developments in their specialty field. If departmental tasks are relatively independent, a high level of functional efficiency is possible. Because of departmental specialization, the functional form relies on a higher level of management for control and coordination. This makes the job of the general manager important and visible to all, but it may not be an efficient use of managerial time.

Extreme specialization, however, creates tunnel vision. People tend to perceive multifunctional problems from the vantage point of their narrow area of expertise. This leads to conflict and turf protecting, which can strain the process of communication and coordination in the absence of a decisive leader. Decisions that are complex or span two or more functions tend to get pushed to the top for resolution, slowing decision responsiveness as the organization becomes larger and more layered. Maintaining quality is difficult, since few people genuinely feel responsible for customer satisfaction or the acceptance of decisions. Functional design also complicates the process of developing broad-based general managerial skills, because functional managers have a limited range of specialized experiences.

━━━━━━ **EXHIBIT 3–6**

Organizational Design by Geography or Territory at OSD

A geographical approach to organization usually occurs as a consequence of size of growth for manufacturing firms. It can be based on regions within the country served, as in the OSD example, or, for multinational firms, organization can be by country or clusters of countries served.

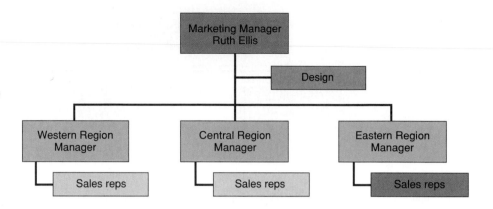

Organizational Design by Geography

Typically, as an organization grows, it spreads its coverage to new geographical regions or territories. In the case of a local manufacturer of customized products such as Office Systems Designs, geographical expansion is into nearby regions. For larger firms or those affected by global competition, geographical expansion might logically be into other countries.

For Charles Simpson, the easiest route to growth meant fielding aggressive sales forces in nearby cities. He asked the sales supervisor, Ruth Ellis, to step up sales calls to potential clients in those cities. Once the sales effort branched beyond St. Louis, sales began growing at greater than 50 percent per year, mostly in Kansas City and Indianapolis. To make sales activities in these regional markets more manageable, Ruth's title was changed to marketing manager, and three regional sales manager positions were created. The western region manager's office was located in Kansas City, the eastern region manager's in Indianapolis, and the central region manager worked out of the home office. Exhibit 3–6 shows the geographic-based structure that supported this shift in sales and marketing strategy. Each sales region now had greater autonomy and focused on increased market penetration in its particular locale.

Advantages and Disadvantages of Design by Geography.   Organizing by location emphasizes local adaptation to market and/or supplier conditions. It is especially well suited to retail chains, the U.S. Postal Service, public accounting partnerships, urban police departments, and fast-food restaurants. For organizations engaged in customer service, a regional structure allows local personnel and managers to be responsive to pressures and opportunities in their region. It promotes competitiveness and quality. Geographic design also makes it possible to create many profit centers where local general managers are responsible for both revenues and expenses.

On the downside, maintaining consistency of image and service can be compromised by a geographic design. The dilemma faced by headquarters managers is how much freedom to allow local managers versus how much control to exercise centrally. This decision typically depends on the size and complexity of the territory to be managed locally. A multinational firm such as pharmaceutical giant Pfizer International (with diverse operations in more than 100 countries) will grant greater autonomy to its business unit managers in foreign countries than Safeway will grant to its supermarket store managers within a single metropolitan

■■■■ **EXHIBIT 3–7**

Organizational Design by Product Line at OSD

When an organization has several product lines, organizing by product line is common. This arrangement enables people to concentrate on providing one type of product very efficiently, often aided by special-purpose technology or equipment.

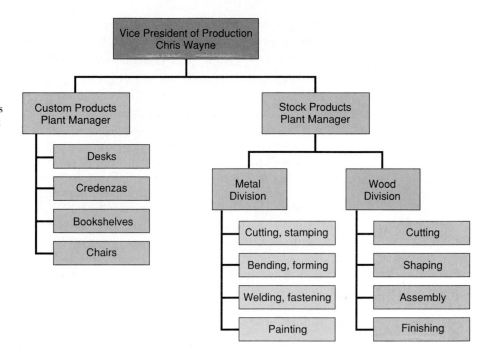

region. The Pfizer managers face more complex and diverse issues due to unique country cultures and different lines of business than those encountered by Safeway store managers in North American suburban communities.

Organizational Design by Product Line

When revenues surpassed $6 million, Office Systems Design began to add a standardized line of products to complement the custom office furniture on which the firm had built its reputation. The combination of increased volume and the addition of the second product line exerted considerable pressure on the production function. The firm continued to function as a *custom job shop,* producing orders to customer specifications. But it now also engaged in *batch processes* to produce for inventory small lots of standardized desks, credenzas, chairs, and computer tables.

The two production operations were separated into independent divisions, each organized, staffed, and equipped appropriately for the two distinct product lines. A newly constructed second building was equipped with heavier-capacity saws, lathes, sanders, and other woodworking machines. These tools were suited for the larger-volume runs of the standardized product line. Less-skilled workers were employed, and jobs were more narrowly defined and routine. The plant manager and his supervisors in the standard products production facility were more directive than in the custom facility. They made daily schedules, reassigned workers among tasks to keep the work flow moving, and gave feedback on productivity and quality.

Once annual sales reached $10 million, the management team decided to add a third product line—standardized steel file cabinets, desks, bookshelves, and so on. A third facility was leased and equipped for fabricating metal furniture from steel and sheet metal. To accommodate the increased complexity, Simpson promoted Chris Wayne to vice president of production and shifted the production operation to organization by product line. Exhibit 3–7 shows the organization now divided into the two primary types of product lines, custom and stock (standardized) products. Stock products are further divided into the wood and metal divisions. Below these manager levels, tasks are still organized by function.

Advantages and Disadvantages of Design by Product Line.   For large, multibusiness firms such as Johnson & Johnson, decentralizing on the basis of products or lines of business promotes entrepreneurial behavior. Even an automotive firm such as General Motors, with its relatively basic cluster of products all derived from a core automotive technology, organizes around product divisions: Chevrolet, Buick, Cadillac, Oldsmobile, Saturn, and so on. Product-line executives typically have profit center responsibility to reinforce accountability.

The potential weakness of decentralized, product-based entities is the difficulty of coordinating related activities across business units. Rivalry is likely to exist—rivalry not only for customers but also for corporate resources, such as investment dollars or additional staff positions. If several business units separately draw on similar core technologies for the research and design of products, they likely forgo economy-of-scale savings and may be slow to share with other units the technological breakthroughs discovered in one unit.

Organizational Design by Customer/Market Channel

Soon after the third product line was added at OSD, Simpson and Ellis realized that their customer requirements and market channels were becoming more diverse. The process of selling customized office furniture to an attorney or consultant is highly personalized, because it includes an original design function. Furthermore, selling stock products to a furniture store or office supply store is different from selling 50 modular office units to an expanding business firm. Within each regional territory, all three types of sales might be made, each requiring a different market channel for serving customers.

Therefore, sales executive Ellis obtained approval to add a second managerial layer below the regional structure, based on the type of customer and the unique sales/service requirements for each channel of distribution. Exhibit 3–8 shows organization by customer, with groupings into custom sales, retail sales (office supply and furniture stores), and institutional sales (large direct sales orders to businesses, schools, and so on). By allowing salespersons to specialize by customer (or market segment), OSD focused on the needs of each type of client.

Advantages and Disadvantages of Design by Customer/Market.   Customer or market-channel-based structures usually are used in combination with one or more other designs. They serve well the needs of the business when product lines can be marketed to very distinct customer segments. Their advantage is that special customer needs can focus quality service throughout each organizational unit. For example, by relying on market feedback from a customer segment, such as offices needing photocopiers, employees serving that segment can make changes in everything from the design of special product features to pricing and methods of providing sales and service.

To create high employee involvement, Edward Lawler believes the customer-based design is optimum. He writes, "A company should usually organize profit centers around customers, for one simple reason: this structure makes it easiest for the organization to align its employees with an external customer who can give feedback and who makes purchasing decisions."[27] Focusing on the customer enables the competitive market—not hierarchical controls or supervisor whims—to

━━━━━ **EXHIBIT 3–8**

Organizational Design by Customer at OSD

When key business activities (such as sales and service) are differentiated on the basis of customers or market segments, a customer-based organizational design makes sense. This allows specialization according to the rather unique needs of particular customer groups.

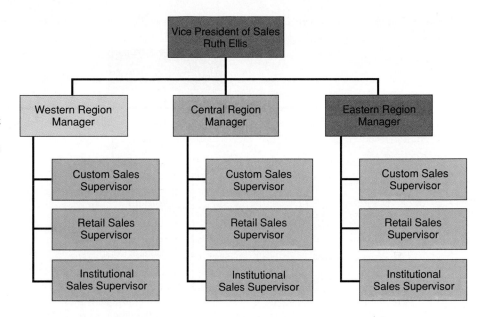

control employee behavior. The challenge for companies offering several lines of products to the same customer is to balance product expertise (a benefit of product-focused designs) with the simplicity of having one voice speak to the customer. Market-focused designs also tend to require duplication of sales and marketing staff, with two or more groups selling the same product line.

Combining Designs over the Organizational Structure Life Cycle

Few businesses enjoy the predictable, sustained growth that a stellar performer like Wal-Mart has demonstrated over the past 30 years. More typically, organizations grow during their early years, then experience contractions as the core business begins to mature and/or as economic cycles disrupt performance. As they *age* and grow in *size,* firms pass through an organizational structure **life cycle** in which they move from simple to progressively more complex structures and systems. Mintzberg's explanation of life cycles suggests that what starts as a simple structure typically becomes either a professional bureaucracy or machine bureaucracy with complex layers and structures of departments.[28] With enough growth, the organization divides quasi-independent activity centers into separate business unit divisions. The ultimate design for a firm diversified into several lines of business is to take on characteristics of a *network,* loosely coupled by central resource allocations.

life cycle
Organization structures progress from simple to complex designs and systems as they age and grow in size.

During both the expansion and contraction phases of the life cycle, reorganizations ("reorgs") are commonplace. The focus of most reorgs is to better align structure with business strategies and competitive forces, although at times "reorganization" is simply a euphemism for reducing headcount by layoffs. Office Systems Design's restructurings are typical of a firm that periodically needs to realign how people, activities, and resources are grouped into work units. We described and provided a separate organization chart for each of the four basic structures. In practice, however, these different designs are combined into a more complex organization structure. A more complete picture of OSD's organization at this point in its life cycle is presented in Exhibit 3–9.

EXHIBIT 3–9   *Integrated Organization Design at OSD*

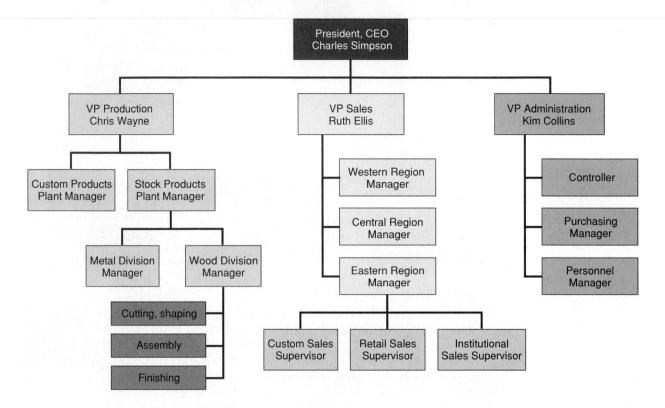

WHAT ARE THE TRADE-OFFS FOR BALANCING ORGANIZATION DESIGN?

The advantages and disadvantages associated with each of the four basic designs suggest the task of organizing is one of making compromises. Except in very small enterprises, organizational design involves striking a balance among opposing forces, needs, and goals. And, once designed, an organization's structure seldom stays in place very long in today's volatile and competitive environment. A long-standing principle is to have structure follow and support strategy rather than allow an out-of-date structure to constrain strategic options.[29] Among the key trade-offs that make organization design challenging is the need to strike an accord between centralization and decentralization. Managers also seek a working balance among autonomy, control, and coordination.

Balancing Centralization and Decentralization

Historically, basic organizational trade-offs come into play when managers consider where in the organization certain decisions should be made. The central trade-off pits pressures for centralization against the need for decentralization. **Centralization** is the concentration of authority and decision making toward the top of an organization. **Decentralization** is the dispersion of authority and decision making to operating units throughout an organization. Most medium-to-large organizations have a degree of both centralization and decentralization in their structures.

centralization
An organizational structure that concentrates authority and decision making toward the top.

decentralization
An organizational structure that disperses authority and decision making to operating units throughout the organization.

Rolled aluminum is one of the many products Alcoa makes. To better meet the needs of its customers, Alcoa recently decentralized by creating 22 business units. Each unit was given authority and responsibility to improve operations, financial performance, and customer satisfaction. (Photo: Alen MacWeeney.)

Larger enterprises with highly competent and skilled employees tend to diffuse decision making, with greater participation and less centralization[30] Large firms that perpetuate centralized management tend to be slower in recognizing how their hierarchical structure restrains organizational effectiveness.[31] Central structures work reasonably well in slow-changing industries but are less adaptable in complex, fast-changing environments. A Microsoft, Intel, Johnson & Johnson, or Intuit could not lead their markets if governed by a highly centralized hierarchy.

As uncertainty and complexity increase, senior managers move incrementally toward decentralized control to promote local adaptability and decision making.[32] In particular, implementation of strategies and operating policies are decision areas normally delegated to local or lower-level managers. Major resource allocation decisions are typically retained by the top management team. As an example, the board of directors of a bank authorizes branch managers to approve auto loans, unsecured consumer loans up to $25,000, and home mortgage loans up to $200,000. Commercial loans and those above the branch limits are reserved for central office approval.

Balancing Autonomy, Control, and Coordination

Managers struggle with the dilemma of how to strike a balance between maintaining control and granting autonomy to others. One facet of *control* grants to managers the power to shape decisions, resource allocations, and actions so that people throughout the organization carry out management's wishes. In contrast *autonomy* means granting power and responsibility to followers to initiate actions that improve processes and achieve organizational goals. Managers consider trade-offs:

Phillips Petroleum is a multidivisional organization whose lines of business include petroleum exploration, drilling, refining and marketing, natural gas processing, plastic and petrochemical production, and research and development. The company restructured many of its businesses and facilities into strategic business units (SBUs). Each SBU acts as a self-directed business with its own management and staff who make most investment and operating decisions and have profit and loss accountability. The goal of centralizing into SBUs is to bring an entrepreneurial approach to each business while maintaining the resources of a large, integrated petroleum company.
(Photo: Phillips Petroleum Company.)

What decisions and responsibilities do I reserve for myself? What decisions do I grant to my people so that I hold them accountable for results without stifling initiative? Even small organizations have difficulty resolving such control–autonomy issues, as entrepreneur Andrea Cunningham discovered (see the accompanying Dynamics of Diversity box).

The control–autonomy conflict is often framed in terms of maintaining consistency versus promoting innovation and flexibility. Managers of sales and R&D departments generally grant considerable autonomy because results require individual initiative. Manufacturing and operations departments tend to be governed by greater control because of the need for efficiency, quality assurance, and conformance to design specifications.

A third issue is intertwined with the control–autonomy trade-off: *Coordination* requires meshing work-related flows across organizational units. Traditionally, it occurs through structural means—decisions are pushed up and actions thrust down the hierarchy. As you learned earlier, the recent use of self-managing teams and cross-functional teams promotes collaborative processes to initiate decisions and integrate actions. Teamwork becomes more pronounced with increased technological complexity, the speedup of product introductions, and the need for flexibility in producing customized products and services for customers.[33] Under these

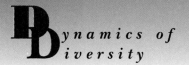

Entrepreneur Andrea Cunningham Moves from Control to Autonomy to Teams

While still in her twenties, Andrea Cunningham launched Cunningham Communication, Inc., (CCI), a public relations firm that serves high-technology firms in the Silicon Valley. Within four years, her agency was billing $3 million annually and employed more than 20 professionals. But Cunningham was troubled that her clients still relied on her personally for advice and creative ideas. She was failing to delegate and lead, and she held too much control unto herself.

To compensate, Cunningham tried (with unfortunate results) to organize the company into small teams (business units), each with its own accounts, profit responsibility, and director. This approach fostered intense team autonomy and identity. But the resulting interteam rivalries killed cooperation among units. To counteract the divisiveness, Cunningham again took control and presented each business unit director with specific goals and responsibilities. Five of the six unit directors quit over the next six months.

When she discovered people wanted to help run the company, Cunningham introduced a new, team-based organization that cut across clients and functions. Six teams were created—marketing, professional development, strategic planning, quality, fun (to stimulate playful creativity), and community relations—and every management task except finance was turned over to the teams. Cunningham gives each team a mission for the year, and the group of 7 to 11 members then comes up with plans, budgets, and strategies for realizing its mission. Everyone serves on at least one team and learns to manage and make difficult trade-offs within the team's budget limits.

By the time the agency employed 50 people, Cunningham had learned to delegate through the team-focused organization, backed up by a "set your own salary" incentive system. Says Cunningham, "I've finally gotten to the point where I don't have to do everything to feel good about myself." Over two years, she had switched from emphasizing control to granting autonomy to coordinating work efforts through team-focused responsibilities and goals.

Source: Leslie Brokaw, "Playing for Keeps," *Inc.* (May 1992), pp. 30–41.

conditions, "work teams simply allow more decisions and more coordination activities to be pushed lower in the organization . . . particularly if the production or service process is complicated and involves a number of steps."[34]

The use of teams to improve quality and speed up decision making brings to the forefront the three-way relationship among control, autonomy, and coordination.[35] Exhibit 3–10 graphically portrays this three-way relationship by identifying the principal trade-offs involved in deciding how to balance the three. The use of coordination (teamwork) promotes flexibility and synergy among activities. Conversely, when control (centralization) is the pivotal organizing strategy, consistency and a more global perspective prevail. Autonomy (decentralization) emphasizes accountability with an overlay of responsiveness to local or unique market conditions.

Bureaucracy versus Organic Organizations

Issues of control–autonomy–coordination spill over into the "look and feel" of organizations. As organizations move toward the twenty-first century, they accelerate movement away from tightly structured, mechanistic approaches to organization

━━━━━ **EXHIBIT 3–10**

Trade-offs among Control, Autonomy, and Coordination

Organizations can't have it all. The interplay among control, autonomy, and coordination involves a series of trade-offs, or compromises. The pairs of arrows show the opposing forces between each set of factors involved in the trade-off. For example, on the left side of the triangle, as an organization becomes more control oriented, it increases consistency at the cost of reducing flexibility.

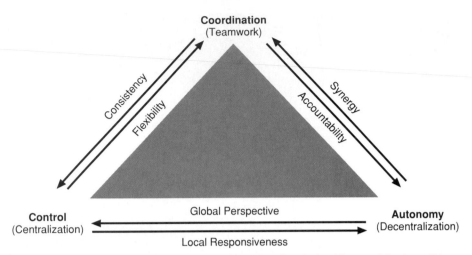

Source: Adapted from Robert W. Keidel, "Triangular Design: A New Organizational Geometry," *Academy of Management Executive* 4 (November 1990), pp. 24, 26.

mechanistic organization
An organization with a traditional "look and feel" that is highly structured and formalized, desiring conformance behaviors to handle routine functions appropriate to stable environments.

organic organization
An organization with a looser "look and feel" that relies on the adaptive capacities of individuals to cope with dynamic internal and external forces, facilitated by empowerment and a collaborative network.

bureaucracy
A classic pyramid shaped structure created as a rational-legal system of authority emphasizing formal roles and rules with the intent of being efficiency oriented.

toward structures and processes that are looser, organic, adaptive networks. A **mechanistic organization** is highly structured and formalized, leading to conforming behaviors to handle routine functions within an essentially stable environment.[36] An **organic organization** relies on the adaptive capacities of individuals, facilitated by empowerment and a collaborative network, to cope with dynamic internal and external forces.[37]

Bureaucracy as a Model.   For decades managers embodied a philosophy in which people were cast into well-defined job roles. The same or similar roles were grouped into work units headed by a supervisor or manager, with groups of work units linked by a hierarchy of reporting relationships. Conceptually, this perspective on the total organization was first advocated by the German scholar Max Weber (see Appendix A for historic detail). As conceived by Weber, **bureaucracy** is an efficiency-oriented system of organization that emphasizes formalization of roles and rules.[38] The classic bureaucracy is shaped like a pyramid and structured on a rational–legal system of authority, key elements of which appeared as questions 1 through 6 in the earlier Your Turn exercise.

As a system of organization, bureaucracy came into being in part to emphasize technical requirements and to rationalize policies without regard to the political patronage and favoritism that had characterized German organizations. By specifying rules and procedures, managers are freed from making routine decisions—such matters can be delegated to subordinates. But because of its formalism and codified protocol, bureaucracy (like power) has become a dirty word to those who don't understand its intent. People often speak with disdain of the "bureaucratic red tape" associated with vast hierarchies. They are critical of routine paper shuffling that stifles creative responses to novel situations and employees who seem uncaring. Conventional wisdom holds that, in bureaucracies, the head appears not to know where the feet are going.

And yet bureaucracies can be very efficient. IBM's was for years but is no more and is being dismantled. A bureaucratic approach to organization can flourish when routine operations are fitted to stable, predictable environments. Bureaucracies enhance predictability and conformance to standards and can be highly

The bureaucratic approach is exemplified by the miles of paper generated by Connecticut Mutual Life Insurance. Bureaucracies enhance predictability and can be highly efficient when handling large volumes of largely repetitive work, in this case insurance claims. Connecticut Mutual stream-lined its operations when it decided to computerize operations. The results of getting rid of paper and reorganizing the work process: response to queries is down from five days to a few hours; 20 percent fewer people are involved; and productivity is up more than 35 percent. (Photo: © Larry Ford.)

efficient when handling large volumes of largely repetitive work. With today's computerized information systems, the bureaucratic organization makes sense for handling much of the work performed in service firms such as banks, insurance firms, and phone companies.

Movement toward Organic, Flexible Organizations. The shortcomings of the bureaucratic, mechanistic model when confronted with turbulent environments has spawned a number of experiments with alternative structures. These go by many names, depending on an author's preferred terminology: organic, temporary, ad hoc, flexible, postmodern, contemporary, postbureaucratic, intelligent, high involvement, and others. Warren Bennis suggests several of the characteristics of alternatives to bureaucracy: "The organizations of the future will be networks, clusters, cross-functional teams, temporary systems, ad hoc task forces, lattices, modules, matrices—almost anything but pyramids."[39] Bennis recounts a story in the Challenge of Change box that views an accelerated rate of change as the threat to bureaucracy's viability.

Organic organizations empower individuals and teams to pursue continuous improvement through flexible adaptation. Task roles are expected to continually change or are ambiguously defined, and organizational design is fluid and features frequent reorganizations. Goals are diverse, complex, less measurable, and more likely to change than in the mechanistic organization. Planning flows up, down, and across organizational units rather than being passed up and down. Structurally, the organization is flatter.

Organic organizations are designed to promote effectiveness in complex, fast-changing environments, especially when technology is a driving force for change. The organic organization promotes high involvement, which helps people provide high-quality products and services at competitive costs and respond quickly to opportunities or threats.[40] Donald Petersen began the transformation of a sluggish

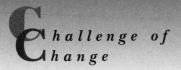

Challenge of Change

Ships On a Stormy Sea: The Coming Death of Bureaucracy

Warren Bennis began his renown article on "The Coming Death of Bureaucracy" with a poignant story:

> Not far from the new Government Center in downtown Boston, a foreign visitor walked up to a sailor and asked why American ships were built to last only a short time. According to the tourist, "The sailor answered without hesitation that the art of navigation is making such rapid progress that the finest ship would become obsolete if it lasted beyond a few years. In these words which fell accidentally from an uneducated man, I began to recognize the general systematic idea upon which your great people (the people of the United States) direct all their concerns."

The foreign visitor was that shrewd observer of American morals and manners, Alexis de Tocqueville, and the year was 1835. He would not recognize Scollay Square today. But he had caught the central theme of our country: its preoccupation, its obsession with change. One thing is, however, new since de Tocqueville's time: the acceleration of newness, the changing scale and scope of change itself.

Source: Warren Bennis, "The Coming Death of Bureaucracy," in Warren Bennis, *An Invented Life: Reflections on Leadership and Change* (Reading, MA: Addison-Wesley, 1993), p. 61.

Ford Motor Co. during the 1980s, a change that accelerated in the 1990s. He is convinced that to revitalize the way people work, it is necessary to change from the traditional top-down organizational design and management practices. In his book, *A Better Idea,* Petersen begins by presenting his ideology:

> *I'm writing this book to express my belief that business can and should be conducted in a better way than it has been in the past. We need to foster an attitude of trust, cooperation, and respect throughout our organizations . . . [to] help the company or organization transform itself from a place where everybody hates to come to work to a place where people trust one another and enjoy working together.*[41]

HOW DO ORGANIZATIONS ACHIEVE LEANER, FLATTER STRUCTURES?

The purpose of organization is to encourage behaviors appropriate to goal and task needs. Given the trend for mental tasks to replace menial ones, a corresponding organizing trend is to flatten the organizational hierarchy, either by breaking businesses into autonomous units or by improving horizontal work-process flows and decreasing the intensity of supervision. Where such structural changes are made, higher involvement results from pushing decisions closer to people with firsthand information—those on the firing line.[42]

During the 1990s it has become popular for managers to streamline organizations by use of the three Rs: restructuring, reengineering, and rightsizing. Unfortunately, these three tend for the most part to be euphemisms for layoffs, for reducing the number of people employed. The goal of all three is to improve financial performance (reengineering also aims to improve customer service), but the human consequences of such programs have been inadequately researched.[43]

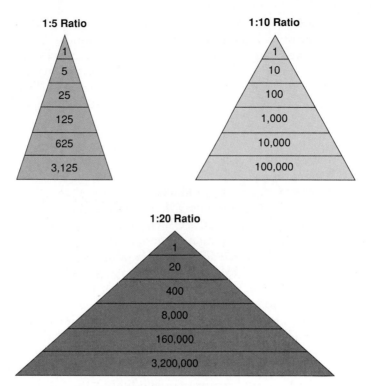

EXHIBIT 3–11

Geometric Effects of "Span-of-Control" Ratios

Each of these three structures (pyramids) have six levels from top to bottom. As the span of control (average number of people reporting to a manager) increases, the organization becomes "flatter," because proportionately fewer managers are required to manage a greater number of people. Simply by doubling the span from 5 to 10, a six-level organization can increase its employee base about thirty-two fold, from 3,125 to 100,000. Another doubling of span (from 10 to 20) increases total employees another thirty-two times (from 100,000 to 3,200,000).

Anytime an organization reduces its work force by 10,000 to 50,000, there are going to be unemployed casualties who do not recover. Nevertheless, organizations will continue to draw on several tactics to flatten structures. We review four such tactics.

Widen the Span of Control

span of control
In describing organizational structures, denotes the number of people supervised by one manager, or the ratio of managers to persons managed.

One way to flatten organizations is to widen the span of control. **Span of control** denotes the number of people supervised by one manager, or the ratio of managers to persons managed. While organizations that seek high involvement may no longer emphasize "control," the span-of-control concept is still useful. Exhibit 3–11 shows the interplay among span of control, hierarchical levels, and organizational size. The only way a large organization, say one with 100,000 or more people, can maintain flexibility without becoming overly hierarchical is to increase the average span of control and reduce the number of management levels (and thus the number of managers). Executives today generally aim to have 7 or fewer levels, in stark contrast to the 14 to 19 levels common to bureaucracies such as General Motors.

In organizations that hold to the old principle of narrow span of control, people are undermotivated and underutilized.[44] When a manager has 5 people in her department (a narrow span), she is likely to interact with them more often—and be more controlling—than if she has a wide span of 15 to 30. AT&T used to believe 6 was the optimum span of control for most managers—a number that allowed the manager to issue directives and expected subordinates to follow them. But as the number of people in a manager's unit increases, the opportunity for the manager to directly control their behavior decreases while the empowerment potential increases.

Ed Lawler, in reflecting on structures at GE, UPS, Union Pacific Railroad, and other organizations in his research, concludes: "I believe that most organizations, even very large ones, should be able to operate effectively with no more than six or seven levels of management. Usually spans of management should never be less than fifteen and, in most cases, should be larger."[45] Ultimately, a manager's span of control is constrained by his or her information-processing capabilities.[46]

Shift Control from Staff to Line

line positions
Job assignments that directly contribute to creating customer value by either designing products, producing them, financing needed resources, marketing to create demand, and/or selling and servicing the product.

staff positions
Jobs that support the line positions through carrying out advisement and internal "overhead" support activities such as accounting, purchasing, and human resource functions.

Organizations historically have two types of members and positions: line and staff. **Line positions** more or less directly contribute to creating value added for the customer by designing products, producing them, financing the needed resources and marketing and selling them. **Staff positions** are supposed to support the line, providing technical advice such as legal counsel or carrying out "overhead" activities such as accounting, purchasing, and human resource functions to relieve managers of specialized administrative burdens.

When staff groups grow in numbers, staff managers often try to expand the scope of their "services" by developing guidelines and rules intended to coordinate (standardize) daily activities ranging from employee evaluations to purchases of supplies. Expanding the scope of staff control carries two costs: the cost of employing staff and the added cost (especially in time) to line people who have to comply with staff procedures.

With the push toward leaner, customer-responsive organizations, many enterprises have cut back on staff and limited their tasks to providing information and advice, not making decisions or requiring reports.[47] Streamlining staff functions with the aim of empowering line people is common at Nordstrom (the high-end department store chain) and SAS (the international airline). Both firms eliminated their detailed procedure manuals (produced by staff) and simply instruct employees to "satisfy the customer."[48]

The elimination of non-revenue-producing staff has been most aggressively pursued by the Europe-based firm, Asea Brown Boveri (ABB).[49] When it acquires businesses, ABB typically reduces their corporate staff by up to 90 percent. To emphasize that it can be done, its corporate home office numbers only about 100 (out of about 250,000 employed). Even IBM concentrated on cutting staff and headquarters employees when it downsized by displacing nearly 100,000 through the early 1990s. IBM's personnel staff shrank 90 percent (from 400 to 40), and the European headquarters was trimmed from 2,000 to less than 200.[50]

Cut Levels of Management

Pyramidal hierarchies shape an environment in which power is not shared. Power firmly held at the top transmits the message that people lower in the organization are not to be trusted to think and act independently. By structuring to eliminate layers of management, an organization pushes power to lower levels and encourages employee involvement. When the board of directors of General Motors pressed Chairman and CEO Robert Stempel to resign and then appointed John F. Smith, Jr., as CEO in the early 1990s, critics stated, "Smith must force a fundamental change in GM's culture by holding managers accountable for their performance while encouraging them to take risks. That means pushing power to make decisions down into the ranks."[51] Many organizations already have. United Parcel

SALLY FORTH • Greg Howard and Craig MacIntosh

Source: Reprinted with special permission of King Features Syndicate.

Service (UPS), with its 200,000 employees, uses only six levels of management. Union Pacific Railroad (UP) flattened its 30,000-employee organization from nine to three levels (before acquiring Southern Pacific).

All of these flattening efforts are not undertaken without difficulty. In the 1980s, General Electric reduced positions and managerial levels but found that most work tasks remained, overtaxing the managers. It then focused on eliminating unnecessary hierarchy-related work, such as reports, meetings, and multiple levels of approval for decisions. In the 1990s, GE acknowledged that the firm has been "pulling the dandelions of bureaucracy for a decade, but they don't come up easily and they'll be back next week if you don't keep after them."[52]

Reengineer from Vertical Flows to Horizontal Work Processes

One of the more widely used approaches to creating a lean organization has been the shift from emphasizing vertical relationships to focusing on horizontal work flows. This shift feeds on changes in high-involvement work teams, the electronic distribution of information, and managing business processes rather than functional departments. For example, in GE's Bayamon, Puerto Rico, plant, 172 hourly employees work in teams with 10 or so others without supervisors, only 15 salaried "advisors" plus one general manager.[53] Each team's representative works with both upstream (distributors, customers) and downstream operations (such as receiving, assembly, and shipping) to ensure that value is added in each link of the horizontal chain of processes. By rotating jobs every six months, employees learn new skills and see how one team's work affects others in the work-flow stream.

Emphasize Cross-Functional Coordination. Reengineering reconfigures work processes to better serve customers. To use the definition popularized by Hammer and Champy, **reengineering** entails the "radical redesign of business processes to achieve dramatic improvements in critical, contemporary measures of performance, such as cost, quality, service, and speed."[54] Reengineering seeks to make two major changes.[55] At the personal level, it aims to shift the mindsets of people caused by working within the "silos," " chimneys," or "smokestacks" of vertical, functionally aligned organizations. At the competitive level, work flows are redesigned to make sense from a customer's perspective. The "reengineering" emphasis is on rearranging business processes so they cut across functions in a

reengineering
The radical redesign of business processes to achieve dramatic improvements in measures such as cost, quality, service, and speed.

Kodak Zebras—employees who make the company's black-and-white film—no longer work in departments but now are organized around the process of making film in what's called "the flow," a horizontal organization. A 25-member leadership team oversees the flow, measuring it for things such as productivity. Within the flow are "streams," which work closely with Kodak business units to cover such operations as creating new products and scheduling production. (Photo: © John S. Abbott.)

horizontal flow. Each set of operational processes should have a definable beginning and end, such as the flow from new product development to customer acquisition, concluding with order fulfillment. The emphasis is on achieving coordination among task interdependencies, for all organizations tend over time to become bureaucratic, allowing routines to become entrenched and turfs to be defended.

Reengineering applies to real work processes, not to single departments. One of Ford Motor's early ventures into redesign began as an initiative to cut costs within the accounts payable department, the unit that paid supplier bills. Ford's breakthrough in thinking occurred when it shifted from accounts payable to examine the entire business process of procurement.[56] Procurement was more encompassing, involving purchasing and receiving as well as accounts payable. Much of account payable's work involved matching up documents: the originating purchase order, the receiving document, and the invoice. Most of the time the documents did not match—the quantity delivered differed from that ordered, or unit costs were different.

In a real sense, Pareto's law of maldistribution was at work. Often known as the 80/20 rule, **Pareto's law** states that 80 percent of an outcome or observed phenomenon is caused by only 20 percent of the input or contributing events. For

Pareto's law
Known as the 80/20 rule, this principle states that 80 percent of an observed result is caused by 20 percent of the activities, or efforts, or people involved.

example, it is not uncommon for 80 percent of an activity's costs to be contributed by 20 percent of the steps involved, or for 80 percent of a firm's accidents to be caused by only 20 percent of the employees.

Ford's new process is largely automated through use of an electronic database accessible by people in all three functions. Instead of paying on receipt and verification of an invoice, payment authorization is now automatically issued when the receiving clerk confirms that an incoming delivery of parts corresponds to the purchase order displayed on the computer screen.

Hallmark, the greeting card company, found that attempting to integrate the work of 700 creative persons in producing some 40,000 cards had stretched the cycle time from preliminary idea to printing of the finished card to two years. It began regrouping into holiday teams—Valentine's Day, Mother's Day, and so on. Now each holiday team combines artists, writers, accountants, lithographers, merchandisers, and others. Rather than being routed from one department to another, the development of each card easily flows within the team so that people can provide their input concurrently rather than sequentially. This change cut *cycle time* (the time to complete a whole task) by more than 50 percent.

But movement toward a horizontal flow of processes does not mean an abdication of management. Especially for innovative companies with fast-changing product lines, management continues to provide direction, balance, and integration: "The view that creative organizations maximize autonomy, individual expression, and open experimentation and prefer egalitarian management simply is not true in such intensely focused, innovation-driven, competitive companies . . . Management's task is to encourage some degree of conformity across individuals, groups, and divisions through the sharing of the company's strategy and culture, while still flirting with anarchy."[57]

Caution: Probabilities of Disappointment and Anxiety Run High.   As firms reengineer and otherwise work to design more flexibility into organizations, the boundaries that once compartmentalized groups of people and effectively insulated most employees from outside forces are breaking up. Before surveying several options for organizational redesign, be aware that it is difficult to successfully change an enterprise, or even major components of it. John Kotter cautions managers about the outcomes of organizational transformation:

> *Over the past decade, I have watched more than 100 companies try to remake themselves into significantly better competitors . . . A few of these corporate change efforts have been very successful. A few have been utter failures. Most fall somewhere in between, with a distinct tilt toward the lower end of the scale . . . The most general lesson to be learned from the more successful cases is that the change process goes through a series of phases that, in total, usually require a considerable length of time. Skipping steps creates only the illusion of speed and never produces a satisfying result.[58]*

Good working relationships don't happen automatically when people are thrust into teams or given more freedom. The struggle to learn new skills begins when senior managers give up some of their authority, encouraging participation and teamwork. Paradoxically, when they do so after years of an authoritarian style, new teams do not know how to constructively confront conflict and disagreements about critical issues.[59] The need to resolve conflict and integrate divergent points of view holds true whether the organization is hierarchical or fluid and boundaryless. Reengineering should help people look at their work from different perspectives: "The task is to allow sufficient boundaries to give individuals and work groups an identity, but to keep them focused outward, not inward . . . The issue is to organize around issues as well as tasks."[60]

Redesigning organizations does not come easy, and the outcomes are not always positive. Research by Kim Cameron of the consequences of 150 corporate restructurings (involving downsizing) found that 75 percent ended up in worse shape.[61] (However, there was no control for the severity of crisis that precipitated the redesign—they could have ended in even worse shape without reconfiguring.) Even reengineering, which reorganizes the way work is done (not just realigns boxes on an organization chart) is not without problems. Michael Hammer, who helped popularize the intervention, estimates between 50 percent to 70 percent of reengineering initiatives fail to achieve their objectives.[62]

Robert Keidel's research finds reengineering arouses organizational anxiety—apprehension and worries about what may happen. He states: "Indeed, the term *reengineering,* as applied to organizations, is unfortunate; it is mechanistic and utterly devoid of human content."[63] Keidel views organizational redesigns, of whatever methodology, as needing to reconceptualize or rethink individually and collectively more than just structure and its financial implications. He concludes:

> *Organizational rethinking . . . means conceptualizing design in a manner that incorporates organizational identity, or character—who we are, and what we stand for; organizational purpose, or constituencies—for whose benefit we exist; and organizational methods, or capabilities—how we satisfy customers/consumers.[64]*

Thus, before launching a top-down redesign using one or more of the three Rs (restructuring, reengineering, and rightsizing), executives might do well to rethink their pending actions by pulling the three Cs noted above to the forefront: character, constituencies, and capabilities. The design of organizations and jobs is, after all, supposed to support and facilitate human effort to carry out business strategies and achieve enterprise purposes.

FORD MOTOR CO. REORGANIZES ITS FINANCE FUNCTION—A SECOND LOOK

In retrospect, you now should realize that when Ford Motor Co. decided to change its finance function, it initiated reorganizations in the way work is performed. It became more team focused, and realigned its basic organizational structure. The concept of organizing product development teams where contributions occur concurrently and interactively was new to Ford. It was a radical departure from past practices where each functional department sequentially made its independent contribution as a new concept vehicle flowed through the process. Cross-functional, fully interactive teams are now the norm at Ford, a change in organization that reduces cycle time (the months required to get a new vehicle into production) and cuts cost by designing out inefficiencies.

Ford's change dramatically altered the entire structure of the organization. The primacy given to independent functions (such as finance, design, engineering) was dethroned and the geographic structure, with four regional divisions, was eliminated. Several layers of management were cut, which improved information exchange and decision making. Now the priority is on the product line, supported by cross-functional teams that streamline the process of bringing new or redesigned vehicles to market. What started as an attempt to diminish the gatekeeping role of finance expanded into a series of organizational restructurings.

SUMMARY

The balance between job design and technology are the two organizational elements that most define the work people do. For over a century, technology has been the major force behind improving standards of living; however, technological advances are dependent on an educated and skilled work force. As developed societies move beyond mass production, a wave of technological change mandates new sciences, which spawns new products and transforms many jobs.

With the increasing complexity of operations, organizations are building in greater participation opportunities for nonmanagers. Groups ranging from quality circles to self-managing and cross-functional teams are involved in continuous improvement projects and running their own operations. Working in teams tends to improve the core job dimensions that affect people's psychological states and motivating potential at work. With high involvement, people are challenged to rethink systems and processes—to eliminate tasks that no longer add value.

On a larger scale, organizational design is the structural arrangement for grouping essential tasks (jobs) and providing a behavioral network for making decisions and coordinating work flows. Managers design the structure of organizations by using variations of four basic forms: design by function, geography, product, or customer. Organizational design supports the strategies of an enterprise and helps focus employee behavior. Managers intend that design will help strike a balance among the needs to control behaviors, allow reasonable autonomy, and coordinate actions across work units.

Because of accelerated shifts in global competition and technology, there is a tendency for organizations to become less mechanistic (or machinelike) and more organic (flexible). Bureaucracy, which for decades promoted efficiency and predictability through rules and control, is yielding to practices that create greater employee involvement and adaptation. With organic involvement come flatter structures and a wider span of control for managers. Reengineering has also promoted the creation of leaner, more cost-efficient organizations by emphasizing the interconnection of process work flows across functional areas. Creating lean structures helps an organization both cope with increasing size and respond to environmental conditions.

Key Concepts

technology, *p. 78*

quality circle (QC), *p. 83*

self-managed team, *p. 83*

sociotechnical systems design, *p. 84*

cross-functional teams, *p. 84*

organizational structure, *p. 85*

organization chart, *p. 85*

organizational design, *p. 85*

life cycle, *p. 91*

centralization, *p. 92*

decentralization, *p. 92*

mechanistic organization, *p. 96*

organic organization, *p. 96*

bureaucracy, *p. 97*

span of control, *p. 99*

line positions, *p. 100*

staff positions, *p. 100*

reengineering, *p. 101*

Pareto's law, *p. 102*

Questions for Study and Discussion

1. The character of work is changing due to dramatic changes in technologies, products, and services. What do you believe to be two significant task–technology challenges facing managers responsible for the work people perform? Explain.

2. What do quality circles, self-managed teams, and cross-functional teams all have in common? How do they differ?

3. Zeta Corp. plans to build a new plant and organize work around the principle of self-managed teams instead of individual jobs. About half the firm's usual work force was born in various Asian and Latin American countries. What are the pros and cons of staffing work teams in the new plant with multicultural versus single-culture groups of employees?

4. Describe and sketch the distinguishing characteristics of the four basic structural forms of organization: design by function, product, geography, and customer. Give at least two reasons why each would be used (advantages) and two limitations.

5. How do the goals of autonomy, control, and coordination affect the design of organizations? How would you expect an organization's managers to deal with each if it was heavily centralized? Decentralized?

6. What were the original purposes of a bureaucratic approach to organization? Why does bureaucracy receive "bad press"? What makes an organization organic? Which gets better results, a bureaucracy or an organic organization? Why?

7. Develop an argument that a span of control of 15 is more effective than a span of 5. What are the behavioral differences involved? Base your argument on an organization built on five levels of management.

EXPERIENTIAL EXERCISE

Visualizing the Ideal Workweek

Purpose. To enable students to visualize the work qualities that most appeal to them and to compare and contrast those ideals with those of peers. The process should draw out considerations of person-job fit and differences in expectations among students.

Time and Procedures. Requires about 40 minutes (less if using two-person groups).

Phase 1. List Individual Work Attributes (5 Minutes). Working alone, list qualities or attributes you would ideally like to experience at work in the first year following academic graduation. Think comprehensively, using the following categories as prompts:

   a. Nature of the job task(s).

   b. Use of technology.

   c. Interactions with others.

   d. Skills required.

   e. Performance measures/indicators.

   f. Personal outcomes/expectations.

   g. Other desired attributes.

Phase 2. Individual Story Preparation (3 Minutes). Now project ahead to fantasize a perfect week at work one year after graduation. Think of what you will be doing, with whom, and with what result. Prepare a framework for a story about the highlights of that week.

Phase 3. Group Formation and Story Telling (7 to 10 Minutes). Team up with two or three other students. Take turns telling your story. Embellish with as much detail as possible. Keep the storyline plausible, even though it is an ideal situation.

Phase 4. Group Introspection and Comparisons (7 to 10 Minutes). Once the stories have been told, discuss the similarities and differences. Probe to understand why people tell the stories they do; look for underlying motives. You might use the following questions to facilitate your discussion:

    a. What job attributes seem to be important to you? To others?

    b. What do the people in your group want out of work?

    c. How do another person's desires compare to your own?

    d. Who within your group seems to be the team player? The individual contributor? Why?

    e. What will likely be required for the ideal to come true?

Phase 5. Class Debriefing (10 Minutes). Discuss as a total class the personal meanings of the exercise. Think along these lines:

    a. Did you (or others) find it difficult to envision your ideal work tasks? Why? How much do you think about future work?

    b. Into what broad job categories did preferences fall? Did anyone desire a routine production job? Managerial work? A career directly providing personal service to others? A career analyzing information?

    c. Which was the most popular job choice? Why?

    d. Was there much interest in self-managed teams? Why?

    e. To what extent do any of the tasks in your stories build on skills learned in school?

    f. Now, think ahead 10 years. Would your stories change substantially? Why? How does experience affect expectations?

EXPERIENTIAL EXERCISE

Nominal Group Technique (NGT) Focuses Person–Organization Fit

Purpose. This exercise helps students relate the behavioral implications of different approaches toward organizing to a match between personal values and expectations. A second bonus is to learn how to employ the nominal group technique (NGT). NGT is a structured, group problem-focusing technique developed by André Delbecq and Andrew Van De Ven that works best when trying to understand a complex question that has many possible answers.[65] Thus, students not only gain insights into organizational design, but also develop a working understanding of NGT as a problem-focusing, problem-solving technique useful when equal participation is desired.[66]

Materials. One or two sheets of newsprint for each group of six to seven persons and one felt-tip marker for each. One roll of masking tape for posting results. Each student will bring a sheet of paper and pen or pencil to the group.

Procedures. It will require about 30 to 45 minutes to complete all six phases of the exercise, longer if debriefing is emphasized.

1. Form Teams and Select Question Theme (3 to 5 Minutes). Organize the class into groups of six to seven persons. Each group then selects (on a first request, first served basis) an organization theme that it will explore during the exercise.

Several theme possibilities are suggested below; others can be chosen, subject to the constraint that a theme must invite a dozen or more possible responses. Your team may select a theme from the list below or originate your own to insert into the following focusing question:

The Focusing Question: *What values, skills, and behaviors do people need to be personally successful and valued organizational contributors in an enterprise characterized by this approach to organization: ____(insert theme)____?*

    Suggested themes:

    a. Organizational design emphasizing functions.

    b. Organization design emphasizing product line.

    c. A mechanistic bureaucracy.

    d. An organic/adaptive organization.

    e. A highly centralized organization.

    f. A highly decentralized organization.

    g. Self-managed teams.

    h. A wide span of control.

    i. A narrow span of control.

Once a theme has been selected, take a couple of minutes to make sure everyone understands the question and theme/concept.

2. Work through the Processes of the NGT (20 Minutes). Your instructor will provide detailed action steps (from the *Instructor's Manual*). The basic sequence is as follows:

    a. Individual brainstorming (3 to 4 minutes).

    b. Round-robin sharing/listing (about 10 minutes).

    c. Clarifying ideas (about 5 minutes).

    d. Individual balloting (3 to 4 minutes).

    e. Pooling of rankings (3 to 4 minutes).

3. Interpretive Discussion and Debriefing (5 to 10 minutes). As a final wrap-up, discuss the implications of the exercise:

The Findings. Why did your team select the theme that it did? What did you discover about this organizational model/characteristic that surprised you or caused you to rethink your attraction to it? To what degree does its personal success factors fit your own expectations?

The NGT Process. Was NGT as satisfying as a general free-for-all discussion? Did it likely produce more detailed results? Under what circumstances might you expect the NGT to be of value as an organizational process tool at work?

CASE

Metric Technology's Latin American Division
By Dave Daetz

As they left the communication forum, Metric Pacific employees breathed a sigh of both relief and dismay. Although many divisions within Metric Technology would be laying off employees to curb expenses during the economic downturn, Ian Fitzsimmonds, president of the Metric Pacific division, had announced his organization would remain unscathed. Nonetheless, he stated clearly that expense growth could not exceed gross margin growth in the coming year because margins had steadily fallen during the past three quarters. In many companies, this would not be a major blow. But at Metric, where expense growth had traditionally exceeded gross margin growth during the company's 14-year history, it signaled the end of an era. Metric employees were expected to become disciplined.

Metric Pacific is one of three major geographic divisions of Metric Technology that span the globe; the other two are Metric Europe and Metric North America. Metric Pacific is further organized into five geographic subdivisions, one of which is Metric Latin America (MLA). Ian Fitzsimmonds's words translated into a difficult challenge for MLA—increase unit revenues 50 percent without adding staff and while continuing to develop employee capabilities.

A lean organization, MLA is organized by function, with the marketing, sales, distribution, finance, and service departments all reporting to a general manager, Roberto Noriega. Sales and marketing are the largest departments, with eight and seven employees, respectively. Employees in both departments are recognized as talented and highly motivated. Outputs from both have been prolific. Communication between these two departments, however, while getting better, needs improvement. Although each group does good work, each operates in a vacuum, and they seldom cooperate to achieve shared objectives.

As Metric Latin America employees returned to their offices from Ian Fitzsimmonds's communication meeting, conversations indicated they were aware of the challenge ahead of them. Only by working together as a team and by focusing on a shared vision could they succeed. But a recent employee survey made visible the obstacles that needed to be overcome. Responses to the survey questions indicated the areas most needing improvement were vision, decision making, communication, compensation, and career development.

Soon after the forum, people assembled for departmental meetings to discuss the cost containment mandate and implications of the survey results. Several issues surfaced during the marketing department's meeting.

Cynthia complained, "We all know we have good people in MLA, and marketing and sales are no exception. But sales only seems to be interested in chasing quarterly quotas. Salespeople are not out there making sure our dealers are using all the marketing materials we provide. And they certainly are not following up on the marketing programs we are developing. Their orientation is so short term that they don't seem interested in spending their time on activities that pave the way to longer-term market leadership."

"I agree," chimed in Hector. "But I think sales is only pursuing Metric Pacific's mandate. Face it, the only vision that exists is a financial vision—you heard Fitzsimmonds.

Without a nonfinancial vision, we're all running off as individual departments doing our own thing—and doing it well—but not pursuing a shared vision."

"Amen!" exclaimed Chris. "We have to work together to define a collective vision and plan. It can't be created at the top and then communicated to the rest of us. Related to this, I've been disenchanted in the last few months because a lot of decisions are not being made at the right level. Decisions I think I should be making are made too high up—I wonder if I make a difference."

"I think you're right," began Marguerite. "I've also felt lately that I can't make a difference. Sales has different priorities than we do, and it doesn't seem to be interested in the latest marketing program I have been working on. If sales doesn't let me know what kind of marketing programs it needs, I'm just shooting in the dark."

"We're already giving 150 percent," stated Don, "and now we have to push even harder this year. Well, it has to be a two-way street. It's no secret that our group is not compensated as well as our peers in Metric North America and Metric Europe. Not only are they on higher pay grades for the same work, but they get bonuses, too. In Latin America, only sales gets the bonuses."

Cynthia jumped in again: "Other divisions allocate some of their budget to team-building activities. Our revenue per employee is well over $1 million, compared to $450,000 or so for the company as a whole. Yet we don't spend money on team building or fun here, other than an occasional end-of-quarter party. Why don't we kick off this year's business planning cycle by going on a retreat as an organization? And I mean all 28 of us, not just the general manager and department heads."

Questions for Managerial Action

1. What organizational concepts are involved in the Metric situation? What clues lead you to these conclusions?

2. What are the behavioral implications of Metric's approach to organizing? What is going well? What is not?

3. What are the obstacles to improved performance?

4. What alternatives does Metric Latin America have for meeting its new performance targets? What must it do to succeed in achieving these goals?

Chapter 4

Organizational Culture

LEARNING OBJECTIVES

After studying this chapter, you should be able to:

- Explain why organizational assumptions are important and identify three types of assumptions that give meaning to culture.
- Identify four steps of organizational cultures based on the origin and content of the underlying cultural value systems.
- Articulate how organizational culture guides behavior.
- Read an organization's culture by observing its physical settings and rituals and by asking questions about its underlying assumptions and values.
- Explain how a founder establishes culture in a new organization and how subsequent leaders adapt cultural elements to promote adaptive change.
- Distinguish four factors useful in comparing and contrasting national cultures.

WAL-MART'S CULTURE INSPIRES REMARKABLE GROWTH

People either love it or hate it. Customers and employees (associates) love it, many small town shopkeepers hate it. The "it" is Wal-Mart, the powerhouse retailing enterprise built on a foundation of commonly shared values that provide consistency and strength to its organizational culture.

The world's largest retail chain began in 1962 when Sam Walton ("Mr. Sam" to associates), at age 50, opened the first Wal-Mart discount store. In the 1960s he experimented with discount retailing, then devised a strategy of locating stores in small communities throughout Arkansas and adjoining states. This small-town strategy enabled Wal-Mart to grow without attracting the wrath of then giants like K-Mart and Sears. By 1980 the chain achieved the $1 billion sales milestone; only 15 years later it was three-fourths of the way to annual sales of $100 billion.

Walton built his success on people, striving to please both customers and associates. To Wal-Mart managers and associates, customer service is a way of life: "Serving one customer at a time with the single-purpose mission of exceeding each customer's expectations" is the goal. Associates actively participate in profit sharing, an incentive that has made many of them very wealth. Said Sam Walton repeatedly before his death, "If you take care of your people, they will take care of you." This was independently validated when *Mass Market Retailers* magazine recognized Wal-Mart associates collectively as the Mass Market Retailer of the Year, commenting: "The Wal-Mart associate. In this decade that term has come to symbolize all that is right with the American worker."

Managers at the headquarters and regional levels are expected to be out in the stores most of the time, not working in their offices. Walton often remarked, "The key is to get out into the store and listen to what the associates have to say. It's terribly important for everyone to get involved. Our best ideas come from clerks." When in stores, managers strive to build a sense of excitement and fun by spontaneously leading cheers, giving out awards, promoting contests, and merchandising products. Store and department managers are given discretion in ordering and merchandising, so they can be sensitive to local needs. Because they are also given financial incentives to become involved in civic activities, each store takes on a "hometown" feel.

With a fixation on customers, quality, and spontaneity, nothing gets stuck in a rut at Wal-Mart—except steady growth. Mr. Sam believed his organization "must have a low resistance to change, we must be flexible and willing to adjust rapidly to stay abreast of the competitive environment. We believe to grow successfully we must continually challenge and test new retailing concepts. . . . We must continually improve." Even though he is no longer around to visit stores, praise people, and lead cheers, the culture shaped by founder Sam Walton endures.

Sources: Sam Walton with John Huey, *Sam Walton: Made in America* (New York: Doubleday, 1992); Wal-Mart *Annual Reports* (January 31, 1989, 1990, 1992, and 1995); and Arthur A. Thompson, Kem Pinegar, and Tracy R. Kramer, "Wal-Mart Stores, Inc.," in A. J. Strickland III and Arthur A. Thompson, Jr., *Cases in Strategic Management* (Chicago: Irwin, 1995), pp. 536–568.

Organizational culture is not always easy to observe and understand, for it tends to subtly permeate most aspects of organizational life. Although culture is one of the newest organizational behavior concepts, it has quickly been recognized as a key predictor of employee satisfaction and competitive performance. The rapid acceptance of its importance in understanding organizational behavior parallels the dramatic growth of Wal-Mart—from obscurity to world-class prominence in about 20 years. Robert Waterman, Jr., even goes so far as to state: "Corporate cultures that tend to put their three constituencies—shareholders, customers, and employees— on the same plane, as opposed to putting shareholders first, are perversely the ones that do best for shareholders."[1]

HOW DO ASSUMPTIONS GIVE MEANING TO ORGANIZATIONAL CULTURE?

culture
The pattern of learned behaviors shared and transmitted among the members of a society.

The concept of culture is about as old as civilization itself. Ralph Linton provides a timeless definition of **culture** as "the configuration of learned behavior and results of behavior whose component elements are shared and transmitted to the members of a particular society.[2] So defined, China has a culture—a commonality of beliefs, experiences, values, and expectations—that sets it apart from Egypt, India, Poland, and Mexico.

For centuries people have expected national or ethnic cultures to cause the people of one region to behave differently form those of neighboring countries. For example, New Zealand's "She'll be right" mentality causes inhabitants to concentrate primarily on enjoying life, believing the natural resources of their country provide the means to do so. This is substantially different from the more competitive and achievement-oriented behavior found in the ancestral homes of most New Zealanders—Australia and England. Similarly, today's managers know the culture of AT&T is distinct from the cultures of IBM, ITT, and GE, and AT&T employees thus behave in predictably different ways.

Organizational Assumptions Guide Behavior

organizational culture
The fundamental assumptions people share about an organization's values, beliefs, norms, symbols, language, rituals, and myths—all of the expressive elements that give meaning to organizational membership and are accepted as guides to behavior.

As a relatively new concept, organizational culture is open to many interpretations. Some managers think of organizational culture as simply "the way we do things around here," while others believe it is a more complex "set of shared values, beliefs, and assumptions that get everyone headed in the same direction."[3] Still others might say that culture inculcates members in the ways of an organization and gives it meaning. Whatever the interpretation, most managers agree that when members are aware of the organizational culture, formal controls are less necessary.

Organizational culture describes the fundamental assumptions about an organization's values, beliefs, norms, symbols, language, rituals, and myths that give meaning to organizational membership and are collectively accepted by a group as

Matsushita Electric Corporation of America, which manufactures and markets Panasonic, Technics, and Quasar, adapts its socialization process to accommodate each culture. Although each U.S. facility has its own management style, principles come from Matsushita's Japanese management culture. One practice is to become partners in activities that benefit local communities. Here employee Jesse Williams assists students in the Panasonic Kid Witness News program, a hands-on video education program to help kids develop talents and organizational skills. (Photo: Matsushita Electric Corporation of America.)

guides to expected behaviors.[4] Patterns of assumptions emerge as a group learns from founders and through discovery or invention to cope with its problems of external adaptation and internal integration.[5] Peter Drucker has even built a theory of business around three key assumptions people make about their organization, assumptions that over time no longer fit reality. He writes: "The assumptions about environment define what an organization is paid for. The assumptions about mission define what an organization considers to be meaningful results . . . Finally, the assumptions about core competencies define where an organization must excel in order to maintain leadership."[6]

As organizational members become aware of core assumptions, they learn the limits of acceptable behaviors. Some behaviors are prescribed and encouraged, such as IBM's tenet of working with customers to help solve problems and extend product applications. Other behaviors are proscribed and are to be avoided, such as the IRS norm that an agent should never accept a free lunch from a client or organization to avoid a potential conflict of interest.

Most organizations develop patterns of cultural assumptions that answer such fundamental questions as: How does our organization relate to its environment? How do we learn and communicate? What do we expect of people and relationships? As answers emerge through actions and behaviors that seem to work, they become incorporated into patterned sets of fundamental assumptions that create an enduring cultural system.[7] Exhibit 4–1 shows two contrasting examples of basic elements woven into internally coherent cultural patterns. We say an organization has a **strong culture** when most members accept a set of interrelated assumptions that forms an internally consistent cultural system.[8]

Assumptions Define Relationships to the Environment

Some environmental assumptions refer to the external environment: Will the organization exploit or seek harmony with nature? More often they refer to the industry environment created by organizational decisions. Each organization shapes or enacts its own unique environment as managers make decisions and selectively

strong culture
Achieved when most members accept the interrelated assumptions that form an internally consistent cultural system.

■■■■■■ **EXHIBIT 4–1**

GEM and MAX: Two Contrasting Cultural Systems

GEM Corporation

The Cultural System

1. People are responsible and motivated to govern themselves.
2. Individuals are the ultimate source of ideas.
3. Truth is pragmatically discovered by using groups to test ideas and competitively try out alternatives.
4. Opposing ideas are healthy because members view themselves as an organizational family who will take care of each other.

The Observable Behaviors

People work in an open office landscape with few doors on offices; there is much wandering around; conversations are intense and at times argumentative; informality prevails.

MAX Corporation

The Cultural System

1. People are disciplined and loyal in carrying out directives.
2. Organizational relationships respect hierarchy; they are linear and vertical.
3. Truth comes from better-educated, older, higher-status members.
4. Each person has a niche or turf that cannot be invaded.
5. The organization will take care of its members within each department unit.

The Observable Behaviors

People work inside their offices with doors closed; there is little conversation except by prearranged appointments; meetings are conducted with strict agendas; deference to authority is respected; formality prevails.
Sources: "Culture in Organizations: A Case Study," by William G. Dyer, Jr. Working Paper #1279-82. Copyright 1983 by the Sloan School of Management. All rights reserved. The MAX example is reprinted from "Coming to a New Awareness of Organizational Culture," by Edgar H. Schein, *Sloan Management Review* (Winter 1984), excerpts from p. 5, by permission of publisher.

respond more to some external elements than to others.[9] Environmentally related assumptions concerning customers, markets, and competitors frame the reason for the organization's existence and make it unique.

Wal-Mart grew rapidly by dominating retailing in the small to medium-size communities where it initially chose to locate. It has created a unique environment by providing customers value in a wide range of branded products in large, clean, modern stores and by bonding employees to the ideals of the firm—putting customers first and making long-term commitments to serve the communities where it locates.

Dollar General Corporation (DG) also operates retail stores in small towns, many within Wal-Mart's territory. Dollar General relates differently to its stores' environments by assuming everything is expendable—nothing should be committed to the long term. DG locates in small, vacant stores on Main Street, where rents are cheap; it stocks manufacturers' closeout or distress merchandise that is bought with deep discounts; and it quickly closes any store that is not profitable.[10] Although these two retailers often share the same markets, their widely divergent patterns of relating to their environments have created entirely different cultures.

Assumptions Promote Learning and Communicating

Learning involves seeking to understand reality and to discover the basis for truth, and "organizations" (the people within them) are capable of learning just as are individuals.[11] Organizations differ in how employees are expected to define reality.

Some organizations seek to learn empirically through experimenting and gathering feedback. Others believe truth is revealed intuitively or comes only from higher management. At a practical level, these issues frame assumptions about management's planning timeframe (short or long term), concepts of space and equity (open or private offices), and beliefs about how to achieve innovation (through individuals or groups).

Language and communication norms also help define organizational reality. In some bureaucracies managers are conditioned that unless they "put it in writing," nothing gets done. In faster-changing, more informal environments, managers expect that once they leave a meeting, their agreed-upon actions will be performed without their having to exchange minutes or memos—a spoken tradition prevails. Depending on what has and has not worked in the past, members of an organization develop an acceptable and somewhat unique basis for learning and communicating.

Assumptions Tell about People and Relationships

Organizations tend to develop common assumptions about human nature and how people are to be treated. Practices within some politically active organizations presume people are self-centered, personally competitive, and willing to sacrifice others for personal gain. In other organizations, people are believed to be team players willing to make self-sacrifices for the common good.

The culture also reflects assumptions about who is to have power and how power is to be used, which affects relationships among people. The late Henry Ford II was a flamboyant executive who perpetuated the tradition that Ford Motor Co. was autocratically managed. Under his long reign, the company was notoriously centralized and capricious, which encouraged political competition among managers. In contrast, while he was CEO of Chrysler, Lee Iacocca (equally flamboyant) initiated practices that delegated more and created a team atmosphere. Chrysler's team climate brought out the best in their people as a way of helping to manage costs, reduce break-even volume levels, and redesign quality cars to meet customer wants.[12]

One disturbing research study found that dimensions of organizational culture were good predictors of the degree to which women would be accepted into management positions.[13] The process of cumulative efforts by the organization to adapt to environmental forces shaped attitudes and behaviors toward women in management. Even though the percentage of management positions filled by women has approximately doubled in the past 25 years (to about 40 percent), the culture in many organizations, especially in manufacturing, perpetuates the stereotype that management is for men.

Such examples and findings dramatize the differences in organizational value systems, and the power of organizational culture in giving each enterprise a unique look and feel—whether based on norms of equality or not.

WHY DO ORGANIZATIONAL VALUE SYSTEMS DIFFER?

values
The enduring beliefs and expectations that a person or group hold to be important guides to behavior.

The assumptions most critical to organizational behavior are those shared values that lie at the heart of human character and societal behavior. **Values** are the enduring beliefs and expectations held to be important guides to behavior by a person or group of people.[14] An individuals' personal values learned from formative early experiences guide his other behavior throughout life. If a certain set of values is held to be very important, it enables the person to behave consistently across different situations. When asked to rank 15 organizational value statements, the 239 respondents (including advertising professionals, CPAs, and business professors) generated high agreement among each group that the top five values are:[15]

1. Provide excellent service to customers.
2. Operate in a highly ethical manner at all times.
3. Provide products and/or services of excellent quality.
4. Consistently make a fair and reasonable profit (not maximize profits).
5. Staff the organization with high-caliber employees from top to bottom.

Just as occurs in business education and training, religious and fraternal or service organizations have long sought to pass along their values to new members or to people generally. People who participated in scouting in their youth may remember the scout oath, that "a scout is trustworthy, loyal, helpful, friendly, courteous, kind," and so on. Or, for many religions, the Ten Commandments serve as reminders that "thou shall not . . ." The laws of a nation usually are based on shared values as to how people ought to behave and what the consequences should be if a person violates those codified values. Before reading on, consider your own values as expressed in elements of organizational culture by completing the Your Turn exercise.

Two Key Factors Define Organizational Value Systems

organizational value system
A core set of values shared by the majority of organizational members, typically differentiated by the origin and content of those enduring values.

Every organization is capable of generating and passing along a set of values that is more or less unique to it. An organization's values convey what behaviors and beliefs are important to its success. A set of values becomes an **organizational value system** when those core values are shared by the majority of organizational members. Values taken on meaning within an organization through what is espoused (what people say) and by inference (what people do).[16] To understand the impact of organizational values on behavior, you need to look both at the origin of those values and at their content or meaning.

charismatic-based values
Values originating from a strong leader, usually the founder, which tend to be internalized by members so long as they look to the leader for guidance and inspiration.

Origins of Organizational Values.   Research by Yoash Wiener suggests organizational values originate from either charismatic leadership or organizational traditions.[17] **Charismatic-based values** originate from a strong leader, usually the founder, and tend to be internalized by members only so long as they identify with the leader, to whom they look for guidance and inspiration. As the pioneer of IBM, Tom Watson is credited with making explicit and inculcating many of the values that help give IBM meaning and guidance today. The same was true of J. Edgar Hoover's long reign and influence on shaping the values of the Federal Bureau of Investigation (FBI). Certainly Sam Walton created an enduring organizational value system for Wal-Mart. For most small firms, the values of the founder–owner directly shape the organizational culture.

tradition-based values
Values deeply rooted in historical practices which provide stability as they are passed from generation to generation.

Alternatively, values can emerge out of organizational traditions that are more anonymous in origin. **Tradition-based values** are deeply rooted in historical practices and lend stability to the organization because they are readily passed from generation to generation of organizational members. Exxon, Delta Airlines, and the U.S. Marine Corps each has a culture that has been passed on largely by tradition. People working for each are well aware of what their organization stands for and how individual members can expect to be treated.

YOUR TURN

What Do You Value in Organizational Culture?

For each question, circle the most valued option.

1. Which would you prefer as an organizational motto?
   a. The customer is king.
   b. We're number one.
2. In discussions with colleagues, which would you value?
   a. A focus on goals, processes, and organizational systems.
   b. Stories of success and superiority over competition.
3. What would you prefer to find in offices and work areas?
   a. An emphasis on function over form and getting work done.
   b. Elegance, attention to symbols of success, clean desks.
4. With which organization would you rather identify?
   a. One with a reputation for conservative stability.
   b. One noted for the bold moves of its leader.
5. How would you like to be socialized in organizational lore?
   a. Hear stories about average people doing good things.
   b. Hear stories about the exploits of founders.
6. On which would you rather base your organizational identity?
   a. A history of providing good service and fair treatment.
   b. Your association with a dynamic industry leader.

Scoring: In each of the four fields identified below, give yourself 1 point for each of the responses you circled:

Functional	1A	2A	3A	= _____	Elitist:	1B	2B	3B	= _____
Traditional:	4A	5A	6A	= _____	Charismatic:	4B	5B	6B	= _____

From your scores in each of the rows above, circle the word that had the highest score in the pair, either functional or elitist, and either traditional or charismatic. Now, turn to Exhibit 4–2 and circle on the model the combination you seem to value the most. The text explains your organizational culture preference.

---

functional values
Express a normative mode of conduct that tells members what they should pay attention to (e.g., customer service, innovation, quality).

elitist values
Focus on the perceived superiority of the organization in comparison to others.

Content of Organizational Values. The content or interpreted meaning of values is based on either functional or elitist ideals. **Functional values** express a normative mode of conduct that tells members what they should pay attention to, such as customer service, innovation, speed, and quality. **Elitist values** focus more on the perceived superiority of the organization in comparison to other organizations. Functional values offer more constructive guidance for members' behaviors. For example, if a firm values quality, everyone should be empowered to make continuous improvements and eliminate dysfunctional practices. Elitist values, on the other hand, attempt to instill pride in membership, creating a "we're number one" mentality. Elitist values can create an aloofness that weakens members' abilities to confront changing realities.

━━━━━ **EXHIBIT 4–2**

Four Types of Organizational Value Systems

When organizational values are strong, one of these four systems typically emerges as the dominant pattern. Since charismatic types are inherently more unstable, the arrows show possible movements toward greater organizational effectiveness (with solid arrows stronger than dashed). Values embedded in tradition with a functional focus are thus more effective in bringing about behaviors necessary for long-term success.

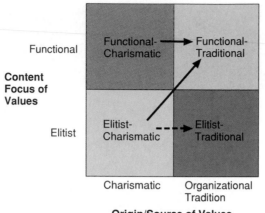

Source: Yoash Wiener, "Forms of Value Systems: A Focus on Organizational Effectiveness and Cultural Change and Maintenance," *Academy of Management Review* 13 (October 1988), pp. 534–545.

Four Alternative Value Systems Define Organizational Cultures

Exhibit 4–2 presents what researchers call a "2 by 2 model" identifying four types of organizational value systems. Of the four, the elitist-charismatic value system is weakest and least stable; the functional-traditional is strongest and most enduring.

Functional-Traditional Values.   "Most likely to contribute to the development of environmentally viable values and, consequently, to organizational effectiveness," functional values that emerge from traditional practices are most supportive of managers' needs to set consistent goals, policies, and strategies.[18] Rather than being pushed from the top down, they evolve slowly through feedback from incremental changes, which both gives these values permanence and makes them difficult for competitors to copy.[19] The values of cooperation, a sense of shared obligations, quality, loyalty, and focused effort that characterize Japanese firms are typical examples. They also are infused in such successful American firms as Lincoln Electric, Nucor (the minimill steel company), and the newly emergent Walt Disney Productions (which has shifted from a functional-charismatic value system).

Elitist-Charismatic Values.   At the opposite end of the long-term effectiveness spectrum are elitist-charismatic values. These values usually come from the flamboyant, eccentric personality of a founder who creates a product or service that meets early market success. Members often revere the charismatic leader's "cause" and what he or she has been able to achieve. Mary Kay Ash imparts such values at Mary Kay Cosmetics. Apple Computer began as a culture based on charismatic leadership (from Steve Jobs and Steve Wozniak) and elitist attitudes ("We're out to change the world"). With changes in leadership, Apple struggled in the early and mid-1990s to refocus organizational values.

Functional-Charismatic Values.   This culture has the potential for longer-term effectiveness and probably represents a transitional phase along the path toward functional-traditional values. Any value system of charismatic origin tends to be temporary, linked to the personal ideals of the founder. But dedication to functional values such as quality and risk taking puts the focus on doing what is right rather than on elitist pride. Wal-Mart recently made this transition, whereas Hewlett-Packard and McDonald's long ago completed the shift.

Challenge of Change — *Allied Signal CEO Refocuses Values to Emphasize Quality*

Lawrence A. Bossidy left his job as vice chairman at GE in July 1991 to take over as CEO at Allied Signal, an industrial supplier with businesses in the chemical, aerospace systems, and automotive parts industries. Since then, the tough-minded, results-oriented Bossidy has sold off assets, reduced headcount, and restructured business. But through the years of transformation, Bossidy emphasized values, goals, and total quality, and led by coaching people to win. He offers a theory: "I believe in the 'burning platform' theory of change . . . The leader's job is to help everyone see that the platform is burning, whether the flames are apparent or not."

What he found at Allied Signal was a company that had grown rapidly through mergers and acquisitions, which left the firm cash poor and with stalled earnings. "We had 58 business units, each guarding its own turf. It was an inner-directed company, focused mainly on itself. Management made all the decisions, and employees' ideas were rarely solicited and therefore rarely offered."

In reflecting back on his first 60 days at Allied Signal, Lawrence Bossidy offers this perspective on culture, values, and quality:

I think you don't change a culture. I think you coach people to win . . . At Allied Signal, each of our three major sectors had its own history as an independent company, its own distinct culture. We didn't want to change that. It makes the company stronger.

But we had to unite ourselves with vision and values. (He began with an off-site meeting of the top twelve managers.) We spent two days arguing—and I mean arguing—about values. That was helpful because at the end of the meeting, we had not only the values, we also had a specific definition of those values. The seven values we settled on are simple: customers, integrity, people, teamwork, speed, innovation, and performance. . .

We made a major commitment to use total quality as the vehicle to drive change . . . TQ does not replace goals; it's the vehicle to facilitate progress toward your goals. And here's where the evaluation of values comes in . . . Think about it. Anybody who makes his numbers (goals) and says "I don't need TQ" has to walk the plank or change. Some people have changed, and some are gone.

Source: Noel M. Tichy and Ram Charan, "The CEO As Coach: An Interview with Allied Signal's Lawrence A. Bossidy," *Harvard Business Review* 73 (March–April 1995), pp. 68–78.

Elitist-Traditional Values. Finally, some organizations use tradition as a way of intentionally sustaining long-term elitism. Usually these are smaller, niche marketers who appeal to clients attracted by snob appeal or the long tradition of being perceived as superior or exclusive. Some universities, law firms, and brokerage houses convey elitist traditions and successfully control client access to uphold the elitist posture. So does Rolls-Royce.

The critical question is how well the culture with its system of values serves the organization during periods of change, especially when environmental forces are shifting. When a new strategy is required, strong cultures that once served an organization well are now likely to inhibit its adaptation. More than a decade following its breakup, AT&T is still struggling to adapt its once dominant "universal service" customer concept to a competitive long-distance telecommunications marketplace. Its long-standing elitist-traditional values, which assume an authoritarian, politicized bureaucracy, complicated its shift to competitive market conditions. Alternatively as noted in the Challenge of Change Box, the new CEO who took over a very distressed Allied Signal sought to focus key values within the prevailing cultures. To do so, he had to convince people the "platform was burning" and then coach them to want to win.

━━━━━ **EXHIBIT 4–3**

Rational and Expressive Elements That Influence Organizational Behavior

The stimuli for behaving consistent with organizational expectations comes from two types of sources. Each can be equally effective in getting things done in organizations. Cultural elements are defined throughout the chapter.

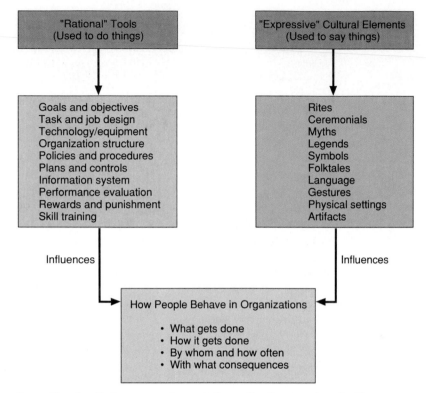

Source: The rational tools are common to organization practice. The expressive cultural forms were suggested by Janice M. Meyer and Jarrison M. Trice, "Studying Organizational Cultures through Rites and Ceremonials," *Academy of Management Review* 9 (October 1984), pp. 653–669.

WHAT FUNCTIONS DOES ORGANIZATIONAL CULTURE SERVE?

Small firms draw on organizational culture to help establish competitive advantages in niche markets. Large firms such as Unilever, IBM, and Sony create global markets and worldwide competition through deliberate strategies and disciplined managerial practices. Across the globe, strategy, technology, organizational structure, information systems, policies, and other rational managerial tools are used by managers to shape corporate direction. Although less overt than such traditional managerial tools, organizational culture also helps guide consistent behavior by reinforcing capabilities and strengthening sources of competitive advantage.

Culture Complements Rational Managerial Tools

Organizations use many tools and processes to channel, guide, and change behavior. Unlike the rational tools in the manager's portfolio, organizational culture cannot provide a quick fix or abruptly change organizational behavior. Culture epitomizes the expressive character of organizations; it is communicated less through objective realism and more through symbolism, feelings, and the meaning behind language, behaviors, and physical settings. Exhibit 4–3 contrasts the elements of organizational culture with the rational tools of management.

Hewlett-Packard (H-P) achieved success as a technology leader with high product reliability in markets focused on calculators, measuring instruments, and computing.

H-P has used management tools to change its organizational structure as it periodically branched into new lines of business. Company policies (more management tools) are extensive and detailed in writing, intended to provide consistency in the performance of routine tasks. But Hewlett-Packard also seeks to influence employee behavior in less direct ways by promoting the "H-P Way," cultural beliefs supported by management that emphasize a disciplined, team approach to innovation. When John Young, the first nonfounder CEO of H-P announced his retirement, he noted that the H-P Way withstands changing times and is transportable worldwide: "The thing that fascinates me as much as anything is to go to China or France or Hungary or Czechoslovakia, and already they have the same team spirit and the value system in place.[20]

Rational tools such as technology and structure are designed to do things. The *expressive practice of culture* reflects more a way of saying things. Managers who just want to get on with the jobs to be done may not perceive the expressive qualities conveyed in organizational rites, rituals, legends, and other cultural elements. But, "to overlook these expressive consequences is to miss much of the significance of what is really happening in organizations."[21]

Culture Supports (or Resists) Strategic Changes

The success or failure of a firm ultimately rides on its strategies—how appropriate they are, given internal and external forces, and how they are implemented. Strategy provides a firm with purpose and direction, encompassing its mission and goals and clarifying where it will focus its efforts and how it will gain competitive advantage. For better or worse, the intended strategy of a firm is affected by the behaviors of the people expected to carry it out. Culture serves as a rudder to keep the firms' strategy on course. Increasingly, managers and consultants are recognizing that "while corporate strategy may control a firm's successes or failure, corporate culture can make or break that strategy."[22]

Strategy Focuses Purpose. Strategy is a rational management process that leads to actions intended to match a firm's product and service offering to a specific market or type of customer. Culture is the expressive backup that influences how well the strategy is implemented. Managers often are blindsided when they try to introduce radical strategic changes that run contrary to cultural expectations. For example, in the mid-1970s, the petroleum industry appeared to face diminished growth and mounting geopolitical pressures. Two CEOs of major oil companies were determined to diversity their businesses to reduce their dependence on oil (a major strategy change). But after five years of flubbing various acquisition attempts, both firms remained firmly committed to oil—and both CEOs were ousted. *Business Week* concluded:

> *Each of the CEOs has been unable to implement his strategy, not because it was theoretically wrong or bad but because neither had understood that his company's culture was so entrenched in the traditions and values of doing business as oilmen that employees resisted—and sabotaged—the radical changes that the CEOs tried to impose . . . If implementing [strategies] violates employees' basic beliefs about their roles in the company, or the traditions that underlie the corporation's culture, they are doomed to fail.[23]*

Culture Focuses Strategy. The two oil executives discovered that, once in place, organizational culture serves as a lens through which members view and evaluate the appropriateness of goals, strategies, and directions. In strong-culture organizations such as Wal-Mart, where core assumptions are widely shared, certain behaviors are honored, even celebrated. The oil CEOs behaved inconsistently with their oil firms' cultures when they pursued diversification strategies that didn't match accepted assumptions about the nature of their business.

Culture truly makes a difference, but what is valued in one organization may be quite different from what is valued in another, even within the same industry. The values, beliefs and other traditions that have made Wal-Mart a stellar performer in the discount world of department store retailing are not the same as those of a Sears, a Macy's, or a Montgomery Ward. Each organization evolves its own cultural underpinnings, which help or hinder future efforts to respond to strategic environmental threats and opportunities. Sears, Macy's, and Montgomery Ward have experienced difficulty changing strategies and improving quality in recent years, in part because of the constraints of cultures that didn't change with the times.

Culture Helps Socialize New Members

socialization
A process by which new members are indoctrinated into the expectations and rituals of the organization—its cultural norms or unwritten codes of behavior.

Many firms try to hire people they believe will be compatible with the culture—that is, who will "fit in." Experienced members then work to socialize newcomers in the ways of the culture, which involves changing attitudes and beliefs to achieve an internalized commitment to the organization.[24] **Socialization** is the process by which new members are indoctrinated in the expectations of the organization and its cultural norms, or unwritten codes of behavior. Jay Galbraith emphasizes that it is the perceived attractiveness of an organization's culture that enables it to recruit and retain the technical talent necessary to build competitive capabilities:

> *The assets of Intel and Motorola are actually the knowledge and energy of the engineers who create the designs. The ability of Intel and Motorola to compete in the new economy depends on their ability to attract, retain, motivate, and coordinate talented engineers.*[25]

To obtain a classic view of how a Japanese bank used to socialize new employees, see the World Watch box. This firm put recruits through a rigorous boot-camp type training program to break down individualism and develop the teamwork expected of Japanese employees.

Socialization Methods.   Organizations with strong cultures devote considerable time to indoctrinating and training the new member in the ways of the organization. Bureaucratic organizations typically devote attention to detailed explanations of rules and procedures. Those who emphasize rules sprinkle their explanations with folklore and myths about the errant soul who tried to introduce personal reforms or who took exception to the rules, only to be castigated for not operating within expected bounds. For such organizations, myths about heroes retell the virtues of paying your dues and being a loyal member over the long term.

By contrast, socialization into smaller, entrepreneurial firms is less formal; it may even appear nonexistent except for introductions all around and perhaps an explanation of benefits. Established members informally tell tales of heroes described either as bandits (nonconforming risk takers who singlehandedly solve difficult problems) or charismatic team leaders with compelling visions. The message is to model the behavior of the hero.

Rites of Passage in a Japanese Bank

How would you like to undergo an intensive military-style boot camp as your indoctrination into a business firm? While uncommon among U.S. firms, that is just what is expected of many university graduates who join Japanese firms. Uedagin Bank has a tradition of expecting new recruits to endure a demanding training program that, much like the military, was designed to throw off past social roles and inculcate in new employees the virtues bank managers hold dear.

To separate new hires from their past, an entrance ceremony welcomes trainees and their parents. Following speeches to praise parents, new recruits are sent for two days to an actual army camp where they are issued used fatigues to diminish ideas of status. A drill sergeant puts them through close-order drill, calisthenics, and an obstacle course. The message: A large firm needs discipline and order, and military-type training helps build those qualities.

Next it's a two-day session in meditation at a Zen temple, complete with tasteless gruel. Here they participate in rituals to help learn the firm's philosophy. A later marathon march emphasizes the need for physical conditioning and teaches a lesson in teamwork. Recruits are told to walk in a single group the first nine miles, which is pleasant and highly social. Then they are segregated into groups, and spontaneous intergroup competition emerges, with each trying to outdistance the other. The faster pace causes many to drop out of what has become a race. The final seven miles is to be completed alone and in silence, with the survivors feeling personal pride in accomplishing what many failed to do.

What the firm sought to teach through experience were the values of self-denial, perseverance, and noncompetition as the means to success collectively. These experiences, combined with living together during the entire training phase (14 hours a day, six days a week), socialize trainees in the ways of Japanese banking.

Source: Condensed from Thomas P. Rohlen, "Spiritual Education in A Japanese Bank," *American Anthropologist* (October 1974). The group bonding practices described by this anthropologist are still evident in some Japanese firms today.

Commitment to Organization or Profession? Sometimes, however, too much "culture shock" or incongruence between individual and corporate beliefs occur. Then, the newcomer is likely either to abandon the organization or to develop personal strategies for coping that enable him or her to save face by upholding personal values.[26] The conflicts between personal–professional and organizational value systems can be especially perplexing. Managers of firms based in the United States generally devote less time to socializing newcomers than do managers in other counties, especially in Asia. Consequently, "U.S. workers often form stronger alliances to their occupations [professional disciplines] than they do their work organizations—an outcome that may be neither desirable nor inevitable.[27]

Culture Promotes Expected Behaviors

Although the expressive character of organizational culture gives it the appearance of being a weak transmitter of values, cultures work best when strong. An organization has a strong culture when members accept and buy into a common set

Breaks for sports are a part of the Microsoft culture as established by founder Bill Gates. His large corporation still has the feel of an entrepreneurial start-up. Employees, like entrepreneurs, are empowered to make business decisions, work intensely for long hours to create or modify a product, and participate in diversions to get the creative juices flowing again. (Photo: © 1991 Steven Bloch/Black Star.)

of beliefs, values, and assumptions, as if their behaviors were guided by an invisible hand. A strong culture has such widely accepted modes of conduct that certain behaviors are expected, and others would never occur.

Culture works best when people forget why they are doing certain things, but keep on doing them. For example, how often are you conscious of why you shake hands when meeting someone? We forget that the origin of shaking hands was to prove that your hand was free of a weapon and therefore extended in peace. But the strong culture that promotes consistent behavior also makes it difficult to adapt when old ways no longer fit new realities. IBM knows well how a strong elitist culture constrains the shift to new, more flexible behaviors.

Where culture is strong, powerful forces spread to all aspects of organizational life. For example, Walt Disney Productions encountered serious cultural rigidities following the death of Walt in 1966.[28] For almost two decades, his successor managers attempted to follow exactly in Walt's footsteps. "What would Walt have done?" was the usually question raised in contemplation of a decision. By trying to second-guess their brilliant founder, they were not only forever mired in the past, but they lacked Walt's creativity and sense of marketing. Not until Michael Eisner was brought in as CEO in 1984 did Disney begin to revitalize both its culture and its strategy.[29] Eisner believed that Disney's cultural strength was dedication to entertainment experimentation and innovation—not rigid adherence to traditional "family entertainment."

Subcultures Allow Organizational Diversity

Few organizations other than small to mid-size enterprises in a single line of business have a uniform, monolithic culture. While central tendencies toward shared assumptions promote a dominant culture throughout a large organization, subcultures coexist as adaptive responses to diverse needs.[30] **Subcultures** are localized subsystems of values and assumptions that give meaning to the common interests of smaller clusters of people within the overall organization. A subculture may identify the members of a specific department, activity center, or division. Or it may emerge when a fairly broad cross section of organizational members share a particular experience or perspective. Perhaps the perspective is the result of having served under a particular leader, or having attended a common university, or sharing a common background such as all being engineers or Italians.[31]

subcultures
Localized subsystems of values and assumptions that give meaning to the common interests of small clusters of people.

Subcultures have three possible impacts on the organization: They can (1) serve to enhance the dominant culture; (2) promote an independence from it, as commonly occurs among divisions of diversified firms; or (3) function as countercultures when they are at odds with it.[32] The counterculture is most problematic for the overall organization.

countercultures
A subculture that rejects the values and assumptions of the host organization and develops opposing beliefs, frequently based on elitist notions of a charismatic leader.

Countercultures reject the values and assumptions of the host organization and develop opposing beliefs, often based on elitist notions that may be promulgated by a charismatic leader.[33] Such groups within an organization function more as adversaries than as partners. When Steve Jobs and his maverick band of programmers and designers developed the original Macintosh computer, there was such rivalry between his elitist group and the rest of Apple Computer that a showdown with John Sculley, then CEO, led to the ouster of Jobs, one of Apple's cofounders. Countercultures such as the Macintosh group can be strong, but they often focus on thwarting the efforts of the larger organization. They demonstrate, however, why cultures are important to organizational performance and why effective managers learn to interpret their organization's culture.

HOW DO MEMBERS READ THEIR ORGANIZATION'S CULTURE?

Cultural clues suggest how a company chooses to succeed. They reveal insights into how problems have been solved and what is held to be important in the conduct of business. Managers need to learn how to read cultural clues, for often there are inconsistencies between what is said and what is done, or between subcultures and the overall culture.[34] They can begin by observing objects—physical settings and artifacts. Then they might probe into the behavioral side by observing clues revealed through rites and people's public actions. Finally, skill in reading culture evolves by asking people questions and listening to how they respond as much as to what they said. The search is less for precise answers than for a general understanding. Analysis of culture is "not an experimental science in search of law, but an interpretative one in search of meaning."[35]

Observe Physical Settings and Artifacts

Any newcomers to an organization—whether just considering employment, reporting the first day on the job, or attending his or her first staff meeting—can pick up clues by observing physical settings and artifacts. Here are a few nonbehavioral clues to watch for.

Facilities. Physical facilities tell a tale of what is important, and not so important, to an organization (see Exhibit 4–4). They reflect values and performance expectations. You might find that although the reception and office areas are reasonably well maintained and tidy, the production facility is cluttered with scrap, chemical stains blotch the floor, heat and noise are excessive, lighting is dim, and paint is peeling from walls and machines. Obviously the physical facilities needed for a manufacturing operation differ from those needed for a sales office. But does one appear the neglected stepchild, as if management has failed to reinvest in its future?[36]

Organizations that function around elitist values tend to convey status differentials in the location and sizes of offices. Status is denoted by being higher up in a building, having a corner office, being located around the perimeter of a floor, and having an office rather than a cubicle. People have been known to fight to get a window office.

Bricks and Mortar

- What is the physical appearance of the facility? Is it well maintained, with an aesthetically pleasing sense of decor, or unkept, dingy, and rundown?
- Do work areas show individual flair (with artwork or awards and other artifacts on display), or does everything appear to be stock issues and monotonously uniform?

Use of Space

- Do space allocations seem equitable and well used, or do some departments seem to have more than they need while others are shoehorned into a corner?
- In office settings, does an open layout invite spontaneous conversations, or are people protected by private offices (behind closed doors)?
- Does the allocation of space clearly reinforce status differences among people in different positions, or does it appear that most people have about the same amount of space?

Equipment, Symbols, and Artifacts

- How ostentatious or spartan are the furnishings and decor? Are the walls painted? Wallpapered? Paneled with inexpensive veneer or solid hardwood?
- What adorns the walls in the reception area, gallery-quality paintings or mass-produced prints? Award plaques and trophies?
- Are the computers, FAX machines, and other technological equipment state of the art?

Dress.   What people wear can say as much about the organization as about them as individuals. Such clues offer insights into the degree of formality expected of people. The conservative white shirts and pinstriped suits of IBM's sales and service force are legendary, in contrast to the informality of T-shirts and jeans within many high-tech firms.[37] Dress also makes a statement about the expected flexibility and individuality encouraged (or discouraged) by the culture. Dress-down Fridays represent attempts by formal organizations to slightly loosen up, to appear more humanistic. As you make inference from physical symbols, you'll begin to see a cultural paradigm emerge.

Find Meaning in Organizational Rites

Rites provide convenient forums for reading an organization's culture based on what is said and done in public.[38] Values, beliefs, and other assumptions typically surface and are reaffirmed at the rites that bring people together for public occasions. A **rite** is a planned public performance where other forms of cultural expression, such as recounting company legends, are woven into a single event. Because rites have a clear beginning and end, they are a good opportunity to observe expressions of cultural assumptions that lie slightly beneath the surface.

rite
A planned public performance or occasion where diverse forms of cultural expression are woven into a single event.

Mary Kay Cosmetics, for example, stages elaborate rites called "national guest nights" and "annual seminars."[39] High-performing saleswomen are awarded gifts of furs, pink Cadillacs and Buicks, and diamonds. Thousands of women sing "I've got that Mary Kay enthusiasm up in my head." Mary Kay Ash and son Richard Rogers tell stories of overcoming personal hardship and succeeding through optimism and determination. The emphasis is on grandstanding high sales achievers, valuing money and materialism as the goals of success, and exalting that which Mary Kay Cosmetics is all about—glamour.

Legends.   Stories and legends are often told at rites. Every IBMer has heard the story about former CEO Tom Watson's being denied access to a secure area by a young security guard. Even though she recognized Watson, he wore the wrong color badge for that area. To his credit, Watson waited patiently while an aide retrieved the proper badge—he made no attempt to pull rank. For IBM members, the message is that all rules and policies apply equally to everyone. This is the stuff legends are made of.

━━━━━ **EXHIBIT 4–5**

How Questions Uncover Cultural Assumptions

To surface underlying cultural assumptions, ask these types of questions. Look both for consistencies and variations in what people tell you. The greater the consistency, the stronger the culture.

1. What is the relevant history of this company? How did it come into being? (Founders always imprint their beliefs on an organization to convey perspectives they want to perpetuate.)

2. What accounts for the success of this company? If growth has been irregular, how has this organization been able to recover from downturns? (Responses suggest beliefs about what accounts for performance and where the firm is going to place its bets.)

3. What kind of people work here? What do you have to do to get ahead? (People usually find it easy to talk about people. Watch for what is said about revered heros, as their behavior indicates what the organization values.)

4. What do you think about this as a place to work? What happens here during a typical day? How do decisions really get made? (While part of the responses will be evaluative, they'll also reveal glimpses into accepted behavior. They also tell something about the rites that are important to stakeholders.)

Source: Terrence E. Deal and Allan A. Kennedy. *Corporate Cultures: The Rites and Rituals of Corporate Life,* pp. 132–133, © 1982 by Addison-Wesley Publishing Company, Inc. Reprinted by permission.

Meetings and Off-Sites. As the most frequently practiced rite in organization, meetings make statements about culture. Some organizations stand on ceremony by meeting at the same time, same place each week, with detailed agendas circulated before the meeting, followed by minutes of who said what. The entire event is a ritual to keep people informed and conforming to predictable behaviors. For other organizations, meetings are impromptu. People get together when someone encounters a problem or perceives an opportunity that needs the ideas of others, and creativity and problem solving are preferred over conformity.

Organizations with turbulent, fast-changing environments frequently engage in "off-site" meetings. The **off-site** is a day-long or multiday forum designed to bring critical players together to question basic assumptions, raise critical issues, and resolve or plan responses to challenges. Some off-sites are held at regular intervals and involve people across the organization, such as a quarterly sales planning session. Others are sessions for issue focusing and problem solving within a single department. Overtly used for rational purposes, both are rich in expressive behaviors that also help socialize newcomers and reinforce beliefs and values.

off-site
A daylong or multi-day forum intended to bring key players together to question basic assumptions, raise critical issues, and plan responses to challenges.

Ask Questions and Observe Responses

When used in isolation, observation often seems an inefficient means of seeking cultural clues. Asking questions is more efficient and direct, even though responses can't always be taken at face value. Managers rely on questioning as a means for interpreting meaning and testing their assumptions about culture on others. The few questions that appear in Exhibit 4–5 are easy to remember and go a long way in preparing you to extract cultural assumptions from organizational members.

Questioning and listening also have practical advantage of providing a database on which personal advancement can be built. At papermaker Fort Howard Corp., Kathleen Hempel advanced from secretary to vice president of human resources in five years, then on to second in command as chief financial officer. Her fast promotions were based in part on her willingness to question and listen to others. As Hempel puts it, "We have to elicit the best thinking from the work force. We want them to take responsibility for solving problems."[40] So, ask questions, then listen and act on what others say—and learn more about culture in the process.

By now you should understand the kinds of assumptions that underlie organizational culture, know how cultures vary, and know how to pick up clues that provide insights into cultures. Now consider what leaders do to build adaptiveness into the culture.

Technicians and robots work together on the assembly line at Apple Computer's manufacturing facility in Singapore, which is one of the exploding Asian economies. The country's ability to accept the future, take risks easily, and tolerate different behaviors in business has made it the kind of place companies look for when they expand overseas, thus contributing to economic growth. (Photo: Milt and Joan Mann/Cameramann International, Ltd.)

HOW DO LEADERS BUILD FLEXIBLE, RESPONSIVE CULTURES?

An organization's founder or founders begin to shape a culture when choosing the first people they hire. Culture really begins to take on meaning as those early hires encounter problems, solve them, and receive feedback from the founder(s) and the environment. Out of responses to crises comes growth, and depending on the lessons learned, certain values and core assumptions take on meaning while others are rejected or become irrelevant. Once established, an organization's culture takes on a life of its own, resisting pressures to change—even if feedback confirms that the firm's relationship to its environment has deteriorated. Yet, over time, cultural modifications often become necessary.

First Generation Managers Develop a Culture

During the formative period when the enterprise is still under the control of the founder(s), culture emerges from two sources: the founder and direct experience. First, founders bring to the start-up firm beliefs about how to succeed in business. Usually assumptions about products, markets, and technology that underlie the business's mission are confirmed or denied rather quickly in the marketplace. Either the business takes hold or it fails. Other assumptions, about styles of decision making and how to compete, take longer to test. Employees who are committed to the founder's concept of doing business seem to tolerate organizational or managerial imperfections as the cost of getting the business established. Founders manifest three important behaviors:

1. The behaviors they deliberately use to role model, teach, and coach.
2. What they pay attention to in the organization or its environment—what they measure and control.
3. How they react to critical events and organizational crises, or their demonstrated methods of coping.[41]

Second, another early source of culture is active experimentation (trial and error), where group members learn what really works and what fails. Whether passed along by the founder or learned through experimentation, only attempted solutions that seem to work are repeated and taught to newcomers. These lessons range from how to treat people, to how to develop creative ideas, to how to secure a foothold in a market environment. As members learn patterns of problem solving, assumptions become confirmed.[42] Employees at Nucor (a steel minimill) and Wabash National (a truck trailer manufacturer) learned that unconventional practices and a willingness to find new ways of doing things quickly enabled their start-up firms to become industry leaders in mature industries.[43]

The Second Generation Adapts a Culture

Culture typically comes under threat once the founder begins to hire into key positions people who are not part of the first generation. While welcomed for their technical or managerial skills, newcomers are viewed by old-timers as less loyal and thus not fully trustworthy. The first generation of employees tends to operate more on the basis of personal relationships than the formal systems more characteristic of the second generation. "The real test of the effectiveness of a corporate culture comes when the organization's environment changes . . . Sometimes a strong culture can be like a millstone around the neck of a firm that is trying to respond to environmental changes."[44]

IBM Encounters Crisis. Unless the culture emphasizes continuous innovation and product-market adaptation, a strong culture makes the introduction of change more difficult. Even IBM, an elitist firm that employees once assumed was invincible, encountered this "millstone around the neck" as it struggled to slough off its mainframe mentality when the market for computers shifted to PCs then to networks between the mid-1980s and mid-1990s. IBMers accepted a sales and marketing orientation as propeling growth, and believed that the cultural element of respect for individuals translated into implicit lifetime employment. And yet IBM's bureaucratic structure (that often imposed nine levels between the CEO and nonsupervisory worker) operated under a cultural norm that if there was "nonconcurrence" on a proposal or project—if not universally acceptable by everyone in the stream of decision makers—the project would be killed or sent back to the drawing board for major revisions.[45] As changes in market forces were accelerating and price competition intensifying, IBM was sluggish in responding to technological and market changes brought about by swifter, smaller competitors. One senior product developer, who quit in frustration, expressed a commonly held view about IBM's decision-making culture: "If it takes you 10 months to figure out what you want to do, and you go through six changes of direction as you develop it, you can expect a 34-month development process."[46]

Hewlett-Packard Adapts. In contrast to IBM, Hewlett-Packard has found that its H-P Way (their name for culture) has permitted reasonably fluid adaptations to business conditions over more than half a century. Although IBM and H-P share some rather common values—such as dedication to the customer—H-P has kept its organization flexible and created a culture in which business units and people who come into contact with customers and technology can act responsively (see the Eye on Ethics box). Writes confounder David Packard, "Ask me to pick what contributed most to H-P's success, and I'll say it was our policy of 'management by objectives.' . . . Management by objectives is the antithesis of management by

Eye on Ethics

The Hewlett-Packard (H-P) Way

Hewlett-Packard has the reputation of being an ethical, quality-focused organization. Its success has been guided by a set of ethical and behavioral principles put in place decades ago by founders William Hewlett and David Packard. Here are eight key elements of the H-P code of conduct, "The H-P Way," as summarized by David Packard several years following his retirement:

1. **Put profits into perspective**—maintain balance between short-term profits and the need to invest for long-term strength and growth.
2. **Act only when you can make a contribution**—expand and diversify only when you can build on strengths and have the capacity to make a contribution.
3. **Put customers first**—every person should think continually about how his activities relate to servicing our customers.
4. **Commit the business to quality**—from the start we had more reason than most to emphasize quality, as customers relied on the accuracy of our measurement instruments.

5. **Have trust in people**—pick the most capable people for each assignment, then keep them enthusiastic about what they are doing.
6. **Keep the organization flexible**—even widely decentralized companies should be alert to signs of cumbersome bureaucracy, the same liability that drags down centralized organizations.
7. **Keep the doors open**—people using the open door must never be subjected to reprisals or other consequences.
8. **Manage by objectives**—overall goals are clearly stated and agreed to, and people are given the flexibility to work toward those goals in ways they determine are best.

Source: David Packard, *The HP Way: How Bill Hewlett and I Built Our Company* (New York: HarperBusiness, 1995)

control, a tightly controlled system in which people are assigned—and expected to do—specific jobs without being taught about the overall objectives of the business. In management by objectives, overall goals are clearly stated and agreed to, and people are given the flexibility to work toward those goals in ways they determine are best."[47]

The alternative to a strong culture such as the H-P Way is to have no consistency of beliefs and values: a weak culture. In **weak cultures,** people are not sure what is expected of them, much less how the organization believes it will succeed. Purposeful change may be even more difficult in weak-culture organizations, but for different reasons: "Without the security and sense of purpose provided by a relatively strong culture, organizational members may feel impotent and unable to act decisively. These are not qualities that foster change."[48]

weak culture
The absence of common assumptions and norms which means people are unsure of what is expected of them or how the organization believes it will succeed.

Growth Prompts Revolutionary Shifts in Culture

Most every period of evolutionary growth in an organization's history is followed by a revolutionary upheaval as systems, people, and structure shift toward a mode that allows another period of growth.[49] "To change the culture is to initiate revolution."[50] Out-of-date cultural assumptions usually are at fault whenever organizational

━━━━ **EXHIBIT 4–6**

Situations Prompting a
Shift in Culture

Cultural changes may be necessary whenever organizations need to:

- Break away from a rigid bureaucratic culture and become more responsive to change.
- Diminish the belief that power or policies gets things done and shift more toward satisfying customers and the marketplace.
- Create an identity and set of values for a mediocre, culturally weak organization.
- Integrate an acquisition (with its own culture) into the ways of a new parent.
- Blend two cultures into one following a merger.
- Establish a unique, autonomous culture after a division is spun off or divested.
- Permit a division or major task unit to develop a subculture supportive of its task.
- Infuse stronger cultural elements into a weak-culture firm through rites and symbols.

members behave unethically, seem unconcerned about quality, intentionally distort the truth, and manipulate each other for personal gain. Several situations that prompt a shift in culture are identified in Exhibit 4–6.

New Leadership, New Practices.   Rather than expect current leadership to change culture incrementally, a revolutionary shift typically requires a change in leadership.[51] With a new management team, new assumptions and practices are introduced. The old ways and beliefs are challenged, and employees question the cultural underpinnings of their organization. Often there is a period of skepticism, resistance, and complaining about "losing our values"—the conditions that enabled growth in the first place. James Champy writes in his book on reengineering management that the power of managers to make significant changes in their organizations "is limited not by the precepts of reengineering but by the very nature of a culture. A company's culture cannot be proclaimed or easily manipulated . . . At best they (managers) can lead the way—that is, they can 'model' the behavior, enable it, and educate it, drawing out what is already there, or what they hope is there."[52] The Challenge of Change box highlights how one second-generation manager transformed a Phoenix auto dealership by using communication practices to shift its culture.

The TQM Transformation.   Organizations that profess a philosophy and process of engaging in total quality management (TQM) must inculcate in people the shared assumption of employee dedication to quality and customer service. This may require a cultural transformation to realign people's beliefs and values toward new norms, often driven by competitive pressure. Pauline Brody, who headed the Xerox Quality Forum that helped Xerox become a winner of the coveted Malcolm Baldrige National Quality Award, writes:

> *TQM requires a change in organizational culture, a fundamental change in the way individuals and groups approach their work and their roles in the organization, that is, from an environment of distrust and fear of reprisal to one of openness and trust where creativity can flourish; from working as individuals to working as teams; from protection or organizational turfs to the breakdown of departmental barriers; from an autocratic management style of direction and control to a softer style of team leader and coach; from power concentrated at the top to power shared with employees; from a focus on results to a focus on continuous improvement of the processes that deliver the results; and finally a change from making decisions based on gut-feel to an analytic, fact-based approach to management.[53]*

Ethnic Diversity Sensitizes Organizational Cultures

Many enterprises, even smaller businesses, are rapidly becoming multiethnic and multicultural because of the imported backgrounds employees bring with them. This is especially true in states such as California and Florida, areas that receive the

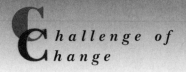

Childress Buick/Kia Shifts Its Culture to Keep People Informed

"Hey buddy, wanna buy a car?" Car dealerships, whether selling new or used stock, are for most customers one of life's greatest apprehensions. Not so at Childress Buick/Kia Co. in Phoenix. But it took a crisis to fix the company and change employee attitudes and values. It started with the installation of a new computer system in 1987 that was bug ridden. This allowed "Rusty" Childress, the owner's son, sporting a new "owner-relations manager" title, to fix the organization—not just the computer.

As he began to peel back the layers of what was troubling Childress Buick (Kia came later), Rusty discovered that the key to transformation emerged from communications. Today he remarks, "By maintaining open communication with customers and employees, not only will you learn exactly what customers need and expect, but employees' job satisfaction will increase as well, which will help perpetuate your department's high level of service quality." Satisfaction with the company rose dramatically in the eyes of many, both customers and employees.

The 122-employee company now relies on all kinds of mediums to move information around the organization: "electronic mail and bulletin boards; hot lines; newsletters and questionnaires and meeting notes; town-hall meetings; and teams and focus groups. Each tool is simple, low cost, and low tech. Each by itself is unremarkable. But taken together, welded into a culture in which you keep hearing the same stories and the same words, the tools are powerful."

Changed communication practices at Childress Buick/Kia has also changed employee behaviors. Instead of the adversarial competition that often permeates the different departments of an auto dealership, at Childress there is active helping across departments. The body-shop group, for example, take time to bring customers to the sales office if their cars have been totally written off by insurance companies, a practice that results in about five new car sales per month. The customer service attitude is so pervasive that over 70 percent of their new-car buyers bring their cars back for routine service—compared to an industry average of 30 percent. Little wonder that other auto dealers as well as hospitals and hotels come to Childress to benchmark their customer service practices.

Source: John Kerr, "Company Profile: The Informers," *Inc.* (March 1995), pp. 50–61

biggest influx of immigrants in the world.[54] Because of closing doors in Europe, the United States now absorbs almost half of the immigrants flowing into developed countries.[55]

What you are learning about managing people's organizational behavior gives you an Americanized view of the world. The managerial approaches that work for us (and a few other Anglo societies) do not necessarily stand up well in other countries. Unfortunately for managers outside North America and the British Commonwealth, the vast majority of what has been researched and written about management during this century originated in English-speaking countries. As an export, North American-based management research and recommendations do not work well unless adapted to fit the local culture.

With our relaxed immigration policies, especially for refugees and immigrants seeking "family reunification," U.S. organizations have taken on a multicultural complexion. Subcultures of various ethnic groups circulate within organizations.

The emphasis is more on diversity than the melting pot of assimilation that prevailed in earlier generations of immigrants. While most rural areas outside the South remain predominantly Caucasian, most urban areas are culturally diverse. California is both the most populous state and the one most in a state of ethnic flux. In 1970, California was 78 percent Caucasian, 12 percent Hispanic, 7 percent African-American, and only 3 percent Asian. By the year 2000, the state's composition is forecast to be 53 percent white, 27 percent Hispanic, 21 percent Asian, and 8 percent African-America. Minority families, especially those with limited English language proficiency, will be responsible for the majority of new births within the state.[56] Such transformation in the ethnic makeup of California was a contributing factor behind the controversial and largely symbolic vote of the University of California Board of Regents to eliminate affirmative action in admitting students and recruiting faculty.[57]

Because of such changes, managers need to know about the central tendencies of the ethnic groups that make up America's work force. Exhibit 4–7 provides a brief glimpse into some of the central characteristics of three minorities that make up the richness of cultural diversity in North American organizations.

Working with people from different ethnic and cultural backgrounds is a challenge for managers and organizational cultures. Although far from perfect, the American culture is more accepting of ethnic and racial diversity than are most cultures of the world. Japan tends to be a very closed ethnic culture, the Eastern European republics tend not to be tolerant of some minorities, and stories of the plight of blacks within South Africa are legion. Such characteristics suggest that as enterprises become global, managers need to understand how national cultures constrain the degree to which an organizational culture can fit within the values and practices of other nations.

HOW DO NATIONAL CULTURES IMPACT GLOBAL BUSINESS?

Most successful firms at times need to rework cultural elements to become more adaptive. One test of organizational culture occurs when a firm moves into a foreign country or when many of its new employee recruits are foreign born. While business people may share some commonality of values across national cultures (such as "providing excellent service to customers"), a country's culture and business environment can cause value elements to differ significantly across national borders. In one study of how accountants from four countries ranked 15 value statements, the most significant variability was found among two business values involving job satisfaction and profit maximization (where low number rankings mean the item is more valued):[58]

	United States	Holland	China	India
Employee motivation and job satisfaction	8	4/5	11	6
Consistently strive to maximize profits	12	14	2	10

Chinese accountants place much less importance on motivation and job satisfaction than do the Dutch, but Indians value it more than Americans. By contrast, the Chinese highly value profit maximization (presumably as a means of economic development), but accountants in the other countries place it rather far down in their rankings of organizationally important values.

─────── **EXHIBIT 4–7**

*Some Cultural
Characteristics of
Hispanics, Asians, and
African-Americans*

Be cautious about cultural stereotyping. Nevertheless, there are some central tendencies found in the major ethnic minorities within U.S. firms. Here are a few:

Hispanics

Spanish-speaking people come from a number of Latin countries, such as Mexico, Chile, Colombia, Puerto Rico, and El Salvador. Because of their predominantly Catholic religious beliefs and cultural values, Hispanics tend to emphasize the extended family more than individuality. Traditionally the father of the Hispanic family has been the authority figure, and the wife has been devoted to husband and children (but this is changing of economic necessity). To say that one is "well educated' in Spanish more often means that the person displays good manners and behaves in accordance with social norms than that the person is well schooled.

Asians

The people of Asia come from more than 30 distinct ethnic groups. Because of early discrimination against immigrants from Asia, people from China, Thailand, Cambodia, Vietnam, and other countries originally tended to congregate in communities of like background, although this behavior diminishes with affluence. People from Asian cultures often value status over wealth. In the Vietnamese culture, having more children typically means greater status. Because of collectivist cultural values, Asians typically emphasize obligation, cooperation, and reciprocity.

Blacks and African-Americans

Black Americans come from several cultures besides those within Africa, including Caribbean and Central and South American cultures. However, the common experience of most blacks has been racism and prejudice combined with a high incidence of educational and economic inequalities. Since 1960, unemployment for blacks in the United States has been at twice the rate for whites, with black household income 60 to 63 percent of white household income. Nearly two-thirds of black families are raised by a single-parent (mother) head of household; however, absentee fathers often are involved in child rearing. Church involvement is often central to black families, with religious values influencing interpersonal relationships.

Sources: Sam Roberts, *Who We Are: A Portrait of America Based on the Latest U.S. Census* (New York: Time Books, 1994); and Lisbeth J. Vincent, Christine L. Salisbury, Phillip Strain, Cecilia McCormick, and Annette Tessier, "A Behavioral-Ecological Approach to Early Intervention: Focus on Cultural Diversity," in Samuel J. Meisels and Jack P. Shonkoff (Eds.), *Handbook of Early Childhood Intervention* (Cambridge, England: Cambridge University Press, 1990), pp. 173–195.

Culture Has International and Ethnic Implications

You are undoubtedly aware of the cultural differences among countries, whether you have traveled outside your home country or simply read and watched TV and movies. Arab cultures differ from Asia, Latin, and Western European cultures. One apparent difference among countries is the symbolism of language. But values and behaviors also have patterned differences, and students of management should be aware of these.

While the productivity differences among countries are largely due to education, national or ethnic values also give people different predispositions toward work and business practices. Cultural differences can influence management styles. For example, Ouchi and Jaeger found that compared to American managers, Japanese managers tend to be more focused on the long term, more involved in group decision making, less likely to delegate responsibilities to an individual, more willing to accept a go-slow approach to career promotions, less focused on a clear career path, more comfortable with informal controls, and more concerned about the welfare of the entire organization.[59] What are some of these systematic differences in national cultures?

National Cultures Program Collective Learning

The landmark research of Geert Hofstede provides an insightful look at the similarities and differences in cultural values among 50 countries. His pathfinding research was drawn from over 100,000 IBM employees in countries throughout the world (excluding the former Soviet republics).[60] The essence of country culture is

The Dr. John H. Lux Total Quality Accomplishment Award established at AMETEK, Inc., a global manufacturer of electrical products and engineered materials, reflects an organizational culture that focuses on innovative technology and customer value. In the photo are members of the award-winning Land Gas Turbine Product Development Team, a cross-functional team that won the award for new business growth, breakthroughs in cycle time and inventory reductions, and focus on customer value and satisfaction. (Source: Courtesy of AMETEK, Inc.)

national mental programming
Geert Hofstede's concept for that part of a country's collective learning that is shared with other members of that nation, region, or group, but not with members of other nations, regions, or groups.

national mental preprogamming, which is that part of our collective learning "that we share with other members of our nation, region, or group but not with members of other nations, regions, or groups." Hofstede provides several examples of national mental programming at work:

> *In Europe, British people will form a neat queue whenever they have to wait; not so, the French. Dutch people will as a rule greet strangers when they enter a small, closed space like a railway compartment, doctor's waiting room, or lift; not so, the Belgians. Austrians will wait at a red pedestrian traffic light even when there is no traffic; not so the Dutch. Swiss (people) tend to become very angry when somebody—say, a foreigner—makes a mistake in traffic; not so the Swedes. All these are part of an invisible set of mental programs which belongs to these countries' national cultures.*[61]

National Cultures Have Four Dimensions

As Hofstede interpreted survey results, he noticed that responses to questions about values were rather stable within nationality groups, but attitudes were not. Values, as defined earlier, are rather permanent desires or beliefs people hold to be important independent of situations. **Attitudes** are temporal beliefs based on valuative interpretations of current conditions. When IBM members responded to attitude questions such as "How do you like your job?" the responses showed no national pattern; they depended on the current situation. In contrast, responses to value questions such as "Describe an ideal job" were similar within but different across nationalities.

attitudes
Temporal beliefs based on evaluative interpretations of current conditions.

Four largely independent dimensions, based on patterns of enduring values, provide the framework for describing national cultures: (1) individualism versus collectivism, (2) centralized versus diffused power, (3) strong versus weak uncertainty avoidance, and (40 masculinity versus femininity.[62]

Individualism versus Collectivism. All societies deal with the relationship between the individual and other people. In highly *individualistic societies,* the individual is expected to look out for his or her own self-interest, and maybe that of the immediate family. At the other extreme, *collectivist societies* assume that close ties exist among people and the interests of the individual are subordinated to the group, be it extended family, tribe, village, and/or employer. Individualistic nations are loosely integrated (do your own thing), collectivist tightly integrated (honor thy group heritage). Interestingly, per capita economic wealth correlates with individualistic behavior—collectivist nations are poorer.

As you might expect, the United States, Great Britain, Australia, and the Netherlands are very individualistic. Some highly collectivist nations are Colombia, Pakistan, Panama, Taiwan, Venezuela, and South Korea. Among those in the middle are Japan, Spain, Israel, Austria, Argentina, and India. However, within any nation can be found individuals tending toward each perspective. Generally, individuals oriented toward a collectivist ideology are more cooperative when working within groups, whereas individualists tend to ignore group needs. Nevertheless, even among individualists, their willingness to cooperate increases if the group size is small, if individual behavior can be identified and evaluated, and if individuals feel that their behaviors are indispensable to the success of the group endeavor.[63] These are the mediating conditions under which strong individualists, as often found in North America, can be team players.

Centralized versus Diffused Power. How to deal with inequalities among people is another fundamental value issue for nations. *Centralized power societies* permit unequal intellectual or physical capabilities to grow into blatant inequalities in the distribution of power and wealth. *Diffused power societies* play down individual differences by sharing or decentralizing power. Societies that deliberately promote greater power differences among people tend to centralize authority. They permit and even promote autocratic leadership as part of their mental conditioning of people.

Nations with distinct power hierarchies are poorer and collectivist. Their people accept unequal distributions of power as almost inevitable, given their psychological dependence on others. Prime examples are the Philippines, India, Venezuela, Guatemala, Pakistan, Panama, and Arab cultures. At the opposite extreme, Anglo nations promote low stratification of power and embrace democratic ideals, just as they believe strongly in individualism. This culture cluster includes the United States, Australia, Great Britain, New Zealand, Canada, and the Netherlands. Japan, Argentina, and Spain score in the middle of the power distance scale.

Strong versus Weak Uncertainty Avoidance. Culture conditions people to cope in different ways with future uncertainty. Societies can avoid the risk of uncertainty by using technology to control nature, laws to discourage deviant behavior, and religion in the broadest sense of the word to promote desired behavior. Nations with a strong need for *uncertainty avoidance* usually claim that absolute truth originates from a dominant religion. To them the future is a challenge to be overcome and is associated with high levels of anxiety, emotionality, and aggressiveness. Strong uncertainty avoidance nations include the Latin European and Latin American countries; Mediterranean countries such as the former Yugoslavia, Greece, and Turkey; and Japan and South Korea.

People in weak uncertainty avoidance countries accept the future and are not troubled by it. They take risks rather easily and are tolerant of different behaviors

Dynamics of Diversity

Women, too, Manage Firefighting

Firefighting has forever been a man's calling. Slowly, however, women are breaking into the ranks of leadership within fire departments. By the mid-1990s, at least 40 women had risen to the positions of division chief, battalion chief, district chief, or chief of fire units within the Untied States, according to the international organization Women in the Fire Service. But the first rung on the ladder is to make the grade to line captain. A line captain is the firegfighter who is first on the scene and who decides how the fire will be handled by fire personnel.

Monique Vanderberg became the first woman to be promoted to line captain in the 50-year history of her fire district, where 35 men were line captains. Vanderberg ventured into firefighting with summer work at a department of forestry before investing six years in her county fire district. She attributes her rapid rise in the department to "hard work, personal faith, and the support of family and fellow firefighters." Says

Vanderberg, "When I first got hired it was like any team sport you go out for. They look to see if you can play your role, if you can do the job. That's true for a man or a woman."

Monique Vanderberg had to pass a battery of tests that included simulated emergency situations, a written exam, and an oral interview. On making the grade and receiving her promotion, Chief Douglas Sporleder remarked, "She's done everything she's needed to do to get to this. I have every confidence she'll perform as well as any of our other captains." Sporleder emphasizes that the captain's position is "the backbone of the department. It's where all the work gets done in emergency scene management." It's where women are finally beginning to lead men in a culture that has for centuries been a man's world.

Source: Michael Cronk, "Firefighter Wins Rank of Captain," *San Jose Mercury News* (August 2, 1995), p. Extra 3.

and opinions since they are relatively secure. Such nations include Denmark and Sweden, Singapore and Hong Kong, and Jamaica. More middle of the road on uncertainty avoidance are the United States and Canada, Finland and Norway, East Africa (Kenya, Ethiopia, Zambia) and West Africa (Nigeria, Ghana, Sierra Leone).

Masculinity versus Femininity. This dimension resolves the division of social roles between the sexes. Some nations make sharp distinctions between roles based on sex, which means men take on the more dominant and assertive roles while women assume the more caretaking, service roles. Nations with such clear sex role divisions are called "masculine" by Hofstede. *Masculine values* permeate societies where the hero is the successful achiever, where showing off and displaying wealth are accepted. Other societies are more tolerant of a wider distribution of roles almost independent of sex and are called "feminine." *Feminine values* include respecting the underdog, putting relationships before wealth, and tending to the quality of life and the environment.

Among nations, the most masculine country is Japan, followed by German-speaking nations and some Latin American countries, such as Mexico and Venezuela. The most feminine are the Scandinavian countries. More nations are clustered toward the middle than on any other dimension, with the United States in this group but leaning toward the masculine side. Only recently have women in the United States begun to break into jobs once the exclusive domain of men (see the Dynamics of Diversity example of firefighters).

=== **EXHIBIT 4–8**

Four Independent Cultural Dimensions: How Select Countries/Regions Score

Country/Region	Approximate Dimension Index Score (0–100)[a]			
	Individualism	Power Distance	Uncertainty Avoidance	Masculinity
Arab countries[b]	40	80	65	50
East Africa[c]	30	60	50	40
Brazil	40	70	75	50
Mexico	30	85	80	70
Panama	10	95	85	45
India	50	80	40	60
Indonesia	15	80	45	45
Korea	20	60	85	40
Japan	45	55	90	95
France	70	65	80	45
Great Britain	90	35	35	65
Germany	65	35	65	65
Sweden	70	30	30	5
United States	90	40	45	65
Canada	80	40	40	55

[a]Hofstede used a series of index scores to plot variables on two-dimensional graphs, with the higher number having higher value for the dimension identified. Numbers in this exhibit represent approximate index scores as interpreted from the graphs, rounded to the closest five points; thus, all values are relative, not absolute.

[b]Arab countries include Egypt, Lebanon, Libya, Kuwait, Iraq, Saudi Arabia, U. A. E.

[c]East African countries include Kenya, Ethiopia, Zambia.

Source: Interpreted form Geert Hofstede, "The Cultural Relativity of Organizational Practices and Theories," *Journal of International Business Studies* 14 (Fall 1983), pp. 75–89.

Comparing Cultural Central Tendencies.   Index scores of Hofstede's four dimensions are shown for several countries in Exhibit 4–8. However, they should be interpreted cautiously. Cultural dimensions exist along a continuum, whether applied to an organization or a nation.[64] The index scores from Hofstede's research represent central tendencies or averages based on a large number of respondents. If you've had a statistics course, you realize there is always variance about the statistical mean. For example, not all American men are 5´9˝ in height, even if this might be a national mean.

Similarly, when describing how nations score on any particular cultural variable, it is easy to stereotype, jumping to the conclusion that a particular behavior or belief describes all the people of a country. In fact, some individuals display very few or even none of the dominant cultural characteristics. One extensive research study of the Hofstede theory examined the extent to which national cultures or organizational cultures created role stress for individuals, whether they were confused by role ambiguity or upset by role conflict. The results of a 21-nation study were clear:

> *Role stress varies substantially more by country than by demographic and organizational factors . . . The power distance and individualism concepts are the ones most closely linked to the role stresses. Overall, managers from high-power-distance countries report greater role overload than managers from low-power-distance countries.*[65]

National Cultures Adapt to Promote Business Activity

The key to effective management practices or quality organizational research is to understand the cultural contexts "in which firms and individuals function and operate."[66] Thus, research documents that the Japanese practice a very different form of capitalism in contrast to the Anglo-American model. Capitalism to the Japanese emphasizes managerial autonomy from the interests of shareholders and employees, economic priorities that emphasize producers over consumers, industrial policy in which government acts as the guiding hand, and a strong state ethic made legitimate more by economic accomplishments than by public consent.[67] Traveling a few thousand kilometers to the west, it will be interesting to see how effective the former Soviet republics (now the Commonwealth of Independent States), including giant Russia, will be in their struggle to become democratic, market-based economies with widespread private ownership of property. To change an economic system without changing cultural values is risky; sustaining that change will be nothing short of revolutionary. So far only the Chinese have attracted free enterprise investment funds on a large enough scale to be on the verge of emerging as a global economic force.[68]

To support these business changes, national cultures will have to change also. People have to experience success with a different system if they are to change their fundamental assumptions and beliefs. So far the old communist system of direct rationing and price setting is believed to produce shortages for the masses and allow the privileged to lead a good life. But the economic infrastructure (factories, roads, etc.) of the former Soviet republics is so rundown that there is insufficient capacity to allow a freer price mechanism to allocate resources.

Even the more gradual shift to the final phase of an economically integrated European community (five decades in the making) has not been problem free. Each European nation has its favorite industries to protect, people to keep employed, beliefs about the role of government in managing business, preferences about distribution systems, desire to preserve the national currency, and so on. But where European firms encounter even greater obstacles is in seeking to establish a multinational presence within the United States. The strong national cultural value of independence and autonomy seeking complicates the integration of U.S. acquisitions into a European multinational corporation. In part this is because most Americans have little or no international experience nor do they seek it because of the large size of the U.S market. Says one French multinational executive with substantial activities in the United States:

> *It is difficult for Americans to develop a world perspective. It's hard for them to see that what may optimize the worldwide position may not optimize the U.S. activities. We have to remind them continually of the need to think globally and encourage exchanges of people. None of this is surprising, because most U.S. firms have not had much international experience.*[69]

The cohesiveness of national cultures constrains the importation of a corporate culture's values, except for multidomestic firms such as ABB (profiled in the World Watch box in Chapter 2). When firms are willing to incorporate elements of the host country national culture into a business unit's corporate culture transfer, the result is a blend of values that promote local adaptability without sacrificing key assumptions that have made the enterprise a global force.

WAL-MART'S CULTURE INSPIRES REMARKABLE GROWTH— A SECOND LOOK

Even without the inspiration and leadership of its founder, Sam Walton, Wal-Mart continues to grow by holding to cultural values and beliefs about how to succeed in business. Each new store, and there are over 3,000 of them, is an opportunity to replicate the cultural elements that Mr. Sam put in place and that CEO David Glass seeks to continue.

With its *1996 Annual Report,* Wal-Mart switched to a magazine format to convey a more personal, intimate feel. The first two "feature stories" were titled, "Creating Value" and "Wal-Mart: A Culture of Service and Value." These reinforce the importance of organizational culture to the 700,000 or so associates who merchandise stores and interact with customers. The second article began, "Becoming the world's largest retailer was never considered. And being big has never been the goal. The objective at Wal-Mart when Mr. Sam and his brother Bud developed their stores in the early 1960s was to provide products of unbeatable value with the best possible customer service."[70]

Although it was never a goal, Wal-Mart's culture and strategy has a significant by-product—it is the most successful job creation firm ever created. Peter Lynch, financial stock picking guru, identified 50 companies who are thriving in the mid-1990s, many after downsizing. In looking at the number of employees in these companies across two decades, compare Wal-Mart's stellar accomplishments to six of the most successful:[71]

Company (with jobs in thousands)	1975	1985	1995
Wal-Mart	7.5	104.0	662.0
International Business Machines	288.6	405.5	225.3
Chrysler	217.6	114.2	126.0
McDonald's	71.9	148.0	212.0
Coca-Cola	31.1	38.5	32.0
Microsoft	–	1.0	17.8
Federal Express	–	34.0	107.0

For Wal-Mart, organizational culture is a principal competitivie advantage in carrying out its corporate and business strategies. And despite the fear of Main Street America, no one can beat Wal-Mart when it comes to creating jobs.

SUMMARY

Culture conveys expected behavior. An organization's culture is a powerful collective force of values, beliefs, assumptions, and norms that are communicated through rites, legends, and other forms of employee socialization and ritual. Organizations develop value systems that can be described as originating either from charismatic leaders or from tradition, and in content either as functional or elitist. Of the four possible combinations, traditional-functional values build the strongest culture, charismatic-elitist the least enduring and adaptable.

Culture is important to organizations not only as the foundation of its strategy, but also because it promotes consistent behavior and helps socialize newcomers in the ways of the organization. Therefore, future managers need to be skilled observers of organizational culture and able to make their culture more responsive to change. You can learn to read corporate cultures by developing the skills of observing and questioning the expressive meanings of organizational rites.

Managers should be aware that the expressive look and feel of organizational culture can be a useful way of influencing behavior and reducing reliance on rational managerial tools such as policies and budgets. However, when an organization has a strong culture (that is, when some members agree on a set of underlying assumptions), people tend to resist adapting to new environmental pressures unless change and experimentation are embedded in cultural values.

Given the increasing globalization of business and governmental relations, managers should be sensitive to the impact of country cultures or ethnic differences on human behavior. One paradigm by Hofstede is useful in comparing national cultures by examining whether they are individualistic or collectivist, hold centralized or diffused power, have strong or weak uncertainty avoidance, and are masculine or feminine. Companies that expand globally find that such dimensions constrain the direct transfer of the organizational culture. Even within domestic organizations, managers need to be sensitive to the ethnic or cultural predispositions of members and customers, especially those whose backgrounds are influenced by Hispanic, African-American, or Asian heritages.

Key Concepts

culture, *p. 112*

organizational culture, *p. 112*

strong culture, *p. 113*

values, *p. 115*

organizational value system, *p. 116*

charismatic-based values, *p. 116*

tradition-based values, *p. 116*

functional values, *p. 117*

elitist values, *p. 117*

socialization, *p. 122*

subcultures, *p. 124*

countercultures, *p. 125*

rite, *p. 126*

off-site, *p. 127*

weak culture, *p. 130*

national mental programming, *p. 135*

attitudes, *p. 135*

Questions for Study and Discussion

1. What does it mean to say organizational culture is "a pattern of basic assumptions that a given group has invented, discovered, or developed"? Identify three basic assumptions that underlie the organizational culture of your school.

2. What are the four types of organizational value systems formed by the interaction of charismatic/tradition and function/elite dimensions? Which is most responsive to change? Least responsive? Why?

3. Why is organizational culture considered an "expressive" way of influencing behavior rather than a "rational" managerial tool?

4. What organizational characteristics provide clues to reading an organization's culture? Which two do you believe to be the most revealing? Why?

5. Why is a strong-culture organization at risk of being unresponsive to change? Why is a change in top management often desirable when an organization's culture is no longer adaptive? Give an example of how leadership can promote culture change.

6. What are Hofstede's four fundamental factors that shape national mental conditioning? Using his framework, what country (or countries) do you believe to be most unlike the United States? Most like the United States?

EXPERIENTIAL EXERCISE

Draw a Culture[72]

Much of what we communicate about organizations depends on language. But other, nonverbal means of expression can transcend the constraints of language. This exercise gives you the opportunity to communicate an abstract idea using the tools of the artist.

Time and Materials Needed.   The exercise can be completed in 10 to 20 minutes, depending on how extensive the debriefing. Drawing time is only 4 to 5 minutes. Each student uses his or her own pen or pencil and one sheet of paper. The instructor brings one roll of masking tape.

Instructions.   Think of an organization you know quite well. It could be your current or past employer. Or you might select a student organization with which you have been actively involved, your church, or your school. Choose a specific organization with which you have had enough experience to form definite impressions about its values, beliefs, rites, and generally accepted assumptions.

Once you have an organization clearly in mind, draw a picture of your organization as a vehicle of transportation. You do not have to literally draw a specific kind of vehicle such as an airplane, automobile, bicycle, tank, or ship. Be creative. Imagine some kind of hybrid vehicle that conveys the characteristics of the organization and will make a statement about its culture. Draw as many features as you can, adding people, symbols, and other images. When you finish your drawing, write the name of the organization somewhere in the margin, with your name under it.

Public Showing.   When finished, bring your drawings to your professor who will tape all pictures to a wall. As pictures are displayed, mill around and observe the drawings of your classmates. Time permitting, you may find out the meanings of some of the more provocative drawings. Your professor may ask a few students to explain what they have drawn and why. Experience suggests that powerful insights into organizational culture often are revealed once you are freed from the confines of language.

EXPERIENTIAL EXERCISE

Oh Say Can You See an Organizational Culture?

Purpose.   This exercise puts students' powers of perception to the test in reading the culture of your educational institution. If time permits, a walk around campus can add focus to what students look for in reading their organizational culture.

Time and Materials.   This activity takes about 15 to 20 minutes without a campus walk, 45 minutes or so with one. In class, it helps to have one blank flip-chart sheet and a marker for each group (of 4 to 6), and masking tape or something to affix charts to a wall.

Procedure.   Organize into groups of 4 to 6 members each.
   Group Work. Your group's task is to develop a list of cultural attributes of your school (university, school, or college) based solely on what you have observed. Time permitting, your instructor may give each group some time (up to half an hour) to walk through the campus, writing down a list of everything that suggests a cultural characteristic based on what can be seen. Without the walk, simply exchange ideas within your group about what you have seen that seems to provide a cultural clue. Here are some questions to prompt your analysis:

- What do the buildings suggest? Tradition (ivy-covered brick) or functional?

- What about equipment, furnishings, and decor? Pristine, elegant elitism, or neglect and impoverishment? State-of-the-art technology, or make do hand-me-downs? Size of classrooms? Are classrooms named?

- What are people wearing? Students? Faculty? Staff?

- What are people doing outside of class? Are people interacting or isolated? Are the doors of professors' offices open? Are they in their offices (when not in class)?

- What story do the bulletin boards tell? Are trophy cases or other symbols of achievement and winning visible?

Class Presentation. After the allotted time, each group displays its flip chart and briefly provides its interpretation of what observable features tell about organizational culture. Then as a class discuss questions such as:

- To what extent are there elements of commonality among the group's conclusions?

- Are there differences of interpretation of what the same observable features mean?

- Do these pictures of your campus confirm your assumptions about its culture?

CASE

AT&T + NCR = Negative Synergy[73]

Will AT&T ever get it right with computers? Ever since the telephone giant was broken up by a federal court order in 1984, it has tried to diversify by manufacturing and selling computers. But so far AT&T's quest has proven illusive, and the long-distance phone company has lost billions of dollars trying to create a presence in the computer industry. On the surface, the idea of a telecommunications firm extending itself into selling computers would "link people, organizations and their information in a seamless, global network" in the words of AT&T Chairman Robert E. Allen. But, in practice, the goal of creating synergy where 2 + 2 = 5 has been more like 2 + 2 = 3.

Background.   The roots of the problem lie both in *organizational culture* and *capabilities*. AT&T lost about $3 billion in its computer business during the last five years of the 1980s. Unable to achieve success on its own, AT&T decided to buy computer business capabilities. Management set their sights on high-flying NCR Corp. NCR had a proud heritage that began as National Cash Register, a business focused on making cash registers for retail establishments. Even Thomas Watson, the founder of IBM, gained early business experience selling business machines for NCR and adopted some of their conservative, white-shirt values into his own enterprise.

As technology changed, NCR began to produce Unix-based "open" computer systems to allow their principal customers, retailers and banks, to manage information originating from transactions performed by the checkout clerk or teller. To AT&T, NCR looked like the right merger partner, and they tendered an unsolicited offer of $6.03 billion in December 1990.

But NCR Chairman Charles Exley did not want to become a mere division of AT&T. He wrote AT&T Chairman Allen, saying, "We simply will not place in jeopardy the important values we are creating at NCR in order to bail out AT&T's failed strategy." Exley played hardball and even gave out inflated profit projections. AT&T upped the ante by an additional $1.4 billion. By September 1991, the merger was consummated with a stock swap worth $7.5 billion.

A Conflict between Two Cultures.   Once the takeover was inevitable, NCR executives began jumping ship, not wanting any part of AT&T. Those who remained were embittered and hostile when AT&T started imposing its own culture on NCR. One NCR manager claimed bluntly, "AT&T destroyed our culture and the esprit de corps we had here."

When NCR Chairman Exley retired as the merger was completed (with a personal settlement of over $35 million), the chief executive leadership of NCR passed to Gilbert Williamson, who had served as NCR's president (R. Elton White took over the position of president). But Williamson and other surviving NCR managers never warmed up to AT&T. In commenting on strained relations between himself and AT&T Chairman Allen, Williamson remarked, "Look, the NCR management team was doing its best to execute the strategy that was in place. That's what AT&T and Bob Allen wanted us to do. We were executing that transition well and making a profit." But Williamson quit NCR early in 1993, which gave AT&T the opening to remake NCR in its image.

AT&T appointed a new CEO, Jerre Stead, who had been CEO of Northern Telecom, then later an AT&T executive who turned around the struggling office-phone-systems business. Stead moved quickly to make NCR into less of a buttoned-down, white-shirt atmosphere and more into an open, "we're all in this together" kind of organization. Slogans such as "Delight your customers" were used in an attempt to motivate workers. The walls of the headquarters conference room in Dayton, Ohio, were torn out and replaced with glass so people could see executives in action.

New titles were introduced. Managers became "coaches" and lower-level employees were "associates." Stead gave out his home phone in a satellite conference call to employees and urged other NCR executives to do the same. He even removed the doors on senior executives' offices to dramatize an "open door" policy. When NCR President R. Elton White returned from a trip to find his door gone, he asked a custodian to replace it. Stead countermanded the order. White quit.

AT&T pressed its culture on NCR in other ways. Workers were made to adhere to AT&T's code of values called the "Common Bond." Many were also cajoled by AT&T "employee resource groups" to recruit and be more sensitive to the groups they represented—women, homosexuals, Asians, blacks, and others. Infuriated, one manager remarked, "If you tried to say anything about [the employee groups] like 'What are they doing here?' or 'They have no business doing this here,' AT&T sent you to sensitivity classes."

Even the townspeople in hometown Dayton rebelled against AT&T. The ultimate blow was when Stead had the NCR sign removed from the headquarters building. He replaced it with AT&T's globe and renamed the division GIS, standing for Global Information Solutions. In reaction to this disregard of a Dayton institution, a public school board awarded a $2.1 million contract for classroom computers to IBM, even though NCR's bid was $200,000 less. Mayor Michael R. Turner, following his first meeting with Stead, questioned whether he was focusing on the right issues. Turner said Stead "acted sort of new age, talking about his glass conference room walls instead of about his products. I wouldn't expect glass walls and casual dressing for employees to be one of the top three things on the mind of a CEO." To the mayor and others, the trappings of symbolic organizational culture and image seemed to be more pressing than strategies for strengthening the business.

Getting Down to Business.   But as NCR soaked up red ink, Jerre Stead did address substantive issues as NCR's CEO. As NCR managers quit, he replaced them with experienced AT&T people. He pushed the business into new products and markets, and set up "customer focus teams" to try to provide customers with access to NCR technical and sales resources. The sales force was reorganized three times in two years. Costs escalated as NCR tried to develop special software and systems for many diverse customer groups. Stead finally reported a $45 million profit in the fourth quarter of 1994, but not from operations. "Profits" came from his sale of NCR real estate in Hong Kong and the Microelectronics division. Then in January, 1995, Stead also quit, attracted by an enticing compensation package offered by Lagent Computer Corp.

AT&T went outside for a CEO replacement of the computer division and brought in Lars Nyberg, a former executive at Phillips Electronics. Nyberg had a reputation for wielding a sharp ax. He was the tenth chief computer executive at AT&T in 11 years and quickly began to dismantle most of what Stead had installed. He split NCR's core businesses in retail and banking into small, self-contained units. Personal computers were discontinued as a line of business. About one-fourth of the 43,000 work force was targeted for separation. NCR, once a proud, widely respected business, looked as if its assets were being groomed for divestiture.

After enduring computer business losses of $8 billion following the 1984 breakup, AT&T, in September 1995, seemed to acknowledge that computers and telecommunications were not necessarily meant for one another. Finally realizing the synergy was not there, AT&T Chairman Robert Allen said, "We have reached the point where the benefits of our size [$75 billion in revenues] are being outweighed by the amount of time and management resources it takes to coordinate." AT&T, this time acting voluntarily rather than under court order, divided itself into three separate companies: Communication Services (the AT&T phone business), Communication Equipment (including former Bell Labs), and Computing (the former NCR). NCR is history.

Questions for Managerial Action

1. Describe how you would react if someone tried to strip away your personal values and replace them with their own.

2. If you had worked for NCR, what would you consider to be the most offensive action by AT&T or their agents once they owned NCR? Why?

3. Why do you believe AT&T was so adamant in pressing its culture on NCR? What do you believe might have happened if NCR had been allowed to function as a subculture within AT&T, preserving its ideology, values, and identity?

4. What should AT&T have learned from this four-year episode with NCR?

Part II

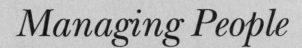

Managing People

5 Perception, Learning, and Personality

6 Motivation and Organizational Learning

7 Motivation Methods and Applications

Chapter 5

Perception, Learning, and Personality

LEARNING OBJECTIVES

After studying this chapter, you should be able to:

- Explain what is meant by person–job fit and the psychological contract.
- Illustrate the impact of perceptions and attributions on people's behavior in organizations.
- Describe three theories of learning and how they apply to organizational settings.
- Contrast four basic individual styles of learning and know in which roles each is effective.
- Illustrate the impact values and attitudes have on perceptions and behavior.
- Describe and illustrate different personality types and traits and their significance for behavior.

MANAGING IN TURBULENT TIMES

Ian McDonald and Alex Gruenwald had been friends for many years. Both worked as middle managers for Thompson Electronics (TE), an old, established manufacturing company. They were college graduates who had each started working for TE 19 years ago. They had done well and progressed to their well-paid, middle-level management jobs. Both Ian and Alex were married and each had three children ranging from 5 to 15 years old. Their wives were homemakers and actively engaged in civic and charitable activities.

Ian called Alex and suggested getting together after work for a drink before going home. Ian had told Alex he needed to talk. He said he was angry, depressed, and worried to pieces. Alex knew why. Both men had been told just a few days ago that they were going to be let go. Profits at TE had plummeted the last couple of years because of strong foreign competition and high costs. Thompson Electronics could not sustain its current size, and a decision was made to downsize. Ian said that it just wasn't fair. He and others had given TE the best years of their working lives. They had worked hard and well and given their unstinting loyalty to the company. Now look what they get in return: a pink slip, six months transition pay, and a "Sorry we have to do this for the good of the company." Ian's reaction was, "What on earth can I do? What I know and can do is only useful to TE. It never occurred to me that I would do anything different. They owe me more than this. It just isn't fair."

Alex admitted that he, too, was surprised and anxious. Yet, somehow, he felt a certain exhilaration. He couldn't quite put his finger on it, but the idea of suddenly being challenged to do something different and unknown was exciting. He was anxious that his wife and kids not be hurt, but deep down he felt optimistic that they would all come through OK. No use looking back. Focus on the adventure ahead. Alex valued Ian's friendship, though he knew that he wasn't looking forward to what might be a depressing after-work talk. He wondered how he should interact with Ian.

Howard Smith was general manager of operations at TE. He had known both Ian and Alex for years and felt terrible about having to let them go. He was even more concerned about the people left at TE. How would they view the downsizing and the departure of people they knew and liked? What would happen to their motivation and loyalty? Would achieving competitive results become even more difficult? He knew the challenges for him and top management were going to grow even bigger.

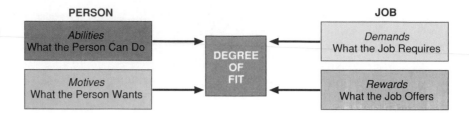

EXHIBIT 5–1

Elements of Person–Job Fit

Howard Smith's job, like that of most managers, is challenging. He will be held accountable for results, including TE's productivity, the satisfaction of its employees, and the overall improvement of results. His challenge will include gaining a high level of cooperation and commitment from individuals with diverse abilities, perceptions, attitudes, and personalities. This chapter will explore some of the important elements that managers should consider in understanding and managing people. Topics include the importance of person–job fit and the impact of perceptions, attributions, learning, values, attitudes, and personality in an organizational setting.

WHAT ARE PERSON–JOB FIT AND THE PSYCHOLOGICAL CONTRACT?

Organizations need to attract people who are able and willing to do the work required to achieve company and unit objectives. People, in turn, hope to work for organizations that help them satisfy their needs and wants. Both organizations and individuals hope to achieve a good fit between them.

Person–job fit is the term we use to describe how well the abilities and motives of an individual fit the job demands and rewards offered by the organization. Exhibit 5–1 illustrates this concept. Until their layoff notices, it appears that both Ian and Alex had good job fits. Their positions required both technical knowledge about electronics, an ability to supervise and interact effectively with people, and an ability to plan, organize, and control operations. The rewards offered them included a good salary, an opportunity to advance, some status and power, and until recently, security. They had the skills and abilities demanded by their jobs, and the rewards offered fit their motives. A manager's job includes making the best fit possible between employees and their jobs.

When people like Ian and Alex enter organizations or jobs, they bring their expectations about what they will have to contribute and what they will receive in response. This set of expectations is called the **psychological contract.** Individuals may not be fully conscious of this "contract"; usually it is implicit and unwritten. People feel satisfied as long as the contract is fulfilled, but if it isn't, they are likely to feel tension and behave in ways that either even up the contract or change it.

Individuals contribute such things as their skills, effort, time, loyalty, and commitment to an organization. In return the organization offers such things as pay, benefits, security, and opportunities to satisfy such motives as the need for achievement, power, status, and affiliation.

Both the individual and the organization will feel satisfied if they perceive the psychological contract as fair. If not, either party can initiate a change. For example, people can withhold effort or quit if they do not get an expected raise. The organization can require employees to exert more effort or to learn a new skill. The psychological contract is dynamic because the expectations and contributions of both the individual and organization change over time. An awareness of

person–job fit
The degree of fit between a person's abilities and motives and a job's demands and rewards.

psychological contract
Workers' implicit expectations about what they are expected to contribute to an organization and what they will receive in return.

psychological contracts can remind mangers of the reciprocal relationship between individuals and the organization and the need to keep those contracts fair, equitable, and up to date.

During the mid-1990s it became apparent that all was not right with many employee–employer contracts. Most companies proclaimed the importance of teamwork, empowerment, participation, and employee loyalty. Yet many of these same companies were downsizing and laying off large numbers of people, many of whom were long-term employees. Mergers and acquisitions also led to many people losing their jobs. These actions were taken to reduce costs and stay competitive. Many companies also began to replace long-term employees with temporary and part-time workers. The chasm between company pronouncements and company actions were obvious. Employees wondered why they should give their loyalty and commitment to companies that did not reciprocate with commitments to long-term relationships.[1]

social contract
Term used to describe collective psychological contracts.

The term **social contract** is sometimes used to describe collective psychological contracts. Although there have always been important variations, the general social contract in the United States for many years included two common elements. One was that employees would give regular attendance and effort along with loyalty to the organization.[2] In return, employers would provide "fair" pay and benefits, advancement based on seniority and merit, and job security within reasonable limits. This social contract was never followed universally, but still it was strongly implied and accepted by large numbers of companies and employees. During recent years that has changed.

Some suggest that a new social contract needs to be developed. Many paradoxes will have to be faced and reconciled. For example, productivity must be enhanced while often the work force is reduced.[3] Companies encourage workers to give their commitment and loyalty without promising the same in return.

A revised social contract will likely include the following in defining new relationships. Employees will be expected to provide a high level of performance, a commitment to the company's objectives, and a willingness to make suggestions and train to improve behavior.[4] Employers, in turn, will provide interesting and challenging work, learning, flexibility, performance-based compensation, and opportunities for participation and involvement. This means that many workers will have to change from their psychological dependence on their employers to a commitment to their craft or profession. Workers will have to develop knowledge and skills that are transferable to other companies and jobs.

In spite of a more ambiguous social contract, one of the manager's key challenges remains making the best possible fit between individuals and jobs. To meet this challenge, managers must understand employees' abilities as they pertain to their daily job tasks.

People's performance depends on their abilities and motives. Ability is about "can do," and motives are about "will do." Both are important to performance, and managers need to know the difference. Some people are able to perform specific tasks but are unwilling to do so; others compensate for their lack of ability by being motivated to learn and work hard. This section focuses on ability; motives will be discussed in Chapter 6.

ability
The capacity to perform physical and intellectual tasks.

Ability versus Aptitude

aptitude
The capacity to learn an ability.

Ability is the capacity to perform physical and intellectual tasks. **Aptitude** is the capacity to learn an ability. People differ both in their abilities and aptitudes. Few, if any, can play basketball as well as Michael Jordan or sing as well as Luciano

Pavarotti. Most of us do not have the aptitude required to match their abilities. Managers should know what abilities are required to perform various jobs and should try to match the jobs with people who have appropriate abilities.

Physical ability can be distinguished from intellectual ability. Physical ability includes such factors as strength, dexterity, coordination, stamina, and quickness. Intellectual ability is the capacity to learn, reason, and apply knowledge to new situations. Intelligence is sometimes thought of as a single factor, but evidence suggests there are multiple intelligences, including linguistic, musical, logical-mathematical, spatial, bodily-kinesthetic, and personal intelligence.[5] Tests have been designed to measure both physical and intellectual skills.

It is useful for managers to understand the difference between ability and aptitude. People who lack either the ability or aptitude to perform a job will likely fail and feel dissatisfied. Those who have the aptitude but not the ability to perform a certain job can learn to do so. Too much ability, however, can also be a problem. Those who are overqualified for certain jobs can become bored and unmotivated. The key is to find the best person–job fit possible.

Managing the person–job fit involves more than simply matching a person's abilities and motives with job requirements and rewards. How an individual performs is also impacted by such variables as perceptions, learning, attitudes, and personality. We now turn to the important impact perceptions have on how people behave in an organization.

WHAT ARE PERCEPTIONS AND ATTRIBUTIONS?

Each of us has experienced perceiving someone or something differently than others do. For example, two subordinates may evaluate their supervisor quite differently. One might perceive the boss as effective because she provides structure and direction, while the other may perceive her as rigid and controlling. Understanding the perceptual process helps explain why such differences occur.

perception
The selection, organization, and interpretation of sensory data.

Perception is the selection, organization, and interpretation of sensory data. It is the critically important process that helps people define their world and guides their behavior. Exhibit 5–2 illustrates the general perceptual process.

People do not see objective reality, but they believe what they perceive is real. Our perceptions are our personal reality, whether they are objective or not, and they influence our behavior.

Imagine a manager named Joel walking into his subordinate's office unexpectedly. His subordinate, Danalo, is leaning back in his chair, feet on the desk and eyes closed. How will Joel react? That will depend on how Joel perceives the situation.

He might respond with anger because he thinks Danalo is sleeping on the job, or he might quietly withdraw because he assumes Danalo is thinking through a problem. Joe's past experience with Danalo will temper his perceptions. For example, he may know Danalo likes to party and stay out late at night, and he may assess him as a below-average employee. Or, instead, he may know that Danalo has been working hard on a difficult project and that in the past he has been productive. Joel knows he himself sometimes leans back and shuts the world out while thinking through a tough problem.

In either case, Joel is noticing certain things and relating them to what he already believes. He then adds meaning and interprets what he sees. The result is his personal perception, which in turn influences his behavior toward Danalo. Joel may behave inappropriately if he misperceives the situation.

━━━━ **EXHIBIT 5–2** *The Perceptual Process: From Stimuli to Behavior*

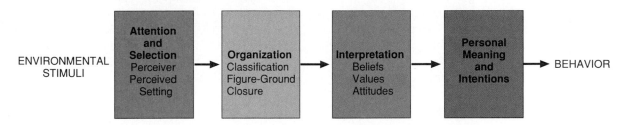

Understanding the perceptual process helps managers know better why people perceive things as they do and why they often perceive things differently. This understanding enables them to better deal with such differences and minimize some of the distortions that occur.

Attention and Selection

Each of us is bombarded with multiple sensory stimuli, and it is impossible to attend to them all. We selectively respond to meaningful stimuli and minimize or ignore others. This part of the process is influenced by the perceiver, the perceived, and the setting.

The Perceiver.   People tend to notice what is important to them. A hungry person is more likely to be aware of food than someone whose stomach is full. An unemployed person is more likely to read a job advertisement than someone gainfully employed. Individuals are more likely to notice positive or negative characteristics of others depending on whether they like them or not. People tend to perceive what they need, want, and expect to see.

The physical, mental, and emotional condition of the perceiver affects attentiveness. A person who is tired, ill, stressed, or emotionally upset may not perceive as accurately as someone who is alert, well, at ease, or calm. Also, the perceiver's beliefs, attitudes, values, motives, and expectations influence what he or she perceives as relevant. For example, a student who values grades more than learning may not pay attention to parts of a classroom lecture but may perk up when the instructor mentions a possible test question.

The Perceived.   Certain general attributes of the perceived object or person influence what is noticed and what is not. These include size, novelty, motion, proximity, and intensity of the stimulus. Loud noises, sudden quietness, unusual motions, and bright colors tend to attract attention. Objects that are novel or unusual stand out. These characteristics also apply to people. Those who are very large or small often attract attention. So do those who are loud, dress in bright colors or unusual styles, and behave in unusual ways. People who are unusually attractive or unattractive are noticed when others are not. The status of a person may also influence attention.

The Setting.   Time and physical conditions such as temperatures, lighting, noise, smell, and clutter are examples of contextual factors that may influence what is noticed and what is not. If an individual is tired and it is late in the day, he or she might be less sensitive to external stimuli that when feeling bright and alert. People generally see more in the light than in the dark, although they might hear more in the dark than in the light.

Fighter pilots are bombarded with stimuli in the cockpit: radio, engine sounds, vibration in the plane, touch of the control stick, visual flight instruments and navigational controls, radar, other air traffic, smells. Pilots are trained to sort out this barrage and respond appropriately. The Air Force is experimenting with a helmet to make this task easier. The helmet, engineered by Wright Aero Labs, allows a pilot to look at a computer-synthesized virtual reality projected onto the inside of the helmet's face shield. Much of the information is displayed so that it can be sensed instead of inferred from instruments, cutting down on some of the stimuli in the cockpit and easing the brain's processing of others. (Photo: © Bruce Frisch.)

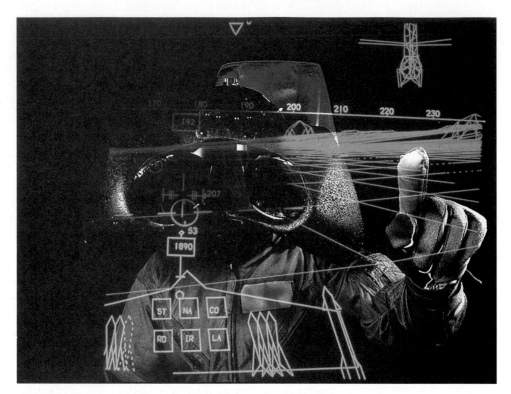

The nature of the setting can also be relevant. Boisterous laughter might be appropriate in a social setting and not noticed as much as it would be in a work setting. A manager might go unnoticed in jeans and a T-shirt at the company picnic but would attract considerable attention dressed that way in the office. The nature of the setting influences what is perceived as appropriate or normal.

Organization

The next step after sensory stimuli have been selected and received is to organize the various stimuli into more meaningful patterns. Three concepts relate to this process: classification, figure–ground differentiation, and closure.

Classification.   We classify people in a variety of categories such as age, gender, race, nationality, physical categories, education, occupation, and status. We also attach the assumptions, beliefs, and attitudes we hold about those groupings. Classifying sensory inputs help us sort and recall sensory data faster than if we did not have an organizational system. However, classification can also lead to stereotypes and inaccurate perceptions. For example, assume a job applicant is directed to visit Robin Taylor, the human resource manager. The applicant approaches two people, a young man and a middle-aged woman, looks at the man, and says, "Mr. Taylor?" The man smiles and replies, "No, I'm Ed Smith. This is Robin Taylor." This embarrassing perceptual error is likely based on the mistaken assumption that men are more likely to be managers and women secretaries. A person who is aware of the perceptual process would recognize the ambiguity in this situation and avoid the mistake.

━━━━ **EXHIBIT 5–3**   *A Figure–Ground Experiment*

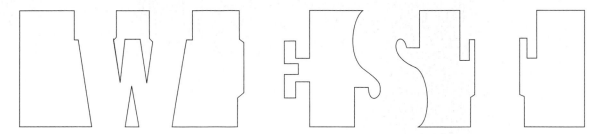

figure
The dominant feature being perceived

ground
The surrounding, competing stimuli being perceived.

Figure–Ground Differentiation.   A key element in perceptual accuracy is the ability to distinguish **figure** (dominant features) from **ground** (surrounding, competing, stimuli). Why, in a crowded and noisy cafeteria, are you are able to hold a meaningful conversation with a friend? Because you are capable of distinguishing the sight and sound of your friend (figure) from the sight and sound of the other people and objects present (ground). Although you perceive the entire scene, you respond selectively to the most relevant stimuli. If you were to respond to all of the stimuli nonselectively, nothing meaningful would result.

It is the same for managers in organizations. People pay more attention to some stimuli than others and run the danger of overlooking relevant clues. For example, the job applicant looking for Robin Taylor might have focused on the ages of Taylor and Smith as well as on their gender. He may have assumed (correctly in this case) that the older of the two was more likely to be the manager. If Joel (in or earlier example) only notices Danolo's shut eyes and relaxed position, he may overlook the piles of work on his desk and his rumpled clothing, which might indicate Danalo had worked all night on a project.

Look quickly at Exhibit 5–3 and then look away. How do you interpret the figure? Most people focus on the individual figures enclosed with lines, and few see any meaning. However, if you focus on the space between the figures, the word WEST appears. If you put a piece of paper along the bottom of the figure, the word becomes even more apparent.

What we see depends on what we see as figure and what we see as ground. We attend selectively to stimuli by focusing on features that capture our attention. A major purpose of studying organizational behavior is to alert you to possible important stimuli. Key theories and concepts (such as power, motivation, and leadership) call attention to variables that affect organizational performance. The trained manager knows what to look for as the dominant figure against a complex background of organizational forces.

perceptual closure
The mind's tendency to fill in missing data when it receives incomplete information.

Closure.   If normal channels of sensory awareness receive incomplete information, the mind often fills in the gaps. **Perceptual closure** occurs when we receive some data that we judge important but incomplete and allow our minds to fill in the missing data, especially if the situation or topic is familiar. Instances of perceptual closure often arise at work when someone in authority delivers a command or instruction but fails to explain it adequately. Typically, the conscientious receiver will think, "What did she mean by that?" or "Why is he making me do this?" Our answers fill the gaps to give us a sense of closure. Sometimes our answers are incorrect! The Eye on Ethics box illustrates another of the complexities of perception, namely, subliminal messages.

Do Subliminal Messages Mess with the Mind?

The mind can be quicker than the eye. Movie makers can exploit this fact by creating subliminal messages in films. *Subliminal* means existing outside the area of awareness or consciousness. Thresholds vary with individuals, but experiments sometimes begin with images lasting just 1/1000th of a second. Director William Friedkin for example, inserted subliminal clues in his murder mystery film titled *Jade*. Friedkin's intent was to create a jarring effect and to provide omens for his audience.

Normal film speeds are 24 frames each second. Friedkin usually uses two or three frames in those 24 to induce a subliminal message. He believes most people cannot perceive a twelfth of a second. However, many are affected by images flashed at that speed even if they are unaware of what they are looking at. His intent is to suggest something, not to show it.

Friedkin has used subliminal messages in two of his prior films, *The Exorcist* (1973) and *Cruising* (1980). *Jade* has the most extensive use of subcutting he has attempted. This technique is controversial. Some experts say audiences should be warned about subliminal images. Gerald Rafferty, president and founder of the Institute for Subliminal Studies, said: "It really is an invasion of privacy. It's fraught with danger." He indicates people's minds get the subliminal message even at a four-hundredth of a second if they are tied into what is expected. This process embeds expectations in the subconscious mind and can trigger emotional reactions. Rafferty cites an example. If there were a picture, let's say, of a beautiful, young, innocent girl on the screen for a long interval of time, and if you are flashing her being brutally murdered, the viewer would get it and probably have an emotional response to that. You'd start feeling uneasy and worried for her."

Friedkin considers using subliminal cuts as a cinematic device and sees no reason to warn moviegoers of its use. Others believe some people will resent being manipulated and will become suspicious that other kinds of messages (for example, "Buy our popcorn") are being directed at them. The Directors Guild of America has no guild rules or policies prohibiting the use of subliminal techniques. The Federal Communications Commission has no rules banning the use of subliminal projects, although broadcasters are required to tell viewers if they are being subjected to subliminal advertising.

Are these techniques ethical? Are they simply interesting communication devices, or are they tools for manipulating people outside their awareness?

Source: Adapted from Amy Harmon and Robert W. Welkos, *Los Angeles Times,* October 12, 1995.

Given sketchy information, people often make assumptions about the missing data. However, if the stimulus is insufficient to effect closure and thus to cope with an ambiguous situation, then frustration, anxiety, and stress may result. Ian Mc-Donald, in our opening vignette, may have been experiencing these feelings caused by his unexpected layoff. Some mangers deliberately assign tasks in an ambiguous manner, believing this will encourage subordinates to develop their own problem-solving skills and become more self-reliant. But if the level of ambiguity is excessive for the individual's job maturity level, this tactic is likely to prove dysfunctional. Lacking closure on the task, and left without clues as to how to proceed, the subordinate may become disoriented, fearful, defensive, and withdrawn. Alert managers watch for these symptoms and help employees work through their feelings by listening and offering suggestions.

Exhibit 5–4 illustrates the perceptual closure concept. Conjecture is easy in the bottom row, but most people would have difficulty completing the top row based on the information given. Closure would not occur.

▬▬▬ EXHIBIT 5–4

Perceptual Closure

It would be difficult to complete the symbols in the top row because of insufficient information. The symbols in the bottom row could be considered complete because sufficient information is provided.

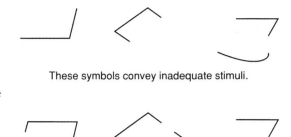

These symbols convey inadequate stimuli.

These symbols are seen as complete.

Interpretation

Keep in mind that the perceptual process happens instantly. It happens much faster than the time it takes you to read about it! Sensory inputs are selected, filtered through our past and present experience, and then interpreted. We add meaning to data we take in. Our past learning and experience as well as our current beliefs, assumptions, attitudes, and values all influence the meaning we add to what we take in. Combined, they form our individual **frame of reference,** which is a mental filter through which perceptions are interpreted and evaluated.

For example, in our earlier example Joel actually interpreted what he saw as Danalo needing a well-deserved break. Although startled at seeing him stretched out with his eyes closed, he knew that Danalo was a conscientious, productive person. He did notice the rumpled clothes and piles of work, and he correctly assumed he had spent the night at his desk. Based on his perception, he quietly withdrew and decided to contact Danalo later.

Fortunately, in this case, Joel perceived correctly. However, the perceptual process is difficult and subject to various errors and distortions. We will identify some of the more common errors.

Perceptual Distortions

People's perceptions become distorted in several ways. These involve selective perception, stereotypes, halo effects, and projection. An understanding and awareness of these distortions can help people avoid them. Each of these distortions tends to obscure individual differences and has the potential to make us oversimplify or misread other people and situations.

People tend to focus on those attributes of people and situations that fit their frame of reference. This is called **selective perception.** Two examples are failing to see the faults of a loved one or the good points about someone we dislike. The potential danger of selective perception is that we miss important data, and the omission causes a distorted view of a person or situation.

Alternatively, we might perceive because of stereotypes. A **stereotype** is a rigid, biased perception of a person, group, object, or situation. We tend to categorize people by their obvious, and sometimes less obvious, differences. Based on their past experiences and learning, those who stereotype think and behave as though all people in that category are the same. Stereotypes can be either positive or negative. People stereotype others on criteria ranging from age, gender, race, religion,

frame of reference
Mental filter through which perceptions are interpreted and evaluated.

selective perception
The tendency to focus on those attributes of people and situations that fit our frame of reference.

stereotype
A rigid, biased perception of a person, group, object, or situation.

and nationality to education level, occupation, and political affiliation. Unwarranted negative stereotypes can lead to bias, which in turn leads to destructive attitudes such as sexism, racism, and nationalism. Managers should be aware of their own inappropriate stereotypes, and they need to confront those of their employees when they lead to destructive relations among a group.

In sharp contrast to stereotyping, at times we attribute a halo effect to others. A **halo effect** is the tendency to overrate a person based on a single trait. An example would be assuming that an attractive person is intelligent without having an objective basis for that judgment. Halo effects can lead to incomplete and inaccurate judgments and, like stereotypes, may prompt someone to miss individual differences.

Another common perceptual distortion is **projection,** which is the attributing to others one's own thoughts, feelings, attitudes, and traits. People sometimes read their own motives or feelings into another. Someone who is very tired or angry may see those same feelings in another person, who in fact may not be feeling that way. A person who tends to be suspicious of others may perceive others as being suspicious, just as someone who is trusting perceives others to be the same way.

Perceiving other people is difficult because of the various kinds of errors we can make. It is even more difficult because we see only behaviors. Much of what causes these behaviors is not observable. We do not see others' thoughts, motives, intentions, attitudes, values, or feelings. We satisfy our need for perceptual closure by making inferences about why others behave as the do. This process—called attribution—is discussed in the following section.

Attribution

Attribution is an assumed explanation of why people behave as they do, based on our observations and inferences. We also make attributions about our own behavior. The study of how people assign causes to and explain behavior has led to the development of attribution theory.[6]

Theories of Attribution.   Attribution theory suggests that when people observe another's behavior, they use certain criteria to determine whether it fits that person's general personality or is affected by other factors. This attribution process is often subconscious.

Assume Fernando Garcia submits an important report a day late. His supervisor, Kris White, must assess the meaning of this behavior. Kris is likely to consider Fernando's past performance, including such things as quality and quantity of work, attendance, promptness, and attitude. She will also be aware of situational factors, including workloads, time pressures, available resources, support, and performance standards. Attribution theory suggests that she will then use three criteria in understanding why Fernando submitted the report late: distinctiveness, consistency, and consensus.

Distinctiveness is used to explain whether a person's behavior fits with other behaviors. If Fernando's analyses are sharp, his writing clear, his presentations professional, and if he has performed effectively and reliably over a range of different assignments, his late submission would be distinctive.

Consistency is used to explain the degree of variance over time. Has Fernando missed other deadlines, or is this an exception? Does he come to work and appointments on time? Is he usually reliable? If Kris decides Fernando's late submission fits a pattern of frequent tardiness, his behavior would be judged consistent.

halo effect
The tendency to overrate a person based on a single trait.

projection
Attributing to others one's own thoughts, feelings, attitudes, and traits.

attribution
An assumed explanation of why people behave as they do, based on our observations and inferences.

distinctiveness
An attribution process used to explain whether a person's behavior fits with other behaviors.

consistency
An attribution process used to explain the degree of variance in behavior over time.

━━━━ **EXHIBIT 5–5** *The Attribution Process*

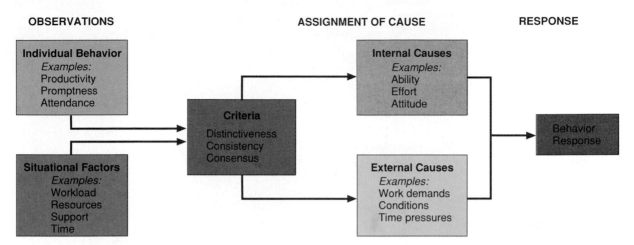

Source: Adapted from T. R. Mitchell and R. E. Wood, "An Empirical Test of an Attributional Model of Leaders' Responses to Poor Perfromance," *Academy of Management Proceedings* (1979), pp. 94–98.

consensus
An attribution process used to determine how others behave in similar situations.

Consensus refers to how others behave in similar situations. Do Fernando's peers submit reports late? How frequently? If they are often late, there is consensus.

After assessing her observations using the above criteria, Kris is likely to attribute the cause of Fernando's behavior to either internal or external factors. Internal causes are those over which the individual is perceived to have control, such as effort or attitude. External causes are those over which the individual is perceived to have little control. Examples include poor or inadequate training, unrealistic workloads and deadlines, poor equipment, and inadequate supervision.

If Kris decides that Fernando was late because he is lazy, incompetent, or has a poor attitude, she is attributing his behavior to internal causes. If instead she thinks Fernando was late because the deadline was unrealistic or the computer file was destroyed, she will attribute Fernando's tardiness to external causes. Of course, a mix of internal and external attributions might be made. Kris's behavior will be influenced by the attributions she makes. Exhibit 5–5 illustrates the attribution process.

Fernando will make self-attributions about being late. He may be more aware than Kris of perceived external factors. Most people tend to give themselves credit for successes but to rationalize failures, based on perceived external factors. This tendency is modified by the degree of the individual's internal or external orientation. Inappropriate attributions can be made by either Kris or Fernando, and we turn now to two errors people commonly make.

attributional error
The tendency to overestimate internal factors and underestimate external factors when making attributions about others.

self-serving bias
The tendency of individuals to attribute their own positive performance to internal factors and their negative performance to external factors.

Attributional Error and Self-Serving Bias. When people make attributions about others, there is evidence that they overestimate internal factors and underestimate external factors.[7] This is called **attributional error.** One study showed that managers are more likely to attribute the poor performance of their subordinates to internal factors, such as ability and effort, than to negative factors inherent in the situation.[8] However, the managers attributed their own poor performance to lack of support, an external factor. This **self-serving bias** is the tendency of individuals to attribute their own positive performance to internal factors and their negative performance to external factors.

Benchmarking, the process by which a company continually measures its goods, practices, and services against those of its toughest competitors and leading firms in other industries, is a form of generalization. Because of L.L. Bean's excellence in filling customer orders reliably and efficiently, the company is regularly visited by other businesses studying Bean's system in order to improve their own. Among U.S. companies, Bean is considered one of the top firms when it comes to customer satisfaction and distribution/logistics. (Photo: © 1993 Jose Azel/Aurora & Quanta Productions.)

Applications of Perception and Attribution.   The behavior of people in organizations is continuously influenced by perceptions and attributions. The interviewer who sizes up an applicant and the manager who evaluates employee performance are basing their judgments on perceptions and attributions. So are people who perceive others, deciding if they like them or not and want to cooperate or compete with them. We should be aware that others are perceiving us differently than we may want to be seen, and vice versa. The need for self-awareness and empathic understanding is clear, as is the need to work continuously to avoid the common errors of perception and attribution.

Perception enables people to learn about and make sense of their worlds. The ability to learn is an important distinguishing characteristic of human beings and is vital to both individuals and organizations. In the next section, we will look at some of the basic theories of how individuals learn.

HOW DO PEOPLE LEARN?

Change pervades businesses and organizations. Individuals must be able to learn new knowledge and skills in order to survive. Recall Ian McDonald and Alex Gruenwald in our opening vignette. When they first started work, they neither had nor were required to use computer skills. This quickly changed as their company integrated personal computers into its procedures. Both Ian and Alex had to learn new skills, just to survive. As each faces his uncertain work future, each will be required to learn many new things. In today's fast-changing world, almost everyone is periodically required to learn new knowledge and skills. The Challenge of Change box illustrates how two managers at Hewlett-Packard had to learn a whole new way of managing in order to solve a complex problem.

learning
The acquisition of knowledge or skill through study, practice, or experience.

An important distinguishing characteristic of human beings is their ability to store information and to learn. **Learning** is the acquisition of knowledge or skill through study, practice, or experience. Learning is usually considered to lead to relatively permanent changes in behavior.

Challenge of Change

At H-P, Learning Moves Outside Existing Structures

Hewlet-Packard's North American distribution organization handles billions of dollars of products from order to delivery. A challenging problem confronting this organization was that it took an average of 26 days for a product to reach the customer. Two experienced managers, Mei-Lin Cheng, 44, and Julie Anderson, 46, were asked to change these results.

Reengineering the existing processes successfully required radically changed perceptions of how to mange change. Cheng and Anderson were up the challenge. They bravely committed to producing significant and measurable improvement in customer satisfaction in less than nine months. In exchange, they received freedom to manage the project without interference from their bosses.

Cheng and Anderson assembled a team of 35 people, including a few members from two outside companies. Their startling approach: They explained the ground rules of the challenge, and then refused to tell anyone what to do. They had thought about how to structure the project, and concluded they shouldn't have a structure. They gave the team members the freedom to define their own goals and roles at work. They had no supervisors, no hierarchy, no titles, no job descriptions, no plans, no step-by-step milestones of progress. They located most of the team members in one office, explained the timeframe and business measures, and then let the team decide how to achieve results. One outcome was that the commitment of team members

intensified and their work became more meaningful personally. Another result was that the team met the deadline and achieved their goals.

The formidable challenge of this team included creating a highly complicated system to create a single, unified database covering everything from the customer order through credit check, manufacturing, shipping, and warehousing to invoicing. They knew they had to have all of the team members looking at the whole system. Cheng and Anderson started with a two-week training and orientation program to help members become familiar with each other and existing processes. After orientation, chaos at first reigned. Slowly, team members began to unravel the blocks and to develop new ways of conceptualizing, designing, and implementing a workable system. One important lesson they learned was to deal with bite-size problems one by one. Another learning experience was they learned to practice. Each morning started with a meeting reviewing what had happened the day before, what had been learned, what were the immediate obstacles, and what were the priorities. In doing this they were building the capacity of the team to learn.

One team member said: "If the intent is to make incremental improvements in business results, the techniques we were taught in school are adequate. If the intent is to fundamentally shift how you deal with problems, then change is a requirement."

Source: Stratford Sherman, "Secrets of HP's 'Muddled' Team", *Fortune,* March 18, 1996, pp. 116–120.

The learning process takes place primarily in the brain. One useful metaphor for the brain is a computer. It has the capacity to receive inputs, organize and store them, and respond to some calls for retrieval. New data can be entered and existing data can be reorganized or deleted. Memory is analogous to computer files, and perception and learning are the processes through which new data are added and old data revised.

Computers differ in their capacity to receive, store, process, and retrieve information quickly and to manipulate the data in order to solve problems. These differing capacities are somewhat analogous to different individuals' intelligence and ability to think. Intelligence is a fuzzy concept. Generally, **intelligence** includes three different aspects: (1) the ability to adapt to novel situations quickly and effectively; (2) the ability to use abstract concepts effectively; and (3) the

intelligence
The ability to adapt to novel situations quickly and effectively, use abstract concepts effectively, and grasp relationships and learn quickly.

ability to grasp relationships and to learn quickly.[9] Daniel Goleman has recently identified another aspect of intelligence he labels "emotional intelligence." It reflects the functioning of a person's emotional brain, which generates and regulates feelings. Goleman suggests emotional intelligence relates to a person's ability to get along with others, exert control over one's life, and think and decide clearly.[10]

Individuals differ in memory, intelligence, and ability to learn. We now turn to some of the basic theories of how individuals learn. The main theories we will consider are (1) behavioral conditioning, (2) social learning, and (3) cognitive discovery. We will also look at different individual styles of learning, because people tend to differ from one another in how they learn.

Behavioral Conditioning

The development of learning theory began in the early twentieth century when the Russian physiologist Ivan Pavlov found he could condition dogs to salivate in response to the sound of a tuning fork, a previously neutral stimulus. Pavlov's work led to the development of **classical conditioning,** which is an experimental approach that associates a conditioned stimulus with an unconditioned stimulus to achieve a conditioned response.

classical conditioning
An experimental approach that associates a conditioned stimulus with an unconditioned stimulus to achieve a conditional response.

Dogs and other animals naturally salivate (*unconditional response—R*) when they are hungry and food (*unconditional stimulus—S*) is present. Pavlov experimented by preceding the presentation of food with the sound of a tuning fork (*conditional stimulus—S˘*) and over time taught the dogs to salivate (*conditional response—R´*) at the sound alone. His experiments provided the intellectual basis for an empirical approach to the study of learning.[11]

People experience classical conditioning in their everyday lives without realizing it. For example, assume you frequently walk by a bakery early in the morning and smell (*S*) the freshly baked bread. If you have not had breakfast, you are likely to salivate and feel hunger pangs (*R*). The odor is an unconditioned stimulus, and your physical reaction is an unconditional response. Assume this happens frequently. Then one day you drive by the bakery and cannot smell the bread, but you salivate and feel hungry anyway. The sight of the shop (*S´*) has become a conditioned stimulus and your physical response, which now occurs without the actual odor, is also conditioned (*R´*)

The late American psychologist B. F. Skinner extended the work of Pavlov and others to develop **operant conditioning,** which is learning in which reinforcement depends on the person's behavior. In operant conditioning, the critical learning element is the direct linkage of significant contingent consequences to an operant behavior.

operant conditioning
Learning in which reinforcement depends on the person's behavior.

A *contingent consequence* is a reinforcer; it may be positive, negative, or neutral. The term *operant* simply means that the individual "operates" in his or her environment to obtain some desired consequences and avoid adverse or negative consequences. Individuals learn to anticipate or expect a certain consequence following specific behaviors. They learn to behave in ways that achieve positive consequences. The more frequently we get the desired consequences or avoid undesirable ones, the firmer the learning.

For example, assume Donna works extra hard on a special project to meet a tight deadline. Her boss is appreciative of Donna's efforts and gives her special praise. Donna enjoys the praise and is likely to work hard again to receive the desired compliments. If she gets no response at all, she will probably feel less inclined to work hard. If Donna is late with her report and is reprimanded, she is likely to work harder the next time to avoid the negative consequence.

The basic assumption underlying conditioning theory is that people tend to repeat those behaviors that lead to desirable consequences and avoid those that lead to negative results.[12] Conditioning theory underlies many of the behaviors

The ability of Richard Teerlink, CEO of Harley-Davidson (photo), and his managers to learn and adapt to change was severely tested in the 1970s and 1980s when customers abondoned Harleys to purchase higher quality Japanese motorcycles. Harley executives recognized the situation and translated what they saw into the development of a successful, high-quality Harley product. Today, Harley's low-slung "Hogs" have more than one-fifth of the market for U.S. bike sales and more than half of the growing $1.3 billion market for heavyweight motorcycles. Approximately 400,000 Harleys appeared with their owners in Daytona Beach, Florida, during Harley-Davidson's annual March Bike Week (photo). (Source: © James Schnepf.)

managers and teachers use in an attempt to motivate people and teach them to behave in certain ways. Today Skinner's principles of operant conditioning are commonly applied in organizational settings to help change the behaviors of a wide range of humanity: drug addicts, students with learning disabilities, smokers, sex offenders, and phobics, as well as employees.[13] The use of reinforcement for purposes of behavior modification is explained in detail in Chapter 7.

Self-Management of Contingencies. It is possible for a person to manage his or her own contingencies. For example, one principle of time management has evolved from the premise that a person will complete "have-to" tasks quite expediently if the reward (positive reinforcement) is engaging in tasks that are more creative, enjoyable, or satisfying. This is known as the **Premack principle** of pairing tasks or events.[14]

Premack principle
The pairing of disagreeable with enjoyable tasks or events to hasten their completion.

Psychologist David Premack based his principle on the finding that when tasks are paired, the more probable (more pleasurable) behavior will tend to reinforce or bring about the less probably behavior; for example, complete the report, then play racquetball or tennis. Well-organized students and workers may find they have adopted the Premack principle without even knowing it had a name. If you have not used if for self-management, try it.

Social Learning Theory

Some psychologists believe that operant conditioning or reinforcement theory is the most valid explanation for how people learn. However, many researchers disagree with B. F. Skinner's contentions that humankind is simply an instrument of society and that people are passively subject to shaping by environmental events and by those in control.[15]

Unwilling to accept the fact that reinforcement alone is the answer, Albert Bandura and others have researched the social learning aspects of human development. **Social learning theory** is based on the process of observational learning through modeling and imitation. It holds that rather than learning exclusively through reinforcement and the shaping of successive approximations toward a desired behavior, we acquire many behaviors simply through imitation. Imitation is especially strong when the learner identifies with and desires to be like the role model. Imitators are in conscious control of whether or not to act like the model.

social learning theory
The belief that we learn many behaviors by observing and imitating others.

Bandura suggests that people are capable of anticipatory control—of choosing how they will respond in various situations.[16] Since people are capable of observing the effects of their behaviors, they can anticipate consequences across a variety of circumstances. For example, Jack's boss may say something in a meeting that angers him. Jack can choose whether or not to express his anger publicly. He is capable of anticipating his boss's response, based on his past experiences with the boss and others in authority positions.

Even though the organizational world acts on them, adults at work still choose what situations to get involved in and how to act in them to produce a desired outcome. We learn through social observation to expect that certain socially desirable behaviors will be reinforced, and we learn the value of the reinforcer.[17] While social learning theory acknowledges and builds on many principles of reinforcement, it moves closer to the concept of learning cognitively through insight and self-discovery.

The Cognitive View: New Patterns of Thought

The perceptual-cognitive view of learning focuses on what happens within the individual: motives, feelings, attitudes, memory, and cognition (thought). Sensory mechanisms are of primary importance in the key cognitive activity, which is observation based. Through speech and a knowledge of language, humans form abstract concepts for organizing perceptions and manipulating ideas. Thus **cognitive learning** involves selective interpretation of perceptual data organized into new patterns of thoughts and relationships. This kind of learning is illustrated by a manager who asks a subordinate if he has a few minutes to talk. The latter says, "Well . . . OK (voice dropping)." Although the words indicate consent, the boss notices a look of frustration and reads into the pause and tone of voice a strong unwillingness. The boss's ability to observe multiple stimuli and to interpret the nonverbal along with the verbal communication can be learned through training and experience.

cognitive learning
Selective interpretation of perceptual data organized into new patterns of thoughts and relationships.

Human beings are capable of rearranging thought patterns into new configurations, or gestalts. *Gestalt* is a German word meaning "shape, configuration, or the arrangement of relationships in a total situation." Patterns of concepts and relationships may occur suddenly, through insight, or they may evolve gradually as elements are linked together with new data.

insight
The sudden discovery of the answer to a problem.

Insight.   Often known as the Eureka! ("I've found it!") or Aha! experience, **insight** is best described as the sudden discovery of the answer to a problem. We achieve insight into a situation, relationship, or problem when we suddenly grasp an idea or see a relationship that helps us to understand the situation better or solve the problem. Insight often comes while doing something and observing what happens.[18]

A labor shortage in the expanding industry has encouraged restaurant managers to utilize social learning theory to hire and retain employees. Manager Kim McManus of the Southern Grille Restaurant in Ellendale, Delaware, acts as a mentor to his employees by helping them focus on job objectives. "I give them honest communication about how they can meet our expectations and how my goals are facilitated by their goals of making more money and having an exciting career." (Source: © 1995 *Nation's Business* / T. Michael Keza.)

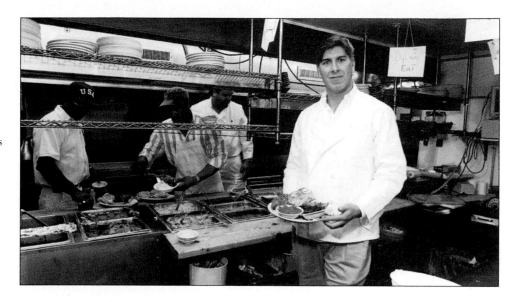

Wolfgang Kohler presented the first experimental evidence on insight in the 1920s, when he demonstrated the results of his work with a chimpanzee named Sultan.[19] The turning point in Kohler's research occurred when he enclosed Sultan and a short stick inside a barred cage, outside of which he placed a longer stick and a banana—both too far away for Sultan to reach. Sultan first picked up the short stick and attempted to rake in the banana. But the elusive banana remained beyond the chimp's extended reach. Unable to obtain results, Sultan sat cowering in the cage, gazing at the objects around him. Suddenly he jumped up and reached for the short stick. With it, he raked in the long stick; then he used the long stick to rake in the banana. Eureka! The chimp had discovered a solution! Today we know that two of the learning processes involved in the phenomenon of insight are discrimination and generalization.

discrimination
The process by which universal or previously unstructured elements are placed into more specific structures.

Discrimination.   Sometimes called differentiation, **discrimination** is the process by which universal or previously unstructured elements are placed into more specific structures.[20] People learn to read by discriminating among symbols—first individual letters, then groupings of letters (words), and finally meaningful groupings of letters separated by spaces and punctuation. Discrimination also occurs when three cars are seen as a Cadillac, a Trans Am, and a Porsche or considered in terms of their components: tires, engines, doors, seats. Managers discriminate a general concept such as "organization" into people, positions, structures, policies, power, leadership, and so on.

generalization
The means through which we transfer learning from one situation to another as well as categorize information.

Generalization.   When concepts, functions, objects, and events are grouped into categories, generalization is at work. **Generalization** is the means through which we transfer leaning from one situation to another as well as categorize information. Whereas discrimination breaks down the general into specific, generalization unites previously separate elements into meaningful universal themes or clusters. Generalization helps people map out and program their memories so that every event does not have to be experienced as something totally new.

Managers generalize when they categorize an organizational behavior problem as one of communication, for example, or of conflict, motivation, job design, or leadership. Then they differentiate its possible causes and probable solutions. They remember the consequences of attempted actions and apply that learning when diagnosing current problems and deciding how they will act. The ability to discriminate, generalize, and develop insight is vital to conceptual skill, which is critically important for successful managers.

Because insight is a human resource, a manager may draw others into a group problem-solving process. An idea offered by Takashi may trigger a thought by Sheila, which prompts a creative suggestion from Shannon. One insight tends to generate another in the search for an effective group solution.

Experiential Learning Styles

One of the most important abilities an individual can possess is the ability to learn. A manager's long-term success depends more on the ability to learn than on the mastery of specific skills or technical knowledge. Research by David Kolb indicates that managers favor a style of learning that differs from that of many other professionals.[21] Managers learn most readily from direct experience and by actively testing the implications of concepts to new situation. Kolb's findings are based on a model of learning that involves four different abilities; they combine to form four distinct styles.

Kolb's experiential learning model distinguishes two primary dimensions of the learning process. If we visualize his model in the form of a compass, one dimension ranges from North (the concrete experiencing of events) to South (abstract conceptualization of ideas). The other dimension extends from West (active experimentation or testing) to East (reflective observations).

These two dimensions are combined to suggest four key learning abilities or processes. As shown in Exhibit 5–6, a complete pattern of learning flows in a circular direction. Beginning at the top, (1) the learner becomes actively involved in new concrete experiences, and (2) through reflective observation examines these experiences from different perspectives (3) to form abstract concepts and generalizations, which (4) lead to theories or assumptions that can be used for active experimentation in problem solving and decision making.

Most people become highly skilled at one or two processes rather than all four. When two adjacent processes are emphasized, a dominant learning style emerges. The four characteristics identified in Exhibit 5–6—divergence, assimilation, convergence, and accommodation—represent distinct personal learning styles.

The Diverger.   Divergers learn best by reflecting on specific experiences and drawing new inferences. The diverger tends to be highly imaginative, excels at brainstorming, and likes involvement in the generation of creative ideas. Divergers have an uncanny ability to view concrete situations from many perspectives. Academically, such learners often are interested in the liberal arts, humanities, and fine arts. Human resource managers are often divergers.

The Assimilator.   With their capability to combine reflective observation and abstract conceptualization, assimilators are good at creating theoretical models. Inductive reasoning is the forte that permits integrating diverse observations into a coherent explanation. Dealing with abstract ideas is the assimilator's domain, more so than seeking practical applications or working with people. Individuals who adopt this learning style are attracted to basic research; in business, you may find them staffing corporate research and planning departments.

━━━━━ **EXHIBIT 5–6**

Kolb's Model of Experiential Learning Styles

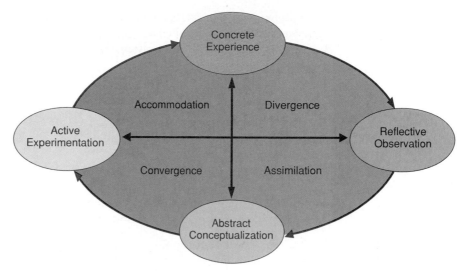

Source: Copyright ©1976 by the Regents of the University of California. Reprinted from *California Management Review,* vol. 18, no. 3, p. 22. By permission of The Regents.

The Converger. Convergers use abstract concepts as a basis for active experimentation. They focus on specific problems, looking for answers and solutions. Like the assimilator, the converger prefers working with ideas and specific tasks more than working with people. Convergers tend to do well in the physical sciences and engineering.

The Accommodator. This style focuses on doing. The accommodator's domain is active experimentation and the carrying out of plans that lead to real experiences. Such people are risk takers, able to adapt quickly to new situations. If a theory does not fit the situation, the accommodator discards the concept and works from the facts. Although at ease with people, accommodators tend to be impatient and assertive. Accommodation is often the dominant style of individuals trained for the business world, especially those who gravitate toward action-oriented management or sales job.

The Need to Combine Skills and Styles

Kolb's research finds managers are oriented toward learning by active experimentation and concrete experience. Many managers are accommodators. By contrast, many business school faculty tend to be strong on reflective observation. This makes them assimilators. Because accommodator managers tend to make fewer inferences from data and are less consistent in their actions than assimilators, both learning styles are necessary within organizations. To blend styles within an organization, David Kolb offers two recommendations.[22]

First, managers and organizations should value and consciously seek learning from experience by budgeting time for the learning process. Second, managers and organizations should value and include those with different learning styles and perspectives. Action-oriented people should be combined with those who are reflective, and those involved in concrete experience should be joined with those who are analytical. Learning can be enhanced when differences are valued.

Two Hemispheres of Learning

One of the emerging thoughts about learning is that brain-hemisphere dominance makes a difference. Neurologists and psychologists have long known that the left hemisphere of the brain controls movements on the right-hand side of the body, and vice versa. Some applied researchers have carried this further by suggesting that our dominant brain hemisphere may play a significant role in how we learn.[23]

The Linear/Systematic Left.   The brain's left hemisphere assimilates information in ordered, systematic ways. The process of analysis and planning (usually a central theme of the business school curriculum) is linear in structure. Accounting systems and management-science quantitative models are based on rational logic. Their underlying assumption is that if data are channeled into a formula or model, a working solution can be found.

Quantification and written language are handled by the left hemisphere of the brain. Many organizational activities are well served by predictability and logic. In stable environments, structured, planned behavior is likely to be effective. However, organizations do not survive and grow without creativity and change.

The Holistic/Relational Right.   Henry Mintzberg suggests that when it comes to running organizations, planning occurs on the left side, managing on the right. He writes, "It may be that management researchers have been looking for the key to management in the lightness of logical analysis whereas perhaps it has always been lost in the darkness of intuition."[24] In fact, Mintzberg adds, "effective managers seem to revel in ambiguity; in complex, mysterious systems with relatively little order."

The world of the right-hemisphere-dominant manager involves holistic, simultaneous, creative learning. In addition, it emphasizes learning from face-to-face verbal exchanges rather than from written reports. Through verbal communication, mangers can interpret nonverbal cues and act simultaneously on real-time data. Synthesis of soft data—impressions, feelings, intuition—provides the basis for acting more than hard-data analysis does.

Hunches and judgment are mental processes from which insights and new possibilities spring forth. With brief time sequences for processing information, action—not reflection—is more the executive norm, as you may recall from Chapter 1. Orderly agendas are atypical in a world beset with interruptions and unplanned activities.

In an article on why and how to develop right-hemisphere intuitive powers, Agor cited the experiences of a number of executives who relied heavily on intuitive decisions. One of them, Paul Cook, founder and president of Raychem Corporation, "replied that nearly all of his decisions were based on intuition, and that the only major decisions he regrets were ones not based on it."[25] Be cautioned, however, that the intuition of which Cook speaks builds on years of experience and learning.

Lifelong Learning

Both the Kolb model of learning styles and the notion of brain-hemisphere specialization emphasize the ongoing nature of individual learning. Life is a series of learning episodes and processes. Those who are managers will find their job involves knowing both how to learn themselves and how to influence the learning of others.

Now that you are familiar with the different ways of learning, you can probably see for yourself why no one theory works all the time across the situations. Applied behavior modification principles, for example, are best used in situations in which reinforcing environmental consequences can be structured. And those who learn best through direct experience are not likely to become reflective/conceptual learners. Each approach and style has its essential place in organizations.

Another special area of learning relates to values and attitudes. In Chapter 4 we discussed the importance of an organization's value system as part of its culture. Here we will focus on individual values and attitudes, which are important because they influence perceptions and impact behavior and performance at work. We turn now to an examination of these two important types of learning.

WHAT ARE PERSONAL VALUES?

Naomi Fujioka was faced with a dilemma. She was about to receive her MBA from a prestigious business school and had two job offers. One offer was to be an investment banker at a very high salary; the other was at a low salary in a nonprofit organization that helps poor children in developing countries. Naomi's choice was heavily influenced by her values. Both jobs were attractive. Naomi valued earning a good income from a challenging position, but she valued even more using her talents to help people in need. She joined the nonprofit organization.

values
Permanent beliefs or ideals held to be important that influence thought and behavior.

Values are stable, enduring beliefs about what is worthwhile that influence thought and behavior. Values are learned, beginning soon after birth, as parents and others indicate that certain behaviors are good an others are bad. Children learn quickly that it is good to be obedient and bad to disobey. They may learn that honesty, cleanliness, politeness, and similar traits and behaviors are good—valuable.

The values of the larger culture and society greatly influence what individuals learn. Parents, teachers, peers, heroes and heroines, the media, art, music, and personal experience also play a role. The country and culture in which one is born, the nature of its economy and political system, and the level of its technology are some of the important variables that influence values. For example, young people in the United States are taught the value of independence, whereas in Japan young people learn the value of dependence and interdependence. In the United States people learn to value individualism, and in Japan they learn to value groups. People in both countries learn to value ambition.

Different cultural values sometimes can create dissonance for those entering a new culture. An illustration of this point is shown in the Dynamics of Diversity box.

Values are relatively stable and deep-seated, and they influence an individual's perceptions of what is good and bad, important and unimportant. For example, if an individual values being on time, he or she will be motivated to behave so as to be on time. The thought of being late may stimulate feelings of stress and a subsequent adrenaline rush to hurry to the appointment.

Types of Values

An early classification of values was developed by Allport and his associates.[26] Their categories included the following:

1. **Theoretical:** Values the discovery of truth and emphasizes critical and rational approaches to problems.
2. **Economic:** Values utility and practicality and emphasizes standard of living.
3. **Aesthetic:** Values form, grace, and harmony and emphasizes the artistic aspects of life.
4. **Social:** Values love of people and altruism and emphasizes concern for others.
5. **Political:** Values power, position, and influence and emphasizes competition and winning.
6. **Religious:** Values unity and people's relationship to the universe and emphasizes high ideals and the search for the purpose of being on earth.

Dynamics of Diversity — *A Woman's Role—Cultural Context Shapes Beliefs*

Reim Men came to the United States from Cambodia in 1974. Because of the upheavals in Cambodia, he lost track of his family. In 1981 they were reunited, and Riem had to make some difficult adjustments in his relationships with his three daughters in America. In Cambodia he and others had learned that women must obey and respect men. Cambodian books, some of which are still read, established rules for a "good woman." She should go to bed later than her husband and get up earlier so that she can perform household tasks. She should acknowledge her husband as always right, even if he is a drunkard, adulterer, or gambler. She should be respectful even if he curses her. The good woman's reward is that she will be considered highly in the community and will go to heaven when she dies. Riem said this all seemed natural and right. Women were considered weak, and their opinions were not valued.

Riem was startled on his arrival in San Francisco to see a young American girl standing on a stage addressing 350 Asian officers at their orientation. She appeared both at ease and competent. This jar to his expectations was just the beginning of many that would alter his views about what was right and natural relative to women and their roles.

It was not until 1980 that Riem could locate his family. His wife, Saphan, a gentle and honest woman who makes friends easily, showed her strength by guiding her five children through several horrible experiences in escaping to the United States. She and her children arrived thin, unkempt, and ill. The children started public school and Saphan took a factory job. His oldest daughter and son, 17 and 18, found part-time work, and his two younger daughters helped with cooking and cleaning. Riem watched startling differences take place in his children. They became extremely happy, as if they had been born anew.

Riem never imagined that his three daughters would grow up to become educated or to run businesses. However, in the Untied States he observed many women doing just that. Today, all of his daughters are independent in the American way. Two own and operate a beauty salon. His youngest daughter worked her way through college and is an interpreter in Superior Court. He says: "I taught them to respect their husbands if their husbands respected them, but to respect themselves first."

Riem says: "Sometimes when Cambodians come here [to the United States] and the wives see other ways, it even can lead to divorce. The husband might say: 'Get me a drink of water.' And the wife might say: 'Get your own water.' And he might say: 'Oh, you've got freedom now, you're a American now!' I tell fathers who come from old ways that if they want their children to respect them, they must earn it. Otherwise the father will end up alone. The old traditions were OK 100 years ago, but not now. This is true not just for the United States or for Cambodia but for the whole world."

Source: "Conversation" (Riem Men with Trin Yarborough), *Los Angeles Times,* March 2, 1996.

Researchers have found that the values people emphasize vary with their occupations. For example, scientists of all kinds are often theoretically inclined; business people—particularly Americans—are high in economic value; artists have a high aesthetic value; psychologists, social workers, and many teachers are inclined toward social values; executives in all fields often have a high political value; and philosophers and the clergy often hold high religious values.

A second way of classifying values was developed by Milton Rokeach.[27] He distinguishes between two sets of values. *Instrumental values* describe desirable beliefs about what behaviors are appropriate in reaching desired goals and ends. Examples include being loving, honest, and ambitious. *Terminal values* describe desirable ends that are worth striving to reach. Examples include a comfortable, prosperous life, world peace, wisdom, and salvation. The Your Turn exercise helps

Instructions: Rank the first column, *ultimate values,* 1 (most important) through 17 (least important). Rank the second column, *means values,* 1 (most important) through 23 (least important). **Suggestion:** Think about what your own past behavior tells about your values. Think about the difference, if any, between what you say you value (ultimate values) and what you do value (means values).

Rank	Ultimate Values	Rank	Means Values
____	Achievement	____	Action-oriented
____	Aesthetics	____	Ambitious
____	Contentment	____	Athletic/physical
____	Equality	____	Brave
____	Excitement	____	Compassionate
____	Harmony	____	Competent
____	Health	____	Considerate
____	Liberty	____	Creative
____	Love	____	Decisive
____	Peace	____	Dependable
____	Pleasure	____	Disciplined
____	Prosperity	____	Energetic
____	Security	____	Friendly
____	Self-esteem	____	Good-natured
____	Social Status	____	Honest
____	Spirituality	____	Intelligent
____	Wisdom	____	Open
		____	Orderly
		____	Outgoing
		____	Rational
		____	Reserved
		____	Spontaneous
		____	Tough-minded

you rank your values. Following Rokeach, rank your ultimate values (similar to what Rokeach calls terminal values). Then rank how you value those traits that help you achieve your ultimate values. Compare your rankings with those of someone who knows you well.

Changes in Values

Although values are relatively enduring, they can and do shift over time.[28] Important local, national, and world events lead to changing attitudes, needs, and values. Young people in the United States during the prosperous 1960s valued their right to rebel against authority and seek individual happiness. Economic conditions grew tighter during the early 1970s, jobs were scarcer, and young people became more conservative and conformed more closely to traditional organizational values. Prosperity returned for many during the 1980s, and people tended to value money and the acquisition of material goods. According to social researcher Daniel Yankelovich, "The shift from the Eighties to the Nineties has turned out to be about as abrupt as you can imagine."[29] He says: "People are tired of one group of people making points off another. And their intuition tells them that the trouble we're in is moral, that there really is such a thing as decadence." Whether this apparent shift in values will be sustained and how it will manifest itself remain to be seen.

An awareness of values can help managers understand and predict the behavior of others. For example, they would know that workers in their thirties, fifties, and sixties are more likely to be accepting of authority than are workers in their forties. They might reasonably predict that older workers are more likely to be loyal to the organization than are those who are younger, although this may be changing as our earlier discussion of a changing social contract indicated.

WHAT ARE ATTITUDES?

attitude
Readiness to respond in a certain way to a person, object, idea, or situation.

When people say "I like my job," or "I'm proud to be a part of this company," or "I'm against unions," they are expressing their attitudes. An **attitude** is a readiness to respond in a certain way to a person, object, idea, or situation. Attitudes differ from values in that they are more specific and can be less stable and enduring. Although some attitudes may remain relatively stable over time, others are subject to change with the accumulation of new information and experience.

Attitudes have three components: cognition, affect, and behavior.[30] The cognitive component is beliefs and values about the perceived target. The affective component includes the feelings associated with the target. The behavioral component stems from the attitude and refers to an intention to behave in a certain way.

These three components can be illustrated by Jon Wainwright's attitude toward his boss. Assume he believes his boss is unfair and authoritarian, and Jon values honesty and independence. Jon's beliefs and values create feelings of dislike for his boss, and he intends to seek a transfer. Jon's attitude (beliefs, values, feelings, and intentions) will influence his behavior.

Although attitudes influence behavior, predictions about actual behavior cannot be made with certainty. For example, although Jon intends to change jobs, he may choose to suppress his feelings and stay on the job because he does not have a good alternative. In such a case, Jon would likely feel frustrated and would experience what is known as cognitive dissonance.

cognitive dissonance
A state of inconsistency between an individuals' attitudes and behavior.

Cognitive dissonance is a term used by Leon Festinger to describe a state of inconsistency between an individual's attitudes and behavior.[31] The discomfort experienced by people feeling cognitive dissonance leads to efforts to reduce the tension by (1) changing the attitude, (2) changing behavior, or (3) rationalizing the inconsistency.

For example, Jon might change his perceptions to emphasize his boss's positive traits and minimize his negative traits, making his overall attitude more positive. Or, he might transfer to another job. Alternatively, he might reason that part of working is putting up with difficult superiors. The effect of each of these three alternatives would be to lessen the tension caused by Jon's conflicting attitudes and behavior.

Attitudes Drive Productivity

It was noted earlier that attitudes influence behavior, but our discussion of cognitive dissonance illustrates that behavior can also influence attitudes. For example, if Jon behaves a certain way to please his boss, the response might be positive and Jon might find his attitude of disliking changing to liking. In this case, his own behavior would have contributed to his change in attitude.

Employee attitudes toward their job and company are important because they can influence productivity and satisfaction. An employee's general attitude toward his or her job is called job satisfaction. Research has shown a negative relationship between job satisfaction and absenteeism and turnover.[32] A similar and even stronger relationship is found between absenteeism and turnover and organization commitment, which is an indication of how strongly an individual identifies with her or his organization.

Employee attitudes are important enough for many companies to periodically measure them by means of attitude surveys. These surveys ask employees to rate their attitudes toward their work, pay and benefits, supervisor, upper management, peer groups, opportunities for advancement, and other items. Effective managers augment these formal survey with informal observations and indirect indicators such as absenteeism and turnover. The value of such surveys will depend largely on how skillfully and effectively managers use these results to improve identified problem areas.

In this chapter so far we have seen that people vary in their abilities, perceive and learn differently from one another, and vary in their values and attitudes. It is not surprising that they also behave differently. We turn now to the concept of personality, which is another factor that managers must consider in managing a diverse work force.

HOW DO PERSONALITIES DIFFER?

personality
The set of traits and behaviors that characterizes an individual.

Personality is the set of traits and behaviors that characterizes an individual. The longer and better we know someone, the more likely we are to recognize the pattern of how that individual responds to various people and situations. The clearer and more enduring the pattern of responses, the more we attribute it to the individual's personality.

In the opening vignette, Ian McDonald and Alex Gruenwald responded differently to their layoffs. Ian felt angry, depressed and anxious. Alex felt more optimistic and even excited. Ian and Alex are different personalities, and their supervisor, Howard Smith, should interact with each differently. Managers and others use personality to understand and predict an individual's behavior and to summarize the essence of an individual.

Heredity and Learning Determine Personality

Personality emerges over time from the interaction of genetic and environmental factors. To a large extent, genes predetermine an individual's physical characteristics, and they contribute to other important personality characteristics such as intelligence and temperament. Gender, race, size, appearance, and even health and energy are influenced significantly by genes.[33]

Although heredity plays a role in the development of personality, it is clear that learning is also vitally important. One of the major characteristics that distinguishes humans from other species is that people have a significantly greater capacity to learn, remember, and think about what has happened in the past, is happening in the present, and might happen in the future. We have already seen how people learn, including how they acquire knowledge, abilities, values, and attitudes. Individuals learn their own motives. Over time, their patterns of behavior become identified as their personalities.

People's personalities become clearer and more stable as they grow older. Personality can change and may do so slowly over the years. The more set an individual's personality becomes, the greater the need for conscious effort to modify it. For example, someone who is used to arguing strongly for her point of view would likely find it difficult to passively listen to those who differed.

The "Big Five" Personality Factors

Because personality is comprised of many elements, psychologists work to identify critical factors that help people observe and understand an individual's style and differences. One such set of factors is referred to by some psychologists as the "Big Five."[34] Each factor represents one aspect of an individual's personality and style. Here are the five factors.

- *Expressive Style:* How individuals express themselves verbally and behaviorally. For example, people's behavior may range from quiet and reserved to talkative and outgoing.

- *Interpersonal Style:* How individuals behave while interacting with others. For example, people's behavior may range from being cool and distant to warm and close.

- *Work Style:* How people work and meet responsibilities. For example, individuals' styles may range from performing work in a detailed and structured manner to a general and spontaneous way.

- *Emotional Style:* How people express their emotions. For example, individuals' behaviors may range from unemotional and stable to highly emotional and volatile.

- *Intellectual Style:* How individuals learn, think, and decide. For example, individuals' styles may range from learning, thinking, and deciding in simple and traditional ways to complex and novel ways.

Each factor helps us to know what behavior patterns to observe in understanding someone's personality. For example, the expressive style factor leads us to observe whether a person is generally quiet and reserved, or talkative and outgoing, or somewhere in between. Each of the other factors helps in similar fashion. Key elements of each factor combine to provide an overall understanding of an individual's personality. This ability to understand different personalities is helpful to managers in being better able to predict an individual's behavior.

For example, assume a manager, Darrel, is deciding which of two people he will appoint as a task force leader. The task will be to develop a new approach to marketing an established product. He has observed one person, Wayne, who is quiet and reserved and interacts relatively little with his work peers. He is very bright, a hard worker, and very reliable in doing detailed, structured work. He has never been observed to express either positive or negative emotion.

The other person, Ursula, is talkative and outgoing. She interacts easily with others and has a warm, outgoing style. She is sometimes careless about details and is easily bored with repetitive, routine work. However, she enjoys solving new problems and makes good decisions in ambiguous situations. Her peers can tell what Ursula is feeling because she is quite expressive, but she has not let her emotions get out of control at work even when under stress. The more difficult the problem, the more she enjoys it.

You are correct if you predict that Darrel decided to appoint Ursula. She fits the team leader role better than Wayne. You can see that Darrel used the "Big Five" personality factors to observe relevant aspects of Wayne's and Ursula's behavior.

Different Psychological Types and Cognitive Styles

One of the earliest theories of personality was developed by Carl Jung.[35] A mother–daughter team, Katherine Briggs and Isabel Briggs-Myers, developed a personality test called the Myers-Briggs Type Indicator (MBTI) to measure the traits posited by Jung.[36] Today it is the most widely used personality test in the United States and is used by many major corporations primarily to develop awareness of and sensitivity to the differences among people.[37]

Basic to Jung's framework is the differentiation between introversion and extroversion. Those who are *introverts* are more oriented toward their inner thoughts and feelings. They like to work quietly and without interruption. *Extroverts* are oriented toward the outer world of people and things. They enjoy communicating verbally with people and prefer to experience life rather than reflect on it.

Jung also differentiates between perceivers and judgers. Those who are *judgers* like to live in an orderly, planned way. They prefer control, structure, and closure. *Perceivers,* on the other hand, prefer flexibility and spontaneity. They enjoy gathering information and adapting to life as it unfolds.

cognitive style
The way an individual perceives and processes information.

Cognitive style describes how individuals perceive and process information. Cognitive style is complex and can be defined and measured several ways. We will concentrate on one way that is based on Carl Jung's theory of psychological types.

According to Jung, individuals develop, mostly unconsciously, preferred ways of gathering information and evaluating it to make decisions. The two opposite ways of gathering information are through a sensing method and by intuition, and the two opposite ways of evaluating information are thinking and feeling. Exhibit 5–7 illustrates these alternative processes.

Obtaining Information by Sensation/Intuition.   Managers who collect information by sensing seek details, hard facts, and quantitative reports. *Sensers* like to apply structures for organizing data logically, step by step. They are especially comfortable working within a structure of organizational policies and rules that provide clear guidelines for action. Senser managers learn best from concrete experience; they can be thought of as left-brain-hemisphere processors.

Intuitive managers disavow routine, structured reports and rely more on hunches and nonverbal perceptions of problems. Data collection by this type of manager often appears to be nonsystematic, with considerable jumping back and forth. *Intuitives* excel at synthesis—that is, taking a large amount of data from a number of sources and drawing seemingly spontaneous conclusions. These managers are imaginative, futuristic, and often good at drawing creative ideas out of others. They are more dependent on the right-brain hemisphere.

EXHIBIT 5–7

*Alternative Processes for
Handling Information*

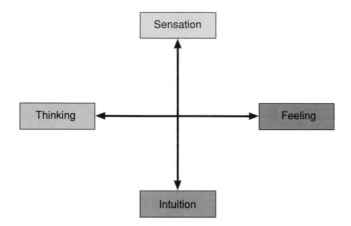

Evaluating Information by Thinking/Feeling.   Two opposite ways of processing and evaluating information are *thinking* and *feeling*. Evaluation is the process of integrating information to solve a problem or to make a decision. Managers who depend on thinking use analysis and rational logic as the basis for problem solving. They tend to be unemotional in applying data to models or problem-solving techniques. The forte of these managers is the use of the scientific method (systematic evaluation of empirical data), devoid of personal considerations.

Managers who arrive at decisions through feeling rely heavily on person-centered values. They personalize their evaluations and are sensitive to the concerns, ideas, and feelings of those around them. Placing major emphasis on the human aspects of problems, these managers dislike creating conflict. They value harmony and tend to conform to the wishes of others rather than consider alternatives based on logic or analysis.

Four Types of Problem-Solving Behaviors.   These different ways of gathering and evaluating information combine to from a matrix of four problem-solving behaviors. Exhibit 5–8 illustrates how these four personality types emerge. Each type has its virtues and shortcomings, but in a complex organization all are necessary The following descriptions are based on research into the problem-solving behaviors of managers.[38]

Sensation Thinkers (ST).   Steve Tinker is the archetypal bureaucrat, concerned with formulating and enforcing rules. Because sensation and thinking dominate his functions, Steve is persistent, yet decisive. He weighs costs and benefits, plans a logical schedule, and has an infinite capacity to absorb and remember details.

Steve is a hard worker, a good coordinator, and a dependable leader. His penchant for analysis and logic makes him quite predictable. However, as a sensation thinker, Steve tends to become impatient with those who aren't equally detailed, organized, and rational. He avoids abstractions and seldom provides feedback to others unless it is based on measured perfromance. Steve is so concerned with preserving acceptable practices and tradition that he overlooks possibilities for creative improvement.

Intuitive Thinkers (IT).   Ida Tucker exemplifies the intuitive thinker. She is a manager who looks ahead, always searching for innovative possibilities. Although she tends to be impersonal, Ida is quick to analyze the power dynamics within an

━━━━ **EXHIBIT 5–8**

Four Cognitive Styles

Functions of gathering and evaluating information combine to identify four personality types.

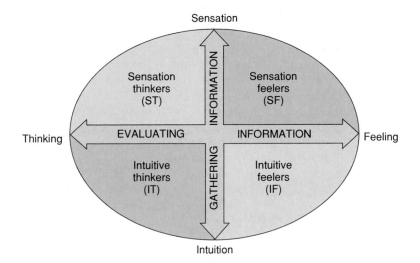

organization. She is noted for her intellectual capabilities and pioneering ideas. Ida is a great designer of new methods and projects. She then depends on her staff to flesh out the details of her proposals.

Once a project has been initiated, Ida relinquishes its administration to someone better suited to establishing organizational routines. Gifted in abstract creativity, Ida sometimes is insensitive to the personal needs and wishes of others. Nevertheless, as an intuitive thinker, she responds to the ideas and problems of others when they are logical and reasonable. She finds it difficult to accept anything other than competent, professional performance. Ida frequently expects more than others are prepared to deliver.

Sensation Feelers (SF). Sensation feelers are exemplified by Shawn Field, who is a methodological manager. She is great at analysis based on detailed observation. Shawn deals efficiently with here-and-now problems. Her decisions and actions result from quick interpretation of the facts. She loves to find the causes of problems in standardized operations and excels at extracting higher efficiency from programmed procedures.

Yet Shawn does not like to see changes sweep too far in new directions. She would rather fix an old system than conceptualize a new approach. Shawn generally gets along well with co-workers. She reinforces good performance by giving praise, writing memos of thanks, and publicly acknowledging others' accomplishments.

Intuitive Feelers (IF). Ian Fuller is the quintessential intuitive feeler. He is a charismatic leader who communicates fluently and is quick to visualize possibilities for improvement. He draws out ideas from others and always consults co-workers before moving ahead on significant actions. Given the freedom to manage, Ian creates a high level of esprit de corps within his team. Ian believes in psychological rewards and makes sure they come in timely response to his workers' emotional needs.

Yet, Ian himself needs recognition from others. He tends to back away from his personal ideas when they appear to conflict with view held by esteemed others. He is very popular among his co-workers, but because he wishes to retain this popularity, Ian is at times hesitant to act. Sometimes the opportunity of the moment is lost as a result of his indecision.

The behavior patterns of these four managers indicate extreme personalities. While managers may tend toward either sensation or intuition, thinking or feeling, usually their dominant combinations do not preclude use of the other functions. In fact, most managers rely on all four functions to some degree.

Still, the message for organizations is clear: To be effective across the entire range of problems—those that demand change and those that require stability, those that call for quantitative analysis and those that require creative thought—an organization needs all four types of managers. In the ideal management team, individual styles complement one another. A built-in system of checks and balances is possible when team members are of different personality types.

Personality Traits

Researchers have identified other personality attributes that are relevant for behavior in organizations.[39] In this section we discuss several of these traits.

locus of control
The degree to which people believe that they, rather than exteral forces, determine their own lives.

Locus of control is a dimension of personality that explains the degree to which people believe that they, rather than external forces, determine their own lives. [40] People who believe that what happens to them depends on themselves are *internals*. Those who believe that what happens is caused by fate, luck, or other external forces are *externals*. For example, assume two employees, one an internal and one an external, both fail to get a raise. The internal is likely to attribute this to his or her own performance, while the external will probably blame an unfair boss or some other outside force. Internals are likely to perform better on jobs that require initiative and offer autonomy. Externals are more likely to seek structured jobs with clear direction.

authoritarianism
The degree to which a person believes that status and power differences are appropriate in an organization.

Authoritarianism is the degree to which a person believes that status and power differences are appropriate in an organization.[41] People high in authoritarianism tend to be autocratic and demanding with subordinates but are likely to accept orders and directions from superiors without question. High-authoritarian types would not fit well in organizations that require flexibility and quick change or sensitivity to people and cooperative behavior. They would fit better in a highly structured organization that values conformity.

dogmatism
The degree of flexibility or rigidity of a person's views.

Dogmatism refers to the degree of flexibility or rigidity of a person's views. Those high in dogmatism tend to be rigid and closed. They often view the world as threatening and cling to their beliefs. People low in dogmatism are more open-minded and receptive to considering views that differ from their own.

Machiavellianism
A personality attribute that describes the extent to which a person manipulates others for personal gain.

Machiavellianism is a personality attribute that describes the extent to which a person manipulates others for personal gain. Named after Niccolo Machiavelli, who authored *The Prince* in the sixteenth century, the concept refers to a rational, pragmatic approach to situations and emotional distance from subordinates.[42] Machiavelli believed that the end justifies the means. Psychologists have developed instruments designed to compare a person's orientation with that of Machiavelli. High "Machs" perform better in loosely structured situations and when they can interact face to face with others.

risk propensity
A person's willingness to take risks.

Risk propensity refers to a person's willingness to take risks. People with a high propensity for risk make decisions faster and are willing to take chances. Risk-aversive people are more cautious, make decisions more carefully, and try to minimize risk. High-risk managers may make costly decisions, although they also may enable their organization to respond quickly to fast-changing environments. Low-risk managers may also make costly decisions if they respond too slowly to changing competitive conditions. The appropriateness of each depends on the organizational situation.

self-esteem
The judgment one makes about one's own worth.

self-monitoring
The degree to which people are sensitive to others and adapt their own behavior to meet external expectations and situational needs.

Self-esteem is the judgment one makes about one's own worth. People with high self-esteem tend to like themselves, have high expectations for success, and feel confident they can achieve their goals. Those with low self-esteem lack confidence and look to others for praise and reinforcement. In so doing, they tend to avoid conflict and conform to expected norms.[43]

Self-monitoring refers to the degree to which people are sensitive to others and adapt their behavior to meet external expectations and situational needs.[44] High self-monitors are similar to actors in that they can assume a personality to satisfy an audience. They are adept at separating their private from their public selves. People who are low self-monitors reveal themselves much more clearly and tend to be themselves regardless of the situation or others' expectations. The high self-monitor may be more flexible in interacting with different types of people.

MANAGING IN TURBULENT TIMES—A SECOND LOOK

Outwardly there are many similarities between Ian McDonald and Alex Gruenwald. Both were 19 years with Thompson Electronics (TE) having joined right out of college, both were married with three children, and both had advanced to mid-level management positions. But the two responded very differently to the same situational stimulus of being laid off from their jobs with TE. Ian reacted bitterly and with anger toward the company. He was depressed and fearful because he perceived that his abilities and talents were only of relevance to TE. Furthermore, he had money worries as his children would start entering universities within two years, and his home mortgage payments were over $3000 per month. Ian felt so panicked that he felt helpless in organizing and undertaking the search for a new career, even though he would be given six months' severance pay. His negative attitudes and self-doubts interfered with his job search and it took nearly a year to finally find a lesser paying job in a non-managerial capacity with a larger company.

Alex, by contrast felt secure in his abilities and perceived his layoff as an opportunity to seek new challenges and develop new competencies. He couldn't wait to use the time off to explore new career possibilities and to enjoy more time with his family. Within four months he had taken a vice presidency with a technology start-up company that was growing fast but facing cash-flow problems. Because the organization was still small (Alex was employee number 22), he assumed a broad range of managerial responsibilities with the expectation that he could contribute in ways that would help create and shape the firm. Although the venture was risky, Alex's attitude was that he would learn and discover if he had what it took to be CEO material.

When Alex and Ian had lunch together some 18 months after being laid off, they had very different stories to tell. Alex could easily see that his friend's outlook on life was even more clouded and confused than when they first heard the news from Howard Smith.

SUMMARY

People enter organizations with different abilities and motives. A manager's role is to achieve the best person–job fit possible, which means matching the individual's abilities and motives with the job requirements and rewards. Each individual develops a psychological contract with the organization, which includes expectations about what each party will give and receive.

The perceptual process includes the selection, organization, and interpretation of sensory stimuli. Individuals often perceive differently from one another, and this makes communication in organizations more difficult. Selective perception, stereotyping, halo effects, and projection are perceptual errors that make managing behavior in organizations more difficult. Attributions are individuals' efforts to explain the reasons for behavior. Externals look for causes outside themselves; internals look within. A common attributional biasing error is for people to blame their own failures on external factors and credit internal factors for their successes.

Individuals learn by responding to positive and negative reinforcers in their environment, by observing others and imitating certain behaviors, and by using their cognitive skills to observe, reason, and choose an appropriate course of action. People develop different styles of learning. Some learn by experiencing and others learn by observing and reflecting. Individuals also favor either the left (linear/systematic) side or the right (holistic/relational) side of their brains in learning and problem solving. Learning is a lifelong activity, made even more important by today's fast-changing world.

Values and attitudes shape people's perceptions and behavior. Values are relatively stable and enduring. They guide people in deciding how to behave and what to seek. Attitudes are more specific and subject to change. They include cognitive, affective, and intentional components and represent how people feel about others, objects, and situations. Attitudes about jobs and organizations influence attendance, turnover, and sometimes commitment and productivity. For this reason, managers should monitor employee attitudes about important organizational variables.

Each individual develops a unique personality, which is the set of traits and behaviors that characterizes a person. Managers who are sensitive to these differences are better able to understand and predict their employees' behavior. However, because people are so complex, complete understanding is an elusive goal.

Key Concepts

person–job fit, *p. 148*

psychological contract, *p. 148*

social contract, *p. 149*

ability, *p. 149*

aptitude, *p. 149*

perception, *p. 150*

figure, *p. 153*

ground, *p. 153*

perceptual closure, *p. 153*

frame of reference, *p. 155*

selective perception, *p. 155*

stereotype, *p. 155*

halo effect, *p. 156*

projection, *p. 156*

attribution, *p. 156*

distinctiveness, *p. 156*

consistency, *p. 156*

consensus, *p. 157*

attributional error, *p. 157*

self-serving bias, *p. 157*

learning, *p. 158*

intelligence, *p. 159*

classical conditioning, *p. 160*

operant conditioning, *p. 160*

Premack principle, *p. 161*

social learning theory, *p. 162*

cognitive learning, *p. 162*

insight, *p. 162*

discrimination, *p. 163*

generalization, *p. 163*

values, *p. 167*

attitude, *p. 170*

cognitive dissonance, *p. 170*

personality, *p. 171*

cognitive style, *p. 173*

locus of control, *p. 176*

authoritarianism, *p. 176*

dogmatism, *p. 176*

Machiavellianism, *p. 176*

risk propensity, *p. 176*

self-esteem, *p. 177*

self-monitoring, *p. 177*

Questions for Study and Discussion

1. a. Give one example of a good person–job fit and give one example of a poor person–job fit. What alternatives can be considered in improving the poor person–job fit?

   b. Assume Joanne Kraus has just been hired as a management trainee with a large regional bank. She is a management major with a 3.6 grade point average from a well-known business school. She is 22 and plans to have a career in banking. What might be some of the elements of her psychological contract?

2. Explain what is meant by this statement: "Some of what you see in me is really in you, and some of what I see in you is in me." Give some examples illustrating the statement.

3. What are some alternative ways of responding to someone who has different perceptions than yours? What is likely to be the impact of each on your interactions with that person?

4. Give one example of a self-attribution and one example of an attribution about another person.

5. Give an example of how the manager of a data processing software unit might apply each of these three learning theories: (1) behavioral conditioning, (2) social learning theory, and (3) cognitive theory.

6. Albert Einstein attributed his famous theory of relativity to sudden insight. Many executives say that when it comes to personnel and product-related problems, their intuition serves them better than objective, rational study. What is your view? Are insight and intuition unrelated to analytical reasoning? Provide illustrations of how differences in the nature of the problems invite either left-brain-hemisphere or right-brain-hemisphere approaches.

7. What are some alternative ways of finding out the values of another person? How about your own? How reliable is each approach?

8. Can attitudes be changed? If so, how? If not, why?

9. Develop a brief job description that would appeal to each of the following types of managers.

   a. sensation thinker

   b. sensation feeler

   c. intuitive thinker

   d. intuitive feeler

EXPERIENTIAL EXERCISE

Exploring Stereotypes

This exercise offers an opportunity to explore both some of your own stereotypes and those of others.

1. As individuals, give three to five one- or two-word responses to each item in the statement below. These are the words/images that come to mind when I think about the following words:

   a. Male
   b. Female
   c. Asian
   d. African-American
   e. Hispanic
   f. Caucasian
   g. Homosexual
   h. Worker
   i. Manager
   j. Executive

2. In groups of four to six people, share and discuss your responses.

EXPERIENTIAL EXERCISE

Diversity Dilemma: A Role Play[45]

Procedure.   Form groups of 4 to 6 people. Read the "situation" described below, then decide who will role play Jeff and who Daneisha as the two meet to discuss her request. (20–30 minutes total.)

Situation.   Jeff Birnbaum faces a dilemma. Daneisha Tinson has just asked him to recommend her for the summer substitute program for upper-management secretaries. Being accepted in that program would give Daneisha both experience and visibility that could help her gain a promotion to an executive secretary position.

Jeff is 42 and the compensation manager for Bunker National Bank, which employs 9,500 people. He values employee development and is a strong advocate of affirmative action and equal employment opportunity. He is Caucasian.

Daneisha is 26 and has worked for five years at Bunker National. She started as a file clerk, was promoted in six months to the word processing department, and two years later was promoted to secretary. Jeff rates her performance as outstanding. She is highly skilled, works hard, and can be trusted to produce top-quality work.

Proud of her African-American heritage, Daneisha enjoys wearing colorful African-style prints, headwraps, and jewelry to work. Jeff knows the senior bank executives, who are all men, are ultraconservative. They wear dark suits, white shirts, and club ties and care about presenting the right image to clients and employees. Their executive secretaries all wear tailored dresses and suits. Jeff wonders if Daneisha would be accepted on the executive floor. He has no doubts about her ability and potential but wonders if her expression of ethnic identification might lead to rejection. If all others must conform, why not Daneisha? Jeff knows the clash between corporate and ethnic culture could lead to trouble. He wonders what he should say to Daneisha.

Role Play.   Two people enact the conversation Jeff has with Daneisha (within your small group). The following questions may provide ideas for the meeting.

1. Should Jeff recommend Daneisha for the summer substitute program? Why or why not?

2. What, if anything, should Jeff tell Daneisha in communicating his opinion?

3. Is this an individual issue or a corporate issue?

The Crowder Company[46]

Fred Ingalls, executive vice president of Crowder Company, felt anxious and tense. He and James Crowder, CEO and president, frequently seemed to clash. They disagreed so much that Fred wondered if he should resign.

Jim Crowder was 51. He started his own machine tool company in 1973. The company grew steadily and became one of the biggest in the industry. Crowder Company was usually profitable, although profits varied with economic conditions and the cycles of the machine tool industry. Jim had personally become quite wealthy when he took the company public. In addition to being CEO, he was the largest shareholder. Jim was seen by most people as focused, determined, and intelligent. He was considered by most to be a "straight talker."

The Promotion and Clash of Views. Fred Ingalls, 38, has a BS in Engineering and an MBA. He was 27 when he started with Crowder. He quickly moved ahead and, until nine months ago, was director of engineering. At that time he was promoted two levels to executive vice president because his predecessor had unexpectedly resigned. Fred had not interacted much with Jim Crowder because Jim had delegated most operational matters to his EVP, and Fred himself had reported to a vice president. Fred's perceptions of Jim had changed during the past months, and he suspected Jim's views of him had also changed.

A major issue between the two dealt with tariffs. Jim believed strongly that the industry needed protection, and he spent large amounts of time with industry groups and in Washington D.C. promoting tariff protection. Fred, on the other hand, contended that Crowder Company could compete without protection, and that it should focus on becoming more efficient and effective in serving customers and in developing new products.

Jim was startled and disappointed with Fred's response to his views. Jim said Fred was naive and inexperienced in strategic matters, and that his ideas were impractical. He indicated clearly that he, as CEO, was the one to be concerned with such decisions. Jim even said that if Fred wanted to question his (Jim's) competence, he should do so directly instead of insinuating indirectly.

Fred Works Quietly Behind the Scenes. Because Jim was so vehement, Fred decided to back away and to avoid discussions in which he differed with Jim. Fred disliked arguments, so he decided to execute his duties by conforming closely to Crowder policies and ways of operating. However, because Jim was gone frequently, Fred interpreted policies rather broadly. He began to quietly take small steps to reshape the organization along the lines he thought appropriate. For example, he had begun to flatten the organization by eliminating a level of management. He also influenced the sales organization to become less product oriented and more focused on meeting customers' changing needs.

When Jim questioned Fred on some of these changes, Fred would back away from the discussion to avoid bombastic arguments. He would focus for awhile on areas of less interest to Jim but which would still help move Crowder toward improved performance.

However, Fred became increasingly aware of how much his own philosophy differed from Jim's. He felt disturbed that he could not talk openly with Jim, and he observed that the two interacted less and less. Fred wondered what the limits of his own authority were. Even though he feared a repeat of previously uncomfortable discussions, he suggested to Jim that they meet to discuss their respective areas of authority and responsibility. Jim agreed and said they would meet as soon as possible. Three weeks passed and Fred had heard nothing.

Jim Begins to Rethink Fred's Appointment. Conversely, Jim was bothered by Fred's behavior since he became EVP. One of Jim's first concerns followed Fred's recommendation to spend large sums of money on new equipment. Jim questioned the payout period and the payoff of such an investment. He also thought Fred exhibited poor judgment in his willingness to abandon Crowder's industry relationships and the protective measures achieved over time in exchange for a gamble on a big investment in a volatile market. Jim decided Fred wasn't willing to support his own case because he quickly backed down when Jim challenged him.

Jim was also irritated at some of the organizational changes that had been made. He would like to have discussed some of these with Fred to help his own thinking on the moves, but he could never pin Fred down to a clear position. Jim was wondering just how much authority he could give Fred. Jim felt particularly annoyed at what he perceived to be Fred's building support for his own ideas behind Jim's back. Changes were made that would be difficult to undo. Jim did not understand why Fred was not as direct with him as he was with Fred. Jim enjoyed an energetic go-at-'em exchange in which viewpoints could be tested. But Fred just didn't seem willing to stand up for his views. Jim pondered how to work with a man like Fred and wondered if he should continue in the executive vice president role.

Discussion Questions

1. What is going on in this case?
2. How do you think Jim and Fred perceive each other? How do they perceive themselves?
3. What do you think each should do? Why?

Chapter 6

Motivation and Organizational Learning

LEARNING OBJECTIVES

After studying this chapter, you should be able to:

- Identify two need-based theories of motivation and describe how each influences approach–avoidance behaviors in a work setting.

- Explain why removing sources of job dissatisfaction will not necessarily rekindle the motivation to work.

- Distinguish among the motives of achievement, power, and affiliation and tell how each affects success as an entrepreneur or manager.

- Relate the three basic factors of expectancy theory to typical work conditions that increase or diminish motivation.

- Distinguish between satisfaction and motivation and indicate how the two are related.

- Explain why equity evaluations (and perceptions of work justice) can alleviate motivational problems.

- Tell why motivation theories based on individual behavior are increasingly inadequate for explaining behavior in multicultural organizations.

- Describe three examples to show the relationship between motivation and learning.

CHUCK MITCHELL OPENS DISPIRITED HEARTS AT GTO

Chuck Mitchell is an idealist and utopian leader. A swimming scholarship brought him to Florida State University, where his academic achievement and senior thesis on utopian communities won him a Wilson Fellowship to undertake a Ph.D. at Yale. But before he could head north, Mitchell became so intrigued with creating utopia that he led a group of students and young professors to buy 240 acres and begin constructing 16 houses that summer. Construction skills learned at the commune and his natural style of leading by doing and building teams propeled him into launching his own construction and real estate development company, which he named Mad Dog.

The success of Mad Dog enabled Chuck Mitchell to invest $60,000 in a friend's start-up business, GTO Inc., a Tallahassee maker of automatic gate openers. Five years later, Lester M. Tabb, the charismatic founder of GTO, died of a heart attack. For five months Tabb's daughter Dana tried to run the company, but at the request of the 16-member board of directors and his own sense of commitment to friends who were GTO investors, Mitchell stepped in to provide leadership.

He found GTO to be an economically troubled and dispirited organization. Average monthly sales of $250,000 was $35,000 short of break-even. Its creditworthiness was nil, and suppliers would ship only on a cash-on-delivery basis. Perhaps worse was the situation among employees on the shop floor. Tabb, it turned out, managed by intimidation. He bicycled through the factory shouting epithets at workers to "work faster." He stressed people and burned them out.

Mitchell first met with all employees on December 7, 1993. In his opening remarks he said, "I want you all to know that I am going to be committed to making GTO a success." He saw employees rolling their eyes; a couple of hands went up and Mitchell nodded at one.

"How long? How long will it take?" the employee wanted to know. This was the question all wanted answered.

"Many of us make the mistake that we feel as if we have to act like we know it all. But the bottom line is that you've got to look within yourself and within the people around you to come up with answers," responded Mitchell. But sensing they wanted more, he summarized, "Give us three months." Mitchell was quickly making a diagnosis that the firm's major inefficiency was its inability to tap the inner reserves of its people. As he investigated more, he found waste everywhere. The company was in a crisis that demanded a triage solution.

Lester Tabb's style was command and control, to tell people what to do. By contrast, Chuck Mitchell managed by asking questions such as, "What aspects of our organization and structure prevent you from being able to do your job better?" He asked for suggestions and advice and quickly gained a sense of the high priority items. But he also took care of the little things, believing, "The little things often mean more to people, and they show that management cares about everybody." He quickly bought coffee, sugar, and creamer to make available to employees; as a health nut Tabb didn't believe in drinking coffee. The roof leaked, so he had it patched. He told employees they could bring in their cars and work on them on weekends using GTO's tools and equipment. He granted people flexibility in their work schedules.

In less than a year profitability was restored, and employee turnover declined substantially. Within two years sales had improved to the point that Mitchell was having employees design a new building. Through his approach to management, Chuck Mitchell took care of employees' basic needs, gave them a sense of belonging to a viable enterprise, rekindled pride and an achievement motive in many, and was emphasizing organizational learning for faster improvement.

Source: Joshua Hyatt, "Real-World Reengineering," *Inc.* (April 1995), pp. 40–53.

What does a person bring to a job and organization? When recruiters interview job applicants, they typically look for indicators that an applicant is both able and willing to perform tasks that contribute to organizational needs and goals. On the able dimension, a person usually is hired because of the competence he or she brings to a particular type of job—the lessons learned from past experiences. The competent person has the aptitude, ability, and self-confidence to perform in that job and to continue learning, as you learned in Chapter 5.

Beyond competence, employers also look for evidence of how willing a person is to undertake required tasks, to learn specific skills and job knowledge, and to enthusiastically tackle assignments. Willingness involves the motivation to focus on the tasks that add value to the organization and to devote enough energy to them that they are done well.

Chuck Mitchell did not hire a new crew of employees when he took over as the chief executive of GTO, the $4 million small business. But he trusted the capabilities of the people he inherited and, in the process of quickly responding to their concerns and suggestions, rekindled their willingness to work diligently and creatively to improve the failing company. Mitchell drew on what they had learned, focused their efforts on reengineering the company, and helped them be motivated to succeed. By tapping into employees' willingness to solve problems and work as a team who had a vested interest in the performance of the organization, GTO turned around from losing $300,000 at the time he took over to recording a profit of nearly $500,000 in Mitchell's first year. In less than two years he was asking employees for ideas on what features to design into a new building, thinking, "Can you imagine the pride they'd feel driving past it."[1]

As demonstrated by Chuck Mitchell's success at GTO, this chapter focuses on the basic motivational factors that can energize a person's work, the distractions that compete for attention, and on how learning affects motives. Several theories have evolved to help explain different facets of motivation. We begin with the concept that people have different needs that direct their behavior. Some of these needs depend on personal circumstances and outside events. Needs can cause people to seek out experiences that enrich their lives. Alternatively, needs can trigger behavior to avoid threatening conditions and feelings of deprivation. Other needs are learned from rewarding experiences. These learned needs become relatively persistent motives that influence a person to seek out experiences that satisfy a particular need, such as the need for achievement or power.

A different explanation of motivation focuses on expectancies, or people's expectations about whether they can affect performance outcomes and how closely desired rewards are linked to performance. People also consider the equity of how they are treated, and those evaluations help determine whether they will appear motivated or not. As you develop in the workplace and perhaps find yourself with managerial responsibilities, you will be more productive if you understand the needs, expectations, and conditions that enable individuals and groups to learn and exhibit qualities of effective motivation.

HOW DO NEEDS AFFECT APPROACH–AVOIDANCE BEHAVIORS?

Throughout most of the twentieth century, managers have tried to find the key that unlocks people's motivation to work. With the help of research, we have come to realize that motivation involves several distinct elements. It is not simply a case of some people having it and others not.

motivation
A conscious decision to perform one or more activities with greater effort than other competing activities.

Motivation involves a conscious decision to perform one or more activities with greater effort than other activities competing for attention. This definition of motivation contains three elements: (1) some need, motive, or goal that triggers action; (2) a selection process that directs the choice of action; and (3) the intensity of effort that is applied to the chosen action. In essence, motivation governs behavior selection, direction, and level of effort.

content theories of motivation
Theories based on identifying specific human needs and describing the circumstances under which these needs activate behavior.

One explanation of human motivation focuses on the content of people's needs. The **content theories of motivation** identify specific human needs and describe the circumstances under which these needs activate behavior. Some theories arrange needs in hierarchical levels, with each level activating a different behavior aimed at satisfying that need. Another theory suggests individuals learn to be strongly attached to certain kinds of needs, typically called motives, because they produce satisfaction whenever they are acted on. Learned motives cause people to be predictable in the choice of tasks and behaviors they undertake.

Before we venture too far into detailed explanations of needs and other sources of motivation, take a couple of minutes to complete the Your Turn exercise. It will get you thinking about personal applications of the motivational theories to be discussed.

Needs Trigger Approach–Avoidance Behaviors

A basic observation about human behavior is that people will make an effort to do or have some things, but they will actively try to avoid or reduce the impact of others. Psychologists refer to this basic human condition as a struggle between *approach and avoidance behaviors*. On the one hand, people willingly seek out or approach desirable conditions—relationships, tasks, events, and so on. Alternatively, they try to minimize or avoid troubling or debilitating conditions. According to the late Abraham Maslow, the opposing behaviors are energized by two very different types of needs. One has to do with reducing threatening deficiencies; the other with seeking personal growth experiences.[2]

YOUR TURN

Motivational Forces That Affect You

For each of the following statements, check the option that appropriately describes you in work or organizational situations.

	Usually	Sometimes	Never
1. I am bothered by lack of creature comforts and security.	☐	☐	☐
2. I need the frequent companionship of others.	☐	☐	☐
3. I seek out novel experiences and learning opportunities.	☐	☐	☐
4. I really get turned on by achievement-related tasks.	☐	☐	☐
5. I delight in building friendships and helping people.	☐	☐	☐
6. I am at my best when in charge and influencing others.	☐	☐	☐
7. My effort and abilities affect my task performance.	☐	☐	☐
8. I am rewarded when I perform well, punished when I fail.	☐	☐	☐
9. I value the rewards and punishments I encounter.	☐	☐	☐
10. I am treated fairly compared to others.	☐	☐	☐
11. I appreciate others rewarding me for my good work.	☐	☐	☐
12. No one needs to acknowledge when I do good things.	☐	☐	☐

Interpretation: This exercise gives you a chance to reflect on what motivates you. Those statements for which you checked "usually" are motivating factors that affect you; those checked "never" probably don't affect you. Here is a summary of the 12 factors described in this exercise and in this chapter: 1. existence needs; 2. relatedness needs; 3. growth needs; 4. achievement motive; 5. affiliation motive; 6. power motive; 7., 8., 9. combine for an expectancy outlook; 10. equity; 11. extrinsic rewards; and 12. intrinsic rewards. As your read about each factor in the chapter, turn back to this exercise to understand your answer within the context of the relevant theory. Which motivated forces do you want to change? Why?

---

deficiency reduction needs
Rather universally-experienced needs that trigger avoidance behaviors where the aim is to find relief from deficiencies, deprivations, or unpleasant tensions.

Deficiency Reduction Needs.   Nobody wants to be hungry, injured, rejected by others, or taken advantage of. **Deficiency reduction needs** trigger behaviors of avoidance—the aim is to find relief from deficiencies, deprivations, or unpleasant tensions and return to a more neutral state of existence free from discomfort. A person who feels hunger pangs will act to relieve that discomfort. The worker troubled over accumulating bills may take a second job to earn extra money and pay off personal debts. Once the normal state has been reattained, the need diminishes, and behavior can be directed to satisfying other needs.

growth aspiration needs
Somewhat unique personal needs influencing choices to seek out goals and experiences that will be meaningful and satisfying.

Growth Aspiration Needs.   Whereas humans generally want to avoid threatening or unpleasant deprivations, growth goals are more personal, even unique. **Growth aspiration needs** motivate people to approach or seek out goals and experiences that they find personally meaningful. Growth needs involve the active pursuit of learning, meaningful personal relationships, and new challenges and experiences. Once a particular growth need or goal has been achieved, people typically direct their behavior toward another challenge or pleasurable experience.

Needs theories of motivation
suggest that most people
such as these, standing in
line to apply for jobs at
a federal job fair, are
motivated by deficiency
reduction needs. Some, who
are underemployed, may be
motivated by growth needs.
(Photo: Rob Crandall/Stock,
Boston.)

Shifts between Growth and Deficiency Reduction Needs. Thinking about these two sets of opposing forces helps explain why a person's behavior changes day to day. We understand the working parent who abruptly leaves work to tend to an injured child or who stays home in bed with the flu. We may also expect the survivors of a mass layoff, who have been reassigned to other departments during the subsequent reorganization, to be disoriented, bewildered, and anxious during the first few days. Under such circumstances, a manager who uses growth "challenges" to motivate isn't likely to receive an enthusiastic response from people trying to protect themselves from the threat of job loss.

This approach–avoidance needs concept also suggests why some people whose essential needs have been met tend to be striving for growth most of the time. Managers should allow such people to channel their energies into solving problems, enhancing their knowledge and abilities, and engaging in new experiences. Typically, people whose careers are advancing, who are financially secure, and who have a satisfying family life focus on growth needs and are seldom distracted by deficiency reduction needs.

Maslow's Hierarchy of Needs

hierarchy of needs
A five-level need theory
proposed by Maslow in
which lower-level basic
needs must be satisfied
before advancing to a
higher-level need.

When managers talk about theories of motivation, almost inevitably they name Abraham Maslow and his "hierarchy of needs" theory. Maslow originally proposed a five-level hierarchy of needs as the basis of his first explanation of needs-based motivation. The **hierarchy of needs** begins with physical well-being as the most basic, then progresses successively through safety, belonging, esteem, and self-actualization needs (see Exhibit 6–1). According to Maslow's hierarchical theory, once a lower-level need has been largely satisfied, its impact on behavior diminishes. The individual then is freed up to progress to the next higher-level need, and it becomes a major determinant of behavior.

Imagine that Theresa, a technical writer and single parent, has been earning a good salary and benefits that enable her to provide for her family's physical well-being—ample food, comfortable housing and clothing, good medical care. Then her company announces it is downsizing (reducing the number of employees),

━━━━━━ **EXHIBIT 6–1**

Maslow's Original Hierarchy of Needs

Abraham Maslow identified five levels of needs as the sources of different motivating behaviors. According to the theory, once a lower-level need has been satisfied, a person can activate the next higher-level need.

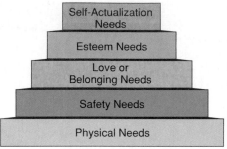

Self-Actualization Needs	The peak of human existence – the ability to develop latent capabilities and realize fullest potential.
Esteem Needs	Psychological well-being, built on the perception of oneself as worthy and recognized by others.
Love or Belonging Needs	Beyond existence needs lies the desire for nurturing, acceptance, respect, and caring relationships.
Safety Needs	Need to be free from harm or danger, to have a secure and predictable life.
Physical Needs	Most basic is the need for relief from thirst, hunger, and physical drives.

Source: Abraham H. Maslow, "A Theory of Human Motivation,"*Psychological Review* 50 (1943), pp. 370–396.

and she fears being laid off (which triggers a safety need). She is unlikely to be overly concerned about the higher-order need of belonging to a group or her own self-esteem need to perform creative and technically accurate work. Rather, she is likely to be motivated to do whatever she believes will enable her to keep her job and/or to begin looking discreetly for other employment. Once the layoffs have been announced and Theresa realizes she is not on the list, she breathes a sigh of relief, then reengages work with a higher-order need energizing her behavior. Interestingly, one research study suggests a moderate threat of layoff leads to a greater increase in work effort than does either high or low job insecurity.[3]

Limitations of the Hierarchy of Needs.   Although popular among managers because of its intuitive appeal, Maslow's theory has been controversial among researchers. When the theory has been applied to industrial environments in North America, results have been mixed at best. Generally they fail to confirm the lockstep sequence of the five hierarchical levels and the principle that lower needs must be gratified before higher needs.[4]

Because of the simplicity of the hierarchy of needs model, managers continue to use it, oblivious to disconfirming evidence. Maslow himself even questioned its applicability to organizational behavior since he based it on a study of neurosis. He wrote, "But I of all people should know just how shaky this foundation is as a final foundation [of motivation in industry]. My work on motivations came from the clinic, from a study of neurotic people."[5]

The theory is perhaps most useful as a reminder of the full range of motivational forces in people. It may, for example, have relevance in developing a work force in developing countries (see World Watch box). A firm from the United States planning to set up a factory in China, where per capita income is less than $500 per year, is likely to find the theory useful as a developmental guide over time.[6] At first, the firm will satisfy basic physical and safety needs; then, as individual workers learn and become more competent, an increasing array of opportunities for fulfilling higher-order needs can be built into job tasks and organizational practices. Particularly those who are university educated can be engaged in challenging jobs that promote organizational growth and well-being.

Existence, Relatedness, and Growth Needs

ERG theory
Alderfer's simplified content theory that identifies **e**xistence, **r**elatedness, and **g**rowth as need categories, and acknowledges multiple needs may be operating at one time without being hierarchically determined.

Clayton Alderfer developed a needs-specific model of motivation that relaxes some of Maslow's original assumptions and combines levels of needs. Alderfer calls his model the **ERG theory**, based on the initials of three categories of motivating needs: existence, relatedness, and growth.[7] Existence needs refer to basic survival

World Watch

A Case of Misdirected Motivation in Mexico?

Kathy Rosenberg was promoted three months ago from reservations supervisor to front-desk manager for Regency Hotel, an independent, 332-room hostelry in Guadalajara, Mexico. Kathy grew up in the United States and became fluent in Spanish while an international business major at the University of New Mexico. She enjoys her new management responsibilities and is pleased that the occupancy rate averaged 94 percent last month, way above the industry average. But at times she feels stressed by the confusion of managing all front-end operations of the hotel, from reservations and cashiering to the bell desk and concierge. She feels most at home handling the reservation function, a task she always enjoyed as a trainee because she likes to help people.

About once a week the staff in the reservation function (all Mexicans) overbook rooms, usually because of incomplete scans of conference sales files. Customers with reservations who arrive late are upset when they have to be referred to nearby hotels. Whenever overbooking occurs, Kathy takes over direct control of the reservations operation herself, often personally handling reservations for two or three days until order seems to return.

But sometimes while Kathy is off focusing on the reservations task, other problems arise. On five days last month, clerks at the reception desk (all Mexicans except one French student intern) checked in every "walk-in" who appeared without reservations. They assumed there would be ample no-shows among those holding reservations. On one occasion, Regency ended up oversold by 24 rooms.

Alex Mendez, the hotel general manager, is concerned about Kathy's development into her new management position. He knows Kathy is proud of the high occupancy levels (which mean greater profits) and doesn't want to destroy that pride. However, he sees her as more interested in individual staff tasks (such as making reservations) than in the complexities of managing, training, and motivating her staff. He has talked with Kathy about balancing her activities as a manager. Alex emphasized that she needs to make sure her staff know the systems and guidelines and be firm with employees who continue to check in guests when the hotel obviously will be overbooked. He plans to meet with her in a three-month performance review to see if he can shift her motivational expectations about the job.

Do Kathy's problems seem to be the result of her personal motivational immaturity or of her lack of motivational attention to her people? Might cultural differences be a contributing factor?

Source: Suggested by Amelya Stevenson, a hotel industry executive.

needs (similar to Maslow's physiological and safety needs) that everyone must satisfy to maintain life. Relatedness needs draw people into interpersonal contact for social-emotional acceptance, caring, and status. Growth needs involve personal development and a sense of self-worth.

Alderfer rejects Maslow's premise that lower-level needs must be satisfied before higher-level needs are activated. He believes a person can seek growth experiences when relatedness and maybe even existence needs have not been adequately met. Artists often are so consumed with their work that creature comforts are unimportant to them, as was the Dutch postimpressionist painter Vincent van Gogh. Alderfer does suggest, however, that the longer lower-level (existence and relatedness) needs go unfulfilled, the more they will be desired. But when growth needs are thwarted, a person will regress toward seeking relatedness or existence needs, which are generally more attainable.

Alderfer also believes that humankind is complex, and more than one need may be operating at a time. During the course of a business day, for example, one person has lunch to eat (existence needs) with two colleagues in part for social interaction (relatedness needs) and in part to obtain support in solving a problem (growth needs). ERG theory seems to provide a more reasonable representation of how individual needs activate dynamic personal behaviors within organizations. Research appears to provide better support for ERG theory than for Maslow's original five-level need hierarchy.[8] Unlike Maslow's clinical study of neurosis, Alderfer was focused on understanding adult behavior in task-oriented organizations.

The needs-based theories discussed so far illustrate the complexity of human behavior. Needs vary within an individual over time, and they vary across people. Approach–avoidance struggles often create ethical dilemmas. Nevertheless, some persons are consistently driven by higher-order needs, while others struggle with lower-order existence needs. This is because people are capable of learning to be guided by specific motives.

HOW DO NEEDS AFFECT WORK-RELATED MOTIVATION?

Two lines of motivational research focus specifically on work-related needs. Frederick Herzberg's research postulates that for workers to be motivated, the content of the job itself must be motivating—simply improving working conditions won't necessarily energize employees' behavior. Douglas McGregor distinguished two approaches to managing employees (Theory X and Theory Y), based on assumptions about employees' willingness to take responsibility for work.

Herzberg's Dual-Factor Theory

A needs-based model intended to provide direct managerial applications evolved from Frederick Herzberg's research into the sources of job-related satisfaction and dissatisfaction. From his research findings about accountants and engineers, Herzberg concluded that (1) job satisfaction and job dissatisfaction derive from different sources and (2) simply removing the sources of dissatisfaction will not cause a person to be motivated to produce better results.

dual-factor theory
Herzberg's motivation content theory based on two independent needs: hygiene and motivator factors.

Herzberg blended these two premises into a dual-factor explanation of motivation. **Dual-factor theory** refers to two different types of needs: (1) hygiene factors, which involve working conditions and can trigger dissatisfaction if inadequate, and (2) motivator factors, which originate from the nature of the job itself and can create job satisfaction.[9]

hygiene factors
Job context factors such as working conditions and benefits that cause dissatisfaction if inadequate.

Dissatisfiers as Hygiene Factors.   Herzberg drew the term hygiene factors from his public-health experience. **Hygiene factors** are those basic factors—job security, working conditions, quality of supervision, interpersonal relationships, and adequacy of pay and fringe benefits—that, if lacking, can cause dissatisfaction. Such factors are largely *extrinsic,* or external to the nature of the job itself; thus they can be thought of as job context features.

Hygiene factors do not produce job satisfaction. If adequate, they simply produce neutral feelings with the realization that basic maintenance needs are taken care of. Like a city's water and sanitation systems, these factors do not cause people to be healthy and robust. They simply prevent disease and unhealthy conditions—they provide good hygiene.

━━━━ **EXHIBIT 6–2**   *Herzberg's Dual-Factor Theory of Motivation*

To improve motivation to work, managers are first advised to provide an adequate job context of working conditions and benefits. This will satisfy lower-level hygiene needs that, if not met, cause dissatisfaction. But to arouse work interest and promote self-directed task motivation, managers also need to ensure that the content of the job itself is reasonably satisfying—that jobs contain responsibility, challenge, and the opportunity to learn and advance.

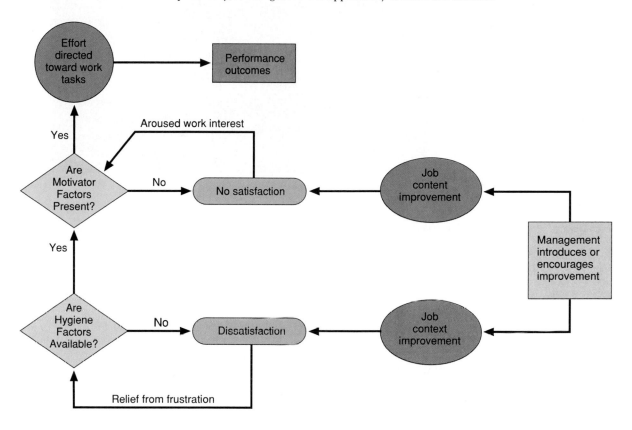

Satisfiers as Motivator Factors.   According to Herzberg, only when a person feels the potential for satisfaction is he or she able to muster significant work motivation. **Motivator factors** such as job challenge, responsibility, opportunity for achievement or advancement, and recognition provide feelings of satisfaction. These are associated with job content and are *intrinsic,* or unique to each individual in his or her own way.

motivator factors
Job content factors such as responsibility and achievement that provide feelings of satisfaction when experienced.

Herzberg's dual-factor theory suggests that if motivators are not present in a job, a person will not necessarily be dissatisfied. However, that person will simply not be in a position to experience satisfaction, since nothing about the work itself is a motivational turn-on. When motivator factors are inherent in the job, satisfaction is perceived as possible, and work-directed energy is aroused or sustained. Only then can a person be consistently motivated, according to Herzberg (see Exhibit 6–2).

Applications and Limitations of the Dual-Factor Theory.   According to the dual-factor theory, the most effective way to stimulate motivation is to improve the nature of work itself. At the time the theory was developed, most jobs were relatively structured and routine (and many still are). Therefore, Herzberg argued that the most appropriate technique for building in motivation factors was to enrich jobs.[10]

Robert Paluck, CEO of Convex Computer, believes in inspiring his workers with special events (extrinsic rewards) to give them a competitive edge. Here Paluck dove into 72 gallons of raspberry Jell-O and was followed by five other executives. Paluck also puts on slide shows demonstrating why team spirit pays off, has paid workers their quarterly profit-sharing in silver dollars, and sends top-performing workers on cruises. (Photo: © 1990 Steven Pumphrey.)

job enrichment
A means to encourage motivation by building greater responsibility and variety into a job.

Job enrichment involves giving a job greater scope (variety) and depth (responsibility for planning and control of the work). Job enrichment means expanding the critical functions and challenges of individual jobs, and yet we know that today's managers are more concerned with structuring work around semiautonomous teams and empowering people to work in a managerless context (as described throughout this book).

Research into the appropriateness of dual-factor theory has been criticized for its original reliance on engineers and accountants as subjects, since these two types of professionals are not as subject to lower-level needs as people working in low-skilled jobs. The theory has been difficult to replicate without asking for self-reports of past events, in which respondents tend to take credit for positive events and blame externalities for negative ones. Some variables, such as quality of supervision or pay, seem to be more unstable than Herzberg specified. Other research has uncovered a link between pay and increasing levels of motivation.[11] Researchers have found that a specific variable can be a source of either satisfaction or dissatisfaction, depending on the person.[12]

McGregor's Theory X and Theory Y

Maslow's ideas about motivation influenced the thinking of Douglas McGregor, who crafted a philosophy based on differing managerial practices. McGregor presented a sharp contrast between two different sets of managerial assumptions about people, reasoning that a manager's ideas about people influence how he or she attempts to manage. He identified these contrasting sets of assumptions with the labels Theory X and Theory Y.[13]

Theory X
A managerial assumption that people act only to realize their basic needs and therefore do not voluntarily contribute to organizational aims.

A **Theory X** set of assumptions about human behavior postulates that people act to realize basic needs, and therefore do not voluntarily contribute to organizational aims. When these are the expected employee characteristics, managers believe that their task is to direct and modify human behavior to fit the needs of the organization. Managers must persuade, reward, punish, and control those who don't naturally strive to learn and grow.

════════ **EXHIBIT 6–3**

*The Contrast between
Theory X and Theory Y*

Managers who subscribe to *Theory X* basically believe that:

1. People dislike responsibility and lack ambition; therefore, they prefer to be led, and management must direct their efforts.

2. The average person is passive, indolent, and works as little as possible; thus, people need to be coerced and controlled.

3. People are self-centered and indifferent to organized needs; therefore, they are by nature resistant to change.

The *Theory Y* assumes that:

1. People seek responsibility and have the capacity to direct and control organizational tasks if they are committed to the objectives.

2. People by nature are not passive or indifferent to organizational needs, for work is as natural as rest or play.

3. Employees at all levels have the ability to be creative and use ingenuity in solving organizational problems.

Source: Douglas McGregor, *Leadership and Motivation* © 1966 Massachusetts Institute of Technology. Used with permission of M. I. T. Press.

Theory Y
A managerial assumption that people are motivated by higher-order growth needs and they will therefore act responsibly to accomplish organizational objectives.

By contrast, a **Theory Y** view of human behavior sees people as motivated by higher-order growth needs. According to Theory Y, management's task is to enable people to act on these needs and to grow in their jobs. Management's essential task is to structure the work environment so that people can best achieve their higher-order personal goals by accomplishing organizational objectives (see Exhibit 6–3).

McGregor's concept was meant to be provocative and was not the product of empirical research. It therefore has not been empirically validated, but rather has served to make managers reflect on how their own assumptions about people affect their behavior toward employees. McGregor intended Theory X and Theory Y to represent extreme ends of a continuum of beliefs. Managers are not expected to function as true "Xs" or "Ys," although most managers appear closer to one than the other.

McGregor stopped short of advocating that all managers become Theory Y managers. His intention was to make managers aware of how stereotyped views of human nature can lead to self-fulfilling prophecies. McGregor saw Theory Y as a way to align manager and employee goals. If people could satisfy their personal goals by accomplishing organizational objectives, their greater productive energy would benefit everyone. The manager who delegates authority and provides people with the resources to do a job often finds that they behave responsibly. According to McGregor, management based primarily on satisfying lower-level needs (Theory X) fails over time to obtain desired results other than maintenance of the status quo.

Limitations of Classic Need Theories

Today's generation of senior managers has had ample exposure to these pioneering attempts to understand motivational forces, and some have tried to relate them directly to their organizations. Exhibit 6–4 shows the pattern of similarities among the theories of Maslow, Alderfer, Herzberg, and McGregor. A knowledge of someone's level of needs provides clues about the likely direction that person's behavior will take. If Katrina is experiencing difficulties with her manager or with a co-worker, she will probably act to minimize contact with the person. If Shuresh

EXHIBIT 6–4   *Parallels among Popular Theories of Motivation*

There are many parallels among the popular theories of Maslow (original hierarchical theory and revised dual-level theory), Alderfer, Herzberg, and McGregor. The needs at the top of the model all lead toward approach behaviors, while those on the bottom propel people toward avoidance behaviors if not adequately obtained. Those in the middle (Maslow's belonging and Alderfer's relatedness) are potentially unstable and can direct behavior, in either direction, depending on the circumstance.

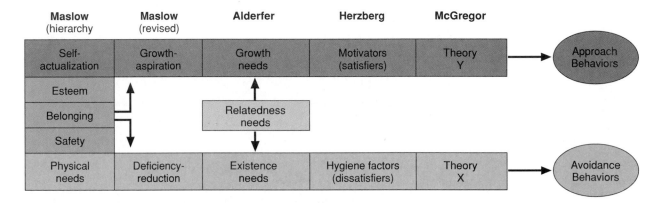

perceives that his growth aspirations can be met by challenging work assignments, he is likely to direct his energy toward job tasks that enable him to learn and to contribute to group goals.

It is more difficult, however, to predict how a person will act when motivated by a lower-level or hygiene need. If Rosabeth perceives her pay as inadequate, how will she behave in response? She might assume the situation will not improve and avoid doing any more work than is absolutely necessary to hold her job. Under similar circumstances, George may become active in union affairs to press for better pay. Kim may work harder to gain the boss's favor, expecting that her efforts will be recognized. So while need theory may provide clues to unsatisfied desires, it doesn't always tell us how an individual is likely to try to satisfy them.

HOW DO LEARNED MOTIVES INFLUENCE WORK BEHAVIOR?

The discussion so far assumes that lower- or higher-level needs are relatively common among humankind. It is simply a person's current circumstances that determine which level of need will be acted on. But a different category of needs is learned or socially acquired. Depending on your personal experience, you may have one or two strong socially learned needs. Learned through repeated experiences, these needs motivate our behavior whenever we perceive an opportunity to satisfy them.

Motives Are Learned from Experience

Some people learn to be consistently energized when they encounter similar circumstances that offer the opportunity of experiencing feelings of satisfaction. People who are aware of a pattern of past satisfactions consistently need or want more of what has become for them a persistent motive. Examples of learned motives include the need for achievement, power, affiliation, competence, status, and autonomy. This learning can be either conscious or unconscious. These learned motives have profound relevance for managers because they directly energize behavior.

Individuals differ in the importance they assign to specific motives. Some people have a clearly dominant motive, such as achievement, power, or affiliation.[14] Regardless of the situation, these individuals are likely to behave consistently with that one dominant motive. Another person might have a balanced mix of motives, making it hard for others to predict how he or she will behave in a certain situation. Yet another person might have a variable hierarchy of motives that depends on the situation. At work her dominant motive might be power or achievement; at home, affiliation; and in social events, status. People who are chronically disadvantaged are unlikely to have developed motives; they unfortunately are driven by lower-order needs.

Managers can motivate others if they are sensitive to the learned motives of individual employees. For this reason we will examine the more important learned motives: achievement, power, and affiliation.

The Achievement Motive.   Many people like to think of themselves as being achievement oriented, undoubtedly because achievement is highly valued in most Western societies. However, people's achievement motives vary in intensity, as do all motives. People who have a high **need to achieve** are usually self-motivated; they seek tasks that will provide them with a sense of accomplishment. They will choose an opportunity to confront a challenging but doable task rather than attend the company's Friday afternoon pizza social (unless they plan to seek ideas from others that promote task accomplishment).

David McClelland and John Atkinson conducted the original research on work-related motives, particularly the achievement motive.[15] They assumed the achievement motive could be measured by what people say, do, or write. Several behavioral characteristics distinguish the achievement-motivated person.

1. Achievers prefer a moderate level of difficulty or challenge. Just as they avoid tasks that are too easy, they also shy away from those that are extremely difficult. Being realistic, they know their limitations. The most desired task is one that requires a high level of exertion but carries a reasonable probability of success.

2. High achievers also like to feel that they are in reasonable control of an outcome. If the element of chance or luck is a primary factor in success, or if others over whom they have little influence are involved, there is reduced incentive to try.

3. Achievement-motivated people also like to receive frequent and specific feedback about how well they are doing. This does not mean they need constant praise from their supervisors. Ideally the task itself should provide enough feedback so they can evaluate themselves; self-approval is good feedback for an achiever.

A high need for achievement has long been associated with entrepreneurial success. It has not been especially predictive of managerial success, except in small organizations. McClelland recently found in a study of PepsiCo, which consists of thousands of reasonably small decentralized business units, that managers with a high need for achievement are more successful than those with a high power motive concerned more with influencing others.[16]

---

need to achieve (or achievement motive)
A learned motive that satisfaction can be found in seeking tasks that will provide a sense of accomplishment.

The Power Motive.   Power is the ability to influence others to behave as we want. People who have a high **need for power,** or power motive, find satisfaction from being in charge and controlling and influencing others. While it is important to have some high achievers in management, an organization will not function effectively without its share of take-charge types for whom power is the dominant motive. These people are willing to specify organizational goals and influence others to achieve them. It is difficult to be a successful manager without a need for power, especially in large organizations. Managers must learn to take satisfaction in acquiring and exercising the means for influencing others.

need for power (or power motive)
A learned motive that finds satisfaction from being in charge and controlling and influencing others.

McClelland and Burnham differentiate managers with strong power needs into two kinds—either personal power managers or institutional power managers.[17] Managers with high *personal power needs* exemplify the stereotypical self-serving, exploitative, dominating boss. Such a need for power reflects the aim of personal gain through manipulation and control of others without exhibiting self-control and inhibition. A personal-power boss may coerce and even threaten subordinates in a forceful attempt to get them to carry out commands. Such a manager then takes credit for their successes. Contrary to what is presented in soap operas, these managers usually don't make it to the top of an organization because people they have stepped on earlier find ways to sabotage their careers.[18]

Managers with high *institutional power needs* temper their influence over others with inhibition and self-control. They are altruistic and believe power should be used more for the good of the organization than for personal advantage. Satisfaction is obtained more from the process of influencing others to carry out their work in pursuit of organizational goals than from their own personal success. Research indicates that higher-level managers in large organizations are more likely to be successful if they possess a high need for power that is institutionalized (with high inhibition and self-control) combined with low affiliation needs.

The Affiliation Motive.   Persons with a high **need for affiliation** find satisfaction in the quality of their social and interpersonal relationships. Affiliators avoid isolation (whereas achievers often welcome it), since interaction with others is so important for them. Such people easily develop wide circles of friends both in and out of the workplace. They are prone to show concern for the feelings of others and to be sympathetic to opposing views. Given the opportunity, they often try to help others work through problems.

need for affiliation (or affiliation motive)
A learned motive to seek satisfaction from the quality of social and interpersonal relationships.

People who are high affiliators often make weak bosses. McClelland and Burnham found that only 20 percent of the "above-average" sales departments in a research sample were supervised by managers whose affiliation needs were more dominant than their power needs.[19] Of the "below-average" departments in their sample, 90 percent were run by affiliation-motivated managers. By contrast, power-motivated managers ran 80 percent of the best and only 10 percent of the worst departments. The researchers concluded that because of their need to be liked, affiliation-motivated managers made "wishy-washy decisions." They bent company rules to make particular individuals happy, and in the process they were seen as unfair.

Attributions and Learning Affect Motive Development

personal attribution
The process of rationalizing causality (either to external or internal [personal] factors) as to why personally-involving events turn out as they do.

A person engages in **personal attribution** when rationalizing causality as to why personally involving events turn out as they do. To develop strong motives, a person learns to see himself or herself as personally responsible. Achievers in particular establish a pattern of *internal attribution* of success.[20] Through repeated opportunities to succeed or fail, high achievers learn to attribute success to their own efforts or abilities. They take on responsibilities because accomplishment of a task provides self-satisfaction and pride. Achievement-motivated employees usually establish their own standards of performance. Often they strive for higher goals than those assigned by supervisors.

When high achievers fail, however, they are reluctant to place all the blame on themselves. Achievers often attribute some of the blame for failure to one or more external circumstances—bad luck, impossible tasks, or interference by powerful others.[21] This helps them retain self-confidence. When they must accept responsibility for an unsuccessful outcome, they engage in problem solving to learn from the experience.

Individuals with low achievement needs perceive success or failure in a different light. To them life is capricious. They tend to attribute their successful outcomes to external factors (good luck, easy tasks, powerful others) and thus feel no personal pride in accomplishment. Conversely, they often accept blame for failures. Given their inability to enjoy success, people with low achievement needs seek out situations where individual achievement is not a factor.

High achievers are attracted to many different types of work, including entrepreneurial and managerial challenges. But being a successful entrepreneur or manager is more complex than simply being motivated to achieve (see Challenge of Change box).[22] In fact, some highly achievement-motivated people are so concerned with their own achievement that they are not very adept at helping others achieve. While they may make good entrepreneurs in start-up companies, high achievers do not necessarily make good managers in large bureaucratic organizations. On balance, the competent manager displays motivational behaviors that include "self-control, self-confidence, an ability to get a consensus from people, and strong motivations for achievement, power, or both."[23]

Motives Help Predict Behavior

Differences in the strength of specific motives help explain why some people are more predictable than others. People tend to develop motivation patterns that represent the needs they consistently seek to satisfy. Motivation patterns are sometimes difficult to infer simply by observing behavior. For example, Savander might have a dominant need for power. He finds that one way to get power is to achieve, so that he will be sought after as an expert. People observing him might assume he has a high achievement motive. However, in his case, achievement is merely a means of satisfying a power need. By contrast, Jennifer has a high need for achievement. In achieving success, she attains considerable power and influence. People might incorrectly assume that she has a high power need because she is promoted to positions of leadership in which she can influence group performance. People use different behavioral strategies to satisfy motive needs.

Be cautious in making attributions about another's motives. However, the better you know another person, the better you are able to identify the motivation patterns underlying his or her behavior. Correctly recognizing another's motive patterns helps a manager select assignments that energize that person. For example, the achiever is excited by his assignment to a challenging project. The power-motivated person enjoys representing her group in a negotiating session.

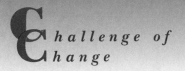

Challenge of Change

Entrepreneurs: Finding Motivation the Second Time Around

Entrepreneurs often have difficulty finding passion in their soul and fire in their belly when they start their second business. Absent is that great motivator, fear of failure. Says two-time entrepreneur John Overby, "With the second company you bring the authority of your experience. You're more confident, and the experience is less stressful." To this, entrepreneur Tom Weldon adds, "I was afraid I didn't have the hunger, the same sense of urgency, the drive it took to succeed the first time. I was no longer terrified on a daily basis. Fear creates urgency."

With entrepreneurs, says psychologist Dennis Jaffe, "The challenge is shifting from the external motivators of the first company—proving to your father-in-law that you're not *really* a slug, attending your 30-year high school reunion clad in head-to-toe Armani—to internal motivators. People who have trouble the second time are not finding intrinsic meaning in what they're doing." Often this means focusing on aspects of the business that are truly enjoyable and meaningful, which may be helping people grow or concentrating on one significant role and letting someone else run the show.

For entrepreneurs, as with anyone pursuing growth goals, a challenge doesn't exist unless it progressively increases in difficulty. As with skiing, the expert is totally bored on the bunny slope. As one progresses from green circles (beginners) to blue squares (intermediate) to black diamonds (expert), to move down to easier terrain is not like skiing at all—there's no challenge. For entrepreneurs there is motivational value in one-upmanship, of doing things faster, with greater impact the second time around. When Gordon Moore and Robert Noyce decided to start Intel after having been part of the cofounders of semiconductor pioneer Fairchild Semiconductor, they were immediately joined by a third defector from Fairchild, Andy Grove. Remarks Moore, "Andy always made it hard for me. I would be all excited that we were under budget or ahead of schedule on a product—and he'd ask why we couldn't do it faster and cheaper." To Grove, current CEO of Intel, "Only the paranoid survive." Call it paranoia, one-upmanship, or challenge—successful entrepreneurs find a way to motivate themselves by upping the ante the second time.

Sources: Christopher Caggiano, "Once More with Feeling," *Inc.* (April 1995), pp. 84–91; and Brent Schlender, "Why Andy Grove Can't Stop," *Fortune* (July 10, 1995), pp. 88–98.

Personal Ideology Promotes Motivational Consistency

ideology
A source of personal consistency based on one's values and conception of his or her place in the world in relation to meaningful activities that promote a sense of self-worth.

Because motives are learned, they promote consistency in motivated behavior. A related, yet different learned source of motivational consistency is one's self-ideology. Shamir notes that a person's values, moral obligations, and sense of self provide a mental image of his or her personal ideology. **Ideology** is a personal conception of one's place in the world, a conception that includes human obligations in relation to meaningful activities that promote a sense of self-worth.

One's concept of ideology influences motivation apart from the interplay between one's needs or motives, and the capacity of the work situation to satisfy them. Unlike needs or motives which vary in strength according to situational forces at the moment, ideology is a stabilizing force behind behavior. This is because it draws on a "concept of values as 'conceptions of the desirable' as distinct from the desired."[24] A person with a strong personal ideology desires to enhance self-concept, self-esteem, and sense of self-consistency. To be true to one's self-image, a person does not always work for direct personal gain; sometimes the emphasis at work is to behave in ways consistent with that image.

Ideological concerns that promote self-consistency may include being respected by colleagues, meeting management expectations, contributing to the production of something of value, sustaining respect by family, feeling pride in being helpful, carrying one's own weight at work, and others. One study in Britain found that even when jobs were threatened by new technology, motivation to do good work did not wane—an outcome attributed to ideological values that linked self-respect with work performance.[25] Even in a factory where employees lacked loyalty to the firm because termination was eminent, they were no less work motivated than employees who were not threatened with job loss.

Ideological beliefs related to work and personal economic values have even been shown to relate to differences in growth rates and income levels across countries—two implicit indices of national motivation. In a study of about 12,000 people in 41 countries, investigators found that individual competitiveness, the desire for money, and a willingness to save are predictors of the growth rate of a region. However, these same three ideological components are negatively associated with per capita income.[26] Competitiveness—the drive to be better than others at what one does—is especially important as a stimulant of growth in less developed nations such as Bangladesh, China, and India. It may be, however, that after a country has become affluent, "cooperativeness" becomes more valued than competitiveness.

HOW DO EXPECTANCIES AFFECT WORK MOTIVATION?

Need-based theories of motivation are accepted by many managers because they seem to provide a specific answer to the question, What needs or motives drive human behavior? Perhaps managers' sustaining belief that needs explain motivation reflects the ongoing search for one best way of managing. This goal began with Frederick Taylor's scientific management movement in the early part of the twentieth century (see Appendix A).[27] Yet researchers have concluded that seeking "one best way" of managing is an illusion.

process theories of motivation
Theories that focus on the ways people think through motivation issues and how they determine whether their actions were successful.

By contrast, another group of theories is not so neat and specific. **Process theories of motivation** explain how and why workers select behaviors and how they determine whether their choices were successful. Since people are creatures of perception, thought, and a certain degree of rationality, they are capable of making informed choices about where and how to channel energy. In making choices, the human tendency is to embrace the most advantageous option or at least avoid functioning at a disadvantage. This premise underlies the process theories based on expectancy and equity.

Expectancy Theory Raises Three Questions

expectancy theory
A theory of motivation based on a person's beliefs about effort–performance–outcome relationships.

Motivation based on expectancy theory focuses on a person's beliefs about the relationships among effort, performance, and rewards for doing a job. **Expectancy theory** was originally expressed as a probability relationship among three variables labeled expectancy, instrumentality, and valence—terms defined in Exhibit 6–5.[28] While these psychological terms mean more to researchers than managers, the concepts and their interrelationship provide the foundation for a useful way of thinking about work motivations.

▬▬▬▬ **EXHIBIT 6–5**

*Three Variables Frame
Expectancy Theory*

The original expectancy theory consists of the interrelationships among three variables:

1. *Expectancy.* The probability (from 0 to 1) that an individual believes his or her work effort directly affects the performance outcome of a task.
2. *Instrumentality.* The probability (from 0 to 1) that an individual anticipates that an attained level of task performance will have personal consequences.
3. *Valence.* The value (from positive to negative) that a person assigns to the personal consequences that follow work performance.

For example, Todd expects he will have a significant influence over the audits he performs as an accountant. He believes that performing high-quality audits will result in substantial pay increases and his promotion to manager. His number one goal is to make manager within five years and to be paid more than his peers.

Source: H. J. Arnold, "A Test of the Multiplicative Hypothesis of Expectancy-Valence Theories of Work Motivation," *Academy of Management Journal* 24 (March 1981), pp. 128–141.

Research supports the validity of expectancy relationships in work settings but acknowledges that the jargon used by psychologists is difficult to apply (see Exhibit 6–5).[29] The basics of expectancy theory for organizational practioners can be converted into a series of three questions that people often ask themselves about their work situation:[30]

1. *Does how hard I try really affect my performance?* To be motivated, you must have a positive answer to this *expectancy question.* You must believe that your personal efforts have the potential to make a positive performance difference. You must also have the capacity for internal attribution, or a willingness to take personal credit or blame for your performance. Positive task motivation begins when you see a link between personal effort and task performance.

2. *Are personal consequences linked to my performance?* In some jobs or roles there is little association between effort and rewards or punishments. To answer this *instrumentality question,* you must believe that task performance results (a first-order outcome) serve to obtain second-order personal consequences or payoffs. Increased motivation is possible when you perceive a positive personal consequence arising from satisfactory task performance.

3. *Do I value the consequences available to me?* Answers to this *valence question* depend on how much you value a particular expected personal outcome or payoff. If you really don't care about the potential payoff, it provides little if any incentive value. Suppose you want recognition, but your boss simply gives you another assignment and sends you off on another trip to the boondocks. You thus discount the value of possible payoffs, and your expectation of being rewarded in a meaningful way diminishes. A person must value the payoff if the expectancy loop is to be positive and motivational.

Think of your own experiences for a moment. Do you often mull over in your mind questions similar to these three? If so, you find yourself in agreement with scholars such as Lyman Porter and Edward Lawler, who find that motivation is enhanced when a person answers yes to all three expectancy-related questions: (1) when effort is believed performance related, (2) when performance is linked to personal consequences, and (3) when the consequences or payoffs available are highly valued.[31] Conversely, when one or more answers is negative, motivation potential diminishes.

It is important for managers to realize that not all people value the available outcomes or rewards in the same way. Managers who want to motivate by expectancies must weigh whether employees place a greater value on extrinsic or intrinsic rewards.

Source: Reprinted with special permission of United Features Syndicate, Inc. (NYC)

Motivational Implications of Intrinsic and Extrinsic Rewards

extrinsic rewards
Rewards externally bestowed, as by a supervisor, teacher, or organization.

intrinsic rewards
Postulates that motivation is moderated by perceived fairness or discrepancies between contributions and rewards.

There are two basic sources of rewards or payoffs. Many people depend on and highly value **extrinsic rewards**—rewards that are externally bestowed, such as praise from a supervisor, a promotion or pay raise, or the grade received on a term paper. Others place a high value on **intrinsic rewards**—their own personal feelings about how well they performed the task or simply the satisfaction they derived from doing it. Managers need to realize the distinction between the two and how their employees view them. For example, in work conditions where employees seek extrinsic rewards but believe their degree of effort is not clearly visible to supervisors, "social loafing" or low effort is likely to occur. However, where there is a high intrinsic involvement in the task, social loafing will be low even when effort is not visible to the manager.[32]

Although most people look for some mix of intrinsic and extrinsic rewards, people clearly differ as to which is the more compelling motivational force.[33] If a manager always praises an achievement-motivated professional who excels largely for the feelings of intrinsic satisfaction, this person will probably begin to look on his manager as shallow or phony. He may think to himself, "I know I did a superb job on this project. Why does she keep stating the obvious? I wish she'd quit being so condescending."

Even within the extrinsic rewards arena, people look for different types of rewards. Praise may be perfectly acceptable to the person motivated by relatedness needs or affiliation, but may do nothing for the person expecting a more tangible payoff—something that can be banked. Typical extrinsic rewards are favorable assignments, trips to desirable destinations, tuition reimbursement for courses in which a good grade is earned, pay raises, bonuses, and promotions. In the cases of some cultures of the world, extrinsic payoffs are in the form of bribes (see Eye on Ethics box).

Managers need to use extrinsic rewards cautiously. People who are internal attributors and achievement motivated need less in the way of extrinsic reinforcement than do people with low self-esteem who are unsure of themselves (assuming there is an underlying equity in financial payoffs). Research initiated by Deci even offers evidence that when too many extrinsic rewards are provided, work effort

Some organizations strive to motivate employees as a cooperative unit. Researchers studying aircraft carrier flight operations discovered that officers strive to build and maintain a completely unselfish devotion among sailors to the tasks. This is necessary because of the life and death nature of the work. One example is the way all personnel, regardless of rank, walk the flight deck picking up everything that could damage a jet's engine. (Photo: U.S. Navy Photo by: McDonnell Douglas Corp.)

declines.[34] He found that the introduction of extrinsic rewards for work previously performed for intrinsic pleasure tends to reduce motivation. Overabundant extrinsic rewards are likely to lessen the need to seek intrinsic satisfaction. People may perceive extrinsic rewards as diminishing their control of the work situation. However, if rewards serve primarily as feedback, this negative effect is minimal.

Managing Motivational Expectancies

A manager does not need to be a psychologist to benefit from applying expectancy theory. First, the theory is most applicable to those jobs in which an individual has discretion as to how and when work is performed. For example, it would have somewhat greater applicability for airline reservation agents (who can either be thorough and helpful or abrupt and indifferent) than for operators on a machine-paced assembly line. But it likely has even greater relevance for professionals such as accountants, market researchers, stockbrokers, and systems analysts.

To get the best from their people, managers should emphasize anticipated reward value, whether extrinsic or intrinsic.[35] The manager's job is to strengthen effort–performance–reward expectancies. For employees who have difficulty attributing outcomes to their performance, managers must make sure they realize performance–reward connections and then provide performance feedback.

Eye on Ethics

Can Koreans Learn to Do Business without Bribes?

The motives that underlie commonly accepted business practices differ because of local values and learned traditions. In South Korea, firms who don't pay bribes don't do business. For more than a decade, a U.S. electronics firm did business in South Korea through a local distributor who made up to $4 million per year. Thinking it could improve margins, the electronics firm dropped its Korean distributor to handle distribution itself. Bad move. In five years since then, the U.S. firm has lost $16 million trying to do business in South Korea. According to the former Korean distributor, the answer is simple: "The Americans refuse to pay bribes to customers to win contracts."

Says the CEO of a medium-sized Korean business: "Any businessman in Korea who has survived the last 30 years is to some degree corrupt, including myself. The whole country was this way. The president was corrupt, the ministers were corrupt, the banks were corrupt. How else could you survive?"

South Korea is no longer an underdeveloped country. Today it is the world's 12th largest economy. But for three decades its spectacular growth came through a highly centralized alliance between government and big businesses, or *chaebols*. Four firms—Hyundai,

Samsung, Daewoo, and LG—account for a third of South Korea's total sales. Korea's political leaders demanded "donations" from companies to gain access to capital and licenses, and businesses in turn expected payments to secure contracts. The locals learn quickly the rules of business survival.

But in late 1991, Hyundai's founder Chung Ju Yung announced that rather than pay off politicians he would form his own political party. Chung's efforts to challenge the tradition of bribery resulted in then President Roh Tae Woo pulling strings to starve Hyundai's access to capital. Bank loans were canceled, attempts to sell more shares were blocked by securities officials, and tax inspectors stormed the company. The isolation strategy continued until Kim Young Sam was elected president in December 1992. Since then, Kim has worked to control widespread corruption and bribery by changing tax laws and making laws to force more disclosure by politicians. It's a start. Can Korea honestly learn to do business without bribery?

Sources: Kevin Sullivan, "Bribes Part of Business in S. Korea," *Washington Post* (November 26, 1995); Laxmi Nakarmi, "Seoul Yanks the *Chaebol's* Leash," *Business Week* (October 30, 1995), p. 58; and Jeffrey A. Fadiman, "Bribery and American Business Ethics: A Resolvable Dilemma," *Northern California Executive Review* 9 (Fall/Winter 1995), pp. 15–22.

Clarify Performance–Reward Linkages. Not all employees know about or understand extrinsic organizational rewards. Survey data also suggest levels of satisfaction with extrinsic rewards are diminishing. The managerial challenge is to clarify rewards available to employees and relate them to personal and team performance.[36] While many organizations provide little performance-based pay differentiation among people of the same salary grade, there are other extrinsic rewards a manager can bestow. For example, a manager can allocate more favorable job assignments to those who meet or surpass performance expectations. The key is to make obvious in advance the payoffs people can expect for certain levels of performance, then follow up on satisfactory performance with feedback and appropriate rewards.[37]

Provide Performance Feedback. Managers need to provide feedback both to demonstrate that they know what others are doing and to acknowledge improved performance or a job well done. Especially for employees who seem unsure of themselves or tend to externally attribute success, a manager should point out ways in which the employee is improving.[38] Praising specific accomplishments or improvements helps bolster employee esteem and promote internal attribution. It helps forge the link between focused effort, performance improvement, and the personal outcome of recognition from powerful others and personal feelings of pride.

HOW DO PERCEPTIONS OF EQUITY AFFECT MOTIVATION?

Along the path to expectancy motivation, things can go wrong. One of the most disruptive situations is when the payoffs or personal outcomes are perceived to be inequitable or unfair. Managers need to be aware of equity perceptions and reduce gaps where possible.

Perceptions of Equity Moderate Motivation

Equity theory
The idea that motivation is moderated by perceived fairness or discrepancies between contributions and rewards

If expectancy motivation is to work, people must perceive an underlying fairness among effort–performance–reward relationships. Stacy Adams popularized this idea in what is called equity theory. **Equity theory** suggests that motivation is moderated by the perceived fairness or discrepancy between personal contributions and rewards relative to others'. There are two basic dimensions to the equity process.

Ratio of Personal Outcomes to Inputs.   People often think in terms of the ratio of their personal outcomes to work inputs. That is, their perceptions of equity depend on how they answer the question, What is the payoff to me (in terms of status, benefits, recognition, money, promotion, and job assignments) relative to my inputs of effort exerted, skills, job knowledge, and actual task performance?

External Comparisons.   People also compare their own outcomes/input ratio to those they perceive for other people doing comparable work. These comparisons may be made on three levels.

1. *Comparisons to specific other individuals.* For example, Bev might conclude, "I guess Kerri really has been outperforming me." Bev would expect Kerri to be getting more in the way of rewards and recognition.
2. *Comparisons to another reference group.* Workers might think, "Our department is getting much better treatment than the shipping department." This comparison recognizes that there are differences in payoffs and "our group" is getting a better deal. But it doesn't indicate if that better treatment is the result of better performance, and therefore deserved. We'll return to this situation in a moment.
3. *Comparisons to general occupational classifications.* At times people compare themselves to people in similar positions in other organizations. A physical therapist at a private hospital might observe, "According to the national salary survey data, my pay is at only the twentieth percentile—way below what someone with my experience should be earning." Another common comparison is across gender within the same occupation, where women often experience discrepancies of earning 20 percent to 40 percent less pay than men.

Adjusting for Equity Gaps

You might think that equity concerns would be activated only when a person believed he or she was being taken advantage of, or was undercompensated relative to others. Not necessarily. While this may be the more common experience, people sometimes conclude that they are overcompensated. This might have been the case in the second comparison listed above if the conclusion had been, "Our group is receiving better treatment but performing no better than the group in shipping."

The equity concept affects motivation whenever a person perceives a meaningful difference in personal or group outcomes and then adjusts behavior or perceptions to reduce the gap.[39] In a research experiment, those who survived a job layoff and thought their co-workers' dismissals were random worked harder than when they believed those caught in the layoff had produced less.[40] Similarly, if Bernice believes she is inequitably overcompensated, she might intensify her efforts to produce more to be worthy of the superior benefits she receives. Or she may simply change her frame of reference to reduce the perceived equity gap, say, by comparing her pay with national rather than company data. Conversely, when people perceive that they are undercompensated relative to the frame of reference (which is more common), they will likely reduce or redirect their efforts in an attempt to beat the system so they end up with a fair deal. These adverse consequences are more pronounced with extrinsic inequities (especially monetary rewards) than intrinsic inequities.[41]

Fairness Involves Distributive and Procedural Justice

distributive justice
The perceived fairness of the amount and allocation of rewards among individuals.

Recent research into the equity issue focuses on the fairness of both distributive and procedural justice. **Distributive justice** refers to the perceived fairness of the *amount* of compensation or rewards employees receive. **Procedural justice** describes the perceived fairness of the *process* used to determine the distribution of rewards among employees. Whereas equity theory historically has focused on the amount individuals receive relative to others (distributive justice), procedural justice shifts attention to the fairness of how managers arrive at those decisions. Although managers might not be as generous to all employees as they would like to be, they remain responsible for determining the process by which reward distributions are made.

procedural justice
The perceived fairness of the means used to determine the amount and distribution of rewards.

Perception of What Might Have Been.   How do employees feel about reward distributions and the procedures used for making them? Research finds that distributive satisfaction impacts primarily on personal outcomes such as satisfaction and attitudes toward pay and promotion decisions. Procedural justice reflects more on organizational outcomes in terms of employee commitment and trust in supervisors.[42]

referent cognitions theory
Postulates that people evaluate their work and rewards relative to "what might have been" under different circumstances.

A related line of research called **referent cognitions theory** indicates that employees are capable of evaluating their work and reward experiences by reflecting on "what might have been" under different circumstances and procedures.[43] For example, would a different process have led to a more favorable personal outcome on a pay raise or expected promotion? Obviously, resentment peaks when the distribution of rewards is perceived as inequitable and the criteria used to arrive at that distribution are believed unfair. Furthermore, there is a cumulative effect when a person "experiences mounting feelings of injustice at work."[44]

Equity Begins with Fair Procedures.   A study of union grievances found that the administration of procedures was more important than the outcomes in influencing workers' satisfaction with their union. Satisfaction with management depended on the extent to which workers found the workplace to be just and moral.[45] Another study (involving a sample of 675 bank employees) also found that procedural justice is the more important of the two.[46]

Leadership style at the Spring-field Corp. in Springfield, Missouri, uses the Theory Y view of human behavior that describes people as motivated by higher-order growth needs. In the photo are Cindy LaRue (left), production worker, and Candy Smalley, a production team leader. Smalley responded to the company's Theory Y orientation from the start: "When I first came here and the CEO not only gave us the financials but expected us to learn them, I was astounded. We felt respected. And now we use those numbers to improve." Source: © Kelly Rodgers.

Such research implies that if an organization's procedures treat employees fairly, they will view the organization as positive even if dissatisfied with personal outcomes such as pay. As long as the procedure is seen as fair, employees find it difficult to envision a more positive alternative for distributing rewards. They therefore are likely to remain committed to the organization and to trust in the fairness of managers. This important bottom-line issue of equity suggests that groups and group perception are important in managing motivation.

SHOULD MOTIVATION FOCUS ON INDIVIDUALS OR GROUPS?

Theories of motivation in Western countries focus on the individual. But not all cultures emphasize the individual. In many cultures, the group (family, tribe, or team) is the center of attention, and individual behavior gets attention only if it deviates from group norms. Even in North America and Europe, organizations are beginning to spotlight the team, not the individual. Given their emphasis on the collective well-being, Canadian firms find this more natural than do firms to the south. In time, motivational theories will become more group based.

Globally, Many Cultures Disregard Individual Motivation

There are major limitations to Western ideas of motivation. Hofstede's investigation of dominant cultural values in 50 countries found that the United States ranks highest in individualism.[47] Americans base their identity more on personal achievements than on family roles or their role within a social group. It is natural for managers in the United States, much of Europe, and even Canada to empha-size individual initiative in evaluating and seeking to motivate employees. And yet, groups are known to be critical to risk-taking propensity in these countries.[48]

In other parts of the world, family connections are the usual way of gaining employment—something that is vilified in the American tradition. Americans expect people to maximize individual gain or personal utility. The Americanized view of motivation overlooks the power of the family and social fabric that dominates collectivist countries, or the impact of the government in assigning people to jobs, as is common in state-owned enterprises in the People's Republic of China.[49] Theories of motivation would be richer if they encompassed cultural forces most Westerners find mystifying.

Innovation Goals Shift Motivation toward Teams

Most of the research about motivation was undertaken in an era of big business, mass markets, and relatively standardized products. The pace of major changes in the design and technology of products was relatively moderate and predictable. During this era (through the third quarter of the twentieth century), management and motivation theory focused on the individual. Researchers asked, "What affects an individual's choice of behaviors and intensity of work effort?" Managers wondered, "How can I get Dick or Jane to vigorously pursue my goals?" Such concerns are useful, but they may be less in tune with today's organizational needs than yesterday's.

In the late 1990s and beyond, the critical motivational task is to energize and empower individuals and teams to improve quality and bring about innovation.[50] Individual behaviors remain important. But producing continuous improvements and innovations is principally a team task. For Honda Motors, the motivation of teams to make continuous improvements flows from its goal to be number one in producing autos.

As managers seek to cope with motivational challenges in the twenty-first century, they are advised to rethink the motivational goals and expectations of their teams and to change their managerial procedures. Using the automotive industry as a case in point, Robert Cole observes that "management has come to recognize that management behavior is the root cause of quality problems."[51] Management consistently underestimates the interest of hourly employees in improving quality; even the United Auto Workers union supports quality improvements.[52] Better technology is not always the answer, for in the late 1980s GM's Buick division achieved dramatic improvements in quality at two plants by reducing automation and initiating in its place plant-level teamwork. Innovation and performance result when teams are motivated to improve. Sometimes that motivational stimulus even comes from deep respect for the honesty of a co-worker who has overcome personal adversity (see the story of Mojo in the Dynamics of Diversity box).

WHAT IS THE INTERACTION BETWEEN LEARNING AND MOTIVATION?

You have already learned that people are capable of learning specific motives, motives such as a need for achievement, power, and affiliation. But learning is not strictly an individual accomplishment. Recently much has been written about organizational learning—most of it extolling the positive virtues of how people learn in the collective as members of a specific organization. But a minority view looks on widespread organizational learning as having negative implications for the organization. To borrow a telecommunications analogy, much of what is learned within an organization has a very narrow bandwidth, whereas what is needed is a broadband channel of learning.

Mojo of the Oilers: An Uncomplicated Life Wins the Hearts of the Team

For 16 years, Bill (Mojo) Lackey was paid by the hour to wash jocks for the Houston Oilers. Mojo was a big man carrying 280 pounds on his 5-foot, 10-inch frame; but he was an uncomplicated man with a slow and innocent nature. With genuine respect, former Houston lineman Carl Mauck described Mojo as "One of life's little people. A simple, wonderful little person." Said Susan Pruett, a close friend whom Mojo called his sister, "Even when you asked him about the Oilers during their bad years, he would say, 'I'm not paid to think about those things, I'm paid to wash clothes.'"

But come game time, Mojo performed a ritual after every Oilers kickoff that was the delight of players and fans. Mojo would gallop onto the field toward the kicking tee, circle around the tee, then pick it up in his left hand and gallop back to the sidelines where he would somersault, spike the tee and scream. When his mother asked him about his ritual of running to retrieve the tee, Mojo replied, "If I go out there slow, then that's how those football players will play."

The respect everyone had for this loving and lovable equipment assistant was put in perspective by lineman Bruce Matthews, a first-round draft choice from USC: "When I joined the team, I had heard of two people there—Earl Campbell and Mojo." When children asked for his autograph, Mojo would sometimes write a page and talk to them for an hour or so. He loved children; friends likened him to a delightful child in an overgrown body.

Mojo spent the last night of his 43-year life on a couch outside the Oiler's locker room—the locker room he considered home. Two days after a massive stroke claimed Mojo, Oiler coach Jeff Fisher ended his Saturday pregame speech by showing his team a video clip of Mojo, then walked out of the room in silence. The next day the Oilers upset Cleveland 37-10. Oilers' players ended the game with chants of "Mo-jo, Mo-jo" as they wept. Nearly 1,000 attended his memorial service. Former teammates came from across the country as if their lives had been touched by an angel in Houston. Mojo was an inspiration to many, including the million dollar players who were central to his uncomplicated but lovable life.

Source: Bill Plaschke, "Life Is Like a Kicking Tee," *Los Angeles Times* (November 23, 1995), pp. C1, C9.

Learning Is Often at a Superficial Level

Learning occurs when, for a given work-related stimulus, employees respond in qualitatively better ways from their responses to similar stimuli in the past.[53] If those new responses result in reduced performance variability or increased productivity, the learning has been economically efficient. To have this occur by design rather than by trial and error, organizational members must question and reassess the relevance of existing work norms, performance standards, and assumptions and beliefs underlying what they do and how they do it.

Chris Argyris used research involving 6,000 people across a wide variety of countries, ages, ethnic identities, educational levels, power levels, experience, and from both sexes to conclude that most modern techniques that promote communication between managers and employees are dysfunctional. Techniques such as TQM, management by walking around, focus groups, organizational surveys, and others inhibit learning. According to Argyris, most learning in organizations is of a single-loop

single-loop learning
Occurs when a manager shifts responsibility from employees to himself or herself by asking simple uni-dimensional questions that produce simple impersonal responses.

character, with the responsibility for learning and action shifted from subordinate to manager. Argyris says: "**Single-loop learning** asks a one-dimensional question to elicit a one-dimensional answer."[54] For example, an executive who asks for the major obstacles to faster product innovation shifts accountability for innovation from employee to the executive, even though on the surface it may appear as if employees are being empowered because their opinions are being asked for.

Shifting Learning to Double-Loop Systems Questioning

double-loop learning
Shifts accountability for actions and learning to employees by having a manager ask complex questions about the employee's motivation for solving a problem.

To enter into double-loop learning, the executive would have to shift accountability back to employees. This might be done by asking tough questions, such as: "How long have you known [about these problems]? What goes on in this company that prevented you from questioning these practices and getting them corrected or eliminated?" **Double-loop learning** turns questions back on people in the form of follow-ups, to ask not only for facts but for the motives behind the facts. But managers are often the problem, for they emphasize positive regard of others, considerateness and morale. Such motives and attitudes "deprive employees and themselves of the opportunity to take responsibility for their own behavior by learning to understand it. Because double-loop learning depends on questioning one's own assumptions and behavior, this apparently benevolent strategy is actually *anti*learning."[55]

In effect, what happens is that managers use socially "upbeat" feedback and behavior to unconsciously inhibit learning. Defensive reasoning protects managers just as it does those who are managed. Organizational members learn a set of rules of dealing with difficult situations in ways that does not embarrass or threaten psychological well-being. Managers end up sending mixed messages when they reply along the lines of "Your recommendation is a good one, but I have to overrule it because . . . " By saving face with subordinates while nevertheless thinking the idea is not a good one, managers are telling employees that your job is to make suggestions, the manager's job is to make decisions and act. Rather than confront others with candor and forthrightness, managers who absolve others are talking the talk but not walking the walk. Rather than promoting empowerment of others, they are creating dependence. Argyris writes:

> *Once employees base their motivation on extrinsic factors—[such as] the CEO's promises—they are much less likely to take chances, question established policies and practices, or explore the territory that lies beyond the company vision as defined by management. They are much less likely to learn.*
>
> *A generation ago, business wanted employees to do exactly what they were told, and company leadership bought their acquiescence with a system of purely extrinsic rewards . . . Today . . . managers need employees who think constantly and creatively about the needs of the organization. They need employees with as much intrinsic motivation and as deep a sense of organizational stewardship as any company executive.*[56]

Organizations Become Learning Systems

Argyris's central thesis is that it is much easier to find out about and treat the symptoms of worker discontent than it is to create learning processes that permit organizational members to probe deeper in solving system-inhibiting problems. Peter Senge, director of the Organizational Learning Center at MIT, has popularized the

learning organization
A deliberate effort by organizational members to develop models, tools, and techniques for their organization to change and grow faster than competitors.

concept of the **learning organization.** He says: "Learning organizations learn faster than the competition, change before they're forced to, and always try to marry personal and financial performance."[57] Learning organizations develop tools and methods to analyze their organizational systems. One firm with successful learning techniques, Royal Dutch Shell, became committed to systematizing learning when its research into older companies found that learning was their key to survival.

Senge reveals limited strategies for substantial double-loop learning.[58] One strategy is to develop a model of how the firm understands the world and can act upon it. Any model must incorporate practical tools and methods that are both substantive—content rich—and provide for behavioral analysis. They "must enable groups of people to develop a better understanding of complex [work] issues and learn how to learn together." Often this means using a learning laboratory that engages computer simulation as a tool to aid systems thinking. A related strategy is to fundamentally redesign work to "inextricably intertwine producing and learning." Like sports teams and the performance arts, organizations need to build in "continual movement between performance and practice." Practice means going off-line from producing output (products, services, decisions, whatever) and experimenting with new plays or working at skill building. GM's Saturn plant has its Worker Development Center adjacent to the assembly line, which contains a mock-up of the assembly process, intended for practice and trying new methods.

As competitive strategies become more driven by speed, flexibility, and agility, the motivation to learn as an organization becomes a critical capability. Firms realize that quick, adaptable responses to customer needs and wants are crucial, as personified by Nissan's "Five A's" vision for the year 2000: anything, anybody, anytime, anywhere, any volume. Other practices that prepare organizations to learn how to learn according to John Slocum and others build on a motivational aspiration to learn as a way of changing:

> *What are these new practices? The first is developing a strategic intent to learn new capabilities. The second is a commitment to continuous experimentation. The third is the ability to learn from past successes and failures. These practices will enable a firm to constantly renew itself and develop new sources of competitive advantage.[59]*

CHUCK MITCHELL AT GTO—A SECOND LOOK

In December 1993, when Chuck Mitchell took over the leadership of GTO, a maker of automatic gate openers, employees were dispirited and doubted the firm would survive. And yet, by energizing and guiding employees' motivation, GTO not only survived but prospered. Mitchell took care of deficiency reduction or hygiene needs by fixing the leaking roof, making coffee available, and granting flexibility in workers' schedules. But at a higher level, he rekindled achievement motives, gave them honest expectancies that if things improved they would materially benefit, and captivated their resourcefulness for organizational learning and innovation.

In February 1994, he raised workers' pay and promised another raise by year's end "if we keep making money." Mitchell left the issue of who got how much up to Payne, one of the administrative managers, who recalled, "I took a printout of all the employees' names and put down what I thought their pay should be. I went to Chuck, and he said, 'If this is what you really feel, then do it.'" Payne did. And the following December when Mitchell handed out the promised profit-sharing checks, each folded inside a company T-shirt in a gift bag, some employees cried.[60] For a change, their ideas were valued, they were trusted, and Chuck Mitchell was managing as if he cared about their well-being as well as company success. He had rekindled motivation, self-confidence, and pride. Employees were eagerly designing the features that would be built into a new, larger, better equipped factory.

SUMMARY

One of life's basic conflicts is whether to approach or avoid a person, task, or event. The direction and intensity of movement toward or away from the situation reflect one's motivation at the moment. Motivation is our conscious decision to direct our effort more toward one or more activities than others and/or to vary the level of effort.

Several theories seek to identify individual needs or motives and suggest how each activates different behaviors. Maslow originally identified five hierarchical levels of needs but later simplified his theory to define needs as either deficiency reduction or growth aspiration forces. Alderfer distilled Maslow's theory into three nonhierarchical needs of existence, relatedness, and growth. This simplification has produced generally favorable research support. Herzberg focused entirely on work motivation and claimed that simply providing for hygiene or maintenance needs will not motivate. Only motivators or the sources of satisfaction found in the nature of work itself will motivate.

Some needs become such compelling sources of satisfaction to an individual that they become socially learned motives. People will consistently engage in activities that satisfy their dominant motive, whether power, achievement, or affiliation. Managers do well to draw on socialized power needs, and entrepreneurs usually have high achievement needs.

The central explanation of motivation as a process is expectancy theory. It explains how individuals evaluate effort–performance–outcome relationships and make behavior choices. Moderating motivation of all kinds are people's perceptions of equity, which are separated into the fairness arenas of distributive and procedural justice.

Theories of motivation popular in North America focus on individual behavior. Yet many organizations are shifting to group-based practices, and in many cultures globally the individual is already subordinate to the group. A new stream of motivation research is expected to focus on providing greater insights into group-based motivation.

Learning affects motivation in more ways than simply shaping the development of motives. Individuals develop an ideology of themselves in relation to their world (including work) that promotes a consistency of task behavior even when motivational stimuli are weak. Organizations are also capable of learning—of solving problems and changing their ways of doing things—if they build in the tools and methods of behavioral analysis that promote a deeper shared commitment toward improvement.

Key Concepts

motivation, *p. 185*

content theories of motivation, *p. 185*

deficiency reduction needs, *p. 186*

growth aspiration needs, *p. 186*

hierarchy of needs, *p. 187*

ERG theory, *p. 188*

dual-factor theory, *p. 190*

hygiene factors, *p. 190*

motivator factors, *p. 191*

job enrichment, *p. 192*

Theory X, *p. 192*

Theory Y, *p. 193*

need to achieve (or achievement motive), *p. 195*

need for power (or power motive), *p. 196*

need for affiliation (or affiliation motive), *p. 196*

personal attribution, *p. 196*

ideology, *p. 198*

process theories of motivation, *p. 199*

expectancy theory, *p. 199*

extrinsic rewards, *p. 201*

intrinsic rewards, *p. 201*

equity theory, *p. 204*

distributive justice, *p. 205*

procedural justice, *p. 205*

referent cognitions theory, *p. 205*

single-loop learning, *p. 209*

double-loop learning, *p. 209*

learning organization, *p. 210*

Questions for Study and Discussion

1. Philosopher Alfred North Whitehead proposed that all human beings seek three purposes: first to be alive, next to live well, and finally to live better.[61] Compare this thought to the theory of motivation you believe most closely parallels it.

2. Under what circumstances do needs serve as reliable motivators at work? Which theory based on needs do you believe to be most useful to managers? Give two ways in which a manager could apply the theory to strengthen the motivation of team members so that they approach rather than avoid essential tasks.

3. Suppose an executive made the statement: "Entrepreneurs are driven by achievement motivation, managers in big firms need to be power motivated, but affiliation-motivated people make lousy managers." Explain the underlying validity of each of the three observations.

4. What are the three key variables of expectancy theory? Give one example of how a person's evaluation of each of the three could lead to a conclusion to increase motivation on a task. Give an example of an evaluation leading to the opposite conclusion.

5. Can a person who is "satisfied" still be motivated? Explain the distinction and relationship between satisfaction and motivation.

6. In what ways might a person adjust if she believed she was unjustly undercompensated? Overcompensated? In considering such equity issues, how does procedural justice differ from distributive justice?

7. Theories of motivation have focused primarily on explaining individual behavior. What are some of the emerging forces that suggest that group-based motivation will become more important in the future?

8. What action would you recommend as a manager to motivate a work group to thrive on organizational learning?

EXPERIENTIAL EXERCISE

What's Your Motive?

Purpose. Managers who are successful at motivating others often pick up clues about the motives of colleagues from their behavior and spoken words. They then try to alter work tasks or elements that direct and energize others. Although brief, this dyad exercise provides practice in reading motive clues from a peer, then responding with intended motivational-enhancing strategies. (Time required: about 15 to 20 minutes.)

Procedure. Form two-person groups. One person takes the position of A, the other B.

1. A begins by describing two recent events: one event in which he or she was really turned on, putting a lot of conscious effort into doing something that was personally meaningful; the other event in which A just couldn't put much into it, where the effort was at most half-hearted (about 2 minutes for each).

2. B then analyzes and describes whatever clues he or she can discern from these scenarios about A's motives or needs. B should draw on whatever theories of motivation that may provide diagnostic insights into the other person's behavior in response to the two different situations—maybe there is an explanation based on achievement, affiliation, or power motives, or perhaps there were underlying unsatisfied needs, expectancies, or equity factors (2 to 3 minutes).

3. Having attempted to analytically interpret clues provided by A, then B describes a work situation in which B is a manager and A is a member of B's group. B now recommends actions he or she would take as a manager to bring out the motivational best in A. Then, A provides feedback about the likely impact of B's strategies or actions on A's behavior (2 to 3 minutes).

4. Reverse roles and repeat steps 1 through 3 with the spotlight on B.

Debriefing. Time permitting, the instructor may want to bring out some best practices by asking for some sharing with the class. Think about the analysis and interpretation your partner offered about your personal situations.

1. Was your partner's interpretation especially insightful, one that accurately reflects one or more of your learned motives or other motivational tendencies? If so, have two or three dyads share those insights. The one making the interpretation should explain how he or she "read" the clues.

2. Did your partner interpret your scenarios based on his or her own motives? In other words, did your partner seem to interpret your stories based on what is important to him or her, in effect reading his or her personal motives into your situation? If so, this is not uncommon for people with highly accentuated learned motives. Have one or two dyads discuss this situation.

3. Would your partner's managerial action recommendations be appropriately motivating for you? If so, have a couple of dyads explain, with the one being "motivated" reflecting on why it would be personally motivating.

EXPERIENTIAL EXERCISE

Team Problem Solving: Lightning Rod Motivation

Purpose. This is a team-based exercise designed to (1) analyze the motivational implications of data generated by a group of engineers working for Lightning Rod Steel (LRS), (2) develop and present to the class a theory-supported action plan for improving motivation of the engineers, and (3) use the same criteria developed by the engineers to assess motivational factors affecting you in a work situation. (Time required: 35 to 45 minutes.)

Procedures. Perform the following five tasks:

1. Assemble the class into teams of five to seven students each.

2. As a team, read the background material, including Exhibit 6–6 (about 3 to 4 minutes).

3. Have each team first analyze the Lightning Rod situation to determine the presumed lack of motivation among engineers. Then, use one established theory of motivation as the basis for developing an action plan of recommendations to "improve the motivation" of the steel company engineers. What specific actions should the managers take? Make sure your plan is feasible and reasonable for the managers to accept (10 to 15 minutes).

4. Have each team member score the 19 motivational factors listed by the engineers in Exhibit 6–6. Determine how much each factor contributes to *your* motivation in an ideal work situation. Assign points from 0 to 5, where 5 means "extremely desirable" and 0 indicates "unimportant." Record your points in the "Your Ideal Scores" section of the exhibit. Then think of any factors important to you that are missing from the list. Compare your responses to those of the engineers and your team members. Plan to comment to the class on why your team scores were similar to or different from the engineers' (about 10 minutes).

5. Present your recommendations and observations to the class. Debrief the activity to look for insights into how motivational expectations and motives differ among your peers (about 15 minutes).

Background of Lightning Rod Steel (LRS). Lightning Rod produces a number of rolled, bar, and tubular steel products from a single mill fueled by two electric hearth furnaces that melt recycled scrap metal. Kent Olsen, the director of manufacturing services, and his two engineering managers are concerned that, given a recession-induced soft market for steel and the constant need

to cut costs by improving efficiencies, "we aren't getting 100 percent from our engineering staff." Engineers number about three dozen and are of two types. Design engineers work on special projects for plant modernization. Industrial engineers update work standards, work method improvements, compensation incentives, and similar projects.

Olsen approaches your consulting group with a couple of questions: "One of the issues we've been unable to resolve among ourselves is how to determine the productivity of engineering professionals, and then how to improve it. Second, why aren't more of our engineers being pirated away by our seven operating general managers for higher paying managerial jobs?" He hands you a page (Exhibit 6–6) developed by the engineers during a recent training session. The data were developed in response to the question, "Brainstorm a list of what you would like to experience more often or have more of in your work situation, then evaluate ideal and actual conditions on a 0- to 5-point scale." Olsen continues, "Maybe this gives you some clues as to what we could do better to motivate engineers."

■■■■■   **EXHIBIT 6–6**

What LRS Engineers Expect at Work

Scores reflect the group mean, with 5 points maximum.

Work Factors	Engineer's Scores		Your Ideal Scores
	Ideal Conditions	Actual Experience	
1. Open and honest communication	4.8	2.2	_____
2. A sense of fairness and justice	4.3	2.0	_____
3. Seeing the results of my work	4.3	2.7	_____
4. The opportunity to get my job done	4.2	2.5	_____
5. Feedback about how I am doing	4.0	2.0	_____
6. Interesting work assignments	4.0	2.2	_____
7. Opportunity for advancement	4.0	0.5	_____
8. Being compensated for performance	4.0	1.5	_____
9. Upward and/or lateral job mobility	4.0	0.8	_____
10. Recognition for work accomplishments	3.8	1.8	_____
11. A say in things that affect me	3.8	1.8	_____
12. A sense of involvement in the company	3.7	2.0	_____
13. Being informed of policies/job openings	3.5	0.7	_____
14. Working for a winning/successful team	3.2	1.7	_____
15. Even work distribution (no peaks/valleys)	3.0	2.0	_____
16. Equitable access to benefits	3.0	2.8	_____
17. A variety of tasks (job rotation)	2.8	1.8	_____
18. Security of not working myself out of job	2.5	1.5	_____
19. Good physical working environment	2.0	1.3	_____

Ralph Henry's Motivational Crisis
By Elaine Chiang

Ralph Henry had worked as a production chemist at Systems Diagnostics Corporation (SDC) for seven years. The last four of those years were with the MED group, during which he received two promotions to become the group's senior chemist. Conscientious and thorough in his work, Ralph was a stickler for details in the lab yet always willing to help others. Co-workers liked Ralph's pleasant, friendly manner and his lively conversations about sports and running (his major avocations). But beyond the immediate group, Ralph was rather private. He interacted with few people outside the MED group and rarely attended social functions and company parties.

Ralph had always enjoyed his career as a chemist. He was particularly pleased with the laboratory environment, which allowed him to work freely and independently, pursuing whatever challenge or idea that came along. It was no big surprise, then, when Ken Chang asked Ralph to become supervisor of the MED group and take over a role Chang had held for three years.

The Reorganization. Systems Diagnostics Corporation makes diagnostic reagent kits and pharmaceutical instrumentation for hospitals, clinical laboratories, and some government agencies. The firm was having difficulties containing costs and had recently announced the third consecutive decline in quarterly profits. Although sales were steady, with the latest announcement of profit erosion, senior management also announced a reorganization to consolidate product lines. As a result of the reorganization, Ken Chang was promoted to production manager of a newly created division, leaving vacant his former position as supervisor of the MED group. While a supervisor, Ken spent much of his time outside the group and, in doing so, granted considerable autonomy to his chemists.

When offered the supervisor's position, Ralph initially balked. He explained to Ken his reluctance to leave the lab bench and his feelings of uneasiness about supervising a group of longtime peers. All of his education was in pure science; he had no management training or experience. Ken promised that Ralph could participate in management training seminars and expressed his confidence that Ralph would quickly master the art of management.

The Promotion. After a week of contemplation, Ralph accepted. When his appointment was announced, members of the MED group were delighted and hosted a congratulatory luncheon for Ralph.

Six months into the supervisory job, Ralph's attitude was as conscientious and upbeat as ever. Much of his time was spent thoroughly checking each group member's work. Unlike Ken in the role of supervisor, Ralph required that all product tests be documented in detail and often requested that routine lab testings be repeated to confirm accuracy. Rather than delegate difficult problems to group members, Ralph took on most of these complex lab tasks himself and often worked late into the evening.

The Crisis. In mid-December a major crisis required Ralph's immediate attention. The deadline on a large naval contract assigned to the MED group was moved from mid-February to mid-January. Management wanted very much to make good on this contract, as the Navy was a potential major customer. But because of technical difficulties, Ralph did not believe MED would meet the deadline, since SDC had a tradition of shutting down during the holidays. To respond to the pressure, Ralph called a meeting of all group members, something he rarely did. He spelled out the situation:

"As you're all aware, we are having a big technical problem with the Navy contract. To compound our troubles, I just got word from management that the deadline has been moved up one month to mid-January. This really puts us in a jam because the plant is scheduled to be shut down for 10 days over the holidays.

"Personally, I know the project is more important than my holiday plans, so I'm canceling them. What I'd like to know is who will be willing to work with me, say, a few of the 10 days. Of course you'll get comp time—or overtime pay, if you prefer. How many of you will be willing to work with me?"

The group was silent. Not one of the 10 members raised a hand or spoke up.

Questions for Managerial Action

1. What motivates Ralph Henry? How do these forces impact on his behavior as a chemist? As a supervisor?

2. What likely motivates the other chemists in the MED group? How well does Ralph understand these motivational forces and adjust his supervisory behavior to bring out their best? Compare the motivational impact on the chemists of Ken Chang's approach to supervision with that of Ralph Henry.

3. Why the "no hands" response to Ralph's request for help? What does it indicate about Ralph's development as a supervisor? Given no volunteers, what does Ralph do now?

Motivation Methods and Applications

LEARNING OBJECTIVES

After studying this chapter, you should be able to:

- Write a simple, clear, challenging goal statement that includes an action verb, key result area, measurement standard, and time frame.
- Identify the desired processes in an effective management by objectives (MBO) program.
- Differentiate among the four alternative forms of behavior-shaping reinforcement (positive, negative, punishment, and omission).
- Tell how to implement an organizational behavior modification program to change a routine behavior.
- Describe three types of incentive or reward plans and explain their links to equity and expectancy motivation.
- Use the principles of task scope and task depth to differentiate among jobs that are classified as routine, technician, enlarged, or enriched.
- Evaluate a job's psychological health (experienced meaningfulness, responsibility, and knowledge of results) using the six core job dimensions that characterize work.
- Illustrate three practices managers can use to empower employees and thereby reduce the need for managerial control.

THE IPO: A MOTIVATIONAL TOOL FOR INNOVATION, FROM SAMUEL ADAMS TO NETSCAPE

Are you motivated by the prospect of innovation, success, and wealth? Are you willing to take risks with the possibility of hitting that grand slam home run, of making it big in business? If so, rather than look to employment with big business, consider venturing into the business that isn't—the start-up. In the world of entrepreneurs who start up businesses with the singular goal of building a better something, the future dream of IPOs has become the extrinsic motivator of the 1990s.

initial public offering (IPO)
Initial sale of a firm's stock on a public security exchange.

Early members of the start-up team typically look forward to the day when their company goes public, when the **initial public offering (IPO)** hits the stock market. Early team members are attracted to the goal of converting their sweat equity into shares of stock that have a market value and can be converted into cash once the public is willing to trade in its shares of stock. The 1990s have produced unprecedented growth in IPOs, propeling innovation as a source of economic growth. *Business Week* writes:

> *Entrepreneur-driven businesses are spreading across the country . . . IPO capitalism is a vital force in the remarkable resurgence in U.S. competitiveness in the global economy, especially in many leading-edge industries . . . IPO capitalism is being propelled by a series of simultaneous, self-reinforcing trends: Successful first-generation high-tech entrepreneurs are funding a new generation of innovators; technology is creating new opportunities for entrepreneurs; hordes of enterprising people are starting their own companies; and pension and mutual funds are increasingly eager to invest in emerging companies. Taken all together, money and ideas are combining at a faster and faster rate, creating new markets and new products which, in turn, replenish the IPO well.*

Just who are these IPO-driven entrepreneurs? Here's a snapshot of two who have been successful at opposite ends of the marketplace, from suds to surfing—two guys named Jim.

Samuel Adams' Jim Koch. Jim Koch (pronounced "Cook") at age 35 quit his $250,000 job with the Boston Consulting Group to follow in his father's footsteps and become a brewer. Koch dusted off an old family recipe he found in his father's attic, drafted a business plan, raised $140,000 to supplant his own $100,000 investment, and launched the Boston Beer Co. (BBC) with a brand he called Samuel Adams. Ironically, in 1985 he sold his first case of Samuel Adams to a pub about a block from the site of its namesake's 1776 brewery. Ten years later, BBC was producing $14 million profits on sales of $180 million, fueled by the demanding goals set by founder Jim Koch. By motivating his sales force with specific improvement goals, this start-up had become the tenth largest beer producer in the United States by its 10th anniversary.

With the success of Samuel Adams' 40 percent annual growth, Koch views his goals as CEO, "To create change, to make Boston Beer a constantly different company. I like challenges; I like building. I get up in the morning to build." While his business goal is to make the perfect beer, Koch patiently waited 10 years to take BBC public to finance sustained growth. Even though venture capitalists and some employees owned considerable founder's stock, Koch retained 42 percent ownership. The balanced success of Boston Beer earned him the distinction of *Inc.* magazine's runner-up entrepreneur of the year.

Netscape's Jim Clark.   While brewing is one of the world's oldest industries and the second most popular drink (after tea), the popularity of web pages on the Internet didn't become an electronic craze until 1995. Like the other Jim, Jim Clark is highly educated and quit his day job—as a professor at Stanford University—to pursue his entrepreneurial passion. James H. Clark had been researching ways to make computer graphics come alive, but he believed he could change computing practices only if he became directly involved in business. Clark the entrepreneur started Silicon Graphics, Inc., the firm that became the premier three-dimensional computer graphics company. But Clark, the computer scientist and entrepreneur, eventually butted heads with managers who opposed his goal of making low-cost machines.

He retired from SGI financially well-off and became a two-time entrepreneurial phenomenon when he created Netscape. Netscape's strategy is to give away the Internet browser and pull in revenue from the software that client firms use to get on the Net. In less than a year, Netscape's software ruled 75 percent of the Web. Netscape placed its IPO in August 1995 at an initial offering price of $28 per share. Within four months, the stock price was trading at more than $160, which made Clark a billionaire and Netscape's earliest team members multimillionaires. Employees are given stock options that can be exercised for as little as $9 per share one year after joining Netscape. In the meantime, they are given specific and challenging goals. The promise of an IPO motivates many.

Sources: Christopher Farrell, "The Boom in IPOs," *Business Week* (December 18, 1995), pp. 64–72; Robert A. Mamis, "Market Maker," *Inc.* (December 1995), pp. 54–64; and "Special Report: Going Public," *Inc.* (May 1966), pp. 34–68.

Organizations have many options for focusing and motivating the behavior of employees. They can set goals, apply selective rewards such as stock options, redesign jobs, create a sense of empowerment to unleash motivation, and even reinforce routine behaviors through the use of organizational behavior modification. The experiences of Jim Koch and Jim Clark suggest that taking a start-up company public with generous stock options for early team members is a motivational inducement for people attracted to entrepreneurial challenges.

Obviously, the prospect of waiting to make it big in the stock market (10 years for Boston Beer, 1 year for Netscape) is not the only motivational driver for people like Koch, Clark, and the partners or employees who join them. Typically, entrepreneurs have a goal of transforming their industry or providing innovative benefits to their customers. Koch's success started a minor revolution in microbrewing, and Clark's businesses made pioneering inroads into computing—first in three-dimensional graphics and then in browsing the Internet. Whatever the goal, undoubtedly there were strong motivational forces stimulating these entrepreneurs and their colleagues.

Chapter 6 surveyed influential theories of motivation and how they affect management. This chapter extends principles of motivation by surveying several techniques designed to direct, focus, and energize human behavior at work. It ranges from goal setting, to reinforcement and systems of rewards, to redesigning jobs and extending capabilities through empowerment.

One of the problems with motivational practices is that many are based on gimmicks, ranging from paying thousands of dollars for a brief inspirational speech by a famous person to handing out premiums that cost a few dollars. At a recent "Motivation Show" in Chicago's McCormick Place, more than 40,000 corporate people looked over the offerings of 3,200 vendor booths selling everything from products to ideas proclaimed to get people to work more productively.[1] Rather than fads and gimmicks, this chapter reviews motivational practices that are widely used and researched to reveal strengths as well as limitations. Flexibility and some variety of approaches are advocated, for people are motivated by different needs and goals.[2]

WHY DO GOALS ENHANCE MOTIVATION?

Work performance is affected by company policies and practices, manager–employee relationships, and organizational goals. Edwin Locke initiated a stream of research that suggests goal striving is a common element in most motivational theories.[3] A **goal** is the desired outcome of an action; it becomes motivational when an individual wants it and strives to achieve it. The goal of a football team is to win the next game, then the league championship. A goal of a marketing department might be to increase global market share three points in the next 12 months.

goal
The desired outcome of an action, which becomes motivational when a person wants it and strives to achieve it.

Difficult Goals Stimulate Effort and Commitment

The use of goals to motivate task accomplishment draws on two primary attributes: the content of the goal and the level of intensity in working toward it.[4] *Content* emphasizes the features of the goal and its level of specificity—which implies a level of difficulty in attaining it. *Intensity* considers the process by which a goal is set—the extent of participation—and the cognitive commitment and intention to bring it about.

Content—Level of Difficulty. Apart from the specificity or tangibility of a goal, most content-related research has concentrated on the relationship between goal difficulty and performance. Using meta-analysis (an analysis of many other studies), two researchers conclude that 175 of 192 laboratory and field research studies produced partial or full support for the hypothesis: Given adequate ability and commitment, more difficult goals stimulate greater effort and performance than easier goals.[5]

To reduce air pollution, the U.S. Environmental Protection Agency uses negative reinforcement: it publishes a list of the top corporate air polluters every five years. In order to stay off that list, Monsanto has cut worldwide toxic air releases from its chemical plants by approximately 90 percent since 1987. (Photo: © Bob Hower/Quadrant)

Intensity—Degree of Participation.   Researchers have examined three types of goal setting: (1) when goals are assigned by management, (2) when members participate in goal setting, and (3) when members are told "Do your best."[6] The results indicate that either having a goal assigned or participating in goal setting are associated with higher performance than the simple instruction to "do your best."

Ironically, while participation often produces greater commitment to goals and perceptions of self-control and fairness,[7] participation does not necessarily lead to higher performance than manager-assigned goals. One workable combination is for managers to assign goals, hold people responsible for results, grant people the autonomy to plan their actions and exercise control over how they do their work, then measure results. People who have the capability to do the task and are committed to achieving it generally will perform well regardless of their degree of participation in setting the goal.[8] Goals that are met motivate higher performance only when they lead to the setting of higher goals.

Participative goal setting can focus on four kinds of goals: Routine goals (an extension of what people are already doing), problem solving to overcome shortcomings, innovation, and personal development to spur greater achievement.[9] By focusing on goals rather than controls, a manager can align people behind organizational purposes and then allow individual initiative without sacrificing coordination.[10] The relaxation of external controls helps people develop a greater capacity for internalizing their commitment to relevant and meaningful tasks. Managers at Birkenstock Footprint Sandals, a company of fewer than 150 employees, encourage people to form task forces to solve complex problems (such as how to use recycling to save energy).[11]

Intentions Combine Goals and Action Plans

intention
Mental awareness of having both a goal and an action plan to obtain the goal.

Understanding intentions is central to fully understanding any cognitive approach to motivation practices, such as goal setting. Intentions encompass more than goal setting alone. A goal represents the desired outcome of action. An **intention** is a

actions
Deliberate choices about where to direct behaviors combined with intense, persistent efforts to achieve a goal over some time period.

"cognitive representation of both the objective [or goal] one is striving for and the action plan one intends to use to reach that objective."[12] Even more explicitly, an intention contains a target combined with some specific action that is focused on bringing about an event within a specified time.[13]

Actions involve choices about the direction of effort, combined with intensity and persistence over some time period. If Todd's goal is to stop his marketing department's warfare with design engineering, he is likely to initiate peacemaking and cooperative behaviors. If he really intends to improve the relationship, Todd likely will continue his cooperative behaviors until the people in engineering realize he is serious about resolving differences between the two. In effect, Todd's goal-setting process builds on the intention to reduce discrepancies between his current situation and a desired future outcome.

The more a manager specifies goals, the easier it is for others to frame their intentions for achieving them. However, if an assigned goal is either too difficult or too easy, personalized intentions are likely to vary from those envisioned by the manager.[14] It also helps if the employee engages in internal attribution and is hopeful of achieving the goal. "Having hope means believing you have both the will and the way to accomplish your goals, whatever they may be . . . Hope has proven a powerful predictor of outcome in every study we've done so far," reports a research psychologist.[15] In a study of 3,920 students at the University of Kansas, researchers found that the amount of hope among entering freshmen was more predictive of academic success than either high school grades or SAT scores, the two conventional predictors.[16] Preliminary data suggest people with high hope tend to be reality centered, set higher goals for themselves, and actively work to attain their expectations. In short, they are motivated.

One such high-hope individual with clear intentions is Allen Breed, who founded Breed Corporation in 1961 to design timing devices for military ordinance. Breed became the visionary evangelist promoting the use of air bags for auto safety. As described in the Eye on Ethics box, he and his small group of engineers labored for nearly 20 years before his air bag technology was accepted by the auto industry.

Management by Objectives (MBO) Sets Priorities

Dave Matthews, former director of training for the Water Council of Scotland, used to open his general management training programs with the statement: "Management by objectives. Ladies and gentlemen, I ask you, is there any other way to manage?" Matthews was speaking of identifying key objectives to be achieved within a specific time period. Throughout the past four decades, organizations have made objective setting a systematic part of their business planning.

management by objectives (MBO)
The practice of manager and subordinate jointly determining time-specific objectives.

The formal process of **management by objectives,** popularly known as **MBO,** is based on the philosophy that the manager and the managed ought to negotiate or collaborate on defining the objectives the subordinate is to pursue over the next time period. The concept originated with management guru Peter Drucker,[17] and was popularized by George Odiorne.[18] Numerous organizations adopt MBO as a formal management practice and link it to performance appraisals and compensation. As a practice, MBO is supposed to provide a cross-check of the purposes pursued by managers at different organizational levels and coordinate objectives from top to bottom.

Saving Lives: Breed Automotive Bags the Big Three

As described by his wife, financier, and business partner, Allen Breed doesn't have a bad day, "He has a good day or a better day." Allen Breed, *Inc.* magazine's "entrepreneur of the year" has been variously described as inventor, visionary, obstinate, optimistic. Breed himself says in matter-of-fact tone, "I never met a rich pessimist."

Breed personifies the entrepreneur's goal of championing a socially desirable product, fighting powerful opposition, and making it big. But it took him and his employees 30 years to become an overnight success. During about 20 of those 30 years, Allen Breed was almost the lone voice in inventing and advocating the use of automobile air bags, the safety device designed to save lives in the instant of a crash. During those years, his small team at Breed Technologies, Inc., of Lakeland, Florida, kept improving on the design of air bag sensors, driving out costs through simplification and improving the speed and reliability of performance.

But Breed's targeted customers, the Big Three auto makers, wanted nothing of air bags. To Detroit executives, air bags wouldn't sell cars, they would only add to costs. Breed, the pioneer and evangelist, was continually rejected by auto makers in North America and abroad from 1967 to 1984. Every time a particular design was rebuffed by an auto executive, he would go back to the drawing board and encourage his team with, "We're going to swing 'em, boys," He continued to turn a deaf ear to the targeted customer, continuing to subsidize his air bag vision with cash flow from producing ordinance sensors for the military.

Breed believes "When something is basically good, you can suppress it for a while, but you can't kill it." He believed auto safety would sell if given a chance. Breed's chance came in 1984, the year the federal government finally mandated the phase-in of air bags.

During the lean years of not winning a single automotive customer, Allen Breed went through three divorces, flirted with bankruptcy, was blacklisted by key customers, mortgaged personal assets, and survived triple-bypass surgery. Once the federal mandate appeared unavoidable to GM and Ford, they tried to persuade Breed to license his technology to someone big such as TRW or Siemens. But Breed was a manufacturer and believed his people could make the parts cheaper in-house than could anyone on the outside. Breed Automotive (Breed's new air bag division) was able to make for 45 cents using hand labor a part that cost TRW $2 as they struggled to debug automated hardware.

"By the early '90s we had 90% of GM's business. In 1992 Ford shut down TRW and gave us all the business." During the first five years of the 1990s, Breed sold nearly 75 million sensors for more than 140 models of cars. In fiscal 1995 his company made $110 million in pretax profits on revenues of $410 million. For Allen Breed, persistence paid off in dollars and lives saved. Commitment to an ethical ideal can have its rewards.

Source: Adapted from Anne Murphy, "Entrepreneur of the Year," *Inc.* (December 1995), pp. 38–51.

The intent of MBO is threefold: (1) to strengthen planning, (2) to encourage participative decision making, and (3) to motivate performance of tasks that have a high payoff for the organization. In a formal MBO process, four steps are typically employed by the manager and subordinate:[19]

1. Agreement on key goals or objectives.
2. Action planning to work on the objectives.
3. Self-control and corrective actions to keep on target.
4. Periodic formal reviews and performance appraisals.

DILBERT • Scott Adams

Source: San Jose Mercury News (June 14, 1995).

The Give and Take of Setting Objectives.   The process is intended to give participants a clearer idea of organizational priorities and of where effort should be concentrated. Ideally, people reporting to a manager who uses MBO are responsible for drafting individual job objectives. The manager then reviews each person's objectives in a face-to-face, give-and-take planning session until they generally agree on the priorities and expected levels of accomplishment. Although some organizations make MBO a formal management practice, today it is common to have some form of MBO practiced in only some parts of the organization or by only some managers.

During their objective-setting review, Arlene, a senior manager, might tell Jay, one of her subordinate managers, "I agree fully with your objectives one through four and number six. These are critical to your department's success. From my point of view, objective five is not necessary, but if you have time and want to pursue it, okay. However, number seven needs to be more challenging and performed sooner. Let's come back to it and see if a higher level of performance isn't possible. But don't waste time on eight, for the company is about to restructure that function so you'd just be spinning your wheels. Now, about that seventh objective . . ."

In theory, this process of agreeing to objectives is one of collaboration. In practice, the manager may veto, change, or impose objectives. Regardless of the degree of participation in objective setting, the important factor is for both people to have a shared expectation of what needs to be done during the next planning cycle. Then it is necessary for both to periodically review progress toward the objectives, and where necessary to make adjustments in the priority or scope of objectives or in the actions taken in pursuit of them.[20]

Limitations versus Benefits.   MBO works well if there is respect and trust between the subordinate and manager, and if the subordinate keeps the manager informed of progress and setbacks. If the relationship is strained or adversarial, or if MBO is required by the organization but not accepted by a manager, then the process is risky. Authoritarian managers seldom change their style and can use MBO as a club. Formula-driven MBO may also reduce flexibility, increase conflict, diminish innovation, and consume time. And in a worst case scenario, some jobs just don't have sufficient flexibility for a person's motivation and ability to really affect performance.[21]

■■■■■■■ **EXHIBIT 7–1**

Four Steps to Writing Clear Goals

Goals need to be clear, specific, and challenging, and one way to achieve this is to *write operational objectives*. A four-step approach is suggested:

1. Begin with an *action verb* preceded by the word "to." Examples: To build, To complete, To present, To learn, To improve, To decrease, To prevent, To sell.

2. Identify a relevant *key result area* that is the performance target. Examples: customer service, reports, orders, inventory, accidents, attendance, accounts receivable.

3. State a *performance indicator* or *measurement standard* that specifies the targeted degree of quality and quantity to be achieved. Indicators can be stated in monetary units, resource units consumed, average time per task, percentages, or changes.

4. Provide a *time frame* by or during which the key result will be produced. Examples: by Friday noon, by the 15th of each month, each week, one week before the IRS deadline.

Here are two brief examples of complete operational objectives:

- To decrease time lost by equipment failure to no more than 10 minutes per day during June.
- To develop marketing forecasts on the gamma product line acceptable to the CEO by December 1.

Source: Demonstrated by Edward J. Harrick at a USAID-sponsored organization development workshop in Bombay, India.

Although the concept of MBO is widely known to managers and has been used by about half the large U.S. corporations, research suggests the success rate is lower than anticipated.[22] As also found in the total quality management (TQM) movement, substance can give way to form when a practice is forced on managers without really becoming part of their working philosophy. But for managers who believe that a shared understanding of priorities is an important precursor of action, MBO can focus and guide behaviors. From an equity viewpoint, it also means that performance reviews and reward processes can be based on results rather than personal characteristics or extraneous variables.[23]

Goals Should Be Clear, Specific, Challenging

To activate energetic, task-focused behavior, a person needs clear, specific, and challenging goals. Especially when delegating tasks, managers should describe clearly what is wanted and provide specific feedback as to the appropriateness of work being done.[24] Suggestions on how to write goals that satisfy the clear, specific, challenging criteria are offered in Exhibit 7–1.

For example, Rose Vasquez, vice president of human resources for a large insurance company, was concerned that Ed Tran, her director of training and development, has been using too many contract training programs from outside consultants, programs that were not central to company needs. During a performance review with Tran 18 months ago, Vasquez stated, "Next year your staff needs to develop and deliver more in-company training for sales agents and cut back on off-the-shelf contract programs."

During the next review, Vasquez expressed disappointment that training originated by the training staff was only 30 percent of the total, although she acknowledged it was up almost 5 percent. She decided to be more explicit: "Ed, for this next year I want you to target 60 percent of your training days for staff-delivered programs and only 40 percent for outside vendors. You develop a plan for achieving it, and let's review it and then meet monthly to review progress toward that plan and the milestones you set." Six months later, Tran was ahead of plan and close to a 50–50 milestone. Participant satisfaction ratings were up nearly 25 percent, a major improvement in the quality of sales training. Vasquez celebrated the progress by taking Tran and his group to a celebration luncheon.

Feedback about performance variables and authority to take corrective action give employees a greater sense of being in control of their jobs. Workers at Milliken's textile plant in Blacksburg, South Carolina, are reminded by signs that they can shut down machines without a supervisor's approval if defects occur (left). Another sign (right), updated daily, reminds workers of the number of days since a late shipment. The message is a subtle hint to get orders out on time so the string of ontime orders continues. (Photos: © Adam Bartos.)

The incident between Vasquez and Tran demonstrates the complex impact of participation in goal setting. When initially given freedom to set his own goals, Tran failed to make the shift Vasquez apparently was looking for. Tran was then assigned a goal by his boss, but he was responsible for planning how to achieve the target, and did so.

HOW DOES REINFORCEMENT MODIFY BEHAVIOR?

A goal requires cognitive or mental involvement by those who pursue it. Let's now consider reinforcement, a less cognitive-dependent technique to modify or shape desired behaviors. **Reinforcement** is the process of managing behavior by having a contingent consequence follow a behavior with the intent of promoting a consistent pattern of behavioral responses.[25] Reinforcement is the product of a *behaviorism* philosophy, meaning that behavior is believed to be shaped by environmental consequences.

There are different types of reinforcement, each designed to promote a specific behavioral response. The buzzing of an alarm clock may send you promptly hopping out of bed to catch a plane or to meet a friend if you anticipate positive consequences. The identical sound may be greeted with less enthusiasm but may still produce the same on-time behavior if you aim to avoid a negative consequence, such as a late start on an exam or a reprimand for showing up late at work. The first incident is an example of positive reinforcement—pleasant consequences promote a desired behavior. The second reflects negative reinforcement—potentially adverse consequences where the desire to avoid something unpleasant promotes the desired behavior.

Behavior Modification Follows an ABC Sequence

Management applications of reinforcement theory rest on the assumption that people in positions of authority can be taught to use environmental consequences to stimulate and shape behaviors of others. Authorities such as teachers and

reinforcement
The use of contingent consequences following a behavior to shape a consistent behavior pattern.

━━━━━━ EXHIBIT 7–2

Four Common Reinforcers

The objective of reinforcement is to apply consequences (reinforcers) following a behavior that will shape a patterned response to a given antecedent condition.

- **Positive reinforcers**—pleasant, rewarding, or otherwise satisfying contingent consequences that are used to initiate or increase a desired behavior. They should increase in frequency as the desired behavior increases. Praise and tangible rewards or gifts are positive reinforcers widely used at work. So are more attractive office space, a more prestigious job title, extra time off, and off-site meetings at resorts.
- **Negative reinforcers**—the removal or reduction of an aversive condition following a desired behavior to initiate or increase the desired behavior. The contingent consequence of the desired behavior is relief or escape from something unpleasant, threatening, or dissatisfying. Negative reinforcement is at work when one person acts to avoid another's wrath or ridicule or to prevent personal harm. It keeps us paying our bills on time and obeying the speed limit.
- **Punishment**—an aversive event or the removal of a positive event following a behavior, designed to reduce the frequency of the behavior or to eliminate it altogether. Punishment in the workplace is less severe than in the criminal justice system and may involve warnings, withdrawal of privileges, or assignment to unpleasant tasks. The most severe punishment is probably dismissal.
- **Omission**—a completely neutral response to a negative behavior to encourage its diminishment. It is often the ideal response to chronic complainers and others with annoying habits, such as telling offensive jokes.

Source: Lee W. Frederikson (Ed.), *Handbook of Organizational Behavior Management* (New York: John Wiley & Sons, 1982).

managers who use reinforcement to shape the behaviors of others apply an $A \rightarrow B \rightarrow C$ *model* structured around *antecedent, behavior,* and *consequence.*

Antecedent.   *A* represents the antecedent condition or cue that precedes a set of behavior alternatives—the stimulus or circumstance that invites a desired behavior. The traffic light turning yellow, the alarm clock ringing, the manager asking for a report, a calendar note about a noon luncheon meeting—these are all antecedent conditions.

Behavior.   *B* is the behavior in response to the antecedent circumstance. Applying the car brakes rather than speeding up, getting out of bed rather than going back to sleep, submitting a comprehensive report on time rather than saying "I was too busy," or showing up for the noontime meeting on time—these behaviors represent the desired responses to the antecedent cues.

Consequence.   *C* represents an environmental consequence that is contingent on behavior. As noted in Exhibit 7–2, the most common consequence is *positive reinforcement,* such as public praise from the manager for an analytically sound report. At times the consequence is *negative reinforcement,* which reduces or avoids a potential negative outcome. Negative reinforcement occurs when a person shows up on time for work to avoid having his or her pay docked. *Punishment* is used to decrease a behavior (for example, when the police officer gives a citation to the speeder). *Omission*—a neutral response, such as ignoring someone who tries to be a comedian at a meeting—also tends to diminish offending behavior.

The **law of effect** advocates that consequences should immediately follow behavior to reinforce the link between the two. With repeated reinforcement over time, the desired behavior becomes systematic.

law of effect
The principle that the consequences of behavior should be immediate to reinforce the link between the two.

organizational behavior modification (OB mod)
Deliberate management application of the antecedent→behavior→consequence sequence to shape desired employee behaviors.

Managing Environments with Organizational Behavior Modification (OB Mod)

When managers deliberately apply the $A \rightarrow B \rightarrow C$ sequence to shape the behavior of others, they are applying what is popularly called **organizational behavior modification,** or **OB mod** for short.[26] OB mod is potentially useful in improving tangible, observable, measurable, repeatable behaviors. It has been

EXHIBIT 7–3

Steps in Organizational Behavior Modification

OB mod requires a systematic planning and strategy process based on data, analysis, and contingent reinforcement. The goal is to establish a desired A → B → C sequence.

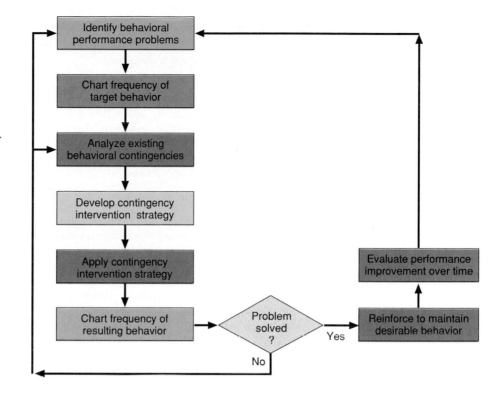

found to help reduce absenteeism, reduce substandard output, increase total output, improve safety (by increasing the number of accident-free days), and decrease costs.

Although simple in principle, OB mod is difficult to consistently apply in most organizational settings if it is left to the manager to apply the contingent reinforcer.[27] Management often lacks systematic control over the workplace environment. Also, it is no easy task to apply timely consequences that are reasonably free from distortion by extraneous feedback. For this reason, some of the most significant behavior modification programs rely on automatic, computer-generated feedback. In fact, feedback alone has been found to be a very useful reinforcer, eliminating the need for any tangible rewards (or punishments).[28] Computer networks are useful in providing employees real-time reports of current output compared to past statistics.

It is also possible for a person to manage his or her own contingencies. One common principle of *time management* is to quickly complete "have to" tasks and then reward yourself by doing something that is more enjoyable or satisfying. This is known as the *Premack principle,* which means that pleasurable tasks or events are paired with less pleasurable tasks to encourage the latter.[29] You may find yourself adopting this principle of self-management without even being aware that it has a name and research support, when you complete an assignment before engaging in a sporting or social activity.

To apply the principles of behavior modification using other than automatic feedback requires planning a multistep process that typically begins with data collection to establish a baseline. This process is best demonstrated with an example. Examine in Exhibit 7–3 the steps of a program described by Luthans and Martinko to modify a common organizational problem—absenteeism.[30] (It is estimated that each year the United States loses over 400 million workdays because of employee absenteeism, or about 5 days per employee.[31])

1. *Establish Baseline Data.* To provide a point of reference, measure or chart the frequency with which the undesirable behavior occurs in the normal, unmodified environment. In many problem situations (absenteeism is only one), existing records will provide an historic database. Frequencies of absence should be charted according to the day of the week, department, and other relevant benchmarks. The objective is to document the problem behavior in a way that reveals the circumstances under which it most frequently occurs.

2. *Analyze Current Behavioral Contingencies.* Examine the current environment to identify any antecedent cues that encourage or discourage the desired behavior. Interviews, group discussions, or a survey are likely to reveal the circumstances that affect attendance. Absenteeism cues might include group norms that encourage or discourage attendance, patterns of family illness, substance abuse, marital problems, lack of day care for children, availability of transportation, lack of an alarm clock, or even the day of the week (Mondays are notorious). Further investigation may show that punitive measures already taken haven't worked. If absenteeism increases following a reprimand, the warning may have actually reinforced the undesirable behavior (which may be seen as a way of gaining attention or getting even).

3. *Develop a Reinforcement Strategy.* Those responsible for correcting the problem evaluate possible reinforcers and select the one(s) thought to be most conducive to improving behavior. Three factors should be considered in structuring a reinforcement program.

   • The reinforcer selected should be meaningful enough to increase the desired behavior and offset the competing reinforcers (of absenteeism).

   • The reinforcers should follow timely evidence of improved behavior to cement the law-of-effect relationship.

   • Criteria for achieving the reinforcer should be realistic, directly related (to attendance), attainable by most employees, and less expensive than the cost (of absences).[32]

   If groups are generally cohesive (meaning people stick together and respect one another), some form of group reward might be appropriate. Some companies allow groups to quit early on Fridays or to build points toward a monthly beer and pizza celebration for perfect group attendance. To reward individuals, the company might pick up more of the cost of health benefits currently borne by the employee. Or, individuals could accumulate points toward a lottery of prizes. Interestingly, a one-in-four chance at a $16 prize has as much reinforcement effect as the certainty of receiving $4. The lottery idea is an example of intermittent, or variable, ratio reinforcement.

4. *Implement the Reinforcement and Chart Results.* A management team might start with posting attendance records and giving praise as a modest first step. If results are not as strong as desired, the managers could move to one of the more substantive reinforcement plans noted above. As attendance improves, the schedule of reinforcement may be shifted to an interval or ratio basis until behaviors become self-reinforcing. An example of a shift from a continuous (daily) to an intermittent reinforcement ratio is shown in the Challenge of Change box, which examines how doughnuts were used to reward and reinforce punctuality.

Challenge of Change   *The Early Birds Get the Goods*

Carol King, director of a public health clinic associated with a midwestern state university, was concerned about the tardiness of her part-time staff. Early morning was a busy time, since the clinic opened at 7:30 and many students sought to obtain services before their 9:00 classes. Seven graduate students worked as counselors, staffing the reception and intake desks. These part-time employees had the annoying habit of drifting in anytime between 7:30 and 8:30. King tried pleas and then warnings; she even docked paychecks to discourage tardiness, but none of these methods worked.

Then King decided to experiment with positive reinforcement. At 7:00 one Monday morning, she arrived with two dozen assorted muffins and placed them next to the coffee pot in the staff room. She set up a small, hand-lettered sign:

GOOD MORNING, EARLY BIRDS!
HELP YOURSELF TO MUFFINS.
—CAROL KING

Promptly at 7:30, King removed all unclaimed muffins but left the sign. Staff members who arrived early or on time that day were rewarded unexpectedly; those who were late saw only the sign. On Tuesday there were more muffins. Again, any not claimed were promptly removed at 7:30. By Wednesday, six of the morning staff arrived on time, partly out of curiosity to see if muffins would be there. King said nothing about punctuality all week.

A muffin or two on one's desk soon became a status symbol—"here works an early bird." During the second week, King began to skip a day or two between muffin deliveries. This, too, was an effective procedure. The uncertainty of intermittent reinforcement kept tardiness at a low level during the remainder of the year.

Source: Thanks to a communication from one of the early birds.

Beware the Folly of Rewarding *A* While Hoping for *B*

Reinforcement practices in industry are controversial; for some industry observers, any form of reward manipulates at best a temporary change in behavior (more about this in the next section).[33] More generally, what management wants, what it rewards, and what it gets from employees are not always the same. "If innovation is espoused, but doing things by the book is what is rewarded, it doesn't take a psychologist to figure out what the firm actually values."[34] This all-too-common practice was originally documented by Steven Kerr in examples ranging from battlefields to orphanages.[35]

Universities typically say they emphasize teaching, but most of the rewards they grant are linked to research, and faculty quickly learn where to channel their energy for maximum payoff. Businesses often say they want to take care of their customers, then reward managers for cutting costs in ways that negatively impact customers. The lesson is that often, without thinking, managers reinforce the wrong behavior. Such errors in judgment suggest that the selective use of rewards should be a key tactic in managers' efforts to motivate employees.

WHAT IS THE LINK BETWEEN REWARDS AND BEHAVIOR?

Bob Clark began working for Wal-Mart as a truck driver in 1972, when the firm had only 15 drivers. He remembers attending a safety meeting his first month, during which Sam Walton proclaimed, "If you'll just stay with me for 20 years, I

Bernard Marcus, chairman of Home Depot, motivates employees with praise and incentives such as stock ownership. Full-time workers receive at least seven percent of their annual salary in company stock in addition to their regular pay. Every salesperson's bright orange apron says, "Hi. I'm _____, a Home Depot stockholder. Let me help you." (Photo: Ann States/SABA.)

guarantee you'll have $100,000 in profit sharing." Clark thought to himself at the time, "Big deal. Bob Clark never will see that kind of money in his life."

Twenty years later, he told Sam Walton: "Well, last time I checked, I had $707,000 in profit sharing, and I see no reason why it won't go up again . . . When folks ask me how I like working for Wal-Mart . . . I tell them about my profit sharing and ask them, 'How do you think I feel about Wal-Mart?' "[36]

The realization of a consistent buildup of monetary rewards increased Bob Clark's commitment to Wal-Mart. But generalized rewards (such as profit sharing) only indirectly related to one's personal actions do not necessarily equitably reinforce individual task-appropriate behaviors. This may seem illogical, but remember: Reinforcement occurs only when some form of consequence increases a desired behavior or decreases an undesired one. If there is no observable change in behavior following a reward, reinforcement has not occurred.

Economic and symbolic "rewards" intended to act as reinforcers frequently fall short of the mark. Sometimes they have no impact, as though employees are saying to themselves as Bob Clark originally did, "Big deal." At other times they may have the opposite impact from that desired (they follow the folly of rewarding A while hoping for B). As expectancy and equity theories of motivation suggest, symbolic rewards such as certificates and recognition luncheons may lead the recipient to question, "Is this all I get for all that I've done?" Feelings of being underappreciated can then lead to a slacking off—the consequences produce a behavior that is contrary to that intended.[37]

Performance Means Behavior Has Been Evaluated

Whenever systematic performance objectives, appraisals, and rewards are lacking in an organization, members usually experience three emotions:

- *Ambiguity:* Exactly what is expected of me as an employee?
- *Uncertainty:* How well am I performing or measuring up to my boss's standards?

At Ford Motor Co.'s North Penn electron assembly plant employees complained that inferior integrated circuits supplied by Harris Semiconductor hurt their productivity and paychecks. Ford managers responded by telling Harris their product would no longer be used. Harris managers and line workers started working closely with Ford to get the new design of integrated circuits to work with Ford's equipment. Harris engineers then made more improvements to increase the chips' reliability. Ford managers were satisfied with Harris and employees felt empowered. Ford made Harris the exclusive supplier of integrated curcuits. (Photo: Courtesy of Harris Corporation, Semiconductor Sector.)

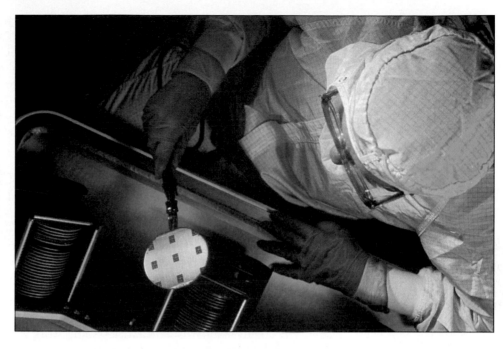

performance
Behavior that has been evaluated or measured as to its contribution to organizational goals.

- *Suspicion:* Are promotions and rewards (or layoffs and discharges) being administered equitably around here?

Many kinds of behaviors occur throughout an organization. But a collection of behaviors does not necessarily produce performance results. Campbell and colleagues emphasize: "Behavior is simply what people do in the course of work (e.g., dictating letters, giving directions, sweeping the floor). **Performance** is behavior that has been evaluated (e.g., measured) in terms of its contribution to the goals of the organization."[38]

The overarching goal is to make as many behaviors as possible be performance contributors. Previously we said that performance can be evaluated on the basis of productivity (including quality), growth, and satisfaction. Research has yet to clearly confirm causality in the performance-satisfaction relationship.[39] That is, we don't yet know if performance causes satisfaction, or vice versa, or if the two occur simultaneously. Even though individuals differ in their sources of motivation, the manager who systematically scts performance objectives, monitors outcomes, and administers reinforcement or rewards is more likely to stimulate task-directed performance than the manager who does not.

The Concept of Pay-for-Performance Rewards

As firms moved into mass production and mass distribution during the industrial era, compensation systems followed suit. They bccame more impersonal, moving toward standardization just like the products being produced. Most employees since the 1950s have been paid on the basis of nonperformance factors, such as their job classification, pay grade, hours worked, and/or seniority. Uniform systems of pay may seem equitable. But from a motivational perspective, such nonperformance payments do not necessarily encourage stellar performance.

By the mid-1990s, nearly 60 percent of firms participating in a national compensation survey are offering "results-sharing" programs.[40] Walt Disney Co. began offering an annual bonus program for animators, directors, and producers who work on its profitable animated movies. A majority of its employees receive bonuses based on division profitability. And in the executive suite, after years of defending shareholder charges of excessive pay, corporations are finally linking executive pay to performance. A major performance benchmark for CEOs is the firm's stock performance. When Quaker Oats Co. stock fell by 13 percent, CEO William D. Smithburg received an 11 percent cut in salary and bonus, to $1.4 million.[41] Such a scenario, with fluctuating rewards, is becoming more commonplace.

As global competitiveness became apparent during the late 1980s, systems of rewards began to incorporate more pay-for-performance factors. Performance-based compensation schemes are consistent with the expectancy theory of motivation. Employees compare rewards received for performance with what they expect to receive. They also compare what they receive with what others receive (the equity factor). Overall satisfaction is likely a composite of how the employee perceives both the extrinsic and intrinsic rewards from the job.[42]

Piecework or Standard-Hour Systems.   The classic performance-based reward system is based on **piecework,** or payment for the amount produced consistent with specified quality standards. Piecework systems work when a person can directly affect his or her rate of output, and the output (quality and quantity) can easily be measured or verified. Some programmers' pay depends on how many lines of code they write; magazine writers are often paid by the number of words in their articles. Shirtmakers in El Salvador are paid a few cents (typically about 7 cents) for each shirt they sew. (See the World Watch box for more on compensation and employment practices in Latin America.)

> **piecework**
> The practice of rewarding performance by paying for the amount produced consistent with quality standards.

A pay-for-performance variation is to use a *standard-hour plan.* Such plans specify the normal time required to complete a task, coupled with a standard rate of pay. For example, the standard for a dental hygienist to clean a patient's teeth may be 45 minutes at a rate of $40. The more skillful technician may be able to serve more patients per day, receiving pay for each at the standard rate.

The Quality–Quantity Trade-Off Dilemma.   The difficult issues in any piece- or standard-rate plan are twofold: One is evaluating work methods to arrive at an equitable standard and rate. Since managers like to periodically adjust one or both compensation factors, the issue of equity can be controversial. The second concern is the quality–quantity trade-off.[43] Without appropriate quality controls, quality may be sacrificed to reach quantity targets. As previously noted, behavior tends to focus on what is measured.

Merit Pay Ties Performance to Add-On Rewards

Rather than tie pay only to output, an alternative is to provide a base salary or hourly wage and then an incentive or bonus based on output. Where the base plus merit incentive system is used, the performance-based portion depends on some measurable level of output over which the employee has control. Output could be measured by volume, defect rate (or quality), or cost savings. Sales representatives often earn a base salary plus commissions based on the level of sales above a set base figure.

Bonus and Profit-Sharing Plans.   Many compensation plans are based on the overall performance of the enterprise rather than the individual's contribution. Profit sharing has become common in many firms including Domino's Pizza, where

Sweatshop Practices in Latin American Apparel Factories

In developing countries, cash-paying jobs are often difficult to obtain, and once obtained, employees work to hold on to them under conditions not tolerated elsewhere. Guatemala, for example, has enacted employment legislation to prevent employment below the age of 14 and with a minimum wage equivalent of $2.80 per *day*. Many North American companies, such as J. C. Penney and Wal-Mart, have required vendors to sign codes of conduct forbidding the violation of any local labor law. And yet, Guatemalan manufacturers in industries such as apparel routinely disregard labor laws, taking advantage of low-skilled workers.

Says Michael Patillo, whose apparel plant in Guatemala City makes shirts under a couple of labels for Penney's, "Penney's? They don't really check" on worker's ages or factory conditions.

"We've never had any request from Penney about how we pay or treat workers—just the quality of our production," reports Dong Joon Kim, manager of the Korean Lindotex SA plant that also makes shirts for J. C. Penney. Where motivation is based on security needs of getting and keeping a job, such plants readily employ workers under age 14, pay them less than the daily minimum wage, and force employees into unpaid overtime as long as 15 hours per day.

Do American retailers have an obligation, moral or economic, to assure that their contract suppliers are operating within the law and complying with the code of conduct they have signed? Says Kenneth Russo, vice president of sourcing at Penney headquarters in Dallas, "We do business in over 50 countries, with literally thousands of individual factories." Company inspectors are primarily trained to check product quality. For them "to be alert and aware of all the issues we're faced with around the world, well, it's just very difficult."

Apparel manufacturers are under pressure to maintain quality and cut costs, if they are to sustain a contract. Says Carlos Arias Macelli, owner of a *maquila* (export factory) making clothes for Penney, "The ethics of the world market are very clear." Retailers and manufacturers "will move wherever it's cheapest or most convenient to their interests."

Ana Mendoza de Riveria, chief of the Labor Ministry's child-worker protection office, remarks, "We don't have the people to investigate" what she believes to be about 300,000 illegally employed minors in Guatemalan industries. Her five-person office has no phone. The gap in "motivational" practices between developed and developing nations is as large as the pay gap.

Source: Bob Ortega, "Conduct Codes Garner Goodwill for Retailers, But Violations Go On," *The Wall Street Journal* (July 3, 1995), pp. A1, A4.

everyone owns stock and profits are distributed back to members.[44] In merit-based pay plans, a pool of money is divided among eligible employees based on some performance evaluation or rating system. The objective of merit plans such as profit sharing, bonuses, and stock options is to link everyone's fate to overall performance, reinforcing corporate cultures that emphasize group results over individual performance. Netscape's IPO and subsequent stock options are intended to attract and hold employees committed to making the firm succeed.

For Wal-Mart, corporate profit growth is a key goal, and the profit-sharing plan is keyed to it.[45] Every employee who works at least 1,000 hours per year is eligible for profit sharing. The firm contributes a percentage of every eligible employee's wages or salary (an average of 6 percent over the last 10 years) into a fund, from which the employee can withdraw cash when leaving the company. This plan helps employees commit to long-term corporate and personal financial growth. Truck driver Bob Clark is but one example—his $700,000-plus share

■■■■■■ **EXHIBIT 7–4**

*Why Gainsharing Plans
Are Growing in Use*

Survey research reveals seven fundamental reasons why gainsharing continues to grow in popularity as a pay-for-performance strategy:

- The basic design of jobs are undergoing fundamental change from individuals to teams.
- Other pay-for-performance systems often lead to disappointing results, especially those that reward individuals (because of the difficulty of untangling individual performance from the contributions of other employees).
- Gainsharing is easy to sell to top management because financial payouts are generally modest and employees share proportionately with the organization the gains of targeted performance improvements.
- Gainsharing has a long history, which makes it easy to imitate successful plans.
- There are many consulting firms that specialize in helping organizations implement gainsharing (and several governmental commissions in the United States and Canada have advocated its widespread implementation).
- Gainsharing provides flexibility in chosing payoff criteria from such diverse factors as profitability, labor costs, material savings, safety records, reject rates, meeting deadlines, and customer satisfaction.
- Gainsharing complements the move toward participative management and employee involvement, as many plans incorporate committee structures to evaluate and act on employee recommendations.

Source: Theresa M. Welbourne and Luis R. Gomez-Mejia, "Gainsharing: A Critical Review and a Future Research Agenda," *Journal of Management* 21 (September 1995), pp. 559+.

of profits provides him financial security. And for 7,800 Philip Morris employees, a recently ratified union contract gives them company stock in lieu of pay increases.[46]

In recent years, executive compensation packages have been loaded with bonuses and stock option add-ons often totaling several million dollars beyond base salary. Compensation specialist Graef Crystal found in his 1994 review of 424 of the largest U.S. corporations that on average CEOs were paid 145 times the pay of the average worker.[47] Such disparities raise questions of equity when contrasted to Ben and Jerry's, the premium ice cream business, where the top pay is only five times more than the lowest salary in the company. With such a narrow compensation spread, it is no surprise that Ben and Jerry's has difficulty recruiting managerial talent.

Beyond their line management teams, companies also have sought to link the compensation of directors to company performance, believing money motivates. Crystal reports that firms as diverse as Scott Paper, Travelers, Ashland Oil, and Johnson & Johnson have devised plans to compensate outside board members in company stock. The assumption is that significant equity ownership assures high motivation to safeguard corporate interests. But will outside directors really change their behavior? Based on stock price changes, Crystal selected 15 high-performing companies and 15 low performers. His question and answer: "Is there any evidence to suggest that companies in which outside directors own lots of stock outperform companies in which outside directors own little stock? The answer is an unequivocal 'no' . . . No matter what the time period chosen . . . there was simply no significant statistical association between outside director shareholdings and subsequent company performance."[48]

gainsharing
A pay-for-performance system that shares financial rewards among all employees based on performance improvements for the entire business unit.

Gainsharing Plans.   Gainsharing is an umbrella for approaches to encourage employees at all levels to be responsible for improving organizational efficiency. **Gainsharing** plans link financial rewards for all employees to improvements in performance of the entire business unit.[49] One survey of 10,000 members of the Society for Human Resource Management found that gainsharing is used in all industries, including the public sector.[50] Another concluded that for the 1990s, except for health care, gainsharing is the most important human resource topic, more important than work design, managing diversity, and other issues.[51] Exhibit 7–4 provides several reasons why gainsharing is increasing in popularity as a motivational incentive, to be made available to all employees in an organizational unit.

YOUR TURN

What Do You Want from Your Job?

Rank the following 16 work-related rewards and outcomes from 1 (most important) to 16 (least important) to you.

Good health insurance and other benefits	_____
Interesting work	_____
Job security	_____
Opportunity to learn new skills	_____
Having a week or more of vacation	_____
Being able to work independently	_____
Recognition from coworkers	_____
Regular hours (no weekends, no nights)	_____
Having a job in which you can help others	_____
Limiting job stress	_____
High income	_____
Working close to home	_____
Work that is important to society	_____
Chances for promotion	_____
Contact with a lot of people	_____
Flexible hours	_____

Interpretation: Compare your rankings with the scores reported in Exhibit 7–5. What factors can you control to increase the probability of satisfaction?

Houston-based Panhandle Eastern Corp. introduced gainsharing following deregulation of the natural gas industry in an effort to make employees more cost and profit conscious. In their plan, if the company achieves earnings per share of $2.00, all Panhandle employees receive a bonus of 2 percent of their salary at year-end. For earnings of $2.10 or more per share, the bonus climbs to 3 percent. Panhandle's gainsharing expectancies reach all organizational levels. Randy Watson, a mailroom employee, has cut mailing costs 43 percent simply by changing "rush" delivery times to arrive at 10:30 A.M. the next day instead of 10:00 A.M.

Rewards as a Cafeteria of Benefits

One method for skirting around the complexities of equitable performance evaluations and merit compensation while maintaining sensitivity to expectancy motivation is to offer cafeteria-style benefits.[52] Historically, compensation was based on the belief that one size fits all, that people could be uniformly rewarded. Today's increasingly popular practice is to let people select from among a portfolio or menu of benefits.

With his nonworking wife and three children, Arthur may be quite concerned that he has comprehensive family medical coverage with minimum deductibles. Fellicia, single and in her early twenties, might opt for increased vacation allowances and educational reimbursement benefits in exchange for a higher deductible in her medical insurance plan. Such flexibility in selecting benefits, while not necessarily related to employee output, helps promote a positive answer to the expectancy question, "Do I value the rewards available to me?"

Individuals want and need different things from their employment. Discover your own preferences by completing the Your Turn exercise. Then compare your profile to the profile of a cross-section of employees shown in Exhibit 7–5 on the next page.

EXHIBIT 7–5

What Employees Want from Their Work

The most important things workers look for in their employment do not necessarily cost the firm money. Providing "interesting work" (rated #2) is inherently less costly for many firms than paying "high income" (rated #11). These data were collected by the Gallup Poll of Princeton, N.J., from a cross-section of employees in differing industries and jobs. The figures reflect responses to the questions: "How important is each of the following characteristics to you? How satisfied are you with it in your current job?"

	Percentage of Workers Who	
	Ranked It as Very Important	Said They Were Satisfied
Good health insurance and other benefits	81%	27%
Interesting work	78	41
Job security	78	35
Opportunity to learn new skills	68	31
Having a week or more of vacation	66	35
Being able to work independently	64	42
Recognition from co-workers	62	24
Regular hours (no weekends, no nights)	58	40
Having a job in which you can help others	58	34
Limiting job stress	58	17
High income	56	13
Working close to home	55	46
Work that is important to society	53	35
Chances for promotion	53	20
Contact with a lot of people	52	45
Flexible hours	49	39

The average "importance" of each characteristic is 61.8%, whereas the average "satisfaction" is only 32.8%. Employers have a long way to go in closing this expectation–satisfaction gap. (Be cautioned that this poll aggregates the answers of people in many types of jobs, so its averages should not parallel your own, except by chance.)

Source: Reprinted with permission, *Inc.* magazine, November 1992. Copyright 1992 by Goldhirsh Group, Inc., 38 Commercial Wharf, Boston, MA 02110.

Controversial Consequences of Incentives and Rewards

Beyond making differential pay adjustments among employees, managers can adjust rewards by varying the assignments they hand out, the praise (or reprimands) they give, the equipment or offices they provide, and the special privileges they grant. Nevertheless, rewards that bear no relationship to personal or team performance invite people to redirect and/or reduce their effort. One typical response of people who experience inequities is to engage more in activities they enjoy than in those that need to be done. Little wonder that managers believe performance should be the most important determinant of compensation, whether the reward is a salary increase or bonus.[53] However, controversy typically surrounds pay plans that rely heavily on performance-based compensation.

Except in cases where performance can be easily measured, employees often believe that the person evaluating them relies too much on subjective judgment. Under such conditions, they question the fairness of merit pay (as do many labor unions). Even though team-based reward plans that provide for gainsharing when groups accomplish strategic goals are on the increase, issues of fairness and equity make them troublesome to administer.[54] Therefore, some managers try to alter a group's perception that it is treated inequitably. For example, managers might present results of a wage and salary survey of comparable jobs that shows the company pays in the top ten percentile of all firms surveyed. Although employees may still desire more money, their opinion of their employer will be more favorable.

On a more general level, some view the use of rewards as unethical and dysfunctional. Alfie Kohn writes, "Most managers too often believe in the redemptive power of rewards" even though some research finds that "rewards typically undermine the very processes they are intended to enhance." He further claims, "Incentives do not alter the attitudes that underlie our behaviors . . . Rewards do not create a lasting commitment. They merely, and temporarily, change what we do." In effect, Kohn views rewards as "bribes" and concludes, "Do rewards motivate people? Absolutely. They motivate people to get rewards."[55] Others claim that Kohn's somewhat valid criticism of behaviorist theory (behavior modification) when generalized to all forms of rewards and incentives is unsubstantiated.[56]

While goals, incentives, and rewards can energize and focus behavior, there are potential pitfalls in using them as motivational systems: Quality may be traded off for quantity and vice versa, dysfunctional inertia may occur if employees cling to ineffectual methods rather than innovate, and behaviors may be focused on the goal only to the disregard of other activities. People may also believe the end justifies the means and engage in illegal or unethical behaviors—as occurred when Sears auto service employees overcharged customers for unnecessary repairs when the retailer instituted product-specific quotas, commissions, and standard job pay rates.[57] Because such potential drawbacks are associated more with individualized reward plans, companies are abandoning individual and departmental pay-for-performance plans in favor of more simplified plans focused on total business performance.[58]

WHAT ARE THE KEY FACTORS IN JOB DESIGN?

job design
The process of incorporating tasks and responsibilities into meaningful, productive, satisfying job responsibilities.

Beyond practices that emphasize goals and rewards, behavioral scientists for decades have concluded that the design of a person's job has significant motivational impact on behavior. **Job design** is the process of incorporating tasks and responsibilities into jobs to make them meaningful, productive, and satisfying. During much of this century, job design has been the responsibility of managers and industrial engineers, who emphasized productivity over meaningfulness or satisfaction. One could even make the claim that managerial work did not begin to be viewed as a profession until bosses recognized that factory jobs could be designed and structured into specific tasks to make it easier for a manager to supervise the work of others.

scientific management
An early twentieth century methodology advocated by Frederick W. Taylor in which work tasks were structured into highly simplified, standardized jobs to simplify hiring, training, and supervision.

As described in Appendix A, one of the breakthrough practices of the early twentieth century was "scientific management." Advocated by Frederick W. Taylor, **scientific management** provided a methodology to structure highly specialized jobs, which simplifed hiring, training, and supervising people with the requisite capabilities. Once trained, the manager's job was to see to it that all those reporting to him were performing according to defined job standards. Scientific management provided an orderliness to the work of organizations.[59] It helped fuel the rise of large businesses producing high volumes of standardized goods—everything from textiles to breakfast cereal to automobiles.

In keeping with the principles of scientific management, job design historically has involved analyzing a complex task, then breaking it down into specific subtasks. One or more of these specific subtasks or jobs are then combined into departmental work units, where managers oversee the work of employees.[60] Managers have been responsible for staffing jobs with competent people, then holding their people accountable for carrying out the assigned tasks.

■■■■   **EXHIBIT 7–6**

Four Combinations of Task Scope and Task Depth

Four distinct types of jobs are identified by the ways in which task scope (variety) and task depth (responsibility) combine. To the employee, jobs are more meaningful as they become less routine and more enriched, since competent, motivated people like to believe that their jobs provide variety and give them responsibility and the resources to carry out tasks.

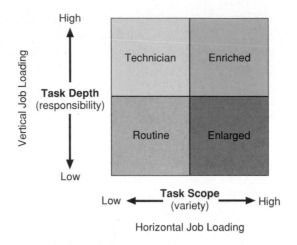

This manager-in-charge, "command and control" approach worked reasonably well during the first three-quarters of the twentieth century, when most jobs were readily defined. Today, however, industrial growth comes more from flexible, smaller firms than from large producers of mass commodities. Giants IBM, GM, and others have become painfully aware of this trend.[61] In Chapter 3 you learned that, increasingly, responsibility for the design of work is shifting to workers themselves and to self-managed teams, rather than residing with managers or industrial engineers. Nevertheless, there are some fundamental concepts involved in designing jobs, whether for individuals or teams, guided by the objective of improving work motivation.

Task Scope and Task Depth

task scope
The degree of task variety built into a job, typically called horizontal job loading when jobs are formally designed.

Two typical dimensions used for defining or describing all types of jobs, from general manager to routine production operator, are task scope and depth. **Task scope** describes the horizontal characteristics of a job, or the degree of variety in the activities a person is expected to perform. A job narrow in scope has few activities. A court reporter, for example, transcribes verbatim what is said during a trial; a lab technician draws blood samples eight hours a day. A janitor who only empties waste cans has a narrow task scope; one who also mops, vacuums, dusts, and washes windows has considerable variety and thus a wider scope.

task depth
The degree of responsibility and autonomous decision authority expected in a job, often thought of as vertical job loading when formally designed.

Task depth addresses how much vertical responsibility or individual accountability is expected in a job. Depth increases when the employee is given responsibility to schedule the sequence of work, to initiate self-control if activities or output begin to get out of balance, to identify and solve problems as they occur, or to originate innovative ways of improving the process or the output. Task depth is shallow when managers determine what jobholders are to do, when they are to do it, and in what quantities, and then monitor results to determine if work output matches the standards handed down.

Combining Scope and Depth into Four Job Profiles

Task scope and depth can be considered ways of "loading" work into jobs. When combined into a 2 × 2 matrix, high or low loadings on each of the two variables identify four types of jobs. Exhibit 7–6 illustrates how these job features produce different work experiences.

Ultimately, managers should ask: Do our job structures and technology fit the capabilities of the people we employ? Do these jobs promote high-quality work? Too often, the answer to both questions will be no. Many jobs still incorporate narrowly defined requirements more common 20 or more years ago. Routine jobs low in scope and depth are prone to underutilize the mental competencies of employees, and thus reduce the quality level attained by the organization.

- *Routine jobs* are programmed to be repetitive and narrow in scope and are often restricted by technology. People in these simplistic and repetitive jobs are expected not to do much independent thinking, just pay attention to detail. Examples of routine jobs include data entry, assembly, clerical, and cashier jobs. Skills are mastered in a matter of hours or days; there is no expectation of career growth.

- *Technician jobs* offer greater opportunities for independent thinking and deciding what to do when but provide employees with little variety in their daily tasks. The technician may have a university education or need professional training to learn how to perform the job, say, of a pharmacist or stock broker. The work may be valued by the client, but research suggests that people such as medical technicians find their repetitive jobs become meaningless over time and offer little growth opportunity.[62]

- *Enlarged jobs* provide an expanded variety or diversity of tasks. At times jobs are deliberately expanded, either by adding on sequential tasks or by allowing employees to rotate among different jobs. Decreasing the number of separate job classifications or titles in a traditional industry typically affords employees enlarged variety or a change of pace.

- *Enriched jobs* enable an individual to feel responsible for whole tasks. Most professional jobs that require analysis and manipulation of symbolic data (managers, scientists, and teachers, for example) are enriched to give the individual responsibility for doing whatever is necessary to get the job done.

Changing Task Scope and Depth

The auto mechanic who is allowed to troubleshoot and correct problems whenever they occur experiences job enrichment. The mechanic who only fixes braking system problems is more technician in character, and the person who simply changes oil probably views the job as routine. Jobs can be changed if they are found to be overly confining and thus fail to utilize the full capabilities of the people employed. Variety in a position can be increased by combining all the separate steps or tasks required to complete a whole job. This process is called **horizontal job loading** because the enlarged job can be viewed as a horizontal chain of multiple work activities performed in a sequence.

horizontal job loading
The process of enlarging jobs by combining separate work activities into a whole job that provides for greater task variety.

Task depth is increased by **vertical job loading,** or the structuring of a job to allow a greater range of responsibility and authority. When management reserves exclusive responsibility for planning and control, employees have little task depth. Companies that subscribe to the principles of quality management and employee involvement actively expand vertical loading for what typically have been routine production or narrowly defined service jobs.[63] They move away from the top-down approach to let employees decide what needs to be done for quality improvement. Many of today's jobs are more complex, subject to change, and require analytic or symbol-manipulation skills. Thus, managers may not be the best people to tell other professionals what to do.

vertical job loading
The process of structuring a greater range of responsibility for planning, control, and decision making authority into a job.

━━━━━━ **EXHIBIT 7–7**

Six Core Job Dimensions for Evaluating Jobs

These core job dimensions are introduced in order of their pervasiveness in affecting the outcome measures of job involvement, motivation, performance, and satisfaction.

1. *Autonomy*—the degree of control a person has over his or her own job actions, such as responsibility for self-governing behaviors to perform the job and the absence of a programmed sequence of activities (essentially, task depth).

2. *Task variety*—the degree to which normal job activities require performing multiple tasks (breadth of task scope).

3. *Task identity*—the extent to which a person has a whole task to complete, with visible starting and ending points.

4. *Feedback*—the frequency and completeness with which the task provides information about work progress and results of personal efforts.

5. *Friendship opportunities*—the extent to which the work setting provides opportunities for close interpersonal contacts.

6. *Dealing with others*—the degree to which task flow or accomplishment requires interaction with others in contributory or collegial ways.

Source: Copyright 1976 by the Regents of the University of California. Reprinted from the *California Management Review*, Vol. 17, No. 4. By permission of The Regents.

HOW DOES JOB DESIGN AFFECT WORK OUTCOMES?

Scope and depth are the most basic descriptors of any job. But other dimensions of a job affect the attitudes of workers, their willingness to perform successfully, the productivity and reliability of their work output, and side effects such as accidents, absenteeism, and job stress.

An Integrating Motivational Theory of Job Design

Hackman and colleagues have developed an integrating theory of job design.[64] The objective is to help managers understand and build into work the conditions that will inspire people to turn in high-quality performances. They used the following three-sequence model to provide recommendations for enriching jobs:

Core job dimensions → Psychological states → Personal/work outcomes

core job dimensions
The underlying characteristics of a job (such as autonomy, task variety) and how they relate to job involvement, motivation, performance, and satisfaction.

Core Job Dimensions.   In the design of jobs, **core job dimensions** are the underlying characteristics of a job and how they relate to a person's job involvement, motivation, performance, and satisfaction.[65] The six original dimensions are described in detail in Exhibit 7–7. These researchers found that the first four of the original core job dimensions (*autonomy, task variety, task identify,* and *feedback*) had greater impact on the outcome measures of job involvement, motivation, performance, and satisfaction than did numbers five and six (*friendship opportunities* and *dealing with others*). As a result of independent research, two other core job dimensions have been added—task significance and task interdependence.[66]

    In considering person–job matches, Hackman and Lawler found all these core dimensions had a better fit and greater meaning for self-motivating individuals who desire opportunity, personal growth, challenge, autonomy, and feedback. Such individuals have high growth needs and tend to be intrinsically motivated, as explained in Chapter 6.

psychological states
Three possible job qualities—experienced meaningfulness, experienced responsibility, knowledge of results—that shape individual job motivation and satisfaction of growth needs.

Psychological States.   To assess the impact of core job dimensions on three **psychological states** that shape individual job motivation and satisfaction, researchers or human resource professionals use a diagnostic instrument, the Job Diagnostic

Survey. Generally people whose jobs enable them to experience the following three psychological states will have a positive "motivating potential" because these cognitions satisfy personal–professional growth needs.

- *Experienced meaningfulness.* Occurs when an individual perceives his or her work as worthwhile or in tune with personal values (influenced by skill variety, task identity, and task significance dimensions).
- *Experienced responsibility.* Realized when a person feels personally accountable for the outcomes of his or her efforts (influenced by the autonomy dimension).
- *Knowledge of results.* Experienced when an individual can determine on a fairly regular basis whether the performance outcomes of his or her work are satisfactory (influenced by the feedback dimension).

Personal/Work Outcomes.   Favorable core job dimensions create a positive motivating potential, which often yields high personal and work outcomes. *Job outcomes* are measured by job involvement, motivation, and satisfaction at the personal level and performance at the work level. For example, Lisa has strong growth needs and perceives her production scheduling job as one of significant responsibility. She receives positive feedback about her results and believes her work to be meaningful both to co-workers and customers. These positive psychological states enable her to enjoy high self-esteem and job satisfaction. She is highly involved in her job and thus internally motivated to excel. Lisa's performance produces high-quality work of a timely and accurate nature, rarely disrupted by absences. We conclude that her job dimensions produce positive psychological states, which in turn lead to high personal and work outcomes. If any of the three psychological states were missing (meaningfulness, responsibility, knowledge of results), her motivating potential would likely be lower than it is.

A manager thinking of enriching jobs to build in more of the positive core job dimensions will find individuals with high growth needs—people turned on by learning and challenges—more receptive to these changes. Another person in Lisa's job who lacks strong growth needs or who has low self-esteem is less likely to accept such changes in the structuring of his or her work. Outcomes will therefore be diminished both for the individual and organization. But jobs with high levels of responsibility and variety are not for everyone. Some want security and structure more than autonomy or challenge.

Interdisciplinary Approaches to Job Design

The approach to job design advocated by Hackman and colleagues clearly emphasizes the motivating potential of work. While popular, there are other philosophies and approaches to job design that affect several other outcomes. Research by Michael Campion and his colleagues distinguishes approaches to job redesign into four distinct fields, each with a rather predictable trade-off of costs and benefits. His four approaches, each based on a different premise or research discipline, are: motivational, mechanistic, biological, and perceptual/motor.[67]

Motivational Approach.   Several theories (including Hackman's) aim to increase the outcomes of job satisfaction, job involvement, and performance by enabling people to realize growth needs by experiencing challenging work. An added benefit of jobs rating high in motivational design are lower boredom and absenteeism. Campion notes, however, that in striving to produce jobs that are stimulating and mentally demanding, the motivational approach may have the unintended consequence of creating staffing difficulties, increasing training times, and having higher mental overload and stress.[68]

Mechanistic Approach.   The earliest techniques for designing jobs emerged from classical industrial engineering with extensions to scientific management. They were based on time and motion studies and work simplification (see Appendix A). Mechanistic approaches are oriented toward efficiency in the use of human resources by simplifying staffing and training requirements through the design of standardized, simplified work tasks that require less experience. Mechanistic jobs have lower mental overload and stress but more boredom and physical demands.

ergonomics
A biomechanic approach to minimize physical strain and stress on a worker based on the healthy design of work methods and technology.

Biological Approach.   From the study of work physiology and biomechanics emerged a concern about job ergonomics. **Ergonomics** emphasizes the minimization of physical strain and stress on the worker based on work methods and technology. Biological methods involve making jobs physically comfortable and matched to physical strength and endurance, combined with attention to noise, climate requirements, and the design of equipment. Where jobs are well-designed biologically, workers report less physical effort and fatigue, fewer aches and pains, and have fewer health complaints. The likelihood of accidents is reduced, employees have more favorable attitudes toward their workstation, and sometimes experience slightly higher job satisfaction. On the cost side, equipment investments are higher and training requirements increase.

Perceptual/Motor Approach.   From human factors engineering, experimental psychology, and human information processing studies, lessons are focused on human processes and performance. Perceptual/motor approaches seek to match job characteristics to human mental capabilities (and limitations) with a primary emphasis on how people concentrate and what helps them pay attention to job requirements. Favorable outcomes from this approach are improved reliability by reducing errors and accidents, and positive worker reactions by reduced fatigue, mental overload, and stress. Staffing and training requirements are reduced, but boredom increases.

Such research about how different disciplines contribute to job design emphasizes that there is no one approach that is best for all types of people and jobs. Like so many other managerial challenges, job design involves seeking a balance among approaches to achieve results that best fit situational realities. Campion concludes:

> *Jobs can be simultaneously high on the mechanistic and perceptual/motor approaches because they both generally recommend design features that minimize mental demands, but the motivational approach gives nearly opposite advice by encouraging design features that enhance mental demands. As such, jobs high on the motivational approach may be more difficult to staff, require more training, have greater error-likelihood, and more mental overload and stress. Jobs high on the mechanistic and perceptual/motor approaches may have less satisfied and motivated employees and higher absenteeism. This suggests a basic trade-off between organizational benefits, such as efficiency and reliability, and individual benefits, such as satisfaction.*[69]

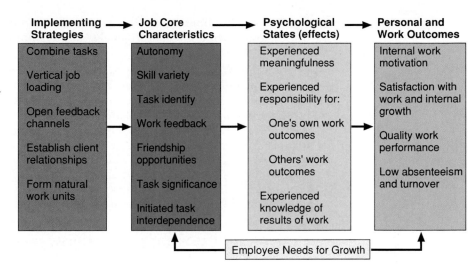

━━━━ **EXHIBIT 7–8**

Integrating the Factors of Job Redesign

Job redesign possibilities may be visualized as a flow of empowering forces that begins with choices among the five implementing strategies and ends with work and personal outcomes. A critical mediating factor is the extent of the employee's need for growth.

Strategies to Enhance Jobs through Redesign

Recent task and process design successes by firms who have won the Malcolm Baldrige National Quality Award suggest actions organizations can take to improve overall job effectiveness. Most of the strategies learned from best practices of such award-winning companies apply mainly to employees who seek growth challenges and enjoy learning. As summarized in Exhibit 7–8, the orientation of such job enhancement strategies is principally through the motivational approach. Five of many strategies are:[70]

- *Combine Tasks.* To improve skill variety, task identity, and interdependence, job enlargement combines tasks that over time have become overly specialized and fragmented. Tasks may be combined by having one individual complete a larger module of work or by establishing teams in which members periodically switch tasks. Critical also is the elimination of tasks that no longer add value to necessary processes.

- *Load Jobs Vertically.* To improve autonomy, empower employees by combining responsibilities for planning, executing, and adjusting work activities. A manager authorizes staff to schedule their own work, decide on work methods, troubleshoot problems, train others, and monitor quality. She also provides them with cost and performance reports.

- *Open Feedback Channels.* To improve interaction with others and clarify task significance, managers should develop systems where employees directly receive all possible feedback about factors that affect their work. The best feedback sources are the job itself, peers, and access to computerized databases, not the manager's perceptions and judgmental comments.

- *Establish Client Relationships.* To improve skill variety, autonomy, interaction with others, and feedback, employees whose actions impact on customers should periodically interact directly with customers. Three steps are suggested: (1) identify a relevant client or customer contact for employees, (2) structure the most direct contact possible, such as on-site visits for commercial customers, and (3) have the work group set up criteria by which the customer can evaluate work quality and channel any remarks directly to the employee or work team.

- *Form Natural Work Teams.* To improve skill variety, task significance, friendship, and interdependence, link people together when the job performed by one person affects others. Regardless of work flow sequences, bringing people together as a team enhances identification with the whole task and creates a sense of shared responsibility. To provide a team project focus, some Hewlett-Packard divisions have moved design engineers into the middle of the production area. They interact with assemblers and manufacturing operators and obtain clues to improving manufacturing processes. Such experiences are expanding the use of teams to engage nonmanagers in wide-ranging problem solving and quality improvement.

HOW ARE PEOPLE MOVITATED BY EMPOWERMENT?

During the 1980s, managers began to discover the motivational power of empowerment. True, some managers have been "empowering" their people for a long time by delegating considerable autonomy, providing ample information, and backing projects that showed creativity or initiative. Likewise, many individuals have learned over the years to be self-motivated and self-empowered—they seize opportunities to make their work more meaningful and are willing to make choices, to experiment, and to have an impact on the organization. But until the term *empowerment* entered the manager's vocabulary, little was done to encourage the practice as a conscious way to promote self-motivation, innovation, and systemwide quality improvements.

Empowerment Enhances Self-Perceptions and Behaviors

empowerment
Describes conditions that enable people to feel competent and in control of their work, energized to take initiative and persist at meaningful tasks.

Empowerment describes conditions that enable people to feel competent and in control, energized to take the initiative and persist at meaningful tasks.[71] Empowerment is a multifaceted and highly personal motivational force. Empowerment can come from within the individual, from peers, or from a manager. As suggested by its definition, empowerment aspires to bring about positive self-perceptions (self-concept, self-esteem, and self-efficacy) and task-directed behaviors. Exhibit 7–9 graphically portrays these forces, and the following text describes some of the interplay among them.

Changed self-perceptions are an important manifestation of empowerment. **Self-concept** is how we think about ourselves, or see ourselves in a role. Our self-concept changes as we shift roles—say, from friend to student to employee. *Self-esteem* is how we generally feel about our own worthiness—our self-acceptance. A specific aspect of self-esteem is self-efficacy, a concept closely linked to empowerment. **Self-efficacy** is an individual's self-perceived ability to perform a certain type of task. A person's feelings about self-efficacy are important because they influence performance and a sense of personal well-being.[72]

self-concept
How we think about ourselves or see ourselves in a role.

self-efficacy
Our self-perceptions about our ability to perform certain types of tasks.

Individuals develop their sense of self-efficacy based on past experience with actual or similar tasks, comparisons with others, and feedback from others. A person's self-assessment of ability (knowledge and skills), general physical and emotional condition, and personality (including overall self-esteem) all influence his or her feeling of task-specific self-efficacy.[73] How skillfully and with how much effort an individual approaches tasks also influences personal performance and the subsequent feeling of self-efficacy. Empowering conditions help strengthen self-efficacy.

■■■■■ **EXHIBIT 7–9**

Empowerment Grows Out of Self-Perceptions and Behavior

Managers encourage empowerment by designing jobs to promote self-reliance, providing challenging goals and meaningful rewards, and exerting considerable leadership. Other people are empowering if they are accepting, provide a model for others to be self-motivated performers, and exert the patience to be mentors.

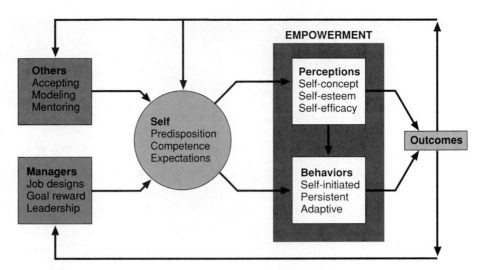

Self-Initiated Empowerment. An individual can initiate personal actions to bring about self-empowerment and greater feelings of self-efficacy. People who are intrinsically motivated internal attributors initiate personal efforts to expand the nature of their jobs and their power. They are willing to take on additional responsibilities and/or creatively work on ways to improve organizational processes or products. Self-empowering people are in effect entrepreneurs who work actively to alter the organization in ways that make them proud of their results.

Empowerment by Others. Colleagues and co-workers have a large impact on work-related self-perceptions. Peers who promote empowerment influence how individuals within a group feel about themselves and the group itself. Within groups, people feel empowered when they are respected and treated as professionals, encourage co-workers to accept responsibility, and have the sponsorship of a personal mentor. Individuals are empowered when peers seek their advice, confide in them, and include them in projects from which they can learn and make contact with others who might help their careers.

Empowerment by Managers. The most talked-about source of empowerment is the behavior of managers or leaders in interacting with staff. The empowering manager actively gives power to individuals and enables them to be self-motivated. This is done by changing employee expectations so they believe they are in control of their destiny and can shape their work and make it meaningful within their organizations. Empowering managers also share information so people can perform their jobs more accurately and confidently. Information technology and systems that allow employees to have on-demand access to whatever information they need is by itself a major empowering factor.

As a management practice, empowerment also means managers open communications, delegate power, share information, and cut away at the debilitating tangles of corporate bureaucracy. The manager who deliberately works to empower his or her employees gives them the license to pursue their visions, to champion projects, and to improve practices consistent with organizational mission and goals. The manager who shares responsibilities with subordinates and treats them as partners is likely to get the best from them.[74] For these reasons, it is common to

Pam Del Duca, CEO of the Delstar Group, a gift and fashion retailing firm in Phoenix, Arizona, leads a raft trip down the Salt River during an offsite, goal-setting meeting of managers. Every employee has an individual sales plan, and those who meet or exceed their goals are rewarded. "The bottom line is, when we grow people, we grow the business," says Del Duca, explaining how the goals they set affect her company's success. (Source: © Don B. Stevenson.)

think of empowerment as a principal quality of leaders. At Sun Microsystems, youthful CEO Scott G. McNealy has built an empowering corporate culture around his motto, "Kick butt and have fun."[75]

Empowerment Results in Personal Changes

The empowered person undergoes two types of personal change. One is a motivational enhancement, especially when the source of empowerment is positive changes initiated by a manager.[76] Empowered people usually intensify their task focus and are energized to become more committed to a cause or goal. They experience self-efficacy, which stimulates motivation by enabling people to see themselves as competent and capable of high performance.

Empowerment also is manifested in active problem-solving behaviors that concentrate energy on a goal. The empowered person is more flexible in behavior, tries alternative paths when one is blocked, and eagerly initiates new tasks or adds complexity to current ones.[77] Behavior becomes self-motivated when the individual seeks to carve out greater personal autonomy in undertaking tasks without the manager's help.

Empowerment Alters Expectations

Although managers often set the stage for empowerment by promoting initiative and relaxing bureaucratic obstacles, ultimately the individual decides whether to act empowered. Because empowerment depends in part on how people perceive reality, not everyone on a team responds the same way to empowerment opportunities.[78]

Naomi, a market analyst, has self-confidence and self-esteem because she believes she can influence organizational outcomes, in part because her manager enthusiastically supports her reports and allows her to present them to top management.[79] Such repeated experiences lead to a personal belief that she is competent, which positively influences her expectations about future events. Naomi believes her competence transfers across situations, and she looks forward to challenging assignments. By contrast, Scott, her accounts receivable colleague, generally sees himself as weak in analytical reasoning and persuasion skills. He has low self-efficacy associated with learned helplessness in these areas. His manager audits his work, points out deficiencies, and hounds him for faster turnaround times. Scott avoids situations that he expects will require analytical or persuasion skills.

Expectancy motivation comes into play in empowerment whenever a person raises questions about himself or herself and the task at hand. Managers help bring about empowerment when they encourage their people to diminish such bureaucratic thoughts as "It's not my responsibility" or "It's beyond my control." One way to overcome self-deluding excuses is to have people identify the customers served by their work, even if customers are other departments within the firm. This shifts the focus away from thinking of one's tasks as trivial busywork toward perceiving one's importance in the flow of interdependent tasks.

THE IPO: A MOTIVATIONAL TOOL FOR INNOVATION, FROM SAMUEL ADAMS TO NETSCAPE—A SECOND LOOK

Boston Beer Company is rather unique among breweries—it outsources to other breweries the production of Samuel Adams and their other brews. Koch attributes the success of Samuel Adams to excellence in attaining two goals. One is care in obtaining exquisite ingredients and in supervising the brewing of a beer that is complex, rich, and fragrant. The second is salesmanship, or rather person-to-person selling. Koch states that in the beginning, "I focused on selling because I couldn't afford advertising or marketing." BBC didn't even add a marketing director until its ninth year in business, when it was far and away the number one "microbrewery."

Jim Koch's emphasis on selling combined with hiring, developing, and motivating talented people gets results. His first employee, Rhonda Kallman, who joined BBC at age 22, was a former secretary in the consulting business that was Koch's first career. She knew the Boston pubs, showed a talent at selling, developed business skills, and was empowered to head up a sales force of more than a hundred that now covers all 50 states. Half of BBC's sales staff are women—unprecedented within the beer industry. Koch observes, "I'm often asked why I hire so many women. The answer is, I don't: I hire talented, resourceful, intelligent, energetic people. It happens that God made half of them women."[80]

Koch likes to manage by invoking simple rules and goals "so people can understand and visualize what you mean." One simple rule that helped produce the highly successful sales force is, "Don't hire anybody unless it improves the average of the company. It's a wonderful rule because administrators can imagine what the average person is like." To keep from drawing down the average means the company interviews vast numbers of people before selecting one. Recently, it took two years to sift through 2,000 applicants before hiring one sales rep for Arizona. One informal indicator (goal) Koch uses to assess motivational commitment is who is willing to volunteer after hours to guide tours at the company's only brewery, a small facility used for experimenting with specialty brews and for public relations. Says Koch, "It's important to get everyone in the company involved in presenting us to the public. When your employees are proud of what they do, and what they make, and the company they're a part of, it shows; it's an unquantifiable asset. So I'm happy when truck drivers ask to do tours."

On the opposite coast, Netscape's Jim Clark seems to motivate by extoling the goals of being "firstust with the mostest" (to use a Peter Drucker strategy). It took Netscape less than one year to go from a concept to the dominant software package for Web browsing and the darling of Wall Street. Clark is almost arrogant in the way he positions his firm in the minds of employees and the public. After Netscape's software ruled 75 percent of the Web, Clark stated, "Ultimately, the Internet will even subsume the phone network."[81] Although it is too early to render a verdict, the early success of Netscape suggests that stock options and other combinations of motivators are getting the job done.   ▬▬▬

SUMMARY

Managers have found many ways to apply and extend the fundamental theories of motivation.

One of the common applications of motivation theory is goal setting. Participation in goal setting helps raise aspirations, but it does not necessarily lead to better performance than when goals are set by management. Once a person has a goal, intentions lead to an action plan to reach the objective. Management by objectives (MBO) is a specific managerial application of goal setting that has been widely used in organizations. People are more likely to perform actions leading to the desired results if they have clear, specific, and challenging goals. This can be done by writing goals that begin with an action verb, identify key result areas, provide a measurement standard, and specify a time for completion.

The most tangible application of motivational theories is organizational behavior modification (OB mod), which uses reinforcement to shape behavior. Reinforcement involves managing the environment, usually by linking a positive consequence to a desired behavior (to increase the likelihood of its being repeated). But OB mod can also rely on negative reinforcement (removal of an aversive or negative condition following a desired behavior) or even punishment or omission of any reinforcement to shape behavior.

Linked to goals are rewards. In pursuit of continuous improvements in quality, organizations are increasing their use of performance-based compensation systems such as gainsharing that focus on the total business unit, rather than on departmental or individual pay-for-performance plans. In addition to bonuses and profit sharing, managers are also allowing employees greater choice in selecting benefits from a cafeteria-style menu. Such a movement recognizes that people have different needs, and compensation systems should reflect those differences.

Historically, jobs have been designed around task depth (autonomy and responsibility) and task scope (variety). As jobs become enriched (by building in greater depth and scope), employees potentially experience greater meaning and satisfaction.

The newest and most conceptually abstract of the applied motivational practices is empowerment. Empowerment enables people to feel competent and in control of their work by granting them authority, providing information, and reducing bureaucratic restrictions. Empowerment leads to a combination of greater motivation and more energetic problem-solving behaviors.

Key Concepts

initial public offering, *p. 217*

goal, *p. 219*

intention, *p. 220*

actions, *p. 221*

management by objectives (MBO), *p. 221*

reinforcement, *p. 225*

law of effect, *p. 226*

organizational behavior modification (OB mod), *p. 226*

performance, *p. 231*

piecework, *p. 232*

gainsharing, *p. 234*

job design, *p. 237*

scientific management, *p. 237*

task scope, *p. 238*

task depth, *p. 238*

horizontal job loading, *p. 239*

vertical job loading, *p. 239*

core job dimensions, *p. 240*

psychological states, *p. 240*

ergonomics, *p. 242*

empowerment, *p. 244*

self-concept, *p. 244*

self-efficacy, *p. 244*

Questions for Study and Discussion

1. Write a comprehensive goal statement of a major task you need to undertake. Include the four elements of an action verb, a key result area, a measurement standard, and a time frame.

2. Different forms of management by objectives (MBO) are widely practiced, yet MBO remains controversial. Place yourself in a familiar work situation and describe what your manager would do to include you in an MBO process. What four objectives would you likely initiate?

3. What are the differences among the four basic types of reinforcement: positive, negative, punishment, and omission? Why is positive reinforcement advocated more than punishment?

4. The management of a health-conscious firm wants to stamp out smoking among its employees. A senior vice president asks you to devise an OB mod program that would use reinforcement to help people stop smoking. What steps would you recommend?

5. Describe each of these types of pay-for-performance systems: piecework, bonuses on top of a base salary, profit sharing, gainsharing, and cafeteria-style benefits. Give an example of each. Why should firms design their compensation systems to maintain equity while at the same time promoting individual expectancies?

6. Examine the 2 × 2 model that characterizes types of jobs by depth and scope (Exhibit 7–6). For each of the four cells, identify a specific type of job that fits that particular cell and explain why. Then, for the cells identified as routine, technician, and enlarged, explain what changes you would make in task scope and/or task depth to enrich each job you have identified.

7. Identify a career-oriented job you would like to hold following graduation. Describe the conditions under which that job would rate favorably on each of the six core job dimensions identified in Exhibit 7–7. Make sure your descriptions reflect job qualities that produce overall positive psychological states of experienced meaningfulness, experienced responsibility, and knowledge of results.

8. "When the managers of an organization actively work to empower their people, there is little need to be concerned about individual motivation." Critically evaluate this statement. In what ways might empowerment shift concerns about motivation away from individuals to the team?

EXPERIENTIAL EXERCISE

Team Feedback and Goal Setting[82]

Purpose.   This exercise gives you and a classmate experience in the give and take of providing feedback and setting goals. Each dyad (two-person team) will have the opportunity to establish a helping relationship for purposes of self-improvement. (Total time required: 30 minutes.)

Materials Needed.   Paper and pen/pencil for each person.

Instructions.   Pair up with a classmate with whom you have had some working experience, perhaps in a previous exercise or another class. Make a managerial decision as to who will be A and who will be B.

A's Self-Disclosure (2 minutes).   At a signal from your instructor, A will have 2 minutes to answer the question "Who am I?" while B listens. A will talk about himself/herself without interruption or questioning from B. A should talk about whatever A is comfortable sharing—family background, relationships with friends, jobs, hobbies, or interests. Any subject is fair game as long as it reveals something about A.

B's Self-Disclosure (2 minutes).   Reverse roles. B tells A about himself/herself.

B's Positive Feedback to A (1 minute).   B now has 1 minute to provide A with feedback on what was heard. The only stipulation is that the feedback should reflect totally positive regard for A. B should not be critical but should emphasize the strengths or interesting qualities perceived about A in the spirit of unconditional positive regard for A.

A's Positive Feedback to B (1 minute).   Now reverse roles and let A tell B the positive attributes heard or perceived.

B's Class Performance Appraisal of A (2 minutes).   Once the dyad is comfortable in making self-disclosures and giving

feedback, the focus shifts to observed classroom behavior. B will assume the role of appraiser and provide candid feedback to A about A's behavior and performance in class. B should try to identify critical incidents or specific events that reflect on A's behavior as a student or team member. This segment opens two-way communication, for A may ask questions or seek clarification. The intent of the feedback is to improve A's future performance as a student. Since criticism often increases defensiveness, move instead to a problem-solving approach.

A's Class Performance Appraisal of B (2 minutes).   Now reverse roles while A gives feedback on B's behavior.

A Sets Objectives with B's Help (5 minutes).   Now it's time to set personal performance objectives. A begins by discussing some aspect of his/her career aspirations that may benefit from better planning and behavior focusing. With B's help, A writes at least two complete objective statements including, as explained in Exhibit 7–1, an appropriate action verb, a key result area, a performance indicator or measure, and a relevant time frame.

B Sets Objectives with A's Help (5 minutes).   Switch roles. The spotlight is now on B, who will develop at least two complete objective statements with A's help.

Conclusion.   The learning value of this exercise rests solely on personal introspection. To some, the exercise—especially the objective-writing phase—may seem tedious, for few people like to write objectives in the presence of others. But with the proper attitude, the outcome should be useful. Just don't close the book on your objectives and forget about them. Remember them next week, next month, next year.

EXPERIENTIAL EXERCISE

How Does the Design of Jobs Affect People?

Purpose.   To quickly bring out individual reactions to different job profiles, and to understand why any one job design profile may appeal to some people while being rejected by others.

Time and Procedures.   Can be completed within about 20 minutes. Preferable if one sheet of newsprint and marker are provided to each team.

Phase 1   (2 to 3 minutes). Form into teams, four persons preferred. At the option of your instructor, either chose or be assigned one of the following job design profiles (assuming at least five teams, each profile should be represented). Four of these profiles are based on the concepts of task scope and task depth (summarized in Exhibit 7–6). The fifth was explained briefly in this chapter and in greater detail in Chapter 3. The profiles are:

- *Routine Jobs* (low scope, low depth)
- *Technician Jobs* (low scope, high depth)
- *Enlarged Jobs* (high scope, low depth)
- *Enriched Jobs* (high scope, high depth)
- *Team-Based Jobs* (high interaction, high interdependence)

Phase 2 *(5 minutes)*. Identify your job profile at the top of the page. Then draw a large "T" with the two subheadings "what turns me on" and "what turns me off." Working as a team, for the next five minutes generate lists of the pros and cons (turn-ons, turn-offs) of the job profile you are describing. Think of the profile as a set of job attributes or characteristics, some of which you may like, some of which you may not. Do not try to get unanimous support for each pro/con—just agreement among a couple of people.

Phase 3 *(2 to 3 minutes)*. Each person on the team now evaluates how strongly each item on the two lists affects you personally. Do so by using a simple plus/minus scoring, with each person's scores marked on the page beside each item. Use two pluses (++) if it is a strong turn-on for you, one plus (+) if moderate; two minuses (−−) if a strong turn-off, one minus (−) if a moderate turn-off. You can assign minuses to items listed in the "turn-on" column, and vice versa. For example, your team may have listed "challenging and constantly changing" under the turn-ons, but you find this threatening and give it one minus.

Phase 4 *(3 to 4 minutes)*. Discuss why individuals on your team felt the same way about some items and differed with others. What accounts for the similarities? The differences?

Phase 5 *(5 to 7 minutes)*. Each team presents to the class its profile and briefly discusses the two or three dimensions that got the most agreement and the two or three that generated diverse reactions. After each team highlights its job profile reaction, engage in a general class discussion of how different job profiles stimulate the reactions that they do.

CASE

Motivation at New United Motor Manufacturing, Inc. (NUMMI)[83]
Gary Convis

Origins of NUMMI. The Fremont plant of General Motors opened in 1965, and after experiencing nearly two decades of labor–management conflict, closed in 1982. At the time of its closing, over 6,000 workers lost their jobs and nearly an equal number of grievances remained unresolved.

Soon after the closing, two forces set in motion events that would lead to a reopening of the plant with very different management philosophies and practices. GM needed to build a compact car for its product line to compete with the popularity of smaller imports, and management wanted to study the production methods of Japanese auto makers. Toyota needed to manufacture automobiles closer to its major off-shore markets and wondered how well its highly efficient Toyota Production System would transfer to American workers and suppliers.

What emerged from these two independent management motives was an agreement to form a 50/50 joint venture to build both GM and Toyota vehicles in the Fremont plant. A separate corporate entity was formed, New United Motor Manufacturing, Inc. (NUMMI—pronounced "new me"), and the plant was reopened in 1984 with a decidedly different approach to management.

The UAW Labor Contract. For starters, the new management team negotiated with the United Auto Workers union a unique contract. While former plant employees would be given first chance at the new jobs, former seniority rights were abandoned. Management focused on a new ideology that targeted building the highest quality vehicles at the lowest possible costs. Workers would be involved in deciding work standards, job allocations and layout, training, job rotation, and other work elements

The dozens of former specialized job classifications were abandoned. Only two classifications are used at NUMMI for hourly workers—skilled trade and nonskilled. Within each classification workers are paid the same hourly rate with only a modest difference between the two classifications. A small 60 cents per hour premium is paid to team leaders who guide the planning and work of four to five people. Even professional people recruited to the firm, such as engineers, occupy their first several weeks on the job working on the line. This helps inculcate in them an appreciation for the tedious and stressful pressures workers face on the line.

A no-strike, no-layoff agreement was part of the contract, a form of job security that Gary Convis, NUMMI's senior vice president, believes "buys the hearts of people." Flexibility prevails instead of the confrontational enforcement of rules.

Management Philosophy and System.

When Convis was recruited into his original position as general manager of the plant, he was advised by a Toyota executive, "Manage as if you had no power." The advice was to forget the command-and-control legacy of Detroit and strive instead to treat people with dignity, to seek consensus in making decisions that directly affect people at work.

The NUMMI system emphasizes human relations, empowerment, and shared responsibility. To emphasize management's philosophy of mutual trust and respect, several key practices form the cornerstones of management–worker relations:

- There are no time clocks, only self-report time sheets.
- An Andon system gives every line employee the right and responsibility to shut down his or her section of the production line to resolve any quality or operating problems.
- A no-fault attendance system does not question an employee's reasons for absence, and no external documentation (e.g., physician's note) is required. However, if people are absent more than the "norm," there are specific steps up to termination that occur. Every effort is made to help people overcome personal problems that might be causing attendance issues.
- An open office environment where no one sits behind a walled-in office. Even Gary Convis has his desk in an open arena with 80 other people.

To further promote a sense of equity, managers and hourly employees eat at the same cafeteria and voluntarily wear the same uniforms provided at company expense. Bonuses are awarded to all employees based on quality, safety, and productivity improvements, with the belief that employees should benefit from performance directly related to production objectives.

Convis wants employees to "do more than just complete your job and then go home." He advocates that employees "Work like your name is on the plant." Such treatment seems to get desirable results. For example, if the robot that installs car seats breaks down, a team of mechanics put some of their people on the job to manually install seats while others work to solve the problem.

Setbacks and Successes.

NUMMI hasn't been without its problems. Its business is only to produce vehicles to specifications and orders generated by Chevrolet and Toy-

ota. By 1995 it was producing over 350,000 vehicles per year. But at an earlier stage its output was erratic. From an output of 205,000 vehicles in 1986 (its second year), it slipped to 187,000 the next year and on down to 128,000 before recovering. At its nadir, NUMMI employed 400 more people that it needed. But true to its no-layoff contract, it engaged people in training and maintenance while keeping them on the payroll.

Such treatment of employees seems to strengthen employee performance. In 1994 NUMMI won the J. D. Powers "Silver Plant Award" (2nd place), and in 1995 won the J. D. Powers "Bronze Plant Award" (3rd place) out of 64 North American vehicle assembly plants. NUMMI's Geo Prizm has received the J. D. Powers highest quality rating of any North American–produced vehicle.

NUMMI management works to include employees in its suggestion and cost management systems programs. As the result of several suggestions, the amount of water used to produce one automobile declined from 1,000 gallons to 680. Teams even have responsibility for planning how to increase line speed. Currently completed automobiles roll off the end of the line at the rate of one every 58 seconds, and pick-up trucks at the rate of 92 seconds per completed vehicle. People are formally recognized for their ideas and dedication, whether improving quality, safety, attendance, or production.

Questions for Discussion

1. What are the lessons to be learned about motivation from the practices of NUMMI?

2. To what extent could the best of management practices at NUMMI be transferred to a multiplant company such as General Motors, Ford, or Chrysler? Under what conditions would such a transfer of practices likely be successful?

3. What would you advise NUMMI management to stop doing, start doing, or do better?

4. Historically auto assembly jobs have been designed to be routine (narrow in both job scope and depth). How would you characterize the design of jobs in NUMMI's manufacturing operation using the variables of variety (scope) and responsibility (depth)? Why?

Part III

Managing Relationships

8 *Communications*

9 *Interpersonal Relationships*

10 *Building Groups into Teams*

11 *Conflict Management and Intergroup Behavior*

Chapter 8

Communications

LEARNING OBJECTIVES

After studying this chapter, you should be able to:

- Explain why communication is so important and how it works in organizations.
- Describe the functions, types, and directions of communication channels in organizations.
- Identify the barriers to effective communication and know how to avoid them.
- Actively listen and obtain feedback to understand others and to build rapport.
- Read nonverbal communication signals.
- Appreciate the diversity of communication styles.
- Improve cross-cultural communication.
- Increase the credibility and clarity of the messages you send to others.

COFFEE-KLATCHING WITH THE CEO

As a part of its efforts to improve communication effectiveness, the management of a company decided to install a $300,000 closed-circuit television system as the most up-to-date way to keep employees informed. During this time, a management consultant was examining the organization's communication efforts and discovered that employees had a common coffee break, during which free pastries were provided and the coffee machines operated without charge.

The consultant suggested that before purchasing the television system, the president might try joining his people during the coffee break to talk with them personally. The president resisted, stating that it would be bad form for executive officers to mingle with employees during breaks and might even be seen as an intrusion.

The consultant persisted, and reluctantly the president agreed to try the radical idea. His first attempt was an abysmal failure. A bystander, seeing him fumble with coins, walked over and told him the coffee was free. Red-faced, he took the cup in hand and looked for someone to engage in conversation. Employees were clustered in little groups quietly talking and glancing curiously at the president. He drank his coffee and walked back into his office.

The president pronounced the experiment a flop because, in his words, "they wouldn't talk to me." The consultant suggested that the president's manner may have been too formal, especially since the workers weren't used to seeing him in their area, and that he should try again. At first the president was emphatic in his refusal to subject himself again to such humiliation. Eventually he agreed to try it one more time, but with his coat off to appear more relaxed. This time he got his coffee without incident and broke into the perimeter of a small gathering. After some conversation about the weather, he asked how things were going and heard some pleasantries indicating that everything was fine.

The following morning, after doing some homework on a current concern of the work force (the opening of a plant in Europe), he raised the subject with a coffee-break group and explained the logic behind the decision. He was surprised to find himself in the middle of an animated discussion about the plant. In the following days, the president continued to venture out for his morning coffee and began to find that he was gaining insights into all kinds of company issues from employees who now felt comfortable enough to air their concerns. The coffee klatches were working so well that he asked his senior staff to begin mingling with their people at coffee time. He also canceled the TV equipment in favor of the simpler and more effective technique of face-to-face communication.

Communication is a crucial aspect of any situation where two or more people interact to accomplish an objective. As just demonstrated with the coffee-klatching CEO, communication is necessary to keep employees informed about what, when, and how to act. It is also a vital tool for enabling managers to discover and solve problems, and to build trust and rapport with employees.

Communication is the one activity that takes up most of a manager's time. Managers rarely find themselves alone at their desks contemplating alternatives to problems. When they are not talking in person with supervisors, peers, or subordinates, they are usually communicating by telephone or reading or writing memos and letters. In fact, it is unusual for a manager to work without interruption more than an occasional half hour two or three times a week.[1] Communicating takes up a major portion of time for nonmanagerial professionals as well.

This chapter examines the all-important impact of communication in organizations. We begin by discussing the importance of communication and how information is processed. After describing the basic communication process, we explore the various channels of communication and their inherent barriers. Finally, we explain how barriers can be overcome and communication effectiveness and efficiency can be increased.

WHAT IS COMMUNICATION?

communication

The process of one person sending a message to another with the intent of evoking a response.

Communication begins when one person sends a message to another with the intent of evoking a response. Effective communication occurs when the receiver interprets the message exactly as the sender intended. Efficient communication uses less time and fewer resources. Communicating with each subordinate individually, for example, is less efficient than addressing all subordinates as a group. The most efficient communication is not necessarily the most effective, however. What a manager wants to achieve is effective communication in the most efficient way.

The Importance of Communication to Organizational Effectiveness

Effective communication is essential for the functioning of any organization. Managers need to transmit orders and policies, build cooperation and team spirit, and identify problems and their solutions. Employees need to clarify directives, provide feedback, and make their problems known. Team members need to share feelings and perceptions to solve problems and resolve conflicts.

Communication breakdowns contribute to a host of organizational problems, from failure to carry out simple directives properly to low productivity and quality. When addressing employees, many managers engage in one-way communication, giving employees the impression that their feelings and input do not matter. To ensure that effective communication occurs, managers should encourage employees to express their feelings, acknowledge such expressions, and be tactful when expressing their own feelings. Poor communication in the workplace costs the economy more than $1 billion annually and contributes to a significant number of employee injuries and deaths, particularly in industries where workers operate heavy machinery or handle hazardous materials.[2]

Communication in organizations serves three major purposes. It allows members to coordinate actions, share information, and satisfy social needs.[3] When employees are happy with how their supervisors communicate with them, their job satisfaction and work output increase[4] and they are more committed to the organization[5]. Simply asking employees for advice can have dramatic payoffs.[6]

At some companies, effective communication begins with the basics: speaking the same language. Linda Lazier, an instructor for Tru Lingua, Inc., teaches English to Hispanic employees of FMI, Inc., a fireplace manufacturer in Santa Ana, California. Tru Lingua's vocational English-as-a-second-language (VESL) program trains workers to use vocabulary and information specifically related to the work they do. Experts say that workers who participate in VESL programs develop confidence and begin to show more initiative in their jobs. (Photo: © 1993 Jim Mendenhall.)

When the senior management at General Motors began to listen to and trust employees by encouraging discussions between managers and employees, output at the company's Buick City plant in Lake Orion, Michigan, increased 8 percent. Over a recent two-year period, the opening up of communication also cut overall defects by 90 percent and assembly hours by 41 percent.[7]

Communication processes within organizations are rapidly changing. In addition to still vital face-to-face, telephone, and written communications, voice mail, electronic mail, video conferencing, faxing, and personal computers make a vast magnitude of complex information immediately available for problem solving and decision making. Knowing how to obtain, transmit, and process information through the multitude of existing communication channels is essential for any manager and most organization members. To do so effectively through any medium, however, requires that managers understand the basic communication process.

The Communication Process

Exhibit 8–1 depicts the interpersonal communication process.[8] The main components of this model are the sender, the receiver, the message, and the channel. The communication process includes the sequential steps of encoding, transmission, and decoding.

▬▬▬▬ EXHIBIT 8–1   *A Model of the Interpersonal Communication Process*

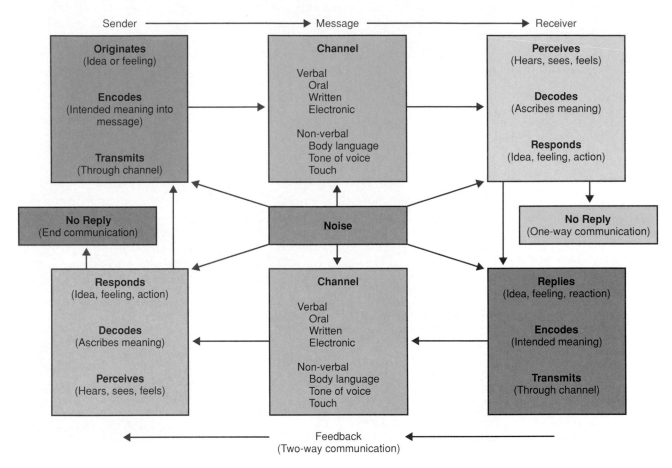

sender
The person communicating a message.

receiver
The person receiving a message.

encoding
Translating information into a message appropriate for transmission.

message
The physical form into which the sender encodes information.

transmission
The act of conveying a communication.

channel
The medium through which a message is transmitted.

Encoding.   Starting in the left-hand column of Exhibit 8–1, the **sender** desires to communicate to the **receiver** some idea, feeling, or intention. Let's imagine that a manager wishes to communicate information about a new deadline. First, the manager must encode the message. **Encoding** is translating the information into a format that will get the idea across. The result is the **message,** which now is ready for **transmission** to one or more of the receiver's senses through speaking, writing, gesturing, or touching.

Transmission Channels.   The **channel** is the medium through which the message is transmitted. Oral communication via sound waves takes place in speeches, meetings, phone calls, or informal discussions. Face-to-face oral communication accounts for 81 percent of a manager's communication each week, of which 45 percent is with subordinates, 15 percent with superiors, 18 percent with peers, and 24 percent with people external to the organization.[9] Sam Walton effectively used oral communication to build Wal-Mart Stores into the nation's largest retail chain with annual sales of over $25 billion and over 90,000 employees by 1990. He personally visited about ten Wal-Mart stores across the United States a week to talk with employees to exchange ideas and solve problems.[10]

nonverbal
All ways of communicating without words, such as tone of voice, facial expression, and gestures.

Nonverbal channels such as touch, facial expression, and tone of voice can convey nuances of meaning mere words are not capable of communicating.[11] Although aware of nonverbal signals, many of us fail to recognize their importance in amplifying, changing, or negating verbal communication.

Written communication channels include letters, memorandums, reports, manuals, and forms. Written materials provide hard copies for storage and retrieval in case documented evidence is needed later.

Electronic channels include E-mail, voice mail, portable telephones, facsimile (fax) machines, telecommuting, computers (integrated databases, modems, etc.), and video conferencing. Electronic mail (E-mail) enables people to exchange messages through their computers. Interpersonal messages can just as easily be transmitted overseas as to an adjacent office. Computer-to-computer communications can also involve bill payments, invoices, or purchase orders. Voice mail is a computer-based answering machine system accessed by telephone to receive or transmit messages. Cellular telephones weighing less than a pound can be utilized while driving, during luncheon meetings, or while walking between appointments. Portable fax machines can be hooked up in a car or other location when hard copies of communications are required. Telecommuting refers to one of the ultimate uses of electronic communications where employees actually work at home while linked to the office through computers, fax machines, and telephones. It is estimated that more than 4 million U.S. employees are already telecommuting and the number is growing rapidly.[12]

On-line technology can improve communication efficiency and result in better productivity. On the other hand, minimizing face-to-face contact and opportunities for soliciting feedback can lead to misunderstandings and lack of nonverbal support, which are often the keys to effective communication and motivation. Face-to-face discussions have the potential for being the most complete and effective channel, followed by telephone conversations, informal letters and memos, electronic mail, formal written documents, and formal quantitative documents such as computer printouts or financial statements.[13] Sam Walton created a way to get the best of both technology and face-to-face communication. Every Saturday morning, Walton and 300 top managers met at Wal-Mart's headquarters where market information was shared and decisions were made. Messages from the managers at these meetings were transmitted via satellite to all Wal-Mart stores, and frequently Sam would appear on television speaking to almost a quarter of a million employees just like he was in the room talking to a handful of people he knew by name.[14]

decoding
The receiver function of perceiving communication stimuli and interpreting their meaning.

Decoding. Communication does not take place if the receiver's senses fail to perceive the sender's message. **Decoding** is the receiver function of perceiving communication stimuli and interpreting their meaning. It encompasses both comprehending the content of the message and determining the sender's intention in transmitting it. The closer the receiver's decoding to the sender's intended message, the more effective the communication has been.

After the message has been decoded into information meaningful to the receiver, how the receiver feels about and responds to the message will depend on the receiver's needs. No matter how clearly information has been encoded, misunderstanding is always possible in its decoding because this process is influenced by the receiver's past experience, personal interpretations, and expectations.

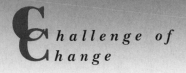

New Electronic Communication Increases Efficiency at Benetton

Benetton, the Italian sportswear company, has established an electronic communication loop linking sales outlets around the world with its factory and warehouse in Ponzano, Italy. If an outlet in Los Angeles needs more red sweaters, the store manager can call in the order to a Benetton sales agent, who enters it on a personal computer that sends it to a mainframe in Italy, where it is transmitted to a knitting machine that automatically makes the sweaters. They are put into a box with a bar code label containing the address of the Los Angeles store and sent to the warehouse, where a computer sends a robot to read the bar codes and sends the order to the Los Angeles store. With this process, Benetton can get the order to Los Angeles in four weeks—one week if the red sweaters are in stock.

Source: B. Dumaine, "How Managers Can Succeed Through Speed," *Fortune,* (February 13, 1989), pp. 54–59.

noise
Anything that interferes with the communication process.

Noise.   **Noise** is anything that interferes, at any stage, with the communication process. A sender may be inarticulate, have an irritating writing style, or speak too softly to be heard. During transmission, extraneous noise from nearby conversations, music, or machines can impede hearing, and irrelevant visual activities may be distracting. Over 23 million people in the United States cannot read this text. A less obvious type of noise occurs when the receiver simply fails to pay attention or is not receptive to the message because of hostile attitudes, past experiences, mental/emotional distractions, or contrary frames of reference. In the international arena, considerable noise and confusion can occur; for example, when Americans, who prefer to get right to the point of a business negotiation, interact with Arabs, who prefer to talk about social topics for a while before addressing the business objective.[15]

The success of the communications process depends to a large degree on overcoming various sources of noise. Some enlightened organizations are providing training to increase communication skills. Adolph Coors, for example, created a reading center, and GTE contributes to the financing of literacy programs in the U.S. communities where potential employees live.[16] Much of the remainder of this chapter addresses ways to overcome communication noise. A basic method to determine if noise has occurred and to correct communication errors caused by noise is to use feedback.

Feedback.   After the sender, or source, has encoded and transmitted the message and the receiver has received and decoded it, the feelings, ideas, and intentions generated in the receiver are usually communicated back to the sender. In this reversal, the receiver now becomes the responder and the original sender becomes the receiver, and the process continues. An important component of the second stage of the communications process is feedback. **Feedback** is the message that tells the original sender how clearly his or her message was understood and what effect it has had on the receiver. Feedback is the manager's primary tool for determining whether or not instructions have been understood and accepted. It can be transmitted through a variety of formal and informal organizational communication channels.

feedback
A message that tells the original sender how clearly his or her message was understood and what effect it has had on the receiver.

Eye on Ethics

Electronic Spying on Employees: Performance Booster or Invasion of Privacy?

Done right, monitoring employee performance by computer or telephone improves service, productivity, and profits. Done wrong, it just bugs the staff—in both senses.

At General Electric Answer Center in Louisville, Kentucky, more than 200 agents field over 14,000 telephone calls a day from potential appliance buyers and fix-it-yourselfers. Ten "coaches" record the agents' calls and later play back some of the conversations to the agents to enhance the quality of their dealings with the public. This silent monitoring, along with other management techniques, pays off in a 96 percent satisfaction rating from its callers. Although it costs GE $4 to answer each call, the center generates an average of $16 a call in appliance sales and service savings. The company can often avoid sending out repair people to fix products under warranty.

Silent monitoring, where the employee doesn't know exactly when the "coach" is listening, is spreading among U.S. companies that use service workers. A 1993 survey of 301 employers found that 22 percent monitor employee voice mail, electronic mail, or computer files, many without their workers' knowledge or consent. At many companies, managers use computerized devices and software programs that count the keystrokes of data entry clerks and telephone operators to gauge productivity. Others secretly watch the screens of desktop computer operators—and have even been accused of reading employees' electronic mail. A manager at a McDonald's restaurant, for example, was fired after steamy voice mail messages to a co-worker he was having an affair with were retrieved and played to his boss.

Low-paid workers engaged in repetitive tasks are not the only ones having their money-making effectiveness monitored. Surveillance is expanding to cover highly paid professionals such as stockbrokers, loan officers, lawyers, and even veterinarians. At Charles Schwab discount brokerage offices, experienced stockbrokers who earn as much as $80,000 a year are routinely monitored through computerized voice-recording systems. The purpose is to improve performance by having supervisors appraise the quality of customer service, as well as to create a permanent record of the transaction.

Surveillance—properly done—can assist people in doing their jobs better. But as employer needs for more information about employee performance bump up against workers' desire for privacy, the negative aspects of electronic monitoring and telephone surveillance are receiving more attention.

American Airlines is installing remote-screen surveillance software to supplement its listening in on telephone calls at its reservation center at the Dallas–Fort Worth airport. American says the idea is to enable supervisors to help agents use its global Sabre reservation system more effectively. In addition to hearing what agents are telling customers on the phone, supervisors will be able to see what agents are entering on their PC screens.

By contrast, executives at GE's Answer Center elected not to buy programs of that sort. "It just goes against our philosophy of professionalism and trust," says manager Bill Waers.

Sources: "Is Office Voice Mail Private? Don't Bet On It," *The Wall Street Journal* (February 28, 1995), p. B1; Junda Woo, "Secret Taping of Supervisors Is on the Rise, Lawyers Say," *The Wall Street Journal* (November 3, 1992), pp. B1–B4; and Gene Bylinsky, "How Companies Spy on Employees," *Fortune* (November 4, 1991), pp. 131–140.

HOW ARE COMMUNICATION CHANNELS USED IN ORGANIZATIONS?

Communication between organizational members can be vertical or lateral, formal or informal. Managers are responsible for establishing and maintaining formal communication channels in downward, upward, and horizontal directions. Just as important in most organizations are informal networks, which convey feelings and reactions among employees.

EXHIBIT 8–2   *Formal Communication Channels*

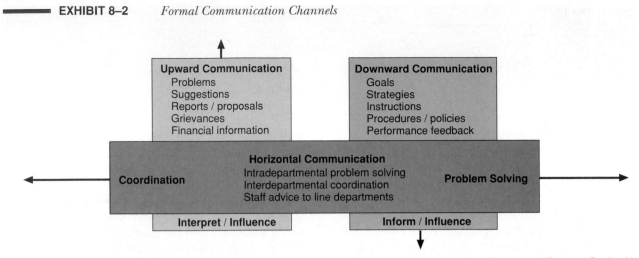

Source: From *Organizations: A Micro/Macro Approach* by Richard L. Daft and Richard M. Steers. Copyright © 1986 by Scott, Foresman and Company. Reprinted by permission of HarperCollins College Publishers.

Formal Communication Channels

Formal communication channels are established within the organization's chain of command in order to accomplish task objectives. Exhibit 8–2 illustrates the three directions of formal communication flow, the types of information conveyed, and the functions they perform.

Downward Communication.   Downward communication is used by managers to assign goals; provide job instructions; inform about policies, procedures, and practices; provide performance feedback; point out problems; and socialize employees. The most costly communication breakdowns occur when instructions are given or received poorly. Even though nearly 90 percent of all instructions are considered routine, it is necessary for managers to confirm them repeatedly.[17] Downward communication can take many forms: speeches, memos, company newsletters, bulletin boards, and policy and procedure manuals. Surveys of employees show that they do not think the information in downward employee reports is relevant to them, and they have difficulty understanding it because it is communicated in head-office language. Employees rely on and trust their supervisors most for relevant downward information.[18]

Upward Communication.   Upward communication provides managers with information about current problems, updates on employees' progress toward goals, suggestions for improvement, proposals for innovations, employee grievances, and feedback about employee attitudes. Upward communication can take the forms of employee surveys, suggestion boxes, face-to-face encounters, open-door policies, or required reports. At Smith & Hawken, a gardening supply company, employees are encouraged to submit to their supervisor every Friday a "5-15 report," which requires no more than 15 minutes to write and 5 minutes to read.[19] By improving upward communication from employees to management, some companies have experienced profit increases of as much as 30 to 40 percent.[20]

Horizontal Communication.   Horizontal communication takes place among peers and can cut across departments and work groups. These lateral communications benefit the organization by more efficiently providing support, coordination, and

World Watch

Meet Me at the Club: Horizontal Communication at Mitsubishi

Communicating in an international conglomerate made up of hundreds of companies is an extremely difficult task. The international conglomerate, Mitsubishi, however, is able to do so effectively, not with formal hierarchical lines of reporting authority, but with relatively informal horizontal communication networks. At the center of the core Mitsubishi policy-making group, or *keiretsu,* are Mitsubishi Corp., Mitsubishi Ban, and Mitsubishi Heavy Industries. Connected to the keiretsu are hundreds of additional companies that network informally, but seriously, with the primary decision makers.

Every evening, more than 30 executives of these companies gather at the Mitsubishi Club for dinner, socialization, and other activities that serve to enhance the communications process. During these hours of business relaxation, deals get made, ideas are shared, and trust is built. Membership is open to members of the board of directors of any Mitsubishi company, and daily attendance at these gatherings is optional. The key to the keiretsu's success may be the open, free, and casual communication fostered by the enduring trust in the relationships that develop.

Some American companies are beginning to tap into this quality-driven, interdependent business strategy by sharing technology, selling and servicing competitors' products, and forming alliances with former or potential market enemies. American keiretsus are applying one of Japan's secret competitive weapons to improve competitive position, market share, and profits for American companies.

Source: David N. Burt and Michael F. Doyle, *The American Keiretsu* (Homewood, IL: Business One Irwin, 1993); and "Maybe the U.S. Could Use a Keiretsu or Two," *Business Week*, September 24, 1990, p. 162.

information than could vertical channels. Some organizations form task forces and committees to facilitate information exchange and coordination between departments. The World Watch box tells how Mitsubishi, an international conglomerate headquartered in Japan, uses informal horizontal communication to help manage its hundreds of associated companies.

Another form of lateral communication occurs outside the walls of any particular organization—communication with customers and suppliers. Boeing Commercial Airplane, for example, buys approximately 60 percent of its airplane parts from outside suppliers. Since Boeing wants to get the highest quality parts, it has recently begun programs to increase lateral communication with suppliers about quality requirements and procedures. Boeing has also asked customers to identify their requirements more specifically and to provide specific feedback so that Boeing can satisfy those requirements.[21]

Informal Communication Channels

Informal communication channels exist to serve the interests of those people who make them up, regardless of their positions in the organization. They are not formally sanctioned by management and do not follow the organization's hierarchy; however, informal communications are often perceived by employees as more believable than communications received through formal organizational channels.[22] Some typical informal channels are the grapevine, social gatherings, informal one-to-one discussions, and small-group networks.

grapevine
The informal communication channel for gossip and rumors.

The Grapevine.   The **grapevine** is the informal communication channel for gossip and rumors and is not controlled by management. It is perceived by most employees as more believable and reliable than top management communication channels.[23] The grapevine satisfies social needs, helps clarify orders and decisions, and serves as a way of getting out information that can't be expressed adequately through formal channels. About 80 percent of grapevine communications is work related, and over 80 percent of the time the grapevine is accurate.[24]

Studies have determined that only about 10 percent of managers actually pass along rumors and gossip—regardless of their importance—to more than one other person. When a manager was contemplating resignation from one company, for example, 81 percent of the other managers knew about it, but only 11 percent shared this information with others.[25] Although managers may not be part of the actual gossip chain, they can keep an ear to the grapevine through loyal subordinates or colleagues who will discreetly share information with them. Then they can pass on news that will improve relationships or act to eliminate gossip that might be harmful to organizational performance.[26]

Social Gatherings.   Each of Tandem Computer's 132 worldwide offices holds a Friday afternoon beer bust to create an informal communication channel for employees. "Over beer and popcorn, employees are more willing to talk openly," says CEO Jim Treybig.[27] Similar social opportunities for informal information exchange can be created at office parties, company picnics, and luncheons.

Management by Wandering Around.   Peter Anderson, when president of Ztel, Inc., a maker of television switching systems, preferred not to personally communicate with employees. By maintaining distance between himself and his employees, however, some analysts think Anderson failed to provide an informal communication channel for employees, which contributed to Ztel's eventual bankruptcy.[28] Anderson's preference is not unusual, but managers don't have to break into ongoing coffee groups or throw beer busts to enter into informal communication with employees. They can simply walk around their organizations and informally chat with all levels of employees to learn about their concerns, ideas, and problems. Informally talking with employees is commonly called *management by wandering around.*[29]

Small-Group Networks.   The pattern and direction of communication flows have important consequences for both task accomplishment and personal satisfaction. The chain network typifies the organization with a strong vertical hierarchy, where information travels only upward and downward. People communicate only with their immediate superior and subordinate. It also exists between people working on a production line. In the circle network, people can only communicate to others on either side. This pattern often occurs between people in departments at the same horizontal level in organizations. The star configuration distributes the flow of communication most evenly. It prevails in informal groups with no assigned leader or tasks to accomplish. The wheel represents the other extreme, where all communications are channeled through a central position. In Exhibit 8–3, the wheel would rely on Kate, who could be the group leader or manager, to make sure that each member has the information he or she needs. Air traffic controllers would be the hub of a circle of airplane pilots attempting to land at the same airport.

The effectiveness of the communication networks varies according to the task.[30] The centralized wheel-type formation provides more efficient and accurate problem solving of simple and routine tasks. For ambiguous and complex problems, however, the more egalitarian star network is much more effective. Overall group

━━━ **EXHIBIT 8–3**   *Communication Networks in Small Groups*

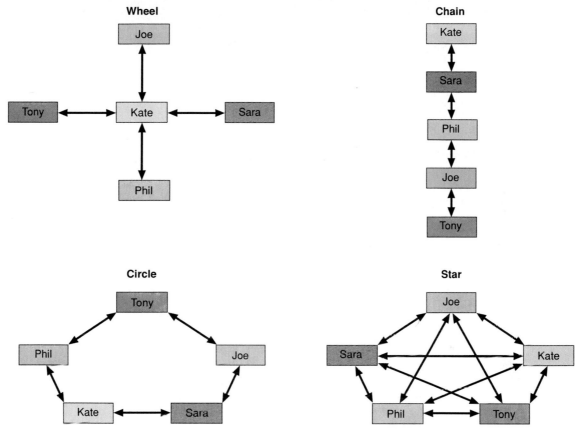

Source: H. J. Leavitt, *Managerial Psychology*, 3rd ed. (Chicago: University of Chicago Press, 1972), pp. 178–180. Used by permission of the University of Chicago Press.

satisfaction is greater in the more egalitarian star networks because group members participate more evenly. In centralized wheel networks, individuals holding the central position are much more active, satisfied, and likely to become leaders than those in peripheral locations.

A frequent problem for women and minorities in organizations is limited access to or exclusion from informal interaction networks. This limited access produces disadvantages such as restricted knowledge of what is going on in the organization and difficulty in forming alliances vital to career advancement and social support.[31]

Actually, a number of barriers exist for all organizational members in each of the communication channels just reviewed. Barriers to effective understanding also can be found within the sender or receiver of information.

WHAT BARRIERS TO COMMUNICATION EXIST?

The image and credibility of the sender, stereotyping, past experiences, overexposure to data, attitudes, mindsets, perceptual filters, trust, and empathy all impact on what receivers of communication "hear" and how they interpret its meaning. These communication barriers occur in everyday business communications.

Dynamics of Diversity   Culture Clash at School and Work

The second-grade schoolteacher posed a simple enough problem to the class: "There are four blackbirds sitting in a tree. You take a slingshot and shoot one of them. How many are left?"

"Three," answered the seven-year-old European with certainty. "One subtracted from four leaves three."

"Zero," answered the seven-year-old African with equal certainty. "If you shoot one bird, the others will fly away."

Who was right and who was wrong? Both, depending on your cultural point of view. For the first seven-year-old, the birds represented a hypothetical situation (structure) that required a literal answer (task). For the second seven-year-old, the birds had a relationship to each other and known behavior could be expected to occur if one was shot.

According to Jo Vanderkloot and Myrtle Parnell, the world can be divided into two communication styles. One is a style that connects people to others through doing things together and revolves around task, structure, and time. This tends to be the Anglo-American approach to work. In Hispanic and African-American cultures, the relationship is what is important. There is a need to have some idea of who that other person is—some common ground—in order to work together. The whole issue of time—get it done now, be here by four o'clock—is Anglo-American. In other cultures, you have an obligation to honor the relationship first, which may mean that deadlines change.

The American workplace (like the American classroom) is changing in gender, color, nationality, and cultural point of view. By the year 2000, women will hold about 48 percent of all jobs, up from 22 percent in 1990. White males are expected to account for only 32 percent of the entering work force by 2000. The organizations that learn to respect and value the perspectives people from different cultures bring to communications and problem solving will be ahead in the twenty-first century.

Source: Audrey Edwards, "The Enlightened Manager: How to Treat All Your Employees Fairly," *Working Woman,* (January 1991), pp. 35–36.

Misinterpretation occurs when the receiver understands the message to his or her own satisfaction but not in the sense that the sender intended. Misinterpretation can be a consequence of sender or channel noise, poor listening habits, erroneous inferences on the part of the receiver, or differing frames of reference. An example of this occurs when unclear instructions lead employees to "hear" the wrong procedures for doing their work.

Frames of Reference

frame of reference
A person's mind-set, based on past experience and current expectations, which determines what is perceived and how it is interpreted.

A combination of past experience and current expectations often leads two people to perceive the same communication differently. Although each hears the actual words accurately, he or she may catalogue those words according to his or her individual perceptions, or **frames of reference.** For example, when someone complains about his or her "dog," some interpret this to refer to a pet, some recall a bad date they have experienced, and others think about an onerous project to which they have been assigned.

Within organizations, people with different functions often have different frames of reference. Marketing people may interpret things one way and production people another. An engineer's interpretation is likely to differ from that of an accountant. An example of how two people might perceive and approach a problem completely differently based on their different cultural frames of reference is provided in the Dynamics of Diversity box.

Technical jargon eases the communication between members of a group but is difficult for outsiders to understand. Here an instructor at Motorola presents technical information on cellular systems design. (Photo: © Scott Goldsmith.)

Semantics

Just as individual frames of reference lend different meanings to identical words or expressions, so can variations in group semantics. *Semantics* pertains to the meaning and use of words. This is especially true when people from different cultures are trying to communicate. Consider, for example, a Japanese businessman who is trying to tell his Norwegian counterpart that he is uninterested in a product. The Japanese politely says, "That would be very difficult." The Norwegian interprets that to mean that there are still problems, not that the deal is off. Since he doesn't understand that the Japanese have more than a dozen subtle ways to say no, the Norwegian responds by asking how his company can help solve the problem. The Japanese, who thinks that he has communicated that the sale is off, is totally confused.[32]

Many professional and social groups adopt a specialized technical language called *jargon* that provides them with a sense of belonging and simplifies communication within the in-group. But sophisticated technical or financial terms can intimidate and confuse outsiders, especially when members of a specialized group use them to project a professional mystique.

The same is true of words that cause emotional reactions in others. The same word does not cause the same reaction in all people. Often only the members of certain groups experience emotional reactions. "Negro" and "girl" (for a grown woman) are words sometimes used by people who did not fight for civil rights, and they can cause very emotional reactions in those who experienced the struggle.

Value Judgments

Value judgments are a source of noise when a receiver evaluates the worth of a sender's message before the sender has finished transmitting it. Often such value judgments are based on the receiver's previous experience either with the sender or with similar types of communications. A professor may tune out when a freshman begins to describe a scheduling problem because "freshmen are always complaining about something." Unfortunately, many managers react similarly in work organizations. When listeners form value judgments, speakers are usually aware of it through verbal and nonverbal feedback. Subsequently, the senders become guarded and defensive, which often inhibits transmission of their real concerns.

Whereas the sender usually knows what he or she intends to communicate, the receiver must infer what is really meant. Because of different frames of reference, the frequent result is a highly distorted understanding of what the sender intended to communicate. A receiver's degree of trust and confidence in the sender directly affects his or her reaction to the words and gestures of the message. In businesses where union leaders are perceived as political exploiters, management will rarely hear their messages without making some inference as to the speaker's intent.

Selective Listening

selective listening
Receiver behavior of blocking out information or distorting it to match preconceived notions.

Value judgments, needs, and expectations cause us to hear what we want to hear. When a message conflicts with what a receiver believes or expects, **selective listening** may cause the receiver to block out the information or distort it to match preconceived notions. Feedback to an employee about poor performance, for example, may not be "heard" because it doesn't fit the employee's self-concept or expectations.

At times people become so absorbed in their tasks that when someone initiates conversation, they are not able to disassociate and listen effectively. Not only is it difficult for a preoccupied person to receive the message the sender intends, but obvious body language may make it appear that the receiver doesn't care about the sender or the message. This can create negative feelings and make future communications even more difficult.

This problem occurs frequently in emotionally charged conversations or philosophical debates, when receivers listen only for an opening to speak, rather than pay attention to the content of the sender's message. Such receivers often miss the sender's entire meaning in their haste to get a personal point across.

Filtering

filtering
The sender's conveying only certain parts of the relevant information to the receiver.

Filtering is selective listening in reverse; in fact, we might call it "selective sending." When senders convey only certain parts of the relevant information to receivers, they are said to be filtering their message. Filtering often occurs in upward communication when subordinates suppress negative information and relay only the data that will be perceived by superiors as positive. Filtering is very common when people are being evaluated for promotions, salary increases, or performance appraisals.

A different kind of filtering occurs in times of information overload or intense time pressure. When managers are deluged with more information than they can process effectively, one response is to screen out and never decode a large number of messages. With time pressure, even the information that a manager has absorbed and processed may not be communicated to all concerned employees. Information overload and time pressures also compound the difficulty of making good decisions and solving complex problems.

Distrust

A lack of trust on the part of either communicator is likely to evoke one or more of the barriers we've just examined. Senders may filter out important information if they distrust receivers, and receivers may form value judgments, make inferences, and listen only selectively to distrusted senders. Such situations are complicated by the fact that the distrust itself may have arisen from earlier communications that were impeded by some of the same barriers. In other words, neither party is dishonest, but their poorly developed communication skills have led them to distrust one another.

Distrust is sometimes caused by status differences. Lower-status employees tend to be intimidated by upper-status job titles, plush offices, sophisticated modes of dress, and perhaps even a particular manager's reputation. Rather than take the risk of being judged incompetent or being ridiculed, subordinates may refrain from seeking help or requesting needed information from a high-status manager.

Many times these barriers to effective communication can be neutralized or avoided altogether if the sender and receiver practice certain communication techniques. The next section addresses how a sender can be more effective. The following section explains how receivers can increase their effectiveness.

HOW CAN MESSAGES BE SENT MORE EFFECTIVELY?

Consistently effective communication requires considerable skill in both sending and receiving information. In this section, we will examine how to achieve better transmission of messages. Later in the chapter, we'll explore the receiver skills that enhance our understanding of the messages others send to us.

Increase the Clarity of Messages

A sender can take the initiative in eliminating communication barriers by making sure a message is clear and credible and that feedback is obtained from the receiver to ensure that understanding is adequate. A number of things can be done to accomplish the goal of effective sending.[33]

Use Multiple Channels.   The impact of a message can be increased by using more than one channel or mode of transmission to send it. Examples are matching facial and body gestures to a message or diagramming it on a piece of paper. This kind of multiple-mode communication of the same message ensures that the receiver has the opportunity to receive the message through more than one sense. A consultant speaking about the need to increase quality of production, for example, may convey the urgency of the message through the multiple channels of words, voice tones, facial expressions, gestures, pictures, postures, and audiovisual presentations.

Be Complete and Specific.   When the subject matter of a message is new or unfamiliar to the receiver, the sender can make the message complete and specific by providing sufficient background information and details. Once the receiver understands

Reliable Cartage Co. believes that employee feedback is an important part of effective communications within its organization. On a regular basis, the company asks all 117 employees to evaluate the company in the areas of wages, benefits, work policies, and work environment. As a result of employee feedback, the company has reviewed its pay scales and has implemented a bonus program tied to performance. (Photo: © David B. Sutton.)

the sender's frame of reference, he or she is more likely to interpret the message accurately. By referring to concrete deadlines and examples, a sender can decrease the probability of misinterpretation.

Claim Your Own Message.   To claim the message as their own, senders should use personal pronouns such as "I" and "mine." This indicates to the receiver that the sender takes responsibility for the ideas and feelings expressed in the message. General statements like "everyone feels this way" leave room for doubt (someone might *not* feel that way). But an "I" message such as "I feel strongly about this" is not ambiguous. The sender is stating a personal opinion. It's better, too, to be up-front rather than put the receiver on the defensive. Say "I think improvement is necessary" if that's what you mean, rather than asking "Don't you think you can do better?"

Be Congruent.   Make sure your messages are congruent with your actions. Being incongruent by saying one thing and doing another confuses receivers. If, for example, managers tell subordinates that they are "always available" to help them but then act condescending and preoccupied when those people come to them with problems, they are communicating something quite different from the verbal message.

Simplify Your Language.   Complex rhetoric and technical jargon confuse individuals who do not use such language. Also, most organizations develop a "lingo," or language distinctly the company's own, made up of words and phrases for people, situations, events, and things. At Walt Disney, for example, all employees are called "cast members." They're "on stage" when they're working and "off stage" when at lunch or taking a break. Any situation or event that's positive is a "good Mickey." Anything less is a "bad Mickey."

Jargon and lingo serve a purpose in an organization. They make the organization more distinctive and unique, which tends to build employees' identity with and commitment to the company. They are also efficient ways to communicate inside the organization. But used with associates outside the company who don't know the jargon, lingo can hinder communication.[34] Effective communicators avoid jargon, slang, clichés, and colorful metaphors when communicating with people outside the industry or those who do not speak the language fluently. By being empathetic and envisioning themselves in the receiver's situation, managers can encode messages in terms that are meaningful to the specific receivers.

Develop Credibility

credibility
The sender's degree of trustworthiness, as perceived by the receiver.

The **credibility** of a sender is probably the single most important element in effective interpersonal communications.[35] Sender credibility is reflected in the receiver's belief that the sender is trustworthy. Factors that increase the clarity of communication, like congruence of verbal and nonverbal messages, contribute to the sender's credibility,[36] as do the additional dimensions discussed below.[37]

Expertise. Receivers will be more attentive when they perceive that a sender has expertise in the area about which he or she is communicating, as when instructions are given by someone authorized to dispense that information.

Mutual Trust. Receivers prefer to have a sender's motives clarified: Are they selfish or altruistic? Owning up to motives at the very beginning of a conversation eliminates the receiver's anxiety about a sender's real intentions and does much to establish common trust.

Reliability. A sender's perceived dependability, predictability, and consistency in providing all relevant information (being consistent in applying performance criteria when evaluating subordinates and treating subordinates fairly and equally, for example) reinforce the sender's perceived trustworthiness.

Warmth and Friendliness. A warm, friendly, supportive attitude is more conducive to managerial credibility than is a posture of hostility and arrogance, especially when subordinates need to tackle new or uncertain tasks.

Dynamic Appearance. A sender who is dynamic, confident, and positive is more credible than one who acts passive, withdrawn, and unsure. Receivers tend to be more attentive to a message when the sender is confident.

Personal Reputation. If other members of the organization have told the receiver that a sender is credible, the receiver usually will tend to believe it. If, on the other hand, a sender's reputation has been tarnished by a history of untrustworthiness, a receiver is likely to believe the negative peer opinions.

Obtain Feedback

Effective communication means both top-down and bottom-up communication. All too often, management concentrates on communicating its message to employees without providing the feedback mechanism for response and input from workers.[38] Boeing Commercial Airplanes applied a number of feedback mechanisms and realized a huge boost in quality improvement, as described in the Challenge of Change box.

Recall that feedback is the receiver's response to the sender's message. Its purpose is to tell the sender what the receiver heard and what the receiver thinks the meaning of this message is. If the receiver's response indicates a lack of understanding, the sender can modify the original message to make sure his

Source: *Profiles in Quality: Blueprints for Action from 50 Leading Companies* (Boston: Allyn and Bacon, 1991), pp. 45–48.

Challenge of Change

Changing Feedback to Improve Quality at Boeing

It doesn't always take a hot new program or the expertise of an expensive consultant to improve quality. Boeing Commercial Airplanes simply improved its feedback communication and quality improvements soared. Jack Wires, vice president of Quality Assurance, believes that to make quality improvements "you really have to know what the job is all about and where the problems are. That's where the employee comes in." Wires says that to get quality feedback about problems you have to develop a relationship between management and employees that will permit workers to tell things to management the way they are.

To discover quality-enhancing ideas, Boeing encourages workers to make suggestions when they see something wrong or something that can be done more efficiently to their supervisors who are trained to act as "enablers" to help workers implement feasible ideas. For example, when shop workers recognized that a change could be made in the way a part was produced, they went to the engineering manager who recognized the merit in their suggestion and made the change. The first-line supervisor later commented that "You won't believe how intelligent the people who run these machines are. You talk to them and ask them how we can improve our operation and they've got all kinds of ideas—they're an untapped resource."

or her intentions are understood. If senders are unable to obtain feedback on how their messages are being received, inaccurate perceptions on the part of a receiver may never be corrected.

When a manager says "Call me later and we'll discuss it" while walking out the door, does the manager mean fifteen minutes from now, two hours from now, to-morrow, or next week? Statements that carry a number of potential meanings are highly susceptible to misunderstanding on the part of their receivers. Unless they are clarified, such ambiguous directions are unlikely to be followed according to the sender's intentions, and the relationship between the parties will be strained.[39] By listening to feedback, managers can transform such highly ambiguous statements into very specific, effective communications.

Verbal feedback allows parties to clarify facts, feelings, and needs. It can also be used to show others that they are recognized and appreciated, as when a manager says, "You did a really good job. I have confidence in you." This kind of feedback prompts others to continue their positive performance.

When someone's behavior requires negative feedback, it can be given construc-tively. Ignoring an inadequate performance or poor work behavior by remaining silent may be construed as tacit approval. Direct comments such as "Sarah told me she's afraid to work with you because you are so aggressive" provide people with the type of verbal feedback they need to correct inadequate behavior.

To ensure that each party understands what the other is trying to communicate, interpretations of received messages can be fed back for confirmation. Clarifying feedback typically begins with a statement, such as "Let me be sure I understand what you have said" or "Let me see if I can summarize the key points we've dis-cussed." Often it ends with a question: "Did I understand you properly?" "Were those your major concerns?" Feedback can provide the needed information for quality and productivity enhancement.

■■■■■ **EXHIBIT 8–4**

Guides for Giving and Receiving Feedback

Criteria for Giving Feedback

1. Make sure your comments are intended to help the recipient.
2. Speak directly and with feeling based on trust.
3. Describe what the person is doing and the effect the person is having.
4. Don't be threatening or judgmental.
5. Be specific, not general (use clear and recent examples).
6. Give feedback when the recipient is open to accepting it.
7. Check to ensure the validity of your statements.
8. Include only things the receiver can do something about.
9. Don't overwhelm; make sure your comments aren't more than the person can handle.

Criteria for Receiving Feedback

1. Don't be defensive.
2. Seek specific examples.
3. Be sure you understand (summarize).
4. Share your feelings about the comments.
5. Ask for definitions.
6. Check out underlying assumptions.
7. Be sensitive to sender's nonverbal messages.
8. Ask questions to clarify.

Source: Summarized from Phillip L. Hunsaker and Anthony J. Alessandra, *The Art of Managing People* (New York: Simon & Schuster, 1986), pp. 209–213. Reprinted by authors' permission.

Through the use of their bodies, eyes, faces, postures, and senses, receivers communicate a variety of positive or negative attitudes, feelings, and opinions that serve as feedback about how they react to a sender's message. All signals communicated back to the sender by the receiver, other than the actual words spoken or written, comprise nonverbal feedback. Examples are eye contact, gestures, facial expressions, and vocal intonations. Although most people react subconsciously to nonverbal feedback, perceptive communicators use it to structure the content and direction of the conversation. By changing the pace of their words, tone of their voice, or their physical position, for example, skilled speakers regain other people's attention and interest.

Feedback can be used to clarify needs and reduce misunderstanding, to improve relationships and keep both parties updated, to determine which issues need further discussion, and to confirm all uncertain verbal, vocal, and visual cues. The proper and effective use of feedback skills can lead to mutual understanding, less interpersonal tension, increased trust and credibility, and higher productivity. Some rules for giving and receiving feedback effectively are summarized in Exhibit 8–4.

HOW CAN MESSAGES BE MORE ACCURATELY RECEIVED?

We have just discussed how a sender can increase the effectiveness of a transmission. Now let's look at how the receiver can ensure understanding through the use of questions, listening, and nonverbal communications.

Ask Questions

Don't be afraid to ask dumb questions. They're easier to handle than dumb mistakes. Only people who know all the answers can dispense with the use of questions. We need to ask questions to obtain the information we need from managers, peers, subordinates, computers, and sometimes even ourselves. Questions motivate communication and open channels of communication, providing an environment in which employees also feel free to state their feelings, which helps managers communicate more effectively with a diverse work force.[40]

Questions allow us to gain information about people and problems. They can help us uncover motives and gain insights about another person's frame of reference, goals, and motives. Questions can convey information—"Did you know we have an education reimbursement program?" They can be used to check understanding or interest and to obtain subordinate participation. Finally, questions can bring attention back to the subject and start others thinking.[41] There are three main types of questions: closed-end, open-end, and clarifying.[42]

Closed-end questions require narrow answers to a specific inquiry. Typical answers will be "yes," "no," or something nearly as brief. Questions of this nature are useful for obtaining specific facts, gaining commitment, or directing the conversation to a desired area. Open-end questions are often used to draw out a wide range of responses to increase understanding or solve a problem. These questions involve other people by asking for feelings or opinions about a topic. They usually cannot be answered by a simple "yes" or "no," begin with "what" or "how," and do not lead others in a specified direction. Clarifying questions are essentially restatements of another person's remarks to determine if you have understood exactly what the speaker meant. These questions are useful for clarifying ambiguities and inviting the speaker to expand on ideas and feelings.

Listen

listening
The intellectual and emotional process in which the receiver integrates physical, emotional, and intellectual inputs in search of meaning.

Listening is an intellectual and emotional process in which the receiver integrates physical, emotional, and intellectual inputs in search of meaning. Listening to others is our most important means of gaining the information we need to understand people and assess situations. Many communication problems develop because listening skills are ignored, forgotten, or just taken for granted.[43] Check your own listening proficiency by completing the following Your Turn exercise.

Listening is not the same as hearing, and effective listening is not easy. People usually hear the entire message, but too often its meaning is lost or distorted. When listening to messages of only 10 minutes in duration, most people are likely to understand and retain only about 50 percent of what is said. Forty-eight hours later, this relatively poor retention rate drops to a still less impressive 25 percent. This means that most people's memory of a particular conversation that took place more than a couple of days ago will always be incomplete and usually be inaccurate.[44]

Poor listeners miss important messages and emerging problems. Consequently, the ideas that they propose are often faulty and inappropriate; sometimes they even address the wrong problems. Failure to listen also creates tension and distrust and results in reciprocal nonlistening by others. The first step to overcoming listening barriers is being aware of them.

Barriers to Effective Listening.[45]   Many people identify listening as a passive, compliant act and develop negative attitudes toward it. From early childhood onward, we are encouraged to put our emphasis on speaking as opposed to listening. We are taught that talk is power. When two people are vying for attention and control, however, they not only fail to listen to each other, but also generate increased tension along with decreased trust and productivity.

YOUR TURN

Listening Inventory

Instructions: Go through the following questions, checking yes or no next to each question. Mark it as you actually behave, not as you think you should behave.

	Yes	No
1. I frequently attempt to listen to several conversations at the same time.	☐	☐
2. I like people to give me only the facts and then let me make my own interpretation.	☐	☐
3. I sometimes pretend to pay attention to people.	☐	☐
4. I consider myself a good judge of nonverbal communications.	☐	☐
5. I usually know what another person is going to say before he or she says it.	☐	☐
6. I usually end conversations that don't interest me by diverting my attention from the speaker.	☐	☐
7. I frequently nod, frown, or whatever to let the speaker know how I feel about what he or she is saying.	☐	☐
8. I usually respond immediately when someone has finished talking.	☐	☐
9. I evaluate what is being said while it is being said.	☐	☐
10. I usually formulate a response while the other person is still talking.	☐	☐
11. The speaker's "delivery" style frequently keeps me from listening to content.	☐	☐
12. I usually ask people to clarify what they have said rather than guess at the meaning.	☐	☐
13. I make a concerted effort to understand other people's point of view.	☐	☐
14. I frequently hear what I expect to hear rather than what is said.	☐	☐
15. Most people feel that I have understood their point of view when we disagree.	☐	☐

Interpretation: The correct answers according to communication theory are as follows: *No* for questions 1, 2, 3, 5, 6, 7, 8, 9, 10, 11, and 14; *Yes* for questions 4, 12, 13, and 15. If you missed only one or two questions, you strongly approve of your own listening habits, and you are on the right track to becoming an effective listener in your role as manager. If you missed three or four questions, you have uncovered some doubts about your listening effectiveness, and your knowledge of how to listen has some gaps. If you missed five or more questions, you probably are not satisfied with the way you listen, and your friends and co-workers may not feel you are a good listener either. Work on improving your active listening skills.

Source: Ethel C. Glenn and Elliott A. Pood, "Listening Self-Inventory," *Supervisory Management* (January 1989), pp. 12–15. Reprinted by permission of publisher, © 1989 American Management Association, New York. All rights reserved.

To listen well, you have to care about the speaker and the message. Disinterest makes listening effectively very difficult. Differences in prior learning and experience between senders and receivers can also detract from listening ability. For example, people with poorly developed vocabularies find it difficult to listen attentively to those with extensive vocabularies. Similar difficulties occur when the parties to a conversation have disparities of language, dialect, or colloquial usage.

Classifying or prejudging the speaker in either positive or negative ways can distort the message accordingly. When we like a speaker, we view the message in a favorable and sympathetic way. When we dislike a speaker, we do just the opposite.

Our beliefs and values also influence how well we listen. If the actual message is in line with what we believe, we tend to listen much more attentively and regard the words in a more favorable light. However, if the message contradicts our current values and beliefs, we tend to criticize the speaker and distort the message.

Lack of concentration and attention often results from the mistaken assumption that we can do two things at the same time. The best you can possibly hope for when doing two things at the same time is to divide your attention equally between them.[46]

People can think nearly four times as fast as they can speak.[47] This leaves the listener with approximately three times again the mental capacity he or she actually needs to hear the message. This "dead space" is used by skilled listeners to summarize and relate data, whereas poor listeners simply let their minds wander.

Skilled listeners attempt to be objective by consciously trying to understand the speaker without letting their personal opinions influence the decoding of the speaker's words. They try to understand what the speaker wants to communicate, not what they want to understand.

Active Listening.   If you refrain from evaluating other people's words, try to see things from their point of view, and demonstrate openly that you are trying to truly understand, you are using the technique of active listening.[48] Active listeners not only are attentive to the words being spoken, but also "put themselves in the other person's shoes." They search for the intent and feeling of the message and indicate their understanding both verbally and nonverbally. Active listeners do not interrupt. They look for verbal and visual cues that the other person would like to say something more. Guidelines for effective listening are provided in Exhibit 8–5.

An active listener practices sensing, attending, and responding. *Sensing* is the ability to recognize the silent messages that the speaker is sending through nonverbal clues such as vocal intonation, body language, and facial expression. *Attending* refers to the verbal, vocal, and visual messages that an active listener sends to the speaker to indicate full attention. These include eye contact, open posture, affirmative head nods, and appropriate facial and verbal expressions.

In *responding,* the active listener summarizes and gives feedback on the content and feeling of the sender's message. He or she encourages the speaker to elaborate, makes the speaker feel understood, and attempts to improve the speaker's own understanding of the problems or concerns.

Read Nonverbal Communication Cues

The amount of nonverbal feedback exchanged is not as important as how the parties interpret and react to it. Very often a person says one thing but communicates something totally different through vocal intonation and body language. These *mixed signals* force the receiver to choose between the verbal and nonverbal aspects

■■■■■ EXHIBIT 8–5

*Guidelines for Effective
Listening*

1. Stop talking. It is impossible to listen and talk at the same time.
2. Listen for main ideas.
3. Be sensitive to emotional deaf spots that make your mind wander.
4. Fight off distractions.
5. Take notes.
6. Be patient. Let others tell their stories first.
7. Empathize with other people's points of view.
8. Withhold judgment.
9. React to the message, not the person.
10. Appreciate the emotion behind the speaker's words.
11. Use feedback to check your understanding.
12. Relax and put the sender at ease.
13. Be attentive.
14. Create a positive listening environment.
15. Ask questions.
16. Be motivated to listen.

Source: Summarized from Phillip L. Hunsaker and Anthony J. Alessandra, *The Art of Managing People* (New York: Simon & Schuster, 1986), pp. 137–141. Used with authors' permission.

of a message. Most often, the receiver chooses the nonverbal aspect.[49] Mixed messages also create tension and distrust because the receiver senses that the communicator is hiding something or is being less than candid.

As much as 93 percent of the meaning that is transmitted between two people in a face-to-face communication can come from nonverbal channels.[50] This means that as little as 7 percent of the meaning we derive from others may come through their words alone. Nonverbal communications actually are more reliable than verbal communications when they contradict each other. Consequently, they function as a lie detector to aid a watchful listener in interpreting another's words. Although many people can convincingly misrepresent their emotions in their speech, focused attention on facial and vocal expressions can often detect leakage of the concealed feelings.[51] Nonverbal communication is made up of visual, tactile, and vocal aspects and the use of time, space, and image.[52]

Visual Aspects of Nonverbal Communication.   The visual component of nonverbal communication has been called *body language,* or *kinesics.* It includes facial expressions, eye movements, posture, and gestures.

The face is the best communicator of nonverbal messages. By "reading" a person's facial expressions, we can often detect unexpressed feelings like happiness, sadness, surprise, fear, anger, and disgust. Caution is advised, however, because different cultures impose emotional restraints to hold back true feelings, and the same facial expression can mean different things in different cultures. For example, agreement or approval are indicated by up-and-down head nods in American culture, but they are expressed by side-to-side head movements in India.[53]

We've all heard the phrases "One glance is worth a thousand words" and "The eyes are the windows to the soul." How do you feel when you are talking to someone wearing mirrored sunglasses? Most of us are uncomfortable because we are cut off from the most significant body expression of that person's mood.

Eye contact allows us to read and communicate a number of things. Direct eye contact, for example, is generally perceived as a sign of honesty, interest, openness, and confidence. If eye contact is avoided, we feel that the other is

Actions speak louder than words. The woman in white in this picture is sending several different messages with her body language. Kinesics, or body language, is a very important part of nonverbal communications. What type of messages is she sending to the people at this meeting? (Photo: © 1991 Steven Bloch/Black Star.)

embarrassed, nervous, or hiding something. As with all body language, eye contact varies by culture. In some Latin American cultures, for example, children are taught not to look directly in the face of an adult (superior)—behavior that, in an adult, could be interpreted by an American manager as a sign of deceit.[54]

Posture provides clues about the attitude of the bearer. How we carry ourselves signals such feelings as self-confidence, aggressiveness, fear, guilt, or anxiety. An example of using posture to appear in charge is when a manager stands up and leans forward over an employee's desk to peer down and give a reprimand. Self-confidence could be portrayed by a relaxed posture, such as sitting back in a chair with legs stretched out and hands behind the head. Contrast this image to that of someone hunched down, looking away, and biting his or her fingernails. A shift in posture means that something is changing, but it is up to the receiver to figure out what.[55]

Gestures combine facial expressions and posture movements to indicate meaning, control conversation, or complement words. Some gestures have universal symbolism. Raising both hands above the head indicates surrender and submission. A salute, a tip of the hat, a handshake, a wave of farewell, a V for victory, an O for okay, and a wink of the eye are just a few of the familiar symbols that transcend most language and cultural barriers.

Most gestures are culturally bound and susceptible to misinterpretation, however. It is very easy for Americans to misread Japanese body language, for example. Japanese try to avoid personal confrontation; they usually exhibit a noncontroversial demeanor and use excessive politeness and tact to smooth over any differences that arise. When negotiating among themselves, this presents no difficulties. But for Americans, serious misinterpretations can arise.[56]

Each isolated gesture is like a word in a sentence and should be considered in light of the other simultaneous forms of communication. When individual gestures are put together in clusters, they paint a more precise picture of what the other person is feeling and thinking.

To the sender of a message, a receiver's gestures serve as feedback; by observing the emotions and attitudes that are expressed nonverbally, he or she can tell how acceptable the message is.[57] For example, disagreement will be evident when someone shakes her head or raises her eyebrows in amazement or doubt. A smile and a nod, on the other hand, will signal agreement.

Tactile Aspects of Nonverbal Communication. Tactile communication is the use of touch to impart meaning, as in a handshake, a pat on the back, an arm around the shoulder, or a push or slap. Gentle touching like a hand on an arm, a kiss, or a hug indicate support, liking, or intimacy. Rough touching like squeezing someone's hand too hard, kicking people under the table, and bumping into them in the hallway is hostile behavior indicating negative sentiment.

Vocal Aspects of Nonverbal Communication. Vocal intonations are how things are said, as exemplified by the common phrase, "It's not what you say but how you say it." The meaning of words can be altered simply by changing the intonation of your voice. Try changing your vocal qualities while you say the word "no." You can express mild doubt, amazement, terror, and anger; you can give a command, decline an invitation, or answer a simple question. Each vocal intonation conveys a separate and unique feeling. Changes in loudness, pitch, rate, rhythm, and clarity all produce different meanings.

Vocal meanings also vary across cultures. For example, if an American raises his or her voice, we assume that the person is excited or angry and usually have a difficult time concentrating on what is being said once the volume has risen beyond what we consider a comfortable level, focusing instead on the projected emotions. In Latin cultures, however, noise level is generally higher than in the United States. The normal American vocal level would be considered too subdued to indicate genuine involvement and appropriate concern for what the Latin American is communicating.[58]

The most important aspect of vocal intonation is a change in vocal quality. When people change their normal vocal qualities, it's a sign that they are communicating something extra.[59] One example is statements tinged with sarcasm, where the vocally transmitted message has a meaning quite different from that of its actual verbal content.

Use of Time as Nonverbal Communication. Time is a continuous and irreversible scarce resource. Consequently, who we spend it with and how much we give communicate our feelings about who and what are important to us.[60] Most men probably try to arrive a little early for a first date with an important woman so that they don't insult her by being late. Yet, in order to hide their eagerness, they probably will not go up to her door until exactly the agreed-upon time. If either party had been very late, a suitable explanation would have been in order to ease the assumption of indifference. Similarly, it is not uncommon for a manager to assume that a subordinate who is frequently late to department meetings does not care about them, whether this is accurate or not.

Use of time also communicates how we view our own status and power in relation to others. If the president of a company calls a junior manager to her office for a meeting, the manager will probably arrive well before the appointed time. Because of the difference in status, most managers would probably feel that any inconvenience in waiting ought to be theirs. The president's time is assumed to be worth more and therefore not to be wasted, as opposed to the less expensive time of subordinates.

proxemics
The use of physical space and things to communicate meaning.

Special Aspects of Nonverbal Communication.   **Proxemics** is the way we use physical space to communicate things about us. How do you feel when you return from a class break and find someone sitting in your seat? Or when someone is standing so close to you that you wonder how long ago he had the tuna sandwich? Or when your boss looks down on you from her plush leather chair behind the expensive oak desk in her large office? Managers need to understand at least three aspects of proxemics for effective communication: territory, things, and personal space zones.[61]

Territory.   Although how space is used to communicate differs by culture, people seek to extend their territory in many ways to attain power and intimacy. We silently say things by manipulating space, as when we intrude on another person's space or guard our own. For example, your office or work area is a *fixed-feature territory* with permanent boundaries such as walls, partitions, and doors. When you walk into a meeting or classroom, you establish a *semifixed feature territory* by fixing movable objects; for example, by laying out notebooks, folders, and a coffee cup or hanging a jacket on a chair. Being assigned fixed-feature territory is a sign of increased status compared to having only semifixed feature space, because a rare resource has been assigned for your exclusive use and you can communicate how important you or others are by shutting people out or holding private meetings. The larger your office, the more status and importance communicated.

People like to protect and control their territory; this is easier to do in fixed-feature areas because you can shut or even lock the door. In semifixed features areas, your best protection is your physical presence, backed up by other people's respect in honoring your territory. If you return from a break and find someone sitting in your seat or, even worse, enter your office and find someone looking for something in your file cabinet, you will probably be angry at the violator.

How Things Communicate.   The things within your space also communicate things to others. A clean desk communicates efficiency versus the disorganization conveyed by a messy one. An attractive reception area communicates that the organization cares about visitors. Expensive things communicate higher status than do cheap ones. Personal things in your space such as trophies, photographs, pictures, plants, and other decorations also convey messages about you to others.

Personal Space Zones.   We all carry an invisible personal territory, much like a private air bubble. We feel a proprietary right to this space and resent others entering it unless they are invited. The exact dimensions of these private bubbles vary from culture to culture and person to person, but adult Americans usually have four personal space zones.

The *intimate zone,* from actual physical contact to about two feet away, is reserved for closest family and friends. A husband and wife often touch and interact enjoyably in this zone, but American businessmen or businesswomen confined to the intimate zone in a crowded subway or elevator would not.

Would you feel comfortable discussing business with someone who is invading your personal space zones? (Photo: © The Stock Market/Dan Dry 1991.)

The *personal zone,* from approximately two feet to four feet, usually is reserved for family and friends. How other people react if you enter into their personal space can be a nonverbal signal about how comfortable they are with you.

The *social zone,* extending from nearly four feet to roughly twelve feet, is where most business transactions, such as sales calls or negotiations, occur. It is far enough away to allow some feeling of security, yet close enough to communicate acceptance and closeness if desired.

The *public zone,* stretching from twelve feet away to the limits of hearing and sight, is most often used for lectures or speeches. It is the most formal zone and represents the farthest limit at which we can effectively communicate face to face.

People can generally be classified into two major proxemic categories. Although space preferences are based on personal and experience factors, Americans and Northern Europeans typify the noncontact group due to the small amount of touching and relatively large space between them during their transactions. Arabs and Latins are in the contact group, who normally stand very close to each other and use a lot of touching when they communicate.

When people do not appreciate differences in personal zones, discomfort, distrust, and misunderstanding can occur. Contact people can unknowingly get too close to or touch noncontact people, as happened when a South American and North American were discussing business at a cocktail party. For the South American, the appropriate zone for interaction was the personal zone, and he used frequent touching to make a point. That was about half the distance (minus touch) that the North American needed to be in his comfortable social zone. The South American would step closer and the North American would back away, in a strange proxemic dance, until both gave up the relationship as a lost cause because of the other's "cold" or "pushy" behavior.

Image as Communication.[62] As irrational as it may seem, people do judge a book by its cover. Through clothing and other dimensions of physical appearance, we communicate our values and expectations. It is the unusual person who can overcome a bad initial impression and reveal genuine assets hidden underneath. People react favorably to an expected image. Consequently, managers who look and act like executives tend to be more successful than those who do not. In *Business Buzzwords,* for example, "suits" is defined as "blue-collar term for white-collar managers, as in: 'look busy. Here come the suits.'"[63]

First impressions made by the initial impact of your clothing, voice, grooming, handshake, eye contact, and body posture are lasting images. Projecting both a depth and breadth of knowledge about your job or area of expertise builds your credibility, commands respect from others, and helps develop rapport. Flexibility, enthusiasm, and sincerity in your work relationships create a positive image that can enhance your communication effectiveness. In terms of dress, colors have meanings (e.g., brown for trusting; white for purity, dark colors for power), as do style (e.g., formal versus casual for more or less status, respectively), and material (e.g., synthetic fibers like polyester convey lower class versus pure fibers like wool for higher class).[64]

Improve Cross-Cultural Communication

Achieving effective communication is a challenge to managers worldwide even when the work force is culturally homogeneous, but when one company includes a variety of languages and cultural backgrounds, it becomes even more difficult. The greater the differences in backgrounds between senders and receivers, the greater the differences in meanings attached to particular words and behaviors. This is equally true for communicators from different countries, different sexes, or different subcultures in the same country.

While most European business people speak several languages, the average American businessperson speaks only English. The same year that 20 million Japanese were studying English, only 23,000 Americans were studying Japanese.[65] The vast majority of people in the world do not understand English, making foreign language training a necessity in today's international business environment.

Even if two communicators are speaking the same language, the same words and phrases may mean different things to people from different cultures. For example, the phrase "That would be very hard to do" means to Americans that some adjustments or extra contributions may be necessary, but the deal is still possible. To a Japanese, the phrase clearly means "No, it won't be possible." For a nonverbal example, Americans think that maintaining eye contact is important and others who don't are dishonest or rude. Japanese, on the other hand, lower their eyes as a gesture of respect when speaking with a superior.[66]

Gender can create subculture communication barriers within the same country. In the United States, for example, men frequently use talk to emphasize status differences because of their need for independence, while women more often use it to create interpersonal connections based on common ground because of their greater need for intimacy. Men frequently complain that women talk a lot about their problems, and women criticize men for not listening. What men are doing is asserting their independence and desire for control by providing solutions that women do not necessarily want in their quest for support, understanding, and connection.[67]

Thousands of successful cross-cultural business communications take place every day. Familiarizing yourself with cultural differences and being aware of your own cultural frame of reference can help you communicate more effectively when working with people from different cultures or subcultures. The following more specific guidelines can facilitate cross-cultural communications.[68]

First, assume differences until similarity is proven. Effective cross-cultural communicators know that they don't know how people with different backgrounds perceive a situation or interpret certain forms of communication. They do not assume that a person from another culture interprets a word or behavior the same way that they do. They avoid embarrassing misinterpretations.

Second, emphasize description rather than interpretation or evaluation. Effective cross-cultural communicators delay judgment until they have observed and interpreted the situation from the perspectives of all cultures involved. Description emphasizes observation of what has occurred rather than interpretation or evaluation, which are based more on the observer's culture and background than on the actual facts.

Third, empathize. When trying to understand the words, motives, and actions of a person from another culture, try to interpret them from the perspective of that culture rather than your own. When you view behaviors from your own perspective, you can completely misinterpret the other's actions if he or she has different values, experiences, and objectives.

Fourth, treat your interpretations as guesses until you can confirm them. Check with others from other cultures to make sure that your evaluation of a behavior is accurate if you are in doubt. Treat your first interpretations as working hypotheses rather than facts, and pay careful attention to feedback in order to avoid serious miscommunications and resulting problems.

COFFEE-KLATCHING WITH THE CEO—A SECOND LOOK

Five years later, the coffee-klatching CEO heads a company with a state-of-the-art communications system. This includes E-mail, Internet, voice mail, cellular telephones, facsimile (fax) machines, modems, and yes, video conferencing. But the coffee klatches still continue to maintain the rapport building, feedback, and creativity that only face-to-face interpersonal communications can provide. In addition, a series of "Update Meetings" are held the last Friday of each month where the president and his staff meet with all employees for one hour regarding current issues. Senior staff also hold mini-update meetings every Friday morning to exchange information and solve problems. Finally, all managers and supervisors are available during their lunch hour on Fridays to consult with employees about their individual concerns.

SUMMARY

Effective communication is essential for transmitting directives, building cooperation and team spirit, optimizing performance and satisfaction, and avoiding and solving problems. Formal communication channels flow in downward, upward, and horizontal directions. Informal networks are more useful when there is a need to tap into current feelings and reactions of employees.

Messages need to be encoded carefully so that they clearly communicate intentions, feelings, and expectations. They should be sent through the most appropriate channels, and feedback should be solicited from the receiver to be sure that the message was decoded as intended.

Communication is complicated by such barriers as frames of reference, value judgments, selective listening, filtering, and distrust. These are especially prevalent in multicultural environments. Barriers can be overcome by sending clear, complete, and specific messages. Credibility can be enhanced by demonstrating expertise, clarifying intentions, being reliable and dynamic, exhibiting warmth and friendliness, and building a positive image. Soliciting and providing specific feedback can also enhance communication effectiveness.

Questions can help a person gain information, uncover motives, give information, obtain participation, check understanding, start others thinking, induce agreement, and refocus attention. Active listening skills build rapport with others and help obtain relevant information.

Body language is useful both in reading the emotions and attitudes of others and in reinforcing your own verbal messages. Understanding vocal qualities can enhance your reading of other people's messages and help to project your own messages more effectively.

Key Concepts

communication, *p. 256*	noise, *p. 260*
sender, *p. 258*	feedback, *p. 260*
receiver, *p. 258*	grapevine, *p. 264*
encoding, *p. 258*	frame of reference, *p. 266*
message, *p. 258*	selective listening, *p. 268*
transmission, *p. 258*	filtering, *p. 268*
channel, *p. 258*	credibility, *p. 271*
nonverbal, *p. 259*	listening, *p. 274*
decoding, *p. 259*	proxemics, *p. 280*

Questions for Study and Discussion

1. Explain why you can't be an effective manager unless you are an effective communicator. How well do you communicate with others now? How can you improve?

2. What are the components of the communications process? Explain how noise can occur within each.

3. What are the barriers to effective communication? How can they be overcome?

4. What is feedback, and why is it such an important factor in effective two-way communication? What can you do to ensure that you transmit productive feedback? How can you get the most out of the feedback that you receive?

5. How can questions be used to enhance the communication process? What types of questions are commonly used?

6. What are the benefits of active listening? What poor listening habits do you currently possess? How can your listening skills be enhanced?

8. How can vocal tones reinforce verbal messages?

9. Why is body language such an important part of effective communications? What are the major ways that you can send messages via your body? What common gestures and gesture clusters are you aware of? What do they mean?

EXPERIENTIAL EXERCISE

Listening to Understand Problems

Purpose.   To practice the skills of active listening under difficult communication conditions.

Format.   Form triads. Each person will play the role of listener, speaker, and observer. Decide who will play each role for the first round.

Procedures (45 to 50 minutes).

1. The speaker chooses an unresolved interpersonal problem to explain to the listener.

2. The speaker explains the problem to the listener and shares his/her personal feelings concerning the problem. (Take no more than 10 minutes.)

3. During this exercise, the listener should attempt to use as many of the active listening skills (attending, paraphrasing, concentrating, and so on) as possible to understand (not solve) the speaker's problem.

4. The observer should remain totally silent during the exercise and take notes on the listener's effective and ineffective listening behaviors.

5. At the conclusion of the exercise, first the observer and then the speaker should give the listener feedback on points they felt indicated effective or ineffective listening skills. (Take no more than 5 minutes for this feedback.)

6. Steps 1 through 5 should be repeated two more times so that each person in the triad has a chance to play each role once.

EXPERIENTIAL EXERCISE

Attending to Help Listen

Introduction. Attending is the process of nonverbally interacting with other people in order to give them your full intellectual and emotional attention. Good attending facilitates your active listening behaviors and demonstrates that you care about and value the other person. The elements of attending include:

1. Facial expression (e.g., smile, serious, frown).
2. Body posture (e.g., open, closed, defensive).
3. Eye contact.
4. Nonverbal prompting (e.g., following the speaker's gestures with your eyes, nodding your head).
6. Verbal prompting (e.g., Wow! Then what? Uh ha).
7. Appropriate proximity (keeping an appropriate distance between people).

Purpose. To practice and experience the effects of variations in attending.

Format. Form dyads. One person is the speaker and the other is the listener.

Procedures (15 minutes).
1. The speaker shares some recent achievement of which he or she is very proud.

2. For one minute the listener does very bad attending—for example, gazes off at something, looks at watch, tries to listen to someone else's conversation. Note the effect it has on the conversation. Does the speaker try to recapture your attention? Does the conversation shift? Does it end prematurely?

3. For the next minute try overattending—for example, use rigid staring, get too close, touch the speaker's arm, nod your head excessively. Note the effect this has. Does the other person become uneasy or move back? Shift his or her gaze away from yours?

4. For the last minute, do your very best attending.

5. Discuss how the speaker felt as the listener underattended, overattended, and attended well.

6. Reverse the speaker and listener roles and repeat the steps.

7. Hold a class discussion on reactions to the various kinds of attending and their implications in business situations.

CASE

The Team-Spirit Tailspin

Richard Johnson, newly appointed president of Century Airlines, knew the company's survival depended on customer service, which in turn depended on motivated employees. So he created the Century Spirit program to build team spirit by encouraging employee participation, individual initiative, and open communication. Among the program's early successes was a newspaper started by a group of flight attendants. The Plane Truth published information about benefits and work conditions as well as feature stories and humorous articles. It quickly became popular not only with flight attendants but with pilots, machinists, and baggage handlers.

As time went on, though, the Plane Truth began to run articles critical of the company. When management cut back workers' hours, the newspaper questioned what sacrifices the executives were making. When the technical services department released figures showing long turnaround times, the paper questioned the machinists' work ethic.

Worried that customers might see the newspaper, Johnson wanted to cancel it. The president of the flight attendants' union also wanted to see it go because it was stirring up trouble with the machinists.

Joan Raffin, Century's human resources director, was asked to stop the publication. But she hesitated. She knew that employee morale was on the brink, but she didn't know whether the newspaper was venting workers' frustrations and reinforcing team spirit or stirring up old animosities and bringing the whole company down. Was it creating more tension than unity or vice versa?

Questions for Managerial Action
1. What communication issues are involved at Century Airlines?
2. What communication channels are being utilized?
3. What are the barriers to this communication vehicle?
4. How can this communication channel be used most effectively?
5. What should Joan Raffin do? Why?

Chapter 9

Interpersonal Relations

LEARNING OBJECTIVES

After studying this chapter, you should be able to:

- Appreciate the importance of good interpersonal relations at work.
- Understand the impact of personality differences on relationships.
- Assess interaction climates.
- Recognize differences in self-presentation.
- Deal effectively with male/female differences in work behaviors.
- Understand the importance of ethics in interpersonal relations.
- Be more aware and understanding of others' behaviors.
- Get along better with people with different interpersonal styles.

CHARM SCHOOLS FOR MANAGERS: IMPROVING INTERPERSONAL SKILLS

On the grounds of Arthur Andersen & Co.'s headquarters outside Chicago, a senior executive jumps off a flagpole and onto a trapeze. Colleagues pass a bucket of water between two nearby trees. Others try to scale a wall.

This is no company circus; the antics are part of a program at the accounting firm to teach employees interpersonal skills. Jumping from the pole teaches confidence; passing the bucket and scaling the wall teach teamwork. The firm also trains its employees in skills such as running meetings and listening to others.

Arthur Andersen is one of the many companies placing a new emphasis on "people skills" for managers and executives. In the past, even ornery managers could succeed just by knowing the business. But increasingly, managers with "people conflicts" are being sent to school to learn how to relate better to others. "Pure technical knowledge is only going to get you to a point," said Lawrence A. Weinbach, Arthur Andersen's chief executive. "Beyond that, interpersonal skills become critical."

The Center for Creative Leadership in Greensboro, North Carolina, estimates that half of all managers have some type of difficulty with people. But discovering such a weakness in a so-called charm school can be humbling. The training doesn't always work, of course. Randall P. White, director of the Center for Creative Leadership's Executive Development Program, estimates that although 10 percent or 15 percent of the participants in his program are highly receptive and change dramatically, an equal amount are hopeless. Some sit in the back of the room and tell counselors they were "forced" to attend and have no problems. When confronted with poor reviews, one manager claimed he was a good manager but all his workers were stupid.

When Richard S. Herlich was promoted to director of marketing for an American Cyanamid Co. division, he saw himself as an enlightened manager. He delegated responsibility, encouraging subordinates to set their own deadlines. "I thought that I had the perfect style," he says. But then he attended the Center's week-long Leadership Development Program. In surveys that his peers, subordinates, and superiors answered before the course, he found that he was too trusting, aloof, and a poor communicator. The diagnosis was confirmed in role playing games by feedback from the other participants. "I was devastated," Herlich says.

When he went back to work, he held a meeting to discuss his problem with his 15 subordinates, who said his aloofness was intimidating. So he became more involved in their work and learned to set deadlines; projects that had taken six to seven months were done in three.

Bethlehem Steel Corp. plant manager Robert Siddall had just the opposite problem. An aggressive and sometimes abrasive leader, he got into damaging clashes with the labor union head, and many of his 170 workers came to view him as dictatorial. "I'm very strong technically," he says, but "I really didn't fit in well on an interactive basis." Instructors taught Siddall to act like a "coach" and to try to listen to and respect other points of view.

He says he gets along with the union leader now. His performance ratings have improved, and his workers now refer to the "old Bob" and the "new Bob." "If I start screaming and yelling, they say, 'old Bob, old Bob'," he says. "We have a lot more fun together." He also believes he's back on track for a promotion.

In the new information era, interpersonal communication is a valuable business tool. Understanding different mind-sets, technical backgrounds, and cultural perspectives is more crucial than ever for managers in the 1990s and beyond. To deal effectively with diversity, managers have to be flexible in how they relate to people from different cultures and backgrounds. No one's personal set of behavioral rules will prevail intact in organizations designed to incorporate diversity and still provide a common integrating culture that promotes the organization's goals.

To make organizations with diverse work forces viable and to be effective leaders, managers need to learn a new respect for differences. As Arthur Andersen's chief executive said in the opening vignette, pure technical knowledge will only get you so far; beyond that, interpersonal skills become critical. According to R. Roosevelt Thomas, Jr., executive director of the American Institute for Managing Diversity at Atlanta's Morehouse College, "This is no longer simply a question of common decency. It is a question of business survival."[1]

And how well are American managers equipped to deal with diverse work forces? Probably not nearly as well as required. Consequently, many managers are being sent to "charm schools" like those described in the opening vignette. This chapter discusses concepts and skills necessary for successfully managing interpersonal relations with different types of people in organizations.

WHAT INFLUENCES INTERPERSONAL RELATIONS?

A recent Gallup survey of executives investigated the biggest challenges management will face by the year 2000. The foremost finding was the importance they placed on interpersonal and communication skills.[2] Possessing interpersonal skills was noted more often than any other response by senior and middle-level executives as a sign that a recent hire had potential to develop into a senior-level executive. A corresponding finding of this and other studies is that, although interpersonal skills are determined to be essential for management development, they are named more often than any other management skill by recent hires as the attribute least emphasized in university and development programs.[3]

Most work either requires or encourages interaction among individuals. The more a job requires two people to work together, the more important becomes the nature of the relationship between them. "There are lots of brilliant people

World Watch

Rule Number 1: Don't Diss the Locals

When deciding who to assign to an important foreign client, many companies select employees who are aces at technical matters or have an outstanding record in management. A recent study by Prudential Relocation Intercultural Services, a subsidiary of Prudential Insurance, discovered a number of horror stories about such selection criteria. One company sent an evangelical Christian to Saudi Arabia where he offended locals by setting up a Bible group and got booted out of the country. An American oil company transferred an executive to Peru where he told jokes deriding the natives' industriousness and excluded them from his parties. Indigenous employees complained to government officials who canceled the company's oil concession. American multinational companies admit that about 90 percent of their overseas placements are mistakes primarily due to their employees' failures to adjust properly to a new culture.

Prudential's survey of 72 personnel managers working at multinationals found that 35 percent agreed that the best trait for overseas success was cultural adaptability, which includes patience, flexibility, and tolerance for others' beliefs. Only 22 percent of the respondents listed technical or managerial skills.

Fortunately, there are a variety of training techniques available to prepare people better for intercultural work. They include (1) reading programs to expose people to the country's sociopolitical history, geography, economics, and cultural institutions; (2) cultural assimilators that expose trainees to specific incidents critical to successful interaction with a target culture; (3) language preparation; (4) sensitivity training to increase people's self-awareness, and (5) exposing trainees to minicultures within their own country during short field exercises.

Sources: "Rule Number 1: Don't Diss the Locals," *Business Week* (May 15, 1995), p. 8; and P. Christopher Earley, "Intercultural Training for Managers: A Comparison of Documentary and Interpersonal Methods," *Academy of Management Journal* 30 (August 1987), pp. 685–698.

who can't relate with others," says Robert LoPresto, an executive recruiter. "We replace that kind of person every day."[4] Even where interaction is only peripheral to the task, relationships can still be a source of satisfaction or frustration and affect the total work effort in many ways. Good interpersonal relations support the work effort; bad ones inhibit it.[5] This can be especially true in international situations, as the World Watch box illustrates.

It can be very frustrating trying to figure out all the possible reasons why people do or don't get along well together. You have already been introduced in previous chapters to some concepts that can help you understand what contributes to interpersonal differences in perception, motivation, and communication. This chapter focuses on personal, behavioral, and situational factors that can create difficulties in relationships. Strategies for effectively managing interpersonal relationships are also described.

The A-B Model[6]

The A-B model in Exhibit 9–1 illustrates the chain of rapid events that occur between two interacting people. Both parties have *needs* they want to satisfy and sets of *values* indicating the most desirable ways of doing so. Sometimes needs are satisfied through defense mechanisms that protect established self-concepts and frames of reference regardless of their current appropriateness. Based on past

For minority entrepreneurs in service industries like Colette Phillips (right), who owns a public relations firm in Massachusetts, interpersonal skills are vitally important for bringing new business and ideas to her company. Phillips believes that a major obstacle to business between white-owned and minority-owned businesses is that owners do not know one another professionally or personally. By forming friendships based on openness and trust, Phillips has found that both satisfaction and productivity improve. Here Phillips meets with retired Boston banker Robert Spiller, one of her clients. (Photo: © Webb Chappell Photography.)

▬▬▬ EXHIBIT 9–1

A-B Model of Interpersonal Behavior

Problem Situation

Person A

Needs → Perceptions

Values →

↓

Assumptions → Evaluations

↓

Feelings → Intentions

(Inter) Actions

Person B

Perceptions ← Needs

↓ ← Values

Evaluations ← Assumptions

↓

Intentions ← Feelings

Consequences

experiences, both people also make *assumptions* about the nature of the other and of the particular kind of situation they are in (e.g., competitive or cooperative). Each person develops positive or negative *feelings* that contribute to enhanced or diminished *perceptions* of self, the other, and the current situation. These perceptions contribute to *evaluations* of the other person in this situation and lead to the formulation of *intentions* to interact in specific ways to accomplish personal objectives. The *consequences* of that behavior and subsequent *interactions* generate new input for another loop of reactions.

Relationships tend to be *reciprocal* in nature, meaning that one person will most often treat another the same way he or she is, or expects to be, treated by that person. In enduring productive relationships, people expect positive **reciprocity**—an exchange of benefits in their interpersonal transactions. For example, physical

reciprocity
The exchange of benefits in interpersonal transactions.

and mental efforts may be "traded" for dollars or recognition. Help and kindness may be exchanged for affection and respect. The exchange need not be equal, but unless it is perceived as fair by both parties, tension likely will rise.

On the other hand, if A assumes that B perceives him or her negatively, A may feel diminished, causing him or her to perceive B negatively and interact with B accordingly. Even if A's first assumption was incorrect, his or her subsequent behavior may make this incorrect assumption come true and a negatively reciprocal relationship may emerge. Many times the stage is set for a particular type of reciprocity by various personality factors or pre-existing interaction climates.

Personality Factors

When trying to understand your feelings and behaviors, it helps to be aware that how you think and feel about yourself and others may be very unlike how they think and feel about themselves and you. These different evaluations and reactions depend on each individual's self-concept, frame of reference, defenses, interpersonal relationship needs, and feelings.

self-concept
Our perception and evaluation of ourselves.

Self-Concept.   Starting with messages from parents, which are later reinforced by significant others, you learn to view and evaluate yourself in a certain way. The identity and evaluation of yourself that you come to accept is your **self-concept,** which may be anything from essentially positive ("I am worthwhile") to negative ("I am worthless"). You protect yourself from any attempts to change your self-concept, even if your view of yourself is a painful one. Even if not ideal, your self-concept allows you to cope, and it's safer to hold on to something known than to let go and take the risk of something new. Yet feedback occurs and learning takes place, causing you to choose between the need to know and the fear of knowing about yourself, especially if the knowledge may force you to change your self-concept.

Through observation and interaction, you learn what significant others think is important. These messages about how you "ought" to feel and behave become your guiding values for later interactions. You also learn what you "ought" to want to achieve, such as graduation from college or freedom from responsibility. Finally, you learn certain techniques that are acceptable to your significant others to gain their approval. These beliefs about what behaviors, feelings, goals, and techniques are desirable become internalized into your **value system.**

value system
Internalized beliefs about what behavior, feelings, goals, and techniques are desirable.

personal frame of reference
How we see the world based upon our past experiences and self concept.

Personal Frame of Reference.   As discussed in Chapter 5, your self-concept and perceptions of other people and things develop into a **personal frame of reference** for perceiving and interpreting experiences. Two people with different frames of reference may do very different things in the same situation to try and satisfy the same needs. For example, two students in a highly interactive seminar may perceive the emphasis on participation very differently. One who has been praised for contributing in classes in the past may feel comfortable and view the situation as potentially rewarding. The other, who has had past class contributions rejected and ridiculed, however, may see the class as very threatening. Consequently, to protect and enhance their self-concepts, these two students are likely to behave in opposite ways in the seminar.

Frames of reference are abstractions of reality, and everyone sees reality differently because of different needs and past experiences. Furthermore, new experiences and changing needs keep the reality changing somewhat. It is very difficult to understand how others perceive their world, especially since we tend to filter

Dynamics of Diversity

Caution! Cultural Blinders at Work

Judy Martinez has no difficulty identifying "the worst day of my career." As to cause, she points to the black male director at the community service agency she worked for in Orlando, Florida.

Martinez, a 34-year-old career counselor, had been nursing a cold. She was seated at her desk sipping from a 12-ounce bottle of malta, a nonalcoholic barley beverage popular in the Spanish-speaking Caribbean. She recalls, "The director kept going back and forth past my office and looking in. The next day I received a memo from him that said 'Alcoholic beverages are not allowed on the premises, and this is an official reprimand . . .' I was in shock. But then, when I tried to talk to him about his memo to get the reprimand removed from my file, he refused to meet with me. To this day, the man has never admitted he was wrong. He has said nothing to me. Nada."

Martinez had to go over the director's head to the executive director, a Panamanian, who personally removed the reprimand from her otherwise unblemished file. Yet Martinez, who is no longer with the agency, still feels hurt by the sting of that cultural misunderstanding. "It was defamation of character," she says angrily.

Why did the director automatically assume that Martinez, a Puerto Rican, was sitting at her desk drinking beer all day? Would he have made the same assumption about an American white man or woman or an African-American?

The problem with assumptions and stereotypes is that they are often the only way we have of processing information. If the only Asians you've seen have been in Kung Fu movies, then that's your understanding of Asians. Managers need to see past their assumptions and stereotypes. If you're going to empower someone different from you in order to get the best out of them, you've first got to understand their behavior.

Source: Audrey Edwards, "The Enlightened Manager: How to Treat All Your Employees Fairly," *Working Woman* 16 (January 1991), p. 45.

their behavior through our own unique frame of reference. Our actions are logical to us given our frame of reference, but so are other people's different behaviors to them, even though they don't make sense to us because of their alternate perception of the situation.

Cultural backgrounds are a frequent source of different frames of reference. Paul Nolan is director of corporate training for the Lincoln Savings Bank in New York, which has a diverse employee mix including young and old men and women who are Hispanic, Chinese, East Indian, African-American, and Italian-American. After going through a number of multicultural training sessions, he believes that he is a better manager. "I've always seen life through white, male eyes," says Nolan. "Even now, when I speak to white males, I'm very structured, very aggressive, succinct. But if I were talking to a Chinese person, I'd ask open-ended questions, such as 'Tell me what you think about this' instead of 'This is what I think.' I've learned that others can perceive me as 'this white man telling me what to do'." Nolan's new, more flexible approach has dramatically increased the participation rate of minorities on the staff.[7] The Dynamics of Diversity box illustrates that it is not just white males who need to increase their sensitivity to culturally diverse groups.

To understand others, you need to understand their frames of reference without judging them in terms of your own values. This does not mean that you must accept for yourself the means they are using to satisfy their needs. Nor should you expect others to always accept your own behavior as the most satisfying for them.

But you can benefit from continuously exploring with others your own perception of reality compared to theirs. Failure to be accepting and understanding can cause defensiveness, inhibit personal growth, and cause conflicts.

Defensiveness.   One response to an interpersonal encounter that threatens your self-concept or frame of reference is to apply one or more psychological defenses. A **defense** is a cognitive distortion that protects the self-concept from being diminished. Defensiveness occurs when you protect yourself by denying, excusing, or rationalizing your actions to protect your self-concept against the threat of being damaged by failure, guilt, shame, or fear.

defense
A cognitive distortion that protects the self-concept against being diminished.

All defense mechanisms involve a degree of distortion of the true relationships between the individual and external reality. Although defense mechanisms provide some relief from tension and anxiety, they do not satisfy underlying needs. Individuals learn defense mechanisms at an early age and continue to use those that have worked for them in the past. Defense mechanisms affect the way individuals relate to each other and the way they understand and adapt to their relationships.[8] Some of the more common defenses are summarized in Exhibit 9–2.

Defenses alleviate painful feelings, but they fail to deal with the causes of the problem. If overused, defenses can be dysfunctional because they inhibit individual growth and interactions with others. Defensiveness may distort ideas, obscure solutions, or hinder interpersonal communication. Individuals can respond nondefensively by acknowledging and accepting the threatening event and then attempting to cope with it by eliminating or moderating their behavior. One way to avoid your own defensive behavior is to acknowledge what is being said as at least partially true. If you are frequently late, for example, and someone criticizes you for it, you could simply acknowledge, "Yes, I often am late" as opposed to trying to convince the other that you're really not always late or that there are always good reasons why you are late.

One way to reduce another person's defensiveness is to use active listening as described in Chapter 8. This means using verbal and nonverbal responses to show that you are listening nonjudgmentally to truly understand the other person. By reflecting back your perception of the other's concerns in a nonjudgmental way, he or she may feel safe and understood enough to reduce defenses.

Interpersonal Relationship Needs.   William Schutz contends that people have three dominant interpersonal needs.[9] The first is *inclusion*—the need to establish and maintain relationships with other people. Inclusion concerns balancing the desire to be part of a group against the desire for solitude. The second is *control*—the need to maintain a satisfactory balance of power and influence in relationships. Control concerns trade-offs between the desires for structure and authority versus the desire for freedom. Finally, there is the need for *affection*—the need to form close and personal relationships with others. Affection concerns balancing desires for warmth and commitment against those for maintaining distance and independence.

Each of these three needs has two subdimensions—the *expressed* desire to give, or impose the need on others, and the *wanted* desire to receive the need from others; for example, the need to invite or include others in our activities, and the need to be invited and included in others' activities. These three interpersonal needs and their two subdimensions are illustrated in Exhibit 9–3. Complete the Your Turn exercise to determine the relative strengths of your interpersonal needs.

EXHIBIT 9–2

Common Defense Mechanisms

Defense	Psychological Process	Illustration
Rationalization "Everybody does it."	Justifying behaviors and feelings that are undesirable by providing explanations that make them acceptable.	You pad your expense account because "everybody does it."
Repression "Motivated forgetting."	"Forgetting" painful and frustrating events by unconsciously putting them out of your memory.	You "forget" to tell the boss about an embarrassing error you made because you feel guilty.
Reaction-Formation "Methinks the lady doth protest too much."	Repressing unacceptable urges and exhibiting the opposite attitudes and behaviors.	The manager who represses the desire to have an affair with his secretary crusades against such activities.
Projection "It's all your fault."	Protecting yourself from awareness of your own undesirable traits or feelings by attributing them to others.	In a crisis, the manager tells employees not to panic to hide his own undesirable feelings of panic.
Regression "Disneyland, here I come."	Responding to frustration by reverting to earlier and less mature forms of behavior; attempting to go back to a more comfortable time.	A manager who cannot get approval for an additional secretary begins typing, filing, and doing other activities more appropriate for subordinates.
Displacement "Kick the dog who bites the cat."	Redirecting pent-up emotions toward persons other than the primary source of the emotion.	You roughly reject a simple request from a subordinate after receiving a rebuff from the boss.
Compensation "Tit for tat."	Engaging in a substitute behavior to make up for a feeling of inadequacy.	A manager who is not advancing professionally works very hard on volunteer activities.
Denial "It ain't true."	Refusing to absorb threatening information.	You are unwilling to accept that others see you as hostile when you are pressed for time.
Withdrawal "If I'm not here, I don't have to deal with it."	Physically or mentally leaving a situation that produces anxiety, conflict, or frustration.	A person's idea is rejected by a committee, so he either is absent from future meetings or fails to participate.
Resignation "If I got to do it, I got to do it, but not too well."	Withholding any sense of emotional or personal involvement in an unpleasant situation.	An employee who hasn't received praise no longer cares whether or not he does a good job.
Conversion "It makes me hurt so bad."	Transforming emotional conflicts into physical symptoms.	A salesman about to meet with a client who is anticipated to say no experiences a headache.
Counterdependence "You can't make me."	Suppressing feelings of dependence and expressing hostile independence.	A boss feeling confused and lost rudely rejects help from subordinates.
Aggression "The best defense is a good offense."	Instigating a hostile attack on another because you are frustrated or uncomfortable.	A manager makes a sarcastic remark to an employee who has just made a minor error.

Sources: Adapted from Timothy W. Costello and Sheldon S. Zalkind, *Psychology in Administration: A Research Orientation,* 1963, pp. 148–149. Reprinted by permission of Prentice Hall, Englewood Cliffs, New Jersey. D. I. Costley and R. Todd, *Human Relations in Organizations* (St. Paul, MN: West Publishing, 1987), pp. 232–235.

If you have strong interpersonal needs, you desire to interact with others and are probably outgoing and gregarious. If you have low interpersonal needs, you don't mind being alone and are more reserved around others. Marketing and human resource majors in business schools have stronger interpersonal needs than accounting and systems analysis students.[10] This indicates that students with higher interpersonal needs tend to select people-oriented careers and vice versa. The findings do not necessarily predict success as a manager, however, because that depends to a large degree on the types of work and people you are supervising.

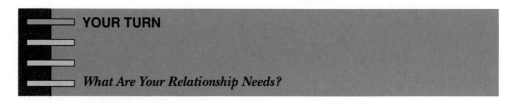

EXHIBIT 9–3

Fundamental Interpersonal Relationship Orientations

| | Interpersonal Needs | | |
Behaviors	Inclusion	Control	Affection
Expressed toward others	I want others to join me	I take charge and influence others	I get close to others
Wanted from others	I want others to include me	I want others to lead me	I want others to get close to me

YOUR TURN

What Are Your Relationship Needs?

Instructions: Allocate between 0 and 9 points to indicate the degree that each of the following six questions applies to you. Place the number of the answer at the left of the statement.

_____ 1. I like to invite people to join social activities.

_____ 2. I feel badly when other people do things without inviting me to join them.

_____ 3. I try to have other people do things the way I want them done.

_____ 4. Other peoples' preferences strongly influence my behavior.

_____ 5. I try to develop close personal relationships with people.

_____ 6. I like people to act close and personal towards me.

_____ **Total Points**

Scoring: Add up the number of points for the six questions to determine your total interpersonal needs score. Your score will fall somewhere between 0 and 54. The point allocations to each of the six questions provides the relative strengths of your interpersonal needs as follows: 1—expressed inclusion; 2—wanted inclusion; and 3—expressed control; 4—wanted control; 5—expressed affection; and 6—wanted affection. You can write these in the boxes in Exhibit 9–3 to visually depict the relative strengths of your interpersonal needs.

Interpretation: There is no "right" score. The value of this information is that it lets you know the relative strength of your own interpersonal needs. The average person, according to national studies, has a total score of 29.[11] Your highest scores on individual questions indicate which interpersonal needs are least satisfied and probably dominate your relationships with others.

Source: Developed by Phillip L. Hunsaker for class discussion, University of San Diego, 1995.

The degree of need compatibility between two or more people can make the difference between a happy and productive team and a dissatisfied and ineffective one. If one person has a high need to express dominance and control, and another had a high need to receive direction, they are likely to get along well. On the other hand, if they both have high needs to express dominance and low needs to receive it, conflict is probable. The key is whether the important needs of each person are complementary and to what degree they are satisfied in the relationship. Compatible individuals usually like each other more and work better together.[12] Awareness of differences in interpersonal needs can help you adapt your own behaviors to let others satisfy their needs, which can enhance your relationships with them.[13]

Feelings.   People continually experience feelings about themselves and others, but many have not learned to accept and use feelings constructively. How you express feelings is a frequent source of difficulty in interpersonal relationships. Problems arise not because emotions are present, but because they are not used well. Rather than express them constructively, people often deny or ignore their own and others' feelings in an attempt to avoid rejection or struggle for control.

For example, you may have experienced immediate rapport or dislike towards someone you just met. What you are feeling has to do with things about the other person and yourself that you are only unconsciously aware of.[14] Immediate liking for a person you have just met is often caused by seeing in them things you like in yourself, or traits you would like to have but don't, like charm or humor.

It's the negative reactions that can cause you the most problems, however, especially if they are directed at a person you will be interacting with for a long time, like your boss or a co-worker. Therefore, it is important to try to understand what caused your reaction and why. It may be that the other person has characteristics that remind you of someone in the past that brought you pain. Or, it might be that the person triggers awareness of your "shadow self," that is, parts of yourself that you are not aware of because you don't like them. Being egotistical, wimpy, or aggressive may be behaviors you repress in yourself, and seeing someone else who dares to act these ways can cause negative reactions.

Maintaining a productive relationship requires that you first look at yourself to understand what it is about you that's causing the negative feelings. You may then see that it is not really the other person you don't like, but a particular characteristic that you also have yourself. Then you may be able to overlook the characteristic in the other, as you do in yourself. If self-analysis isn't enough, it can be helpful to tactfully express personal feelings so that you and the other party can try to work out potential difficulties in a productive way.[15] The Challenge of Change box illustrates how companies sometimes turn to outside therapists to improve interpersonal relationships.

Interaction Setting

Often, what appear to be personality changes may just be two people's varying responses to different and incompatible job requirements. This frequently happens when people work in different parts of the organization, under different organizational cultures, for different bosses, and in different jobs that make different demands.

Job Requirements.   Job requirements determine how psychologically close or distant two people need to be to perform their work. The depth of interpersonal relationships required by a job depends on how complex the task is, whether the people involved possess different kinds of expertise, the frequency of interaction in the job, and the degree of certainty with which job outcomes can be predicted.[16]

Work situations that are simple and familiar to both workers, don't require strong feelings, demand little interaction, and have a high certainty of outcomes call for minimal task relationships. Complex situations that require different knowledge from each person, high trust, much interaction, and have an uncertain outcome call for more intense interpersonal relationships closer to colleagueship.[17] An example of a minimal task relationship would be an operating room nurse and a surgeon, whose only required exchange regards information about the patient's welfare and the surgeon's need for instruments. Colleagueship requires that people collaborate in a complex task situation demanding trust and mutual support, like when two police detectives are attempting to arrest an armed criminal.

Challenge of Change

Battling Executives Seek Out Therapists

David Hammer, president of Community Benefits Corporation, and Stanley Ham, his top-producing branch manager, were avoiding each other. Both were walking on eggshells when they had to interact and were fuming over hidden resentments. The situation finally resulted in a letter of resignation from Mr. Ham, which prompted Mr. Hammer to call in an expert before accepting the resignation: a psychiatrist.

The president did not want to lose Mr. Ham, but he was also very angry and convinced that Mr. Ham was "sitting on his hands" in a hot market. Mr. Ham, on the other hand, did not think that he was getting enough credit for the business he brought in.

They both agreed to visit a psychiatrist individually and in joint sessions in the neutral turf of the doctor's office. This venue was designed to put superior and subordinate on an equal footing psychologically. The psychiatrist summarized how each viewed the problems, reinterpreted the executives' statements so they could hear their own reactions or biases, and acted to "dilute and cushion" the anger that emerged. Both men came away with new understandings of why they saw and

reacted to each other's behaviors as they did. They developed action plans to help them "stop playing games" and interact more effectively with each other.

Such one-on-one confrontations with a neutral moderator are the essence of corporate therapy, a blend of management consulting with the techniques of marriage and family counseling. Executives are allowing therapists to probe not only their different management styles, but also how their personal emotions and backgrounds exacerbate interpersonal problems. Executives have traditionally said, "If you're below me, it's your problem to get along with me." With counseling, however, the person higher in the power hierarchy learns to take appropriate responsibility for interaction difficulties.

As with Hammer and Ham, the counselor usually meets with the individuals involved to hear their complaints, get their personal histories, and build trust. Then joint sessions are held where the counselor listens, serves as a buffer, and asks questions intended to get participants to face the issues and find solutions.

Source: Jolie Solomon, "Battling Executives Seek Out Therapists," *The Wall Street Journal* (November 7, 1988), p. B1.

Organizational Culture.   As discussed in Chapter 4, the organization's culture influences the general nature of employee relationships. People take cues from the culture they work in and usually respond to what they perceive as general expectations. Some cultures discourage intimacy and only allow distant, impersonal relationships. The more culture fosters competitiveness, aggressiveness, and hostility, the greater the likelihood people will be cautious and on guard with each other. Other cultures encourage familylike closeness. The more sociable and personal the culture, the more people are likely to share nonwork information and feelings.[18] Different interaction patterns can be distinguished by four primary factors:[19]

- *Openness* is the degree to which participants share their thoughts and feelings with others.
- *Trust* is the degree that you believe someone else is honest and supportive.
- *Owning* refers to taking responsibility for a problem to which you are a contributor versus blaming someone else.
- *Risk to experiment* is the degree to which you are punished for trying something new, especially if it fails, versus doing things in safe, approved-of ways.

regenerative interaction patterns
Cooperative and caring relationships which promote openness, trust, rapport and intimacy.

degenerative interaction patterns
Competitive and destructive relationships resulting in lack of openness, low trust, blaming, and defensiveness.

trust
The feeling of confidence that someone will act to benefit rather than harm you.

In **regenerative interaction patterns,** people are open with each other, which develops trust and promotes rapport and intimacy. This is a "win-win" relationship where people are "for each other"; they want to help each other grow and consequently cooperate for their mutual benefit. Owning is high because people want to understand each other and learn from mistakes. The risk associated with trying new behaviors is low because trust and goodwill promote constant growth and improvement. If there are problems in a regenerative relationship, the parties try to understand and learn from past mistakes in order to develop an even more satisfying and productive relationship.

In **degenerative interaction patterns,** on the other hand, any problems that develop result in blaming others, defensiveness, lack of trust, and decreased openness. In such a "win-lose" relationship, lack of trust leads to reduction of openness, risking new behaviors that may fail, and owning up to past mistakes, because all of these can make you more vulnerable. Most people try to escape degenerative climates if they want to grow and relate productively with others. If they stay, it is usually because of a high need for power and dominance or a very low self-esteem and high insecurity.

Trust Levels.   Trust is a key ingredient in any win-win relationship, whether personal or business. **Trust** exists whenever you choose to let yourself be dependent on another person whose future behavior can affect your well-being. Trust occurs to the degree that you are aware that another's behavior can benefit or harm you, and you feel confident that the other person will act to benefit you.[20] An example of trust occurs when a working mother leaves her baby at a day-care center. She is aware that her choice could lead to harmful or beneficial consequences and feels relatively confident that the staff will behave to bring about beneficial consequences.

Relationships do not grow and develop until individuals trust each other. Trust is learned from past interactions with another. Trust is earned as the parties self-disclose personal information and learn that they will not be hurt by making themselves vulnerable to each other. Increased trust leads to the sharing of more personal information between the parties, which enhances regenerative interaction patterns and contributes to improved problem solving and productivity.[21] Read the World Watch box to see how trust contributes to the Japanese success story.

Whenever trust is broken, the relationship suffers. The damage may be temporary or permanent, depending on the nature of the relationship. The way Richard Nixon handled the Watergate scandal by denying responsibility and withholding information, for example, cost him the trust of the American people and the possibility of a second term in office.[22]

In his best-selling book, *The Seven Habits of Highly Effective People,* Stephen Covey uses the metaphor of an "emotional bank account" to describe the amount of trust that has been built up in a relationship.[23] To Covey, trust refers to the overall feeling of safeness that you have with another person. You make "deposits" into an emotional bank account with another person through kindness, honesty, and keeping commitments. These acts build up a reserve trust account that promotes confidence in you even if your communication is sometimes ambiguous or you make an occasional mistake. But, if you show disrespect, fail to honor commitments, or take advantage of the other person, your trust account becomes depleted. The relationship then becomes degenerative, with hostility and defensiveness making it difficult to build up trust again.

World Watch

The Trusting Japanese

Trust has contributed greatly to the Japanese success story of the 1980s. In contrast to the adversarial labor–management relations typical of U.S. factories, the Japanese approach to production—with its flexible team, just-in-time deliveries, and top priority on quality—demands extremely high employee loyalty and trust. Workers given responsibility for running the production line will only care about and catch mistakes if they trust management. And that trust must be mutual, for just-in-time delivery systems depend on a steady stream of components and are easy to sabotage.

Starting in the early 1990s, Japanese organizations struggled in facing for the first time in four decades the realization that their growth machine was not to last forever. Problems of prolonged recession in the 1990s, the breakdown of lifetime employment, and changing expectations of young and female workers have put a crack in the trust mirror. The remainder of this decade will demonstrate if their trust bond can hold under adverse conditions.

Source: Aaron Bernstein, "The Difference Japanese Management Makes," *Business Week* (July 14, 1986), p. 48

Covey suggests six major deposits to build up emotional bank accounts:[24]

- *Understand and honor other peoples' needs and priorities,* which may be very different than our own.
- *Attend to little things,* like showing kindness and being courteous, because they make big positive deposits in relationships.
- *Keep commitments.* Breaking a promise can be a massive withdrawal that may prevent future deposits because people won't believe you.
- *Clarify expectations* so that others don't feel cheated or violated if you don't behave in ways that they assumed you knew they desired, even though they never overtly told you.
- *Show personal integrity* by keeping promises, being honest, fulfilling expectations, and being loyal to all people equally, including those not present.
- *Apologize sincerely when you make a withdrawal,* without rationalizing or trying to shift some of the blame to the other.

As trust builds in our emotional bank account, it becomes the foundation of regenerative relationships with others. People learn to put all their cards on the table to deal with issues and solve problems without wasting energy focused on differences in personality or position. Without trust, you lack the credibility and safety for open communication, creativity, problem solving, or mutual learning.

WHY DO PEOPLE HAVE DIFFERENT STYLES OF RELATING?

interpersonal effectivenss
The degree that the consequences of your behavior match your intentions.

When interacting with others, sometimes you get the reactions you want, but other times you don't. Your **interpersonal effectiveness** is the degree to which the consequences of your behavior match your intentions. You can improve interpersonal effectiveness by disclosing your intentions, receiving feedback on your behavior, and modifying your behavior until it has the consequences you intend it to have.[25]

When G. Rives Neblett took over Shelby Die Casting in Mississippi, he organized workers into teams and changed the company's degenerative climate to a regenerative one. Initially there was turmoil while they learned to conduct meetings democratically and managers learned not to dominate. This resulted in a trusting climate where teams worked cooperatively, pinpointing problems and working to solve them. (Photo: © 1996 Nation's Business/T. Michael Keza.)

■■■■■ **EXHIBIT 9–4**

Johari Window

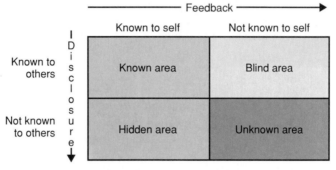

Source: From *Group Processes: An Introduction to Group Dynamics,* by Joseph Luft, by permission of Mayfield Publishing Company. Copyright © 1984, 1970, 1963 by Joseph Luft.

Important aspects of your behavior to be aware of include your self-presentation, orientation towards others, behavioral style, ethics, and reactions to people who differ in gender or ethnic background.

Differences in Self-Presentation

How well do other people know you? Are you easy to get to know? Do you feel free to tell others what you feel and think? In order to know you and be involved with you, I must know who you are and what you need. For that to happen, you must **self-disclose** how you perceive, think, and feel about the present situation, along with any relevant information from your past. Without self-disclosure, you cannot form a meaningful relationship with another person.

self-disclose
The process of revealing how you perceive and feel about the present.

Johari Window
A model of the different degrees of openness between two people based on their degree of self-disclosure and feedback solicitation.

The Johari Window.   The **Johari window,**[26] diagrammed in Exhibit 9–4, is a model of the different degrees of openness between two people. It is based on the degrees of self-disclosure and solicitation of feedback when sharing information with another person. The model presents four windowpanes of awareness of ourselves and others.

■■■■■ **EXHIBIT 9–5**

Different Self-Presentation Styles

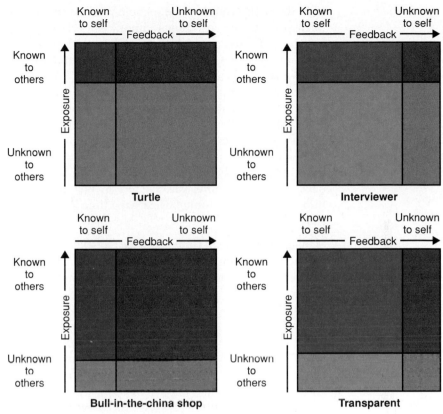

Turtle

Interviewer

Bull-in-the-china shop

Transparent

Source: Reprinted from *Group Processes: An Introduction to Group Dynamics* by Joseph Luft, by permission of Mayfield Publishing Company. Copyright © 1963, 1970, 1984 by Joseph Luft.

In the *open area,* information is disclosed and known by both parties; mutually shared perceptions confirm both parties' frames of reference. In the *hidden area* lie things that you are aware of but do not share because you may be afraid that others will think less of you, use the information to their advantage, or chastise you because they may hurt the other's feelings. The *blind area* encompasses certain things about you that are apparent to others but not to yourself, either because no one has ever told you or because you defensively block them out. Blind spots, however, make you less effective in interactions with others. A certain team member may be terrible at running meetings, for example, but may not know it because no one has given her any feedback. Finally, in the *unknown area* lie repressed fears and needs or potential that neither you nor the other are aware of.

Different Styles of Self-Disclosure.[27] In important intimate and trusting relationships, aboveboard behavior is called for and people self-disclose freely with each other. This is the *transparent style* of interacting illustrated in Exhibit 9–5, characterized by the large "open" area. Transparent styles are appropriate for significant relationships in regenerative climates. They would not be appropriate with casual acquaintances, in competitive situations, or where trust and goodwill have not been established.

A person with a relatively large "hidden" area uses an *interviewer style* because this person asks a lot of questions when soliciting feedback but does not self-disclose to others. Consequently, others have a difficult time knowing how the person feels or what she wants. After a while, people can become irritated at continually being asked to open up and share things without any reciprocation from the interviewer. They may become suspicious about how the information will be used, and may begin to shut down on the quantity and quality of information they are willing to share.

People with large "blind" areas give a lot of feedback but solicit very little from others. People with this *bull-in-the-china-shop style* frequently tell others what they think and feel and where they stand on issues, but they are insensitive to feedback from others. Since they do not "hear" what others say to and about them, they do not know how they come across and what impact their behavior has on others.

A person with a large "unknown" area does not know much about himself—nor do others. He may be the silent observer type, who neither gives nor asks for feedback. This is the *turtle,* who carries an imaginary shell around him that insulates him from others. People have a hard time knowing where he stands or where they stand with him.

Managing Openness: Guidelines for Self-Disclosure.[28]   Because openness is risky—having both potential costs and rewards—it can be difficult to decide how open to be and with whom. Sharing your feelings and needs with others can build strong relationships in which you feel understood and cared about and have your needs satisfied. With the wrong parties, however, your openness could be used against you. With closed behavior, you don't risk rejection or being taken advantage of, but you incur the costs of possibly not satisfying your needs and goals. It is difficult to establish meaningful relationships if you don't let yourself be known to significant others. Both too much or too little openness can be dysfunctional in different types of interpersonal relationships.

Managing your openness means choosing when and how to be more open and authentic in your relationships with others. It means thinking before acting. In choosing how open to be in any situation, consider your own motives, the probable effects of your remarks on the other, and the recipient's readiness to hear your views. This includes an assessment of the degree of trust between you to determine if self-disclosure would be too risky.[29] In mature relationships, for example, the bonds of trust between parties causes them to assume that the other will not use disclosed personal information in ways that risk negative consequences.

Different Behavioral Styles[30]

Many times two people who cannot get along with one another (whether they be peers or boss and subordinate) have no difficulty interrelating with other people. Sometimes these differences can be accounted for by different frames of reference, needs, goals, or self-presentation styles. Often they occur, however, because people have different preferred ways of being treated by others. If two people's preferred ways of interacting don't match, there is a high likelihood of conflict and tension.

behavioral style
A person's habitual way of interacting with other people.

A person's **behavioral style** is his or her habitual way of interacting with other people. It can be determined by examining two dimensions. *Responsiveness* is a person's degree of readiness to show emotions and develop relationships. *Assertiveness* refers to the amount of control a person tries to exercise over other people. Exhibit 9–6 summarizes the four primary behavioral styles determined by different levels of responsiveness and assertiveness.

Source: Reprinted with special permission of King Features Syndicate.

People with different behavioral styles often irritate each other and have incompatible work methods. A key interpersonal skill is knowing how to adapt your own behavioral style to others' in order to avoid alienation. This is practicing *behavioral flexibility:* treating others the way they want to be treated. American corporations are realizing the importance of being more considerate of others and are sending their managers to "charm schools," as described in the opening vignette. But before you polish your charm, you need to understand your own behavioral style and be able to determine that of others.

The Expressive Style.   *Expressives* are animated, intuitive, and lively, but they can also be manipulative, impetuous, and excitable. They are fast paced, make spontaneous decisions, and are not very concerned about facts and details. They thrive on involvement for others. They are very verbal and good at influencing and persuading. They are the cheerleaders: "I can, you can, we can make a difference." They like to be recognized.

Expressives are very emotional and are relatively comfortable sharing their own feelings and hearing about the feelings of others. To maintain productive relationships with them, it helps not to hurry a discussion and to be entertaining. When striving for an agreement with an expressive, make sure that you both fully understand all the details and summarize everything in writing so it won't be forgotten.

The Driving Style.   *Drivers* are highly assertive but not very responsive. They are firm with others and make decisions rapidly. They are oriented toward productivity and concerned with bottom-line results, so drivers can be stubborn, impatient, and tough minded. Drivers strive to dominate and control people to achieve their tasks.

═══════ **EXHIBIT 9–6**

Characteristics of the Four Behavioral Styles

High Responsiveness	
Amiable Style	**Expressive Style**
Slow at taking action and making decisions	Spontaneous actions and decisions
Likes close, personal relationships	Likes involvement
Dislikes interpersonal conflict	Dislikes being alone
Supports and "actively" listens to others	Exaggerates and generalizes
Weak at goal setting and self-direction	Tends to dream and get others caught up in the dream
Has excellent ability to gain support from others	Jumps from one activity to another
Works slowly and cohesively with others	Works quickly and excitingly with others
Seeks security and belongingness	Seeks esteem and belongingness
Good counseling skills	Good persuasive skills

Low Assertiveness ◄──────────────────► **High Assertiveness**

Analytical Style	**Driver Style**
Cautious actions and decisions	Firm actions and decisions
Likes organization and structure	Likes control
Dislikes involvement with others	Dislikes inaction
Asks many questions and specific detail	Prefers maximum freedom to manage self and others
Prefers objective, task-oriented, intellectual work environment	Cool and independent; competitive with others
Wants to be right and therefore relies heavily on data collection	Low tolerance for feelings, attitudes, and advice of others
Works slowly and precisely alone	Works quickly and impressively alone
Seeks security and self-actualization	Seeks esteem and self-actualization
Good problem-solving skills	Good administrative skills

Low Responsiveness

Source: P. L. Hunsaker and A. J. Alessandra, *The Art of Managing People* (New York: Simon & Schuster, 1986), p. 36. Copyright © 1980 by Phillip L. Hunsaker and Anthony J. Alessandra. Reprinted by permission of Simon & Schuster, Inc.

Drivers like expressing and reacting to tough emotions, but are uncomfortable either receiving or expressing tender feelings. You can maintain a productive relationship with a driver if you are precise, efficient, and well organized. You should keep the relationship businesslike. To influence a driver in the direction you desire, provide options you are comfortable with, but let the driver make a decision.

The Analytical Style.   *Analyticals* are not very assertive or responsive. They are persistent, systematic problem solvers who sometimes appear aloof, picky, and critical. They need to be right, which can lead them to rely too heavily on data. In their search for perfection, their actions and decisions tend to be extremely cautious. They do not shoot from the hip, avoid being confrontational, and think before they speak.

Analyticals suppress their feelings because they are uncomfortable with any type of emotion. To get along with an analytical, try to be systematic, organized, and prepared. Analyticals require solid, tangible, and factual evidence. Do not use gimmicks or push them for a fast decision. Take time to explain the alternatives and the advantages and disadvantages of your recommendations.

"Sensitive to what needs?"

Source: *Parade Magazine.* (April 12, 1992), p. 8.

The Amiable Style.   *Amiables* are very responsive, but unassertive, causing them to be supportive and reliable. Sometimes they appear to be complaining, soft hearted, and acquiescent. They are slow to take action and want to know how other people feel about a decision before they commit themselves. Amiables dislike interpersonal conflict so much that they often tell others what they think others want to hear rather than what is really on their minds.

Amiables like expressing and receiving tender feelings of warmth and support, but abhor tough emotions like anger or hostility. They are good team players and have no trouble recognizing the person in charge, unlike drivers, who always act as if they are the boss. To get along with amiables, support their feelings and show personal interest in them. Move along in an informal manner and show the amiable that you are "actively listening."

Male/Female Differences

No one denies that males and females are different. Because of these differences, most people interact differently with same-sex than with different-sex communicators. Some of the most common sexual differences in interpersonal relationships concern communication styles, relating strengths, interaction preferences, and social-sexual behavior.

Communication Differences.   Male managers' communication behaviors are often characterized by task orientation, dominance, challenges to others, and attempts to control the conversation. For example, males talk more and interrupt more often than do females. Females are usually more informative, receptive to ideas, focused on interpersonal relations, and concerned for others. They are more reactive and show more emotional support.[31]

Women are more precise in their pronunciation than men, who, for example, tend to shorten the ends of words (using "in" instead of "ing").[32] Males and females also differ in word choice. Females tend to select more intense adverbs, such as "awfully friendly," whereas males use words that are more descriptive and defining.

Women more often use *qualifying terms,* which are phrases that soften or qualify the intent of our communication. They make language less absolute and less powerful. Examples include "maybe," "you know what I mean," "it's only my opinion," and so on.[33]

Women also frequently use *tag questions,* which are qualifying words at the end of a sentence that ask the other for confirmation of the statement presented. When using these, they automatically defer to others: "It's really time for a break now, right?" "We did the job right, didn't we?" By adding the tag question, the speaker gives the impression of being unsure and surrenders decision-making power.[34]

Relating Strengths.   Different interacting psychological and social forces place women's early development in a context of *communion,* emphasizing expressiveness, connection, and relatedness, whereas men's early development occurs in a context of *agency,* emphasizing independence, autonomy, and instrumentality. This early emphasis on relatedness and connection causes women to develop, more highly than men, the qualities of vulnerability, empathy, and an ability to empower and enable others.[35]

Men are socialized to deny feeling vulnerable and are encouraged to strive for self-reliance, strength, and independence, while women are expected to attend to their own and others' feelings and connect emotionally with others. By being better able to comfortably recognize and respond to feelings of self-doubt, inadequacy, and vulnerability, women are better able to nonjudgmentally address weaknesses in themselves and others, which are preconditions to personal growth, healthy interdependence, and helping others.

Women learn to listen with empathy and to be responsive and sensitive to others' emotions. Men, on the other hand, are encouraged to be rational and strong and to deny feelings in order to maintain rationality and control. Women's stronger empathy is thought to be valuable in maintaining collaborative, growth-enhancing relationships.

Finally, women grow up expecting a two-directional pattern of relational growth, where contributing to the development of others will increase their feelings of effectiveness and competence and where others will be motivated to reciprocate. This is opposed to men's early training, which emphasizes independence and competitiveness. Consequently, women are more naturally adaptable to helping others at work in coaching or mentoring relationships.[36]

Interaction Preferences.   Males and females differ in their reactions to authority figures and how they prefer to deal with conflict. These issues have grown in importance as more women have assumed positions of authority in organizations. In terms of supervisor preference, females tend to have more positive attitudes towards female managers than do males. They also perceive female managers as more competent than males perceive them.[37] Although female college students report that they would prefer a female boss upon graduating, more females with work experience prefer male supervisors.[38]

With respect to conflict, more female than male managers have been socialized to avoid confrontations altogether or to seek help in resolving them. More women than men settle for noninfluential roles rather than become involved in

Because of differences in male/female communication behaviors, Chicago attorney Laurel G. Bellows advises women in business to learn two styles of negotiating: nonpositional and confrontational. She suggests that female traits such as building relationships and being creative work well in nonpositional negotiations— situations in which parties use creative and cooperative methods to reach agreements helpful to both sides. In confrontational negotiations, women must realize it is okay to be adversarial and argue with the other parties— typical traits that men learn as young boys playing sports. (Photo: © 1992 John Zich.)

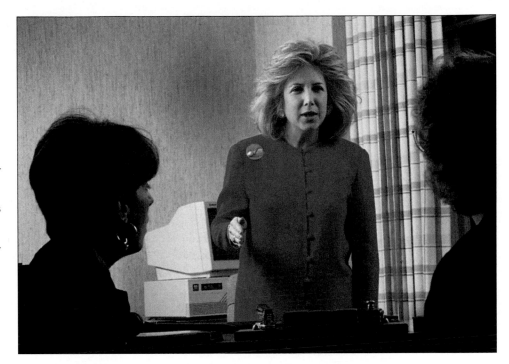

power struggles and conflicts. In contrast, many men have been taught to overemphasize power and strive for one-upmanship even when it is unnecessary or counterproductive.

Social-Sexual Behavior.   Social-sexual behavior is any non-work-related behavior having a sexual component; it includes things like sexual harassment, flirting, and office romances. Analyses of office romances and sexual harassment have suggested that over half of all employees have received some kind of sexual overture from a co-worker of the other gender. About 10 percent of all women have actually quit a job because of sexual harassment,[39] which includes all unwelcome verbal or physical sexual advances.[40]

More than half of U.S. women executives say they have suffered sexual harassment, a problem reported by 70 percent of Japanese working women and 50 percent of women working in European countries. In addition, 15 percent of men say they have been harassed by either female or male co-workers. Harassment results in stress, absenteeism, productivity declines, turnover, and lawsuits, which cost companies an average of about $300 per employee per year. Solutions include raising awareness, providing training, and consistent enforcement of clearly communicated rules and penalties.[41]

The existence of genuine attraction between men and women in the workplace can't be ignored. When men and women work closely and intensely together, they often become attracted to each other even if they didn't intend it to happen. Sex goes to work with us every day, and we are naive if we assume that management can hand down an edict stating, "We'll have no attraction here." Since people do choose whether or not to act on these feelings, it is better to give people guidelines and help in managing attraction productively. Effectively managing sexual attraction in relationships involves learning to communicate directly, setting personal boundaries, and having a sense of ethics.[42]

Different Communication Ethics

Interpersonal communications are ethical when they facilitate a person's freedom of choice by presenting accurate, relevant information. They are unethical when they prevent another person from securing information relevant to a choice. Unethical communications force a choice the other person would not normally make, or decline to make choices that the person's would normally make, or both.[43]

Deception is the conscious alteration of information to significantly influence another's perceptions.[44] Deception includes lying, which is concealing or distorting truthful information, and behaviors that do not reflect our true feelings or beliefs, like smiling at people we dislike or acting busy to avoid more work.

An *overt lie* is a false statement made with deliberate intent to deceive. Covert lying occurs when you omit something relevant, leading others to draw incorrect inferences. Lying or hiding the truth is unethical because it prevents another person from getting complete and correct information to fully explore all possible alternatives.

Interpersonal deception is very prevalent in the workplace. It is mainly used to avoid punishment,[45] but also serves to present a better image, protect others' feelings, attain personal goals, and avoid embarrassment.[46] Since honesty and trust are so important for productive interpersonal relationships, however, deception can be a serious flaw.

Deception can be detected by noticing behavioral changes. When people are practicing deception, they display more vagueness, uncertainty, and reticence; their messages are less plausible; and their speech contains more errors and is less fluent.[47] Liars avoid eye contact and have a tendency to squirm more than honest people.[48] The Eye on Ethics box discusses how some companies are obtaining hidden information without being open themselves.

Ethical behavior has very important consequences. In every national poll, the most important thing people want in a leader, friend, partner, or workmate is honesty. The biggest cost of lying is that you may lose the trust of other people who depend on you and on whom you depend.[49] Working with others in organizations involves interdependence, so lying should be confronted and eliminated in order to maintain mutual trust.[50]

CHARM SCHOOLS FOR MANAGERS—A SECOND LOOK

Feedback from others at the "charm schools" described in the opening vignette enables managers to eliminate blind spots in their interpersonal styles. How can charm schools help managers learn how to satisfy the interpersonal relationship needs of themselves and others; build trust with others; interact productively with different behavioral styles; deal effectively with male and female differences; and act ethically?

The importance of mastering these interpersonal skills has recently been demonstrated in Daniel Goleman's 1995 book, *Emotional Intelligence*,[51] where he shows that they can matter more than I.Q. Drawing on recent behavioral

Eye on Ethics

Obtaining and Using Interpersonal Information without Permission

A growing number of class action lawsuits by employees accuse employers of overstepping the bounds of decency and privacy in the workplace by scrutinizing electronic mail or eavesdropping on telephone calls. Some employers face suits for firing workers supposedly because bosses didn't like electronic mail messages they had read—sometimes after assuring employees of privacy.

Some employers monitor their employees' use of desktop computers. A PC may be personal, but it's far from private, especially if it's part of a network. The Norton-Lambert Co. of Santa Barbara, California, which makes *Close UP* networking software, takes out trade journal ads to urge employers to "look in on Sue's computer screen from your own terminal . . . In fact, Sue doesn't even know you're there! Hit the shift key again and off you go on your rounds monitoring other people in the company. Viewing one screen after another, helping some, watching others. All from the comfort of your chair."

Conversely, labor lawyers say secret taping of supervisors by employees is also on the rise. Spurred by employees' efforts to protect their jobs in a tight economy and aided by the availability of cheap, miniature recorders, taping is typically done to buttress legal claims. But it outrages and exasperates employers who may have thought they were speaking to an employee in confidence.

Defenders counter that the secret recording sometimes is the only way to bring out the truth. "If Anita Hill had a tape recorder, we wouldn't have had that stupid hearing," says Craig M. Cornish, a lawyer who represents employees. Defenders of taping also say the recordings spare not only employees but companies from costly lawsuits. In one instance this year, a Colorado woman recorded harassing phone calls by her supervisor at a high-tech company. After giving him transcripts of the tapes, the woman noticed the harassment stopped. Not only was no lawsuit filed, but the woman still works at the company.

Sources: Gene Bylinsky, "How Companies Spy on Employees," *Fortune* (November 4, 1991), pp. 131–140; and Junda Woo, "Secret Taping of Supervisors Is on the Rise, Lawyers Say," *The Wall Street Journal* (November 3, 1992), pp. B1–B4.

---

research, Goleman points out that people with high emotional intelligence, that is, self-awareness, empathy, impulse control, and social deftness, are stars in the workplace whose relationships flourish. Lack of emotional intelligence, on the other hand, can ruin relationships and sabotage careers. The good news is that emotional intelligence is not fixed at birth and it can be nurtured and strengthened in families, schools, and even the kind of executive training described in the opening vignette.

SUMMARY

Executives emphasize the critical importance of interpersonal skills in achieving organizational objectives and managerial success. A good starting place for improving your competence in interpersonal relations is to understand the personality factors that influence them. These include things like self-concept, frame of reference, defenses, feelings, and need compatibility.

Sometimes where interactions take place determines how effective they are. Job requirements determine the depth and range of possible interpersonal relationships. Organizational culture determines how people interact emotionally, and the specific interaction climate between two people influences their degree of trust and intimacy.

How people relate is affected by how openly they share information, their preferred behavioral styles, their comfort level in expressing emotions, and their tendencies to deceive one another. Men and women also exhibit differences in their communication styles, interaction preferences, and social-sexual behaviors.

Key Concepts

reciprocity, *p. 290*

self-concept, *p. 291*

value system, *p. 291*

personal frame of reference, *p. 291*

defense, *p. 293*

regenerative interaction pattern, *p. 298*

degenerative interaction pattern, *p. 298*

trust, *p. 298*

interpersonal effectiveness, *p. 299*

self-disclosure, *p. 300*

Johari window, *p. 300*

behavioral style, *p. 302*

Questions for Study and Discussion

1. Why are interpersonal relationships in the workplace important? What are some relationships you have had that affected your productivity and satisfaction positively? Negatively?

2. What is your present self-concept? Describe times when you had a diminished self-concept and what caused it. Have you experienced an inflated self-concept? Describe what happened.

3. Describe a negative relationship you have had with someone in terms of the A-B model. Do the same for a positive relationship. What are the key differences between the factors in each situation?

4. Describe a relationship with someone in whom you place great trust. What conditions create and maintain that trust? Describe a relationship with someone in whom you place little trust and the conditions that created it. What are the differences between the trusting and distrusting relationships?

5. What is your behavioral style? How does it influence your relationships with other people at work, at school, and in your personal life? How can your knowledge of behavioral styles be applied to improve your relationships in these different settings?

6. What are the main relationship differences between females and males? Think of your most important relationship with a male and a female. How do the different relating preferences affect your specifically in these relationships?

7. Draw a Johari window with the four quadrants reflecting your personal degrees of self-disclosure and solicitation of feedback. How does your Johari window influence your relationships with others?

EXPERIENTIAL EXERCISE

Comparing Interpersonal Needs

Preparation.   Complete the Your Turn exercise—*What Are Your Relationship Needs* assessment—presented earlier in this chapter. Then form discussion groups of three to six.

Time.   30 to 60 minutes (depending on size of the discussion groups).

Activity.   Share your scores with others in your small group and discuss the implications for your interpersonal relationships according to the following questions. (10 to 15 minutes for each student.)

1. Examine your scores on each need category as they relate to each other. Your highest scores indicate which interpersonal needs probably dominate your relationships with others. How well do these scores describe your interpersonal behavior in the various aspects of your life?

2. How do the other people in your group react to your scores in terms of how they experience you?

3. Examine how different you are relative to others on the six different interpersonal need scores. How are these differences perceived by others?

4. Your scores are also good indicators of how others are likely to react to you. Compare your scores to others in your group.

   a. Who are you compatible with, that is, one person wants what the other expresses?
   b. Who are you incompatible with, that is, one person expresses something another does not want, or both parties express the same thing (for example, if you have control, or neither wants something that is necessary, such as control)?
   c. What happens when two people emphasize the same need, (for example, affection), as opposed to situations where they emphasize different needs (for example, control versus affection)?

5. Discuss the implications of your interpersonal needs for inclusion, control, and affection for you as a manager.

6. Reflect back on the previous discussion with your group members. Do you behave in ways that you want to change? Share the changes you propose and see how others react.

EXPERIENTIAL EXERCISE

Getting to Know You: Connecting by Rubber Bands

Preparation.   Requires a room with space to move about freely.

Time.   35 to 40 minutes.

Activity 1.   All members of the class stand up and silently mill around greeting each other nonverbally. After you have greeted everyone (about three minutes) you nonverbally choose a partner for activity 2.

Activity 2.   Stand about two feet apart facing your partner. Put your hands out in front of you, almost touching the hands of your partner. Pretend that your hands are connected by rubber bands and that you are facing your partner in a mirror. Nonverbally move your hands around in a creative way (3 to 5 minutes).

Activity 3.   Stay in your hand-mirroring position. Now pretend that your feet are also connected by rubber bands. Again, nonverbally move your hands and feet around. Be creative: See if you can move around the room, encounter other dyads, and so on (3 to 5 minutes).

Activity 4.   With your partner, nonverbally choose another dyad. Sit down together and share what you learned about your partner from participating in activities 1, 2, and 3 with the other dyad. Rotate sharing until all are finished (10 minutes), then discuss the following questions in your group (15 minutes):

1. Who invited the other to be his or her partner? What did you learn about needs for including or being included about yourself and your partner?

2. What did you learn about your own and your partner's need for control from how your movements were initiated in the hand and feet mirroring?

3. Was there reciprocity with your partner, or did one person take charge?

4. What kind of behavioral style do you think your partner has from sharing this exercise with him or her?

5. What else did you learn about yourself and your partner?

CASE

The Bill and Mary Show: Bendix to Morrison Knudsen[52]

Mary Cunningham was a hot topic at Bendix Corporation long before September 1980, when Bill Agee stood before more than 600 employees and denied that her rapid advancement had anything to do with "a personal relationship that we have." Cunningham joined the company in the previous June as executive assistant to the CEO, Bill Agee, after a three-hour interview in New York at the Waldorf-Astoria. "A meeting of kindred spirits," she said. Exactly one year later, Agee gave her a bigger title—vice president for corporate and public affairs. Three months after that came the promotion to vice president for strategic planning. Agree tried to confront the uproar that immediately followed by announcing to employees that his new vice president and he were "very, very good friends" but not romantically involved. The comment backfired, creating a national media furor so intense and so focused on Cunningham's youth, blond hair, and shapely figure that in the fall of 1980 the Bendix board of directors forced her resignation.

Inside Bendix, gossip about the relationship between Cunningham and Agee began to reach crescendo after her June promotion, and all sorts of things helped keep the noise level up. A TV camera focusing on former President Gerald Ford at the Republican National Convention happened to find Agee and Cunningham sitting next to him. Some Bendix people suggested that Agee was less accessible than he had once been, and Cunningham's growing influence with him did not help to allay suspicions. She had called herself his "alter ego" and "most trusted confidante"; he said she was his "best friend." Then in August, Agee and his wife of 25 years divorced so quickly it surprised even top officials at Bendix.

Top corporate executives in the United States had been accused of almost everything imaginable except having romances with one another. But, what was one to think? Here were two young, attractive, unattached people working together, traveling together, even staying in the same two-bedroom suite at the Waldorf Towers. They had to be having an affair—and that would explain Cunningham's sprint up the ranks. Or was Cunningham, as Gail Sheehy portrayed her in a four-part newspaper series, a brilliant, idealistic corporate missionary destroyed by jealous cynics. Barbara Walters interviewed Cunningham, and feminist leaders like Gloria Steinem rallied to her defense asking if this meant that young, talented, attractive, ambitious, and personable female executives were permitted only slow climbs upward, lest they invite gossip?

Insisting that their relationship had been platonic until after she left Bendix, Agee and Cunningham married in June 1982. By then, Agee had converted to Catholicism and divorced his wife of 25 years. Cunningham's six-year marriage to Howard Gray, a black executive with American Express, was annuled. The same year, after resurfacing as a vice president at Seagram's, Cunningham acted as Agee's unpaid adviser during Bendix's attempted takeover of the Martin Marietta Corporation. But their ambitious plan collapsed when Bendix was swallowed by the Allied Corporation in a merger that cost hundreds of Bendix employees their jobs. The fiasco was blamed, in part, on the chair's young wife, the strategic planner.

The couple escaped to Cape Cod and started a small venture capital firm. In 1983, Mary Agee founded the Nurturing Network, a nonprofit organization that helps single working and college-age women with unplanned pregnancies. In 1988, Bill Agee was named CEO of the Morrison Knudsen Corporation in Boise, Idaho.

In 1994 Morrison Knudsen posted losses of $310 million and lurched toward bankruptcy. In February 1995, Bill Agee was ousted as MK stock fell from $30 a share to $5 1/2; employees and retirees alike watched their futures evaporate. In February, too, Mary Agee resigned as executive director of the nonprofit Morrison Knudsen Foundation, a position critics say she used to benefit the Nurturing Network. Once more, the Agees were at the center of a corporate ethics controversy—and this one seemed no less vitriolic than the last.

The Boise community has not regretted the Agee's demise. It wasn't only the shareholders' losses and the hundreds of MK workers Bill Agee fired, but the fact that the Agees rubbed Boise the wrong way almost from the start—so much so that after being excluded from the town's private clubs and most prestigious boards, the couple and their two children abruptly relocated three years ago to a $3.4 million estate in Pebble Beach, Calif. From that Pacific Coast setting 600 miles away from their offices, Mary Agee managed her charity and Bill Agee ran Morrison Knudsen by phone, fax, and FedEx, and from a $17 million corporate Falcon jet that peeved MKers dubbed "Mary's taxi."

Now, with more than a dozen lawsuits filed by shareholders, charging that Bill Agee and the Morrison Knudsen board wasted assets and managed the company recklessly, Mary Agee's role is under legal as well as public scrutiny regarding the use of MK assets to benefit the Nurturing Network. The lawyers are also eyeing the close relationship linking MK and its foundation with the Nurturing Network—a complex web of friendships, business interests, and moral commitments. In 1992, half the

MK board members had wives on the Nurturing Network board, while Bill Agee served on both boards. "Once so many of the directors and their wives had joined with the Agees in . . . a moral crusade," the *New York Times* pointedly asked, "how likely was it that they would challenge Mr. Agee in the boardroom?"

Questions for Managerial Action

1. Was Mary Cunningham/Agee unfairly victimized by a society suspicious that attractive women advance on their wiles, not their wits?

2. Is any 29-year-old fresh from business school, no matter how smart, qualified to be the chief planning executive of a multibillion-dollar corporation in the throes of a major restructuring?

3. Are the personal lives of Agee and Cunningham—or any other corporate officials—anybody's business?

4. Once such an embarrassing controversy surfaces, how should a corporation deal with it?

5. What ramifications do romantic relationships at work have for other organizational members and for organization effectiveness in general?

6. What are the probable reasons why people reacted the way they did to the Bill and Mary developments?

7. What mechanisms could organizations institute to avoid these kinds of problems?

8. What could Bill and Mary have done differently to avoid the negative outcomes?

Chapter 10

Building Groups into Teams

LEARNING OBJECTIVES

After studying this chapter, you should be able to:

- Explain the primary characteristics of groups.
- Compare the contributions of different types of groups.
- Describe the stages of group development.
- Discuss how group norms are developed and enforced.
- Determine sources of group cohesiveness.
- Understand threats to group performance.
- Explain how to develop a group into a team.
- Discuss the characteristics of high-performing teams.
- Define key team member roles.
- Assess and improve team performance.

NEW TEAMS ENHANCE QUALITY AT CHRYSLER

At Chrysler's assembly plant at Brampton, Ontario, Don Callahan and Brian Large huddled around a half-built Dodge Intrepid, trying to figure out why the warning light on the instrument panel was on even though the air conditioner was working fine. Both are members of the LH cars' "platform team": Callahan, a hourly assembly-line worker, and Large, a product engineer, have worked together since the Intrepid prototype was first built. In a few hours, they managed to fix the electrical glitch and send their car down the line.

If Chrysler had developed the LH like most U.S. vehicles have been developed, Callahan wouldn't have contacted Large about the problem, because the two would never have met. And the early production cars would likely have reached customers' hands with the electrical system still on the fritz. But the workers, designers, and engineers who collaborated in developing the first test batch of cars thrashed out the final stages of a vehicle development process that sought to blur the traditional lines between people in different functional work units—all in the name of building a better car.

The platform team, long the standard way of putting cars together among Japanese auto makers, has been officially embraced by Chrysler executives as superior to the compartmentalized functional system still prevalent throughout the U.S. auto industry. Simplification is the goal of the platform team. When designers, product engineers, manufacturing engineers, purchasing agents, suppliers, and line workers make decisions together from the beginning, it saves time, money, and untold hassles when the car finally goes into production.

So far, the team approach appears to be paying off. The LH team has shaved a full year off Chrysler's average vehicle-development cycle, historically 4 1/4 years. And team members did it with 40 percent fewer engineers than a typical product program would use. At a price tag of just over $1 billion, the LH budget came in well under those of two other well-known team efforts, Ford's $3 billion Taurus/Sable and GM's $3.5 billion Saturn.

Source: Amy Harmon, "TEAMWORK: Chrysler Builds a Concept as Well as a Car," *Los Angeles Times* (April 26, 1992), pp. D1–D3.

Chrysler's investment in teamwork paid handsome dividends during the development of its LH cars. Many other specific team efforts have paid off as well or better, like the Medical Products Group at Hewlett-Packard that revitalized a health care business that most others had written off, or the small band of rebel railroaders that took on most of the top management of Burlington Northern and created a multibillion-dollar business in "piggy-backing" rail services despite widespread resistance, even resentment, within their own company. For each of these success stories of outstanding team performance, however, there are many times more about work groups that didn't work at all.[1] What makes the difference between high-performing teams and group failures is the subject of this chapter.

Most of you have, or surely will have, the opportunity to experience teamwork with the popular business school learning tool: the group project. Faced with a group task, many students protest: "Is there any way I can get out of doing this as a group project? I don't want to have to coordinate and depend on other people. I could do it better and faster by myself!" Similar thoughts often go through the minds of managers and professionals when they are placed on committees, task forces, work teams, quality circles, and other organizational groups.

Most of us enter team situations cautiously because ingrained individualism (a hallmark of the American culture) and experience discourage us from putting our fates in the hands of others or accepting responsibility for others. This is with good reason. If members do not overcome their natural reluctance to trust their fate to others, the price of "faking" a team approach is high: At best, members get diverted from their individual goals, costs outweigh benefits, and people resent the imposition on their time and priorities; at worst, serious animosities develop that undercut even the potential personal bests of individuals.[2]

Working with others is not easy. Nevertheless, groups constitute the basic building blocks of any organization. In today's complicated and rapidly changing business environment, few individuals in an organizational setting can successfully go it alone. For many tasks, teams accomplish much more work in less time than the same number of individuals can working separately. Employees can also grow more quality conscious through group interaction as they learn about others' experiences, problems, and solutions as work in process flows through the organization.[3] When groups do not act like teams and are nonproductive and dissatisfying, it is usually because their members lack necessary attitudes, knowledge, and skills to work together effectively. Or, they have not been provided with clear objectives, structures, and appropriate environments by management.

Although there is no guaranteed "how-to" recipe for building high team performance, there are a number of findings from studying successful teams that provide insights to the essential ingredients. One objective of this chapter is to enhance your awareness, appreciation, and understanding of how groups function and contribute to organizations. Another is to provide you with the tools to participate as an effective group member. Finally, you will learn how to manage groups, develop them into high-energy teams when needed, and intervene when your team gets off track.

WHAT ARE GROUPS AND WHAT FUNCTIONS DO THEY PERFORM?

We all spend a great deal of time in group interactions long before we take jobs in organizations. Most of us are born into a family group, become part of one or more play groups, and soon enter the academic world of multiple-classroom

Pat Lancaster (second from left), president of Lantech, a family-owned manufacturing company in Louisville, Kentucky, invested thousands of hours in training the company's 330 employees and managers in teamwork skills and TQM. A cross-functional process improvement team made up of floor workers, managers, and engineers redesigned the process for building the company's semi-automatic machines that stretchwrap large items in plastic. (Photo: © Pat McDonogh.)

groups. Later we may join clubs and teams and become members of fraternal or religious groups, while for others a gang may become their dominant group. Some of these group memberships are mandatory, others are undertaken voluntarily. Work groups are the manager's main vehicle for accomplishing organizational tasks.[4] Groups also satisfy personal needs for friendship, self-esteem, and identity.[5]

People riding an elevator, watching a movie, or waiting in a doctor's office may constitute a physical gathering of individuals, but they lack the basic psychological characteristics of a group. A **group** can be defined as two or more people who regularly interact with and influence one another over a period of time, perceive themselves as a distinct entity distinguishable from others, share common values, and strive for common objectives.[6]

In most organizations, several different types of groups exist, and most employees are likely to be members of more than one. Groups can be classified as formal or informal.

Formal Groups

Formal groups such as committees, maintenance crews, and task forces are established by management and charged to perform specific tasks and accomplish organizational objectives. Some of the most common contributions that formal groups make to their two primary beneficiaries, the organization and its individual members, are summarized in Exhibit 10–1.

A **command group** is permanently specified in the formal organization structure and consists of a supervisor who exercises formal authority over direct subordinates. Specific departments such as accounting, quality control, or shipping are examples of command groups. **Task groups** are temporary formal groups that are created to solve specific problems. Examples include a product development team, a university curriculum revision committee, or a political candidate's campaign advisors. Task groups don't report to any particular department but are often made up of people from different command groups who possess complementary areas of expertise to solve the assigned problem. When the problem is solved, the task group usually disbands and members return to their command groups. Examples of task groups in action are given in the World Watch box.

---

group
Two or more people who perceive themselves as a distinct entity, regularly interact and influence one another over a period of time, share common values and strive for common objectives.

formal group
A group intentionally established by a manager to accomplish specific organizational objectives.

command group
A permanent group in the organization structure with a formal supervisor and direct subordinates.

task group
A temporary formal group created to solve specific problems.

━━━━━ **EXHIBIT 10–1**

What Formal Groups Contribute

Contributions to Organizations

1. Accomplish complex, interdependent tasks that are beyond the capabilities of individuals.
2. Create new ideas.
3. Coordinate interdepartmental efforts.
4. Solve complex problems requiring varied information and perspectives.
5. Implement action plans.
6. Socialize and train newcomers.

Contributions to Individuals

1. Satisfy needs for affiliation.
2. Confirm identity and enhance self-esteem.
3. Test and share perceptions of social reality.
4. Reduce feelings of insecurity and powerlessness.
5. Provide mechanism for solving personal and interpersonal problems.

Source: Adapted from E. H. Schien, *Organizational Psychology,* 3rd ed. (Englewood Cliffs, NJ: Prentice Hall, 1980), pp. 149–151.

World Watch

Japanese Quality Circles

The Japanese tend to do things in groups, to place a high value on group membership, and to strive to be as cohesive as possible. This group orientation is exemplified by the now famous quality control (QC) circles instituted in Japanese industries right after World War II. Even in 1983 there were more than 100,000 such groups formally registered with the Japanese Quality Circle Association and more than a million others that were unregistered.

A typical QC group in Japan consists of from two to ten employees from a natural working group in which all members know one another's duties. The groups focus on any production or service problems or improvements that fall within the scope of their jobs. It is estimated that the average QC circle in Japan produces about 55 implemented suggestions per worker per year. The record is 99 implemented suggestions per worker in one year. Because the tremendous success and quality of Japanese products have been largely attributed to QC groups, many U.S. firms are now using or experimenting with QC circles.

One such firm is the Society National Bank of Cleveland, where more than 130 officers and employees have been involved in a quality circle program for the last 10 years. Teams of four to twelve members, plus a group leader, meet one hour each week to help solve problems. Management believes that the program has improved communications throughout the bank, increased the total awareness of all employees, decreased turnover and absenteeism, and generally aided the development of human resources and customer relations.

More specifically, the branch team reduced the time required for balancing accounts at the end of the day from 45 minutes to 20 minutes. The domestic collection team developed new ways of processing redemption coupons in-house for a savings of $45,000. And the customer service team reduced customer calls from 3 percent to 1 percent and reduced the percentage of calls answered by recorded messages from 5 percent to 2 percent.

Source: "Quality Circles Solve Problems at Society National Bank," *American Bank* (May 6, 1983), pp. 5–10.

Informal Groups

informal group
A group that emerges through the efforts of individuals to satisfy personal needs not met by the formal organization.

Informal groups emerge through the efforts of individuals trying to satisfy personal needs for support, friendship, growth, and recreation. Membership in informal groups is based on common interests and mutual attraction versus being assigned, as it is in formal groups. Examples of work-related informal groups are the "lunch bunch," the bowling team, and the car pool. The subtle influence of informal groups over their members' behaviors often turns out to be more powerful than the vested authority of formal groups.[7]

interest group
An informal group consisting of individuals who affiliate to achieve an objective of mutual interest.

An **interest group** is made up of individuals who affiliate to achieve an objective of mutual interest that may have nothing to do with their formal command or task group memberships. Working mothers who lobby together to get their organization to facilitate their multiple roles by providing day care facilities on the premises, flexible working hours, and shared job assignments is an example. Another is the Hispanic Association of AT&T employees, which was formed for the purpose of furthering the professional growth of AT&T's Hispanic employees.[8]

friendship group
An informal group based on common characteristics which are not necessarily work related.

Friendship groups also develop based on common characteristics such as marital status, political views, college affiliations and sports. Friendship groups are important for their own sake because they satisfy the affiliation needs of their members. Enlightened managers maintain good relations with friendship groups because these groups have tremendous influence on their members that managers would prefer to have directed towards organizational goals.[9]

reference group
A group with which an individual identifies to form opinions and make decisions regardless of whether he or she is an actual member.

A **reference group** is any group with which an individual identifies for the purpose of forming opinions, making decisions, or determining how to act. Reference groups are the bases for many friendship and interest groups, but they may also exist outside of the organization and still influence a person's behavior at work. Reference groups are based on things like race, gender, politics, religion, social class, education level, and profession. Reference groups provide values for individuals on which to base personal decisions and norms that justify social behavior, both of which may or may not be congruent with organizational preferences.[10] Most of us have seen examples when individuals are more influenced by reference groups than organizations about how to dress or interact with others at work. See the Dynamics of Diversity box for examples of how some homosexual employees have formed reference groups to enhance their feelings of acceptance regardless of others' reactions.

Although informal groups exist to satisfy individual needs, they also provide contributions to the formal organization. Examples of some of the primary contributions of informal groups are given in Exhibit 10–2.

HOW DO GROUPS DEVELOP?

Groups have life cycles similar to people. They are born, grow, and develop, and often die. A group's effectiveness is influenced by its stage of development and how well its members have learned to work together. A newly formed task group reacts much differently to threatening changes than does an older, more stable command group.[11] To become stable, cohesive, and effective, a group must resolve issues about goals, power, and intimacy as it progresses through several stages of maturation.

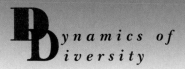

ynamics of
iversity   *Support Groups for Homosexual Employees*

Gay employees are a clear example of a reference group that historically has remained hidden. In recent years, however, gay employees have insisted on recognition, and, as a group, they are having a profound impact on how institutions view other key groups both at work and in the home.

Gay men and women are rapidly forming employee groups such as the one whose huge banner recently greeted all those on their way to the elevators at Levi Strauss's San Francisco headquarters: LESBIAN AND GAY EMPLOYEE ASSOCIATION CELEBRATES PRIDE WEEK. In the mid-1980s, Apple and Digital Equipment were among the first companies to have gay employee

groups. Since then, homosexual employees at AT&T, Boeing, Coors, DuPont, Hewlett-Packard, Lockheed, Sun Microsystems, US West, and many other corporations have joined together for fellowship and to lobby top management on issues that are important to them. These include eliminating overt workplace hostility, extending employee benefits to all domestic partners (not just spouses), and making sure partners are welcome at company social events the same way husbands and wives are.

Source: "Gay in Corporate America," *Fortune* (December 16, 1991), pp. 43–50.

EXHIBIT 10–2

What Informal Groups Contribute

Without informal group memberships, individuals often feel lonely, insecure, and alienated. They also have no way to verify their perceptions of events, expectations, or contributions.

Contributions to Individuals

1. Satisfaction of social and affiliation needs.
2. Satisfaction of needs for security and support.
3. Enhanced status for members if the group is perceived by others as prestigious.
4. Enhanced feelings of self-esteem if a member is valued by other group members.
5. Feeling more competent by sharing the power of the group to influence and achieve.

Contributions to Organizations

1. Solidify common social values and expectations congruent with organizational culture.
2. Provide and enforce guidelines for appropriate behavior.
3. Provide social satisfaction unlikely for anonymous individual workers to experience.
4. Provide a sense of identity that often includes a certain degree of status.
5. Enhance members' access to information.
6. Help integrate new employees into the informal expectations of the organization.

Sources: Summarized from P. K. Lunt, "The Perceived Causal Structure of Loneliness," *Journal of Personality and Social Psychology* (July 1991), pp. 26–34; and Keith Davis, *Human Relations at Work,* 2nd ed. (New York: McGraw-Hill, 1962), pp. 235–257.

The Five-Stage Model of Group Development

Several research-based theories suggest that most groups progress in sequence through the five stages of forming, storming, norming, performing, and adjourning.[12] Different groups will remain at various stages of development for different lengths of time, and some may remain permanently stalled at any stage. By being aware of a group's process, its leader can facilitate members' functioning at each stage and the transition to the next one. This five-stage model of group development is illustrated in Exhibit 10–3.

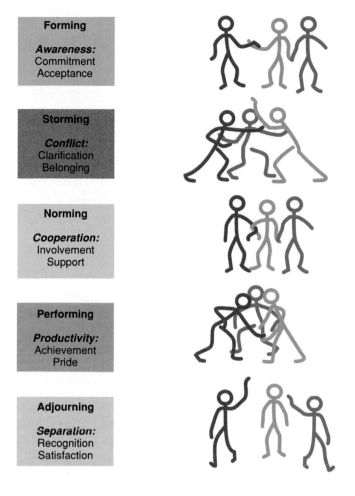

*Stages of Group
Development*

Forming.   In a newly formed group, a lot of uncertainties exist about the group's purpose, structure, and leadership. Members are concerned about exploring friendship and task potentials. They don't have a strategy for addressing the group's task. They don't know yet what behaviors are acceptable as they try to determine how to satisfy needs for acceptance and personal goal satisfaction. As awareness increases, this stage of group development is completed when members accept themselves as a group and commit to group goals.

Storming.   The next stage involves intragroup conflict about the clarification of roles and behavioral expectations. Disagreement is inevitable as members attempt to decide on task procedures, role assignments, ways of relating, and power allocations. One objective at this stage is to resolve the conflicts about power and task structure. Another is to work through the accompanying hostility and replace it with a sense of acceptance and belonging that is necessary to progress to the next stage.

Norming.   Cooperation is the theme of the norming stage, which involves the objectives of promoting open communication and increasing cohesion as members establish a common set of behavioral expectations. Members agree on a structure that divides work tasks, provides leadership, and allocates other roles. Desired outcome for this stage of group development are increased member involvement and mutual support as group harmony emerges. If groups become too contented, however, they can get stalled at this stage because they do not want to create conflict or challenge established ways of doing things.

Performing.   In this stage of development, group members are no longer conflicted about acceptance and how to relate to each other. Now members work interdependently to solve problems and are committed to the group's mission. Productivity is at its peak. Desired outcomes are achievement and pride, and major concerns include preventing loss of enthusiasm and sustaining momentum. For permanent work groups, this is hopefully the final and ongoing state of development.

Adjourning.   The adjournment or separation phase occurs when temporary groups like task forces and committees disband after they have accomplished their goals. Feelings about disbanding range from sadness and depression at the loss of friendships to happiness and fulfillment due to what has been achieved. The leader can facilitate positive closure at this stage by recognizing and rewarding group performance. Ceremonial events bring closure to the desired emotional outcome of a sense of satisfaction and accomplishment.

Moderators to the Five-Stage Sequence of Group Development

In task groups created to develop solutions to immediate problems within prescribed time periods, these developmental phases are less separate and distinct than the five-stage model of group development suggests. Two factors that affect the process are task deadlines and group composition.

Task Deadlines.   Given a deadline for task completion, a group will develop its own distinctive approach to problem solving until about halfway through the allotted time. At this midpoint, most groups change their approach to the task and apply a burst of concentrated energy, reexamining assumptions and ineffective behaviors and replacing them with new approaches that usually contribute to dramatic gains in progress. These more productive behaviors are maintained until close to the deadline, when a final burst of activity to finish the job occurs.[13]

Group Composition.   Other developmental differences have been found between culturally diverse and homogeneous groups.[14] Newly formed homogeneous groups are more effective than heterogeneous ones through the first part of the task (performing) stage. After settling into the performing stage, however, heterogeneous groups catch up and perform comparable to homogeneous ones. More diverse groups actually become slightly more proficient at identifying problems and generating solution alternatives if they continue to work together for long periods of time.

HOW ARE GROUPS STRUCTURED?

After a group has progressed through the stages of development previously described, certain stable patterns of relationships exist among its members. Communication networks have been established, bonds of intimacy and interpersonal attraction have emerged, powerful and influential members have been identified, agreement regarding appropriate behavior has been reached, and the relative esteem for each team member has been established in a hierarchy. These patterns of relationships constitute the group's structure and directly impact each member's behaviors.

When Chrysler began work on a new compact called the Neon in 1990, it formed a team of engineers, marketers, purchasing agents, and financial people to work together from the start to avoid later delays. To keep production costs low, the team sought early input from companies that would supply parts for the car. In 1991 Chrysler approved the team's budget, and production began in January 1994. (Photo: Don B. Stevenson Photography.)

━━━ **EXHIBIT 10–4**

Group Roles

Task Roles	Maintenance Roles	Personal Roles
Initiating	Encouraging	Blocking
Giving information	Harmonizing	Recognition seeking
Seeking information	Setting group standards	Dominating
Summarizing	Gatekeeping	Avoiding
Elaborating	Compromising	Seeking help
Consensus testing	Providing feedback	

Functional Group Roles[15]

role
An expected set of recurring behaviors that are expected from a member by others in a group.

A **role** is an expected set of recurring behaviors that are expected from a member by others in the group. Some group roles are functional in that they help the group achieve its goals. Other roles, which are usually motivated by specific individual needs, are dysfunctional and interfere with group effectiveness. After a group has matured to the performing stage, personal behaviors detrimental to the group are mostly eliminated and members adopt behaviors beneficial to group performance.

task roles
Roles that directly help accomplish group goals.

maintenance roles
Roles that help establish and maintain good relationships among group members.

It is necessary for two types of functional roles to emerge for a group to continue to exist and accomplish its objectives in a satisfactory manner. **Task roles** directly help accomplish group goals. **Maintenance roles** help establish and maintain good relationships among group members. Examples of these roles are listed in Exhibit 10–4, along with some frequent **personal roles,** which are sets of behaviors that meet individual needs and are usually detrimental to the group's interaction. Personal roles need to be replaced with maintenance and task roles before a group can become an effective team.

personal roles
Roles which only meet individual needs and are usually detrimental to the group.

Norms

norms
Commonly held expectations about appropriate group member behavior.

Groups develop common expectations, called *norms,* to reinforce functional role behaviors and prevent dysfunctional personal behaviors. **Norms** are expectations about appropriate individual and group behavior commonly agreed on by members.[16] They are established over time for behaviors that have significant impact on a group, like facilitating its survival, increasing predictability of member behaviors, ensuring member satisfaction, expressing values important to the group's identity, and preventing embarrassing interpersonal problems.[17]

Types of Norms.   Norms tell group members how to behave in certain situations. *Formal norms* exist as written rules and procedures for all employees to obey. Most norms, however, are *informal* in that they develop from group members' own experiences of what behaviors help and hinder their performance and satisfaction. Some informal norms are *functional* and others are *dysfunctional* in facilitating the achievement of organizational goals.

There are common classes of norms that appear in most work groups.[18] Perhaps the most common are about *performance-related processes* that provide members with guidelines about things like how hard to work, how to do a job, how much to produce, and how to communicate. There usually are norms about *appearance* that indicate appropriate dress standards, how to look busy, and how to appear loyal to the company. *Informal social arrangements* are also dictated by norms regulating with whom members should joke around, eat lunch, and become friendly. Finally, norms relegate the *allocation of resources* like overtime pay, assignment of onerous jobs, and who gets new tools.

How Norms Develop.[19]   Norms usually develop gradually and informally as group members learn what behaviors are necessary to function effectively. They may also be established more rapidly in one or more of the following ways.

Explicit statements by supervisors or influential co-workers about actions that facilitate group success can define specific role expectations, determine acceptable personal behaviors, (e.g., how colleagues address each other, lateness, personal phone calls), and define legitimate ways of accomplishing work. *Critical events* can establish important precedents that become accepted norms. For example, if a member tells people in other units about hiring plans, which results in the new position being lost, norms about secrecy might develop to protect the group in similar situations in the future.

Primacy refers to the first behavior pattern that emerges in a group that often sets group expectations. People usually continue to sit in the same seats they sat in at their first meeting even though original seats were not assigned and people could change where they sit at every meeting. On the other hand, some group norms emerge because members bring expectations with them from other work groups in previous organizations. Such *carry-over behaviors* from past situations increase the predictability of group members' behaviors in new settings. For example, students and professors bring with them relatively constant sets of expectations to each class. Consequently, students do not have to continually relearn their roles from class to class.

How Norms Are Enforced.   Groups want their members to conform to norms and can apply a wide variety of techniques to pressure individuals to change their behaviors. If a member strongly desires to be accepted by the group, just being informed of group norms is often enough to cause compliance. Praising the member who exactly meets the group's production norms will reinforce commitment.

When a member is observed deviating from agreed on behaviors, the group usually applies pressure to enforce conformance to its norms. The member is first reminded of the range of behaviors acceptable to the group and then perhaps teased. If norms are greatly exceeded, the deviant member may be ostracized.

Common goals
Success experience
Small size
Interpersonal attraction
Challenge of a common enemy
High status
Cooperation among members
Female composition

A group is more likely to reject a person who violates its norms when he or she has not conformed or performed adequately in the past. On the other hand, a member can build "idiosyncrasy credits" by previously behaving consistently with group expectations and contributing effectively to group goals. These credits are spent when the person performs badly or violates norms. When credits are expended, the person will most likely be punished for violated norms.

Status within Groups

status
The measure of relative worth and respect conferred upon an individual by the group.

As a group proceeds in its work, some members will contribute more to the group's productivity and camaraderie, earning them greater respect or making them better liked than others. **Status** is a measure of relative worth and respect conferred on an individual by the group. Early in a group's life, status rankings are temporarily determined by each person's status outside the group based on things like education, income, occupation, or title. Over time a more permanent status pattern develops based on each member's role and contribution to group goals.[20]

Higher status is more likely to be awarded to members who are willing to put in long hours to make the group successful. Members who intentionally violate group norms for personal benefit are usually ranked at the bottom of the social hierarchy because they pose a threat to the group's security and integrity.

Cohesiveness

cohesiveness
The degree of attractiveness of a group to its members and the closeness of the interpersonal bonds between group members.

Successful performance of both task and maintenance roles contributes directly to positive feelings about membership in a group. When members like one another and the group itself, the group is **cohesive**—that is, held together by the close interpersonal bonds of its members who highly value their association and want to maintain it.[21] The more cohesive a group, the more effective it will be in meeting member needs and the more conformity it can demand from its members.

Sources of Cohesiveness.[22]   Group cohesiveness springs from many sources. Eight of the factors that make membership attractive to group members are listed in Exhibit 10–5.

Cohesion is likely to be high if the *goals* of the group are clearly *specified and compatible* with member needs. Lack of agreement on goals or incompatibility of personal and group goals will disrupt cohesiveness. Successful *accomplishment* of goals generates positive feelings about the group and its members. Continued failure, on the other hand, can cause continued frustration or member withdrawal from the group. Losing sports teams, for example, frequently suffer from dissension and finger pointing borne of frustration from lack of wins.

As group *size* increases, both interactions and communications begin to break down and cohesiveness decreases. Groups of five to seven are large enough to provide diverse inputs and small enough to give members the opportunity to voice

At Bread Loaf Construction, a 150-employee full-service construction company, executive vice president John Leehman and president Maynard McLaughlin work hard to build a sense of teamwork among employees. Employees, 12 at a time, participate in outdoor adventure programs designed to stretch participants beyond their personal limits and build teams. Here several employees work as a team to balance on a wire between two trees. During the day participants, wearing harnesses, climb 30-foot trees then dive into a net; at night they are taught how to build their personal visions and discuss how to build the company so people can use it to reach their goals. (Photo: Bread Loaf Construction.)

their opinions, make contributions, and be recognized.[23] Groups of more than fifteen members generate feelings of anonymity ("who needs me?") in all but a few members.

If the group has a *charismatic leader* or consists of members who are personally attracted to one another, cohesiveness is likely to be high. Attraction may be based on common values, willingness to support one another, physical characteristics, common interests, or any number of other factors that members find desirable in one another.

Attacks from external entities that are perceived as threatening to the group's fundamental purpose create a shared resistance, increased commitment to the group, and tighter bonds among its members. Internal differences are minimized under these conditions, and cohesiveness increases as members dedicate themselves to common causes. Japanese business leaders are adept at creating cohesiveness based on an almost warlike vision of competing firms as "enemies" to be defeated. Labor unions often use the same tactic against management.

Membership in a *high-status* group is valued more than membership in a group that others disdain. Group status may depend on past success, the importance of group activities, the group's level in the organization, or the standards for admission. A simple example is the status ranking of fraternities and sororities on campus. Membership at the "best" house is highly prized.

Competition within a group tends to decrease cohesiveness, while working together toward a common goal increases it. Tasks and reward systems that promote cooperation among members promote feelings of goodwill and discourage competitive win/lose situations and the resulting negative feelings.

Women are thought to be more cooperative and less competitive with people whom they see as friends or teammates than are men. Studies have consistently reported that all-female groups are more cohesive than all-male or mixed-sex groups.[24]

The Crips and Bloods may rule the streets, but the Lunada Bay Pirates rule the waves. Ask any surfer from San Diego to Santa Cruz if he or she would dare trespass on the gang's turf, and the answer is a resounding "No way, dude!" One Huntington Beach surf rider who attempted to enter the Pirate turf on a dare remembers that "halfway there, they hosed me down with bad vibes and I split."

Bad vibes? Other than letting the air out of an intruder's tires or occasionally throwing a rock or fist, the Lunada Bay Pirates rarely resort to violence to defend their turf. It is significant enough, however, that a group of Torrance surfers filed a $6 million claim against the city of Palos Verdes Estates for failing to stop the harassment of visitors by locals.

Lunada Bay, barely a third of mile wide, lies beneath two cliffs in Palos Verdes Estates and is one of the best surfing areas in Southern California. More than 150 Palos Verdes surfers are allowed to surf the bay, and it is nearly impossible for outsider to slip in unnoticed. An established pecking order limits the number of Pirates in the surf to less than two dozen. Palos Verdes surfers can identify themselves at a distance because they all wear basic black wet suits and they know each other's board makers and cars. Whenever the surf is good, a half dozen Pirates guard the trail entrance at the top of the cliffs.

"There are just too many surfers for too few waves in California," says one Pirate. "If we stood back, this place would be overrun." Because of these hordes of common enemies seeking some of their limited resource, the Lunada Bay Pirates are an extremely cohesive group dedicated to the goal of preserving their surfing area.

A more cooperative approach is suggested by Hoyt Smith, 35, a lifelong La Jolla surfer who feels surfers should repair the dings to their sport by displaying the aloha spirit: the friendly-no-matter-what attitude exemplified by Duke Kahanamoku, the late "father of modern surfing" who brought the sport here from Hawaii. "When you're out there on a moving playing field with no referees, you have to depend on people acting in the common interest," says Smith.

Sources: "Surfing Lethal Weapons," *San Diego Union-Tribune* (June 7, 1995), p. B2; and Danny Garcia. *Los Angeles Times Magazine* (May 3, 1992), p. 18.

Cohesive groups come in many styles and sizes. Consider the effectiveness of the Lunada Bay Pirates described in the Eye on Ethics box. Which sources of cohesiveness do the Pirates share?

Consequences of Group Cohesiveness.   Like the Lunada Bay Pirates, members of cohesive groups have common goals and values and satisfy their needs by being together. Members value their membership highly and want to maintain it. The result is a high degree of conformity to group norms and a high degree of group influence over individual members. High cohesiveness, however, can have either positive or negative consequences for group productivity, job satisfaction, and growth.

Productivity.   Highly cohesive groups have the potential to be more productive than groups with low cohesiveness, but this potential is not always realized. Much depends on whether the group identifies with the organization's goals and whether its norms support high productivity.[25] Highly cohesive groups tend to have more uniform output among members than do less cohesive groups because cohesive group members adhere closely to production norms. Consequently, productivity will be high if a group's norms support organizational goals, but productivity will be low if its norms oppose the organization's goals.[26] These relationships between cohesiveness, group norms, and productivity are illustrated in Exhibit 10–6.

━━━━━ **EXHIBIT 10–6**

*Relationships between
Cohesiveness, Group
Norms, and Productivity*

Performance Norms

	High	Low
High	High Productivity	Low Productivity
Low	Medium Productivity	Medium to Low Productivity

Cohesiveness

Satisfaction.   Cohesive groups place high value on themselves and their tasks, which raises the group's status in its members' eyes. The high degrees of acceptance and mutual attraction among group members result in less internal tension and more genuine camaraderie. Consequently, satisfaction of individuals' needs and feelings of well-being tend to run high in cohesive groups, regardless of whether this synergy is focused for or against organizational objectives.

Growth.   If they are not cohesive, groups offer little support for sharing knowledge and teaching skills. In highly cohesive groups members share and learn from one another because members like one another and take pride in group performance. It is possible, however, that high degrees of enforced compliance to group norms and standards may prevent members from achieving their task and interpersonal potential. If, for example, a highly cohesive group maintains low output norms and adheres to a rigid social structure, the development of an individual's technical and interpersonal skills may be thwarted.

Group versus Individual Problem Solving

Although groups often take more time than individuals to make decisions, well-managed ones usually are more creative, produce better quality decisions, generate more acceptance of decisions, and have more commitment to effective implementation.[27] However, groups do have characteristics that, if not managed properly, can impede their effectiveness. Some of the important advantages and disadvantages of group versus individual decision making are summarized in Exhibit 10–7.[28]

WHAT ARE THE THREATS TO GROUP EFFECTIVENESS?

The potential disadvantages of groups contribute to four well-studied threats to effectiveness. Inappropriate conformity and groupthink are directly related to members' needs for acceptance. Social loafing can be tied to ambiguous responsibilities. Individualism is a competing goals issue.

Inappropriate Conformity

When individual members go along with group decisions they believe are clearly wrong, they are conforming inappropriately.[29] Most of us can think of at least a couple of times when we have gone along with the group against our better judgment. Plenty of examples exist of how business groups too often do the same thing in accounts of practices like sexual harassment, insider trading, and illegal hazardous waste disposal.

■■■■■■ **EXHIBIT 10–7**

Advantages and Disadvantages of Group Problem Solving

Advantages Groups Have over Individuals	Disadvantages Groups Have Compared to Individuals
• *More knowledge and information.* A group of people meeting together to solve a problem has more breadth and, quite often, more depth of experience and knowledge than any one individual. This is especially true if members come from diverse backgrounds.	• *Competing goals.* Group members often have prior commitments to other reference groups or have personal agendas that conflict. These differences can lead to disagreement about alternative solutions and destructive conflict.
• *Diversity of viewpoints.* A number of people with different experiences can generate more options and creative alternatives. They also bring a greater number of approaches to solving the problem.	• *Time consuming.* People have to plan and coordinate group meetings and then wait for everyone to arrive. The processes of being understood, resolving interpersonal conflicts, and irrelevant side conversations also detract from group problem-solving efficiency.
• *Increased understanding.* By participating in the problem-solving process, group members have a better understanding of the decision and why it was made.	• *Social pressure to conform.* Especially in highly cohesive groups, members often conform to majority opinions that are not optimal in order to gain liking and acceptance.
• *Increased acceptance.* Group members are also more likely to accept a decision they understand. Also, a participative decision, in North American democratic-type societies, is often perceived as more legitimate than an autocratic decision by a single manager, which might be considered arbitrary.	• *Domination by a few.* High status, power, or just an assertive personality can cause certain members to dominate group discussions and influence decisions that they prefer. If the dominating people do not have the best ideas and those who do are kept silent, the quality of the group decision will suffer.
• *Better implementation.* Participation in a decision creates a feeling of ownership of "our decision" versus one by some authority figure. People want to show that they are right and consequently will work hard to implement it themselves as well as encouraging others to do the same.	• *Ambiguous responsibility.* Since no one individual is held responsible for a group's decision, there is often uncertainty about who is accountable for implementing decisions and who gets the credit or blame for outcomes. Often this can lead to decisions that are more risky than appropriate for the organization, because no one in particular will be held accountable if the decision falls.

The Groupthink Phenomenon

groupthink
A state in groups where the pressures for conformity are so great that they dominate members' ability to realistic appraise alternative decision options.

Groupthink exists when pressures for conformity are so great that they dominant members' concerns for realistic appraisal of alternative courses of action.[30] The term was created by Irvin Janis as a result of his study of top-level U.S. government groups' foreign policy decision fiascoes.[31] Groupthink occurs in highly cohesive groups when they desire to agree. Classic examples of groupthink occurred when President John F. Kennedy and his cabinet decided on the Bay of Pigs invasion fiasco as a strategy for dealing with Cuba; when President Lyndon B. Johnson's White House advisors decided to escalate the Vietnam War; when the U.S. Navy failed to prepare for the Pearl Harbor disaster; and when the United States decided to invade North Korea.

Eight dominant symptoms of groupthink can be gleaned from such disastrous situations. All of these decision-making groups endeavored to avoid disagreements, overlooked disturbing information, rejected valuable criticism, and failed to voice dissenting opinions. Exhibit 10–8 highlights the symptoms of groupthink.

Studies of successful policy decisions reveal that effective groups do not exhibit these symptoms.[32] It appears that groupthink can be avoided if a leader remains neutral, encourages criticism, asks for new ideas, and brings in outside consultants to raise alternative views.

━━━━━ **EXHIBIT 10–8**

Symptoms of Groupthink

- *Illusions of group invulnerability*. Members of the group feel they are invincible, resulting in risk taking (e.g., Pearl Harbor).
- *Collective rationalization*. Refusal to consider contradictory data or to consider unpleasant alternatives thoroughly (e.g., failure to consider engineers' warnings about the O-rings in the Challenger disaster).
- *Illusion of group morality*. Members of the group feel it is "right" and morally correct (e.g., religious or ethnic wars like the Arabs and Jews, or Serbs, Croats, and Muslims).
- *Stereotypes of competitors*. Shared negative opinions of treating groups as weak, evil, and stupid (e.g., communists versus capitalists, Muslims versus Christians).
- *Pressure to conform*. Direct pressure to conform is applied to a member who suggests other alternatives or that the group may be wrong (e.g., L.A. police officer hitting Rodney King because the others expected him to even though he thought it was wrong).
- *Self-censorship*. Members do not share personal concerns if contrary to overall group opinion (President Kennedy's cabinet members with doubts about the Bay of Pigs invasion remaining silent).
- *Illusions of unanimity*. Erroneously believing that all are in agreement and accepting consensus prematurely (e.g., if one person would have opposed the Bay of Pigs invasion, Kennedy would have canceled it, but no one did and consensus was assumed).
- *Mind guarding*. Members of the group protect the group from hearing disturbing ideas or viewpoints from outsiders (e.g., keeping new conflicting test results suppressed just before the FDA approves a new drug).

Source: Irving L. Janis, *Groupthink: Psychological Studies of Policy Decision and Fiascoes,* 2nd ed. (Boston: Houghton Mifflin Company, 1982).

Social Loafing

Common logic says that the productivity of a group should at least equal the sum of the productivity of each individual member, and the research on the advantages of groups over individuals suggests that they may be even more productive than the sum of individual member outputs in problem-solving situations. Research studies have determined, however, that individual efforts actually decline as group size increases.[33] This tendency for individuals to exert less effort when working in a group than working individually is called **social loafing.**

social loafing
The tendency of individuals to exert less effort when working in a group than working individually.

One reason for social loafing is the possibility that if you perceive that other group members are not contributing their fair share, you might reduce your own input to reestablish a perceived equity of effort.[34] Another possibility is that if members think that individual inputs are not identifiable, this dispersion of responsibility will cause some to become "free riders."[35] Finally, if the group task is perceived as unimportant or is boring, and the previous two conditions exist, motivation may decrease even more.[36] This research has important implications for managers of groups, since social loafing does not seem to occur when group members expect their outputs to be measured.[37]

Group Composition

Social loafing has been found to be more prevalent in *individualistic cultures* like the United Stated or Great Britain, where people are competitive and motivated by personal gain, than in collective societies like Japan, China, or Israel, which support group goals over self-interest.[38] Consequently, groups in collective societies usually perform better than groups in individualistic societies.

Heterogeneous groups composed of dissimilar members are likely to have more *diversity* in experiences, information, and viewpoints that can enhance their problem-solving effectiveness.[39] This group advantage may be modified, however, if the group diversity is generated from differences in cultural background (racial, religious, or national), which can promote lack of identification with the group and difficulties in communicating and solving conflicts.[40] These interpersonal

Teams of executives from General Foods try to build a raft from 50-gallon drums, two by fours, and rope. With too much management intervention, the executives discover, the team cannot accomplish its goals. But when the teams are allowed to devise their own solution, success is achieved! The goal of such exercises is to get managers to transfer positive team building behavior back to the work situation. (Photo: Photograph by Taro Yamasaki.)

problems can detract from task effectiveness and result in ambiguity, confusion, and miscommunication, unless members learn how to be more open to different perspectives and manage their disagreements productively.[41]

Although men and women most often work well together in groups, *gender* differences can cause problems in group effectiveness. In mixed-gender groups, for example, men interrupt women significantly more than other men. Women, on the other hand, interrupt less often and less effectively, but don't discriminate between men or other women. This difference contributes to decreased power and influence for women.[42]

It can be even worse if women move into professions previously dominated by men. Men more often than women want to keep the other sex out and put up resistance that can manifest itself in discrimination and harassment.[43] Group leaders need to be aware of sexual tensions in mixed-gender groups and be ready to prevent sexual harassment and discrimination.

HOW CAN GROUPS BECOME MORE EFFECTIVE?

Being aware of and compensating for the above threats to group effectiveness can go a long way towards improving group functioning. Effective leadership in facilitating the group process and running effective meetings can also help immensely. Finally, team building activities that transform work groups into high performance teams can boost group effectiveness where appropriate.

Leadership Facilitation

Whether a group will be effective or ineffective depends primarily on the skills of its members and its leader's ability to facilitate the process. For example, lower-status group members usually defer to those with higher status, even though they

AFFIRMATIVE DISTRACTION

Source: *Working Woman,* October 1995.

━━━━━ **EXHIBIT 10–9**

Guidelines for Conducting Productive Meetings

Although most meetings have well-deserved reputations for being both inefficient and ineffective, there are some well-established guidelines that can help improve the process. Running a meeting productively requires the following actions:

1. *Preparing and distributing an agenda well in advance of the meeting.* This allows participants to know who should attend, how to prepare, and what the objectives are.

2. *Consulting with participants before the meeting.* This ensures that all participants have properly prepared and do not forget anything.

3. *Establishing specific time parameters.* To avoid wasting time and allow participants to plan other activities, meetings should begin and end on time.

4. *Maintaining focused discussion.* Disruptions, interruptions, and irrelevant discussions should be discouraged so that the discussion can be directed to the issues at hand.

5. *Encouraging and supporting participation by all members.* The best ideas may be in the heads of silent members who need to be encouraged to participate.

6. *Encouraging the clash of ideas.* Critical thinking, constructive disagreement, and reality testing are necessary to avoid premature decisions.

7. *Discouraging the clash of personalities.* Personal attacks cause anger and hostility that detract from meeting effectiveness.

8. *Facilitate careful listening.* Model and encourage concentrated listening where the speaker is empathized with and receives responses from others to ensure understanding.

9. *Bringing proper closure.* Meetings should be ended by summarizing accomplishments and allocating follow-up assignments.

Source: Adapted from S. R. Robbins and P. L. Hunsaker, *Training in Interpersonal Skills,* 2nd ed. (Englewood Cliffs, NJ: Prentice Hall, 1996), pp. 171–184.

may be the ones with the best ideas.[44] Group leaders need to ensure that all participants feel free to contribute. They should avoid trying to persuade others in the problem-solving group to adopt their own preference. The leader's role is to establish a cooperative environment in which all opinions are heard and evaluated before a solution is reached.[45] If the leader is not aware of the dynamics of the group process or is not effective in the role of facilitator, a cohesive group may succumb to threats like social loafing and groupthink.

Meeting Guidelines

Despite numerous jokes and complaints about the time they waste, meetings are the group process used on a regular basis by most organizations to combine expertise and solve organizational problems. The attitudes, qualifications, and behaviors of the people attending a meeting are important contributors to its effectiveness. All of these factors can be influenced by the meeting leader who sets up formal procedures to control the process. Some established guidelines for facilitating meeting effectiveness are summarized in Exhibit 10–9.

One way of increasing meeting efficiency is to allow participants to remain at their desks and interact through *electronic meeting systems (EMSs).* EMSs consist of sophisticated computer software that keeps meetings on track and moves the group toward clear, well-thought-out decisions by allowing meeting participants to follow structured, nonpersonal procedures on personal computers to rapidly solve problems, generate new ideas, assess opinions, make decisions, and resolve conflicts. EMSs allow for anonymous inputs so that participants can be completely honest without fear of reprisal, and they can cut the meeting time in half because they eliminate digressions, allow several participants to talk at once, and structure the process. On the other hand, the lack of emotional elements and, nonverbal inputs, and differences in keyboard skills can be drawbacks.

Motorola uses EMS tools for planning, ranking and rating employee performance, and plotting strategies for the future. At Westinghouse, EMSs are used for any kind of meeting where the need is to gather information and stimulate new ideas, rather than simply disseminate existing information. Westinghouse applies EMSs to develop strategic plans for international marketing, to collect and evaluate utility-customer opinions on proposed R&D funding options, to evaluate progress in customer satisfaction, and to plot areas for achieving competitive advantages.[46]

Team Building

team building
All activities aimed at improving the problem-solving ability of group members by resolving task and interpersonal issues that impede the team's functioning.

Team building includes all activities aimed at improving the problem-solving ability of group members by working through task and interpersonal issues that may impede the team's functioning. Team building can be applied when forming groups or as an intervention to improve existing groups.

Forming New Groups. For both task and interpersonal effectiveness, it is usually easier to form a completely new group than to deal with the resistance that must be overcome when trying to change existing groups. New groups do not have to break down any barriers, bad habits, harmful attitudes, inappropriate working relations, or procedures. Addressing the following questions before the group begins to work can get a new group off to a productive start.[47]

- *Where are we going?* Personal and team goals should be clarified so that members share a common vision, purpose, and goals. Realistic priorities should be clarified for each person so he or she knows how participation on the team fits in with other commitments.

- *Who are we?* Members should share their expectations and concerns about working with the team. As group members share their strengths, weaknesses, work preferences, values, and beliefs, diversity can be dealt with before it causes conflicts.

- *Where are we now?* Members can use the first two steps and determine their existing situation (where are we now) compared to their goals (where are we going?), to determine the final step.

- *How will we get there?* This includes establishing operating guidelines about decision making, work methods, participation, conflict resolution, work completion, and team improvement.

Symptoms Indicating Needed Improvement of Existing Groups. A team-building program usually is not initiated unless someone (the leader, a higher-level manager, a team member, or consultant) recognizes that the group is having problems working productively as a team.[48] Symptoms of ineffective groups[49] include *communicating outside the group* instead of expressing disagreements and concerns during group meetings; *overdependency on the leader* versus members moving ahead when it is clear that action is needed; *unrealized decisions* that are made but not carried out; *hidden conflicts* causing tension and decreased productivity and satisfaction; *fighting without resolution* evident in continual open arguments, and attempts to put down, deject, or hurt others; the formation of *self-interest subgroups* that put themselves before the needs of the total unit.

Determining How to Improve Group Performance. Chapter 12 provides an in-depth discussion of the problem solving process, tools, and techniques. The same sequential problem-solving steps can be applied to solve group problems, improve

	Groups	Criteria	Teams
▬▬▬▬ **EXHIBIT 10–10** *Differences between Groups and Teams*	Formal established Individual Sum of individual outputs Diverse	**Leadership** **Accountability** **Performance** **Skills**	Shared roles Shared and individual Collective and synergistic Complementary

their effectiveness, and build them into high performance teams. After identifying problems through data gathering (interviews, questionnaires, or observations), they are analyzed, prioritized, and assigned to task groups to solve. The resulting action plans are then implemented, results are evaluated, and follow-ups are continually applied to ensure that problems are effectively solved.[50] If this process reveals that traditional work groups are not appropriate to achieve objectives, high performance teams may need to be developed because they often better utilize employee skills and are more adaptable to changing organizational demands.[51]

HOW DO TEAMS DIFFER FROM GROUPS?

We defined a *group* as two or more people who regularly interact with and influence one another over a period of time, perceive themselves as a distinct entity distinguishable from others, share common values, and strive for common objectives. Group members may share information, make decisions, and help each other, but they produce individual outputs within individual areas of accountability. A work group's performance is the sum of what its members accomplish as individuals. Committees and task forces composed of individuals who work together, therefore, are not necessarily teams.

team
Relatively permanent work group whose members share common goals, are interdependent, and are accountable as a functioning unit to the organization as a whole.

As summarized in Exhibit 10–10, a **team** is a type of group that can be defined as a "small number of people with complementary skills, who are committed to a common purpose, set of performance goals, and approach for which they hold themselves mutually accountable."[52] A team engages in collective work produced by coordinated joint efforts that result in more than the sum of the individual efforts, or *synergy*. Members are accountable for performance both as individuals and as a group.

Types of Teams: Sports Analogies

Peter Drucker distinguishes among three kinds of teams that differ in structure, member behavior requirements, strengths, vulnerabilities, limitations, and requirements. To be effective, each should be used for different types of tasks.[53] It doesn't work to change the fields or make hybrids. The results are frustration and low performance, like playing baseball on a tennis court, or vice versa. Work groups and teams are tools designed for specific tasks. The key to effectiveness is to match up team characteristics with situational demands.

The first type of team is really like our definition of a group, where players are nominally *on* a team, but do not directly depend on or interact with each other to achieve objectives. Players have fixed positions and specialties that they perform alone. An example is a *track team* where group performance is the summation of individual accomplishments. In industry, it might be a traditional Detroit automobile assembly line.

Advantages of track-style teams are that each member is accountable for specific goals and is evaluated individually (like major-league baseball statistics). Because no one has to adapt to anyone else on the team, each position can be staffed by "stars" no matter how ego-centered they are, and they do their jobs their own ways.

The second is like a *football team,* where players have fixed positions but also need to coordinate efforts as a team. The design teams originated by Japanese auto makers are football-type teams, where engineers, manufacturing staff, and marketing people work in parallel. Other examples are a symphony orchestra or an emergency room hospital unit.

Third is the *tennis doubles team,* where players have a primary rather than fixed position and are required to cover for their teammate by adjusting to their partner's strengths and weaknesses and the constantly changing demands of the game. Examples are a jazz combo or the General Motors team of cross-trained members that designed and produced the Saturn automobile.

Football and doubles tennis teams have flexibility and synergy, but they require more organizational factors than track teams. Football teams need a game plan, and everyone in the orchestra puts the Mozart symphony on his or her music stand. Stars are only featured if a solo is called for; otherwise, they subordinate themselves to the team. The "flexible-manufacturing" plant at GM's Saturn Division, for example, developed small teams consisting of less than seven cross-trained members who were allowed flexibility with respect to individual member's work style as long as everyone contributed only to the one clear goal for the entire team.

Types of Team: Actions Taken

In most organizations there are essentially three types of groups that meet these descriptions of true teams.[54] They can be classified by their objectives to recommend, do, or run things.[55]

Teams That Recommend Things.   After studying and solving specific problems, some teams *recommend things.* They are usually temporary and disband after analyzing problems, recommending solutions, and formulating action plans for others to implement. Examples of these *problem-solving teams* are task forces, project groups, and quality circles. As described in Chapter 3, quality circles, for example, are small groups (seven or eight people) from the same work area who voluntarily get together to identify, analyze, and recommend solutions for problems related to quality, productivity, and cost reduction.

Teams That Make or Do Things.   Teams that *make or do things* are permanent work groups responsible for ongoing, value-added activities like manufacturing, marketing, sales, or service. Examples of such *work teams* that produce things are interacting command groups, like airline flight crews,[56] or **autonomous, self-managed work teams** that are given the authority for their own planning, scheduling, monitoring, and staffing.[57] One of the first experiments with autonomous work teams was in the 1970s when Saab built a new engine plant set up with teams that were allowed to decide how to assemble engines, establish their work pace, and schedule their own breaks instead of the usual production line form of manufacturing. Results were that the previous annual 70 percent turnover and 20 percent absenteeism rates were practically eliminated and productivity increased to one engine per person every 30 minutes.[58]

By 1987, 27 percent of the *Fortune 1000* companies had some employees in autonomous work groups, and by 1990 the number had increased to 46 percent.[59] By the year 2000, it is estimated that close to half of the workers in the United States will be on self-managed work teams.[60]

autonomous work team (self-managed)
Self-managed group of workers who are given authority for planning, scheduling, monitoring, and staffing themselves.

As illustrated by the Saab new plant design, it is easier to install autonomous work teams when a new organization is being created than to impose them on an existing structure because appropriate applicants and technology can be selected for the new system. In well-established organizations, training and socialization are required and reward systems need to be adapted to the new situation.[61]

Companies such as General Motors, Hewlett-Packard, General Mills, and Texas Instruments also report successful applications of self-managed work teams.[62] Some organizations have been disappointed however.[63] A review of 70 studies on autonomous work groups found that they generally had a positive impact on productivity and responsibility but no significant impact on satisfaction, commitment, absenteeism, or turnover.[64]

cross-functional team
A team composed of persons from several different functional units who work together to the accomplishment of a task.

Another type of team that does things is the **cross-functional team,** which unites people from several different units at the same hierarchical level to accomplish a task. Boeing, the world's largest airplane manufacturer, uses cross-functional teams made up of marketing, engineering, manufacturing, finance, and service representatives so that each department knows what the other is doing. The result is better coordination of technical specialists, which increases the efficiency of product design and delivery.[65]

General Motors used cross-functional teams in the development of the Saturn automobile to coordinate the entire project from the very beginning.[66] Rubbermaid assembled a cross-functional team composed of engineers, designers, and marketers who went to customers together to determine the features preferred in a new portable "auto office." Contributions from several different functions ensured that all important design questions were answered, and first-year sales were running 50 percent above projections.[67]

The following Challenge of Change box demonstrates an extraordinarily successful example of cross-functional teams at McCormick & Company.

Teams That Run Things. Teams that *run things* are made up of top managers of an organization or its major subunits.[68] These groups are responsible for determining the organization's mission, goals, strategic plan, and operating procedures, and then overseeing the activities of those reporting to them to ensure successful implementation and desired results. Teams run things at any level, from the total organization down through divisions, departments, and programs to ongoing functional activities.

HOW DO GROUPS DEVELOP INTO TEAMS?

Effective teamwork has been found to be a key characteristic of America's 100 best companies.[69] Nevertheless, it doesn't just automatically happen. Without proper preparation, quality circles, autonomous work groups, cross-functional teams, and other types of teams may not live up to expectations.[70] If members don't trust or support each other, meetings easily degenerate into fighting and arguing, and cooperation is nil.[71]

Newly assembled groups, be they football players or production workers, go through the same stages of group development described earlier until they reach the performing stage. Even at that stage they need to possess the following characteristics: the team mission is agreed by all; leadership is a shared activity; accountability is both individual and shared collectively; problem solving is ongoing; and effectiveness is measured by the group's collective accomplishments.[72]

Challenge of Change

Cross-Functional Advice Teams at McCormick

Multiple Management, the participative management program of spice maker McCormick & Company, has enjoyed 60 years of successful application. In November 1932, Charles Perry McCormick established the first Multiple Management board from a group of employee volunteers to provide innovative ideas for packaging, sales, and product development. The program achieved immediate success: At a time when 14 million people were out of work and the national economy was greatly depressed, McCormick moved from losses to profits within a single year. Between 1932 and 1937, some 2,000 Multiple Management board suggestions were accepted.

Multiple Management is a network of small groups of up to 20 managers and employees who meet every other week for two to three hours on a voluntary basis to discuss innovative ideas and procedures. There are 13 Multiple Management boards at McCormick, roughly one for each major unit of the company. Each group functions as a junior board of directors to identify, analyze, and solve work-related problems. The range of focus includes (but is not restricted to) new product development, quality control, safety, productivity, cost reduction, and inventory control. In addition, members commonly spend several hours of their own time each week on board work.

Eighty percent of the boards' recommendations are accepted and adopted by senior management. More significant is that a group of individuals work together toward a common goal. Even if a project is abandoned, it often inspires other investigations that are successful.

A typical Multiple Management board might be composed of a research chemist, an auditor, a member of the human relations department, an engineer, and a marketing administrator. Board members frequently find themselves working on problems involving areas of the business that are new to them. Often their fresh, unprejudiced ideas prove valuable.

The influence of these hard-working boards does not mean that senior managers abdicate authority and accountability. On the contrary, they meet those responsibilities more effectively because of the shared decision-making process.

Source: Robert E. Sibson, *The Sibson Report* (Spring 1992), pp. 2–5.

Exhibit 10–11 provides some guidelines for managers desiring to build high team performance. Some related considerations are team values, organizational conditions, interpersonal skills, and the match of team roles with member work preferences.

Team Values

Group members need to possess certain core values that reinforce collective accountability for cooperative outputs. Such key values encourage listening and responding constructively to others, giving the benefit of the doubt, providing support, recognizing the interests of others, and acknowledging their accomplishments.[73]

Organizational Conditions

Overall, teams work best if the following four conditions are met: management visibly support teams; the team, in turn, support the organization's goals; team leaders are skilled at running team meetings; and the organization can afford to lose time and defer productivity while team members learn to work together.[74]

This Hong Kong transit system team is photographed during a training session where their leader helps them develop the technical, problem-solving, and decision-making skills needed to become successful. Interaction during such training sessions (and socially) helps team members bond, developing the interpersonal skills required to establish and achieve common goals. (Source: © Jeff Smith/The Image Bank.)

EXHIBIT 10–11

How Managers Can Improve Team Performance

- Determine performance goals that can be immediately achieved to create early success.
- Make sure that members have the appropriate skills.
- Establish demanding performance standards and provide direction.
- Create a sense of urgency in the first meeting.
- Set clear rules of behavior.
- The leader should model appropriate behaviors.
- Members spend lots of time together bonding as a team socially and while working.
- Continually give the team and individual members positive feedback and rewards.
- Regularly challenge the team with new projects or problems to solve.

Source: J. R. Katzenback and D. K. Smith, "The Discipline of Teams," *Harvard Business Review* (March–April 1993), pp. 118–119.

Member Skills

Successful teams are usually composed of members who possess a complementary mix of skills required to do the team's job. *Technical skills* are necessary to meet the team's functional requirements. *Problem-solving* and *decision-making skills* are needed to identify problems and opportunities, evaluate options, make necessary trade-offs, and decide how to proceed. Finally, *interpersonal skills*, like openness, active listening, feedback, support, trust, mutual influence, and constructive confrontation, are required to establish common goals and collaborate to achieve them.[75]

Matching Team Roles and Preferences

If you were the coach of a football team, you would want to get your players into their best positions. You would find out quickly what skills they had and where they felt they could play best. Then you would assign them to specific defensive or offensive roles. During the game, you would want your individual players to coordinate their specialized roles as blockers, passers, and runners, rather than have each player try to do all the work alone. These basic principles are the same for managing a work team. Like a coach, a manager tries to accomplish a common goal by linking differentiated roles held by motivated team members.[76]

Team Work Roles

Team work roles are sets of behaviors that contribute to team goal achievement. The following nine work roles need to be present if a team is to optimize its performance.[77]

Advising.   Advising concerns gathering and disseminating information about things like new products or services or competitors' activities. Examples of advising jobs in organizations include librarian, researcher, forecaster, planner, and communication officer.

Innovating.   Innovating involves thinking up new ideas or new ways of tackling old problems. Scientists in research and development spend practically all of their time specializing in innovation. With the push for total quality management, the need for innovation to improve productivity at all job levels and functions is becoming universal.

Promoting.   Promoting centers on selling ideas to those with the resources to implement them. Promoters persuade decision makers to invest in a new idea or pursue a new potential market. All teams need to promote themselves to ensure adequate financing, staffing, and resources to survive and grow. The most obvious promoting jobs are in sales and marketing, but department managers, project team leaders, and anyone with a new idea to implement needs to promote.

Developing.   Developing involves assessing and developing ideas for practical implementation. Once an idea has been generated and accepted by management, developers on task teams analyze how to produce the product or service and market it. New product engineers and project managers have developing responsibilities.

Organizing.   Organizing means setting up a structure so that the product or service can be produced or provided. It involves deciding who will do what when. Organizing is a basic responsibility for any manager to ensure that subordinates are coordinated, productive, and efficient.

Producing.   Producing goods and services is the profit generator of all teams. Production departments are the obvious place to observe tangible products being made, but all teams produce something, whether it is a report, a problem solution, a new design, a staffing plan, or the close of a sale. Producing is the primary function of anyone who actually does a task—such as assemblers, salespeople, designers, or accountants.

Inspecting.   Inspecting ensures that high quality has been maintained and that accurate records are kept. All details need to be checked and verified, typically by people such as accountants or quality control inspectors.

Maintaining. Maintaining ensures that the infrastructure is in place so the team can work with maximum efficiency. This function is usually associated with support service roles such as found in human resources, finance, and maintenance.

Linking. Linking is the coordination and integration of all work roles to ensure maximum cooperation and interchange of ideas, expertise, and experience. Managers are formally assigned this function in most organizations, but, in reality, any team member may contribute to this role.

Work Preferences

Although most people can operate in any of the team roles, they are most comfortable in only three or four. Since people are more motivated to perform functions that they prefer, matching preferences and work functions can produce better performance.

Amiables. *Amiables* function best in advisor and maintainer roles. They like to make information available and give advice so that others can make the decisions. They are excellent listeners, which makes them well liked by others and prepares them to act as natural facilitators to the team. Amiables take pride in maintaining both the physical and social sides of work. They are supportive (e.g., back-room helpers) and provide stability for others on the team by reminding them of standards and agreements.

Expressives. *Expressives* often are involved in new developments outside the organization and bring back ideas that may challenge the existing way of doing things. They are very capable at pushing ideas forward and getting people enthusiastic about them. Consequently, they are effective in the innovating and promoting roles.

Drivers. *Drivers* prefer developing and organizing roles. They look for ways to make ideas work in practice. They are task oriented and like to set up operating procedures to get things done. They set objectives, establish plans, organize people, and establish systems to ensure things get done by set deadlines.

Analyticals. *Analyticals* take pride in producing a product or service to a standard. They enjoy doing detailed inspecting work and concentrate carefully on facts and figures to uncover variances or errors.

To perform at their optimum, work teams need to have all of the nine work functions performed by individuals whose skills and preferences match up with role requirements. When these role holders are linked together in a coordinated manner, team synergy will be at its peak.[78]

When Lee Iacocca took over at Chrysler, he discovered that not only did they not have the right mix on their management team, but there also was no linking, that is, everyone worked independently. He was quick to realize that Chrysler's business and financial problems were, to a large extent, a result of its lack of teamwork: "All of Chrysler's problems really boiled down to the same thing. Nobody knew who was on first. There was no team, only a collection of independent players, many of whom hadn't yet mastered their positions." It was this key organizational problem that Iacocca set out to resolve because it was the basis for the long-term improvement of the organization.[79]

HOW DO TEAMS MAINTAIN AND IMPROVE THEIR EFFECTIVENESS?

To win games, a sports team must coordinate the efforts of individual players. A sports team practices hours each week for that one hour of critical playing time where its performance counts. Members review films of past games, identify mistakes, set goals, and plan strategies for the next game. Then the team practices until weaknesses are eliminated and it is skilled at implementing its new action plans.

Work teams also need to coordinate the efforts of individual members to be effective. Most work teams, however, seldom take time to review their past actions to determine what worked and what didn't. They don't spend time learning from past mistakes, nor do they consistently revise goals, plan new strategies, practice new ways of behaving, or get coaching on new methods of communicating and working together.

Even teams effective in the performing stage of development can lose their momentum and develop problems as they mature. Success and familiarity can lead to complacency, groupthink, and decreased creativity.[80] Let's address some actions that maintain and rejuvenate team effectiveness.

Maintaining Balanced Roles and Preferences

Sometimes teams can correct imbalances by moving people around in the organization or bringing new people in with new skills to fill in the gaps. It is also sometimes possible for team members to "stretch" into areas not currently high on their list of preferences through appropriate skill training. In addition, people from other groups can be brought in to temporarily fill a certain role. Three more sophisticated techniques are sometimes used to clarify role expectations and obligations of team members.

role analysis technique
Clarifies role expectations and obligations of team members through a structured process of mutually defining and delineating role requirements.

Role Analysis Technique.   With the **role analysis technique,** each individual defines the rationale, significance, and specific duties of his or her role with the inputs of other team members. The final result is a mutually agreed on set of written "role profiles" summarizing the activities, obligations to others, and expected contributions from others for each role on the team.[81]

role negotiation technique
A controlled negotiation process between team members that results in written agreements to change specific behaviors by conflicting parties.

Role Negotiation Technique.   The **role negotiation technique** is a controlled negotiation process between team members who have problems based on power and authority. It requires team members to focus on work behaviors, not on personal feelings about each other, and to write down what they want others to do more of, do less of, stop doing, and maintain unchanged. The result is a written agreement to change specific behaviors by conflicting parties.[82]

responsibility charting
A technique for clarifying who is responsible for what on various decisions and actions with the team.

Responsibility Charting.   **Responsibility charting** clarifies who is responsible for which decisions and actions by having team members construct a grid with the types of team decisions and actions in a vertical column on the left side and the specific team members who are involved across the top. Then each team member is assigned one of five following behavioral expectations for each of the actions: responsibility to initiate action, approval or veto rights, support for implementation, right to be informed (but with no influence), and noninvolvement in the decision.[83]

Maintaining Trust and Openness

Team members can't begin to improve their interpersonal relations unless they are made aware of the impact of their behaviors on others and how they can make these behaviors more productive. When individuals feel secure enough to ask others to explain how they perceive their behaviors and to provide suggestions for improvement, other team members can disclose their perceptions in constructive and supportive ways to help eliminate blind spots. By helping each other improve, team members start to trust each other more, become more open, feel better about others, and form a cohesive team.[84]

One way to do this is through **sensitivity training.** This is a series of unstructured meetings with no formal agenda, where participants share observations and feelings about team processes, relationships, and unspoken consequences, to help each other understand and enhance team performance.[85] There are also **structured feedback procedures** that facilitate the sharing of similar data when group members are more reticent and need more guidance. For example, team members can write what they perceive to be each other's role preferences, style strengths and weaknesses, and other data of interest. Then, each individual reads his or her list to the group and receives clarification.[86]

Another approach is to administer **self-assessment inventories** that measure things like behavioral styles, Type A personality, or conflict management style. These can be scored, interpreted, and published for all group members to see. The team can then analyze the scores to better understand why others prefer certain ways of doing things and behave as they do. Incongruencies between personal styles and task assignments and relationship-style differences can be discussed and action plans generated to manage them more appropriately.

Finally, **exercises and simulations** can be utilized to analyze behavior in a non-threatening setting. How observed behaviors might help and hinder goal accomplishment and team development can then be discussed.

sensitivity training
Unstructured feedback meetings where members share observations and feelings about each other to help improve sensitivity of behavior on others and the team's ability to function.

structured feedback procedures
Meetings where members share feedback with each other by using a prepared format.

self-assessment inventories
Paper and pencil tests that reveal participant characteristics.

exercises and simulations
Activities participants engage in to generate behavior for feedback that can be analyzed and used to develop improvement plans.

NEW TEAMS ENHANCE QUALITY AT CHRYSLER— A SECOND LOOK

As the LH team at Chrysler discovered, it takes more than throwing a disparate bunch of people into one space to get them to surrender jealously guarded turf and a value system based on individualism. The first six months for the LH team at Chrysler were the roughest. Instead of sitting next to people with the same professional background and similar duties, the 850 LH team members found themselves surrounded by co-workers they had never met, doing things they had never heard of. Hourly worker Don Callahan puts it bluntly: "I thought they were a bunch of snobs," he says of cerebral engineer types such as his friend Brian Large, who admits to rarely setting foot in a plant before the LH project. "But once you get them to talk your language, they're all right."

Plant manager John Franciosi says there are remnants of "turf protection syndrome" and pockets of resistance to Chrysler's new order, especially among older employees. But he insists that a combination of peer pressure and recognition that this workplace revolution has solid support from on high is slowly bringing the skeptics around. "We would point fingers at each other over timing," Franciosi recalled at a recent staff meeting. "One guy would say, 'Well, that's the best I can do.

If you want better, go talk to the dumb metal-stamping guys.' And I would say 'Wait a minute. The dumb stamping guys are on the team, so bring the dumb stamping guys in and we'll talk together.' "

Some team managers decided that anybody who pointed a finger at or blamed a fellow team member would be called in front of the whole team and publicly embarrassed. A few red-faced examples later, the LH crew began to get the message, and the handful that didn't were asked to leave. But such hard-nosed tactics were the exception compared to trust-building exercises and an emphasis on consensus decision making that helped minimize resentment and reduce friction in the ranks. As the launch for the new car neared, it was hard to find anyone on the team who would prefer to go back to the old way of doing things.

Top managers gave recognition and support to the LH team and ran interference for them. Often, these executives signaled their support by simply staying out of the team's way. One of the LH team members' goals was to hash out their problems among themselves rather than lodge time-consuming appeals with top management. But even silent allies in high places were useful when company veterans began to feel threatened by the LH team's deviations from the norm.[87]

SUMMARY

The majority of an organization's work is accomplished by people working on teams such as quality circles, project groups, or autonomous production teams. However, some groups work like a dream team, appearing to accomplish miracles, while others generate nightmares. What makes the difference? The answer lies in appropriate group membership, structures, processes, and training. If group members with appropriate skills and attitudes are trained to understand their own and others' role requirements, they can develop to collaborate without dysfunctional conflicts to achieve common objectives. There are several paradoxes to be continually managed, however.

One is that the cohesiveness that groups develop when members value their association with one another and their common goals can promote enhanced satisfaction and extra synergy, but it can also reinforce resistance to change and underachievement if members need to relinquish behaviors that are accepted as group norms.

Also, the very conformity that standardizes behavior and makes life comfortably predictable may also serve to stifle constructive conflict and creativity. In striving for group acceptance, many members show far less initiative and independent thought than they are capable of demonstrating as individuals. Deviates who intentionally violate group norms are often resented and forced back in line, but at times their behaviors can be breakthroughs for productive change.

To transform groups into high-performing teams, they need to develop high degrees of trust, open communication, participation, and constructive confrontation skills. Group members must perform all of the key work functions of advising, innovating, promoting, developing, organizing, producing, inspecting, maintaining, and linking. Also, individuals with appropriate skills and interests need to be matched to their preferred work function.

Finally, high-performance teams need to apply team-building techniques aimed at improved working relationships. The process of improving team effectiveness includes continual data gathering and analysis to assessment areas needing improvement; problem solving to determine sources and solutions to problems; training and exercises to build the skills and processes necessary for continual high performance.

Key Concepts

group, *p. 317*

formal group, *p. 317*

command group, *p. 317*

task group, *p. 317*

informal group, *p. 319*

interest group, *p. 319*

friendship group, *p. 319*

reference group, *p. 319*

role, *p. 323*

task roles, *p. 323*

maintenance roles, *p. 323*

personal roles, *p. 323*

norms, *p. 323*

status, *p. 325*

cohesive, *p. 325*

groupthink, *p. 329*

social loafing, *p. 330*

team building, *p. 334*

teams, *p. 335*

autonomous, self-managed work teams, *p. 335*

cross-functional teams, *p. 337*

role analysis technique, *p. 342*

role negotiation technique, *p. 342*

responsibility charting, *p. 342*

sensitivity training, *p. 343*

structured feedback procedures, *p. 343*

self-assessment inventories, *p. 343*

exercises and simulations, *p. 343*

Questions for Study and Discussion

1. Think about the groups you belong to. What types of formal and informal groups are they? What are your primary reference groups? What effects do they have on your behavior in actual groups?

2. Think about some groups of which you are or have been a member. Cite their specific norms. What group functions do these norms serve? How are these group norms enforced?

3. Think of a successful sports or project team you have been on. What key characteristics made it so effective?

4. Think of a team you have been on that was not effective. How did you feel being a part of this team? What were the main problems? What did you do about the situation? Why?

5. How would you go about forming a new team to complete a class project worth one-third of your grade? What questions would you want members to address? What work functions would you want to be certain to cover? What balance of member preferences would you desire?

6. How would you practice continual process improvement in your class project team? What interventions and techniques would you apply and why? How would you go about gaining their acceptance and implementation by other team members?

7. What factors would you consider in forming a new automobile joint venture team made up of American, Japanese, and German managers? What processes would you recommend for building cohesion and avoiding conflicts?

EXPERIENTIAL EXERCISES

These exercises can be completed independently, or the second exercise can build on the first, depending on class time available. Either, or both exercises can also be followed up by the Your Turn inventory to generate feedback about the team process during the exercise(s).[88]

The Way Things Work in Most Organizations

Analyzing Work Group Structure (30 minutes). Analyze the first illustration as an analogy to a traditional task group.[89]

   a. Break into groups of four and determine metaphors for the following questions (15 minutes).
     1. Who is represented by the person at the front?
     2. Who are the people at the rear of the wagon?
     3. What is represented by the wagon?
     4. What is represented by the square wheels?
     5. What is represented by the rope at the front?
     6. What is represented by the pushers' hands?
     7. What do the round wheels represent?
   b. As a class, share your ideas about the meaning of the illustration and its implications for teamwork (15 minutes).
   c. *(Optional)* Complete the team self-evaluation in the following Your Turn exercise. Each member is to evaluate the team independently, using his or her own form (30 minutes).

Working Together As a Problem-Solving Team (45 minutes). In your groups of four, decide among yourselves which character in the second illustration below each of you will be to complete this exercise. If you have more than four people in your group, then more than one person will have to play each character (or, if you'd prefer, somebody can be the horse). If you have fewer than four people in your group, one of your group members will have to play the role of two of the characters.

   a. As a group, create your own story about what happened to lead up to the events in the second illustration, and decide how your character behaved in the time leading up to what you see occurring in this illustration. Be creative and have some fun in making up an interesting story about your team. Instead of referring to the characters as "the guy holding the rope" or "the one who's sweating," give each character a name. The names can be fictitious, or maybe you'd prefer to give them your names (15 minutes).
   b. Each team presents its story to the class and fields questions (20 minutes).
   c. The class as a whole compares stories and determines implications to real task team situations (10 minutes).
   d. *(Optional)* Complete the team self-evaluation in the following Your Turn exercise. Each member is to evaluate the team independently, using his or her own form (30 minutes).

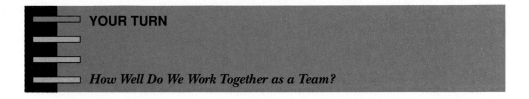

YOUR TURN

How Well Do We Work Together as a Team?

Instructions. Think of a team that you have recently been a member of (e.g., class project group, student body committee, volunteer group), and complete the following team self-evaluation by circling the number representing your evaluation for each question.

How Well Are We Working Together?

	Strongly Disagree	Disagree	Neither Agree nor Disagree	Agree	Strongly Agree
1. The team knows exactly what it has to get done.	1	2	3	4	5
2. Team members get a lot of encouragement for new ideas.	1	2	3	4	5
3. Team members freely express their real views.	1	2	3	4	5
4. Every team member has a clear idea of the team's goals.	1	2	3	4	5
5. Everyone is involved in the decisions we have to make.	1	2	3	4	5
6. We tell each other how we are feeling.	1	2	3	4	5
7. All team members respect each other.	1	2	3	4	5
8. The feelings among team members tend to pull us together.	1	2	3	4	5
9. Everyone's opinion gets listened to.	1	2	3	4	5
10. There is very little bickering among team members.	1	2	3	4	5

Scoring and Interpretation.
To find your total score, add the numbers in the circles. _____
To find your average score, divide the total score by 10. _____
If your average score is 4 or higher, teamwork is strong. If your average is between 3 and 4, teamwork is healthy, but there's room for improvement. If your average is 2 or lower, something is getting in the way of teamwork.

Whatever the score, discussing these issues together with an open mind is likely to improve teamwork. If possible, meet with your other team members. Compare evaluations and identify which of the 10 items your team agreed were strengths of the team (ratings of 4 or 5) and those that you agreed were weaknesses (ratings of 1 or 2). Discuss what the team needs to do to work more effectively together.

Source: Table from John H. Zenger, et al., *Leading Teams: Mastering the New Role* (Homewood, IL: Business One Irwin, 1994). Used with permission.

CASE

Self-Directed Work Teams at the San Diego Zoo[90]

San Diego Zoo has been undergoing a metamorphosis from a traditional functional hierarchy where 50 departments, like animal keeping, horticulture, and maintenance, worked in parallel without venturing out of their narrowly defined job responsibilities. In an effort to provide a healthier environment for plants and animals, better educate visitors about conservation issues, and enhance visitor experience by immersion into natural habitats, the zoo developed bioclimatic zones that grouped together plants and animals in cageless enclosures that visitors walk through. Examples of these "bioclimatic zones" are Tiger River, Gorilla Tropics, Kopjhe Corner, and Sun Bear Forest.

Zoo personnel quickly discovered that the separate departments did not work well for the coordinated operations required by the bioclimatic zones. The zoo's response was to develop separate self-managing teams of seven to ten members whose goal is to work together to successfully operate their bioclimatic zone. The teams are cross-trained and made up of specialists in horticulture, mammals, bird, fish, maintenance, and construction from the old departments. Because all now share responsibility for their zone, jobs blend together and team members all pitch in to do whatever kind of work is necessary regardless of their former department designation. Teams meet regularly to analyze the work required, set goals for themselves, manage their budgets, and monitor their progress.

In the beginning, teams only operated in the bioclimatic zones, while the rest of the staff continued to operate in the traditional way. As the zoo completes additional renovations, the remaining zones will also be staffed by self-managed teams of employees from the original 50 functional departments.

The challenge for the zoo's department managers is to let go of their traditional managerial practices and learn new ones that better facilitate the new team-zone-based organization. Managers now take on a coach/advisor role and use their technical expertise and big-picture perspective to support teams and act as liaisons for them.

So far the results have been exemplary. Zoo attendance is up 20 percent and workmen's compensation claims within the self-managed teams have been significantly reduced.

Questions for Managerial Action

1. How did the switch to bioclimatic zones challenge the specialists and managers of these separate departments?

2. What should the management of the San Diego Zoo have considered before deciding to change to a self-managed team type of organizational structure (e.g., managers' loss of power, compensation and reward systems)?

3. What could have gone wrong with this type of change? Why?

4. Would being on one of these zone teams increase or decrease your job satisfaction versus being a part of a traditional functional department? Why?

Chapter 11

Conflict Management and Intergroup Behavior

LEARNING OBJECTIVES

After studying this chapter, you should be able to:

- Define and describe the conflict process.
- Identify factors that contribute to conflict situations.
- Recognize symptoms of conflict.
- Differentiate between functional and dysfunctional conflict.
- Know when to use interpersonal conflict styles appropriately.
- Bargain and negotiate.
- Explain the factors that cause intergroup conflict.
- Suggest strategies for managing intergroup conflicts.

RESTRUCTURING PROMOTES QUALITY AT GM'S SATURN PLANT

When Saturn was first envisioned in 1985 by a seminal group of management and United Autoworkers Union (UAW) representatives at General Motors, the contract called for UAW representatives to be equal partners in making all start-up decisions for Saturn, including where to put the plant, how it would be set up, and even which advertising agency to retain. At first, both management and union officials found it difficult to jettison the familiar confrontational ways in favor of a spirit of cooperation. But that gradually changed as Saturn engineers traveled around the world looking for world-class approaches to the process of building a car, and UAW production workers went with them.

"There are still conflicts, but they are managed differently than before," says Mike Bennett, the local union president. "It's not adversarial. It's more advocacy in terms of finding a better solution or better options." An example of such conflict came last fall when GM's chairman, Robert Stempel, arrived for a visit and found a demonstration by union people wearing black-and-orange armbands to protest a plan to increase production—because they thought it would compromise quality. The workers thought that adding teams to the production line too quickly would hinder ongoing efforts to work out all the problems and improve the quality of the cars. The union protesters made—and won—their case. Instead of increasing production quickly to 700 cars a day to try to meets the strong demand in the marketplace, GM increased production slowly as kinks in the process were worked out. Today, the line produces 1,000 cars a day—90 percent of capacity.

Plant manager Robert Boruff recalls this incident with awe: "Think about an organization where you've got people coming from 146 GM locations, all of whom have been raised with a bias that the members are first and quality is second. They aren't protesting line speedup. They're not protesting health and safety issues. They just want to ensure the quality of the product. That's not a problem, that's a gift from God."

Source: Adapted from Beverly Geber, "Saturn's Grand Experiment," *Training* (June 1992), pp. 27–35. ▬▬▬

Every relationship contains conflict, disagreement, and opposed interests. Conflict has the potential to destroy relationships, put companies out of business, and ruin careers, but these outcomes are not inevitable. Negative consequences usually

━━━━━ **EXHIBIT 11–1**   *Stages of the Conflict Process*

Stage 1: Latent Conflict	Stage 2: Perceived Conflict	Stage 3: Felt Conflict	Stage 4: Manifest Conflict	Stage 5: Conflict Outcome
Antecedent conditions: Interdependence Different goals Ambiguity	Aware of a problem Incompatibility is perceived Tension begins	Emotionally involved Focus on differences Opposing interests	*Conflict behaviors:* Disagreeing Verbal attacks Ultimatums	*Functional:* Positive outcomes Creative problem solving Complacency avoidance *Dysfunctional:* Negative outcomes Aggression and hostility Inability to cooperate

arise from failure to handle conflict in constructive ways. As demonstrated by the union and management cooperation in the General Motor's Saturn opening vignette, constructive conflict management produces creative solutions to problems, higher-quality relationships, and constructive change. Unless relationships of any type are able to withstand the stress involved in inevitable conflicts, and manage them productively, they are not likely to endure.[1] This chapter provides a game plan for understanding and managing conflict productively in both personal and organizational situations.

WHAT IS CONFLICT?

conflict
A disagreement between two or more parties who perceive that they have incompatible concerns.

Conflict is a disagreement between two or more parties—for example, individuals, groups, departments, organizations, countries—who perceive that they have incompatible concerns. Conflicts exist whenever an action by one party is perceived as preventing or interfering with the goals, needs, or actions of another party. Conflicts can arise over a multiple of organizational experiences, such as incompatible goals, differences in the interpretation of facts, negative feelings, differences of values and philosophies, or disputes over shared resources.[2]

The Conflict Process

Although a conflict does not exist until one party perceives that another party may negatively affect something that the first party cares about,[3] the development of antecedent conditions marks the start of the process. Conflict usually proceeds through the five stages diagrammed in Exhibit 11–1.[4]

Stage 1: Latent Conflict.   When two or more parties need each other to achieve desired objectives, there is potential for conflict. Other antecedents of conflict, such as interdependence, different goals, and ambiguity of responsibility, are described in the next section. They don't automatically create conflicts, but when they exist, they make it possible. Latent conflict often arises when a change occurs. Conflict might be caused by a budget cutback, a change in organizational direction, a change in a personal goal, the assignment of a new project to an already overloaded work force, or an expected occurrence (such as a salary increase) that doesn't happen.

Stage 2: Perceived Conflict.   This is the point at which members become aware of a problem. Incompatibility of needs is perceived and tension begins as the parties begin to worry about what will happen. At this point, however, no one feels that anything that they care about is actually being overtly threatened.

Stage 3: Felt Conflict. Now the parties become emotionally involved and begin to focus on differences of opinion and opposing interests, sharpening perceived conflict. Internal tensions and frustrations begin to crystallize around specific, defined issues, and people begin to build an emotional commitment to their particular position. What emotions are felt is important because negative ones produce low trust and negative perceptions of the other party's position, which can result in destructive win–lose tactics.[5] More positive feelings, on the other hand, can contribute to a more balanced view of the situation and more collaborative endeavors.[6] In either case, the result is a defining of what the conflict is actually about that will determine the alternatives available for later resolution.

Stage 4: Manifest Conflict. The obvious display of conflict occurs when the opposing parties plan and follow through with acts to achieve their own objectives and frustrate the other. Actions can range from minor disagreeing, questioning, and challenging at one end of the conflict-intensity continuum, to verbal attacks, threats, ultimatums, physical attacks, and even efforts to destroy the other party at the other end.[7]

Stage 5: Conflict Outcome. The results of the interactions of the conflicting parties in the manifest conflict stage result in outcomes that can be functional or dysfunctional for one or both parties. As conflict proceeds through the stages, functional resolution becomes more difficult. The parties become more locked into their positions and more convinced that the conflict is a win or lose situation. It is usually easier to achieve positive collaboration and win–win outcomes when the conflict is recognized early before frustration and other negative sentiments set in.

Functional versus Dysfunctional Conflict

The traditional view of conflict assumed that it was undesirable and led to negative outcomes like aggression, violence, and hostility. This *dysfunctional view* of conflict implied that managers should determine the causes of conflict and eliminate them, and make sure that future conflicts were prevented.

This was the view of the board of directors of Sunbeam-Oster, which fired its CEO, Paul Kazarian, in 1993, three years after he had been hired to save the company from bankruptcy. Most would think that Kazarian took a high risk and failed, but that was not the case. In fact, he saved the company, turning its multimillion-dollar losses into multimillion-dollar profits in one year. His success continued until even the day before he was fired, when quarterly profits were reported to have increased 40 percent. Mr. Kazarian's problem was that he created dysfunctional conflicts for other influential people in the company. Although Kazarian rationalized his approach by saying "You don't change a company in bankruptcy without making a few waves," others viewed him as creating more work for people that were already working beyond capacity, pitting people against each other, and intimidating managers, employees, and even outside suppliers and customers.[8]

If Kazarian was right however, as his economic results verified, conflict can be viewed as *functional* because of its potential to stimulate creative resolution of problems and corrective actions and to keep people and organizations from slipping into complacency. Perhaps it shouldn't matter if individuals don't like conflict. If it increases performance and is beneficial to the group or organization as a whole, it is functional.

━━━━━ **EXHIBIT 11–2**

Factors Causing Conflict

Goal Incompatibility

- Mutually exclusive goals
- Lack of resources
- Different time orientations

Structural Design

- Interdependence
- Lack of substitutability
- Power differentials

Different Role Expectations

- Role ambiguity
- Role conflict
- Uncertainty reduction

Degenerative Climate

- "Win–lose" attitudes
- People with different values and expectations
- Merged cultural differences

Personal Differences

- Different values
- Different preferred way of behaving
- Different views of the world

This outcome of the conflict is the criterion for determining if it is functional or dysfunctional, that is, whether it has positive or negative outcomes for the decision-making group (e.g., department, organization, stockholders). Perhaps the most appropriate attitude toward conflict is that it is inevitable and has the potential to be dysfunctional, but if managed constructively, conflict can be functional and enhance performance.

WHY DOES CONFLICT OCCUR?

When conditions exist that create opportunities for conflict to arise, the latent stage of conflict is present. When these conditions actually do create conflict, they become causes. The primary causes of conflict in organizations can be condensed into the five general categories summarized in Exhibit 11–2: goal incompatibility, structural design, role expectations, degenerative climate, and personal differences.

Goal Incompatibility

An ideal situation exists when two parties perceive their goals as mutually enhancing and view each other's behaviors as contributing to the achievement of both sets of goals. In such a case, a high degree of cooperation is likely to result. Design research and marketing departments, for example, will probably enjoy a cooperative relationship because a new line developed by the former will provide the latter with the products it needs to meet its increased sales objectives. Several things can get in the way, however.

Mutually Exclusive Goals.   When one party's goal achievement is perceived as threatening to another's, the resulting conflict is likely to engender win–lose competition. For example, both design research and marketing departments may interrelate poorly with a production department that has a goal of eliminating new and low-volume production runs. Another classic case of goal conflict often exists between sales departments who want increased volume and market share versus credit departments who want to limit sales to customers with the ability to pay.

Robert Harvey (in red), manager of the Office of Capital Projects at the Port Authority of New York and New Jersey, and his staff planned and organized the rehabilitation of New York's World Trade Center after the bombing in February 1993. Harvey used project-management and risk-analysis computer software to analyze and streamline the operations of builders, engineers, support personnel, and law enforcement agents. (Photo: © Bill Swersey/Gamma-Liaison.)

Insufficient Shared Resources.   Most organizations operate with a finite amount of money, personnel, and equipment. As parties compete for their share of the organizational pie, conflict often results. If one party receives more power, higher status, better work assignments, or more material resources, the remaining parties often get less. Dysfunctional conflict results from the win/lose competition that limited resources foster.[9] An interesting example of top management being compensated extremely well at the expense of the workers who actually made the profits available appears in the Eye on Ethics box.

Different Time Orientations.   Another potential source of conflict is the different timespans needed by parties to achieve their goals. Some parties have relatively short time orientations. Production crews, for example, may require hourly feedback about results. Marketing departments often focus on weekly sales volume, while research and finance departments may have to look several years ahead when developing new products or forecasting interest rates and other economic trends.

When parties suboptimize and focus only on accomplishing their own goals, their different time orientations can cause considerable conflict. The marketing department's goal of introducing new products immediately, for example, can conflict with the research department's need for at least six months to design and develop them and production's minimum two-month manufacturing period.

Structural Design

interdependence
The degree to which interactions between parties must be coordinated in order for them to perform adequately.

Differences in goals, resource demands, and time orientations are related to **interdependence,** or the degree to which interactions between parties must be coordinated in order for them to perform adequately. How relationships between parties are structured by the organization determines how they interact to facilitate or hinder each other in accomplishing goals.

Eye on **E**thics

General Dynamics Gives Execs Big-Bucks Bonuses but Workers Get Pink Slips

In 1991, General Dynamics shareholders approved a gainsharing compensation plan for the company's top 25 executives that provided them with bonuses of over $18 million, or an average of $700,000 apiece in the first six months of the plan's operation. The rank-and-file workers at General Dynamics questioned whether the executives were worth that much money. This episode occurred at a time when governmental and academic critics were questioning whether executive performance warranted such lofty rewards relative to those received by rank-and-file workers.

There was also considerable suspicion about the rapid rise in stock prices to which the executive gainsharing plan was indexed. Stock prices rose quickly after the new gainsharing plan was instituted because

management cost cutting increased the company's cash position by around $600 million, much of which was returned to stockholders. Employees, unfortunately, did not benefit as had the executives and stockholders— especially the 12,000 employees that management decided to lay off to achieve the cost savings.

From the employees' perspective, management awarded itself bonuses for achieving stock-price increases that it brought about by letting go 13 percent of the work force. It just didn't make sense for the 25 top management people to receive windfall profits at the expense of the people who had worked in the trenches for many years.

Source: J. E. Ellis, "Layoffs on the Line, Bonuses in the Executive Suite," *Business Week* (October 21, 1991), p. 34.

Interdependence.   The relationships between parties can be visualized on a continuum, ranging from complete dependence to complete independence. When one party has the power to determine the performance outcomes and goal achievements of another, the second party is relatively dependent on the first. Two parties are independent only when their respective activities have no impact whatsoever on each other.

Most relationships fall somewhere between complete dependence and independence and are characterized by the need to coordinate certain activities for successful task performance. The more two parties share responsibilities and need to coordinate schedules and to cooperate in decision making, the more interdependent they are. Exhibit 11–3 illustrates three distinct types of interdependent relationships: pooled, sequential, and reciprocal.[10]

pooled interdependence
Exists when two parties are independent of each other for their own performance outcomes, but each makes a contribution to the overall organization that affects the well-being of both parties.

Pooled interdependence exists when two parties are independent of each other for their own performance outcomes, but each makes a discrete contribution to the overall organization that affects the well-being of all parties. At Marshall Industries, the electronic components processing company in our video, for example, the finance department and the shipping department handle completely separate functions. They rarely have cause to interact directly with each other, so no direct conflict is likely to occur. Both departments' performances, however, independently contribute to the overall profitability of the company, which affects profit sharing for employees in all departments.

sequential interdependence
Occurs when the output of one party provides necessary inputs for another to accomplish its goals.

Sequential interdependence occurs when the output of one party provides necessary inputs for another to accomplish its goals. An example of this is when the "pickers" at Marshall Industries pull the specified electronic components out of

━━━ **EXHIBIT 11–3**

Types of Interdependence

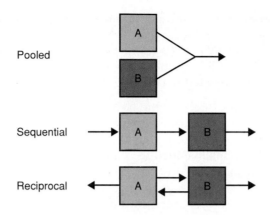

the warehouse that are needed for the "value added" department to use in assembling packages for customers. The receiving groups in these situations are dependent on the providing groups for the timing and quality of goods or services needed to do their jobs. This one-way flow of activity can cause considerable anxiety for receiving parties because their goal attainment is dependent on inputs from the supplying party, and they have no real leverage to ensure that their needs are met.

reciprocal interdependence
Exist if the outputs of two parties are inputs for each other.

Reciprocal interdependence exists if the outputs of two parties are inputs for each other. In such symbiotic relationships, each party supplies necessary inputs to the other. The Marshall Industries salespeople, for example, relay information to the value-added department so that they can create packages of components that meet customer requirements. If the value-added packages do not satisfy customer demands, salespeople will have a more difficult time securing orders in the future. The potential for conflict between reciprocating groups is great because of the high need for coordination. Success requires effective communication and joint decision making.

Awareness of the nature of interdependence is necessary to manage potential conflict and ensure optimal performance of interacting parties at any level: interpersonal, group, intergroup, and multiorganizational. The complexity of relationships depends on the type of interdependence experienced by two groups. Pooled interdependence is the least complex relationship, while reciprocally interdependent interactions require the most coordination and collaboration.

When groups are dependent on one another for the completion of their tasks, the potential for conflict is high. This is especially true when effective task performance depends on reciprocal interaction. Imagine the potential for disaster if control tower personnel were to experience conflict with flight crew members on aircraft. The potential for conflict also exists among sequentially dependent subgroups. An assembly-line delay in the production of furniture, for example, can cost workers in the finishing department the opportunity to earn their incentive bonus.

Lack of Substitutability. The more alternative sources of needed resources and services available to a party, the greater its degree of substitutability. Many organizations require that parties use the services of certain other parties within the organization in order to ensure full utilization of resources. This policy creates a sequential dependency relationship because the supplying party has power over the receiving party. The lack of available alternatives is often perceived as a conflict by the dependent party because differences in goals and time orientations could be dysfunctional for them. Intergroup conflict could occur, for example, when a marketing department wants to introduce a wide variety of new products but is required to work only with the company's own small design research department, which is already stretched to capacity.

Power Differentials. Each of the factors examined so far has the potential to create differences in influence and dependence between parties, which in turn contribute to differences in power. In December 1995, 8,700 United Auto Workers at Caterpillar, Inc., finally ended a 17-month strike with nothing gained and about $32,000 lost in wages per worker because, as one striker said, "The company's in complete control. We have to accept defeat."[11]

If party A makes certain decisions that impact on party B's ability to accomplish its goals, party A has power over party B. The more dependent party C is on receiving vital inputs from party D, the more power supplier party D has over receiver party C. The more important party A's function in an interdependent situation, the more all other parties need it, and the more influence party A will command. Since most groups, like most individuals, do not like to be completely dependent on someone else, power differences can cause intergroup conflict, especially when areas critical to goal achievement or satisfaction are involved.

Different Role Expectations[12]

role
A set of related tasks and behaviors that an individual or group is expected to perform.

A **role** is a set of related tasks and behaviors that an individual or group is expected to carry out. A **role set** is all the people who interact with a person or group in a specific role and have expectations about appropriate behavior. A role set for a manager would include his or her supervisor and subordinates plus members of other groups who attempt to influence the manager's behavior. Since all members of a role set depend on the incumbent's performance in some manner, they actively attempt to bring about behavior consistent with their needs. Identifying a role set helps explain who influences a particular person or group to behave in certain ways.

role set
All the people who interact with a person or group in a specific role and have expectations about appropriate behavior.

Role Ambiguity. Role sets need to make clear what they expect from parties who fulfill specified roles. When members of a role set fail to transmit enough information about their expectations, incumbents experience **role ambiguity.** It is difficult to behave acceptably when it is not clear what others expect.

role ambiguity
Exists when role sets do not make clear their expectations of role holders.

Role ambiguity has several causes. Sometimes those in the role set aren't clear themselves about what should be required, so they don't say anything or the expectations that are communicated are vague. A role holder may, for example, receive feedback to be a "better" group member but fail to glean any specifics as to what "better" actually means. "Better" may apply to standards of productivity, but it could just as easily apply to interpersonal relationships within the group. The resulting uncertainty can have paralyzing effects. Another source of confusion is contradictions between communicated expectations and reactions after complying. Suppose a group member is told that teamwork is what counts but later is denied a salary increase on the grounds that he or she didn't exhibit "outstanding individual achievements" relative to others.

role conflict
Exists when the behavioral expectations of the role holder and/or those of others in the role set do not agree.

Role Conflict. When a party's own expectations and those of other role set members differ, **role conflict** occurs. Japanese managers who join U.S. firms, for example, often face social ostracism from the close-knit community of Japanese expatriates when they adopt behaviors and customs expected in their American organizations that are contrary to Japanese customs.[13] There are four types of role conflict.[14]

Intrasender Conflict.   When prescriptions and proscriptions that come from a single member of the role set are inconsistent or conflicting, intrasender role conflict occurs. If, for example, a team leader is asked by the company's president to add the president's cousin to the staff, but at the same time to follow all equal opportunity guidelines, intrasender conflict may result. The team leader will be legitimately confused about the president's motives, the firm's commitment to equal opportunity, and how he or she should act.

Intersender Conflict.   When pressures from one member of a party's role set conflict with those from one or more others in the same role set, intersender conflict results. A classic example occurs when a group member is promoted to a formal leadership position and finds it impossible to satisfy all the old peers' expectations as well as the new managerial mandates. A first-line supervisor supervising former peer-group members will surely receive pressures from "old buddies" for favors that conflict with the goals of upper-level management.

Interrole Conflict.   When different roles held by the same party require mutually exclusive behaviors, interrole conflict exists. For example, to meet an impending deadline, a project team's boss may request that everyone work late on a night when a team member has an important social engagement with his or her spouse (a conflict between work and personal roles).

Person-Role Conflict.   When your role requires you to do something you don't want to do or feel you shouldn't do, person-role conflict exists. Conflict between a person's needs and values and the demands of a role set is exemplified when an individual is asked by other group members to restrict production. If doing so is contrary to the group member's personal code of ethics, person-role conflict will result.

role overload
Occurs when role expectations exceed a party's ability to respond effectively.

Role Overload.   **Role overload** occurs when role expectations exceed a party's ability to respond effectively. This often occurs when multiple role senders have legitimate expectations for a person's behavior that are all impossible to fulfill within a given time limit. Mid-December, for example, is a time of role overload for many college students, especially those working their way through school. They must prepare for final examinations and typically write term papers for four or five courses simultaneously. It is also the height of the holiday shopping season, so those working in retail stores or associated businesses must cope with their employers' demands to work longer hours. Others may feel the self-imposed pressure to work more hours to meet their own increased financial needs. In addition, relatives and friends expect that students will be available for holiday activities. Unfortunately, these conflicting expectations cause frustration and stress for students that offset the prevailing holiday cheer.

Managing Role Problems.   Anyone can experience any or all of these role conflicts. Different types of role problems are more likely to occur at different levels of an organization, however. At lower levels of the organization, role conflict is more prevalent. The first-line supervisor, for example, has to deal with conflicting expectations from subordinates, peers, union representatives, and upper management.

At higher levels, role ambiguity is more likely to be a problem. A new company president, for instance, must somehow cope with the task of "making the company more profitable" without really knowing what the relevant factors are or how to restructure them. Regardless of their specific source, role difficulties frequently cause dysfunctional conflict.[15]

The pressures and negative consequences of role conflicts can be reduced in several ways. Both role ambiguity and conflict can be reduced by identifying who legitimate role-set members are, reducing interdependencies, and establishing more explicit role expectations. The role difficulties of a working single parent cannot be reduced appreciably, for example, but the roles of many organization members can be streamlined by clarifying role expectations from above and delegating specific tasks downward. A legal secretary who works for three attorneys, one senior and two junior associates, can ask for clear guidelines as to how to prioritize her tasks.

Uncertainty Reduction.   There is a paradox to what we have just recommended: Some role clarification can actually create dysfunctional conflicts. Uncertainty is the difference between what is actually known and what needs to be known in order to make correct decisions and perform adequately. Eliminating uncertainty requires establishing task clarity; making sure that the responsibilities of parties are clearly stated and understood. It is fairly easy to eliminate task uncertainty for groups in routine jobs such as manufacturing by establishing policies, standard operating procedures, and rules. Groups responsible for nonroutine tasks, such as developing new products or marketing strategies, however, experience much higher levels of uncertainty and require customized responses.

Some groups are assigned the responsibility of reducing uncertainty for other groups by making decisions or creating rules and procedures that establish operating standards for them. A good example is when an accounting department provides regulations that control how sales representatives must handle expense accounts. Intergroup conflict often results from power differences created when the group assigned to reduce uncertainty imposes rules or procedures perceived to interfere with another group's goal accomplishment.

Degenerative Climate

degenerative interaction climate
An organizational climate that encourages dysfunctional conflict.

As discussed in Chapter 4, the organization's culture influences the general nature of employee relationships. In Chapter 9, we demonstrated how some cultures encourage a **degenerative interaction climate** where *"win–lose" attitudes* set the stage for dysfunctional conflict relationships to flourish. Degenerative climates are easy to establish and difficult to overcome. All it would take to destroy a cooperative overall organizational climate, for example, would be an accounting department that flaunts its power by reporting all expense-account errors to higher management and disclosing publicly the names of those "caught" violating the established procedures.

Another way that climate can create dysfunctional conflict is in cases where *people with different values and expectations* established from experiences in previous organizational cultures must interact together. Many production workers, for example, have little formal education and are concerned with the pragmatic aspects of specific tasks in highly structured environments. Scientists in research

━━━━━ **EXHIBIT 11–4** *An Overview of Conflict Management*

Sources of Conflict	Stages of the Conflict Process	Consequences	Methods of Managing Conflict	Performance Outcome
Mutually exclusive goals Lack of resources Different time orientations Interdependence Lack of substitutability Power differentials Role ambiguity Role conflict Uncertainty reduction Degenerative climate Personal differences Lack of cooperation	Latent Perceived Felt Manifest	*Functional* Problem awareness Increased group cohesion Motivation to improve Creative change *Dysfunctional* Suboptimization Negative feelings Distorted perceptions Negative stereotypes Decreased communication	*Interpersonal* Competing Accommodating Avoiding Collaborating Compromising *Intergroup* Superordinate goals Increase communication Problem solving Negotiation Expansion of resources Third-party judgment Changing structure Smoothing Avoidance	*Increased* *Decreased*

and development groups, on the other hand, may have many years of formal education and spend most of their relatively unstructured work hours engaged in esoteric, future-oriented activities. These differences may make it virtually impossible for such groups to understand one another's values, expectations, and priorities.

Another example of culture clash occurred when General Electric acquired Kidder, Peabody & Company. There were big *merged cultural differences* between GE's organization men, with their generous pension plans, and the entrepreneurial prima donnas of Kidder, who chafed at any management controls and made so much money they didn't need a pension plan. The differences in previous cultures caused the Kidder and GE Capital groups to dislike each other intensely. The Kidder group referred to the GE people as "credit clerks," and the GE Capital group thought the Kidder people were overpaid, arrogant, and undertalented. Consequently, just about everything that could go wrong did, including destructive competition and loss of profitable business.[16]

Personal Differences

As we discussed in Chapter 9 on interpersonal relations, there are some people you have an instant affinity to while others you immediately dislike. There is a high potential for conflict between people with *different values, different preferred ways of behaving,* and *different views of the world.*

Exhibit 11–4 presents a model that summarizes the sources of conflict, how it progresses, its positive and negative consequences, and ways of managing it (interventions for reducing, preventing, or handling it productively). Since conflict can often be functional for organizations, management should first try to understand why it exists by examining its sources and then look at its impact on the parties involved and the organization. After the sources and consequences of the conflict are well understood, management is in a position to intervene to manage it productively.

WHAT ARE THE CONSEQUENCES OF CONFLICT?

As mentioned earlier, some conflict is inevitable in any organization where individuals and groups must interact to produce complex outputs. Although conflict can often be destructive, at other times it may stimulate creativity, encourage flexibility, and even be satisfying because it provides an interesting environment to work in.[17] The key is to determine whether the conflict is functional or dysfunctional, and then to manage it appropriately.

Functional Conflict

functional conflict
Conflict between groups that stimulates innovations and production.

If you have grown up in the United States, you are well aware of the value of the kind of competition that stimulates individuals and groups to greater efforts that yield superior results. Spectators pay millions of dollars annually to share the excitement of skilled athletic competitive conflict. In the business world, competition inspires the creation of new products and establishes affordable pricing structures. International competition stimulates nations to advance their technology and develop their resource bases. These examples of **functional conflict** are between competing groups that are not part of the same formal organizational structure. These competing groups do not have to work together to solve common problems or achieve common goals. The reward system provides for one winner and one loser. But in situations where the competing groups are part of the same organizational structure and must work together to achieve organizational goals, the objective is a win–win, as opposed to a win–lose, outcome.

conflict-positive organization
An organization in which participants perceive conflict as an opportunity for personal and organizational growth.

   Conflict is inevitable even between departments that are supposed to cooperate to accomplish organizational goals. To manage it so that motivation increases and the quality of work improves, managers need to make sure that departments have cooperative goals and that procedures, attitudes, and skills are in place to productively deal with conflict. A number of benefits can result in a **conflict-positive organization** in which participants perceive conflict as an exciting opportunity for personal and organizational growth:[18]

- Discussing conflict openly can make organization members more aware and better able to cope with problems.
- Attention is drawn to issues that may interfere with productivity, and organizational practices may be challenged and improved as a result.
- Successfully resolved conflict can strengthen relationships because organizational members understand each other better, release built-up tensions, and learn that relationships are strong enough to work through problems productively.
- Personal development occurs as participants learn about their own conflict styles and increase their competencies in managing interpersonal and interdepartmental problems.
- As a break from standard operating procedures, conflict can be stimulating and fun as participants become involved in solving interesting interdependent problems.

Functional Change within Groups.   One of the most important places to observe these positive results are within a group experiencing conflict with another group. Four changes occur in groups experiencing intergroup conflict: increased cohesion, increased loyalty, increased emphasis on task accomplishment, and acceptance of autocratic leadership.[19]

Increased Cohesiveness.   When groups are threatened by other competing groups, members put aside their interpersonal differences and band together against the common enemy, and group membership becomes more attractive. This phenomenon is often seen when nations that traditionally compete economically and politically band together against a common aggressor in wartime. Examples are the Arab nations' cooperation against the common Israeli threat and the European allies' coming together during the world wars.

Increased Loyalty.   Group goals take precedence over individual gain or satisfaction as members sacrifice for the common good. Members rigidly adhere to established rules and strictly enforce new ones to eliminate potential conflicts among members that might detract from task accomplishment.

Acceptance of Autocratic Leadership.   In the face of a crisis, group members are more willing to accept the autocratic decisions of a central leader because they are more timely than democratic methods and other members are free to consolidate energy for winning the conflict.

Emphasis on Task Accomplishment.   Personal goals and satisfaction are put aside so that all energy can be concentrated on meeting the challenge put forth by the competing groups. There is a sense of urgency, with no time for goofing off or performing unrelated activities.

Research Findings Confirming the Functionality of Intragroup Conflict.   As we saw in Chapter 10, conflict can improve the quality of decision making by eliminating groupthink and allowing all points of view to be considered.[20] Janis's analysis of major decisions made by four American presidents demonstrated that constructive conflict resulted in high-quality decisions, whereas decisions where all advisors easily conformed to majority opinion were often disaster.[21] Research scientists have also been found to be most productive when intellectual conflict exists.[22]

Conflict has been demonstrated to be positively related to productivity in well-established, permanent groups as well. One study found that high-conflict groups outperformed low-conflict groups by 73 percent.[23] As described in Chapter 10, culturally diverse groups that experience more conflict about different values, perspectives, and approaches generally are more creative and produce higher-quality decisions than do homogeneous groups.[24]

Functional Changes between Groups.   Even dysfunctional intergroup conflict can produce positive consequences if participants learn from the experience and manage conflicts better in the future. Research has demonstrated that conflict can actually promote coordination between departments and contribute to task accomplishment, efficient use of resources, and customer service if the interacting departments have cooperative, but not competitive, goals.[25] Potential positive consequences for relations between groups include:[26]

- Increased problem awareness.
- Decreased tensions after disagreements have been resolved.
- More appropriate readjustments of tasks and resources.
- Establishment of mechanisms for obtaining feedback about intergroup problems.
- Clarification of priorities and tasks.

A joint Zenith–AT&T research team has worked together since 1989 to develop a digital high-definition television (HDTV) system. They wanted the Federal Communications Commission to select theirs for setting the technical standards that all TV manufacturers and broadcasters must meet. At the same time the team was competing against two other teams also trying to create a standard-setting system. As the contest neared completion, the teams decided to form one grand alliance to develop a single HDTV system. To work successfully together the groups had to subordinate their individual goals and work cooperatively to get the combined system operating. (Photo: Zenith Electronics Corporation.)

Dysfunctional Conflict

dysfunctional conflict
Conflict between groups in the same organization that hinders the achievement of group and organizational goals.

Dysfunctional conflict occurs when the interaction between two or more parties hinders the achievement of individual, group, or organizational goals.[27] Conflict with lose–lose outcomes such as the labor–management dispute at Eastern Airlines in 1989, which contributed to the company's bankruptcy, can be catastrophic.

Dysfunctional Changes between Groups.   Four common intergroup consequences of conflict are hostility, distorted perceptions, negative stereotyping, and decreased communication. All serve to exacerbate negative outcomes in intergroup conflict.[28]

Hostility.   Hostility between groups (a "we–they" attitude) often develops, causing each group to see itself as virtuous and the other groups as incompetent or unprincipled enemies. The intense dislike that develops makes reconciliation more difficult.

Distorted Perceptions.   Groups in conflict often develop distorted perceptions emphasizing the negative and ignoring the positive traits of competing groups. At the same time, members often develop higher opinions of their own group.

Negative Stereotypes.   The resulting negative stereotypes of other groups contribute to decreased and distorted communication, suboptimization, and lack of coordination. Members perceive fewer differences within their own group and greater differences between their group and the "enemy" than really exist, creating even greater conflict between groups and further strengthening cohesiveness within each group.

━━━━━ **EXHIBIT 11–5**

Interpersonal Conflict-Management Styles

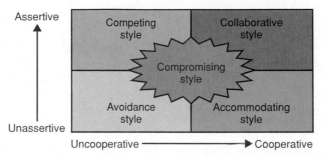

Source: Adapted from Thomas I. Ruble and Kenneth W. Thomas, "Support for a Two-Dimensional Model of Conflict Behavior," *Organizational Behavior and Human Performance* 16 (1976), p. 145.

Decreased Communication.   These negative attitudes and stereotypes usually cause communication breakdowns between conflicting groups. Although groups often increase surveillance to detect the plans and weaknesses of competing groups, no real sharing of information takes place, and this void is filled by the distorted perceptions and negative stereotypes already mentioned. Decreased communication is especially dysfunctional where sequential or reciprocal interdependence exists between groups.

Dysfunctional Changes within Groups.   Many of the same problems that two individuals experiencing conflict must contend with manifest themselves within groups—lack of trust, decreased cooperation, decreased communication, and so on. Also, in a group, as member satisfaction decreases, so does cohesion and productivity, which can eventually threaten the very survival of a group.[29]

HOW CAN CONFLICT BE MANAGED?

The first part of this chapter has shown how conflict can have negative and/or positive consequences for individuals, groups, and organizations. The key variable that determines its outcome is how the conflict is managed. The next section describes approaches that individuals take to interpersonal conflicts. Then organizational methods of handling intergroup conflicts will be discussed.

Interpersonal Conflict-Management Styles

Individuals usually have two main concerns when engaged in an interpersonal conflict: getting what they want for themselves, and the kind of relationship they want to maintain with the other party. When people are primarily concerned for themselves, they are assertive in trying to satisfy their own needs. When they care about the other person and want to maintain a positive relationship, people are cooperative and concerned about making sure the other's needs are satisfied. The different degrees of emphasis that people place on these two basic concerns can be expanded into five specific **conflict management styles:** competing, accommodating, avoiding, collaborating, and compromising[30] These are diagrammed in Exhibit 11–5.[31]

conflict-management styles
The different combinations of assertiveness and cooperation that people emphasize when in a conflict situation.

Competing.   Competing is assertive and uncooperative behavior, embodied in individuals' pursuit of their own concerns at others' expense. Competing behavior is often used by power-oriented people who will use every technique available to win their point or defend their position.

Competing can be beneficial when quick, decisive action is vital, as in emergencies. It is also useful when unpopular actions, such as discipline or cost cutting, must be implemented. Finally, competing is sometimes necessary to protect against people who take advantage of noncompetitive behavior. If you are too competitive, however, you may find yourself surrounded by yes-men who have learned that it is unwise to disagree with you, which cuts you off from sources of important information.

Accommodating.   Accommodating is the opposite of competing. It consists of unassertive and cooperative behavior. The accommodating individual frequently neglects his or her own concerns to satisfy the needs of others in order to maintain a positive relationship.

Accommodating is an appropriate strategy when the issue at stake is much more important to the other person. Satisfying another's needs as a goodwill gesture will help maintain a cooperative relationship, building up social credits for use in later conflicts. Accommodating is also appropriate when a manager wishes to develop subordinates by allowing them to experiment and learn from their own mistakes. Too much accommodation, however, can deprive others of your personal contributions and viewpoint.

Avoiding.   Avoiding is unassertive and uncooperative behavior. Individuals with this conflict management style pursue neither their own concerns nor those of others. To avoid conflict altogether, a person might diplomatically sidestep an issue, postpone it, or withdraw from the threatening situation.

Avoiding is appropriate when the issue involved is relatively unimportant to you. Also, if you have little power or are in a situation that is very difficult to change, avoiding may be the best choice. Similarly, avoidance may be wise if the potential damage from confronting a conflict outweighs its benefits or you need to let people cool off a little in order to bring tensions back down to a reasonable level. On the other hand, you should not let important decisions be made by default or spend a lot of energy avoiding issues that eventually must be confronted.

Collaborating.   Collaborating is the opposite of avoiding; it consists of both assertive and cooperative behavior. It involves working with the other person to find a solution that fully satisfies both parties. This is a joint problem-solving mode involving communication and creativity on the part of each party to find a mutually beneficial solution.

Collaborating is a necessity when the concerns of both parties are too important to be compromised. Collaborating merges the insights of people with different perspectives. It allows you to test your assumptions and understand others', to gain commitment by incorporating others' concerns, and to work through hard feelings. Not all conflict situations, however, deserve this amount of time and energy. Trivial problems often do not require optimal solutions, and not all personal differences need to be worked through. It also does little good to behave in a collaborative manner if others will not.

Compromising.   Compromising falls somewhere between assertive and cooperative behaviors. The objective is to find a mutually acceptable middle ground that partially satisfies both parties. This expedient conflict management style splits the difference and makes concessions.

A compromise is appropriate when goals are moderately important but not worth the effort of collaboration or the possible disruption of competition. If a manager is dealing with an opponent of equal power who is strongly committed to a mutually exclusive goal, compromise may be the best hope for leaving both of them in relatively satisfactory positions. Compromise is also wise when a temporary settlement needs to be achieved quickly. It can be a useful safety valve for gracefully getting out of mutually destructive situations. On the other hand, too much compromising might cause you to lose sight of more important principles, values, and long-term objectives. Too much compromise can also create a cynical climate of gamesmanship.

None of these conflict management approaches is better or worse than any other per se. Their effectiveness depends on how appropriate they are for any particular situation. Most individuals, however, have a "dominant" style that they most often use because it has been successful in the past and they are comfortable with the required behaviors. If their dominant style is not appropriate or does not work, people revert to "backup" styles in attempting to resolve conflicts. To determine your dominant and backup style hierarchy, complete the following Your Turn exercise.

If it is important to you to resolve a conflict in a way that enhances the relationship involved, collaboration or compromise are far more effective than avoidance or competitive strategies. As described in the earlier chapters on communications and interpersonal relations, effective communications and constructive feedback are necessary to support more collaborative efforts and to work through confrontations that may develop.[32] It is also necessary to be flexible and be able to bargain with the other party.

Bargaining. Bargaining, or negotiating, is the practical application of collaborating and compromising approaches to conflict management. Collaboration results in *integrative bargaining*, where the parties assume that it is possible to create a win–win solution. If successful, the result is satisfaction and positive long-term relationships. Compromise, on the other hand, results in *distributive bargaining*, where zero-sum conditions exist: There is a fixed pie, and what one party gains is at the other party's expense—for example, a used car negotiation. Tips for successful bargaining are summarized in Exhibit 11–6.

Approaches to Managing Intergroup Conflict

Groups that are able to cooperate with other groups are usually more productive than those that are not.[33] But there are many areas of potential conflict. Conflict erupted at Apple Computer in the early 1980s, for example, even though groups were in independent divisions. The newly created Macintosh division was assigned the task of developing a creative breakthrough product as quickly as possible and was receiving a disproportionate share of the company's publicity and resources. At least this was how the Apple II division, which was bringing in most of the company's profits, saw it. This situation lead to jealousy, resentment, and name calling between the two divisions.

Since dysfunctional intergroup conflict can have destructive organizational consequences, it is important to detect, reduce, and act to prevent its recurrence. On the other hand, even dysfunctional conflict is useful in that it signals needed

Consider conflict situations in which your wishes differed from those of another person or group. Indicate how often you applied each of the following tactics.

	Rarely				Always
1. I argue to prove my position.	1	2	3	4	5
2. I negotiate for a compromise.	1	2	3	4	5
3. I try to meet others' expectations.	1	2	3	4	5
4. I try to find a mutually acceptable solution.	1	2	3	4	5
5. I firmly pursue my position.	1	2	3	4	5
6. I keep conflicts to myself to avoid hassles.	1	2	3	4	5
7. I hold on to my solution no matter what.	1	2	3	4	5
8. I compromise through give-and-take tactics.	1	2	3	4	5
9. I share information to reach a joint decision.	1	2	3	4	5
10. I keep my differences to myself.	1	2	3	4	5
11. I accommodate the wishes of others.	1	2	3	4	5
12. I try for the best solution for everyone.	1	2	3	4	5
13. I propose middle-ground agreements.	1	2	3	4	5
14. I go along with the suggestions of others.	1	2	3	4	5
15. I avoid hard feelings by not sharing my disagreements.	1	2	3	4	5

Scoring: To determine your primary conflict-handling style, transfer the number you assigned to each statement on the questionnaire to the scoring key below, and then add the columns. Your conflict-handling style is the category with the highest total. See Exhibit 11–5, and the previous discussion for a complete description of these styles.

Competing	Accommodating	Avoiding	Collaborating	Compromising
1. _____	3. _____	6. _____	4. _____	2. _____
5. _____	11. _____	10. _____	9. _____	8. _____
7. _____	14. _____	15. _____	12. _____	13. _____

Total:

Sources: M. A. Rahim, "A Measure of Styles of Handling Interpersonal Conflict," *Academy of Management Journal* (June 1983), pp. 368–376; and K. W. Thomas and R. H. Kilmann, *Thomas-Kilmann Conflict Mode Instrument* (Sterling Forest, NY; XICOM, Inc., 1977).

changes. Also, functional intergroup conflict that serves to improve the quality of decision making and stimulate creative breakthroughs should be judiciously managed to achieve the most beneficial results for the organization.[34] Consequently, the critical issue is not how to eliminate conflict but how to manage it productively to obtain positive change and avoid negative consequences.

As with interpersonal conflict, attempts to manage intergroup conflict can result in win–lose (competing and accommodating), lose–lose (avoiding), win–win (collaborating), or compromise (bargaining) outcomes. Win–lose outcomes are brought about by all-or-nothing competitive strategies that encourage one group to win at the expense of the other. Since organizations consist of ongoing relationships, zero-sum strategies create destructive political environments. Avoiding strategies don't solve problems, they leave them to fester and erupt later. At best, they allow

■■■■ **EXHIBIT 11–6**

Guidelines for Effective Bargaining

1. **Consider the other party's situation.** Acquire as much information as you can about your opponent's interests, goals, needs, wants, constituencies, and strategy. This information will help you to counter his or her arguments with the facts and figures that support your position.

2. **Have a concrete strategy.** Have a strategy. Know ahead of time how you will respond to any given situation.

3. **Begin with a positive overture.** Establish rapport and mutual interests before starting the negotiation. Begin, perhaps, with a small concession that will probably be reciprocated and lead to agreements.

4. **Address problems, not personalities.** Concentrate on the negotiation issues, not on the personal characteristics of your opponent. Avoid the tendency to attack your opponent, which will make him or her feel threatened, and concentrate on defending his or her self-esteem as opposed to solving the problem.

5. **Maintain a rational, goal-oriented frame of mind.** Use the previous guideline in reverse if your opponent attacks or gets emotional with you. Let the other person blow off steam without taking it personally while you try to understand the problem or strategy behind the aggression.

6. **Pay little attention to initial offers.** Initial offers tend to be extreme and idealistic. Treat them as such.

7. **Emphasize win–win solutions.** Assume a zero-sum game means missed opportunities for trade-offs that could benefit both sides. Look for an integrative solution. Create additional alternatives, especially low-cost concessions you can make that have high value to the other party.

8. **Insist on using objective criteria.** Agree on objective criteria that can aid both parties in assessing the reasonableness of an alternative. Don't succumb to emotional pleas, assertiveness, or stubbornness if their underlying rationale does not meet these criteria.

Source: S. P. Robbins and P. L. Hunsaker, *Training in Interpersonal Skills: Tips for Managing People at Work,* 2nd ed. (Upper Saddle River, NJ: Prentice Hall, 1996), pp. 244–245.

Mediator John Bates (in shirt and tie) watches as two parties shake hands and resolve their dispute. The Bates Edwards Group is a San Francisco company that provides alternative dispute resolution. The for-profit company helps parties settle disputes without using the courts, thus saving huge amounts of money and relieving the overburdened judicial system. (Photo: © 1992 Robert Holmgren.)

temporary productivity until the groups can address the conflict more effectively. Compromise strategies allow both groups to gain a little, but neither to obtain all that its members desire. Since win–win strategies allow both groups to obtain their goals through creative integration of their concerns, the best practice is to try a win–win strategy first. If this does not work, a compromise strategy can provide some benefits to both groups. Organizations with effectiveness intergroup coordination strategies can often manage conflict effectively without it becoming destructive.

Intergroup Coordination Strategies. Exhibit 11–7 identifies seven of the most frequently used methods for coordinating intergroup performance to avoid dysfunctional conflicts. The seven strategies are listed on a continuum of increasing

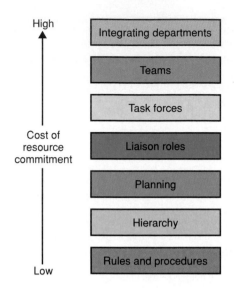

━━━━━ **EXHIBIT 11–7**

Strategies for Coordinating Intergroup Performance

High

Integrating departments

Teams

Task forces

Cost of resource commitment

Liaison roles

Planning

Hierarchy

Rules and procedures

Low

cost in terms of resource and energy commitment. The strategies are not mutually exclusive. In most organizations, the simpler strategies listed at the low end of the continuum are used in conjunction with the more complex strategies listed at the high end.[35] For example, managers using task forces to coordinate intergroup performance are likely to be using rules and procedures in conjunction with the higher-level task force strategy.

Rules and Procedures.   One of the simplest and least costly ways of coordinating intergroup performance is to spell out in advance the required activities and behaviors in the form of rules and procedures. Written standards tell members of interacting groups what to do in specific situations to ensure adequate performance and avoid having to work things through each time. If the typing pool is tied up with the finance department's quarterly report, for example, and if the personnel department knows ahead of time that under such conditions it is free to hire temporary help from an outside agency, no confrontational interaction between personnel and finance will be necessary.

The problem with rules and procedures is that they only help when intergroup activities can be anticipated in advance and recur often. When uncertainty and change characterize the task environment, however, rules and procedures alone may not guarantee effective coordination of intergroup relations.

Hierarchy.   When rules and procedures are not sufficient for coping with intergroup problems, conflict can be passed up the hierarchy to a common superior for resolution. If conflict arises between copywriters and graphic designers in an advertising department, for example, the advertising production manager may intervene as mediator. But if the sales force perceives conflict with the entire advertising operation, the vice president in charge of marketing may have to resolve the issue.

Planning.   In more complex situations, coordinating group activities requires more than rules, procedures, or hierarchies. Planning can be essential to task accomplishments when it is necessary to determine in advance the goals, roles, and responsibilities of all groups that need to cooperate.

Task Forces Let Labor into the Boardroom

Task forces have been formed into more permanent teams of labor and management representatives in Europe to help reach agreements without strikes and other damaging results of conflict. The most common way is to integrate labor representatives into the board of directors, either with or without veto power, as occurred at Chrysler's former U.K. facilities.

In Germany, workers elect representatives to serve on their companies' work councils, which make decisions on social matters such as employee conduct, work hours,

and safety. If the labor director of a company disagrees with the council's decision, an arbitrator settles the dispute. The councils include an equal number of shareholders in economic and financial decisions, but the chairman, who is elected by the shareholders, has the tie-breaking vote.

Source: J. D. Daniels and L. H. Radebaugh, *International Business: Environments and Operations,* 5th ed. (Reading, MA: Addison-Wesley, 1989), p. 690.

A classic example of the need for planning is in building construction. Most interactions can be anticipated and the behaviors of various groups controlled in a programmed fashion. All groups—diggers, concrete pourers, bricklayers, carpenters, plasterers, painters—must know in advance what they are supposed to do and when. Activities are controlled by a master plan that coordinates the efforts of the interacting groups.

Liaison Roles. When the number of interactions between two or more groups become more frequent or complex, organizations often establish coordinating personnel to handle these ongoing interaction requirements. A **liaison** expedites lateral communication much more effectively than could a cumbersome formal information system alone. Because liaisons are well acquainted with the nature of the work in both groups, they can cut through the bureaucracy to provide quicker, more effective communication. An example would be an MBA with an undergraduate degree in engineering who acts as a liaison between the engineering and production departments.

liaison
A party that expedites lateral communication between interacting groups by circumventing formal organizational boundaries.

Task Forces. When several groups interact over time in a complex situation, another way of facilitating intergroup cooperation is to establish a temporary **task force** made up of one or more individuals from each of the interacting units. This group investigates problems, suggests solutions, and facilitates communication among all groups involved. When the problem or task has been completed, the task group disbands and members return to their respective groups and resume their normal activities. A task force of a new product for a major customer, for example, might consist of individuals from production, research, and marketing, along with the customer's representatives. The World Watch box describes how shareholders and labor and management representatives serve on more permanent task forces to codetermine labor policies in Europe.

task force
A temporary group made up of individuals from interacting groups that resolves problems, facilitates cooperation, and promotes integration of efforts.

Teams. When several groups must interact in a complex situation over a long period of time, more permanent teams can be formed to manage intergroup activities. Team members maintain their original roles in their functional department

Challenge of Change

Tracking Product Teams at Hewlett-Packard

The costs of designing a new product are less important to its ultimate success than the time it takes to get the product to market. Hewlett-Packard has developed the concept of the "Return Map" as a way of speeding up product development through interfunctional teamwork. People from different functional departments are required to triangulate on the product development process as a whole by estimating and re-estimating the amount of time it will take to perform critical tasks.

The Return Map graphically represents the time and money contributions of all teams to the moment when a project breaks even. The time line is divided into three

phases: investigation, development, and manufacturing and sales. Costs are plotted against time, as are revenues, after manufacturing releases the product. All metrics are estimated at the beginning of a project to determine its feasibility, then they are tracked while the project evolves to keep it on target. Estimates are team responsibilities, and deviations provide valuable information that spurs continuous investigation and improvement.

Source: Charles H. House and Raymond L. Price, "The Return Map: Tracking Product Teams," *Harvard Business Review* (January–February 1991), p. 164.

in addition to their new ones as coordinating team members. Task teams are established at universities to function as standing committees that periodically make decisions about such things as granting tenure to faculty members or allocating annual budgets. At International Paper Company, the United Paper Workers Union and management agreed to create a team made up of the union president, company president, and three members of each group, whose goal was to enhance cooperation and avoid confrontation. This team has provided benefits such as an agreement that the company would steer clear of attempts to eliminate the union from certain plants in return for the union's willingness to grant cheaper pension formulas.[36]

Integrating Departments.   When the complexity of information flows between several interacting groups is beyond the capacity of plans, temporary task forces, or permanent teams, an entire integrating department can be established. These are permanent departments with full-time individuals whose only responsibility is the effective coordination of intergroup activities. Since this is a very expensive method, it is usually used only if an organization's business requires a lot of ongoing cooperation between groups with conflicting goals or if recurring, nonroutine problems can significantly impact overall organizational success.

Integrating departments is the most complex mechanism for managing intergroup coordination. If problems beyond the capabilities of such departments arise, a major organizational redesign is probably called for. For these reasons, Hewlett-Packard was forced to redesign its product teams, as described in the Challenge of Change box.

■■■■■■ **EXHIBIT 11–8**

International Conflict Resolution Approaches

	North Americans	Arabs	Russians
Primary negotiating style and process	Factual: Appeals made to logic	Affective: Appeals made to emotions	Axiomatic: Appeals made to ideals
Opponent's arguments countered with . . .	Objective facts	Subjective feelings	Asserted ideals
Making concessions	Small concessions made early to establish a relationship	Concessions made throughout as a part of the bargaining process	Few, if any, small concessions made
Response to opponent's concessions	Usually reciprocate opponent's concessions	Almost always reciprocate opponent's concessions	Opponent's concessions viewed as weakness and almost never reciprocated
Relationship	Short term	Long term	No continuing relationship
Authority	Broad	Broad	Limited
Initial position	Moderate	Extreme	Extreme
Deadline	Very important	Casual	Ignored

Source: Nancy J. Adler, *International Dimensions of Organizational Behavior*, 2nd ed. (Boston: PWS-Kent, 1991), pp. 179–217.

Strategies for Preventing and Reducing Dysfunctional Intergroup Conflict

Persistent dysfunctional intergroup conflict needs to be confronted.[37] Techniques that can prevent[38] and reduce[39] intergroup conflict are presented in this section. It should be kept in mind, however, that different cultures prefer different approaches to resolving conflicts. Some of these cultural differences are shown in Exhibit 11–8.

Superordinate Goals. One of the most effective ways to reduce intergroup conflict is to determine an overriding goal that requires the cooperative effort of the conflicting groups. Such a goal must be unattainable by either group alone and of sufficient importance to supersede all their other goals. One fairly common superordinate goal is *survival* of the organization. This usually requires the elimination of suboptimal strategies on the part of conflicting groups. In the airline industry, for example, several unions have agreed to forgo pay increases and have even accepted temporary pay reductions when the survival of an airline was threatened.

This strategy *eliminates win–lose situations* as groups shift efforts towards cooperation so they all can pull together to maximize organizational effectiveness. Setting up an appraisal system that *rewards total organizational effectiveness* rather than individual group accomplishments also supports these efforts. Marshall Industries, in our video, did this to promote cooperation rather than competition between groups, resulting in the virtual elimination of conflicts and increased profits and stock prices.

A derivative strategy to restore alliances and increase cooperation is focusing on a *common enemy*. At the international level, bickering nations unite against a common adversary in times of war or natural catastrophe. Players on athletic teams that normally compete in a particular league join together to produce an all-star team and challenge another league. Nothing halts the squabbles of Democrats faster than a reminder that the Republicans are gaining strength. Like all these factions, warring groups will suppress their conflicts and join together to help their organization compete successfully against another. Sometimes, however, they must be reminded that the opposition is out there.

Increased Communication.   In cases where groups are not competing for scarce resources or trying to achieve inherently conflicting goals, devising means to increase communication can do much to correct misunderstandings, reduce negative stereotypes, and develop more positive feelings among group members. Requiring groups to meet together to solve common problems can reduce stereotypical images, faulty perceptions, and contribute to mutual understanding. NCR Corp. (formerly National Cash Register Company) began tearing down the walls between its engineering and manufacturing groups by putting people from design, purchasing, manufacturing, and field support in adjacent cubicles to allow them to communicate with one another throughout the design and manufacturing process. This process reduced assembly time from 30 minutes to 5 and permitted assembly without special tools. The free flow of information across groups enabled NCR to get better products to market much faster.[40]

Problem Solving.   Problem solving is a more structured means of bringing together conflicting groups for a face-to-face confrontation. The purpose of a problem-solving meeting is to identify and solve conflicts through a mutual airing of differences, complaints, and negative feelings. An effort is made to work through differences and bring about a greater understanding of the opposing group's attitudes, perceptions, and position. Although diversity can create problems, it can also solve them, as described in the Dynamics of Diversity box.

The problem-solving approach requires considerable time and commitment, but it can be effective when conflicts stem from misunderstandings or differences in perceptions. Specific problem-solving strategies and techniques can be found in Chapter 12.

negotiation
A form of problem solving where two groups with conflicting interests exchange things in order to reach a mutually agreeable resolution.

Negotiating.   **Negotiating** is a form of problem solving in which two groups with conflicting interests exchange things in order to reach a mutually agreeable resolution. One of the most publicized forms of negotiating is when unions bargain for better wages, working conditions, benefits, and job security, while management bargains for lower labor costs and increased efficiency. Many other, more informal forms of intergroup bargaining go on constantly, as when one department agrees to stay in an old office space in exchange for new computer equipment.

When choosing representatives, groups should be aware that personality, experience, training, and chosen strategy make a difference in how well a negotiator does.[41] Tips for successful negotiating were provided in Exhibit 11–6. Negotiating styles also vary across national cultures, as illustrated in Exhibit 11–9.

Expansion of Resources.   When the major cause of intergroup conflict is limited resources, the likely outcome is a win–lose situation in which one group succeeds at the expense of another. If at all possible, the organization should eliminate this source of conflict by expanding its resource base. Additional investments may pay off handsomely in terms of increased productivity.

Third-Party Judgment.   Groups may appeal to a common boss or an outside judge to serve as a mediator in resolving their conflict. Often this is easier, less time consuming, and less expensive than working through every issue with intergroup problem-solving techniques. At other times, more collaborative approaches have failed, and mediation is the last resort.

Dynamics of Diversity

Diversity Can Help Solve Cross-Cultural Problems

Diversity of employees—composed of differences in sex, religion, race, national origin—have led to historical conflicts in the workplace for years. In 1964, discrimination based on these factors was declared illegal. Today, awareness of work force diversity has expanded to include age, disability, and sexual orientation.

These factors have led to a variety of conflicts based on perceived discrimination, which can result in costly lawsuits. No organization ever "wins" a discrimination suit, even if defending a litigation is successful, because it still costs executive time and distraction and incurs considerable legal fees. Potential trouble areas arise when larger pools of qualified people compete for fewer managerial jobs in an environment of biased hiring policies, wrongful dismissal, discriminatory relocation, and sex discrimination or harassment suits. The Department of Labor's *Glass Ceiling Initiative* report cites these "artificial barriers as a significant cause for why minorities and women have not advanced further in corporate America."

Managers need to be able to detect and handle different perceptions and assumptions about work force issues and either prevent grievances or handle them at the first step in order to avoid costly discrimination suits. Conflict resolution is perhaps the key skill needed to manage a diverse work force.

Conflict-resolution processes that take into consideration cross-cultural and cross-gender differences include sharing information about issues and interests; exploring divergent values, expectations, and assumptions; understanding different perspectives; and reframing and reaching agreement. By applying these processes, cross-cultural problems often lend themselves to mutually beneficial solutions because of the different preferences of the parties involved. Say a company wants employees to take different holidays so that the plant can remain open at all times. This can be a problem for managers if employees are all from the same culture. Christians will all want off Christmas week, for example. If some employees are Jewish, however, they will be happiest with a vacation the week of Hanukkah, which rarely coincides with Christmas week. Cross-cultural differences can facilitate mutually beneficial solutions to problems that are all but unsolvable when all employees share similar cultural and religious backgrounds.

Source: Sybil Evans, "Conflict Can Be Positive," *HR Magazine* (May 1992), pp. 49–51.

Professional arbitrators are commonly brought in to resolve disputes between unions and management. In November 1993, the highest manager to intervene was President Clinton, who engineered binding federal arbitration to brake a disastrous strike that grounded two-thirds of American Airlines' flights over the busy Thanksgiving season. Another example is the National Conference of Commissioners on Uniform State Laws statute that lets most fired workers who feel their terminations were unjustified take their cases to a neutral arbitrator who can decide disputes in a few weeks, as opposed to the other common option of expensive and time-consuming lawsuits.[42]

Within organizations, common superiors are often called in to recommend solutions to conflicts between departments. Managers acting as third-party mediators have significant clout because the warring parties agree before the arbitration begins to abide by the mediator's decision. Depending on the criteria established for successful dispute resolution (e.g., fairness, performance effectiveness) managers may select a variety of intervention strategies ranging from investigation of facts to adversarial (e.g., trial-like) confrontation meetings.[43]

━━━━ **EXHIBIT 11–9**   *Cross-Cultural Negotiation Styles*

Japanese	North American	Latin American
Emotional sensitivity highly valued.	Emotional sensitivity not highly valued.	Emotional sensitivity valued.
Hiding of emotions.	Dealing straightforwardly or impersonally.	Emotionally passionate.
Subtle power plays; conciliation.	Litigation not as much as conciliation.	Great power plays; use of weakness.
Loyalty to employer. Employer takes care of its employees.	Lack of commitment to employer. Breaking of ties by either if necessary.	Loyalty to employer (who is often family).
Group decision-making consensus.	Teamwork provides input to a decision maker.	Decisions come down from one individual.
Face-saving crucial. Decisions often made on basis of saving someone from embarrassment.	Decisions made on a cost-benefit basis. Face-saving does not always matter.	Face-saving crucial in decision making to preserve honor, dignity.
Decision makers openly influenced by special interests.	Decision makers influenced by special interests but often not considered ethical.	Execution of special interests of decision maker expected, condoned.
Not argumentative. Quiet when right.	Argumentative when right or wrong, but impersonal.	Argumentative when right or wrong; passionate.
What is down in writing must be accurate, valid.	Great importance given to documentation as evidential proof.	Impatient with documentation as obstacle to understanding general principles.
Step-by-step approach to decision making.	Methodically organized decision making.	Impulsive, spontaneous decision making.
Good of group is the ultimate aim.	Profit motive or good of individual ultimate aim.	What is good for group is good for the individual.
Cultivate a good emotional-social setting for decision making. Get to know decision makers.	Decision making impersonal. Avoid involvements, conflict of interest.	Personalization necessary for good decision making.

Source: Nancy J. Adler, *International Dimensions of Organizational Behavior,* 2nd ed. (Boston: PWS-Kent, 1991), pp. 179–217.

The advantages of arbitration can carry a hidden cost. An arbitrator usually hands down a win–lose decision that is unlikely to receive the loser's full commitment. Like a parental decision on who is "right" when two children fight over a toy, an arbitrated outcome may solve the immediate problem but increase hostility between the conflicting factions. No one is left with an enhanced understanding of what caused the basic conflict or how future clashes can be prevented. When an arbitrator hands down a compromise solution that only partially fulfills the demands of both sides, neither group is totally satisfied with the outcome. Although this may be slightly preferable to a win–lose decision, the sources of conflict are likely to remain.[44]

Changes in Organizational Structure.   When the reasons for intergroup conflict are scarce resources, status differences, or power imbalances, changes in organizational structure may be the answer.[45] Structural changes include things like those in the above section on coordinating intergroup relations: rotating group members on a semipermanent basis, creating liaison or coordinator positions, and eliminating special-interest groups that exist within the organization. Marshall Industries rotates new employees through a variety of assignments in different groups to ease the competitive effects of single-group identification, enhance understanding of interaction in the whole system, and provide a total organization identification. Marshall Industries essentially regrouped people from different departments with different specialties into overlapping, cross-trained teams. This decreased identity with one particular department and increased understanding of the requirements and needs of other groups. In other situations, conflicting groups can be relocated, task responsibilities can be redefined, and hierarchies

"Hoteling" is a form of resource sharing recently initiated at some sales and service-based companies such as IBM, AT&T, and major accounting firms. The companies actually do away with private offices and provide temporary spaces such as sound-proof cubby holes or a conference room for workers when they are on-site. At Ernst & Young's Washington office, workers recieve help from a company concierge (photo). Name tags for temporary offices and family photos as computer screen savers add a personal touch for the resource-sharing employee. (Source: © Mark Richards/CONTACT.)

can be decentralized. Sometimes two conflicting groups can be merged into one. If the conflict clearly centers around the personal animosities of two or more strong individuals, the key instigators can be removed.

Restructuring has produced increased quality, productivity, and cooperation for companies such as Corning Glass Works, Ford Motor, and Hewlett-Packard, which are shifting their focus from how individual departments function to how different departments work together. Companies such as Conrail, Dun & Bradstreet Europe, Du Pont, and Royal Bank of Canada have created network groups of department managers with appropriate business skills, personal motivations, resource control, and positions to shape and implement organizational strategy. The free flow of information to all network group members who need it and the emphasis on horizontal collaboration and leadership have clarified joint business goals and helped meet deadlines.[46]

Smoothing.   Smoothing is a means of providing conflicting groups with some incentive to repress their conflict and avoid its open expression. The smoothing process plays down the differences between the groups and accentuates their similarities and common interests. The rationale is that eventually the groups will realize they are not as alienated from one another as they initially believed. Because this approach circumvents full confrontation of the sources of conflict, they will probably resurface in the future and possibly cause a more serious disturbance. Smoothing is at best a temporary solution.

Avoidance.   Some groups may be able to ignore dysfunctional situations temporarily by looking the other way or disregarding the threatening actions of others in the hope that the situation will resolve itself. But most conflicts don't fade away; usually, they worsen with time. Although avoidance is ineffective in the long run, certain controlled conditions can be established to lessen the short-term consequences of conflict. Sometimes conflicting groups can be physically separated, or the amount of interaction between them can be limited. Procrastination, disregard for the demands of others, and attempts at peaceful coexistence are all variations of the avoidance process.

RESTRUCTURING PROMOTES QUALITY AT GM'S SATURN PLANT—A SECOND LOOK

General Motors' objective for creating Saturn was to develop a quality compact car that could compete well with Japanese imports from Honda, Toyota, and Nissan. In 1994, the average Saturn dealer in the United States sold almost twice as many cars per month (more than 100) than its Japanese competitors. Part of this success has been due to high quality (lowest defect rates of any U.S. brand) and customer satisfaction (e.g., only Lexus and Infinity were better in the 1994 J. D. Power survey). But the main input for Saturn's success has been attributed to the "gift from God" referred to in the opening vignette: the cooperation between the union and management.

From the start, human factors were always as important as financial ones. Union management collaboration was invaluable as Saturn developed from a vision to a new style of organization where old competitive behaviors were left behind in favor of more cooperative ones. Previously competing groups were united behind the common vision of a team-oriented organization outside the traditional GM hierarchy. To achieve their superordinate goal and compete against the common enemy (i.e., Japanese imports), Saturn developed improved communications, ensured sufficient resources for all, and abolished win–lose climates—for example, they even eliminated reserved parking places and executive dining rooms to establish a sense of common community.[47]

SUMMARY

Organizations are made up of interacting individuals and groups with varying needs, objectives, values, and perspectives that naturally lead to the emergence of conflicts. When conflict occurs it can either stimulate new positive changes or result in negative consequences. Members of a group in conflict with another group, for example, often experience increased cohesion, loyalty, task concentration, and autocratic leadership. Between themselves, however, the conflicting groups can experience dysfunctional hostility, distorted perceptions, negative stereotypes, and decreased communication.

Conflicts need to be managed appropriately to provide positive outcomes and avoid the negative possibilities. Interpersonal conflict management styles include competing, avoiding, accommodating, collaborating, and compromising. Interacting groups can be coordinated through rules and procedures, hierarchy, planning, liaison roles, task forces, teams, or integrating departments. Strategies for preventing and reducing dysfunctional intergroup conflict include emphasizing the total organization by focusing on superordinate goals or a common enemy, increasing communication, joint problem solving, negotiating, expanding resources, obtaining a mediator, changing organization structure, smoothing things over, and avoiding potential win–lose conflict situations.

Key Concepts

conflict, *p. 352*
interdependence. *p. 355*
pooled interdependence,*p. 356*
sequential interdependence, *p. 356*
reciprocal interdependence, *p. 357*
role, *p. 358*
role set, *p. 358*
role ambiguity, *p. 358*
role conflict, *p. 358*
role overload, *p. 359*

degenerative interaction climate, *p. 360*
functional conflict, *p. 362*
conflict-positive organization, *p. 362*
dysfunctional conflict, *p. 364*
conflict management style, *p. 365*
liaison, *p. 371*
task force, *p. 371*
negotiating, *p. 374*

Questions for Study and Discussion

1. What major factors cause intergroup conflict? Think of a group to which you currently belong and determine how these factors influence your behavior and feelings towards other groups with which your group interacts.

2. Describe situations from your personal experience in which conflict between groups was functional and dysfunctional.

3. Discuss the mechanisms for resolving intergroup conflicts between students and faculty on your campus. Are they effective or not? Why or why not? What mechanisms do you suggest to better resolve such conflicts?

4. Explain this statement: "An organization can experience too little or too much conflict."

5. Define pooled interdependence, sequential interdependence, and reciprocal interdependence. In which situation is conflict most likely to occur? Why? Which type of interdependence exists between groups with which you are familiar?

6. Suggest the appropriate conflict reduction strategies for a collective bargaining stalemate in which both management and union groups have a record of hostility and noncooperation. Could such potential conflict be prevented by the design chosen for a new industrial organization? How?

7. What is the predominant intergroup conflict at your school or place of work? What is being done to resolve this conflict? What could be done?

8. What is your dominant conflict management style? How did you develop it? When does it work best for you? When doesn't it work?

EXPERIENTIAL EXERCISE

Win As Much As You Can[48]

Goals.
1. To diagnose and manage a potential conflict situation within an organization competing with another organization.
2. To provide opportunities for practicing negotiation skills.
3. To explore trust building and collaboration in a potential conflict situation.

Time. 55 to 75 minutes (Preparation: 10 to 15 minutes; exercise: 35 minutes; debriefing: 10 to 25 minutes).

Directions. Divide the class into two or more organizations. Then divide each organization into four, one- to five-person departments. The four departments in each organization should be far enough apart from each other so that members of each department can communicate without being overheard by other departments.

The exercise consists of seven rounds of decision making in which each department selects either P (profit) or Q (quality) based on its prediction of what the other departments in its organization will do and the payoff schedule. Winnings or losses depend on what is negotiated and what the other departments decide to do.

Process.
1. Each player invests $1.00 in his or her company (gives the money to instructor). If any student is uncomfortable risking a dollar, or if it is a very large class, one option is to have each department assign an observer to help the instructor (a) collect and announce decisions; (b) observe internal and intergroup dynamics; (c) handle negotiations; (d) lead department debriefing; and (e) lead class debriefing.
2. Participants study the payoff schedule, the scorecard, and profit distribution matrix. (5 minutes)
3. There is to be no talking between departments, only within departments, except during negotiations.
4. There are opportunities to negotiate with other departments before the rounds with bonuses; that is, after rounds 2, 4, and 6. Departments must direct requests to negotiate to the instructor (or observer), and other departments can agree or refuse. If departments agree to negotiate, one representative from each department meets with one from another department in a private place. Negotiators are not allowed to show their score sheets to each other. Departments pick different members to negotiate with each of the other departments so that all get a chance to negotiate. Actual decisions for the next round can only be made through consensus of department members after they return from negotiations.
5. Departments have 10 minutes to get organized and determine their goals and strategy. Each decision round is three minutes. Each negotiation period is five minutes.
6. *Scoring:* Departments keep their own cumulative scores on their scorecard. The instructor or observer duplicates a scorecard for each organization on the board and keeps total organization scores for each round (i.e., sum of scores for the four departments in each organization).
7. *Payoff Schedule Directions.* At the beginning of each of the seven successive rounds, choose either a P to maximize profit margin or a Q for highest quality. The payoff for each round depends on the pattern of choices made by other departments in your organization. The payoff schedule, scorecard, and profit distribution summary are included on the following Decision Tally Sheet. Scores can be kept on this sheet in the book, but it should be duplicated and passed out to participants separately for easier use.

Profit Distribution. At the end of the seven rounds of play, add up the cumulative organization and department scores. Write these on the board and distribute the total pot as follows:

- The organization with the largest balance gets 40 percent (equally distributed among the four departments).
- The department with the largest balance gets 30 percent (can be either the winning or losing organization).
- The department with the second-largest balance gets 20 percent.
- The department with the third-largest balance gets 10 percent.
- If there is no positive payoff for either organization, there will be no distribution, even if departments have positive balances. The instructor keeps all of the money.

Discussion Questions.
1. How would you describe the behavior of the departments in your organization?
2. How would you describe your own behavior?
3. Is this real-life behavior?
4. How do you feel about the way you played the game? How do you feel about how the other departments played the game?
5. What did you learn about yourself? About others?

DECISION TALLY SHEET

Directions. At the beginning of each of the seven successive rounds choose either a P to maximize profit margin, or a Q for highest quality. The "payoff" for each round is dependent upon the pattern of choices made by other departments in your company.

Payoff schedule.

4 Ps:	Lose $1.00 each
3 Ps:	Win $1.00 each
1 Q:	Lose $3.00
2 Ps:	Win $2.00 each
2 Qs:	Lose $2.00 each
1 P:	Win $3.00
3 Qs:	Lose $1.00 each
4 Qs:	Win $1.00 each

Scorecard.

Round	Your Choice (Circle)	Group's Pattern of Choices	Your Payoff	Cumulative Balance	
1	P Q	___ Ps ___ Qs			
2	P Q	___ Ps ___ Qs			
3	P Q	___ Ps ___ Qs			Bonus (×3)
4	P Q	___ Ps ___ Qs			
5	P Q	___ Ps ___ Qs			Bonus (×5)
6	P Q	___ Ps ___ Qs			
7	P Q	___ Ps ___ Qs			Bonus (×10)

Profit Distribution.

- Company with largest balance gets 40 percent (equally distributed).
- Department with largest balance gets 30 percent.
- Department with second-largest balance gets 20 percent.
- Department with third-largest balance gets 10 percent.
- If no positive payoff for any company, there will be no distribution.

EXPERENTIAL EXERCISE

Used Car Negotiation[49]

Directions. This is a role play designed to help you develop your compromise approach to conflict resolution through practicing negotiation skills. The class should first break into pairs. Then decide which person will play the role of the seller and which person will play the role of the buyer. You have five minutes to read the situation, your role, and to prepare your targets. Do not read the other person's role. The negotiation should not take longer than 15 minutes. After that the class will compare outcomes and discuss the various strategies utilized.

Situation. You are about to negotiate the purchase/sale of an automobile. The buyer advertised the car in the local newspaper. Before advertising it, the buyer took the car to the local Volkswagon dealer, who has provided the following information.

- 1988 VW Rabbit convertible; standard shift.
- White with red upholstery, tinted glass.
- AM/FM, cassette. 30,450 miles.
- Steel-belted radial tires expected to last to 65,000 miles.
- 35 miles per gallon.
- No rust; dent on passenger door barely noticeable.
- Mechanically perfect except exhaust system, which may or may not last another 10,000 miles (costs $300 to replace).
- "Blue book" retail value, $5,000; wholesale, $4,400.
- Car has spent its entire life in the local area.

Buyer's Role. Your car was stolen and wrecked two weeks ago. You do a lot of traveling in your job, so you need a car that is economical and easy to drive. The Rabbit advertised looks like a good deal, and you would like to buy it right away if possible. The insurance company gave you $4,000 for your old car. You have only $700 in savings that you had intended to spend on a trip with an extremely attractive companion—a chance you really don't want to pass up.

Your credit has been stretched for some time, so if you borrow money, it will have to be at an 18 percent interest rate. Furthermore, you need to buy a replacement car quickly, because you have been renting a car for business purposes, and it is costing you a great deal. The Rabbit is the best deal you've seen, and the car is fun to drive. As an alternative, you can immediately buy a used 1989 Ford Escort for $3,800 (the wholesale value), which gets 28 miles per gallons and will depreciate much faster than the Rabbit.

The seller of the Rabbit is a complete stranger to you. Before beginning this negotiation, set the following targets for yourself:

1. The price you would like to pay for the car: _____
2. The price you will initially offer the seller: _____
3. The highest price you will pay for the car: _____

Seller's Role. You have bought a used Mercedes from a dealer. The down payment is $4,700 on the car, with steep monthly payments. You are stretched on credit, so if you can't make the down payment, you will have to borrow at 18 percent. You're going to pick up the Mercedes in two hours, so you want to sell your old car, the Rabbit convertible, before you go.

You advertised the car (which is in particularly good condition) in the newspaper and have had several calls. Your only really good prospect right now is the person with whom you are about to bargain—a stranger. You don't *have* to sell it to this person, but if you don't sell the car right away, you will have to pay high interest charges until you do sell it.

The Mercedes dealer will only give you $4,400 for the Rabbit, since he will have to resell it to a Volkswagen dealer. The local VW dealer is not anxious to buy the car from you since he just received a shipment of new cars; in any case, he probably would not give you more than $4,400 either.

Before beginning this negotiation, set the following targets for yourself:

1. The price you would like to receive for the car: _____
2. The price you will initially request: _____
3. The lowest price you will accept for the car: _____

CASE

Goal Setting at the Kimberly Toy Company

The Kimberly Toy Company board of directors called a meeting of all department heads and announced its goal for next year: a company profit increase of 20 percent. On the basis of this organizational goal, the managers were requested to establish goals for their own departments and to report them at the next week's meeting.

Each department head in turn requested suggestions from employees and held numerous meetings with operating managers. The process turned out to be more difficult than it had seemed. The board's new directive had to be considered in the context of many individual departmental objectives already established for the year, and any changes had to uphold the integrity of those goals. It also became apparent that a department's activity in achieving a new goal either might enhance or threaten the well-being of other departments. Thus, their reactions had to be considered as well.

The following objectives were established independently and presented a week later at the corporate goal-setting meeting:

- Marketing department: increase sales by 25 percent, mainly through the introduction of new products.
- Production department: decrease costs and increase efficiency by eliminating new and low-volume production runs and providing safety training for all workers.

- Design research department: create and develop a new line based on currently popular trends in television and motion pictures.
- Personnel department: cut back on nonessential training and redesign jobs to reduce turnover and subsequent new hires.
- Finance department: reduce interest costs by instituting a 30 percent cutback on short-term debt; expedite receipts by changing the due date on accounts receivable from 45 days to 30 days after billing.

Questions for Managerial Action

1. How will each department's goal most likely be perceived by each of the other departments?

2. How do you think the factors of time orientation, uncertainty, substitutability, interdependence, resource sharing, power, and climate will shape the consequences of the goal-setting meeting?

3. How successfully do you think each of these departmental goals will contribute to achieving the board of directors' organizational goal of increasing Kimberly's profits by 20 percent? Explain your answers.

4. What conflict resolution strategies would be most appropriate in this situation?

Part IV

Leading and Managing Practices

12 Ethics and Problem Solving

13 Power and Organizational Politics

14 Leaders and Managers

Chapter 12

Ethics and Problem Solving

LEARNING OBJECTIVES

After studying this chapter, you should be able to:

- Explain the nature of managerial problem solving.
- Identify the five steps of the rational problem-solving process.
- Appreciate the value of ethics and morality in decision making.
- Describe the strengths and weaknesses of different decision styles.
- Utilize quality management tools for problem solving.
- Apply techniques to stimulate creativity and innovation.

PUTTING PORSCHE IN THE PINK. BANZAI!

Not too long ago, the production floor of Porsche's factory was not a pretty sight. Workers would storm off in a huff. Managers would fume. Voices would rise above the hum and bang of the line. Porsche's assembly line looked like a dark warehouse. On either side were shelves eight-feet high with huge parts bins filled with 28 days of inventory. To get a part, workers often had to climb ladders, wasting enormous amounts of time. Half-built engines sat on the side of the assembly line while workers left their work spaces to dig for parts, and others stood around waiting until they returned.

Porsche could afford this type of inefficiency in the early 1980s when the economic boom fueled sales to more than 50,000 vehicles a year. But then the recession of the early 1990s hit, and Porsche sales plummeted to 14,000 units in 1993, including a paltry 3,000 in the United States, its largest market. From the dizzying heights of the mid-1980s when American yuppies, not to mention staid German executives, had to have one, Porsche went to the brink of bankruptcy in 1992. Recession had crippled sales, and costs were out of control. That was when the company's family owners called in 43-year-old Mr. Wendelin Wiedeking to be Porsches's chief executive and solve its problems.

From the beginning, Wiedeking's idea was to bring in the Japanese. First, he eliminated one-third of his managers and gave those remaining new assignments, so that they would be struggling to learn new jobs "rather than waiting for me to make a mistake." Next, he took his management team on extensive tours of Japanese auto plants. They benchmarked by timing precisely how long it took Porsche to assemble body parts and engines and install carpeting and dashboards, then studied comparable times in Japan. On most tasks, Porsche was taking almost twice as long. These comparisons gave Porsche management a dramatic understanding of what had to be done.

In late 1992, Wiedeking brought the Shin-Gijutsu group, a cadre of former Toyota engineers, to the Porsche plant and gave them carte blanche to revitalize the system. It was a painful process. The Japanese engineers unleashed demanding explanations—scolding, lecturing, and browbeating some of Germany's finest automobile craftsman—about how poorly they were doing their jobs. But the result was the salvation of Porsche A.G., Germany's ultimate symbol of racing car performance and autobahn freedom.

With help from the Japanese engineers, assembly time for a car was reduced from 120 hours to 72. The number of errors per car fell 50 percent, to an average of three. The work force has shrunk 19 percent, to about 6,800 employees from more than 8,400 in 1992. Parts bins have been entirely eliminated and assemblers now only take the parts needed for each stage of assembly. The line itself has been shortened, and inventories have been cut back so much that factory space has been reduced by 30 percent. All of this means Porsche is making more cars at lower cost. And, the company recently reported its first profit in four years, after $300 million in losses.

Source: N. C. Nash, "Putting Porsche in the Pink: German Craftsmanship Gets Japanese Fine-Tuning," *The New York Times* (January 20, 1996), pp. 17–18.

Individual, managerial, and organizational success all depend on making the right decisions at the right times.[1] But decision making is just one component of the problem-solving process. Unless a problem has been defined and its root causes identified, managers are unlikely to be able to make an appropriate decision about how to solve it. Effective managers, like Porsche's Wiedeking, know how to gather and evaluate information that clarifies a problem. They know the value of generating more than one action alternative and weighing all the implications of a plan before deciding to implement it. And they acknowledge the importance of following through. This chapter explains decision making and problem solving and offers some guidelines for eliminating barriers to effective problem solving.

WHAT ARE THE STEPS FOR RATIONAL PROBLEM SOLVING?

problem solving
The process of eliminating the discrepancy between the actual and desired state of affairs.

Problem solving is the process of eliminating the discrepancy between actual and desired outcomes. Although sometimes subconsciously, most people confront problems by first acknowledging that they exist. Next, the problem needs to be defined and analyzed. Then alternative solutions need to be generated. **Decision making**—selecting the best solution from among feasible alternatives—comes next. Finally, the solution needs to be implemented, which Europeans call "taking" a decision. For optimal problem solving, social scientists advocate the use of the rational problem-solving approach outlined in Exhibit 12–1.[2]

decision making
The step in the problem-solving process that entails choosing the best solution from several alternatives.

A problem exists whenever the actual situation is not what is needed or desired. For example, when a work project needs to be done by a certain deadline and information needed to complete the assignment has not been supplied, a problem exists.

Problem Awareness

A major responsibility for all managers is to maintain a constant lookout for actual or potential problems. Managers do this by keeping channels of communication open, monitoring employees' current performance, and examining deviations from present plans as well as from past experience.[3] Four situations usually alert managers to possible problems: when there is a deviation from past experience, when there is a deviation from a set plan, when other people communicate problems to the manager, and when competitors outperform the overall organization.[4]

Being aware that problems exist is not always easy, however. People may be genuinely unaware of a problem's source or reluctant to acknowledge that a negative situation actually exists. The problem may appear threatening to them, they may fear reprisal from a supervisor for their share of the responsibility, or they may not want to be considered inept. The Dynamics of Diversity box shows just how threatening problems brought on by change can sometimes be. Several factors help managers become aware of problems, beginning with trust.

EXHIBIT 12–1

The Rational Problem-Solving Process

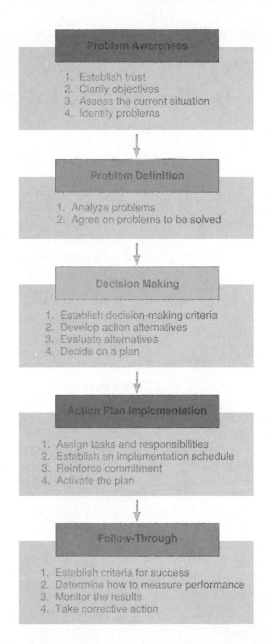

Problem Awareness

1. Establish trust
2. Clarify objectives
3. Assess the current situation
4. Identify problems

Problem Definition

1. Analyze problems
2. Agree on problems to be solved

Decision Making

1. Establish decision-making criteria
2. Develop action alternatives
3. Evaluate alternatives
4. Decide on a plan

Action Plan Implementation

1. Assign tasks and responsibilities
2. Establish an implementation schedule
3. Reinforce commitment
4. Activate the plan

Follow-Through

1. Establish criteria for success
2. Determine how to measure performance
3. Monitor the results
4. Take corrective action

Establish Trust. When a problem involves others, they need to feel understood and accepted; they must have confidence that the problem can be resolved; they must trust management to see the problem as a learning experience and not as an excuse to punish someone.[5] People need to feel secure enough to acknowledge that a problem exists and to acknowledge their own contributions to it.

Clarify Objectives.

"*Puss,*" *Alice began, "would you tell me, please, which way I ought to walk from here?*

"*That depends a good deal on where you want to get to,*" *said the Cat.*
"*I don't care where,*" *said Alice.*
"*Then it doesn't matter which way you walk,*" *said the Cat.*

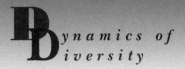

ynamics of Diversity

Culture Clash in the L.A. Fire Department

Historically throughout America, fire departments have been made up of very homogeneous employees—white males, with no women, few men of color, and no known gay men. Because fire fighting requires round-the-clock coverage, fire fighters work three 24-hour shifts and share common living quarters at most urban fire stations. Fire fighters depend on each other in life-threatening situations and grow very close, almost becoming extended families. Each station also has its own rituals, traditions, and rules for conduct and safety, which make them small societies with highly enforced expectations and norms.

In the past, men of color who became fire fighters were assigned to segregated stations. In 1953, for example, all blacks in Los Angeles were assigned to two stations in predominantly black neighborhoods, and although 80 percent requested transfers, their requests were routinely turned down. Since the passage of the Civil Rights Act and affirmative action, firehouses have been challenged by women and people of color wishing to join. These changes have been viewed as threatening and confusing by existing fire fighters.

The Los Angeles City Fire Department, which serves one of the most diverse communities in the United States, has experienced a disproportional set of problems. In 1988, when fire fighters of diverse racial identities were expected to live and work together, a swastika was discovered in a station that was experiencing racial tensions. Although a federal judge put

the chief and 60 officers on probation, they were defended by the union, which claimed that "since the station was the fire fighter's home, it was not a place to carry out social experiments."

When another station's first woman recruit refused to perform a demeaning sexual act as part of the initiation ritual, she was informed that she would be treated as an outcast if she did not comply. Finally she was pressured into performing the ritual, and someone else complained to the chief, who investigated and reprimanded the male fire fighters involved. Shortly afterwards, the woman was transferred to another station, where she was greeted by a sign soliciting donations for the reprimanded fighters who had lost wages because of the incident. Her outcast role caused her resignation shortly thereafter.

These examples demonstrate that many organizations view multicultural changes as a threatening and confusing problem. As attitudes change, however, organizations are beginning to assess the "problem" differently and recognize that diversity can add value and opportunities. When Los Angeles Fire Department Chief Donald Manning was recently asked how he viewed the changes generated by the influx of diverse others into the department, he replied, "There is strength in the new heterogeneity to meet the diverse needs of a diverse community."

Source: M. Loden and J. B. Rosener, *Workforce America: Managing Employee Diversity as a Vital Resource* (Homewood, IL: Business One Irwin, 1991), pp. 128–131.

---

objective
The desired state of affairs resulting from the problem-solving process.

Unlike Alice, most of us have an **objective** or desired outcome that we want to achieve. If you don't know what your objectives are, it is difficult to know what your problems are, let alone what to do about them. Therefore, objectives must be set and clarified before a current situation can be assessed.

Setting objectives serves four main purposes.[7] First, it provides a clear, documented statement of what you intend to accomplish. Written objectives are a form of acknowledgment and reminder of commitment. Second, setting objectives establishes a basis for measuring performance. Third, knowing what is expected and desired provides positive motivation to achieve goals. And fourth, knowing exactly where you're going is much more likely to get you there than trying many different solutions in a haphazard way.

GTE Telephone Operations had nearly $16 billion in revenues in 1992. But, faced with increasing competition and the need to reduce costs, GTE has begun the process of re-engineering the entire company to better serve the customer with improved technology and more efficient business processes. One example of a re-engineered process is the new GTE Customer Care Center, where "front-end technicians" now have the ability to access customer records, remotely test lines, and fulfill most customers' repair requests while they are still on the telephone. (Photo: Courtesy GTE.)

The manager's responsibility is to make sure that set objectives support overall organizational goals. To obtain commitment from employees, managers must define organizational objectives and point out how they support each employee's personal goals. Finally, the objectives for any particular person or group should mesh with the objectives of others who might be affected by them. One way to address these constraints is to conduct team goal-setting meetings so that all concerned parties can participate openly.

There is little motivational value in setting objectives that require nothing more than maintenance of present performance levels. On the other hand, very difficult objectives may appear unattainable and therefore be demoralizing. While objectives should foster an improvement over present performance, they should also be clearly *achievable*.

Assess the Current Situation.   When evaluating the current situation, participants must focus on both the "what" and the "how" of performance from two viewpoints: that of the organization and that of the people involved. The immediate need is to determine if goals are met by the current situation. Do actual conditions match desired ones? If not, what are the differences? Mismatches usually show up clearly, but sometimes an inadequate current situation is taken for granted because it is how things have been for so long. If the matching process reveals discrepancies, the next step is to determine why.

Identify Problems.   Serious mistakes can be made if managers act before they accurately identify all of the sources of a problem. To identify a problem accurately, it must be understood from all points of view.

The full determination of how a particular problem prevents people from accomplishing desired goals can be made only when all parties are free to participate in its identification without fear of being blamed or criticized. If problem solving is perceived as a joint learning experience, people will be much more likely to contribute needed information than if they fear punishment for disclosing information that may indicate they have made mistakes.

Problem identification and solution are much easier in routine than nonroutine situations. Routine problems are those that arise on a regular basis and can be solved through *programmed decisions*—standard responses based on procedures that have been effective in the past. One example of a programmed decision is a student's automatic probationary status when his or her grade point average sinks below a predetermined level. Another is the reordering of supplies as soon as inventory on hand falls below a certain quantity. Most routine problems are anticipated, which allows managers to plan in advance how to deal with them and sometimes to delegate problem solving to their subordinates.

Nonroutine problems are ones not anticipated by managers. They are unique. No standard responses to them exist. These types of problems require *nonprogrammed decisions*—innovative solutions tailored to fit specific dilemmas. The petroleum shortage of the late 1970s was a nonroutine problem that required new ways of distributing gasoline and transporting goods and people. Catastrophes always pose nonroutine problems. When an American Airlines DC-10 crashed in 1979, all the nation's DC-10s were grounded. Stranded ticket holders, shortages of long-range aircraft, and idle pilots and flight crews were just some of the nonroutine problems faced by decision makers at many levels.

One way to be prepared for potential problems and to be able to quickly identify their causes is to thoroughly understand the process involved. A **flow chart** is a pictorial representation of all the steps of a process. Flow charts document a process and help demonstrate how the various steps relate to each other. See Exhibit 12–2 for a sample flow chart involving quality inspection of incoming parts.

The flow chart is widely used in problem identification. The people with the greatest amount of knowledge about the process meet to first draw a flow chart of what steps the process actually follows. Then they draw a flow chart of what steps the process should ideally follow. By comparing the two charts they find differences, because that is where the problems arise.[8]

flow chart
A pictorial representation of all the steps of a process.

Problem Definition

If the problem is not defined clearly, any attempt at solving it will be doomed to fail because the parties involved won't really know what they are working on. All the remaining steps will be distorted because they will be based on insufficient or erroneous information. Lack of information often inhibits the generation of adequate alternatives and exploration of potentially negative consequences.

All necessary information should be gathered so that all relevant factors can be analyzed to determine the exact problem that must be solved. The goal is to determine the root causes of the problem. If instruction forms are constantly misinterpreted, for example, are the forms incomplete, or is the required information poorly supplied? Causes should not be assumed; instead, all plausible alternatives should be investigated before settling on the most probable cause(s).

Hasty assumptions can also result in symptoms being mistaken for sources of problems. When symptoms are eliminated, it is often mistakenly assumed that the problem has also been eliminated. This is like receiving medication from your doctor to control a skin rash, which is only a symptom that something is wrong. The medication clears the rash, but the actual cause of the problem isn't identified

▄▄▄▄ **EXHIBIT 12–2**

Process Flow Diagram:
Receiving Inspection

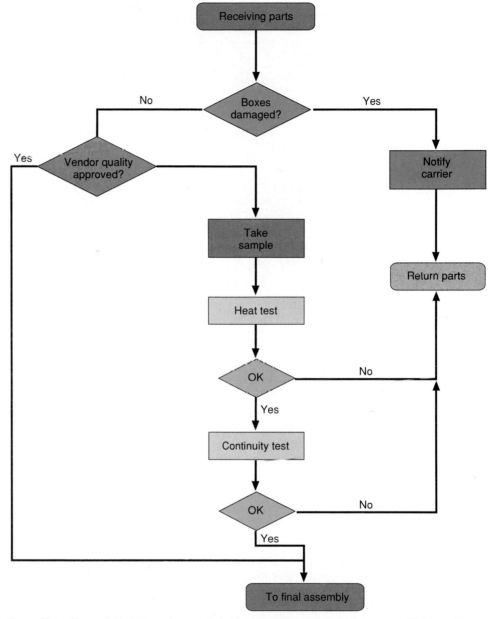

Source: Michael Brassard. *The Memory Jogger: A Pocket Guide of Tools for Continuous Improvement* (Methuen, MA: GOAL/QPC, 1988), p. 10.

until you and/or the physician look for clues. When you discover that the onset of the rash coincided with the arrival of a new plant in your living room, you have identified the problem: an allergy to that plant.

Analyze Problems.   Checking to make sure that the problem is defined accurately and analyzed completely provides a safeguard against incorrect assumptions, treatment of symptoms only, and incomplete understanding. The way a problem is actually defined has a major impact on what alternatives are considered, what

A TQM team at George Washington University Medical Center identified and analyzed a problem in the hospital's oncology unit: patients could sometimes wait up to 12 hours for elective chemotherapy. When the team dissected the process of admitting a patient to the hospital, they found it to be much more complicated than they had imagined. Team-suggested changes in the admissions process were implemented, and the average time between admission and start of chemotheraphy decreased from 11 hours to less than 2 hours. (Photo: © Terry Ashe.)

decision is reached, and how the action plan is implemented. Failure to define an identified problem accurately can impede consideration and eventual application of the best solution.

Failure to thoroughly diagnose a problem can result from inadequate time and energy available to review all the possible causes and implications. Other times, underlying psychological reasons come into play, such as not wanting to know what the real problems are, fearing that we ourselves are to blame, being concerned that a close associate will be hurt, or anticipating that the problem will prove too enormous for us.

One technique for facilitating a thorough problem analysis is the cause-and-effect diagram.[9] A *cause-and-effect diagram,* or fishbone chart, is constructed to represent the relationship between some "effect" and all possible "causes" influencing it. As illustrated in Exhibit 12–3, the effect or problem is stated on the right side of the chart, and the major influences or causes are listed to the left. Although a problem may have various sources, the major causes can usually be summarized under the four "M" categories of *manpower, methods, machines,* and *material.* Data can then be gathered and shared to determine the relative frequencies and magnitudes of contribution of the different potential causes.

Agree on Problems to Be Solved.   If more than one problem has been identified and defined, the next step is to set priorities regarding which problem will be worked on first and which ones will be put aside temporarily or indefinitely. One criterion for rank ordering multiple problems is how much their solutions will contribute to desired objectives. The most important problems should be dealt with first, even if their solutions seem more difficult. One quality management tool that can help management do this is called Pareto analysis.

━━━━ **EXHIBIT 12–3**

*Cause-and-Effect Diagram
(Fishbone Analysis)*

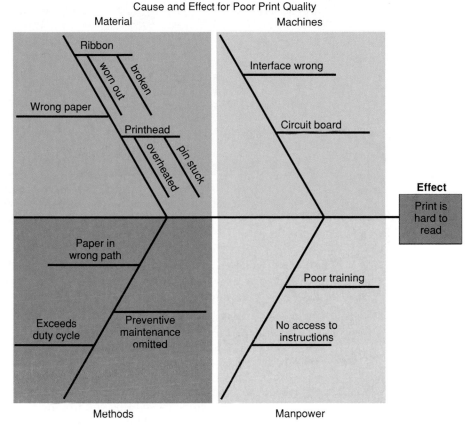

Source: Michael Brassard. *The Memory Jogger: A Pocket Guide of Tools for Continuous Improvement* (Methuen, MA: GOAL/QPC, 1988), p. 26.

Pareto chart
A vertical bar graph that indicates which problems should be solved first.

A **Pareto chart** is a vertical bar graph that indicates which problems, or causes of problems, should be solved first. To construct a Pareto chart, the problems to be compared and rank ordered are determined by brainstorming and analyzing existing data. Then a standard for comparison, such as annual cost or frequency of occurrence, and the time period to be studied are selected. After necessary data for each category have been gathered, the frequency or cost of each category is compared to that for other categories. The categories are listed from left to right on the horizontal axis in order of decreasing frequency or cost.[10] A Pareto chart of field service customer complaints is illustrated in Exhibit 12–4.

Decision Making

After information has been gathered and goals have been clarified, situations assessed, and problems identified, the next step is to develop a particular course of action that will either restore formerly acceptable conditions or improve the situation in a significant way. Since there is usually more than one way to solve a problem, it is critical to keep open to all possible solutions and arrive at several alternatives from which to choose.

▬▬▬▬ EXHIBIT 12–4

Pareto Chart: Field Service Customer Complaints (Rank Order by Frequency of Occurrence)

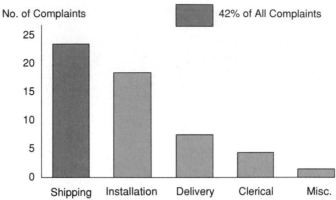

No. of Complaints   ▮ 42% of All Complaints

Used with permission from GOAL/QPC, 13 Branch Street, Methuen, MA 01844–1953. Tel: 508–685–3900. Source: *The Memory Jogger: A Pocket Guide of Tools for Continuous Improvement.* Copyright © 1988 GOAL/QPC.

criteria
Statements of objectives that need to be met for a problem to be solved.

Establish Decision-Making Criteria.   Decision-making **criteria** are statements of objectives that need to be met for a problem to be solved. Effective criteria should possess the following characteristics:

- *Specific, Measurable, and Attainable.* "I need to reduce scrap material waste by 10 percent, avoid a reduction in product quality, and increase production by 5 percent," is an example of a concise decision-making criteria statement. Decision-making criteria should be *specific:* "I will increase productivity by 5 percent," not just "I want to increase productivity." Second, they should be *measurable:* Saying you want to increase employee morale is not as good a criterion statement as saying that you will increase employee morale as indicated by a 4 percent reduction in absenteeism over the next three months. Third, to gain commitment to meeting criteria, there should be sufficient time, resources, and expertise available to make them *attainable.*

- *Complementary.* The criteria must also complement one another. The achievement of one should not reduce the likelihood of achieving another. For example, you would not improve the quality and detail of your written reports at the expense of spending the necessary time with those who must interact with you.

- *Ethical.* Decision criteria should conform to what is considered morally right by society. Criteria should be legal, fair, and observant of human rights. Organizations need to establish a commonly agreed on set of ethical standards to guide decisions when individuals are confronted with conflicting obligations, cost-benefit trade-offs, and competing value choices. The following section on ethical decision making expands on the many dilemmas of applying moral criteria.

- *Acceptable.* Even the best technical decision will not be workable if it is unacceptable to the parties involved. You may be convinced, for example, that the best solution for meeting a production deadline without increasing costs is to have the department work weekends for the next month without additional compensation. But this is not a viable action plan because it will not be acceptable to those on whom its implementation depends. Negative reactions to changes can create more problems than are solved. Sensitivity to emotional factors, personal values, and individual objectives is vital in choosing a successful action plan.

Develop Action Alternatives. The value, acceptance, and implementation of an action plan are enhanced by involving all affected parties in the generation and analysis of alternatives. Acceptance can be tested by soliciting feedback to determine if those involved understand the potential benefits and to assess their readiness to make the necessary commitment. As many solutions as possible should be generated to avoid picking a premature solution that doesn't meet all long-run criteria. Techniques to facilitate this step are provided in the following section on how problems can be solved more effectively.

Evaluate Benefits and Risks of Alternatives. It is important to look at all the long-run consequences of the alternatives being considered. This is sometimes overlooked because of our tendency to avoid spending extra time and energy and our fear of discovering negative consequences in preferred solutions.

Important criteria to consider in evaluating action alternatives are each alternative's *probability of success* and the associated *degree of risk* that negative consequences will occur. If the chance of failure is high and the related costs for an alternative are great, the benefits of an alternative may not justify its use. Risk can be personal as well as economic—just ask the person whose reputation is on the line or who is soon to undergo a performance review. The degree of risk can be separated into four categories: certainty, known risk, uncertainty, and turbulence.[11]

Certainty exists if the exact results of implementing a problem solution are known in advance. Certainty (of return) exists if you put your money in a savings account for one year, whereas it does not exist if you invest it in real estate or the stock market. Certainty is the exception rather than the rule in most managerial decision-making situations. Complete information and guaranteed outcomes are rare.

Known risk is present when the probability that a given alternative will produce specific outcomes can be predicted. For example, an executive may know that by taking a commercial airline flight tonight, he or she has a 99.5 percent probability of arriving on time for a business meeting in New York tomorrow morning. If the executive lives in San Diego, he or she will also know for certain that if the last flight is missed, the meeting tomorrow will also be missed. Probabilities based on historical records or statistical analyses are sometimes assigned to risky alternatives. At other times, probabilities are simply estimated through managerial intuition.

Uncertainty exists when decision makers are unable to assign any probabilities to the consequences associated with an alternative. Choices among uncertain alternatives are often based on intuition and hunches.

Turbulence occurs when the environment is rapidly changing and decision makers are not even clear about relevant variables, available solution options, or potential consequences of decisions. In times of recession, economic reforms, or military conflict, turbulence usually prevails.

Decide on a Plan. As alternatives are evaluated according to these criteria, many will be clearly unsatisfactory and can be eliminated. Sometimes the evaluation will reveal that one alternative is decidedly superior to all others. At other times none of the proposed action plans will be acceptable, signaling a need to develop additional alternatives. Most often, however, several alternatives will appear feasible, and the best one must be selected. Exhibit 12–5 illustrates a decision-making grid that summarizes the above criteria for evaluating alternatives. Such a grid can help to visualize which alternative offers the maximum benefits with minimal risks and

Alternatives	Criteria					
	Benefits	Probability of Success	Costs	Risks	Associated Consequences	Timing
Alternative A						
Alternative B						
Alternative C						

costs. The decision-making goal is to select the best solution alternative for solving the entire problem without creating any additional negative consequences for anyone else in the organization.

Perfect Rationality.   In a world of perfect rationality, all problems can be clearly defined, all information and alternatives are known, the consequences of implementing each alternative are certain, and the decision maker is a completely rational being who is concerned only about economic gain. These conditions of *classical decision theory* allow for an optimal solution to every problem and provide the basics for ideal management decision making. The real world, however, is made up of real people with real problems, and it rarely conforms to these ideal conditions.

Bounded Rationality.   *Behavioral decision theory* has questioned the classical assumptions and recognized the real-world limitations to obtaining and processing all relevant information that might optimize decision making. Administrators exhibit bounded rationality when they reach satisfactory rather than "perfect" decisions. Bounded rationality is necessary in the face of constraints on time, money, and intellectual resources.[12] While the goal of the decision model presented here is to optimize decision outcomes, **satisficing**—choosing the first satisfactory alternative that meets minimal requirements—probably describes the majority of daily managerial decision making. Fortunately, this was not the approach taken by President John F. Kennedy's decision-making group to resolve the Cuban missile crisis described in the World Watch box.

satisficing
Choosing the first satisfactory decision alternative that meets minimal requirements.

Action Plan Implementation

A decision and action plan are of little value unless they are effectively implemented. How the action plan is to be accomplished connects the decision with reality. Implementation includes assigning tasks and responsibilities and establishing an implementation schedule.

Assign Tasks and Responsibilities.   It is important to clarify both verbally and in writing what each person involved will do to make the new action plan work. To avoid misunderstandings, it is essential to specify who is to do what, by when, and how.

Establish an Implementation Schedule.   To be effectively implemented, all necessary tasks need a specified time schedule for completion. One way to do this is to start at an end point (the date by which the objective should be completed) and

World Watch

The Cuban Missile Crisis Revisited

The subject was how the United States should counter menacing communist moves on a Caribbean island. The president's advisors were sorely perplexed: Every idea they could think of posed the gravest dangers, but in the end they hit on a successful course of action.

As American troops were invading Grenada, the John F. Kennedy Library in Boston released tapes and transcripts of two meetings between President Kennedy and his top aides at the start of the Cuban missile crisis 21 years earlier. That confrontation, immensely more ominous than the Grenada conflict, posed a lesson for management planners facing unexpected trouble. George Ball, who participated in the meetings as undersecretary of state, spelled it out in a *Washington Post* article published just before the release of the tapes: "Had we fixed on a response within the first 48 hours," Ball wrote, "we would almost certainly have made the wrong decision." Crisis planners, he said, must "carefully examine all the consequences and look far beyond our initial action."

The tapes establish that JFK and his advisors did exactly that on October 16, 1962, the day after the U.S. photo reconnaissance proved that the Soviets were installing nuclear missiles in Cuba. Initially, the planners more or less assumed that the United States would have to take military action. President Kennedy at one point described an air strike, at least on the missiles, as something "we're certainly going to do." His primary question then was whether the action could be kept limited or would have to be expanded, possibly to include an eventual U.S. invasion of Cuba.

Joint Chiefs of Staff Chairman Maxwell Taylor and Secretary of Defense Robert McNamara were dubious

about the prospects for a "surgical" strike limited to the missiles. If the United States wanted to "knock out" all Soviet weapons capable of hitting American soil from Cuba, said McNamara, it would have to bomb "airfields, plus the aircraft . . . plus all potential nuclear warhead storage sites." The president's brother, Attorney General Robert F. Kennedy, fretted that such extensive bombing would "kill an awful lot of people," in which case it would be "almost incumbent on the Russians" to threaten a strong counterblow, perhaps far from Cuba. Moreover, the secrecy necessary for successful military action would preclude consultation with allies, and that worried Secretary of State Dean Rusk. He warned that if the United States took "an action of this sort without letting our closer allies know of a matter which could subject them to a very great danger . . . we could find ourselves isolated and the NATO alliance crumbling at a moment of maximum peril."

Toward the close of the evening meeting, McNamara eloquently pleaded that the planners consider "what kind of world we live in after we've struck Cuba . . . how do we stop at that point?" Instead of an air strike, McNamara began talking of a blockade, accompanied by "an ultimatum" to the Soviets, which he conceded would have dangers also. He said, "This alternative doesn't seem to be a very acceptable one, but wait until you work on the others." That provoked grim laughter, but after many more meetings, a blockade was decided on. It ultimately drew overwhelming public support from around the world and induced the Soviets to pull their missiles out of Cuba without any necessity for the United States to fire a shot.

Source: *Time* (November 7, 1983), p. 50.

Gantt chart
A graphic planning method that breaks down a project into separate tasks and estimates the time needed for their completion.

work backward. Action implementation steps can be listed in priority order and assigned reasonable time periods for completion, starting with the last step before the objective is accomplished.

One of the earliest scheduling techniques was developed by Harry Gantt in the early 1900s. A **Gantt chart** is a graphic planning and control method that breaks down a project into separate tasks and estimates the time needed for their

IDS Financial Services, the nation's top financial planning firm, was plagued by high employee turnover and growing competition. The company established a 30-person design team, recruited from all areas of the company, to redesign the company with four objectives in mind: retain 95% of clients; retain 80% of IDS planners with four years of service; achieve 18% annual revenue growth; and bolster IDS's position as the industry leader. The team broke into 10 committees. Final design recommendations were planned for testing in 1993 with full roll out in 1994. (Photo: © 1993 Doug Knutson.)

completion. The chart has a space for planned starting and completion dates and for actual dates filled in as implementation occurs. A sample Gantt chart appears in Exhibit 12–6.

Gantt charts help to make certain that all implementation tasks are considered in relationship to each other and that appropriate people are assigned to each task. They provide checkpoints for all tasks to ensure that they are finished on time. Gantt charts are developed by defining goals and setting completion dates and then bracketing time blocks based on the time required and completion date of each task.

Once an action plan is implemented, managers often move on to another task. It is of key importance, however, to follow through to be sure that the solution is working effectively and that no additional problems have been created. Follow-through is the final stage of the problem-solving process.

Follow-Through

Following-through entails the development and maintenance of positive attitudes in everyone involved in the implementation process. There are several guidelines to help establish the positive climate necessary for the implementation steps that follow:

- Visualize yourself in the position of those doing the implementing so that you understand their feelings and perspectives.
- Establish sincere respect and concern.
- Make sure necessary resources are available.

With this kind of positive climate set up, there are several sequential steps in the follow-through process. They include establishing the criteria for measuring success, monitoring the results obtained, and taking corrective action when necessary.

Establish Criteria for Measuring Success.   Unless the circumstances have changed, the criteria for measuring problem-solving success are the time, quality, and quantity goals already developed in the action-planning stage. These criteria serve as *benchmarks* for measuring and comparing the actual results.

EXHIBIT 12–6 *Sample Gantt Chart*

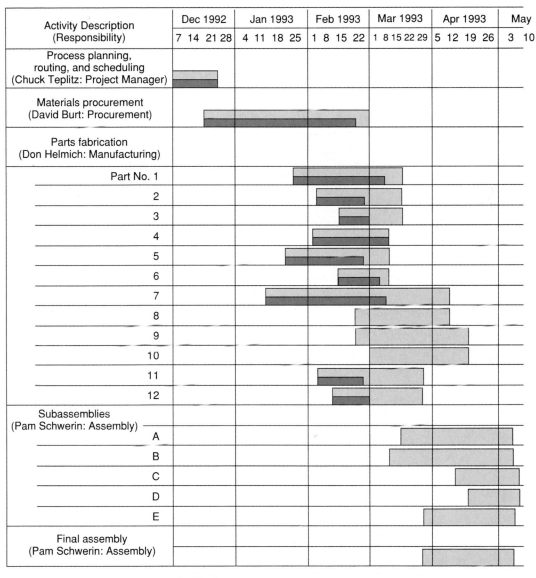

Activity Description (Responsibility)	Dec 1992	Jan 1993	Feb 1993	Mar 1993	Apr 1993	May
	7 14 21 28	4 11 18 25	1 8 15 22	1 8 15 22 29	5 12 19 26	3 10
Process planning, routing, and scheduling (Chuck Teplitz: Project Manager)						
Materials procurement (David Burt: Procurement)						
Parts fabrication (Don Helmich: Manufacturing)						
Part No. 1						
2						
3						
4						
5						
6						
7						
8						
9						
10						
11						
12						
Subassemblies (Pam Schwerin: Assembly) A						
B						
C						
D						
E						
Final assembly (Pam Schwerin: Assembly)						

Planned starting and completion dates
Work completed

Source: L. W. Rue and L. L. Byars, *Management Skills and Applications,* 6th ed. (Homewood, IL: Richard D. Irwin, 1992), p. 210. Adapted from Elwood S. Buffa, *Modern Production Management,* 4th ed. (New York: John Wiley & Sons, Inc., 1973), p. 576.

Monitor the Results. The data on the results can be compared with the established criteria. If the new performance meets the criteria, no further action is necessary other than continued monitoring. If the new results do not measure up, the next step is to determine why. Each implementation step may alter the problem situation in unanticipated ways.

Take Corrective Action.   The problem-solving process is a *closed-loop system*. If performance fails to match the success criteria, the problem needs to be identified by again applying the problem-solving process. For any new corrective action plan, new measures and schedules need to be determined and new data need to be gathered and tested against the criteria.

WHAT IS ETHICAL DECISION MAKING?

A large majority of American managers agree that unethical practices occur in business, and a substantial portion (about 65 percent) report that they have been pressured to compromise their own ethical standards when making organizational decisions.[13] Some of the underlying causes for individuals and organizations making poor choices when considering ethical issues are: [14]

- Individuals and/or organizations are sometimes immature.
- Economic self-interest is overwhelming.
- Special circumstances outweigh ethical concerns.
- Lack of education in the areas of morality and ethics.
- Potential rewards outweigh possible punishments for unethical behavior.
- The culture or mindset is that "All's fair in love, war, and business."
- Organizational pressure on individuals to commit unethical acts.

ethics
The discipline dealing with moral duty and obligations regarding what is good and bad.

ethical behavior
Behavior that conforms to accepted standards of conduct.

ethical reasoning
Sorting out principles that determine what is ethical.

ethical dilemma
A problem that involves complex and conflicting principles of ethical behavior.

Ethics is the discipline dealing with what is good and bad and with moral duty and obligations. **Ethical behavior** is that which conforms to accepted standards of conduct. **Ethical reasoning** involves sorting out the principles that help determine what is ethical when faced with an ethical dilemma. An **ethical dilemma** is a situation or problem facing an individual that involves complex and often conflicting principles of ethical behavior. A classic example of an ethical dilemma would be the submarine commander who has to decide whether to stay afloat to save a downed pilot or to submerge immediately to avoid enemy aircraft. In business, ethical dilemmas often arise when managers face conflicting values. For example, a salesperson might face the dilemma of telling the truth about a product and thus losing a sale and his or her commission.

To prevent these ethical dilemmas, organizational decision makers need to prioritize all competing values and standards of behavior. A commonly agreed on set of ethical standards can then be developed to guide decisions when conflicting obligations, cost-benefit trade-offs, and competing value choices are present.[15] When thinking through particular dilemmas, the following questions can sharpen ethical sensitivity and moral awareness:[16]

- Does this decision or action meet the highest societal standards about how people should interact with each other?
- Does this decision or action agree with my religious teachings and beliefs (or with my personal principles and sense of responsibility?
- How will I feel about myself if I do this?
- Do we (or I) have a rule or policy for cases like this?
- Would I want everyone to make the same decision and take the same action if faced with these same circumstances?
- What are my true motives for considering this action?

Ethical Decision Making in International Environments

The United States hoped that other countries would follow its 1977 passage of the Foreign Corrupt Practices Act with similar laws. None have, however, which places American companies at a major disadvantage when operating in foreign countries with different business ethics. Many other countries actually consider payoffs to win business not only legal but tax deductible. In Thailand, for example, payoffs are taken for granted, and in China, corruption among government officials is widely acknowledged. In Malaysia, companies routinely turn out blatant copies of American products, even stamping U.S. logos on the goods.

For American companies to operate successfully in East Asia, the world's fastest-growing region, they must somehow develop business relationships without violating U.S. ethics laws. Some companies think this is impossible and don't even try. Other companies try to operate under the spirit of the law without actually circumventing it themselves by enlisting intermediaries to handle the local business practices in any way they can. These practices frequently backfire, however.

Los Angeles–based Teledyne, for example, was accused of hiring a former Egyptian general to make illegal payments to buy influence for the aerospace company's business in Egypt. Teledyne allegedly paid the general more than $1.5 million for the illegal "purchase of influence." Teledyne never disclosed to the Securities and Exchange Commission and Defense Department authorities as required by federal law that it hired a foreign agent in the Middle East, an act verified by the Teledyne chairman's signature on a lease for the general's apartment.

The 10-year career of a senior manager at Mattel Toy Company came crashing to the ground when he was jailed for two years and fined $300,000 for soliciting bribes from two of Mattel's Taiwanese fabric suppliers to place Mattel's textile orders with the firms. These penalties were administered even though the judges stated publicly that "a culture of corruption" existed in Taiwan and that "Taiwan witnesses gave the impression that paying illegal commissions was a necessary irritant in business deals."

Sources: "Manager Jailed For Barbie Bribe," *HongKong Standard* (January 13, 1996), p. 2; "Ex-Mattel Manager Sent to Jail," *South China Morning Post* (January 13, 1996), p. 6; Ralph Vartabedian, "Teledyne Is Accused of Bribery," *Los Angeles Times* (October 29, 1992), pp. D1 and D5; and Ford S. Worthy, "When Somebody Wants a Payoff," *Fortune* (Fall 1989), pp. 117–122.

Public Justification Criteria. One dilemma in determining ethical criteria concerns differences of opinion regarding what behaviors are appropriate. The rule of thumb in North American business culture is whether you would feel proud about your behavior if every detail was published in the newspaper the next day. Specific questions to ask yourself when contemplating an action using *public justification criteria* are:[17]

- How would I feel (or how will I feel) if (or when) this action becomes public knowledge?
- Will I be able to explain adequately to others why I have taken this action?
- Would others feel that my action or decision is ethical or moral?

This test does not eliminate ethical dilemmas between subcultures or different countries, however, because there are "readers" with very different values. An international example concerning different expectations about bribery is given in the Eye on Ethics box.

Four Types of Values As Benchmarks. Since neither the home or host country values are absolute or hold for both countries, some type of transitional, or compromise criteria, need to be established in these situations that satisfy all parties concerned with the interactions. Nevertheless, there are some moral values that might be so important to a party that they should never be compromised. These are core values, or *absolute values,* like those established by the United Nations regarding basic human rights. *Compatible values* are statements of desirable ways of behaving that support absolute values. One example is a credo statement of a company that states how members should behave to live up to the company's absolute values. *Transitional values* are those that bend somewhat from absolute and compatible values to be more compatible with the different values of another culture. For example, the limits established for gift giving in the United States might be less than those allowed for Japan, where the custom is to be more extravagant. These are values in tension, which may or may not endure depending on the consequences. Finally, there are *intolerable values* that are so opposed to our core values that no interaction with the people holding them is possible. Countries allowing slave labor or dangerous procedures with high death rates would not be viable business partners for a company in a Judeo-Christian country.[18]

Example of an Ethical Dilemma Personified. Competing ethical criteria can also create ethical dilemmas within the same culture. Take the dilemma faced by John Higgins in the following situation.

John Higgins is director of research for a large electronics industry company. He recently promoted Mary Fernandez to head the design team charged with developing a critical component for a new radar system. He evaluated Mary as having superior knowledge of the technical elements in the project. However, he had begun to hear that the members of the all-male team were complaining about a woman leading them. There was evidence that some team members were subtly sabotaging the project. John knew it was fair to give Mary this job based on her merits, but he also knew that the successful and quick completion of the project was essential both for the company's success and his own reputation. He wondered if he should remove Mary as team leader.[19]

John Higgins's problem is typical of the complex decisions managers face much of the time. These problems can be viewed from different points of view, including the economic, legal, and moral frameworks.[20] A strictly *economic* framing of this problem would consider what is most efficient and effective in terms of minimizing costs and maximizing efficiency and profits. From this point of view, Higgins would likely opt to remove Mary Fernandez as team leader. The *legal* view is concerned with whether or not a given act violates the law. Using a legal framework, Higgins would ask such questions as Would removing Fernandez be illegal because of gender discrimination? Does management have the legal right to assign duties? From this viewpoint, Higgins may need legal advice in making his decision. Viewing this problem from a *moral* framework raises a different set of questions. Two basic ones are: Would such a move be right? Would it be fair and just? A decision might be both economically wise and legal and still be immoral.

Some people believe that moral considerations apply to their personal lives but not to their business decisions. Those with this viewpoint believe that economic and legal considerations are the only relevant basis for making sound business decisions. What is most profitable overrides moral considerations, assuming legality.

This does not mean such people believe business is an immoral activity. Rather, they would see it as amoral, which means business runs according to its own rules. They assume that laws provide the necessary rules for conducting business, so the relevant questions are: Is the behavior profitable? Is it legal? If John Higgins held this amoral view, he would likely replace Mary. However, he might believe that moral issues are relevant for work as well as for personal behavior. Managers face difficult decisions when they must balance moral considerations and organizational goals.

Morality

morality
A set of principles defining right and wrong behaviors.

What, then, is a moral viewpoint? **Morality** is a set of principles defining right and wrong behaviors. A behavior is considered moral if it conforms to a standard of right behavior.[21] The concept of ethics is closely related to morality, and the terms moral and ethical are frequently used synonymously.

Some educators say ethics cannot be taught.[22] Their point, partially, is that people may be taught ethical behavior, but that there is no guarantee they will behave ethically. While this is true, the starting point is to teach people to recognize the ethical dimensions of a problem and to reason with ethical principles to decide on an ethical solution in a particular situation. A framework for applying moral principles to ethical dilemmas is presented below.

Moral Principles

When individuals are confronted with ethical dilemmas—situations that involve conflicting or competing moral interests—it is helpful to have guiding principles for reasoning through the dilemma. Three major sets of moral principles are utilitarianism, rights, and justice.

utilitarianism
Achieving the greatest good for the greatest number.

Utilitarianism. **Utilitarianism** means to act in such a way that the greatest good is achieved for the greatest number.[23] To use utilitarianism for reasoning through an ethical dilemma, begin by identifying alternative courses of action.[24] Then determine the benefits and harm resulting from each alternative for all relevant stakeholders. A *stakeholder* is any person or group that would be affected by the behavior resulting from a decision being made. Next select the alternative that encompasses the most benefits and least harm for the most stakeholders. This principle is similar to cost-benefit analysis, which is commonly used in business decision making. Utilitarianism guides the decision maker to choose the alternative that produces the greatest net social good when all the stakeholders are considered.

social good
Decision outcomes resulting in the most happiness and benefits.

In the context of a moral decision, **social good** is defined in general terms such as happiness, benefit, or least harm.[25] The broad nature of this definition sometimes makes application of the concept difficult, and people may differ in their assessments. It is easier to use the economics term, **utility,** but it has a narrower meaning, referring to only the economic benefits realized in transactions. It is much more difficult to measure happiness, benefit, or good. The greater the number of stakeholders affected by a decision, the more difficult is such measurement.

utility
The economic benefits of a decision outcome.

Another weakness of utilitarianism is its focus on outcomes and not on the means for achieving the ends. If utilitarianism is the only principle applied, some courses of action may be suggested that conflict with other ethical principles such as rights and justice. The Higgins-Fernandez case exemplifies this point. Higgins might reason that he, the other employees, and the company would best be served if the conflict surrounding Mary Fernandez were eliminated by removing her. However, such a decision would appear to violate Fernandez's rights, and many would question the fairness or justice of such a decision.

In spite of these limitations, the utilitarian principle can be useful. Its main value is that it helps guide decision makers to act in ways that lead to the greatest social good. Appropriate application of utilitarianism requires considering the impact of decisions on all stakeholders and reaching decisions that benefit the largest number. Questions to ask when applying utilitarianism might include:[26]

- What will be the short- and long-term consequences of this action?
- Who will benefit from this course of action?
- Who will be hurt?
- How will this action create good and prevent harm?

right
A justified claim for others to behave toward a person in a certain way.

Rights. A second philosophical approach to reasoning about ethical dilemmas focuses on the rights of individuals. This approach is grounded in the work of Immanuel Kant, the eighteenth century German philosopher who believed that each individual has a right to be treated with dignity and respect and as a free and equal person. A **right** is a justified claim or entitlement that an individual can make to behave or to have others behave toward him or her in a certain way.[27] The justification for such a claim is based on a standard accepted by a society. Sometimes these rights are explicitly stated. The Declaration of Independence identifies life, liberty, and the pursuit of happiness as "unalienable rights," and the United States Constitution sets forth the "Bill of Rights," which includes such things as the right of free speech and the "right to a speedy and public trial by an impartial jury" if accused of a crime. Interpretations of these specific rights have led to many additional legal and socially accepted moral rights.

Legal rights are codified in law, whereas *moral rights* are justified by society's generally accepted moral standards. An important basis for moral rights is Kant's principle that humanity must always be treated as an end, not merely as a means.[28] This implies that treating another as a means is to use that person for one's own gain. Treating the individual as an end implied respect by allowing the person to choose for herself or himself in order to satisfy personal needs and goals.

Rights impose corresponding duties. These duties may either be to refrain from certain behavior or to act out certain behavior. For example, an individual's right to privacy imposes on others the duty to refrain from violating that privacy. Kant's notion that each individual should be treated with respect suggests that each individual has a corresponding duty to treat others with respect. If society accepts that each individual has a right to education or medical care, there are corresponding duties to provide them for those who cannot provide for themselves.

The rights approach suggests that actions are wrong that violate the rights of individuals. However, individual rights sometimes conflict. For example, the right to associate freely with whomever one wants may conflict with the right not to be discriminated against. For example, should a private club be able to determine that only men can be members? In such cases the decision maker needs to determine which right is more important for sustaining human dignity. Is it free association or equality?[29]

The rights approach to ethical dilemmas indicates that it is morally wrong to interfere with the moral rights of an individual. However, consideration of individual rights alone is insufficient for ethical decision making because social costs must also be considered. Individual rights should not be achieved at an unreasonable cost to others in the society. The difficulty of defining, measuring, and balancing these rights sometimes make specific ethical decisions difficult. Both individual rights and the common good must be considered. Questions to ask when using the rights approach to solve ethical dilemmas include:[30]

- Would this action infringe or impinge on the moral rights or dignity of others?
- Would this action allow others freedom of choice in this matter?
- Would this action involve deceiving others in any way?

justice
Fairness in the distribution of rewards and punishments.

Justice. Justice has been connected with ethics and morality more than any idea in western civilization.[31] **Justice** is fairness. It means giving each person what he or she deserves.[32] Conflicts often develop when people disagree over how benefits and burdens should justly be distributed. The challenge is to determine morally what each person or group justly deserves.

One widely accepted principle that helps reason about such issues was stated by Aristotle over two thousand years ago. He postulated that equals should be treated equally and unequals unequally. Today, that principle is interpreted as meaning that "individuals should be treated the same, unless they differ in ways that are relevant to the situation in which they are involved."[33] For example, two people of different gender or race who perform equally should be compensated equally. However, two people who perform and contribute differently should be paid differently, even if they are of the same gender or race. Differences based on such criteria as contribution, need, and what one deserves are sometimes used to justify unequal treatment. For example, it is widely accepted that it is just for the government to treat poor people differently than those who are wealthy. However, many would agree that it is not just, or fair, to treat Mary Fernandez differently than her male colleagues only because of gender.

distributive justice
The fair distribution of benefits and burdens across a group or society.

retributive justice
Fairness of compensation awarded to injured parties.

compensatory justice
Fairness of blame or punishment for wrongdoers.

There are different types of justice.[34] The kind we have been talking about so far is **distributive justice,** which refers to the fair distribution of benefits and burdens across a group or society. A second kind of justice is **retributive justice,** which is the fairness of blame or punishment for wrongdoers. For example, most would say that firing an employee for making a relatively small mistake the first time would not be fair. On the other hand, if that employee had been adequately trained and had made a similar mistake before, and if the mistake was relatively expensive, termination might be just.

Compensatory justice is concerned with the fairness of compensation awarded to those who have been injured. For example, an employee who is terminated illegally is entitled to compensation for having been wronged. The extent of a compensation that is just depends on such factors as how long the employee goes without getting work, how long the employee had been with the employer, and how much hardship the illegal termination caused the employee.

Key questions to ask when making moral decisions are: Am I treating all people equally? If not, is such action justified? In business and other organizations people are often treated differently in terms of their pay, job responsibilities, and authority.

If these differences are based on morally acceptable criteria, such as performance or experience, such unequal treatment is considered just. Differences of treatment based on such things as race, gender, religion, or age are not considered just in the United States. Morally acceptable criteria, however, are different in different countries. Questions to apply when deciding how to be just include:[35]

- Would I feel that this action was just (ethical or fair) if I were on the other side of the decision?
- How would I feel if this action were done to me or to someone close to me?
- Would this action or decision distribute benefits justly?
- Would it distribute hardships or burdens justly?

Cultural differences will make a difference in what is considered just, which can cause ethical dilemmas in international business transactions like those previously described in the Eye on Ethics box. The issue of bribery, for example, is one of the toughest to resolve in the international context. It regularly occurs in government as well as business even though it violates all of the economic, legal, and moral frameworks just discussed. The free market system is the best in the world for promoting efficient productivity, but it only works if transactions are based solely on price and quality considerations. No country in the world has laws that sanction bribery, so it is universally illegal. Furthermore, it violates the moral principles of justice (it is not fair), rights (those who produce the best quality with the lowest price are not necessarily rewarded), and utilitarianism (the greatest net social good for all stakeholders is not obtained).[36]

Arthur Andersen & Company, one of the major U.S. accounting firms, is trying to help solve this type of business ethics dilemma. Brainstorming with ethics experts from academia and business, it has developed a program promoting ethics education in business schools and in employee training programs. The sessions cover ethical issues in finance, marketing, management, and accounting, such as accepting gifts and tips, truthfulness in advertising, and sexual harassment.[37]

As we have seen, however, not all issues can be unequivocally solved by applying previously agreed on standards of conduct because such agreement is impossible. In such situations, the best that one can do is to refer to personal intuition and insight. Some questions to ask yourself when dealing with these ambiguous ethical dilemmas are:[38]

- Have I searched for all alternatives? Are there other ways to look at this situation? Have I considered all points of view?
- Even if I can rationalize this decision or action, and even if I could defend it publicly, does my inner sense tell me this is right?
- What does my intuition tell me is the ethical thing to do in this situation? Have I listened to my inner voice?

WHAT ARE INDIVIDUAL DIFFERENCES IN DECISION STYLES?[39]

Individuals do not always follow ethical guidelines or the rational problem-solving process just described. Even when they do, there are variances due to individual information-processing habits. Some differences involve satisficing versus optimizing preferences. Others are determined by the amount of information people prefer and the criteria they focus on when making decisions.

When these maintenance and operating workers at Union Carbide's Taft, Louisiana plant threw out their old process flowchart and created a new one, they found savings worth more than $20 million—50% more than management expected. Union Carbide's top management made the decisions to redesign operations at the plant and ratified goals as to how the new design should work. But management left the details of the new design—how to set up shifts, for example—to the plant employees. (Photo: © John Chiasson/ Gamma-Liaison.)

decision styles
Learned habits for processing decision-making information.

Decision styles refer to our learned habits for processing decision-making information. Whether one style is "better" than another depends on the particular situation in which it is used. There are two primary ways that people differ in their decision-making habits: (1) in the amount of information they use and (2) in the number of alternatives they develop to potentially solve a problem.

Amount and Focus of Information Processing

Some people use a great deal of information in generating and evaluating alternatives, while others use very little. When faced with a problem, a *satisficer* uses just enough information to arrive at a feasible solution. The satisficer knows that more information about the problem might be available but decides that it is not worth the additional effort to obtain it.

A *maximizer,* on the other hand, continues to gather information until nothing new can be learned about the problem. A maximizer knows that a workable solution might be reached with less information but decides that important aspects of the problem might not be recognized unless all available information is considered.

Both methods are valuable in the appropriate situations. For example, the satisficer has an advantage when time is important, whereas the maximizer has an advantage when problems are complicated and there is little time pressure.

EXHIBIT 12–7

Individual Decision Styles

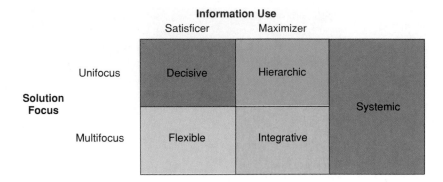

Solution focus refers to the number of alternatives that a person develops for dealing with a problem. *Unifocus* people are committed to one dominant criterion and consequently favor a single solution to a problem. *Multifocus* people, on the other hand, apply several criteria and generate several solutions to a problem. The unifocus approach has an advantage when efficiency is important, when it is possible to adopt only one solution, or when rules and regulations narrowly limit the range of choices. The multifocus approach has an advantage when there is a need to find new ways of doing things or it is important to "cover all the bases."

The Five Dominant Decision Styles

From these differences in amount of information used and solution focus, five fundamentally different decision styles emerge. Exhibit 12–7 illustrates the relationships among the five decision styles.

Decisive Style.   Decisive persons use just enough information to reach one workable solution. Decisives are fast-thinking, action-oriented people who place high importance on efficiency, promptness, and reliability. They usually stick to one course of action for dealing with a particular problem.

Flexible Style.   People with this style also use a minimal amount of information, but they are multifocused and so produce several solutions for a problem. Like Decisives, Flexibles are action oriented, but they place greater importance on adaptability than on efficiency. They like to keep their options open.

Hierarchic Style.   People with the hierarchic style analyze a large amount of information thoroughly to develop a single best solution to a problem. They place great emphasis on logic and quality. Hierarchics tend to be slow to make decisions the first time they encounter a particular problem, but they speed up substantially after they develop a method for handling that type of problem.

Integrative Style.   People with this style utilize a very large amount of information to produce multiple solutions to problems. Integratives value exploration, experimentation, and creativity. They look at problems from many points of view and see numerous options for dealing with a single problem. Consequently, they sometimes have difficulty deciding on only one solution, which makes them appear indecisive. To counter this tendency, Integratives sometimes try to implement several courses of action simultaneously.

Systemic Style. This two-stage decision style combines both integrative and hierarchic patterns. A person using the systemic style initially approaches a problem in the integrative way, viewing it from many points of view and exploring multiple solutions. After examining many options, however, the person becomes more hierarchic, subjecting various alternatives to a rigorous analysis that ends with a clearly prioritized set of solutions. The Systemic usually develops a very broad understanding of a problem. In many cases, Systemics examine multiple problems simultaneously to understand the broader implications of situations. Because of the thoroughness of their analyses, Systemics tend to be slow decision makers.

Backup Styles

Although most people have a clear predisposition toward one dominant decision style, many shift to a different "backup" style occasionally. The shift between dominant and backup styles is related to how much pressure a person experiences when making decisions.

Under the pressure of tight deadlines, high risk, and significant consequences, people tend to shift to the less complex decisive or flexible styles, which are easier and faster to use. These styles are also frequently used under low pressure if there is not enough information to employ a more complex style. Under moderate pressure, people tend to use the more complex systemic, integrative, or hierarchic styles because there is a lot of information available and sufficient time to analyze it in depth.

WHEN IS PARTICIPATION IMPORTANT FOR DECISION MAKING?

Who should be involved in the problem-solving process? Just the manager? A committee? A coalition of key individuals? The entire department? In 1992, General Motors was losing $2.5 million a day. To turn this negative trend around, employees were encouraged to participate wholeheartedly with GM management in a $3 billion gamble to build a tight, light, high-quality, peppy subcompact in competition with Tercel, Civic, and the rest of Japan's best. GM's approach was to merge management and labor into a team where they would make decisions and share the pains, gains, and profits. The result was a lean production facility, a familial management–labor structure, and an obsession with quality control. The product was the Saturn, which during its first nine months sold at twice the rate of Toyotas or Hondas.[40]

Degrees of Decision Participation

There is evidence that participation can enhance morale, satisfaction, and productivity, but in emergencies or when others do not have sufficient information, an autocratic decision may be more appropriate.[41] Degrees of decision participation can be grouped into the following three broad levels. [42]

- **Autocratic.** The manager solves the problem alone using only information personally available or solicited from subordinates. Subordinates are not involved in analyzing the problem or generating solutions.
- **Consultative.** The manager shares the problem with subordinates either individually or as a group and solicits their ideas and suggestions. The manager then makes an independent decision that may not reflect subordinates' inputs.

- **Group.** The manager shares the problem with subordinates as a group. Together the manager generates and evaluates alternatives with subordinates and attempts to reach a consensus agreement on a solution that the manager accepts and implements.

Criteria for Participation

When deciding how much participation to use when making a decision, several factors need to be considered. Three of the most important are the quality requirements, the degree that it is necessary for subordinates to accept the decision, and the time required to make the decision.

Quality Requirements.   Whether a decision is best made by an individual or a group depends on the nature and importance of the problem. Important decisions that have large impacts on organizational goal achievement need to be the highest quality possible. In a complex situation, it is unlikely that any one individual will have all the necessary information to make a top-quality decision. Therefore, the decision maker should at least consult with others who are either closer to the problem or more "expert" in dealing with it. One person with appropriate knowledge and experience, on the other hand, can decide what to do to solve simple routine problems.

Acceptance Requirements.   The effectiveness of the action plan decided on is a combination of its quality and the effort put into implementing it. A top-quality decision, if not implemented appropriately, will not be effective. A lower-quality decision that receives enthusiastic support from all involved may be more effective than a higher-quality alternative that implementers do not "buy into."

Those affected by a decision are usually more highly motivated to implement the action plan if they have had an opportunity to influence it. Being involved usually increases participants' understanding and generates a feeling of commitment to make "our" decision work, whereas an arbitrary, autocratic decision that is handed down often results in passive acceptance or even active resistance to implementation. This will be elaborated on in Chapter 16.

Time Requirements.   Allocating problem solving and decision making to a group requires a greater investment of time in meetings that is unavailable for usual tasks. But the level of acceptance and probability of efficient execution is greater for participative decisions than autocratic methods. Also, a higher-quality decision may result from the inclusion of a variety of perspectives and approaches. It is important to determine if this additional time investment produces significantly higher degrees of quality, acceptance, and commitment.

HOW CAN PROBLEMS BE SOLVED MORE EFFECTIVELY?

Techniques for avoiding groupthink and the liabilities of group decision making discussed in Chapter 10 can enhance group problem-solving effectiveness. Other methods for solving problems better include encouraging creativity, structured processes for guiding interaction, and electronic information processing.

Encouraging Creativity

For organizations to creatively solve problems, managers must demonstrate that they value it and know how to deal with innovations when they are suggested. The Center for Creative Leadership has determined some characteristics of managers who generate creativity in their organizations.

Fighting dyslexia while growing up, Chic Thompson concentrated on getting his ideas across verbally and visually. His ability to overcome his problems led Thompson to start Creative Management Group, a small business that helps companies, business groups, and governmental agencies think creatively. Some techniques include brainstorming, idea mapping, and thinking in opposites—he says seeing what a problem is *not* can produce interesting ideas that assist people in resolving problems. (Photo: © 1996 Nation's Business/ T. Michael Keza.)

Characteristics of Managers Who Generate Creativity.[43]   Managers who encourage creativity are willing to *absorb risks* taken by subordinates. They allow their people freedom, expect some errors, and are willing to learn from inevitable failures. Managers who are afraid of mistakes, on the other hand, restrict the freedom of their subordinates to experiment and be creative.

Productive managers of creativity can live with *half-developed ideas.* They do not insist that an idea be 100 percent proven before supporting its development. They are willing to listen to and encourage subordinates to press on with "half-baked" proposals that hold promise. They know that criticism can kill an innovation.

Creative managers have a feel for the times when the company rule book needs to be ignored and will *stretch normal policies* for the greater long-term good. Managers that permit no deviation from standard operating procedures will make predictable progress and avoid mistakes, but they will not obtain giant breakthroughs that calculated risk taking can promote.

Productive managers are *good listeners.* They listen to their staff, try to pull out good ideas, and build on suggestions. They do not try to impose new policies or procedures on people without listening to the other side first.

Creative managers *don't dwell on mistakes.* They are more future oriented than past oriented. They don't hold the mistakes of others against them indefinitely. They are willing to begin with the world as it is today and work for a better future. They learn from experience, but they do not wallow in the past.

When good ideas are presented, productive managers are willing to decide on the spot to try them without waiting for further studies. They are courageous enough to *trust their intuition* and commit resources to implementing promising innovations.

Finally, productive managers are *enthusiastic and invigorating.* They encourage and energize others. They enjoy using the resources and power of their position to push projects forward and make improvements.

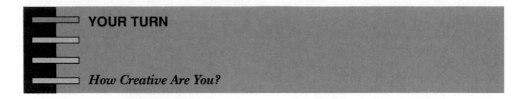

YOUR TURN

How Creative Are You?

Place a check mark by the 10 words in the following list that best characterize you.

energetic	persuasive	observant	fashionable	self-confident
persevering	original	cautious	habit-bound	resourceful
egotistical	independent	stern	predictable	formal
informal	dedicated	factual	open-minded	forward-looking
tactful	inhibited	enthusiastic	innovative	poised
acquisitive	practical	alert	curious	organized
unemotional	dynamic	polished	courageous	clear-thinking
helpful	efficient	perceptive	quick	self-demanding
good-natured	thorough	impulsive	determined	understanding
realistic	modest	involved	flexible	absent-minded
sociable	well-liked	restless	retiring	

Scoring Key. For each of the following adjectives that you checked, give yourself 2 points:

energetic	resourceful	original	enthusiastic	dynamic
flexible	observant	independent	perceptive	innovative
persevering	dedicated	courageous	curious	self-demanding
involved				

For each of the following adjectives that you checked, give yourself 1 point:

thorough	determined	restless	informal	self-confident
alert	open-minded	forward-looking		

The rest of the adjectives receive no points.

Add up your total number of points: _____

Interpretation

16–20	Very creative
11–15	Above average
6–10	Average
1–5	Below average
0	Noncreative

Source: Copyright © 1981 Eugene Raudsepp, Adapted from *How Creative Are You?* (New York: Putnam, 1981), pp. 22–24.

To determine how creative you are, complete the Your Turn exercise. If your score is not as high as you would like, a number of ways to enhance creativity are described in the next section.

Promoting Creative Thinking in Organizations.   To encourage creativity, a manager needs to provide a bureaucracy-free environment that tolerates diverse behavior. When a wealthy patron once asked Pablo Picasso what he could do to help him, Picasso looked at him and said succinctly, "Stand out of my light."[44] Several examples of how universities and businesses have promoted creativity by eliminating organizational barriers follow.[45]

In a course at the University of Houston, nicknamed Failure 101, students are requested to build the tallest structure possible out of ice-cream-bar sticks and then look for "the insight in every failure. Those who end up with the highest projects went through the most failures. Whoever followed a fixed idea from the outset never finished first."

Training students to learn from mistakes and try, try again may be good training for future careers in business. But "you can't just order up a good idea or spend money to find one," points out Jon Henderson, director of Hallmark's Creative Resources Center. "You have to build a supportive climate and give people the freedom to create things."

One famous example of how a creative climate can pay off is 3M in Minneapolis, where employees are encouraged to devote about 15 percent of their work time to non-job-related creative thinking. Doing "skunkworks duty," as it is known at 3M, has resulted in such creative products as Post-It notes, three-dimensional magnetic recording tape, and disposable medical masks. About 30 percent of total revenues is from new products developed in the past five years, and 3M figures that nearly 70 percent of its annual $12 billion in sales comes from creative ideas that originated with the work force.

At W. L. Gore & Associates, the company that brought us Teflon products, employees are urged to take risks. The feeling is that if they are not making mistakes, they are doing something wrong. This philosophy has propelled W. L. Gore from a glorified mom-and-pop operation to a company with 37 plants worldwide that turns out everything from electronics to dental products.

Despite the obvious benefits creative risk taking has brought to companies like 3M and W. L. Gore, not all managers are comfortable with the adjustments necessary for creating a climate that nurtures creativity. The Conference Board, a business research group, found that managers with negative feelings about creativity feel that it is uncontrollable, which is anathema for a manager whose job is to control. Consequently, many managers are fearful and unwilling to give up their power and control. But, according to founder Vieve Gore, it was the absence of direct control and deliberate structure that contributed to W. L. Gore's phenomenal creative success.

For managers who see the necessity for creativity but are still apprehensive, several structured alternatives to promoting problem-solving creativity exist that do not entail giving up control in the work environment.[46] Among them are brainstorming, the nominal group technique, and the Delphi technique.

Brainstorming

brainstorming
A small-group decision-making process in which members freely generate ideas in a noncritical environment.

Brainstorming is a demonstrated approach for achieving high participation and increasing the number of action alternatives.[47] To engage in brainstorming sessions, people meet in small groups and feed off one another's ideas, which provide stimuli for more creative solutions. Rules for effective brainstorming promote the goal of quantity of ideas no matter how far fetched, allow no criticism or evaluation of ideas as they are generated, allow only one idea at a time from each person, and encourage people to build on each other's ideas.

Brainstorming groups are encouraged to be freewheeling and radical. Through use of a nonevaluative environment that is intentionally fun, brainstorming ensures involvement, enthusiasm, and a large number of solution alternatives.

Challenge of **C**hange *Electronic Brainstorming*

Electronic brainstorming is similar to the nominal group technique except that group members exchange ideas on interactive computer terminals instead of writing their ideas on paper. It is especially effective in groups larger than five members, where experiments have demonstrated that more unique and high-quality ideas are generated and members are more satisfied than when they use verbal brainstorming. Electronic brainstorming is not a face-to-face medium, which reduces the negative effects of ideas being blocked due to apprehension about their rejection.

Electronic brainstorming also enables widely dispersed group members to generate ideas interactively. In this application, electronic brainstorming is a sophisticated form of computer conferencing, wherein group members' ideas are automatically sent to each other's screens during the idea generation session. This process may be particularly helpful when people's schedules differ markedly because of time zones and workloads. It may offer an attractive alternative to conference calls that require everyone to be available to interact at the same time.

Finally, the simultaneity of input in electronic brainstorming also prevents one individual from dominating the idea generation process. Inputs tend to be evenly distributed over group members, which helps increase not only the number of ideas generated but also people's satisfaction with the process.

Source: R. Brent Gallupe et al., "Electronic Brainstorming and Group Size," *Academy of Management Journal* 35, no. 2 (1992), pp. 350–369.

Brainstorming generally works well in a participative, team-oriented climate where people are comfortable with each other and are committed to pulling together toward a common goal. In some situations it may not be effective, however. One example occurred in Paris, France, where the expatriate general manager from the United States attempted a brainstorming session with department managers and, instead of a number of excited ideas, was met with a room full of frowns and complete silence. When he inquired why there were no responses, he was told very seriously that he was the director general, and it was his job to tell them what to do. The staff's job was to follow orders and accept his suggestions, not to do his job for him.

At other times, a hostile or political climate might inhibit the free flow of ideas. In restrictive interpersonal climates, more structured techniques like the nominal group or Delphi group technique may be more effective. The recent development of electronic brainstorming, described in the Challenge of Change box, can also circumvent the need for face-to-face brainstorming meetings.

Nominal Group Technique

nominal group technique
A structured group problem-solving method in which members write down ideas, present them round-robin fashion, and rank proposals.

In the **nominal group technique,** participants meet together in a highly structured format that governs the decision-making process.[48] First, participants independently write down their ideas about the problem. Second, each presents one idea to the group in a round-robin fashion without discussion. These ideas are summarized and written on a flip chart or blackboard so all can see them. After a group discussion to clarify and evaluate the ideas, an independent ranking of the proposals takes place. These rankings are pooled to determine the proposal with the highest aggregate ranking, which is the group's decision.

The nominal group technique offers the advantages of multiple idea generation, balanced participation, and participant satisfaction. It is time consuming and does require participants to meet together at a common location. In any group decision-making situation, the advantages and disadvantages of a proposed technique should be weighed with respect to the nature of the participants and the specific decision being made.

Delphi Technique

Delphi technique
A group problem-solving method in which participants interact through a series of written suggestions rather than face to face.

In the **Delphi technique,** participants do not meet together but interact through a series of written judgments and suggestions.[49] After each participant has been presented with the problem, he or she writes down comments and possible solutions and sends them to a central location for recording and reproduction. Each participant then receives a copy of all other comments and solutions to use as a springboard for additional ideas or comments. These also are returned to the central location for compilation and reproduction, and an independent vote on solution priority is taken.

The Delphi technique allows for the pooling of a variety of ideas, viewpoints, independent feedback, and criticism at minimal expense, since participants do not have to congregate at a common meeting place. It does, however, take an extended period of time, and there is really no control over the decision-making process. Depending on the nature of the decision group, participants' lack of face-to-face interaction can be either an asset or a liability.

Group Decision Support Systems

group decision support systems
Computer-supported data processing tools that facilitate group decision making.

Group decision support systems are electronic and computer-supported data processing tools that can facilitate group decision making in certain situations. "Same time–same place" interactions among team members can be facilitated by software tools such as mathematical models, spreadsheets, graphics packages, and electronic brainstorming activities. "Same place–different time" interactions are supported by such tools as retrieval systems for information sharing and display software. "Same time–different place" group interactions can be accomplished through videoconferencing, which combines audio and video communications. "Different time–different place" decision making can be helped by such mechanisms as electronic mail and groupware. Group decision support system tools have been shown to increase the efficiency of group problem solving, better document it, and produce higher-quality decisions.[50]

PUTTING PORSCHE IN THE PINK—A SECOND LOOK

In 1996 peace prevails on the Porsche line. The production changes imposed by the Shin-Gijutsu group three years ago produce more cars faster with fewer people without losing technical sophistication and road performance. Putting the losses behind it, the company can now concentrate on developing new models and new markets. Porsche already had orders for 10,000 of its new roadster, the Boxster, which it plans to introduce later as its least expensive 1997 model. The company is also in discussions with other auto makers about possibly producing a high-performance off-road vehicle, a minivan and a small low-priced sports car.

The team of Japanese consultants now returns only about four times a year because the innovations they initiated are being continued by the German engineers. Workers on the line submit 2,500 suggestions a month. Porsche still hopes to strip another 10 hours off car-assemble time, making the company comparable to the best Japanese auto makers. Porsche is also working with its suppliers to cut costs and improve quality and deliveries. While it works away at this goal, Porsche has formed Porsche Consulting to spread to other German manufacturers the Japanese manufacturing concepts it has learned.

Source: N. C. Nash, "Putting Porsche in the Pink: German Graftsmanship Gets Japanese Fine-Tuning," *The New York Times* (January 20, 1996), pp. 17–18.

SUMMARY

The rational problem-solving process includes identifying the problem, clarifying objectives, analyzing alternatives, deciding on a solution, implementing the solution, and following through to ensure its effectiveness. To begin solving a problem, the current situation needs to be diagnosed to understand and define the problem as accurately as possible. Hasty assumptions often contribute to a failure to distinguish a problem's symptoms from its sources.

When making decisions, the immediate and long-term effects of all alternative solutions on other people and situations should be considered. Decisions should also be ethical, meaning that the decision maker has an obligation to ensure that the alternative chosen conforms to accepted standards of conduct. Useful criteria when making ethical decisions include public justification, moral principles, legal rights, and distributive and retributive justice. Effective action plans contain measurable criteria and time lines. Involving the people affected by the plan in the analysis of alternatives and in decision making will build their commitment to its implementation. When evaluating action plan alternatives, benefits are weighed against possible negative consequences. Other considerations include probability of success; associated risk factors; potential money, time, and energy costs; and the possible reactions of those affected.

Effective implementation of an action plan depends on the parties' commitment to make it work. Commitment to the agreed-on solution usually is gained when problems, needs, and objectives are identified mutually, and solutions are reached through participation and consensus of all involved. Specific tasks and responsibilities are assigned, schedules are established, and personal commitment is reinforced as the plan is activated.

The follow-through process involves the development of procedures to monitor and assist the implementation of the new action plan. A control process is applied to measure performance, monitor results, and take corrective actions when needed.

Individuals learn different habits for processing information when making decisions resulting in decisive, flexible, hierarchic, integrative, or systemic decision styles. Participation in decision making is important when there are quality, acceptance, and time requirements. The group process can be made more effective by encouraging creativity and applying techniques such as brainstorming, the nominal group technique, the Delphi technique, and decision support systems.

Key Concepts

problem solving, *p. 388*

decision making, *p. 388*

objective, *p. 390*

flow chart, *p. 392*

Pareto chart, *p. 395*

criteria, *p. 396*

satisficing, *p. 398*

Gantt chart, *p. 399*

ethics, *p. 402*

ethical behavior, *p. 402*

ethical reasoning, *p. 402*

ethical dilemma, *p. 402*

morality, *p. 405*

utilitarianism, *p. 405*

social good, *p. 405*

utility, *p. 405*

right, *p. 406*

justice, *p. 407*

distributive justice, *p. 406*

retributive justice, *p. 406*

compensatory justice, *p. 406*

decision styles, *p. 409*

brainstorming, *p. 415*

nominal group technique, *p. 416*

Delphi technique, *p. 417*

group decision support systems, *p. 417*

Questions for Study and Discussion

1. Explain why it is so important to establish an atmosphere of trust in situations of group problem solving. Can you cite situations where you have not trusted others with whom you were involved in solving a problem? Compare them with situations in which you have felt trust. Have you ever felt that others in a group distrusted you? Why?

2. What four purposes are served by clarifying objectives early in the problem-solving process? Whose objectives should be considered?

3. Explain this statement: "No problem solution can be better than the quality of diagnosis on which it is built."

4. With regard to selecting an action plan, indicate whether you agree or disagree with each of the following statements and why: (1) Experience is the best teacher. (2) Intuition is a helpful force. (3) Advice from others is always beneficial. (4) Experiment with several alternatives.

5. What difficulties might you anticipate when using the rational problem-solving process? Why? What additional difficulties might arise because of personal attributes? Which of these have you experienced? Explain. What were the consequences? How can these difficulties be avoided?

6. Which decision style would be most effective at each stage of the rational problem-solving process? Why? Explain which decision style would be best for making decisions under emergency circumstances. Which is best for solving a complex problem requiring considerable creativity?

7. Explain under what circumstances you would want to use participation to solve a problem. When would you rather solve the problem individually?

8. How can a manager encourage creative problem solving by department members?

EXPERIENTIAL EXERCISE

Ethical Decision Making [51]

Purpose. To practice stretching and expanding your moral reasoning and ethical judgment and to sharpen your ethical sensitivity and moral awareness. (Total time required is 55 to 110 minutes, depending on the number of cases assigned and the degree of class discussion.

Procedure. Participants assume that they are managers at Martin Marietta Corporation who are undertaking an ethics training session. The exercise consists of deciding on ethical courses of action for 10 minicases. (Time: 50 minutes: 5 minutes per case. If time is limited fewer cases can be used.)

Instructions. Form groups of 4 to 6 people and select a group leader who will lead the discussion of the first case. Your group will have 5 minutes to reach a decision for each case before moving on to the next one. Rotate leaders for the case discussions.

Note. These cases reflect real-life situations. Consequently, you may sometimes feel that a case lacks clarity or that the precise choice you would have made is not available. Some cases have more than one satisfactory solution and others have no good solutions. In all cases, however, you must **decide on the one best solution** from those presented.

Debriefing: After the decisions have been made for all of the cases, the class should discuss each case in order. For each case, groups share their decisions and explain why they think their choice is the best. Then the instructor provides the point values and rational assigned for each option by the Martin Marietta Corporation trainers. Each group keeps track of its score for each case. At the end of the discussion, groups add their points for all 10 cases and the group with the highest score wins. (Time: 60 minutes. Less time is required if fewer cases are assigned or the total class discussion of group answers is omitted).

Minicase 1. A defense program has not yet been formally approved nor have the funds been allocated. Nevertheless, because it all looks good and you need to get started in order to meet schedule, you start negotiating with a supplier. What do you tell the supplier?

Potential Answers.
  A. "This is a 'hot' program for both of us. Approval is imminent. Let's get all the preliminary work under way."
  B. "The program is a 'go.' I want you under contract as soon as possible."

  C. "Start work and we will cover your costs when we get the contract."
  D. "If you want to be part of the team on this important, great program, you, like us, will have to shoulder some of the start-up costs.

Minicase 2. Two of your subordinates routinely provide their children with school supplies from the office. How do you handle this situation?

Potential Answers.
  A. Lock up the supplies and issue them only as needed and signed for.
  B. Tell these two subordinates that supplies are for office use only.
  C. Report the theft of supplies to the head of security.
  D. Send a notice to all employees that office supplies are for office use only and that disregard will result in disciplinary action.

Minicase 3. Your operation is being relocated. The personnel regulations are complex and might influence your employees' decisions about staying on the "team." Relocating with no experienced staff would be very difficult for you. What do you tell your employees about their options?

Potential Answers.
  A. State that the relocation regulations are complex: you won't go into them right now. However, you tell them that everything probably will come out OK in the end.
  B. Suggest that they relocate with you, stating that a job in hand is worth an unknown in the bush.
  C. Present them with your simplified version of the regulations and encourage them to come along.
  D. Tell them only that you'd like them to relocate with you and conserve the team, which has worked so well together.

Minicase 4. Your price is good on a program contract you are bidding, but you think it will take you several months longer than your competitor to develop the system. Your client, the U.S. Army, wants to know the schedule. What do you say?

Potential Answers.
  A. Tell the Army your schedule is essentially the same as what you believe your competitor's will be.
  B. Show the Army a schedule the same as what you believe your competitor's is (but believing you can do better than what your engineers have told you).

C. Explain to the Army the distinct advantage of your system irrelevant of schedule.

D. Lay out your schedule even though you suspect it may cause you to lose points on the evaluation.

Minicase 5. A friend of yours wants to transfer to your division, but he may not be the best qualified for the job. You do have an opening, and one other person, whom you do not know, has applied. What do you do?

Potential Answers.

A. Select the friend you know and in whom you have confidence.

B. Select the other person, who you are told is qualified.

C. Request a qualifications comparison of the two from the human resources department.

D. Request the human resources department to extend the search for additional candidates before making the selection.

Minicase 6. Your new employee is the niece of the vice president of finance. Her performance is poor, and she has caused trouble with her co-workers. What do you do?

Potential Answers.

A. Call her in and talk to her about her inadequacies.

B. Ask the human resources department to counsel her and put her on a performance improvement plan.

C. Go see her uncle.

D. Maybe her problems are caused by the newness of the job; give her some time to come around.

Minicase 7. You work in finance. Another employee is blamed for your error involving significant dollars. The employee will be able to clear himself, but it will be impossible to trace the error back to you. What do you do?

Potential Answers.

A. Do nothing. The blamed employee will be able to clear himself eventually.

B. Assist the blamed employee in resolving the issue but don't mention your involvement.

C. Own up the error immediately, thus saving many hours of work.

D. Wait and see if the matter is investigated and at that time disclose your knowledge of the case.

Minicase 8. After three months you discover that a recently hired employee who appears to be very competent falsified her employment application in that she claimed she had a college degree when she did not. As her supervisor, what do you do?

Potential Answers.

A. You are happy with the new employee, so you do nothing.

B. Discuss the matter with the human resources department to determine company policy.

C. Recommend that she be fired for lying.

D. Consider her performance, length of service, and potential benefit to the organization before making any recommendation to anyone.

Minicase 9. A close relative of yours plans to apply for a vacancy in the department that you head. Hearing of this, what would you say to that person?

Potential Answers.

A. "Glad to have you. Our organization always needs good people."

B. "I would be concerned about the appearance of favoritism."

C. "It would be best if you did not work for me."

D. "If you get the job, expect no special consideration from me."

Minicase 10. A current supplier contacts you with an opportunity to use your expertise as a paid consultant to the supplier in matters not pertaining to your company's business. You would work only on weekends. You could:

Potential Answers.

A. Accept the job if the legal department poses no objection.

B. Accept the job.

C. Report pertinent details to your supervisor.

D. Decline the position.

EXPERIENTIAL EXERCISE

None of Us Is As Smart As All of Us[52]

Purpose.   To compare the effectiveness and efficiency of group versus individual problem solving. (Time: 30 to 45 minutes.)

Procedure.   Break the class into groups of 4 or 5 people each. If there are any rebels in the class who believe they can solve problems better than a group, let them work alone to challenge the company slogan of Stanley Bostitch, Inc.: "None of is as smart as all of us." At least 3 or 4 people should try to solve the problem individually for comparison purposes.

Instructions.   The problem is to find 47 triangles in the figure below. Three answers are provided to get you started. Each team, or individual, should record the time it takes to find the 47 triangles. Be careful to check your work for accuracy because 15 seconds will be added to your final time for each error you make in completing the assignment. It will help you to avoid duplicating a triangle you've already listed if you always write your three letters in alphabetical order. For example, when you find triangle HBG, write it as BGH.

Debriefing.   The instructor will provide the correct answers for the 47 triangles. Add appropriate penalties for each error. Then average the final times for all groups (time to complete the exercise plus penalties). Do the same for individuals. Compare the results. Did individuals or groups do better? Why? Discuss the following questions:

1. How do you account for the results of this exercise?

2. When would it be more appropriate to use groups instead of individuals to solve problems? Why?

3. What differences were there between problem-solving groups? What contributed to them?

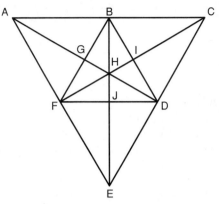

Source: Edward E. Scannell and John W. Newstrom. *Still More Games Trainers Play* (New York: McGraw-Hill, Inc., 1991), p. 251. © 1991. Reproduced with permission of McGraw-Hill, Inc.

1. ABD	11.	21.	31.	41.
2. ABE	12.	22.	32.	42.
3. ABF	13.	23.	33.	43.
4.	14.	24.	34.	44.
5.	15.	25.	35.	45.
6.	16.	26.	36.	46.
7.	17.	27.	37.	47.
8.	18.	28.	38.	
9.	19.	29.	39.	
10.	20.	30.	40.	

Time: _____

Number of incorrect answers: _____ (add 15 seconds to original time for each error)

Final Time (including all 15 second penalties): _____

CASE

Dealing with Academic Dishonesty[53]

Someday it will happen to every professor. A student will turn in such an excellent, well-written paper that its authenticity is in serious doubt. Or, during a test, the professor looks up and sees one student copying from another, or from crib notes lying on the floor. Studies show that about 40 percent of students cheat in a given term, and it isn't only the lazy student looking for a shortcut. In fact, overachievers are more likely to cheat than underachievers when a professor springs a test on them and they feel they're losing control of their ability to prepare for class. For example, a student who is taking 16 course-hours, working 30 hours a week, and still trying to have a social life may not feel adequately prepared for a test and feel pressured to cheat. The question for professors is—what can be done about it?

It seems unthinkable that a professor would ignore students whispering answers to one another during a test, or obviously copying from crib notes, yet some admit that they frequently overlook such dishonesty. Although cheating rates are rising nationwide, many professors turn a blind eye to it because it puts them in the uncomfortable role of police officer instead of educator. Most universities' academic dishonesty policies scare professors with onerous, ambiguous regulations. Professors typically don't know what to expect of the policies and often avoid dealing with them. Many fear that complex legal proceedings will hurt their reputations and feel that it's their word against the student's. Others have trouble with the penalties. Some believe that lowering students' grades is unlikely to stop them from cheating again, but having them expelled from the university is too severe.

University administrators are worried about these faculty attitudes towards cheating, and some feel that "academic dishonesty is one of the most serious problems facing higher education today." They know that many professors are anxiety-ridden about it and believe that it is reducing the validity of the education students are receiving.

Students at universities with honor codes are much less likely to cheat than those at schools without such codes. Many students report that there is a confusing lack of set rules about what professors define as cheating, which makes cheating seem unimportant. Others, however, report that they rely on faculty to stop their classmates from cheating and express disappointment in the professors who let them get away with it.

Questions for Managerial Action

1. What types of student cheating behavior have you observed?
2. Whose responsibility is it to control cheating?
3. How can cheating be prevented?
4. How should cheating be dealt with when it is detected?

Chapter 13

Power and Organizational Politics

LEARNING OBJECTIVES

After studying this chapter, you should be able to:

- Define power and explain why it is useful in organizations.
- Describe at least two forms of power that come with position, two from personal characteristics, and two from situational forces.
- Explain why social networks create opportunities for managers to establish power.
- Identify four situational factors that affect power and explain why power is context specific.
- Describe the differences among four forms of political manipulation: persuasion, inducement, obligation, and coercion.
- Identify at least five tactics for developing political power.
- Differentiate among moral, immoral, and amoral modes of handling power.
- Explain why centralization diminishes political behavior.

POWER PLAYS TAKE A BITE OUT OF APPLE COMPUTER INC.

Apple Computer is an organization that marches to the beats of different drummers. As one of the most visible and colorful corporations in the world, Apple Computer has historically been a rebel, nonconforming firm focused on individual empowerment of both customers and employees. But the power plays at the top are responsible for abrupt shifts in strategy and organization that have caused Apple to yo-yo with considerable ups and downs.

The first power struggle occurred between cofounder Steve Jobs and John Sculley. Jobs recruited Sculley from Pepsi-Cola in 1983 to be president and CEO, while Jobs retained the title of chairman and provided technological leadership. As a young rebel with a cause, Jobs' brashness clashed with the professional managerial style of Sculley. Cofounder Steve Wozniak described the clash: "Steve . . . left bad sentiments all over the company. I think a lot of managers were upset over Steve wanting to direct what they were doing, being very rude, and talking to people in a way that didn't make them feel like they were smart and respected—like they didn't know what they were doing unless they did it his way. All this came up to John, and I think he started having to take actions to save the company." In 1985, with board backing, Sculley ousted Jobs and took on the role of chairman as well as CEO.

Sculley's penchant was marketing, not technology, and he tended to lead by shifting executives in frequent structural reorganizations. One 14-year Apple veteran complained that productivity of researchers was often derailed by management decisions that switched the direction of projects in mid-stream. With a cluttered product line and rapidly declining margins and market share, in June 1993 Sculley was pushed aside by the board and the reins of power shifted to Michael Spindler. Spindler, a German-born engineer who helped Apple establish an international strategy, was brought to the United States by Sculley two years earlier to be his number two executive.

Spindler made the technology transition to the Power PC microprocessor and was deeply involved in nitty-gritty details. But he was not seen as a leader or motivator of people. He did not like to hear bad news, and, when a task force predicted financial losses if sweeping changes were not made, he sat on the report rather than passing it on to the board. This inaction started a brain drain of key people and rumors of a takeover, and within six months it resulted in the reality of a $69 million quarterly loss when Apple failed to produce the computer models customers were demanding during the 1995 holiday season. In reflecting on the struggles for control of Apple, one engineer remarked, "Apple has a lot of extremely talented people, but it's a question of how they are led. I think the senior management team played a lot of country club politics."

By February 1996, Spindler was pushed out after his staunchest supporter, board chairman A. C. "Mike" Markkula, relinquished his title to bring in Gilbert Amelio. Markkula, who was Apple's earliest professional manager and its largest individual stockholder, appeared to realize that a power play by Sun Microsystem to buy out Apple would yield a depreciated price, that retail sales would continue to deteriorate, and that a Spindler proposed reorganization was criticized by almost everyone—ingredients for a change in who would wield power at Apple.

Will Gil Amelio, a Ph.D. educated physicist who has 16 patents to his credit, be able to save Apple? More than a scientist and technologist, Amelio is a leader with a history of transforming organizations. His institutional power motive quickly surfaced in his first management position at Fairchild Semiconductor, as recounted by George Wells, a former Fairchild boss and now CEO of Exar Corp: "I'll never forget the time we were riding in a car together. Gil said to me, 'I want to get out of this pigeonhole I'm in as a technologist and become known as a businessman'." Amelio demonstrated his "businessman" capabilities several times over, first at Fairchild, then at Rockwell, and most recently as CEO of National Semiconductor. When he took the reins at National, he quickly concluded the company needed a vision to guide its future and a cultural transfusion to revitalize morale and focus effort. Similar challenges await him at Apple.

Gilbert Amelio certainly has the power to transform Apple, for Markkula relinquished his title as chairman so that all power could be concentrated in Amelio as chairman of the board as well as chief executive officer. Will Amelio energize that power with actions that shift Apple back onto the profitable growth curve? One thing is sure—that his actions will be closely watched and that whatever he does, Amelio and Apple will make news.

Sources: One of your textbook authors had two of the principals in this vignette appear before his "company exclusive" MBA classes. John Sculley, while CEO of Apple, spoke to three classes in the Apple-SJSU MBA program, and Gilbert Amelio, while CEO of National Semiconductor, spoke to student-employees in the National-SJSU MBA program. Published sources: Guy Kawasaki, *Hindsights* (Hillsboro, OR: Beyond Words Publishing), p. 215; Lee Gomes and Mike Langberg, "Did Apple Find a Savior?" and Dean Takahashi, "Man for the Job: Amelio Relishes a New Challenge," both in *San Jose Mercury News* (February 3, 1966), pp. 1A and 20A; Dean Takahashi, "R&D Costs a Top Priority for Amelio," *San Jose Mercury News* (February 5, 1996), p. 10E; and Peter Burrows, "How Much for One Apple, Slightly Bruised?" *Business Week* (February 12, 1996), p. 35.

"Power is America's last dirty word," according to Professor Rosabeth Kanter.[1] If power elicits social disapproval, politics can't be too far behind. Power (and its companion, politics) is a force that people try to keep under wraps. People who have power generally feel obliged to deny that they have it or at least not to flaunt it. And those who want it often try to give the impression that they don't. (There are, of course, exceptions!) Such behaviors indicate that power is a very misunderstood phenomenon.

Power is neutral. It is neither inherently evil nor inherently good. The executives responsible for Apple in its first two decades used their power with the goal of building for Apple a dominant position in the world of personal computing—an industry whose origin flourished with the early successes of Apple. Although powerful managers and leaders often have big egos, those at Apple wanted to use their power for the good of the organization. Each of the key players—Steve Jobs, John Sculley, Michael Spindler, Mike Markkula, and Gilbert Amelio—knew that to be successful in his role, he would have to exercise power to change the realities and behaviors of others.

Information can be power.

MRS. GELLERMAN SEIZES AN OPPORTUN-
ITY TO SNAP A FEW PICTURES OF THE
BOSS NAPPING ON THE JOB WHICH SHE'LL
FILE FOR FUTURE JOB PROTECTION USE.

Source: Reprinted by permission: Tribune Media Services.

Most of us realize that sometimes power is pivotal to a successful outcome. You have already read about using empowerment, organizational culture, and job design to enrich the lives of employees and to improve the problem-solving capabilities of teams. These are examples of how increasing the power of people at work produces positive outcomes.

WHAT IS POWER AND HOW DO WE GAIN IT?

Society expects parents to influence their children's social and moral development. Teachers and professors are expected to influence the intellectual and ethical development of students. Salespeople are rewarded when they influence customers' buying decisions.

In most social contexts, being influential is viewed as a positive quality, something that is expected if not admired. But people often feel uneasy with power. We view it negatively if we feel manipulated, exploited, or squelched, like a pawn in another person's game. Power is a basic social force that alters the reality of those influenced by the power holder.[2] Yet power can be a vital and positive change force within organizations.

Power Goes Beyond Influence

Power is the ability to alter circumstances so that another person does what the power holder wants done.[3] If A has power over B, A can get B to do something

power
The ability of A (the power holder) to alter circumstances impacting on B so that B does what A wants done.

that B might not otherwise do.[4] A has power if he or she can overcome B's resistance to achieve A's objective. The outcome can be beneficial for both. A manager, for example, can place a subordinate who develops a proposal supportive of the manager's goals in an assignment that gives her visibility and access to senior management—a career enhancing move.

Power has greater force than influence. Power is the ability to alter reality by changing the cause-and-effect relationships. *Influence* is the ability to alter another person's perceptions of the cause-and-effect relationships in a situation.[5] Power is the currency that buys changes in organizational outcomes. Power shapes goals and resource allocations, influences promotional decisions, underlies most conflicts and their resolution, and brings about change in organizational structure.[6] Managers, in particular, need to be both powerful and influential—influential in the sense that they get colleagues to cooperate without resorting to formal authority or position power.[7]

Power can be abused and used selfishly, or it can be used constructively to revitalize the quality of life in organizations and subsequently the quality of products and services produced. The intentions of power determine its positive or negative effect. Sam Walton used power constructively to instill a philosophy that employees "value the customer," and in doing so, he created the largest retailing chain in the world—Wal-Mart. He empowered managers to be responsive to local customer and community needs. By contrast, Leona Helmsley, the self-proclaimed queen of New York hotels, ran roughshod over employees and flagrantly used corporate resources for her own pleasure until convicted of tax fraud. Her desire for personal power and contempt for the average person and the law are captured in her infamous statement, "Only little people pay taxes." Here we have two ambitious executives, two different intentions for using power, and two very different outcomes.

Power arises from three non–mutually exclusive primary sources—position, personal behavior, or situational forces. Exhibit 13–1 summarizes key power elements in these three power sources. A person's *formal position* may convey the power to exercise legitimate authority or control rewards.[8] Alternatively, some people have *personal sources of power,* such as expertise, reference to others, or networks of alliances—all essentially unrelated to organizational position. Finally, a person may seize a *situational opportunity* to exercise power, often drawing on associations with powerful persons, control of information, or even coercion. As suggested by the overlapping circles in the drawing, a person often combines two or more power sources to gain greater leverage in altering the behavior of others. Two of these power sources are potentially enhanced if an organization empowers people at work.

Power Often Comes with Organizational Position

position power
A form of power that originates from the rights a person holds by virtue of the organizational hierarchy—the legitimate authority to reward and punish.

Although many sources of position power exist, a most common one stems from B's dependence on A for something that B strongly desires.[9] This dependence may stem from A's ability to provide advancement, recognition, security, information, acceptance, favorable positions, or vital resources. **Position power** originates from the rights a person holds in the organizational hierarchy, such as legitimate authority, the ability to reward, and the capacity to punish. For managers, power usually goes with the job. They use a variety of position power tactics originally documented in a classic study by French and Raven.[10] Managers need to realize, however, that position power is relative—commanding obedience is risky if the manager's performance depends on the creative action or expertise of subordinates.[11]

━━━━━ **EXHBIT 13–1**

Alternative Sources of Power

The diagram helps answer the questions "Where does power come from?" and "Why do some people have more power than others?" The overlapping circles emphasize that the three primary sources are not mutually exclusive—a person can enhance their power by drawing on two or even all three sources. Empowered nonmanagers are likely to experience increased power from personal and situational forces.

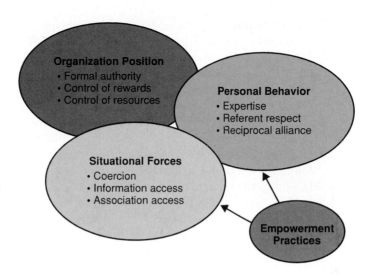

formal authority

Legitimate power derived directly from a person's title and position in the organizational hierarchy.

reward power

Demonstrated when a person offers to reward others for doing something he or she wants.

Formal Authority. The right to command is called **formal authority.** This type of power derives directly from a person's title and position in the organizational hierarchy.[12] When people comply with orders issued from someone with formal authority, they do so because they have accepted the power associated with that person's job as legitimate to organizational governance. The effectiveness of authority ultimately depends on subordinates' acceptance of a manager's right to command.

If subordinates are willing to risk personal consequences and refuse to obey the directives of someone in a position of authority, then that person lacks legitimate power—their authority is questioned. Requests or directives believed to be within a legitimate "zone of acceptance" will be obeyed, but orders falling outside the legitimate range of acceptable expectations will be questioned, if not rejected.[13] An executive assistant, for example, may comply readily with requests to handle correspondence, schedule appointments, maintain documents, and greet visitors but may refuse to shop for gifts for the manager's family, pad the boss's expense account, or work Sundays.

If legitimate authority alone is used to influence behavior, others will likely seek to gain counterbalancing power. Even the mere possession of formal authority isolates the manager from subordinates who inherently resist influence, fear possible punishment, or are simply uncomfortable with authority figures.[14] Nevertheless, formal authority is often necessary to resolve complex differences of opinion, as when a higher level manager dictates a solution to how differences are to be resolved between two or more battling departments.

Reward Power. Managers are usually perceived as having the ability to supply desired rewards such as promotions, pay raises, or sought-after job assignments. **Reward power** is demonstrated when a person actually or implicitly offers to provide others with rewards for doing something he or she wants. Its strength rests on the desirability and magnitude of the rewards and on the perception of others that the manager can (and will) provide the rewards if they comply with directives or requests.

Reward power impacts motivation (a lesson introduced in Chapters 6 and 7). Problems develop if the actual rewards do not match expectations. Furthermore, some peers who do not receive equitable rewards may feel that the manager is "playing favorites."[15]

Control of Resources.   Managers typically are given budgets or authority to allocate resources in carrying out the work of their units. But the position one occupies often gives them power beyond what is formally intended simply because they are in a position to control access to resources that others need. A purchasing technician (not even a manager), because of where she is in the flow of processing purchase requisitions, can restrict or delay access to goods and services sought by people at higher levels within the organization. Peer managers or even managers lower within the organizational hierarchy can use their control of special equipment or services to bargain for actions favorable to their goals.

Power gained by controlling access to resources others need or want often provokes ethical issues. Who is going to be better or worse off as a result of someone having resource control power? What will Michael Eisner, Walt Disney's chief executive, do with his power to decide the entertainment and informational content of multimedia programming now that Disney owns ABC Television? The Eye on Ethics box raises questions about the ways in which Disney's CEO could potentially use his resource power to alter ABC's programming.

Power Can Originate from Personal Behavior

Respect does not arise merely because a person occupies a pivotal position in the hierarchy or can dole out certain rewards or sanctions. The kind of respect that inspires high-quality performance is the respect people feel for those whom they admire and in whom they have confidence.[16] Even a recent university graduate, new to an organization, is likely to influence managers with state-of-the-art technical knowledge. Such personal power originates with expertise and personality, a connection originally discovered by French and Raven.[17]

expert power
Originates when a person is perceived to have superior knowledge, experience, or judgment that others need and do not possess themselves.

Expert Power.   A person has **expert power** when he or she is perceived to have knowledge, experience, or judgment that other people need and do not possess themselves. Given the increased complexity and technology throughout society, we have become dependent on experts.[18] When advised by someone with expert knowledge of computers, taxation, or the law, we usually accept their advice.

Your degree of expert power depends on your performance record over time, the importance of your area of expertise, and the alternative sources of such knowledge available to others. If you exercise poor judgment or offer faulty advice, or if others find ways to solve problems without your help, your potential power over others diminishes.[19] Expert power may also decrease if you make the receiver feel inferior or if you train others so well that they can carry on without you. A person who develops a reputation as a **mentor**—one to whom others turn for sustained personal coaching and guidance—enjoys expert power.

mentor
A person with more expertise who helps those with less.

referent power
Comes from being respected, likable, and worthy of emulating.

Referent Power.   **Referent power** is found in a person who is respected, likable, and worthy of emulating. When others identify with and are attracted to someone they look up to, that person is said to have **charisma**.[20] People with charisma are admired and often serve as role models for others, as John F. Kennedy did for Bill Clinton. Most people can develop referent power by demonstrating friendly, supportive, and considerate behaviors toward others. You will learn in Chapter 14 that being considerate is one of the basic ways of enacting leadership style.

charisma
A quality of admiration when others identify with and are attracted to a leader they look up to.

Eye on Ethics

Disney—World of MultiMedia Power?

To people worldwide who have access to television and movies, Disney is almost like one of the family. Parents have for three generations believed that entertainment from Walt Disney reflects a simple, moral way of approaching life. They encourage their children to assimilate Disney values and the goodness of their artistic products—from Mickey Mouse to Aladdin to Lion King.

Then, in 1995, Walt Disney Co. acquired ABC television (about the same time Westinghouse Electric Corp. acquired CBS). Such a takeover raises perplexing power questions. Will Disney management exercise power over the news programming of ABC? Will new products from Disney be featured more frequently and favorably on ABC broadcasts? Will ABC's news division assimilate the entertainment ideology of Disney into stories and features that transmit "infotainment"? Will ABC managers and editors suppress inconvenient news or select stories that are less controversial, less graphic in the display of extremes within society?

Bigness is not in and of itself bad. But when giants in two industries combine, it causes managers, employees, and customers to question the accountability of power. A century ago, the U.S. government, fearing price control, broke up the businesses of oil, steel, and railroad "robber barons" to prevent monopoly power. Today's issues are less with price but more with mind control—as multimedia big businesses shape the information and images that feed into public opinions—our thoughts and attitudes.

The pundits of power are especially protective when the product impacts the way people think, whether the holder of power be a Michael Eisner, Rupert Murdock, Bill Gates, or Steven Spielberg. Says Kathryn Montgomery, president of the Center for Media Education in Washington, D.C., "They're the moguls of the consciousness industry." To this, Bartley Brennan, a Bowling Green University professor specializing in antitrust and securities laws and ethics, adds: "There's a distinct possibility that they will become the censors and controllers of ideas coming across the satellites and software in the next century. And I'm afraid the diversity of ideas will be lost. We're dealing with the possibility of a monopoly situation here—an oligopoly of ideas."

Eisner may have no intent to use his authorized power as CEO to dictate, say, a philosophy of the kinds of stories to be broadcast by ABC's news division. However, ABC managers likely realize that with Eisner's power to allocate resources (and to reward and punish), their careers might be more secure by self-selecting artistic and journalistic content they believe more in accord with Disney's tradition of family values. Under either scenario, some would celebrate the outcomes, others would damn the centralization of power.

Sources: Richard Scheinin, "Welcome to Disneyworld," *San Jose Mercury News* (August 5, 1995), pp. 1E, 11E; and Mike Antonucci, "Even Mega-Media Corporations Must Bow to Consumer Demands," *San Jose Mercury News* (August 5, 1995), pp. 1E, 12E.

People are motivated to comply with requests from those who hold referent power because they want to please them and gain their approval. Some requests may be beyond the zone of acceptance, however, and asking too much too often may cause a reduction of referent power. To retain referent power, its holders are under constant pressure to maintain their exemplary images and live up to others' expectations.

reciprocity
The trading of power or favors for mutual gain—you help me, I'll help you.

Reciprocal Alliances. Most power bases, especially those of personal origin, work best if part of an ongoing, reciprocal exchange. People who engage in mutually beneficial exchanges and build alliances or networks will, over time, increase their power. **Reciprocity** is the trading of power or favors for mutual gain. Repayment

Ben & Jerry's makes great natural ice cream. But the most popular tourist attraction in Vermont also exemplifies the morality of good management. Imbued with the social ideals of the 1960s, one of the company's many values is to "make great ice cream but not at the expense of social good." (Photo: Courtesy Ben & Jerry's Homemade, Inc.)

coercive power
Based on the ability to withhold desired resources or make life unpleasant for those who do not comply with the power holder's requests.

information power
Stems from the ability to control access to critical information and its distribution.

need not occur at the time of a transaction, since payments can be banked for later exchange. According to Cohen and Bradford, "Using reciprocity requires stating needs clearly without 'crying wolf', being aware of the needs of an ally without being manipulative, and seeking mutual gain rather than playing 'winner takes all'."[21]

Once people work together on successful projects, they have colleagues on whom they can call for future help. The scientist, accountant, or marketer who heads a group for one project may the next time be in a supportive role. To promote reciprocal networks ("I'll help you if you'll help me"), Xerox CEO Paul Allaire valued the "superordinate" or higher-level goal: "You can't get people to focus on only the bottom line. You have to give them an objective like 'satisfy the customer' that everyone can relate to. It's the only way to break down those barriers and get people from different functions working together."[22] Reciprocal alliances build on expanded social networks of give-and-take influence within the organization.

Power Can Originate from Situational Forces

Whereas power from organizational and personal sources seems to be rather specific as to why it originates, the situational category is less definitive. Situational forces typically involve more a blending of organizational and personal sources with opportunistic elements brought about by an event or circumstance. As Jeffrey Pfeffer reminds us, power often involves the fit between situational requirements and personal traits.[23]

Coercive Power.   A person can influence others by threatening to deprive them of things they value. **Coercive power** is the ability to withhold desired resources or make life unpleasant for people who do not comply with the power holder's requests. Coercive power is based on fear and is likely to arouse anger, resentment, and even retaliation. One common reaction is "malicious obedience," in which resentful associates soothe their hurt feelings by doing "exactly" what the coercer told them to do—no less, but certainly no more. If the mission fails, it's the power wielder who ends up looking bad when the associate truthfully says, "I did exactly what you told me to do!"

Coercion is one of the most commonly used forms of power.[24] Yet some experts believe that it is useful only in limited situations.[25] A manager is most likely to be obeyed when both reward and coercive power are perceived as legitimate and used in combination. Coercion that is used like blackmail invites coercive reciprocity if given a chance.

Information Power.   Information becomes power when we possess information others need but do not have. **Information power** stems from the ability to control access to critical information and its distribution. You need not be an expert to assimilate, overhear, or read important information. People in accounting, information systems, or purchasing often have access to information others seek. They can develop power through selective distribution of information and guarded communication.

If you control information, the likelihood that your decisions will be challenged by others is reduced.[26] Control over the distribution of critically needed information enables you to define reality for others in ways that serve your own objectives. Control over information also means that it can be selectively filtered and packaged to influence decisions made by persons dependent on this information.[27] For

The Colgate-Palmolive Company and the National Dental Association (NDA), an association of African-American dentists, have used their combined power to positively influence children in underserved inner city communities. Together they developed the "Bright Smiles, Bright Futures" van program to promote good dental health. The two organizations have also awarded 686 scholarships totaling more than $800,000 to eliminate some of the economic barriers for African-American dental students. (Source: Courtesy of the Colgate-Palmolive Company.)

example, a computer facilities manager could influence his firm's computer selection decision by providing information favoring one option and discrediting others. Risks of using information in this manner, however, include the decreased trust and loss of respect of those who find out they have been unfairly influenced. They will likely develop alternative sources of information.

Association Power.   Some people manage to develop considerable power simply by being associated with a powerful person, even though they may have no personal or positional power of their own. **Association power** arises when one person has influence with another who possesses power. Family members, confidantes, and close aides of public officials have association power. In some organizations, so do staff members who have developed close advisory relationships with the manager.

association power
Arises when one person has influence with another who possesses power.

An executive's assistant handles phone calls, correspondence, and appointments. The loyal assistant also serves as a sounding board for the executive's ideas and frustrations and knows who currently is in and out of favor with the boss. Association power has its place in organizations because it can help cut through the bureaucracy, as if an informal power structure exists in the shadow of the formal organization.

Power Can Be Enhanced by Empowerment

Organization position, personal behavior, and situational forces are the three traditional sources of power in organizations. As described in Chapter 7, empowerment has recently emerged as a form of power for people unaccustomed to having power. Empowerment has become a popular topic of discussion and practice because of the widespread use of electronic information systems and the competitive pressure to flatten organizational structures. The result has been that employees are asked increasingly "to accept responsibility for the definition of the content of their jobs and the quality of their work."[28] Employees have been granted authority to resolve problems encountered on the job as managers shift decision-making responsibility from themselves to the ones who directly engage problems.

Empowerment is more than delegation. It involves sharing information and knowledge with employees and rewarding performance. Empowerment encompasses job enrichment by giving a person a whole job with decision responsibility, and providing him or her sufficient information to know how that job fits into the organization's purpose. One potential impact of empowered employees is to enhance their personal power and increase the likelihood they will experience situational power.

HOW DO SOCIAL NETWORKS AFFECT A MANAGER'S POWER?

Managers and subordinates are linked in social networks infused with power expectations. Over time, subordinates learn to expect that their behavior will be altered by their manager.[29] Realizing this, they then tend to go with the flow rather than ignore, disobey, or resist the manager's attempts to exercise power.

People Expect Social Control

With social acceptance, power becomes normalized: Social control of one's behavior by others becomes an accepted part of organizational life.[30] Even though lower-level members might have the countervailing power to resist requests or directives from managers (by virtue of their expertise or control over access to needed information, materials, people), they seldom do so once the pattern of acceptance has been established.

Social control expectations are in part a product of cultural socialization. We next examine how different cultures create different expectations of social control and power sharing.

Power Acceptance Is a Western Belief.   Industrial systems in Europe, North America, and Australia/New Zealand have been built on the generally accepted belief that managers are the ones who make key decisions in organizations. This expectation of social control by managers has cost Western society dearly—our organizations are not as internally cooperative and productive as they could be. Group problem-solving talent has often been underutilized because traditional practices keep significant decision power in the hands of the managerial hierarchy.[31] When power is expected to be a managerial prerogative rather than a force that also flows up from front-line employees, self-initiated problem solving for continuous improvement does not occur.[32] One alarming study of nonmanagerial American employees reported that:

- Three-fourths said they could be significantly more effective than they are.
- One-half said they put no more effort into their job than that necessary to hold it.
- Sixty percent said they "do not work as hard as they used to."[33]
- Such statistics suggest that top-down position power is costly.

After negotiating since 1994, the pilots union and Federal Express Corp. agreed on a contract and, pending union member agreement, averted a strike. The principle behind union/management negotiations is reciprocity: two sides mutually benefit from harmonious relations and suffer from disharmony. A strike would not only cost the company and workers income but could result in potential job loss as customers seek delivery from other services. (Source: © Lisa Waddell.)

Power Diffusion Is an Eastern Practice. Large businesses in Japan and some other Asian cultures are widely recognized as built on a bottom-up decision model and group consensus. Power tends to be more diffused through widely shared information and involvement in contributing to a gradual course of action. Inequalities in status and rewards between top managers and first-rung employees are much less pronounced in Japanese than in U.S. firms,[34] except between men and women, as you'll learn in a moment. Except at the top, Japanese managers hold less formal authority and draw more on expertise than equal-level managers in the United States. Consequently, managers in Japanese firms usually seek the counsel of group members and build communication networks with a minimum of reliance on position power.[35] However, the recent necessity to increase the speed, flexibility, and magnitude of decisions has shifted more power to top executives in Japanese firms, a top-down shift that has unknown implications in the long run.[36]

Western managers are slowly moving toward participatory and group-based models of decision making in an effort to make the workplace more Eastern in character. But quality circles, self-directed teams, and gainsharing plans are still not widespread.[37] Nevertheless, when managers move in the direction of power sharing, people feel empowered that they can make a difference, and quality usually improves. Not only that, but managers who share power generally increase their own power by strengthening the self-control of others.[38] Exhibit 13–2 shows how power expands as a manager shares it.

Central Positions Enhance Power

The position a person occupies within a social network shapes that person's access to information and people. People holding central positions in an informal network have the potential for greater power because of this access.[39] Central positions, such as occupied by middle and top managers, give people an opportunity

━━━━━ **EXHIBIT 13–2**

Decision Power Sharing Increases Subordinates' Self-Efficacy and Manager's Reputational Power

The classic Tannenbaum and Schmidt model portrayed power as largely a zero-sum game, bounded within the rectangle ABCD. As the manager shared decision power, presumably he or she gave up power to others. But as power is shared (by shifting decision behaviors toward the right), subordinates perceive themselves as more in control of their environment, thanks to their manager. The manager thus does not lose power but potentially continutes to hold power (the areas bounded by A'C'ED). It is even likely that with strengthened relations between manager and subordinates, the manager's power will increase (the slope of DE will become steeper).

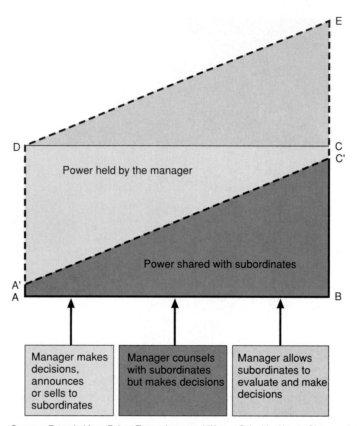

Sources: Extended from Robert Tannenbaum and Warren Schmidt, "How to Choose a Leadership Pattern," *Harvard Business Review* 36 (March–April 1958), pp. 95–102; and Kenneth W. Thomas and Betty A. Velthouse, "Cognitive Elements of Empowerment: An 'Interpretative' Model of Task Motivation," *Academy of Management Review* 15 (October 1990), pp. 666–681.

to know who holds power and how powerful they are. They also provide more opportunities to cross-check information against multiple sources, making for more accurate perceptions of what goes on within the company. And the more accurate a person's perception of the social network and of information, the more likely that person is to be influential.

People in central positions are sought after for advice, which becomes a source of power.[40] People feed useful information to those who have reputations for being powerful. For example, a corporate controller may be seen by managers in other departments as centrally connected and accessible. People therefore seek her out for advice and special requests. These interactions are likely to provide her with even more information about people, events, resources, and opportunities within the firm. As her information base and experience in getting things done increase, so will her reputational power.

Diversity Is Threatened by Power Relationships

social exchange theory
Assumes that power and outcomes within a group are unevenly distributed, yet expects that each individual in a web of power relationships aims for positive outcomes.

Power involves interactions among people in a group or network, with one central person exerting dominant influence over time. Sociologists refer to **social exchange theory** as the expectation that each individual caught in the dependency web of power relationships aims for positive outcomes.[41] But exchanges are not equal, not even positive for some. Social exchanges (the interplay of requests, ideas, and commands) are always asymmetrical, meaning that there is an uneven distribution of power and unequal valuation of outcomes or benefits.[42] Because of this, some players experience negative outcomes.

One negative outcome occurs when ethnic minorities or women are confined to the low end of the power spectrum. In part, such imbalances are caused by their fewer numbers and by token dynamics, in which the token minority or female complies with power strategies used by the majority.[43] The abuses suffered range from sexual harassment to personal humiliation through choice of language. For example, the dominant male might refer to a woman as "girl" or "sweet young thing." Or the boss might say, "I want you boys to . . ." This off-hand remark may be taken as a racial put-down by the African-American in the group, who associates the term "boy" with the historical oppression of his race. In doing business with Japanese men, Western women are at a disadvantage unless they deliberately use power-equalizing tactics.

In some cases, language is used as a power tactic to put down a minority or to be condescending. In others, offensive language is unintentional. Ironically, powerful managers who put down minorities and women may still accept their ideas and contributions. Unfortunately, those who are underrepresented cannot go to the wall each time a slur occurs. To do so throws the relationship into a win–lose contest, and power often wins. One study reports, however, that where women are able to break into the male-dominated coalition, they can end up being perceived as more central to the power network than their male counterparts.[44] This occurs in Chinese cultures when a wife inherits a family business or a daughter takes control of a firm because there are no brothers available or willing to do so (see Dynamics of Diversity box).

Sexism Sustains Power Imbalances/Inequities

White males continue to dominate the power hierarchy in most North American organizations, and even more so in Japan, China, and several Asian cultures. Women are subjected to games and inequities that keep many discouraged if not angry about the imbalances of power. Evidence of sexism ranges from subtleties of how women are treated in meetings to blatant harassment. Sexual harassment builds on the unequal distribution of power; for some men, harassment is a tactic that preserves the power separation.

But sexism need not consist strictly of sexual innuendo. Kathleen Reardon presents a thoughtful picture of the sexist atmosphere that pervades organizations in her *Harvard Business Review* case study, "The Memo Every Woman Keeps in Her Desk."[45] The memo is a plea to the male CEO (of hypothetical Vision Software) to open his eyes to the abuses women suffer in the organization. It reads in part:

Despite Vision's policies to hire and promote women and your own efforts to recognize and reward women's contributions, the overall atmosphere in this company is one that slowly erodes a woman's sense of worth and place. I believe that top-level women are leaving Vision Software not because they are drawn to other pursuits but because they are tired of struggling against a climate of female failure. Little things that happen daily—things many men don't even notice and women can't help but notice—send subtle messages that women are less important, less talented, less likely to make a difference than their male peers.

The critical question for women managers who actually write such a memo is whether they risk sending it before they quit, or whether they simmer while it remains in their desks. To send the memo risks the backlash of becoming

Dynamics of Diversity

Chinese Women Face Tough Obstacles in Business

Women in Chinese cultures have made great strides in becoming accepted within the professions, academia, and especially local politics. But women are seldom in executive positions in firms, where Chinese family businesses dominate private enterprises throughout nations such as Taiwan, Singapore, Malaysia, Hong Kong, and China. Usually the only way a woman can make it to the top of a business organization is either through inheritance or having no brothers willing to take over the business. Says University of Hong Kong Professor S. Gordon Reddy, "Chinese Confucianism accords power and authority to the father figure. The woman is always the fallback." But when a fallback occurs, daughters and wives often make the family proud. Here are two successes.

Jade Chow. After completing her MBA at the University of Southern California, Jade Chow was two years into work at a regional accounting firm and had just gotten married when her mother phoned. Her mother, an exception in her own right, was running the family's small silk factory. She needed help for about three months. That was in 1990. Today, Jade Chow is picked up in Hong Kong by her driver every morning and taken across the border into Shenzhen, China. At work she manages nearly 1,000 workers in the family's silk garment factory— office staff, cutters, sewers, dyers, and salespeople. Jade

Chow has achieved personal and business success by serving as the dutiful child, helping the family by taking over the business from aging parents.

Nina Wang. Since the kidnapping and presumed death of her husband in 1990, Nina Wang assumed the title of "chairlady" (her preference) of the Chinachem Group, a firm in which she owns 90 percent of the stock. She has imprinted her own style on the property development firm—from wearing fire-engine-red vinyl miniskirts and patent-leather platform shoes to being highly intolerant of convention and tradition. Wang is also willing to take risks and be adventuresome in business. She is most excited about a project to build the Nina Tower, a skyscraper that resembles the Chrysler Building, only much taller. Her goal is to build and own the world's tallest building, over 500 meters (1,640 feet) high. To finance construction of the tower, estimated at $1 billion, Nina Wang simply intends to use cash generated from her business. She already owns or has financial interests in about 200 buildings in Hong Kong, plus investments in companies elsewhere, including North America. Little wonder that the Chinachem Group is the largest privately held business in Hong Kong.

Source: Edward A. Gargan, "Female Empire Builders," *San Jose Mercury News* (January 21, 1996), pp. 1E, 2E.

stigmatized as someone who is a complainer, not part of the team, or a feminist. Power repercussions can haunt the woman who attempts to call attention to sexist practices, short of harassment, that keep women from advancing.

In meetings, women are more likely to be talked over and interrupted than men. They have to be more persistent to get a fair hearing of their ideas. Women are less often invited into the closed door sessions that follow meetings, sessions where political alliances are bonded and off-line decisions are struck to deal with sensitive issues. Women often feel they have to downplay their nonworking role as mothers, whereas men can be boastful whenever they "play mom," as if doing so is a real sacrifice, but one that wins them points for being human. Today as women have moved into management, the distinction between the "mommy track" and the "fast track" needs to be broken. According to Friedan, even in organizations that do offer parental leave to either spouse there is an unspoken message that anyone who takes advantage of child care and family programs won't get ahead.[46] Such institutional thinking retards equal gender access to power.

Biased Negotiations Limit Power Effectiveness

negotiation
A decision-making process
for resolving differences
and allocating resources between
independent parties who do
not share common outcome
preferences.

Negotiations are a give-and-take part of everyday life in organizations. **Negotiation** is a decision-making process for resolving differences and allocating resources between interdependent parties who do not share common outcome preferences.[47] An effective negotiation reaches a good agreement that is in the best interest of the negotiator. But often negotiation biases originating from a narrow or distorted frame of reference reduces the negotiator's rationality and limits outcome effectiveness. Listed below are seven biases that block effective negotiations.

1. Having a singular frame of reference that limits consideration of new information.
2. Escalating commitment to a previously selected course after it is no longer reasonable.
3. Assuming one's gain must come at the expense of the other party and missing opportunities for mutually beneficial trade-offs.
4. Anchoring judgments on irrelevant information, such as an initial offer.
5. Relying on readily available information rather than expanding the search.
6. Failing to consider available information by being opposed to the opponent's perspective.
7. Remaining overconfident about the likelihood of attaining a favored outcome.

The above biases stem from the negotiator holding too rigidly to an initial frame of reference, usually one that assumes win–lose trade-offs. Negotiations where diversity issues are involved historically have triggered stereotyped frames of reference. Overcoming these biases increases the power of a negotiator by opening possibilities to consider a wider range of information. Doing so increases the probability of an equitable resolution.

HOW DO SITUATIONAL AND PERSONAL FACTORS AFFECT POWER?

Power is situationally dependent. A person may be able to influence people in some situations but not in others, which means power depends on the context or relationship.[48] In fact, the balance of power can be reversed, depending on the circumstances. At the office, a manager may be recognized by her subordinates as having power over the group. But if the boss joins other members of the department for a weekend of backpacking, it may well be that the subordinate who was once a forest ranger will end up telling everyone what to do—even her! The context changed.

Not everyone desires to be in a position of power. Even those who do have strong needs for power differ in why they believe power is important and how they use it. To understand organizational power, it is necessary to be sensitive to different situations and to individual power needs.

Situational Factors Determine Power Relationships

Power in organizations stems from many situational factors, including specialization and task importance, perceptions of competence, the dependence of others, ambiguous roles, organizational uncertainty, organizational culture, and resource scarcity.

Specialization and Task Importance.   A fundamental characteristic of all organizations is division of tasks to create specialization of roles, functions, and departments. In the process, not all jobs or departments are created equally. Because of

Powerful people sometimes bluff and create artful illusions.

Source: *San Jose Mercury News* (June 19 and 20, 1995).

their contribution to performance, some demonstrate greater importance than others, and power is in part based on the importance of the role within the organization.[49] In a brokerage house, the critical function might be credit analysis; in a bank, market development; in a software firm, programming; and for an aircraft manufacturer, engineering.

Perceptions of Competence.   People who perform well at organizationally critical tasks establish power for themselves. People who fail to perform up to the expectations of others fall short of their power potential. Power also is established by the person who convinces others that his or her work is both necessary and valuable.[50] When one manager replaces another in the same position, a shift in perceived power often follows. Depending on the perceived skills and competence of the new manager, he or she will be seen as more or less powerful than the former manager.

Dependence of Others.   A person's degree of power is also a function of other people's dependence on him or her to satisfy their needs. If Bob thinks he is dependent on Alice to attain his goal, Bob will be more apt to cooperate with Alice's wishes. The power of Alice over Bob has long been defined as "equal to the dependence of B on A."[51] Consider a personal example. Suppose you need a specific course to attain the degree necessary for the job you want after graduation. Further suppose that Professor Kirk is the only one who teaches that course. Surely Professor Kirk now has more power over you than if several others taught the course or the course were not required. Dependence is often based on the number of alternatives available and the importance of the outcomes the power holder controls.

Ambiguous Roles.   Power plays are unlikely to affect workers in highly specific, routine jobs. But when job roles are ambiguous or professional in nature—when employees have discretion in decisions and actions—people are vulnerable to power overtures by others. The financial analyst who prepares an analysis of a proposed acquisition may skew the results to favor the position of the chief financial

SALLY FORTH • Greg Howard and Craig MacIntosh

officer, who dangles the carrot: "What you recommend could speed you onto a fast-track managerial career." By contrast, the assembler who installs wiring harnesses in minivans as they pass her station is less likely to be the target of power plays by the team leader.

Organizational Uncertainty. Managers in organizations that are economically volatile or that are frequently buffeted by crisis rely more on power than do managers in stable organizations.[52] In a stable organization with a largely predictable future, employees expect their behavior will be governed primarily by bureaucratic systems and standard operating procedures.

Organizations in turbulent environments are constantly changing—grasping for better product features and practices to increase reliability while cutting activities that add to costs. In this climate of uncertainty, managers and technical professionals resort to power plays to push for their favorite programs. Power is more likely to be a factor influencing decisions in high-tech firms than in supermarkets, for example.

Organizational Culture. Organizations differ in their predispositions to use power to influence behavior. In some organizations, such as many public utilities, employees accept power-based decisions and political actions as a way of life. Because managers in high-power organizations act as power brokers to block or advance the careers of others, making the boss look good helps an employee's career progress. By contrast, in highly task-focused organizations, position power has less influence on behavior.[53]

Resource Scarcity. Shortages, cutbacks, and general conditions of scarcity stimulate power tactics. Companies with abundant resources—a rarity these days—experience fewer power plays, provided members perceive the distribution of resources to be equitable. But take away the resources, and power struggles intensify for whatever remains.[54] This is especially apparent when a firm shifts from periods of growth to cyclical periods of austerity, as is common during economic recessions.

When once-successful computer and software firms shift to layoffs and cutbacks in departmental and program budgets during periods of declining gross margins (recall Apple), survival instincts whet appetites for power and politics. This has been a contributing factor to the turmoil at Apple Computer. Managers and professionals use whatever influence they can muster to keep themselves and their groups insulated from layoffs and downsizing.

By applying Japanese principles of continuous improvement called *Kaizen*, Patricia Lewis and William Schwartz (photo) greatly improved the production of dolls at the Alexander Doll Company in New York City. *Kaizen* is a process of evaluating a manufacturing system and involving workers in improvements to become more efficient and promote quality. The process develops a dedicated and knowledgeable work force that participates in problem solving. (Source: © 1995 Tom Sobolik/Black Star.)

In addition to the situational factors we've discussed, personal needs drive power practices. Not all people need power, and those who do have different motives.

People Have Different Power Needs

power motive
The socially acquired or learned desire to have strong influence or control over others.

Who wants power? On the surface, it seems that everyone might find it beneficial to have control over others. In actuality, individuals have different comfort levels concerning power over others. The **power motive** is the learned desire to have strong influence or control over others. David McClelland found the power motive to be a reliable personality characteristic that varied from person to person.[55] Think of your friends. Don't some like to take control and make decisions for the group more than others? What you see is differences in the need for power.

Dual Face of the Power Motive.

People with a high need for power are more likely to seek out and remain in positions of authority because they enjoy influencing others to accomplish objectives. They will exercise personal power tactics to speed their promotion to positions that convey greater power. People with a low need for power, on the other hand, do not gain satisfaction from influencing others. They may lack the assertiveness and confidence necessary to direct others or to defend their group's interests in

Challenge of Change

Mary Mueller Builds Power from Networking

Mary Mueller relied on networking to land her job as senior director of marketing at Kid Rhino, the start-up children's music division of Rhino Records. She continued to use networking as a source of power to quickly convert a concept into a commercial success in the early 1990s.

For Mueller, "Networking doesn't just mean calling somebody up and name dropping in the hope of getting a job [or closing a deal]. You have to add value to each meeting by demonstrating your expertise, so that the time spent is worthwhile for both parties . . . What you need is a sense of vision and determination to capture people's imaginations."

The founders of Rhino Records, as flexible industry mavericks, granted Mueller the freedom to create a children's music market. "That meant I had to develop distribution channels for an as-yet-undefined market. Do you realize how challenging it is to distribute a product with limited exposure in a nebulous market?" She decided to talk to anyone who would listen—toy stores, drugstores, supermarkets, and museum stores, in addition to traditional channels.

In a matter of months, she landed the second-largest order in Rhino's history, a deal that required many meetings with decision makers. "These negotiations reinforced the importance of networking and the need to bring value to those networking efforts. Networking can play a much bigger role than helping your personal advancement. It also can benefit your company. It's what helps you put deals together and even decide with whom you want to do deals."

What Mary Mueller calls networking is a dramatic example of seizing and applying personal power based on expertise and information. She is on her way to becoming a powerful force in an emerging industry segment, creating for Kid Rhino a presence among entertainment giants.

Source: Marc Sharma, "The Charge of Kid Rhino," *USC Business* 3 (Fall/Winter 1992), pp. 40–41

dealings with superiors and hostile outsiders. The power motive has been found to be predictive of a manager's probability of rising through the hierarchy in bureaucratic organizations.[56] But it is less critical in technical or professional settings.[57]

You may recall from Chapter 6 that a person's power needs can be personalized or socialized. People with personalized power needs exercise power to dominate others and keep them weak and dependent. They are often rude, sexually exploitive, aggressive, and concerned with acquiring symbols of power and status. A person with socialized power needs is more emotionally mature and exercises power for the benefit of others and of the organization, much as Mary Mueller has done on behalf of Kid Rhino (see Challenge of Change box). The socialized power wielder minimizes coercion, playing favorites, and using power for personal gain.[58]

While men and women have similar needs for power, women have a higher need for socialized power than do men.[59] A person with a high need for socialized power is more likely to achieve visible managerial success than a person without a power need or with a personalized power need, although gender bias is a complicating factor. Strong personal power needs may improve short-run performance but bring about a later fall from power.

Power Avoidance and Powerlessness. Because of the responsibility it entails and the interpersonal conflicts associated with it, many people have no need for power. To them it is easier and less anxiety provoking not to always live up to the expectations that go along with being a powerful person. Using power inevitably embroils a person in conflict, where actions and motives are confronted and challenged. Many people would just as soon avoid emotionally charged confrontations at work.

Others publicly deny their desire for power—and sometimes even deny it to themselves—for several reasons. One is the widely held belief that power corrupts, which is supported by the way people with power have abused it in the past. Adolf Hitler is certainly a grim example. Leona Helmsley and Michael Milken are more typical. Richard Nixon is a special case of a president doing good on an international scale but failing personally by believing he was above the law. Another reason for denial is that when people acquire power for its own sake, they may be covering up feelings of inferiority, compensating for deprivations, or substituting power for lack of affection.[60] These are not images that readily fit most people's self-concepts.

Power avoidance notwithstanding, most people fear powerlessness, a key source of alienation.[61] People realize power is one of the valid mechanisms for reality testing and getting things done in organizations.[62] Powerlessness and organizational ambiguities contribute to a person's use of political behaviors. People who feel powerless invest their energy in dysfunctional behavior like protecting their turf, avoiding difficult issues, covering up mistakes, avoiding risks, and resorting to self-serving politics.

HOW DO PEOPLE ENGAGE IN ORGANIZATIONAL POLITICS?

Contrary to popular opinion, "politics" originally referred to actions that served society. In the eighteenth century, being political meant engaging in public service. But times and meanings have changed. Even the ideology underlying the formation of the Democratic and Republican political parties—that of serving large interest groups—has largely faded from political reality.[63]

organizational politics
The deliberate management of influence to achieve outcomes not approved by the organization, or to obtain sanctioned outcomes through non-approved methods.

Organizational politics has been defined as the deliberate "management of influence to obtain ends not sanctioned by the organization or to obtain sanctioned ends through nonsanctioned influence means."[64] Whereas power can be a latent force (a capability), politics involves deliberate actions to develop and use power to counter the goals, ideas, or plans advanced by competing interests.[65] Because it functions outside the official system, the purpose of politics is to shift otherwise ambiguous outcomes to one's personal advantage.[66] Politics has been found to be an integral part of industrial life and critical to the management of change and innovation.[67] Jeffrey Pfeffer even writes: "Accomplishing innovation and change in organizations requires more than the ability to solve technical to analytic problems. Innovation almost invariably threatens the status quo, and consequently, innovation is an inherently political activity."[68]

While politics at times may be deceitful and even illegal, politically motivated employees often have the best interests of the organization at heart. Political behavior can still be service oriented, true to the original meaning of "politics." Politics invokes strategies intended to trip the balance of power and influence the outcome in one's favor. For example, imagine that a compensation manager believes he has a design for a better performance evaluation system. Knowing his ideas will appear radical, he meets several times with each individual who serves on the compensation policy committee to influence each to buy into the new scheme. His political actions are outside the required system, but his vision aims to benefit the organization.

Organizational Uncertainty Increases Conflict and Politics

Conflict often results when performance criteria are ambiguous, goals inconsistent or dissimilar, rewards uncertain, work flows interdependent, communication lacking, or organizational participants highly competitive. Conflict among these variables is amplified when the stakes are high or power is diffused. Political behaviors are likely to be intense under such conditions.[69] By contrast, when performance standards are explicit and rewards rationally allocated, political activity usually declines.

Other conditions incite conflict and political behaviors. They emerge, for example, when resources are scarce or insufficient, so that people are motivated to maneuver outside the formal system to get their "fair share." Furthermore, it is difficult to avoid political behavior when interacting with authoritarian personalities or people who externally attribute outcomes. Since authoritarian personalities are less aware of their behavior, they may take greater political risks wanting to squash those who get in their way.[70] Politics is also likely when there is little trust among members and rewards are allocated on a zero-sum basis.[71] But perhaps most significant, political behavior often occurs when peers work in lateral relationships in which no one has authority over the others.[72]

As a means of dealing with inconsistent and uncertain conditions, organizational politics serves several positive functions. Political behavior can help get the job done in spite of personnel inadequacies by working around the weak link. Politics can also be a force for change when qualified, politically active people tackle problems that resist formal solutions. A political network also serves as a grapevine for communicating with and influencing individuals throughout the organization.

Important, Decentralized Decisions Invite Politics

As shown in Exhibit 13–3, people are more likely to become political when the decision outcome is important to them or to their group. But because political behavior often has costs, people tend to be selective. They don't waste their chips by becoming embroiled in issues where the potential outcome is insignificant.[73]

The other factor moderating the use of politics is the extent to which power is dispersed or centralized. When power is concentrated toward the top of an organization (or bureaucratic rules are widely accepted), there is less incentive to use political power to influence decisions. Politics comes into greater play when power is widely dispersed and decision-making processes are ad hoc. Coalitions then emerge, with each group supporting the position most favorable to its members.

Alternative Forms of Political Behavior

Political capacity is the ability and inclination to behave politically, to exercise power and influence. It has been stated that "the sum of someone's power and influence represents that person's capacity for political action."[74] Although techniques for gaining power and influence vary, manipulating the behavior of others is at the heart of political behavior. Exhibit 13–4 shows that political manipulation

▬▬ EXHIBIT 13–3

Conditions That Set the Stage for Political Behavior
Conditions that produce conflict are likely to stimulate political behaviors when the stakes are high and power is widely diffused throughout the organization. People then maneuver outside the formal system to "get their fair share."

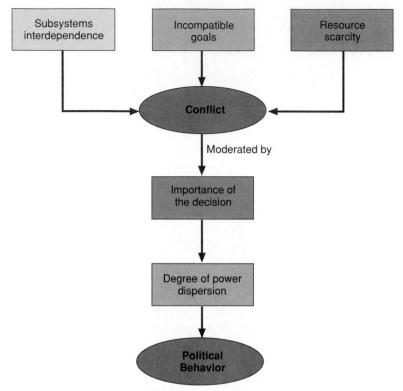

Source: Suggested by Jeffrey Pfeffer, *Power in Organizations* (Marshfield, MA: Pitman Publishing, 1981), pp. 67–96.

▬▬ EXHIBIT 13–4

Different Forms of Political Manipulation
For purposes of this model, the subtle differences between power and influence need to be clarified. As defined by Beeman and Sharkey, power is the capacity to change situational realities. Influence works by altering a person's perception of the situation.

Basis of Manipulation

	Power	Influence
Positive	Inducement	Persuasion
Negative	Coercion	Obligation

Type of Manipulation

Source: Reprinted from *Business Horizons,* March–April 1987. Copyright 1987 by the foundation for the School of Business at Indiana University. Used with permission.

can be positive or negative and based on power or influence. It identifies four forms of political manipulation: inducement, persuasion, obligation, and coercion. Of the four, persuasion is the most gentle, coercion the most forceful.

When using *persuasion*, the manipulator tries emotion and logic to influence the way others perceive the situation. Successful persuasion leaves the other person feeling better off, but not necessarily better off. For example: "If you'll write this proposal today, we'll probably be able to secure the contract."

Inducement is a stronger positive force that relies on the use of power. The manipulator offers some form of reward in exchange for compliance—perhaps more desirable assignments, greater autonomy, a larger budget, or the promise of a more favorable performance review. To illustrate: "If you back my plan with the general manager, I'll push for the capital investment you want for your lab." But since providing rewards may cost the manipulator, persuasion alone is often attempted first.

Obligation is a negative form of political manipulation that draws on feelings of owing the manipulator something. For example, Alex will remind Bess of the personal investment he has made in her welfare over the years. Alex may attempt to convince Bess that unless she does as he wants, she will be worse off. He might say, "Remember how I saved your Taiwan joint venture? You've got to help me with this Singapore alliance or our entire Far East business goes down the drain."

By contrast, in applying outright *coercion,* Alex will alter the situation so that Bess actually is worse off unless she complies. Alex might say, "If you don't issue a purchase order for this industrial robot, I'll let management know you are contracting with a vendor who illegally disposes of toxic wastes." Coercion can backfire, so it must be used infrequently and exercised with caution. Experienced politicians often delegate coercive tactics to a committee or subordinate so they don't appear to be the "heavy."

Successful managers use a variety of other political tactics. One study asked people to describe incidents in which they succeeded in getting a superior, subordinate, or co-worker to do what they wanted. It found that the variety of tactics used to influence another is fairly extensive. Examples of eight of these tactics appear in the Your Turn exercise. Take a moment to complete it right now.

Which specific influence tactic to use depends on the objective of the political attempt and the nature of the situation. Exchange and ingratiation tactics, for example, are likely to be used to obtain personal favors. Rational appeals and coalition tactics are likely to be used to gain acceptance of work-related changes. Assertiveness and sanctions are used to influence subordinates, while rational appeals are used to influence superiors. Ingratiation tactics, exchange tactics, and upward appeals are often used to influence peers.

Political Tactics Are Learned Skills

One of the more interesting realities of organizational politics is its reciprocal nature. "I'll help you if you help me" provides the foundation for a political power base, so long as both are not direct adversaries. There probably will come a time in your career when achieving your goal hinges more on political activity than on your technical expertise. At the very least, you must be aware of how those around you use power so you avoid being negatively manipulated.[75] The tactics that follow are common in many settings and can be learned.[76] They may initially seem contrary to your behavioral preferences, but be forewarned—others will use them. Tactical skills include:

1. *Maintain alliances with powerful people.* Forming coalitions and networking is basic to gaining power in any organization (recall Mary Mueller's success at Kid Rhino). Coalitions are important not only in making committee decisions but also in day-to-day encounters. Maintain close alliances with those on whom you depend to accomplish your tasks. In addition to your boss and peers, establish working relationships with staff people who have expert or information power and with people in other departments whose work affects your own. An accommodating purchasing agent, shipper, or accountant can make a big difference in how readily you get things done.

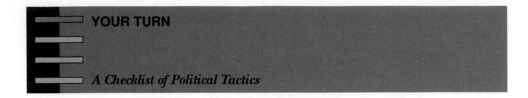

YOUR TURN

A Checklist of Political Tactics

Which of these behaviors have you used in your attempts to get others to do your bidding? Which have others used on you? Why did they succeed or fail? Check those used and make a note of the result.

	I Have Used on Others	Others Have Used on Me	Result and Why
Assertiveness			
• Point out that the rules require the person to do it.	_____	_____	_____
• Repeatedly remind the person what is wanted.	_____	_____	_____
Ingratiation			
• Act polite and humble while making the request.	_____	_____	_____
• Sympathize about the hardships the request causes.	_____	_____	_____
Rational appeals			
• Write a detailed plan justifying a request.	_____	_____	_____
• Explain the reasons for your request.	_____	_____	_____
Sanctions			
• Threaten to expel the person from the group.	_____	_____	_____
• Threaten to complain to a higher authority.	_____	_____	_____
Exchanges			
• Propose an exchange of favors.	_____	_____	_____
• Remind the person of past favors you provided.	_____	_____	_____
Upward appeals			
• Appeal to higher levels to support a request.	_____	_____	_____
• Send the person to see a superior.	_____	_____	_____
Blocking			
• Threaten to stop working with the person.	_____	_____	_____
• Ignore the person and stop being friendly.	_____	_____	_____
Coalitions			
• Obtain support of co-workers to back a request.	_____	_____	_____
• Make request at meeting where others will back it.	_____	_____	_____

Source: David Kipnis, Stuart M. Schmidt, and Ian Wilkinson, "Intraorganizational Influence Tactics: Explorations in Getting One's Way," *Journal of Applied Psychology* 65 (1980), pp. 440–452. Copyright 1980 by the American Psychological Association. Adapted by permission.

2. *Avoid alienation.* In keeping with the tactic of maintaining alliances, don't injure someone who is or might soon be in a position to take revenge. The same principle applies to burning bridges that may be needed to cross future raging currents.

3. *Use information as currency.* Politically astute organizational members understand the power implications of obtaining and carefully disseminating

information. Sharing information with someone who needs it and has no other means of acquiring it enhances your power base. That person now owes you a favor and may perceive you as someone on whom he or she is dependent for future information.

4. ***Withdraw from petty disputes.*** Some issues are so critical they are worth fighting for. But some conflicts are so petty that it makes more sense to concede and walk away. Be gracious in yielding on an issue that is important to another person but not to you. Doing so builds credibility and an indebtedness that might be reciprocated at a later date.

5. ***Avoid decisive engagement.*** By advancing slowly toward a political end, it may be possible to progress undetected or at least remain sufficiently inconspicuous to avoid alarming and arming others. If an adversary's proposal appears to be gaining momentum and cannot be thwarted immediately, for example, it may be possible to refer it to a committee for further discussion. This gains a delay and a wider bargaining arena.

6. ***Avoid preliminary disclosure of preferences.*** Appearing overly eager for a certain outcome may leave you in a vulnerable position. If the outcome of a situation is uncertain, it may be advisable to support the aggressive efforts of someone else rather than take the lead yourself. This way you can get off the ship if it begins to sink. And if an impasse does occur, your timely "fresh perspective" may be the approach that allows others to compromise.

7. ***Make a quick but successful showing.*** Make a big, successful splash early in the game to get the right people's attention, especially if you're a newly appointed manager. Being visible, available, and an apparent expert means you're likely to receive assignments and positions with more power and potential. Even once you are established in the organization, sometimes it pays to "shoot for the moon" on a project, so that you can later settle for less but in the process move people and programs closer to your way of thinking.

8. ***Collect IOUs.*** The "Godfather" of book and film fame used IOUs to extend his realm of influence. He would do favors for "family" members, but he made it clear that they owed him something in return. When these IOUs were called in, the debtor was expected to pay up—usually with interest. Extending favors or support to another is like depositing in a savings account, as long as you trust the person to reciprocate later.

9. ***Exploit possible negative outcomes.*** Sometimes things must get worse before they get better. Bad news demands attention and may be the catalyst for desired change. A CEO could not convince the board to fund the acquisition of a supplier until the firm's sole source of supply was threatened by a vendor's cash-flow problems. By focusing on likely negative outcomes, those who would otherwise resist may switch to your side.

10. ***Divide and rule.*** The assumption behind this principle is that those who are divided will not form coalitions themselves. One way to divide and rule is to approach individual members of your opponent's coalition and point out your common interests. Sociologists call this "cooptation." Another tactic is to identify your adversaries' weaknesses and publicize them or reveal their behaviors that run contrary to organizational norms.

These ten tactics can be learned, and there are sound reasons for using them. As a rule, political tactics are more successful if they are subtle and non-threatening—blatant power plays often lead to resistance, defensive reactions, and retaliation. Because unobtrusive political tactics do not threaten other people's self-esteem or resource base, they are less likely to cause negative reactions.[77]

The merger between Aetna Life & Casualty Company and US Healthcare, Inc., cost Aetna $8.9 billion and left Aetna CEO Ronald Compton (right) and US Healthcare Chairman Leonard Abramson (left) with the task of melding "inherently different" cultures. Aetna, known as a stodgy insurer, is joining with a health-maintenance company recognized for aggressive cost controls and sophisticated systems. Creating such an unstable climate will likely cause organizational uncertainty as employees in both merging firms cope with the changes. (Source: © Jim Leynse/ SABA.)

HOW CAN POWER AND POLITICS BE MORAL?

The use of power and politics within organizations invites a test of moral judgment. A morally ethical manager or professional seeks to behave not just in compliance with the letter of the law or company policy, but within the spirit of it as well.[78] Power and politically motivated behavior need not be applied in an immoral or unethical fashion.

Morality and Power Are Not Mutually Exclusive

When it comes to using power, a person's actions can be classified as moral, amoral, or immoral (see Exhibit 13–5). You can evaluate your actions using this three-level classification scheme. It helps you to see whether you are applying or thinking of applying power too far beyond the boundaries of ethical propriety.

moral manager
One who strives to develop and adhere to ethical goals, motives, standards, and general operating strategies.

Moral Management.   The **moral manager** strives to develop and adhere to ethical goals, motives, standards, and general operating strategies. Power is exercised to pursue fair and just ends. The manager views laws as minimum standards of conduct. Moral management is essentially unselfish and not prone to self-serving politics. Moral management does not have to compromise performance; ethical behavior promotes enduring self-interest.

Moral management is consistent with innovation and continuous improvement. You can see this in the power-sharing, self-policing, continuous improvement redesigns that Japanese and German auto manufacturers apply to their products to constantly upgrade quality, safety, and operating performance. This has not always been the standard of conduct for U.S. auto manufacturers, who at times have compromised safety to save a few dollars per auto in redesign costs.[79] Moral managers support their people, recognize their accomplishments, are sensitive to their fears and needs, and communicate confidence in the organization's purpose and products.

━━━━━━ **EXHIBIT 13–5**

*Three Standards of
Managerial Ethics*

ETHICAL STANDARDS

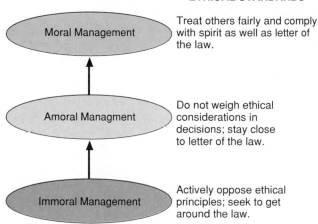

Moral Management — Treat others fairly and comply with spirit as well as letter of the law.

Amoral Managment — Do not weigh ethical considerations in decisions; stay close to letter of the law.

Immoral Management — Actively oppose ethical principles; seek to get around the law.

Source: Reprinted from *Business Horizons,* March–April 1987. Copyright 1987 by the Foundation for the School of Business at Indiana University. Used with permission.

immoral manager
One devoid of ethical principles and who is actively opposed to doing what is ethical.

Immoral Management. The **immoral manager** is not only devoid of ethical principles, but also actively opposed to what is ethical.[80] Selfishness is paramount for the immoral manager, whether focusing on using power for personal gain or maximizing short term gains for the firm. Senior managers of Beech-Nut, the baby food company, deliberately moved inventories of bottled sugar water (deceptively labeled as apple juice) from warehouse to warehouse in efforts to evade Food and Drug Administration investigators. They were knowingly engaging in immoral (and illegal) behavior.[81] Cutting corners and concealing facts are common tactics for immoral managers obsessed with personal power. This seems to be the case in tobacco industry executives proclaiming that their product is nonaddictive, and yet their proprietary research has revealed for decades the addictive capacity of tobacco.

Amoral Management. Perhaps even more troubling than outright immoral management is the **amoral manager** who lacks any moral sensibility whatsoever. Managers who are amoral can be intentional or unintentional in approaching ethical issues. The intentionally amoral manager knowingly keeps ethics out of personal decisions within the organization. The unintentionally amoral manager doesn't think about ethics at all. He or she may lack ethical principles and thus not reflect on the broader consequences of how power is used.

amoral manager
One who lacks any moral sensibility whatsoever; one who doesn't think about the moral implications of actions, or who chooses to keep ethics out of decisions.

The amoral manager will operate within the letter of the law to the extent that it is known. However, one of the greatest dangers of amoral management is that decisions are made without anticipating negative consequences. Several well-known cases include PepsiCo's TV promotion of Frito corn chips using the "Frito Bandito" theme that Mexican-Americans found offensive; Nestlé's decision to market concentrated baby formula in underdeveloped countries with impure water; or police departments' height and weight requirements that effectively exclude many persons from ethnic groups that on average are slight in stature.[82]

Technology poses a new ethical challenge. Technology now permits supervisors to eavesdrop on their staff's phone conversations and to secretly observe computer screens or even type in warnings when they see something they don't like.[83]

Whether the employee is a reservation agent or stockbroker, such use of power invades privacy with an aura of "Big Brother is watching you." Electronic eavesdropping is not only a questionable use of power, but it can accentuate negative feedback and lead to the overuse of punishment to boost performance.

Pluralistic Positive Politics

Active political behavior can be healthy because it forces the clash of ideas. Although the "best" idea may not always prevail, at least people are encouraged to defend their views. Professors Greiner and Schein refer to this as the "pluralistic/political model," which they contend is the most realistic way to describe how organizational actors arrive at decisions. "The pluralistic/political model sees organizations as composed of differing interest groups. Each party pursues its own goals, sometimes on selfish grounds but often for well-intended reasons based on its view of what is best for the organization as a whole."[84]

Organizational politics require dispersion of power throughout an organization, which means people are free to disagree. The same holds true for nation-states and political entities. Since 1989 there has been a cry for freedom around the world—a rush for pluralistic power diffusion. Once the Berlin Wall began to crumble and the Cold War with the former USSR thawed, there was no holding back the drive to diffuse power away from all-powerful central governments. Political activism has increased worldwide in spite of totalitarian regimes because freedom is preferable to oppression and lack of choice, even in the face of transitional chaos—provided basic needs are cared for. However, as described in the World Watch box, efforts to make businesses more market-sensitive within Russia have been a struggle in the transitional years since the communists fell from grace.

When power is tightly centralized within a hierarchy, decisions are protected from politics. This applies to nations as well as to organizations. Professor Pfeffer observes, "There is more political activity in democratic countries with relatively equal political parties than there is in countries which are run by strong dictatorships. Ironically, when power is dispersed, decisions become worked out through the interplay of various actors with more equal power in a political process."[85]

Only with a knowledge of how political behaviors work can you analyze your own dependencies, assess the sources and strength of your power, and recognize when political tactics are being used to influence you. The degree to which you apply political skills depends on the nature of your situation and your personality. But an awareness of their use and consequences will enhance your personal and organizational effectiveness.

POWER PLAYS TAKE A BITE OUT OF APPLE COMPUTERS, INC.—A SECOND LOOK

One of life's devastating emotions is to be told that one's work has been judged to be unacceptable. How a person reacts to being fired is a reflection on character, especially if the termination is carried out in the popular press. Michael Spindler, when fired from Apple Computer, wrote a melancholy E-mail to all who worked for Apple that closed with the words:

> *Those of you who—through all these long years—have helped me, supported me and even guided me—I thank you sincerely from the bottom of my soul for the friendship and being together. In fading away from the place which I loved and feared, I will become whole again—hopefully renew the father, husband and self I am.*[86]

*Managing in Russia—Uneasy Transition
from Bear to Bull*

From 1917 to 1991, managers of Russian organizations worked under a communist set of rules and policies that concentrated power (with unquestioned authority) in the senior administrator of each enterprise. This created a self-defeating situation in which Russian executives were forced to micromanage as people waited for a top-down decision. Rather than risk blame if something went wrong, action was delayed until authorized by the senior manager. Although managers were expected to be honest in interpersonal conduct, of necessity they routinely ignored the 80,000 or so rules and regulations that were supposed to govern the average enterprise. Following rules would have bogged down decisions for managers who were already overworked and overstressed.

During *perestroika* reforms of the late 1980s, there was a brief experiment with shared power administered through elected councils of workers within each enterprise. The 1987 Law on the Soviet State Enterprise was intended to encourage collective participation in decision making, but it was abandoned in 1989. Senior executives complained workers elected representatives who would make life easier for them rather than more productive for the firm.

By 1991, the power of the Communist Party over management of enterprises was broken, and the strength of

the former USSR collapsed as individual republics seized their independence. Managers of once state-owned enterprises are struggling to learn how to manage by relinquishing their autocratic power grip and sharing power with employees and owners (sometimes one and the same). Younger entrepreneurs create their own businesses, but investment capital remains difficult to come by.

In the troublesome transition toward a market economy, a new legal system has to be built, but it has not yet been done. Vast middle-management bureaucracies strangle decisions in large companies, and payoffs to the mafia (described as a nongovernment tax) or bribes to government officials are necessary to keep a business running. Managers routinely use *blat*, or influence and the trading of favors, to lubricate business transactions—from obtaining licenses to securing supplies of critically needed parts. Add to this a work force unmotivated to produce much less to innovate, and it is understandable that Russian managers are facing a slippery uphill climb toward a market economy.

Sources: Interview with Dr. Nikolai Yasenev, vice-rector of international relationships, Ural State Technical University, Ekaterinburg, Russia (February 5–8, 1996); and Shelia M. Puffer, "Understanding the Bear: A Portrait of Russian Business Leaders," *Academy of Management Executive* 8 (February 1994), pp. 41–54.

As Spindler's replacement, Gil Amelio views himself as an organizational transformer who, as described in his 1995 book, *Profit from Experience,* likes to learn from the past to prepare for new challenges. After leaving his lab bench as a scientist for AT&T Bell Laboratories, Amelio joined in 1971 one of the original Silicon Valley companies, Fairchild Semiconductor, where he was in charge of the microprocessor division. He got a real opportunity at exercising power in 1983 when he was recruited to Rockwell International to rescue its $120 million semiconductor products division, which had a $2 million a month negative cash flow. He refocused the business on its strongest products, changed its business plan, and took steps to change attitudes and morale.[87] To date, his most substantial exercise of power has been as CEO of National Semiconductor, a firm that ironically was bogged down in trying to integrate the acquisition of Fairchild and, to make matters worse, had lost money in 8 of its previous 11 years.

In Amelio's five years at National, he led people and organizational resources through five visions in Phase I (restoring financial viability) and was starting Vision 6.0 in Phase II (quantum growth), with the strategic intent of becoming "the world's leading supplier of semiconductor-intensive products for moving and shaping information."[88] But rather than complete the transformation of National, a firm nearing $3 billion, Amelio chose the challenge of charting a new course for the more controversial and visible Apple Computer with sales of almost $13 billion.

Exactly how he uses his formal authority and personal power as a charismatic leader, we aren't sure, for this is written the day he takes over as Apple's CEO. But we are sure that he will act quickly, for his motto is "speed is life." If Apple reaches the year 2000 as an independent company, it will have the look and feel of a different business from the pre-Amelio Apple. Apple will have become strategically focused—probably more of a software than a hardware company—and employees will once again have become empowered, but result focused.

Like Spindler, Amelio sent an e-mail to the people of the Apple community. But rather than a reflection on the past, his message emphasized the future. It said in part:

> I look forward to working with all of you . . . Let's work together to strengthen Apple's technology leadership, to serve our loyal customers and to enhance our reputation as one of the most respected and recognized brands in the world. Together, let's resolve to build a business as great as our products.[89]

SUMMARY

Power is the basic force managers use to change organizational realities by getting others to do what they want done. Anyone can have power, but managers and leaders have power advantages since their positions in social networks place them at the center of information and decision exchanges; people thus expect them to act powerfully.

Power can arise from a person's position (as do formal authority and reward power) or personal behavior (as do expert and referent power). But situational forces allow other power possibilities (such as coercion and access to information), which affect the degree to which a person can alter the realities of others and thus exercise power. Some people's socialized power needs energize them to act in keeping with organizational purposes. Others with high personal power needs have more self-serving aims. Some seek to avoid power altogether, not wanting the responsibility and potential conflict often associated with it.

Organizational politics occur when people or groups seek to alter resources or outcomes in their favor. Political behaviors increase when conditions are uncertain, complex, and competitive. Political manipulation can take the form of inducement, persuasion, obligation, or coercion. Political tactics such as maintaining coalitions with powerful people, using information as currency, avoiding premature disclosure of preferences, and collecting IOUs are learned skills.

But the practice of being political or exercising power does not need to be immoral or even amoral. Moral managers act fairly and legally to do that which is ethically right in service of the organization. Across nations as well as organizations, political activities abound when power is disbursed and multiple interest groups jockey for position. Tightly centralized power limits people's freedom to act politically.

Key Concepts

power, *p. 427*

position power, *p. 428*

formal authority, *p. 429*

reward power, *p. 429*

expert power, *p. 430*

mentor, *p. 430*

referent power, *p. 430*

charisma, *p. 430*

reciprocity, *p. 431*

coercive power, *p. 432*

information power, *p. 432*

association power, *p. 433*

social exchange theory, *p. 436*

negotiation, *p. 439*

power motive, *p. 442*

organizational politics, *p. 444*

moral manager, *p. 450*

immoral manager, *p. 451*

amoral manager, *p. 451*

Questions for Study and Discussion

1. Power has been defined as the ability to alter another person's behavior. In what ways can a manager use position power to alter someone's behavior? How can a nonmanager use personal power?

2. Why does position power seem to be more accepted in Western societies such as the United States than in Eastern societies such as Japan? Relate your answer to the concept of centrality within a social network.

3. Create a scenario that describes the ideal conditions under which a manager will have power over a group. Incorporate at least four situational factors into the picture of power you paint.

4. How do people's power needs differ? How do the different orientations toward power of people with high power needs influence their chances for personal and organizational success?

5. How do inducement, persuasion, obligation, and coercion differ? If you were a manager, which form of political manipulation would you use most? Why?

6. Suppose your boss suggested that your contribution to the department would be stronger if you could draw on a more versatile portfolio of political behaviors. Identify four political tactics you would feel comfortable using and describe situations in which you might use each.

7. What is the difference between an immoral and an amoral manager? Comment on how you could use the political tactics you identified in Question 6 and still be a moral manager.

8. Why are political activities less likely to occur in a tightly centralized system? Do you foresee an increase or decrease in political behaviors in Third World countries? Why?

EXPERIENTIAL EXERCISE

Power Plays within Universal Care, Inc.: A Role Play

Purpose. This role-playing exercise enables class members, working in groups of 7 to 10, to experience political behaviors when confronted with obvious differences in power. You will assume the position of a vice president who sits on the board of directors. Because a variety of crises have been plaguing the firm, the CEO just resigned and you and other company vice presidents must now elect a replacement from among your peers.

The exercise serves three purposes: (1) to create complex and realistic roles from sketchy data; (2) to confront issues and negotiate decisions when actors have explicit power differences; and (3) to stimulate introspection about your personal reactions to having more or less power than other group members and the behaviors you use to deal with power discrepancies.

Time Required. 45 to 60 minutes.

Materials. One index card per student (5" × 7" suggested) and one felt-tip marker per group.

Background on Universal Care, Inc. Universal Care, Inc., was founded 15 years ago by a physicist, a biologist, a chemist, and an engineer. The company has grown erratically into what is now a $5 billion multidivisional firm. UCI branched beyond its entrepreneurial beginnings in molecular research into diverse lines of business, all related to health care. The firm currently has products in pharmaceuticals, genetic engineering, medical instrumentation, residential nursing, and prosthetics (including a mechanical heart).

During the past year, UCI has increasingly come under a variety of pressures, even attacks. Several lawsuits against the firm for alleged product malfunctions that resulted in injury or death were won by the plaintiffs. Fortunately, no class action suits have yet been settled against the company, although two are pending—one involving a heart implant valve alleged to be associated with three patient deaths. Three suits have been filed by other biotech firms alleging infringement of patents on DNA-related products. Several of these incidents have made the front pages of major daily newspapers, each raising questions about the propriety of the firm's products and/or operations.

Management is faced with the likelihood of a significant fourth-quarter loss that is expected to result in negative earnings for the year (which ends in two months). This stems from a combination of legal judgments against UCI; reserves set aside for possible future legal losses; intensified competitive action in several product segments, causing loss of market share; and the difficulty in assimilating seven recent acquisitions (especially in the residential nursing segment). Additionally, a number of key employees in research and management have recently defected, leaving human resource gaps in some key areas. (A few of these former employees left after blowing the whistle on questionable company practices.)

Under these intense pressures, the CEO announced today a personal decision to resign and take early retirement, effective in two weeks. Because of the rapid growth of the firm in the past few years, no serious effort had been given to developing a successor. Now, however, there is a pressing need to elect a new CEO, and the corporate bylaws are explicit on the process. According to the wishes of the founders (who withdrew from active management within two years of UCI's going public six years ago), the bylaws state that a new CEO must be elected from the ranks of incumbent managers who sit on the board of directors.

You are a vice president of UCI and a member of the board of directors. You are quite concerned by the sudden resignation of the CEO and the need to quickly elect a replacement. A special board meeting has been scheduled solely for the purpose of electing a new CEO. You have a little time to prepare for that meeting and to communicate selectively with some of your peers on the board.

Role-Play Procedures. Your instructor will guide you through the preliminary steps necessary to prepare for this role-playing exercise. When told by your instructor, your group will assemble as a board of directors to nominate, discuss, and eventually to elect the new CEO using the bylaws of UCI. Following the board meeting and election, you will then discuss what you learned.

EXPERIENTAL EXERCISE

Triads Learn from Personal Power Situations

Purpose.   To revisit recent personal attempts to exercise power, evaluate personal motives, and analyze the appropriateness of strategy (power source) relative to outcome.

Time Required.   15 to 20 minutes.

Materials Needed.   None.

Procedures.   This is a relatively quick in-class exercise that emphasizes learning by reflection and shared insight.

Phase 1.   Group the class into triads (groups of three members each).

Phase 2.   (10 minutes) Each of you should recall and describe two recent personal attempts to exercise power. Think of someone (or several people) whose behavior you wanted to influence or control—you wanted the person (persons) to do something he/she would not have otherwise done without your intervention. The target of your power could have been someone in your family, a friend, a student group, someone at work, and so on. For each situation described, your group should do two things.

First, describe what you wanted done and how you went about attempting to get the other person(s) to go along with your wishes? How did you know the person(s) was not originally prepared to do this? How successful were your efforts?

Second, as a group analyze this attempt at power. What kind of power strategy (source of power) was being used (see the list below)? What factors affected power effectiveness in this situation? Why did the power strategy seem to work, or, if it did not, what alternative actions might have been used? As a refresher, the principal power sources are:

A.   *Organization position* (authority, control of rewards or resources).

B.   *Personal behavior* (expertise, referent respect, reciprocal alliances).

C.   *Situational forces* (coercion, access to information or associations).

Once stories have been told and analyzed, as a final triad task attempt to analyze each person's power needs. Who among you seems to have a strong power motive, a need to influence or control others across several situations? For those with power needs, does it seem to be directed toward control of others for purely personal advantage or are there clues that power is exercised for some common or higher order good?

Phase 3.   As a class, follow the guidance of your professor to briefly answer the questions and discuss:

1.   How many of you experienced successful outcomes? (Show of hands, both if two successes.)

2.   Which of the primary power strategies (sources) was most used? (Show of hands for each of the three summarized above, A, B, or C.) How about specific types of strategies, say expertise? Control of access to information? Coercion?

3.   Why do you believe some power sources are more available to you at this stage in your life than others? Which seem to be more difficult, perhaps even dangerous, to use?

4.   What are the pros and cons of deliberately trying to develop your power motive or need for power? Those of you who do have a reasonably strong power motive, what would you advise your lower-power-need classmates to do to feel more comfortable with a need for power?

CASE

Power Tactics at Old Line Bank and Trust

Robert Wagley, Wright State University (Dayton, Ohio)

The Setting.   Old Line Bank and Trust is located in the Northeast. The bank has experienced a phenomenal level of growth because of the boom in travel and leisure activities in the area. As a result of this growth, many young professionals have recently been added to the work force. Most of these new hires have university degrees and come from outside the local area.

The community is one of the most staid areas in the northeast. Its inhabitants refer to newcomers as "outsiders." Even families who have lived in the community for three generations are still referred to by locals as outsiders and experience difficulties being accepted into the local power elite. In all respects, the community is firmly conservative.

Organization and Company Practice.   Joseph Edwards has been the senior vice president of administration and human relations for 32 years. Samuel Henderson has served as senior vice president of commercial banking for 27 years. The president and CEO is Warren Briggs, who has 24 years of experience in the position. Briggs is the great-grandson of the bank's founder. These three executives are also members of the board of directors and active members of the community's social elite.

It has been the practice of these three individuals, as well as other senior officers, to refer to younger members of the bank's staff as "girls" or "boys." For several years this has annoyed most of the young people working in the bank. Although senior executives were aware this practice irritated some of the staff, they continued it without offering apologies or justifications.

The Recent Incident.   Last week, three women managers took the newest member of the bank's management team, an African-American male, to lunch at one of the "in" dining establishments. The four ranged in age from 26 to 32 and all shared a common bond, having earned degrees from well-respected business schools. During lunch Samuel Henderson passed by their table and as a quick greeting asked, "What are you girls telling our new boy?" It was meant as a lighthearted joke, but nobody at the table laughed or smiled.

After Henderson went on his way, the group discussed his remark. That afternoon the four of them filed a complaint with both Edwards and Briggs. Both executives responded that the comment was meaningless and just intended to convey that they were part of the bank family. In closing, Briggs gave the four this advice: "If you want to progress in this firm, you had better spend less time with this silly stuff and more time making money for the bank."

Questions for Managerial Action

1. Would you go along with Briggs's advice to "grin and bear it" or would you persist in trying to change condescending executive behaviors?

2. What power/political issues are involved in this incident?

3. How could the practice of calling employees "boys" and "girls" be part of a deliberate power ploy by senior officers?

4. What impact does the use of such "titles" have for those who are called "boys" and "girls"? What options do the younger employees have for dealing with this common bank practice? Where do they draw the battle line?

Chapter 14

Leaders and Managers

LEARNING OBJECTIVES

After studying this chapter, you should be able to:

- Distinguish between the art of leadership and the practice of management.
- Critique the premise that personality traits separate leaders from nonleaders.
- Contrast two types of group-centered leadership theories—those based on cognitive styles and those focused on observable behaviors.
- Explain why most current theories of leadership are based on situational contingencies.
- Contrast transformational leadership with group-centered leadership.
- Show why leadership is not necessary for all organizational circumstances.

LARRY BOSSIDY: GROWTH SEPARATES WINNERS FROM LOSERS

Fortune magazine proclaims Larry Bossidy "the most sought-after CEO in America." Bossidy left the number two position at General Electric in 1991 to take the helm at ailing Allied-Signal, and has since been courted by IBM, Kodak, Westinghouse, and others. Brutally demanding and seldom satisfied, Bossidy sets challenging growth targets for his managers, helps them lay out strategies, provides resources, then grills them to make sure they follow through. "Growth," he says, "is the biggest challenge. For managers it will separate the winners from the losers."

Allied-Signal generates over $15 billion in revenue from the sale of auto parts, engineering metals, airplane engines, chemicals, and other mundane products. Bossidy understands that cost cutting alone will not enable a business to prosper during periods of slow economic growth. He would rather provide leadership for growth than rely on downsizing and cost cutting to hold up economic performance. In leading people in diversified enterprises, Bossidy drives a simple vision of success to his managers: "Business is really just two things. You increase sales, and you improve productivity. But the two go together." Productivity and efficiency provide for lower prices and faster deliveries, which attract new customers and ignite growth and profits.

As a leader of other leaders and managers, Larry Bossidy promotes growth as a motivational force: "The biggest payoff from growth is with people." Expanding opportunities are necessary to attract and encourage talented people. Without growth, he believes firms resort to seeking productivity, which means laying off people. "Restructuring [with layoffs] is negative. You get a frightened work force. Eventually you need to maintain or create jobs, not destroy them."

Bossidy is not a leader who stays in his executive suite to make only the big decisions. He immerses himself in the operating details of Allied-Signal's 20 businesses and guides unit managers in crafting business strategies. He claims, "A strategist divorced from operations is an incomplete person. You make far better judgments doing both." Because of his breadth of experience, keen insight, and no-nonsense feel for opportunities, subordinate managers don't see him as micromanaging. Says one reporting executive, "He's the most experienced guy at the table. With his help, we definitely make better decisions."

Source: Shawn Tully, "So, Mr. Bossidy, We Know You Can Cut. Now Show Us How to Grow," *Fortune* (August 21, 1995), pp. 70–80.

Herb Kelleher is the cofounder, chief executive, and leader of Southwest Airlines. Known for his flamboyant zaniness like dressing in clown costumes and painting three of the company's planes to look like Shamu the whale, Kelleher encourages his employees to enjoy themselves which in turn makes them happier and more productive. His leadership has been well received. Southwest employees showed their approval of Kelleher's vision for the company when, after fuel costs began to skyrocket in the wake of Iran's invasion of Kuwait, one-third of the company's employees took voluntary deductions from their pay to buy aviation fuel. Kelleher learned of the "Fuel from the Heart" program when he received a banner signed by those who pledged. (Photo: © Pam Francis.)

Leaders such as Larry Bossidy are the people who create, grow, and transform organizations. But as environmental events are anticipated and unfold, people like Bossidy are caught in a dilemma. On the one hand, they have to lead change processes and redirect people's energies together with other resources. They have to lead transformations of products, technologies, and organizational practices that produce growth. Conversely, they must manage to preserve order and achieve productivity. They have to manage costs and timetables and coordinate tasks across departments so that quality and efficiency are achieved.

Bossidy is able to excel as a manager at driving out costs and developing innovative processes for getting work done more efficiently. He is also a visionary leader who provides a clear sense of direction for transforming ideas into commercial successes, and he energizes others by challenging them to help make possibilities come true. Larry Bossidy is both an accomplished manager and a superlative leader. But are these terms synonymous? Or do "leader" and "manager" mean different things?

WHAT DISTINGUISHES MANAGERS FROM LEADERS?

Managers are common at all levels of organizations, whether they are called supervisors, managers, directors, administrators, or executives. Managers typically devote most of their day to managing resources, projects, deadlines, and so on. Leaders excite people about visions of opportunities and empower them to innovate and excel. Like managers, leaders can be found at all levels. Unlike managers, leaders don't necessarily need a title to effectively exert leadership—in fact, the leader may not be a manager at all. By contrast, managers are always given titles symbolic of their scope of responsibilities.

Managers Have Authority to Be in Charge

As discussed in Chapter 1, a manager is a person granted formal authority to be in charge of an organization or one of its subunits. **Managers** diagnose and influence systems and are responsible for controlling activities to keep the flow of work running smoothly. They keep activities and programs on track, maintain system predictability, and balance revenues against costs to achieve reasonable productivity and profitability. **Authority** is the right to make decisions and commit organizational resources based on one's position within the organizational hierarchy. Managers draw on their position authority to initiate problem solving, decision making, and action. But with authority come responsibility and accountability. **Accountability** means the manager is answerable for the setting of appropriate goals, the efficient allocation of resources, and task accomplishment within the unit.

Leaders Influence Others to Follow

How do you recognize a leader? It is easy to think of a few public figures who have made the news—Michael Eisner, Lee Iacocca, Ted Turner, Colon Powell, or Bill Clinton. These we may recognize as *formal leaders* because they also hold position authority as a president, commander, or other title. Or you may work with a visible professional who seems to be stirring up new ideas, championing new causes, and inspiring co-workers to pursue strategic visions. Such *informal leaders* do not have the advantage of formal authority; their spheres of influence are unrelated to organizational position. This commonly occurs when a mid-level manager of one department influences peers in other departments to support a favored program or a pilot project.

But how about people lower down in the hierarchy? Leaders can be found at all levels of an organization, but not all immediately stand out from the crowd. When several nonmanagerial people are put together on a "leaderless" task force or assigned to a self-managed team, one or two are likely to emerge as informal leaders. Such emergent leaders keep goals defined, agendas moving, and ideas integrated so the project is completed on schedule. In ad hoc groups and in interactions with peers, leadership is observable even in the absence of formal managerial authority.

Leadership has been called the most studied and least understood topic of any in the social sciences.[1] **Leadership** is the process of providing direction, energizing others, and obtaining their voluntary commitment to the leader's vision. A **leader** creates a vision and goals and influences others to share that vision and work toward the goals. A vision is an articulated picture of the future that conveys purpose, direction, and priorities. It illuminates the conditions, events, products, and qualities that could be attained through focused human energy and selective use of resources. Leaders are thus concerned with bringing about change and motivating others to support that vision of change.

In his years as CEO of Allied-Signal, Larry Bossidy has influenced the direction of its portfolio of businesses and serves as a leader model for people beyond his direct supervision. Bossidy is certainly a leader who has transformed organizations because of his leadership, but he has also been a manager of systems, resources,

managers
Persons granted authority to be in charge of an organizational unit and thus responsible for diagnosing and influencing systems and people to achieve appropriate goals.

authority
The right to make decisions and commit organizational resources based on position within the organization.

accountability
Holding a person with authority answerable for setting appropriate goals, using resources efficiently, and accomplishing task responsibilities.

leadership
The act of providing direction, energizing others, and obtaining their voluntary commitment to the leader's vision.

leader
A person who creates a vision and goals, then energizes others to voluntarily commit to that vision.

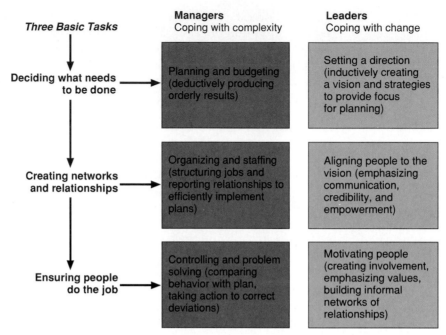

Source: Summarized from John Kotter, "What Leaders Really Do," *Harvard Business Review* 68 (May–June 1990), pp. 103–111.

and product lines. On a global level, the international statesman Nelson Mandela has cajoled and inspired political leaders to work toward reducing oppression and sharing political power. His goal has been to achieve racial equality in his historically segregated South Africa homeland. Mandela as President of South Africa is definitely a leader. But a manager? Probably not.

Managers Do Things Right, Leaders Do the Right Things

Managers can be leaders. Leaders don't have to be managers. But to understand the distinction between the two, compare their organizational impact. While one person might fill the roles of both manager and leader, those roles exhibit distinct systems of action. Professor John Kotter observes that management involves coping with complexity, while leadership is about coping with change.[2] He states that "each system of action involves deciding what needs to be done, creating networks of people and relationships that can accomplish an agenda, and then trying to ensure that those people actually do the job."[3] Exhibit 14–1 provides Kotter's basic distinction between how managers and leaders accomplish these three tasks.

In their book, *Leaders,* Warren Bennis and Burt Nanus provide a slightly different perspective on the difference between managers and leaders that nonetheless agrees with Kotter's basic theme. Although the distinction may sound trite, it suggests a difference in how efforts are focused:

> *To manage means to bring about, to accomplish, to have responsibility for, to conduct. Leading is influencing, guiding in direction, course, action, opinion. The distinction is crucial. Managers are people who do things right and leaders are people who do the right thing. The difference may be summarized as activities of vision and judgment— effectiveness [leading]—versus activities of mastering routines—efficiency [managing].[4]*

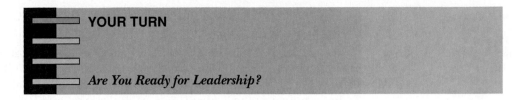

YOUR TURN

Are You Ready for Leadership?

For each statement, circle the number on the scale that best describes you.

	Strongly Disagree				Strongly Agree
1. I like to stand out from the crowd.	1	2	3	4	5
2. I feel proud and satisfied when I influence others to do things my way.	1	2	3	4	5
3. I enjoy doing things as part of a group rather than achieving results on my own.	1	2	3	4	5
4. I have a history of becoming an officer or captain in clubs and/or organized sports.	1	2	3	4	5
5. I try to be the one who is most influential in task groups at school or work.	1	2	3	4	5
6. In groups, I care most about good relationships.	1	2	3	4	5
7. In groups, I most want to achieve task goals.	1	2	3	4	5
8. In groups, I always show consideration for the feelings and needs of others.	1	2	3	4	5
9. In groups, I always structure activities and assignments to help get the job done.	1	2	3	4	5
10. In groups, I shift between being supportive of others' needs and pushing task accomplishment.	1	2	3	4	5

Interpretation: Add the scale values you circled on items 1 through 5. If your total score on these five items is 20 or more, you are likely to enjoy being a leader. If 10 or less, at this time in your life you are likely more interested in personal achievement. If you score in the middle range, your leadership potential could go either direction, depending on events.

As a leader, your style is suggested by your responses to items 6 through 10. For items 6 and 7, if your score is higher on 6 (than 7), you may be more concerned about relationships; a higher score on 7 suggests task motivation. For items 8 and 9, a higher score on 8 implies greater use of relationship-building behaviors; a higher score on 9 suggests an emphasis on task behaviors. A score of 4 or 5 on item 10 suggests you may adapt to circumstances as you see the need. Read on to learn about qualities that distinguish exemplary leaders.

In attempting to manage complexities, managers emphasize systems, structures, controls, and actions intended to achieve predictability and order. Leaders engage in extensive communication to elicit and act on ideas. Ultimately, leaders articulate thoughts in simplified visions that provide people with a sense of direction. Leaders promote change and are the trendsetters of organizational life. They empower others to work on causes, in part as a way of gaining commitment to the organization. All organizations need both managers and leaders.

Are you ready for leadership? Answer the questions in the Your Turn exercise to gain insights into whether you should strive to become a more influential leader.

Qualities That Distinguish Leaders from Followers?

Vance Packard provided an enduring perspective on leadership when he wrote, "Leadership appears to be the art of getting others to want to do something that you are convinced should be done."[5] Leadership prompts followers to behave in ways they would not necessarily without the leader's influence. To understand this art, it helps to look at the leader's traits, cognitive style, and behavior with group members.

In ancient times, it was assumed great leaders were born into an upper-class heritage. Today, we recognize that leaders develop; they learn from and are formed by life's experiences. Professor Abraham Zaleznik even contends that "leaders grow through painful conflict during their developmental years, while managers confront few of the experiences that generally cause people to turn inward." Leaders are thus "twice born," since they have encountered adversity that causes them to look inward "to reemerge with a created rather than an inherited sense of identity."[6] Andy Grove, CEO of Intel, credits the paranoia he endured as a refugee in war-torn Europe (WWII) as driving him to take risks to make bold, innovative moves that keep his company number one in the world of microprocessors.[7]

Leaders May Be Perceived As Having Distinguishing Personalities

Beginning around the turn of the century and extending into the 1940s, the search to discover the keys to leadership focused on trying to identify personal traits that would separate leaders from followers or effective leaders from ineffective leaders.[8] The hoped-for combination of characteristics that separate leader from follower, strong leader from weak, never really materialized. And yet, successful leaders do stand out from other people. Researchers now believe that traits such as drive and self-confidence by themselves are not sufficient to predict leadership success. They are only preconditions or enablers from which leaders must initiate actions such as clarifying a vision, setting goals, and role modeling.[9]

social-cognitive theory
A line of research that finds people do use idealized personal traits or characteristics as a way to distinguish leaders from nonleaders.

Notwithstanding the controversial history about the role of traits, there has been a resurgence of interest in the personal qualities of leaders. Recent research confirms that followers do attribute distinguishing characteristics to leaders, and these perceptions are important in their own right. **Social-cognitive theory** holds that people use idealized personal traits to distinguish leaders from nonleaders. Read the World Watch box and try to picture Ricardo Semler interacting with people in his Brazilian organization. Perhaps you can visualize how a leader's personality enables others to perceive in him effective leadership qualities.

Contemporary research returned to the classic personality trait studies, reinterpreted the data, and found that six traits were shown to influence perceptions about leaders: intelligence, adjustment, sensitivity, masculinity, extroversion, and dominance.[10] Personality traits help followers organize perceptions about leaders, which in turn influences their behavior. For example, if group members see Roseabeth as having the qualities of a leader (they believe she is sensitive, yet willing to exert her will), it is easier for her to influence the group. By contrast, if a mid-level manager such as Enrique does not possess traits group members typically associate with leaders (they believe he is introverted and does not adjust well to changes), the group is likely to see him only as a manager, not as a leader.

credibility
One of the most characteristic traits of leaders, which refers to being honest, competent, forward-looking, and inspiring.

Research also found that above all, followers look most for credibility in their leaders.[11] **Credibility** refers to being honest, competent, forward looking, and inspiring. Another stream of recent research concludes that six stand-out traits distinguish leaders from nonleaders: drive, leadership motivation, honesty and

Brazilian Firm *"Hunts the Woolly Mammoth"*

By age 30, Ricardo Semler was president of Semco S/A, Brazil's largest marine equipment and food-processing machinery manufacturer. He had also authored a best-selling book, *Turning the Tables*. Semler is proud that his organization functions more on the basis of leadership than management. He took over a small family business, expanded it to serve global markets, and increased employment to over 800, making Semco one of Brazil's fastest-growing companies.

Unlike traditional Brazilian firms where paternalism creates a powerful, centralized family fiefdom, Semco is guided by three fundamental values: democracy, profit sharing, and information. Semler states, "One of my first moves when I took control of Semco was to abolish norms, manuals, rules, and regulations" and replace them with common sense and reasonableness. As a highly participatory leader, Semler did a number of things that seem unconventional. He promoted "civil disobedience" so people would challenge anything that was not working. Staff departments and specialized jobs were eliminated so that people either make or sell products—there is no one in between. He abolished all policies on things like travel expenses, allowing employees to charge whatever they thought reasonable. He has subordinates evaluate managers twice a year, and subordinates earn more than managers if they are more indispensable. Everyone gets an equal vote on key decisions such as where to locate a new plant.

Semler personifies a radical brand of leadership. He delights in portraying his organization using the metaphor of a prehistoric woolly mammoth hunt. Hunting roles were filled by whoever was able to perform a task first or best in the hunt, giving the semblance of order without formal organization. "What I am saying is put ten people together, don't appoint a leader, and you can be sure that one will emerge. So will a sighter, a runner [for the hunt], and whatever else the group needs. We form the groups, but they find their own leaders. That's not a lack of structure, that's just a lack of structure imposed from above."

Source: Ricardo Semler, "Managing without Managers," *Harvard Business Review* 67 (September–October 1989), quotes pp. 79, 82.

---

integrity, self-confidence, cognitive ability, and knowledge of the business.[12] Exhibit 14–2 elaborates on these qualities. When followers look to leaders for direction and inspiration, they expect to find certain characteristics. Leaders "need to have the 'right stuff' and this stuff is not equally present in all people."[13] Personal characteristics are important; however, they are merely a precondition for leadership. The leader's behavior patterns and cognitive style are also important and have been widely studied.

Behavior As a Characteristic of Leadership

Personality traits feed into behavior. Ultimately people evaluate leaders on the basis of their behavior and decide if they want to voluntarily follow their lead. In the late 1950s and the 1960s, the emphasis of research on leadership effectiveness shifted from traits to the identification of behavior patterns displayed by leaders. Two approaches dominated the research of this period. Although they used different terms, these studies essentially differentiated between behaviors that focus on task production and behaviors that focus on building employee relationships.

University of Michigan Research.   Rensis Likert and others at the University of Michigan undertook a series of investigations aimed at differentiating leadership behaviors. From their interviews with managers at Prudential Insurance Company,

━━━━━ **EXHIBIT 14–2**

Traits That Distinguish Leaders from Nonleaders

As you read the following descriptions of these six traits, try to create an image of a leader at work. Does this describe you?

- *Drive*—has the need for achievement through challenging assignments, the desire to get ahead, high energy to work long hours with enthusiasm, tenacity to overcome obstacles, and initiative to make choices and take action that leads to change.
- *Leadership motivation*—exemplifies a strong desire to lead, the willingness to accept responsibility, the desire to influence others, and a strong socialized desire for power (which means the desire to exercise power for the good of the organization).
- *Honesty and integrity*—demonstrates truthfulness or nondeceitfulness (honesty) and consistency between word and deed, is predictable, follows ethical principles, is discreet, and makes competent decisions (integrity).
- *Self-confidence*—gains the trust of others by being sure of own actions (and not being defensive about making mistakes), being assertive and decisive, maintaining emotional stability (not losing one's cool), and remaining calm and confident in times of crisis.
- *Cognitive ability*—has a keen mind and thinks strategically, reasons analytically, and exercises good judgment in decisions and actions; has the ability to reason deductively and inductively.
- *Knowledge of the business*—beyond formal education, develops technical expertise to understand the concerns of followers, comprehends the economics of the industry, and knows the organization's culture and behavior.

Source: Shelley A. Kirkpatrick and Edwin A. Locke, "Leadership: Do Traits Matter?" *Academy of Management Executive* 5 (May 1991), pp. 48–60.

---

task-oriented behavior
An approach to leadership that focuses on supervision of group members to obtain consistent work methods and job accomplishments.

employee-oriented behavior
An approach to leadership that aims at satisfying the social and emotional needs of group members.

they concluded that two approaches to leadership behavior prevail at the group level: the task oriented and the employee oriented.[14] **Task-oriented behavior** focuses on careful supervision of group members to obtain consistent work methods and accomplishment of the job. **Employee-oriented behavior** aims at satisfying the social and emotional needs of group members.

The Michigan researchers believed these two behavioral orientations were mutually exclusive—a leader exhibits either one or the other. They concluded that groups led by employee-oriented leaders had better work attitudes and higher productivity. A follow-up study supported the association of positive group member attitudes with employee-oriented leadership; however, productivity was found to be higher within groups supervised by task-oriented leaders.[15] Trying to predict group outcomes based only on one or the other leader behavior is complicated because leaders are complex, changing people. (The Eye on Ethics box reveals such dynamic qualities in one leader, Steve Wozniak, developer of the original Apple computer, in his reflections on success and how to enjoy a meaningful life.)

Ohio State University Research.　Edwin Fleishman and colleagues at Ohio State used a leadership behavior description questionnaire to narrow the dimensions of leader behavior. The list of hundreds of possibilities was eventually narrowed to two dominant and contrasting behaviors: initiating structure and showing consideration.[16] **Initiating structure** was defined as leader behavior intended to establish "well-defined patterns of organization, channels of communication, and methods of procedure" between leader and group. **Showing consideration** was defined as leader behavior that brings out "friendship, mutual trust, respect, and warmth in the relationship between the leader and members of his staff."[17]

initiating structure
Leader behavior intended to establish well-defined patterns of organization, channels of communication, and work procedures between leader and group.

showing consideration
Leader behavior to bring out friendship, mutual trust, respect, and warmth in leader-member relationships.

Although there are obvious parallels between the Michigan and Ohio State measures of leadership behavior, the Ohio State researchers did not see their two leader behaviors as mutually exclusive. A leader might score high or low on both dimensions; in fact, it was initially hypothesized that the effective leader engages both in initiating structure and showing consideration. Early research at International Harvester (later reorganized and renamed Navistar) found that initiating structure was not clearly related to either productivity or group member attitudes,

Steve Wozniak: Inventor, Educator, Humanitarian

Apple began as a fruit, crisp and juicy, to be picked from a tree. Then Steve Wozniak, known to friends as Woz, began to connect chips and write code to create a new Apple, the Apple II, the first commercially successful personal computer—the machine that created a major new industry. But once Apple Computer, the corporation, went public and began to grow, Woz cashed out his millions, left the company, and turned to helping others. In reflecting on his life, Woz offers insights into how to lead a meaningful and ethical life:

> *I had my happiness before I had money. I had a whole big internal religion—no church or anything—but a whole line of thoughts and philosophies about how to live life and how to be happy forever. I had that down. I was a real healthy, pure person . . . .*
>
> *I am doing what I grew up being taught was right. I read books to my young children, and in all the books there are good people who are doing things for others—Goofy wins a big race over Big Bad Pete, and he gives the money he won to build a baseball diamond for the orphans. If you are lucky enough to be successful, then try to do something to help your community . . . .*

> *In the sixth grade, I decided I was going to be an engineer, and then I was going to be an elementary school teacher. That's what I've done. I could have had a lot of fun in Apple and been involved in some great things going on in the world, but I really feel better about what I am doing . . . .*
>
> *Find something you are good at, work on it, and eventually you can succeed and make your life. Don't just slack off and think you will just go through life doing a job. You should try to do incredible things—put a lot of hours into making a lot of things very, very good . . . .*
>
> *If you are starting out in a company, spend the extra hours. Talk to people and get that report just right. You have a lot of free time when you are young, so put it into what you are good at before you wind up with a life with many commitments, meetings, bills, and mortgages. Spend time when you are young, and that will give you a lot more freedom when you are older.*

Today Steve Wozniak is an electronics tinkerer, philanthropist, and teacher of fifth-graders.

Source: Guy Kawasaki, *Hindsights: The Wisdom and Breakthroughs of Remarkable People* (Hillsboro, OR: Beyond Words Publishing, 1993), pp. 209–218.

whereas showing consideration had some relationship to positive employee attitudes but not to productivity.

In extensive follow-up research, neither behavior ensured maximum performance effectiveness and work-group satisfaction.[18] Although leaders high in *both* initiating structure and showing consideration tended to have better follower performance and satisfaction than leaders low in either or both, there were enough negative side effects (absenteeism and grievances) that the positive outcomes were not unconditional. Trying to predict group performance solely on the basis of leader behavior once again turned out to be a futile endeavor.

Leader Behavior and Decision Styles. As early as the late 1930s, Kurt Lewin and others at the University of Iowa were studying the leader's role in decision making and its impact on productivity and satisfaction. Their three principal decision styles were identified as autocratic (takes charge, gives assignments), democratic (is easygoing, suggests, encourages), and laissez-faire (is passive, noncommittal). Independently, a fourth decision style—the human relations approach (is participative, emphasizes group cohesiveness) became associated with the other three.[19]

■■■■■■   **EXHIBIT 14–3**

Classic Descriptors of Leaders's Decision Behaviors
This figure combines two classic ways of viewing leadership. The matrix itself is created by using the Ohio State leadership behavior variables—initiating structure and showing consideration. The four cells are a useful framework for identifying the four leader decision behaviors that emerged from research at the University of Iowa.

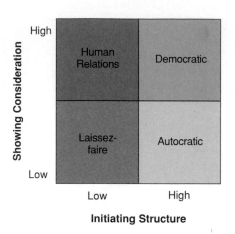

These concepts are now in common use and are considered classic ways of identifying leaders.[20] Exhibit 14–3 shows how these four descriptors of a leader's decision style can be distinguished when superimposed on the two broad behavioral dimensions of initiating structure and showing consideration.

Leadership Style As a State of Mind

leadership style
The thoughts held to be important to a leader (motives, attitudes, goals, sources of satisfaction) in guiding how the leader interacts with group members.

Beyond personality traits and observable behaviors, how the leader views himself or herself when in a leadership role is also important. **Leadership style** involves the cognitions (the motives, attitudes, goals, and sources of satisfaction that exist in the mind of the leader) that guide interactions with group members. Four decades of leadership style research have applied variations of the task accomplishment and employee relationship concepts to the thoughts and concerns of leaders. Some leaders think primarily about getting the job done; they are production focused and driven to achieve successful results whatever the task they choose or are assigned. Other leaders are concerned primarily about gaining cooperation from their people and building relationships based on mutual respect—they believe high morale produces reasonable performance.

Leadership Grid®
A matrix used by Blake and Mouton to identify five leadership styles based on concerns for people and/or production.

The Leadership Grid®.   One of the most popular explanations of cognitive style is the Leadership Grid® by Robert Blake and Jane Mouton.[21] The **Leadership Grid®** is a matrix that identifies five leadership styles by interpreting leaders' attitudes about concern for production and concern for people. A leader's style is diagnosed by a battery of questions that assigns point values ranging from 1 (low) to 9 (high) on the independent production and people attitudes. The five dominant styles are identified by points on the grid (see Exhibit 14–4).

For example, a leader who scores 9,1 subscribes to the authority-compliance style. Such task-focused leaders have great concern for output and presume that people obediently accept the influence of authority figures. By contrast, the 1,9 or country club style manifests a belief that if people's needs are thoughtfully attended to, they will feel comfortable and friendly with co-workers and as a result will cooperate. The impoverishment, or 1,1 style, seeks simply to get by with minimal effort (a condition more commonly associated with abdication, not leadership).

Blake and Mouton typically find that most respondents score toward the 5,5 middle-of-the-road style, one characterized by compromise and a desire to do things right by keeping divergent interests in balance. Organizations that employ the grid

EXHIBIT 14–4

Blake and Mouton's Leadership Grid®

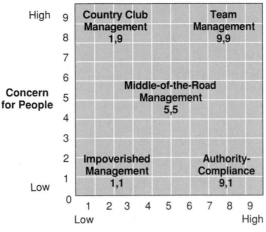

Source: The Leadership Grid® Figure from *Leadership Dilemmas—Grid Solutions*, by Robert R. Blake and Anne Adams McCanse (formerly the Managerial Grid Figure by Robert T. Blake and Jane S. Mouton), Houston: Gulf Publishing Company, p. 29. Copyright © 1991 by Scientific Methods, Inc. Reproduced by permission of the owners.

in leadership training do so with the goal of moving participants toward the 9,9 team style, purported to be the ideal. Empirical research does not necessarily support the abundant testimonials about the effectiveness of such "ideal" styles.[22] Some even claim that the 9,9 ideal leader, with equal concern for both production and people, is a myth.[23] You'll see why in the subsequent discussion. The power to predict leader effectiveness improves when one considers the leader in interaction with changing situations, which is known as the contingency approach.

HOW DO LEADERS AND MANAGERS ADJUST TO SITUATIONAL CONTINGENCIES?

Some leaders exert influence over large numbers of people without having to interact with them on an interpersonal level. The president of a large company or the chief of a metropolitan police force can through personal credibility and position power influence members of the organization to follow their lead without having to personally talk with most members. We'll examine this as a form of transformational leadership that people at the top of an organization need if they are to change the direction of values, strategies, and culture. Not all leaders are transformational. Yet one characteristic that is shared among all leaders is that at times they work directly with members of their immediate support team or group. We now discuss several explanations of the thought processes and behaviors of leaders as they interact with immediate group followers over the course of changing circumstances. These theories apply equally to chief executives, store managers, or department managers, and their lessons serve as the starting point for developing managers.

While it is probable that a leader will rely on one pattern of behavior more than on others, an effective leader's behavior is not as rigid as implied by the behavioral labels we've discussed so far. Let's say that Michelle is observed to interact infrequently with members of the graphic design group that she heads. When she does, it is usually to exchange a brief pleasantry or to inquire about or comment on a designer's project. Her dominant behavior outwardly appears to be neither task nor relationship oriented, suggesting that she is a "laissez faire" type, or "impoverished," to use grid terminology.

However, on occasion Michelle devotes considerable time to helping a group member through a stressful project or personal situation. She listens, questions, counsels, provides encouragement, and conveys empathy and understanding. This behavior is high relationship, low task. Occasionally Michelle can also be seen working closely with some of her group on a project. She clarifies goals, defines priorities, provides guidelines for how a job is to be done, asks for progress reports, and provides feedback about their performance. Such behavior is high task, low relationship.

The general observation that Michelle most often uses what classical theorists call "laissez faire" leadership does not mean that Michelle is failing to do her job. In fact, Michelle may be a strong "team-style" leader, with high concern for both people and tasks. But she perceives that her group is capable and usually effective without her direct intervention. Michelle may be correctly adjusting her leadership behavior to the contingencies of changing member needs and other circumstances by usually staying out of their way—she empowers them. Granting her group members autonomy also frees her to work more on influencing peers (over whom she has no direct authority) and external groups of customers and suppliers.

Contingency Theory Variables

Under what circumstances is a leader effective? This question long has piqued the curiosity of leaders as well as scholars. In *The Human Side of Enterprise,* Douglas McGregor observed, "Managers who are successful in one function are sometimes, but by no means always, successful in another. The same is true of leadership at different organizational levels."[24]

contingency theory
The perspective that a leader's effectiveness is dependent on how he or she interacts with various situational factors—there is no one best universal approach.

Contingency theory emphasizes that a leader's effectiveness is not independent from situational factors that impact on the tasks to be undertaken. Leadership occurs within a task context—typically, a challenge to turn into an organizational advantage, a goal that must be accomplished, or simply a job needing to be done. Any of these can vary in degree of specificity and complexity. Also involved in any leadership situation are people factors such as variations in the leader's style or behavior in interaction with the capabilities and readiness of subordinates to perform a task.

Exhibit 14–5 identifies four principal contingency factors associated with leadership effectiveness. As suggested by the arrows in the diagram, these four factors interact to shape the leader–follower relationship. They apply whether the perceived leader is appointed as a manager or emerges from the group. Two contingency factors identified in Exhibit 14–5 relate to the leader personally—his or her cognitive style and his or her actual observable behavior. By now these variables should seem familiar. The two remaining contingency factors are new to the discussion. They include work-related elements of the situation and the behavior of followers.

The Leader's Cognitive Style.   Much of the research knowledge about leadership focuses on the leader's motives, concerns, knowledge, and personality. People differ in how they want to be perceived as leaders and what they seek to get out of

A Four-Factor Model of Leadership Contingencies

Leadership research usually focuses on how the leader interacts with others—the leader's behavior. But leader behavior does not occur in a vacuum. The figure suggests that the cognitive structures or mind-sets of leaders influence chosen behaviors. Similarly, effective leaders also consider the people with whom they are working, as well as other situational factors embodied in either the organization or the task itself.

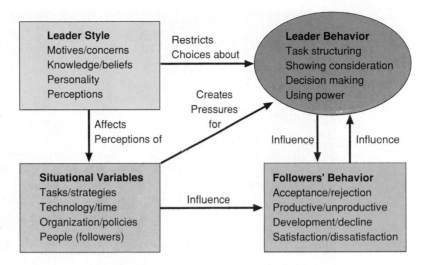

being a leader. As we have seen, some adopt a people-centered leadership style aimed at building trusting and caring relationships. Others assume a task-centered leadership style that embraces goal accomplishment and productive results. These approaches are learned from experience, are highly personal, and tend to be consistent over time. The leader's mind-set or cognitive style serves two purposes. It affects the leader's perception of the situation, and it constrains the range of personal behaviors the leader chooses to use.[25]

The Leader's Observable Behavior. While thoughts, personal motives, and attitudes (that is, a leader's style) are not always transparent, a leader's behavior is directly observable. Some leaders devote a great deal of time to structuring and directing task activities. Others concentrate on showing consideration, making people feel accepted and aware that their well-being is important. Some leaders handle power autocratically; others work to share power with their subordinates, empowering them to perform up to their potential. A leader's outward behavior is the public face of leadership and is directly interpreted by those with whom the leader interacts.

Work-Related Situational Variables. The effective leader does not behave independently of situational realities.[26] The nature of the job to be done (for example, whether it is routine and unchanging or complex and ambiguous), the technology and resources or time available, the organization's culture, and the leader's power or managerial authority within the organization—these and other issues set the stage for determining if leadership methods will be effective.

The Behavior of Followers. People who are targets of influence become critical forces in determining how to lead. People differ in their competencies, motivation, attitudes, and goals. A leader should consider these human idiosyncrasies, since they affect receptiveness to the leader's attempts to influence. They also affect the reciprocal influence others have over the leader. Especially when group members are from different ethnic, racial, or cultural backgrounds, expectations about leadership and the willingness to accept authority can differ greatly.

We now review four influential contingency theories of leadership: Fiedler's style and favorableness factors, Hersey and Blanchard's situational leadership theory (SLT), House and Mitchell's path-goal theory, and Vroom and Yetton's group decision tree.

By combining different leadership styles, Kay Unger and Jon Levy together have built Gillian, a women's clothing company, into a $125 million business employing 300 people. Levy attributes their leadership differences to the type of operations each oversees and their individual personalities. Unger oversees design and production and describes herself as fluid, spontaneous, and flexible because she deals with creative people. Levy is responsible for sales, marketing, and finance and is described by Unger as more strict and rigid because his responsibilities require more structure. (Photo: © Wayne Sorce.)

A Leader's Motives Predict Style and Effectiveness

Fred Fiedler maintains that leadership style remains stable across time and across various leadership experiences.[27] Style to him refers to the underlying motivation of the leader—the personal sources of satisfaction the leader seeks out by being a leader. Leaders who have a strong **task-motivated style** enjoy the feeling of pride in accomplishing a task or having their group do a job well. The **relationship-motivated style** leaders seek more to realize respect in interpersonal relationships and to experience satisfaction in helping a group to develop as a team.

task-motivated style
Used by Fiedler to describe leaders whose satisfaction comes from pride of task accomplishment and group success in doing a job well.

relationship-motivated style
Fiedler's way of characterizing leaders who are principally concerned with respect in interpersonal relations and in helping the group develop as a team.

Style and Circumstance Predictors of Effectiveness.

Fiedler and colleagues found that measures of leadership style held up as predictors of group performance, but with different outcomes in different situations. They structured a model of leadership effectiveness that uses three critical contingency factors to define the circumstances affecting the leadership situation:[28]

1. *Task structure*—ranging from high (specific) to low (ambiguous).
2. *Position power*—ranging from high (formal authority) to low (informal authority).
3. *Leader-member relations*—ranging from good (cohesive) to poor (hostile).

These three factors combine to produce situations that range from favorable to unfavorable for the leader. Very favorable conditions for leader influence occur when all three factors are in the high, strong, or good range. Conversely, the most unfavorable leadership situation exists when all three factors are low, weak, or poor.

The crucial question is how style and circumstance relate to effectiveness. Research indicates that a task-motivated leadership style is likely to produce effective group results under leadership circumstances that are either favorable or very unfavorable. For example, in the very unfavorable situation, the task-motivated leader is willing to take charge and structure the situation and members' tasks.

A relationship-motivated style is expected to be effective under mid range or mixed circumstances—those that are moderately favorable. In these situations, achieving team coordination and realizing group synergy are more productive than handing out detailed task assignments to individual group members. Independent research generally supports the validity of Fiedler's theory[29] although other research suggests measures of style using an instrument called the LPC tend to be unstable when readministered to the same respondents.[30]

A Contrast between Two Leaders. Jan is a task-motivated automotive sales manager who derives satisfaction principally from successful group performance, such as surpassing quotas, setting seasonal records, maintaining profit margins, and outselling competitive agencies. Javier, a sales manager at a competitor across the street, is a leader with a relationship-oriented style. He finds satisfaction through good interpersonal relations: building camaraderie among his sales force, following up on customer service, establishing a positive image for his firm in the community, and winning repeat customers.

Having a dominant leadership style does not mean, however, that a task-motivated leader like Jan will be unfriendly and autocratic toward her sales representatives or potential customers. It simply suggests that she will find greater personal satisfaction in achieving sales and profit (task) success than in caring for the needs of others. But if Jan perceives that a group member is discouraged by three days without a sale, she may engage in friendly, sympathetic (relationship-building) conversation rather than reemphasize sales techniques or demand improvement (task behaviors). Similarly, relationship-motivated Javier may reprimand a member of his sales force and demonstrate how to close a sale if he feels that the salesperson's relaxed attitude is resulting in lost sales.

Since style is a consistent personal motive, Fiedler recommends engineering job contingencies to fit the leader rather than trying to change the leader.[31] But administratively and politically, it is difficult to engineer such a precise fit. And what happens if the situation changes, possibly as a result of the leader's success? Given these limitations, it is useful to define leadership style, as explained by Fiedler, as a cognitive preference that constrains actual leader behavior. That is, a leader's motives (style) restrict his or her ability to change behaviors or be flexible as situational factors shift.

A Leader's Behavior Should Be Matched to Followers' Needs

situational leadership theory (SLT)
The Hersey and Blanchard model of leadership effectiveness based on combinations of the leader's task and relationship behaviors as moderated by the job maturity of followers.

Although a leader's motives and concerns are important preconditions, followers respond to what a leader actually does rather than to his or her intentions. At least, that is the premise behind Paul Hersey and Kenneth Blanchard's situational leadership theory. In **situational leadership theory (SLT),** combinations of leader task and relationship behaviors are moderated by the job maturity of followers. Hersey and Blanchard's model uses a 2×2 matrix in which leader behaviors are described by two variables:

- *Task behavior*—The extent to which leaders are likely to organize and define the roles of group members (followers) and to explain what activities each is to do and when, where, and how tasks are to be accomplished; characterized by endeavoring to establish well-defined patterns of organization, channels of communication, and ways of getting jobs accomplished.

- *Relationship behavior*—The extent to which leaders are likely to maintain personal relationships with members of their groups (followers) by opening channels of communication, providing socioemotional support (psychological strokes), and facilitating behaviors.[32]

Adapting to Followers' Job Maturity.   Whereas Fiedler uses three factors to define situation contingencies, Hersey and Blanchard use a single integrative factor—the follower's maturity, or job readiness, in relation to tasks to be performed. They define follower job maturity/readiness as "the capacity to set high but attainable goals, willingness and ability to take responsibility, and education and/or experience of an individual or a group."[33] Maturity ranges along a continuum according to the degree to which followers are willing and able to complete tasks on their own. Hersey and Blanchard emphasize that an individual's maturity varies with the task: "A saleswoman may be very responsible in securing new sales but very casual about completing the paperwork necessary to close on a sale. As a result, it is appropriate for her manager to leave her alone in terms of closing on sales, but to supervise her closely in terms of her paperwork until she can start to do well in that area too."[34]

Applications over a Job Maturity Life Cycle.   Ideally, as a follower's job maturity changes, the leader's behavior toward that person should change also. The key pattern of effective leader behaviors in relation to follower maturity is presented in Exhibit 14–6. Leadership behaviors should be adjusted over time to develop subordinate competencies as well as to guide and control current performance.

Consider a leader who has two subordinates low in job maturity—for example, inexperienced supermarket cashiers both of whom are in their first full-time job. The assistant store manager begins their socialization by emphasizing responsibilities and training them in how tasks should be performed (high concentration on task, or "telling"). As the cashiers begin to demonstrate that they can handle basic jobs, the leader shifts to also providing reassurance and praise and making each worker feel valued (high-relationship, or "selling" behaviors).

Over time, the leader's task guidance diminishes as the two's performance becomes self-sustaining. Once the cashiers reach a high level of competence, the leader grants greater autonomy (for example, to cash checks without approval by the manager). Interaction then occurs on an as-needed, or "participating" basis. In professional occupations, such a pattern often occurs between a mentor and protégé as the younger person gains professional skill, stature, and reputation, ultimately becoming independent of the mentor.[35]

However, if the job maturity of a person or group regresses, the leader needs to move backward along the bell-shaped curve in an effort to help followers regain their previous level of demonstrated maturity. One of the cashiers in our illustration may slip from a condition where "participating" leadership is effective back to where more "selling" is needed when new computerized equipment is introduced.

Research Supports SLT within Job Categories.   The most significant conclusion from research on the SLT model is that leaders are unlikely to find a full range of job maturities among employees within a single job category or work group. Different levels of maturity are most directly associated with various classes of jobs, among the ranks of unskilled, semiskilled, craft, or professional. For example, professionals generally are "capable of and desirous of greater self-direction," whereas unskilled workers tend to "expect and may prefer greater direction and less social-emotional attention on the part of supervisors."[36]

━━━━━ **EXHIBIT 14–6**

Hersey and Blanchard's Situational Leadership Theory
SLT matches leader behaviors to follower readiness (job maturity). Select one of the four boxes above the "follower readiness" scale. Note where the dashed vertical line intersects the normal curve in the matrix. That point of intersection indicates the appropriate leader behavior.

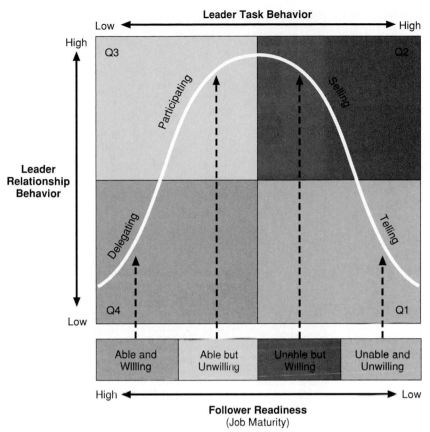

Source: Based on Paul Hersey and Kenneth H. Blanchard. *Management of Organizational Behavior*, 6th ed. (1993), p. 186. Adapted by permission of Prentice Hall, Inc., Englewood Cliffs , NJ. Situational Leadership® is a registered trademark of the Center for Learning, Escondido, CA.

Leaders Clarify the Path to a Goal

Another practical guide for motivating followers' behaviors focuses on helping them find the most viable path to organizational goals. This leadership approach takes its roots from expectancy motivation theory. Recall that expectancy approaches to motivation are based on the actor's belief that his or her personal efforts affect performance and lead to expected payoffs.

path-goal leadership theory
The perspective that a leader should clarify goals, show acceptable paths for attaining goals, make the path easier to travel, and reward satisfactory performance.

The **path-goal leadership theory** describes what the leader should do to motivate followers: clarify performance goals, show the acceptable paths or means for attaining them, make the path easier to travel, and provide reinforcing consequences for those who achieve satisfactory performance.[37] As originated by House and Mitchell, the major concern of this theory is how a leader helps clarify subordinate pathways to challenging organizational goals and personal rewards.[38] Leaders need to guide followers toward paths that reduce resistance to change, based on an analysis of the environmental forces for change.[39] The Dynamics of Diversity box summarizes one executive's actions to lead women up the path to career success in her organization.

Path-Goal Leadership Behaviors.   Like many theories about leadership at the group level, the path-goal approach involves two fundamental alternatives: instrumental (task) behaviors and supportive (relationship) behaviors.

When Sam Rivera became an assistant foreman at Fel-Pro Inc., an auto-parts maker, his supervisor expected Rivera to be very tough. Rivera found that he was much happier being himself: easy going and accommodating as long as the work gets done, showing supportive leadership. Rivera has given emergency leave to an employee who needed to get professional help for his son, and he found a new job for an employee who was unable to do the job he was hired for. Rivera tries to put himself in his employees' shoes. The outcome of his leadership? His group routinely exceeds its objectives. (Photo: © Alice Q. Hargrave.)

instrumental leader behaviors
Path-goal leader behaviors (such as setting goals and targets, teaching, and coaching) that reduce task uncertainty either by being directive or by encouraging followers to become achievement oriented.

supportive relationship leader behaviors
Path-goal leader behaviors that focus on group emotional well-being by showing concern, providing encouragement, and giving reinforcement.

Instrumental leader behaviors are task focused in the sense that the leader sets goals, builds teams, teaches, coaches, sets measurement criteria, provides evaluative feedback, and helps reduce task uncertainty by either being directive or encouraging followers to become achievement oriented. Their purpose is to focus on the management of teams, structures, and processes that show followers how achieving organizational goals is consistent with realizing their own personal goals.[40]

Supportive relationship leader behaviors involve showing concern, providing encouragement, and giving reinforcement to make the path easier to travel. The focus is on emotional well-being.

These two fundamental alternatives combine in four specific leader behaviors that make the path-goal approach operational:[41]

- *Directive leadership* (highly instrumental) lets followers know what is expected of them, provides guidance as to what is to be done and how, clarifies performance standards and time schedules, and calls attention to work procedures and policies.
- *Achievement-oriented leadership* (highly instrumental) establishes challenging goals, seeks performance improvement, and displays confidence that people will exert high levels of effort.
- *Participative leadership* (moderately instrumental and supportive) involves consulting with and soliciting the ideas of others in decision making and action taking.
- *Supportive leadership* (highly supportive) shows concern for the needs and goals of others and strives to make the work situation pleasant and equitable.

Dynamics of Diversity — *One Woman Executive Shows Others the Paths to the Top*

Women and other minorities historically have not progressed to the upper rungs of the corporate ladder. Yet there are examples of breakthroughs. One senior vice president of human resources, herself a woman, spoke about how she helped women in her organization get on appropriate paths to senior management positions:

As women began to appear in greater numbers in business schools in the sixties, companies hired them. They were good women, but they didn't make it; they plateaued. The recruiters didn't make it clear that the career path to senior management required several relocations, including international ones. When it came time to take a new assignment, the women said, "We can't do that." Two issues were at stake. First, these women were in dual-career couples and their husbands were unwilling or unable to interrupt their career paths. Second, the women were not sure the moves would pay off. They told management, "We don't see any women at the top."

Because of my experience at another company, I was brought in to change this situation. I realized that a number of systems needed to be changed. We
revised our selection procedures. Now the women we hire have backgrounds that include cross-cultural experience, and they often have language skills. We tell them clearly that the route to senior management will involve relocation. We reorganized our development program to include experience in several field locations. We built relocation in early.

We addressed the management side, too. We hired women from the outside for both line and staff positions at the senior level to be role models . . . .

We also dealt with the perception bias by making sure that the board of directors includes women. I arrange for a group of our high-potential women to have breakfast with them each time the board meets. This informal opportunity for visibility and networking has been important in changing perceptions.

In other words, we looked for several ways to attack this issue, not just one.

Source: Ann M. Morrison, *The New Leaders: Guidelines on Leadership Diversity in America* (San Francisco: Jossey-Bass, 1992), pp. 201–202.

Contingencies for Path-Goal Leadership. The path-goal approach aims to enhance members' motivation to achieve group goals. In working with any kind of group, the type of path-goal leadership behavior most likely to yield favorable results depends on a number of contingency forces. Exhibit 14–7 presents some of these contingencies, dividing them into follower variables (perceptions, experience) and task or working environment variables. Researchers have found the most useful application of path-goal leadership occurs when the follower's task is perceived to be ambiguous, ill-defined, and lacking in routine or standardization, as in jobs in product development or marketing research.[42] Task-focused instrumental leader behavior helps followers clarify ambiguous roles. Under conditions of low task structure (complex and/or ambiguous jobs), instrumental leaders have higher follower job satisfaction and goal attainment.

But in highly structured tasks—in purchasing or accounts payable jobs, for example—group members view instrumental leader behavior as an attempt to exert added, unnecessary structure and control over their lives—too much management. In well-defined and routine situations, supportive relationship behavior from the leader is more appropriate. Like other forms of relationship-building behavior, supportive transactions aim to increase morale and cooperation by building on a base of consideration.

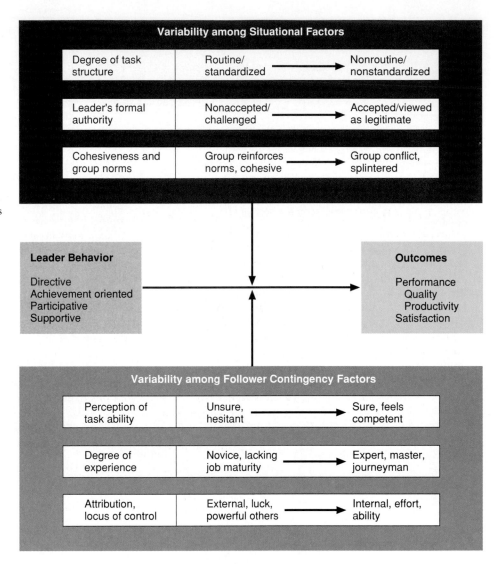

Key Factors and Variables in the Path-Goal Model of Leadership
The outcome or effectiveness of the leader's behavior depends on the interaction between situational variables (identified in the top of the diagram) and variations among followers (identified in the bottom). The leader's four basic behavioral options (the middle box on the left side) depend on these six key situational and follower variables.

If the leader's path-goal behavior is effective, then those who are being influenced are likely to:

- Be accepting of the leader.
- Expect that personal effort leads to better performance.
- Expect that effective performance leads to relevant rewards.
- Be satisfied with their work and work situation.

Decision Style Influences Group Behavior

How a leader makes decisions affects the likelihood that influence efforts will be positive. In earlier eras a boss's power tended to be absolute when workers were relatively unskilled and tasks were usually routine and simple. Then, a manager (more than a leader) could get results by being autocratic, by being the sole decision maker. But in many of today's work environments, tasks are complex and employees are highly educated and often more technically competent than the manager or leader. Participation by group members in decisions often produces better quality decisions and increases commitment for effective implementation.

Tannenbaum and Schmidt's Power-Sharing Model. One of the earliest contingency theories emphasized the extent to which the leader shared power with group members in making decisions. As previously pictured in Exhibit 13–2, the process of making decisions within a group can be described as a sliding ratio scale between "leader held power" and "leader shared power." At one extreme are decisions in which all power is held by the leader (a "make and announce" style). Power sharing increases if the leader "sells" the decision, and increases more when she asks for feedback about possible alternatives before making the decision. Power sharing reaches its pinnacle when the leader delegates to the group the right to analyze challenges and make decisions subject only to broad parameters.

A key lesson of this contingency theory by Tannenbaum and Schmidt is not that delegated decisions are necessarily better than unilaterally made ones.[43] Rather, effectiveness all depends on forces in the leader, forces in the followers, and forces in the task situation. For example, if group members are not accustomed to making complex decisions and a life-threatening crisis faces the organization needing a quick response, then a "make and announce" decision by the leader is likely to be most effective. Where members are highly talented and effectiveness is a function of group creativity and innovation, the effective leader probably helps crystalize a vision and involves group members in evaluating alternatives and collaboratively taking a decision.[44]

The Vroom and Yetton Decision Tree Model. The concept that decision style shapes outcome effectiveness was extended by Victor Vroom and colleagues. Their normative model is based on the premise that decisions affecting the group need to be timely, of high quality, and accepted by group members. The Vroom and Yetton model (with extensions by Jago) presents three basic decision styles.[45]

- Autocratic (where the leader unilaterally makes decisions).
- Consultative (where the leader solicits member inputs before deciding).
- Group (where the leader collaborates with members to arrive at a joint decision).

To guide leaders through the process of decision making, the model uses a decision tree to structure the branching of decisions depending on considerations such as whether it affects an individual or the group, its complexity, and how quickly it must be made. A computer-assisted version allows the leader to assign ratings or probabilities in working through the branching issues. Efforts to empirically validate the structured Vroom-Yetton (Jago) model support the premise that working through a sequence of situational considerations leads to better decisions, both in the minds of leaders who evaluated past decisions[46] and from independent raters.[47]

But decision making is only part of a leader's job. Another important dimension—at least for some leaders—is visionary path finding or organizational transformation.

HOW DO LEADERS TRANSFORM ORGANIZATIONS?

transformational leader
A leader who energizes others with visions and strategies of how to refocus and revitalize the larger organization so that change meets people's enduring needs.

If you are inclined toward leadership, the early stages of your career will likely build on the concepts of leading groups already discussed. However, leadership beyond the face-to-face group level involves learning other qualities. When leaders seek to influence the entire organization or one of its major units, they draw on transformational leadership. **Transformational leaders** energize others with visions and strategies of how to refocus and revitalize the larger organization.

During her tenure as executive director of Girl Scouts of America, Frances Hesselbein created a vision, mobilized commitment, institutionalized change, and transformed the Girl Scouts from an institution in danger of becoming irrelevant into an innovative, customer-driven enterprise. Propelled by her mission of helping girls reach their highest potential, she re-focused the energies of three-quarters of a million adult volunteers onto getting the scouts interested in projects involving science, the environment, and business instead of traditional household skills. Membership is now on the rebound, especially among minority girls. (Photo: 1990 Louis Psihoyos/Matrix.)

The concept of the transformational leader is credited to James MacGregor Burns, who emphasizes that leadership involves changing organizations: "The ultimate test of practical leadership is the realization of intended, real change that meets people's enduring needs."[48] Leaders at the head of an organization mobilize influence across the organization so that others follow the path they envision without the necessity for interpersonal interaction.

Pathfinding Precedes Problem Solving and Implementing

Organizations need three types of managers and leaders: pathfinders, problem solvers, and implementers. As envisioned by Harold Leavitt, these three types have trouble coexisting, for each sees the world very differently.

The *implementing manager/leader* is pervasive in organizations. Implementing involves action, getting things done through people, making things happen. With a focus on getting people to do what he or she wants, the implementing leader works through social and emotional behaviors, whether building teams or cajoling, persuading, influencing, or commanding.

The *problem-solving manager/leader* engages in planning, organizing, and making decisions. Of the three types of manager/leader, the problem solver is the most definitive—he or she is rational, systematic, and gives the appearance of being highly organized. Problem-solving managers make order out of chaos. While the

Above all, a leader must communicate.

Dilbert □ Scott Adams

Source. *San Jose Mercury News* (October 22, 1995).

pathfinding leader
The entrepreneur and charismatic leader who is a visionary and dreamer concerned with pointing to where an organization ought to try to go.

implementing leader thrives on the use of emotion to energize people, the calm, cool, collected problem-solving manager resists allowing emotions to creep into systematic equations. Reason and logic prevail in these natural managers of systems.

The *pathfinder* is the most ill-defined and scarce of the three types of manager/leader. A **pathfinding leader** is a visionary and dreamer concerned about charting a mission and direction; the pathfinder is an entrepreneur and charismatic leader who lives in a world of values and aesthetics, who puts "faith before evidence." Leavitt emphasizes the pathfinder's unique qualities: "Pathfinding is about getting the right questions rather than the right answers. It is about making problems rather than solving them. It is not about figuring out the best way to get there from here, not even about making sure that we get there. It is rather about pointing to where we ought to try to go."[49]

Pathfinding leaders who also have a capability for implementing provide the entrepreneurial stimulus to start new businesses and transform old ones. Pathfinders make the breakthroughs, take the risks, and commit themselves to developing the newer and better. They are the divergent thinkers who, rather than converge on the "one best answer," push people to consider creative possibilities from which choices can be made. Pathfinders are personified by General Electric's Jack Welch (see the Challenge of Change box). Welch strategically refocused GE into 14 core businesses, departing from the unrelated conglomerate type of diversification that characterized GE in the 1970s. In undertaking this transformation, Welch practiced the productivity improvements later confirmed by research as necessary for periodic organizational refocusing.[50]

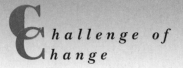

Challenge of Change

GE's Jack Welch: The Pathfinder Personified

General Electric is synonymous with Jack Welch ("Neutron Jack" to colleagues), who is credited with the reinvention of this diversified firm since taking over as CEO in 1981. Despite a triple bypass in 1995 at age 59, Welch plans on staying at the helm until the year 2000. Welch has steered a determined course for GE, propelled by his twin goals of being at least number one or two in global market share and the low-cost producer in every one of its many business sectors. In reflecting on his success in an interview, he gave this response when asked, "What makes a good manager?"

I prefer the term business leader. Good business leaders create a vision, articulate the vision, passionately own the vision, and relentlessly drive it to completion. Above all else, though, good leaders are open. They go up, down, and around their organization to reach people. They don't stick to the established channels.

They're informal. They're straight with people. They make a religion out of being accessible. They never get bored telling their story.

Certainly Welch has not become bored with telling his story, as he has created and shared the visions that began to transform GE in the early 1980s from hundreds of splintered businesses into a coherent core of industries where GE had real strengths. He is now leading a transformation of attitudes within GE, called "Work Out," to release creative emotional energy. Says Welch, "Ultimately, we're talking about redefining the relationship between boss and subordinate" so that people challenge their boss to eliminate wasteful practices, confront controversial issues, and improve quality.

Sources: Noel Tichy and Ram Charan, "Speed, Simplicity, Self-confidence: An Interview with Jack Welch," *Harvard Business Review* 67 (September–October 1989), p. 113; and Tim Smart, "Who Could Replace Jack Welch?" *Business Week* (May 29, 1995), p. 32.

Pathfinding makes managing and leading a very personal process rather than simply a role. In transforming organizations, the pathfinding leader unsettles people with difficult questions such as: What do we really want to do with this company? What do we value? What kind of organization would we love to build? Such strategic questions force soul searching and the possibility that people could do something uniquely different with their time and resources. Pathfinding leadership enables quality and continuous improvement to become the driver.

Behavioral Strategies for Transformational Leaders

Leaders draw on at least three behavioral strategies in transforming organizations:[51]

- *They create a vision.* Depending on personal style (and through some combination of intuition, analysis, creativity, learning from others, and deductive thinking), the leader articulates and champions a vision of a desired future state that is challenging, meaningful, and credible. Visions give direction to organizational members in ways congruent with the leader's style and philosophy and consistent with environmental pressures and organizational resources and constraints. The best visions are ones that take root within the organization, which build enduring capabilities that transcend changes in leaders and market conditions.[52] Sam Walton had a clear vision of bringing mass merchandising at low prices to rural communities when he created Wal-Mart, a vision that prospered even after his death.

- *They mobilize commitment.* Acceptance by others is critical to making the new vision happen. Leaders demonstrate personal excitement and promote the vision to groups at every opportunity, replacing managing by dictate with articulating a message that is highly motivational.[53] Lee Iacocca transformed near-bankrupt Chrysler Corporation into a downsized but robust organization that by the 1990s had become the most cost-efficient automobile firm in the entire global industry. He did so by using his direct and decisive style to create high visibility through advertisements and internal communications. He even gained the commitment of the United Auto Workers union to the layoff of 60,000 employees during the worst of Chrysler's troubles in the 1980s.

- *They institutionalize change.* Rather than apply the quick fix or one-minute management solution, the transforming leader oversees systemwide shifts in problem-solving and decision-making processes. This involves seeing that new practices pervade the organization instead of being limited to a handful of elite managers. The transforming leader enables others to act on the vision and conveys the confidence to meet challenges. Michael Eisner did this when he took over as CEO of ailing Walt Disney Productions and shifted perceptions, standards, and decision criteria to transform Disney into a powerful, diversified entertainment giant once again.[54]

Transformation through Dedication and Continuous Improvement

Given the fast and far-reaching rate of competitive, technical, and geopolitical change, organizational strategies and practices that were effective five years ago have limited applicability in many industries today. This reality was driven home by Louis V. Gerstner, Jr., two years into his transforming experience as CEO of IBM (a firm that in the first three years of the 1990s had net losses of $16 billion): "One of the great things about this industry is that every decade or so, you get a chance to redefine the playing field. We're in that phase of redefinition right now, and winners or losers are going to emerge from it."[55] One winner is likely to be Silicon Graphics, led by Ed McCracken, who draws energy from the entertainment industry to keep his three-dimensional computing products at the forefront of innovation (see the Challenge of Change box).

Such turbulent conditions demand transformational change to lead strategies that develop new lines of business and deepen a commitment to quality and continuous improvement. Yet former university president Warren Bennis believes that many visions lack impact and staying power because they overlook two fundamental human needs that undergird change in today's organizations: quality and dedication. He writes:

> *Modern industrial society has been oriented to quantity, providing more goods and services for everyone. Quantity is measured in money; we are a money-oriented society. Quality often is not measured at all but is appreciated intuitively. Our response to quality is a feeling. Feelings of quality are connected intimately with our experience of meaning, beauty, and value in our lives.*
>
> *Closely linked to the concept of quality is that of dedication to, even love of, our work. This dedication is evoked by quality and is the force that energizes high-performing systems.*[56]

Challenge of Change   *Silicon Graphics Thrives on Fantasy and Chaos*

Silicon Graphics is the computer graphics provider behind the special effects in Steven Spielberg films and the animation in Disney's Epcot Center Aladdin simulated carpet ride. Ed McCracken is chairman and CEO of the $2 billion organization—a firm that completely changed its visualization of its customer base and line of products before it was even 10 years old. As described by McCracken, Silicon Graphics started as a university spin-off, making the hardware and software that enable dynamic three-dimensional visualizations on a flat-panel screen. Its first customer was NASA Ames, providing the computer-based technology that made possible animated flight simulations and mission planning mapping. But the power users of computers shifted from defense in the 1980s to entertainment in the 1990s. The computing power and systems behind Aladdin's magic carpet ride (where each guest steers his own flying carpet) are much more sophisticated than required to pilot a simulated F-16 fighter jet.

The firm's managers have found that the entertainment industry is much more fanciful in their uses of computing power. Customers such as Lucas Films, Steven Spielberg, and Dream Works vividly articulate the limitations of current technology and provide rich fantasies of the future they expect in simulated animation. Listening to imaginative customers in the film and entertainment industries provides McCracken and his Silicon Graphics team with more challenging future product possibilities than does talking to automotive people at General Motors, who simply want cheaper and faster computing. This is why Silicon Graphics entered into a joint venture with Lucas Films to push the technology frontier in film making from analog photography to digital editing.

In looking ahead, McCracken talks about two visions of the computing industry. One sees the hardware as a commodity, little more than a price product with innovation largely a matter of history. The other foresees ever faster change and innovation. Ed McCracken personifies the second mode, which reveals his leadership perspective: "Silicon Graphics thrives on change and chaos." Blossoming from that chaos is the world-class market leader in making fantasy appear larger than life. McCracken's visions—leadership of the firm, leadership of an industry.

Source: Ed McCracken, "The Information Super Highway: How Entertainment Will Drive Its Technological Development into the 21st Century," Business Alumni Executive Briefing (San Jose State University, June 22, 1995).

Bennis asserts that too many men and women in positions of high leadership fail to exercise needed transformational leadership. They get entrapped in managing daily routines and never lead the reform toward total quality through continuous improvement. Bennis as well as other researchers such as Kouzes and Posner also conclude that transformational leadership is a skill that can be learned[57] (see Exhibit 14–8). One develops leadership skills by learning from the best practices of others and from personal mistakes or setbacks.

Sam Walton led the transformation of Wal-Mart from a one-store operation in 1962 to the largest retail chain in the world by learning from constantly observing and acting on the best management and merchandising practices of others. He also learned from setbacks how to be better prepared for the next event. He began his road to fame and fortune by signing a five-year lease on his first variety store. He turned it into the most successful Ben Franklin franchise in the nation, only to lose it after five years when the property owner (aware of its success) would not renew the lease. Never again did Sam Walton lease without a contractual option to renew. He learned, he led, he transformed.

<table>
<tr><td>

────── **EXHIBIT 14–8**

*How Leaders Get
Extraordinary Things Done*

</td><td>

Researchers Kouzes and Posner focused on what leaders do whenever they are at their personal best and concluded that there are five behavioral practices common to successful leaders:

- *They challenge the process.* They are willing to take risks to change the status quo. They make mistakes to push innovation.
- *They inspire a shared vision.* They have a dream—a purpose, mission, goal, or agenda. They live their lives backwards by starting with a picture in their mind, then enlisting others to share passionately in that vision and make it happen.
- *They enable others to act.* They focus on "we" to build coalitions and encourage collaboration. They build teams and empower others. (This is the most significant of the five practices.)
- *They model the way.* They are clear about their business beliefs and behave consistently with those beliefs. They show others their values by behaving as they expect others to act.
- *They encourage the heart.* They use celebrations to offer dramatic encouragement and rewards. They show team members they can win and winning is exciting. They love their customers, their products, their people, and their work.

Source: James M. Kouzes and Barry Z. Posner, *The Leadership Challenge: How to Get Extraordinary Things Done in Organizations* (San Francisco: Jossey-Bass, 1995).

</td></tr>
</table>

IS LEADERSHIP ALWAYS NECESSARY?

Thus far we have assumed leadership to be an active, positive force in stimulating group and organizational performance. But by now you probably realize that leadership is a complex process, one in which it is all too easy to make errors in judgment that precipitate inappropriate behaviors. Two concepts shed additional light on some of the complications that often accompany the process of leadership. One is the observation that leadership does not usually occur on a level playing field—leaders do play favorites. Furthermore, there are times when leadership is not necessary—other factors can substitute for leadership.

Playing Favorites: Leader–Member Exchange Theory

leader–member exchange theory
Realizes that leaders seldom treat followers equally: in-group members experience mutual trust and reciprocal influence while out-group members are merely supervised.

Leaders seldom treat followers equally. **Leader–member exchange theory** holds that interactions between a leader and group members depend on who is in the leader's *in-group* and who is in the *out-group*.[58] Research finds that a manager as a person in authority may "lead" some subordinates (the "trusted cadre," the in-group members) and merely "supervise" others (the "hired hands," the out-group).[59]

In one observational study of 60 leader–member dyads (pairs), researchers found two classes of exchanges between leaders and members.[60] The in-group exchange was described as a partnership with mutual trust, respect and liking, reciprocal influence, and a sense of "being in this together." The out-group exchange was characterized by downward influence, defined role relationships, the leader as overseer, and no sense of common outcomes. Another study found that followers who have attitudes similar to the leader's and who are extroverted are more likely to develop closer leader–member exchanges.[61] As leaders seek to discover follower talents and motivations, the more extroverted follower makes these qualities obvious to leaders more so than introverted co-workers.

More critical than the complex issue of what attracts leaders to some members and not to others is the question of the consequences of playing favorites. How do the distinctions between in-group and out-group affect a member's experience?[62] Interestingly, in-group and out-group members do not report differences in the quality of group experience—with factors such as job enrichment, satisfaction with the leader, or influence.[63] It may be that while leaders do have their favorites, the differences in leader–member exchanges "do not necessarily affect members' feelings of equity, cohesiveness, or conflict."[64]

━━━━ **EXHIBIT 14–9**

Three Substitutes for Leadership

Leadership interventions are needed less, if at all, when the following conditions are found within a group:

- *Individual job expertise.* The highly mature individual in a profession, a craft, or a technical job knows when and how to perform the task. Years of experience and training and working with a number of supervisors enable the individual to work without dependence on a leader except when receiving assignments or new goals.
- *Intrinsic task satisfaction.* People who obtain high personal satisfaction from working on a particular task do not need a supervisor's influence to keep them productive. When satisfaction comes from the task itself rather than from extrinsic rewards administered by a manager, the best leadership role is largely supportive, not interfering.
- *Formalized rules and procedures.* Tightly structured tasks with specific understood procedures reduce worker dependency on supervisors. Leadership may be superfluous when the employee does not have to exert judgment in order to perform the task successfully.

Source: Steven Kerr and John M. Jermier, "Substitutes for Leadership: Their Meaning and Measurement," *Organizational Behavior and Human Performance* 22 (December 1978), pp. 375–403. Used by permission of Steven Kerr, visiting professor, University of Michigan.

There Are Substitutes for Leadership

Some researchers take issue with theories that assume leadership will always be useful.[65] One study found that leadership theories fail to systematically account for much of the change in group performance.[66] While group members need guidance and psychological strokes or emotional support, they may not necessarily be dependent on the manager or leader for them. Quite simply, there are substitutes for leadership; three are described in Exhibit 14–9.

The first two substitutes (personal expertise and intrinsic task satisfaction) reflect professionalism or a high degree of job maturity, to use the Hersey and Blanchard terminology. The third condition (rules and procedures) may occur when job technology acts as a control even when job maturity is not advanced. These and other conditions that substitute for leadership further support the contingency philosophy. They confirm that the extent of the need for leadership and leader behavior are situationally dependent.

The originators of the path-goal theory of leadership also note that when a group's goals as well as the paths to goals are clear, leadership is not really necessary. Under these conditions—when employees know what to do, how to do it, and when to do it—"attempts by the leader to clarify paths and goals will be both redundant and seen by subordinates as imposing unnecessary, close control."[67] Leaders should be aware of a group's situational needs, for there are times when influence need not be exerted.

The Dilemma of Women and Minorities in Leadership

Within North American organizations, white males have had a decided advantage for rising to prominent leadership positions. Few women and people of color have been able to break the barriers for entry into the ranks of senior management and its opportunities to exert broad, transforming leadership. When Dee Bodine, a 52-year-old black woman, director of marketing for the northwest region of AMM Enterprises, was interviewed and asked if people of color face barriers or special problems in advancing into top management, she replied:

> *Yes, absolutely, there are barriers to moving into senior management. It starts at the one-on-one level. People see us as weaker, less qualified, and a bigger risk. Therefore, we don't get picked for key assignments that would give us visibility and credibility. The few of us who do get chosen live in a very nonsupportive, lonely, pressure cooker kind of environment. The personal perceptions translate into both formal and informal practices that exclude us.[68]*

This same study by Ann Morrison found that the most critical barriers to advancement by women and people of color are:

1. Prejudice, of treating stereotyped differences as weaknesses.
2. Poor career planning, where minorities are blocked from high-profile, challenging jobs.
3. A lonely, hostile, unsupportive working environment for nontraditional (minority) managers.
4. A lack of organizational savvy of knowing "how to play the game" of politics.
5. Career comfort by executives in dealing with their own kind (the inside group).
6. Difficulty in balancing family and career, especially for women.[69]

On this last point, one story was told where a woman on the verge of being promoted opted instead to be demoted because her husband was critical of the amount of travel she was doing. She also reported that no man within the company had accepted a demotion rather than be promoted within at least the last five years. Another meta study concluded that "management jobs are still dominated by men and that, given the option, many organizations still prefer to hire or promote men into administrative and management positions."[70]

And yet, surprisingly, an increasing number of women who make it into responsible management positions, even senior management, are reassessing their lives and opting to leave their posts rather than be bored or unfulfilled. A survey by Yankelovich Partners of 300 career women (94 percent managers and executives) between the ages of 35 to 49 found that 87 percent had made or were seriously considering making a significant change in their lives.[71] In contrast to common perceptions, it was not motherhood or glass ceilings that pulled these women away from corporate leadership. Many were striking out on their own to become entrepreneurs, consultants, or involved in philanthropic pursuits—quests to become more fulfilled and satisfied.

Typical of many, Claire Irving left her career in corporate mergers and acquisitions to start her own detective agency. She gave this reason for her change: "It wasn't burnout, it was boredom." Satisfied with her switch, she remarked, "I am doing it for me." Ironically, at the very time society begins to expect more women in positions of corporate leadership, it seems that significant numbers of those who achieve business success redirect their lives so that life is more manageable and personally meaningful. Perhaps the lesson is that from the viewpoint of leader satisfaction, there can be as much (or more) joy in leading 5 as in leading 500 or 5,000.

LARRY BOSSIDY: GROWTH SEPARATES WINNERS FROM LOSERS—A SECOND LOOK

A firm cannot prosper by productivity alone. Productivity implies cutting back on people and other resources used to produce revenues. To sustain a vibrant outlook toward the future, leaders must grow the enterprise. At Allied-Signal, Larry Bossidy is blunt and unrelenting in his drive for growth. Reflecting on his leadership style as his Lear jet heads from Indiana to Alabama, Bossidy remarks, "I was always candid. For years, being totally direct wasn't regarded as a plus. Then under Jack Welch (of GE), it came into vogue."

As an example of his candidness, earlier that day at a South Bend plant that makes auto braking systems for Chrysler and Ford, Bossidy addressed a large gathering of employees: "In manufacturing we're still 3 on a scale of 10." Everyone was put on notice. In a private meeting, Bossidy lets plant managers know they aren't growing profits fast enough to meet his goals. The managers insist they will meet the targets. Unconvinced, Bossidy retorts, "You better hardwire your hopes, or we'll have a discussion in a few months nobody will be comfortable with." But after the meeting, he admits to being more pleased with progress than he lets on: "Remember, these are tough stretch targets. You can't punish managers for not getting 100%." Even if the braking business comes close to achieving its goals, Bossidy acknowledges that its managers will deserve fat bonuses. Unrelenting, yes; but also fair and concerned about people's motivation.[72]

SUMMARY

Managers carry out a broader set of functions than do leaders. Managers focus on using their authority to cope with complexity, see that things are done right, and assure resources are used efficiently. Leaders emphasize change and continuous improvement, and they seek to visualize the right thing to do by questioning practices and possibilities.

Leaders seek to influence followers so they will want to work toward the leader's goals. Leaders also appear to have certain traits in common that help others to have confidence in their credibility, a phenomenon explained by social-cognitive theory.

Several streams of research have focused on the leader's style or behavior as he or she interacts directly with the group to be influenced. Although many labels have been employed to describe this behavior, in essence, they distinguish between the leader's task-oriented and relationship-oriented behaviors or between the leader's underlying cognitive styles (motives and concerns).

Because predictions of effectiveness based solely on the leader's behavior or style have generated inconsistent results, most contemporary models incorporate one or more situational variables. These are called contingency theories. Fiedler equates effectiveness to task versus relationship styles in combination with three contingency variables. Hersey and Blanchard pay attention to how the leader's task and/or relationship behaviors are adapted to followers' job maturity competencies. House and Mitchell view the leader's behavior as clarifying goals and showing the path to them. Vroom and Yetton consider leadership effectiveness options by working through a decision tree of group and situational factors.

A different form of leadership is necessary at the level of the larger organization, where the leader acts as a visionary pathfinder and a transformer of organizational strategies and practices. At this level, leaders must learn the skills of creating a vision, mobilizing commitment, and institutionalizing change. They get extraordinary things done by being dedicated to continuous improvement and enabling others to act.

Some research suggests that there are times when leadership is not necessary or may even get in the way. Leaders often play favorites; they have a preference over in-group members over out-group members. There are even conditions that may be substitutes for leadership. Finally, women and people of color face the dilemma that while they have more obstacles to overcome to break into responsible leadership positions, many who do succeed find the experience less than fulfilling. They choose to downsize the complexities in their lives by breaking away from big organizations to follow other more personal pursuits.

Key Concepts

managers, *p. 463*

authority, *p. 463*

accountability, *p. 463*

leadership, *p. 463*

leader, *p. 463*

social-cognitive theory, *p. 466*

credibility, *p. 466*

task-oriented behavior, *p. 468*

employee-oriented behavior, *p. 468*

initiating structure, *p. 468*

showing consideration, *p. 468*

leadership style, *p. 470*

Leadership Grid®, *p. 470*

contingency theory, *p. 472*

task-motivated style, *p. 474*

relationship-motivated style, *p. 474*

situational leadership theory (SLT), *p. 475*

path-goal leadership theory, *p. 477*

instrumental leader behaviors, *p. 478*

supportive relationship leader behaviors, *p. 478*

transformational leaders, *p. 481*

pathfinding leader, *p. 483*

leader–member exchange theory, *p. 487*

Questions for Study and Discussion

1. Both leadership researchers and corporate executives contend that too many organizations are overmanaged and underled. In your own words, what are the differences between managers and leaders? Why do organizations need both?

2. The idea of identifying leaders on the basis of personality traits was once popular, became discarded, and now has rising popularity once again. What are some of the reasons why personal characteristics are useful in thinking about leaders and how they are perceived? What are some of the traits or characteristics that seem to distinguish leaders from the rest of the crowd, in the minds of followers?

3. Many of the popular theories of leadership generated over the past four decades incorporate a task and a relationship dimension to describe the leader (although several labels have been used). Even though they use similar terms, what is the difference between the behavior-based theories and those that apply a cognitive style interpretation? Why have efforts to predict group effectiveness using only the leader's behavior or style produced inconclusive results?

4. Draw a four-cell matrix using "initiating structure" (task) and "showing consideration" (relationship) as your two behavior axes. Add "high" and "low" labels on each axis. In each of the cells, write examples of how a leader would behave. Then describe the circumstances that would allow each set of behaviors to be effective.

5. Compare and contrast the leadership-style model of Fiedler with the situational theory of Hersey and Blanchard. Both are contingency theories, but how does their use of the concepts "task" and "relationship" differ? Which one seems most useful? Why?

6. How does a transformational leader bring about change? What personal behaviors help the transformation process?

7. What are the circumstances when leadership may not really be necessary? Comment on the observation that the relationship between leaders and followers is not always an equitable one.

EXPERIENTIAL EXERCISE

What Does the Leader Do Now? (A Role Play)

Purpose.   What would you do as a leader as you encounter changing situations? This role play gives several members of the class the opportunity to test out their approach. (Total time required: 20 minutes.)

Procedure.   Form into groups of 6 to 8 members. Select two members, one to be the leader for situation A, the other for B. Now, everyone read the background in situation A. Then, leader A, engage your group in a meeting for 7 to 8 minutes to review the issues generated by the grand opening of your computer store. After concluding A, then leader B will engage the members of the group in a discussion for 7 to 8 minutes pertaining to situation B issues. (As an alternative, your instructor may ask that the same leader work with group members for both situations.)

Situation A.   You are the newly appointed manager of a new computer store, the twenty-first in a fast-growing regional chain. The grand opening just concluded, which turned in a better-than-expected sales performance. But it was a week scarred by confusion and numerous problems serving customers. With two exceptions, the seven full-time sales-service staff you hired have no previous computer sales experience. You personally did all the hiring two to three weeks before the store opened, looking for people experienced in working with computers. The glitches during the last week were a combination of the staff not knowing the technical specifications of inventory items they had not personally used and at times resorting to faking their recommendations to customers—or acting with indifference toward customers. You decide to meet with your entire staff before the store opens on Monday morning to share with them the sales success of opening week, and to begin correcting the types of customer-related problems that caused you to be less than pleased with their overall performance during the opening.

Situation B.   Your store is now into its second quarter of operation. You have hired four more staff. With a couple of exceptions, the staff has settled into their roles quite nicely. People have learned the technical side of the business and have generally become versatile across several brands of equipment. They demonstrate a basic knowledge of most software products. Paul, however, continues to generate two to four customer complaints per week, usually about his impatient, condescending attitude in working with customers who lack technical expertise. Samantha has proven to be a capable technician, especially in configuring hardware and installing software, but she is often hesitant to make specific recommendations when serving customers. You have decided to hold your first staff meeting of the quarter to review progress to date and engage your people in a quest for continuous improvement.

Debriefing.   Discuss in small groups (or as a class, at the direction of your instructor):

1. What did leader A do that seemed effective? Not so effective?
2. Which leadership theories seem to have relevance for the way leader A handled the group? What is your assessment of the job maturity of group members in situation A? Did the leader's behavior seem to take this into account? How?
3. What did leader B do that was effective? Not so effective?
4. Again, what leadership theories appear to have relevance for leader B's handling of the situation? To what degree has employee job maturity changed in situation B? Did the leader seem to take this into account? How?

EXPERIENTIAL EXERCISE

Dividing Up Leadership (A Role Play)

Purpose.   This role-playing exercise initially involves all class members and gives everyone an opportunity to exert leadership influence in one of six groups. Through the two-phase dynamics of the exercise, students form impressions about their own leadership tendencies and learn through social observation what leadership behaviors do and do not work in the present situation. The first phase focuses on emergent leadership within self-selected groups; in the second phase, representatives from each group vie to influence others as to the merits of their group's recommendation and their share of a $500,000 budget. (Total time required, about 45 minutes.)

Materials Needed. Six group background notes are provided by the instructor from the *Instructor's Guide.* Each note represents one of the six major activity centers for the Multi-Phase Products company: Research, Manufacturing, Marketing, Administration, Scientific Instruments Division, and Medical Instruments Division.

Pre-Group Preparation: A Background Note on Multi-Phase Products Co. Everyone please read the following background material before beginning phase 1:

Multi-Phase Products, Inc., is a midsize firm in the medical and scientific instruments industries that has begun to experience difficulties. The firm is organized along functional lines, and it has two business divisions that produce and sell products. Now 12 years old, the firm currently employs about 700 people. Last year it generated revenues of $120 million with profits before taxes of $3 million. Now three months into the fiscal year, managers within the firm are troubled by declining profit margins. Three years ago, net profit margins before taxes peaked at 10 percent of gross revenues; this quarter a loss is projected. Gross margins have also declined (from 55 percent three years ago to 40 percent this quarter). In part, this is because of higher costs involved in introducing a new technology within the Medical Instruments Division. There has also been an erosion of price points in the maturing Scientific Instruments Division, which is facing intensified competition in both domestic and foreign markets. In several specific product market areas, customers have the perception that the quality of Multi-Phase products has slipped relative to that of competitors.

Procedure for Phase 1: Group Selection and Recommendations. After everyone has read the background note, progress through the following three steps:

1. The instructor asks for six volunteers whose job is simply to act as resource persons and pass along information to group members once groups form. Each volunteer is handed one of the six group background information notes (by the instructor, obtained from the *Instructor's Manual*) and a sign indicating the group's organizational unit. The six then stand around the perimeter of the room (at the four corners and midpoints of the two longest sides) and hold up their organizational unit sign.

2. All others in the class then stand and move to one of the six locations. Use any criteria you wish in selecting a group, such as its function, the people who seem to be attracted to it, or the number of people in the group. Groups need not be equal in numbers, but the largest must have no more than twice as many members as the smallest.

3. Now the work begins. The resource volunteer shares verbally (by paraphrasing, not reading) information contained in the "group note" with his or her group. Members discuss ideas for improving the firm, restoring quality, and selecting an approach that seems reasonable. They also decide what share of a $500,000 "quality improvement budget" they believe their recommendation merits. They then select one member to represent their interests as a leader at the "task force" meeting. (Instructor will allocate time—about 10 minutes.)

Procedure for Phase 2: Task Force Budget Meeting. The six task-force leaders now assemble in front of the room (seated, if movable chairs are available). Each presents his or her group's recommendations and discusses them with the other five. This is a leaderless group in the sense that no one is appointed to officiate as chairperson.

The six-person group will then decide on the merits of the six proposals by allocating the $500,000 quality improvement pool of funds the CEO has budgeted for this purpose. The allocation that is finally accepted by the task force group should be proportionate to the perceived value of the six proposals for improving Multi-Phase Products. (The instructor may call an end to negotiations if the group seems to be in an impasse—about 15 minutes.)

Debriefing. The instructor guides a discussion of questions such as:

1. Why did you choose to volunteer (or not to volunteer) as a resource person? To what extent did resource persons become group leaders at the multigroup negotiations?

2. What behaviors were influential in deciding on the group's recommendations? Were the behaviors of influential persons examples of leaders showing consideration, or were they instrumental in nature? Did some people actively seize the opportunity to influence the group? For people who were influential, what were you seeking to accomplish by both the content and manner of expressing your ideas?

3. Why were some of the leaders apparently more able to convey a vision of their plan in the budget negotiations? Did the most visionary exert greater influence on the task force?

4. What was the basis for leadership at the phase 1 group level? To what extent was the outcome of the budget allocation process in phase 2 a reasonable reflection of the pathfinding leadership qualities of the group leaders?

CASE

Troubling Leadership Issues in the Panamanian Agency[73]

Latin America Deputy Director Bob Grollin was four months into his job as regional chief for a bureau of the U.S. Agency for International Development. From his sixth-floor office in Panama City, Bob spoke candidly about the leadership of his predecessor, about his own recent move into general management, and about the effectiveness of the bureau director in Washington, DC.

Julio [my predecessor] was an independent and highly respected leader. He provided an excellent role model for learning good management practices, even though by nature I put more emphasis on paperwork than he does. Julio was a people person. Everything seemed easy to him—he never sweated the details or deadlines. He spent much of his time politicking with bureaucrats in Latin American agencies. I was, thus, very anxious when I first took over this job, mainly because Julio had run the office so successfully. I've always thought it important to nail down contract terms and work with all parties to get them to live up to their agreements. It took two months before I really began to sleep at night.

The Washington staff respect me, but they don't always appreciate the unstable and chaotic conditions we must contend with in Latin America. A new government can come in overnight, or a minister of finance may be ousted abruptly, and such events mean that we have to virtually start over on pending projects. My field staff are technically competent, but at times they're remiss on the managerial and bureaucratic aspects of their jobs—that is, the paperwork. U.S. staffers seem to adjust to the local pace, where things are more relaxed and informal. But I don't get much feedback about my own leadership from my staff in the field offices throughout Latin America. I'm never sure how they read my intentions.

Paul Kerlinger, the director of our Washington bureau, is a strong, take-charge leader. People are loyal to him because he has a brilliant way of personalizing our entire organization. He has a lot of political and bureaucratic clout in Washington; he calls a lot of the shots and plays the network well. But this creates a weakness too, I believe, as everyone tends to depend on him too much. Many senior staff in the Washington office avoid decision responsibility. They try to second-guess Paul, or they lean on him because his decisions are usually right. But this means that results aren't as prompt as we in the field need.

Paul likes to be everywhere, keeping dozens of balls in the air. But more balls are passed to him than he hands off to others. I don't think this is necessarily his intention. But as a matter of practice, top staffers expect the chief to work his miracles.

Three days after Grollin made these observations in Panama, two bureau staffers met by chance and had lunch together in Washington, DC. Linda Galvin, the Latin American field officer assigned to Honduras, and Larry Lamarre, the Central American liaison officer in Washington, soon found themselves venturing into a discussion of their supervisors. With some hesitation, Linda noted:

My boss, Bob Grollin, typically thinks my initial judgment is incorrect. We have different personalities and goals and we differ in our approach to handling projects. I can't do things his way, and vice versa. Bob doesn't realize that Hondurans think differently from Panamanians and have a different sense of priorities. He seems determined to imprint his style throughout the Americas. In one meeting, he complained that I was not listening and not supporting him.

Larry had experienced different frustrations in Washington:

When I came to this office from Jamaica, there was no provision for helping me learn the most elementary aspects of the job. For example, I went to Gordon Davis, my supervisor, to ask how to send an international cable. He said he didn't know how! Gordon manages by stress. He once told me, "If you ever think you are in control, you are mistaken." And yet Gordon's very thoughtful about personal problems, and he can be articulate and really effective in meetings. But he's afraid of his boss [Paul Kerlinger] and tries to second-guess him. I have yet to see him initiate a firm stand on anything.

Questions for Managerial Action

1. What leadership styles or behaviors are suggested by these conversations? What specific clues lead to your conclusions?

2. Where is transformational leadership taking place within the agency? In what ways? Does it have any negative effects?

3. In what ways does there seem to be an appropriate contingency relationship between leaders and their situations? Where are there poor fits between leaders and situations?

4. Does the vertical relationship between any leaders and subordinates suggest an in-group versus out-group situation? Who do you see in each type of situation? What are the likely consequences over time?

Part V

Managing Change

15 Stress at Work

16 Change and Organizational Development

Appendix A Origins and Methods of
                   Management and OB Theories

Appendix B Managing Your Career

Chapter 15

Stress at Work

LEARNING OBJECTIVES

After studying this chapter, you should be able to:

- Define stress and list its symptoms.
- Track the general adaptation syndrome's three phases.
- Identify the major causes of stress.
- Discuss consequences of stress.
- Describe strategies for coping with stress.

THE STRESS OF SUCCESS

"A lot of people think I'm completely nuts," said Nancy Bauer two years after walking away from a successful five-year career in marketing communications. Why leave a prestigious client list, a healthy income, and a midtown Manhattan office at age 38? In a single word, stress. The harder Bauer tried to be a corporate superwoman, the more her stress level increased. "I was handling 15 accounts, had 12 people working for me, and at a minimum was dealing with 30 people at a time." On top of all the work stress, Bauer wanted to get pregnant. "I was 38 years old and didn't have any children." Bauer said she was a product of "male-held perceptions" that rule the corporate world—"the value system of produce, produce, produce and work, work, work."

As the grip of stress tightened, her weight fluctuated. She began to lose strands and then clumps of hair. She spent her weekends sleeping. "I would come home and sleep all weekend as a way to replenish myself. I was that drained." Her doctor told her she needed a break. But in her company, "people who take pit stops are looked at as if they are not cut out to be this superperson. And New York tends to glorify people who live on just four hours' sleep a night . . . always doing, doing, doing. Its a sense of being invincible, rather than being vulnerable, yet strong," Bauer said.

"I forgot my own definition of success," she recalls, "and started living according to one that fit the circumstances, no matter how disagreeable." Other people in the company had ulcers and cholesterol problems, and they were still working at outrageous levels. But, her doctor told her, "You've got to take a leave from your job, to save your life. Go away. Get out of New York. Reflect for a while."

Source: Used with permission of the American Marketing Association. H. Schlossberg, "Meditation Uplifts Her Life on the Fast Track," *Marketing News* (October 1, 1990), pp. 10–11.

The real-life case of Nancy Bauer demonstrates that work stress can have disastrous effects on the quality of life. Work stress knows no boundaries. It affects men and women, executives and secretaries, Americans and Japanese. Forty-six percent of workers and 70 percent of managers believe that stress is a huge and growing problem in the workplace.[1] Stress is created by a multitude of overlapping factors such as overwhelming work loads, ethical dilemmas, difficult relationships with bosses and colleagues, and international uncertainties. Although stress can some-times stimulate and challenge us, too much stress for too long a time has negative effects on both our work quality and personal life. Work stress will not go away, but it can be managed productively.

As you read this chapter, think back to the plight of Nancy Bauer. What were the sources of her stress? What could she have done to cope with them more productively?

WHAT IS STRESS?

Taking a final exam, having a serious accident, giving a formal speech, ending a significant relationship, and missing a deadline can all be stressful. But different people have different feelings and reactions in response to the same event: some negative and some positive. **Stress** refers to the body's psychological, emotional, and physiological responses to any demand that is perceived as threatening to a person's well-being. These are natural changes that prepare a person to cope with **stressors,** which are threatening environmental conditions, either by confronting them (fight) or by avoiding them (flight).

Think of how you would react to seeing an automobile speeding straight at you as you were crossing an intersection. Your emotional reaction would be fear, which would cause you to psychologically experience increased tension, anxiety, and alertness brought on by hormones released from the pituitary, thyroid, and adrenal glands. These hormonal changes would then cause physiological increases in your metabolism, blood pressure, heart rate, breathing rate, muscle tension, and pupil dilation to prepare you to cope with the threatening situation. These same reactions might occur when you are faced with a nonphysical stressor like giving a speech, making a deadline, or resolving a disagreement, when the threat is to your self-esteem or relationship with others.

The degree of stress experienced depends on several factors.[2] First, the demand must be *perceived* (people must be aware that it exists) as *threatening* (having the po-tential to hurt them if they do not react appropriately). Second, the threat must be to something that is *important* to people (has the potential to substantially affect their well-being). Finally, people experiencing the threatening demand must be *uncertain* about the outcome (not sure if they can deal with it effectively). Nancy Bauer, in the opening vignette, probably would not have experienced any stress if she was invited to lunch with an established client to put the final touches on a ad-vertisement that was already approved. On the other hand, if her boss asked her to sign five new accounts in the next month, she might not have escaped from her job without a nervous breakdown.

The General Adaptation Syndrome

Dr. Hans Selye, a pioneer of stress research, determined that the usual response to stressful events that continued for some time follows a fairly consistent pattern known as the **general adaptation syndrome (G.A.S.).**[3] The G.A.S. refers to the de-fensive reactions designed to help a person cope with any environmental demand perceived as threatening. The stressor could be an illness, extremely high job de-mands, an extreme temperature, an insult, or a deadline. Exhibit 15–1 illustrates the three stages of the G.A.S.: alarm, resistance, and exhaustion.

stress
The body's reaction to a demand that is perceived as threatening.

stressor
An environmental demand that is perceived as threatening.

general adaptation syndrome
A consistent pattern of defensive behavioral reactions that a person uses to cope with a continuing stressor.

EXHIBIT 15–1   *The General Adaptation Syndrome: Stress-Coping Effectiveness over Time*

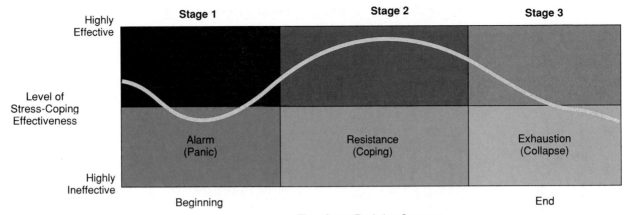

Source: Hans Selye, *Stress without Distress* (Philadelphia: J. B. Lippincott, 1974).

Stage 1: Alarm.   Imagine that it is 4:00 P.M. and you have just been told to prepare an important presentation for a key client for 8:00 tomorrow morning. Like many people, you may initially panic and react ineffectively by denying that this could really be happening, complaining to others, or trying to come up with a number of reasons why you can't make the deadline.

This is the *alarm stage* of the G.A.S., in which the body mobilizes to meet the challenge posed by the stressor. The brain sends out a biochemical message to all the body's systems, causing blood pressure to rise, respiration to increase, pupils to dilate, and muscles to tense up. Because the initial shock causes a panic, there is a minor loss of coping effectiveness until the body can rally its defenses.

Stage 2: Resistance.   If you are able to summon your resources to begin preparing for the presentation (cope with the stressor), you are in the *resistance stage,* when you actually fight (dig into the presentation and resign yourself to a night at the office) or flee from the stressor (delegate the job to someone else). The panic of the alarm stage shifts to an effort to devise a rational game plan. Your energy is channeled into coping effectively.

If the resistance stage is successful and you manage to delegate the job or complete the presentation before dawn, you can head home for a few hours of sleep with a feeling of satisfaction. If, however, morning is approaching and you are still working on the presentation, tension, anxiety, and fatigue set in, and symptoms of the alarm stage return.

Stage 3: Exhaustion.   People have a limited source of energy for fighting stress, and prolonged exposure to the stressor without resolution can bring on the *exhaustion stage*. At this point, you collapse, perhaps by falling asleep at your desk while working on the presentation or just giving up.

Adaptation to stressors is a costly effort. Activation of the G.A.S. places extraordinary demands on the body. If resistance to a particular crisis is high, and the crisis continues for an extended time, little energy is left for coping with other stressors. When prolonged exposure to stress uses up available adaptive energy, exhaustion can take the forms of depression, mental breakdown, or simply being unable to cope any longer.[4] We will discuss this type of "burnout" in the following section on the consequences of stress.

Constructive versus Destructive Stress[5]

distress
Stress that has a negative consequence on a person's well-being.

In its everyday usage, the word *stress* connotes something unpleasant and undesirable. We often use the word to refer to the aggravation brought about by traffic jams, troubled relationships, dwindling finances, or heavy work loads. This uncomfortable state of mind and disturbing physical symptoms are all forms of **distress,** that is, stress that has a negative impact. Later in this chapter we will elaborate on some of its destructive consequences, such as ulcers, heart attacks, depression, murders, and suicide, to name a few.

On the other hand, stress can have positive effects, such as the feeling of excitement before an athletic contest or speech that arouses us to "get up" for the event and perform in a superior way. Some degree of emotional and physiological arousal is necessary to motivate us for most of our daily activities. This positive stress gives us the energy we need to get up in the morning, to excel at work, and to be creative.[6]

Stress itself is neither good or bad. It depends on the existing conditions how we perceive and react to it. Stress can be conceptualized as akin to body temperature. It's always there, and maintaining the optimal degree is an essential component of health. A temperature that climbs too high or dips too low signals some physical malfunction that needs to be attended to.

Episodic versus Chronic Stress

Early in the morning, our stress level may be very low. If we encounter traffic on the way to work and expect to be late to an important meeting, our stress level will increase. If we find that the meeting has been postponed, our stress drops back to a more comfortable level. Throughout a normal day, week, month, or year, we are likely to experience a whole range of stress levels, from crises to relaxation, as we react to deadlines, emergencies, weekends, and vacations.

episodic stress
A pattern of high stress followed by intervals of relief.

A pattern of high degrees of stress followed by intervals of relief is referred to as **episodic stress.** We endure the anxiety, cope with the challenge, and then relax. This is the kind of stress that was functional for our ancestors, who at times needed to run to escape a saber-toothed tiger or to physically fight off an enemy. Elevated stress was functional because it created a state of readiness to fight or flee. After the stressor had been dealt with, relaxation and renewal followed.

Unfortunately, the stressors many people face in the 1990s—job insecurity, the rising cost of living, constant deadlines, poor interpersonal relationships with bosses or co-workers—are continual. These types of stressors put a person in a state of readiness to deal with threats that they can neither fight nor flee. They produce **chronic stress,** which is constant and additive. Each stressor contributes to increasing tension that cannot be released productively. Although some people may snap and punch their boss in the nose or even kill someone because of these conditions,[7] most people just grin and bear the pressure because there is no way to productively relieve it. The cost of maintaining continuous high levels of chronic stress, however, is often a serious health breakdown.[8]

chronic stress
The stress caused by continual confrontation of stressors without relief.

EXHIBIT 15–2

Model of the Stress Process

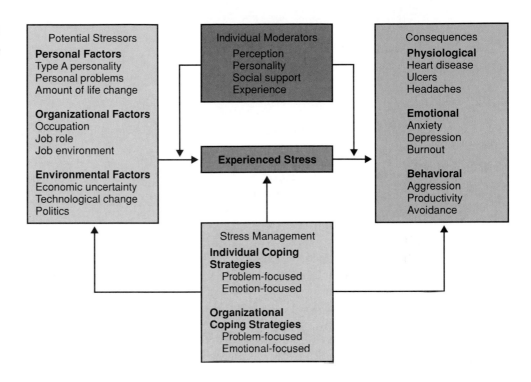

Potential Stressors
Personal Factors
Type A personality
Personal problems
Amount of life change

Organizational Factors
Occupation
Job role
Job environment

Environmental Factors
Economic uncertainty
Technological change
Politics

Individual Moderators
Perception
Personality
Social support
Experience

Experienced Stress

Consequences
Physiological
Heart disease
Ulcers
Headaches

Emotional
Anxiety
Depression
Burnout

Behavioral
Aggression
Productivity
Avoidance

Stress Management
Individual Coping Strategies
Problem-focused
Emotion-focused

Organizational Coping Strategies
Problem-focused
Emotional-focused

WHAT CAUSES STRESS?

Karen Richards, a 37-year-old vice president who supervises bond trading and underwriting at First Eastern Bank Corp. of Wilkes-Barre, Pennsylvania, has to sell twice as many municipal bonds as she did five years ago to make the same profit. She's also concerned about her job. Her employer is the last large bank in eastern Pennsylvania that hasn't been acquired by a bigger rival. She figures she would lose her job if the bank were bought out. Meanwhile, her schedule is so full that she has little free time for stress-alleviating activities, such as exercise.[9]

Many factors contribute to the stress experienced by people such as Karen Richards. The organizational environment may provide a host of potential stressors. Others are due to changes in our personal lives, and some are the result of personality characteristics. These multiple contributors to work stress are diagrammed in Exhibit 15–2.

Personal Factors

A particularly dangerous type of stress is generated internally by individuals who place constant demands on themselves. House of Seagram President Frank S. Berger, for example, gets up at 4:15 A.M., is at the office at 5:35 A.M. "at the latest," and grabs a sandwich in the office at lunch "if it's possible." Berger says that he keeps two meetings going on at once and just goes from one to the other, schedules a business appointment for dinner at 10:00 P.M., and goes home at 11:30 P.M. If he doesn't have a dinner meeting, he goes home between 10:00 and 11:00 P.M. Adds Berger: "I only sleep three and a half to four hours a night; I start to get tired if I cut it below three."[10] Berger is a prime example of the Type A personality.

■■■■ **EXHIBIT 15–3**

Characteristics of Type A and Type B People

Type A	Type B
Competitive	Relaxed
Achiever	Easygoing
Aggressive	Seldom impatient
Fast worker	Takes more time to enjoy avocational pursuits
Impatient	Not easily irritated
Restless	Works steadily
Hyperalert	Not preoccupied with social achievement
Explosive of speech	Moves and speaks slower
Tense facial muscles	Seldom lacks time for others
Feeling of being under pressure	

Type A personality

Personality characterized by impatience, restlessness, competitiveness, aggressiveness, and a sense of intense time pressure

Type B personality

A personality that does not feel under pressure, is easy going, and seldom impatient.

Type A Personality.   Cardiologists Meyer Friedman and Ray Rosenman have identified two distinct personality patterns and labeled them Type A and Type B.[11] They contend that Type A individuals like Frank Berger are three times more likely to suffer from coronary disease than are their opposites, Type B people. Typically, people with **Type A personality** are impatient, restless, competitive, aggressive, under intense perceived time pressure, and always attempting to accomplish several things at once. The **Type B personality,** on the other hand, does not feel under pressure; Type B's take things much more slowly and enjoy a variety of non-work-oriented activities. Type A and Type B characteristics are compared in Exhibit 15–3.

Because Type A's thrive in an environment of tight deadlines and devote long hours to accomplishing volumes of work, they often achieve rapid promotions through the middle level of management. If they perceive a high degree of control over their job environment, Type A's experience high job satisfaction and performance, although they do report high incidents of health complaints.[12] Unfortunately, they seldom manage to remain in good health and only a few obtain top-level management positions. Part of the problem is that Type A's don't slow down enough to make thoughtful analyses of complex issues. In addition, their impatience and hostility produce stress and discomfort among those with whom they work. Consequently, most successful top executives are Type B individuals, who have the patience and more amiable interpersonal style required to maintain organizational harmony.[13]

Of the Type A characteristics, hostility and anger are the most "toxic" contributors to coronary heart disease for both men and women.[14] Since 61 to 76 percent of managers in most organizations are Type A's,[15] they need to be open to feedback that they are hostile, and then do something about it. Suggestions include reducing cynical mistrust of the motives of others; reducing the frequency and intensity of their anger, frustration, and rage; and learning to treat others with kindness and consideration.[16] To determine if you are a Type A personality, complete the Your Turn exercise.

Most Type A individuals are unaware of or refuse to acknowledge their problem or their need to change. Many attribute their past successes to Type A behaviors and others fear that seeking help to change their behavior will be viewed as a sign of weakness.[17] If it continues in this manner, Type A behavior could become a major social problem, as described in the World Watch box about work-obsessed Japan.

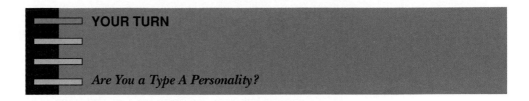

YOUR TURN

Are You a Type A Personality?

To estimate your behavior type, answer the following questions by indicating the "yes" or "no" response that most often, though not always, applies to you.

	Yes	No
1. When you are under pressure or stress, do you usually do something about it immediately?	——	——
2. Has anyone ever told you that you eat too fast?	——	——
3. When someone takes too long to come to the point in a conversation, do you often "put words in his or her mouth" in order to speed things up?	——	——
4. Do you often find yourself doing more than one thing at a time, such as working while eating, reading while dressing, figuring out problems while driving?	——	——
5. Do you feel irritated if someone interrupts you while you are in the middle of something important?	——	——
6. Are you always on time or a little bit early for appointments?	——	——
7. Do you feel impatient or restless when forced to wait in line, such as at a restaurant, store, or post office?	——	——
8. Do you find competition on the job or in outside activities enjoyable and stimulating?	——	——
9. Do you consider yourself to be definitely hard driving and competitive?	——	——
10. Would people who know you well rate your general level of activity as "too active" and advise you to "slow down"?	——	——
11. Would people who know you well agree that you tend to get irritated easily?	——	——
12. Would people who know you well agree that you tend to do most things in a hurry?	——	——
13. Would people who know you well agree that you have more energy than most people?	——	——
14. Do you enjoy competition and try hard to win?	——	——
15. Is it very difficult for you to relax after a hard day?	——	——
16. In your opinion, do top executives usually reach their high positions through hard work rather than social skills and the luck of "being in the right place at the right time"?	——	——
17. During the average busy workweek, do you usually spend over 50 hours working?	——	——
18. Do you usually go to your place of work when you are not expected to be there (e.g., evenings or weekends) at least once a week?	——	——

continued

continued

19. Do you bring work home or study work-related materials more than once a week?   ___ ___

20. Do you often stay up later than you prefer or get up early in order to get more work done?   ___ ___

21. Do you regularly keep two jobs moving forward at the same time by shifting back and forth rapidly from one to the other?   ___ ___

22. Do you often set deadlines or quotas for yourself at work or at home?   ___ ___

23. Rather than plan in advance for a holiday, do you prefer to take it as it comes?   ___ ___

24. In the past three years, have you ever taken less than your allotted number of vacation days?   ___ ___

25. Did you ever hold more than one job at the same time?   ___ ___

Scoring: Add up the number of checks you have in the "Yes" column to obtain your Type A personality score. All of the questions in this questionnaire represent characteristics of Type A personalities. A rough interpretation of your score is as follows:

Score	Approximate Degree of Type A Affliction
20–25	Extreme Type A
10–20	Moderate Type A
1–10	Low Type A
0	Type B

Personal Problems. *Family difficulties* can create a lot of stress. One example is when a two-career family balances conflicting demands concerning child care, career moves, time conflicts, priorities, and expectations. Stress can also be created by *financial problems* or *health problems*. In addition, *poor relationships* with spouses or children can be a major source of job and life dissatisfaction. For an extreme example, Japanese-Americans who have abandoned their traditional way of life with its inherent social support both at home and at work have a stress-related death rate from coronary heart disease over double that of Japanese still in Japan.[18] When people feel that they are surrounded by others that really care, stressors are perceived as being less severe, and much anxiety is alleviated.[19] This is true whether the support is from a cohesive work group or an understanding family.[20]

Amount of Life Change.   Research suggests that positive and negative life changes combine to create stress as the individual strives to adjust to each new situation.[21] Too much change in too short a period of time increases a person's chances of developing serious health problems. The stress of changes adds up in a cumulative fashion and eventually overloads the endocrine system, thereby depleting stress-coping resources and suppressing the immune system, which makes the body more susceptible to certain types of disease. To determine if the amount of change in your life has the potential to contribute to stress-related illness, complete the Life Change Unit Scale in Exhibit 15–4.

Overwhelming amounts of change can be very stressful. But the research does not indicate that it will always lead to major health problems for everyone. Some people experience high levels of change in their lives without any illness at all.[22] If your score alarms you and you are experiencing difficulties, however, postpone any further changes that are under your control until your score settles down.

World Watch

Stressed to Death in Japan

In Japan, *karoshi* is recognized as a fatal mix of apoplexy, high blood pressure, and stress that doctors relate directly to too many hours on the job. Its victims, which some estimates put in the tens of thousands, often are middle managers and supervisors in their forties and fifties who are known in the companies as *moretsu sha-in* (fanatical workers) and *yoi kigyo senshi* (good corporate soldiers).

Millions of Japan's 55 million workers routinely put in 13- and 14-hour workdays, mainly because it is expected. Despite a recent revision of the labor standards law that reduced the 48-hour workweek to 46 hours, Japanese workers spend an average of 2,250 hours annually on the job—about six weeks more than most Americans.

A recent Health Ministry report called *karoshi* the second leading cause of death (after cancer) among Japanese workers. "Our research shows that there are conservatively at least 30,000 *karoshi* victims every year in Japan," said Hiroshi Kawahito, an attorney with the Defense Council of Victims of Karoshi, a legal support group for victims. "And the number is growing." A survey

conducted late in 1989 by the Fukoku Mutual Life Insurance Co. revealed that 46 percent of all Japanese aged 30 to 60 consider it likely they will die from the effects of *karoshi*.

Some men respond to the pressure by dropping from sight. Japan's National Police Agency said 9,964 men were reported missing last year. Authorities say investigations of each case showed the men apparently simply chose to disappear. "These men appeared to have gone underground rather than face the grind of their jobs. They just couldn't take it anymore," a police official said.

Still others immerse themselves in their office life, said Toru Sekiya, director of a Tokyo neuropsychiatric clinic and author of the best-selling book *Daddy Cannot Come Home!*

"The stress and the long hours spent on the job result in an irrational feeling of alienation from their families and a phobia about going home and staying home," Sekiya said. "Many remain in their offices or spend the night in hotels and 24-hour coffee shops."

Source: Ronald E. Yates, *Chicago Tribune*. Used with permission.

Organizational Factors

Exhibit 15–5 compares the frequency with which 15 different stressors are experienced by managers in 10 different countries. Time pressures and deadlines, mentioned by over one-half of the respondents, were the most frequently cited source of work stress, closely followed by work overload.

High Stress Occupation. High-stress occupations allow incumbents little control over their jobs, impose relentless time pressures, have threatening or unpleasant physical conditions, or carry weighty responsibilities. High-stress jobs, such as manager, foreman, and secretary, possess these high-stress characteristics, while low-stress jobs such as stock handler, artisan, and college professor do not. Jobs in the top 10 percent for stress have 4.8 times the heart-attack risk of those in the bottom 10 percent.[23] Even managers and professionals can only bob and weave for so long through the successive waves of downsizings, acquisitions, consolidations, and recessionary layoffs typical of the early 1990s.[24]

Job Role. Whatever the occupation, certain negative characteristics of a person's role at work can increase the likelihood of his or her experiencing stress. Job role stressors include impossible work loads, idle periods of time, job ambiguity, and conflicting performance expectations.[25]

EXHIBIT 15–4

Life Change Unit Scale*

Fill in the mean values for the life events you have experienced in the past twelve months, then total your personal points.

Rank	Life Event	Mean Value	Personal Points
1.	Death of spouse or significant other	100	_____
2.	Divorce	73	_____
3.	Marital (or significant other) separation	65	_____
4.	Jail term	63	_____
5.	Death of close family member	63	_____
6.	Personal injury or illness	53	_____
7.	Marriage	50	_____
8.	Fired from work	47	_____
9.	Marital (significant other) reconciliation	45	_____
10.	Retirement or quit job	45	_____
11.	Change in health of family member	44	_____
12.	Pregnancy (or of wife/significant other)	40	_____
13.	Sex difficulties	39	_____
14.	Gain of new family member (sibling, step parent, etc.)	39	_____
15.	Business readjustment (decrease in income)	39	_____
16.	Change in financial state	38	_____
17.	Death of a close friend	37	_____
18.	Change to different line of work	36	_____
19.	Change in number of arguments with significant other	35	_____
20.	Loan over $10,000 (for car, college tuition, etc.)	31	_____
21.	Foreclosure on loan	30	_____
22.	Change in responsibilities at work	29	_____
23.	Son or daughter leaving home (or leaving parents' home)	29	_____
24.	Trouble with nuclear family members (e.g., in-laws)	29	_____
25.	Outstanding personal achievement	28	_____
26.	Wife/husband/roommate begin or stop work	26	_____
27.	Begin or end school	26	_____
28.	Change in living conditions	25	_____
29.	Revision of personal habits	24	_____
30.	Trouble with boss or professor	23	_____
31.	Change in work hours or conditions	20	_____
32.	Change in residence	20	_____
33.	Change in schools	20	_____
34.	Change in recreation	19	_____
35.	Change in church activities	19	_____
36.	Change in social activities	18	_____
37.	Loan less than $10,000	17	_____
38.	Change in sleeping habits	16	_____
39.	Change in number of family get-togethers	15	_____
40.	Change in eating habits	15	_____
41.	Vacation	13	_____
42.	Christmas	12	_____
43.	Minor violations of the law	11	_____

Total Points

Interpretation: Holmes and Rahe found that people with points totaling less than 150 generally have good health the following year. Those with scores between 150 and 199 have a 37 percent chance of developing health problems while those with scores between 200 to 300 have a 51 percent chance. People scoring over 300 points have a 70 percent chance of having a major illness.

* This scale was first published as "The Social Readjustment Rating Scale" in an article by Thomas H. Holmes and Richard H. Rahe in the *Journal of Psychosomatic Research* 11 (1967), pp. 213–218.

Poor work relationships can mean the end of a business partnership. When Kenneth Ryan and Edward LeBeau faced conflict over each other's personal traits and management style, they sought help from a Chicago psychologist who counsels business partners. The psychologist helped the owners of Airmax Inc., a cargo-management firm based at Chicago's O'Hare International Airport, reconsider and revise their attitudes toward one another, take time out when talk gets heated, and improve trust. (Photo: © John Zich.)

Overload. When people are expected to accomplish more than their ability or time permits they feel pressured and under stress. This is role overload, which was shown in Exhibit 15–5 to be the number one source of work stress around the world. For both upper- and middle-level managers, unreasonable deadlines and constant pressure are the most frequent stressors in their jobs.[26] This *quantitative role overload* exists whenever people are required to produce more work than they can comfortably complete in a given period of time. *Qualitative role overload* exists when the requirements of the job are greater than the skills or knowledge of the employee.

In a lawsuit by his father, work overload was blamed for the suicide of 27-year-old Charles McKenzie who jumped off a building during his first year as an associate at the New York law firm of Cleary, Gottlieb, Steen, & Hamilton. New attorneys at large law firms are routinely expected to work between 60 to 80 hours per week, with only two weeks off for vacations and sick days, which most do not take because of the billable hours they would miss.[27]

Underutilization. Most people prefer a job that has enough tasks to keeps them busy and enough challenges to keep them involved. *Underutilization* occurs when people have insufficient work to fill their time or are not allowed to use enough of their skills and abilities. White-collar workers fair best in having good job-ability fits, followed by skilled blue-collar workers. Unskilled workers experience the most boredom and apathy with their jobs because of underutilization of skills and abilities, low levels of responsibility, lack of participation, and uncertain futures.[28] The resulting stress symptoms include weariness, frequent absence, and proneness to injury. Machine-paced assembly lines are an example of such a work environment.

━━━━━━ **EXHIBIT 15–5**   *Global Comparison of Work Stressors*

Source of Stress	Percentage of Respondents Mentioning Source	Most Often Mentioned by Managers In	Least Often Mentioned by Managers In
1. Time pressures and deadlines	55.3%	Germany (65.4%)	Japan (41.8%)
2. Work overload	51.6	Egypt (76.7%)	Brazil (38.1%)
3. Inadequately trained subordinates	36.4	Egypt (65.0%)	Britain (13.1%)
4. Long working hours	29.0	Nigeria (40.5%)	Brazil (19.6%)
5. Attending meetings	23.6	South Africa (28.5%)	United States (16.3%)
6. Demands of work on my private and social life	22.1	Sweden (31.7%)	Singapore (12.9%)
7. Demands of work on my relationship with my family	21.4	Nigeria (29.7%)	Brazil (8.2%)
8. Keeping up with new technology	21.4	Japan (32.8%)	Egypt (10.0%)
9. My beliefs conflicting with those of the organization	20.6	United States (30.2%)	Egypt (13.3%)
10. Taking my work home	19.7	Egypt (30.0%)	Japan (13.4%)
11. Lack of power and influence	19.5	United States (46.5%)	Sweden (11.0%)
12. Interpersonal relations	19.4	Japan (29.8%)	Singapore (12.9%)
13. The amount of travel required by my work	18.4	Nigeria (29.7%)	Brazil (9.3%)
14. Doing a job below the level of my competence	17.7	Brazil (23.7%)	Sweden (10.3%)
15. Incompetent boss	15.6	United States (30.2%)	Britain (9.1%)

Source: Reprinted with permission. © *International Management* 1993. Reed Business Publishing.

Operating nuclear power plants involves periods of boredom that must be endured simultaneously with sufficient alertness to respond to potential emergency situations. Awareness of the costs of an ineffective response to an emergency makes these jobs all the more stressful.[29]

Role Ambiguity.   *Role ambiguity* exists when people work without a clear understanding of their job definition, performance expectations, preferred methods of meeting those expectations, or consequences of their behaviors. The incidence of role ambiguity is greater among managers than among many other occupations because managerial tasks are often hard to define, and a high degree of freedom and autonomy goes with the job.[30]

Role Conflict.   *Role conflict* exists when a job function contains duties or responsibilities that conflict with one another. It is most commonly found among middle managers, who find themselves caught between top-level management and lower-level managers.[31] A classic example of role conflict is that of the worker who is caught between a supervisor's demand for increased output and the pressure of peers for restricted output. Another type of role conflict occurs when an individual is told by superiors to ignore some legal or ethical practice.

Role conflict not only causes increased interpersonal tension and decreased job satisfaction, but also destroys trust and respect for those who exert the conflicting role pressures. The resulting social and psychological withdrawal can be costly for both the individual and the organization.[32]

Responsibility for Others.   A job that carries responsibility for either the well-being or task performance of others is likely to cause stress. People in supervisory positions are more susceptible to such disorders as ulcers and hypertension than are the people they supervise.[33]

Poor Working Conditions. Prolonged continuous exposure to extreme heat, cold, noise, or crowding can be very stressful. So can high visibility and lack of privacy. Workers on rotating work shifts experience more stress than do those on regular shifts.[34]

Organizational Politics. A survey of over 2,500 managers found that the political climate of the organization was the third most frequently cited stressor (following heavy work load and differences between what managers had to do and would like to accomplish).[35] A by-product of power struggles within an organization is heightened competition and increased stress for participants. Managers caught up in power games and political alliances also pass on pressure to subordinates.[36]

Poor Work Relationships. Stress can be generated from poor relationships with other co-workers, whether they can be the boss, peers, subordinates, or workers in other departments. In study after study, across organizations, occupations, geographical locations, and time periods, at least 60 percent of workers report that the most stressful aspect of their job is their immediate supervisor.[37] The Eye on Ethics box demonstrates how mismanagement can generate stress.

Difficult peers can also be unpleasant to work with for a variety of reasons. This is especially true for women, who are often encumbered by major stresses on the job rarely encountered by men, such as sexual harassment, role overload, role conflict, pay inequality, and discrimination based on sex.[38]

Environmental Factors

People can't just ignore what is going on in the world around them. Most of us read newspapers, look at news broadcasts on the television and radio, talk to colleagues about what is going on, and notice what is happening in the physical environment. These varying elements cause us stress because they are uncertain and may affect us in some important ways. The anxiety aroused by uncertain environmental factors carries over into the workplace and our personal lives.

Economic Uncertainty. Downsizing, rightsizing, reductions in head count, and so on are all in the name of efficiency and cost reduction to increase profitability. The problem is that we may be the ones made redundant and forced to find another means of sustenance. Even if it is only the stock market that is declining, that is where our pension funds are invested, and we have all at least heard of the Great Depression of the 1930s.

Technological Change. Automation, computers, and robots have contributed greatly to productivity, but also have displaced workers and forced them to relearn skills for different occupations. Even if a worker's skills are not made completely obsolete by technological advances, they usually necessitate learning new ones to be able to remain a viable contributor in the workplace. How many of your fellow students don't possess computer skills today? Probably not one. That was not the case 15 years ago, and older employees are often uptight about learning necessary computer age skills and competing against younger employees who have mastered them.

Politics. The jobs for many people directly depend on which party is in political office. For others, indirect relationships exist because of employment in government-funded organizations like aerospace, defense, and science. Even unemployed persons can feel the stress about political uncertainties as they might affect

Eye on Ethics

Facing the Legalities of Job Stress

Feeling stress on the job? File a claim! Many workers are doing just that, and they're winning workers' compensation payments for emotional illness traced to the pressure of their jobs. Stress-related complaints now are the fastest-rising type of job disability claim in the state of California and are costing hundreds of millions of dollars annually.

In California, claims of mental stress resulting in lost work time rose from just 1,178 incidents in 1979 to 9,368 in 1988 and were approaching 35,000 in 1990, according to the state Workers' Compensation Institute. "Job pressures" were most frequently cited by employees as the cause of mental stress (69 percent), followed by harassment (35 percent), being fired (15 percent), discrimination (7 percent), demotion, and other grievances.

Are stress claims valid? Answers vary. Consider some cases in which workers won compensation. They include the case of a former cake decorator for Albertson's, a California supermarket chain, who said her supervisor had been very curt with her and told her to "get her butt in gear."

The Michigan Supreme Court recently granted lifetime workers' compensation to a General Motors Corporation parts inspector who was considered to be a "compulsive perfectionist." He suffered mental strain when assembly-line workers purposefully installed automobiles parts he had labeled defective to get even with his constant corrections of their work.

A Burroughs Corporation secretary became hysterical when her boss constantly criticized her for going to the restroom too often. She said he also asked prying questions about her new husband's family. The state workers' disability compensation bureau awarded her $7,000. Her attorney hopes to get a larger settlement from an appeal board.

A Maine state trooper became severely depressed because he was on call 24 hours a day. He claimed his sex life deteriorated because he never knew when the phone would ring. The State Supreme Court approved the officer's claim for total, permanent disability, but the attorney general asked the court to reconsider—and then settled out of court for $5,000.

Helen Kelly had 22 years of seniority when she suffered a nervous breakdown after being transferred to another department at Raytheon Co. She collected $40,000 in workers' comp benefits.

Sources: Based on "Job Stress Claims Increase Dramatically in California," *Los Angeles Times* (March 31, 1990), pp. A23–25; R. Zemke, "Workplace Stress Revisited," *Training* (November 1991), pp. 35–39; R. W. King and I. Pave, "Stress Claims Are Making Business Jumpy," *BusinessWeek* (October 14, 1985), p. 152.

their social security, welfare, or student aid. The Challenge of Change box describes how President Clinton's standoff against Republican leaders over how to balance the budget adversely affected federal employees and the economy.

Individual Stress Moderators

The same stressor will not cause the same reaction in all people. The demands of something that will overwhelm one person will challenge another to produce a brilliant performance. Some of the factors that moderate the degree of stress experienced by different individuals to the same potential stressor are perception, personality, social support, and experience.

Perception.   For people to experience stress, they must first perceive an environmental demand, to which they are not sure they can respond adequately, that has the potential to significantly hurt their well-being. Students who are absent and

Challenge of Change

The People Costs of a Balanced Budget

The New Year of 1996 was not a happy one for 260,000 federal employees who had been furloughed during a two-week shutdown of parts of the federal government because of President Clinton's standoff against Republican leaders over how to balance the budget. Just the week before, Speaker Newt Gingrich proposed declaring all furloughed federal employees "essential," which would require them to return to work, but without pay.

The deadlock over the federal budget also affected 760,000 other federal employees who only received partial pay, and thousands of and private contractors as well. Yellowstone National Park, for example, was shut down on December 18, 1995, along with other national parks, and lost over $1 million a day. The private concessions company that owns the hotels stopped paying salaries for employees, and since there were no visitors, other private businesses that depended on tourism were also devastated. Alpen Guides Company complained that "usually we have taken 300 to 400 people into the park by now. So far we have taken in zero. This week alone, we refunded $21,000."

Budget negotiations also created stress for people who had planned on closed governmental services and could not get passports issued or visit national parks, museums, and monuments as they had planned for vacations. Other serious consequences involved the uncertainties about what would happen as furloughed workers missed mortgage payments, students were unable to obtain federal loans, and the elderly worried about cuts in Medicare and Medicaid.

Source: Jerry Gray, "Democrats Reject a Plan to Return Federal Workers," *The New York Times* (December 30, 1995), pp. 1, 9; and James Brokke, "Federal Shutdown Hits Hard in Area Around Yellowstone" *The New York Times* (December 30, 1995), pp. 1, 9.

miss an oral report assignment for the following week, for example, will not experience any stress because they do not even know about it. Of the students present, some will not experience much stress because they are already getting an A, have many friends in the classroom, were on their high school debate team, and already know the topic well. At the other end of the spectrum might be foreign transfer students with no friends yet, who are not doing well in the class, have never given a speech before, know little about the topic, and doubt their ability to gather the necessary information and present it in an articulate manner. While the first type of student may do little more than brush up on the subject matter and go about business as usual, the second type may agonize about little else but the dreaded presentation for days. The different students are faced with the same demand but have much different perceptions of its importance, impending rewards, and costs because of their different perceptions of their own situation in the class, level of coping skills, and self-confidence that they can prepare in time.[39]

Personality. Differences in personality characteristics have been found to moderate the degree of stress experienced. We have already discussed how Type A personalities create and experience more stress than do Type B personalities. In the discussion of the big five personality factors in Chapter 5, it was evident that people whose personality styles were not very expressive, were not open to new experiences, and had negative emotions experienced more stress than their opposites.[40] In fact, almost all the different personality types, styles, and traits discussed in Chapter 5 are potential stress moderators. We will illustrate with the following predominant ones below—self-esteem, locus of control, extroversion, and hardiness.

Willis Berrios, owner of Berrios Construction Company in San Francisco, believes that employees' individual growth and self-discipline influence how they perform their jobs. One afternoon when his staff's stress point was raised to where it was interfering with the smooth flow of work, Berrios called an impromptu meeting to discuss taking control of work time. The session helped make everybody stop what they were doing and rethink the way they were trying to get their jobs done. Here, Berrios leads a session on time management for his staff. (Photo: Linda Sue Scott.)

High *self-esteem* causes people to feel good about themselves and have high confidence in their abilities to cope effectively. Consequently, people with high self-esteem experience less stress when experiencing threatening situations than do those with low self-esteem.[41]

People with an internal *locus of control* believe that they make a difference and that their destinies are primarily under their own control. Those with an external locus of control believe that whatever happens is either a matter of chance or determined by forces external to them. Internal attributors tend to perceive their jobs as less stressful and more satisfying than do external attributors, regardless of their education level, length of time on the job, or managerial level.[42] Externals are more likely to feel helpless to deal productively with stressors, so they experience more stress.[43]

Introverts are inner-directed, private, reserved people who spend time in their inner world of thoughts. *Extroverts* are more outer directed, friendly, and expressive. Consequently, introverts experience more stress when attempting to cope with the interpersonal aspects of role conflict.[44]

Hardiness is a combined personality characteristic of people who believe that they are in control of their lives, have the ability to respond to and transform potentially negative situations, and actively seek out novelty and challenge. They welcome change and have a high tolerance for ambiguity. Consequently, "hardy" managers experience far lower-than-average rates of illness in high-stress environments than do others.[45]

hardiness
A personality characteristic of people who are more immune than most to the negative consequences of experiencing stress.

Social Support. Positive relationships with colleagues and supervisors can lessen the impact of stress.[46] The same is true for supportive relationships outside of the job with family members and friends. Social support provides comfort and assistance, which buffers the people from the negative consequences of stress.[47]

Experience. Experience teaches people how to deal with recurring situations that originally were threatening because of their novelty, uncertainty, and threats to self-esteem and well-being. Research has verified common sense and demonstrated that more experience on a specific job is negatively correlated with stress because those who remain in a stressful job are either more hardy, or they have learned to cope with it productively.[48]

Another reason for this effect is that people who do not enjoy a job probably resign. The fit between a person's abilities and needs and the demands of the job assignment is inversely related to the degree of stress experienced.[49] The more a person's needs are satisfied and the greater his or her ability to perform effectively, the less stress is likely to be experienced on the job.

WHAT ARE THE CONSEQUENCES OF STRESS?

A wide variety of physiological, psychological, and behavioral changes can affect a person who is experiencing unhealthy, chronic stress. These symptoms may not be obvious at first. People who adopt a fast-track lifestyle may forget how it feels to be free of stress and accept their harried state as a fact of life. Because the symptoms of stress are so varied, they may be overlooked or mistaken. Special attention should be given to prolonged headaches, elevated blood pressure, fatigue, and depression.[50]

Physiological Consequences

Early physiological symptoms of stress include elevated blood pressure, increased heart rate, sweating, hot flashes, headaches, and gastrointestinal disorders. Chronic stress is often accompanied by more severe disorders like increased cholesterol levels and hypertension, two conditions that precipitate a number of serious health impairments.[51] Medical experts attribute between 50 and 75 percent of all illness, including ulcers, arthritis, and allergies, to stress-related sources. Perhaps the most significant stress-related illness is coronary heart disease, which kills one in four American males. In fact, significant correlations between job dissatisfaction and heart disease have been discovered among workers from more than 40 different occupations.[52]

Gender studies show that, on average, American women experience lower mortality rates from stress-related illness than do men and exhibit a lower incidence of heart disease, cirrhosis, and suicide. Men are more likely to develop serious illnesses, but women are likely to experience higher rates of psychological distress.[53]

Psychological Consequences

Chronic stress can also cause boredom, dissatisfaction, anxiety, depression, tension, and irritability, all of which detract from feelings of well-being and contribute to poor concentration, indecision, and decreased attention spans.[54] If they are unable to alter or escape from their stressors, people may resort to psychological substitutes such as negativism, anger, feelings of persecution, criticism, displacement, denial, apathy, fantasy, hopelessness, withdrawal, forgetfulness, or procrastination.[55]

When prolonged exposure to stress uses up available adaptive energy, exhaustion can take the forms of depression, mental breakdown, or what is termed *burnout*. **Burnout** is a feeling of exhaustion that develops when an individual simultaneously experiences too much pressure and too few sources of satisfaction.[56] Over 18 percent of business owners, managers, professionals, and technical personnel in the United States suffer from burnout.[57] When we confront continual

burnout
Exhaustion that develops from experiencing too much pressure and too few sources of satisfaction.

Factor	Who Burns Out More
Sex	Females more than males
Age	Younger more than older (especially beyond age 50)
Pay	Lower paid more than higher paid
Position	Lower status more than higher status
Ethnicity	Hispanics more than any other race
Customer contact	Those with direct customer contact more than those with no customer contact
Seniority	Longer-term employees more than those with less than 10 years of service
Job preference	Those in a nonpreferred job more than those in a preferred job
Marital status	Singles more than married
Potential	Those with low promotion potential more than those with high potential

Source: R. T. Golembiewski and R. F. Munzenrider, *Phases of Burnout: Developments in Concepts and Applications* (New York: Praeger, 1988), pp. 132–138. An imprint of Greenwood Publishing Group, Inc., Westport, CT. Reprinted with permission.

role ambiguity, performance pressures, interpersonal conflicts, or economic problems while simultaneously trying to fulfill our own and the organization's expectations, the most likely effects are fatigue, frustration, helplessness, and literal exhaustion.[58]

A 1991 Northwestern National Life Insurance study found that one in three Americans seriously thought about quitting work in 1990 because they were afraid they would "burn out" if they didn't. The women who felt "constantly under pressure, trying to accomplish more than they can handle" outnumbered the men 35 percent to 23 percent.[59] People in occupations requiring them to protect and help other people—like doctors, counselors, police officers, nurses—also have high probabilities of burnout.[60] Results from the study presented in Exhibit 15–6 provide some additional factors that contribute to high risk of burnout.

Behavioral Consequences

Some of the first behavioral consequences for individuals experiencing chronic stress are sleep disorders, changes in eating habits, increased smoking, more alcohol consumption, and nervous mannerisms such as rapid speech, fidgeting, and rudeness towards others. When normally very agreeable people quit interacting politely with peers and start yelling at subordinates and secretaries, it is often because of negative stress. The most extreme cases of excessive stress result in workplace violence, where a person ends up physically attacking or even killing co-workers. Postal workers in Royal Oak, Michigan, experienced intense stress, for example, after a former letter carrier killed five co-workers, wounded four others, and then shot himself after failing to get his job back.[61]

Performance decline is perhaps the most studied behavioral consequence of stress. It is estimated that 75 percent of all work loss is due to stress.[62] Not all stress is bad for performance, however. For example, athletes "get up" for critical performances, performers experience nervousness before going on stage, and the stress students feel during final exams energizes them to work harder to achieve their goals.

The relationship between stress and performance resembles an inverted U-curve, as shown in Exhibit 15–7.[63] Stress is like a violin string: The optimal degree of tension is essential to obtaining the proper performance. A string that is too tight or too loose will not produce the desired effect. Insufficient stress leads to

━━━━ **EXHIBIT 15–7**

Stress and Performance

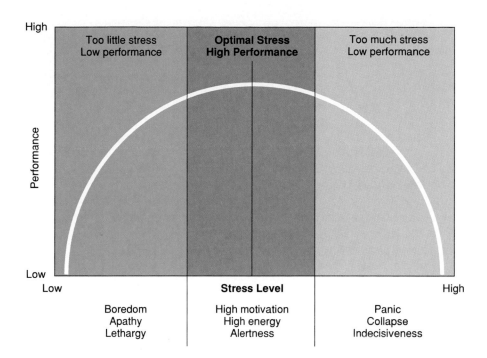

boredom, apathy, and decreased motivation. Increasing stress from an insufficient level yields better performance through increased arousal and concentration—up to an optimal point. Problem-solving groups, for example, become more receptive to new information provided by others when the group is under increased stress.[64] After that, if stress continues to increase and persists for long periods of time, the ability to perform effectively will decrease because of depleted energy, overload, and anxiety.[65] Examples of performances impaired by excessive stress are when students suffer from test anxiety and cannot remember material they know well for their answer, athletes who "choke" during critical contests, and performers who make mistakes while on stage.

Organizational Costs

In addition to the very expensive decreases in productivity, organizations suffer from a number of indirect stress-related costs. Stress-related absenteeism, turnover, compensation claims, lawsuits, medical insurance, and other medical expenses are estimated to cost organizations $150 billion per year. Stress-related incidents account for 12 percent of all workers' compensation claims nationwide. They rose 700 percent between 1979 and 1988. Some factors contributing to worker stress in the last decade include the recession-induced dislocation of many workers, computers that "de-skill" many jobs, and the use of more contract workers to lower the cost of health benefits.[66]

Another harmful employee response to stress is the use of alcohol and other drugs, leading to more accidents, costly errors, and decreases in task performance levels. Employees who use drugs and alcohol are far less productive than their co-workers, miss 10 or more times as many workdays, and are three times as likely as nonusers to injure themselves or someone else.[67]

Eye on Ethics   *Stress on Wall Street*

Michael Milken generated tremendous stress for subordinates in his ruthless quest for profits in the now-infamous junk bond scandal. While working for Milken, head trader Warren Trepp began smoking four packs of cigarettes a day. Bruce Newberg started taking blood pressure medicine after chewing through a phone line on one hysterical day. Gary Winnick complained he was developing a brain tumor and began seeing a psychiatrist as he requested a transfer to another office.

It was reported that Milken badgered traders for not squeezing the most out of a trade, heckled employees who tried to leave after only 12 hours of work, and chided people who requested sick leave. The results were financial collapses, ruined careers, destroyed health, and devastated relationships.

Source: J. B. Stewart, "Scenes from a scandal: The secret world of Michael Milken and Ivan Boesky," *The Wall Street Journal* (October 2, 1991), pp. B1 and B8.

Frustration and stress can also result in aggression and sabotage. If employees blame the organization for the stress-induced symptoms, they may adopt aggressive behaviors in an effort to "get even." Such aggression can take the forms of verbal or physical abuse, intentional slowdowns, and acts of sabotage such as making intentional mistakes, damaging products, and starting negative rumors. Left unchecked, such reactions to stress can cause irreparable harm to an organization.[68] See the Eye on Ethics box for a discussion of the legal aspects of job-induced stress.

HOW CAN STRESS BE MANAGED PRODUCTIVELY?

Stress is an unavoidable condition of life. Although we can't eliminate it, we can use our understanding of stress to control its effects and thereby enjoy more productive, satisfying lives both at work and elsewhere. In this section, we'll prescribe techniques that organizations and individuals can implement to reduce the likelihood of stressful situations and to cope with those that will inevitably arise.

Stress management at both individual and organizational levels consists of three steps. The first step is *awareness* of negative stress symptoms such as the individual and organizational consequences just discussed—decreased performance, irritability, absenteeism, and so on. The second step is *determining the source*—what are the stressors contributing to the distress and its negative consequences? The third step is *doing something constructive to cope* more effectively with the stress. There are two types of coping: problem-focused coping, where the stressors are dealt with directly by either removing or changing them; and emotion-focused coping, where people learn how to modify or manage their stressful feelings and reactions in more constructive ways.[69]

Individual Coping Strategies

Because stress is such a multidimensional phenomenon, the ultimate responsibility for stress management rests with the individual. There are a number of things people can do by themselves to better cope with stress. Some of these proven strategies are discussed below.

Problem-Focused Strategies. Problem-focused strategies for coping with individual stress need to attack the specific stressor directly. If a graduating senior is worried about finding a job after graduating, stress will start to be reduced to the extent that he or she starts the job search process. Once several job possibilities have been located, interviews set up, and information on the companies gathered, the stress level will start to decrease. The same is true for a worker who has just been given an assignment that is not clear and has an impossible deadline. Once the worker shares these concerns with management and gets help and an extended deadline, stress levels drop. There are several general strategies that can aid in dealing with most stressors that can be decreased by solving a problem: time management, seeking help, and if all else fails, changing jobs.

Time Management. Not being in control of your time can generate serious anxiety, frustration, and even panic. Time management consists of applying the principles of management to yourself—in other words, planning, organizing, and controlling the use of your time. It means using schedules and other control mechanisms to keep your performance flowing smoothly along some desired time line. General time management strategies entail deciding on exactly what goal is to be accomplished by what date or time, making a list of all the activities necessary to accomplish the goal, prioritizing the tasks from most important to least important, estimating how long it will take to accomplish the tasks, and then planning activities starting with the most important task first until the goal is accomplished.[70]

Seeking Help. Getting help from a colleague, advice from your boss, or training from the human resources department can provide a stressed person with the knowledge and skills to deal with a stressor productively. Just knowing that such support is available from others is helpful in coping with stress. Longer-term support systems can be set up through **mentoring,** where a junior employee is personally coached by a more senior and proven performer. Mentoring has been found to relieve stress caused by high-performance demands, pressures for change, and low job challenge.[71]

mentoring
The process of a senior performer coaching a junior one.

If the cause of stress is due to improper employee training, classes, coaching, or another appropriate form of instruction should be undertaken. Not only will proper training eliminate qualitative job overload, but it also increases self-esteem and confidence as employees begin to perform more effectively on the job.

Change of Jobs. If, after exhausting all available problem-solving techniques job-related stress is still not reduced to a satisfactory level, changing the nature of your job or even leaving the organization in favor of alternative employment may be the answer. Sometimes renegotiating your job role can eliminate the stress caused by role ambiguity, conflict, overload, or underload.[72] If this doesn't work, however, no job is worth the sacrifice of physical and mental health, and it may be best to seek other job opportunities. Hanging in there until burnout occurs only compounds the stress.[73]

Emotion-Focused Strategies. If the stressor can't be reduced or eliminated through problem-focused strategies, or if an individual decides to live with the stressor for some reason, emotion-focused strategies can be used to decrease the level of stress experienced to more healthy and comfortable levels. Certain emotion-focused strategies work better for some people than others. Anything that works to reduce stress for you in a healthy, productive manner should be used. Some common emotion-focused strategies include relaxation, exercise, psychological strategies, recreation, and companionship.

Relaxation.   Relaxation decreases muscle tension, which in turn decreases heart rate, breathing rate, and blood pressure.[74] Herbert Benson suggests that to elicit the relaxation response, you must find a quiet place, then assume a comfortable position, close your eyes, and concentrate on relaxing all your muscles while you listen intently to your own breathing for 20 minutes.[75] A study of 126 employees at the Converse Rubber Company found that after just a month of two daily 15-minute relaxation breaks using Benson's relaxation response, employees demonstrated significant increases in work performance and sociability and decreases in stress, blood pressure, and sick days.[76] A similar study of the relaxation response at two high-tech corporations in San Diego found that participating employees demonstrated significant decreases in anxiety, depression, and hostility and better coping skills.[77]

To practice *meditation,* sit comfortably with your eyes closed for about 20 minutes and engage in the repetition of a special sound, called a *mantra.* Those who practice meditation can vouch for the fact that following this procedure twice a day reduces your heart rate, oxygen consumption, and blood pressure.[78]

An easy way to start meditation is to breathe in a full and relaxed manner. Every time you exhale, calmly let the word "one" float through your mind. You may also want to imagine that you are in a safe place while you continue this process for 15 minutes.[79]

To get high-tech help for relaxing, there is the *biofeedback process,* which involves detecting small changes in body tension through galvanic skin responses picked up by electrodes attached to the body. When these responses are amplified and displayed to individuals connected to the biofeedback machine, they can learn how to control their body responses in ways that reduces stress.[80]

John Manuso has calculated that at the New York offices of Equitable Life Assurance Company, the weekly cost of employing a highly distressed employee before biofeedback-assisted stress management training was $70. After treatment, the additional stress-related cost was only $15 per distressed employee per week. For every dollar invested in such a program, it was estimated that the employer received a $5.52 return per person per year.[81]

Exercise.   Medical science has shown that the physiological and biochemical changes resulting from exercise reduce the effects of stress.[82] Exercisers experience lower degress of anxiety, depression, and hostility than do nonexercisers.[83] Regardless of whether you choose jogging, biking, tennis, walking, swimming, or one of countless other activities, the evidence is unequivocal that proper exercise enhances physical health and mental well-being.

Psychological Strategies.   There are a number of psychological strategies that can control the amount of stress experienced and its impact on an individual. Two of these are increased self-awareness and perceptual adaptation.

Increased self-awareness about how you normally behave on the job and in social situations and an ability to recognize early signs of tension make up the first step in managing personal stress. Your self-awareness will signal you to withdraw from overload situations and seek help when necessary.

Through perceptual adaptation, or reframing, individuals can learn to condition their minds to handle those stressors they are not able to control or eliminate.[84] The "thousand-year test," for example, can help you reduce tension by asking yourself, "A thousand years from now, will anyone really care if I miss this

Training horses in precision riding is one of Karen Horn's hobbies. Horn is CEO of Banc One, one of the largest financial companies in the United States. Horn also takes singing lessons and skeet-shooting instruction. She finds great pleasure being totally consumed in a world different from her corporate job; she believes it helps her bring a fresh approach to her CEO duties. (Photo: © 1993 Chris Buck.)

deadline?" Or, "What is the worst thing that can actually happen to me if things do go wrong, and can I cope with it?" Often, you can reduce stress just by realizing that you will be able to survive even if the worst happens.

Recreation.   If all you do is work, you're bound to experience stress, no matter how much you love your job. Everyone needs hobbies and recreational interests that have no purpose beyond the relaxation and pleasure they bring. It's especially important that Type A personalities take their minds off work and relax with some sport or hobby that forces them to forget their job-related troubles. It doesn't matter what they do, so long as it is enjoyable and not related to work.

Companionship.   Stress tends to intensify when a person is alone. If you live by yourself, invite others to share in your leisure pursuits. People who develop close, supportive relationships have a powerful antidote to stress. One study of middle-age men who lost their jobs found that those who had social support from wives, family, or friends survived the resulting stress relatively unharmed. Those without such support, however, suffered physical as well as mental problems.[85]

Organizational Coping Strategies

Organizations have plenty of incentive to decrease stress at work. In addition to humanitarian reasons, there are financial ones, since work-related stress costs billions of dollars each year through sickness, accidents, turnover, and absenteeism.

Stress is multidimensional.

DILBERT® by Scott Adams

Source: DILBERT reprinted by permission of United Feature Syndicate, Inc.

Problem-Focused Strategies.   There are many things that organizations can do to directly eliminate stressors or prepare employees to deal with them productively. Some of them are job redesign, selection and placement, training, team building, and day care facilities.

Job Redesign.   Careful job analysis can reveal role ambiguity, overload, underload, and conflict, as well as poor working conditions. Then jobs can be redesigned to eliminate these problems and reduce the distress they cause. For example, people with Type A personalities have been found to have higher performance and job satisfaction when their perceived control is increased by reductions in role ambiguity and role conflict, participation in setting goals, placement in relatively autonomous jobs, and assignment of tasks in which they have a high degree of control over work scheduling and work methods.[86] Job analysis can also reveal where job enrichment may be beneficial and set accurate job requirements for better matching of employee abilities to job demands. Finally, organizations can provide flexible work schedules and job sharing so that employees can divide up tasks and working hours to attend to outside commitments.[87]

Selection and Placement.   Most current selection and placement procedures aim to prevent qualitative role overload by ensuring that employees' education level, abilities, and experience match the requirements of the job.[88] Personality factors can also be assessed to ensure a good person–job fit. Examples are tolerance for ambiguity, level of self-esteem, and introversion versus extroversion. Both organizations and job applicants need to beware of the tendency to take the "only option" regardless of fit, which strains the individual from the onset.

Training.   When employees have been trained properly, a major source of stress is eliminated. Training should include role clarification—the specifying of job duties—to reduce the likelihood of role ambiguity and conflict. Training in stress management has been instituted in a number of companies, and human relations skills can do much to alleviate the stress associated with interpersonal conflict.

Team Building.   When jobs require group interaction, their design should include incentives to cooperate rather than compete. By building team spirit and providing a supportive climate, an organization can prevent many common stressors from occurring at all.

Day Care Facilities.   The "three o'clock syndrome" refers to the productivity drop, increase in errors, and rise in accidents that occur to working parents as thoughts turn to their children at the end of the school day. In the past, some companies even banned phone calls home in hopes of eliminating jammed phone lines as children and parents try to make contact. But now, companies like John Hancock Financial Services are providing on-site facilities for emergencies and encouraging employees to check on their children in other locations. S. C. Johnson & Son offers after-school programs at its own on-site child-care center. Other companies are financing improvements in after-school care in communities where their employees live.[89]

Emotion-Focused Strategies.   Organizations can offer facilities and training to help employees cope with the negative emotional states they must cope with when stressors cannot be prevented, eliminated, or modified. Some of the things that organizations can do are to provide open communication, employee assistance programs, mentoring, fitness promotion, and personal time off.

Open Communication.   Stress levels run high when rumors or newspaper articles hint of an impending layoff, but employees are not given clues as to who may be affected or when the event will occur. When employees are kept informed about what is going on or is about to happen, ambiguity and conflict decrease, and so does the general level of anxiety.

When upper-level managers are open to communication from below, employees feel more accepted and better understood. Mutual trust and respect along the hierarchy means far less counterproductive behavior. This is especially true when employees are allowed to participate in decisions that affect their work so that they feel more in control and less threatened.

Employee Assistance Programs.   Many companies support employee assistance programs that offer free counseling in-house or by referral. By providing and encouraging the use of such services for stress management purposes, an organization acknowledges the existence of such problems among personnel and demonstrates its support of those who suffer from them. Assistance is usually also provided for non-work-related problems relating to health, finance, and family problems because the resulting stress is carried over into the job.

Mentoring.   Companies can provide formal mentoring programs where senior, more experienced employees are paired up with junior ones to help show them the ropes and provide emotional support and encouragement. Mentors not only reduce the stress caused by uncertainty about how to do things and deal with challenging assignments, but they are a source of comfort when newer employees just need to let off steam.

Wellness Promotion.   Many organizations offer physical exams as well as counseling programs for their employees. Others provide employees with personal days and, for high-level administrators and professionals, sabbaticals of several months that they can take to help reduce or recover from negative stress. Some provide physical fitness facilities designed to promote health through exercise and relaxation.

Employees of Safeway's Bakery Division routinely work out in the company's gym. Providing such outlets can go a long way to reducing employee stress levels and decreasing absenteeism rate among employees. (Photo: Steven Bloch/Black Star.)

American firms spend billions of dollars each year on fitness and recreational programs. Kimberly-Clark alone has spent $2.5 million in a health-testing and physical fitness facility staffed by 15 health care personnel. McDonald's Corporation even provides biofeedback facilities and allows managers to take relaxation breaks to use the equipment to lower their respiration and heart rate.[90] The Federal Reserve Bank of Boston has spent $25,000 to convert a 4,000-square-foot storage room into an employee fitness center, complete with a 10-station universal gym, ballet bars, a punching bag, exercise mats, showers, and lockers. A relatively inexpensive option described in the Challenge of Change box is the provision of lunchtime counselors like those at Chase Manhattan.

At first glance, it might seem that such facilities are a poor use of space and a drain on corporate profits. But proponents of fitness centers say that they can improve employee morale and save money by getting a company's "walking time bombs"—those with cardiovascular problems—on a proper exercise schedule and diet.[91] A secondary benefit is the potential reduction of stress-related workers' compensation claims. Finally, such "wellness programs" are credited with decreasing absenteeism rates.

THE STRESS OF SUCCESS—A SECOND LOOK

With her hair falling out, her physiology a wreck, her professional life in turmoil, and still childless, Bauer actually flew to India for several weeks of meditation, where she successfully got back on track. She no longer works 90 hours a week.

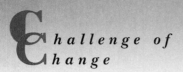

Challenge of Change

Employees See Plays, Eat Brownies to Relieve Stress

To combat anxiety attacks, employers have embraced a myriad of therapies. As Chase Manhattan prepared to pare the payroll 12 percent, management initiated a program of lunchtime support groups, led by professional therapists, for employees feeling stress.

Citicorp has also made extensive use of lunchtime counselors. One, Dr. Art Ulene of NBC's "Today" show, recently advised employees to "change the way you think about some of the things that drive you crazy" as one method for lowering stress. Standing in line at the supermarket, which Dr. Ulene once found intolerable, can be less annoying if it's viewed as an opportunity to meet interesting people, he told the audience amid laughter.

Linda Schoenthaler, a financial planning consultant and senior partner at Circle Consulting Group in New York, treats colleagues to matinee outings on Broadway, while her firm sponsors brownie-tasting bake-offs.

Meanwhile, at Hoffmann-La Roche, Inc., in Nutley, New Jersey, employees receive after-hours instruction in a variety of stress management methods. They include meditation, breathing exercises, feeling awareness, and biofeedback.

Source: "Fear and Stress in the Office Take Toll," *The Wall Street Journal* (November 6, 1990), Section B, p. 1.

She resigned from her corporate position to start her own free-lance business and again have time for her husband and even herself.[92] Meditation was responsible for allowing her to find appropriate balance in her life.

SUMMARY

Work-related stress is a major concern in the 1990s. Never before have people been so concerned about "burning out" at work. Successive waves of downsizing, acquisitions, and consolidations have added to the traditional stressors of overwork, time deadlines, and ambiguity. Yet stress in the workplace has always been with us, and it often serves as the motivator for outstanding accomplishments.

As our natural reaction to threatening situations, stress is our ally in survival. Either too much or too little stress, however, can negatively affect our performance and well-being. Monitoring our stress symptoms can help us know how well we are coping and when to do something constructive about the challenge we are experiencing. Failure to monitor and react appropriately to chronic stress can lead to immense organizational costs, including significant health problems and even death.

Although stress may originate from a variety of organizational sources, such as work overload and time pressures, it can also be caused by problems in a person's home life or personality makeup. A variety of factors, such as social support and personal ability, moderate the consequences of stress for various individuals.

It may be impossible or even undesirable to eliminate stress, but it can be managed productively. Organizations can help by providing personal assistance and applying appropriate management principles. Of course, it is the individuals who are experiencing the stress who must personally manage it for themselves using both organizational and personal resources.

Key Concepts

stress, *p. 498*
stressor, *p. 498*
general adaptation syndrome, *p. 498*
distress, *p. 500*
episodic stress, *p. 500*
chronic stress, *p. 500*

Type A personality, *p. 502*
Type B personality, *p. 502*
hardiness, *p. 512*
burnout, *p. 513*
mentoring, *p. 517*

Questions for Study and Discussion

1. What are your most common stress symptoms? How do these symptoms affect your performance, interpersonal relations, and happiness?

2. What are the major stressors contributing to the stress symptoms you are currently experiencing? If you are not currently experiencing stress symptoms, how do you account for this state of affairs?

3. How do you and other students you know cope with the stress of final examinations? What are the short-term and long-term consequences of these various methods?

4. How do you react to the stress of giving a speech? Check out how five of your friends feel about public speaking. Why is it considered stressful? Why do some people perceive it as more stressful than do others?

5. Think back to the case of Nancy Bauer in the vignette. What were the stressors she experienced? What were the consequences for her performance and satisfaction? What could her organization have done to improve the situation? What other alternatives did Bauer have to manage her stress more productively?

EXPERIMENTAL EXERCISE

Diagnosing Stress and Its Causes

Purpose. To diagnose the stress symptoms, causes, and coping strategies that you have experienced and compare them with the experiences of others in similar situations to gain a broader perspective of the stress process and increase your repertoire of stress management options.

Time. The total time for all four steps is 50–75 minutes. If time is limited, step 4 can be omitted and smaller groups can be formed.

Step 1. Individually think about a stressful situation you have experienced. Then write down your answers to the following questions. (5 minutes)

1. What caused the stress (what were the stressors)?
2. What symptoms of stress did you experience?

3. What were the consequences of the stress?
4. How did you try to cope with the stress?

Step 2. In groups of four to six, compare your answers to the questions in step 1 in round-robin fashion (10–15 minutes). When all have shared their experiences, compare them according to the following guidelines (20 minutes).

Step 3.
1. Identify common elements in the stressful situations just described by your group members. Write them down for later class sharing.

2. List all of the symptoms of stress that individuals in your group experienced in the stressful situations they shared. Note the common symptoms across situations.

3. Specify the causes of stress and their frequency of occurrence in group members' experiences.

4. Describe the different processes that group members used to reduce the stress in the situations they reported.

5. Suggest additional ways for reducing the stress in the original situations described and for managing stress in similar situations in the future.

Step 4. Choose a spokesperson from your group to share your group's answers with the entire class. Discuss, as a class, the groups' summaries just shared. Use the following questions as guidelines. (30 minutes)

1. What are the most common symptoms of stress?

2. What are the most common causes of stress?

3. What means of stress reduction are effective?

4. What have you learned from this exercise that can help you cope with current or potential stressors?

EXPERIMENTAL EXERCISE

Tensing Muscles Relaxation Technique

Purpose. To experience a stress reduction technique.

Time. 10 minutes.

Instructions. It is recommended that the instructor or class member is selected to read the following instructions to the class while they are relaxing with their eyes closed. Students can read the exercise and do it on their own in class or elsewhere if preferred.

1. Select a comfortable sitting or reclining position.

2. Loosen any tight clothing.

3. Tense your toes and feet (curl the toes; turn your feet in and out). Hold and study the tension. Relax.

4. Now tense your lower legs, knees, and thighs. Hold the tension, and study the tension, then relax your legs.

5. Now tense your buttocks. Hold and study the tension. Relax your buttocks.

6. Tense the fingers and hands. Hold and study the tension, then relax.

7. Tense your lower arms, elbows, and upper arms. Hold and study the tension, then relax.

8. Tense your abdomen. Hold and study the tension, then relax.

9. Now tense your chest. Hold and study the tension, then relax. Take a deep breath, and exhale slowly.

10. Tense your back. Hold and study the tension, then relax.

11. Now tense your shoulders. Hold and study the tension, then relax.

12. Finally, tense your neck. Hold and study the tension, then relax.

13. Now relax every part of your body and be as quiet as possible for a couple of minutes.

14. How do you feel?

Debriefing. After the exercise is finished, simply ask participants to share how they feel and what they experienced during the exercise. Participants can also share other relaxation techniques with each other that they have experienced such as deep breathing, visual fantasies, and meditation.

CASE

A Hectic Day at Alcala Savings and Loan Association[93]

Tadeus Kadetsky awoke to the ring of the telephone next to his bed. It was after midnight. Tad thought instantly of his aging mom and dad in Minneapolis and reached for the receiver with a feeling of dread. But it was the desk sergeant at police headquarters downtown, making what was to him a routine call.

"Mr. Kadetsy. The back door down here at Alcala Savings and Loan is unlocked. You're gonna have to come down and check the place out with our officer and lock up the building."

Tad was both relieved and agitated. "So what else can go wrong at work?" he asked himself as he grappled in the dark for jeans and a sweatshirt.

Tad was vice president of Alcala Savings and Loan Association, a small financial institution that had come into its own in the 10 years since Tad had started work there. At that time there were only two employees: the managing officer, Mario Picconi, and himself. Now there were eighteen.

As Tad drove toward town, he began to recall the events of the preceding day at work. It had been one of those days that were becoming increasingly common. Such days left him exhausted—so much so that at home he had begun to argue with his wife and to scold his three children for minor things that had once left him unruffled.

Yesterday the turmoil had started early in the morning when the chairman of the board burst into his office and created a disturbance because she had not yet received last month's statistical data. She had to review it prior to that afternoon's board of directors' meeting, she informed him. Tad had intended to get the statistical information together, but in what little spare time he could find between customers he had made out the monthly report for the Federal Home Loan Bank instead. That deadline could not be ignored.

After the chairman of the board departed, Tad went to tell Picconi that he needed another clerical person to help relieve his workload. Picconi asserted that the association was currently overstaffed and that more efficient use of the personnel on board would solve the problem. Tad agreed with him that the present number of personnel should be adequate, but their efficiency was poor. Picconi took this as a direct criticism of the niece and two cousins he had hired, and a heated argument developed between the two men. Eventually their tempers cooled, and Tad returned to his office and resumed his work.

About two o'clock in the afternoon, Tad stepped out of his office and spotted two customers waiting at the counter. Not a single teller was in evidence. His quick investigation disclosed three tellers downstairs having coffee. Another had gone out for cigarettes, and the fifth was in the supply room stocking up on forms for his window. Tad called Picconi out of his office and quickly pointed out the situation. Picconi snapped, "You take care of it!" Then he ducked back into his office and slammed the door. Tad herded the tellers out of the lunchroom with a sharp reprimand and then went to see Anita Farelli, who was supposed to supervise them.

Anita was in her middle twenties and had worked for Alcala Savings and Loan for nearly five years. At first she had shown marginal interest in her work, but after she got married and her husband entered law school, her interest picked up; now she was progressing quite rapidly.

Tad asked Anita for an explanation of the teller situation. Anita advised him that she had no real control over the tellers. She told Tad that she had asked Picconi for help but got none, and that on occasions when she had attempted to discipline certain tellers, Picconi had reprimanded her for doing so. By this time Tad was sorely frustrated, but he managed to keep himself under control.

Just before five o'clock, Tad's secretary (a Picconi cousin) brought him the typed letters that he had dictated earlier that day. As Tad prepared to sign them, he noted two contained so many errors that he decided to stay late and retype them himself.

Now, as the steeple clock in the center of town struck a single gong, Tad Kadetsky drove into the parking lot pondering why the back door was unlocked. Hadn't Picconi been the last person to leave? "But Mario always checks both doors before he leaves the building . . . could I myself have forgotten?"

Questions for Managerial Action

1. What symptoms of stress is Tad exhibiting in this case?

2. What are the sources of his stress? Is Tad himself responsible for any of these?

3. What could Tad do to improve his management of stress in this situation?

4. How could Tad apply time management techniques to help him regain control and reduce stress?

5. What kind of role conflict exists here? From Tad's perspective, what would be the most effective mode of dealing with it?

Chapter 16

Change and Organizational Development

LEARNING OBJECTIVES

After studying this chapter, you should be able to:

- Identify what factors cause change.
- Understand why people and organizations resist change.
- Discuss the phases of change.
- Describe how change can be planned and implemented.
- Explain the processes of organizational development.
- Describe the tools used in organizational development.
- Explain the characteristics of learning organizations.

FORD PROSPERS BY EMBRACING CHANGE

In the early 1980s, all U.S. automakers were losing ground, and Ford was in the worst shape. Ford was posting record losses of over $3 billion, while its market share was being eaten away by both domestic and foreign competitors. Donald Peterson was named Ford's president in 1980 and decided that if Ford was to again be successful, it had to gain a styling and design advantage over its competitors, and it had to boost the quality level of its products. Peterson decided that to reach these objectives, he had to change the entire culture of the firm into one that would both appreciate and nurture its people. His ace was the installation of participative management from the top to the bottom of the firm.

On May 4, 1983, Ford introduced the first new product of Peterson's participative decision management sold as the Ford Tempo and Mercury Topaz with only minor styling differences. By the end of the 1980s, Ford Motor Company increased its market share from 17 percent to 22 percent while its American rivals, General Motors and Chrysler, lost market share. Many analysts give credit for Ford's success to Chairman Donald E. Petersen, who saw the need for change throughout the entire organization—in Ford's culture, processes, and approach to management. Quality became the key corporate value. Attention shifted to customers and what they wanted in an automobile.

According to Petersen, benchmarking was one of the most important steps Ford took in an effort to improve overall quality. Benchmarking means Ford found out how the best companies conducted critical activities and then compared Ford operations to the way these successful companies did business. Manufacturing processes, design, marketing, financial management, and quality were all compared. The need for change was apparent.

Petersen knew the importance of gaining support for change from all groups within the organization. He included union representatives as well as managers in the benchmarking and idea-generating processes. Ford people learned from a visit to a Mazda factory in Japan the value of simplifying management controls and reducing bureaucracy. They learned that Mazda utilized simpler accounting, inventory management, and information operations. Mazda had fewer managers and levels of management.

Petersen also emphasized teaming, which means bringing together people from several areas within the company to solve problems. The highly successful Ford Taurus illustrates the value of teaming. Ford learned from the Japanese how to include marketing people and accountants with product planners to design and build better cars that appeal to buyers. Team

Taurus sought widespread participation by showing prototypes to workers, who in turn provided more than 1,400 suggestions. Half of these ideas were accepted and implemented in making the Taurus. In an effort not to discourage workers whose ideas were not accepted, explanations as to why their suggestions were not used were given to them personally.

Although implementing change was not easy, Ford management and employees realized that improving quality by making changes throughout the organization was essential for survival and improved sales and profits. The result of these planned efforts was that Taurus became the best-selling car in the United States at the time.

Source: Adapted from *Boardroom Reports* (June, 15, 1992).

change
The process of moving from one condition to another.

Individuals, groups, and organizations must constantly cope with change in order to survive.[1] **Change** is the coping process of moving from the present state to a desired state that individuals, groups, and organizations undertake in response to dynamic internal and external factors.

Fortune magazine first published its list of America's top 500 companies in 1956. Sadly, only 29 companies from the top 100 on the original list remain today. The other 71 have disappeared through dissolution, merger, or downsizing. Survival, even for the most successful companies, cannot be taken for granted. Giants such as General Motors, Ford, and Chrysler know that, to survive, they must adapt to accelerating and increasingly complex environmental dynamics. As the opening vignette suggests, Ford was more successful than General Motors at managing change during the 1980s.

Why is change important to managers and organizations? Simply stated, organizations that do not bring about change in timely ways are unlikely to survive. One reason that the rate of change is accelerating is that knowledge and technology feed on themselves, constantly creating new innovations at exponential rates.

One of the social changes businesses face is accommodating the physically disabled, especially since the Americans with Disabilities Act went into effect in July 1993. Joe Schmidtberger, owner of Alvin's IGA food store in Lawrence, Kansas, helped train his 39 employees to serve customers with disabilities by having those patrons explain their special needs. For example, employees learned from shoppers who use wheelchairs that they need help reaching for merchandise. (Photo: © Chuck Kneyse/Black Star.)

━━━ EXHIBIT 16–1

Forces and Examples of Change

Technology
  Genetic engineering
  Computers and robots
  Total quality management techniques

Economic Conditions
  Recession or expansion
  Interest rate fluctuations
  International labor rates

Global Competition
  Southeast Asia's economic success
  Unification of the European Common Market
  Mergers and consolidations

World Politics
  The collapse of the Soviet Union
  Hong Kong's change from British to Chinese governance
  World sanctions applied to countries violating human rights

Social and Demographic Changes
  Increasing environmental concerns
  Increasing cultural diversity
  Increased education levels of the work force

Internal Problems
  Behavioral problems: high turnover, absenteeism, strikes, sabotage
  Process problems: communications and decision-making breakdowns
  Destructive politics and conflict

WHAT FACTORS CAUSE CHANGE?

Changes in organizations are stimulated by multiple external and internal forces, often interacting to reinforce one another. Managers' responses to these factors, in turn, often have a significant impact on individuals within the organization. Some of the dominant forces that stimulate change in organizations are summarized in Exhibit 16–1.

To survive and prosper, organizations must respond and adapt to these multiple forces. They must innovate and continuously improve their products and services to meet changing customer demands and competition. Technologies must be updated, and new and better ways to organize and manage must be found. As the American automobile industry found out decades ago, complacency and the status quo are dangerous. In the following World Watch, Motorola provides an example of how an American company can proactively take advantage of international changes.

Although external factors can mandate adaptation, the internal changes that occur in organizations sometimes severely and negatively affect the individuals who work in them. For example:

- An aerospace engineer employed for 20 years by a large defense contractor may be suddenly confronted with a layoff because his company's business is declining.
- A semiskilled factory worker who lacks technical skills and knowledge to operate new, high-technology machinery finds her employment terminated.
- The 50-year-old manager employed 25 years is no longer needed because her company eliminated two managerial levels from its structure.
- The fear instilled in those who are still working after 4,000 people have been let go because of a major merger as they wonder if they will be next.

World Watch

Motorola Participates in China's Changing Economy

China is changing from a moderately important economic force to a potential economic powerhouse. China has 1.2 billion people and offers potential for huge markets, low cost production, and technical development. The city of Changan is an example. Its population was 30,000 in 1993, and the city was so poor that many people left to find jobs elsewhere. Today, more than 100,000 people are employed in the 700 factories in the Changan area. The city earned $40 million renting plants to foreign ventures that made products ranging from dolls to precision tools.

Many economists predict that China will average a 7 percent or greater growth rate over the next decade. It is likely China will significantly impact global trade, investment, and raw material flows. Motorola is an example of an American company adapting to change by participating in China's developing economy.

In 1992 Motorola started a small plant in Tianjin that produced paging devices. At first management assumed most of the output would be sold outside China. However, by mid-1993 the entire weekly output of 10,000 units was being sold in China, and it found that total demand within China had increased from 1 million units in 1991 to a projected 4 million units in 1993. Motorola is adapting quickly by investing in expansion. It spent $120 million in 1993 to build a first-phase plant that will produce pagers, simple integrated circuits, and cellular phones. It plans to develop a second-phase plant to manufacture automotive electronics, advanced microprocessors, and walkie-talkie systems. Motorola's total investment will exceed $400 million.

These changes are fraught with problems, including political uncertainties, inflation, and lack of qualified engineers and accountants. Motorola is cooperating with schools by providing scholarships and equipment to help develop an inside track to securing necessary talent. It also is spending millions on its own training programs, including sending Chinese engineers to its Schaumberg, Illinois, headquarters for training. By successfully adapting to changing world markets and sources of product, Motorola is enhancing its own performance and contributing to the development of China. According to Lai Chi-sun, general manager of Motorola-China Ltd., "We no longer talk of the 'potential' market. That market has arrived."

Source: Joyce Barnathan, Pete Engardio, et al., "The Chinese Are Rushing Toward Prosperity—and There Seems No Stopping Their Momentum," *Business Week,* May 17, 1993, pp. 54–69, and personal communication with a Tianjin plant engineering manager.

Changing work force demographics also impact companies. Increasing numbers of women and minorities in managerial and professional positions enhance the human resources available to companies but raise ethical issues about advancement opportunities and pay. The Eye on Ethics box documents examples of inequality issues.

The norm of pervasive change brings problems, challenges, and opportunities. Those individuals, managers, and organizations that recognize the inevitability of change and learn to adapt to and manage it will be most successful. Both people and organizations frequently resist change, even if it is in their best interests. In the next section, we will identify some of the reasons for this resistance.

WHY IS CHANGE OFTEN RESISTED

It is not difficult to recognize resistance to change when explicitly manifest through things like strikes, slowdowns, and complaints. It is more difficult to

Eye on Ethics

Inequality Lingers for Women at Work

One of the important changes in the work world in the past 20 years is the role of women in management. Although nearly one-half of the overall labor force is female and 43 percent of managers are women, only 3 percent are senior executives. These data indicate increasing opportunities for women in management, but many feel the playing field is still not level, especially for higher management levels. They believe that sexual discrimination still creates obstacles for women moving into the executive suits. A *Business Week* poll indicated a majority of women managers believe that a glass ceiling exists in the workplace, and 70 percent believe that a male-dominated culture impedes their progress. A majority (57 percent) believe that the rate of progress for women in corporations has slowed down or stopped altogether.

There is also strong evidence that an across-the-board dollar disparity exists between the pay of men and women. A Census Bureau study estimated that women earn only 70 cents for every dollar earned by men. A Bureau of Labor Statistics study showed that the median wage for women financial managers was 62 percent of that of men, and for women managers of marketing, advertising, and public relations it was 68 percent. One obstacle to addressing the pay gap is salary secrecy. It has been suggested that in many companies pay is a topic more taboo than sex. Some women find out about pay differences through friends in payroll, but most have to use their own clues.

One woman who worked for a well-known bank for eight years observed that her male colleagues could afford expensive homes and things that she could not. Although she ranked number 1 or 2 in profits, her pay did not reflect that performance. When she asked for a raise, she was told a single woman does not need as much money as a man.

Another woman, a geologist, learned by chance that a newly hired male co-worker earned the same as she, even though she had five years of experience. Further investigation revealed that workers with her credentials averaged $40,000 compared with the $26,000 she was being paid. Some believe that many women are at a disadvantage because they are not as skilled at confrontation and salary negotiation. Clearly these data suggest several ethical issues, including those of unequal advancement opportunity, disparity of pay, and secrecy that obscures the differences.

Sources: *Business Week,* June 8, 1992, pp. 74–83; and *The Wall Street Journal,* June 9, 1993, p. B1.

---

detect and cope with implicit resistance, like decreased motivation or loyalty, errors, and absenteeism. Once resistance is detected, however, this does not mean that it should be immediately eliminated. Resistance to change is sometimes beneficial because it promotes functional conflict and debates that can promote more thorough analyses of alternatives and their consequences. On the other hand, excessive or irrational resistance can hinder progress and even survival. Many times, however, change is resisted even when its benefits outweigh its costs. Why does this happen? There are several overlapping reasons why people and organizations resist change.

Why Individuals Resist Change[2]

Individuals at all organizational levels are prone to resisting change. The leaders of many of the companies dropped from the Fortune 500 lists failed to recognize the need to change and adapt in order to survive.

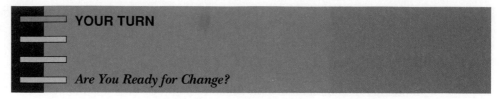

YOUR TURN

Are You Ready for Change?

People vary in their comfort with change. By answering the following questions you can get insight on one aspect of your readiness for change.

Instructions: Circle the number after each question that represents your response. Key: SA = strongly agree; MA = moderately agree; A = agree; N = neither agree nor disagree; D = slightly disagree; MD = moderately disagree; SD = strongly disagree.

	SA						SD
1. An expert who doesn't come up with a definite answer probably doesn't know too much.	7	6	5	4	3	2	1
2. I would like to live in a foreign country for a while.	7	6	5	4	3	2	1
3. There is really no such thing as a problem that can't be solved.	7	6	5	4	3	2	1
4. People who fit their lives to a schedule probably miss most of the job of living.	7	6	5	4	3	2	1
5. A good job is one where what is to be done and how it is to be done are always clear.	7	6	5	4	3	2	1
6. It is more fun to tackle a complicated problem than to solve a simple one.	7	6	5	4	3	2	1
7. In the long run it is possible to get more done by tackling small, simple problems rather than large and complicated ones.	7	6	5	4	3	2	1
8. Often the most interesting and stimulating people are those who don't mind being different and original.	7	6	5	4	3	2	1
9. What we are used to is always preferable to what is unfamiliar.	7	6	5	4	3	2	1
10. People who insist on a yes or no answer just don't know how complicated things really are.	7	6	5	4	3	2	1
11. A person who leads an even, regular life in which few surprises or unexpected happenings arise really has a lot to be grateful for.	7	6	5	4	3	2	1
12. Many of our most important decisions are based on insufficient information.	7	6	5	4	3	2	1
13. I like parties where I know most of the people more than ones where all or most of the people are complete strangers.	7	6	5	4	3	2	1
14. Teachers or supervisors who hand out vague assignments give one a chance to show initiative and originality.	7	6	5	4	3	2	1
15. The sooner we all acquire similar values and ideals the better.	7	6	5	4	3	2	1
16. A good teacher is one who makes you wonder about your way of looking at things.	7	6	5	4	3	2	1

Earlier chapters concerning personality, perception, learning, and motivation provide the basic characteristics of individuals that make them inclined to resist change. The following discussion summarizes five of the main reasons why individuals resist change. You can assess your own comfort level with change by completing the Your Turn exercise.

Interpretation: The instrument you have just completed assesses your tolerance of ambiguity, which is the ability to cope with uncertain, conflicting, or complex situations. People who feel comfortable with sudden change, novelty, and uncertainty have a high tolerance for ambiguity, and those who feel uncomfortable have a low tolerance for ambiguity. The quiz on the previous page measures three dimensions. One is your tolerance for novelty—new and unexpected situations. The second is your tolerance for complexity—lots of information that may not all be relevant and organized, and which may be conflicting or incomplete. The third dimension is your tolerance of problem-solving situations in which answers are not readily discovered. People with a high tolerance of ambiguity are better able to cope with unstructured and dynamic situations characterized by uncertainty and ambiguity. It is not surprising that effective managers usually have a high tolerance for ambiguity. The level of an individual's tolerance for ambiguity is a fairly fixed personality trait, but it can be modified and changed with conscious effort by those who want to make such a change. Becoming more accepting of ambiguity as a natural condition in the world today helps to cope with the change and uncertainty that inevitably faces each of us.

Scoring Instructions for Tolerance and Ambiguity:
1. Reverse the scores for even-numbered items. This means for the even-numbered items only, 7 = 1, 6 = 2, 5 = 3, 4 = 4, 3, = 5, 2 = 6, and 1 = 7.
2. Sum the scores for all 16 items (using the reverse scores from step 1) to get your total score.
3. Compute your subscores using the following:
   (N) Novelty Score (2, 9, 11, 13)
   (C) Complexity Score (4, 5, 6, 7, 8, 10, 14, 15)
   (I) Insolubility Score (1, 3, 12)

Total Score:
The average range is 44 to 48. Scores below 44 indicate high tolerance for ambiguity. Scores above 48 indicate high intolerance for ambiguity.

Source: From *Journal of Personality* 30 (1962), pp. 29–50. Duke University Press. Reprinted with the permission of the publisher.

Selective Perception. In Chapter 5, we observed that people sometimes perceive the same thing differently. When changes are initiated, individuals tend to focus on how they will be personally affected rather than seeing the big picture for the entire organization. For example, assume a manager announces that members of his group will henceforth be paid on a piecework rather than an hourly basis. Irma, who is fast and highly skilled, may eagerly embrace the change as an opportunity to increase her pay. Angelo, a new employee, may object for fear he will fall behind the others. At other times, individuals may perceive that change is incompatible with personal beliefs and values.

Lack of Information. People will resist change if they lack knowledge as to what is expected or why the change is important. Many people take the attitude that "if it's not broken, don't fix it." If the reasons for change are not clearly presented, they tend to fill in the missing pieces with speculation, which often assumes the worst in terms of initiator intentions and personal impact. In addition, if people don't have enough information about how to change, they may fear making mistakes, so they will not try.

Fear of the Unknown.   Individuals resist change when they are uncertain about how it will affect their well-being. They ask themselves, for example, How will downsizing or new automation affect my job security?[3] Other fears include uncertainties about not knowing how to change or of not being able to perform as well as before the change, losing position, income, status, or power. There is also the possibility that work will be less convenient or more difficult, and the potential of losing desirable social interactions.

Habit.   People prefer familiar actions and events, even if they are not optimal. Have you ever tried to break a bad habit like smoking, drinking too much coffee, or not exercising? Breaking a habit is difficult because it takes hard work and involves giving up perceived benefits from the habit, even if the new behavior has more desirable consequences.

Resentment toward the Initiator.   If a change seems arbitrary or unreasonable, or its timing and manner of implementation lack concern for the people, resentment and anger are often directed toward those initiating the change. People also resent being controlled and losing autonomy over their work lives when their thoughts and feelings are not considered by change initiators. Finally, without trust in the initiators' intentions, people may resist the change out of resentment or fear of possible unknown consequences.

Why Organizations Resist Change

Organizations resist change for many of the same reasons individuals do. In addition, many organizational practices minimize risk taking; if a process is working satisfactorily, they quite often won't change it until they are forced to.[4] There are also many forces inside an organization that create resistance to changes initiated by environmental conditions.[5] Some of the main ones are summarized below.

Power Maintenance.   Changes in decision making authority and control of resource allocations threaten the balance of power in organizations. Units benefiting from the change will endorse it, but those losing power will resist it, which can often slow or prevent the change process. Managers, for example, often resist the establishment of self-managed work teams. Or, manufacturing departments often resist letting purchasing departments control input quality.

Structural Stability.   Recall from Chapter 4 that organizations create hierarchies, subgroups, rules, and procedures to promote order and guide behaviors. People who "fit" these desired behavioral criteria are hired and shaped to conform further through the socialization process and organizational conditioning. These organizational structures, rules, and conditioning are designed to develop consistent, predictable behaviors. Such behaviors resist change. Furthermore, as we described in Chapter 1, an organization is a system of interrelated structures or subsystems. A change in any one area will have effects on others, which may not be acceptable.

Functional Suboptimization.   Differences in functional orientation, goals, and resource dependencies can cause changes that are seen as beneficial to one functional unit to be perceived as threatening to another. Functional units usually think of themselves first when evaluating potential changes. They support those that enhance their own welfare, but resist the ones that reduce it or seem unequitable.

━━━━ **EXHIBIT 16–2** *Methods for Dealing with Resistance to Change*

Approach	Commonly Used	Advantages	Drawbacks
Education and communication	Where there is a lack of information or inaccurate information and analysis.	Once persuaded, people will often help with the implementation of the change.	Can be very time consuming if lots of people are involved.
Participation and involvement	Where the initiators do not have all the information they need to design the change, and where others have considerable power to resist.	People who participate will be committed to implementing change, and any relevant information they have will be integrated into the change plan.	Can be very time consuming if participants design an inappropriate change.
Facilitation and support	Where people are resisting because of adjustment problems.	No other approach works as well with adjustment problems.	Can be time consuming, expensive, and still fail.
Negotiation and agreement	Where someone or some group will clearly lose out in a change, and where that group has considerable power to resist.	Sometimes it is a relatively easy way to avoid major resistance.	Can be too expensive in many cases if it alerts others to negotiate for compliance.
Manipulation and co-optation	Where other tactics will not work, or are too expensive.	It can be a relatively quick and inexpensive solution to resistance problems.	Can lead to future problems if people feel manipulated.
Explicit and implicit coercion	Where speed is essential, and the change initiators possess considerable power.	It is speedy, and can overcome any kind of resistance.	Can be risky if it leaves people mad at the initiators.

Organizational Culture. Chapter 4 discussed how organizational culture, that is, established values, norms, and expectations, acts to promote predictable ways of thinking and behaving. Organizational members will resist changes that force them to abandon established and approved of ways of doing things.

Group Norms. As discussed in Chapter 10, groups develop their own norms to promote desirable behaviors. Most members conform to these norms, especially in cohesive groups. Consequently, any change that disrupts group norms, tasks, or role relationships will probably be resisted. Groups also suboptimize to ensure their own self-interests, often at the expense of the larger organization. This means that groups will often resist changes that do not directly benefit them individually.

Managers sometimes mistakenly assume that subordinates will perceive the desired changes as they do; thus, they have difficulty understanding the resistance. As we have just discussed, there are more reasons to assume that people will perceive the desired change differently. A key task is to determine and understand the reasons behind people's resistance when it occurs. Then the challenge is to find ways to reduce or overcome that resistance.

Overcoming Resistance to Change

Research has identified six general strategies for overcoming resistance to change.[6] Exhibit 16–2 illustrates the kinds of situations in which these approaches might be used, along with the advantages and disadvantages of each. It is the manager's job to match the demands of a change situation with the best approach to overcoming resistance with minimum disruption.

As manager of Aetna Life & Casualty Co.'s Work/Family Strategies unit, Michelle M. Carpenter promotes the benefits of flexible schedules. Before the Work/Family Strategies unit was created in 1988, hundreds of female employees quit after taking maternity leave. Between July 1991 and June 1992, 88% of workers who took family leave returned to work. Roughly 2,000 of Aetna's 44,000 employees work part-time, share a job, work at home, or work a compressed work-week. Carpenter opted for the compressed week, leaving more time with her sons. (Photo: © Rob Kinmonth.)

Education and Communication.   Help people learn beforehand the reasons for the change, how it will take form, and what the likely consequences will be. Even if the consequences of a change are generally perceived as positive, extensive communication is required to reduce anxiety and ensure that people understand what is happening, what will be expected of them, and how they will be supported in adapting to change.[7]

Participation and Involvement.   Encourage those involved to help design and implement the changes in order to draw out their ideas and to foster commitment. Participation increases understanding, enhances feelings of control, reduces uncertainty, and promotes a feeling of ownership when change directly affects people. It is difficult for people to resist changes that they themselves have helped bring about.

Facilitation and Support.   Provide encouragement, support, training, counseling, and resources to help those affected by the change adapt to new requirements. By accepting people's anxiety as legitimate and helping them cope with change, managers have a better chance of gaining respect and the commitment to make it work.

Negotiation and Agreement.   Bargain to offer incentives in return for agreement to change. This tactic is often necessary when dealing with powerful resisters, like bargaining units. Sometimes specific things can be exchanged in return for help in bringing about a change. Other times, general perks can be widely distributed to help make the change easier to undertake.

Manipulation and Co-optation.   *Manipulation* is framing and selectively using information and implied incentives to maximize the likelihood of acceptance. An example would be if management tells employees that accepting a pay cut is necessary to avoid a plant shutdown, when plant closure would not really have to

Under corporate pressure to be number one in its markets, GE's Electric Motors Division needed to restructure to better compete in the marketplace. In the late 1980s the company demanded pay cuts from its hourly workers and closed 2 of its 12 motor plants. They guaranteed the remaining 5,400 workers jobs for three years and spent $200 million for new equipment and product development. GE's strategy of change caused morale and productivity to dive. GE is now rethinking its strategies along the lines of teamwork, quality, and just-in-time work flows. (Photo: © 1993 Joe McNally.)

occur. *Co-optation* is influencing resistant parties to endorse the change effort by providing them with benefits they desire and noninfluencial roles in the process.

Explicit and Implicit Coercion. Some managers use authority and the threat of negative incentives to force acceptance of the proposed change. Management might decide that if employees do not accept proposed changes, then it will have to shut the plant down, decrease salaries, or lay off people.

HOW DO MANAGERS PREPARE FOR PLANNED CHANGE?

planned change
The process of preparing and taking actions to move from one condition to a more desired one.

Change can be planned or unplanned. Unplanned change just happens in the natural course of events or is imposed on an organization by external forces. Organizations and individuals then react to these unplanned changes in order to maintain or improve their situation. On the other hand, **planned change** is the result of consciously preparing for and taking actions to reach a desired goal or organizational state. It involves proactively making things different rather than reacting to changes imposed from outside the organization. The key questions to be answered when planning change are:

1. *What* do we want to achieve? What are our goals?
2. *Why?* What are our performance gaps?
3. *Who* will be the change agents responsible for making the change?
4. *How* do we plan to make that happen? What targets do we want to change and what process will we apply to change them?
5. What organizational *consequences* do we anticipate from the change?

Goals of Planned Change

Planned changes attempt to accomplish two general types of outcomes. The first type is aimed at improving the organization's ability to cope with unplanned changes that are thrust on it. Changes in this area include increasing the effectiveness of information gathering and forecasting systems, and the organization's flexibility so that it can adapt in appropriate and timely ways. Advanced knowledge of competitors' new products, changes in governmental regulations, or supply limitations can prepare organizations for what they need to do to adapt.

A second type of planned change is targeted at changing employees' behaviors to make them more effective contributors to the organization's goals. Changes in this category include instilling new attitudes, values, and ways of visualizing the organization and employee roles in it, as well as training to improve productivity, interpersonal relationships, and creative contributions.

Performance Gaps between Present and Desired Future

To sharpen the focus in determining why to change, various processes can be used to dramatize the difference between the status quo and the desired new standard of performance or desired organizational state. Previously, the six-panel photo essay in Chapter 2 showed the steps some managers use to engage those involved in the change in creating a visual gap analysis. And recall in the opening vignette that Donald Petersen saw a significant performance gap between Ford's quality of output and what which was essential for competing with the Japanese and other auto companies.

Change Agents

change agent
An individual or group responsible for changing behavior and systems.

Individuals or groups who assume responsibility for changing behavior and systems are called **change agents.** Ford's CEO Donald Petersen was the chief change agent responsible for significantly transforming the way people performed at Ford Motor Company in the 1980s. But often it is the managers or staff at lower levels in organizations who serve as change agents. Their role is to recognize the need for altering the status quo and to plan and manage the implementation of the desired changes. Psychologists and consultants are frequently called into organizations as quasi-independent change agents to help members devise new ways to cope and even thrive with dramatic changes.[8]

Targets and Process of Change

Change agents identify the level at which their efforts will be directed. Levels can be targeted to change individuals, groups, and/or entire organizations. Each represents a different level, or unit, of change. Change efforts may even be directed toward the *transorganizational level,* which means the relationships between one company and others. For example, Ford Motor Company worked to change its relationships with several of its suppliers during the 1980s to develop just-in-time (JIT) delivery schedules. But the General Motors experience of 1996 demonstrated that taking less than a systemwide approach at changing to an efficient JIT inventory flow can leave the organization vulnerable. Strikes in two GM brake plants quickly caused closures of 23 of GM's 29 assembly plants and layoffs of over 100,000 employees because of parts shortages.[9]

Change agents also must focus on specific targets to alter in attempting to close performance gaps and reach desired objectives. Organizational targets for change include people, technology, jobs and work flows, organizational structure and processes, culture, and management. Exhibit 16–3 shows examples of how each of these targets can be changed.

Targets	Examples
Individual	• Fire a person and replace him or her with someone new. • Change knowledge, skill, attitude, or behavior.
Technology	• Replace existing technology with a more modern machine or way of doing work.
Structure	• Change from a functional structure to a product division structure. • Add a new department or division, or consolidate two existing ones.
Processes	• Change the pay system from hourly wages to salaries.
Culture	• Implement a program to encourage valuing quality and service.
Management	• Encourage participation in the diagnosis and solution of problems by people at lower levels to replace a top-down approach.

After the level and target have been decided on, the change agent needs to determine what will actually be changed—the *content,* and what *process* will bring it about. For example, assume a manager is concerned about decreasing productivity among the clerical staff. She thinks the cause might be excessive talking among staff members. In order to discourage talking among the clerical staff, she may decide to move their desks farther apart or place partitions between them. This is a content change.

How this manager introduces and implements the change is the process. For example, she may decide to announce the change by memo or in a staff meeting, or she might have the desks moved during the night so that the clerks find out about the change when they come to work the next day. Each of these three approaches to process might lead to different results, some quite unintended—including more serious morale problems within the organization.

More change efforts fail, or achieve less-than-expected results, because of inadequate process than because of poor content. Successful change often requires as much thought given to process as to content. Top-level managers and staff people sometimes neglect process because they are often removed from the day-to-day happenings in a particular work unit. They focus on the logic and quality of the content and forget or underestimate the importance of how people will perceive and react to any change they decide to implement. Managers sometimes assume that others will perceive the logic and value of the change just as they do. Often they are badly mistaken.

When planning change and evaluating alternatives, managers must pay attention both to the quality of the proposed content and to the probability of its acceptance. For instance, in the desk-arranging example, the manager should assess whether the benefits of the change in desk arrangement will outweigh potential costs. She should also predict the probability of acceptance of the change by employees. If that probability is too low and the benefits of the idea are marginal, she should look for a different approach.

Anticipating Organizational Consequences: The Systems Approach

Because these various elements are all part of an interdependent system, a change in any single target often leads to changes in the others. For example, when companies introduced networked computers to improve productivity, a series of changes followed. First, people had to learn new skills because of the new technology. Often, a new data processing department was introduced into the structure.

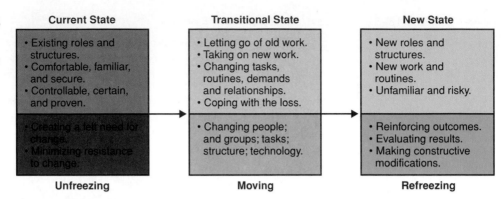

EXHIBIT 16–4

Three Phases of Planned Change in Organizations

Current State	Transitional State	New State
• Existing roles and structures. • Comfortable, familiar, and secure. • Controllable, certain, and proven.	• Letting go of old work. • Taking on new work. • Changing tasks, routines, demands and relationships. • Coping with the loss.	• New roles and structures. • New work and routines. • Unfamiliar and risky.
• Creating a felt need for change. • Minimizing resistance to change.	• Changing people; and groups; tasks; structure; technology.	• Reinforcing outcomes. • Evaluating results. • Making constructive modifications.
Unfreezing	**Moving**	**Refreezing**

Source: Adapted from Kurt Lewin's model of change.

People throughout the organization had to learn a new vocabulary, and the way information was processed began to change. Over time, jobs were altered. For example, the need for middle managers decreased in some companies as computers facilitated the organization and flow of information and made possible decision making at lower levels.

Not all change is as pervasive as the introduction of computer technology, but it is common for changes to ripple throughout an entire organization. Managers sometimes make a "simple" change without considering the systems implications. This often leads to unintended consequences.

For example, assume that manager Jean Cohen wants to improve her assistant's attendance record. Cohen offers to let her have one day off for every two months of perfect attendance. Indeed, her effort is successful in that her assistant seldom misses a day of work. However, she also tells the other assistants in the department, who complain to their bosses that they do not have a similar incentive. Their bosses in turn complain to Cohen's supervisor, who reprimands her. This result might have been avoided if Cohen had discussed her approach with her peers and supervisor before unilaterally making the change.

WHAT ARE THE PHASES OF PLANNED CHANGE?

One of the earliest and most utilized ways of identifying the phases of planned change was developed by Kurt Lewin, a noted social psychologist. His model, illustrated in Exhibit 16–4, contains three phases: unfreezing, changing, and refreezing.[10]

unfreezing
Raising awareness that current conditions are not satisfactory and reducing resistance to desired change.

Unfreezing involves helping people to see that a change is needed because the existing situation is not adequate. Existing attitudes and behaviors need to be altered during this phase so that resistance to change is minimized. The manager in the previous desk-arranging example must give some thought to how employees should be prepared for the change. She may do this by explaining how the change can help increase productivity, but she will also probably have to convince the clerks that their social satisfaction will not be lowered or that this cost will be worth some other gain they care about. The manager's goal is to help the clerks see the need for change and to increase their willingness to make the change a success.

moving
Letting go of old ways of doing things and adopting new behaviors.

The second phase involves **moving,** or making the change, which involves letting go of old ways of doing things and initiating relationships for new ones. This is difficult because of the anxiety involved in letting go of the comfortable and familiar to

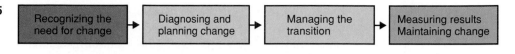

━━━ EXHIBIT 16–5

The Planned Change Process

| Recognizing the need for change | → | Diagnosing and planning change | → | Managing the transition | → | Measuring results Maintaining change |

learn new ways of behaving, with new people, doing different tasks with perhaps more complex technology. In the desk example, that means moving the desks and reinforcing the desired attitudes and behaviors of the clerks. In more complex changes, several targets of change may need to be changed simultaneously.

The third phase, **refreezing,** involves reinforcing the changes made so that the new ways of behaving become stabilized. If people perceive the change to be working in their favor, positive results will serve as reinforcement. If they perceive the change as not working in their favor, it may be necessary for the manager to use external reinforcers, which can be positive or negative.[11] For example, the manager might encourage the employees to keep working at the change by predicting that desired positive results will come. Or she might even promise a small reward, such as a lunch or an afternoon off, when the change has been completed successfully. Sometimes a more coercive approach to reinforcement is either necessary or appropriate. The goal of this phase of the change process is to cause the desired attitudes and behaviors to become a natural, self-reinforcing pattern.

refreezing
Reinforcing the changes made to stabilize new ways of behaving.

HOW IS THE PLANNED CHANGE PROCESS MANAGED?

Building on Lewin's three phases of planned change, Exhibit 16–5 shows the steps required in planning and implementing change. In real situations, these steps are not always followed in sequence, but effective change normally includes each of them.

Recognizing the Need for Change

The need for change is sometimes obvious, as when results are not in line with expectations, things clearly are not working well, or dissatisfaction is apparent. As the "pain" in such situations increases, so does the incentive to change.

On the other hand, sometimes the need for change is less obvious. If all appears to be going well, there is little or no incentive to change. This applies to both individuals and companies. For example, assume that Jack is performing satisfactorily in his accounting job but has neglected to update his computer skills. Without warning, Jack's manager announces a change in the programs being used that requires skills Jack lacks. Frances, on the other hand, has completed a specialized computer skills course and knows the new program. The manager decides that Frances will take over Jack's position, and Jack is moved to a lower-level job. Jack mistakenly assumed that his ability to handle his current job translated into future security. He failed to anticipate the changing demands created by changes in technology. Frances anticipated the change and was better prepared to adapt when change came.

Companies also miss signals in changing markets, and because they are performing successfully, assume all is well. Significant changes can suddenly occur, causing serious trouble. IBM, for example, epitomized success in the computer industry in the 1980s. Unfortunately, its leaders failed to recognize the speed and scope of changes occurring both in its customer base and among competitors. Constant changes in microchip technology led to progressively powerful personal computers that could do the work done previously by larger mainframe computers for many types of tasks. IBM executives failed to appreciate the impact the more powerful personal computers would have on IBM's mainframe business.

Both individuals and top management need to monitor their environments to anticipate and recognize changes that might affect them. These changes can occur in knowledge, skills, and technology. Companies also face changes in customers, regulators, competitors, and suppliers. One of the key roles of top managers is to monitor environments and to adapt strategies to achieve success. Review the previous World Watch box on how Motorola adapted to change by participating in China's developing economy.

Diagnosing and Planning Change

Once the need for change has been recognized and a decision made to make a change, a series of questions needs answering.

- What are our specific goals?
- Who are the involved stakeholders?
- What are the forces driving and restraining change?
- What contingencies should be considered?
- What process strategies will we use?
- What interventions will we use?
- How will we measure success?

Goals.   The general planned change goals of preparing an organization to cope with external changes and enhancing its employees' competencies were discussed in the above section on planning change. The first thing a change agent needs to do is determine what specific things need to be changed to achieve the desired situation. In doing so, it is important to distinguish between immediate and longer-term objectives and between means and objectives.

For example, assume that a production manager needs to achieve greater output. He may assume that the way to accomplish this is to add machines. If he mistakenly defines his goal to be adding more machines without evaluating other options, he decreases the chances of making the best decision. Another option would be to add people and operate a second shift. Another would be to reengineer existing processes to achieve greater output with existing machines and people. Both of the latter options offer more flexibility in case the need for increased output is temporary. It helps a manager choose the appropriate alternative if both short-term and long-term goals are clearly defined.

Stakeholders.   When planning a change, all groups of people who might be affected by the change should be considered. They are the stakeholders discussed in Chapter 1. Such groups might include employees, managers, owners/stockholders, suppliers, customers, and even regulators. For example, management might decide to increase employees' pay to encourage motivation, but in doing so might irritate stockholders who view the increase as an unnecessary expense that cuts into earnings. Or a manager might eliminate a step in his department's procedures to increase his group's efficiency, but thereby cause the work of another department to increase.

EXHIBIT 16–6

Example Force-Field Analysis for the Automobile Industry of the 1970s

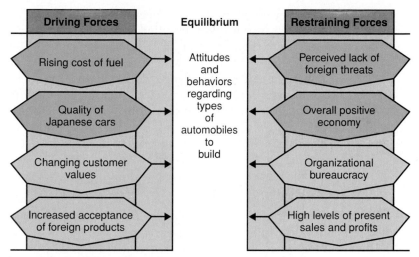

Source: R. D. Gatewood, R. R. Taylor, and O. C. Ferrell, *Management: Comprehension, Analysis, and Application* (Chicago: Richard D. Irwin, 1995), p. 562.

Driving and Restraining Forces. Kurt Lewin envisioned any potential change situation as an interplay of multiple opposing forces.[12] Social systems tend toward a state of equilibrium, or balanced stability. For change to occur, it is necessary to trip the balance of forces so that the system (be it an individual, group, or organization) can move toward a new level of balance. Lewin developed the model of a force field to promote comprehensive and systematic analysis of potential factors that should be considered when evaluating alternative ways to promote positive changes.

force-field analysis
The process analyzing the forces that drive change and those that restrain it.

Force-field analysis is the process of analyzing the forces that drive change and the forces that restrain it. *Driving forces* push toward courses of action that are new or different from the status quo. *Restraining forces* exert pressure to continue past behaviors or to resist new actions. If these opposing forces are approximately equal, there will be no movement away from the status quo. For change to occur, the driving forces must be increased (in number or intensity) and/or the restraining forces must be reduced. An example of a force-field analysis is diagrammed in Exhibit 16–6.

Force-field analysis is a useful diagnostic tool for the change agent. First, it assumes multiple forces, thus preventing oversimplified cause-and-effect thinking. Second, it recognizes that change can be brought about by different strategies, including increasing driving forces, reducing restraining forces, or combining the two strategies. It can be especially useful if the manager as change agent analyzes forces from two different perspectives—first, relative to his or her own goals, then from the point of view of those who are expected to implement change. This exercise typically reveals overlooked forces.

Considering Contingencies to Determine the Best Processes and Interventions.
The best way to change a given situation depends on various contingency factors—the critical factors in the situation that make one strategy more appropriate than another. Key contingent factors to consider include time; importance; anticipated resistance; power positions; ability, knowledge, and resources required; and source of relevant data.[13]

For example, if a change needs to be made quickly, is not critically important, and resistance is not anticipated, using direct authority may be appropriate. However, if the change is important, resistance is anticipated, and the power position of the "changees" is relatively high, a participative approach might be more suitable. The key point is that change agents should consider the situation in terms of its contingent factors and then select the most appropriate strategy for intervention.

intervention
A planned process that introduces change.

Social, structural, and technical change techniques that are guided by a change agent are referred to as *interventions*. An **intervention** is a planned process of introducing change involving an individual, group, or organization, usually with its help. It must be decided who will do what, when, where, and how. We will discuss several interventions in the following section on organizational development interventions.

Measuring Results.   The last step in the diagnostic and planning process includes deciding the criteria for success, how results will be measured, and what will determine when the change effort can cease.

Managing the Transition[14]

Introducing and implementing a change seldom leads immediately to the desired results because people often require time to learn how to behave differently. Individual performance often declines during the learning period, sometimes inducing fear and anxiety among employees. During this period, there may be a strong desire to return to more familiar and proven behaviors. This doubt and fear may be reinforced if individuals share their concerns and complaints with one another.

Change agents can help people get through the transition period by anticipating subpar performance and attitudinal problems and being ready with increased support, education, encouragement, and resources to help employees adapt. As people learn how to perform under the changed conditions and as they begin to perceive positive results, the external supports given by the change agent can be reduced. People begin to internalize their newly learned behaviors.

During the transition, the change agents need to set up managing structures to monitor results and keep actions on track. Usually special project managers, committees, and interest groups are set up to assess and manage the change transition.

Measuring Results and Maintaining Change[15]

The change agent needs to determine if the change is progressing as planned and accomplishing desired results. Information needs to be gathered through feedback mechanisms such as surveys, sensing groups, or interviews, and then compared to desired outcomes. If, as it is often discovered, initial enthusiasm has faded as changes encounter operating problems, change agents need to intervene to sustain the momentum by providing assistance, training, and resources. It also helps to develop support groups, set up special meetings and off-site retreats, and provide the means for steady reinforcement (e.g., praise, bonuses, award dinners) of those changing.

organizational development (OD)
The systemwide application of behavioral science knowledge to the planned change process to improve organization effectiveness.

WHAT IS ORGANIZATIONAL DEVELOPMENT (OD)?

A special subset of planned change is organizational development (OD). OD started out as an eclectic set of behavioral science tools and practices but has now become a professional field of social action and scientific inquiry. **OD** can be

Radical changes are taking place in the health-care industry. In response to those changes, US Pharmaceuticals, a Bristol-Myers Squibb Group, has dramatically restructured its sales force to meet the needs of new customers who are often large-volume buyers like managed care plans and hospital systems. To better serve the Rutgers Health Plan, sales respresentative Cynthia Banks (photo) uses a laptop computer to dial into a central database to obtain information on products, prices, and inventory. (Source: Courtesy of Bristol-Myers Squibb Company.)

defined as a systemwide application of behavioral science knowledge to the planned development and reinforcement of organizational strategies, structures, and processes for improving an organization's effectiveness.[16]

The Nature of Organizational Development

OD encompasses a wide variety of planned-change interventions, built on participative values, that seek to improve organizational effectiveness and employee well-being. Organizational effectiveness includes productivity (efficiency and effectiveness), people's satisfaction with the quality of their work life, and the ability of the organization to revitalize and develop itself over time. OD can be differentiated from change in the following ways:

- Generally, OD focuses on changing an entire system in contrast to only one or a few components. (A system might include a group, department, division, organization, or even a group of organizations.)
- OD involves the application of behavioral science knowledge and techniques in contrast to operations research, industrial engineering, or other deterministic disciplines.

- OD focuses on helping people and organizations learn how to diagnose and solve their own problems in contrast to relying on others for solutions.
- OD is often more adaptive and less rigid than structural-mechanistic change approaches. Although it does include a formal planning component, OD is a flexible, ongoing process of diagnosing and solving people-related problems, which can change with new discoveries and developments.

The difference between focusing on changing just one component and changing a whole system can be illustrated by comparing management development to OD. Assume that a successful manager is sent to a training program sponsored by a leading business school or consulting firm. Assume that she gains new insights as a result of the training and decides to change. She then returns to her workplace, only to find that her boss, subordinates, peers, structure, processes, and culture all remain unchanged. Before long, she is likely to revert to those behaviors she previously found successful in that system. In order to achieve significant change, it is likely that several of the components will need to be altered simultaneously. OD looks at the total system.

OD Values

OD is a value-driven process.[17] It emphasizes human and organizational growth, collaborative and participative processes, and a spirit of inquiry.[18] The underlying OD meta-values include:[19]

- *Respect for people.* People should be treated with dignity and respect because they are perceived as responsible, conscientious, and caring.
- *Trust and Support.* Effective organizations have regenerative interaction climates (see Chapter 9). They are characterized by trust, authenticity, openness, and support.
- *Power equalization.* To achieve the best collaboration, organizations should emphasize egalitarian participation and deemphasize authority and control hierarchies.
- *Confrontation.* Problems should be shared and confronted so that they can be openly dealt with by all concerned.
- *Participation.* Those who will be living with the change should be involved in planning and implementing it. If they understand it, and participate in planning it, they will be more committed to implementing it.

OD Practitioners

OD is usually carried out by a professional change agent who is either a consultant from outside the organization or from an internal staff department within it that is separate from the unit being assisted.[20] External consultants offer their services to many organizations, while internal consultants provide their services to units within a single organization. Both kinds of OD consultants help individuals and groups to diagnose their own problems, develop solutions, and take action to improve processes and outputs.

In addition to the full-time professionals, some managers and staff people have developed sufficient knowledge and skill to be able to apply OD approaches to their own work areas.[21] A growing number of companies, including General Motors, Hewlett-Packard, Polaroid, TRW, Honeywell, and General Electric, have programs to train managers how to develop and change their own work units.[22] Other

OD Practices Revive Ailing Xerox

Xerox introduced the first plain-paper copier in 1959, and a new industry was born. Xerox's growth was spectacular, and its name became synonymous with all photocopying. Apparently growth and success came too easily, and Xerox became complacent. This state abruptly ended during the early 1980s, when low-cost Japanese competition cut Xerox's market share of copiers in half.

In the mid-1980s, Xerox started a major change effort to regain its premier market position. A comprehensive program based on total quality was applied to all areas, including product development, manufacturing, and customer service. Titled "Leadership through Quality," its success was evidenced by Xerox's becoming the first

major U.S. company to win back market share from the Japanese. It also increased its return on assets from 9 percent to 14 percent.

Xerox learned its lesson, and it shuns complacency. When Paul Allaire became CEO, he started a systematic, methodical organizational redesign to help implement a new strategy positioning Xerox as "the document company." Managerial roles, selection systems, reward systems, values, and other organizational elements were all redefined and changed. Xerox is well positioned for success in a quickly changing, competitive global environment.

Source: Robert Howard, "The CEO as Organizational Architect: An Interview with Xerox's Paul Allaire," *Harvard Business Review* (September–October 1992), pp. 106–121.

managers develop competence in specialized areas such as reward systems, stress management, or career planning and development. This has enabled some organizations to manage change both faster and more effectively. Other companies, like Procter & Gamble, have programs that develop managers' OD skills by rotating them into full-time OD roles.[23] See the Challenge of Change box to learn how CEO Paul Allaire acted as a change agent when he tackled change head on to pull Xerox out of a dangerous slump.

OD Processes

OD processes have emerged from four primary sources originating in both the United States and Europe.[24] These have been combined to an eclectic approach today that is centered around the action research model described below.

Sources. The first source was the development of *sensitivity training groups* by the National Training Laboratories (NTL) as a way of giving individuals feedback about themselves in unstructured situations. Over time, more structured approaches developed into what we know today as team building, which was discussed in Chapter 10.

A second source was the development of *survey research* and feedback. The thrust of this approach is to survey people at various levels in organizations to ascertain their attitudes toward work, supervision, working conditions, pay and benefits, and other related job factors. The results are then fed back to managers. In many cases, the survey data are shared with supervisors and workers, who use them to decide how to work more effectively.

The emergence of OD can also be traced to the new focus on productivity and quality of work life. One important contributor to this new emphasis was London's

Tavistock Institute of Human Relations. Professor Eric Trist and others developed what was to become known as a *sociotechnical systems* approach to organizational development, discussed in Chapter 3. This approach combines the existing interest in human satisfaction at work with the technical aspects that increase efficiency and productivity—for example, reward systems, work flows, the physical work environment, and management styles.[25]

A fourth source of OD is *action research,* which combines research findings with action applications to help organizational members change and become more effective. Action research emphasizes the collaboration of social scientists and organizational members in designing and measuring efforts to improve organizational effectiveness.[26]

Today OD practitioners use two basic strategies to achieve their objectives of helping to improve organization effectiveness and to enhance the welfare of organization members—the human process and technostructural approaches.[27] The *human process approach* emphasizes human needs and values and focuses on improving interpersonal, group, and intergroup relationships and processes. The *technostructural approach* emphasizes efficiency and productivity and focuses primarily on work flows and processes, organization structure, the integration of technology and people, and performance. Most OD practioners work with both approaches. They are adept at helping managers change organizational structure and culture, which requires an understanding of a client organization's strategy, technology, organizational values, and of the business itself.[28]

action research
Data collection, analysis, and problem diagnosis, the results of which are provided to the client system to help decide on plans for improvement.

Action Research.   The heart of the OD process is **action research.** Before a change agent intervenes, a client system is at least symptomatically aware of a problem. It is important for the change agent to thoroughly diagnose and analyze problems so that the data can be fed back to participants. Then they can collaboratively decide on an action plan. After implementation, outcomes are evaluated to determine if any further actions are needed. The action research model is an extension of the planned change process and is diagrammed in Exhibit 16–7.

In actual practice, these steps overlap, and they provide only a general guide to what must be done. OD is not an exact science, and part of the art is developing steps to be taken as the process moves along. Rigid, standardized approaches are seldom successful, and the best practitioners are adept at innovating and adapting to the unfolding situation.

Example of OD in Action

The general OD process can be illustrated by the following actual experience, which shows some of the steps taken by one organization to manage change.

Elsie White, a superintendent (second-level supervisor) at General Insurance Company, called Rob Henry, who had worked with the company for several years on a variety of management problems. Elsie asked Rob if he would conduct a two-hour team-building session for the clerical staff. She said she was on a committee of four other superintendents, and they had decided a team-building seminar was needed.

Sensing and Identifying the Problem.   Rob asked Elsie what the committee hoped to achieve with the seminar. She explained that morale was low, absenteeism was rather high, cooperation was lacking, and people were having trouble

━━━ **EXHIBIT 16–7**

Action Research Method

◆ Sensing and Identifying the Problem

◆ Engaging an OD Practitoner

◆ Collecting Data

◆ Feeding Data Back to Client Group

◆ Joint Diagnosis of Problem

◆ Implementing the Action Plan

◆ Evaluating Results and Deciding on Further Steps

getting along. After additional conversation, Rob sensed that more than a two-hour seminar was needed to improve this situation. He suggested he meet with the committee to discuss the problem in more depth before holding any seminar for the clerical staff.

During this early step, it is important for the OD practitioner or change agent to listen carefully and to avoid making hasty judgments about the nature of the problem. Experienced OD professionals know that perceptions differ from person to person. They also know a manager's initial diagnosis may not be complete or accurate. During this early period, the OD agent keeps an open mind about the nature of the situation. The goal is to learn more and to understand as much as possible about the system involved.

Engaging an OD Practitioner.   Rob met with the committee a few days later. As the supervisors talked, he learned the following:

- The supervisors were all members of Claims Section A, which consisted of 12 units, each with a superintendent, five or six professional-level claims representatives, and two clerical people.

- One of the two clerical people in each unit was a secretary, grade 4; the other was a mail and file clerk, grade 3.

- Until a few months ago, the mail and file clerks were all grouped together under one supervisor, and this unit did all of the filing and mail collection and delivery for the 12 units. The change was made to help foster a feeling of being a team and to improve productivity.

- The supervisors indicated that in several units the secretaries and mail and file clerks did not like each other.

- The clerks and secretaries were mostly women with diverse ethnic backgrounds. Most were relatively young and had less than 5 years' seniority, although a few were older and had as many as 15 years with the company.

During the discussion, Rob confirmed his tentative diagnosis that the problem involved more than people getting along better. He said that if the goal was to give the clerical staff a break from work, a two-hour seminar would be appropriate. But if they wanted to change attitudes and behavior, much more would be required. The committee members agreed the goal was to improve the situation by changing some of the clerks' attitudes and behavior.

Rob suggested that the next step would be for him to talk to some of the clerical staff individually to get their perceptions. The committee agreed, and they assumed responsibility for picking a sample of secretaries and clerks representative of the group.

Rob also checked with Elsie and the committee to ensure that they were keeping their manager and other superintendents informed about what was happening in this situation. Those people had an important stake in this effort, and it was important they be informed and given an opportunity to make suggestions or to agree to the process.

During this stage, Rob played the role of listener and stimulator. He communicated to the committee members that they were in charge. He helped them clarify their goals and he suggested initial steps for action. However, he made it clear that the final decisions rested with the committee members. The role of the OD consultant is to help people diagnose and solve their own problems, not to tell them what to do or do it for them.

Collecting Data.   Not surprisingly, Rob found that perceptions varied among the clerical staff he interviewed. Interviews lasting about 45 minutes were conducted individually in a conference room. Rob found that one pair got along very well, two were in considerable conflict, and one had a neutral relationship. He learned several other important things, which included the following:

- The grade 4 secretaries regarded the grade 3 clerks as subordinates, and some clearly treated them that way.

- The grade 3 clerks ended up doing most of the menial tasks in each unit.

- The grade 3 clerks all wanted to learn the grade 4 jobs, but some of the secretaries resisted and complained that the grade 3 clerks needed to do their own work better. Many of the clerks felt they could already do the secretaries' job, and the others believed they would be able to do it with more training and experience.

- Some of the pairs were not very cooperative. For example, secretaries were to answer the many phone calls that came into the unit. Some clerks would help out when the secretary was overly busy, but others said, "That's her job!"
- There was too much work in each section for one person, but not enough for two.
- Two of those interviewed had been absent on workers' compensation leave because of stress.
- The desks of some of the pairs were placed close to one another, but in some cases the pairs could not even see each other because of partitions.
- Some pairs interacted frequently and others hardly at all, and there were some personality clashes.

Rob met at a later date with the committee and reported his findings, most of which were not surprising to the supervisors. However, they had not noticed the significance of some of the factors. For example, the pair that cooperated and worked best together were the same age and had their desks near each other. The pair that cooperated least, especially on sharing phone duty, could not even see each other. This meant that if the secretary were on the phone, the clerk would not realize she should answer a second call.

Feeding Data Back to the Client Group and Joint Problem Diagnosis. The committee members discussed the data reported by Rob, and it became clear that the various problems were partly about relationships and partly about the structure within the unit. For example, explicit job descriptions made it easy for one or the other to say, "That's not my job." The different grade levels created a perceived status difference that interfered with cooperative behavior. Several of the clerks felt frustrated that they could not be promoted even though they were fully capable of doing the secretary's job. Some thought the fact that there was not enough work for two people contributed to the secretaries' not sharing some of their work with the clerks. That is, they were afraid of losing status and possibly their jobs.

Most of the information Rob provided was known by the committee members; however, some was new. For example, although some had sensed there was not enough work for both a secretary and a clerk, they had not articulated that possibility. Some were surprised their subordinates admitted this information.

Joint Action Planning. The committee decided as a result of this discussion to pursue the possibility of promoting the clerks to a grade 4 level as soon as they were qualified. The committee made a convincing argument to upper management, and it was agreed each unit could have two grade 4 employees. The supervisors also agreed that an effort would be made to redesign the work and organization so that fewer people would be needed. They agreed this should be accomplished through attrition so that no one would be punished for helping to improve efficiency. These were structural interventions.

It was also agreed that Rob would conduct a half-day team-building session for all of the clerical staff in Claims Section. Following that session, the superintendents would host a special luncheon in a nearby restaurant. The goals of this event were to let the workers know they were appreciated, to stimulate their thought processes about their jobs, and to obtain their input on how to build more cooperative, productive, and enjoyable relationships.

This planning session also revealed the need for some individual counseling. The committee members talked about how this would be done with the goal of maximizing useful results.

The committee also decided to plan a session for all 12 superintendents and their manager to focus on how to build better teams in each of the units. This involved making plans for the superintendent, claims representatives, and clerical staff to spend some time discussing how they could help each other perform better.

One key to successful intervention is that the people involved develop an understanding of what must be done and why. This results when they participate in diagnosing the situation and planning the interventions. Often the participants will make the interventions, although sometimes the OD agent also helps. In this case, it was decided Rob should lead the team-building exercise because of his experience and because he might be viewed by the clerical staff as less threatening than some of the supervisors. The committee decided the team-building seminar would be held without any management people present.

Implementing the Action Plan.   The team-building exercise turned out to be both fun and stimulating for most of the participants. They viewed the event as appreciation for their efforts, which was management's intention. The participants also made several useful suggestions for improving work processes, which were communicated to the superintendents. In fact, some of the suggestions were subsequently implemented.

Evaluating Results and Deciding on Further Steps.   Within six months, several positive results occurred. Five grade 3 clerks were promoted to grade 4 secretaries, and the motivation and morale of the other grade 3 clerks improved significantly. The grade 3s and 4s, with the exception of two pairs, were working well together. Some rearrangements of desks facilitated their helping each other out, and complaints about lack of cooperation were greatly reduced. Several ideas as to how the work could be accomplished with fewer people had been provided by the clerical people. These were in the process of being implemented, and one grade 4 secretary who had been promoted to another unit was not replaced. Absenteeism was down significantly. Many of the superintendents were pleased because they could devote more of their time to improving operational results in their units.

The original committee decided that efforts to reduce the total number of clerks should continue, with the active participation of those involved. They decided that individual superintendents should continue to monitor results and to reinforce evidence of positive attitude and behavior changes with recognition and thanks. Rob was thanked, and it was agreed he need no longer be involved. The group felt good about the progress that had been made.

OD Interventions

The above example demonstrates how managers and OD practitioners make interventions to improve organizational processes and outputs, resulting in better performance and satisfaction. The interventions also helped people and the organization become more effective in diagnosing and solving their own problems.

Characteristics.   OD interventions have three major characteristics.[29] First, they are based on an understanding of how the organization or unit actually functions, not just on how it is supposed to function according to charts and manuals. We saw previously that data collection and diagnosis was an important early step in the OD process.

Second, the interventions must reflect the organizational members' free and informed choices. OD practitioners don't order people to intervene in a certain way. Instead, as we saw in the last section, they strive to help organization members participate in both the diagnosis of problems and the decisions about what interventions to make.

Third, to be successful, the interventions must gain the internal commitment of those affected, not just their outward compliance. Internal commitment usually results from people having been involved in diagnosing the problem and determining interventions. This participation leads to their feeling some ownership of and responsibility for actions taken and results achieved.

Types of OD Interventions.   OD interventions can be classified in different ways. One is by what organizational *issues* they are intended to resolve.[30] Another is by the organizational *level* (individual, group, organization) at which the intervention is made. Exhibit 16–8 shows types of OD interventions and some of the issues they help resolve. Exhibit 16–9 summarizes the interventions by level. Some of the following specific interventions overlap levels and issues.

T-group

A training group designed to help individuals learn about themselves and group dynamics by studying their own interactions.

Sensitivity Training.   This intervention (often called **"T-group"** for training group) is designed to help individuals learn more about themselves, group dynamics, and leadership by studying their own interactions in a seemingly unstructured setting. The learning usually takes place in groups of 10 to 15 individuals and a professional trainer. The session is mainly unstructured, and individuals focus on here-and-now issues that occur between themselves. Individuals are encouraged to express their perceptions and feelings—sessions often become quite intense. Possible outcomes for the people involved include increased self-awareness, greater empathy and sensitivity to the behavior of others, better listening skills, and better understanding of group processes. When participants are from regular work teams, T-groups can also result in increased openness, tolerance of individual differences, conflict resolution skills, and cohesiveness. As more and more companies shift to team building, sensitivity training is starting to become a more structured part of that process.

Process Consultation.   In this intervention a OD practitioner first observes various organization or group processes, like goal setting, problem solving, and conflict resolution. The trainer then provides feedback to the client group and helps group members diagnose and solve process problems. Structured exercises are sometimes used to create processes that are observed and diagnosed with the intent to help group members work together more effectively.

Third-Party Peacemaking.   This intervention is similar to process consultation, but its focus is on interpersonal relationship problems. The OD practitioner helps individuals in a dysfunctional relationship to resolve conflicts. Acting as an impartial third party, the OD practitioner listens and helps those involved to gain insights about each other's perceptions and needs. The goal is to solve interpersonal problems by increasing understanding, developing empathy, and bargaining.

Role Negotiation.   When there is evidence of friction or misunderstanding among group members about who should do what, this intervention can be helpful. Role negotiation clarifies individual or group responsibilities and what each person is to give to and receive from others so that all may perform effectively.

EXHIBIT 16–8   *OD Interventions and Organizational Issues*

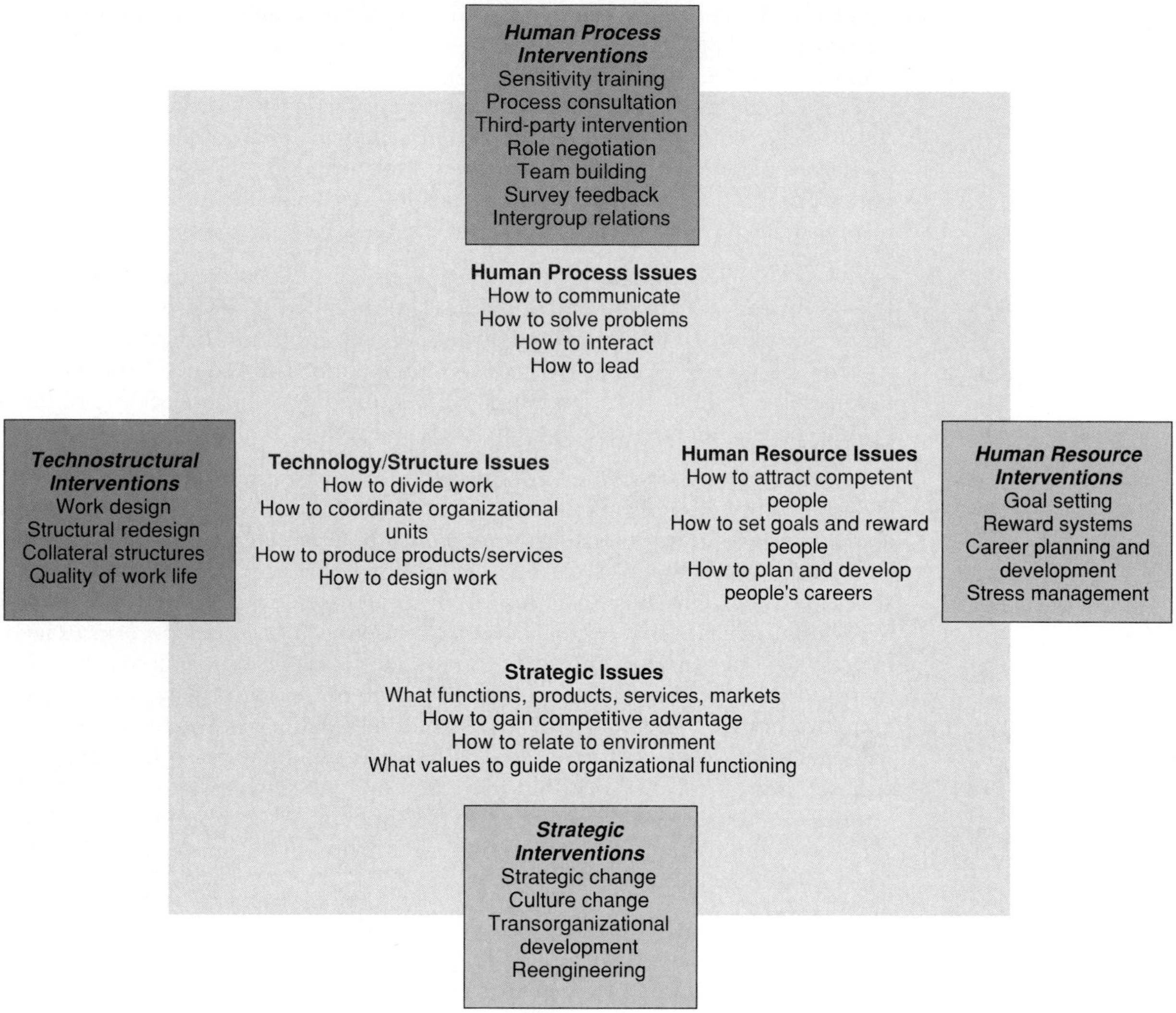

Human Process Interventions
Sensitivity training
Process consultation
Third-party intervention
Role negotiation
Team building
Survey feedback
Intergroup relations

Human Process Issues
How to communicate
How to solve problems
How to interact
How to lead

Technostructural Interventions
Work design
Structural redesign
Collateral structures
Quality of work life

Technology/Structure Issues
How to divide work
How to coordinate organizational units
How to produce products/services
How to design work

Human Resource Issues
How to attract competent people
How to set goals and reward people
How to plan and develop people's careers

Human Resource Interventions
Goal setting
Reward systems
Career planning and development
Stress management

Strategic Issues
What functions, products, services, markets
How to gain competitive advantage
How to relate to environment
What values to guide organizational functioning

Strategic Interventions
Strategic change
Culture change
Transorganizational development
Reengineering

Source: Adapted from Thomas G. Cummings and Edgar F. Huse, *Organization Development and Change* (St. Paul, MN: West Publishing, 1989), p. 128.

Team Building.   This intervention, discussed previously in Chapter 11, is intended to help work groups improve both their processes and outputs. Group members help to identify areas for improvement and how progress can be made. Typical areas of concern are goals, norms, roles, work processes and strategies, communication, and decision making.

Survey Feedback.   The purpose of this intervention is to collect data and feed it back to managers and employees with the intent of helping them identify problems and solutions. Information is usually collected by questionnaires. The OD practitioner helps facilitate the process, but the emphasis is on having those involved in a problem design ways to improve their performance and satisfaction.

Intergroup Relations.   This intervention is used when there is evidence of dysfunctional relationships between groups. The OD practitioner works with representatives

━━ **EXHIBIT 16–9**	Intervention	Individual	Group	Organization
OD Interventions by Organizational Level	Sensitivity training	✓	✓	
	Process consultation		✓	
	Third-party intervention		✓	
	Role negotiation		✓	
	Team building		✓	
	Survey feedback		✓	✓
	Intergroup relations			✓
	Work design	✓	✓	
	Structural redesign			✓
	Collateral structures			✓
	Goal setting	✓	✓	✓
	Reward systems	✓	✓	✓
	Career planning and development	✓		
	Stress management	✓		
	Strategic change			✓
	Culture change			✓
	Transorganizational development			✓
	Reengineering			✓

Source: Adapted from Thomas G. Cummings and Edgar F. Huse, *Organization Development and Change* (St. Paul, MN: West Publishing, 1989), p. 130.

of the groups to develop supportive relationships that lead to improved performance and satisfaction. Each group is helped to understand how each sees the other, what each needs and expects from the other, and how conflicts can be resolved and cooperation enhanced.

Job Redesign. Job design was discussed in Chapter 3. The goal of job redesign is (1) to achieve a good fit between the job's demands and rewards and the individual's skills and motives while (2) simultaneously achieving and improving group and organizational output goals. The OD practitioner helps identify the core characteristics of jobs and how they might be redesigned to better fit an individual's needs and skills.

Structural Redesign. The characteristics of this intervention were also discussed in Chapter 3. The intent is to find the optimum way to divide and integrate work in the organization or unit, thus improving overall performance and the quality of people's work life. This requires an ongoing analysis of changing organizational system components and how they best fit together. Components include the environment, strategy, structure, technology, resources, culture, people, and management. Structural redesign is usually a major, large-scale intervention.

Collateral Organizations. The collateral organization is temporary and supplements the formal organization. It is designed to focus on specific problems or opportunities without interfering with the formal organization's productivity. Members are drawn from the formal organization to form a parallel, or collateral, organization. They meet periodically in problem-solving sessions. This OD intervention facilitates creativity and directs attention to specific needs and opportunities. An example would be the formation of a temporary task group to determine a better process to introduce new products.

Goal Setting.   The intent of this intervention is to improve the alignment between individual and organizational goals. The goal-setting process helps clarify goals and facilitates communication between managers and subordinates. It focuses on what is to be achieved, how it will be achieved, and what might interfere with goal accomplishment. This intervention is often formally introduced across the entire hierarchy and all units.

Reward Systems Redesign.   This intervention was discussed in Chapter 7. OD practitioners help managers design better fits between what they want people to do and how they reward them. The goal is to improve worker productivity and satisfaction. Reward systems include all those things that people regard as positive responses to their work efforts, although the focus is usually on formal pay, promotion, and benefit systems. OD interventions most often concentrate on ways to increase intrinsic motivation by providing rewards like challenge, chances for recognition and increased self-esteem, and so on.

Career Planning and Development.   Emphasized are interests and competence building designed to help individuals choose and follow satisfying career paths in line with personal goals. OD and human resource management (HRM) practitioners help individuals look ahead to see what opportunities exist and what preparation is required to move toward opportunities.

Stress Management.   Stress is a common component of many jobs, particularly those at the managerial and professional levels. Organizations can incur heavy losses because of stress, so OD and HRM practitioners design programs and disseminate information that helps individuals manage their own stress. This topic was discussed in depth in Chapter 15.

Culture Change.   The importance of organizational culture was discussed in Chapter 4. An OD intervention directed toward modifying culture is designed to change cultural norms, beliefs, and values. Such an intervention occurs when existing cultures get out of line with changes in the environment and organization strategies. For example, when AT&T changed from a regulated organization focused on service to a nonregulated company dependent on profit in a competitive environment, there was a need for a culture change. U.S. auto companies had to convert their cultures from valuing low costs and mass production to valuing quality and production lots as small as one vehicle. This intervention is a major one and requires the full support of top management.

Transorganizational Development.   This is a relatively new intervention that arises from the need to develop different kinds of relationships than have existed in the past with groups outside the organization such as suppliers, customers, and even competitors. The increased focus on quality and time has stimulated companies to cooperate more closely and even develop partnerships with suppliers in planning and interacting. Many companies now undertake joint ventures with foreign competitors, and the challenges of developing these relationships and bridging different organizational cultures requires this special kind of intervention.

reengineering
The redesign of a work process to achieve more quality, efficiency, and effectiveness.

Reengineering.   A relatively new concept, **reengineering** describes the total rebuilding of important organizational processes. Reengineering involves fundamental rather than gradual change. The goal is to analyze critical work processes (e.g., purchasing, accounting, product design, sales) in detail so that they can be redesigned to achieve more quality, efficiency, and cost effectiveness. Reengineering usually leads to significantly changed processes that look little like the originals. Effective reengineering includes consideration of key human resource systems such as rewards, appraisal, and participation.

Ethical Concerns in Organizational Development

Whether consultants or managers, OD practitioners focus on helping people and organizations change. This process of influencing change sometimes leads to ethical dilemmas. A few years ago, an informal group of leaders from the various associations developed a set of ethical guidelines for OD practitioners. Some of the key areas of ethical concern are described below.[31]

- **Interventions.** One area in which OD practitioners face ethical dilemmas is in their choice of interventions. We have already seen that OD practitioners are value oriented. Many have also developed specialized skills. It is not considered ethical for the OD practitioner to choose an intervention he or she is not fully qualified to administer. It is also not ethical to use a favorite intervention familiar to the OD practitioner when it is neither appropriate for nor desired by the client.

- **Information.** A second area of critical concern relates to information gathered by the OD practitioner during the change process. Some of this information is personally and organizationally sensitive. OD practitioners must scrupulously avoid the misuse of such information. Misuses include revealing confidential information to the wrong parties and misusing confidential information to manipulate the client system for personal advantage. One example of an ethical dilemma is whether or not to share information confidentially revealed by subordinates when asked by the person who hired the OD practitioner.

- **Dependency.** The very nature of a helping relationship often leads to dependency. It is considered unethical for OD practitioners to prolong that dependency relationship. The role of the OD person is to help the client become independent by developing her or his own ability to manage the change and other processes involved.

- **Informed Choice.** Another area with ethical implications involves clients having neither an understanding of the processes being proposed nor a say in whether those interventions will be used. The OD practitioner is obligated as much as possible to inform clients of interventions that might be suitable and to help them understand what they entail. Then the client should have the freedom to choose whether a particular intervention is used.

A natural goal of OD is to transform the organization into a self-sufficient, problem-solving and learning organization. A successful "learning organization" continues the OD process internally on an independent, ongoing basis.

WHAT ARE LEARNING ORGANIZATIONS?

Learning organizations change before they're forced to and integrate personal and financial performance requirements faster and more effectively than the competition.[32] "Learning disabilities" can be fatal to organizations, causing them to prematurely shorten their life span. Like individuals, organizations that don't know how to learn may survive but never live up to their potential. Only those firms that become effective learners can succeed in the increasingly turbulent, competitive global market.[33] According to Ron Hutchinson, vice president of

══════ **EXHIBIT 16–10**

Characteristics of a Learning Organization

- **Systems Thinking.** Members perceive their organization as a system of interrelated processes, activities, functions, and interactions. Any action taken will have repercussions on other variables in the system. It is important to see the entire picture in the short and long run.
- **Shared Vision.** Belief and commitment towards a goal deeply desired by all. Sublimation of competing departmental and personal interests for the achievement of the shared vision.
- **Personal Mastery.** Continual learning and personal growth by all organizational members. Individuals are willing to give up old ways of thinking and behaving to try out possible better ones for themselves and the organization.
- **Mental Process Models.** Shared internal images of how individuals, the organization, and the world work. Willingness to reflect on the reasoning underlying our actions and to change these assumptions when necessary to create a more appropriate process for doing things.
- **Team Learning.** Organization members openly communicate across departmental and hierarchical boundaries to help all members solve problems and learn from each other. Decreasing the need for personal wins in order to increase the search for the truth for the good of the entire team.

customer service for Harley-Davidson Motor Company, Inc., "To be effective long term, we must have an organization in place that understands what caused prior mistakes and failures—and most importantly what caused successes. Then, we need to know how we can inculcate the successes and inculcate the preventive measures to avoid additional failures."[34]

organizational learning
Improving organizational procedures based on analysis of basic assumptions, values, and objectives.

In Chapter 6, we said that **organizational learning** occurs when employees respond more effectively to the same work-related stimulus than they did in the past. This definition implies more than merely applying present procedures to solving erupting problems (i.e., single-loop learning). Effective organizational learning (i.e., double loop learning) entails modifying the procedures themselves and maybe even the assumptions, values, and objectives on which they were based to not only solve current problems, but to prevent their recurrence in the future.[35]

learning organization
An organization skilled at creating, acquiring, and transferring knowledge to improve its behavior.

A **learning organization** is an organization skilled at creating, acquiring, and transferring knowledge and at modifying its behavior to reflect new knowledge and insight.[36] Human resources manager Laura Gilbert says her Minnesota Educational Computing Corporation has become "a place that has a proactive, creative approach to the unknown, encouraging individuals to express their feelings, and using intelligence and imagination instead of just skills and authority to find new ways to be competitive and manage work."[37]

The Characteristics of Learning Organizations

Five characteristics required for a learning organization are summarized in Exhibit 16–10. They are personal mastery, mental process models, shared vision, team learning, and systems thinking. Systems thinking is the most important because all the others are a part of it. In a learning organization, people are willing to let go of old defenses and ways of behaving in order to learn with others how their organization really works. Then they can form a common vision of where they want to go, develop mental models of how organizational processes work, design a plan to get there, and implement it as a committed team.[38]

Armed with these characteristics, learning organizations are better equipped to cope with traditional organizational problems of fragmentation, competition, and reactiveness. Instead of separating different organizational functions into competing fragments, learning organizations emphasize the total system and how each function contributes to the whole process. Instead of competing for resources and trying to prove who is right or wrong, learning organizations promote cooperation and sharing of knowledge for the benefit of all. Finally, instead of reacting to problems like a fire fighter, learning organizations encourage innovativeness and continual improvement so that problems don't occur in the first place, or will not recur in the future.[39]

Types of Organizational Learning

As we discussed in Chapter 6, individuals prefer different learning styles. So do organizations. Research has identified four basic types of organizational learning: competence acquisition, experimentation, continuous improvement, and boundary spanning.[40]

Competence Acquisition. Organizations that learn by competence acquisition cultivate new capabilities in their teams and individuals. They demonstrate public commitment to learning by continuously seeking new ways to work and by promoting learning as a fundamental part of their business strategies.

Experimentation. Organizations that learn by experimentation try out new ideas. They are innovators who attempt to be the first to market with new processes or products.

Continuous Improvement. Organizations that learn by continuous improvement strive to master each step in the process before moving on to the next. Their goal is to become the recognized technical leader for a particular product or process.

Boundary Spanning. Organizations that learn by boundary spanning continuously scan other companies' efforts, benchmarking their processes against competitors. In Chapter 12's opening vignette, for example, Porsche sent engineering teams to Japanese car factories to compare assembly times and discover how to improve their own processes.

Research has found that, in general, companies that learn by experimentation are better able to compete and change than those that rely on the other learning methods.[41] This doesn't mean that experimentation is best for all companies. To maximize competitiveness, an organization's dominant type of learning should match its culture. For instance, a bureaucratic organization proud of tradition would have a difficult time trying to learn by experimentation.

Creating Learning Organizations

How can a traditional reactive organization be changed into a continual learner? Instituting any process that enlarges the organization's knowledge base and improves the way knowledge is interpreted and put to use will help.[42] Three specific actions are to establish a learning strategy, redesign organization structure, and modify the organization's culture.

Establish a Learning Strategy. Management needs to develop and make explicit a strategic intent to learn. This includes a commitment to experimentation, a willingness to learn from experiences, and a willingness to implement necessary changes in the spirit of continuous improvement.[43] Strategic alternatives were described above.

Redesign Organizational Structure. Traditional hierarchical organizational structures that emphasize authority, separate departments into competing domains, and enforce formal communication networks impede organizational learning. To enhance organizational learning, communication can be increased by encouraging informal face-to-face interaction and electronic distribution to all concerned parties. Competition can be replaced with cooperation through the establishment of common performance measures and rewards. Authority levels are reduced by instituting cross-functional teams and eliminating departmental boundaries.[44]

Modify the Organization's Culture.   Learning happens best in the context of organizational cultures that value growth, openness, trust, and risk taking. Known as the regenerative climate (described in Chapter 9), emphasis is on high openness, trust, and owning of responsibility. Managers promote experimentation, trying new things, constructive criticism, learning from past mistakes, and bringing functional disagreements into the open. Management establishes regenerative climates by publicizing what is desired, acting accordingly themselves, and rewarding desired behaviors. The organizational development process is concerned with developing learning organizations to improve individual and organizational effectiveness.[45]

AUTO MAKERS PROSPER BY EMBRACING CHANGE —A SECOND LOOK

Although Donald Peterson was awarded much of the acclaim, he continuously stressed that Ford's success was achieved because of the full team of organization members working together in a participative way. Today, quality circles and other forms of employee decision involvement are working throughout Ford to improve quality and productivity. Ford's Taurus, Thunderbird, Probe, and Escort are at the forefront of styling, and quality continues to improve.

Ford's success has not been overlooked by other U.S. auto makers. We have already discussed the development of Chrysler's LH teams in Chapter 10, which shaved a full year off Chrysler's vehicle-development cycle of 4 1/4 years with 40 percent fewer engineers. More recently, Chrysler has used concurrent engineering teams made up of people from engineering, marketing, purchasing, and finance: They form at the start of a project to avoid delays from disagreements and misunderstanding. It took the Neon Team 3 1/2 years to deliver this new model at a cost of $1.3 billion. Contrast this to Ford's newest Escort that took 5 years to deliver at a cost of $2 billion, or GM's Saturn, discussed in Chapter 11, that took 7 years and cost $5 billion.[46]

SUMMARY

Pervasive change has become the norm as organizations and individuals adapt to rapid and often unexpected change to survive and prosper. External change forces include technology, economic conditions, global competition, world politics, and social and demographic factors.

People seek change that is favorable and resist change perceived as harmful or ambiguous. They make cost/benefit assessments of potential changes, which influence their degree of acceptance or resistance. To be skilled at managing change, managers and other change agents begin by identifying performance gaps and the targets of their change efforts. They must understand both the content and process of change and how their efforts affect their organizational system.

Three phases of change are unfreezing, changing, and refreezing. Planned change involves (1) recognizing the need for change, (2) diagnosing and planning, (3) considering contingencies, (4) taking action and measuring results, and (5) managing the transition.

Organizational development (OD) is a systemwide application of behavioral science knowledge designed to improve organizational effectiveness and people's satisfaction and quality of work life. OD practitioners include both professionals and managers who have specialized knowledge, skills, and experience. OD is concerned with both the technical and social aspects of work and system design and improvement. Increasingly, OD practitioners work on strategy, culture development, and technology integration.

The OD process is similar to that of planned change. The steps include (1) sensing the problem and engaging an OD practitioner, (2) entering and contracting, (3) collecting data and diagnosing, (4) planning and implementing interventions, and (5) evaluating results and deciding on further steps. A variety of specific OD interventions are available to OD practitioners and change agents. Nevertheless, the process of influencing change is potentially open to ethical dilemmas, and OD practitioners have developed guidelines to deal with them.

In the long run, OD and planned change intervention seeks to create learning organizations that are skilled at creating, acquiring, and transferring knowledge and at modifying behavior to reflect new knowledge and insights. Five characteristics required for a learning organization are personal mastery, mental process models, shared vision, team learning, and systems thinking.

Key Concepts

change, *p. 530*

planned change, *p. 539*

change agents, *p. 540*

unfreezing, *p. 542*

moving, *p. 542*

refreezing, *p. 543*

force-field analysis, *p. 545*

intervention, *p. 546*

organizational development (OD), *p. 546*

action research, *p. 550*

T-group, *p. 555*

reengineering, *p. 558*

organizational learning, *p. 560*

learning organization, *p. 560*

Questions for Study and Discussion

1. Think of an organization you know and identify what you think is the most significant change it has made in the last five years. What factors influenced the change? Was the change resisted? If so, by whom and why? Apply a force-field analysis to your example.

2. The manager of the business office for a 250-bed hospital wants to improve the handling of patient record keeping. She shows you a proposed reorganization of the department in which several currently specialized functions (admitting, third-party payment, and the like) are combined into "patient representative" positions. The 30 restructured roles will handle patient files almost from entry to exit. The manager plans to announce the change at the next staff meeting. What would you communicate to her to minimize resistance to the proposed change?

3. Think of an organization or group to which you belong. Identify a change you think would improve the organization. How would you go about planning and implementing the change? Include Lewin's three phases of change in your answer. Also, distinguish between content and process in developing your plan.

4. OD practitioners use two basic strategies to achieve their objectives: the human process and the technostructural approaches. Distinguish between these two and give an example of each.

5. Select two OD interventions for each level (individual, group, organization) and give examples of when and how they might be used appropriately. What limits might each have?

6. What are one or two examples of ethical dilemmas that change agents or OD practitioners might encounter? How would you suggest they think about those dilemmas?

7. Give examples of learning organizations that you have been a part of or heard about. How would these types of organizations benefit or harm individual members compared to traditional organizations?

EXPERIENTIAL EXERCISE

Changing the Grading System

Purpose.
- To practice stakeholder analysis.
- To practice making a force-field analysis.
- To plan briefly what needs to be done to bring about change.

Background. Assume that several students have petitioned your instructor to grade your current course in organizational behavior on a pass-fail basis. Your instructor has reservations about this, but was willing to ask the dean if there was a possibility of changing the grading in this course from an A through F basis to pass-fail. The dean expressed willingness to consider the question but asked for a more detailed proposal, including the pros and cons and how such a plan might be implemented. Your instructor, in turn, has asked your group to develop a preliminary analysis of how such a change might be made. (Total time required: 35 to 55 minutes.)

Specific Instructions.
Step I. You are to join a group of four to seven students to do the following:

1. Develop a stakeholder analysis. Identify all stakeholders and their interests and concerns (5 to 10 minutes).

2. Prepare a force-field analysis. Identify the pushing and restraining forces and estimate the intensity and importance of each (10 to 15 minutes).

3. Prepare a preliminary plan for introducing and implementing the change. Identify who will do what and when. Be specific about the order and priority of actions (5 to 10 minutes).

4. Prepare a brief recommendation indicating whether or not your group thinks your instructor should proceed (5 minutes).

Note. This is a simulated exercise and is not intended to influence your instructor to change the grading system!

Step II. Entire class reconvenes. As time permits, do the following:

1. Each group reports its recommendation.

2. Class discussion. Class discusses learning from this experience and how this process would be similar to and different from analyzing and planning a change at work.

3. Compare the analyses (10 to 20 minutes for all of Step II).

EXPERIENTIAL EXERCISE

Personal Force-Field Analysis[47]

Purpose. Problems can be understood as the difference between a current situation and a desired situation. Discussing problems is beneficial when it (1) helps to reduce our anxiety, (2) leads to a reduction of the problem or discomfort caused by it through a redefinition of the problem, or (3) leads to constructive action that alleviates the problem. This exercise is designed to accomplish all three purposes. Force-field analysis is based on the concept that there are opposing forces in equilibrium that keep us stuck in our current situations when we want to move to a more desirable situation. (Total time required for the personal force field is about 25 minutes. Another 30 minutes is necessary if dyads are formed to provide feedback.)

Directions. *Step 1:* Individually complete the force-field problem-solving module below for a current problem you are experiencing personally. The problem could be a habit you are trying to break (e.g., drinking coffee, smoking, procrastination), or something you want to improve in but have trouble working on (e.g., public speaking skills, learning a foreign language, mastering a new computer program) or any other type of problem you are putting off solving for some reason (e.g., looking for a new job, breaking off a dysfunctional relationship, starting a diet or exercise program to get in shape) (20 to 30 minutes).

1. **Describe the current situation that you want to change.** Often, part of the problem is that no one knows exactly what the problem is. To start the process, describe a current situation as accurately and briefly as possible.

2. **Describe the desired situation.** This is not necessarily the ideal situation that can often be an impractical solution. Indicate the direction and realistic change you desire.

3. **List the opposing or restraining (negative) forces** that resist improvement in the situation in the following force-field diagram.

4. **List the driving or pushing (positive) forces** that are motivating you to change in the following force-field diagram.

5. **Review the driving and restraining forces** and number them according to their impact on the situation (1 is most important, 2 is second in impact, 3 is third, etc.).

Force-Field Analysis

Current Situation ⇨ ⇨ ⇨		Desired Situation
Driving Forces	↔	Restraining Forces
_____	↔	_____
_____	↔	_____
_____	↔	_____
_____	↔	_____

6. **Procedures.** These are *action steps* aimed at directly changing the forces that maintain the current problem situation. Change procedures modify the strength of the forces, keeping the current situation as it is. You may either (1) increase the strength of or add driving forces, or (2) decrease the strength of or take away restraining forces. Concentrate on the most important forces (underlined in step 5) and brainstorm as many *action steps* as possible.
   A. Add driving forces.
   B. Increase the strength of driving forces.
   C. Eliminate restraining forces.
   D. Reduce the strength of restraining forces.

7. **Priorities.** Arrange actions listed in A through D in order of priorities. Use ease of implementation and possible effect as two criteria.

8. **Organization of resources.** For the five top priority action steps (step 7), list the materials, people, and other resources available.

   Action Step   **Resources**

9. **Agenda.** Action implementation steps for each strategy:
   • *What is going to be done?*
   • *Who is going to do it?*
   • *When is it going to be done?*
   • *Evaluation. How will you determine when the step is completed and accomplished?*

10. **Commitment.** Make a personal statement about your intentions and desired consequences.

Step 2: When you complete all the steps in your force-field analysis, pick a partner who is also finished, and share your work. Your partner's job is to ask for clarification, provide you with feedback about additional information you may want to add, and reality-test your plans so that you can make sure that you have the best possible chance of success for implementation (15 minutes).

Step 3: Reverse the procedure in step 2. Now the second partner shares the force-field analysis and gets feedback (15 minutes).

CASE

Rebuilding Metro East's Department of Housing and Urban Development

The mayor of Metro East appointed Carolyn Baker commissioner of the city's Department of Housing and Urban Development (D-HUD). Metro East is a predominantly African-American urban community located across a navigable river from a major midwestern city. At the turn of the century, Metro East boasted a strong industrial base with residential showplaces. But over the years the city developed a reputation for harboring crime and vice. An active syndicate made bribes, payoffs, and corruption a normal government practice. Today, Metro East is a city on the decline.

The new mayor, still in his late twenties, sought to change the tradition of graft and reverse the city's decline. He persuaded Baker to resign her appointed job at the state capital and accept the challenge of revitalizing the city's D-HUD. Carolyn Baker is a vibrant African-American woman in her mid-forties and brings to the commissionership a diverse experience in government administration. She shares the mayor's commitment to reform and reorganize city government.

Carolyn Baker assumed her new position by taking decisive actions. In her second week at D-HUD, she eliminated all its previous decisions (subunits). She perceived that the department had evolved structurally by tacking on new subunits as grants were obtained. In place of the grant-based structure, she created four new divisions: economic development, housing, community planning, and special projects.

Additionally, Baker acted at once to sift out redundant and nonproductive staff members. Today only half the original 70 people remain employed. This mass exodus occurred through a process of "self-destruction." Baker simply required everyone to submit to her a weekly activities report (no special form, simply a documentation of activities). Some submitted nothing the first week; others wrote a few words on a scrap of paper. Those who did not present evidence of productivity were discharged.

In the old organization, everyone had done his or her own thing. Budgets for various grants had been, in Baker's words, "badly raped." Several of the twenty-odd programs in D-HUD had budget overruns. When she took over, the department was operating financially on a "reimbursement" status from state and federal offices of HUD. What this means is that D-HUD is paid only after it submits bills of incurred expenses.

This week Baker received acknowledgment that her department can shift to a "letter-of-credit" status if it can show that internal accounting and control systems are in order. Such a change would mean that Metro East could operate on money advanced to the department while work is in process. Several actions are necessary to show intent and demonstrate actual progress to higher-level HUD administrators (see Exhibit 16–11). Baker has already (1) enforced building codes, (2) removed the time clock (most staff hold master's degrees), and (3) instituted a system for maintaining permanent records of building permits and inspection reports.

Carolyn Baker reflects on her first seven weeks in the commissioner's office: "I'm a great delegator. I do little correspondence personally. I usually assign it to someone else. Most of the people who remain here are competent and capable of acting like professionals, if they are given a chance. They know the answers, but not necessarily the questions. Now that several changes have been made, it is probably time to begin rebuilding our systems and the talents of our staffers."

Questions for Managerial Action

1. Evaluate the "self-destruction" concept carried out in the form of the required weekly activities report.
2. What should Commissioner Baker do now? Be specific.
3. What should be the role of outsider help, if any?

EXHIBIT 16–11

Necessary Changes at D-HUD

1. Analysis and documentation of work flow among divisions.
2. An operational statement of mission segmented by function.
3. Incentives to attract and hold businesses within the city.
4. Development of a systematic policy-and-procedures manual.
5. A current position description and resumé for every employee.
6. A process for competitive performance appraisals.
7. A rational salary policy related to jobs and performance.

Origins and Methods of Management and OB Theories

In his study of the origins of management thought, Jack Duncan identifies 1886 as the year Henry Towne proposed to a meeting of the American Society of Mechanical Engineers that management should have a body of theory.[1] In the audience was Frederick Taylor, whose subsequent research, writing, and principles created the "scientific management" movement and the first serious study of managing behavior in organizations. From these engineering origins, the study of management has branched out and became more formalized over the last century. This appendix provides a perspective on the history of management and organizational behavior theories and how they have shaped what we know and appreciate about organizations. It concludes with a brief note on the methods of conducting behavioral research.

THE CLASSICAL PERSPECTIVES

In the first 20 years of the twentieth century, several streams of thought independently emerged that focused on the revolutionary idea that management could be systematically learned and codified. This was an era when mass production and economies of scale first became the accepted path to business success. Henry Ford introduced his moving assembly line in 1914, enabling production of a Model T Ford in two hours. The price of a Model T dropped from $850 in 1908 to about $400.[2] Among the notables to leave a permanent mark on the study of behavior in organizations and the practice of management during this emerging industrial era were the Americans Frederick Taylor and Lillian Gilbreth, the Frenchman Henri Fayol, and the German Max Weber.

scientific management
An early 1900s movement that elevated the status of managers and held that scientific observation of people at work would reveal the one best way to do any task.

Scientific Management.   **Scientific management** emerged from Frederick Taylor's assumption that the interests of management and employees could be integrated through the principle of economically motivated self-interest. He clearly distinguished between managerial and nonmanagerial work. Taylor believed scientific observation of people at work (through time and motion studies) would reveal the one best way to do any nonmanagerial task. Once the best way had been determined and the requisite skills identified, managers could hire appropriate people and train them to perform the specialized job. With performance requirements and tools specified, Taylor also established a "differential piece-rate" pay system that rewarded work output in excess of established standards.

Taylor placed his emphasis on the "task," or the tangible elements of a job, which he saw as the "most prominent single element in modern scientific management."[3] He replaced haphazard rules of thumb with systematic, measured, empirically derived *principles*. Taylor was the first to emphasize the prediction of behavior, followed by goals, training, and other management techniques to influence work outcomes. But he espoused a rather mechanistic view of workers. He wrote that successful pig-iron handlers were so "stupid and so phlegmatic" that they appeared to resemble more in "mental makeup the ox than any other type" of animal.[4] Nevertheless, Taylor's contributions to the emergence of management are legendary, and several of his original concepts still provide the foundation for current management practices.

Lillian Gilbreth, one of the first women to earn a Ph.D. in the field of psychology, took the "task" concept of scientific management and embellished it as a goal-setting process. She viewed task determination as a means-ends process of *analysis* (separating complex things into their constituent elements) and

■■■■■ **EXHIBIT A–1**

Henri Fayol's Functions of Management

To build "unity through management," Fayol described how managers administer operations through five functional activities.

- **Planning**—studying the future and arranging the means for dealing with it, which encompasses forecasting, setting goals, and determining actions.
- **Organizing**—designing a structure to assist in goal accomplishment that effectively relates human and nonhuman resources to the tasks of the enterprise.
- **Coordinating**—uniting all activities that take place within the organization so that elements are given proper resources and the means to accomplish goals.
- **Commanding**—(directing)—engaging in those activities that ensure effective operation, including leadership and motivation of employee action toward goals.
- **Controlling**—ensuring that everything is carried out according to the plan.

Sources: Henri Fayol's *General and Industrial Management* (1949), as summarized in W. Jack Duncan, *Great Ideas in Management* (San Francisco: Jossey-Bass, 1990), pp. 91–97.

synthesis (putting the elements back together into a logical system). This interaction between analysis and synthesis became the basis for empirically based goal setting. To Lillian Gilbreth, a goal was not an idealized aspiration, but the result of an objectively determined study of work tasks based on what "has actually been done and what can be expected to be repeated."[5] Her pioneering 1914 work on analysis and synthesis as the basis of goal setting provided the foundation for later management practices such as *management by objectives (MBO)* and the use of rewards to reinforce behavior.

Administrative Principles. Administrative management principles were first developed by a French industrialist, Henri Fayol. He published *General and Industrial Management* in bulletin form in 1916, although it was not available in an English translation within North America until 1949.[6] Fayol elevated the study of management from the shop floor (Taylor's emphasis) to the total organization. He viewed business as a composite of six subsystems: purchasing, production, sales, finance, accounting, and administration. To handle the subsystems, he described the five *management functions* of planning, organizing, coordinating, directing, and controlling (see Exhibit A–1).

These management functions remain the basic platform for the principles of management texts in use today (an approach that is not followed in this text). The first part of Fayol's book emphasized that *management principles* (a theory of management) needed to be developed so that they could be taught to managers. Fayol complemented his five functions with fourteen principles of administrative management, which included such teachings as *division of labor* to achieve specialization for maximum efficiency and *unity of command* so that workers receive directives from only one superior to eliminate confusion.

Bureaucracy Theory. Although conventional wisdom associates the word *bureaucracy* with inefficiency and indifference to clients, it was originally put forth by Max Weber as an ideal design for efficiency. A sociologist concerned about society in Germany, Weber introduced several underlying structural principles for organizational effectiveness under the umbrella of the concept of bureaucracy.[7] To Weber, **bureaucracy** meant:

bureaucracy
Max Weber's rational-legal authority structure for organizing specialized functions and standardizing procedures to achieve efficiency.

- A hierarchy of command based on a rational-legal authority structure established by a person's rank in the hierarchy.
- Specialization and division of labor by organizational function, such as engineering, production, and sales.

- An explicit system of rules and policies that standardizes how things are to be done to ensure equitable treatment of everyone.

- Promotion and tenure based on competence, developed through training and experience, and measured by objective standards.

- Impersonal treatment of people through consistent application of rules and decisions to prevent favoritism.

Weber assumed work was not necessarily meant to be pleasant but rather to be efficient, with minimum conflicts of interest. Managers were expected to be unemotional and treat people as though they were interchangeable.

Although he wrote as a sociologist concerned about preserving social order, one of Weber's most significant contributions to management was his *focus on authority*.[8] He believed organizations require order to regulate human behavior, and employees accept directives and guidelines from management to improve harmony and productivity. The most significant source of authority is from the legal system, giving the manager legitimate authority; the weakest is charismatic authority based on the esteemed personal qualities of the leader or manager. In Weber's view, people comply with authority because it is in their best interest to do so, which suggests a passive human nature. This impersonal treatment of people was seen as a limitation of Weber's theory once groups were recognized as social systems.

THE BEHAVIORAL APPROACHES

Regardless of whether practiced in the United States, France, or Germany, the classical theories of management held a limited view of people as employees. They all viewed the rank-and-file worker as rather passive and lacking in self-direction, motivated mainly by economic self-interest. Three forces combined to hasten the decline of the mechanistic point of view in favor of a more human-centered orientation: The hardship of the Great Depression, enactment of progressive legislation such as the social security and wage-and-hours acts, and an intellectual climate that raised social consciousness. The original shift in focus away from a rational–economic picture of employees to a more social–behavioral perspective came from an attempt to refine and extend scientific management.

Hawthorne Studies Spawn Human Relations Movement.   The theoretical turning point in management philosophy and practice was the work of Elton Mayo in his famous Hawthorne studies. Mayo's 1924 research project to determine the relationship between physical working conditions and worker productivity at Western Electric's Hawthorne Works near Chicago yielded puzzling results.[9] The productivity of the initial work groups selected for observation seemed to increase constantly, regardless of changes in a variety of physical variables such as temperature, lighting, or duration of work. What seemed to be important were social elements such as involvement in decision making, work relationships, and group attitudes and values.

Hawthorne effect
The unintentional biasing of research outcomes due to the possibility that simply paying attention to the experimental subjects causes their behavior to change.

The Hawthorne Works research methodology has been widely criticized. Some allege that simply because the experimental subjects (the employees) were being paid attention, their behavior changed—a research-confounding effect called the **Hawthorne effect.** Yet more than any other single body of research, the decade of Western Electric experiments (involving more than 20,000 workers) shifted the management paradigm from largely mechanistic principles to a human relations orientation built around the behavioral complexities of people with diverse needs functioning in a complex, informal social system. Organizational behavior became important as a field of study and a concern of management.

Toward a Humanistic Psychology.   During the era of the late 1940s and the 1950s, a popular (but widely misunderstood) theory of motivation was expressed by Abraham Maslow[10] and his followers, such as Douglas McGregor.[11] They pushed the humanistic frontier even further in focusing on the complexities of human behavior as a critical variable in organizational effectiveness. Maslow defined human motivation as "the study of ultimate human goals" in his 1954 book *Motivation and Personality*.[12] He emphasized the uniqueness of human needs and at the same time called attention to the different ways cultures impact the satisfaction of those needs.

As explained in Chapter 6, Maslow recognized that some needs deal with overcoming basic human deficiencies, whereas others pull us in the direction of individualistic, growth-motivated goals. This concept shifted management attention away from simply providing basic needs toward an awareness that people's growth needs could be achieved at work, benefiting both the individual and the organization. Many present-day practices such as empowerment, team building, and building high-commitment organizations are based on the humanistic realities originally advocated by Maslow and refined by many others.

SYSTEMS THEORIES WITH CONTINGENCY ADJUSTMENTS

The last half of the twentieth century has seen a proliferation of theoretical refinements largely consistent with the systems concept of organizations. Several contributors helped create the concept of contingent-based administrative behavior within an open system.

systems theory
Emphasizes that the whole is greater than the sum of the parts, and that the parts or subsystems are related to each other and to the whole.

Systems Theory.   Systems theory holds that the whole is greater than the sum of the parts, and that all parts or subsystems are related to one another and to the whole. Two works were especially notable for examining organizations as social systems. The first was George Homan's *The Human Group*, which presented a social systems model of group behavior.[13] The other milestone was *The Social Psychology of Organizations* by Katz and Kahn,[14] which built on the work of Parsons[15] to emphasize the close relationship between the organization and its supporting environment. The systems approach allows the level of analysis to run up and down the hierarchy and from the outside environment to individual behavior, depending on the behavior that is the focus of attention. More than any other model, the systems perspective examines growth and decline in terms of predicted patterns of effectiveness.

Administrative Behavior.   Mary Parker Follett wrote across a number of management topics. The essence of her most important ideas was recorded in *Freedom and Coordination* (1949), a series of lectures edited by Lyndall Urwick. In seeking to develop a more enlightened theory of administration, "Follett maintained that there are two basic qualifications for a profession: It must be founded on science, and its knowledge must be used in the service of others."[16] One of her major contributions was to articulate the reciprocal nature of power. Unlike Weber, who had a hierarchical view of authority, Follett believed that power came from the nature of the task performed. Power is thus function based, or embedded in the plan of the organization, not in the individual.

To Follett, the exercise of power simply makes things happen, and managers use power as an agent of change. She did not accept the prevailing belief that managers have "power over" other people. Rather, she introduced the concept of "power with" others as a process for jointly developing solutions and coactive behaviors as opposed to power as a lever of coercion.[17] By both influencing others and accepting the influence of others, a genuine environment of participation is possible.

Follett favored replacement of authority with careful education of people in the best practices for carrying out work. She emphasized the "law of the situation," cautioning managers to think through the total situation before issuing commands—to think holistically before acting impulsively. When possible, commands should not be directed toward individuals. Directives can provide guidance in a non-finger-pointing way if people understand why they must do certain things that are in their best interest.

Herbert Simon broke new ground with publication of his *Administrative Behavior* in 1946.[18] In this and other works, Simon introduced the concept that managers are decision makers who are not always rational because they do not have "the wits to maximize." Instead, the administrator works within a realm of subjective rationality to maximize outcomes subject to what is known about the decision situation. Thus, the decision maker is limited by *bounded rationality* rather than perfect knowledge and ends up making *satisficing* (acceptable) instead of maximizing decisions.

Cyert and March extended Simon's lead in their 1963 book, *A Behavioral Theory of the Firm* to observe that managers engage in sequential searches of alternative solutions, often with ill-defined outcome preferences.[19] Collectively, this body of research shifted attention away from the people being managed to the imperfections and limitations of those who manage and who are responsible for decisions to better the organization.

The Contingency Perspective.   For the first fifty-plus years of management research, scholars and practitioners alike tried to uncover universal principles that would hold up regardless of circumstances. These proved to be elusive. More recently, researchers and managers have recognized that organizational behavior cannot be engineered by consistently applying one theory to solve a particular problem. In most situations, multiple sources influence outcomes, so the contingency approach within a systems model is viewed as more workable. The contingency approach builds an "it all depends" perspective into the applications of management theory.

contingency theories
Theories that identify the circumstances in which a particular practice is more likely to obtain desired results.

But contingency does not mean simply that anything goes. Rather, useful **contingency theories** identify the circumstances in which a particular practice is more likely to obtain desired results. For example, if employees are new and unsure of themselves, the manager is hypothesized to get better results by being considerate yet firmly task directed; if employees know how to handle their job, being more relationship focused and less intense about task directives is more likely to promote effective performance.[20] The lesson from contingency approaches is that the manager must examine the situation to discover its relevant variables, diagnose the problem, and then adapt some independent variable (often the manager's own behavior) to fit the need. This discussion invites a brief overview of research methods.

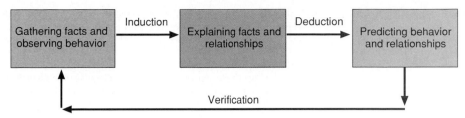

■■■■■ **EXHIBIT A–2**

The Scientific Method

Research that employs the scientific method results in a cycle of ever expanding knowledge based on the empirical verification of predicted hypotheses and models.

Source: Based on Eugene F. Stone, *Research Methods in Organizational Behavior* (Glenview, IL: Scott, Foresman, 1978).

RESEARCH AND METHODOLOGICAL FOUNDATIONS

The study of management and organizational behavior has evolved from industrial engineering and the various behavioral and social sciences to serve practical purposes. It provides knowledge that can be applied in organizational settings to improve performance and to increase efficiency and effectiveness at three levels of analysis: that of the individual, the small group, and the entire organization.

Beyond *industrial engineering* (which gave birth to scientific management), five social science disciplines have been major contributors to management and organizational behavior knowledge. *Psychology* focuses directly on understanding and predicting individual behavior. *Sociology* studies how individuals interact with one another in social systems. *Social psychology* is a behavioral science hybrid that integrates psychology and sociology to study why individuals behave as they do in groups. *Anthropology* studies the relationship between individuals and their environments and how a person or a group adapts to its environment. *Political science* studies individuals and groups in governmental and public policy–making environments and has relevant OB applications through its focus on power, conflict, and rivalry.

scientific method
The use of theory to guide systematic, empirical research from which generalizations can be made to influence applications.

The Scientific Method.   Although the behavioral sciences may appear to lack the universal precision of the physical sciences, they all embrace the fundamentals of the scientific method. The **scientific method** uses a theory to guide systematic, empirical research from which generalizations can be made to influence applications. Rather than rely on intuition or a few ad hoc observations, the scientific method draws on facts through theory-guided investigations of behavior in organizations. It works only because behavior is caused rather than random. Research based on the scientific method progresses through four stages: from description to understanding to prediction and finally to control to bring about predicted outcomes. These stages parallel those managers go through as they learn to become more skilled and ultimately to influence behavioral outcomes.

Exhibit A–2 portrays the flow of the scientific method as applied to the study of organizational behavior. Some researchers begin with observing and gathering facts from the real-world behavior of individuals, groups, and organizations. From their specific preliminary observations, they inductively reason possible general explanations or theories of the cause of behavior and/or its effects. Or researchers can apply deductive logic by building on their logical-rational thoughts about phenomena to state testable hypotheses or models of predicted behavior in general organizational situations. In reality, there is no separation of inductive and deductive approaches to theory development, but rather an essential continuity.[21] The

━━━━━ **EXHIBIT A–3**

Research Designs for Studying Behavior

The empirical investigation of behavior in organizations draws on four primary alternatives for collecting data: interviews, questionnaires, observation of a sample of respondents, and secondary sources (such as company records). Researchers have a number of design options to chose from to provide answers to the questions (hypotheses) being investigated. Here are the basics of four common research designs:

- **Case study.** The researcher focuses on a single organization and does an in-depth study using a variety of data collection methods, including interviews, observation, and reviews of existing records. Case studies are useful in uncovering new insights into behavioral phenomena or making a limited exploration of a deductive model. Generalization of results is limited.

- **Field survey.** This method gathers data about perceptions, feelings, and opinions through interviews and questionnaires administered to people in their actual work setting. Large numbers of people should be surveyed to obtain valid conclusions from the sample that will apply to the general population. Data tend to be correlational in nature (indicating that relationships exist); surveys lack cause-effect conclusions.

- **Field experiment.** Field experiments allow the researcher to manipulate independent variables in actual organizations in an attempt to control variables and explain causality. At times, the subjects know they are being observed under experimental conditions (as in the Hawthorne studies). In other situations, the experimental treatment is part of an actual management pilot program and less influenced by the Hawthorne effect.

- **Laboratory experiment.** Control of independent variable manipulation without intervening environmental effects is at its maximum in lab experiments conducted in artificial settings. Conclusions of causality can be highly reliable, but generalization is often difficult because the artificial conditions are devoid of organizational complexities.

interplay between conceptualizing general explanations of phenomena (deductive reasoning) and empirically studying the relationships among specific phenomena (inductive reasoning) is "the essence of modern scientific method."[22]

Managers can also apply the scientific method. For example, in making appraisals of employees, a manager can study multiple performance events over a period of time instead of drawing inferences from a single event. An inference based on a single snapshot can lead to an erroneous conclusion if the employee is having an off day (or a superior day). Similarly, if only one dimension of behavior were observed (such as friendliness), the conclusion might be equally misleading. Instead, the more reliable approach is to use multiple criteria with episodes documented at different intervals of time. Documentation at the time of the event is important, for lapsed time between events and evaluations tends to blur the details of what actually happened.

Hypothesized Relationships among Variables. Once a model or hypothesis has been specified, then the researchers verify (or disconfirm) hypothesized relationships by means of systematic data collection and analysis using experimentation, survey methods, or field investigations of an appropriate sample. (See Exhibit A–3 for notes on research methods.) Most research is conducted to establish relationships between two or more variables. A **hypothesis** is a statement about the proposed relationship between the variables. An **independent variable** (also called the treatment, experimental, or antecedent variable, represented by the symbol X) is thought to cause an effect on one or more **dependent variables** (often called the criterion or predicted variable, symbolized by Y). It might be hypothesized, for example, that leaders who are more considerate and team centered will realize higher group output and higher employee satisfaction than leaders who are directive and task centered. The research design to test such a hypothesis would treat variation in leadership style as the independent variable and group output and employee satisfaction as the dependent variables.

In some research designs, a **moderating variable** might be specified—one that is believed to influence the effects of the independent variable on the dependent variable. For example, working conditions may moderate the effect of leadership

hypothesis
A statement about the proposed relationship between independent and dependent variables.

independent variable
The variable thought to affect one or more dependent variables.

dependent variable
The outcome studied through research and believed to be caused or influenced by an independent variable.

moderating variable
A variable believed to influence the effects of the independent variable on the dependent variable.

on output. (In the Hawthorne research, working conditions such as lighting were hypothesized as independent variables thought to directly cause a change in output—a hypothesized relationship that was difficult to prove.)

reliability
The consistency of the data obtained from a particular research method.

Reliability is the consistency of the data obtained from a particular research method. A performance evaluation is reliable, for example, if it gives the same score to people who perform at the same level, or to the same person who performs consistently over several evaluation periods. Different performance scores for truly equivalent performers mean that the research method or data-gathering instrument is not reliable.

Before basing research conclusions on the data collected by a particular instrument, it needs to be proven reliable. If your bathroom scale displays a different weight reading each of five times you step on it during a one-minute reliability trial, you will certainly dismiss the data as unreliable. The same reliability expectations should hold for research instruments or methods of measuring organizational performance.

validity
The degree to which a research method actually measures what it is supposed to measure.

Validity is the degree to which the research actually measures what it is supposed to measure. A research design or instrument has *internal validity* if the independent variable really did produce a change in the dependent variable. The research has *external validity* if the findings can be generalized to populations beyond the sample. A researcher might find, for example, that differences in leadership style (as measured by a particular instrument) among a sample of university juniors did produce predictable outcomes in groups participating in an experiment (that is, internal validity might be high). However, generalizing the results to managers in actual work settings might be questionable. The external validity would be low because the experimental findings are not generalizable beyond a population of university students.

Research Implications for Managers. Managers obviously can learn from the results of published research. But like scientists, managers need to control for extraneous events that distort conclusions about particular circumstances or people. For example, managers need to consider the factors beyond the control of an employee when evaluating his or her performance. Without being aware of moderating forces, the manager risks a distorted perception of the extent to which a person's or group's behavior contributed to observed or measured performance outcomes.

In a different application, when managers act as change agents, they can think like scientists by conceptualizing a model or hypothesizing relationships among critical variables. By thinking through mutual dependencies or cause-effect relationships, the manager should also be able to identify appropriate measures of key outcomes before and after the change. The practice of measuring organizational variables has become more common in the last few years as firms adopt benchmarking and continuous improvement techniques. Measurements, statistical process controls, and model building are all indicators that the scientific method can be applied by managers as well as researchers.

Key Concepts

scientific management, *p. 568*

bureaucracy, *p. 569*

Hawthorne effect, *p. 570*

systems theory, *p. 571*

contingency theories, *p. 572*

scientific method, *p. 573*

hypothesis, *p. 574*

independent variable, *p. 574*

dependent variable, *p. 574*

moderating variable, *p. 574*

reliability, *p. 575*

validity, *p. 575*

Managing Your Career

YOU CAN START YOUR OWN BUSINESS

In 1982, Tami Simon was a broke, disillusioned Swarthmore College dropout. Today, she runs a $6 million business that reflects her long-standing interest in philosophy and spirituality. Simon, 33, is founder and president of Sounds True, a mail order company in Boulder, Colorado, that produces audiotapes on personal and spiritual development.

In 1983, Tami Simon moved to Boulder to study Eastern mysticism at the Naropa Institute. She began working as a volunteer at a public radio station, KGNU, and ended up as host of an interview show. Most of her guests were writers, psychologists, or inspirational speakers. "I loved being able to ask them the burning questions that were in my heart," Simon recalls.

When Simon's father died in 1984, leaving her $50,000, she decided to "invest in myself, in something I wanted to do."

She began taping conferences on personal and spiritual development in the Denver area. By 1987, she had about 1,000 recordings of such New Age speakers as Ram Dass, author of *Be Here Now!,* a classic work based on Eastern mysticism, and Stephen Levine, an expert in the field of death and dying. With the help of Devon Christensen, 41, who designed a mail-order catalog and packaging for Simon's audiotapes, Sounds True was launched. Sales rose slowly at first, then shot up to $3 million annually between 1989 and 1993.

Soon, Simon was able to build a recording studio to produce original recording tapes. An early guest was Clarissa Pinkola Estes, then director of the C. G. Jung Center in Denver. Estes had been trying for 17 years to find a publisher for a book she had written when Simon produced a tape on it. After the tape came out, publishers approached Estes. The result was the best-seller *Women Who Run with the Wolves.*

Source: Judith Valente, "You Can Start Your Own Business," *Parade Magazine* (June 23, 1996), pp. 8–11.

It used to be that most people went to work for large companies and expected to stay with them for most of their careers. People were loyal to companies and vice versa. Career ladders were clearly designed. Managers, specialists, and those with the company for many years could count on holding their jobs. People who obtained a good education, worked hard, and were loyal were normally assured of a job and opportunity to build a career.

But not today. *Business Week* says, "The traditional corporate career, which was once the cornerstone of American middle-class life, is rapidly disappearing."[1] Many higher-level managers, technical specialists, and employees with twenty or more years of service are being released from their jobs and companies. An American Management Association survey of 1,100 companies found that 17 percent of those laid off were middle managers, although they constituted only 5 percent to 8 percent of workers.[2]

Today most people expect to work at several different jobs in several different organizations; often, they expect to totally change careers several times. Others, like Tami Simon, opt to start their own businesses. Success in today's culture is no longer measured by money, position, and status alone, but also by family, life-style, geographic location, and personal autonomy. No longer do people assume that the organization has unilateral control over their career. Today people are counseled to assume responsibility for their own career development.[3]

WHAT FACTORS ARE DRIVING CAREER TRENDS?

Many factors have contributed to these changes. Competition has intensified as the nations of the world move closer to a global economy. Technological advances continue to enhance productivity and spur new product development. Employees are better educated and more empowered to make decisions and take actions at work.

These and other factors have stimulated many companies to become leaner, flatter, and more efficient, thus reducing the number of jobs. That trend, in turn, has eroded the feelings of loyalty among workers, managers, and technical people at all levels. Many people are wary of trusting or identifying too closely with a company. People suddenly out of work have difficulty finding jobs comparable to those they left—or in some cases any job at all.[4] For some, the impact on their self-esteem and aspirations is devastating.

The accelerating rate of change stimulated by technological advancements means that in the future people will change companies and even careers more frequently than in the past. Rather than planning for a career in one field, industry, or company, young people would do better to assume they will work in three or more companies and career areas and to focus on developing transferable skills. Not only are advancement paths unclear, so are career opportunities.

Jerre Stead of AT&T provides an example of today's nontraditional career ladder. Succession at AT&T had been quite predictable in past years, with most executives moving up through the telephone operating companies. Stead moved rapidly to the top in his 21-year career, but not at AT&T. He started his career at Honeywell, then joined Square D Co., where he was promoted to president and CEO in 1989. When Square D was acquired by another company in 1991, Stead moved to AT&T as president of AT&T's Global Business Communications Systems.[5]

Today companies like AT&T increasingly value people with different views and experiences. AT&T apparently valued Stead's varied background more than that of managers who climbed the traditional AT&T ladder. Managers who cruise along under the old rules of climbing through a single discipline within one company may find only disappointment. The path to the top is much more ambiguous than it used to be.

WHAT IS A CAREER?

To most people, a career is a series of separate but related experiences that occur in the process of moving upward in their chosen occupation or profession. Traditionally

Individuals may differ in the age at which they transition from one stage to the next, but for most people the role of work in their lives progresses through rather predictable career stages.

Age	Stage	Description
0–14	Early childhood	Parents, schools, peers, and experiences influence attitudes, values, and expectations about work.
15–24	Exploration and initial jobs	Temporary jobs and first full-time job to earn money, develop independence, test self and learn own strengths and weaknesses, and investigate possibilities and limits of specific jobs.
25–34	Trial work period	Move from testing self to clearer view of self and direction in work context. Individuals can feel confident and successful or confused, uncertain, frustrated.
35–44	Establishment	Find and accept role and career path that is satisfying, or resign self to not fully achieving aspirations and accepting what must be endured, or trying a different path.
45–65	Stability and maintenance	For some, continuing advancement and growth; for many, plateauing and stabilizing and making contributions in a satisfying way; for some, frustration; and for some, trying a different path.
65+	Postretirement	Letting go and finding new activities and outlets for satisfaction.

this process involved increases in salary, responsibility, status, prestige, and power. But today an individual can remain in the same job, developing new skills, without necessarily moving upward in an organization. It is also becoming common for people to move laterally among various jobs in different fields and different organizations.

The concept of "career" applies not only to work for pay, but a variety of other life pursuits, such as homemaking and volunteer work. Hall defines **career** as "the individuality perceived sequence of attitudes and behaviors associated with work-related experiences and activities over the span of the person's life."[6]

career
The work-related experiences and activities over the span of a person's life.

Career Stages

Many people begin to prepare for a career without even thinking about it. As children's personalities develop and they go through school, they begin to fantasize about what they will do when they get older. Their thoughts are usually influenced by their socioeconomic status, family background, and educational environment.

Many young people enter the work world through part-time jobs, and they begin to learn more about what they like and don't like to do and what they hope to achieve. These young people are in the first of several career stages, shown in Exhibit B–1. Most people progress through these stages, although the exact timing of each varies.

HOW DO I PLAN MY CAREER?

Planning your career requires that you determine your life priorities, values, and interests. We turn to these topics in this section.

Know Yourself Well

Not everyone aspires to be president of the company, nor does everyone want to be a manager. However, virtually all people want to be successful and happy. Definitions of success and happiness are elusive, largely because both are self-defined.

YOUR TURN

Valuing Selected Aspects of Life

Allocate a total of 100 points among these different aspects of life according to how much you value each. If one aspect is very important, you might give it 30 to 50 points. Some might receive zeros. Your total should be 100.

____	Work/career/profession	____	Intellectual growth
____	Family	____	Spiritual growth
____	Wealth (money)	____	Social life (friends)
____	Material possessions	____	Physical fitness/health
____	Political/societal concerns	____	Recreation

What constitutes success to one person may not to another, and what brings happiness is also highly personal. *Success is achieving your objectives.* Happiness is feeling satisfied with your situation. Thus, one of the first steps in career planning is to begin identifying your goals, values, and aspirations. Career planning should be approached in the context of your whole life.

Life planning is deciding how you want to live your life. Although some people value career and work highly, most believe there is more to life than work. Other important factors include family, leisure-time activities, social life, spiritual development, education and personal development, and civic and philanthropic involvement. **Life planning** includes making choices about what mix of these various aspects of life most closely matches your values and aspirations. Some people emphasize career and work over the other factors. Others focus on family or spiritual development or social life. Some try to achieve a relatively even balance.

life planning
Making choices about what activities you want to spend your time on in your life.

The first Your Turn exercise shows selected aspects of life. How important is each to you?[7] This exercise can help you gain perspective on your values and so help you plan a more satisfying life.

Making these choices can be difficult because each choice involves costs as well as benefits. Each person has the same amount of time each day, and it is impossible to do everything. Choosing one activity often means another cannot be pursued. For example, a poll conducted by Louis Harris and Associates in 1993 found that Americans are ambivalent about the value of a two-paycheck family. Although 80 percent of those surveyed said they accepted women holding paying jobs while raising children, 50 percent said the trend toward both parents working had a negative effect on families.[8]

The pain of making such choices is illustrated by women and men who must choose between career and family. Both pursuing a career and raising a family are time and energy consuming. Time spent at work to "get ahead" often means time away from children, who need parental attention, guidance, and love. The conflict, especially for mothers, can be intense.

Tim Burke, a former All-Star relief pitcher, illustrates the conflicting pull of work and family.[9] In February 1993, he resigned from the Cincinnati Reds and gave up his major league baseball salary so that he could spend more time with his family. He had averaged more than $2 million in salary during the last three

YOUR TURN

This Has Been My Life

Write answers to the following questions. This exercise helps you sort out your main values, motives, and aspirations to this stage of your life.

1. What have I liked to do most? Least?
2. What successes have I had? Failures?
3. What have been my most important relationships, and what impact have they had on me?
4. How important have relationships been to me?
5. What were the most important incidents in my life and what meaning do they have for me?
6. Have there been any turning points in my life so far?
7. When did I feel happiest and most fulfilled? Discontented and least fulfilled? What was the context of these feelings?
8. How does my past experience help me understand my present feelings about myself? My degree of self-esteem? My present personality and behavior?

---

seasons. What drew Burke away from the glamour and income of the big leagues? Tim and his wife, Christine, had adopted two physically handicapped daughters from Korea and a handicapped son from Guatemala. At the time of his resignation, they were about to adopt a fourth handicapped child. Burke said, "You know something? When it comes down to it, it wasn't even close. My place is no longer on the baseball field. It's at home."

Where Have I Come From?   One way of getting to know yourself, including what motivates you, what you like and dislike doing, and what is important to you, is to answer the question: Where have I come from? What is my background and how does it relate to how I think and feel about myself? One way to answer these questions is to write your autobiography.[10]

Set aside some uninterrupted time during which you can give exclusive attention to writing freely about yourself. Just start writing what comes to mind without worrying about organization or whether you are getting the "right" things down. When finished, review your results to analyze what areas seem most and least important to you. A more structured alternative is to complete the second Your Turn exercise above. You could also use the questions in the exercise to help diagnose your autobiography.

Know Your Values.   The previous exercises have already required that you identify your values to some extent. You can expand your awareness by completing the third Your Turn exercise, which is designed to help you rank your values.

Now that you have identified the relative importance of different aspects of your life and their associated values, it is helpful to identify your interests.

Determine Your Interests

Your autobiography and responses to the Your Turn exercises probably pointed toward some of your interests. By the time people are in college or beginning to choose their occupations, they have developed predispositions toward various clusters of jobs.[11] What you liked and did not like doing reveals your interests.

YOUR TURN

What Do I Value?

Place a + (plus sign) in front of any item that you value—that is so important to you that you consistently try to experience it. For any item that you disdain or seek to avoid, put a − (minus sign). Skip any item that is neutral, or does not influence you. When finished, study your results to find patterns that suggest what you might want to experience in your career.

_____ Achieving		_____ Advancing
_____ Being logical		_____ Being relaxed
_____ Being creative		_____ Being challenged
_____ Being alone		_____ Being close
_____ Being higher than others		_____ Being praised
_____ Being independent		_____ Being secure
_____ Being safe		_____ Being expert
_____ Competing		_____ Controlling
_____ Cooperating		_____ Creating ideas or things
_____ Directing others		_____ Doing mental work
_____ Enjoying work		_____ Experiencing stability
_____ Feeling comfortable with ambiguity and uncertainty		_____ Feeling in control
_____ Finishing a job		_____ Focusing on one job at a time
_____ Having routine		_____ Having variety
_____ Having work structured		_____ Having unstructured work
_____ Having order		_____ Having several balls in the air
_____ Helping others		_____ Receiving clear direction
_____ Taking risks		_____ Working with simple ideas
_____ Working with things		_____ Working with people
_____ Working with hands		_____ Working outdoors
_____ Working in groups		_____ Working alone
_____ Working with general ideas		_____ Working with details
_____ Working with complex ideas and problems		
_____ Others? _____		_____ Others? _____

One source of help is the Strong Interest Inventory (SII), which is a widely used vocational interest test. Most campus career counseling centers can help you obtain the SII and have it scored.[12] The SII relates your interests to major occupational groups and selected jobs. It is based on John Holland's theory that most occupations can be grouped in one of six major categories. Exhibit B–2 describes the characteristics of people attracted to each. Individuals may be interested in and suitable for more than one theme area. For a list of some basic interest areas and selected jobs associated with these major occupational themes, see Exhibit B–3. Exhibit B–3 is only suggestive and is not a substitute for the Strong Interest Inventory, which gives much more complete information.

EXHIBIT B–2	**Themes**	**Partial Characteristics and Interests—Person Tends to Be:**
Six Occupational Themes Defined by the Strong Interest Inventory	Realistic (R)	Rugged, practical, often aggressive. Enjoys outdoors. Prefers working with hands and things. Good physical skills. Less adept at expression in words and expressing emotions. Reserved. Conventional.
	Investigative (I)	Task oriented. Wants to understand the physical world. Enjoys solving abstract problems. Dislikes highly structured situations and enjoys ambiguous challenges. Often has unconventional values and attitudes. Frequently creative.
	Artistic (A)	Artistically oriented. Enjoys artistic settings and opportunities for self-expression through artistic media. Likes to work alone. Individualistic. Assertive. Tends to be sensitive and emotional. Creative and highly original.
	Social (S)	Sociable, responsible, humanistic, concerned with welfare of others. Usually expresses self well and gets along with others. Likes attention and working in groups. Little interest in physical work and working with things.
	Enterprising (E)	Dominant. Leader. Facile with words. Good at selling. Energetic, enthusiastic, confident. Enjoys persuading and leading. Impatient with detail and work that involves long intellectual effort. Likes power, status, and material wealth.
	Conventional (C)	Likes highly ordered activities. Fits well in large organizations and chains of command. Dislikes ambiguity and wants to know what is expected. Stable, controlled, dependable. Little interest in intense relationships. Values material possessions and status.

Know Your Skills

Knowing your values and interests helps in determining *what you want* from a job and career. Knowing your abilities and skills helps in determining *what you can give* to an organization. Begin recording your personal inventory of skills. Avoid comparing yourself to others. One suggestion is to brainstorm on this subject, listing as many skills as you can. Then you can rank them according to those you feel best about and those you want to improve. Keep your list where you can add to it as you identify new skills or more fully develop existing skills. An excellent source of help in identifying your skills is Richard Bolles's *What Color Is Your Parachute?*[13] (revised annually).

Skills can be developed through school, training, and experience. A good career plan identifies current skills, those needed for the next job, and those likely to be required in the future. The plan can then provide for when and how the needed skills will be developed. The next step is to plan how to find the right position to move you along in your career.

HOW DO I GET WHAT I WANT?

Finding your ideal job can be difficult because some factors are out of your control. Economic conditions, the availability of jobs, and the number of people looking for similar jobs are a few of those factors. This leads some people to settle for taking any job they can get, at least temporarily, and sometimes that may be appropriate. However, a better approach is to get a clear picture in your mind of the kind of job and career you want, and then seek diligently to find and obtain that job.

━━━━ **EXHIBIT B–3**

Basic Interests and Selected Occupations

Occupational Theme	Interest Areas	Job Examples
Realistic	Agriculture	Farmer
	Nature	Forester
	Adventure	Police officer
	Military activities	Air Force officer
	Mechanical activities	Engineer
Investigative	Science	Physicist
	Mathematics	Computer programmer
	Medical science	Physician
	Medical service	Physical therapist
Artistic	Music/Dramatics	Musician
	Art	Commercial artist
	Writing	Advertising executive
Social	Teaching	School administrator
	Social service	Social worker
	Athletics	Recreation leader
	Domestic arts	Home economics teacher
	Religious activities	Minister
Enterprising	Public speaking	Elected public official
	Law/Politics	Lawyer
	Merchandising	Marketing executive
	Sales	Life insurance agent
	Business management	Store manager
Conventional	Office practices	Accountant

Define What You Want to Do. You have already laid the groundwork for defining the kind of job and career you want through the preceding self-assessment process. Your results can help you answer questions that will further define the job you want:

- What are your best skills, and where do you want to use them?
- What kinds of people would you like to work with or help?
- In what kind of place would you like to work?
- What fields or industries feel compatible with your skills and interests?
- What salary level do you want?
- What developmental and advancement opportunities do you want?

In answering these and similar questions, you can begin to define the specific jobs or careers that will enable you to use your skills and fulfill your interests and aspirations.

Identify Potential Organizations. Begin to identify specific organizations that have the kinds of jobs you want. Do this by word of mouth, by reading business periodicals, and by using school career guidance services. Read the help wanted ads in the business section of your local paper and the *The Wall Street Journal.* List specific organizations that have potential for you. Then request information about these companies. You may even want to visit some. Such a visit is not to secure a position, but to obtain information that will help you assess the fit with your own skills and interests. If you have an informational interview, go with questions in mind and keep the meeting brief. Inquire about the company's employment needs and the goals it is trying to reach.

network
Contacts who can help
provide information, advice,
and help in your career.

Build a Network of Contacts.   Start your career planning immediately, even if you have some years of school ahead of you. Begin to build a **network** of contacts who can help you obtain information, give you advice, and help you get introductions into the companies of your choice. Talk with the successful friends of your parents and the parents of your friends. Ask them for the names of others who might help. Become acquainted with the people in your school who can give you information and advice and can serve as references. You will be surprised how wide a network you can develop if you work at it.

Intern.   Summer and part-time work can be just a source of money or it can provide important skills and information. Look for work that fits your job and career interests. Such a job may be more valuable to you in the long run than one that pays more. Above-average performance may be rewarded by valuable contacts and references.

Design Your Resumé.   Carefully design a one-page resumé that effectively describes your goals, qualifications, and skills. You may want to have more than one resumé for use in trying to achieve different types of jobs. The basics should stay the same, but the goals and emphasis on skills might vary. Refine your resumé until you feel it represents you in the best manner possible.

Prepare and Practice for Interviews.   Prepare and practice. Those are the keys to successful interviews. Your preparation is already far along if you have carefully assessed your values, goals, interests, and skills and determined the kinds of jobs you want. List the questions you think an interviewer might ask, and write answers to them. Ask a few interviewers what questions they ask and what they look for in an applicant. Then practice interviewing. Professors, business people, and career services personnel may be willing to conduct a mock interview with you. This kind of practice and accompanying feedback can improve your chances of receiving job offers.

Obtain Interviews.   Unless you work for yourself, an interview is likely to be essential in obtaining a job. Do some research and try to discover the decision process in the companies you have targeted. If you can, try to have your interview with the decision maker. This is not always possible, and you should be careful not to antagonize people you might be trying to bypass. However, sometimes it is possible through contacts to get an interview directly with the person who makes the decision. Remember, the interview is a two-way process. The organization is interviewing you, and you are interviewing the organization. Your mutual goal is to decide if you have a good fit. Some people make the mistake of selling themselves into a job and company they later discover they dislike. Exhibit B–4 suggests a few caveats for interviewing.

To obtain the job you want, you can use either a shotgun or a rifle approach. The first involves sending out lots of letters and resumés, often blindly, hoping someone responds positively. The rifle approach involves targeting those organizations that have a high probability of having jobs that fit your values, interests, and skills. It requires that you take the basic career planning steps described in this appendix.

Obtaining the right job to move your career along is important, although keep in mind that this is not a life-and-death situation! You are not making a lifetime decision. If you make a mistake, you can profit from what you have learned and find another position that suits you better. Nevertheless, the more carefully you have followed the steps previously described, the more likely you are to obtain a position that fits you well. Obtaining your job is only a door-opener, however. The real challenge is to perform well, develop, and progress. We turn now to a few ideas on how to keep your career moving along toward your goals.

■■■■■■■■ **EXHIBIT B–4**

*Suggestions for
Employment Interviews*

To increase your chances of success:

- Research the company before your interview.
- Focus on the employer's needs and how you meet them.
- Listen carefully, respond succinctly, and always be courteous.
- Be early, appropriately dressed, and be considerate of the interviewer's time.
- Ask about salary and developmental opportunities near the end of the interview if those subjects have not been addressed; avoid being the first to introduce these subjects.
- Be clear on what followup is appropriate.
- Send a thank-you note.
- Follow up by phone or letter if appropriate.
- Sometimes it is appropriate to ask for feedback and advice after an unsuccessful interview.

HOW DO I MANAGE MY CAREER?

Think of managing your life and career as a part-time task you will perform for the rest of your life. This section is designed to stimulate you to think about some important steps to take in managing your own career.

Make a Mission Statement.   Think of yourself metaphorically as a small company. Develop a mission statement that expresses your philosophy and central values. In your statement, include who you want to be, what you want to do, and your most central values.[14] Who you are describes your character; what you do describes the contributions you want to make.

Establish and Visualize Your Goals.   Stephen Covey urges people to "begin with the end in mind."[15] He points out that all things are created twice. First there is the mental creation, or visualization, of what might be. Second there is the actual creation. People who have a clear vision of their values and goals tend to direct their behavior toward fulfilling their mission. Peak performers frequently are visualizers.[16]

Be Aware of Career Stage.   Keep in mind the opportunities and pitfalls related to each of the career stages you will pass through. The first stage usually runs from your twenties into your thirties. In this stage, your goal should be to gain a variety of experiences and to develop basic skills that will be transferable to other positions. Often a big company is a good place to go through this stage, but some small companies also have advantages. Avoid overspecialization. One suggestion is that by your mid-thirties you have a "T-shaped experience profile: a wide array of general managerial skills with at least one deep groove of expertise."[17]

Communicate a Positive Attitude.   Enthusiasm and a positive outlook are contagious. For some people, expressing these traits comes easily. Others have to work at it. The effort is worth the benefits.

Perform.   This is as obvious as it is crucial. Yet some people lope rather than run in their first jobs, and some focus so much on the jobs ahead they forget to perform in the present. Excellent performance becomes a habit, just as does mediocre performance.

Capitalize on Luck and Build on Setbacks.   Luck often comes to those who have worked hard and prepared themselves for unexpected events. Do not count on luck to help implement your life and career plans, but if it should come, rejoice and be ready to capitalize on it. Setbacks come to everyone, but successful people respond positively to them. They find ways to learn from and build on the setbacks to help them get back on track toward reaching their goals.

Develop a Network.   Some people concentrate so much on their job at hand that they fail to develop relationships throughout the organization. Usually some conscious effort has to be directed toward building such a network. Those who have established relationships enjoy the benefits of being hooked into informal communications. Also, friends in strategic places can help you achieve results that might be difficult if you rely only on the formal organization.

mentor
An experienced person who helps a less experienced person achieve career goals.

Find a Mentor, Be a Mentor.   A **mentor** is someone, usually older and more experienced, who helps another person achieve his or her career goals. The mentor serves as a guide, coach, advisor, and counselor. Some companies, such as IBM, have formal mentoring programs. Others, such as AT&T, rely on informal mentoring because they think it more effective.[18]

If there is no formal mentoring program, find someone in your organization you trust and like. However, remember that a mentor is no substitute for performance. Often a mentor is not a direct superior but someone who cares enough about you to share his or her accumulated wisdom and experience. As you develop experience, look for opportunities to serve as a mentor. Helping others achieve success is an important attribute of successful managers and professionals.

WHAT SPECIAL SITUATIONS SHOULD I BE AWARE OF?

We now turn to three topics important in many people's careers. They are the "mommy and daddy tracks," the "glass ceiling," and plateauing.

Mommy and Daddy Tracks

In 1989, Felice N. Schwartz wrote a *Harvard Business Review* article in which she suggested that companies should recognize that not all women are alike and that different career paths should be open to them.[19] She suggested that those who opted to devote time to having and caring for children should be given opportunities to work but with lower expectations of rewards. This article initiated an intense controversy, out of which came the term **mommy track,** which is a career path for mothers that provides opportunities to work without the pressure of striving to advance as high as others.

mommy track
A career path for mothers with less advancement pressure and less rewards so that mothers can spend more time with their families.

To balance family and career demands, Schwartz suggested that people should stop trying to "have it all." The implication was that women choosing this track should be willing to give up getting to the top because they had chosen to spend some time and energy with their families. Some critics suggested that women should not have to make such choices and should have full access to the top without being penalized for devoting time to families.

daddy track
A career path for fathers with less advancement pressure and less rewards so that fathers can spend more time with their families.

There was little evidence that men had to make such choices, the implicit assumption being that women were charged with raising children even if they worked, while men were free to pursue their careers full time. However, today there is some indication that some men are on the **daddy track.**[20] They find they have to choose between family and career, a dilemma that has always faced working mothers. Some fathers are basing their career decisions on how their children will be affected more than on their own advancement. Remember our earlier example of Tim Burke, the baseball player?

This painful dilemma of choosing between family and career faces many people today. The increasing numbers of women in advanced positions and professions and the number of married couples with dual careers pose a host of challenges not encountered by past generations. Pressure is growing for organizations to recognize these problems and help solve them. Flexible schedules, telecommuting, child care, family leaves, and reduced pressure for mobility as a criterion for advancement are things organizations can do to alleviate some of the new problems. The payoff for the organization is an expanded talent pool and image of caring about its employees.

The "Glass Ceiling"

glass ceiling
An invisible barrier that limits the advancement of women and minorities.

The **"glass ceiling"** is an invisible barrier that limits the advancement of women and minorities.[21] This ceiling is supported by inappropriate stereotypes about gender, race, and age. For example, some assume that women who behave as men do are unfeminine, that women who emphasize family are not committed to their careers, and that women will not move to new career opportunities.[22] The lack of female and minority managers at higher levels indicates that organizations must take positive steps to break the barriers holding back qualified women and minorities.

The U.S. Labor Department conducted an 18-month study in the early 1990s that found the height of the glass ceilings varied from company to company.[23] In some, the ceiling was not much above the supervisory level, which may account for women holding only 6.6 percent and minorities only 2.6 percent of corporate executive positions. The Labor Department study found that minorities hit the glass ceiling even earlier than women.

One common stereotype is that women will not stay with their companies. Yet a recent study showed that many women left their jobs out of frustration with career progress, not because of home or children. During the 1980s, the number of women-owned startups grew at twice the rate of all U.S. business startups, and one study showed that 73 percent of women who quit large companies moved to another organization. Only 7 percent quit to stay at home.[24]

A related problem is that women and men are paid differently for comparable work. One recent study showed that women lagged men relative to salary progression and job transfers although the women were fully and comparably qualified.[25]

The pressure to break this artificial ceiling is building, and the best companies are beginning to take proactive steps to ensure that women and minorities are extended full and fair opportunities to advance.

Plateauing

plateauing
The ending of career advancement.

Virtually everyone who works for a company eventually reaches a plateau beyond which he or she does not advance. For some, this is frustrating because they both want to continue advancing and are qualified to do so. But in pyramidal organizations, the openings at the top become increasingly scarce. Some find **plateauing** a normal experience and continue to contribute and find satisfaction in their work. Expectations and attitude have much to do with how employees experience plateauing. Those who find a great gap between their expectations and reality are likely to feel dissatisfied and frustrated.

The trend toward downsizing with its attendant layoffs of people at all levels has forced many to find alternatives to working for large companies. They have often found the changes positive and satisfying.[26] Some bought a franchise, did consulting, joined a small business, or started a new business. Many people, though not all, found the career changes energizing and satisfying, and some even found their new careers more lucrative.

YOU CAN START YOUR OWN BUSINESS: A SECOND LOOK

Tami Simon's motto is, "You have to have people who believe in you, and you have to be dedicated and serious and exemplify that in everything you do." But she had a critical challenge: she considers her employees friends. She had difficulty asking them to improve their performance. Her solution was to establish quantifiable performance goals for each worker.

In 1996, Simon expects sales to reach $6 million this year. Her company now has 35 employees and an inventory of 300 tapes. Two years in a row, *Inc.* magazine named Sounds True as one of the 500 fastest-growing private companies in America.[27]

SUMMARY

Some people leave their careers to chance. Wiser people plan, which is especially important now because careers are likely to be quite different in the future. Career paths are likely to be more variable and less predictable.

Planning your career requires that you understand how future changes will impact it. Intense worldwide competition, fast-changing technology, and changing organizational forms and management will cause people to change jobs, organizations, and even careers more frequently than in the past. You should expect change and uncertainty and be prepared to manage your own career.

Career planning is part of life planning, which means prioritizing the work, family, social, financial, and spiritual aspects of life. Decide what kind of person you want to be and what you want to do. Identify your values, interests, and skills so that you can decide how well they fit particular jobs and careers.

To achieve your career goals and get the job you want, define what you want to do. Then initiate a process of identifying potential organizations, building a network of contacts, working part time, designing your resumé, and preparing for interviews. The final step is to conduct interviews until you find a job and organization that fit you best.

Assume responsibility for managing your own career. Develop your personal mission statement and clearly establish and visualize your goals. Be aware of which career stage you are in, as each has its own opportunities and pitfalls.

Women and minorities face special problems. Women who value both careers and families often feel the pressure of juggling the conflicting demands of family and work. Organizations need to learn how better to help with such problems. Both minorities and women encounter the "glass ceiling," which is an invisible barrier that blocks advancement. All people reach plateaus in their careers; the critical factor is how each individual reacts to and manages that stage. For some, the experience is frustrating and discouraging; others take it in stride and continue to contribute and find satisfaction.

Key Concepts

career, *p. 579*	mommy track, *p. 587*
life planning, *p. 580*	daddy track, *p. 587*
network, *p. 585*	glass ceiling, *p. 588*
mentor, *p. 587*	plateauing, *p. 588*

Notes

Chapter 1

1. Alessandra Bianchi, "Breaking Away," *Inc.* (November 1995), p. 36.

2. Peter F. Drucker, *Management: Tasks, Responsibilities, Practices* (New York: Harper & Row, 1974), p. 61.

3. G. T. Lumpkin and Gregory G. Dess, "Simplicity as a Strategy-Making Process: The Effects of Stage of Organizational Development and Environment on Performance," *Academy of Management Journal* 38 (October 1995), pp. 1386–1407.

4. Peter F. Drucker, "The Information Executives Truly Need," *Harvard Business Review* 73 (January–February 1994), pp. 54–62.

5. Anne B. Fisher, "Market Value Added: Creating Stockholder Wealth," *Fortune* (December 11, 1995), pp. 105–116.

6. Amy Cortese, "The Software Revolution," *Business Week* (December 4, 1995), pp. 78–90.

7. Ian I. Mitroff, Richard O. Mason, and Christine M. Pearson, "Radical Surgery: What Will Tomorrow's Organizations Look Like," *Academy of Management Executive* 8 (May 1994), pp. 11–21.

8. Both missions quoted in James C. Collins and Jerry I. Porras, "Organizational Vision and Visionary Organizations," *California Management Review* 34 (Fall 1991), pp. 30–52.

9. Noel Tichy and Ram Charan, "Speed, Simplicity, Self-Confidence: An Interview with Jack Welch," *Harvard Business Review* 67 (September–October 1989), pp. 112–120.

10. "A Conversation with Roberto Goizueta and Jack Welch," *Fortune* (December 11, 1995), p. 96.

11. Jon L. Pierce, Stephen A. Rubenfeld, and Susan Morgan, "Employee Ownership: A Conceptual Model of Process and Effects," *Academy of Management Review* 16 (January 1991), pp. 121–144.

12. Raymond F. Zammuto, "A Comparison of Multiple Constituency Models of Organizational Effectiveness," *Academy of Management Review* 9 (October 1984), pp. 606–616.

13. Mary Eisenhart, "Baldrige Award Winner Solectron Sets the Standard for Manufacturing," *Microtimes* (June 8, 1992), pp. 94–102.

14. David A. Garvin, "How the Baldrige Award Really Works," *Harvard Business Review* 69 (November–December 1991), p. 80.

15. "Sears Loses $4 billion, Not Fazing Wall Street," *New York Times* (February 10, 1993).

16. Matt Nauman, "Sears Auto Fraud Case Is Settled," *San Jose Mercury News* (September 3, 1992), pp. 1A, 26A; and Kevin Kelly, "How Did Sears Blow This Gasket?" *Business Week* (June 29, 1992), p. 38.

17. Edward L. Thorndike, *Animal Intelligence: Experimental Studies* (New York: Hafner, 1965 [orig. 1911]), p. 244.

18. Pioneering work in general systems theory appeared in Kenneth E. Boulding, "General Systems Theory—The Skeleton of Science," *Management Science* 2 (April 1956), pp. 200–201; and L. von Bertalanffy, *General Systems Theory: Foundations, Development, Applications* (New York: George Braziller, 1968). Early applications to organizations were by Daniel Katz and Robert L. Kahn, *The Social Psychology of Organizations* (New York: John Wiley & Sons, 1966); and C. West Churchman, *The Systems Approach* (New York: Dell, 1968).

19. Paul S. Goodman, Mark Fichman, F. Javier Lerch, and Pamela R. Snyder, "Customer-Firm Relationships, Involvement, and Customer Satisfaction," *Academy of Management Journal* 38 (October 1995), pp. 1310–1324.

20. Raymond E. Miles and Charles C. Snow, "Fit, Failure, and the Hall of Fame," in Barry M. Staw (Ed.), *Psychological Dimensions of Organizational Behavior* (New York: Macmillan, 1991), pp. 632–646.

21. Henry Mintzberg, "The Manager's Job: Folklore and Fact," *Harvard Business Review* 90 (March–April 1990), p. 163.

22. Henri Fayol, *General and Industrial Management* (London: Pitman, 1949 [orig. 1916], translated by C. Storrs).

23. Marco Iansite, "Shooting the Rapids: Managing Product Development in Turbulent Environments," *California Management Review* 38 (Fall 1995), pp. 37–58.

24. David L. Bradford and Allan R. Cohen, *Managing for Excellence* (New York: John Wiley & Sons, 1984), p. 17.

25. Tom Peters, *Thriving on Chaos: Handbook for a Management Revolution* (New York: Harper & Row, 1987).

26. *Fortune* (April 5, 1993).

27. John P. Kotter, *The General Managers* (New York: Free Press, 1982).

28. Mintzberg, "The Manager's Job," (1990), p. 168.

29. Alvin Toffler, *The Third Wave* (New York: Bantam Books, 1981).

30. Robert L. Katz, "Skills of an Effective Administrator," *Harvard Business Review* 33 (January–February 1955), pp. 33–42.

31. Warren Boeker and Jerry Goodstein, "Organizational Performance and Adaptation: Effects of Environment and Performance on Changes in Board Composition," *Academy of Management Journal* 34 (December 1991), pp. 805–826.

32. Associated Press (September 5, 1992).

33. Christopher Farrell with Michael J. Mandel, "Productivity to the Rescue," *Business Week* (October 9, 1995), pp. 134–146.

34. M. T. Iaffaldano and P. M. Muchinsky, "Job Satisfaction and Job Performance: A Meta-Analysis," *Psychological Bulletin* (March 1985), pp. 251–273.

35. M. M. Petty, G. W. McGee, and J. W. Cavender, "A Meta-Analysis of the Relationship between Individual Job Satisfaction and Individual Performance," *Academy of Management Review* 9 (October 1984), pp. 712–721.

36. Edward E. Lawler III, *The Ultimate Advantage: Creating the High-Involvement Organization* (San Francisco: Jossey-Bass, 1992).

37. Henry P. Sims, Jr., and Peter Lorenzi, *The New Leadership Paradigm* (Newbury Park, CA: Sage, 1992), Chapter 13.

38. Harper's Index," *Harper's* (September 6, 1992).

39. Mary B. Teagarden and 13 others, "Toward a Theory of Comparative Management Research: An Idiographic Case Study of the Best International Human Resources Management Project," *Academy of Management Journal* 38 (October 1995), pp. 1261–1287.

40. J. J. Servan-Schreiber, *The American Challenge* (New York: Athenaeum, 1967).

41. "The 1990 Census Will Show . . . ," *American Demographics* (January 1990), p. 25.

42. Patricia A. Galagan, "Tapping the Power of a Diverse Workforce," *Training & Development Journal* (March 1991), pp. 39–44.

43. Arthur M. Schlesinger, Jr., *The Disuniting of America: Reflections on a Multicultural Society* (New York: W. W. Norton, 1992).

44. Roosevelt Thomas, Jr., "From Affirmative Action to Affirming Diversity," *Harvard Business Review* (March–April 1990), pp. 107–117.

45. Alessandra Bianchi, "Breaking Away," *Inc.* (November 1994), p. 39.

46. Inspired by a classic, "The Dashman Company," in Paul R. Lawrence and John A. Seiler, *Organizational Behavior and Administration: Cases, Concepts, and Research Findings* (Homewood, IL: Irwin, 1965), pp. 16–17.

Chapter 2

1. David A. Nadler, Robert B. Shaw, A. Wlise Walton, and Associates, *Discontinuous Change: Leading Organizational Transformation* (San Francisco: Jossey-Bass, 1995).

2. Henry Mintzberg, "Crafting Strategy," *Harvard Business Review* 65 (July–August 1987), pp. 66–75.

3. Ibid.

4. Peter F. Drucker, *Management: Tasks, Responsibilities, Practices* (New York: Harper & Row, 1974), p. 61.

5. "Dr. Strangelove?" *Financial World* (January 1995); and Gilbert M. Gaul and Susan Q. Stranahan, "From Warfare to Corporate Welfare," *San Jose Mercury News* (July 2, 1995), pp. 1E–2E.

6. M. S. S. El-Namaki, "Creating a Corporate Vision," *Long Range Planning* 25, no. 6 (1992), p. 25.

7. James C. Collins and Jerry I. Porras, "Organizational Vision and Visionary Organizations," *California Management Review* 34 (Fall 1991), pp. 30–52; and James C. Collins and Jerry I. Porras, "Building a Visionary Company," *California Management Review* 37 (Winter 1995), pp. 80–100.

8. Compression Labs, Inc., *1994 Annual Report*.

9. Wal-Mart *1995 Annual Report*.

10. Laurie Larwood, Cecilia M. Falbe, Mark P. Kriger, and Paul Miesing, "Structure and Meaning of Organizational Vision," *Academy of Management Journal* 38 (June 1995), pp. 740–769.

11. M. P. Kriger, "Towards a Theory of Organizational Vision: The Shaping of Organizational Futures," paper presented at the Academy of Management annual meeting (San Francisco, 1990); James G. Hunt, *Leadership: A New Synthesis* (Newbury Park, CA: Sage, 1991); Royston Greenwood and C. R. Hinings, "Understanding Strategic Change: The Contribution of Archetypes," *Academy of Management Journal* 36 (October 1993), pp. 1052–1081; and Burt Nanus, *Visionary Leadership: Creating a Compelling Sense of Direction for Your Organization* (San Francisco: Jossey-Bass, 1992).

12. James M. Kouzes and Barry Z. Posner, *The Leadership Challenge* (San Francisco: Jossey-Bass, 1995).

13. Raymond E. Miles, Henry J. Coleman, Jr., and W. E. Douglas Creed, "Keys to Success in Corporate Redesign," *California Management Review* 37 (Spring 1995), pp. 128–145.

14. For a similar question-based concept for the individual strategist, see Hans H. Hinterhuber and Wolfgang Popp, "Are You a Strategist or Just a Manager?" *Harvard Business Review* 70 (January–February 1992), pp. 105–113.

15. Sumantra Ghoshal, Breck Arnzen, and Sharon Brownfield, "A Learning Alliance between Business and Business Schools: Executive Education as a Platform for Partnership," *California Management Review* 35 (Fall 1992), pp. 50–67.

16. William E. Halal, "From Hierarchy to Enterprise: Internal Markets Are the New Foundation of Management," *Academy of Management Executive* 8 (November 1994), p. 73.

17. Andrew Bartmess and Keith Cerny, "Building Competitive Advantage through a Global Network of Capabilities," *California Management Review* 35 (Winter 1993), pp. 78–103.

18. David A. Aaker, "Managing Assets and Skills: The Key to a Sustainable Competitive Advantage," *California Management Review* 31 (Winter 1989), pp. 91–106.

19. Robert A. Irvin and Edward G. Michaels III, "Core Skills: Doing the Right Things Right," *The McKinsey Quarterly* (Summer 1989), pp. 1–19.

20. Dave Ulrich and Dale Lake, "Organizational Capability: Creating Competitive Advantage," *Academy of Management Executive* 5 (February 1991), pp. 77–91.

21. Pickup Lawsuit to Dog GM," *Gannett News Service* (February 5, 1993).

22. Kenneth R. Andrews, *The Concept of the Corporation*, 3rd ed. (Homewood, IL: Irwin, 1987), Chapter 3.

23. Mintzberg, "Crafting Strategy," pp. 74–75.

24. A. W. Clausen, "Strategic Issues in Managing Change: The Turnaround at BankAmerica Corporation," *California Management Review* 32 (Winter 1990), pp. 98–105.

25. Jay Finegan, "Taking Names," *Inc.* 14 September 1992), pp. 121–130.

26. Peter F. Drucker, *The New Realities* (New York: Harper & Row, 1989), p. 230.

27. James A. Welch and P. Ranganath Nayak, "Strategic Sourcing: A Progressive Approach to the Make-or-Buy Decision," *Academy of Management Executive* 6 (February 1992), pp. 23–31.

28. Raymond F. Zammuto and Edward J. O'Connor, "Gaining Advanced Manufacturing Technologies' Benefits: The Roles of Organization Design and Culture," *Academy of Management Review* 17 (October 1992), pp. 701–728.

29. Robert H. Hayes and Gary P. Pisano, "Beyond World-Class: The New Manufacturing Strategy," *Harvard Business Review,* 72 (January–February 1994), pp. 77–86.

30. Ralf Boscheck, "Competitive Advantage: Superior Offer or Unfair Dominance?" *California Management Review* 37 (Fall 1994), pp. 132–151.

31. Hayes and Pisano (1994), p. 78.

32. Hayes and Pisano (1994), p. 79.

33. Andrew Bartmess and Keith Cerny, "Building Competitive Advantage through a Global Network of Capabilities," *California Management Review* 35 (Winter 1993), pp. 78–103.

34. Michael E. Porter, "The Competitive Advantage of the Inner City," *Harvard Business Review* 73 (May–June 1995), pp. 55–71; and Michael E. Porter, *Competitive Advantage* (New York: Free Press, 1985).

35. Mark Maremont, "Kodak's New Focus," *Business Week* (January 30, 1995), pp. 62–68.

36. Michael E. Porter, "From Competitive Advantage to Corporate Strategy," *Harvard Business Review* 64 (May–June 1982), pp. 43–59.

37. John Pound, "Beyond Takeovers: Politics Comes to Corporate Control," *Harvard Business Review* 70 (March–April 1992), pp. 83–93.

38. Mary C. Lacity, Leslie P. Willcocks, and David F. Feeny, "IT Outsourcing: Maximize Flexibility and Control," *Harvard Business Review* 73 (May–June 1995), pp. 84–93.

39. William E. Halal, "From Hierarchy to Enterprise: Internal Markets Are the New Foundation of Management," *Academy of Management Executive* 8 (November 1994), p. 72.

40. Andrew Bartmess and Keith Cerny, "Building Competitive Advantage Through a Global Network of Capabilities," *California Management Review* 35 (Winter 1993), pp. 78–103.

41. David A. Aaker, "Managing Assets and Skills: The Key to a Sustainable Competitive Advantage," *California Management Review,* 31 (Winter 1989), pp. 91–106.

42. Michael E. Porter, "The Competitive Advantage of Nations," *Harvard Business Review* 68 (March–April 1990), p. 74.

43. Ibid., quotes sequentially from pp. 84, 73, and 75.

44. Manab Thakur and Luis Ma R. Calingo, "Strategic Thinking Is Hip, But Does it Make a Difference?" *Business Horizons* 35 (September–October 1992), p. 48.

45. Arie de Geus, "Planning as Learning," *Harvard Business Review* 66 (March–April 1988).

46. Henry Mintzberg, "The Fall and Rise of Strategic Planning," *Harvard Business Review* 72 (January–February 1994), pp. 107–114.

47. Peter F. Drucker, *Managing in Turbulent Times* (New York: Harper & Row, 1980), pp. 43–45.

48. Tom Peter's remarks were directed toward Silicon Valley leaders at the "High Tech Summit Visioning Conference," sponsored by Joint Venture: Silicon Valley, presented at Santa Clara, Calif., October 14, 1992.

49. L. L. Cummings, "The Logics of Management," *Academy of Management Review* 8 (October 1983), pp. 532–538.

50. Ibid., p. 533.

51. Ibid., pp. 533–534.

52. Ian H. Wilson, "Environmental Scanning and Strategic Planning," *Business Environment/Public Policy Conference Papers* (St. Louis: American Assembly of Collegiate Schools of Business, 1980), pp. 159–163.

53. James B. Thomas, Shawn M. Clark, and Dennis A. Gioia, "Strategic Sensemaking and Organizational Performance: Linkages among Scanning, Interpretation, Action, and Outcomes," *Academy of Management Journal* 36 (April 1993), pp. 239–270.

54. Michael Cowley currently is a consultant and trainer for Goal/QPC, following retirement from Hewlett-Packard. The processes described in the following section were used by Dr. Cowley in bringing together business executives and faculty to facilitate academic program planning.

55. Laurie Larwood, Cecilia M. Falbe, Mark P. Kriger, and Paul Miesing, "Structure and Meaning of Organizational Vision," *Academy of Management Journal* 38 (June 1995), pp. 740–769.

56. Ed McCracken, "The Information Super Highway: How Entertainment Will Drive Its Technological Development Into the 21st Century," Business Alumni Association Executive Breakfast Briefings (San Jose State University, June 22, 1995).

57. Quoted in James M. Kouzes and Barry Z. Posner, *The Leadership Challenge* (San Francisco: Jossey-Bass, 1995).

58. Scott A. Snell, "Control Theory in Strategic Human Resource Management: The Mediating Effect of Administrative Information," *Academy of Management Journal* 35 (June 1992), p. 293.

59. Alan L. Wilkins and William G. Ouchi, "Efficient Cultures: Exploring the Relationship between Culture and Organizational Performance," *Administrative Science Quarterly* 28 (September 1983), pp. 468–481.

60. Charles O'Reilly, "Corporations, Culture, and Commitment: Motivation and Social Control in Organizations," *California Management Review* 31 (Summer 1989), p. 11.

61. Jan Carlzon, *Moments of Truth* (Cambridge, MA: Ballinger, 1987).

62. O'Reilly, "Corporations, Culture, and Commitment," pp. 9–25.

63. Ibid., p. 12.

64. M. A. Maguire and William G. Ouchi, "Organizational Control and Work Satisfaction," Research paper no. 278, Graduate School of Business, Stanford University, 1975.

65. Gerald R. Salancik, "Commitment and the Control of Organizational Behavior and Belief," in Barry M.

Staw, *Psychological Dimensions of Organizational Behavior* (New York: Macmillan, 1991), p. 310.

66. Stephen F. Jablonsky, Patrick J. Keating, and James B. Heian, *The Management Communication and Control Systems Diagnostic Questionnaire: Core Values and Organizational Learning* (New York: Financial Executives Research Foundation, 1992).

67. Patrick J. Keating and Stephen F. Jablonsky, *Changing Roles of Financial Management: Getting Close to the Business* (New York: Financial Executives Research Foundation, 1990).

68. Jablonsky, Keating, and Heian, *The Management Communication and Control Systems Diagnostic Questionnaire.*

69. William C. Taylor, "Control in an Age of Chaos," *Harvard Business Review* 72 (November–December 1994), pp. 64, 65.

70. Jablonsky, Keating, and Heian (1992) found only 25 percent of the 805 managers in their study to have the competitive team orientation.

71. Tracy Robertson Kramer and Arthur A. Thompson, Jr., "Philip Morris Companies, Inc.," in A. A. Thompson, Jr., and A. J. Strickland III, *Strategic Management: Concepts and Cases* (Burr Ridge, IL: Irwin, 1995), pp. 703–751; Philip Morris, Inc., *Annual Report* (1989); and Bruce Horovitz, "Hot New Products Line Grocery Shelves," *USA Today* (February 16, 1995), p. 1B.

Chapter 3

1. Quoted in Thomas A. Stewart, "Managing in a Wired Company," *Fortune* (July 11, 1994), p. 44.

2. *Economic Report of the President* (Washington, D.C.: U.S. Government Printing Office, published annually). See tables on employment.

3. Alvin Toffler, *The Third Wave* (New York: Bantam, 1981); and "Riding the Wares," *Worth* (June 1996), pp. 94–100.

4. Andrew S. Grove, "Technology Industries Outlook," 1992 Outlook Conference (San Francisco: The Bay Area Council, March 11, 1992).

5. Peter F. Drucker, "The New Productivity Challenge," *Harvard Business Review* 69 (November–December 1991), pp. 69–79.

6. Steve Kaufman, "Superstores' Low Prices Leave Retailing's Independents Dazed," *San Jose Mercury News* (July 10, 1995), p. 5D.

7. Robert B. Reich, *The Work of Nations* (New York: Alfred A. Knopf, 1991), pp. 84–85.

8. Neal Templin, "Team Spirit: Response to Crisis Made Ford Factories in U.S. More Efficient," *The Wall Street Journal Europe* (December 17, 1992), pp. 1, 7.

9. Edward E. Lawler III, *The Ultimate Advantage: Creating the High-Involvement Organization* (San Francisco: Jossey-Bass, 1992), p. 112.

10. Richard J. Schonberger, "Human Resource Management Lessons from a Decade of Total Quality Management and Reengineering," *California Management Review* 36 (Summer 1994), pp. 109–123.

11. Ian I. Mitroff, *Break-Away Thinking: How to Challenge Your Business Assumptions* (New York: John Wiley & Sons, 1988), p. 21.

12. M. Hossein Safizadeh, "The Case of Workgroups in Manufacturing Operations," *California Management Review* 33 (Summer 1991), p. 62.

13. Robert E. Cole, *Strategies for Learning: Small-Group Activities in American, Japanese, and Swedish Industry* (Berkeley, CA: University of California Press, 1989).

14. Consultative participation is more an informal decision practice, and a task force allows only part-time involvement—they are discussed elsewhere.

15. Donald L. Dewar, *The Quality Circle Handbook* (Red Bluff, CA: The Quality Circle Institute, 1980), pp. F1–F7.

16. Kevin Anderson, "Dramatic Turnaround," *USA Today* (April 10, 1992), p. 5B.

17. Richard L. Daft and Richard M. Steers, *Organizations: A Micro/Macro Approach* (Glenview, IL: Scott, Foresman and Company, 1986), pp. 273–274.

18. William Pasmore, Carol E. Francis, and Jeffrey Haldeman, "Sociotechnical Systems: A North American Reflection on Empirical Studies of the 70s," *Human Relations* 35 (1982), pp. 1179–1204.

19. Joseph T. Vesey, "The New Competitors: They Think in Terms of 'Speed-to-Market'," *Academy of Management Executive* 5 (May 1991), pp. 23–33.

20. Ibid., p. 24.

21. Kathleen Kerwin, "The Shape of a New Machine," *Business Week* (July 24, 1995), p. 63.

22. Mary Ann Von Glinow and Susan Albers Mohrman (Eds.), *Managing Complexity in High Technology Organizations* (New York: Oxford University Press, 1990).

23. Susan Albers Mohrman and Thomas G. Cummings, *Self-Designing Organizations: Learning How to Create High Performance* (Reading, MA: Addison-Wesley, 1989); David P. Hanna, *Designing Organizations for High Performance* (Reading, MA: Addison-Wesley, 1988); and Edward E. Lawler III, *High-Involvement Management* (San Francisco: Jossey-Bass, 1988).

24. Lawler, *The Ultimate Advantage*, p. 51.

25. The organizational designs of Office Systems Design represent illustrative simplifications of an actual firm's designs.

26. Expanded arguments of the advantages and disadvantages of organizational designs can be found in Arthur A. Thompson, Jr., and A. J. Strickland III, *Strategy Formulation and Implementation: Tasks of the General Manager*, 5th ed. (Homewood, IL: Irwin, 1992), pp. 223–233.

27. Lawler, *The Ultimate Advantage*, p. 65.

28. Henry Mintzberg, *Structure in Fives: Designing Effective Organizations* (Englewood Cliffs, N.J.: Prentice Hall, 1983).

29. Alfred D. Chandler, *Strategy and Structure: Chapters in the History of the Industrial Enterprise* (Garden City, NY: Anchor, 1962).

30. Patrick E. Connor, "Decision-Making Participation Patterns: The Role of Organizational Context," *Academy of Management Journal* 35 (March 1992), pp. 218–231.

31. Micheline Maynard, James R. Healey, and Michael Clements, "Board Gives Tough Task to Fresh Talent," *USA Today* (November 3, 1992), pp. B1–B2.

32. Jeffrey A. Alexander, "Adaptive Change in Corporate Control Practices," *Academy of Management Journal* 34 (March 1991), pp. 162–193.

33. James W. Dean, Jr., and Gerald I. Susman, "Organizing for Manufacturable Design," *Harvard Business Review* 67 (January–February 1989), pp. 28–36.

34. Lawler, *The Ultimate Advantage*, p. 113.

35. Robert W. Keidel, "Triangular Design: A New Organizational Geometry," *Academy of Management Executive* 4 (November 1990), pp. 21–37.

36. William Pasmore, Carol E. Francis, and Jeffrey Haldeman, "Sociotechnical Systems: A North American Reflection on Empirical Studies of the 709s," *Human Relations* 35 (1982), pp. 1179–1204.

37. J. Richard Hackman (Ed.), *Groups That Work (And Those That Don't): Creating Conditions for Effective Teamwork* (San Francisco: Jossey-Bass, 1989).

38. Joseph T. Vesey, "The New Competitors: They Think in Terms of 'Speed-to-Market'," *Academy of Management Executive* 5 (May 1991), pp. 23–33.

39. Warren Bennis, *An Invented Life: Reflections on Leadership and Change* (Reading, MA: Addison-Wesley, 1993), p. 105.

40. Lawler, *The Ultimate Advantage*.

41. Vesey, "The New Competitors," p. 24.

42. Lawler, *The Ultimate Advantage*.

43. Hugh M. O'Neill, "Restructuring, Re-engineering, and Rightsizing: Do the Metaphors Make Sense?" An introduction to the special issue of the *Academy of Management Executive* 8 (November 1994), pp. 9–11.

44. Lawler, *The Ultimate Advantage*, p. 61

45. Ibid., p. 62.

46. Charles W. L. Hill and Robert E. Hoskisson, "Strategy and Structure in the Multiproduct Firm," *Academy of Management Review* 12 (April 1987), pp. 331–341.

47. Michael Goold, "Strategic Control in the Decentralized Firm," *Sloan Management Review* (Winter 1991).

48. J. Carlzon, *Moments of Truth* (New York: Ballinger, 1987).

49. William Taylor, "The Logic of Global Business: An Interview with ABB's Percy Barnevik," *Harvard Business Review* 69 (March–April 1991), p. 92.

50. David Kirkpatrick, "Breaking up IBM," *Fortune* 126 (July 27, 1992), p. 53.

51. Kathleen Kerwin and Thane Peterson, "Fixing GM: Pages from a Radical Repair Manual," *Business Week* (November 16, 1992), p. 46.

52. General Electric, *Annual Report* (1990).

53. Thomas A. Stewart, "The Search for the Organization of Tomorrow," *Fortune* (May 18, 1992), pp. 92–98.

54. Michael Hammer and James Champy, *Reengineering the Corporation: A Manifesto for Business Revolution* (New York: Harper Business, 1993), p. 32.

55. Robert W. Keidel, "Rethinking Organizational Design," *Academy of Management Executive* 8 (November 1994), pp. 12–27.

56. Hammer and Champy, *Reengineering the Corporation*, pp. 39–44.

57. Joseph E. McCann, "Design Principles for an Innovating Company," *Academy of Management Executive* 5 (May 1991), p. 89.

58. John P. Kotter, "Why Transformation Efforts Fail," *Harvard Business Review* 73 (March–April 1995), p. 59.

59. Larry Hirschhorn and Thomas Gilmore, "The New Boundaries of the 'Boundaryless' Company," *Harvard Business Review* 70 (May–June 1992), pp. 104–115.

60. McCann, "Design Principles for an Innovating Company," pp. 87–88.

61. Kim S. Cameron, cited in Richard A. Melcher, "How Goliaths Can Act Like David," *Business Week/Enterprise* (1993), p. 193.

62. Michael Hammer, quoted in Thomas A. Stewart, "Reengineering: The Hot New Managing Tool," *Fortune* (August 23, 1993), p. 42.

63. Keidel, "Rethinking Organizational Design," p. 17.

64. Ibid.

65. André L. Delbecq, Andrew H. Van de Ven, and D. H. Gustafson, *Group Techniques for Program Planning* (Glenview, IL: Scott, Foresman, 1975).

66. Curtis W. Cook, "Nominal Group Methods Enrich Classroom Learning," Charles M. Vance (Ed.), *Mastering Management Education: Innovations in Teaching Effectiveness* (Newbury Park, CA: Sage, 1993), pp. 179–186.

Chapter 4

1. Quoted in Rahul Jacob, "Corporate Reputations," *Fortune* (March 6, 1995), p. 54, from Robert Waterman's book *What America Does Right: Learning From Companies That Put People First*.

2. Ralph Linton, *The Cultural Background of Personality* (New York: Appleton-Century Crofts, 1945), p. 32.

3. Richard Pascale, "Fitting New Employees into the Company Culture," *Fortune* (May 28, 1984), p. 28.

4. Andrew M. Pettigrew, "On Studying Organizational Cultures," *Administrative Science Quarterly* 24 (December 1979), p. 574.

5. Edgar H. Schein, *Organizational Culture and Leadership* (San Francisco: Jossey-Bass, 1985).

6. Peter F. Druker, "The Theory of the Business," *Harvard Business Review* 72 (September–October 1994), p. 100.

7. Edgar H. Schein, "The Role of the Founder in Creating Organizational Culture," *Organizational Dynamics* (Summer 1983), pp. 13–28. Schein's original five assumptions are combined here into three that are more general.

8. Edgar H. Schein, "Coming to a New Awareness of Organizational Culture," *Sloan Management Review* (Winter 1984), p. 4.

9. Karl Weick, *The Social Psychology of Organizations* (Reading, MA: Addison-Wesley, 1969).

10. Jim Kennedy, "Dollar General Corporation," in A. J. Strickland III and Arthur A. Thompson, Jr., *Cases in Strategic Management*, 3rd ed. (Homewood, IL: Richard D. Irwin, 1988), pp. 23–51.

11. Peter Senge, *The Fifth Discipline: The Art and the Practice of the Learning Organization* (New York: Doubleday, 1990).

12. Jerry Flint, "The New Team's Plans for Moving Iron," *Forbes* (October 1, 1990), p. 78.

13. Terry C. Blum, Dail L. Fields, and Jodi S. Goodman, "Organization-Level Determinants of Women in Management," *Academy of Management Journal* 37 (April 1994), pp. 241–268.

14. M. Rokeach, *The Nature of Human Values* (New York: The Free Press, 1973), p. 5. Rokeach wrote the classic definition: "A value is an enduring belief that a specific mode of conduct or end-state of existence is personally or socially preferable to an opposite or converse mode of conduct or end-state of existence."

15. Fred J. Thumin, Julius H. Johnson, Jr., Charles Kuehl, and William Y. Jiang, "Corporate Values as Related

to Occupation, Gender, Age, and Company Size," *The Journal of Psychology* 129 (1995), pp. 389–400.

16. George England, "Organizational Goals and Expected Behavior of American Managers," *Academy of Management Journal* 10 (June 1967), pp. 107–117.

17. Yoash Wiener, "Forms of Value Systems: A Focus on Organizational Effectiveness and Cultural Change and Maintenance," *Academy of Management Review* 13 (October 1988), pp. 534–545.

18. Ibid., p. 538.

19. Robert H. Hayes, "Strategic Planning—Forward in Reverse?" *Harvard Business Review* 63 (November–December 1985), pp. 111–119.

20. "Life after Young" 'H-P Way' Will Thrive," *San Jose Mercury News* (July 19, 1992), p. 3E.

21. Janice M. Beyer and Harrison M. Trice, "How an Organization's Rites Reveal Its Culture," *Organizational Dynamics* 15 (Spring 1987), p. 7.

22. Bernard C. Reimann and Yoash Wiener, "Corporate Culture: Avoiding the Elitist Trap," *Business Horizons* 31 (March–April 1988), p. 36.

23. "Corporate Culture: The Hard-to-Change Values That Spell Success or Failure," *Business Week* (October 27, 1980), p. 148.

24. John P. Wanous, *Organizational Entry: Recruitment, Selection, and Socialization of Newcomers* (Reading, MA: Addison-Wesley, 1980), p. 171.

25. Jay R. Galbraith, *Designing Organizations* (San Francisco: Jossey-Bass, 1995), pp. 2–3.

26. J. E. Hebden, "Adopting an Organization's Culture: The Socialization of Graduate Trainees," *Organizational Dynamics* 14 (Summer 1986), pp. 54–72.

27. Beyer and Trice, "How an Organization's Rites Reveal Its Culture," p. 13.

28. David M. Boje, "Stories of the Storytelling Organization: A Postmodern Analysis of Disney as 'Tamara-Land," *Academy of Management Journal* 38 (August 1995), pp. 997–1035.

29. William E. Fulmer and Robert M. Fulmer, "Walt Disney Productions," in A. J. Strickland III and Arthur A.

Thompson, Jr., *Cases in Strategic Management,* 3rd ed.(Homewood, IL: Richard D. Irwin, 1988), pp. 71–94.

30. W. Jack Duncan, "Organizational Culture: 'Getting a Fix' on an Elusive Concept," *Academy of Management Executive* 3 (August 1989), pp. 229–236.

31. K. L. Gregory, "Native-View Paradigms: Multiple Cultures and Culture Conflicts in Organizations, *Administrative Science Quarterly* (September 1983), pp. 359–376.

32. Suggested by Caren Siehl, University of Southern California.

33. R. A. Cooke and D. M. Rousseau, "Behavioral Norms and Expectations: A Quantitative Approach to the Assessment of Organizational Culture," *Group and Organizational Studies* 13 (1988), pp. 245–273.

34. Andrew M. Pettigrew, "On Studying Organizational Cultures," *Administrative Science Quarterly* 24 (December 1979), p. 574.

35. C. Greetz, *The Interpretation of Cultures* (New York: Basic Books, 1973), p. 5.

36. The idea that physical environments convey meanings about organizational beliefs and suggestions for what to observe were prompted by William B. Wolf, "The Nature of Organizations," in W. B. Wolf (Ed.), *Management: Readings toward a General Theory* (Belmont, CA: Wadworth, 1964), pp. 18–23; Robert E. Coffey, Anthony G. Athos, and Peter A. Raynolds, *Behavior in Organizations: A Multidimensional View,* 2nd ed. (Englewood Cliffs, NJ: Prentice Hall, 1985), pp. 38–52; and Terrence E. Deal and Allan A. Kennedy, *Corporate Cultures: The Rites and Rituals of Corporate Life* (Reading, MA: Addison-Wesley, 1982), pp. 129–139.

37. Kevin Maney, "Workplace Dresses Down in '90s," *USA Today* (July 24, 1992), p. B-1.

38. Beyer and Trice, "How an Organization's Rites Reveal Its Culture," pp. 5–24.

39. Robin Romblad and Arthur A. Thompson, Jr., "Mary Kay Cosmetics, Inc," in A. J. Strickland III and Arthur A. Thompson, Jr., *Cases in Strategic Management,* 3rd ed. (Plano, TX: Business Publications, Inc., 1988), pp. 456–498.

40. Marcia Berss, "Real Time Testing," *Forbes* (January 21, 1991), p. 61.

41. Schein, "The Role of the Founder," p. 22.

42. Ibid., p. 14.

43. Charles Stubbart, Dean Schroder, and Arthur A. Thompson, Jr., "Nucor Corporation," in A. J. Strickland III and A. A. Thompson, Jr., *Cases in Strategic Management,* 4th ed. (Homewood, IL: Richard D. Irwin, 1992), pp. 215–248; and Edward O. Welles, "Least Likely to Succeed," *Inc.* (December 1992), pp. 74–86.

44. Reimann and Wiener, "Corporate Culture: Avoiding the Elitist Trap," p. 40.

45. John E. Gamble, "Lexmark International, Inc.," in A. J. Strickland III and Arthur A. Thompson, Jr., *Cases in Strategic Management,* 5th ed. (Chicago: Richard D. Irwin, 1995), pp. 605–629.

46. Quoted in Paul Carroll, "Hurt by a Pricing War, IBM Plans Write-Off and Cut of 10,000 Jobs," *The Wall Street Journal* (December 6, 1989), p. A1.

47. David Packard, "Lessons for All Companies from Hewlett-Packard," *Bottom Line Business* 24 (October 1, 1995), p. 3.

48. Harrison M. Trice and Janic M. Beyer, "Studying Cultures through Rites and Ceremonials," *Academy of Management Review* 9 (October 1984), pp. 666.

49. Larry E. Greiner, "Evolution and Revolution as Organizations Grow," *Harvard Business Review* 50 (July–August 1972), pp. 37–46.

50. William G. Dyer and W. Gibb Dyer, Jr., "Organization Development: System Change or Culture Change?" *Personnel* (February 1986), p. 14.

51. George C. Rubenson and Anil K. Gupta, "Replacing the Founder: Exploding the Myth of the Entrepreneur's Disease," *Business Horizons* 35 (November–December 1992), pp. 53–57.

52. James Chapmy, *Reengineering Management: The Mandate for New Leadership* (New York: Harper Business, 1995), p. 35.

53. From an internal document cited in Richard Blackburn and Benson Rosen, "Total Quality and Human Resources Management: Lessons Learned from Baldridge Award-Winning Companies," *Academy of Management Executive* 7 (August 1993), p. 50.

54. Sam Roberts, *Who Are We: A Portrait of America Based on the Latest U.S. Census* (New York: Time Books, 1994).

55. Peter Brimelow, *Alien Nation* (New York: Random House, 1995).

56. Lisbeth J. Vincent, Christine L. Salisbury, Phillip Strain, Cecilia McCormick, and Annette Tessier, "A Behavioral-Ecological Approach to Early Intervention: Focus on Cultural Diversity," in Samuel J. Meisels and Jack P. Shonkoff (Eds.), *Handbook of Early Childhood Intervention* (Cambridge, England: Cambridge University Press, 1990), pp. 173–195.

57. B. Drummond Ayres, Jr., "Obstacles Arise to Switch by California on Diversity," *New York Times* (July 24, 1995), p. A1.

58. Julius H. Johnson, Jr., Fred J. Thumin, Charles Kuehl, and William Y. Jiang, "Toward Harmonization: A Cross-Cultural Empirical Study Examining Managerial Values of Accountants from Four Countries," *The Journal of Global Business* (1995).

59. William G. Ouchi and Alfred M. Jaeger, "Type Z Organization: Stability in the Midst of Mobility *Academy of Management Review* 3 (April 1978), pp. 305–314.

60. Geert Hofstede, *Culture's Consequences: International Differences in Work-Related Values* (Beverly Hills, CA: Sage Publications, 1980); and G. Hofstede, "Management Scientists Are Human," *Management Science* 40. (Number 1, 1994), pp. 4–13.

61. Geert Hofstede, "The Cultural Relativity of Organizational Practices and Theories," *Journal of International Business Studies* 14 (Fall 1983), p. 76.

62. Ibid., pp. 75–89.

63. John A. Wagner III, "Studies of Individualism-Collectivism: Effects on Cooperation in Groups," *Academy of Management Journal* 38 (February 1995), pp. 152–172.

64. A. A. Oritz, "The Influence of Locus of Control and Culture on Learning Styles of Language Minority Students," in J. J. Johnson and B. A. Ramierez (Eds.), *American Indian Exceptional Children and Youth* (Reston, VA: ERIC Clearinghouse on Handicapped and Gifted Children, Council for Exceptional Children, 1987), pp. 9–16.

65. Mark F. Peterson and 22 others, "Role Conflict, Ambiguity and Overload: A 21-Nation Study," *Academy of Management Journal* 38 (April 1995), p. 446.

66. P. Christopher Earley and Harbir Singh, "International and Intercultural Management Research: What's Next?" *Academy of Management Journal* 38 (April 1995), p. 338.

67. Chalmers Johnson, "Comparative Capitalism: The Japanese Difference," *California Management Review* 35 (Summer 1993), pp. 51–67.

68. Bo Burlingham, "China, Inc." *Inc.* (December 1992), pp. 110–121.

69. Quoted in Philip M. Rosenzweig, "The New American Challenge: Foreign Multinationals in the United States," *California Management Review* 36 (Spring 1994), p. 117.

70. *Wal-Mart, 1996 Annual Report*, p. 5.

71. Peter Lynch, "In Defense of the Invisible Hand," *Worth* (June 1996), pp. 86–92.

72. Originally presented at an Organization Behavior Teaching Conference and passed through the collegial network. Author unknown.

73. Adapted from John J. Keller, "Why AT&T Takeover of NCR Hasn't Been a Real Bell Ringer," *The Wall Street Journal*, September 19, 1995, pp. A1, A6; and "AT&T to Break Up into Three Separate Firms," *San Jose Mercury News*, September 21, 1995, pp. 1A, 22A.

Chapter 5

1. Robert Kuttner, "Talking Marriage and Thinking One-Night Stand," *Business Week* (October 18, 1993), p. 16; and Louis S. Csoka, "A New Employer-Employee Contract?" *Employee Relations Today* (June 22, 1995), p. 21ff.

2. Mrury Weidenbaum, "A New Social Contract for the American Workplace," *Challenge* (January, 1995), p. 51ff.

3. Ibid.

4. Ibid. Csoka, "A New Employer-Employee Contract?"

5. Howard Gardner, *Frames of Mind: The Theory of Multiple Intelligences* (New York: Basic Books, 1983).

6. H. H. Kelley and J. L. Michela, "Attribution Theory and Research," *Annual Review of Psychology* (1980), pp. 457–501; Barry M. Staw, "Attribution of the Causes of Performance: A General Alternative Interpretation of Cross-Sectional Research on Organizations," *Organizational Behavior and Human Performance* (1975), pp. 414–432; James R. Bettman and B. A. Weitz, "Attributions in the Board Room: Causal Reasoning in Corporate Annual Reports," *Administrative Science Quarterly* (June 1983); pp. 165–813; and H. H. Kelley, *Attribution in Social Interaction* (Morristown, NJ: General Learning Press, 1971).

7. A. G. Miller and T. Lawson, "The Effect of an Informational Option on the Fundamental Attribution Error," *Personality and Social Psychology Bulletin* (June 1989), pp. 194–204.

8. John R. Schermerhorn, Jr., "Team Development for High Performance Management," *Training and Development Journal* 40 (November 1986), pp. 38–41.

9. J. P. Chaplin, *Dictionary of Psychology*, rev. 2nd ed. (New York: Bantam Doubleday Dell, 1985), pp. 233–234.

10. Daniel Goleman, *Emotional Intelligence* (New York: Bantam Books, 1994).

11. Ivan P. Pavlov, *Conditional Reflexes;* G V Anrep (trans.) (London: Oxford University Press, 1927).

12. This is a paraphrasing of E. L. Throndike's "Law of Effect." See Edward L. Thorndike, *Educational Psychology: The Psychology of Learning* (New York: Columbia University Press, 1913), II, 4.

13. B. F. Skinner, *The Shaping of a Behaviorist* (New York: Harper & Row, 1964), Chapter 8.

14. David Premack, "Toward Empirical Behavior Laws: 1. Positive Reinforcement," *Psychological Review* 66 (1959).

15. B. F. Skinner, *Beyond Freedom and Dignity* (New York: Bantam-Vintage Books, 1971).

16. Abert Bandura, "Behavior Theory and the Models of Man," *American Psychologist* 29; and no. 12(1974), pp. 859–869.

17. Albert Bandura and Richard H. Walters, *Social Learning and Personality Development* (New York: Holt, Rinehart & Winston, 1963), p. 2.

18. Morris L. Bigge, *Learning Theory for Teachers* (New York: Harper & Row, 1964), p 214.

19. Wolfgang Kohler, *The Mentality of Apes* (New York: Harcourt Brace and World, 1925).

20. Kenneth E. Blaker, *Behavior Modification* (Morristown: NJ: General Learning Press, 1976), pp. 19–20.

21. David A. Kolb, "Management and the Learning Process," *California Management Review* 18 (Spring 1976), pp. 21–31.

22. Ibid., p. 30.

23. Robert E. Ornstein, "Right and Left Thinking," *Psychology Today* (May 1973), pp. 87–92.

24. Henry Mintzberg, "Planning on the Left Side and Managing on the Right," *Harvard Business Review* 54 (July–August 1976), p. 53.

25. Weston H. Agor, "Using Intuition to Manage Organizations in the Future," *Business Horizons* 27 (July–August 1984), p. 51.

26. G. W. Allport, P. E. Vernon, and G. Lindzey, *Study of Values* (Boston: Houghton Mifflin, 1951).

27. M. Rokeach, *The Nature of Human Values* (New York: Free Press, 1973); M. Rokeach and S. J. Ball-Rokeach, "Stability and Change in American Value Priorities, 1968–1981," *American Psychologist* (May 1989), pp. 775–784.

28. John Huey, "Finding New Heroes for a New Era," *Fortune* (January 25, 1993), pp. 52–69; Myron Magnet, "The Money Society," *Fortune* (July 6, 1987), pp. 26–31; Daniel Yankelovich, "New Rules in American Life: Searching for Self-Fulfillment in a World Turned Upside Down," *Psychology Today* (April 1981), pp. 35–86; M. R. Cooper et al., "Changing Employee Values: Deepening Discontent?" *Harvard Business Review* (January–February 1979), pp. 117–125.

29. Huey, "Finding New Heroes," p. 62.

30. S. J. Breckler, "Empirical Validation of Affect, Behavior, and Cognition as Distinct Components of Attitude," *Journal of Personality and Social Psychology* (May 1984), pp. 1191–1205.

31. Leon Festinger, *A Theory of Cognitive Dissonance* (Palo Alto, CA: Stanford University Press, 1957).

32. Hom, Katerberg, and Hulin, "Comparative Examination of Three Approaches to the Prediction of Turnover," *Journal of Applied Psychology* (June 1979), pp. 280–290; R. T. Mowday, L. W. Porter, and R. M. Steers, *Employee Organization Linkages: The Psychology of Commitment, Absenteeism, and Turnover* (New York: Academic Press, 1982).

33. Thomas J. Couchard, Jr., et al., "Sources of Human Psychological Differences: The Minnesota Study of Twins Reared Apart," *Science* 250 (October 12, 1990), pp. 223–228; "How Genes Shape Personality," *U.S. News & World Report* (April 13, 1987), pp. 58–62.

34. Lewis Goldberg originally used this term. See Keith Harary and Eileen Donahue, "Who Are You?" *Psychology Today* (May–June 1992), p. 69.

35. Carl G. Jung, *Psychological Types* (New York: Harcourt, 1933).

36. "Myers-Briggs Type Indicator" (Palo Alto, CA: Consulting Psychologists Press, Inc., 1987).

37. Thomas Moore, "Personality Tests Are Back," *Fortune* (March 30, 1987), pp. 74–82.

38. John W. Slocum, Jr., and Don Hellriegel, "A Look at How Managers' Minds Work," *Business Horizons* 26 (July–August 1983), pp. 58–68.

39. Lawrence Pervin, "Personality," in Mark Rosenzweig and Lyman Porter (Eds.), *Annual Review of Psychology* 36 (Palo Alto, CA: Annual Reviews, 1985).

40. J. B. Rotter, "Generalized Expectancies for Internal versus External Control of Reinforcement," *Psychological Monographs* 80, no. 609 (1966).

41. T. W. Adorno et al., *The Authoritarian Personality* (New York: Harper & Row, 1950); and "Who Becomes an Authoritarian?" *Psychology Today* (March 1989), pp. 66–70.

42. Niccolo Machiavelli, *The Prince*, George Bull (trans.) (Middlesex: Penguin, 1961); and Richard Christie and Florence L. Gies, *Studies in Machiavellianism* (New York: Academic Press, 1970).

43. Barbara Foley Meeker, "Cooperation, Competition, and Self-Esteem: Aspects of Winning and Losing." *Human Relations* (March 1990), pp. 205–220.

44. M. Snyder, *Public Appearance/Private Realities: The Psychology of Self-Monitoring* (New York: W. H. Freeman, 1987).

45. Based on a case described by Jeffrey Goldstein and Marjorie Leopold, "Corporate Culture vs. Ethnic Culture," *Personnel Journal* (November 1990), pp. 83–92.

46. Adapted from a classic case, "The Gage Company," Harvard Business School, 1968, in Robert E. Coffeys, Anthony G. Athos, and Peter A. Raynolds, *Behavior in Organizations: A Multimensional View* (Englewood Cliffs, NJ: Prentice Hall, 1975).

Chapter 6

1. Joshua Hyatt, "Real-World Reengineering," *Inc.* (April 1995), pp. 40–53.

2. Abraham H. Maslow, *Motivation and Personality*, 2nd ed. (New York: Harper & Row, 1970); and Abraham H. Maslow, "Deficiency Motivation and Growth Motivation," in M. R. Jones (Ed.), *Nebraska Symposium on Motivation* (Lincoln: University of Nebraska Press, 1955).

3. Joel Brockner, Steven Grover, Thomas F. Reed, and Rocki Lee Dewitt, "Layoffs, Job Insecurity, and Survivors' Work Effort: Evidence of an Inverted-U Relationship," *Academy of Management Journal* 35 (June 1992), pp. 413–425.

4. M. A. Wahba and L. G. Bridewell, "Maslow Reconsidered: A Review of Research on the Need Hierarchy," *Organizational Behavior and Human Performance* 15 (1976), pp. 121–140; and J. Rauschenberger, N. Schmitt, and J. E. Hunter, "A Test of the Need Hierarchy Concept by a Markov Model of Change in Need Strength," *Administrative Science Quarterly* 25 (December 1980), pp. 654–670.

5. Abraham H. Maslow, *Eupsychian Management: A Journal* (Homewood, IL: Richard D. Irwin, 1965), p. 55.

6. *The China Daily* (January 23, 1992), p. 3.

7. Clayton P. Alderfer, "An Empirical Test of a New Theory of Human Needs," *Organizational Behavior and*

Human Performance 4 (May 1969), pp. 142–175; and C. P. Alderfer, *Existence, Relatedness, and Growth* (New York: Free Press, 1972).

8. J. P. Wanous and A. Zwany, "A Cross-Sectional Test of Need Hierarchy Theory," *Organizational Behavior and Human Performance* 18 (May 1977), pp. 78–97; and C. P. Schneider and Clayton P. Alderfer, "Three Studies of Measures of Need Satisfaction in Organizations," *Administrative Science Quarterly* (December 1973), pp. 489–505.

9. Frederick Herzberg, *Work and the Nature of Man* (Cleveland: World, 1966).

10. Frederick Herzberg, "One More Time: How Do You Motivate Employees?" *Harvard Business Review* 46 (September–October 1987), pp. 109–120.

11. Edward E. Lawler III, *Pay and Organizational Development* (Reading, MA: Addison-Wesley, 1981); Robert J. House and Lawrence A. Wigdor, "Herzberg's Dual-Factor Theory of Job Satisfaction and Motivation: A Review of the Evidence and a Criticism," *Personnel Psychology* 20 (Winter 1967), pp. 369–389; and M. Fein, "Work Measurement and Wage Incentives," *Industrial Engineering* (September 1973), pp. 49–51.

12. D. A. Whitsett and E. K. Winslow, "An Analysis of Studies Critical of the Motivation-Hygiene Theory," *Personnel Psychology* (1967), pp. 391–416.

13. Douglas McGregor, *The Human Side of Enterprise* (New York: McGraw-Hill, 1960).

14. M. J. Stahl, *Managerial and Technical Motivation: Assessing Needs for Achievement, Power, and Affiliation* (New York: Praeger, 1986); and David C. McClelland and David H. Burnham, "Power Is the Great Motivator," *Harvard Business Review* 73 (January–February 1995), pp. 126–139.

15. David C. McClelland, *The Achieving Society* (New York: Van Nostrand Reinhold, 1961); D. C. McClelland, "Achievement Motivation Can Be Developed, *Harvard Business Review* 43 (November–December 1965), pp. 6–8+; and John W. Atkinson, *An Introduction to Motivation* (Princeton, NJ: Van Nostrand, 1964).

16. David C. McClelland, "Retrospective Commentary" to McClelland and

Burnham, *Harvard Business Review* 73 (January-February 1995), pp. 138–139.

17. McClelland and Burnham, "Power Is the Great Motivator;" and D. C. McClelland, *Power: The Inner Experience* (New York: Irvington, 1975).

18. Charles M. Kelly, "The Interrelationship of Ethics and Power in Today's Organizations," *Organizational Dynamics* 5 (Summer 1987).

19. McClelland and Burnham, "Power Is the Great Motivator."

20. Bernard Weiner, *Achievement Motivation and Attribution Theory* (Morristown, NY: General Learning Press, 1974).

21. Ruth E. Cook, "Why Jimmy Doesn't Try," *Academic Therapy* 19, no. 2 (1983), pp. 153–163.

22. D. C. McClelland and D. G. Winter, *Motivating Economic Achievement* (New York: Free Press, 1969).

23. McClelland, "Retrospective," p. 139.

24. Boas Shamir, "Meaning, Self and Motivation in Organizations," *Organization Studies* 12 (1991), pp. 405–424.

25. Ysanne M. Carlisle and David J. Manning, "The Concept of Ideology and Work Motivation," *Organization Studies* 15 (December 1994), pp. 683–700.

26. Adrian Furnham, Bruce D. Kirkcaldy, and Richard Lynn, "National Attitudes to Competitiveness, Money, and Work Among Young People: First, Second, and Third World Differences," *Human Relations* 47 (January 1994), pp. 119+.

27. Frederick W. Taylor, *Principles of Scientific Management* (New York: Harper, 1911).

28. Victor H. Vroom, *Work and Motivation* (New York: Wiley, 1964).

29. John P. Wanous, Thomas L. Keon, and Jania C. Latack, "Expectancy Theory and Occupational/Organizational Choices: A Review and Test," *Organizational Behavior and Human Performance* (August 1983), pp. 66–86.

30. Curtis W. Cook, "Guidelines for Managing Motivation," *Business Horizons* 23 (April 1980), pp. 61–69.

31. Lyman W. Porter and Edward E. Lawler III, *Managerial Attitudes and*

Performance (Homewood, IL: Richard D. Irwin, 1968); and Edward E. Lawler III, *Motivation in Work Organizations* (Monterey, CA: Brooks/Cole, 1973).

32. Jennifer M. George, " Extrinsic and Intrinsic Origins of Perceived Social Loafing in Organizations," *Academy of Management Journal* 35 (March 1992), pp. 191–202.

33. Richard M. Steers and Lyman W. Porter, *Motivation and Work Behavior,* 4th ed. (New York: McGraw-Hill, 1987).

34. E. L. Deci, "Effects of Externally Mediated Rewards on Intrinsic Motivation," *Journal of Personality and Social Psychology* 18 (1971), pp. 105–115; E. L. Deci, *Intrinsic Motivation* (New York: Plenum, 1975); and P. C. Jordan, "Effects of an Extrinsic Reward on Intrinsic Motivation: A Field Experiment," *Academy of Management Journal* 29 (June 1986), pp. 405–412.

35. Jeffrey A. Bradt, "Pay for Impact," *Personnel Journal* 70 (May 1991), pp. 76–79.

36. Thomas L. Quick, "Simple Is Hard, Complex Is Easy, Simplistic Is Impossible," *Training and Development Journal* 44 (May 1990), pp. 94–99.

37. Jay T. Knippen and Thad B. Green, "Boost Performance Through Appraisals," *Business Credit* 92 (November–December 1990), p. 27.

38. Maurice F. Villere and Sandra J. Hartman, "The Key to Motivation Is in the Process: An Examination of Practical Implications of Expectancy Theory," *Leadership and Organization Development Journal* 11, no. 4 (1990), pp. i–iii.

39. Richard T. Mowday, "Equity Theory Predictions of Behavior in Organizations," in Richard M. Steers and Lyman W. Porter (Eds.), *Motivation and Work Behavior,* 4th ed. (New York: McGraw-Hill, 1987), pp. 91–113.

40. Joel Brockner, Jeff Greenberg, Audrey Brockner, Jenny Bortz, Jeanette Davy, and Carolyn Carter, "Layoffs, Equity Theory, and Work Performance: Further Evidence of the Impact of Survivor Guilt," *Academy of Management Journal* 29 (June 1986), pp. 373–384.

41. Pradeep K. Tyagi, "Inequities in Organizations, Salesperson Motivation and Job Satisfaction,"

International Journal of Research in Marketing 7 (December 1990), pp. 135–148.

42. R. Folger and M. A. Konovsky, "Effects of Procedural and Distributive Justice on Reactions to Pay Raise Decisions," *Academy of Management Journal* 32 (March 1989), pp. 115–130.

43. R. Folger, "Rethinking Equity Theory: A Referent Cognitions Model," in H. W. Bierhoff, R. L. Cohen, and J. Greenberg (Eds.), *Justice in Social Relations* (New York: Plenum, 1986), pp. 145–162.

44. Bruce Fortado, "The Accumulation of Grievance Conflict," *Journal of Management Inquiry* 1 (December 1992), p. 288.

45. Gerald E. Fryxell and Michael E. Gordon, "Workplace Justice and Job Satisfaction as Predictors of Satisfaction with Union and Management," *Academy of Management Journal* 32 (December 1989), pp. 851–866.

46. Dean B. McFarlin and Paul D. Sweeney, "Distributive and Procedural Justice as Predictors of Satisfaction with Personal and Organizational Outcomes," *Academy of Management Journal* 35 (August 1992), pp. 626–637.

47. G. Hofstede, "Dimensions of National Cultures in Fifty Countries and Three Regions," in J. B. Deregowski, S. Dziurawiec, and R. C. Annis (Eds.), *Explanations in Cross-Cultural Psychology* (Lisse, Netherlands: Swets and Zeitlinger, 1983), pp. 335–355.

48. Sim B. Sitkin and Amy L. Pablo, "Reconceptualizing the Determinants of Risk Behavior," *Academy of Management Review* 17 (January 1992), pp. 9–38.

49. Nakiye A. Boyacigiller and Nancy J. Adler, "The Parochial Dinosaur: Organizational Science in a Global Context," *Academy of Management Review* 16 (April 1991), pp. 274–276.

50. W. Alan Randolph and Barry Z. Posner, *Getting the Job Done! Managing Project Teams and Task Forces for Success* (Englewood Cliffs, NJ: Prentice Hall, 1992).

51. Robert Cole, "U.S. Quality Improvement in the Auto Industry: Close but No Cigar," *California Management Review* 32 (Summer 1990), p. 72.

52. Helen Fogel and David Sedgwick, "UAW May Bid for GM 'Quality' Strikes," *The Detroit News* (March 21, 1990), p. 3e.

53. Augustine A. Lado and Mary C. Wilson, "Human Resource Systems and Sustained Competitive Advantage: A Competency-Based Perspective," *Academy of Management Review* 19 (October 1994), pp. 699–727.

54. Chris Argyris, "Good Communication that Blocks Learning," *Harvard Business Review* 72 (July–August 1994), pp. 77–85.

55. Argyris, "Good Communication that Blocks Learning," p. 79, provided all quotes in this paragraph.

56. Ibid., pp. 84–85.

57. Michael Pellecchia, "The Fifth Discipline's Sequel Still Is Formidable Reading," *Star Tribune* (February 24, 1995), 2D, quote by Richard Ross, coauthor of Peter Senge, Charlotte Roberts, Richard B. Ross, Bryan J. Smith, and Art Kleiner, *The Fifth Discipline Fieldbook: Strategies and Tools for Building a Learning Organization* (New York: Currency Doubleday, 1995).

58. Ideas and quotes in this paragraph are from Peter M. Senge, "Letters to the Editor: Communication and Learning," *Harvard Business Review* 72 (November–December 1994), p. 182; and Senge, "Executive Update CEO Briefing: The Learning Organization," *Investor's Business Daily* (November 29, 1994), p. A4.

59. John W. Slocum, Michael McGill, and David T. Lei, "The New Learning Strategy: Anytime, Anything, Anywhere," *Organizational Dynamics* 23 (September 1994), p. 36.

60. Joshua Hyatt, "Real-World Reengineering," *Inc.* (April 1995), pp. 40–53.

61. Alfred North Whitehead, *The Function of Reason* (Boston: Beacon Press, 1929).

Chapter 7

1. Ronald E. Yates, "Can Motivational Techniques Release Corporations Within? Firms Take New Age Approach to Finding Success in Workplace," *Chicago Tribune* (October 15, 1995), p. 1C.

2. Patricia Buhler, "Motivating the Employee of the 90s: Managing in the 90s," *Supervision* 55 (July 1994), pp. 8–10.

3. Edwin A. Locke, "The Ubiquity of the Technique of Goal Setting in Theories and Approaches to Employee Motivation," *Academy of Management Review* 3 (July 1978), pp. 594–601; with more recent integration in Edwin A. Locke and Gary P. Latham, *A Theory of Goal Setting and Task Performance* (Englewood Cliffs, NJ: Prentice Hall, 1990).

4. Shawn K. Yearta, Sally Maitlis, and Rob B. Briner, "An Exploratory Study of Goal Setting in Theory and Practice: A Motivational Technique that Works?" *Journal of Occupational and Organizational Psychology* 68 (September 1995), pp. 237+.

5. R. E. Wood, A. J. Mento, and Edwin A. Locke, "Task Complexity as a Moderator of Goal Effects: A Meta-Analysis," *Journal of Applied Psychology* 72 (1987), pp. 416–425.

6. Locke and Latham, *A Theory of Goal Setting and Task Performance.* Their pioneering paper was Gary P. Latham and Edwin A. Locke, "Goal Setting—A Technique that Works," *Organizational Dynamics* 8 (Autumn 1969), pp. 68–80.

7. M. Erez, P. C. Earley, and C. L. Hulin, "The Impact of Participation on Goal Acceptance and Performance: A Two-Step Model," *Academy of Management Journal* 28 (February 1985), pp. 50–66.

8. Gary P. Latham and H. A. Marshal, "The Effects of Self-Set, Participatively Set and Assigned Goals on the Performance of Government Employees," *Personnel Psychology* 35 (1982), pp. 399–404.

9. Thomas L. Quick, "Using the 'Three Rs' to Achieve Your Goals," *Sales and Marketing Management* 142 (September 1990), pp. 170–171.

10. D. E. Berlew, "Managing Human Energy: Pushing Versus Pulling," in S. Srivastva (Ed.), *Executive Power* (San Francisco: Jossey-Bass, 1986), pp. 35–50.

11. Howard Rothman, "The Power of Empowerment," *Nations Business* 81 (June 1993), pp. 49–52.

12. Mark E. Tubbs and Steven E. Ekeberg, "The Role of Intentions in Work Motivation: Implications for Goal-Setting Theory and Research," *Academy of Management Review* 16 (January 1991), pp. 180–199.

13. I. Ajzen, "From Intentions to Actions: A Theory of Planned Behavior," in J. Kuhl and J. Beckman (Eds.), *Action Control: From Cognition to Behavior* (Berlin: Springer–Verlag 1985), pp. 11–39.

14. Locke and Latham, *A Theory of Goal Setting and Task Performance.*

15. Quoted from Charles Snyder in "To Succeed, You Gotta Have Hope, Studies Show," *New York Times* (December 26, 1991).

16. Charles Snyder, *Journal of Personality and Social Psychology* (November 1991); and Timothy Elliott, *The Journal of Personality and Social Psychology.*

17. Peter F. Drucker, *The Practice of Management* (New York: Harper & Row, 1954).

18. George S. Odiorne, *Management by Objectives* (New York; Pitman, 1965); and G. S. Odiorne, *MBO II: A System of Managerial Leadership for the 80s* (Belmont, CA: Pitman, 1979).

19. Jack N. Kondrasuk, "Studies in MBO Effectiveness," *Academy of Management Review* 6 (July 1981), pp. 419–430.

20. Jerry L. Roslund, "Evaluating Management Objectives with the Quality Loss Function," *Quality Progress* (August 1989), pp. 45–49.

21. Charles M. Kelly, "Remedial MBO," *Business Horizons* 26 (September–October 1983), pp. 64–65.

22. F. E. Schuster and A. F. Kindall, "Management by Objectives, Where We Stand—A Survey of the Fortune 500," *Human Resource Management* 13 (Spring 1974), pp. 8–11.

23. E. J. Seyna, "MOB: The Fad that Changed Management," *Long-Range Planning* (December 1986), pp. 116–123.

24. Gilda Dangot-Simpkin, "Getting Your Staff to Do What You Want," *Supervisory Management* 36 (January 1991), pp. 4–5.

25. A. E. Kazdin, *Behavior Modification in Applied Settings* (Homewood, IL: Dorsey Press, 1975), pp. 33–34.

26. Fred Luthans and Robert Kreitner, *Organizational Behavior Modification and Beyond: An Operant and Social Learning Approach* (Glenview, IL: Scott, Foresman, 1985), pp. 46–49.

27. Judi Komake, "Why We Don't Reinforce: The Issues," *Journal of Organizational Behavior Management* (Fall–Winter 1982), pp. 97–100.

28. Kirk O'Hara, C. Merle Johnson, and Terry A. Beehr, "Organizational Behavior Management in the Private Sector: A Review of Empirical Research and Recommendations for Further Investigation," *Academy of Management Review* 10 (October 1985), pp. 848–864.

29. David Premack, "Toward Empirical Behavior Laws: Positive Reinforcement," *Psychological Review* 66 (1959).

30. Fred Luthans and Mark Martinko, "An Organizational Behavior Modification Analysis of Absenteeism," *Human Resource Management* 15 (Fall 1976), pp. 11–18.

31. Richard M. Steers and Susan R. Rhodes, "Major Influences on Employee Attendance: A Process Model," in Barry M. Staw (Ed.), *Psychological Dimensions of Organizational Behavior* (New York: Macmillan, 1991), pp. 151–164.

32. Colette A. Frayne and Gary P. Latham, "Application of Social Learning Theory to Employee Self-Management of Attendance," *Journal of Applied Psychology* (August 1987), pp. 387–392.

33. Alfie Kohn, "Why Incentive Plans Cannot Work," *Harvard Business Review* 71 (September–October 1993), pp. 54–63.

34. Charles O'Reilly, "Corporations, Culture, and Commitment: Motivation and Social Control In Organizations," In Arthur A. Thompson, Jr., William E. Fulmer, and A. J. Strickland III, *Readings in Strategic Management,* 4th ed. (Homewood IL: Irwin, 1992), p. 465.

35. Steven Kerr, "On the Folly of Rewarding A, While Hoping for B," in Barry M. Staw (Ed.), *Psychological Dimensions of Organizational Behavior* (New York: Macmillan, 1991), pp. 65–75. Originally in *Academy of Management Journal* 18 (1975), pp. 769–783.

36. Sam Walton with John Huey, *Sam Walton: Made in America* (New York: Doubleday, 1992), pp. 132–133.

37. Dean B. McFarlin and Paul D. Sweeney, "Distributing and Procedural Justice as Predictors of Satisfaction with Personal and Organization Outcomes," *Academy of Management Journal* 35 (August 1992), pp. 626–637.

38. John P. Campbell, Marvin D. Dunnette, Richard D. Arvey, and Lowell V. Hellervik, "The Development and Evaluation of Behaviorally Based Rating Scales," *Journal of Applied Psychology* (February 1973), p. 15.

39. John M. Ivancevich, "High and Low Task Stimulation Jobs: A Causal Analysis of Performance-Satisfaction Relationships," *Academy of Management Journal* 22 (June 1979), p. 220.

40. "Employers Spice Up Their Compensation Packages with Special Bonuses," *The Wall Street Journal* (October 24, 1995), p. A-1.

41. "Deliver—or Else: Pay for Performance Is Making an Impact on CEO Paychecks," *Business Week* (March 27, 1995), p. 36.

42. Edward E. Lawler III, *Pay and Organizational Development* (Reading, MA: Addison-Wesley, 1981).

43. C. W. Hamner, "How to Ruin Motivation with Pay," *Compensation Review* 21 (1975), pp. 88–89.

44. "When Are Employees Not Employees? When They're Associates, Stakeholders . . . ," *The Wall Street Journal* (November 9, 1988, p. B1.

45. Walton with Huey, *Sam Walton: Made in America,* p. 132.

46. "At Philip Morris, Blue Chips for Blue Collars," *Business Week* (March 27, 1995), p. 38.

47. Graef Crystal, "Growing the Pay Gap," *Los Angeles Times* (July 23, 1995).

48. Graef Crystal, "Paying Directors in Company Stock Doesn't Boost Performance," *Los Angeles Times* (March 12, 1995).

49. Theresa M. Welbourne and Luis R. Gomez-Mejia, "Gainsharing: A Critical Review and a Future Research Agenda," *Journal of Management* 21 (September 1995), pp. 559+.

50. S. E. Markham, K. D. Scott, and B. L. Little, "National Gainsharing Study: The Importance of Industry Differences," *Compensation and Benefits Review* 24, no. 1 (1992), pp. 34–35.

51. Alexander Consulting Group, "Health Care Costs, Quality Top List of Human Resources Concerns," *Employee Benefit Plan Review* 47, no. 3 (1992), pp. 38–39.

52. "More Benefits Bend with Workers' Needs," *The Wall Street Journal* (January 9, 1990), p. B1.

53. Edward E. Lawler III, "Managers' Attitudes Toward How Their Pay Is and Should Be Determined," *Journal of Applied Psychology* 50 (1966), pp. 273–279.

54. Edward J. Ost, "Team-Based Pay: New Wave Strategic Incentives," *Sloan Management Review* (Spring 1990); and in Arthur A. Thompson, Jr., William E. Fulmer, and A. J. Strickland III, *Readings in Strategic Management*, 4th ed. (Homewood, IL: Irwin, 1992), pp. 485–499.

55. Kohn, "Why Incentive Plans Cannot Work."

56. Charles M. Cumming, "Incentives that Really Do Motivate," *Compensation and Benefits Management* 26 (May 1994), pp. 38–40.

57. Patrick M. Wright, "Goal Setting and Monetary Incentives: Motivational Tools that Can Work Too Well," *Compensation and Benefit Review* 26 (May 1994), pp. 41–50.

58. Peter Nulty, "Incentive Pay Can Be Crippling," *Fortune* (November 13, 1995), p. 235.

59. Charles D. Wrenge and Amedero G. Perroni, "Taylor's Pig-Tale: A Historical Analysis of Frederick W. Taylor's Pig-Iron Experiments," *Academy of Management Journal* 17 (1974), pp. 6–27.

60. Michael Hammer, "Reengineering Work: Don't Automate, Obliterate," *Harvard Business Review* 68 (July–August 1990), p. 107.

61. Michael W. Miller, "IBM Shares Tumble by 7.6% on Pessimism Over Actions," *The Wall Street Journal Europe* (December 17, 1992), p. 4.

62. F. Lengel, "The Existence and Impact of Alienating Job Conditions in the Hospital Medical Laboratory," a master's degree report, Wayne State University, Detroit, 1976.

63. Edward W. Lawler III, "Total Quality Management and Employee Involvement: Are They Compatible?" *Academy of Management Executive* 8 (February 1994), pp. 68–76; and Richard Blackburn and Benson Rosen, "Total Quality and Human Resources Management: Lessons Learned from Baldrige Award-Winning Companies," *Academy of Management Executive* 7 (August 1993), pp. 49–66.

64. J. Richard Hackman, Greg R. Oldham, Robert Janson, and Kenneth Purdy, "A New Strategy for Job Enrichment," *California Management Review* 17 (Summer 1976), pp. 57–71.

65. J. R. Hackman and Edward E. Lawler III, "Employee Reactions to Job Characteristics," *Journal of Applied Psychology* 55 (1971), pp. 259–286, defines the first six core job dimensions. See also J. Richard Hackman, "The Design of Work Teams," in Jay W. Lorsch (Ed.), *Handbook of Organizational Behavior* (Englewood Cliffs, NJ: Prentice Hall, 1987), pp. 315–342.

66. Moses N. Kiggundu, "Task Interdependence and the Theory of Job Design," *Academy of Management Review* 6 (July 1981), pp. 499–508.

67. Michael A. Campion, "Interdisciplinary Approaches to Job Design: A Constructive Replication with Extensions," *Journal of Applied Psychology* 73 (1988), pp. 467–481; and Michael A. Campion and Carol L. McClelland, "Interdisciplinary Examination of the Costs and Benefits of Enlarged Jobs: A Job Design Quasi-Experiment," *Journal of Applied Psychology* 76 (1991), pp. 186–198.

68. Michael Campion, "Ability Requirement Implications of Job Design: An Interdisciplinary Perspective," paper presented at 95th conference of the American Psychological Association, New York (August 1987).

69. Campion, "Interdisciplinary Approaches to Job Design."

70. Blackburn and Rosen, "Total Quality and Human Resources Management."

71. Jay A. Conger and Rabindra N. Kanungo, "The Empowerment Process: Integrating Theory and Practice," *Academy of Management Review* 13 (July 1988), pp. 471–482.

72. Albert Bandura, *Social Learning Theory* (Englewood Cliffs, NJ: Prentice Hall, 1977); and A. Bandura, "Self-Regulation of Motivation and Action Through Goal Systems," in V. Hamilton, G. H. Bower, and N. H. Frijda (Eds.), *Competence Considered: Perceptions of Competence and Incompetence Across the Lifespan* (Dordrecht, Netherlands: Luwer Academic Publishers, 1988), pp. 37–61.

73. Marilyn E. Gist and Terence R. Mitchell, "Self-Efficacy: A Theoretical Analysis of Its Determinants and Malleability," *Academy of Management Review* 17 (April 1992), pp. 183–211.

74. Allan R. Cohen and David L. Bradford, *Managing for Excellence: The Guide to High Performance in Contemporary Organizations* (New York: John Wiley & Sons, 1984).

75. Robert D. Hof, "Scott McNealy's Rising Sun," *Business Week* (January 22, 1996), pp. 66–73.

76. Leon A. Kappelman and Victor R. Prybutok, "A Small Amount of Empowerment Pays Off Big in a Regional Bank," *National Productivity Review* 14 (September 22, 1995), pp. 39–42.

77. Kenneth W. Thomas and Betty A. Velthouse, "Cognitive Elements of Empowerment: An 'Interpretative' Model of Intrinsic Task Motivation," *Academy of Management Review* 15 (October 1990), p. 673.

78. Ibid., pp. 666–681.

79. Albert Bandura, *Social Foundations of Thought and Action: A Social-cognitive View* (Englewood Cliffs, NJ: Prentice Hall, 1986).

80. This and the next several quotes are from Robert A. Mamis, "Market Maker," *Inc.* (December 1995), pp. 54–64.

81. Christopher Farrell, "The Boom in IPOs," *Business Week* (December 18, 1995), p. 69.

82. Exercise demonstrated by Edward J. Harrick as an organization development exercise for Housing Development Finance Corporation, Bombay, India.

83. Contributed by Gary Convis, senior vice president, NUMMI, based on his presentation, "Team Member Involvement: How Kaizen, Problem Solving Circles and Suggestions Empower Team Members and Help Make NUMMI a Lean, Efficient Manufacturing Facility," San Jose State University College of Business Alumni Breakfast Briefings, Fairmont Hotel, December 14, 1995.

Chapter 8

1. B. L. Reece and R. Brandt, *Effective Human Relations in Business,* 3rd ed. (Boston: Houghton Mifflin, 1987), p. 97.

2. Ibid., p. 27.

3. Otis W. Baskin and Graig E. Aronoff, *Interpersonal Communication in Organizations* (Santa Monica, CA: Goodyear, 1980), p. 2.

4. J. David Pincus, "Communication Satisfaction, Job Satisfaction, and Job Performance," *Human Communication Research* (Spring 1986), pp. 395–419.

5. J. M. Putti, S. Aryee, and J. Phua, "Communication Relationship, Satisfaction, and Organizational Commitment," *Group and Organizational Studies* (1990), pp. 44–52.

6. D. Nichols, "Bottom-Up Strategies: Asking the Employees for Advice," *Management Review* (1989), pp. 44–49.

7. J. M. Schlesinger and P. T. Ingrassia, "GM Woos Employees by Listening to Them, Talking of Its Team," *The Wall Street Journal* (January 12, 1989), p. 1.

8. Everett M. Rogers and Rekha Agarwala-Rogers, *Communication in Organizations* (New York: Free Press, 1976), pp. 10–14.

9. Fred Luthens and Janet K. Larsen, "How Managers Really Communicate," *Human Relations* (February 1986), pp. 167–168.

10. "Leaders of the Most Admired," *Fortune* (January 29, 1990), pp. 40–54.

11. Walter Kiechel III, "Breaking the Bad News to the Boss," *Fortune* (April 9, 1990), pp. 111–112.

12. J. N. Goodrich, "Telecommuting in America," *Business Horizons* (July–August 1990), pp. 31–37.

13. L. K. Trevino, R. H. Lengel, W. Bodensteiner, E. A. Gerloff, and N. Kanoff-Muir, "The Richness Imperative and Cognitive Style: The Role of Individual Differences in Media Choice Behavior," *Management Communication Quarterly* 4 (1990), pp. 176–197.

14. "Wal-Mart's Store of the Future Blends Discount Prices, Department Store Feel," *The Wall Street Journal* (May 17), 1991, p. B1.

15. L. Copeland and L. Griggs, *Going International* (New York: Random House, 1985), p. 103.

16. David Smart, "When Johnny's Whole Family Can't Read," *Business Week* (July 20, 1992), pp. 68–70.

17. Al Howell, "Communicating for Productivity," *Bobbin,* 3, no. 4 (December 1991), pp. 20–21.

18. Peter Maud, "Dialogue with Employees: Why Most Well-Intentioned Efforts Fail," *Practicing Manager,* 11, no. 3 (October 1991), pp. 33–36.

19. Paul Hawken, *Growing a Business* (New York: Simon & Schuster, 1987).

20. James Brassil, "Communication in Business: Encouraging Upward Communication," *Pace* (November/December 1984), p. 39.

21. *Profiles in Quality: Blueprints for Action from 50 Leading Companies* (Boston: Allyn and Bacon, 1991), pp. 45–48.

22. S. J. Modic, "Grapevine Rated Most Believable," *Industry Week* (May 15, 1989), p. 14.

23. Ibid.

24. Donald B. Simmons, "The Nature of the Organizational Grapevine," *Supervisory Management* (November 1985), pp. 39–42.

25. K. Davis, "Management Communication and the Grapevine," *Harvard Business Review* (September–October 1953), pp. 43–49.

26. W. Kiechel III, "In Praise of Office Gossip," *Fortune* (August 19, 1985), pp. 253–256.

27. Thomas F. O'Boyle and Carlo Hymowitz, "More Corporate Chiefs Seek Direct Contact with Staff, Customers," *The Wall Street Journal* (February 27, 1985), pp. 1 and 12.

28. Lois Therrien, "How Ztel Went from Riches to Rags," *Business Week* (June 17, 1985), pp. 97–100.

29. Tom Peters and Robert Waterman, *In Search of Excellence* (New York: Harper & Row, 1982), pp. 173–174.

30. Harold J. Leavitt, *Managerial Psychology,* 3rd ed. (Chicago: University of Chicago Press, 1972), pp. 189–196.

31. Herminia Ibarra, "Personal Networks of Women and Minorities in Management: A Conceptual Framework," *Academy of Management Review,* 18, no. 1 (1993), pp. 56–87.

32. N. J. Adler, *International Dimensions of Organizational Behavior* (Boston: Kent, 1986), p. 53.

33. L. L. Tobias, "Twenty-Three Ways to Improve Communication," *Training and Development Journal* (1989), pp. 75–77.

34. Michael W. Miller, "At Many Firms, Employees Speak a Language That's All Their Own," *The Wall Street Journal* (December 29, 1987), p. 15.

35. D. W. Johnson, *Reaching Out,* 2nd ed. (Englewood Cliffs, NJ: Prentice Hall, 1981), pp. 65–66.

36. Sandra G. Garside and Brian H. Kleiner, "Effective One-to-One Communication Skills," *Industrial & Commercial Training,* 23, no. 7 (1991), pp. 24–28.

37. Johnson, *Reaching Out,* pp. 65–67.

38. Evelyn Lewis and Barry K. Spiker, "Tell Me What You Want Me to Do," *Manufacturing Systems,* 9, no. 12 (December 1991), pp. 46–49.

39. Phillip L. Hunsaker and Anthony J. Alessandra, *The Art of Managing People* (New York: Simon & Schuster, 1986), pp. 202–213.

40. Eleanor Davidson, "Communicating with a Diverse Work Force," *Supervisory Management,* 36, no. 12 (December 1991), pp. 1–2.

41. Hunsaker and Alessandra, *The Art of Managing People,* pp. 97–102.

42. Ibid., pp. 102–111.

43. Om P. Kharbanda and Ernest A. Stallworthy, "Listening: A Vital Negotiating Skill," *Journal of Managerial Psychology,* 6, no. 4 (1991), pp. 6–9, 49–52.

44. Gerald M. Goldhaber, *Organizational Communication,* 4th ed. (Dubuque, IA: William C. Brown, 1980), p. 189.

45. Hunsaker and Alessandra, *The Art of Managing People,* pp. 131–137.

46. P. L. Hunsaker and C. A. Frayne, "More and Better Results through Concentration," *Supervisory Management* (February 1983), pp. 14–19.

47. P. L. Hunsaker and C. W. Cook, *Managing Organizational Behavior* (Reading, MA: Addison-Wesley, 1986), p. 216.

48. Hunsaker and Alessandra, *The Art of Managing People*, pp. 129–131.

49. A. Mehrabian, "Communication without Words," *Psychology Today* (September 1968), pp. 53–55.

50. Ibid.

51. Paul Ekman, "Facial Expression and Emotion," *American Psychologist* (April 1993), pp. 384–392.

52. F. Williams, *The New Communications* (Belmont, CA: Wadsworth, 1989), p. 45.

53. J. W. Gibson and R. M. Hodgetts, *Organizational Communication: A Managerial Perspective* (Orlando, FL: Academic Press, 1986), p. 95.

54. Ibid.

55. Albert Mehrabian, *Nonverbal Communication* (Chicago: Aldine/Atherton, 1972), pp. 25–30.

56. Om P. Kharbanda and Ernest A. Stallworthy, "Verbal and Non-Verbal Communication," *Journal of Managerial Psychology*, 6, no. 4 (1991), pp. 10–13, 49–52.

57. G. I. Nierenberg and H. H. Calero, *How To Read a Person Like a Book* (New York: Pocket Books, 1973).

58. Gibson and Hodgetts, *Organizational Communication*, pp. 103–105.

59. R. Rosenthal et al., "Body Talk and Tone of Voice: The Language without Words," *Psychology Today* (September 1974), pp. 64–68.

60. Hunsaker and Alessandra, *The Art of Managing People*, Chapter 12.

61. P. L. Hunsaker, "The Space Case," *Registered Representative* (April 1984), pp. 67–72.

62. Hunsaker and Alessandra, *The Art of Managing People*, pp. 144–155.

63. M. Johnson, *Business Buzzwords* (Cambridge, MA: Blackwell, 1990).

64. Anat Rafaeli and Michael G. Pratt, "Tailored Meanings: On the Meaning and Impact of Organizational Dress," *Academy of Management Review*, 18, no. 1 (1993), pp. 32–55.

65. Phillip Harris and Robert Moran, *Managing Cultural Differences*, 3rd ed. (Houston: Gulf Publishing, 1991), p. 13.

66. Jeswald Salacuse, *Making Global Deals* (Boston: Houghton Mifflin, 1991), pp. 14–15.

67. Deborah Tannen, *You Just Don't Understand: Women and Men in Conversation* (New York: Ballantine Books, 1991), pp. 24–25.

68. N. J. Adler, *International Dimensions of Organizational Behavior,* 2nd ed. (Boston: Kent Publishing, 1991), pp. 83–84.

Chapter 9

1. Audrey Edwards, "The Enlightened Manager: How to Treat All Your Employees Fairly," *Working Woman* 16, no. 1 (January 1991), pp. 38–39.

2. The Gallup Organization, *Challenge to Management Education: Avoiding Irrelevancy* (Morristown, NJ: Financial Executives Research Foundation, 1991), pp. 5–9.

3. S. P. Robbins and P. L. Hunsaker, *Training in Interpersonal Skills,* 2nd ed. (Englewood Cliffs, NJ: Prentice Hall, 1996), p. 1.

4. Kurt Sanholz, *National Business Employment Weekly* (Fall 1987).

5. A. R. Cohen, S. L. Fink, H. Gadon, R. D. Willits, and N. Josefowitz, *Effective Behavior in Organizations,* 5th ed. (Homewood, IL: Irwin, 1992), p. 253.

6. This model was adapted from ideas in A. N. Turner and G. F. F. Lombard, *Interpersonal Behavior and Administration* (New York: The Free Press/Collier-Macmillan, 1969); and R. E. Coffey, A. G. Athos, and P. A. Raynolds, *Behavior in Organizations: A Multidimensional View,* 2nd ed. (Englewood Cliffs, NJ: Prentice Hall, 1975), pp. 150–151.

7. Edwards, "The Enlightened Manager," pp. 38–39.

8. D. L. Costley and R. Todd, *Human Relations in Organizations* (Los Angeles: West Publishing Company, 1987), pp. 232–235.

9. William C. Schutz, *FIRO: A Three Dimensional Theory of Interpersonal Behavior* (New York: Rinehart & Co., 1958).

10. R. E. Hill, "Interpersonal Needs and Functional Areas of Management," *Journal of Vocational Behavior,* 4 (1974), pp. 15–24.

11. David A. Whetton and Kim S. Cameron, *Developing Managerial Skills,* 3rd ed. (New York: HarperCollins, 1995), p. 81.

12. N. J. DiMarco, "Supervisor-subordinate Life Style and Interpersonal Need Compatibilities as Determinants of Subordinate's Attitudes Toward the Supervisor," *Academy of Management Journal,* 17 (1974), pp. 575–578; and W. W. Liddell, and J. W. Slocum, Jr., "The Effects of Individual-role Compatibility Upon Group Performance: An Extension of Schutz's FIRO Theory," *Academy of Management Journal,* 19 (1976), pp. 413–426.

13. Robbins and Hunsaker, *Training.*

14. Loraine O'Connell, "Gut Reactions Tells About Self," *The San Diego Union-Tribune* (September 26, 1994), p. E-3.

15. Ibid.

16. Cohen, Fink, Gadon, Willits, and Josefowitz, *Effective Behavior in Organizations*, p. 256.

17. W. G. Bennis, D. E. Berlew, E. H. Schein, and F. I. Steele, *Interpersonal Dynamics,* 3rd ed. (Chicago: Dorsey Press, 1973), pp. 495–518.

18. F. Steele and S. Jenks, *The Feel of the Work Place* (Reading, MA: Addison-Wesley Publishing, 1977), pp. 157–163.

19. R. T. Golembiewski, *Renewing Organizations: The Laboratory Approach to Planned Change* (Itasca, IL: F. E. Peacock Publishers, 1972), p. 31.

20. D. W. Johnson, *Reaching Out: Interpersonal Effectiveness and Self-Actualization,* (Needham Heights, MA.: Allyn and Bacon, 1993), pp. 32–47.

21. Blaine Goss and Dan O'Hair, *Communicating in Interpersonal Relationships* (New York: Macmillan Publishing Company, 1988), pp. 47–48.

22. Ibid., p. 48

23. Stephen R. Covey, *The Seven Habits of Highly Effective People* (New York: Simon & Schuster, 1989), pp. 188–189.

24. Ibid., pp. 190–199.

25. Johnson, *Reaching Out*, p. 18.

26. J. Luft, *Group Processes*, 3rd ed. (Palo Alto, CA: Mayfield Publishing Company, 1984), pp. 11–20.

27. P. C. Hanson, "The Johari Window: A Model for Soliciting and Giving Feedback," in *The 1973 Annual*

Handbook for Group Facilitators (San Diego: University Associates, 1973), pp. 114–119.

28. Much of this discussion is based on Coffey, Athos, and Raynolds, *Behavior in Organizations,* pp. 155–157.

29. Goss and O'Hair, *Communicating in Interpersonal Relationships,* pp. 47–48.

30. This discussion is based on P. L. Hunsaker and A. J. Alessandra, *The Art of Managing People* (New York: Simon & Schuster, 1986), pp. 32–49.

31. J. Bard and P. Bradley, "Styles of Management and Communication: A Comparative Study of Men and Women," *Communication Monographs* 46 (1979), pp. 101–111.

32. J. Hunsaker and P. Hunsaker, *Strategies and Skills for Managerial Women* (Cincinnati: South-Western Publishing, 1991), pp. 252–253.

33. B. Eakins and R. Eakins, *Sex Differences in Human Communication* (Boston: Houghton Mifflin Company, 1978), pp. 117–119.

34. Hunsaker and Hunsaker, *Strategies and Skills for Managerial Women,* p. 139.

35. Joyce K. Fletcher, "Castrating the Female Advantage: Feminist Standpoint Research and Management Science," *Journal of Management Inquiry* (March 1994), pp. 74–82.

36. K. Kram, "Mentors in the Workplace," in D. T. Hall (Ed.), *Career Development in Organizations* (San Francisco: Jossey-Bass, 1986), pp. 29–47.

37. V. Wheeless and C. Berryman-Fink, "Perceptions of Women Managers and Their Communicator Competencies," *Communication Quarterly* 33 (1985), pp. 137–148.

38. R. Liden, "Female Perception of Female and Male Managerial Behavior," *Sex Roles* 12 (1985), pp. 421–432.

39. B. A. Gutek, A. G. Cohen, and A. M. Konrad, "Predicting Social-Sexual Behavior at Work: A Contact Hypothesis," *Academy of Management Journal,* 33, no. 3 (1990), pp. 560–577.

40. Chris Lee, "Sexual Harassment: After the Headlines," *Training* (March 1992), pp. 23–31.

41. J. Castro, "Sexual Harassment: A Guide," *Time* (January 20, 1992), p. 37.

42. Lee, "Sexual Harassment: After the Headlines," pp. 23–31.

43. J. A. DeVito, *The Interpersonal Communication Book,* 6th ed. (New York: Harper Collins Publishers, 1992), p. 77.

44. M. Knapp and M. Comadena, "Telling It Like It Isn't: A Review of Theory and Research on Deceptive Communication," *Human Communication Research* 5 (1979), pp. 270–285.

45. D. McLellan, "That's a Lie," *Los Angeles Times* (February 9, 1993), p. E3.

46. Goss and O'Hair, *Communicating in Interpersonal Relationships,* pp. 258–266.

47. M. Cody, P. Marston, and M. Foster, "Deception: Paralinguistic and Verbal Leakage," in R. Bostrom, (Ed.) *Communication Yearbook* (Beverly Hills, CA: Sage Publications, 1978).

48. R. Kraut, "Verbal and Nonverbal Cues in the Perception of Lying," *Journal of Personality and Social Psychology* 36 (1978), pp. 380–391.

49. McLellan, "That's a Lie," p. E3.

50. Roger C. Mayer and James H. Davis, "An Integrative Model of Organizational Trust," *Academy of Management Review* (July, 1995), pp. 709–734.

51. Daniel Goleman, *Emotional Intelligence* (New York: Bantam Books, 1995).

52. This case was prepared from materials in Laura Berman, "The Gospel According to Mary," *Working Woman* (August 1995), pp. 47–49, 68–72; and P. W. Bernstein, "Things the B-School Never Taught," *Fortune* (November 3, 1980), pp. 53–56.

Chapter 10

1. Jon R. Katzenback and Douglas K. Smith, *The Wisdom of Teams: Creating the High-Performance Organization* (Boston: Harvard Business School Press, 1993); and Peter F. Drucker, "There's More Than One Kind of Team," *The Wall Street Journal* (February 11, 1992), p. A16.

2. John R. Katzenback and Douglas K. Smith, "The Discipline of Teams," *Harvard Business Review* (March–April, 1993), pp. 111–120.

3. Michael Gates, "The Quality Challenge: Can Managers and Workers See Eye to Eye?" *Incentive* 163, no. 8 (August 1989), pp. 20–22.

4. F. J. Yammarino and A. J. Dubinksy, "Salesperson Performance and Managerially Controllable Factors: An Investigation of Individual and Work Group Effects," *Journal of Management* 16 (1990), pp. 87–106.

5. B. E. Ashforth and F. Mael, "Social Identity Theory and the Organization," *Academy of Management Review* (January 1989), pp. 20–39.

6. M. E. Shaw, *Group Dynamics: The Psychology of Small Group Behavior,* 3rd ed. (New York: McGraw-Hill, 1981), pp. 11–12.

7. J. Meer, "Loafing Through a Tough Job," *Psychology Today* (January 1985), p. 72; and G. R. Ferris and K. M. Rowland, "Social Facilitation Effects on Behavioral and Perceptual Task Performance Measures: Implications for Work Behavior," *Group & Organization Studies* (December 1983), pp. 421–438.

8. Oscar Suris, "Hispanic Group Meets with Chief Executive," *The Orlando Sentinel* (August 11, 1990), pp. c1, c6.

9. R. T. Hussein, "Informal Groups, Leadership, and Productivity," *Leadership and Organization Development Journal* 10, no. 1 (1989), pp. 9–16.

10. R. W. Napier and M. K. Gershenfeld, *Groups: Theory and Experience,* 5th ed. (Dallas: Houghton Mifflin, 1993), pp. 81–84.

11. Bob Hughes, "25 Stepping Stones for Self-Directed Work Teams," *Training* 28, no. 12 (December 1991), pp. 44–46.

12. B. W. Tuckman and M. A. C. Jensen, "Stages of Small Group Development Revisited," *Group and Organizational Studies* 2 (1977), pp. 419–427; M. F. Maples, "Group Development: Extending Tuckman's Theory," *Journal for Specialists in Group Work* (Fall 1988), pp. 17–23; and C. Kormanski and A. Mozenter, "A New Model of Team Building: A Technology for Today and Tomorrow," in J. W. Pfeiffer and J. E.

Jones (Eds.), *The 1987 Annual: Developing Human Resources* (San Diego: University Associates, 1987), pp. 255–268.

13. C. J. G. Gersick, "Marking Time: Predictable Transitions in Task Groups," *Academy of Management Journal* 32 (1989), pp. 274–309; C. J. G. Gersick, "Revolutionary Change Theories: A Multilevel Exploration of the Punctuated Equilibrium Paradigm," *Academy of Management Review* 16 (1991), pp. 10–36; and E. Romanelli and M. L. Tushman, "Organizational Transformation as Punctuated Equilibrium: An Empirical 'Test'," *Academy of Management Journal,* 37 (October 1994), pp. 1141–1166.

14. W. E. Watson, K. Kuman, and L. K. Michaelson, "Cultural Diversity's Impact on Interaction Process and Performance: Comparing Homogeneous and Diverse Task Groups," *Academy of Management Journal* 36 (1993), pp. 590–602.

15. Adapted from David A. Kolb, Irwin M. Rubin, and Joyce M. Osland, *Organizational Psychology: An Experiential Approach,* 5th ed. (Englewood Cliffs, NJ: Prentice Hall, 1991), pp. 213–214; Thomas A. Kayser, *Mining Group Gold* (El Segundo, CA: Serif Publishing, 1990); and K. D. Benne and P. Sheats, "Functional Roles of Group Members," *Journal of Social Issues* 4, no. 2 (Spring 1948), pp. 41–49.

16. Daniel C. Feldman, "The Development and Enforcement of Group Norms," *Academy of Management Review* (January 1984), pp. 47–53.

17. Ibid.

18. P. S. Goodman, E. Ravlin, and M. Schminike, "Understanding Groups in Organizations," in L. L. Cummings and B. M. Staw (Eds.), *Research in Organizational Behavior,* Vol. 9 (Greenwich, CT: JAI Press, 1987), p. 159.

19. Feldman, "The Development and Enforcement of Group Norms."

20. Napier and Gershenfeld, *Groups: Theory and Experience,* p. 520.

21. J. Keyton and J. Springston, "Redefining Cohesiveness in Groups," *Small Group Research* (May 1990), pp. 234–254.

22. I. Summers, T. Coffelt, and R. E. Horton, "Work-Group Cohesion," *Psychological Reports* (October 1988), pp. 627–636.

23. P. Yetton and P. Bottger, "The Relationships Among Group Size, Member Ability, Social Decision Schemes, and Performance," *Organizational Behavior and Human Performance* (October 1983), pp. 145–159.

24. K. L. Bettenhausen, "Five Years of Groups Research: What We Have Learned and What Needs to be Addressed," *Journal of Management* (June 1991), p. 362.

25. B. Mullen and C. Copper, "The Relation Between Group Cohesiveness and Performance: An Integration," *Psychological Bulletin* (March 1994), pp. 210–227.

26. R. T. Keller, "Predictors of the Performance of Project Groups in R&D Organizations," *Academy of Management Journal* (December 1986), pp. 715–726.

27. M. E. Shaw, *Group Dynamics,* 3rd ed. (New York: McGraw-Hill, 1981), p. 78.

28. Norman R. F. Maier, "Assets and Liabilities in Group Problem Solving," *Psychological Review* 74 (July 1967), pp. 239–249; and A. E. Schwartz and J. Levin, "Better Group Decision Making," *Supervisory Management* (June 1990), p. 4.

29. For an example of the strength of inappropriate conformity, see S. E. Asch, "Effects of Group Pressure upon the Modification and Distortion of Judgments," in H. Guetzkow (Ed.), *Groups, Leadership and Men* (Pittsburgh: Carnegie Press, 1951), pp. 177–190.

30. R. J. Aldag and S. Riggs Fuller, "Beyond Fiasco: A Reappraisal of the Groupthink Phenomenon and a New Model of Group Decision Processes," *Psychological Bulletin* (May 1993), pp. 533–552.

31. Irving L. Janis, *Groupthink: Psychological Studies of Policy Decisions and Fiascoes,* 2nd ed. (Boston: Houghton Mifflin, 1982).

32. Ibid.

33. J. A. Shepperd, "Productivity Loss in Performance Groups: A Motivation Analysis ," *Pscyhological Bulletin* (January 1993), pp. 67–81.

34. J. M. Jackson and S. G. Harkins, "Equity in Effort: An Explanation of the Social Loafing Effect," *Journal of Personality and Social Psychology* (November 1985), pp. 1199–1206.

35. K. Williams, S. Harkings, and B. Latane, "Identifiability as a Deterrent to Social Loafing: Two Cheering Experiments," *Journal of Personality and Social Psychology* (February 1981), pp. 303–311; and Robert Albanese and David D. Van Fleet, "Rational Behavior in Groups: The Free-Rider Tendency," *Academy of Management Review* 10 (April 1985), pp. 244–255.

36. J. M. George, "Extrinsic and Intrinsic Origins of Perceived Social Loafing in Organizations," *Academy of Management Journal* (March 1992), pp. 191–202.

37. S. G. Harkins and K. Szymanski, "Social Loafing and Group Evaluation," *Journal of Personality and Social Psychology* (June 1989), pp. 934–941.

38. P. C. Earley, "Social Loafing and Collectivism: A Comparison of the United States and the People's Republic of China," *Administrative Science Quarterly* (December 1989), pp. 565–581.

39. R. A. Guzzo and G. P. Shea, "Group Performance and Intergroup Relations in Organizations," in M. D. Dunnette and L. M. Hough, (Eds.), *Handbook of Industrial & Organizational Psychology,* 2nd ed., Vol. 3 (Palo Alto, CA: Consulting Psychologists Press, 1992), pp. 288–290.

40. Watson, Kumar, and Michaelsen, "Cultural Diversity's Impact on Interaction Process and Performance."

41. N. J. Adler, *International Dimensions of Organizational Behavior,* 2nd ed. (Boston: PWS-Kent, 1991), p. 99.

42. L. Smith-Lovin and C. Brody, "Interruptions in Group Discussions: The Effects of Gender and Group Composition," *American Sociological Review* (June 1989), pp. 424–435.

43. E. M. Ott, "Effects of the Male-Female Ratio at Work," *Psychology of Women Quarterly* (March 1989), p. 53.

44. J. E. Driskell and E. Salas, "Group Decision Making Under Stress," *Journal of Applied Psychology* (June 1991), pp. 473–478.

45. A. E. Schwartz and J. Levin, "Better Group Decision Making," *Supervisory Management* (June 1990), pp. 319–342.

46. Michael Finley, "New Technology Is Changing How Meetings Are Conducted," *Office Systems* (May 1992), pp. 44–47.

47. These steps are summarized from C. Margerison and D. McCann, *Team Management Systems: The Team Development Manual* (Toowong, Queensland, Australia: Team Management Resources, 1990), pp. 19–36.

48. W. G. Dyer, *Team Building: Issues and Alternatives,* 2nd ed. (Menlo Park, CA: Addison-Wesley, 1987), pp. 97–108.

49. William G. Dyer, Robert H. Daines, and William C. Giauque, *The Challenge of Management* (New York: Harcourt Brace Jovanovich, 1990), pp. 346–350.

50. M. J. Driver, K. R. Brousseau, and P. L. Hunsaker, *The Dynamic Decisionmaker* (New York: Jossey-Bass, 1993), pp. 216–231.

51. See for example, D. Tjosvold, *Team Organization: An Enduring Competitive Advantage* (Chichester, England: Wiley, 1991); and J. R. Katzenback and D. K. Smith, *The Wisdom of Teams* (Boston: Harvard Business School Press, 1993).

52. Katzenback and Smith, *The Wisdom of Teams,* p. 45.

53. Peter F. Drucker, "There's More Than One Kind of Team," *The Wall Street Journal* (February 11, 1992), p. A16.

54. Ibid.

55. J. R. Katzenback and D. K. Smith, "The Discipline of Team," *Harvard Business Review* (March–April 1993), pp. 116–118.

56. E. Sundstrom, K. P. De Meuse, and D. Futrell, "Work Teams," *American Psychologist* (February 1990), pp. 120–133.

57. Ibid.

58. J. R. Barker, "Tightening the Iron Cage: Concertive Control in Self-Managing Teams," *Administrative Science Quarterly* (September 1993), pp. 408–437; and M. A. Verespej, "Worker-Managers," *Industry Week* (May 16, 1994), p. 30.

59. W. F. Dowling, "Job Redesign on The Assembly Line: Farewell to Blue-collar Blues?" *Organizational Dynamics* (Autumn 1973), pp. 51–67.

60. Brian Dumaine, "Who Needs a Boss?" *Fortune* (May 7, 1990), pp. 52–60.

61. Bob Hughes, "25 Stepping Stones for Self-Directed Work Teams," *Training* 28, no. 12 (December 1991), pp. 44–46; C. C. Manz, D. E. Keating, and A. Donnellon, "Preparing for an Organizational Change to Employee Self-Management," *Organizational Dynamics* (Autumn 1990), pp. 15–26.

62. See, for example, J. S. Lublin, "Trying to Increase Worker Productivity: More Employers Alter Management Style," *The Wall Street Journal* (February 13, 1992), p. B1. J. Hillkirk, "Self-Directed Work Teams Give TI Lift," *USA Today* (December 20, 1993), p. 8B; M. A. Verespel, "Workers-Managers," *Industry Week* (May 16, 1994), p. 30; and Dumaine, "Who Needs a Boss?"

63. R. Zemke, "Rethinking the Rush to Team Up," *Training* (November 1993), pp. 55–61.

64. P. S. Goodman, R. Devadas, and T. L. Griffith Hughson, "Groups and Productivity: Analyzing the Effectiveness of Self-Managing Teams," in J. P. Campbell, R. J. Campbell, and Associates (Eds.), *Productivity in Organizations* (San Francisco: Jossey-Bass, 1988), pp. 295–327.

65. D. J. Yang and M. Oneal, "How Boeing Does It," *Business Week,* (July 9, 1990), p. 49.

66. "The Role of OD in General Motors' Saturn Project," Symposium at the 1987 Academy of Management Meeting in New Orleans, October 11, 1987.

67. Dumaine, "Who Needs a Boss?" p. 54.

68. "Should the CEO be One Person?" *World Executive Digest* (February 1993), pp. 22–24.

69. Wendell L. French and Cecil H. Bell, Jr., *Organization Development: Behavioral Science Interventions for Organization Improvement* (Englewood Cliffs, NJ: Prentice Hall, 1990), p. 127; M. Mascowitz, "Lessons from the Best Companies to Work For," *California Management Review* (Winter 1985), pp. 42–47; and William G.

Dyer, Robert H. Daines, and William C. Giauque, *The Challenge of Management* (New York: Harcourt Brace Jovanovich, 1990), p. 343.

70. Robert D. Smither, "The Return of the Authoritarian Manager," *Training* (November 1991), p. 40.

71. Dyer, Daines, and Giauque, *The Challenge of Management,* pp. 343–344.

72. Katzenback and Smith, *The Wisdom of Teams,* p. 214.

73. Ibid., p. 112.

74. Robert D. Smither, "The Return of the Authoritarian Manager," *Training* (November 1991), p. 40.

75. Katzenback and Smith, "The Discipline of Teams," pp. 114–116.

76. R. V. Davies, *The Team Management Systems Research Manual* (York, United Kingdom: Team Management Systems, 1990), pp. 1–2.

77. Charles Margerison and Dick McCann, *Team Management: Practical New Approaches* (London: Mercury Books, 1990).

78. Ibid., p. 16.

79. L. Iacocca, *Iacocca—An Autobiography* (New York: Bantam Books, 1986).

80. M. Kaeter, "Repotting Mature Work Teams," *Training* (April 1994) (Supplement), pp. 4–6.

81. French and Bell, *Organization Development,* pp. 133–134.

82. Roger Harrison, "When Power Conflicts Trigger Team Spirit," *European Business* (Spring 1972), pp. 27–65.

83. Richard Beckhard and Reuben T. Harris, *Organizational Transitions: Managing Complex Change* (Reading, MA: Addison-Wesley, 1977), pp. 76–82.

84. J. Luft, *Group Processes,* 3rd ed. (Palo Alto, CA: Mayfield Publishing Company, 1984).

85. W. A. Pasmore and M. R. Fagans, "Participation, Individual Development, and Organizational Change: A Review and Synthesis," *Journal of Management* (June 1992), pp. 375–397.

86. Herbert A. Otto, *Group Methods to Actualize Human Potential: A Handbook* (Beverly Hills, CA: The Holistic Press, 1970), pp. 50–59.

87. Amy Harmon, "TEAMWORK: Chrysler Builds a Concept as Well as a Car," *Los Angeles Times* (April 26, 1992), pp. D1–D3.

88. This exercise combines ideas from others in R. D. Gatewood, R. R. Taylor, and O. C. Ferrell, *Management: Comprehension, Analysis, and Application* (Homewood, IL: Austen Press, 1995), pp. 422 and 456–457.

89. Scott J. Simmerman, *The Book of Square Wheels: A Tool Kit for Facilitators and Team Leaders,* 3rd ed. (Taylors, SC: Performance Management Company, 1994), pp. 1–2.

90. H. Allender, "Self-Directed Work Teams: How Far is Too Far?" *Industrial Management,* (September–October 1993), pp. 13–15; Nancy K. Austin, "Making Teamwork Work," *Working Woman,* January 1993, p. 28; S. Cauldron, "Are Self-Directed Teams Right for Your Company?" *Personnel Journal* (December 1993), pp. 76–94; "What a Zoo Can Teach You," *Fortune* (May 18, 1992), and Tomas Stewart, "The Search for the Organization of Tomorrow," *Fortune* (May 18, 1992).

Chapter 11

1. D. W. Johnson, *Reaching Out: Interpersonal Effectiveness and Self-Actualization* (Boston: Allyn and Bacon, 1993), pp. 205–207.

2. Adapted from M. A. Rahim, *Managing Conflict in Organizations,* 2nd ed. (Westport, CT: Praeger, 1992).

3. K. W. Thomas, "Conflict and Negotiation Processes in Organizations," in M. D. Dunnette and L. M. Hough (Eds.), *Handbook of Industrial and Organizational Psychology,* 2nd ed., Vol. 3 (Palo Alto, CA: Consulting Psychologists Press, 1992), pp. 651–717.

4. Louis Pondy, "Organizational Conflict: Concepts and Models," *Administrative Science Quarterly* 12 (1967), pp. 296–320.

5. R. Kuman, "Affect, Cognition and Decision Making in Negotiations: A Conceptual Integration," in M. A. Rahim (Ed.), *Managing Conflict: An Integrative Approach* (New York: Praeger, 1989), pp. 185–194.

6. P. J. D. Carnevale and A. M. Isen, "The Influence of Positive Affect and Visual Access on the Discovery of Integrative Solutions in Bilateral Negotiations," *Organizational Behavior and Human Decision Processes* (February 1986), pp. 1–13.

7. F. Glasl, "The Process of Conflict Escalation and the Roles of Third Parties," in G. B. J. Bomers and R. Peterson (Eds.), *Conflict Management and Industrial Relations* (Boston: Kluwer-Nijhoff, 1982), pp. 119–140.

8. G. DeGeorge, "Why Sunbeam Is Shining Brighter," *Business Week* (August 29, 1994), pp. 74–75; G. Smith, "How to Lose Friends and Influence No One," *Business Week* (January 25, 1993), pp. 42–43; and "Sunbeam-Oster will pay $173 million to Paul Kazarian and two partners to settle litigation over his ouster," *New York Times* (July 23, 1993), p. c15.

9. B. Kabanoff, "Equity, Equality, Power, and Conflict," *Academy of Management Review* (April 1991), pp. 416–441.

10. J. D. Thompson, *Organizations in Action* (New York: McGraw-Hill, 1967), pp. 54–55.

11. "UAW strike against Caterpillar called off: latest offer rejected," *The San Diego Union-Tribune* (December 4, 1995), p. B-2.

12. The concepts in this section are from R. L. Khan, D. Wolfe, R. Quinn, and J. Snoek, *Organizational Stress: Studies in Role Conflict and Ambiguity* (New York: Wiley, 1964).

13. J. S. Lubin, "Japanese Are Doing More Job Hopping," *The Wall Street Journal* (November 18, 1991), p. B1.

14. Khan, Wolfe, Quinn, and Snoek, *Organizational Stress.*

15. J. R. Rizzo, R. J. House, and S. I. Lirtzman, "Role conflict and ambiguity in complex organizations," *Administrative Science Quarterly* 15 (1970), pp. 150–163.

16. Steve Swartz, "Costly Lesson: GE Finds Running Kidder Peabody & Co Isn't All that Easy," *The Wall Street Journal* (January 27, 1989), p. B1.

17. Robert E. Quinn, *Beyond Rational Management: Mastering the Paradoxes and Competing Demands of High Performance* (San Francisco: Jossey-Bass, 1988), p. 2.

18. Dean Tjosvold, *Working Together to Get Things Done* (Lexington, MA: D.C. Heath, 1986), pp. 111–112.

19. D. H. Schein, *Organizational Psychology,* (Englewood Cliffs, NJ: Prentice Hall, 1965), pp. 80–86.

20. R. A. Cosier and C. R. Schwenk, "Agreement and Thinking Alike: Ingredients for Poor Decisions," *Academy of Management Executive* (February 1990), pp. 69–74.

21. Irving L. Janis, *Groupthink: Psychological Studies of Policy Decisions and Fiascoes,* 2nd ed. (Boston: Houghton Mifflin, 1982).

22. D. C. Pelz and F. Andrews, *Scientists in Organizations* (New York: John Wiley, 1966).

23. J. Hall and M. S. Williams, "A Comparison of Decision-Making Performances in Established and Ad-Hoc Groups," *Journal of Personality and Social Psychology* (February 1966), p. 217.

24. C. Kirchmeyer and A. Cohen, "Multicultural Groups: Their Performance and Reactions with Constructive Conflict," *Group & Organizational Management* (June 1992), pp. 153–170; and S. A. Lobel and P. L. McLeod, "Effects of Ethnic Group Cultural Differences on Cooperative Behavior on a Group Task," *Academy of Management Journal* (December 1991), pp. 827–847.

25. Dean Tjosvold, Valerie Dann, and Choy Wong, "Managing Conflict Between Departments to Serve Customers," *Human Relations,* 45, no. 10 (1992), pp. 1049–1050.

26. Robert H. Miles, *Macro Organizational Behavior* (Santa Monica, CA: Goodyear, 1980), p. 123.

27. M. Sherif and C. Sherif, *Groups in Harmony and Tension* (New York: Harper, 1953), pp. 229–295.

28. Schein, *Organizational Psychology.*

29. K. Jehn, "Enhancing Effectiveness: An Investigation of Advantages and Disadvantages of Value Based Intragroup Conflict," *International Journal of Conflict Management* (July 1994), pp. 223–238.

30. M. A. Rahim and N. R. Magner, "Confirmatory Factor Analysis of the Styles of Handling Interpersonal Conflict: First-Order Factor Model and Its Invariance Across Groups," *Journal of Applied Psychology,* 80, no. 1 (1995), pp. 122–132.

31. Thomas, "Conflict and Negotiation Processes in Organizations."

32. A. J. Alessandra and P. L. Hunsaker, *Communicating at Work* (New York: Simon & Schuster, 1993), Chapter 7.

33. D. G. Ancona, "Outward Bound: Strategies for Team Survival in an Organization," *Academy of Management Journal* (June 1990), pp. 334–356.

34. R. A. Cosier and C. R. Schwenk, "Agreement and Thinking Alike: Ingredients for Poor Decisions," *Academy of Management Executive* (February 1990), pp. 69–74.

35. J. R. Galbraith, *Designing Complex Organizations* (Reading, MA: Addison-Wesley, 1973), p. 103–117.

36. "Paper Avoids a Replay of J. P. Stevens," *Business Week* (June 1983), pp. 33–34.

37. W. L. Ury, J. M. Brett, and S. Goldberg, *Getting Disputes Resolved: Designing Systems to Cut the Costs of Conflict* (San Francisco: Jossey-Bass, 1988).

38. Schein, *Organizational Psychology*, pp. 177–178.

39. M. Afzalur Rahim, (Ed.), *Managing Conflict: An Interdisciplinary Approach* (New York: Praeger Publisher, 1989; and R. Likert and J. Likert, *New Ways of Managing Conflict* (New York: McGraw-Hill, 1976).

40. "A Smarter Way to Manufacture," *Business Week* (April 30, 1990), pp. 110–117.

41. R. J. Lewicki, J. A. Litterer, J. W. Minton, and D. M. Saunders, *Negotiation*, 2nd ed. (Burr Ridge, IL: Irwin, 1994), pp. 45–128.

42. A. Bernstein and Z. Schiller, "Tell It to the Arbitrator," *Business Week* (November 4, 1991), p. 109.

43. A. R. Elangovan, "Managerial Third-Party Dispute Intervention: A Prescriptive Model of Strategy Selection," *Academy of Management Review* (October 1995), pp. 800–830.

44. For a current prescriptive model of third-party dispute intervention, see A. R. Elangovan, "Managerial Third-Party Dispute Intervention: A Prescriptive Model of Strategy Selection," *Academy of Management Review*, 20, no. 4 (1995), pp. 800–830.

45. Galbraith, *Designing Complex Organizations*, p. 15.

46. Ram Charan, "How Networks Reshape Organizations for Results," *Harvard Business Review* (September–October 1991), p. 179, and "Theory P Stresses How Departments Interact," *The Wall Street Journal* (December 13, 1991), p. B1.

47. "The Saturn Story: Building a Brand," *California Management Review* (Winter 1994).

48. J. A. DeVito, *The Interpersonal Communication Book*, 6th ed. (New York: HarperCollins, 1982), pp. 360–361; and J. W. Pfeiffer and J. E. Jones (Eds.), *A Handbook of Structured Experiences for Human Relations Training*, rev. ed., vol. III (1974).

49. S. P. Robbins and P. L. Hunsaker, *Training in Interpersonal Skills: Tips for Managing People at Work*, 2nd ed. (Upper Saddle River, NJ: Prentice Hall, 1996), pp. 253–254.

Chapter 12

1. B. M. Bass. *Organizational Decision Making* (Homewood, IL: Richard D. Irwin, 1983).

2. E. R. Archer, "How to make a business decision: An analysis of theory and practice," *Management Review* (February 1980), pp. 289–299.

3. W. F. Pounds, "The Process of Problem Finding," *Industrial Management Review* II (Fall 1969), pp. 1–19.

4. Ibid.

5. P. L. Hunsaker and A. J. Alessandra, *The Art of Managing People* (New York: Simon & Schuster, 1986), pp. 224–226.

6. Lewis Carroll, *Alice's Adventures in Wonderland* (New York: Viking Press, 1975), p. 22.

7. G. L. Morrisey, *Management by Objectives and Results for Business and Industry*, 2nd ed. (Reading, MA: Addison-Wesley, 1977).

8. Michael Brassard, *The Memory Jogger: A Pocket Guide of Tools for Continuous Improvement* (Methuen, MA: GOAL/QPC, 1988), pp. 9–13.

9. Ibid., pp. 24–29.

10. Ibid., pp. 17–23.

11. S. M. Natale, C. F. O'Donnell, and W. R. C. Osborne, Jr., "Decision Making: Managerial Perspectives," *Thought* 63, no. 248 (1990), pp. 32–51.

12. H. A. Simon, *Administrative Behavior*, 2nd ed. (New York: Free Press, 1957).

13. J. Tsalikis and D. J. Fritzsche, "Business Ethics: A Literature Review with a Focus on Marketing Ethics," *Journal of Business Ethics* 8 (1989), pp. 695–743.

14. O. C. Ferrell and G. Gardiner, *In Pursuit of Ethics: Tough Choices in the World of Work* (Springfield, IL: Smith Collins Company, 1991), pp. 9–13.

15. Linda S. Klein, "Ethical Decision Making in a Business Environment," *Review of Business* 13, no. 3 (Winter 1991/1992), pp. 27–29.

16. Sherry Baker, "Ethical Judgment," *Executive Excellence* (March 1992), pp. 7–8.

17. Ibid., pp. 7–8.

18. T. Donaldson, "Values in Tension: Ethics Away From Home," Kenneth Robinson Fellowship Lecture, University of Hong Kong (January 9, 1996).

19. Adapted from an example in John R. Boatright, *Ethics and the Conduct of Business* (Englewood Cliffs, NJ: Prentice Hall, 1993), p. 1.

20. Ibid., pp. 4–19.

21. Ibid., p. 8.

22. James R. Rest, "Can Ethics Be Taught in Professional Schools? The Psychology Research," *Easier Said Than Done* (Winter 1988), pp. 22–26.

23. John E. Fleming, "Business Ethics: An Overview," (University of Southern California: Unpublished paper, 1994), p. 2.

24. "Thinking Ethically," in *Issues in Ethics* 1, no. 2 (Winter 1988), (Santa Clara University, Center for Applied Ethics) p. 2.

25. Ibid.

26. Baker, "Ethical Judgment," pp. 7–8.

27. "Rights Stuff," *Issues in Ethics* 3, no. 2 (Spring 1990), (Santa Clara University, Center for Applied Ethics), pp. 1, 6; and Fleming, "Business Ethics," p. 3.

28. Ibid., p. 6.

29. Ibid.

30. Baker, "Ethical Judgment," pp. 7–8.

31. "Justice and Fairness," *Issues in Ethics* 3, no. 1 (Fall 1990), (Santa Clara University, Center for Applied Ethics), pp. 1, 7.

32. Ibid.

33. Ibid.

34. Ibid.

35. Baker, "Ethical Judgment," pp. 7–8.

36. T. Donaldson. "Values in Tension: Ethics Away From Home." Kenneth Robinson Fellowship Lecture, University of Hong Kong (January 9, 1996).

37. M. A. C. Fusco, "Ethics Game Plan: Taking the Offensive," *Business Week Careers* (Spring/Summer 1989), p. 51.

38. Baker, "Ethical Judgment," pp. 7–8.

39. The material in this section is summarized from M. J. Driver, K. R. Brousseau, and P. L. Hunsaker, *The Dynamic Decisionmaker* (New York: Jossey-Bass, 1993), pp. 1–36.

40. Paul Dean. "Open-and-Shut for Value," *Los Angeles Times* (October 30, 1992), pp. E1 and E6.

41. John L. Cotton, David A. Vollrath, and Kirk L. Froggatt, "Employee Participation: Diverse Forms and Different Outcomes," *Academy of Management Review* (January 1988), pp. 8–22.

42. V. H. Vroom and A. J. Jago, *The New Leadership: Managing Participation in Organizations* (Englewood Cliffs, NJ: Prentice Hall, 1988).

43. David Campbell, "Some Characteristics of Creative Managers," *Center for Creative Leadership Newsletter* 1 (February 1978), pp. 6–7.

44. Ibid., p. 7.

45. The company examples in this section are from Jay Cocks, "Let's Get Crazy," *Time* (June 11, 1990), pp. 40–41.

46. Maryam Alari, "Group Decision Support Systems: A Key to Business Team Productivity," *Journal of Information Systems Management* 8, no. 3 (Summer 1991), pp. 36–41.

47. A. F. Osborn, *Applied Imagination* (New York: Scribners, 1957).

48. A. H. Van de Ven and Andre Delbecq, "The Effectiveness of Nominal, Delphi, and Interacting Group Decision-Making Processes," *Academy of Management Journal* 17 (1974), pp. 605–621.

49. N. C. Dalkey and Olaf Helmer, "An Experimental Application of the Delphi Method to the Use of Experts," *Management Science* 9 (1963), pp. 458–467.

50. Alari, "Group Decision Support Systems," pp. 36–41.

51. George Sammet, *Gray Matters: The Ethics Game* (Orlando, FL: 1992).

52. E. E. Scannell and J. W. Newstrom, *Still More Games Trainers Play* (New York: McGraw-Hill, 1991), p. 251.

53. The case was prepared based on material appearing in Bridget Murray, "Are Professors Turning a Blind Eye to Cheating?" *The APA Monitor* (January 1996), pp. 1, 42; and Don McBurney, "Cheating: Preventing and Dealing With Academic Dishonesty," *APS Observer* (January 1996), pp. 32–35.

Chapter 13

1. Rosabeth M. Kanter, "Power Failure in Management Circuits," *Harvard Business Review* 67 (July–August 1979), pp. 69–79.

2. Don R. Beeman and Thomas W. Sharkey, "The Use and Abuse of Corporate Politics," *Business Horizons* 30 (March–April 1987), p. 27.

3. Rosabeth Moss Kanter, *Men and Women of the Corporation* (New York: Basic Books, 1977), Chapter 7.

4. Harold J. Leavitt, *Managerial Psychology*, 4th ed. (Chicago: University of Chicago Press, 1978), pp. 148–155.

5. Beeman and Sharkey, "The Use and Abuse of Corporate Politics," p. 27.

6. Virginia E. Schein, "Organizational Realities: The Politics of Change," *Training and Development Journal* (February 1985), pp. 37–41.

7. Allan R. Cohen and David L. Bradford, *Influence without Authority* (New York: John Wiley & Sons, 1991), Chapter 1.

8. Gary Yukl and Tom Taber, "The Effective Use of Managerial Power," *Personnel* 60 (1983), pp. 37–44.

9. Richard M. Emerson, "Power-Dependence Relations," *American Sociological Review* 27 (1962), pp. 31–40.

10. John R. P. French, Jr., and Baertram Raven initiated this line of research in their classical article, "The Bases of Social Power," in Dorwin Cartwright (Ed.), *Group Dynamics: Research and Theory* (Evanston, IL.: Row, Peterson, 1962), pp. 607–623.

11. Nicole Woolsey Biggart, "The Power of Obedience," *Administrative Science Quarterly* 29 (1984), pp. 540–549.

12. Samuel B. Bacharach and Edward J. Lawler, *Power and Politics in Organizations* (San Francisco: Jossey-Bass, 1980), Chapter 3.

13. The term originates from the classic book by Chester Barnard, *The Functions of the Executive* (Cambridge, MA.: Harvard University Press, 1938), Chapter 12.

14. Sik Hung Ng, *The Social Psychology of Power* (London: Academic Press, 1980), Chapter 3.

15. Dennis Duchon, Stephen G. Green, and Thomas D. Taber, "Vertical Dyad Linkage: A Longitudinal Assessment of Antecedents, Measures, and Consequences," *Journal of Applied Psychology* (February 1986), pp. 55–60.

16. Mauk Mulder, Leendert Koppelaar, Rendel de Jong, and Jaap Verhage, "Power, Situation, and Leader's Effectiveness: An Organizational Field Study," *Journal of Applied Psychology* 71 (1986), pp. 566–570.

17. French and Raven, "The Bases of Social Power," pp. 607–623.

18. Robert J. Thomas, "Bases of Power in Organizational Buying Decisions," *Industrial Marketing Management* 13 (October 1984), pp. 209–217.

19. Edward P. Hollander, "Leadership and Social Exchange Processes," in K. J. Gergen, M. S. Greenberg, and R. H. Willis (Eds.), *Social Exchange: Advances in Theory and Research* (New York: Winston-Wiley, 1979).

20. Arthur Schweitzer, *The Age of Charisma* (Chicago: Nelson-Hall, 1984).

21. Allan R. Cohen and David L. Bradford, "Influence without Authority: The Use of Alliances, Reciprocity, and Exchange to Accomplish Work," in Barry M. Staw (Ed.), *Psychological Dimensions of Organizational Behavior* (New York: Macmillan, 1991), p. 384.

22. Brian Dumaine, "The Bureaucracy Busters," *Fortune* (1991), p. 42.

23. Jeffrey Pfeffer, *Managing with Power: Politics and Influence in Organizations* (Boston: Harvard Business School Press, 1992).

24. David Kipnis, *The Powerholders* (Chicago: University of Chicago Press, 1976), pp. 77–78.

25. Dorwin Cartwright, "Leadership, Influence, and Control," in James G. March (Ed.), *Handbook of Organizations* (Chicago: Rand-McNally, 1965), pp. 1–47.

26. Dale E. Zand, *Information, Organization, and Power* (New York: McGraw-Hill, 1981).

27. Kenneth N. Wexley and Gary A. Yukl, *Organizational Behavior and Personnel Psychology*, rev. ed. (Homewood, IL.: Richard D. Irwin, 1984), pp. 228–229.

28. Robert C. Ford and Myron D. Fottler, "Empowerment: A Matter of Degree," *Academy of Management Executive* 9 (August 1995), pp. 21–29.

29. A. J. Grimes, "Authority, Power, Influence, and Social Control: A Theoretical Synthesis," *Academy of Management Review* 3 (October 1978), pp. 724–735.

30. Jeffrey Pfeffer, *Power in Organizations* (Marshfield, MA.: Pitman, 1981), p. 5.

31. Robert E. Cole, "U.S. Quality Improvement in the Auto Industry: Close but No Cigar," *California Management Review* 32 (Summer 1990), p. 77.

32. Dan Ciampa, *Total Quality: A User's Guide for Implementation* (Reading, MA.: Addison-Wesley, 1992), pp. 175–202.

33. Daniel Yankelovich and Associates, *Work and Human Values* (New York: Public Agenda Foundation, 1983), pp. 6–7.

34. James C. Abegglen and George Stalk, Jr., *Kaisha: The Japanese Corporation* (New York: Basic Books, 1985).

35. James R. Lincoln, "Employee Work Attitudes and Management Practice in the U.S. and Japan: Evidence from a Large Comparative Survey," *California Management Review* 32 (Fall 1989), pp. 89–106.

36. Tomasz Mroczkowski and Masao Hanaoka, "Continuity and Change in Japanese Management," *Human Resources* (Winter 1989), p. 52.

37. David I. Levine, "Participation, Productivity, and the Firm's Environment," *California Management Review* 32 (Summer 1990), p. 86.

38. Kenneth W. Thomas and Betty A. Velthouse, "Cognitive Elements of Empowerment: An 'Interpretative' Model of Interpretative Task Motivation," *Academy of Management Review* 15 (October 1990), p. 673.

39. Daniel J. Brass, "Being in the Right Place: A Structural Analysis of Individual Influence in an Organization," *Administrative Science Quarterly* 29 (1984), pp. 518–539.

40. David Krackhardt, "Assessing the Political Landscape: Structure, Cognition, and Power in Organizations," *Administrative Science Quarterly* 35 (June 1990), pp. 342–369.

41. Bacharach and Lawler, *Power and Politics in Organizations,* Chapter 2.

42. David A. Baldwin, "Power and Social Exchange," *The American Political Science Review* 72 (1978), pp. 1229–1242.

43. Kanter, *Men and Women of the Corporation,* Chapters 7 and 8, introduced token dynamics. Also see Gail Theus Fairhurst and B. Kay Snavely, "Majority and Token Minority Group Relationships: Power Acquisition and Communication," *Academy of Management Review* 8 (April 1983), pp. 293–300.

44. Daniel J. Brass, "Men's and Women's Networks: A Study of Interaction Patterns and Influence in an Organization," *Academy of Management Journal* 28 (June 1985), pp. 327–343.

45. Kathleen Reardon, "The Memo Every Woman Keeps in Her Desk," *Harvard Business Review* 71 (March–April 1993), pp. 16–22.

46. Kathleen K. Reardon, "Betty Friedan on 'The Second Stage' in Business," *Journal of Management Inquiry* 2 (March 1993), pp. 8–11.

47. This section, including the seven biases, draws from Margaret A. Neale and Max H. Blazerman, "Negotiating Rationally: The Power and Impact of the Negotiator's Frame," *Academy of Management Executive* 6 (August 1992), pp. 42–51.

48. Pfeffer, *Power in Organizations*, p. 3.

49. Ibid.

50. Ibid., p. 98.

51. Emerson, "Power-Dependence Relations," pp. 31–41.

52. Jeffrey Pfeffer, "Power and Resource Allocation in Organizations," in R. Miles and W. Randolph, (ed.), *The Organizational Game* (Santa Monica, CA.: Goodyear, 1979), pp. 232–246.

53. Rosabeth Moss Kanter, *When Giants Learn to Dance* (New York: Simon and Schuster, 1989), Chapter 6.

54. Pfeffer, "Power and Resource Allocation in Organizations."

55. David C. McClelland, *Power: The Inner Experience* (New York: Irvington, 1975).

56. David G. Winter, *The Power Motive* (New York: Collier Macmillan, 1973).

57. Edwin T. Cornelius and Frank B. Lane, "The Power Motive and Managerial Success in a Professionally Oriented Service Industry Organization," *Journal of Applied Psychology* 69 (1984), pp. 32–39.

58. David C. McClelland and D. H. Burnham, "Power Is the Great Motivator," *Harvard Business Review* 54 (March–April 1976), pp. 100–110.

59. Leonard H. Chusmir, "Personalized vs. Socialized Power Needs among Working Women and Men," *Human Relations* 39 (February 1986), pp.149–159.

60. Kipnis, *The Powerholders.*

61. Rosabeth Moss Kanter, "Power Failure in Management Circuits," in Allen and Porter, *Organizational Influence Processes* (New York: Scott, Foresman, 1983), pp. 87–104.

62. Gerald R. Salancik and Jeffrey Pfeffer, "Who Gets Power—and How They Hold on to It: A Strategic-Contingency Model of Power," *Organizational Dynamics* (Winter 1977).

63. Peter F. Drucker, *The New Realities* (New York: Harper & Row, 1989), pp.76–105.

64. Bronston T. Mayes and Robert W. Allen, "Toward a Definition of Organizational Politics," *Academy of Management Review* 2 (October 1977), pp. 672–677.

65. Michael P. Allen, Sharon K. Panian, and Roy E. Lotz, "Managerial Succession and Organizational

Performance: A Recalcitrant Problem Revisited," *Administrative Science Quarterly* 24 (1979), p. 177.

66. Jeffrey Pfeffer, *Managing with Power: Politics and Influence in Organizations* (Boston: Harvard Business School Press, 1992), p. 7.

67. Robert J. Thomas, *What Machines Can't Do: Politics and Technology in the Industrial Enterprise* (Berkeley, CA: University of California Press, 1994).

68. Pfeffer, p. 7.

69. Beeman and Sharkey, "The Use and Abuse of Corporate Politics," pp. 26–27.

70. G. Biberman, "Personality and Characteristic Work Attitudes of Persons with High, Moderate, and Low Political Tendencies," *Psychological Reports* (October 1985), pp. 1303–1310.

71. P. M. Fandt and G. R. Ferris, "The Management of Information and Impressions: When Employees Behave Opportunistically," *Organizational Behavior and Human Decision Processes* (February 1990), pp. 140–148.

72. Larry E. Greiner and Virginia E. Schein, *Power and Organizational Development: Mobilizing Power to Implement Change* (Reading, MA.: Addison-Wesley, 1988), pp. 18–23.

73. Dan Ferrell and James C. Petersen, "Patterns of Political Behavior in Organizations," *Academy of Management Review* 7 (July 1982), pp. 403–412.

74. Beeman and Sharkey, "The Use and Abuse of Corporate Politics," p. 27.

75. David Kipnis, "The Use of Power," in Allen and Porter (Ed.), *Organizational Influence Processes* (Glenview, IL.: Scott, Foresman, 1983), pp. 17–32.

76. Greiner and Schein, *Power and Organizational Development;* John B. Miner, *The Management Process: Theory, Research, and Practice,* 2nd ed. (New York: Macmillan, 1978), pp. 179–180; and Henry Mintzberg, *Power In and Around Organizations* (Englewood Cliffs, NJ: Prentice Hall, 1983).

77. M. W. McCall, Jr., *Power, Influence, and Authority: The Hazards of Carrying a Sword* (Greensboro, NC: Center for Creative Leadership, Technical Report No. 10, 1978).

78. Gerald F. Cavanagh, Dennis J. Moberg, and Manual Velasquez,

"The Ethics of Organizational Politics," *Academy of Management Review* 6 (July 1981), pp. 363–374.

79. The leader in exposing purported business malfeasance has been Ralph Nader and his Center for the Study of Responsive Law. Nader gained notoriety with his book on auto safety, *Unsafe at any Speed.*

80. Archie B. Carroll, "In Search of the Moral Manager," *Business Horizons* 30 (March–April 1987), p. 9.

81. Chris Welles, "What Led Beech-Nut Down the Road to Disgrace," *Business Week* (February 22, 1988), pp. 103–106.

82. Carroll, "In Search of the Moral Manager."

83. Gene Bylinsky, "How Companies Spy on Employees," *Fortune* (November 4, 1991), pp. 131–140.

84. Greiner and Schein, *Power and Organizational Development,* p. 17.

85. Pfeffer, *Power in Organizations,* p. 87.

86. Dean Takahashi and Mike Langberg, "E-mail Rallies Apple's Troops," *San Jose Mercury News* (February 6, 1996), pp. 1C, 2C.

87. Dean Takahashi, "Man for the Job: Amelio Relishes a New Challenge," *San Jose Mercury News* (February 3, 1995), pp. 1A and 20A.

88. "Phase II Special Edition," *Inter National News* (October 1995), a 26-page publication by the people of National Semiconductor.

89. Takahashi, San Jose Mercury News.

Chapter 14

1. Warren Bennis and Burt Nanus, *Leaders: The Strategies for Taking Charge* (New York: Harper & Row, 1985), p. 20.

2. John P. Kotter, "What Leaders Really Do," *Harvard Business Review* 68 (May–June 1990), pp. 103–111. For a more expansive distinction, see Kotter's *A Force for Change: How Leadership Differs from Management* (New York: Free Press, 1990).

3. Kotter, "What Leaders Really Do," p. 104.

4. Bennis and Nanus, *Leaders: The Strategies for Taking Charge,* p. 21.

5. Vance Packard, *The Pyramid Climbers* (New York: McGraw-Hill, 1962), p. 170.

6. Abraham Zaleznik, "The Leadership Gap," *Academy of Management Executive* 4 (February 1990), p. 9.

7. Brent Schlender, "Andy Grove Can't Stop," *Fortune* 131 (July 10, 1995), pp. 88–98.

8. Ralph M. Stogdill, "Personal Factors Associated with Leadership: A Survey of the Literature," *Journal of Psychology* 25 (1948), pp. 35–71; or Ralph M. Stogdill, *Handbook of Leadership: A Survey of Theory and Research* (New York: Free Press, 1974), pp. 49–63. A second milestone article was R. D. Mann, "A Review of the Relationships between Personality and Performance in Small Groups," *Psychological Bulletin* 56 (1959), pp. 241–270.

9. Shelly A. Kirkpatrick and Edwin A. Locke, "Leadership: Do Traits Matter?" *Academy of Management Executive* 5 (May 1991), pp. 48–60.

10. Robert G. Lord, Christy L. De Vader, and George M. Alliger, "A Meta-Analysis of the Relation between Personality Traits and Leadership Perceptions: An Application of Validity Generalization Procedures," *Journal of Applied Psychology* 71 (1986), pp. 402–410, found that Mann (1950) misinterpreted his survey findings, in part because his simple correlational analysis failed to pick up the strong relationships between traits and the respondent's perceptions of leadership.

11. Warren H. Schmidt and Barry Z. Posner, *Managerial Values and Expectations: The Silent Power of Personal and Organizational Life* (New York: American Management Association, 1982).

12. Kirkpatrick and Locke, "Leadership: Do Traits Matter?"

13. Ibid., p. 59.

14. Rensis Likert, *New Patterns of Management* (New York: McGraw-Hill, 1961), p. 36.

15. N. C. Morse and E. Reimer, "The Experimental Change of a Major Organizational Variable," *Journal of Abnormal and Social Psychology* 52 (1956), pp. 120–129.

16. Ralph M. Stogdill and A. E. Coons, *Leader Behavior: Its Description and Measurement* (Columbus, OH: Ohio State University, Bureau of Business Research, 1957), p. 75.

17. Andrew W. Halpin, *The Leadership Behavior of School Superintendents*

(Chicago: Midwest Administration Center, The University of Chicago, 1959), p. 4.

18. A. K. Korman, "Consideration, Initiating Structure, and Organizational Criteria—A Review," *Personnel Psychology* (Winter 1966), pp. 349–361.

19. Leonard Berkowitz, "Group Standards, Cohesiveness, and Productivity," *Human Relations* 7 (1954), pp. 509–514; and Stanley E. Seashore, *Group Cohesiveness in the Industrial Work Group* (Ann Arbor: University of Michigan Survey Research Center, 1954).

20. Kurt Lewin and Ronald Lippitt, "An Experimental Approach to the Study of Autocracy and Democracy: A Preliminary Note," *Sociometry* 1 (1938), pp. 292–300.

21. Robert R. Blake and Jane S. Mouton *The Managerial Grid* (Houston: Gulf Publishing, 1964); see also Blake and Mouton, "An Overview of the Grid," *Training and Development Journal* 5 (May 1975), pp. 29–36; and, more recently, Blake and Mouton, *The Managerial Grid III* (Houston: Gulf Publishing, 1985).

22. Michael Beer and S. Kleisath, "The Effects of the Managerial Grid on Organizational and Leadership Dimensions," in Sheldon S. Zalkind (Ed.), *Research on the Impact of Using Different Laboratory Methods for Interpersonal and Organizational Change* (Washington, DC: Symposium of the American Psychological Association, September 1967).

23. L. L. Larson, J. G. Hunt, and R. N. Osborn, "The Great Hi-Hi Leader Behavior Myth: A Lesson from Occam's Razor," *Academy of Management Journal* 19 (December 1976), pp. 628–641; and P. C. Nystrom, "Managers and the Hi-Hi Leader Myth," *Academy of Management Journal* 21 (June 1978), pp. 325–331.

24. Douglas McGregor, *The Human Side of Enterprise* (New York: McGraw-Hill, 1960); see also D. McGregor, *Leadership and Motivation* (Cambridge, MA: The MIT Press, 1966).

25. Bernard Weiner, Sandra Graham, Shelley E. Taylor, and Wulf-Uwe Meyer, "Social Cognition in the Classroom," *Educational Psychologist* 18 (Summer 1983), pp. 109–124.

26. Contingency realities were first popularized by Robert Tannenbaum and Warren Schmidt, "How to Choose a Leadership Pattern," *Harvard Business Review* 38 (March–April 1958), pp. 95–102.

27. Dorwin Cartwright and Alvin Zander, *Group Dynamics: Research and Theory* (New York: Harper & Row, 1960).

28. See, for example, Fred E. Fiedler and M. M. Chemers, *Leadership and Effective Management* (Glenview, IL: Scott, Foresman, 1974), p. 70.

29. L. H. Peters, D. D. Hartke, and J. T. Pohlmann, "Fiedler's Contingency Theory of Leadership: An Application of the Meta-Analysis Procedures of Schmidt and Hunter," *Psychological Bulletin* (March 1985), pp. 274–285.

30. J. K. Kennedy, J. M. Houston, M A. Korgaard, and D. D. Gallo, "Construct Space of the Least Preferred Co-Worker (LPC) Scale," *Educational and Psychological Measurement* (Fall 1987), pp. 807–814. LPC refers to a semantic differential instrument that asks leaders to describe their "Least Preferred Co-Worker" using pairs of bipolar adjectives (such as pleasant/unpleasant).

31. Fred E. Fiedler, "Engineering the Job to Fit the Manager," *Harvard Business Review* 43 (September–October 1965), pp. 115–122.

32. Paul Hersey and Kenneth H. Blanchard, *Management of Organizational Behavior: Utilizing Human Resources*, 3rd ed. (Englewood Cliffs, NJ: Prentice Hall, 1977), pp. 103–104.

33. Ibid., p. 161.

34. Ibid.

35. K. E. Kram, *Mentoring at Work* (Glenview, IL: Scott, Foresman, 1984).

36. Robert P. Vecchio, "Situational Leadership Theory: An Examination of a Prescriptive Theory," *Journal of Applied Psychology* 72 (August 1987), pp. 444–451, quote p. 450.

37. Curtis W. Cook, "Guidelines for Managing Motivation," *Business Horizons* 23 (April 1980), p. 63.

38. Robert J. House and Terence R. Mitchell, "Path-Goal Theory of Leadership," *Journal of Contemporary Business* 3 (Autumn 1974), pp. 81–97.

39. Paul Strebel, "Choosing the Right Change Path," *California Management Review* 36 (Winter 1994), pp. 29–51.

40. David A. Nadler and Michael L. Tushman, "Beyond the Charismatic Leader: Leadership and Organizational Change," *California Management Review* 32 (Winter 1990), pp. 77–97.

41. House and Mitchell, "Path-Goal Theory of Leadership," pp. 81–97.

42. Chester Schriesheim and Mary Ann Von Glinow, "The Path-Goal Theory of Leadership: A Theoretical and Empirical Analysis," *Academy of Management Journal* 20 (September 1977), pp. 398–405.

43. Robert Tannenbaum and Warren Schmidt, "How to Choose a Leadership Pattern," *Harvard Business Review* 36 (March–April 1958), pp. 95–102.

44. Kenneth W. Thomas and Betty A. Velthouse, "Cognitive Elements of Empowerment: An 'Interpretative' Model of Task Motivation," *Academy of Management Review* 15 (October 1990), pp. 666–681.

45. Victor H. Vroom and Philip W. Yetton, *Leadership and Decision Making* (Pittsburgh: University of Pittsburgh Press, 1973); and Victor H. Vroom and Arthur G. Jago, *The New Leadership: Cases and Manuals for Use in Leadership Training* (New Haven, CN: 1987).

46. Vroom and Yetton, *Leadership and Decision Making*, p. 12.

47. R. H. Field, "A Test of the Vroom-Yetton Normative Model of Leadership," *Journal of Applied Psychology* 67, pp. 523–532.

48. James M. Burns, *Leadership* (New York: Harper & Row, 1978), p. 461.

49. Harold J. Leavitt, *Corporate Pathfinders* (New York: Penguin, 1987), p. 3.

50. Constantinos C. Markides, "Consequences of Corporate Refocusing: Ex Ante Evidence," *Academy of Management Journal* 35 (June 1992), pp. 298–412.

51. These and other strategies have been described by many, including: James M. Kouzes and Barry Z. Posner, *The Leadership Challenge: How to Get Extraordinary Things Done in Organizations* (San Francisco: Jossey-Bass, 1995); and Warren Bennis and

Burt Nanus, *Leaders: The Strategies for Taking Charge* (New York: Harper & Row, 1985).

52. James C. Collins and Jerry I. Porras, "Building a Visionary Company," *California Management Review* 37 (Winter 1995), pp. 80–100.

53. Jay A. Conger, "Inspiring Others: The Language of Leadership," *Academy of Management Executive* 5 (February 1991), pp. 31–45.

54. David M. Boje, "Stories of the Storytelling Organization: A Postmodern Analysis of Disney as 'Tamara-Land'," *Academy of Management Journal* 38 (August 1995), pp. 997–1035.

55. Ira Sager, "The View from IBM," *Business Week* (October 31, 1995), p. 142.

56. Warren Bennis, *Why Leaders Can't Lead* (San Francisco: Jossey-Bass, 1990), pp. 23–24.

57. Warren Bennis, *An Invented Life: Reflections on Leadership and Change* (Reading, MA: Addison-Wesley, 1993), pp. 19–22; and Kouzes and Posner, *The Leadership Challenge*.

58. George Graen and J. Cashman, "A Role Making Model of Leadership in Formal Organizations: A Developmental Approach," in J. G. Hunt and L. L. Larson (Eds.), *Leadership Frontiers* (Kent, OH: Kent State University Press, 1975), pp. 143–165.

59. Arthur G. Jago, "Leadership: Perspectives in Theory and Research," *Management Science* 28 (March 1982), p. 331.

60. F. Dansereau, George Graen, and W. Haga, "A Vertical Dyad Linkage Approach to Leadership within Formal Organizations," *Organizational Behavior and Human Behavior* 13 (1975), pp. 46–78.

61. Antoinette S. Phillips and Arthur G. Bedeian, "Leader-Follower Exchange Quality: The Role of Personal and Interpersonal Attributes," *Academy of Management Journal* 37 (August 1994), pp. 990–991.

62. Dennis Duchon, Stephen G. Green, and Thomas D. Taber, "Vertical Dyad Linkage: A Longitudinal Assessment of Antecedents, Measures, and Consequences," *Journal of Applied Psychology* (February 1986), pp. 56–60. These differences in leader behaviors were originally

called vertical-dyad linkages, but the language has been simplified to leader–member exchange.

63. K. I. Kim and Dennis W. Organ, "Determinants of Leader-Subordinate Exchange Relationships," *Group and Organizational Studies* 7 (1982), pp. 77–89.

64. Duchon et al., "Vertical Dyad Linkage," p. 59.

65. Steven Kerr and John M. Jermier, "Substitutes for Leadership: Their Meaning and Measurement," *Organizational Behavior and Human Performance* 22 (December 1978), pp. 375–403.

66. Ibid., p. 375.

67. House and Mitchell, "Path-Goal Theory of Leadership," pp. 81–97.

68. Ann M. Morrison, *The New Leaders: Guidelines on Leadership Diversity in America* (San Francisco: Jossey-Bass, 1992), p. 29.

69. Ibid., pp. 34–52.

70. Terry C. Blum, Dail L. Fields, and Jodi S. Goodman, "Organization-Level Determinants of Women in Management," *Academy of Management Journal* 37 (April 1994), p. 241.

71. This study and experiences cited in the remainder of this section are from Betsy Morris, "Executive Women Confront Midlife Crisis," *Fortune* 132 (September 18, 1995), pp. 60–86.

72. Shawn Tully, "So, Mr. Bossidy, We Know You Can Cut. Now Show Us How to Grow," *Fortune* (August 21, 1995), pp. 70–80.

73. An actual situation uncovered by one of the authors during field research in Latin America. Names have been changed.

Chapter 15

1. J. Bales, "Work Stress Grows, But Services Decline," *The APA Monitor* 22, no. 11 (November 1991), p. 32.

2. R. S. Lazrus and S. Folkman, *Stress, Appraisal, and Coping* (New York: Springer, 1984).

3. Hans Selye, *The Stress of Life* (New York: McGraw-Hill, 1956).

4. D. A. Girdano, G. S. Everly, Jr., and D. E. Dusek, *Controlling Stress and*

Tension: A Holistic Approach, 3rd ed. (Englewood Cliffs, NJ: Prentice Hall, 1990), p. 37.

5. J. C. Quick and J. D. Quick, *Organizational Stress and Preventive Management* (New York: McGraw-Hill, 1984), p. 8.

6. A. E. Schwartz and J. Levin, "Combatting Feelings of Stress," *Supervisory Management* 35 (February 1990), pp. 4–5.

7. "Trigger Happy—A False Crisis: How Workplace Violence Became a Hot Issue," *The Wall Street Journal* (October 13, 1994), pp. A1, A10.

8. J. A. Archer, Jr., *Managing Anxiety and Stress* (Muncie, IN: Accelerated Development, Inc., 1991), pp. 12–13.

9. "Fear and Stress in the Office Take Toll," *The Wall Street Journal* (November 6, 1990), p. B1.

10. C. Barnett, "Workaholics: They're Not All Work Enthusiasts," *Republic Scene* (January 1982), p. 39.

11. Meyer Friedman and Ray Rosenman, *Type A Behavior and Your Heart* (New York: Alfred A. Knopf, 1974).

12. C. Lee, S. J. Ashford, and P. Bobko, "Interactive Effects of Type A Behavior and Perceived Control of Worker Performance, Job Satisfaction, and Somatic Complaints," *Academy of Management Journal* 33 (December 1990), pp. 870–882.

13. "Type-A Managers Stuck in the Middle," *The Wall Street Journal* (June 17, 1988), p. 17.

14. R. B. Williams, Jr., "Type A Behavior and Coronary Heart Disease: Something Old, Something New," *Behavior Medicine Update* 6 (1984), pp. 29–33.

15. A. P. Brief, R. S. Schuler, and M. Van Sell, *Managing Job Stress* (Boston: Little, Brown and Co., 1981), p. 138.

16. R. Williams, "The Trusting Heart," *Psychology Today* (January/February 1989), pp. 35–42.

17. Meyer Friedman and Diane Ulmer, *Treating Type A Behavior and Your Heart* (New York: Alfred A. Knopf, 1984), pp. 236–239.

18. A. W. Riley and S. J. Zaccaro, *Occupational Stress and Organizational Effectiveness* (New York: Praeger, 1987), pp. 60–66.

19. Daniel Katz and Robert Kahn, *The Social Psychology of Organizations,* 2nd ed. (New York: Wiley, 1978).

20. D. A. Revicki and H. J. May, "Occupational Stress, Social Support and Depression," *Health Psychology* 4 (1985), pp. 61–77.

21. Thomas H. Holmes and Richard H. Rahe, "The Social Readjustment Rating Scale," *Journal of Pscychosomatic Research* 11 (1967), pp. 213–218.

22. Scott M. Monroe, "Major and Minor Life Events as Predictors of Psychological Distress: Further Issues and Findings," *Journal of Behavioral Medicine* (June 1983), pp. 189–205.

23. "Low-control, high-stress jobs raise heart-attack risk, study shows," *San Diego Tribune* (August 1, 1988), p. D-2.

24. R. Zemke, "Workplace Stress Revisited," *Training* (November 1991), p. 35.

25. M. T. Matteson and J. M. Ivancevich, *Controlling Work Stress,* (San Francisco: Jossey-Bass, 1987),pp. 41–52.

26. Zemke, "Workplace Stress Revisited," p. 36.

27. A. Stevens, "Suit Over Suicide Raises Issue: Do Associates Work Too Hard?" *The Wall Street Journal* (April 15, 1994), pp. B1, B7.

28. *Employee Burnout: America's Newest Epidemic,* (Milwaukee: Northwestern Life Insurance Company, 1991), p. 8.

29. C. L. Cooper, "The Experience and Management of Stress: Job and Organizational Determinants," in A. W. Riley and S. J. Zaccaro (Eds.), *Occupational Stress and Organizational Effectiveness* (New York: Praeger, 1987), pp. 53–69.

30. Girdano et al., *Controlling Stress and Tension,* pp. 140–141.

31. Ibid.

32. Ibid., p. 141.

33. Riley and Zaccaro, *Occupational Stress and Organizational Effectiveness,* pp. 56–59.

34. Ibid., pp. 56–57.

35. A. Kiev and V. Kohn, *Executive Stress: An AMA Survey Report* (New York: AMACOM, 1979).

36. Matteson and Ivancevich, *Controlling Work Stress,* pp. 48–49.

37. R. Hogan and J. Morrison, "Work and Well-Being: An Agenda for the '90s," paper presented at the American Psychological Association and National Institute for Occupational Safety and Health Conference, Washington, DC, November 1990.

38. B. Gutek, "Women's Fight for Equality in the Workplace," paper presented at the American Psychological Association and National Institute for Occupational Safety and Health Conference, Washington, DC, November 1990.

39. Gary L. Cooper and Roy Payne, *Causes, Coping and Consequences of Stress at Work* (New York: Wiley, 1988), pp. 216–220.

40. M. J. Burke, A. P. Brief, and J. M. George, "The Role of Negative Affectivity in Understanding Relations Between Self-Reports of Stressors and Strains: A Comment on the applied Psychology Literature," *Journal of Applied Psychology* 78 (1993), pp. 402–412.

41. Girdano et al., *Controlling Stress and Tension,* pp. 114–115.

42. Gary R. Gemmill and W. J. Heisler, "Fatalism as a Factor in Managerial Job Satisfaction, Job Strain, and Mobility," *Personnel Psychology* 25 (1972), pp. 241–250.

43. L. R. Murphy, "A Review of Organizational Stress Management Research," *Journal of Organizational Behavior Management* (Fall–Winter 1986), pp. 215–227.

44. R. W. Kahn, D. M. Wolfe, R. P. Quinn, J. D. Snoek, and R. A. Rosenthal, *Organizational Stress* (New York: Wiley, 1964), pp. 72–95.

45. Matteson and Ivancevich, *Controlling Work Stress,* pp. 88–91.

46. R. C. Cummings, "Job Stress and the Buffering Effect of Supervisory Support," *Group and Organization Studies* (March 1990), pp. 92–104; J. J. House, *Work Stress and Social Support* (Reading, MA: Addison-Wesley, 1981).

47. J. G. Anderson, "Stress and Burnout Among Nurses: A Social Network Approach," *Journal of Social Behavior and Personality* 6, no. 7 (1991), pp. 251–272.

48. S. J. Motowidlo, J. S. Packard, and M. R. Manning, "Occupational Stress: Its Causes and Consequences for Job Performance," *Journal of Applied Psychology* (November 1987), pp. 619–620.

49. J. R. P. French and R. D. Caplan, "Organizational Stress and Individual Stress," in A. J. Marrow (Ed.), *The Failure of Success* (New York: AMACOM, 1973), pp. 30–36.

50. D. Schwimer, "Managing Stress to Boost Productivity," *Employee Relations Today* (Spring 1991), pp. 23–27.

51. K. Matthews, E. Cottington, E. Talbott, L. Kuller, and J. Siegel, "Stressful Work Conditions and Diastolic Blood Pressure among Blue-Collar Factory Workers," *American Journal of Epidemiology* (1987), pp. 280–291.

52. B. Fletcher, "The Epidemiology of Occupational Stress," in C. L. Cooper and R. Payne, *Causes, Coping and Consequences of Stress at Work* (New York: John Wiley & Sons, 1988), pp. 3–52.

53. T. D. Jick and L. F. Mitz, "Sex Differences in Work Stress," *Academy of Management Review* 10 (1985), pp. 408–420.

54. D. Watson and A. Tellegen, "Toward a Consensual Structure of Mood," *Psychological Bulletin* 98 (1985), pp. 219–235.

55. Fletcher, "The Epidemiology of Occupational Stress," pp. 3–52.

56. R. T. Golembiewski and R. F. Munzenrider, *Phases of Burnout: Developments in Concepts and Applications* (New York: Praeger, 1988), pp. 6–10.

57. D. P. Rogers, "Helping Employees Cope with Burnout," *Business* (October–December 1984), pp. 3–7.

58. S. E. Jackson, R. L. Schwab, and R. S. Schuler, "Toward an Understanding of the Burnout Phenomenon," *Journal of Applied Psychology* 71 (1986), pp. 630–640.

59. Zemke, "Workplace Stress Revisited," pp. 35–39.

60. C. Maslach, *Burnout: The Cost of Caring* (Englewood Cliffs, NJ: Prentice Hall, 1982).

61. T. DeAngelis, "Psychologists Aid Victims of Violence in Post Office," *APA Monitor* (October 1993), pp. 144–145.

62. J. Bell, "Managing Stress," *Accountant's Magazine* 94 (August 1990), pp. 14–16.

63. Archer, *Managing Anxiety and Stress,* pp. 9–10.

64. J. E. Driskell and E. Salas, "Group Decision Making under Stress," *Journal of Applied Psychology* 76 (June 1991), pp. 473–479.

65. M. Jamal, "Relationship of Job Stress to Job Performance: A Study of Managers and Blue-Collar Workers," *Human Relations* (May 1985), pp. 409–424.

66. Bales, "Work Stress Grows, but Services Decline," p. 32.

67. J. Castro, "Battling the Enemy Within," *Time* (March 17, 1986), p. 53.

68. Ann Japenga, "Sabotage at Work," *Los Angeles Times* (May 3, 1990), pp. E1 and E16.

69. S. Folkman and R. S. Lazarus, "Coping as a Mediator of Emotion," *Journal of Personality and Social Psychology,* 54 (1988), pp. 466–475.

70. A. Lakein, *How to Get Control of Your Time and Your Life* (New York: Peter H. Wyden, 1973).

71. K. E. Kram and D. T. Hall, "Mentoring as an Antidote to Stress during Corporate Trauma," *Human Resource Management* (Winter 1989), pp. 493–511.

72. W. L. French and C. H. Bell, Jr. *Organizational Development: Behavioral Science Interventions for Organization Improvement* (Englewood Cliffs, NJ: Prentice Hall, 1990).

73. H. Schlossberg, "Meditation Uplifts Her Life on the Fast Track," *Marketing News* (October 1, 1990), pp. 10–11.

74. J. C. Smith, *Cognitive-Behavioral Relaxation Training* (New York: Springer Publishing Company, 1990).

75. Herbert Benson, *The Relaxation Response* (New York: William Morrow, 1975).

76. K. E. Hart, "Managing Stress in Occupational Settings: A Selective Review of Current Research and Theory," in C. L. Cooper (Ed.), *Stress Management Interventions at Work* (Rochester, England: MCB University Press Limited, 1987), pp. 11–17.

77. Ibid., p. 14.

78. R. L. Woolfold, R. Lehrer, B. McCann, and A. Ronney, "The Effects of Progressive Relaxation and Meditation on Cognitive and Somatic Manifestations of Daily Stress," *Behavioral Research and Therapy* 20 (1982), pp. 325–338.

79. J. C. Smith, *Stress Scripting: A Guide to Stress Management* (New York: Praeger, 1991), pp. 162–163.

80. Girdano et al., *Controlling Stress and Tension,* pp. 280–295.

81. J. S. J. Manuso, "Management of Individual Stressors," in M. P. O'Donnel and T. A. Ainsworth (Eds.), *Health Promotion in the Workplace* (New York: John Wiley, 1984).

82. K. Mobily, "Using Physical Activity and Recreation to Cope with Stress and Anxiety: A Review," *American Corrective Therapy Journal* (May/June 1982), pp. 62–68.

83. Reported in Matteson and Ivancevich, *Controlling Work Stress,* p. 221.

84. J. S. Shepherd, "Manage the Five C's of Stress," *Personnel Journal* 69 (July 1990), pp. 64–68.

85. Daniel C. Ganster, Marcelline R. Fusilier, and Bronston T. Mayes, "Role of Social Support in the Experiences of Stress at Work," *Journal of Applied Psychology* 71, (1986), pp. 102–110.

86. D. L. Nelson and C. Sutton, "Chronic Work Stress and Coping: A Longitudinal Study and Suggested New Directions," *Academy of Management Journal* 33, no. 4 (1990), pp. 859–869.

87. "Workplace Flexibility Is Seen as Key to Business Success," *The Wall Street Journal* (November 23, 1993), p. A1.

88. Randall S. Schuler and Susan E. Jackson, "Managing Stress through PHRM Practices: An Uncertainty Interpretation," in K. Rowland and G. Ferris (Eds.), *Research in Personnel and Human Resources Management* 4 (Greenwich, CN: JAI Press, 1986), pp. 183–224.

89. "Helping Parents Cope with Latchkey Anxiety," *The Wall Street Journal* (November 1, 1991), p. B1.

90. Matteson and Ivancevich, *Controlling Work Stress,* pp. 214–215.

91. Robert Guenther, "Employers Try In-House Fitness Centers to Lift Morale, Cut Cost of Health Claims," *The Wall Street Journal* (November 10, 1981), p. 31.

92. Schlossberg, "Meditation Uplifts Her Life on the Fast Track," pp. 10–11.

93. P. L. Hunsaker and C. W. Cook, *Managing Organizational Behavior* (Reading, MA: Addison-Wesley, 1986), pp. 259–261.

Chapter 16

1. C. Argyris, R. Putman, and D. M. Smith, *Action Science* (San Francisco: Jossey-Bass, 1985).

2. R. Likert, *The Human Organization* (New York: McGraw-Hill, 1967).

3. C. Argyris, *Personality and Organization* (New York: Harper and Row, 1957).

4. R. H. Hall, *Organizations: Structures, Processes, and Outcomes,* 4th ed. (Engelwood Cliffs, NJ: Prentice Hall, 1987), p. 29.

5. R. M. Kanter, *When Giants Learn to Dance: Mastering the Challenges of Strategy* (New York: Simon and Schuster, 1989).

6. John P. Kotter and Leonard A. Schlesinger, "Choosing Strategies for Change," *Harvard Business Review* 57 (March–April 1979), pp. 106–114.

7. Jean B. Keffeler, "Managing Changing Organizations: Don't Stop Communicating," *Vital Speeches* (November 15, 1991), pp. 92–96.

8. Tori DeAngelis, "Psychologists Balance Company Needs," *Monitor* (November 1994), pp. 34–35.

9. Bill Vlasic, "Bracing for the Big One," *Business Week* (March 25, 1996), pp. 34–35.

10. K. Lewin, *Field Theory in Social Science* (New York: Harper & Row, 1951).

11. Thomas G. Cummings and Christopher G. Worley, *Organization Development and Change,* 5th ed. (St. Paul, MN: West Publishing Company, 1993), p. 63.

12. Lewin, *Field Theory in Social Science.*

13. Kotter and Schlesinger, "Choosing Strategies for Change."

14. Jacqueline M. Groves, "Leaders of Corporate Change," *Fortune* (December 14, 1992), pp. 104–114.

15. Cummings and Worley, *Organization Development and Change,* p. 155.

16. Ibid., p. 2. For other definitions of OD, see J. I. Porras and P. J.

Robertson, "Organizational Development: Theory, Practice, and Research," in M. D. Dunnette and L. M. Hough (Eds.), *Handbook of Industrial & Organizational Psychology*, 2nd ed., Vol. 3 (Palo Alto: Consulting Psychologists Press, 1992), pp. 721–723.

17. Thomas L. Case, Robert J. Vandenberg, and Paul H. Meredith, "Internal and External Change Agents," *Leadership and Organizational Development Journal* 11, no. 1 (1990); and Warren Bennis, *Organization Development: Its Nature, Origins, and Prospects* (Reading, MA: Addison-Wesley, 1969).

18. L. D. Brown and J. G. Covey, "Development Organizations and Organization Development: Toward an Expanded Paradigm for Organization Development," in R. W. Woodman and W. A. Pasmore (Eds.), *Research in Organizational Change and Development*, vol. 1 (Greenwich, CT: JAI Press, 1987), p. 63

19. W. A. Pasmore and M. R. Fagans, "Participation, Individual Development, and Organizational Change: A Review and Synthesis," *Journal of Management* (June 1992), pp. 375–97.

20. P. L. Hunsaker, "Role of the Inside Change Agent: Strategies for Changing Organizations," in D. D. Warrick (Ed.), *Contemporary Organizational Development* (Glenview, IL: Scott, Foresman, & Company, 1983), pp. 123–137.

21. M. Beer and E. Walton, "Organization Change and Development," *Annual Review of Psychology* 38 (1987), pp. 229–272.

22. See Rosabeth Kanter, *The Change Masters* (New York: Simon and Schuster, 1983).

23. Cummings and Worley, *Organization Development and Change*, p. 22.

24. Ibid., pp. 5–13.

25. Ellen A. Fagenson and W. Warner Burke, "Organization Development Practitioners' Activities and Interventions in Organizations during the 1980s," *The Journal of Applied Behavior Science* 26, no. 3, pp. 285–297.

26. Edward E. Lawler III et al., *Doing Research That Is Useful for Theory and Practice* (San Francisco: Jossey-Bass Publishers, 1985).

27. M. Beer and A. E. Walton, "Developing The Competitive Organization: Intervention and Strategies," *American Psychologist* 45 (1990), pp. 154–161.

28. Fagenson and Burke, "Organization Development Practitioners' Activities," p. 295.

29. Cummings and Worley, *Organization Development and Change*, p. 126.

30. Ibid.

31. Ibid., pp. 32–38.

32. Chris Argyris, "Good Communication that Blocks Learning," *Harvard Business Review* 72 (July–August 1994), pp. 77–85.

33. Dorothy Marcic, "Summary of *The Fifth Discipline* by Peter Senge," in Jon L. Pierce and John W. Newstrom (Eds.), *The Manager's Bookshelf: A Mosaic of Contemporary Views*, 4th ed. (New York: Harper Collins), 1996, pp. 105–112.

34. Charlene M. Solomon, HR Facilitates the Learning Organization Concept," *Personnel Journal* 73, no. 11 (November 1994).

35. Augustine A. Lado and Mary C. Wilson, "Human Resource Systems and Sustained Competitive Advantage: A Competency-Based Perspective," *Academy of Management Review* 19 (October 1994), p. 699.

36. David A. Garvin, "Building a Learning Organization" *Harvard Business Review* 71, no. 4 (1993), pp. 78–91.

37. Solomon, "HR Facilitates the Learning Organization Concept," p. 56

38. Peter Senge, *The Fifth Discipline: The Art and Practice of the Learning Organization* (New York: Doubleday, 1990).

39. F. Kofman and P. M. Senge, "Communities of Commitment: The Heart of Learning Organizations" *Organizational Dynamics*, (Autumn 1993), pp. 5–23.

40. Helen Rheem, "The Learning Organization: Building Learning Capability," *Harvard Business Review* (March–April 1995), pp. 3–12.

41. Ibid.

42. Greg Richards, "Organizational Learning in the Public Sector: From Theory to Practice," *Optimum* 25, no. 3 (December 22, 1994), p. 3.

43. John W. Slocum, Jr., Michael McGill, and David T. Lei, "The New Learning Strategy: Anytime, Anything, Anywhere," *Organizational Dynamics*, 23, no.2 (September 22, 1994), p. 33.

44. Greg Richards, "Organizational Learning in the Public Sector."

45. J. I. Porras and P. J. Robertson, "Organizational Development: Theory, Practice, and Research," in M. D. Dunnettte and L. M. Hough (Eds.), *Handbook of Industrial & Organizational Psychology*, 2nd ed., Vol. 3 (Palo Alto: Consulting Psychologists Press, 1992), p. 734.

46. John H. Zenger et al., *Leading Teams: Mastering the New Role* (Homewood, IL: Business One Irwin, 1994), pp. 11, 97.

47. Based on Kurt Lewin's force-field analysis model.

Appendix A

1. W. Jack Duncan, *Great Ideas in Management* (San Francisco: Jossey-Bass, 1990), p. 3.

2. Ibid., pp. 18–19.

3. Frederick W. Taylor, *The Principles of Scientific Management* (New York: Harper & Row, 1914), p. 39.

4. Ibid., p. 59.

5. Lillian M. Gilbreth, *The Psychology of Management* (Easton, PA: Hive Publishing, 1914, republished 1973), p. 130.

6. Henri Fayol, *General and Industrial Management*, C. Storrs, trans. (London: Pitman, 1949).

7. Max Weber, *The Theory of Social and Economic Organization*, A. M. Henderson and T. Parsons, eds. and trans. (New York: Free Press, 1947).

8. This interpretation is from Duncan, *Great Ideas in Management*, pp. 204–207.

9. G. Elton May, *The Human Problems of an Industrial Society*, 2nd ed. (New York: Macmillan, 1933).

10. Abraham Maslow's pioneering study was "A Theory of Human Motivation," *Psychological Review* (July 1943), pp. 370–396.

11. Douglas McGregor, *The Human Side of Enterprise* (New York: McGraw-Hill, 1960).

12. Abraham Maslow, *Motivation and Personality* (New York: Harper & Row, 1954).

13. George C. Homans, *The Human Group* (New York: Harcourt Brace & World, 1950).

14. Daniel Katz and Robert L. Kahn, *The Social Psychology of Organizations* (New York: John Wiley & Sons, 1966).

15. Talcot Parsons, *The Social System* (New York: Free Press, 1951).

16. Duncan, *Great Ideas in Management*, quote from p. 259; other interpretations in this section on Follett from pp. 207–210.

17. Pauline Graham (Ed.), *Mary Parker Follet: Prophet of Management* (Boston: Harvard Business School Press, 1995).

18. Herbert A. Simon, *Administrative Behavior* (New York: Free Press, 1946).

19. Richard M. Cyert and James G. March, *A Behavioral Theory of the Firm* (Englewood Cliffs, NJ: Prentice Hall, 1963). A second edition was published in 1992 by Blackwell (Cambridge, MA).

20. Robert P. Vecchio, "Situational Leadership Theory: An Examination of a Prescriptive Theory," *Journal of Applied Psychology* 72 (August 1987), pp. 444–451.

21. Arvind Parkhe, " 'Messy' Research, Methodological Predispositions, and Theory Development in International Joint Ventures," *Academy of Management Review* 18 (April 1993), p. 237.

22. Gilbert Sax, *Empirical Foundations of Educational Research* (Englewood Cliffs, NJ: Prentice Hall, 1968), p. 31.

Appendix B

1. *BusinessWeek* (October 7, 1991), p. 158.

2. Anne B. Fisher, "Morale Crisis," *Fortune* (November 18, 1991), p. 71.

3. Kenneth Labich, "Take Control of Your Career," *Fortune* (November 18, 1991), pp. 87–96.

4. *The Wall Street Journal* (April 20, 1993), p. A-1, reporting a study by Harvard Professor James Medoff.

5. Amanda Bennett, "Path to Top Job Now Twists and Turns," *The Wall Street Journal* (March 15, 1993), pp. B-1, B-3.

6. Douglas T. Hall, *Careers in Organization* (Pacific Palisades,CA: Goodyear, 1976).

7. This exercise is based on James Clawson et al., *Self-Assessment and Career Development*, 2nd ed. (Englewood Cliffs, NJ: Prentice Hall, 1985), pp. 39–43.

8. *The Wall Street Journal* (June 11, 1993), p. B-1.

9. Bill Plaschke, "Real Life Relief," *Los Angeles Times* (March 13, 1993), p. C1ff.

10. See James G. Clawson et al., *Self-Assessment and Career Development*, 3rd ed. (Englewood Cliffs, NJ: Prentice Hall, 1992).

11. John Holland, *Making Vocational Choices: A Theory of Careers* (Englewood Cliffs, NJ: Prentice Hall, 1973).

12. For further information, contact Consulting Psychologists Press, Inc., 577 College Avenue, Palo Alto, CA 94306; (415) 326–4448. The cost of scoring a single profile is about $25, and group rates lower that amount considerably.

13. Richard N. Bolles, *(The 1993) What Color Is Your Parachute?*, (Berkeley, CA: Ten Speed Press, 1993), pp. 194–228.

14. See Stephen R. Covey, *The 7 Habits of Highly Effective People* (New York: Simon & Shuster, 1989), pp. 106–139.

15. Ibid., p. 99.

16. Ibid., p. 134.

17. Labich, "Take Control of Your Career," p. 88.

18. "Labor Letter," *The Wall Street Journal* (March 24, 1992), p. A1.

19. Felice N. Schwartz, "Management Women and the New Facts of Life," *Harvard Business Review* (January–February 1989), pp. 65–76.

20. Elizabeth Mehren, "On the Daddy Track," *Los Angeles Times* (June 30, 1993), p. E1ff.

21. See Ann M. Morrison, Randall P. White, and Ellen Van Velsor, *Breaking the Glass Ceiling* (Reading: MA: Addison-Wesley, 1987).

22. See Schwartz, "Management Women and the New Facts of Life"; and "Women as a Business Imperative," *Harvard Business Review* (March–April 1992), pp. 105–113.

23. Susan B. Garland, "Throwing Stones at the 'Glass Ceiling'," *BusinessWeek* (August 19, 1991), p. 29.

24. "How to Keep Women Managers on the Corporate Ladder," *BusinessWeek* (September 2, 1991), p. 64.

25. Linda Stroh, Jenne Brett, and Anne Reilly, "All the Right Stuff: A Comparison of Female and Male Managers' Career Progression," *Journal of Applied Psychology* 77, no. 3 (1992), pp. 251–260.

26. Bruce Nussbaum et al., "Corporate Refugees," *BusinessWeek* (April 12, 1993), pp. 58–65.

27. Judith Valente, "You Can Start Your Own Business," *Parade Magazine* (June 23, 1996, pp. 8–11).

Glossary

ability The capacity to perform physical and intellectual tasks.

accountability Holding a person with authority answerable for setting appropriate goals, using resources efficiently, and accomplishing task responsibilities.

action research Data collection, analysis, and problem diagnosis, the results of which are provided to the client system to help decide on plans for improvement.

actions Deliberate choices about where to direct behaviors combined with intense, persistent efforts to achieve a goal over some time period.

amoral manager One who lacks any moral sensibility whatsoever; one who doesn't think about the moral implications of actions, or who chooses to keep ethics out of decisions.

aptitude The capacity to learn an ability.

association power Arises when one person has influence with another who possesses power.

attitude Readiness to respond in a certain way to a person, object, idea, or situation.

attitudes Temporal beliefs based on evaluative interpretations of current conditions.

attribution An assumed explanation of why people behave as they do, based on our observations and inferences.

attributional error The tendency to overestimate internal factors and underestimate external factors when making attributions about others.

authoritarianism The degree to which a person believes that status and power differences are appropriate in an organization.

authority The right to make decisions and commit organizational resources based on position within the organization.

autonomous work team Self-managed group of workers who are given authority for planning, scheduling, monitoring, and staffing themselves.

behavioral style A person's habitual way of interacting with other people.

boundary-spanning transactions Those actions that link an organization to specific external sectors, exchanges that make the system dynamic and open.

bureaucracy A classic pyramid shaped structure created as a rational-legal system of authority emphasizing formal roles and rules with the intent of being efficiency oriented.

bureaucracy Max Weber's rational-legal authority structure for organizing specialized functions and standardizing procedures to achieve efficiency.

burnout Exhaustion that develops from experiencing too much pressure and too few sources of satisfaction.

business advocate A control profile focused on competitiveness built upon core values of service and involvement.

career The work-related experiences and activities over the span of a person's life.

centralization An organizational structure that concentrates authority and decision making toward the top.

change The process of moving from one condition to another.

change agent An individual or group responsible for changing behavior and systems.

channel The medium through which a message is transmitted.

charisma A quality of admiration when others identify with and are attracted to a leader they look up to.

charismatic-based values Values originating from a strong leader, usually the founder, which tend to be internalized by members so long as they look to the leader for guidance and inspiration.

chronic stress The stress caused by continual confrontation of stressors without relief.

classical conditioning An experimental approach that associates a conditioned stimulus with an unconditioned stimulus to achieve a conditional response.

closed systems Systems that operate without environmental or outside disturbances.

coercive power Based on the ability to withhold desired resources or make life unpleasant for those who do not comply with the power holder's requests.

cognitive dissonance A state of inconsistency between an individuals' attitudes and behavior.

cognitive learning Selective interpretation of perceptual data organized into new patterns of thoughts and relationships.

cognitive style The way an individual perceives and processes information.

cohesiveness The degree of attractiveness of a group to its members and the closeness of the interpersonal bonds between group members.

command and control orientation A manager's approach to control that emphasizes chain-of-command structures for operating efficiencies and conservation of resources.

command group A permanent group in the organization structure with a formal supervisor and direct subordinates.

communication The process of one person sending a message to another with the intent of evoking a response.

competitive advantage Occurs whenever a business is able to sustain an edge over its rivals by attracting customers and defending itself against competitive forces.

competitive strategy Actions at the level of a specific line of business intended to create a competitive advantage by planned actions about where to compete and how to compete.

competitive team orientation A manager's approach to control focused on adding value to the market by enhancing core competencies and strategic competitiveness.

conflict A disagreement between two or more parties who perceive that they have incompatible concerns.

conflict-management styles The different combinations of assertiveness and cooperation that people emphasize when in a conflict situation.

conflict-positive organization An organization in which participants perceive conflict as an opportunity for personal and organizational growth.

conformance orientation A manager's approach to control found in organizations doing business with governments where the emphasis is on compliance to rules and procedures.

consensus An attribution process used to determine how others behave in similar situations.

consistency An attribution process used to explain the degree of variance in behavior over time.

content theories of motivation Theories based on identifying specific human needs and describing the circumstances under which these needs activate behavior.

contingency theory The perspective that a leader's effectiveness is dependent on how he or she interacts with various situational factors—there is no one best universal approach.

contingency theories Theories that identify the circumstances in which a particular practice is more likely to obtain desired results.

control Any process to help align actions of people and systems with the goals and interests of the organization.

control system Evaluative and feedback processes to let people know their managers are paying attention to what they do and can tell when undesired deviations occur.

controlling The process of evaluating the degree to which outcomes match objectives; and when they do not, analyzing why and taking corrective action.

core capabilities The critical skills and processes that an organization executes so well in carrying out its intended strategy that its reputation builds around them.

core job dimensions The underlying characteristics of a job (such as autonomy, task variety) and how they relate to job involvement, motivation, performance, and satisfaction.

corporate policeman A control profile focused on budgets that emphasizes administering and checking up on rules and procedures.

corporate strategy For multibusiness firms, the highest-level decisions and actions about what lines of business to be in and how to manage them.

countercultures A subculture that rejects the values and assumptions of the host organization and develops opposing beliefs, frequently based on elitist notions of a charismatic leader.

credibility leadership One of the most characteristic traits of leaders, which refers to being honest, competent, forward-looking, and inspiring.

credibility communication The sender's degree of trustworthiness, as perceived by the receiver.

cross-functional team A team composed of persons from several different functional units who work together to the accomplishment of a task.

cross-functional teams A way of organizing that pulls people together from several different functions or

disciplines to emphasize coordination of separate but interrelated tasks in achieving product and service quality.

culture The pattern of learned behaviors shared and transmitted among the members of a society.

daddy track A career path for fathers with less advancement pressure and less rewards so that fathers can spend more time with their families.

decentralization An organizational structure that disperses authority and decision making to operating units throughout the organization.

decoding The receiver function of perceiving communication stimuli and interpreting their meaning.

defense A cognitive distortion that protects the self-concept against being diminished.

deficiency reduction needs Rather universally-experienced needs that trigger avoidance behaviors where the aim is to find relief from deficiencies, deprivations, or unpleasant tensions.

degenerative interaction climate An organizational climate that encourages dysfunctional conflict.

degenerative interaction patterns Competitive and destructive relationships resulting in lack of openness, low trust, blaming, and defensiveness.

dependent variable The outcome studied through research and believed to be caused or influenced by an independent variable.

discrimination The process by which universal or previously unstructured elements are placed into more specific structures.

distinctiveness An attribution process used to explain whether a person's behavior fits with other behaviors.

distress Stress that has a negative consequence on a person's well-being.

distributive justice The perceived fairness of the amount and allocation of rewards among individuals.

dogmatism The degree of flexibility or rigidity of a person's views.

double-loop learning Shifts accountability for actions and learning to employees by having a manager ask complex questions about the employee's motivation for solving a problem.

dual-factor theory Herzberg's motivation content theory based on two independent needs: hygiene and motivator factors.

dynamic system Any system that changes over time as structures and functions adapt to external disturbances and conditions.

dysfunctional conflict Conflict between groups in the same organization that hinders the achievement of group and organizational goals.

effectiveness Producing the right output or doing things right to create value for stakeholders.

efficiency Doing something right or getting the most output for the least input.

elitist values Focus on the perceived superiority of the organization in comparison to others.

employee-oriented behavior An approach to leadership that aims at satisfying the social and emotional needs of group members.

empowerment Describes conditions that enable people to feel competent and in control of their work, energized to take initiative and persist at meaningful tasks.

encoding Translating information into a message appropriate for transmission.

environmental scanning The monitoring of current and anticipated trends and events in the external environment through quantitative data and qualitative perceptions.

episodic stress A pattern of high stress followed by intervals of relief.

equity theory The idea that motivation is moderated by perceived fairness or discrepancies between contributions and rewards

ERG theory Alderfer's simplified content theory that identifies existence, relatedness, and growth as need categories, and acknowledges

multiple needs may be operating at one time without being hierarchically determined.

ergonomics A biomechanic approach to minimize physical strain and stress on a worker based on the healthy design of work methods and technology.

exercises and simulations Activities participants engage in to generate behavior for feedback that can be analyzed and used to develop improvement plans.

expectancy theory A theory of motivation based on a person's beliefs about effort-performance-outcome relationships.

expert power Originates when a person is perceived to have superior knowledge, experience, or judgment that others need and do not possess themselves.

extrinsic rewards Rewards externally bestowed, as by a supervisor, teacher, or organization.

feedback A message that tells the original sender how clearly his or her message was understood and what effect it has had on the receiver.

figure The dominant feature being perceived.

filtering The sender's conveying only certain parts of the relevant information to the receiver.

force-field analysis The process of analyzing the forces that drive change and those that restrain it.

formal authority Legitimate power derived directly from a person's title and position in the organizational hierarchy.

formal group A group intentionally established by a manager to accomplish specific organizational objectives.

frame of reference Mental filter through which perceptions are interpreted and evaluated.

frame of reference A person's mind-set, based on past experience and current expectations, which determines what is perceived and how it is interpreted.

friendship group An informal group based on common characteristics which are not necessarily work related.

functional conflict Conflict between groups that stimulates innovations and production.

functional values Express a normative mode of conduct that tells members what they should pay attention to (e.g., customer service, innovation, quality).

gainsharing A pay-for-performance system that shares financial rewards among all employees based on performance improvements for the entire business unit.

general adaptation syndrome A consistent pattern of defensive behavioral reactions that a person uses to cope with a continuing stressor.

generalization The means through which we transfer learning from one situation to another as well as categorize information.

glass ceiling An invisible barrier that limits the advancement of women and minorities.

goal The desired outcome of an action, which becomes motivational when a person wants it and strives to achieve it.

grapevine The informal communication channel for gossip and rumors.

ground The surrounding, competing stimuli being perceived.

group Two or more people who perceive themselves as a distinct entity, regularly interact and influence one another over a period of time, share common values and strive for common objectives.

groupthink A state in groups where the pressures for conformity are so great that they dominate members' ability to realistic appraise alternative decision options.

growth aspiration needs Somewhat unique personal needs influencing choices to seek out goals and experiences that will be meaningful and satisfying.

halo effect The tendency to overrate a person based on a single trait.

hardiness A personality characteristic of people who are more immune than most to the negative consequences of experiencing stress.

Hawthorne effect The unintentional biasing of research outcomes due to the possibility that simply paying attention to the experimental subjects causes their behavior to change.

hierarchy of needs A five-level need theory proposed by Maslow in which lower-level basic needs must be satisfied before advancing to a higher-level need.

horizontal job loading The process of enlarging jobs by combining separate work activities into a whole job that provides for greater task variety.

hygiene factors Job context factors such as working conditions and benefits that cause dissatisfaction if inadequate.

hypothesis A statement about the proposed relationship between independent and dependent variables.

ideology A source of personal consistency based on one's values and conception of his or her place in the world in relation to meaningful activities that promote a sense of self-worth.

ideology Beliefs and values held by a manager about how to succeed in business, encompasses economic assumptions and ethical ideals.

immoral manager One devoid of ethical principles and who is actively opposed to doing what is ethical.

independent variable The variable thought to affect one or more dependent variables.

informal group A group that emerges through the efforts of individuals to satisfy personal needs not met by the formal organization.

information power Stems from the ability to control access to critical information and its distribution.

initial public offering (IPO) Initial sale of a firm's stock on a public security exchange.

initiating structure Leader behavior intended to establish well-defined patterns of organization, channels of communication, and work procedures between leader and group.

insight The sudden discovery of the answer to a problem.

instrumental leader behaviors Path-goal leader behaviors (such as setting goals and targets, teaching, and coaching) that reduce task uncertainty either by being directive or by encouraging followers to become achievement oriented.

intelligence The ability to adapt to novel situations quickly and effectively, use abstract concepts effectively, and grasp relationships and learn quickly.

intention Mental awareness of having both a goal and an action plan to obtain the goal.

interdependence The degree to which interactions between parties must be coordinated in order for them to perform adequately.

interest group An informal group consisting of individuals who affiliate to achieve an objective of mutual interest.

interpersonal effectiveness The degree that the consequences of your behavior match your intentions.

intervention A planned process that introduces change.

intrinsic rewards Postulates that motivation is moderated by perceived fairness or discrepancies between contributions and rewards.

job design The process of incorporating tasks and responsibilities into meaningful, productive, satisfying job responsibilities.

job enrichment A means to encourage motivation by building greater responsibility and variety into a job.

Johari Window A model of the different degrees of openness between two people based on their degree of self-disclosure and feedback solicitation.

justice Fairness in the distribution of rewards and punishments.

law of effect The principle that the consequences of behavior should be immediate to reinforce the link between the two.

leader A person who creates a vision and goals, then energizes others to voluntarily commit to that vision.

leader-member exchange theory Realizes that leaders seldom treat followers equally: in-group members experience mutual trust and reciprocal influence while out-group members are merely supervised.

leadership The act of providing direction, energizing others, and obtaining their voluntary commitment to the leader's vision.

Leadership Grid® A matrix used by Blake and Mouton to identify five leadership styles based on concerns for people and/or production.

leadership style The thoughts held to be important to a leader (motives, attitudes, goals, sources of satisfaction) in guiding how the leader interacts with group members.

learning The acquisition of knowledge or skill through study, practice, or experience.

learning organization An organization skilled at creating, acquiring, and transferring knowledge to improve its behavior.

liaison A party that expedites lateral communication between interacting groups by circumventing formal organizational boundaries.

life cycle Organization structures progress from simple to complex designs and systems as they age and grow in size.

life planning Making choices about what activities you want to spend your time on in your life.

line positions Job assignments that directly contribute to creating customer value by either designing products, producing them, financing needed resources, marketing to create demand, and/or selling and servicing the product.

listening The intellectual and emotional process in which the receiver integrates physical, emotional, and intellectual inputs in search of meaning.

locus of control The degree to which people believe that they, rather than exteral forces, determine their own lives.

Machiavellianism A personality attribute that describes the extent to which a person manipulates others for personal gain.

maintenance roles Roles that help establish and maintain good relationships among group members.

management The practice of organizing, directing, and developing people, technology, and financial resources to provide products and services through organizational systems.

management by objectives (MBO) The practice of manager and subordinate jointly determining time-specific objectives.

manager A systems diagnoser and influencer who works with people and other resources to perform tasks that achieve goals.

managers Persons granted authority to be in charge of an organizational unit and thus responsible for diagnosing and influencing systems and people to achieve appropriate goals.

mechanistic organization An organization with a traditional "look and feel" that is highly structured and formalized, desiring conformance behaviors to handle routine functions appropriate to stable environments.

mentor An experienced person who helps a less experienced person achieve career goals.

mentoring The process of a senior performer coaching a junior one.

message The physical form into which the sender encodes information.

milestones Future dates by which certain events are planned to occur.

mission An organization's fundamental purpose, articulated to define the nature of the business and unify human and other resources.

moderating variable A variable believed to influence the effects of the independent variable on the dependent variable.

mommy track A career path for mothers with less advancement pressure and less rewards so that mothers can spend more time with their families.

moral manager One who strives to develop and adhere to ethical goals, motives, standards, and general operating strategies.

motivation A conscious decision to perform one or more activities with greater effort than other competing activities.

motivator factors Job content factors such as responsibility and achievement that provide feelings of satisfaction when experienced.

moving Letting go of old ways of doing things and adopting new behaviors.

national mental programming Geert Hofstede's concept for that part of a country's collective learning that is shared with other members of that nation, region, or group, but not with members of other nations, regions, or groups.

need for affiliation (or affiliation motive) A learned motive to seek satisfaction from the quality of social and interpersonal relationships.

need for power (or power motive) A learned motive that finds satisfaction from being in charge and controlling and influencing others.

need to achieve (or achievement motive) A learned motive that satisfaction can be found in seeking tasks that will provide a sense of accomplishment.

negotiation A decision-making process for resolving differences and allocating resources between independent parties who do not share common outcome preferences.

negotiation A form of problem solving where two groups with conflicting interests exchange things in order to reach a mutually agreeable resolution.

network Contacts who can help provide information, advice, and help in your career.

noise Anything that interferes with the communication process.

nonverbal All ways of communicating without words, such as tone of voice, facial expression, and gestures.

norms Commonly held expectations about appropriate group member behavior.

off-site A daylong or multi-day forum intended to bring key players together to question basic assumptions, raise critical issues, and plan responses to challenges.

open systems Systems influenced by external pressures and inputs, making them more complex and difficult to control than closed systems.

operant conditioning Learning in which reinforcement depends on the person's behavior.

organic organization An organization with a looser "look and feel" that relies on the adaptive capacities of individuals to cope with dynamic internal and external forces, facilitated by empowerment and a collaborative network.

organization A group of people working toward a common objective.

organization chart The symbolic structure of boxed titles and lines that represent positions and reporting of relationships.

organizational behavior OB for short, refers to the behaviors of individuals and groups within an organization, and the interactions between the organization and environmental forces.

organizational behavior modification (OB mod) Deliberate management application of the antecedent—behavior—consequence sequence to shape desired employee behaviors.

organizational culture The fundamental assumptions people share about an organization's values, beliefs, norms, symbols, language, rituals, and myths—all of the expressive elements that give meaning to organizational membership and are accepted as guides to behavior.

organizational design The process managers go through to create meaningful structures, decision and information networks, and governance systems.

organizational development (OD) The systemwide application of behavioral science knowledge to the planned change process to improve organization effectiveness.

organizational learning Improving organizational procedures based on analysis of basic assumptions, values, and objectives.

organizational politics The deliberate management of influence to achieve outcomes not approved by the organization, or to obtain sanctioned outcomes through non-approved methods.

organizational structure The networked arrangement of positions and departments through which the essential tasks of an enterprise are subdivided and grouped to create the systems, decision centers, and behavioral linkages that carry out business strategies.

organizational value system A core set of values shared by the majority of organizational members, typically differentiated by the origin and content of those enduring values.

outsourcing The strategy of purchasing services or components from suppliers to prevent overextending the firm beyond its core capabilities.

Pareto's law Known as the 80/20 rule, this principle states that 80 percent of an observed result is caused by 20 percent of the activities, or efforts, or people involved.

pathfinding leader The entrepreneur and charismatic leader who is a visionary and dreamer concerned with pointing to where an organization ought to try to go.

path-goal leadership theory The perspective that a leader should clarify goals, show acceptable paths for attaining goals, make the path easier to travel, and reward satisfactory performance.

perception The selection, organization, and interpretation of sensory data.

perceptual closure The mind's tendency to fill in missing data when it receives incomplete information.

performance Behavior that has been evaluated or measured as to its contribution to organizational goals.

personal attribution The process of rationalizing causality (either to external or internal [personal] factors) as to why personally-involving events turn out as they do.

personal frame of reference How we see the world based upon our past experiences and self concept.

personal roles Roles which only meet individual needs and are usually detrimental to the group.

personality The set of traits and behaviors that characterizes an individual.

person-job fit The degree of fit between a person's abilities and motives and a job's demands and rewards.

piecework The practice of rewarding performance by paying for the amount produced consistent with quality standards.

planned change The process of preparing and taking actions to move from one condition to a more desired one.

planning The process of establishing objectives and specifying how they are to be accomplished in a future that is uncertain.

plateauing The ending of career advancement.

pooled interdependence Exists when two parties are independent of each other for their own performance outcomes, but each makes a contribution to the overall organization that affects the well-being of both parties.

position power A form of power that originates from the rights a person holds by virtue of the organizational hierarchy—the legitimate authority to reward and punish.

power The ability of A (the power holder) to alter circumstances impacting on B so that B does what A wants done.

power motive The socially acquired or learned desire to have strong influence or control over others.

Premack principle The pairing of disagreeable with enjoyable tasks or events to hasten their completion.

procedural justice The perceived fairness of the means used to determine the amount and distribution of rewards.

process theories of motivation Theories that focus on the ways people think through motivation issues and how they determine whether their actions were successful.

productivity Ratio of acceptable quality outputs to inputs consumed, a measure of how well the organization achieves its goals.

projection Attributing to others one's own thoughts, feelings, attitudes, and traits.

proxemics The use of physical space and things to communicate meaning.

psychological contract Workers' implicit expectations about what they are expected to contribute to an organization and what they will receive in return.

psychological states Three possible job qualities—experienced meaningfulness, experienced responsibility, knowledge of results—that shape individual job motivation and satisfaction of growth needs.

quality circle (QC) A group process that operates apart from but parallel to the traditional managerial structure by involving volunteers in analyzing problems and recommending solutions.

receiver The person receiving a message.

reciprocal interdependence Exist if the outputs of two parties are inputs for each other.

reciprocity The trading of power or favors for mutual gain—you help me, I'll help you.

reengineering The redesign of a work process to achieve more quality, efficiency, and effectiveness.

reference group A group with which an individual identifies to form opinions and make decisions regardless of whether he or she is an actual member.

referent cognitions theory Postulates that people evaluate their work and rewards relative to "what might have been" under different circumstances.

referent power Comes from being respected, likable, and worthy of emulating.

refreezing Reinforcing the changes made to stabilize new ways of behaving.

regenerative interaction patterns Cooperative and caring relationships which promote openness, trust, rapport and intimacy.

reinforcement The use of contingent consequences following a behavior to shape a consistent behavior pattern.

relationship-motivated style Fiedler's way of characterizing leaders who are principally concerned with respect in interpersonal relations and in helping the group develop as a team.

relative quality degradation Occurs when an enterprise's rate of improvement falls behind that of competitors, which relegates it to second-class performance.

reliability The consistency of the data obtained from a particular research method.

responsibility charting A technique for clarifying who is responsible for what on various decisions and actions with the team.

results An external acceptance or rejection of what an organization does—satisfied customers are the hallmark of positive results.

revitalization Ability to take care of tomorrow's problems as well as today's by renewing strategies, resources, technology, and skills.

reward power Demonstrated when a person offers to reward others for doing something he or she wants.

risk propensity A person's willingness to take risks.

rite A planned public performance or occasion where diverse forms of cultural expression are woven into a single event.

role A set of related tasks and behaviors that an individual or group is expected to perform.

role ambiguity Exists when role sets do not make clear their expectations of role holders.

role analysis technique Clarifies role expectations and obligations of team members through a structured process of mutually defining and delineating role requirements.

role conflict Exists when the behavioral expectations of the role holder and/or those of others in the role set do not agree.

role negotiation technique A controlled negotiation process between team members that results in written agreements to change specific behaviors by conflicting parties.

role overload Occurs when role expectations exceed a party's ability to respond effectively.

role set All the people who interact with a person or group in a specific role and have expectations about appropriate behavior.

satisfaction Positive feelings people have about an organization, whether as an employee, customer, supplier, or regulator.

scientific management An early 1900s movement that elevated the status of managers and held that scientific observation of people at work would reveal the one best way to do any task.

scientific method The use of theory to guide systematic, empirical research from which generalizations can be made to influence applications.

selective listening Receiver behavior of blocking out information or distorting it to match preconceived notions.

selective perception The tendency to focus on those attributes of people and situations that fit our frame of reference.

self-assessment inventories Paper and pencil tests that reveal participant characteristics.

self-concept Our perception and evaluation of ourselves.

self-disclose The process of revealing how you perceive and feel about the present.

self-efficacy Our self-perceptions about our ability to perform certain types of tasks.

self-esteem The judgment one makes about one's own worth.

self-managed team A work unit whose members are granted responsibility and authority to take the decisions and actions necessary to produce a product or service.

self-monitoring The degree to which people are sensitive to others and adapt their own behavior to meet external expectations and situational needs.

self-serving bias The tendency of individuals to attribute their own positive performance to internal factors and their negative performance to external factors.

sender The person communicating a message.

sensitivity training Unstructured feedback meetings where members share observations and feelings about each other to help improve sensitivity of behavior on others and the team's ability to function.

sequential interdependence Occurs when the output of one party provides necessary inputs for another to accomplish its goals.

showing consideration Leader behavior to bring out friendship, mutual trust, respect, and warmth in leader-member relationships.

single-loop learning Occurs when a manager shifts responsibility from employees to himself or herself by asking simple uni-dimensional questions that produce simple impersonal responses.

situational leadership theory (SLT) The Hersey and Blanchard model of leadership effectiveness based on combinations of the leader's task and relationship behaviors as moderated by the job maturity of followers.

social-cognitive theory A line of research that finds people do use idealized personal traits or characteristics as a way to distinguish leaders from nonleaders.

social contract Term used to describe collective psychological contracts.

social exchange theory Assumes that power and outcomes within a group are unevenly distributed, yet expects that each individual in a web of power relationships aims for positive outcomes.

social learning theory The belief that we learn many behaviors by observing and imitating others.

social loafing The tendency of individuals to exert less effort when working in a group than working individually.

socialization A process by which new members are indoctrinated into the expectations and rituals of the organization—its cultural norms or unwritten codes of behavior.

sociotechnical systems design A systems approach to enhance motivation and productivity by structuring work groups to achieve a balance between technical and human subsystems.

span of control In describing organizational structures, denotes the number of people supervised by one manager, or the ratio of managers to persons managed.

staff positions Jobs that support the line positions through carrying out advisement and internal "overhead" support activities such as accounting, purchasing, and human resource functions.

stakeholders Members of identifiable clusters of people who have economic and/or social interests in the behaviors and performance of a specific organization.

status The measure of relative worth and respect conferred upon an individual by the group.

stereotype A rigid, biased perception of a person, group, object, or situation.

strategic thinking A process of envisioning and planning to create a workable fit between organizational competencies (and limitations) and external opportunities (and threats) with the goal of better serving customers.

strategy The planned fit between an organization's capabilities and its evolving environment, crafted to achieve a favorable position within the competitive marketplace.

stress The body's reaction to a demand that is perceived as threatening.

stressor An environmental demand that is perceived as threatening.

strong culture Achieved when most members accept the interrelated assumptions that form an internally consistent cultural system.

structure Organizational groupings of people and tasks into departments providing for coordination among workflows and decision authority.

structured feedback procedures Meetings where members share feedback with each other by using a prepared format.

subcultures Localized subsystems of values and assumptions that give meaning to the common interests of small clusters of people.

superordinate goals The highest goals of an organization, fundamental desired outcomes that enable managers to assess performance relative to its mission.

supportive relationship leader behaviors Path-goal leader behaviors that focus on group emotional well-being by showing concern, providing encouragement, and giving reinforcement.

SWOT analysis An assessment of internal resources and competence in relation to conditions in an organization's external environment.

system An integrated whole formed by a set of interrelated elements and interacting subsystems.

systems Guidelines or structured processes for handling recurring transactions and events in a standardized or consistent way.

systems theory Emphasizes that the whole is greater than the sum of the parts, and that the parts or subsystems are related to each other and to the whole.

T-group A training group designed to help individuals learn about themselves and group dynamics by studying their own interactions.

task depth The degree of responsibility and autonomous decision authority expected in a job, often thought of as vertical job loading when formally designed.

task force A temporary group made up of individuals from interacting groups that resolves problems, facilitates cooperation, and promotes integration of efforts.

task group A temporary formal group created to solve specific problems.

task roles Roles that directly help accomplish group goals.

task scope The degree of task variety built into a job, typically called horizontal job loading when jobs are formally designed.

task-motivated style Used by Fiedler to describe leaders whose satisfaction comes from pride of task accomplishment and group success in doing a job well.

task-oriented behavior An approach to leadership that focuses on supervision of group members to obtain consistent work methods and job accomplishments.

team Relatively permanent work group whose members share common goals, are interdependent, and are accountable as a functioning unit to the organization as a whole.

team building All activities aimed at improving the problem-solving ability of group members by resolving task and interpersonal issues that impede the team's functioning.

technology The scientific knowledge, processes, systems and equipment used to create products and services and to help people carry out their tasks.

Theory X A managerial assumption that people act only to realize their basic needs and therefore do not voluntarily contribute to organizational aims.

Theory Y A managerial assumption that people are motivated by higher-order growth needs and they will therefore act responsibly to accomplish organizational objectives.

tradition-based values Values deeply rooted in historical practices which provide stability as they are passed from generation to generation.

transformational leader A leader who energizes others with visions and strategies of how to refocus and revitalize the larger organization so that change meets people's enduring needs.

transmission The act of conveying a communication.

trust The feeling of confidence that someone will act to benefit rather than harm you.

Type A personality Personality characterized by impatience, restlessness, competitiveness, aggressiveness, and a sense of intense time pressure.

Type B personality A personality that does not feel under pressure, is easy going, and seldom impatient.

unfreezing Raising awareness that current conditions are not satisfactory and reducing resistance to desired change.

validity The degree to which a research method actually measures what it is supposed to measure.

value system Internalized beliefs about what behavior, feelings, goals, and techniques are desirable.

values The enduring beliefs and expectations that a person or group hold to be important guides to behavior.

vertical job loading The process of structuring a greater range of responsibility for planning, control, and decision making authority into a job.

vision A desired future image of the organization and its processes and products that integrates current realities and expected future conditions within a specific time frame.

weak culture The absence of common assumptions and norms which means people are unsure of what is expected of them or how the organization believes it will succeed.

Name Index

Aaker, David A., 591, 592
Abbott, John S., 102
Abegglen, James C., 610
Abramson, Leonard, 450
Adams, Scott, 201, 223, 520
Adams, Stacy, 204
Adler, Nancy J., 373, 376, 599, 602, 603, 605
Adorno, T. W., 597
Agor, Weston H., 166, 597
Agway, 47
Ajzen, I., 600
Alari, Maryam, 609
Albanese, Robert, 605
Alcoa, 46
Aldag, R. J., 605
Alderfer, Clayton P., 188, 190, 597, 598
Alessandra, Anthony J., 273, 277, 304, 602–604, 608
Alexander Doll Company, 442
Alexander, Jeffrey A., 593
Allaire, Paul, 432, 549
Allen, Michael P., 610
Allen, Robert E., 143, 144
Allen, Robert W., 610
Allender, H., 607
Allied Signal, 119
Alliger, George M., 611
Allport, G. W., 167, 597
Amelio, Gilbert, 426, 453, 454
American Airlines, 261
Ancona, D. G., 608
Anderson, Julie G., 159, 614
Anderson, Kevin, 593
Anderson, Peter, 264
Andreas, Mick, 13
Andrews, F., 607
Andrews, Kenneth R., 591
Annis, R. C., 599
Antonucci, Mike, 431
Apple Computer, 125, 128, 367, 425, 452–454
Archer Daniels Midland Co., 13
Archer, E. R., 608
Archer, J. A., Jr., 613, 615
Argyris, Chris, 208, 209, 599, 615, 616
Arnold, H. J., 200
Arnzen, Breck, 591
Aronoff, Graig E., 602
Arthur Andersen & Company, 287, 408
Arvey, Richard D., 600
Aryee, S., 602
Asch, S. E., 605
Asea Brown Boveri, 51, 52, 100

Ash, Mary Kay, 118, 126
Ashe, Terry, 394
Ashford, S. J., 613
Ashforth, B. E., 604
AT&T, 99, 143, 144, 319, 364, 558, 578, 587
Athos, Anthony G., 595, 597, 603, 604
Atkinson, John W., 195, 598
Austin, Nancy K., 607
Ayres, B. Drummond, Jr., 596
Azel, Jose, 158

Bacharach, Samuel B., 609
Baker, Sherry, 608, 609
Baldwin, David A., 610
Baldwin Locomotive, 25
Bales, J., 613, 615
Ball, George, 399
Ball-Rokeach, S. J., 597
Bandura, Albert, 161, 162, 596
BankAmerica, 48
Banks, Cynthia, 547
Bard, J., 604
Barker, J. R., 606
Barnard, Chester, 609
Barnathan, Joyce, 532
Barnett, C., 613
Barnevik, Percy, 52
Bartmess, Andrew, 591, 592
Basil, Douglas C., 65, 78
Baskin, Otis W., 602
Bass, B. M., 608
Bates, John, 369
Bates Edwards Group, 369
Bauer, Nancy, 497, 522, 523
Beckhard, Richard, 606
Beckman, J., 600
Bedeian, Arthur G., 613
Beech-Nut, 451
Beehr, Terry A., 600
Beeman, Don R., 446, 609, 611
Beer, Michael, 612, 616
Bell, Cecil H., Jr., 606, 615
Bell, J., 614
Bellows, Laurel G., 307
Ben & Jerry's, 432
Benetton, 260
Benne, K. D., 605
Bennett, Amanda, 617
Bennett, Mike, 351
Bennis, Warren, 98, 464, 485, 486, 594, 603, 611–613, 616
Benson, Herbert, 518, 615

Berger, Frank S., 501
Berkowitz, Leonard, 612
Berlew, D. E., 599, 603
Berman, Laura, 604
Bernstein, Aaron, 299, 608
Bernstein, P. W., 604
Berrios, Willis, 511
Berryman-Fink, C., 604
Berss, Marcia, 595
Bettenhausen, K. L., 605
Bettman, James R., 596
Beyer, Janice M., 595
Bianchi, Alessandra, 4, 590, 591
Biberman, G., 611
Bierhoff, H. W., 599
Biggart, Nicole Woolsey, 609
Bigge, Morris L., 597
BioInstruments, 16
Birkenstock Footprint Sandals, 220
Blackburn, Richard, 601
Blake, Robert R., 470, 471, 612
Blakeley, Ann, 63
Blaker, Kenneth E., 597
Blanchard, Kenneth H., 475–477, 612
Blazerman, Max H., 610
Bloch, Steven, 124, 278, 522
Blum, Terry C., 594, 613
Bobko, P., 613
Bodensteiner, W., 602
Bodine, Dee, 488
Boeing Commercial Airplanes, 45, 263, 271, 272, 337
Bocker, Warren, 590
Boje, David M., 596, 613
Bolles, Richard N., 583, 617
Bomers, G. B. J., 607
Bortz, Jenny, 598
Boruff, Robert, 351
Boscheck, Ralf, 592
Bossidy, Lawrence A., 119, 461, 489, 490
Boston Beer Co., 218, 247
Bottger, P., 605
Boulding, Kenneth E., 590
Bower, G. H., 601
Bowermaster, David, 6
Boyacigiller, Nakiye A, 599
Boynton, Andrew C., 52
Bracharach, Samuel B., 610
Bradford, David L., 432, 590, 601, 609
Bradley, P., 604
Bradt, Jeffrey A., 598
Brandt, R., 602
Brass, Daniel J., 610
Brassard, Michael, 393, 395, 608

Brassil, James, 602
Bread Loaf Construction, 326
Breckler, S. J., 597
Breed, Allen, 221, 222
Breed Corporation, 221, 222
Brennan, Bartley, 431
Brett, Jenne M., 608, 617
Bridewell, L. G., 597
Brief, A. P., 613, 614
Briggs, Katherine, 173
Briggs-Myers, Isabel, 173
Brimelow, Peter, 596
Briner, Rob B., 599
Brockner, Audrey, 598
Brockner, Joel, 597, 598
Brodsky, Norm, 58
Brody, C., 605, 339
Brody, Pauline, 131
Brokke, James, 511
Broklaw, Leslie, 95
Brousseau, K. R., 606, 609
Brown, L. D., 616
Brownfield, Sharon, 591
Buck, Chris, 519
Buffa, Elwood S., 401
Buhler, Patricia, 599
Burak, Marshall J., 22
Burke, M. J., 614
Burke, Tim, 580, 581
Burke, Warner W., 616
Burlingham, Bo, 58, 596
Burlington Northern, 316
Burnham, David H., 196, 598, 610
Burns, James MacGregor, 482, 612
Burrows, Peter, 426
Burt, David N., 263
Byars, L. L., 401
Bylinsky, Gene, 261, 309, 611

Caggiano, Christopher, 198
Calero, H. H., 603
Calingo, Luis Ma R., 592
Callahan, Don, 315, 343
Cameron, Kim S., 104, 594, 603
Campbell, David B., 583, 609
Campbell, John P., 600, 606
Campbell, R. J., 606
Campion, Michael A., 241, 601
Caplan, R. D., 614
Carlisle, Ysanne M., 598
Carlzon, Jan, 64, 592, 594
Carnevale, P. J. D., 607
Carpenter, Michelle M., 538
Carroll, Archie B., 611
Carroll, Lewis, 608
Carroll, Paul, 595
Carter, Carolyn, 598
Cartwright, Dorwin, 609, 610, 612
Case, Thomas L., 616
Cashman, J., 613
Castro, J., 604, 615
Cauldron, S., 607
Cavanagh, Gerald F., 611
Cavender, J. W., 591
Cerny, Keith, 591, 592

Champy, James, 101, 131, 594, 595
Chandler, Alfred D., 593
Chaplin, J. P., 596
Charan, Ram, 55, 119, 484, 590, 608
Chase Manhattan, 523
Chemers, M. M., 612
Cheng, Mei-Lin, 159
Chiasson, John, 409
Childress, Rusty, 132
Childress Buick/Kia Co., 132
Chow, Jade, 438
Christie, Richard, 597
Chrysler, 315, 323, 341, 343
Chung Ju Yung, 203
Churchman, C. West, 590
Chusmir, Leonard H., 610
Ciampa, Dan, 610
Citibank, 24
Citicorp, 523
Clark, Bob, 229, 230
Clark, James H., 218, 248
Clark, Shawn M., 592
Clausen, A. W., 591
Clawson, James, 617
Clements, Michael, 593
Clinton, Bill, 375, 430, 511
Coca-Cola, 6
Cocks, Jay, 609
Cody, M., 604
Coffelt, T., 605
Coffey, Robert E., 595, 597, 603, 604
Cohen, Allan R., 432, 590, 603, 607, 609
Cohen, R. L., 599
Cole, Robert E., 207, 593, 599, 610
Coleman, Henry J., Jr., 591
Colgate-Palmolive Company, 433
Collins, James C., 590, 591, 613
Collins, Kim, 92
Comandena, M., 604
Compaq Computer, 25
Compression Labs, Inc., 43
Compton, Ronald, 450
Conger, Jay A., 601, 613
Connor, Patrick E., 593
Convis, Gary, 601
Cook, Curtis W., 22, 65, 78, 594, 598, 602, 612, 615
Cook, Paul, 166
Cook, Ruth E., 598
Cook, William J., 6
Cooke, R. A., 595
Coons, A. E., 611
Cooper, C. L., 614, 615
Cooper, Gary L., 614
Cooper, M. R., 597
Copeland, L., 602
Copper, C., 605
Cornelius, Edwin T., 610
Cornish, Craig M., 309
Cortese, Amy, 590
Cosier, R. A., 607, 608
Costello, Timothy W., 294
Costley, D. L., 294, 603
Cottington, E., 614
Cotton, John L., 609
Couchard, Thomas J., Jr., 597

Covey, J. G., 616
Covey, Stephen R., 298, 299, 586, 603, 617
Cowley, Michael, 57, 592
Crandall, Rob, 187
Creative Management Group, 413
Creed, W. E. Douglas, 591
Cronk, Michael, 137
Crystal, Graef, 600
Csoka, Louis S., 596
Cumming, Charles M., 601
Cummings, Larry L., 56, 592, 605
Cummings, R. C., 614
Cummings, Thomas G., 556, 557, 593, 615, 616
Cunningham, Andrea, 95
Cunningham Communication Inc., 95
Cyert, Richard M., 572, 617

Daemmrich, Bob, 63
Daetz, Dave, 108
Daft, Richard L., 262, 593
Daines, Robert H., 606
Dalkey, N. C., 609
Dangot-Simpkin, Gilda, 600
Daniels, J. D., 371
Dann, Valerie, 607
Dansereau, F., 613
Davidson, Eleanor, 602
Davies, R. V., 606
Davis, James H., 604
Davis, Keith, 320, 602
Davy, Jeanette, 598
de Geus, Arie, 592
de Jong, Rendel, 609
De Meuse, K. P., 606
De Vader, Christy L., 611
Deal, Terrence E., 127, 595
Dean, James W., Jr., 593
Dean, Paul, 609
DeAngelis, Tori, 614, 615
Deci, E. L., 202, 598
DeGeorge, G., 607
Del Duca, Pam, 246
Delbecq, André L., 594, 609
Deregowski, J. B., 599
Dess, Gregory G., 590
Devadas, R., 606
DeVito, J. A., 604, 608
Dewar, Donald L., 593
Dewitt, Rocki Lee, 597
Dickson, Reginald D., 28
DiMarco, N. J., 603
Dollar General Corporation (DG), 114
Domino's Pizza, 232
Donahue, Eileen, 597
Donaldson, T., 608, 609
Dong Joon Kim, 233
Donnellon, A., 606
Dorrow, Alan, 25
Dowling, W. F., 606
Doyle, Michael F., 263
Driskell, J. E., 605, 615
Driver, M. J., 606, 609
Drucker, Peter F., 5, 41, 48, 54, 79, 113, 221, 248, 335, 590–594, 600, 606, 610
Dubinsky, A. J., 604

Duchon, Dennis, 609, 613
Dumaine, Brian, 260, 606, 609
Duncan, W. Jack, 568, 595, 616, 617
Dunnette, Marvin D., 600, 607, 616
Dusek, D. E., 613
Dyer, William Gibb, Jr., 114, 595, 606
Dziurawiec. S., 599

Eakins, B., 604
Eakins, R., 604
Earley, P. Christopher, 289, 596, 605
Earth Resources Corp., 63
Eastman Kodak, 50
Edwards, Audrey, 266, 292, 603
Eisenhart, Mary, 590
Eisner, Michael, 124, 431, 485
Ekeberg, Steven E., 599
Ekman, Paul, 603
El-Namaki, M. S. S., 591
Elangovan, A. R., 608
Elliott, Timothy, 600
Ellis, J. E., 356
Ellis, Ruth, 88, 90, 92
Emerson, Richard M., 609, 610
Engardio, Pete, 532
England, George, 595
Erez, M., 599
Erlich, Donald J., 54
Estes, Clarissa Pinkola, 577
Evans, Sybil, 375
Everly, G. S., Jr., 613
Exley, Charles, 143

Fadiman, Jeffrey A., 203
Fagans, M. R., 606, 616
Fagenson, Ellen A., 616
Fairhurst, Gail Theus, 610
Falbe, Cecilia M., 591, 592
Fandt, P. M., 611
Farone, William A., 67
Farrell, Christopher, 218, 591, 601
Fayol, Henri, 17, 569, 590, 616
Federal Express Corp., 44, 45, 435
Federal Reserve Bank of Boston, 522
Feeny, David F., 592
Fein, M., 598
Feldman, Daniel C., 605
Ferrell, Dan, 611
Ferrell, O. C., 607, 608
Ferris, G. R., 604, 611, 615
Festinger, Leon, 170, 597
Fichman, Mark, 590
Fiedler, Fred, 474, 612
Field, R. H., 612
Fields, Dail L., 594, 613
Finegan, Jay, 592
Fink, S. L., 603
Finley, Michael, 606
Fisher, Anne B., 590, 617
Fisher, George, 51
Fisher, Jeff, 208
Fleishman, Edwin, 468
Fleming, John E., 608, 609
Fletcher, B., 614
Fletcher, Joyce K., 604

Flint, Jerry, 594
Fogel, Helen, 599
Folger, R., 599
Folkman, S., 613, 615
Follett, Mary Parker, 571, 572
Ford Motor Co., 75, 76, 82, 84, 102–104,
    231, 529, 540, 562
Ford, Henry, 44
Ford, Henry, II, 115
Ford, Robert C., 610
Fort Howard Corp., 127
Fortado, Bruce, 599
Foster, M., 604
Fottler, Myron D., 610
Franciosi, John, 343
Francis, Carol E., 593, 594
Francis, Pam, 462
Frayne, Colette A., 600, 602
Frederikson, Lee W., 226
French, John R. P., Jr., 428, 430, 609, 614
French, Wendell L., 606, 615
Friedkin, William, 154
Friedman, Meyer, 502, 613
Frijda, N. H., 601
Frisch, Bruce, 151
Fritzsche, D. J., 608
Froggatt, Kirk L., 609
Fryxell, Gerald E., 599
Fuller, S. Riggs, 605
Fulmer, Robert M., 595
Fulmer, William E., 595, 600
Furnham, Adrian, 598
Fusco, M. A. C., 609
Fusilier, Marcelline R., 615
Futrell, D., 606

Gadon, H., 603
Galagan, Patricia A., 591
Galbraith, Jay, 122, 595, 608
Gallo, D. D., 612
Gallupe, R. Brent, 416
Galvin, Linda, 494
Gamble, John E., 595
Ganster, Daniel C., 615
Gantt, Harry, 399, 400
Garcia, Danny, 327
Gardiner, G., 608
Gardner, Howard, 596
Gargan, Edward A., 438
Garland, Susan B., 617
Garside, Sandra G., 602
Garvin, David A., 590, 616
Gates, Bill, 6, 7, 124
Gates, Michael, 604
Gatewood, R. D., 607
Gaul, Gilbert M., 591
Geber, Beverly, 351
Gemmill, Gary R., 614
General Dynamics, 356
General Electric, 7, 8, 55, 101, 261, 361,
    539
General Foods, 331
General Motors, 6, 23, 25, 46, 90, 100,
    257, 337, 351, 378, 411, 540
George, Jennifer M., 598, 605, 614
George Washington University, 394

Gergen, K. J., 609
Gerloff, E. A., 602
Gershenfeld, M. K., 604, 605
Gersick, C. J. G., 605
Gerstner, Louis V., Jr., 485
Ghoshal, Sumantra, 591
Giauque, William C., 606
Gibson, J. W., 603
Gies, Florence L., 597
Gilbert, Laura, 560
Gilbreth, Lillian M., 568, 569, 616
Gilmore, Thomas, 594
Gingrich, Newt, 511
Gioia, Dennis A., 592
Girdano, D. A., 613, 614, 615
Gist, Marilyn E., 601
Glasl, F., 607
Glass, David, 139
Glenn, Ethel C., 275
Goldberg, Lewis, 597
Goldberg, S., 608
Goldhaber, Gerald M., 602
Goldsmith, Scott, 267
Goldstein, Jeffrey, 597
Goleman, Daniel, 160, 308, 309, 596, 604
Golembiewski, R. T., 514, 603, 614
Gomes, Lee, 426
Gomez-Mejia, Luis R., 235, 600
Goodman, Jodi S., 594, 613
Goodman, Paul S., 590, 605, 606
Goodrich, J. N., 602
Goodstein, Jerry, 590
Goold, Michael, 594
Gordon, Michael E., 599
Goss, Blaine, 603, 604
Graef Crystal, 234
Graen, George, 613
Graham, Pauline, 617
Graham, Sandra, 612
Gray, Jerry, 511
Green, Stephen G., 609, 613
Green, Thad B., 598
Greenberg, Jeff, 598, 599
Greenberg, M. S., 609
Greenlar, Michael, 47
Greenwood, Royston, 591
Greetz, C., 595
Gregory, K. L., 595
Greiner, Larry E., 452, 595, 611
Griggs, L., 602
Grimes, A. J., 610
Grollin, Bob, 494
Grove, Andrew S., 6, 198, 466, 593
Grover, Steven, 597
Groves, Jacqueline M., 615
GTE Telephone Operations, 391
Guenther, Robert, 615
Guetzkow, H., 605
Gupta, Anil K., 595
Gustafson, D. H., 594
Gutek, B. A., 604, 614
Guzzo, R. A., 605

Hackman, J. Richard, 240, 594, 601
Haga, W., 613
Halal, William E., 52, 591, 592

Haldeman, Jeffrey, 593, 594
Hall, Douglas T., 615, 617
Hall, J., 607
Hall, R. H., 615
Hallmark, 103
Halpin, Andrew W., 611
Ham, Stanley, 297
Hamilton, V., 601
Hammer, David, 297
Hammer, Michael, 101, 104, 594
Hamner, C. W., 600
Hanaoka, Masao, 610
Hanna, David P., 593
Hansen, Jo-Ida C., 583
Hanson, P. C., 603
Harary, Keith, 597
Hargrave, Alice Q., 478
Harkings, S., 605
Harkins, S. G., 605
Harley Davidson, 161
Harmon, Amy, 154, 315, 607
Harrick, Edward J., 224, 601
Harris, Phillip, 603
Harris, Reuben T., 606
Harrison, Roger, 606
Hart, K. E., 615
Hartke, D. D., 612
Hartman, Sandra J., 598
Harvey, Robert, 355
Hawken, Paul, 602
Hayes, Robert H., 592, 595
Healey, James R., 593
Hebden, J. E., 595
Heian, James B., 67, 593
Heisler, W. J., 614
Hellervik, Lowell V., 600
Hellriegel, Don, 597
Helmer, Olaf, 609
Helmsley, Leona, 428, 444
Hempel, Kathleen, 127
Henderson, Jon, 415
Henkoff, Ronald, 13, 24
Herlich, Richard S., 287
Hersey, Paul, 475–477, 612
Herzberg, Frederick, 190, 191, 598
Hesselbein, Frances, 482
Hewlett, William, 130
Hewlett-Packard, 7, 51, 120, 121, 129, 130, 159, 372
Hill, Charles W. L., 594
Hill, R. E., 603
Hillkirk, J., 606
Hinings, C. R., 591
Hinterhuber, Hans H., 591
Hirshhorn, Larry, 594
Hitler, Adolf, 444
Hodgetts, R. M., 603
Hof, Robert D., 6, 601
Hoffmann-La Roche, Inc., 523
Hofstede, Geert, 134, 135, 137, 138, 206, 596, 599
Hogan, R., 614
Holland, John, 582, 617
Hollander, Edward P., 609
Holmes, Thomas H., 506, 614
Holmgren, Robert, 369

Homans, George C., 571, 617
Honda Motors, 207
Hoover, J. Edgar, 116
Horn, Karen, 519
Horovitz, Bruce, 39, 593
Horton, R. E., 605
Hoskisson, Robert E., 594
Hough, L. M., 607, 616
House, Charles H., 372
House, Robert J., 598, 607, 612, 613
Houston, J. M., 612
Howard, Greg, 303, 440, 441
Howard, Robert, 549
Howell, Al, 602
Hower, Bob, 220
Huey, John, 112, 597, 600
Hughes, Bob, 604, 606
Hughson, T. L. Griffith, 606
Hulin, C. L., 597, 599
Hunsaker, Phillip L., 273, 277, 295, 304, 333, 369, 602–604, 606, 608, 609, 615, 616
Hunt, James. G., 591, 612, 613
Hunter, J. E., 597
Huse, Edgar F., 556, 557
Hussein, R. T., 604
Hutchinson, Ron, 559
Hyatt, Joshua, 184, 597, 599
Hymowitz, Carlo, 602

Iacocca, Lee, 115, 341, 485, 606
Iaffaldano, M. T., 591
Iansite, Marco, 590
Ibarra, Herminia, 602
IBM, 24, 97, 100, 126, 129, 135, 543, 587
IDS Financial Services, 400
Intel, 6, 7
International Harvester, 47
International Paper Company, 372
Irvin, Robert A., 591
Irving, Claire, 489
Isen, A. M., 607
Ivancevich, John M., 600, 614, 615

J.C. Penney, 233
Jablonsky, Stephen F., 66, 67, 593
Jackson, J. M., 605
Jackson, Susan E., 614, 615
Jacob, Rahul, 594
Jaeger, Alfred M., 134, 596
Jaffe, Dennis, 198
Jago, Arthur G., 609, 612, 613
Jamal, M., 615
Janis, Irving L., 329, 330, 363, 605, 607
Janson, Robert, 601
Japenga, Ann, 615
Jehn, K., 607
Jenks, S., 603
Jensen, M. A. C., 604
Jermier, John M., 488, 613
Jiang, William Y., 594, 596
Jick, T D., 614
Jobs, Steve, 7, 118, 125, 425
John Hancock Financial Services, 521

Johnson, C. Merle, 600
Johnson, Chalmers, 596
Johnson, D. W., 602, 603, 607
Johnson, Julius H., Jr., 594, 596
Johnson, Lyndon B., 329
Johnson, M., 603
Johnson & Johnson, 86
Jones, J. E., 604, 605, 608
Jones, M. R., 597
Jordan, P. C., 598
Josefowitz, N., 603
Jung, Carl G., 173, 597

Kabanoff, B., 607
Kaeter, M., 606
Kahanamoku, Duke, 327
Kahn, Robert L., 571, 590, 614, 617
Kanoff-Muir, N., 602
Kant, Immanual, 406
Kanter, Rosabeth Moss, 426, 609, 610, 615, 616
Kanungo, Rabindra N., 601
Kappelman, Leon A., 601
Katz, Daniel, 571, 590, 614, 617
Katz, Robert L., 590
Katzenback, John R., 339, 604, 606
Kaufman, Steve, 593
Kawahito, Hiroshi, 505
Kawasaki, Guy, 426, 469
Kayser, Thomas A., 605
Kazarian, Paul, 353
Kazdin, A. E., 600
Keating, D. E., 606
Keating, Patrick J., 66, 67, 593
Keffeler, Jean B., 615
Keidel, Robert W., 96, 104, 594
Kelleher, Herb, 462
Keller, John J., 596
Keller, R. T., 605
Kelley, H. H., 596
Kelly, Charles M., 598, 600
Kelly, Helen, 510
Kelly, Kevin, 590
Kennedy, Allan A., 127, 595
Kennedy, J. K., 612
Kennedy, Jim, 594
Kennedy, John F., 329, 399, 430
Kennedy, Robert F., 399
Keon, Thomas L., 598
Kerr, John, 132
Kerr, Steven, 229, 488, 600, 613
Kerwin, Kathleen, 593, 594
Keyton, J., 605
Keza, T. Michael, 163, 300, 413
Khan, R. L., 607
Kharbanda, Om P., 602, 603
Kiddler, Peabody & Company, 361
Kiechel, Walter, III, 602
Kiev, A, 614
Kiggundu, Moses N., 601
Kilmann, R. H., 368
Kim Young Sam, 203
Kim, K. I., 613
Kimberly-Clark, 522
Kindall, A. F., 600
King, Carol, 229

King, R. W., 510
Kinmonth, Rob, 538
Kipnis, David, 448, 610, 611
Kirchmeyer, C., 607
Kirkcaldy, Bruce D., 598
Kirkpatrick, David, 594
Kirkpatrick, Shelley A., 468, 611
Klein, Linda S., 608
Kleiner, Art, 599
Kleiner, Brian H., 602
Kleisath, S., 612
Knapp, M., 604
Kneyse, Chuck, 530
Knippen, Jay T., 598
Knutson, Doug, 400
Koch, Jim, 217, 218, 247
Kodak, 102
Kofman, F., 616
Kohler, Wolfgang, 163, 597
Kohn, Alfie, 237, 600
Kohn, V., 614
Kolb, David A., 164, 165, 597, 605
Komake, Judi, 600
Kondrasuk, Jack N., 600
Konrad, A. M., 604
Koppelaar, Leendert, 609
Korgaard, M. A., 612
Korman, A. K., 612
Kormanski, C., 604
Kotter, John P., 18, 103, 464, 537, 590, 594, 611, 615
Kouzes, James M., 486, 487, 591, 592, 612, 613
Krackhardt, David, 610
Kram, K. E., 604, 612, 615
Kramer, Tracy Robertson, 39, 112, 593
Kraut, R., 604
Kreitner, Robert, 600
Kriger, Mark P., 591, 592
Kuehl, Charles, 594, 596
Kuhl, J., 600
Kuller, L., 614
Kuman, R., 605, 607
Kuttner, Robert, 596

L.L. Bean, 158
Labich, Kenneth, 617
Lacity, Mary C., 592
Lackey, Bill (Mojo), 208
Lado, Augustine A., 599, 616
Lai Chi-sun, 532
Lake, Dale, 591
Lakein, A., 615
Lamarre, Larry, 494
Lancaster, Pat, 317
Lane, Frank B., 610
Langberg, Mike, 426, 611
Lanier, Jaron, 339
Large, Brian, 315, 343
Larsen, Janet K., 602
Larsen, Ralph, 86
Larson, L. L., 612, 613
Larwood, Laurie, 591, 592
Latack, Jania C., 598
Latane, B., 605
Latham, Gary P., 599, 600

Lawler, Edward E., III, 82, 83, 86, 90, 100, 200, 240, 591, 593, 594, 598, 600, 609, 610, 616
Lawrence, Paul R., 591
Lawson, T., 596
Lazarus, R. S., 615
Lazier, Linda, 257
Lazrus, R. S., 613
Leavitt, Harold J., 265, 482, 483, 602, 609, 612
Lee, Chris, 604, 613
Leehman, John, 326
Lehrer, R., 615
Lei, David T., 599, 616
Lengel, R. H., 601, 602
Leopold, Marjorie, 597
Lerch, Javier, 590
Levin, J., 605, 606, 613
Levine, David I., 610
Lewicki, R. J., 608
Lewin, Kurt, 469, 542, 612, 615, 616
Lewis, Evelyn, 602
Lewis, Patricia, 442
Liddell, W. W., 603
Liden, R., 604
Likert, R., 615
Likert, Rensis, 467, 611
Lincoln, James R., 610
Lindzey, G., 597
Linton, Ralph, 112, 594
Lippitt, Ronald, 612
Lirtzman, S. I., 607
Litterer, J. A., 608
Little, B. L., 600
Lobel, S. A., 607
Locke, Edwin A., 468, 599, 600, 611
Loden, M., 390
Logan, F. Daniel, Jr., 3, 31, 32
Lombard G. F. F., 603
LoPresto, Robert, 289
Lord, Robert G., 611
Lorenzi, Peter, 591
Lorsch, Jay W., 601
Los Angeles City Fire Department, 390
Lotz, Roy E., 610
Lublin, J. S., 606, 607
Luft, Joseph, 300, 301, 603, 606
Lumpkin, G. T., 590
Lunada Bay Pirates, 327
Lundy, J. Edward, 75
Lunt, P. K., 320
Luthans, Fred, 227, 600, 602
Lynch, Peter, 139, 596
Lynn, Richard, 598

McBurney, Don, 609
McCall, M. W., 611
McCann, B., 615
McCann, Dick, 606
McCann, Joseph E., 594
McCanse, Anne Adams, 471
McClelland, Carol L., 601
McClelland, David, 195, 196, 442, 598, 604, 610
McCormick, Cecilla, 134, 596
McCormick, Charles Perry, 338

McCormick & Company, 338
McCracken, Ed, 62, 485, 486, 592
McDonald's, 5, 522
McDonogh, Pat, 317
Macelli, Carlos Arias, 233
McFarlin, Dean B., 599, 600
McGee, G. W., 591
McGill, Michael, 599, 616
McGregor, Douglas, 190, 192, 193, 472, 571, 598, 612, 616
Machiavelli, Niccolo, 176, 597
MacIntosh, Craig, 303, 440, 441
Mckenzie, Charles, 508
McLaughlin, Maynard, 326
McLeod, P. L., 607
McManus, Kim, 163
McNally, Joe, 539
McNamara, Robert, 75, 399
McNealy, Scott G., 246
Mael, F., 604
Magner, N. R., 607
Magnet, Myron, 597
Maguire, M. A., 65, 592
Maier, Norman R. F., 605
Maitlis, Sally, 599
Mamis, Robert A., 218, 601
Mandel, Michael J., 591
Mandela, Nelson, 464
Maney, Kevin, 595
Mann, Milt and Joan, 19, 128
Mann, R. D., 611
Manning, David J., 598
Manning, Donald, 390
Manning, M. R., 614
Manuso, John S. J., 518
Manz, C. C., 606
Maples, M. F., 604
March, James G., 572, 610, 617
Marcic, Dorothy, 616
Marcus, Bernard, 230
Maremont, Mark, 592
Margerison, Charles, 606
Markham, S. E., 600
Markides, Constantinos C., 612
Markkula, A. C. Mike, 426
Marpac Industries, Inc., 25
Marriott Corporation, 46
Marshal, H. A., 599
Marshall Industries, 356, 373, 376
Marston, P., 604
Martinez, Judy, 292
Martinko, Mark, 227, 600
Mary Kay Cosmetics, 126
Mascowitz, M., 606
Maslach, C., 614
Maslow, Abraham H., 185, 187, 188, 571, 597, 616, 617
Mason, Richard O., 590
Matsushita Electric Corporation of America, 113
Mattel Toy Company, 403
Matteson, M. T., 614, 615
Matthews, Bruce, 208
Matthews, Dave, 221
Matthews, K., 614
Maud, Peter, 602

May, G. Elton, 616
May, H. J., 614
Mayer, Roger C., 604
Mayes, Bronston T., 610, 615
Maynard, Micheline, 593
Mayo, Elton, 570
Medoff, James, 617
Meeker, Barbara Foley, 597
Meer, J., 604
Mehrabian, Albert, 603
Mehren, Elizabeth, 617
Meisels, Samuel J., 134
Melcher, Richard A., 594
Mendoza de Riveria, Ana, 233
Mento, A. J., 599
Merck, 7
Meredith, Paul H., 616
Meyer, Janice M., 120
Meyer, Wulf-Uwe, 612
Michaels, Edward G., III, 591
Michaelson, L. K., 605
Michalowski, Nancy, 3
Michela, J. L., 596
Microsoft, 6, 7, 15, 124
Miesing, Paul, 591, 592
Mikawa, Eiji, 24
Miles, Michael A., 39
Miles, Raymond E., 590, 591
Miles, Robert H., 607
Milken, Michael, 444, 516
Miller, A. G., 596
Miller, Michael W., 601, 602
Milliken, 226
Miner, John B., 611
Minton, J. W, 608
Mintz, S. L., 76
Mintzberg, Henry, 16, 18, 19, 48, 53, 65,
    91, 166, 590–593, 597
Mitchell, T. R., 157
Mitchell, Terence R., 601, 612, 613
Mitroff, Ian I., 82, 590, 593
Mitsubishi, 263
Mitz, L. F., 614
Moberg, Dennis J., 611
Mobily, K., 615
Modic, S. J., 602
Mohrman, Susan Albers, 83, 593
Monroe, Scott M., 614
Montgomery, Kathryn, 431
Moore, Gordon, 198
Moore, Thomas, 597
Moran, Robert, 603
Morris, Betsy, 613
Morrisey, G. L., 608
Morrison, Ann M., 479, 489, 613, 617
Morrison, J., 614
Morse, N. C., 611
Motorola, 334, 532
Motowidlo, S. J., 614
Mouton, Jane S., 470, 471, 612
Mowday, Richard T., 597, 598
Mozenter, A., 604
Mroczkowski, Tomasz, 610
Muchinsky, P. M., 591
Mueller, Mary, 443
Mulder, Mauk, 609

Mullen, B., 605
Munzenrider, R. F., 514, 614
Murphy, Anne, 222
Murphy, L. R., 614
Murray, Bridget, 609

Nader, Ralph, 611
Nadler, David A., 591, 612
Nakarmi, Laxmi, 203
Nanus, Burt, 464, 591, 611, 613
Napier, R. W., 604, 605
Nash, N. C., 388, 418
Natale, S. M., 608
Nauman, Matt, 590
Nayak, P. Ranganath, 592
NCR Corp., 143, 144, 374
Neale, Margaret A., 610
Neblett, G. Rives, 300
Nelson, D. L., 615
Nestle, 451
Netscape, 218, 248
Newberg, Warren, 516
The New England (TNE) insurance
    company, 3, 4, 31
Newstrom, John W., 609, 616
Nichols, D., 602
Nierenberg, G. I., 603
Nixon, Richard, 298, 444
Nolan, Paul, 292
Norfolk General Hospital, 83
Norton-Lambert Co., 309
Noyce, Robert, 198
Nulty, Peter, 601
Nussbaum, Bruce, 617
Nyberg, Lars, 144
Nystrom, P. C., 612

O'Boyle, Thomas F., 602
O'Connel, Loraine, 603
O'Connor, Edward J., 592
O'Donnell, C. F., 608
O'Hair, Dan, 603, 604
O'Hara, Kirk, 600
O'Neill, Hugh M., 594
O'Reilly, Charles, 64, 65, 592, 600
Odiorne, George S., 221, 600
Office Systems Design, Inc., 86–92
Oldham, Greg R., 601
Oneal, M., 606
Organ, Dennis W., 613
Oritz, A. A., 596
Ornstein, Robert E., 597
Ortega, Bob, 233
Osborn, A. F., 609
Osborn, R. N., 612
Osborne, W. R. C., Jr., 608
Osland, Joyce M., 605
Ost, Edward J., 601
Ott, E. M., 605
Otto, Herbert A., 606
Ouchi, William G., 65, 134, 592, 596
Overby, John, 198

Pablo, Amy L., 599
Packard, David, 129, 130, 595
Packard, J. S., 614
Packard, Vance, 466, 611
Paluck, Robert, 192
Panhandle Eastern Corp., 234
Panian, Sharon K., 610
Paré, Terence P., 55
Parkhe, Arvind, 617
Parsons, Talcot, 571, 617
Pascale, Richard, 594
Pasmore, William A., 593, 594, 606, 616
Patillo, Michael, 233
Pave, I., 510
Pavlov, Ivan P., 160, 161, 596
Payne, Roy, 614
Pearson, Christine M., 590
Pellecchia, Michael, 599
Pelz, D. C., 607
PepsiCo, 451
Perot, H. Ross, 62
Perroni, Amedero G., 601
Pervin, Lawrence, 597
Peters, L. H., 612
Peters, Tom, 18, 590, 592, 602
Petersen, James C., 611
Peterson, Donald, 97, 98, 529, 562
Peterson, Mark F., 596
Peterson, R., 607
Peterson, Thane, 594
Pettigrew, Andrew M., 594, 595
Petty, M. M., 591
Pfeffer, Jeffrey, 432, 444, 446, 452, 604,
    608, 610, 611
Pfizer International, 88
Philip Morris, Inc., 39, 47, 67
Phillips, Antoinette S., 613
Phillips, Colette, 290
Phillips Petroleum, 94
Phua, J., 602
Pierce, Jon L., 590, 616
Pincus, J. David, 602
Pinegar, Kim, 112
Pisano, Gary P.., 592
Plaschke, Bill, 208, 617
Pohlmann, J. T., 612
Pondy, Louis, 607
Pood, Elliott A., 275
Popp, Wolfgang, 591
Porras, Jerry I., 590, 591, 613, 615, 616
Porsche, 387, 417
Porter, Lyman, 200, 597, 598
Porter, Michael E., 52, 592
Posner, Barry Z., 486, 487, 591, 592, 599,
    611, 613
Pound, John, 592
Pounds, W. F., 608
Pratt, Michael G., 603
Premack, David, 161, 596, 600
Price, Raymond L., 372
Procter & Gamble, 46
Prybutok, Victor R., 601
Psihoyos, Louis, 482
Puffer, Shelia M., 453
Pumphrey, Steven, 192
Purdy, Kenneth, 601

Putti, J. M., 602

Quaker Oats Co., 232
Quick, J. C., 613
Quick, J. D., 613
Quick, Thomas L., 598, 599
Quinn, R. P., 614
Quinn, Robert E., 607

Radebaugh, L. H., 371
Rafaeli, Anat, 603
Rahe, Richard H., 506, 614
Rahim, M. Afzalur, 368, 607, 608
Randall, Jim, 13
Randolph, W. Alan, 599
Raudsepp, Eugene, 414
Rauschenberger, J., 597
Raven, Baertram, 428, 430, 609
Ravlin, E., 605
Raynolds, Peter A., 595, 597, 603, 604
Reardon, Kathleen K., 437, 610
Reddy, Gordon S., 438
Reece, B. L., 602
Reed, Thomas F., 597
Reich, Robert, 80, 593
Reichenstein, Murray, 75
Reilly, Anne, 617
Reim Men, 168
Reimann, Barnard C., 595
Reimer, E., 611
Reliable Cartage Co., 270
Rest, James R., 608, 609
Revicki, D. A., 614
Rheem, Helen, 616
Rhino Records, 443
Rhodes, Susan R., 600
Richards, Greg, 616
Richards, Karen, 501
Richards, Mark, 377
Riley, A. W., 613, 614
Rivera, Sam, 478
Rizzo, J. R., 607
Robbins, S. P., 333, 369, 603, 608
Roberts, Charlotte, 599
Roberts, Sam, 134, 596
Robertson, P. J., 615, 616
Rogers, D. P., 614
Rogers, Everett M., 602
Rogers, Richard, 126
Rohlen, Thomas P., 123
Rokeach, Milton, 168, 594, 597
Romanelli, E., 605
Romblad, Robin, 595
Ronney, A., 615
Rosen, Benson, 601
Rosener, J. B., 390
Rosenman, Ray, 502, 613
Rosenthal, R. A., 603, 614
Rosenzweig, Mark, 597
Rosenzweig, Philip M., 596
Roslund, Jerry L., 600
Ross, Richard, 599
Rothman, Howard, 599
Rotter, J. B., 597
Rousseau, D. M., 595

Rowland, K. M., 604, 615
Royal Dutch Shell, 210
Rubenfeld, Stephen A., 590
Rubenson, George C., 595
Rubin, Irwin M., 605
Ruble, Thomas I., 365
Rue, L. W., 401
Rusk, Dean, 399
Russo, Kenneth, 233
Ryan, Kenneth, 507
Ryder, 12

S. C. Johnson & Son, 521
Saab, 336
Safeway, 522
Safizadeh, M. Hossein, 593
Sager, Ira, 613
Salacuse, Jeswald, 603
Salancik, Gerald R., 592, 610
Salas, E., 605, 615
Salisbury, Christine L., 134, 506
Sammet, George, 609
San Diego Zoo, 348
Sanholz, Kurt, 603
Saunders, D. M., 608
Sax, Gilbert, 617
Scannell, E. E., 609
Schein, Edgar H., 114, 594, 595, 603, 607, 608
Schein, Virginia E., 452, 609, 611
Scheinin, Richard, 431
Schermerhorn, John R., Jr., 596
Schiller, Z., 608
Schlender, Brent, 611
Schlesinger, Arthur M., Jr., 29, 591
Schlesinger, J. M., 602
Schlesinger, Leonard A., 537, 615
Schlossberg, H., 497, 615
Schmidt, Stuart M., 448
Schmidt, Warren H., 436, 481, 611, 612
Schmidtberger, Joe, 530
Schminike, M., 605
Schmitt, N., 597
Schneider, C. P., 598
Schnepf, James, 161
Schoenthaler, Linda, 523
Schonberger, Richard J., 593
Schriesheim, Chester, 612
Schroder, Dean, 595
Schuler, Randall S., 613–615
Schuster, F. E., 600
Schutz, William C., 293, 603
Schwab, R. L., 614
Schwartz, A. E., 605, 606, 613, 617
Schwartz, Felice N., 587, 617
Schwenk, C. R., 607, 608
Schwimer, D., 614
Scott, K. D., 600
Scott, Linda Sue, 511
Sculley, John, 125, 425
Sears, Roebuck and Co., 11, 24, 46
Seashore, Stanley E., 612
Sedgwick, David, 599
Seiler, John A., 591
Sekiya, Toru, 505
Sell, M. Van, 613

Selye, Hans, 498, 499, 613
Semier, Ricardo, 467
Senge, Peter, 210, 594, 599, 616
Servan-Schreiber, J. J., 28, 591
Seyna, E. J., 600
Shamir, Boas, 598
Sharkey, Thomas W., 446, 609, 611
Sharma, Marc, 443
Shaw, M. E., 604, 605
Shaw, Robert B., 591
Shea, G. P., 605
Sheats, P., 605
Shelby Die Casting, 300
Shepherd, J. S., 615
Shepperd, J. A., 605
Sherif, C., 607
Sherif, M., 607
Sherman, Stratford, 159
Shonkoff, Jack P., 134
Sibson, Robert E., 338
Siddall, Robert, 288
Siegel, J., 614
Sik Hung Ng, 609
Silicon Graphics, 62, 486
Simmerman, Scott J., 607
Simmons, Donald B., 602
Simon, Herbert A., 572, 608, 617
Simon, Tami, 577, 589
Simpson, Charles, 86–92
Simpson, Robert L., 76
Sims, Henry P., Jr., 591
Singh, Harbir, 596
Sitkin, Sim B., 599
Skinner, B. F., 160, 161, 596
Slocum, John W., Jr., 210, 597, 599, 603, 616
Smart, David, 602
Smart, Tim, 484
Smith, Bryan J., 599
Smith, Douglas K., 339, 604, 606
Smith, G., 607
Smith, Hoyt, 327
Smith, J. C., 615
Smith, John F., Jr., 100
Smith, Richard, 44
Smith & Hawken, 262
Smith-Lovin, L., 605
Smithburg, William D., 232
Smither, Robert D., 606
Snavely, B. Kay, 610
Snell, Scott A., 592
Snoek, J. D., 607, 614
Snow, Charles C., 590
Snyder, M., 597
Snyder, Pamela R., 590
Sobolik, Tom, 442
Solectron Corp., 11
Solomon, Charlene M., 616
Solomon, Jolie, 297
Southern Grille Restaurant, 163
Spiker, Barry K., 602
Spiller, Robert, 290
Spindler, Michael, 425, 426, 452
Sporleder, Douglas, 137
Springston, J., 605
Srivastva, S., 599

Stahl, M. J., 598
Stalk, George, Jr., 610
Stallworthy, Ernest A., 602, 603
Staw, Barry M., 592, 593, 600, 605, 609
Stead, Jerre, 143, 144, 578
Steele, F. I., 603
Steers, Richard M., 593, 597, 598, 600
Stempel, Robert, 100, 351
Stevens, A., 614
Stevenson, Amelya, 189
Stevenson, Don B., 246, 323
Stewart, J. B., 516
Stewart, Thomas A., 593, 594
Stewart, Tomas, 607
Stodgill, Ralph M., 611
Stone, Eugene F., 573
Strain, Phillip, 134, 596
Stranahan, Susan Q., 591
Strebel, Paul, 612
Strickland, A. J., III, 39, 112, 593–595, 600
Stroh, Linda, 617
Stubbart, Charles, 595
Sullivan, Kevin, 203
Summers, I., 605
Sun Microsystems, 50
Sunbeam-Oster, 353
Sundstrom, E., 606
Suris, Oscar, 604
Susman, Gerald I., 593
Sutton, C., 615
Sutton, David B., 270
Swartz, Steve, 607
Sweeney, Paul D., 599, 600
Swersey, Bill, 355
Sykes, Donald and Suzanne, 25
Synder, Charles, 600
Szymanski, K., 605

Taber, Thomas D., 609, 613
Takahashi, Dean, 426, 611
Talbott, E., 614
Tandem Computer, 264
Tandy/Radio Shack, 50
Tannen, Deborah, 603
Tannenbaum, Robert, 436, 481, 612
Tavistock Institute, 84
Taylor, Frederick W., 199, 237, 568, 598, 616
Taylor, Maxwell, 399
Taylor, R. R., 607
Taylor, Shelley E., 612
Taylor, William C., 52, 593, 594
TDK Corp., 64
Teagarden, Mary B., 591
Teerlink, Richard, 161
Teledyne, 403
Tellegen, A., 614
Templin, Neal, 76, 593
Tessier, Annette, 134, 596
Thakur, Manab, 592
Therrien, Lois, 602
Thomas, James B., 592
Thomas, Kenneth W., 365, 368, 436, 601, 607, 610, 612
Thomas, R. Roosevelt, Jr., 29, 288, 591
Thomas, Robert J., 609, 611

Thompson, Arthur, A., Jr., 39, 112, 593–595, 600
Thompson, Chic, 413
Thompson, J. D., 607
Thorndike, Edward L., 590, 596
3M, 415
Thumin, Fred J., 594, 596
Tichy, Noel, 55, 119, 484, 590
Tjosvold, D., 606, 607
Tobias, L. L., 602
Todd, R., 294, 603
Toffler, Alvin, 79, 590, 593
Towne, Henry, 568
Trepp, Warren, 516
Trevino, L. K., 602
Treybig, Jim, 264
Trice, Harrison M., 120, 595
Trinity Communications, 4, 32
Trist, Eric, 550
Tru Lingua, Inc., 257
Tsalikis, J., 608
Tubbs, Mark E., 599
Tuckman, B. W., 604
Tully, Shawn, 461, 613
Turner, A. N., 603
Turner, Michael R., 144
Tushman, Michael L., 605, 612
Tyagi, Pradeep K., 598

Uedagin Bank, 123
Ulene, Art, 523
Ulmer, Diane, 613
Ulrich, Dave, 591
Union Carbide, 409
United Pacific Railroad (UP), 101
United Parcel Service (UPS), 100, 101
U.S. Environmental Protection, 220
US Healthcare Inc., 450
US Pharmaceuticals, 547
U.S. Steel, 14
Urwick, Lyndall, 571
Ury, W. L., 608

Valente, Judith, 577, 617
Van de Ven, Andrew H., 594, 609
Van Fleet, David D., 605
van Gogh, Vincent, 189
Van Hook, Ben, 339
Vance, Charles M., 594
Vandenberg, Robert J., 616
Vanderberg, Monique, 137
Vanderkloot, Jo, 266
Vartabedian, Ralph, 403
Vecchio, Robert P., 612, 617
Velasquez, Manual, 611
Velthouse, Betty A., 436, 601, 610, 612
Verespej, M. A., 606
Verhage, Jaap, 609
Vernon, P. E., 597
Vesey, Joseph T., 593, 594
Villere, Maurice F., 598
Vincent, Lisbeth J., 134, 596
Vlasic, Bill, 615
Vollrath, David A., 609
von Bertalanffy, L., 590

Von Glinow, Mary Ann, 593, 612
Vroom, Victor H., 612

W.L. Gore & Associates, 415
Wabash National, 54
Waddell, Lisa, 435
Wagley, Robert, 458
Wagner, John A., III, 596
Wahba, M. A., 597
Wal-Mart, 43, 111, 114, 139, 140, 233
Walt Disney Co., 124, 232, 431
Walters, Richard H., 596
Walton, A. E., 616
Walton, A. Wlise, 591
Walton, Sam, 43, 111, 112, 116, 139, 258, 259, 428, 485, 486, 600
Wang, Nina, 438
Wanous, John P., 595, 598
Warrick, D. D., 616
Waterman, Robert, Jr., 112, 594, 602
Watson, D., 614
Watson, Tom, 116, 126, 143
Watson, W. E., 605
Wayne, Chris, 89, 92
Weber, Joseph, 86
Weber, Max, 97, 569, 616
Weick, Karl, 594
Weidenbaum, Mrury, 596
Weinbach, Lawrence A., 287
Weiner, Bernard, 598, 612
Weitz, B. A., 596
Welbourne, Theresa M., 235, 600
Welch, James A., 592
Welch, John "Jack", 7, 8, 24, 55, 483, 484
Welkos, Robert W., 154
Welles, Chris, 611
Wells, George, 426
Westinghouse, 334
Wexley, Kenneth N., 610
Wheeless, V., 604
Whetton, David A., 603
Whitacre, Mark, 13
White, Elton, 143
White, Randall P., 287, 617
Whitehead, Alfred North, 599
Whitsett. D. A., 598
Wiedeking, Wendelin, 387
Wiener, Yoash, 116, 118, 595
Wigdor, Lawrence A., 598
Wiley, John & Sons, 590
Wilkins, Alan L., 592
Willcocks, Leslie P., 592
Williams, F., 603
Williams, Jesse, 113
Williams, K., 605
Williams, M. S., 607
Williams, R. B., Jr., 613
Williamson, Gilbert, 143
Willis, R. H., 609
Willits, R. D., 603
Wilson, Ian H., 592
Wilson, Mary C., 599, 616
Wilson, Terry, 13
Winnick, Gary, 516
Winslow, E. K., 598

Winter, David G., 598, 610
Wolf, William B., 595
Wolfe, D. M., 607, 614
Wong, Choy, 607
Woo, Junda, 261, 309
Wood, R. E., 157, 599
Woodall, Marvin, 86
Woodman, R. W., 616
Woolfold, R. L., 615
Worley, Christopher G., 615, 616
Wozniak, Steve, 118, 469
Wrenge, Charles D., 601
Wright, Patrick M., 601

Xerox, 549

Yamasaki, Taro, 331
Yammarino, F. J., 604
Yang, D. J., 606
Yankelovich, Daniel, 170, 597, 610
Yarborough, Trin, 168
Yasenev, Nikolai, 453
Yates, Ronald E., 505, 599
Yearta, Shawn K., 599
Yetton, Philip W., 605, 612
Young, John, 121
Yukl, Gary A., 609, 610

Zaccaro, S. J., 613, 614
Zake, Bruce, 54
Zaleznik, Abraham, 466, 611
Zalkind, Sheldon S., 294, 612
Zammuto, Raymond F., 590, 592
Zand, Dale E., 610
Zander, Alvin, 612
Zemke, R., 510, 606, 614
Zenger, John H., 347, 616
Zenith Electronics Corporation, 364
Zich, John, 307, 507
Ztel Inc., 264
Zwany, A., 598

Subject Index

A-B model of interpersonal behavior, 289–291
Ability, 149–
Absenteeism, 228
Absolute values, 404
Accommodating, 366
Accommodators, 165
Accountability, 463
Achievement motive, 195
Achievement-oriented leadership, 478
Action research, 550, 551
Actions, 221
Active listening, 276
Adjourning, 321
Administrative management principles, 569
Aesthetic values, 167
Affiliation motive, 196
Affinity map, 59
Affirmative action, 29
African Americans, 134
Amiables, 304, 305, 341
Amoral manager, 451
Analyticals, 304, 341
Anthropology, 573
Aptitude, 149
Arbitration, 375, 376
Asians, 134
Assertiveness, 302
Assimilators, 164
Association power, 433
Attending, 276
Attitude, 170
Attitudes, 135
Attribution, 156–158
Attributional error, 157
Authoritarianism, 176
Authority, 463
Autonomous, self-managed work teams, 336
Avoiding, 366

Bargaining, 367, 369
Behavioral conditioning, 160
Behavioral decision theory, 398
Behavioral flexibility, 303
Behavioral style, 302–305
Benchmarking, 158
Big Five, 172
Bill of Rights, 406
Biofeedback process, 518
Blacks, 134
Blind area, 301
Body language, 277, 278
Book
  overview, 30, 31
  themes, 27–30

Boundary spanning, 561
Boundary-spanning transactions, 15
Bounded rationality, 398
Brain-hemisphere dominance, 165, 166
Brainstorming, 415, 416
Bribery, 403
Bull-in-the-china-shop style, 301, 302
Bureaucracy, 95–98, **97, 569**
Burnout, **513,** 514
Business advocate, 66

Cafeteria-style benefits, 234
Career, 579
Career management, 576–589
  planning your career, 579–585
  process, 586, 587
  special situations, 587, 588
  starting your own business, 577, 589
  Strong Interest Inventory, 582–584
  trends, 577, 578
Career stages, 579
Carry-over behaviors, 324
Case study, 574
Cause-and-effect diagram, 394, 395
Cellular telephones, 259
Center for Creative Leadership, 287
Centralization, **92,** 93
Centralized power societies, 136
Certainty, 397
Change, 530
  causes of, 531, 532
  individual resistance to, 533–536
  OD, distinguished, 547, 548
  organizational resistance to, 536, 537
  overcoming resistance to, 537
  planned, 539–543
  planning/implementation, 543–546
  targets of, 540, 541
  unplanned, 539
Change agents, 540
Change options, 21, 22
Channel, 258
Charisma, 430
Charismatic-based values, 116
Charm schools, 287, 303, 08
Chronic stress, 500
Clarifying questions, 274
Classical conditioning, 160
Classical decision theory, 398
Closed-end questions, 274
Closed systems, 15
Co-optation, 539
Coercion, 447
Coercive power, 432
Cognitive dissonance, 170
Cognitive learning, 162
Cognitive style, 173–175

Cohesive, 325
Collaborating, 366
Collateral organizations, 557
Collectivist societies, 136
Command and control orientation, 66
Command group, 317
Communication, 254–285, **256**
  barriers to, 265–269
  cross-cultural, 281, 282
  formal communication channels, 262, 263
  gender, and, 282, 305, 306
  importance, 256, 257
  informal communication channels, 263–265
  interpersonal communication process, 257–260
  listening, and, 274–277
  nonverbal communications, 276–281
  personal space zones, and, 280, 281
  physical appearance, and, 281
  physical space, and, 280
  questions, and, 274, 275
  sending the message, 269–273
  time, and, 279, 280
Compatible values, 404
Compensation systems, 231–235
Compensatory justice, 407
Competence acquisition, 561
Competing, 365, 366
Competitive advantage, 49–53, **50**
Competitive strategy, 52, 53
Competitive team orientation, 66
Compromising, 366, 367
Conditioning theory, 160, 161
Conflict, 352
Conflict management, 350–383
  causes of conflict, 354–361
  conflict process, 352, 353
  functional vs. dysfunctional conflict, 353, 362–365
  intergroup coordination strategies, 369–372
  international aspects, 373
  interpersonal conflict-management styles, 365–369
  organizational uncertainty, and, 445
  overview, 361
  reduction/prevention strategies, 373–377
Conflict management styles, 365
Conflict-positive organization, 362
Conflict process, 352, 353
Conformance orientation, 66
Consensus, 157
Consistency, 156
Content theories of motivation, 185
Contingency theories, 572

Contingency theory, 472
Contingent consequence, 160
Control, 62
Control-autonomy-coordination, 93–95
Control system, 63–66
Controlling, 55
Convergers, 165
Core capabilities, 46
Core job dimensions, 240
Corporate policeman, 66
Corporate strategy, 51
Countercultures, 125
Covert lying, 308
Creative thinking, 412–415
Credibility, 271, 466
Criteria, 396
Critical events, 324
Cross-cultural communication, 281, 282
Cross-functional teams, 84, 337, 338
Culture, 112; *see also* Organizational
    culture
Cycle time, 103

Daddy track, 587
Day care facilities, 521
Decentralization, 92, 93
Deception, 308
Decision making, 388, 395–398, 411, 412
Decision-making skills, 339
Decision participation, 411, 412
Decision styles, 409
    backup style, 411
    information processing, and, 409, 410
    types of, 410, 411
Decoding, 259
Defense mechanisms, 293, 294
Defense, 293
Deficiency reduction needs, 186
Degenerative interaction climates, 360
Degenerative interaction patterns, 298
Delphi technique, 417
Dependent variable, 574
Diffused power societies, 136
Digital revolution, 77
Directive leadership, 478
Discrimination, 163
Distinctiveness, 156
Distress, 500
Distributive bargaining, 367
Distributive justice, 205, 407
Distrust, 269
Divergers, 164
Diversity, 29
    conflict, and, 375
    organizational culture, and, 131–133
    power, and, 436, 437
Dogmatism, 176
Double-loop learning, 209
Downward communication, 262
Drivers, 303, 304, 341
Driving forces, 545
Dual-factor theory, 190–192
Dynamic system, 15
Dysfunctional conflict, 364

Economic values, 167
Effectiveness, 25
Efficiency, 25
80/20 rule, 102
Electronic brainstorming, 416
Electronic channels, 259
Electronic eavesdropping, 309, 451, 452
Electronic mail (E-mail), 259
Electronic meeting systems (EMSs), 333,
    334
Electronic surveillance, 261
Elitist-charismatic values, 118
Elitist-traditional values, 119
Elitist values, 117
Emotional intelligence, 160
Emotional style, 172
Employee assistance programs, 521
Employee attitudes, 171
Employee-oriented behavior, 468
Employment interviews, 585, 586
Empowerment, 244–247, 433, 434
Encoding, 258
Enlarged jobs, 239
Enriched jobs, 239
Entreprenuers, 198
Environmental scanning, 57
Episodic stress, 500
Equity theory, 204
ERG theory, 188–190
Ergonomics, 242
Ethical behavior, 402
Ethical dilemma, 402, 404
Ethical reasoning, 402
Ethics, 29, 30, 402
    benchmarks, 404
    bribery, 403
    interpersonal communications, 308
    morality, 405–408
    obtaining interpersonal information
        without permission, 309, 451, 452
    organizational development, 559
    price fixing, 13
    public justification criteria, 403
    subliminal messages, 154
Exercises and simulations, 343
Existence needs, 188
Expectancy, 200
Expectancy theory, 199, 200
Experiential learning styles, 164, 165
Expert power, 430
Expressive practice of culture, 120, 121
Expressive style, 172
Expressives, 303, 304, 341
External validity, 575
Externals, 176
Extrinsic rewards, 201–204
Extroverts, 173, 512
Eye contact, 277, 278

Federal budget deadlock, 511
Feedback, 260, 271–273
Feelings, 296
Felt conflict, 353
Feminine values, 137
Field experiment, 574

Field survey, 574
Figure, 153
Filtering, 268
First impressions, 281
Fishbone chart, 394, 395
Fixed-feature territory, 280
Flattening organizational structure,
    98–104
Flowchart, 392, 393
Football team, 336
Force-field analysis, 545
Formal authority, 429
Formal communication channels, 262,
    263
Formal groups, 317, 318
Formal leaders, 463
Formal norms, 324
Formal position, 428
Forming, 321
Frames of reference, 155, 266, 291
Free riders, 330
Friendship groups, 319
Functional-charismatic values, 118
Functional conflict, 353, 362, 363
Functional-traditional values, 118
Functional values, 117

Gainsharing, 234, 235
Gantt chart, 399, 400
Gay employees, 320
Gender; *see* Male/female differences
General adaptation syndrome (G.A.S.),
    498, 499
Generalization, 163
Gentle touching, 279
Gestalt, 162
Gestures, 278, 279
Glass ceiling, 587
Globalization of business, 28
Goal, 219, 220
Grapevine, 264
Group decision support systems, 417
Groups, 317
    cohesiveness, 325–328
    composition, 330, 331
    development of, 319–322
    effective, 331
    formal, 317, 318
    functional group roles, 323
    gender differences, 331
    group vs. individual problem solving,
        328, 329
    groupthink, 329, 330
    inappropriate conformity, 328
    informal, 319, 320
    leadership facilitation, 331, 333
    meeting guidelines, 333
    norms, 323–325
    social loafing, 330
    status within, 325
    structure of, 322–328
    team building, 334, 335, 337–339
    teams, contrasted, 335
    threats to effectiveness, 328–331

Groupthink, 329, 330
Growth aspiration needs, 186
Growth needs, 189

Halo effect, 156
Hardiness, 512
Hawthorne effect, 570
Hawthorne studies, 570
Hidden area, 301
Hierarchy of needs, 187, 188
Hispanics, 134
History of OB theories, 567–575
Homosexual employees, 320
Horizontal communication, 262, 263
Horizontal job loading, 239
Horizontal organization, 101, 102
Hoteling, 377
Hygiene factors, 190
Hypothesis, 574

Ideology, 56, 198, 199
Immoral manager, 451
Implementing manager/leader, 482
Independent variable, 574
Individualistic societies, 136
Inducement, 446
Industrial engineering, 573
Influence, 128
Informal communication channels, 263–265
Informal groups, 319, 320
Informal leaders, 463
Informal norms, 324
Informal social arrangements, 324
Information power, 432
Initial public offering (IPO), 217
Initiating structure, 468
Input-transformation-output system, 14
Insight, 162
Institutional power, 196
Instrumental leader behaviors, 478
Instrumental values, 168
Instrumentality, 200
Integrative bargaining, 367
Intellectual style, 172
Intelligence, 159
Intention, 220
Interdependence, 355–357
Interest group, 319
Internal attribution, 197
Internal validity, 575
Internals, 176
Interpersonal effectiveness, 299
Interpersonal relations, 286–313
  A-B model, 289–291
  behavioral style, 302–305
  charm schools, 287, 303, 308
  defensiveness, and, 293, 294
  ethics, 308, 309
  feelings, and, 296
  influencing factors, 288–299
  interaction setting, and, 296–299
  interpersonal needs, 293–295
  job requirements, and, 296

Interpersonal Relations—*Cont.*
  male/female differences;
    see Male/female differences
  organizational culture, and, 297
  personality factors, and, 291–296
  self-presentation/self-disclosure, 300–302
  trust, and, 298, 299
Interpersonal skills, 339
Interpersonal style, 172
Interrole conflict, 359
Intersender conflict, 359
Interventions, 546, 554–559
Interviewer style, 301
Intimate zone, 280
Intolerable values, 404
Intrasender conflict, 359
Intrinsic rewards, 201
Introverts, 173, 512
Intuitive feelers, 175
Intuitive thinkers, 174, 175
Intuitives, 173

Jargon, 267
Job design/redesign, **237**–244
Job enrichment, 192
Job outcomes, 241
Johari window, 300
Judgers, 173
Justice, 407

Kaizen, 442
Kinesics, 277, 278
Knowledge workers, 80
Known risk, 397

Laboratory experiment, 574
Latent conflict, 352
Law of effect, 12, 226
Leader, 463
Leader-member exchange theory, 487
Leadership, 460–494, **463**
  behavior, 467–470
  contingency theories, 474–481
  decision style, 469, 470
  distinguishing characteristics, 466–468
  favoritism, and, 487
  group decision tree, 481
  management, distinguished, 462–465
  need for, 487–489
  observable behavior, 473, 474
  path-goal theory, 477–480
  situational contingencies, and, 471–481
  situational leadership theory, 475–477
  style/favorableness factors, 474, 475
  substitutes for, 488
  transformational, 481–487
  women/minorities, and, 488, 489
Leadership Grid, 470, 471
Leadership style, 470, 471
Learning, 158–167, **158**
  behavioral conditioning, 160, 161
  brain hemispheres, and, 165, 166
  cognitive view of, 162–164

Learning—*Cont.*
  experiential styles of, 164, 165
  lifelong process, as, 166
  motivation, and, 207–210
  social learning theory, 161, 162
Learning organization, 210, 559–562, **560**
Left-hemisphere dominance, 166
Legal rights, 406
Liaison, 371
Life change unit scale, 506
Life cycle, 91
Life planning, 580
Line positions, 100
Listening, 274–277
Locus of control, 176, 512
Lunchtime counselors/support groups, 523
Lying, 308

Machiavellianism, 176
Maintenance roles, 323
Malcolm Baldrige National Quality Award, 11
Male/female differences; *see also* Women
  communication differences, 282, 305, 306
  interaction preferences, 306
  relating, 306
  social-sexual behavior, 307
Management by ideology, 56
Management by information, 56
Management by objectives (MBO), 221–224
Management by wandering around, 264
Management themes, 27–30
Management, 10
Managerial ethics, 451
Managers, 16, **463**
  chaotic view of, 18
  decisional roles, 20, 21
  influence on organization systems, 21–26
  informational roles, 20
  integrating responsibility of, 23
  interpersonal roles, 18–20
  rational heroic view of, 16–18
  skills, 79
  stakeholders, and, 9
Manifest conflict, 353
Manipulation, 538
Mantra, 518
Masculine values, 137
Maximizer, 409
Mechanistic organization, 96
Mediation, 374, 375
Meditation, 518
Meetings, 333
Mentor, 430, 587
Mentoring, 517, 521
Merit plans, 232, 233
Message, 258
Milestones, 48
Misinterpretation, 266
Mission, 7, 42, 43
Mixed signals, 276

Moderating variable, 574
Mommy track, 587
Moral manager, 450
Moral rights, 406
Morality, 405
Motivation, 182–215, **185**
  behavior, and, 197
  content theories of, 185
  dual-factor theory, 190–192
  equity, and, 204–206
  ERG theory, 188–190
  expectancy theory, 199, 200
  hierarchy of needs, 187, 188
  individual vs. group, 206, 207
  intrinsic/extrinsic rewards, 201–204
  learned motives, 194–196
  learning, and, 207–210
  needs theories of, 185–204
  performance feedback, and, 204
  personal attribution, and, 196, 197
  personal ideology, and, 198, 199
  process theories of, 199
  theory X/Y, 192, 193
  work-related needs, 190–193
Motivation methods/applications,
    216–252
  behavior modification, 225–229
  empowerment, 244–247
  goal-setting, 219–221
  initial public offering, 217, 218
  job design/redesign, 237–244
  management by objectives, 221–224
  reinforcement, 225–229
  rewards, 229–237
Motivator factors, 191
Moving, 542
Multifocus, 410
Myers-Briggs Type Indicator (MBTI), 173

National cultures, 133–139
National mental preprogramming, 135
Need for affiliation, 196
Need for power, 196
Need to achieve, 195
Needs theories of motivation, 185–194
Negative reinforcement, 225, 226
Negotiating, 374, 376
Negotiation, 439
Network, 585
Networking, 443
Noise, 260
Nominal group technique, 416, 417
Nonprogrammed decisions, 392
Nonverbal, 259, 276–281
Norming, 321
Norms, 323–325

Objective, 390
Obligation, 447
Occupational themes, 583
Off-site, 127
Omission, 226
Open area, 301
Open-end questions, 274
Open systems, 15, 16

Openness, 297
Operant conditioning, 160
Organic organization, 96, 97
Organization, 5
  mission/goals, 7
  purpose, 5–9
  social responsibility of, 11
  stakeholders in, 8
Organization chart, 76, **85**
Organization star, 76, 77
Organizational assumptions, 112–115
Organizational behavior (OB), **9**
**Organizational behavior modification
    (OB mod)**, **226**, 227
Organizational culture, 23, 110–144, **112**
  analysis of, 125–127
  assumptions, and, 112–115
  clues to, 125–127
  development, 128–133
  ethnic diversity, and, 131–133
  functions of, 120–125
  international aspects, 133–139
  interpersonal relations, and, 297
  national cultures, and, 133–139
  shifts in, 130, 131
  values, and, 115–119
Organizational design, 85
  balancing, 92–98
  customer/market, by, 90, 91
  function, by, 86, 87
  geography/territory, by, 88
  participative team management, and,
    80–85
  product line, by, 89, 90
  technology, and, 77–80
Organizational development (OD), **546**
  action research, 550, 551
  ethical concerns, 559
  example, 550–554
  interventions, 554–559
  nature of, 547, 548
  practitioners, 548, 549
  process, 550, 551, 563
  sources, 549, 550
  values, 548
Organizational learning, 560
Organizational politics, 444–449, 452, 509
Organizational structure, 85
Organizational value system, 116
Origins of OB theories, 567–575
Outsourcing, 32, **51**
Overload, 508
Overt lie, 308
Owning, 297, 298

Pareto chart, **395**, 396
Pareto's law, 102
Participative leadership, 478
Participative team management, 82–85
Path-goal leadership theory, **477**
Pathfinding leader, **483**, 484
Pay-for-performance rewards, 231–234
Perceived conflict, 352
Perceivers, 173
Perception, **150**

Perception—*Cont.*
  applications of, 158
  attention and selection, 151, 152
  distortions in, 155, 156
  interpretation, 155
  organization, 152–154
Perceptual closure, **153**, 155
Perceptual process, 151
Perfect rationality, 398
Performance, **231**
Performance-based rewards, 231–234
Performance-related processes, 324
Performing, 321
Person-job fit, **148**
Person-role conflict, 359
Personal attribution, **196**
Personal frame of reference, **291**
Personal ideology, **198**
Personal power, 196
Personal roles, **323**
Personal sources of power, 428
Personal space zones, 280, 281
Personal zone, 281
Personality, 171–177, **171**
Personality factors, 172, 173
Personality traits, 176, 177
Persuasion, 446
Physical appearance, 281
Piecework, **232**
Planned change, **539**–543
Planning, 53–57, **55**
  business start-up, for, 57, 58
  group process, as, 57–61
  visual approaches, 62
Plateauing, 587
Pluralistic/political model, 452
Political capacity, 445
Political science, 573
Political tactics, 447–449
Political values, 167
Politics; *see* Organizational politics
Pooled interdependence, **356**, 357
Position power, **428**
Positive reinforcement, 225, 226
Posture, 278
Power, **427**
  diversity, and, 436, 437
  empowerment—*Cont.*, and, 433, 434
  morality, and, 450–452
  need for, 442–444
  organizational position, and, 428–430
  personal behavior, and, 430–432
  power sharing, and, 435, 436, 481
  sexism, and, 437, 438
  situational forces, and, 432, 433,
    439–442
  social networks, and, 434–439
  sources of, 428, 429
  what is it, 427, 428
Power avoidance, 444, 445
Power distance, 136, 138
Power motive, **196**, **442**
Power sharing, 481
Powerlessness, 445
Premack principle, **161**, 227
Primacy, 324
Problem solving, **388**

Problem solving—*Cont.*
  action plan implementation, 398–400
  brainstorming, 415, 416
  conflict management, and, 374
  creative, 412–415
  decision making, 395–398
  Delphi technique, 417
  follow-through, 400–402
  group decision support systems, 417
  group vs. individual, 328, 329
  nominal group technique, 416, 417
  problem awareness, 388–392
  problem definition, 392–395
  steps in process, 389
Problem-solving behaviors, 174, 175
Problem-solving manager/leader, 482
Problem-solving skills, 339
Problem-solving teams, 336
Procedural justice, 205
Process consultation, 555
Process theories of motivation, 199
Productivity, 24, **25**, 327
Profit sharing, 232, 233
Programmed decisions, 392
Projection, 156
Proxemics, 280
Psychological contract, 148
Psychological states, 240, 241
Psychology, 573
Public justification criteria, 403
Public zone, 281
Punishment, 225, 226

Qualifying terms, 306
Qualitative role overload, 508
Quality circle (QC), 83, 318
Quantitative role overload, 508
Questions, 274

Radar chart, 61
Rational managerial tools, 120, 121
Rational problem-solving process; *see*
    Problem solving
Receiver, 258
Reciprocal alliances, 431, 432
Reciprocal interdependence, 357
Reciprocity, 290, **431**
Reengineering, 101–104, **558**
Reference group, 319
Referent cognitions theory, 205
Referent power, 430
Refreezing, 543
Regenerative interaction patterns, 298
Reinforcement, 225–229
Reinvention, 26
Relatedness needs, 189
Relationship-motivated style, 474
Relative quality degradation, 51
Relaxation, 518
Reliability, 575
Religious values, 167
Research and methodological
    foundations, 573–575
Responding, 276
Responsibility charting, 342
Responsiveness, 302

Restraining forces, 545
Restructuring, 376, 377
Results, 48
Retributive justice, 407
Revitalization, 26
Reward power, 429
Rewards, 229–239
Right, 406
Right-hemisphere dominance, 166
Risk propensity, 176
Risk to experiment, 297
Rite, 126
Role, 323, 358
Role ambiguity, 358, 508
Role analysis technique, 342
Role conflict, 358, 359, 508
Role negotiation, 555
Role negotiation technique, 342
Role overload, 359, 508
Role set, 358
Rough touching, 279
Routine jobs, 239

Satisfaction, 26
Satisficer, 409
Satisficing, 398
Scientific management, 237, 568
Scientific method, 573
Selective listening, 268
Selective perception, 155
Self-assessment inventories, 343
Self-concept, 244, **291**
Self-disclosure, 300–302
Self-efficacy, 244
Self-empowerment, 245
Self-esteem, 177, 244, 512
Self-managed team, 83
Self-monitoring, 177
Self-presentation, 300–302
Self-serving bias, 157
Semantics, 267
Semifixed feature territory, 280
Sender, 258
Sensation feelers, 175
Sensation thinkers, 174
Sensers, 173
Sensing, 276
Sensitivity training, 343, 555
Sequential interdependence, 356, 357
Sexism, 437, 438
Sexual harassment, 307
Showing consideration, 468
Silent monitoring, 261
Single-loop learning, 209
Situational leadership theory (SLT),
    475–477
Situational opportunity, 428
Skills, 79, 80, 339
Small-group networks, 264, 265
Smoothing, 377
Social-cognitive theory, 466
Social contract, 149
Social control expectations, 434
Social controls, 65
Social exchange theory, 436
Social gatherings, 264

Social good, 405
Social learning theory, 161, **162**
Social loafing, 330
Social psychology, 573
Social values, 167
Social zone, 281
Socialization, 122
Sociology, 573
Sociotechnical systems design, 84
Solution focus, 410
Span of control, 99
Staff positions, 100
Stakeholders, 8, 405
Standard-hour plan, 232
Statement of purpose, 43
Status, 325
Stereotype, 155
Storming, 321
Strategic management
    add value to customers, 40–42
    mission statement, 42, 43
    questions to explore, 45–48
    structures/systems, 44, 45
    vision, 43, 44
Strategic thinking, **40**
Strategy, 44
Stress, 496–526, **498**
    behavioral consequences, 514, 515
    causes of, 501–510
    consequences, 513–516
    constructive vs destructive, 500
    environmental causes, 509
    episodic vs. chronic, 500
    general adaptation syndrome, 498, 499
    individual coping strategies, 516–519
    individual stress moderators, 510–513
    international aspects, 505, 507
    management of, 516–523
    organizational causes, 505–509
    organizational coping strategies,
        519–523
    organizational costs, 515, 516
    personal causes, 501–504
    physiological consequences, 513
    psychological consequences, 513, 514
    workers' compensation, and, 510
Stressors, 498
Strong culture, 113
Strong Interest Inventory (SII), 582–584
Structure, 44
Structured feedback procedures, 343
Subcultures, 124
Subliminal messages, 154
Superordinate goals, 7, 373
Supportive leadership, 478
Supportive relationship leader behaviors,
    478
SWOT analysis, 47
System, 12
Systems, 45
Systems theory, 571

T-group, 555
Tactile communication, 279
Tag questions, 306
Task depth, 238

Task force, 371
Task groups, 317
Task-motivated style, 474
Task-oriented behavior, 468
Task roles, 323
Task scope, 238
Tasks, 21
Team building, 334, 335, 337–339, 521
Team-based participation models, 82–85
Teams, 335
    actions taken, 336, 337
    conflict management, and, 371, 372
    development of, 337–339
    effective, 342, 343
    groups, contrasted, 335
    matching roles/preferences, 340
    organizational conditions, 338
    skills, 339
    sports analogies, 335, 336
    values, 338
    work preferences, 341
    work roles, 340, 341
Technical jargon, 267
Technical skills, 339
Technician jobs, 239
Technology, 22, **78**
    change, and, 77–80
    global competition, and, 80
Telecommuting, 259
Tennis doubles team, 336
Terminal values, 168
Theoretical values, 167

Theory X, **192**, 193
Theory Y, **193**
Third-party peacemaking, 555
Thousand-year test, 518
Three o'clock syndrome, 521
Time management, 227, 517
Total quality management (TQM), 24, 25,
    131
Track team, 335
Tradition-based values, 116
Transformational leaders, 481
Transitional values, 404
Transmission, 258
Transorganizational development, 558
Transparent style, 301
Trust, 297, **298**
Turbulence, 397
Turtle, 301, 302
Type A personality, 501–504, **502**
Type B personality, **502**

Uncertainty, **397**
Uncertainty avoidance, **136**
Uncertainty reduction, **360**
Underutilization, **508**
Unfreezing, **542**
Unifocus, 410
Unknown area, 301
Upward communication, 262
Utilitarianism, **405**
Utility, **405**

Valence, 200
Validity, **575**
Value judgments, 268
Value system, **291**
Values, 115, **167**
Vertical job loading, **239**
Vision, **43**, 44, 463
Vocal intonations, 279
Vocal meanings, 279
Vocal quality, 279
Vocational English as Second Language
    (VESL) program, 257
Voice mail, 259

Wall Street Journal, 584
Weak culture, **130**
Wellness promotion, 521, 522
Women; *see also* Male/female differences
    competitiveness, 326
    glass ceiling, 588
    inequality at work, 533, 588
    leadership, and, 488, 489
    sexism, 437, 438
Work style, 172
Work teams, 336, 337
Written communication channels, 259